Lecture Notes in Computer Science

Lecture Notes in Artificial Intelligence   14001

Founding Editor

Jörg Siekmann

Series Editors

Randy Goebel, *University of Alberta, Edmonton, Canada*
Wolfgang Wahlster, *DFKI, Berlin, Germany*
Zhi-Hua Zhou, *Nanjing University, Nanjing, China*

The series Lecture Notes in Artificial Intelligence (LNAI) was established in 1988 as a topical subseries of LNCS devoted to artificial intelligence.

The series publishes state-of-the-art research results at a high level. As with the LNCS mother series, the mission of the series is to serve the international R & D community by providing an invaluable service, mainly focused on the publication of conference and workshop proceedings and postproceedings.

Pablo García Bringas · Hilde Pérez García ·
Francisco Javier Martínez de Pisón ·
Francisco Martínez Álvarez ·
Alicia Troncoso Lora · Álvaro Herrero ·
José Luis Calvo Rolle · Héctor Quintián ·
Emilio Corchado
Editors

Hybrid Artificial Intelligent Systems

18th International Conference, HAIS 2023
Salamanca, Spain, September 5–7, 2023
Proceedings

 Springer

Editors
Pablo García Bringas ⓘ
University of Deusto
Bilbao, Spain

Hilde Pérez García ⓘ
University of Leon
León, Spain

Francisco Javier Martínez de Pisón ⓘ
University of La Rioja
Logroño, La Rioja, Spain

Francisco Martínez Álvarez ⓘ
Pablo de Olavide University
Seville, Spain

Alicia Troncoso Lora ⓘ
Pablo de Olavide University
Seville, Spain

Álvaro Herrero ⓘ
University of Burgos
Burgos, Spain

José Luis Calvo Rolle ⓘ
University of A Coruña
Ferrol - Coruña, Spain

Héctor Quintián ⓘ
University of A Coruña
Ferrol - Coruña, Spain

Emilio Corchado ⓘ
University of Salamanca
Salamanca, Spain

ISSN 0302-9743 ISSN 1611-3349 (electronic)
Lecture Notes in Artificial Intelligence
ISBN 978-3-031-40724-6 ISBN 978-3-031-40725-3 (eBook)
https://doi.org/10.1007/978-3-031-40725-3

LNCS Sublibrary: SL7 – Artificial Intelligence

This Springer imprint is published by the registered company Springer Nature Switzerland AG
The registered company address is: Gewerbestrasse 11, 6330 Cham, Switzerland

Preface

This volume of *Lecture Notes in Artificial Intelligence (LNAI)* includes accepted papers presented at the *18th International Conference on Hybrid Artificial Intelligence Systems (HAIS 2023)*, held in the beautiful city of Salamanca, Spain, in September 2023.

HAIS has become an unique, established and broad interdisciplinary forum for researchers and practitioners who are involved in developing and applying symbolic and sub-symbolic techniques aimed at the construction of highly robust and reliable problem-solving techniques, and producing the most relevant achievements in this field.

The hybridization of intelligent techniques coming from different computational intelligence areas has become popular because of the growing awareness that such combinations frequently perform better than the individual techniques such as neurocomputing, fuzzy systems, rough sets, evolutionary algorithms, agents and multiagent systems, and so on.

Practical experience has indicated that hybrid intelligence techniques might be helpful to solve some challenging real-world problems. In a hybrid intelligence system, a synergistic combination of multiple techniques is used to build an efficient solution to deal with a particular problem. This is, thus, the setting of the HAIS conference series, and its increasing success is the proof of the vitality of this exciting field.

The HAIS 2023 International Program Committee selected 65 papers, which are published in these conference proceedings, yielding an acceptance ratio of about 54%.

The reviewing process consists of a single-blind review for at least three reviewers for each submitted paper was extremely rigorous in order to maintain the high quality of the conference and we would like to thank the Program Committee for their hard work in the reviewing process. This process is very important in creating a conference of high standard and the HAIS conference would not exist without their help.

The large number of submissions is certainly not only a testimony to the vitality and attractiveness of the field but an indicator of the interest in the HAIS conference itself.

HAIS 2023 enjoyed outstanding keynote speeches by distinguished guest speakers: Oscar Cordón of University of Granada (Spain), Michał Woźniak of Wroclaw University of Technology (Poland), and Hujun Yin of University of Manchester (UK).

HAIS 2023 has teamed up with "Neurocomputing" (Elsevier) and "Logic Journal of the IGPL" (Oxford University Press) for a suite of special issues, including selected papers from HAIS 2023.

Particular thanks go as well to the conference's main sponsors, Startup Olé, the CYL-HUB project financed with NEXT-GENERATION funds from the European Union, and channelled by Junta de Castilla y León through the Regional Ministry of Industry, Trade and Employment, BISITE research group at the University of Salamanca, CTC research group at the University of A Coruña, and the University of Salamanca. They jointly contributed in an active and constructive manner to the success of this initiative.

We want to thank all the contributing authors, members of the Program Committee, and the Local Organizing Committee for their hard and highly valuable work. Their work has helped to contribute to the success of the HAIS 2023 event.

We thank the staff of Springer for their help and collaboration during this demanding publication project.

September 2023

José Luis Calvo Rolle
Francisco Javier Martínez de Pisón
Pablo García Bringas
Hilde Pérez García
Francisco Martínez Álvarez
Alicia Troncoso Lora
Álvaro Herrero
Héctor Quintián
Emilio Corchado

Organization

General Chair

Emilio Corchado   University of Salamanca, Spain

International Advisory Committee

Ajith Abraham   FLAME University, India
Antonio Bahamonde   University of Oviedo, Spain
Andre de Carvalho   University of São Paulo, Brazil
Sung-Bae Cho   Yonsei University, Korea
Juan M. Corchado   University of Salamanca, Spain
José R. Dorronsoro   Autonomous University of Madrid, Spain
Michael Gabbay   King's College London, UK
Ali A. Ghorbani   UNB, Canada
Mark A. Girolami   University of Glasgow, UK
Manuel Graña   University of País Vasco, Spain
Petro Gopych   Universal Power Systems USA-Ukraine LLC,
                                   Ukraine
Jon G. Hall   Open University, UK
Francisco Herrera   University of Granada, Spain
César Hervás-Martínez   University of Córdoba, Spain
Tom Heskes   Radboud University, The Netherlands
Dusan Husek   Academy of Sciences of the Czech Republic,
                                   Czech Republic
Lakhmi Jain   University of South Australia, Australia
Samuel Kaski   Helsinki University of Technology, Finland
Daniel A. Keim   University of Konstanz, Germany
Marios Polycarpou   University of Cyprus, Cyprus
Witold Pedrycz   University of Alberta, Canada
Xin Yao   University of Birmingham, UK
Hujun Yin   University of Manchester, UK
Michał Woźniak   Wroclaw University of Technology, Poland
Aditya Ghose   University of Wollongong, Australia
Ashraf Saad   Georgia Southern University, USA
Fanny Klett   German Workforce Advanced Distributed
                                   Learning Partnership Laboratory, Germany

Paulo Novais	Universidade do Minho, Portugal
Rajkumar Roy	EPSRC Centre for Innovative Manufacturing in Through-Life Engineering Services, UK
Amy Neustein	Linguistic Technology Systems, USA
Jaydip Sen	Tata Consultancy Services Ltd, India

Program Committee Chairs

Jose Luis Calvo Rolle	University of A Coruña, Spain
Francisco Javier Martínez de Pisón	University of La Rioja, Spain
Pablo García Bringas	University of Deusto, Spain
Hilde Pérez García	University of León, Spain
Francisco Martínez Álvarez	Pablo de Olavide University, Spain
Alicia Troncoso Lora	Pablo de Olavide University, Spain
Álvaro Herrero	University of Burgos, Spain
Héctor Quintián	University of A Coruña, Spain
Emilio Corchado	University of Salamanca, Spain

Program Committee

Álvaro Michelena Grandío	University of A Coruña, Spain
Anca Andreica	Babes-Bolyai University, Romania
Ángel Arroyo	University of Burgos, Spain
Antonio Díaz-Longueira	University of A Coruña, Spain
Antonio Jesús Díaz Honrubia	Polytechnic University of Madrid, Spain
Arkadiusz Kowalski	Wrocław University of Technology, Poland
Borja Sanz	University of Deusto, Spain
Camelia Serban	Babes-Bolyai University, Romania
Carlos Carrascosa	Polytechnic University of Valencia, Spain
Carlos Pereira	ISEC, Portugal
Damian Krenczyk	Silesian University of Technology, Poland
David Iclanzan	Sapientia University, Romania
Dragan Simic	University of Novi Sad, Serbia
Eiji Uchino	Yamaguchi University, Japan
Eneko Osaba	TECNALIA Research & Innovation, Spain
Enol García González	University of Oviedo, Spain
Enrique De La Cal Marín	University of Oviedo, Spain
Enrique Onieva	University of Deusto, Spain
Esteban Jove	University of A Coruña, Spain
Federico Divina	Pablo de Olavide University, Spain

Pablo García Bringas	University of Deusto, Spain
Paula M. Castro	University of A Coruña, Spain
Peter Rockett	University of Sheffield, UK
Petrica Pop	Technical University of Cluj-Napoca, North University Center at Baia Mare, Romania
Robert Burduk	Wroclaw University of Technology, Poland
Ruben Fuentes-Fernandez	Complutense University of Madrid, Spain
Sean Holden	University of Cambridge, UK
Urszula Stanczyk	Silesian University of Technology, Poland

HAIS 2023 Organizing Committee Chairs

| Emilio Corchado | University of Salamanca, Spain |
| Héctor Quintián | University of A Coruña, Spain |

HAIS 2023 Organizing Committee

Álvaro Herrero Cosio	University of Burgos, Spain
José Luis Calvo Rolle	University of A Coruña, Spain
Ángel Arroyo	University of Burgos, Spain
Daniel Urda	University of Burgos, Spain
Nuño Basurto	University of Burgos, Spain
Carlos Cambra	University of Burgos, Spain
Leticia Curiel	University of Burgos, Spain
Beatriz Gil	University of Burgos, Spain
Raquel Redondo	University of Burgos, Spain
Esteban Jove	University of A Coruña, Spain
José Luis Casteleiro Roca	University of A Coruña, Spain
Francisco Zayas Gato	University of A Coruña, Spain
Álvaro Michelena	University of A Coruña, Spain
Míriam Timiraos Díaz	University of A Coruña, Spain
Antonio Javier Díaz Longueira	University of A Coruña, Spain

Contents

Deep Learning

Evolutionary Computation and Optimization

HAIS Applications

Image and Speech Signal Processing

Agents and Multiagents

Biomedical Applicatons

Anomaly and Fault Detection

One-Class Reconstruction Methods for Categorizing DoS Attacks on CoAP

Álvaro Michelena[1], Antonio Díaz-Longueira[1], Míriam Timiraos[1,2],
Esteban Jove[1(✉)], Jose Aveleira-Mata[3], Isaías García-Rodriguez[4],
María Teresa García-Ordás[4], José Luis Calvo-Rolle[1],
and Héctor Alaiz-Moretón[3]

[1] Department of Industrial Engineering, CTC, CITIC, University of A Coruña,
Calle Mendizábal s/n, 15403 Ferrol, A Coruña, Spain
{alvaro.michelena,a.diazl,miriam.timiraos.diaz,
esteban.jove,jlcalvo,hector.quintian}@udc.es
[2] Department of Water Technologies, National Technological Center,
Fundación Instituto Tecnológico de Galicia, Cantón Grande 9,
Planta 3, 15003 A Coruña, Spain
mtimiraos@itg.es
[3] Research Institute of Applied Sciences in Cybersecurity (RIASC), MIC,
University of León, Campus de Vegazana, s/n, 24071 León, Spain
{jose.aveleira,hector.moreton}@unileon.es
[4] Department of Electrical and Systems Engineering, University of León,
Campus de Vegazana, s/n, 24071 León, Spain
{isaias.garcia,mgaro}@unileon.es

Abstract. Denial of Service (DoS) attack over Internet of Things (IoT) is among the most prevalent cyber threat, their complex behavior makes very expensive the use of Datagram Transport Layer Security (DTLS) for securing purposes. DoS attack exploits specific protocol features, causing disruptions and remaining undetected by legitimate components. This paper introduces a set of one-class reconstruction methods such as autoencoder, K-Means and PCA (Principal Component Analysis) for developing a categorization model in order to prevent IoT DoS attacks over the CoAP (Constrained Application Protocol) environments.

Keywords: Anomaly detection · IoT · CoAP · autoencoders · PCA · K-Means

1 Introduction

The Constrained Application Protocol (CoAP) is a web-like transfer protocol specifically designed to facilitate communication at the application layer for energy-constrained IoT devices [25]. CoAP operates over the User Datagram Protocol (UDP) and adheres to the Representational State Transfer (REST) architectural framework. CoAP's architecture comprises two distinct layers: (1) the message layer and (2) the request/response layer. The message layer is

P. García Bringas et al. (Eds.): HAIS 2023, LNAI 14001, pp. 3–14, 2023.
https://doi.org/10.1007/978-3-031-40725-3_1

responsible for managing communication over the UDP protocol, while the request/response layer transmits the corresponding messages, using specific codes to mitigate and circumvent functional issues, such as message loss [17,21].

One of the notable advantages of CoAP is its ability to seamlessly integrate with HTTP, thus enabling integration with existing web infrastructure while satisfying the specific demands of constrained environments. This integration is achieved by addressing specialized requirements such as support for multicast communication, minimization of overhead, and simplicity in constrained settings. The primary purpose of CoAP is to facilitate machine-to-machine (M2M) communication, particularly in domains like smart energy and building automation. As well as the request/response interaction model, the protocol also encompasses built-in discovery mechanisms for services and resources, aligning itself with the fundamental concepts of the Web [2,20].

The security of CoAP primarily relies on the implementation of the Datagram Transport Layer Security (DTLS) protocol at the transport layer. DTLS ensures confidentiality, integrity, and non-repudiation of information and services [23,30]. However, not all IoT devices and environments can make use of DTLS due to the computationally expensive cryptographic operations required by this technology or the necessary additional bytes for message encryption and integrity checks. These needs produce a higher energy consumption, reduced network throughput, and increased latency, which can negatively impact the overall performance of the IoT network [4,22]. A number of research is being conducted in order to find lighter implementations for DTLS or new techniques that can jointly be used with these cryptographic approaches. One such techniques is the development of model-based intrusion detection systems that can help securing IoT environments while relieving devices from the burden of the task [9,11]. These models can be based on simple known rules, however, these cannot be used to solve a categorization problem. As a result, the classifier implementation must go through a process of learning from a set of training items.

This work is devoted to develop a convenient model-based IDS for detecting DoS attacks on IoT scenarios, trying to find the best techniques to achieve this objective. DoS attacks based on amplification is one of the most usual and dangerous ones, as it can be performed even in secured encrypted scenarios where DTLS is used [6,18]. The objective of this work is to get a good detector for this kind of specific attacks. This approach introduces an scalability issue, as the model training should be performed for each different IoT ecosystem where it is needed. Also, the approach is only useful for amplification-based DoS attacks and so different models should be trained for detecting other anomalies, if needed. Currently, a number of efforts are being carried out in order to achieve more generic and zero-day attack detectors [8,13,24], but these solutions are more prone to both false positives and false negatives. Also, these approaches may require more computational resources and processing time.

One-class makes reference to a specific situation in which the classifier must distinguish between a known class (target class) and an unknown class (non-target class) [10,28]. One-class classifiers can be implemented through three approaches: using density estimation functions to approximate the system behavior, delimiting the boundaries of the target set, or applying reconstruction methods. This method implements a model from the training data to minimize the reconstruction error. Then, objects from the non-target class would lead to high reconstruction error, thus facilitating the outlier detection [15].

The paper is divided into a number of sections. The case study, which details the particular IoT CoAP ecosystem and dataset being used, is described in the second section. The third part discusses the techniques that will be used, including information on the auto-encoder, K-Means and PCA (Principal Component Analysis). The experiments that were carried out and their outcomes are covered in section four. Section five addresses the results of set of experiments while the findings and recommendations for further research are presented in the concluding part.

2   Case Study

In the preceding section, the general features of CoAP were discussed, along with the cybersecurity challenges it faces. This section delves deeper into the workings of CoAP and elaborates on the implementation of a DoS attack.

CoAP works like client/server model, much like HTTP, and makes use of the REST API architecture for communication. This structure employs a REST API, where resources are identified by unique URLs and can be manipulated through HTTP methods such as GET, POST, PUT, and DELETE. Additionally, CoAP includes the "Observe" functionality [5], which allows a client to keep track of a server resource. The server delivers periodic updates of the resource to registered clients, enabling bidirectional communication among devices.

To generate a dataset, a testing environment is deployed to create genuine traffic within the CoAP framework, wherein DoS attack will be performed to assess the protocol's debility, as delineated in RFC7252 [25]. This environment comprises a "Node.js" server furnished with the "node-coap" library to facilitate the CoAP protocol. A "DHT11" sensor is interfaced with a "NodeMCU" board, which is programmed using the "ESP-CoAP" library [19] to deliver temperature and humidity services. A JavaScript client presents the sensor data on the terminal, while a pair of "Copper4cr" clients facilitate the dispatching of requests and the reception of responses [16].

A DoS attack will be executed on the CoAP protocol within the devised environment, with the objective of generating a valuable dataset to aid in the identification of anomalies in the protocol and the mitigation of such threats.

When a request is received, CoAP servers produce a response packet. The size of this response packet can be considerably larger than the request packet, due to CoAP's capability to transmit multiple blocks in various sizes, even remarkably small ones during an attack. This characteristic makes CoAP clients susceptible to Denial of Service (DoS) attacks [29].

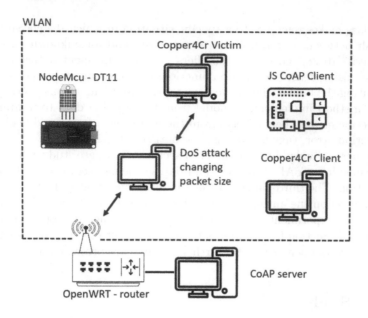

Fig. 1. CoAP environment with DoS attack

An attacker can launch an amplification attack by provoking a denial of service and falsifying the victim's IP address as the source address in a request packet. This action prompts the server to dispatch a larger packet directed at the victim. To perform this attack within the environment, the attacker poses as a Copper4Cr client, spoofing the client's IP address, leading the server to reply to their requests instead of the legitimate client's. To impede the client's service, the attacker adjusts the response packet to employ exceptionally small block sizes. As a consequence, the server is compelled to deliver an increased volume of response packets to the client. Figure 1 shows how the DoS attack is carried out in the CoAP environment.

All traffic is meticulously captured with the intent of procuring a pcap file, which is subsequently employed to analyze the frames of the generated traffic and extract universally shared fields among them. These fields encompass system times, relative capture times, and all fields pertinent to the CoAP protocol. The frames are labeled in accordance with their timestamp at the time of capture, signifying whether they correspond to a DoS attack or typical traffic.

The dataset collected for this study contains three types of fields: frame level fields, CoAP protocol fields, and a particular "type" field used to identify frames under DoS attack. The frame level fields allow for easy pattern recognition in the generated data. The CoAP protocol fields provide information specific to the frames using this protocol and can be found in the CoAP section of the Wireshark Display Filter Reference. The "type" field is used to indicate the type of attack and frames under DoS attack are labeled with the "DoS" tag. The dataset is stored in a CSV file and contains a total of 30,319 frames, with 21,269 frames representing normal traffic and 9,050 frames representing traffic under attack.

3   One-Class Reconstruction Methods

This section describes the different reconstruction methods applied to the training set to develop anomaly detection. It is important to emphasize that only information about normal operations is registered.

3.1   Autoencoders

Autoencoder is a type of supervised neural network that is based on the dimensional reduction or compression of information, which is later decompressed to recreate the original input data so that the final representation is as close as possible to the original one. Figure 2 shows the architecture of an autoencoder network that presents two stages:

- Coding stage: it is made up of the input layer, in which the data is entered; one or more hidden layers of dimensional reduction and a last bottleneck layer, in which there is a compressed representation of the original data.
- Decoding stage: from the bottleneck layer, the information is decompressed by passing it through one or more hidden layers to be displayed in the output layer with the same dimension as at the network's input.

The hidden bottleneck layer contains a number of hidden h_{auto} neurons [28,31]. Once the network is trained, it is assumed that test instances that do not belong to the target set will present a great reconstruction error. It is calculated through Eq. 1, where $f_{auto}(p; w)$ represents the reconstructed output of the network.

$$e(p) = \parallel f_{auto}(p; w) - p \parallel^2 \qquad (1)$$

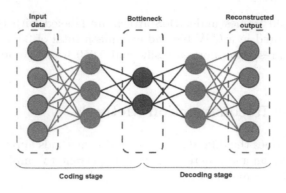

Fig. 2. Autoencoder topology

3.2 K-Means

The K-Means is an unsupervised algorithm commonly used for machine learning problems [27,28]. This clustering algorithm is based on the distances between objects to determine their memberships. It assumes that the data is grouped into *clusters* that must be selected by the user, and that they can be characterized by a series of θ_k prototype objects located after minimizing the function in Eq. 2. These prototypes create a partition of the entire feature space.

$$\varepsilon_{K-means} = \sum_i \left(\min_k \| x_i - \theta_k \|^2 \right) \tag{2}$$

The use of K-Means for one-class purposes lies in the calculation of the reconstruction error. Once the different centroids are determined, a test instance p reconstruction error is the minimum Euclidean distance from the object to its closest prototype, as shown in Eq. 3.

$$e(p) = \min_k \| p - \theta_k \|^2 \tag{3}$$

An example of K-Means application in a two-dimensional dataset is shown in Fig. 3. The target set is separated into two clusters. The test point p_1 is considered anomalous since the distance to its nearest centroid (blue cross) is greater than all maximum distances of blue points to that centroid. On the contrary, p_2 belongs to the target set because it is closer to the green cross than many green points.

3.3 Principal Component Analysis

Principal Component Analysis (PCA) is a statistical method commonly applied to analyze multivariate data. Its use extends to many branches as a tool for dimensional reduction, clustering, and classification problems to anomaly detection. PCA focuses on finding the relationship between data by obtaining the

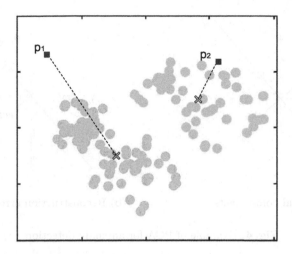

Fig. 3. Clasificador K-Means vs K-Centers (Color figure online)

orthonormal subspace that reflects the greatest variation between the different variables [1, 26, 28]. Then, the eigenvectors of the covariance matrix of the training data are calculated, whose eigenvalues are maximum, to later build a base $\mathcal{W}$ of the generated subspace with them, onto which the data will be projected. From a test object p, the reconstruction error will be calculated to check if it belongs to the target data set. To do this, its projection in the subspace will be calculated first (see Eq. 4). The reconstruction error is calculated as the difference between the original and projected points, as shown in Eq. 5.

$$p_p = \mathcal{W}(\mathcal{W}^T\mathcal{W})^{-1}\mathcal{W}^T z \qquad (4)$$

$$e(p) = \| p - p_p \|^2 \qquad (5)$$

By default, the k eigenvectors with the largest eigenvalues are commonly used, although there it is possible to use eigenvectors with the smallest eigenvalues. Figure 4(a) shows an example of how two principal components are represented in two dimensions. In this case, PC1 corresponds to a greater eigenvalue. To check whether a test point p (red square) belongs to the target class, the square of the distance d from that point to its projection on the principal component p_p (purple square), as shown in Fig. 4(b). The point belongs to the target set if this value is below the limit established during the training stage. Otherwise, it will be considered as non-target [12, 14].

4   Experiments

The dataset is divided into two general groups, normal operation and Denial of Service situations. Considering that the training stage is based on data from nor-

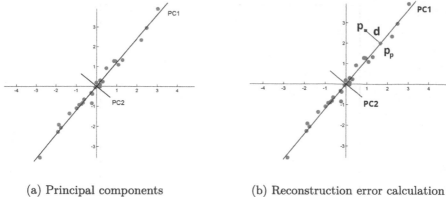

(a) Principal components   (b) Reconstruction error calculation

Fig. 4. Example of PCA for anomaly detection

mal operations, a k-fold iteration is followed to validate the classifiers. Figure 5 shows an example with three folds, where the green sets are used to learn the target class patterns, and the gray and yellow sets represent the normal and DoS operation, respectively. These last two sets determine the performance of the classifier for each technique and configuration during the classifier test.

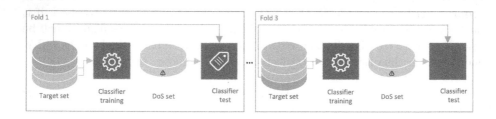

Fig. 5. Example of k-fold with $k = 3$

The well-known Area Under the Receiving Operating Characteristics Curve (AUC) measurement is used to assess each classifier configuration's performance. The true positive and false positive rates are combined to provide the AUC, which provides an interesting idea of the classifier performance. From a statistical perspective, this number represents the possibility that a random positive event will be classified as positive [7]. Furthermore, AUC presents the advantage of not being sensitive to class distribution, particularly in one-class tasks, when compared to other measures like sensitivity, precision, or recall [3]. The times needed to train the classifier and to label a new test sample are also registered as a measure of the classifier goodness.

Furthermore, to seek the best classifier performance, the algorithms were trained with raw data, with a 0 to 1 normalization and with a Z-Score normalization. Besides these three different configurations, several hyperparameters were swept for each technique.

Autoencoders: The number of neurons in the hidden layer was tested from 1 to 11, that is the number minimum dimensional reduction of the coding stage. Furthermore, the threshold is tested considering different anomalies percentage in the target set: 0%, 5%, 10%, 15%.

K-Means: The number of clusters in which the data is grouped was tested from 1 to 15. Furthermore, the threshold is tested considering different anomalies percentage in the target set: 0%, 5%, 10%, 15%.

PCA: The components tested from 1 to 11 are the number of features minus one. Furthermore, the threshold is tested considering different anomalies percentage in the target set: 0%, 5%, 10%, 15%.

5 Results

Table 1 summarizes the results achieved by Autoencoders classifiers. It is important to remark that the training times are greater than the ones obtained with K-Means and PCA. This fact is especially significant when the dataset is not preprocessed. However, the raw data leads to the best Autoencoder results, with 8 neurons in the hidden layer and considering outliers 15% of the training data.

Table 1. Results achieved by Autoencoders classifiers

Normalization	Hidden size	Outlier (%)	AUC (%)	train (s)	label (μs)
Raw	8	15	80.4	246.5	5.3
0 to 1	9	10	68.5	29.9	4.7
Zscore	5	0	76.0	17.5	3.6

The greatest AUC values correspond to a K-Means classifier with 13 clusters, with an AUC of 82.72% (Table 2). Significant differences are also noticeable in terms of training times between classifiers. They are derived from the number of clusters; a greater number of clusters results in a slower training process.

Finally, PCA results are shown in Table 3, with Zscore normalization, seven principal components, and 10 (%) of outlier fraction as the best configuration, although it does not overcome K-Means results.

Table 2. Results achieved by K-Means classifiers

Normalization	Clusters	Outlier (%)	AUC (%)	train (ms)	label (μs)
Raw	13	10	82.72	72.15	1.90
0 to 1	11	15	59.97	51.67	1.48
Zscore	5	0	50.01	20.65	1.04

Table 3. Results achieved by PCA classifiers

Normalization	Component	Outlier (%)	AUC (%)	train (ms)	label (μs)
Raw	8	15	67.09	77.57	1.76
0 to 1	8	10	66.42	65.71	1.17
Zscore	7	10	81.03	47.25	1.03

6   Conclusions and Future Works

The significance of security in IoT devices has grown in recent times, making it increasingly important to employ systems for knowing networks behavior in order to help identify and categorize emerging attack methods, particularly in industrial processes and communication protocols such as CoAP. Early detection of these attacks is essential to ensure the resilience of these processes.

In the current study, was employed a DoS CoAP dataset for developing a model based on the training data with the aim of minimizing the reconstruction error. As a result, instances belonging to the non-target class will yield high reconstruction errors, making it easier to detect outliers. Being, the best way the implementation of a K-Means classifier with 13 clusters.

Future research will explore the application of the set of methods studied in this paper to other CoAP datasets, which consist of Man-in-the-Middle and Cross-Protocol family attacks.

Acknowledgments. Álvaro Michelena's research was supported by the Spanish Ministry of Universities (https://www.universidades.gob.es/), under the "Formación de Profesorado Universitario" grant with reference FPU21/00932.

Míriam Timiraos's research was supported by the Xunta de Galicia (Regional Government of Galicia) through grants to industrial Ph.D. (http://gain.xunta.gal), under the Doutoramento Industrial 2022 grant with reference: $04_I N606 D_2 022_2 692965$. CITIC, as a Research Center of the University System of Galicia, is funded by Consellería de Educación, Universidade e Formación Profesional of the Xunta de Galicia through the European Regional Development Fund (ERDF) and the Secretaría Xeral de Universidades (Ref. ED431G 2019/01).

References

1. Basurto, N., Arroyo, A., Cambra, C., Herrero, A.: A hybrid machine learning system to impute and classify a component-based robot. Log. J. IGPL **31**(2), 338–351 (2022). https://doi.org/10.1093/jigpal/jzac023
2. Bormann, C., Castellani, A.P., Shelby, Z.: CoAP: an application protocol for billions of tiny internet nodes. IEEE Internet Comput. **16**(2), 62–67 (2012)
3. Bradley, A.P.: The use of the area under the roc curve in the evaluation of machine learning algorithms. Pattern Recogn. **30**(7), 1145–1159 (1997)
4. López, V., et al.: Intelligent model for power cells state of charge forecasting in EV. Processes **10**(7), 1406 (2022)
5. Correia, N., Sacramento, D., Schutz, G.: Dynamic aggregation and scheduling in CoAP/observe-based wireless sensor networks. IEEE Internet Things J. **3**, 923–936 (2016)
6. Crespo Turrado, C., Sánchez Lasheras, F., Calvo-Rollé, J.L., Piñón-Pazos, A.J., de Cos Juez, F.J.: A new missing data imputation algorithm applied to electrical data loggers. Sensors **15**(12), 31069–31082 (2015)
7. Fawcett, T.: An introduction to roc analysis. Pattern Recogn. Lett. **27**(8), 861–874 (2006)
8. Fernandes, B., Silva, F., Alaiz-Moreton, H., Novais, P., Neves, J., Analide, C.: Long short-term memory networks for traffic flow forecasting: exploring input variables, time frames and multi-step approaches. Informatica **31**(4), 723–749 (2020)
9. Fernandez-Serantes, L., Casteleiro-Roca, J., Calvo-Rolle, J.: Hybrid intelligent system for a half-bridge converter control and soft switching ensurement. Rev. Iberoamericana Autom. Inform. Industr. (2022)
10. Gonzalez-Cava, J.M., et al.: Machine learning techniques for computer-based decision systems in the operating theatre: application to analgesia delivery. Log. J. IGPL **29**(2), 236–250 (2020). https://doi.org/10.1093/jigpal/jzaa049
11. Granjal, J., Silva, J.M., Lourenço, N.: Intrusion detection and prevention in CoAP wireless sensor networks using anomaly detection. Sensors **18**(8) (2018). https://www.mdpi.com/1424-8220/18/8/2445
12. Jove, E., et al.: Comparative study of one-class based anomaly detection techniques for a bicomponent mixing machine monitoring. Cybern. Syst. **51**(7), 649–667 (2020)
13. Jove, E., Casteleiro-Roca, J.L., Quintián, H., Zayas-Gato, F., Vercelli, G., Calvo-Rolle, J.L.: A one-class classifier based on a hybrid topology to detect faults in power cells. Log. J. IGPL **30**(4), 679–694 (2021). https://doi.org/10.1093/jigpal/jzab011
14. Jove, E., et al.: Hybrid intelligent model to predict the remifentanil infusion rate in patients under general anesthesia. Log. J. IGPL **29**(2), 193–206 (2021)
15. Khan, S.S., Madden, M.G.: One-class classification: taxonomy of study and review of techniques. Knowl. Eng. Rev. **29**(3), 345–374 (2014)
16. Kovatsch, M.: Github - mkovatsc/Copper4Cr: Copper (Cu) CoAP user-agent for chrome (javascript implementation) (2022). https://github.com/mkovatsc/Copper4Cr
17. Mali, A., Nimkar, A.: Security schemes for constrained application protocol in IoT: a precise survey. In: Thampi, S.M., Martínez Pérez, G., Westphall, C.B., Hu, J., Fan, C.I., Gómez Mármol, F. (eds.) SSCC 2017. CCIS, vol. 746, pp. 134–145. Springer, Singapore (2017). https://doi.org/10.1007/978-981-10-6898-0_11

18. Mattsson, J.P., Selander, G., Amsüss, C.: Amplification attacks using the constrained application protocol (CoAP). Internet-Draft draft-irtf-t2trg-amplification-attacks-02, Internet Engineering Task Force (2023). https://datatracker.ietf.org/doc/draft-irtf-t2trg-amplification-attacks/02/. Work in Progress

19. lovelesh patel: Commits · automote/esp-coap · github (2021). https://github.com/automote/ESP-CoAP/commits?author=lovelesh

20. Porras, S., Jove, E., Baruque, B., Calvo-Rolle, J.L.: A comparative analysis of intelligent techniques to predict energy generated by a small wind turbine from atmospheric variables. Log. J. IGPL **31**, 648–663 (2022). https://doi.org/10.1093/jigpal/jzac031

21. Quintian Pardo, H., Calvo Rolle, J.L., Fontenla Romero, O.: Application of a low cost commercial robot in tasks of tracking of objects. Dyna **79**(175), 24–33 (2012)

22. Radoglou Grammatikis, P.I., Sarigiannidis, P.G., Moscholios, I.D.: Securing the internet of things: challenges, threats and solutions. Internet Things **5**, 41–70 (2019). https://www.sciencedirect.com/science/article/pii/S2542660518301161

23. Rahman, R.A., Shah, B.: Security analysis of IoT protocols: a focus in CoAP. In: 2016 3rd MEC International Conference on Big Data and Smart City (ICBDSC), pp. 1–7 (2016)

24. Rodríguez, E., et al.: Transfer-learning-based intrusion detection framework in IoT networks. Sensors **22**(15), 5621 (2022). https://dx.doi.org/10.3390/s22155621

25. Shelby, Z., Hartke, K., Bormann, C.: The constrained application protocol (CoAP). RFC 7252 (2014). https://www.rfc-editor.org/info/rfc7252

26. Simić, S., et al.: A three-stage hybrid clustering system for diagnosing children with primary headache disorder. Log. J. IGPL **31**(2), 300–313 (2022). https://doi.org/10.1093/jigpal/jzac020

27. Simić, S., Simić, S.D., Banković, Z., Ivkov-Simić, M., Villar, J.R., Simić, D.: Deep convolutional neural networks on automatic classification for skin tumour images. Logic J. IGPL **30**(4), 649–663 (2021). https://doi.org/10.1093/jigpal/jzab009

28. Tax, D.M.J.: One-class classification: concept-learning in the absence of counter-examples [Ph. D. thesis]. Delft University of Technology (2001)

29. Thomas, D.R., Clayton, R., Beresford, A.R.: 1000 days of UDP amplification DDoS attacks. eCrime researchers Summit, eCrime, pp. 79–84 (2017)

30. Zayas-Gato, F., et al.: Intelligent model for active power prediction of a small wind turbine. Log. J. IGPL **31**, 785–803 (2022). https://doi.org/10.1093/jigpal/jzac040

31. Zayas-Gato, F., et al.: A novel method for anomaly detection using beta Hebbian learning and principal component analysis. Log. J. IGPL **31**(2), 390–399 (2022). https://doi.org/10.1093/jigpal/jzac026

Application of Anomaly Detection Models to Malware Detection in the Presence of Concept Drift

David Escudero García[1]([✉])[iD] and Noemí DeCastro-García[2][iD]

[1] Research Institute of Applied Science in Cybersecurity, Universidad de León,
Campus de Vegazana s/n, 24071 León, Spain
[2] Department of Mathematics, Universidad de León, Campus de Vegazana s/n,
24071 León, Spain
{descg,ncasg}@unileon.es

Abstract. Machine learning is one of the main approaches to malware detection in the literature, since machine learning models are more adaptive than signature based solutions. One of the main challenges in the application of machine learning to malware detection is the presence of concept drift, which is a change in the data distribution over time. To tackle drift, online models that can be dynamically updated passively or by actively detecting change are applied. However, these models require new instances to be labelled to update the model. Usually, labels are scarce, cannot be obtained immediately and the presence of imbalance in the data make the construction of an effective model difficult. It has been studied that concept drift has a lower impact on benign instances, so we test the effectiveness of anomaly detection models to detect malware in the presence of concept drift. Anomaly detection models only need benign instances for training, and therefore may be less affected by the scarcity of labelled malicious instances. The results show that anomaly detection models achieve better results than supervised online models in conditions of heavy data imbalance and label scarcity.

Keywords: Machine learning · Malware detection · Concept drift · Cybersecurity · Anomaly detection

1 Introduction

Malware classification is a problem that has received a lot of attention because of the yearly increase in threats [11]. Antiviruses and other signature based methods provide quick identification of suspicious samples, but they require the sample to have been previously identified, which limits their application to new threats. Therefore, research efforts are directed to address this problem by proposing different strategies of malware identification. One of the most common solutions

Supported by Spanish National Cybersecurity Institute (INCIBE).

proposed in the literature is to apply ML (Machine Learning) techniques. However, some hurdles must be overcome in order to effectively apply ML solutions to the problem of malware detection.

Anomaly detection provides organizations and Security Operations Centers (SOCs) with a mechanism to detect cybersecurity attacks. Since modeling the data systematically, without expert knowledge, is a complex problem, anomaly detection models are used to automatically detect potential events of interest with minimum human intervention. However, implementing ML-based anomaly detectors for malware is a challenge [17].

One of the main problems in malware detection is the change in data distribution of both malware and benign samples. This change in data distribution, known as concept drift, decreases the performance of the models. Different concept drift detection techniques have been applied to create effective machine learning models [5].

In addition, malicious samples are relatively rare compared to benign ones. This imbalance invites framing malware detection as an anomaly detection problem where the goal is to build a model that has learned to characterize behavior considered normal or benign under the no intrusion hypothesis. Then, malicious samples can be detected due to their divergence from normal behaviour.

Malware detection has been framed as an anomaly detection problem or from the point of view of concept drift adaptation, but not many works have taken both approaches into account. Some works use anomaly detection methods to deal with concept drift [5, 20], but they are not focused on malware detection. Therefore, we formulate the problem of malware detection as a novelty detection problem, in which benign samples constitute normal data and malware samples are anomalous, taking into account that concept drift mainly affects malware samples and has a smaller magnitude in benign ones [14]. This may be useful for two reasons. Since drift affects mainly malicious samples, anomaly detection models should be less affected by concept drift and will need fewer labeled instances to be updated. Secondly, data imbalance should have a lower impact. Benign samples will be abundant compared to malicious ones, and anomaly detection models should have less difficulty constructing effective models. Also, we have carried out a comparative study in which several anomaly detection models are involved.

In this work we assess the usefulness of anomaly detection models to detect malware in the presence of concept drift and data imbalance with label scarcity. We will compare the performance of different anomaly detection algorithms and traditional online ML models with different degrees of data imbalance and available labels for model updating. All experiments are carried out using the KronoDroid dataset [13], which spans both benign and malicious apps from 2008 to 2020. Our hypothesis is that anomaly detection models may provide better predictive performance when the degree of imbalance is high and the number of available labels for updating the models is small, which is common in realistic scenarios [11].

2   Related Work

First, we provide a brief description of concept drift and then we introduce other works that deal with concept drift in malware detection.

2.1   Concept Drift

One of the main assumptions in the field of machine learning is that the model operates over a stationary data distribution, that is, the distribution of the data does not change over time. This is an unrealistic assumption not only in the field of malware detection [11], but in others such network attack detection [28]. New malware families may appear with new ways of exploiting system vulnerabilities [30]. Malware authors also implement evasion techniques [9] in order to make detection more difficult. The result is that the samples modify both their dynamic and static features. These changes in data distribution over time are know as concept drift [22] and compromise the predictive performance of the models, because the knowledge they acquired from training on past samples may not generalize well to new samples.

Concept drift is a change in the distribution of data over time [22]. A machine learning model seeks to assign a label $y_i \in Y$ to an observation $x_i \in \mathcal{R}^d$ that contains a numerical representation of certain features of interest to the problem. For example, in malware detection, the vectors x_i can contain information such as API calls of the sample and each instance will be assigned a label in $\{malicious, not\ malicious\}$. Following the nomenclature proposed in [10], a concept is a joint distribution $Concept = P(X,Y) = P(Y \mid X)P(X)$ over the set of features of the data and the space of labels.

$P_t(X)$ denotes the marginal distribution of the data at an instant of time t, and by $P_t(Y \mid X)$ the conditional distribution of the data at that same instant. Concept drift appears when at a later instant u any of the two previous distributions changes: $P_t(y \mid X) \neq P_u(y \mid X)$ and/or $P_t(X) \neq P_u(X)$ [10].

In machine learning problems it is common to assume that the concept is the same at any pair of time instants t and u: $P_t(X,Y) = P_u(X,Y)$. If this condition is not met, and it is not commonly met in real problems [22], the performance of the models will tend to decrease over time. In general, concept drift is divided into real when $P_t(Y \mid X) \neq P_u(Y \mid X)$ and virtual in the case that $P_t(X) \neq P_u(X)$ [22]. The distinction is made because it is understood that a change in the marginal distribution of the data, although it implies a change in the concept, does not necessarily affect the predictive performance of the model, as illustrated in Fig. 1.

The goal of concept drift detection and adaptation techniques is to limit the impact of distribution changes through different mechanisms.

2.2   Concept Drift in Malware Detection

Several works apply different techniques to adapt models to concept drift. Drift adaptation techniques focus on keeping the model updated to the current data

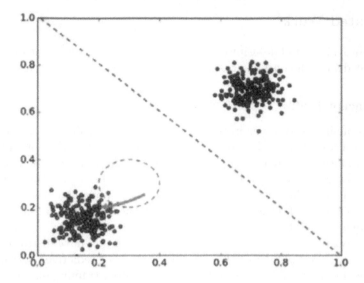

Fig. 1. Change in the marginal distribution of the data. The dashed green line represents the decision frontier of a model. (Color figure online)

distribution. Some works use ensemble techniques that substitute outdated models with new data [14]. In other works a single model is updated when a drift detection algorithm signals change in the data [4]. To keep the model updated, it is necessary to have access to labels in the new data. Several works make use of a prequential evaluation scheme [10], in which the label of an instance is immediately made available after the model makes a prediction. Nevertheless, manual labeling of new samples is a costly and time-consuming process that requires expert knowledge to be effective. Consequently, there probably will be only a limited amount of labeled new data to retrain or update the model, which may be insufficient to make effective predictions. In addition labels will probably be available only after a certain amount of time has passed. Finally, data in malware detection applications is usually unbalanced [11], with a limited amount of malicious samples. This imbalance is particularly disadvantageous in models which are updated online, since it may lead to underweighting minority classes [19].

Some works follow a passive strategy of adaptation, in which the occurence of drift is not explicitly detected. Instead, the model is updated with new instances. In [14] the method works in batches: processing a certain number of instances at once instead of one by one. In this case, there is no explicit drift detection: an ensemble of models is maintained and for each new batch, the model with the worst performance is replaced. This keeps the ensemble constantly up to date. This scheme improves the accuracy rate by an average of 0.3 compared to a static model trained on the first batch of data.

Another approach is the use of dynamic models (such as those proposed in [12,16]) combined with some drift detection algorithm proposed in the literature. This is the case of [4,8]. The drift detection algorithms used in these works monitor the evolution of the prediction error, so it is necessary that all instances have labels. In [8] dynamic models are updated (but not retrained from scratch) with the received instances while the drift detection algorithm signals an alarm. If there are no alarms, it is understood that the classifier is adjusted to the current distribution and it is not necessary to update. In [4] the strategy is different: the models are constantly updated. When the drift detection algorithms signal an alarm, instances are accumulated, which are used to retrain the models. This work includes a comparison with other strategies without drift detection. In this case, the f1-score improves by 0.15 by including drift detection with online models.

A limitation in these works is that they assume the availability of labels in new instances, following the prequential model of evaluation, which is unlikely to happen in many cases.

The work in [18] stands out because it proposes a model that does not require labels to be updated. The ensemble consists of a fixed number of linear models. Concept drift detection of the models is carried out by a reserved set of representative instances. If the confidence of the model in the predictions of the representative samples is far enough from the confidence in the prediction of the current instance, then the model is marked as aged: it is not taken into account in the ensemble to predict and is updated with each new instance, using the ensemble prediction as a pseudo-label. This mechanism improves the accuracy rate by 0.1 compared to a traditional online model. The main advantage of this model is that does not need labels, it can be applied to environments with label scarcity. The main problem is that there is no mechanism to determine the reliability of the pseudo-labels. This is analyzed and in certain cases the accuracy rate can be worse than that of a static model: in some cases it shows a decreasing trend when new instances are processed due to accumulation of errors. If the pseudo-label assignment is unfavourable, the effectiveness of the model is compromised and the presence of imbalance in the data may contribute to a decrease in pseudo-label quality.

The approach in this work is based on the application of anomaly detection models, using a passive adaptation strategy: drift is not explicitly detected and the anomaly detection models are kept updated through available labels.

3   Materials and Methods

The goal of this work is to determine whether anomaly detection models can provide competitive performance compared to supervised learning models in situations of data imbalance and label scarcity in an online setting.

In this section, we describe the dataset used in the experiments, the applied models and evaluation protocol.

3.1 Dataset

We use the KronoDroid dataset [13], which contains malicious and benign Android applications obtained from other datasets and public repositories. We have selected it because it contains dated samples from a wide interval of time: from 2008 to 2020. In addition, it contains 240 different malware families. Therefore, it provides a reasonably good approximation of a real sample of apps. Since the apps are dated it is easy to simulate a data stream by processing samples ordered by date. The collected apps are dynamically and statically analyzed using both an emulator and a real device. For this work we use the real device dataset that contains a total of 78137 samples, 41382 malware and 36755 benign.

The dataset contains 489 features both obtained from dynamic (frequency of API calls) and static analysis (permissions and intents). These two feature sets are commonly used in the literature of Android malware [21]. For simplicity, we will discard list-like features such as the list of intent filters and services defined by the application. We also discard non-informative features such as the SHA-256 of the sample or its associated timestamps. We will make use of a total of 477 of features, summarized in Table 1.

Table 1. Summary of features in the KronoDroid dataset

Description	Count
Frequency of system calls during execution	288
Binary feature that indicates whether a standard permission was requested	166
Number of activities, actions, services declared in intent filters	7
Compressed and uncompressed filesize	2
Total number of files	1
Number of normal, dangerous, signature, custom and standard permissions requested	5
Total number of services, activities, intent filters, and others	8

To date the apps, the dataset includes 4 different timestamps for each app: earliest modification, last modification, first seen on VirusTotal and first seen in the wild. According to the authors [13], the date of last modification is preferred, so we will use it to order the samples. As a preprocessing step, we remove all samples whose last modification date is inconsistent, that is, outside of the time interval of the dataset. For example, some samples have their date set as 1980 or 2032, which are clearly erroneous. This leaves a total of 76720 samples, 40936 malicious and 35784 benign.

3.2 Models

We have tried to select commonly used algorithms for both supervised learning and anomaly detection. Since we use the Python language, we make use of existing libraries. From River [25] we obtain all the supervised learning models used in the experiments: Adaptive Hoeffding Tree (AHT) [2], Extremely Fast Decision Tree (EFDT) [23], Logistic Regression (LR) [7] and Adaptive Random Forest (ARF) [12]. We also use two online anomaly detection algorithms: Half-Space Trees (HST) [29] and One-Class SVM (OSVM) [27]. We apply a grid search to tune the hyperparameters of all models. In Table 2 we list the models and search spaces for their hyperparameters. All other parameters are left at the default values used by each library. We report the results of the best hyperparameter configuration.

Table 2. Models and their hyperparameters

Model	Hyperparameter	Search space
AHT	split criterion	$[gini, hellinger, information\ gain]$
	max depth	$[8, 10, 12, 14]$
EFDT	split criterion	$[gini, hellinger, information\ gain]$
	max depth	$[8, 10, 12, 14]$
ARF	split criterion	$[gini, hellinger, information\ gain]$
	number of models	$[10, 25, 50, 100]$
	max depth	$[8, 10, 12, 14]$
LR	l2 regularization	$[0, 0.001, 0.025, 0.05, 0.1, 0.125]$
HST	number of trees	$[10, 25, 50, 100, 150, 250, 500]$
	max tree height	$[8, 10, 12, 14]$
	window size	$[5000, 6000, 7000, 8000]$
OSVM	nu	$[0.5, 0.4, 0.3, 0.2, 0.1, 0.05, 0.04, 0.03, 0.02, 0.01]$

3.3 Experimental Protocol

In the experiments, different proportions of malicious samples and available labels for model updating are tested. To set the proportion of malicious samples, we apply a random downsample to adjust their number. The number of instances of the dataset is reduced as a side effect. The proportion of available labels for model updating is also controlled with a random sample that determines which instances will have a label available. For fairness, the sample will be the same for all models. Finally, to simulate that instance labels may not be immediately available we introduce a delay of 2000 instances before they are used to update the models.

The process is as follows:

- First, we use the corresponding downsampled dataset according to the selected malware proportion.
- The first 10% of instances, sorted by date as mentioned in Sect. 3.1 is assumed to be fully labelled and used to train the models. This corresponds roughly to applications in the interval from 2008 to 2010.

– The model makes predictions on instances one by one and updates itself with each instance after the set delay if its label is available.

This process is repeated for each model, proportion of malware and labels.

The area under ROC curve(AUC) is a common metric to measure the effectiveness of anomaly detection models. ROC curves plot the recall $\frac{TP}{TP+FN}$ against the false positive rate $\frac{FP}{FP+TN}$ using different thresholds on the prediction score. TP corresponds to true positives, FP to false positives, TN to true negatives and FN to false negatives. We consider "malicious" to be the positive class. Although AUC has been shown to be consistent with other evaluation metrics such as Matthews correlation coefficient [24] in both balanced and unbalanced datasets [15], it may provide skewed evaluations when imbalance is present [6]. In fact, in our experiments, HST achieves an AUC of 0.95 with a malware proportion of 0.05 and a proportion of labels of 0.1. This is an overly optimistic view of the model's performance. This is why we use the average precision score (APS), which is related to precision-recall curves [3]. The precision-recall curves measure precision $\frac{TP}{TP+FP}$ against recall and can be more informative in the data is imbalanced [6]. We use the scikit-learn [26] implementation, which defines APS as $APS = \sum_n (R_n - R_{n-1})P_n$ where P_n and R_n are the values of precision and recall at the nth threshold.

4   Results and Discussion

The performance of tested models with different proportions of malware and availability of labels are shown in Table 3.

There are clear differences in the performance of the anomaly detection models. OSVM performs consistently worse that any other of the tested models and shows a decreasing trend in its performance when adding more labels to update the model with. In particular, its performance is more than 50% worse than other models with a malware proportion of 0.05. The one-class SVM is known to be sensitive to outliers [1], so fluctuations in data distribution probably compromise its effectiveness in an online learning setting.

On the other hand, HST achieves the best results amongst all models when the data is imbalanced and few labels are available. It has an improvement of 16% and 9% for a malware proportion of 0.05 and label proportion of 0.1 and 0.25 respectively and of 18% and 9% for a malware proportion of 0.1 with label proportions of 0.1 and 0.25. When the number of labelled instances increases HST is outperformed by other supervised models. In addition, when the degree of imbalance is lower, supervised models obtain better results regardless of the proportion of labelled instances. With a malware proportion of 0.534 HST is outperformed by most models for any proportion of labels greater than 0.1.

HST, like OSVM, also suffers from a reduction in performance when more labels become available to update the models, particularly when imbalance is greater: when the proportion of malicious instances is 0.05 the reduction in APS is of 0.1 when going from a proportion of labelled instances of 0.1 to fully labelled.

Table 3. APS of models with different proportions of malware and available labels. The best result in each row is bolded.

malware proportion	label proportion	ARF	EFDT	HST	AHT	LR	OSVM
0.05	0.1	0.363	0.336	**0.566**	0.259	0.487	0.175
	0.25	0.421	0.336	**0.534**	0.442	0.49	0.239
	0.5	0.468	0.367	0.483	0.322	**0.516**	0.129
	0.75	0.446	0.389	0.454	**0.477**	0.419	0.116
	1	0.457	0.405	0.466	0.282	**0.507**	0.124
0.1	0.1	0.543	0.558	**0.731**	0.603	0.619	0.275
	0.25	0.576	0.560	**0.664**	0.607	0.610	0.228
	0.5	0.600	0.617	0.641	**0.643**	0.603	0.278
	0.75	**0.638**	0.566	0.632	0.540	0.632	0.242
	1	0.644	0.551	**0.684**	0.552	0.683	0.183
0.25	0.1	0.865	0.686	**0.892**	0.750	0.891	0.402
	0.25	**0.883**	0.820	0.812	0.781	0.872	0.472
	0.5	0.872	0.767	0.819	0.733	**0.879**	0.442
	0.75	0.879	0.794	0.809	0.792	**0.884**	0.371
	1	0.882	0.802	0.817	0.774	**0.885**	0.321
0.534	0.1	**0.974**	0.914	0.932	0.892	0.966	0.722
	0.25	**0.978**	0.940	0.927	0.937	0.966	0.754
	0.5	**0.984**	0.941	0.918	0.921	0.968	0.661
(Unmodified)	0.75	**0.978**	0.946	0.929	0.931	0.967	0.696
	1	**0.974**	0.945	0.919	0.936	0.970	0.611

This is mostly caused by an increase in false positives: the shift in distribution in benign instances causes the anomaly scores assigned to benign instances to increase and malicious instances become less distinguishable. A lower amount of labelled instances reduce the impact of this shift since the model is less updated. HST and OSVM are unsupervised models, so they cannot directly make use of malicious instances to update the model like LR through gradient descent or ARF, EFDT and AHT, through drift detection and modification of their tree structures. Therefore, some kind of mechanism to better update the models could be useful.

To further analyze the performance of HST in favourable settings, in Tables 4 and 5 we present the confusion matrices of HST and LR with a malware proportion of 0.05 and label proportion of 0.1. These are the two best models for this settings and illustrate some differences in performance between the anomaly detection models and supervised models. The main difference is the amount of false positives and false negatives. HST has a lower false negative rate than LR (0.316 and 0.485 respectively) and LR a lower false positive rate than HST (0.013

Table 4. Confusion matrix of HST with malware proportion of 0.05 and label proportion of 0.1. In parenthesis the percentage of instances per row.

True label	Predicted label		Total
	Benign	Malicious	
Benign	30948 (96.54%)	1111 (3.46%)	32059
Malicious	582 (31.60%)	1260 (68.40%)	1842

Table 5. Confusion matrix of LR with malware proportion of 0.05 and label proportion of 0.1. In parenthesis the percentage of instances per row.

True label	Predicted label		Total
	Benign	Malicious	
Benign	31651 (98.72%)	408 (1.28%)	32059
Malicious	894 (48.53%)	948 (51.47%)	1842

and 0.035 respectively). Although there are some differences, these trends hold for other cases in which HST performs better than supervised models: high imbalance and scarce labels. Whether the increased false positive rate in exchange for lower false negatives of HST is appropriate will depend on the application.

5   Conclusion

In this work, we have carried out an evaluation of anomaly detection models applied to the problem of malware detection in the presence of concept drift in a publicly available dataset of Android apps. The results show that in situations of heavy imbalance (less than 10% percent of malicious instances) and with low label availability in new instances (lower than 25%), some anomaly detection models such as Half-Space Trees can outperform other supervised online learning models such as Adaptive Random Forest or Logistic Regression with improvements of 10% in the average precision score. Therefore in scenarios with data imbalance and scarce labels, which tend to be more common in real applications, anomaly detection models may prove effective.

However, when more labels are available or the data is reasonably balanced, supervised models are more effective, since anomaly detection models tend to be unsupervised and benefit less from additional labelled instances, since they make no use of malicious instances for updating.

These results however, are obtained in a single dataset, so as future work we intend to include different, related malware datasets in the study to verify whether anomaly detection models may be effective in different drift settings. In addition, studying different strategies to make use of labelled malicious instances to update anomaly detection models could prove effective to improve their performance in settings with abundant labels or less data imbalance.

References

1. Amer, M., Goldstein, M., Abdennadher, S.: Enhancing one-class support vector machines for unsupervised anomaly detection. In: Proceedings of the ACM SIGKDD Workshop on Outlier Detection and Description, pp. 8–15 (2013)
2. Bifet, A., Gavaldà, R.: Adaptive learning from evolving data streams. In: Adams, N.M., Robardet, C., Siebes, A., Boulicaut, J.-F. (eds.) IDA 2009. LNCS, vol. 5772, pp. 249–260. Springer, Heidelberg (2009). https://doi.org/10.1007/978-3-642-03915-7_22
3. Buckland, M., Gey, F.: The relationship between recall and precision. J. Am. Soc. Inf. Sci. 45(1), 12–19 (1994)
4. Ceschin, F., Botacin, M., Gomes, H.M., Pinagé, F., Oliveira, L.S., Grégio, A.: Fast & furious: on the modelling of malware detection as an evolving data stream. Expert Syst. Appl. 212, 118590 (2023). https://doi.org/10.1016/j.eswa.2022.118590
5. Choras, M., Wozniak, M.: Concept Drift Analysis for Improving Anomaly Detection Systems in Cybersecurity, pp. 35–42 (2017). https://doi.org/10.18690/978-961-286-114-8.3
6. Cook, J., Ramadas, V.: When to consult precision-recall curves. Stand. Genomic Sci. 20(1), 131–148 (2020)
7. Cox, D.R.: The regression analysis of binary sequences. J. R. Stat. Soc. Ser. B (Methodol.) 20(2), 215–242 (1958)
8. Darem, A.A., Ghaleb, F.A., Al-Hashmi, A.A., Abawajy, J.H., Alanazi, S.M., Al-Rezami, A.Y.: An adaptive behavioral-based incremental batch learning malware variants detection model using concept drift detection and sequential deep learning. IEEE Access 9, 97180–97196 (2021). https://doi.org/10.1109/ACCESS.2021.3093366
9. Galloro, N., Polino, M., Carminati, M., Continella, A., Zanero, S.: A systematical and longitudinal study of evasive behaviors in windows malware. Comput. Secur. 113, 102550 (2022). https://doi.org/10.1016/j.cose.2021.102550
10. Gama, J., Žliobaite, I., Bifet, A., Pechenizkiy, M., Bouchachia, A.: A survey on concept drift adaptation. ACM Comput. Surv. 46(4) (2014). https://doi.org/10.1145/2523813
11. Gibert, D., Mateu, C., Planes, J.: The rise of machine learning for detection and classification of malware: research developments, trends and challenges. J. Netw. Comput. Appl. 153 (2020). https://doi.org/10.1016/j.jnca.2019.102526
12. Gomes, H.M., et al.: Adaptive random forests for evolving data stream classification. Mach. Learn. 106, 1469–1495 (2017)
13. Guerra-Manzanares, A., Bahsi, H., Nõmm, S.: KronoDroid: time-based hybrid-featured dataset for effective android malware detection and characterization. Comput. Secur. 110, 102399 (2021). https://doi.org/10.1016/j.cose.2021.102399
14. Guerra-Manzanares, A., Luckner, M., Bahsi, H.: Android malware concept drift using system calls: detection, characterization and challenges. Expert Syst. Appl. 206, 117200 (2022). https://doi.org/10.1016/j.eswa.2022.117200
15. Halimu, C., Kasem, A., Newaz, S.S.: Empirical comparison of area under ROC curve (AUC) and Mathew correlation coefficient (MCC) for evaluating machine learning algorithms on imbalanced datasets for binary classification. In: Proceedings of the 3rd International Conference on Machine Learning and Soft Computing, pp. 1–6 (2019)

16. Hulten, G., Spencer, L., Domingos, P.: Mining time-changing data streams. In: Proceedings of the Seventh ACM SIGKDD International Conference on Knowledge Discovery and Data Mining, KDD 2001, pp. 97–106. Association for Computing Machinery, New York (2001). https://doi.org/10.1145/502512.502529
17. Jordaney, R., et al.: Transcend: detecting concept drift in malware classification models. In: 26th USENIX Security Symposium (USENIX Security 2017), Vancouver, BC, pp. 625–642. USENIX Association (2017)
18. Kan, Z., Pendlebury, F., Pierazzi, F., Cavallaro, L.: Investigating labelless drift adaptation for malware detection. In: Proceedings of the 14th ACM Workshop on Artificial Intelligence and Security, AISec 2021, pp. 123–134. Association for Computing Machinery, New York (2021). https://doi.org/10.1145/3474369.3486873
19. Kegelmeyer, W.P., Chiang, K., Ingram, J.: Streaming malware classification in the presence of concept drift and class imbalance. In: Proceedings of 12th International Conference on Machine Learning and Applications, vol. 2, pp. 48–53 (2013). https://doi.org/10.1109/ICMLA.2013.104
20. Kermenov, R., Nabissi, G., Longhi, S., Bonci, A.: Anomaly detection and concept drift adaptation for dynamic systems: a general method with practical implementation using an industrial collaborative robot. Sensors **23**(6) (2023). https://doi.org/10.3390/s23063260
21. Liu, K., Xu, S., Xu, G., Zhang, M., Sun, D., Liu, H.: A review of android malware detection approaches based on machine learning. IEEE Access **8**, 124579–124607 (2020). https://doi.org/10.1109/ACCESS.2020.3006143
22. Lu, J., Liu, A., Dong, F., Gu, F., Gama, J., Zhang, G.: Learning under concept drift: a review. IEEE Trans. Knowl. Data Eng. **31**(12), 2346–2363 (2019). https://doi.org/10.1109/TKDE.2018.2876857
23. Manapragada, C., Webb, G.I., Salehi, M.: Extremely fast decision tree. In: Proceedings of the 24th ACM SIGKDD International Conference on Knowledge Discovery & Data Mining, KDD 2018, pp. 1953–1962. Association for Computing Machinery, New York (2018). https://doi.org/10.1145/3219819.3220005
24. Matthews, B.: Comparison of the predicted and observed secondary structure of T4 phage lysozyme. Biochimica et Biophys. Acta (BBA) - Protein Struct. **405**(2), 442–451 (1975). https://doi.org/10.1016/0005-2795(75)90109-9
25. Montiel, J., et al.: River: machine learning for streaming data in Python (2021)
26. Pedregosa, F., et al.: Scikit-learn: machine learning in Python. J. Mach. Learn. Res. **12**, 2825–2830 (2011)
27. Schölkopf, B., Platt, J.C., Shawe-Taylor, J.C., Smola, A.J., Williamson, R.C.: Estimating the support of a high-dimensional distribution. Neural Comput. **13**(7), 1443–1471 (2001). https://doi.org/10.1162/089976601750264965
28. Shahraki, A., Abbasi, M., Taherkordi, A., Jurcut, A.D.: A comparative study on online machine learning techniques for network traffic streams analysis. Comput. Netw. **207**, 108836 (2022). https://doi.org/10.1016/j.comnet.2022.108836
29. Tan, S.C., Ting, K.M., Liu, T.F.: Fast anomaly detection for streaming data. In: Proceedings of the Twenty-Second International Joint Conference on Artificial Intelligence, IJCAI 2011, vol. 2, pp. 1511–15160. AAAI Press (2011)
30. Yang, L., et al.: CADE: detecting and explaining concept drift samples for security applications. In: 30th USENIX Security Symposium (USENIX Security 2021), pp. 2327–2344. USENIX Association (2021)

Identification of Anomalies in Urban Sound Data with Autoencoders

Laura Melgar-García[1(✉)], Maryam Hosseini[2], and Alicia Troncoso[1]

[1] Data Science & Big Data Lab, Pablo de Olavide University, 41013 Seville, Spain
{lmelgar,atrolor}@upo.es
[2] Massachusetts Institute of Technology, Massachusetts, USA
maryamh@mit.edu

Abstract. The growing population in the metropolises is influencing the need to plan cities to be safer for people. Several Smart Cities initiatives are being implemented in the cities to achieve this goal. A network of acoustic sensors has been deployed in New York City thanks to the SONYC project. Sounds of the city are being collected and analyzed. In this research work, acoustic signal data are represented with Mel-spectrogram images with mel-scale frequency versus time on a decibel scale. Traditional autoencoders and variational autoencoder models are deployed to detect anomalies in the mel-spectrogram images. The obtained results demonstrate that the variational autoencoder model finds anomalies accurately in the acoustic records.

Keywords: Autoencoders · Anomaly detection · Acoustic sensor network · Urban sound data

1 Introduction

It is expected that 66% of the world's population will live in urban areas by 2030 [5]. This increase in population in the metropolises is causing the concept of Smart Cities to gain more attention in recent years. Numerous studies and research projects focus on improving the management and efficiency of these environments to make them safer for people [25].

The World Health Organization has ranked air pollution and traffic noise as the two most important diseases in Western Europe, respectively [2]. Focusing on noise pollution, it is estimated that nine out of ten New York City citizens are exposed to noise levels above those considered harmful by the EPA Environmental Protection Agency. The SONYC project, or Sounds of New York City [4], focus on analyzing and mitigating urban noise pollution in this city. During the development of the project, a network of acoustic sensors has been deployed. This Smart City initiative works together with machine learning to effectively use sound records to improve citizen's safety and health [4].

Audio machine learning, also known as machine listening, is the specific application of machine learning models to audio or sounds data. It covers different

P. García Bringas et al. (Eds.): HAIS 2023, LNAI 14001, pp. 27–38, 2023.
https://doi.org/10.1007/978-3-031-40725-3_3

fields such as voice recognition, music tagging, music generation or anomaly detection. This last application has mainly focused on machinery to identify problems that may affect automatic industrial machines.

In this research work, anomaly detection is applied to the sounds of New York City with the primary goal of identifying and mitigating noise pollution. The main contributions of this work are: 1) An automatic deep learning model is proposed to determine whether a sound record is an anomaly or not; 2) Each record has an anomaly score; 3) Analysis of the city's anomalies; and 4) Useful methodology for the community of the project [4] that tags the sound records one by one. The rest of the article is organized as follow: Sect. 2 presents the previous studies made in the field of anomaly detection with sounds, Sect. 3 introduces the different machine learning methods used, Sect. 4 focuses on the results after the study of the sounds in the city and Sect. 5 mentions the conclusions and future works.

2　Related Works

The application of machine learning solutions in audio and music signal processing has caught more attention in the last two decades [12]. In [8] convolutional neural networks were used to recognize uncommon speech signals, i.e., tonal signals. Authors in [22] created a new algorithm for audio classification following the segmentation-by-classification model with convolutional neural networks for log-mel spectrograms. Authors in [18] used traditional machine learning models to detect COVID-19 using cough samples. In [1] a prediction of the emotions perceived from sounds was carried out.

Thanks to the development of Smart Cities, sensor networks are being deployed in urban areas. Authors of [7] proposed a system to identify the presence of UAVs unmanned aerial vehicles in complex urban scenarios to improve safety in urban areas using the spectrogram representation of the sounds and convolutional neural networks. A study on air pollutant concentrations and noise levels in the low emissions zones implemented in Madrid was presented in [11]. Authors in [17] studied the data recorded by an acoustic sensor network in Barcelona clustering them to identify different urban acoustic environments.

Anomaly detection in audio data is a very interesting topic. Anomalies were described as patterns in data that do not conform to a well-defined notion of normal behaviour in [6]. Machinery condition monitoring is one of the most common applications in anomaly detection in audio data. Generally, they focus on trying to detect an early machinery failure to trigger an alarm and react early with maintenance [14]. In most cases, this problem follows an unsupervised learning approach because historical machine data refers to normal working data that is used to train the model. Anomalies are identified in the testing process when there are outliers from the normal sounds [23]. Authors in [20] studied statistical, machine learning and deep learning techniques for anomaly detection in an interactive quadruple tank and in a continuous stirred tank reactor system. The best results were achieved with Mahalanobis distance and LSTM-Autoencoder. Authors in [24] used an autoencoder model based on anomaly detection for indoor air quality data. Once their decoder produced an output, a reconstruction loss metric was computed between the obtained output and the original input. In addition, an anomaly score was given to each data point. The model considered a data as an anomaly when its score was higher than a defined threshold.

Anomaly detection has been extensively studied for failure applications in industrial machinery. However, much research remains to be done for its application to urban sounds. In [19] near one hour of traffic sounds of the city of Salerno, Italy, was analyzed. The model used auto-regressive variational autoencoders and interval-valued fuzzy sets to detect anomalies in the data.

3   Methodology

This Section presents the transformations applied to the audio signals used as dataset and the models and methodology used to detect anomalies.

3.1   Audio Data Preprocessing

Audio data is a representation of temporal waveforms that can be described by different physical measures, such as amplitude, over a period of time. In order to extract additional information from the one-dimensional raw data, audio waveforms are transformed into a different domain. This Section explains the preprocessing methodology applied to raw audio data to transform them to the frequency domain and obtain the corresponding mel-spectrograms.

Spectrograms are an alternative way of representing the traditional audio signal in the frequency domain using a Fourier Transformation to decompose the signal into its frequencies, such as the STFT Short Time Fourier Transformation. Specifically, spectrograms are representations of frequency versus time [16].

The transformation of spectrograms into mel-spectrograms is motivated by the fact that humans hear frequencies on a scale of pitches called mel-scale. In addition, humans hear sounds in a logarithmic way rather than linear. This variation of spectrograms leads to a representation of the mel-scale versus time on a decibel-scale. This latter mentioned scale serves the same purpose as the amplitude representation in spectrograms [15]. When acquiring such representations, the same reference value needs to be set for all files and the whole dataset needs to be normalized in the same way. The reference value used for the mel-scale with the decibel scale (*dB_scale*) is zero and the normalization is performed by dividing the data by 255 to work with data in the range 0–1. This ensures that all mel-spectrograms are in the same range and referenced in the same way.

3.2   Deep Learning Models

This Section presents the deep learning models implemented to detect anomalies using the mel-spectrograms obtained after the preprocessing of the audio data.

Deep Autoencoders. An autoencoder is an unsupervised deep learning algorithm consisting of two architecturally symmetric networks, i.e., the encoder and the decoder. The complete network is made up of an input layer, a hidden layer and an output layer. In the encoding phase, the input data is mapped into a reduced feature representation space by the hidden layer, also referred to as latent space. The decoding phase maps the encoder output to the input space using the hidden layer weights. Since the goal of the decoder is to reconstruct the input data, the number of neurons in the input and output layer must be the same [10]. Figure 1 represents graphically its architecture.

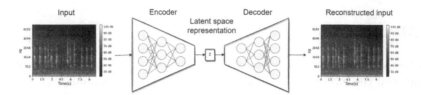

Fig. 1. Traditional deep autoencoder representation

In summary, the general procedure of traditional autoencoders (AE) is to work with a very low dimensional latent space without losing significant information. In other words, their goal is to achieve the maximum compression of the input data in the hidden layer of the network, maintaining the maximum information when encoding but also maintaining the lowest possible error when decoding. An autoencoder can be represented as:

$$H = \sigma_1(W_1 x + b_1) \widehat{x} = \sigma_2(W_2 H + b_2) \tag{1}$$

where variables denoted with 1 refers to the encoder and 2 to the decoder, H are the hidden layer variables, σ_i are the activation functions, W_i are the weighted matrices, b_i are the bias, x refers to the input data and $\widehat{x}$ is the output of the autoencoder. It tries to minimize the loss function to obtain the most accurate reconstruction of the input data x comparing with the final prediction $\widehat{x}$ [3].

Convolutional Autoencoders. Autoencoders based on convolutional layers offer the advantage of preserving spatial relationships, which is very useful when working with two-dimensional patterns such as images. Convolutional autoencoders (CNN AEs) have the same goal as traditional AEs: extracting features to reconstruct the input data with the added advantage of retaining the information between the pixels of the images.

CNN AEs maintain the same architecture as traditional autoencoders and add convolutional layers, with convolutional filters, at the encoder and decoder. They follow the AE's Eq. 1 where W_1 and W_2 are the weight matrices of the convolutional filters for the encoder and decoder, respectively, which enforce local connectivity patterns between neurons of adjacent layers.

Variational Autoencoders. One of the main limitations of traditional autoencoders is the non-regularized latent space. An intuitive idea of this non-regularized space is that similar data is clustered together, however, there is an uneven distribution of data in the latent space. This non-regularization causes the autoencoder to provide erroneous information when a test sample (with different characteristics from the training samples) cannot be represented by any of the points in the existing latent space. Variational autoencoders (VAE) solve this issue of the traditional autoencoders working with a regularized latent space.

Variational autoencoders follow the same two steps as traditional autoencoders: an encoding phase and a decoding phase. The main modifications are applied during the first phase to introduce regularization in the latent space. Input data is not encoded as single points, as in the traditional methodology, but as probability distributions over the latent space for each latent attribute. Distributions are forced to be standard normal distributions, based on the means and standard deviations obtained as output of the encoder. The decoding phase uses the latent vectors and decompresses them in order to obtain the lowest error in its output, i.e., the reconstructed input data.

The loss function in variational autoencoders consists of two components. The first component is the reconstruction loss that must be minimized. The second component is the KL divergence which stands for Kullback Leibler Divergence. This component is not considered in the loss function of traditional autoencoders, since it refers to the regularization of the VAE latent space distribution. The KL divergence measures the difference between two probability distributions. Considering z a latent representation and x the input data, the probabilistic encoder is represented as $p(z|x)$ and the probabilistic decoder as $p(x|z)$. Variational autoencoders use the statistical variational inference technique or variational Bayes to infer intractable distributions. This technique is applied in VAEs by ensuring that $q(z|x)$ is similar to $p(z|x)$, represented as: $minKL(q(z|x)||p(z|x))$ with the goal of using q to infer the variables in the latent space. Taking into account these constraints, the loss function is :

$$loss_f = reconstruction\_error + regularizer = L(x, \hat{x}) + \sum_j KL(q_j(z|x)||p(z))$$

(2)

where $L(x, \hat{x})$ is a traditional error metric, in this research work is the mean square error (defined in Sect. 3.3), and the regularizing term focuses on making $q(z|x)$ similar to $p(z)$ which follows a unit Gaussian distribution $p(z) = N(z; 0, I)$. Figure 2 illustrates the general architecture of a VAE model.

3.3   Anomaly Detection Model

In this research work, each deep learning model defined in Sect. 3.2 is trained with its corresponding parameters after a validation phase. Training data for an autoencoder-based model with anomaly detection objectives needs to be made of normal data, considering normal data as non-anomalies and abnormal data as anomalies [9]. In this way, the model is trained with normal data so that it

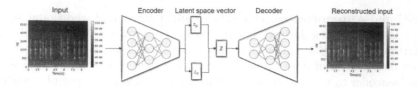

Fig. 2. Traditional variational autoencoder representation

can learn the general ideas from it. Therefore, it can identify different patterns when the data presents some kind of anomaly during the test phase. Both the training and test records need to be preprocessed as defined in Sect. 3.1.

Once the autoencoder-based model is trained, the test phase starts. The model produces the reconstructed mel-spectrogram image of each test record data. These images are denormalized to bring them back to their original range of values before evaluating the error of its reconstruction. The error between the original representation and the reconstructed one is computed. The error metrics used are the mean square error $MSE = \frac{1}{m}\sum_{i=1}^{m}\sum_{r=1}^{rows}\sum_{c=1}^{cols}(y_{r,c}^i - \widehat{y}_{r,c}^i)^2$, the mean absolute error $MAE = \frac{1}{m}\sum_{i=1}^{m}\sum_{r=1}^{rows}\sum_{c=1}^{cols}|y_{r,c}^i - \widehat{y}_{r,c}^i|$ and the mean absolute percentage error $MAPE = \frac{1}{m}\sum_{i=1}^{m}\sum_{r=1}^{rows}\sum_{c=1}^{cols}\left|\frac{y_{r,c}^i - \widehat{y}_{r,c}^i}{y_{r,c}^i}\right| \times 100$, where m is the number of sound images in the set, $rows$ is the number of pixels in the horizontal axis and $cols$ is the number of pixels in the vertical axis. Therefore, $y_{r,c}^i$ refers to the r pixel on the horizontal axis and c on the vertical axis of the $i-th$ image in the set and $\widehat{y}_{r,c}^i$ is the predicted value of the (r, c) pixel of that i image. Each sound file has an associated mean error.

Therefore, the model should provide a low reconstruction error for normal test data and a high reconstruction error for abnormal test data. In this research work, the reconstruction threshold is defined considering the average MSE error metric of the training phase of each model (the motivation for this decision can be found in Sect. 4). If the reconstruction error is greater than the threshold, then, the sound is identified as an anomaly, otherwise the sound is identified as normal. The testing phase is presented in Algorithm 1 where reference is made to the procedures detailed in Sects. 3.1, 3.2 and 3.3.

4   Results

This Section presents the open source dataset used, the process of tuning the parameters for the deep learning models, the results obtained and an analysis of the automatic identification of urban sound anomalies in New York City.

4.1   Dataset Description

The dataset used for this research work is part of the open source data from a network of urban acoustic sensors in New York City, deployed by the SONYC

Algorithm 1: Test phase: detection of anomalies in sound data

---

Result: Sound record identified as anomaly or not

$M \leftarrow$ Autoencoder-based trained model

$E \leftarrow$ Mean Square Error MSE metric

$\alpha \leftarrow$ Reconstruction threshold error

for *each x^i in test_set* **do**

  $mel^i \leftarrow$ mel_spectrogram(x^i, dB_scale, $normalization_{value}$)

  $reconstructed\_mel^i \leftarrow M(mel^i)$

  $reconstructed\_mel^i \leftarrow denormalization(reconstructed\_mel^i)$

  $mse^i \leftarrow E(mel^i, reconstructed\_mel^i)$

  if $error^i \geq \alpha$ **then**

   | x^i is an anomaly sound

  else

   | x^i is a normal sound

  end

end

---

project [4]. The dataset is available online at [21]. There are 18510 audio files of 10-second records. Each record has its longitude and latitude in the city, and the hour, day, week and year associated. All data are labeled by volunteers following a defined taxonomy of 8 different coarse-grained classes (engine, machinery-impact, non-machinery impact, powered-saw, alert signal, music, human voice and dog) that are subdivided at a more specific classification level, resulting in 23 fine-grained classes. For this research, all audio files are preprocessed following the methodology described in Sect. 3.1 to obtain a mel-spectrogram representation for each file with 128×432 pixels, following the specifications of the Python librosa library [13] and the project itself [21].

The whole dataset has a variable in the taxonomy document that associates a split set for each file, i.e., training, validation or test set. This division is maintained for this study, considering that all files labeled as "alert signals" and all its sub-classes (car-horn, car-alarm, siren, reverse-beeper and other unknown alert signal) need to be included in the test set, as mentioned in Sect. 3.3. The final division of the data is 13507 samples for the training set, 4200 for the validation set and 803 for the test set. The test set consists of 534 samples without anomalies and 269 with anomalies.

4.2 Parameter Tuning

The grid search strategy is used to refine the models and obtain the optimal network structure. After the tuning process, the models with the lowest evaluation error and lowest loss are selected. In all three models, the most accurate performances on the validation set are models trained with 64, 32, 16 and 8 filters. The best traditional AE is reached with 0.001 for the learning rate, 32 for the batch size and 6 epochs. The best CNN AE model is obtained with 0.001 for the learning rate, 64 for the batch size and 5 epochs. The most accurate VAE is achieved with the Adam optimizer, 0.0003 for the learning rate, 32 for the batch size and 25 epochs.

4.3 Models Performance

The performance of the models is validated in two phases. The first phase considers the reconstruction errors of the mel-spectrograms representations of the audio clip. The second phase is discussed in Sect. 4.4 and focuses on the understanding of the detected anomalies.

Table 1 includes the MSE, MAE and MAPE error for each selected model after the tuning phase. These metrics represent the average value for the whole training set, i.e., the training and the validation set together, the whole test, i.e., including anomaly and non-anomaly data, and only the instances that were labeled as anomalies by the experts.

Table 1. Results metris

Data	MSE			MAE			MAPE		
	AE	CNN AE	VAE	AE	CNN AE	VAE	AE	CNN AE	VAE
Training	0.99	17.65	19.48	0.86	3.04	3.27	1.48	5.51	5.88
Test	0.77	16.66	17.64	0.78	2.86	3.01	1.45	5.54	5.75
Anomalies	0.96	24.21	27.81	0.83	3.27	3.68	1.46	6.03	6.70

The errors of the whole training and test sets are very close, confirming the accurate performance of the models. In addition, results show a higher error value for all the cases when anomalies are evaluated, leading to the interpretation that the models perform as expected, i.e., models fit and learn the normal data and, therefore, they are able to identify any anomaly pattern.

The average error rate of the traditional autoencoder is significantly lower than that of the convolutional autoencoder and the variational autoencoder. The reason of this huge difference is that the traditional autoencoder over-fits during the training of the data, providing very accurate results but not being able to identify the general characteristics of the sound representations. In other words, the reconstructed images are very accurate but this model cannot learn the general patterns of data, and so, cannot identify anomalies correctly.

The latent space is the main difference between the proposed models. Models using the traditional AE approach encode input data as single points. However, VAE encode input data as distributions that provide a regularized latent space. Figures 3a, 3b and 3c depict the latent space representation of the traditional AE, CNN AE and VAE models, respectively, using the t-SNE t-Distributed Stochastic Neighbor Embedding algorithm. Specifically, this algorithm is computed over a two-dimensional embedded space that is initialized with the PCA algorithm. Figures 3a and 3b illustrate an uneven representation of the latent space that is more likely to provide poor results for test images that are not very similar to the training data. Figure 3c represents the opposite case, i.e., the latent space is regularized and can cover any test image providing better results. This feature can be seen not only in the spatial representation, but also in the ranges of each Figure. Figure 3c covers a wider space, i.e., a larger range, than the traditional AE and CNN AE.

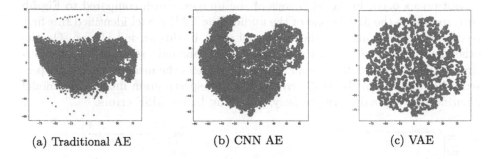

(a) Traditional AE   (b) CNN AE   (c) VAE

Fig. 3. Latent space representation

4.4   Anomalies Identified with Variational Autoencoder

Considering the results of each model and their latent space representation, the variational autoencoder model is selected as the best model to identify anomalies in the data. The errors for this VAE model in Table 1 are larger for the anomalies than for the training and test set. This suggests that the model learns the general patterns of normal data accurately. However, when there are anomalies in the data, the model provides worse results. Although it may be contrary to our general thinking, the main objective of this research is achieved. In other words, the model provides larger errors to anomalies and thus, they can be identified.

In the dataset there are records in which the full 10-seconds are alert signals and there are some of the files with only one millisecond of alert signal, but both of them are categorized as anomalies. To analyze this feature, the standard deviation of the MSE error is computed, since it is the error metric that shows the most difference between the sets. The anomaly set provides a mean MSE of 27.81 and a standard deviation of 82.73. The test set without anomalies provides a mean MSE of 13.24 and a standard deviation of 26.47. This very large difference between the standard deviations values is due to the fact that in the case of anomalies there are pixels in which a large error is achieved. This does not occur in the set without anomalies and therefore the standard deviation of this set is smaller. Figures 4a and 4b illustrate the average MSE of each file as a blue dot and its standard deviation with light blue lines for the anomalous data and non-anomalous data of the test set, respectively. The red dashed line is the selected threshold to identify anomalies that corresponds to the VAE mean MSE of the whole training set (see Table 1). Each test data obtains an anomaly score based on the Z-score parametric measure considering the mean and standard deviation.

Figure 5 depicts the anomaly record with the lowest anomaly score and the anomaly record with the largest anomaly score, showing in both cases the raw time series representation, the mel-spectrogram representation and the corresponding MSE error heat map. Regarding the record with the lowest anomaly score, during its first second a horn is recorded, and so it is correctly labeled as an anomaly. The rest of the audio does not represent any anomaly sound. Its raw representation is in Fig. 5a. The anomaly is correctly identified in Fig. 5c. The largest errors occur in the left pixels of the images, which compared to Fig. 5b corresponds to the first second of the audio. The VAE model identified this first second as an anomaly, i.e., the computed error in this second is high. On the other hand, the audio record with the highest anomaly score is a continuous siren. Figure 5d shows the raw audio, Fig. 5e depicts the mel-spectrogram representation and Fig. 5f the MSE error of the mel-spectrogram image. The model identifies the anomaly very precisely, providing higher MSE errors.

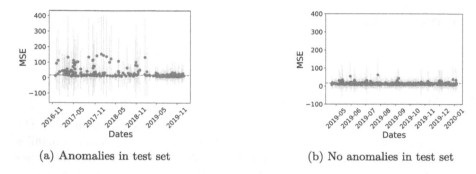

(a) Anomalies in test set   (b) No anomalies in test set

Fig. 4. MSE average and standard deviation for variational autoencoder.

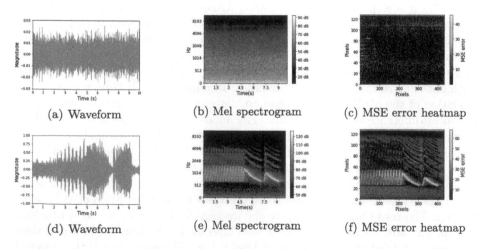

(a) Waveform   (b) Mel spectrogram   (c) MSE error heatmap

(d) Waveform   (e) Mel spectrogram   (f) MSE error heatmap

Fig. 5. Anomaly audio record with less MSE error in Figs. 5a, 5b, 5c and anomaly audio record with larger MSE error in Figs. 5d, 5e, 5f.

5 Conclusions

The analysis of the urban sounds of the city of the New York can provide interesting insights about noise pollution in the city. This research work focuses on the study of urban sound anomalies in order to obtain a neural network model that is able to identify them. Sound records have been transformed from their waveform representation to a mel-spectrogram representation. Three different models based on autoencoders have been implemented for this work. Models based on autoencoders are commonly applied to anomaly identification applications. They have been trained on non-anomalous data so that they could learn the general characteristics of this type of data and identify any anomalous test sample that has different patterns. In this work, the variational autoencoder has been the most accurate model. The anomaly test data has provided very large mean errors, and especially very large standard deviation errors. This shows that the model learns the characteristics of normal data and therefore obtains large errors for the anomalies, which can trigger an alarm. The future works will be focused on a wider study of anomalies in acoustic urban data considering spatio-temporal information of each record.

Acknowledgements. The authors would like to thank the Spanish Ministry of Science and Innovation for the support under projects PID2020-117954RB-C2 and TED2021-131311B-C22, the European Regional Development Fund and Junta de Andalucía for PY20-00870, P18-RT-2778 and UPO-138516 and the US-Spain Fulbright grant.

References

1. Abri, F., Gutiérrez, L.F., Siami Namin, A., Sears, D.R.W., Jones, K.S.: Predicting emotions perceived from sounds. In: 2020 IEEE International Conference on Big Data (Big Data), pp. 2057–2064 (2020)
2. Agency, E.E.: Noise pollution is a major environmental health concern in Europe (2022). https://www.eea.europa.eu/themes/human/noise. Accessed 30 Apr 2023
3. Altan, G., Kutlu, Y.: Chapter three - generalization performance of deep autoencoder kernels for identification of abnormalities on electrocardiograms. In: Das, H., Pradhan, C., Dey, N. (eds.) Deep Learning for Data Analytics, pp. 37–62. Academic Press (2020)
4. Bello, J.P., et al.: SONYC: a system for monitoring, analyzing, and mitigating urban noise pollution. Commun. ACM **62**(2), 68–77 (2019)
5. Camero, A., Alba, E.: Smart city and information technology: a review. Cities **93**, 84–94 (2019)
6. Chandola, V., Banerjee, A., Kumar, V.: Anomaly detection: a survey. ACM Comput. Surv. **41**(3), 1–58 (2009)
7. Ciaburro, G., Iannace, G.: Improving smart cities safety using sound events detection based on deep neural network algorithms. In: Informatics, vol. 7, no. 3 (2020)
8. Dua, S., et al.: Developing a speech recognition system for recognizing tonal speech signals using a convolutional neural network. Appl. Sci. **12**, 6223 (2022)

9. Ehsani, N., Aminifar, F., Mohsenian-Rad, H.: Convolutional autoencoder anomaly detection and classification based on distribution PMU measurements. IET Gener. Transm. Distrib. **16**(14), 2816–2828 (2022)
10. Kunapuli, S.S., Bhallamudi, P.C.: Chapter 22 - a review of deep learning models for medical diagnosis. In: Machine Learning. Big Data, and IoT for Medical Informatics, pp. 389–404. Academic Press, Intelligent Data-Centric Systems (2021)
11. Lebrusán, I., Toutouh, J.: Using smart city tools to evaluate the effectiveness of a low emissions zone in Spain: Madrid central. Smart Cities **3**(2), 456–478 (2020)
12. Lerch, A., Knees, P.: Machine learning applied to music/audio signal processing. Electronics **10**(24), 3077 (2021)
13. Librosa: Documentation (2023). https://librosa.org/doc/latest/index.html. Accessed 20 Apr 2023
14. Murphree, J.: Machine learning anomaly detection in large systems. In: 2016 IEEE AUTOTESTCON, pp. 1–9. IEEE (2016)
15. Müller, R., Illium, S., Ritz, F., Schmid, K.: Analysis of feature representations for anomalous sound detection. In: Proceedings of the 13th International Conference on Agents and Artificial Intelligence. Science and Technology Publications (2021)
16. Natsiou, A., O'Leary, S.: Audio representations for deep learning in sound synthesis: a review. 2021 IEEE/ACS 18th International Conference on Computer Systems and Applications (AICCSA), pp. 1–8 (2021)
17. Pita, A., Rodriguez, F.J., Navarro, J.M.: Cluster analysis of urban acoustic environments on Barcelona sensor network data. Int. J. Environ. Res. Public Health **18**(16), 8271 (2021)
18. Ren, Z., Chang, Y., Bartl-Pokorny, K.D., Pokorny, F.B., Schuller, B.W.: The acoustic dissection of cough: diving into machine listening-based COVID-19 analysis and detection. J. Voice **22** (2022)
19. Rovetta, S., Mnasri, Z., Masulli, F., Cabri, A.: Anomaly detection based on interval-valued fuzzy sets: application to rare sound event detection. In: WILF. CEUR Workshop Proceedings (2021)
20. Singh, K.: Anomaly detection and diagnosis in manufacturing systems: a comparative study of statistical, machine learning and deep learning techniques. In: PHM Society, vol. 11 (2019)
21. (SONYC-UST), S.U.S.T.: A multilabel dataset from an urban acoustic sensor network (2020). https://zenodo.org/record/3966543#.YznJ93ZByUk
22. Venkatesh, S., Moffat, D., Miranda, E.R.: You only hear once: a YOLO-like algorithm for audio segmentation and sound event detection. Appl. Sci. **12**(7), 3293 (2022)
23. Wang, Y., et al.: Unsupervised anomalous sound detection for machine condition monitoring using classification-based methods. Appl. Sci. **11**(23), 11128 (2021)
24. Wei, Y., Jang-Jaccard, J., Xu, W., Sabrina, F., Camtepe, S., Boulic, M.: LSTM-autoencoder based anomaly detection for indoor air quality time series data (2022)
25. Zhao, F., Fashola, O.I., Olarewaju, T.I., Onwumere, I.: Smart city research: a holistic and state-of-the-art literature review. Cities **119**, 103406 (2021)

Revisiting Histogram Based Outlier Scores: Strengths and Weaknesses

Ignacio Aguilera-Martos[✉], Julián Luengo and Francisco Herrera

Department of Computer Science and Artificial Intelligence, Andalusian Institute of Data Science and Computational Intelligence (DaSCI), University of Granada, Granada, Spain
nacheteam@ugr.es, {julianlm,herrera}@decsai.ugr.es

Abstract. Anomaly detection is a crucial task in various domains such as finance, cybersecurity or medical diagnosis. The demand for interpretability and explainability in model decisions has revived the use of traceable models, with Histogram Based Outlier Scores being a notable option due to its fast speed and commendable performance. Histogram Based Outlier Scores is a well-known and efficient unsupervised anomaly detection algorithm. Despite its popularity, it suffers from several limitations, including the inability to update its internal knowledge, model complex distributions, and consider feature relations. This work aims to provide a comprehensive analysis of the Histogram Based Outlier Scores algorithm status and its limitations. We conduct a comparative analysis of Histogram Based Outlier Scores with other state-of-the-art anomaly detection algorithms to identify its strengths and weaknesses. Our study shows that while Histogram Based Outlier Scores is efficient and computationally inexpensive, it may not be the best option in scenarios where the underlying data distribution is complex or where variable relations play a significant role. The presented alternatives and extensions to Histogram Based Outlier Scores provide valuable insights into the development of future anomaly detection methods.

Keywords: Anomaly detection · explainable AI · HBOS

1 Introduction

Anomaly detection is a fundamental task in data analysis and machine learning that aims to identify deviations from the expected behavior within a dataset. It involves detecting rare and unusual observations that differ significantly from the majority of normal data points. This process is crucial for uncovering novel patterns, outliers, and abnormal events, providing valuable insights across various domains such as network intrusion detection [10], fraud detection [17], system monitoring [16], quality control [7], and outlier identification in complex datasets. Anomaly detection techniques have gained widespread adoption due to the increasing volume of data and the need for automated decision-making systems.

P. García Bringas et al. (Eds.): HAIS 2023, LNAI 14001, pp. 39–48, 2023.
https://doi.org/10.1007/978-3-031-40725-3_4

Among the various methods developed, Histogram Based Outlier Scores (HBOS) [5] stands out for its simplicity, efficiency, and accuracy along with the interpretability that the model provides. HBOS creates histograms for each feature and computes the anomaly score based on the probability of each sample in the histograms. Despite its advantages, HBOS has several limitations, such as the inability to handle complex distributions, lack of update mechanisms, and the assumption of independence between variables.

In this contribution, we revisit the HBOS algorithm, providing a comprehensive analysis of its strengths and weaknesses, as well as comparing it to other state-of-the-art anomaly detection algorithms. We also present several extensions and alternatives to HBOS that address its limitations, such as Multi-step Histogram Based Outlier Scores (MHBOS) [2], Light Online Detector of Anomalies (LODA) [11] or Empirical-Cumulative-distribution-based Outlier Detection (ECOD) [8]. We analyze the performance of these methods using various datasets and metrics and provide insights into the suitability of each approach for different types of data and applications. Our work aims to provide practitioners with a better understanding of the HBOS algorithm and its extensions, and to guide the selection of the most appropriate method for a given anomaly detection task, where explainability is a key factor.

The rest of the text is structured as follows: in Sect. 2 the anomaly detection problem is presented. Section 3 introduces the HBOS algorithm as well as related algorithms. In Sect. 4 the experimental framework, results and analysis are presented. Section 5 presents the main strengths and weaknesses of HBOS. Finally Sect. 6 summarizes the lessons learned from this study.

2   Anomaly Detection

Anomaly detection [4] is a classical Machine Learning task consisting on identifying data points that deviate significantly from the norm or expected behavior of a given dataset. Unsupervised anomaly detection methods are particularly useful when labeled data is scarce or not available, as they do not require prior knowledge. This type of detection is only required to assume that the proportion of anomalies is low in relation to the number of normal data points.

Anomalies can be classified as contextual or collective [1]. Contextual anomalies occur in a specific situation which gives the anomaly the relevance, such as a high-priced item in a low-cost store. Collective anomalies are groups of data points that exhibit anomalous behavior as a whole piece, such as a group of hot days in winter.

Distinguishing between noise and anomalies is essential to ensure the accuracy and reliability of the results. Noise refers to random or irrelevant variations with no meaningful information. The main sources where noise comes from are measurement errors, data acquisition artifacts or environmental factors. In contrast, anomalies are observations that significantly deviate from the normal behavior of the data and contain useful information from unusual events. Removing noise and anomalies from the data is crucial for accurate data analysis and the enhancement of the applied techniques afterwards.

3   Histogram Based Outlier Scores: Analysis

This section is dedicated to discussing HBOS and the extensions that have been proposed to enhance the algorithm. Section 3.1 will provide an overview of the original HBOS algorithm, while Sect. 3.2 will introduce the MHBOS algorithm, which aims to overcome the limitation of updating histograms. In addition, Sect. 3.3 will explain the LODA algorithm as a means of addressing the issue of feature interaction within the model. Finally, Sect. 3.4 will provide an explanation of the ECOD algorithm, which to addresses the problems associated with the use of histograms in the HBOS algorithm.

3.1   Histogram Based Outlier Scores

Histogram are a graphical representation that divide the domain of a variable into fixed-sized intervals or bins and counts the number of values that fall within each bin. This structure provides the practitioner with the frequency or probability, if scaled, of a certain value range.

The HBOS [5] algorithm leverages histograms to determine if a value is rare or anomalous. To this end, the algorithm generates one histogram for each feature, scales the frequencies to reach the maximum value of one, and combines the information using the formula $HBOS(p) = \sum_{i=1}^{d} \log_2\left(\frac{1}{histogram(p_i)}\right)$.

The logarithmic function, when applied to the inverse of the histogram frequency of the corresponding bin, is an increasing monotonic function. The logarithmic function reaches its minimum when the frequency is one, resulting in a value of zero. In contrast, if the frequency is less than one, the fraction becomes greater than one, resulting in a positive number. Hence, a higher value is obtained for samples with lower frequency, which corresponds to more anomalous samples. Finally, the information from all histograms is aggregated.

3.2   Updating the Histograms: MHBOS

MHBOS [2] is a novel algorithm that addresses the inability of HBOS to handle data streams. This algorithm introduces several update mechanisms for both static and dynamic histograms, which maintain the performance of HBOS while enhancing the algorithm's flexibility.

MHBOS defines an initial histogram for each feature with the available data. By means of one of the update mechanisms the histogram values (bin edges and frequencies) are updated with the incoming data slice. Thefore the algorithm is able to train iteratively on the available data and therefore face streams of data.

3.3   Modeling Relationships Across Features: LODA

LODA [11] leverages weighted and random one-dimensional projections of the features in the dataset. By doing so, it transforms the variables into a single feature that contains mixed information from all of them. Histograms are then constructed over these projections to represent joint distributions, and probabilities are computed in the same manner as with HBOS. This process is repeated multiple times to obtain several histograms and represent as many feature interactions as possible.

This algorithm tackles one of the key weaknesses of HBOS. The original algorithm assumes that the features are independent and therefore histogram modelling each feature is enough to detect anomalies. This is not the case in all datasets and therefore LODA extends the behavior to solve this problem.

3.4   Histograms Aside: ECOD

ECOD [8] is a probabilistic detector that uses the empirical cumulative distribution function to score the samples based on the assumption that rare events occur in the tail of the distribution. The algorithm checks if the distribution of the data is right or left skewed and analysis the corresponding cumulative distribution function to evaluate the probability of each sample. The bigger the cumulative probability the more anomalous the value is as more data points are present to the right or left.

While ECOD has its own weaknesses the method gets rid of histograms. HBOS suffers from modelling certain types of distributions such as distributions with holes and heavy tails. When using ECOD the holes in the distribution do not matter as the important value is the cumulative probability of the sample.

4   Experimental Analysis

In this section, we present the experimental framework used to analyze the impact of the modifications implemented in the alternative methods compared with HBOS, as well as recent Deep Learning approach. First, we describe the experimental setup used to evaluate the performance of the algorithms (Sect. 4.1. Then, we present the experimental results and study the performance of HBOS with state-of-the-art anomaly detection algorithms (Sect. 4.2) checking whether HBOS is still competitive against their alternatives or Deep Learning approaches or not.

4.1   Experimental Framework

In this study, a set of state-of-the-art algorithms for anomaly detection are opposed to HBOS. For this purpose MHBOS, LODA and ECOD are included as they were presented as solutions to the limitations of HBOS. In order to perform an updated comparison, a Deep Learning approach based on an Autoencoder is included. Autoencoder models [6] have been applied for anomaly detection as well as many other tasks. These neural networks learn to encode and reconstruct normal data. This process of dimensionality reduction learning enable a good reconstruction of normal samples yielding high error in anomalous instances.

To provide a comprehensive context for HBOS within the classical algorithm landscape, we have incorporated a range of algorithms for comparison. Our selection encompasses Principal Component Analysis [15] (PCA), One-class Support Vector Machine [13] (OCSVM), Local Outlier Factor [3] (LOF), K-Nearest Neighbors [12] (KNN), and Isolation Forest [9] (IForest). These algorithms represent a diverse set of anomaly detectors, encompassing distance-based, density-based, and decision tree-based approaches.

The benchmark datasets are obtained from ODDS Library [14], that collects classic labeled datasets for anomaly detection using distance-based methods. For our experimentation, we employed 6 datasets from the ODDS Library, which encompassed a broad range of instances and features, enabling us to obtain more generalized conclusions. The chosen datasets are: Arrhythmia (Arr) with 452 instances and 274 features, Breastw (Br) with 683 instances and 9 features, Glass (Gl) with 214 instances and 9 features, Letter (Lt) with 1,600 instances and 32 features, Thyroid (Th) with 3,772 instances and 6 features and finally Vertebral (V) with 240 instances and 6 features.

4.2   Experimental Results

The analysis of Table 1 reveals that HBOS algorithm outperforms other algorithms on most datasets, with MHBOS, OCSVM and LOF as the only algorithm that come close. HBOS demonstrates consistent performance across all datasets, achieving the highest F1 score on the Breastw dataset and the highest AUC on the Thyroid and Arrhythmia datasets. However, HBOS does not perform well on three out of the six datasets, namely Glass, Vertebral, and Letter.

Table 1. F1 and AUC for each algorithm. Datasets abbreviations in Sect. 4.1.

Datasets	Gl		Br		Lt		Th		Arr		V	
	F1	AUC	F1	AUC	F1	AUC	F1	AUC	F1	AUC	F1	AUC
HBOS	0.111	0.705	**0.949**	0.990	0.12	0.623	**0.860**	**0.995**	**0.530**	**0.814**	0.066	0.328
AutoEncoder	0.111	0.601	0.933	0.973	0.18	0.724	0.387	0.961	0.424	0.775	0.1	0.524
ECOD	0.111	0.620	0.928	0.991	0.09	0.572	0.548	0.977	0.484	0.805	0.133	0.42
LODA	0	0.715	0.937	0.988	0.15	0.628	0.290	0.951	0.393	0.779	0.066	0.352
MHBOS	**0.444**	0.727	**0.949**	**0.993**	0.18	0.637	0.806	0.991	0.515	0.801	0.1	0.548
PCA	0.111	0.635	0.934	0.959	0.1	0.496	0.526	0.978	0.424	0.775	0.133	0.569
OCSVM	0.111	0.824	0.907	0.957	0.08	0.710	0.376	0.955	0.424	0.770	**0.233**	**0.694**
LOF	0.285	0.784	0.213	0.486	**0.538**	**0.912**	0.092	0.713	0.365	0.747	0.072	0.522
KNN	0.125	**0.839**	0.924	0.980	0.395	0.910	0.346	0.965	0.409	0.780	0.037	0.378
IForest	0.111	0.665	0.933	0.991	0.13	0.661	0.591	0.980	0.484	0.797	0	0.248

In order to gain further insight on why HBOS is having problems in those datasets, we analyzed the histograms of HBOS in the datasets where its performance was poor. We selected four histograms to summarize the internal state of the model, which are presented in Figs. 1a, 1b, 2a, and 2b. Our findings indicate that the performance of HBOS decreases when it encounters spaces in a distribution that has already been filled, resulting in a poor representation of the underlying domain. In contrast, we can observe an informative histogram in Fig. 1b as a comparison.

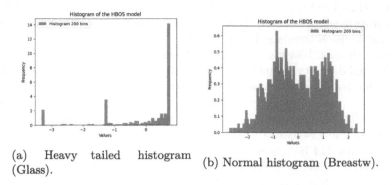

(a)   Heavy   tailed   histogram (Glass).

(b) Normal histogram (Breastw).

Fig. 1. Borderline situations on histograms

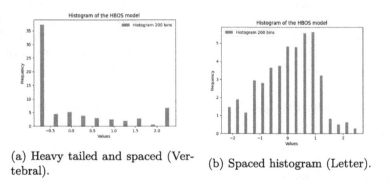

(a) Heavy tailed and spaced (Vertebral).

(b) Spaced histogram (Letter).

Fig. 2. Borderline situations on histograms

Table 2 presents the execution times of the algorithms. Based on the results, it can be inferred that AutoEncoder require a significant amount of time to execute, owing to its high complexity. On the other hand, MHBOS exhibit moderate execution times across most datasets. Notably, HBOS demonstrate remarkably low execution times for most datasets, being the fastest PCA, LOF or OVSVM depending on the dataset. Consequently, HBOS can be regarded as a well-balanced algorithm, exhibiting good performance with low execution times.

Table 2. Time consumed for each algorithm in execution (time in seconds).

Datasets	Gl	Br	Lt	Th	Arr	V
HBOS	1.733	2.197	4.262	1.450	7.075	2.128
AutoEncoder	53.991	102.025	470.736	596.141	240.764	66.344
ECOD	1.694	2.144	4.261	1.636	32.205	1.418
LODA	5.097	4.297	5.578	7.265	4.039	5.466
MHBOS	2.531	4.782	9.735	7.823	32.126	5.789
PCA	1.238	1.344	**1.714**	**1.247**	3.95	1.835
OCSVM	**1.172**	1.359	3.515	15.400	1.929	**1.128**
LOF	1.123	**1.226**	2.665	4.596	**1.428**	1.186
KNN	3.836	11.051	138.535	233.417	11.501	4.103
IForest	28.887	90.344	92.455	87.549	87.792	34.203

4.3   Algorithm Analysis

The performance and limitations of the HBOS algorithm are presented in this study. The algorithm exhibits fast processing time and consistently produces high-quality results, with computational efficiency measured at $O(B \cdot F)$, where B represents the number of histogram bins and F denotes the number of features.

However, limitations of the algorithm were identified in three datasets due to gaps that occur in the histograms. These gaps contribute to an increased number of false positives in the output, particularly impacting the F1 metric. False positives in anomaly detection may imply a very sensitive algorithm which raises too many alarms.

While neural networks are considered the state-of-the-art for many problems, it is not always the case that they outperform other methods for a given dataset or problem. In our study, we found that the Autoencoder model was not the best performer, with HBOS proving to be superior. This result may be triggered by the number of instances and features present in datasets, as deep neural networks require larger volumes of data to train properly and therefore lighter algorithms could be more suitable. Although neural networks offer greater flexibility and the ability to update their knowledge as new data arrives, they can be difficult to interpret due to their black-box nature. On the other hand, simpler methods like HBOS can achieve comparable results to neural networks in certain scenarios and offer a more interpretable output that can be easily understood by practitioners.

5   Considerations About Strengths and Weaknesses

HBOS has established itself as a prominent algorithm for anomaly detection, utilizing histograms as a simple yet effective tool. The algorithm's main strengths lie in its straightforward design, high performance, and low execution times as discussed in the previous section. Furthermore, due to its reliance on histograms,

HBOS is highly interpretable, providing insights into the specific features that determine whether a sample is anomalous and how they are related to the underlying distribution.

Notwithstanding the aforementioned advantages, HBOS suffers from significant limitations. The algorithm assumes that the variables are independent and do not have any correlation. As a result, the histograms generated by the algorithm only capture information about individual variables not considering any relationships between them. Consequently, the algorithm is unable to detect collective anomalies, identifying only contextual anomalies. This is clearly visible in the Letter data set, in which the relationships between variables are fundamental to understanding the letter to be recognized.

The primary drawback of using histograms as a distribution modeling tool in HBOS relates to distributions with non-covered spaces by bins and/or heavy tails, resulting in suboptimal algorithm performance. Due to the fixed bin size, some empty bins may be present between non-empty bins, leading to poor density estimation of the distribution. Consequently, the probability assigned to a sample may be non-conclusive, and an anomaly may be placed in a normal bin. Similarly, dynamic histograms with a high number of repeated values may result in distorted bins, further reducing the algorithm's accuracy. Vertebral is a good example of this, as we have been able to observe and corroborate by means of the histograms shown in Figs. 1a, 1b, 2a and 2b. Lastly, the lack of a histogram update mechanism renders HBOS inflexible and unresponsive to new data, making it unsuitable for dynamic datasets.

The importance of explainability and interpretability in machine learning has been increasingly recognized in recent years. Being able to understand and explain the reasoning behind a model's predictions is crucial for building trust and ensuring accountability. Regarding HBOS this is a valuable characteristic, as it enables users to understand how the model works and identify potential weaknesses or biases. In the future, it will likely become even more important as more complex models are developed, and regulatory requirements around explainability continue to evolve.

6   Conclusions

In this contribution, we have conducted a thorough analysis of the HBOS algorithm and identified its key strengths and limitations. Additionally, we have compiled recent proposals such as MHBOS, LODA, and ECOD, which address some of the exposed limitations. The study has pursued to prove whether these alternatives are effective, which has been accomplished specially with MHBOS proving to be more performant than the rest of the extensions.

Our results have led us to conclude that more complex Deep Learning models do not necessarily perform better than classical alternatives in simpler datasets. Furthermore, while deep neural network models lack explainability, the HBOS model offers a straightforward interpretation of results.

We conclude that HBOS is a reliable and fast tool that provides easy-to-interpret results. While the extensions discussed in this work address some issues with the algorithm, they do not solve all of them simultaneously. LODA is unable to update histograms dynamically, MHBOS maintains problems associated with histogram usage, and ECOD assumes independence between variables. We suggest that the development of probabilistic detectors has ample room for improvement by addressing these issues in combination or by integrating new tools beyond or along with the use of histograms.

Acknowledgment. This work has been supported by the Ministry of Science and Technology of Spain under project PID2020-119478GB-I00 and the project TED2021-132702B-C21 from the Ministry of Science and Innovation of Spain. I. Aguilera-Martos was supported by the Spanish Ministry of Science under the FPI programme PRE2021-100169.

References

1. Aggarwal, C.C.: An introduction to outlier analysis. In: Outlier Analysis, pp. 1–34. Springer, Cham (2017). https://doi.org/10.1007/978-3-319-47578-3_1
2. Aguilera-Martos, I., et al.: Multi-step histogram based outlier scores for unsupervised anomaly detection: arcelormittal engineering dataset case of study. Neurocomputing **544**, 126228 (2023)
3. Breunig, M.M., Kriegel, H.P., Ng, R.T., Sander, J.: LOF: identifying density-based local outliers. SIGMOD Rec. **29**(2), 93–104 (2000)
4. Chandola, V., Banerjee, A., Kumar, V.: Anomaly detection: a survey. ACM Comput. Surv. (CSUR) **41**(3), 1–58 (2009)
5. Goldstein, M., Dengel, A.: Histogram-based outlier score (HBOS): a fast unsupervised anomaly detection algorithm
6. Hinton, G.E., Salakhutdinov, R.R.: Reducing the dimensionality of data with neural networks. Science **313**(5786), 504–507 (2006)
7. Leigh, C., et al.: A framework for automated anomaly detection in high frequency water-quality data from in situ sensors. Sci. Total Environ. **664**, 885–898 (2019)
8. Li, Z., Zhao, Y., Hu, X., Botta, N., Ionescu, C., Chen, G.: ECOD: unsupervised outlier detection using empirical cumulative distribution functions. IEEE Trans. Knowl. Data Eng. (2022)
9. Liu, F.T., Ting, K.M., Zhou, Z.H.: Isolation forest. In: Proceedings of the 2008 Eighth IEEE International Conference on Data Mining, pp. 413–422 (2008)
10. Moustafa, N., Hu, J., Slay, J.: A holistic review of network anomaly detection systems: a comprehensive survey. J. Netw. Comput. Appl. **128**, 33–55 (2019)
11. Pevný, T.: LODA: lightweight on-line detector of anomalies. Mach. Learn. **102**(2), 275–304 (2016)
12. Ramaswamy, S., Rastogi, R., Shim, K.: Efficient algorithms for mining outliers from large data sets, pp. 427–438 (2000)
13. Schölkopf, B., Williamson, R., Smola, A., Shawe-Taylor, J., Platt, J.: Support vector method for novelty detection. In: Proceedings of the 12th International Conference on Neural Information Processing Systems, pp. 582–588 (1999)
14. Shebuti, R.: ODDS Library (2016). http://odds.cs.stonybrook.edu
15. Shyu, M.L., Chen, S.C., Sarinnapakorn, K., Chang, L.: A novel anomaly detection scheme based on principal component classifier. In: Proceedings of International Conference on Data Mining (2003)

16. Xue, Q., Li, G., Zhang, Y., Shen, S., Chen, Z., Liu, Y.: Fault diagnosis and abnormality detection of lithium-ion battery packs based on statistical distribution. J. Power Sources **482**, 228964 (2021)
17. Zhang, G., et al.: eFraudCom: an e-commerce fraud detection system via competitive graph neural networks. ACM Trans. Inf. Syst. (TOIS) **40**(3), 1–29 (2022)

Data Mining and Decision Support Systems

Model Performance Prediction: A Meta-Learning Approach for Concept Drift Detection

Fernanda A. Melo[1]($\boxtimes$)(iD), André C. P. L. F. de Carvalho[2]($\boxtimes$)(iD),
Ana C. Lorena[3]($\boxtimes$)(iD), and Luís P. F. Garcia[1]($\boxtimes$)(iD)

[1] Department of Computer Science, University of Brasília, Brasília 70910-900, Brazil
melo.fernanda@aluno.unb.br, luis.garcia@unb.br
[2] Institute of Mathematical and Computer Sciences, University of São Paulo, São Carlos 13560-970, Brazil
andre@icmc.usp.br
[3] Aeronautics Institute of Technology, São José dos Campos 12228-900, Brazil
ana.lorena@gp.ita.br

Abstract. Data stream applications in highly dynamic environments often face concept drift problems, a phenomenon in which the statistical properties of the variables change over time, which can degrade the performance of Machine Learning models. This work presents a new model monitoring tool through the use of Meta Learning. The algorithm was conceived for data streams with concept drift and large target arrival delay. Additionally, a new set of Meta Features is proposed based on the use of unsupervised concept drift metrics. Unlike related Meta Learning approaches, a regressor was used at the meta level to predict the predictive performance of the base model. These predictions can be used to generate concept drift alerts before the arriving objects are labelled. Experimental results show that the proposed approach obtains, on average, a classification error reduction of 12.8%, when compared to the traditional Meta Learning approaches, and 38%, when compared to the baseline, the last known performance, in predicting the performance of the base model.

Keywords: Data Streams · Concept Drift · Meta Learning

1 Introduction

Data streams can be associated with highly dynamic and non-stationary environments [6,7,15]. Their analysis allows the extraction of useful information that can reveal what is currently happening in a given dynamic application.

Often, in a data stream scenario, the statistical properties of the target variable change over time, leading to a phenomenon called concept drift, which can impair the performance of predictive models [11]. The concept drift between

© The Author(s), under exclusive license to Springer Nature Switzerland AG 2023
P. García Bringas et al. (Eds.): HAIS 2023, LNAI 14001, pp. 51–62, 2023.
https://doi.org/10.1007/978-3-031-40725-3_5

two distinct points in time t_0 and t_1 can be formally defined according to Eq. 1, where X is the set of input attributes and y is the target variable.

$$\exists X : p_{t_0}(X, y) \neq p_{t_1}(X, y) \tag{1}$$

Alternatives to deal with the challenges associated with concept drift detection have been investigated in several publications [8,27,32]. There are several concept drift detection techniques, from easy-to-implement statistical measures, such as the Population Stability Index (PSI) [16], to complex measures that make use of Machine Learning (ML) models, such as Margin Density Drift Detection (MD3) [22]. Most of the existing works in the literature focus on the solution of supervised learning problems, although most real world problems have a delay in the arrival of the target variable [8].

The no free lunch theorem [31] states that different data concepts may better suit models with different biases, making the algorithm selection emerge as an adequate solution to improve the overall ML system performance. In particular, algorithm selection figures as a promising strategy for handling concept drift and avoiding performance loss. However, while its value is demonstrated for problems where the performance of the algorithms are similar over long periods of time, this behavior might be very different when analyzing over small time windows [19–21], like the usual data stream approaches.

Meta Learning (MtL) is an advanced framework that can be used to learn the pattern of existing changes in the data in a systemic way to recommend the most suitable model for each situation [2,3,25,28,30]. It has been largely employed in the literature to support algorithm selection [25].

This research introduces a novel approach in concept drift detection by utilizing MtL, which has never been employed for this purpose before. The key innovation lies in a novel MtL architecture that predicts ML model performance, incorporating modifications to the conventional framework. Another distinguishing aspect of this work is the consideration of a substantial target delay, leading to the exclusive utilization of unsupervised Meta Features (MFe). Additionally, a fresh set of MFe is proposed, leveraging unsupervised concept drift metrics.

This paper is structured as follows: Section 2 presents a review over relevant background. Section 3 details the MtL framework for data streams. Section 4 introduces the methodology used in this research. Section 5 presents the results and Sect. 6 presents the obtained conclusions.

2   Background

The highly dynamic environment of data stream problems introduces new challenges for ML [15]. The high data generation speed in this type of problem leads to frequent changes in the way of accessing and processing data, and to concerns on the efficient usage of available computing resources [29]. As recent information is generally more relevant than historical data, the data streams are analyzed in temporal windows.

The concept drift is a major obstacle for data stream problems because of the difficulty in maintaining an accurate model in non-stationary environments [7,27]. A common approach to deal with this problem is the use of incremental learning strategies [15], through continuous training of ML models that allow incremental adaptations in their internal parameters.

The most common approach is to adapt the models at regular intervals. However, a more interesting approach consists of monitoring concept changes in order to detect the ideal moment for retraining or adjusting the ML model. Gama *et al.* (2012) [6] cites two different approaches to monitor data streams. The first involves monitoring performance indicators associated with statistical process control and the second approach involves comparing distributions at different points in time. In this research, both approaches will be used.

2.1   Concept Drift Detection

Although the growing number of publications on concept drift detection indicates the relevance of this area, most of them are focused on the solution of supervised problems, where the real value of the target variable is discovered at the same time, or slightly later, than the arrival of the input features [9]. However, in many real-world problems, there is a large delay in the arrival of the target variable. In these situations, solving the concept change detection problem in an unsupervised way would be a more realistic approach.

Most concept drift detection metrics make a comparison between a reference distribution, a base that is known to have no concept drift, such as the training dataset, and the monitoring distribution, the window being evaluated to attest to the existence or not of concept drift.

The Population Stability Index (PSI) [23] is a widespread used technique for detecting drift, with easy implementation and interpretation. The PSI measures the similarity between two distributions and is calculated individually for each attribute of the dataset. This makes PSI prone to false positives resulting from the detection of change of virtual concepts since the alteration of the distribution of input attributes does not necessarily imply a real concept change, despite being a strong indication. In addition, PSI is a univariate measure, and does not scale well for a large number of input features.

In contrast, there is the Domain Classifier (DC) [24], a technique that deals with the drift problem in a multivariate way. It builds a binary classifier to discriminate instances coming from the reference and monitoring windows. If the data distribution is different enough among both windows, the classifier can discriminate them and exhibits high accuracy.

The Unsupervised Change Detection for Activity Recognition (UDetect) [1] is based on the premise that the high variance of instances of a certain class in relation to the training instances of that same class indicates a concept drift. It is implemented by dividing the data into fixed-size groups, calculating the average distance to the class centroid. Finally, the reference and monitoring distances are compared.

The Stream Quantification by Score Inspection with Instance Selection (SqsiIs) [13] uses the similarity of the reference and detection model scores as a concept drift measure. It is implemented by applying a two-sample *Kolmogorov Smirnov* (KS) test between the reference and detection model scores after a transformation to make both distributions have the same mean and standard deviation.

Finally, the Online Modified Version of the Page-Hinkley Test (OmvPht) [14] is used to detect concept drift by assuming that the predictions distributions can be modeled as two Gaussian curves and employs the overlap between them as a measure of concept change.

2.2 Meta Learning

MtL uses ML algorithms to deal with the Algorithm Selection Problem (ASP), which is the recommendation of the algorithm, and hyperparameter values, that best satisfy the objectives of a given problem. Rice (1976) *et al.* [17] defines the ASP using four spaces: problem P, algorithm A, performance metrics Y and attribute F.

The problem space P consists of the set of databases $x \in P$, used in the study. As this research addresses the study of data flows, which are by nature sequences of data without a defined size, only one database was used per experiment. The algorithm space A consists of the set of all algorithms $\alpha \in A$, which can be used to solve a given problem. The performance metrics space Y consists of the set of metrics that can be used to measure the performance of algorithms α on a given problem. Finally, the attribute space F consists of the set of characteristics that can be used to describe the problem, such as statistical or descriptive measures that represent the dataset and its attributes.

Based on these sets, the MtL can be formally defined as: for a given instance of the problem $x \in P$, with attributes $f(x) \in F$, find the selection mapping $S(f(x))$ on algorithm space A such that the algorithm selected $\alpha \in A$ maximizes the performance $y(\alpha(x)) \in Y$.

In MtL problems, characterization measures are named Meta Features (MFe). Rivolli, A. *et al.* (2022) [18] standardize data characterization measures for classification databases used in MtL into seven categories: Simple, Statistical, Clustering, Information Theory, Model-based, Landmarking and Miscellaneous.

The Simple MFe category is composed of measures that are easily extracted from the data and do not require significant computational resources, such as the number of observations, dimensionality and sparsity. The Statistical MFe group extracts information about the distribution of the numerical features, such as mean, minimum, maximum and standard deviation. The Clustering MFe are calculated from the outputs of a clustering algorithm using the input features, such as compactness or inertia. The Information Theory MFe group refer to measures that capture the amount of information in the data using variability and redundancy measures, such as entropy and mutual information. The Model-Based group contains MFe based in models induced using the data, such as number of leaves, nodes and depth of tree-based models. The Landmarking group use the performance of fast learning algorithms as characterization metrics, as Naive Bayes (NB) or k-Nearest Neighbors (KNN). Finally, the Miscellaneous group refers to the other MFe that do not belong to any other group. Some examples are the uniqueness of a feature and the dataset sparsity.

This work assumes that there is a long delay in the target variable arrival. Therefore, only unsupervised MFe were used in the experiments. In addition, some unsupervised concept drift detection measures were used, as it is assumed that these attributes can add relevant information to the meta model. For the same reason, the base model prediction and its performance in the last window with a known target variable were also used.

2.3   Meta Learning for Data Streams

Using MtL on data streams, also known as *metaStream*, involves periodically recommending algorithms in non-stationary environments [5,19–21]. In metaStream, some changes are made to the original MtL process. First, the problem space P is composed only of the data stream, while the performance $y \in Y$ of the algorithms $\alpha \in A$ and the MFe $f(x) \in F$ are extracted from the data of each time window.

Rossi *et al.* (2014) [19] divide the architecture of the solution into two levels: at the base level, a sliding window of fixed size is applied to the data stream; this is a forgetting mechanism that discards old instances of the base. The base level objective is to train a set of models $\alpha \in A$ which can be used in the algorithm selection problem. The meta level consists of training a new ML algorithm, called meta model, whose objective is to find the relationship between the data at the base level and the performance of the algorithms. This meta model is then used to predict the most suitable algorithm for each data window.

Jader *et al.* (2020) [5] propose an improvement based on the meta model incremental training and the usage of the set of MFe defined by Rivolli, A. *et al.* (2022) [18]. They conclude that several of these MFe have become highly important attributes for the meta model. On the other hand, the incremental training gain results were not satisfactory, so it will be disregarded in this research.

3   MetaStream Framework

The MetaStream architecture [5,19–21] is split into two stages: the offline phase consists of hyperparameter optimization, training and validation of base-level algorithm. Then, the online phase starts, acting dynamically on the data stream by predicting the base model performance at each window.

The offline phase starts when a set of labeled historical data accumulates. This batch is used to train the base model and evaluate its performance. Besides that, it is used as the reference window to calculate the concept drift measures that will compose the MFe. Finally, it is also used to build the first meta base and train the first meta model. The target variable of the meta base is called meta label and consists of the base model performance in each window.

The online phase takes place in the data stream as illustrated in Fig. 1. The upper part shows the data stream handling at the base level, where the green colored instances represent the most recent data whose target variable is unknown, assuming that there is a large delay in its arrival. The orange region of the image represents the labeled instances of the data stream, which are used to calculate the performance of the base model in the last windows with known target variable. This value is used as the experimental baseline.

The bottom part of Fig. 1 illustrates how the algorithm works at the meta level, where MFe are constantly created as new data arrives at fixed size windows η. Only unsupervised MFe were included, therefore the step represented with green color does not depend on the target variable arrival. On the other hand, the orange region represents the labeled instances of the meta-base, whose meta labels are updated as the target variable reaches the base level, enabling the calculation of the base model performance. Finally, when a set of labeled data in the metabase is accumulated, the meta model is retrained with the new information.

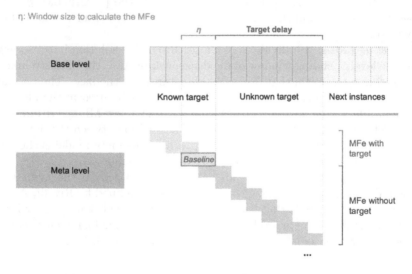

Fig. 1. MetaStream architecture (Color figure online)

4   Methodology

All data sets used in this research refer to balanced classification problems. Four real databases commonly used in the data stream literature were chosen: Electricity, Airlines, Rialto and Powersupply [26]. The data sets information including number of instances, attributes and classes are described in Table 1.

Traditional classification metrics, such as recall, precision and F1 score were used to evaluate the base model performance. Since the traditional evaluation

Table 1. Data sets main characteristics

	Electricity	Airlines	Powersupply	Rialto
Number of instances	45.312	539.383	29.928	82.250
Number of attributes	6	6	2	27
Number of classes	2	2	24	10

measures are not sufficient in the data stream scenario, the Cohen's Kappa [4] was also included in this analysis [10].

In order to validate the proposed architecture for models with different biases, four algorithms were chosen at the base level: Support Vector Machines (SVM), Random Forest (RF), Decision Tree (DT), and Logistic Regression (LR). For handling multiclass problems with LR, the One-vs-rest decomposition strategy was used, in which each class is taken as positive against the others.

The LightGBM [12] was the meta regressor used in all experiments, with hyperparameter optimization performed with Time Series Cross Validation. The high number of MFe generated makes MtL highly prone to overfitting, therefore, a feature selection experiment was made during the offline phase. For this, the meta model was trained with a percentage of all available MFe for each base.

The meta model evaluation used the Mean Squared Error (MSE), usual metric for evaluating regression problems. In addition, the accumulated MSE gain in each window was also measured as a way to observe how the regressor compares with the baseline over the data stream.

The elapsed time is measured to validate whether the performance gain compensates the increase in latency given the time limitations of data stream applications. Finally, the feature importance for the meta regressor is calculated as a way of understanding the individual contribution of the proposed MFe.

5 Results

In order to understand the contribution of the proposed MFe, two meta models were trained in each experiment: the first will be called "proposed MtL" and uses both the existing and proposed MFe. The second was trained without the inclusion of the new MFe, such as the attributes based on the base model prediction and the concept drift detection measures. This version will be called "original MtL" throughout this Section.

In Fig. 2, the y-axis illustrates the average MSE across all windows. The x-axis represents the three ways of grouping the executions: by database (Fig. 2a), by meta label (Fig. 2b) and by base model (Fig. 2c). Finally, the bar colors represents the model: orange refers to the baseline, blue to the original MtL and gray to the proposed MtL. In all cases, the error of the proposed MtL algorithm is always smaller than the original one. In addition, both MtL algorithms have smaller error than the baseline in all cases, except for the Airlines database.

The next analysis will be focused on the results obtained with the Electricity and Airlines databases, in which MtL presented the best and worst performance, respectively. In addition, more detailed analyzes will be carried out with the Kappa meta-label, since this is a traditional metric from the data stream literature [10] and was the one in which MtL outperformed the baseline.

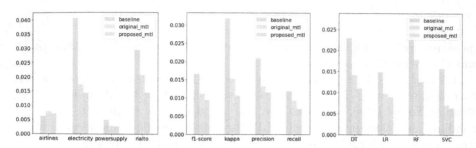

(a) Mean MSE per database (b) Mean MSE per meta label (c) Mean MSE per base model

Fig. 2. Mean MSE of proposed MtL algorithm, original MtL and baseline (Color figure online)

Figures 3 and 4 illustrate the cumulative gain chart with the Kappa as meta label, for the Airlines and Electricity databases, respectively. The x-axis represents the window used to calculate the MSE and the y-axis represents the window's accumulated gain with respect to the baseline. In these charts, the baseline is being compared with the proposed algorithm, with the original MtL and with an "ideal regressor", usually called oracle, which presents zero MSE in all windows. The larger the area under the curve, the greater is the gain of the algorithm in relation to the baseline, with the upper limit being the oracle gain, represented by the gray curve.

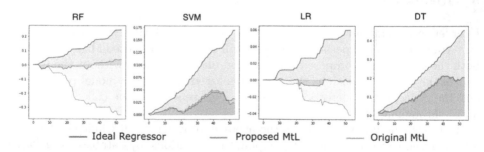

Fig. 3. Cumulative gain of proposed MtL algorithm in Airlines database with Kappa meta label (Color figure online)

Figure 3 shows the results of the Airlines database. The performances of the proposed and original MtL systems are very similar when SVM and DT are used as the base model, indicating that the proposed MFe did not present great gains for these cases, although the performance of both MtL models was superior to the baseline. On the other hand, when RF and LR are used as the base model, the proposed MtL performed much better with the use of the new MFe. Even so, both had poor results in relation to the baseline, indicating that MtL is not indicated for these cases.

Figure 4 shows the results for the Electricity database. The performance of both proposed and original MtL were good, reaching, on average, 76% and 66% of the performance of the oracle, respectively. Therefore, the new proposed MFe were responsible for an average increase of 10% in the original MtL gain for this base. In addition, the ascending cumulative gain chart indicates that the MtL is more suitable than the baseline in most of the evaluated windows for the Electricity database.

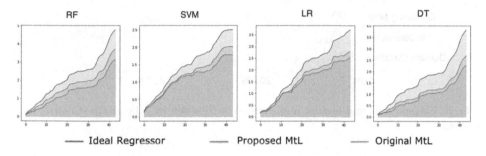

Fig. 4. Cumulative gain of proposed MtL algorithm in Electricity database with Kappa meta label (Color figure online)

5.1   Meta Feature Importance and Elapsed Time

MtL is a computationally expensive technique and is being applied in data stream problems where processing time is restricted. Therefore, in addition to evaluating the proposed MFe in terms of accuracy gains, the elapsed time is measured. Figure 5 illustrates the average execution time and feature importance for each MFe group. The red circles on the left highlight the groups referring to the new MFe proposed in this research.

The concept drift detection metric Domain Classifier and the clustering MFe group correspond to more than half of the total processing time. In addition, the concept drift detection measures PSI and OmvPht represent the groups with the shortest execution time. The clustering MFe corresponds to only 1.5% of the total importance, despite the long execution time, while the Domain Classifier had practically no impact and took 22.5% of the execution time, indicating that it is not a suitable metric for use in MtL.

In contrast, the other groups presented satisfactory results, highlighting the statistical and score based MFe, which correspond to approximately 80% of the mean importance and only 12% of the elapsed time. In addition to these, the concept drift detection measures OmvPht and PSI also showed interesting results with 7% and 5% of importance and only 1.2% and 3% of the execution time, respectively.

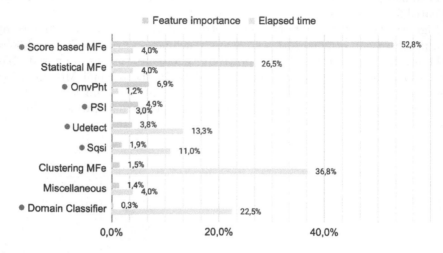

Fig. 5. Elapsed time and feature importance contribution by MFe group (Color figure online)

6   Conclusions

The experiments demonstrate that MtL can be used in predicting the performance of base-level models with various biases, as well as in real data stream databases with the presence of concept change. The application of the proposed algorithm presented, on average, a MSE reduction of 12.8% in relation to the traditional MtL and 38% in relation to the baseline. In the end, the proposed MtL outperformed the baseline in all experiments except for the Airlines data set when RF or LR were used as the baseline model.

In addition, the proposed MtL obtained better results than the original MtL in most cases, attesting that the proposed MFe are able to increase the predictive power of the meta model, even though there is an increase in the execution time. The choice of whether or not to use the new MFe depends on the latency requirements of each problem. Even so, some concept drift detection measures look promising with high importance and low processing time, such as the PSI and the OmvPht. Finally, the inclusion of the score based MFe proved to be a significant contribution to the choice of meta attributes.

Future work will involve the implementation of concept drift alerts based on the performance prediction of the base model. The proposed technique will be compared with other detection measures in databases with labeled concept drift.

The final objective is to propose a robust tool capable of detecting the concept drift before the arrival of the target variable, even in problems with high arrival delay.

Acknowledgment. This study was financed in part by the Coordenação de Aperfeiçoamento de Pessoal de Nível Superior - Brasil (CAPES) - Finance Code 001.

References

1. Bashir, S.A., Petrovski, A., Doolan, D.: A framework for unsupervised change detection in activity recognition. Int. J. Pervasive Comput. Commun. **13**(2), 157–175 (2017)
2. Brazdil, P.: Metalearning: Applications to Automated Machine Learning and Data Mining. Springer, Cham (2022). https://doi.org/10.1007/978-3-030-67024-5. Cognitive Technologies
3. Brazdil, P., Giraud-Carrier, C.: Metalearning and algorithm selection: progress, state of the art and introduction to the 2018 special issue. Mach. Learn. **107**, 12 (2017)
4. Cohen, J.: A coefficient of agreement for nominal scales. Educ. Psychol. Measur. **20**(1), 37–46 (1960). April
5. Jáder M. C. de Sá, Andre, L.D., Rossi, Gustavo E. A. P. A. Batista, and Luís P. F. Garcia. Algorithm recommendation for data streams. In: 2020 25th International Conference on Pattern Recognition (ICPR), pp. 6073–6080, 2021
6. Gama, J.: A survey on learning from data streams: current and future trends. Prog. Artif. Intell. **1**(1), 45–55 (2012). January
7. Gama, J., Medas, P., Castillo, G., Rodrigues, P.: Learning with drift detection. In: Bazzan, A.L.C., Labidi, S. (eds.) SBIA 2004. LNCS (LNAI), vol. 3171, pp. 286–295. Springer, Heidelberg (2004). https://doi.org/10.1007/978-3-540-28645-5_29
8. Gemaque, R.N., Costa, A.F.J., Giusti, R., Dos Santos, E.M.: An overview of unsupervised drift detection methods. Wiley Interdisc. Rev. Data Min. Knowl. Discov. **10**, e1381 (2020)
9. Gemaque, R.N., Costa, A.F.J., Giusti, R., Dos Santos, E.M.: An overview of unsupervised drift detection methods. WIREs Data Min. Knowl. Discov. **10**(6), e1381 (2020)
10. Janardan and Shikha Mehta: Concept drift in streaming data classification: algorithms, platforms and issues. Procedia Comput. Sci. **122**, 804–811 (2017)
11. Kadam, S.V.: A Survey on Classification of Concept Drift with Stream Data. working paper or preprint (2019)
12. Ke, G., et al.: Lightgbm: a highly efficient gradient boosting decision tree. In: Proceedings of the 31st International Conference on Neural Information Processing Systems, NIPS 2017, pp. 3149–3157, Red Hook, NY, USA, Curran Associates Inc (2017)
13. Maletzke, A.G., dos Reis, D.M., Batista, G.E.: Combining instance selection and self-training to improve data stream quantification. J. Braz. Comput. Soc. **24**(1), 1–17 (2018)
14. Mouss, H., Mouss, D., Mouss, N., Sefouhi, L.: Test of page-hinckley, an approach for fault detection in an agro-alimentary production system, vol. 2, no. 08, pp. 815–818 (2004)

15. Nguyen, H.-L., Woon, Y.-K., Ng, W.-K.: A survey on data stream clustering and classification. Knowl. Inf. Syst. **45**(3), 535–569 (2014). December
16. du Pisanie, J., Allison, J.S., Visagie, J.: A proposed simulation technique for population stability testing in credit risk scorecards. Mathematics **11**(2), 492 (2022)
17. Rice, J.R.: The algorithm selection problem**this work was partially supported by the national science foundation through grant gp-32940x. this chapter was presented as the george e. forsythe memorial lecture at the computer science conference, february 19, 1975, washington, d. c. volume 15 of Advances in Computers, pp. 65–118. Elsevier (1976)
18. Rivolli, A., Garcia, L.P., Soares, C., Vanschoren, J., de Carvalho, A.C.: Meta-features for meta-learning. Knowl. Based Syst. **240**, 108101 (2022)
19. Rossi, A.L.D., de Leon Ferreira, A.C.P., Soares, C., De Souza, B.F.: MetaStream: a meta-learning based method for periodic algorithm selection in time-changing data. Neurocomputing, **127**, 52–64 (2014)
20. Rossi, A.L.D., De Souza, B.F., Soares, C., de Leon Ferreira de Carvalho, A., Ponce, C.: A guidance of data stream characterization for meta-learning. Intell. Data Anal. **21**(4), 1015–1035 2017
21. Rossi, A.L.D., Soares, C., de Souza, B.F., de Leon Ferreira, A.C.P.: Algorithm selection for time-changing data. Inf. Sci. **565**, 262–277 (2021)
22. Tegjyot Singh Sethi and Mehmed Kantardzic: Don't pay for validation: detecting drifts from unlabeled data using margin density. Procedia Comput. Sci. **53**, 103–112 (2015)
23. Siddiqi, N.: Credit Risk Scorecards: Developing and Implementing Intelligent Credit Scoring. Wiley, Hopboken (2005)
24. Maggio, D.P.S.: A Primer on Data Drift & Drift Detection Techniques. Dataiku (2020)
25. Smith-Miles, K.A.: Cross-disciplinary perspectives on meta-learning for algorithm selection. ACM Comput. Surv. **41**(1), 1–25 (2009)
26. Souza, V.M.A., Reis, D.M., Maletzke, A.G., Batista, G.E.A.P.A.: Challenges in benchmarking stream learning algorithms with real-world data. Data Min. Knowl. Disc. **34**, 1805–1858 (2020)
27. Tsymbal, A.: The problem of concept drift: definitions and related work (2004)
28. Vanschoren, J., Soares, C., Brazdil, P., Kotthoff, L.: Meta-Learning and Algorithm Selection (2014)
29. Verma, D., Nashine, R.: Data mining: next generation challenges and futureDirections. Int. J. Model. Optim. **2**(5), 603 (2012)
30. Vilalta, R., Giraud-Carrier, C., Brazdil, P.: Meta-learning - concepts and techniques. In: Maimon, O., Rokach, L. (eds.) Data Mining and Knowledge Discovery Handbook, pp. 717–731. Springer, Boston (2009). https://doi.org/10.1007/978-0-387-09823-4_36
31. Wolpert, D.H., Macready, W.G.: No free lunch theorems for optimization. IEEE Trans. Evol. Comput. **1**(1), 67–82 (1997)
32. Žliobaitė, I., Pechenizkiy, M., Gama, J.: An overview of concept drift applications. In: Japkowicz, N., Stefanowski, J. (eds.) Big Data Analysis: New Algorithms for a New Society. SBD, vol. 16, pp. 91–114. Springer, Cham (2016). https://doi.org/10.1007/978-3-319-26989-4_4

Reinforcing Assessment Processes Using Proactive Case-Based Reasoning Mechanisms

Jaime Leite(ID) and Orlando Belo(✉)(ID)

ALGORITMI R&D Centre/LASI, University of Minho, Campus of Gualtar, 4710-057 Braga, Portugal
obelo@di.uminho.pt

Abstract. The integration of case-based reasoning mechanisms into E-learning systems is not a recent option. These mechanisms allow us to implement reasoning systems using similar experiences in a retrospectively way, which is quite attractive for problem solving in some application areas. Its application promotes the achievement of very interesting solutions, especially when an interesting case base exists *a priori*, integrating knowledge and appropriate problem-solving methods. In this paper, we present and describe a hybrid reasoning system especially developed to support student knowledge assessment processes in an E-learning platform. The system integrates two autonomous reasoning modules, which combine their functioning during knowledge assessment processes, combining rule-based and case-based knowledge, respecting a set of assessment restrictions defined a priori by a human supervisor.

Keywords: E-Learning Systems · Rule-based Reasoning · Case-based Reasoning E-learning User Assessment · Supervised Reasoning

1 Introduction

The development of reasoning systems [1] has evolved systematically over the past few years. It is one of the most active areas in the field of Artificial Intelligence. It has provided various types of solutions for a large number of application areas, which directly or indirectly require the transposition of problem-solving methods used by people into software systems. Several relevant applications of systems with reasoning capacity have been developed in learning, covering a large number of situations of teaching and learning processes. Some intelligent systems have been integrated and exploited in these processes, as innovative initiatives promoted by the institutions or, simply, by the most visionary teaching professionals. They are a "step forward" in learning processes and knowledge assessment [2]. Many different techniques have been used in the process of designing and implementing intelligent teaching systems, both in terms of knowledge representation structures and reasoning mechanisms. For some time, rule-based systems had great relevance and impact in the development of intelligent systems, due to their simplicity and "fast" implementation. However, its performance was not always the best. In some cases was due to the rigidity of the knowledge representation model or due to the functioning of its reasoning system, which often revealed the same behavior, induced by their static production rules, obviously. Subsequently, in another range of applications, case-based reasoning systems began to be studied and adopted. It comes to fill some of the limitations revealed by previous systems, providing a new way of acting for teaching processes, both in tutoring activities or in knowledge assessment processes.

Case-based reasoning (CBR) systems [3, 4] appear in a large diversity of application areas [5]. Their ability to use similar experiences retrospectively is quite attractive for many practical problem-solving cases. They allow for achieving very effective solutions, in particular when we have a base of experiences (of cases) of resolution with interest and dimension. Despite the diversity of the CBR application areas, we focused our attention mainly to its application to E-learning problem solving. In this area, we easily find CBR systems applications in many practical domains, for teaching students, based on previously carried out teaching processes [6], establishing student profiles for the implementation of personalized teaching systems [7], or preparing training lessons [8], among other applications. The knowledge we extracted from studying these applications contributes to improve the performance of a knowledge assessment system we have been developing over the last few years [9]. In a first stage of the development, this system supported knowledge assessment processes using production rules, which we mapped in a specific decision-making program. This program operates dynamically, adjusting its behavior accordingly the information provided by a set of specific profiling mechanisms, which define and calculate the values of various assessment properties (knowledge domain, student knowledge status, level of learning, student difficulties, etc.) at each moment of the assessment process. Despite the efficiency of the process implemented, taking into account the goals of the system, we needed to make it a little more "creative" in the assessment processes in which it generates questions about a domain and gets the corresponding answer from a student. We decided to incorporate in the system another reasoning system, supported by CBR mechanisms, in order to enrich system's assessment processes, making it more versatile and generating questions from previously assessment cases, not being restricted to the knowledge previously defined.

In this paper, we present and discuss the work we done for incorporating a set of CBR mechanisms into the E-learning system referred previously. We will pay particular attention to all the aspects related to the implementation of the CBR mechanisms, system functioning and quiz session support, and question generation process. We structured the remaining part of this paper as follows: Sect. 2, describes some related work in the area of E-learning and reasoning systems integration, as well as exposes and describes the system developed and how it works, during a specific student assessment process; and, finally, Sect. 3, presents some conclusions and future work.

2 Reinforcing Reasoning Mechanisms with CBR

The development of E-learning systems has evolved a lot in recent years, involving a very wide spectrum of techniques and models in the construction of knowledge representation structures and reasoning mechanisms. However, whenever E-Learning systems require the use of knowledge acquired in past teaching or learning processes or the adaptation of existing solutions to similar problems, CBR appeared as the most appropriate technique to be use in their inception and implementation. CBR [10] can be seen simultaneously as a hybrid method especially oriented for solving similar problems and gathering knowledge about new experiences, having an immediate application in problem solving. CBR has been applied in a wide variety of areas, with particular success in decision support systems. We can witness several CBR applications in E-learning. Khamparia and Pandey [11], for example, addressed the integration of CBR mechanisms in an eLearning system oriented to the teaching of programming languages, having the ability to provide study material to users, according to their state in the learning process. Huang et al. [12], integrated CBR jointly with genetic algorithms into an E-Learning System, in order to develop examination or assessment analysis processes. However, of all the works we analyzed, the McSherry's approach [13] captured our attention. This author used CBR for addressing the automatic generation of multiple-choice questions problem for supporting an evaluation system. Through a set of cases, describing experiences and events of a given domain of knowledge, the system generated a set of multiple-choice questions based on a set of cases whose rates of interest and similarity satisfied the criteria of the question generation process. Complemented with some specific work, the approach of McSherry served as a guide in the integration of CBR mechanisms in a rule-base assessment system developed for the E-Learning system previously referred. In the next section, we will present and describe how we made the CBR integration.

2.1 The E-learning System

During the last years we have been developing, an artificial tutor [9] especially oriented to improve teaching and learning processes of students in various fields of study within a curricular unit of an institution, through the realization of knowledge assessment process supported by interactive quiz sessions. Throughout these sessions, the system monitors and records the behavior of students, measuring the expertise and knowledge demonstrated, so that it can establish learning profiles for each one that performs these sessions. Having this knowledge, the system can adjust its behavior throughout assessment sessions, according to the performance of the students, while storing various data elements (knowledge domains covered, number of questions presented, number of correct or incorrect answers, response times, etc.), which are essential for the establishment of the learning profiles. The system was designed for helping students in their preparation by customizing learning sessions and providing them with behavior indicators conceived for improving their performance. However, it is also a useful tool for teachers, since they can adjust their teaching and assessment processes in a personalized way, since they can have access to students' profiles and knowledge assessment results.

The system was designed following some learning experiences acquired during lecturing on different courses in many years of professional activities and inspired on some of the best learning and assessment practices. To materialize that, we conceived a specific inference engine that works over a knowledge base containing assessment data structures, evaluation heuristics, student profiles, assessment constraints, and other auxiliary structures. The system works with all these elements to define what is the best strategy for evaluating students' knowledge during an assessment quiz session. The system's evaluation model was designed accordingly to the requirements of various fields of knowledge, independently of their characteristics and domain's specificities. We used quiz tests for support assessment sessions. It is one of the most widely used format for evaluation large community of students. In a quiz session, the system may launch several sequences of multiple answer questions – the system works based on multiple-choice / single-answer format [14] –, which are generated automatically by the reasoning system. In every assessment cycle, the system collects and evaluates the learning profile of a student and accordingly its properties (level of expertise, level of knowledge, domains approached, quiz sessions, questions launched, correct answers, answering times, etc.) it decides what questions will be launched and presented to students.

2.2 Knowledge Assessment

Initially, the user that is in charge of the studying domain configures knowledge assessment sessions. He has the competence to define all the assessment parameters, like the initial competence level, the expected performance, the minimum sequence of hits, etc., for the selected knowledge domain and to specify the questions that he intends to use as a working basis. This configuration serves to define the evaluation criteria that should be apply to the knowledge assessment process. At an early stage, when the student is new to the system and its profile is unknown, the system uses the domain configuration and the basic questions specified to trigger the process. However, even in these circumstances, the system's profiler initiates the generation of the student's profile, recording all the actions taken since the launch of the first selected question. This action history allows for tracking all knowledge level transitions that the student had over time. The student's profile will be used in all the stages of an assessment process. As the assessment session evolves, having the student correct answers or not, his profile is updated and the new version used next for indicating to the system how to behave in the selection and launch of a new question. Let us see, in a more concrete way, how the system acts in this process.

As we can see in Fig. 1, the assessment process occurs in four different stages. They are: 1) configuration of the student assessment process ("Configure Assessment Process"); 2) selection and gathering of candidate questions ("Gather Valid Questions), 3) definition of an adequate question to be launched, following the requisites of the knowledge domain evaluation process ("Select a Question"), and 4) presenting the question to the student and receive an answer ("Present Question and Receive Answer"). All like a regular quiz process. The first tasks has already been explained previously, when we refer to the initial configuration of the system before starting an assessment process.

The assessment system acts like a conventional selection and decision program, applying dynamically a set of rules throughout the various stages of an assessment session, activating different actions for selecting questions and deciding which one of them will be the most appropriate to launch, according the triggered rules. In practice, the system acts as a conventional rule-based system, despite being incorporated in a block of autonomous programs. After checking the status of the student, the system collects its current profile, in order to obtain some elements that are necessary for selecting the next question, such as the student's knowledge level and expertise, the questions already used and their precedencies, or the student's response time average. Having these elements, the reasoning system collects a set of candidate questions in the system's document store, evaluates them and decides what the next question to launch is. In the decision

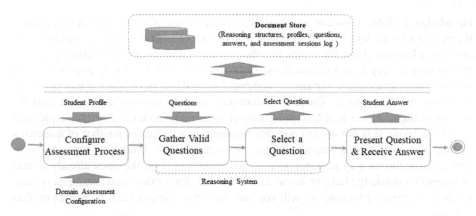

Fig. 1. Functioning schema of the reasoning system.

process, the reasoning system analyzes the previous answered questions, to verify the size of the sequence of answers given correctly (a positive backlog), the knowledge level of the, its expertise in terms of response times and precedence of the questions. All these elements are essential to define the level of difficulty of the new question. The backlog is used to avoid fortuitous rises or unlucky descents of the student's knowledge level. In addition, the system controls the precedence and repetition of questions to respect the way they were configured. The level of difficulty of a question will increase (or decrease) over time according to the performance of the student and the rules that were previously established by the knowledge domain manager.

Table 1. A selected group of properties of a student's profile.

Property	Description	Domain
User Id	*Student's identification*	INT
Knowledge Domain	*Description of the knowledge domain*	STRING
User Level	*Student's knowledge level within the knowledge domain*	INT (1..5)
User Performance	*Student's performance*	INT (1..5)
User Expertise	*Percentage of efficiency of the student in the knowledge domain*	INT (1..5)
Correct Answers	*Number of right answers given by the student*	INT
Wrong Answers	*Number of wrong answers given by the student*	INT
User Hit Rate	*Knowledge domain hit rate*	DECIMAL
Answering Time	*Total time spent by a student answering questions*	INT
Positive Back Log	*Longer sequence of correct answers given by the student*	INT

The profile of a student increases over time according to the number of assessment sessions he has taken, and the number of questions he answered in a given domain of knowledge. In Table 1, we can see the description of some of the properties that defines the profile of a student in a given domain of knowledge. This will allow getting very concrete elements about the topics that the student know or reveals difficulties. This information is very useful for teachers. After selecting and presenting a question to a student, the system collects the answer and evaluates if it is correct. Then, this data will be sent to the profiling system. The process continues until the moment the student ends the session or the system is unable to present more questions. In fact, the system's question "stock" is finite. It is not always possible to maintain a sufficient number of questions to support very long assessment sessions. To overcome this limitation, we decided to find an expeditious way to generate new questions based on the ones already stored in system's knowledge base or in the data collected during the knowledge assessment sessions. In the next section, we will see how the integration of CBR helped us on this process.

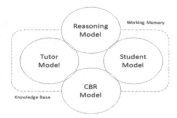

Fig. 2. Models and working structures illustration of the reasoning system.

2.3 CBR Integration

Using CBR in the system imposed some modifications in the previously adopted reasoning model (Fig. 2), which included a tutor model, a student model and a reasoning model, which incorporate the definition of parameters and action modes, respectively, of the manager of the knowledge domain, the student and the system, during a knowledge assessment process. To these models, we added a new CBR model, inspired by the work developed by McSherry [13]. This author presented a mechanism, called AutoMCQ, for generating automatically multiple-choice questions, following a case-based approach. The construction of the sentence of a question is carried out through the instantiation of templates, which regulate its own structure and contents. Then, the sentence reinforced using the information contained in the case base, for getting the various answering options. To the option defined as the correct answer, the system includes several other incorrect answering options, designed as distractors, which have a high degree of similarity with the correct one.

The system only applies the CBR model at the end of a quiz session, when it can no longer evolve further in the process of knowledge assessment, when it can no longer select a new question according to the requirements of the ongoing process. The CBR system acts in a conventional way, generating the new questions in four main stages, similarly to those that characterize a conventional CBR process, namely: retrieve, reuse, revise

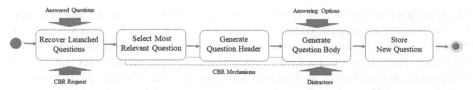

Fig. 3. The main tasks of the CBR system.

and retain. In Fig. 3 we can see the main tasks we have implemented to accommodate the CBR process and its main tasks.

The retrieve phase is activated when the CBR System receives a request to generate a new question ("CBR Request"). At this stage, the system select an initial collection of cases ("Recover Launched Questions") – the most interesting cases to sustain the formation of the new question – to obtain the most appropriate case to define the new question ("Select Most Relevant Question"). In practice, the most appropriate question is selected, with the greater interest, from the questions answered previously having a certain level of difficulty, a domain and a subdomain of knowledge. To calculate the interest (i) of the new question (Eq. 1), we combined and weighted three data elements maintaining in the system's document store, for each question used in knowledge assessment sessions. These elements are the number of times the question has been answered (a), the number of answering choices (o), and the number of correct answering choices (c). The influence of each of these elements in the calculation of the interest of the answer was defined based of its relevance, and the weights of the referred elements defined with the values of 0.6, 0.3 and 0.1, respectively.

$$i \leftarrow (0.6 \times a) + (0.3 \times o) + (0.1 \times c) \tag{1}$$

The reuse phase is the next. At this stage, the new question is prepared modifying the "Header" and "Body" attributes of the question having the greater interest value. Changing these attributes allows to present new elements for studying to users in the form of a new question. The modification of the "Header" ("Generate Question Header") implies the replacement of words in its sentences, in particular, nouns and adjectives, by some of their synonyms. To accomplish this task, we used the spaCy library [15]. This is a natural language processing tool, which is available in the Python programming language. One of the most important working elements in this process is the spaCy's natural language model. This model allows for getting the various grammatical characteristics of a word, such as the gender or the syntactic category (noun, adjective, etc.). It is also possible to associate the words that have the same meaning and then the various meanings associated with each of them. Using spaCy, we modified nouns and adjectives contained in the header of the question, using the gender and plurality of each word (singular and plural) the library provides, as well as the lemmas associated with each word and the lemma whose gender and plurality are equal to those of the word to be replaced. Still in the reuse phase, we also change the body of the question ("Generate Question Body"), to obtain a more interesting and diverse set of answering options for the question. When modifying the body of a question, we also introduce distractors, which are incorrect answer options, having a high similarity level to the correct options.

The verification of the similarity between answering options is performed also by spaCy. For each incorrect answer, its degree of similarity is added to the degree of similarity of the correct answer. Then we calculate their average to get the similarity degree of the option we select. Thus, the question's body will integrate a correct answer and a group of incorrect answers having the best similarity average. The "Validate New Question" task is the next. This task analyzes the various elements of the new question that may introduce some kind of redundancy or incoherence in the case base of the system. The correction of anomalies is ensured by a specific module of the system that verifies if the identification of the question is repeated, checks if knowledge domains' names are poorly defined, and verifies if there are very similar answering options and if the element of interest of the question is updated, among other things. The incorrect answering choices having the same answering options sentences are eliminated and the values of the correct, mandatory, and elimination attributes being different from '0' or '1' assume the default value of '0'.

Finally we enter the retain phase, performing the "Store New Question" task. This task inserts the new question into the system's document store, introducing it into the question collection. Like all data element management or manipulation operations in the system, this insertion is performed by a MongoDB query – `mongo.db.questions.insert(self.working_memory[New_Question])`. In this query, the parameter "New_Question" transports to the document store management system the new question, in a specific JSON structure, with a format quite similar to the one presented in Fig. 4. The JSON structure is developed gradually during the assessment process and kept active in the working memory of the system before being sent to the document store for updating the system's knowledge base.

```
"_id":ObjectId("61a8ea6f8859b5ca37ebca9d"),
"id":"PTEINSBDSQL023",
"language":"pt",
"study_cycle":"Ensino Superior",
"scholarity":"Engenharia Informática",
"domain":"Sistemas de Bases de Dados",
"subdomain":"SQL",
"subsubdomain":"",
"difficulty_level":"1",
(...)
"header":"Como é que poderemos tornar mais clara e compreensível a escrita de instruções SQL?",
"body":[
    {
        "answer":"Utilizando uma abordagem combinada de identação e de lineação.",
        "correction":"1",
        "mandatory":"1",
        "eliminative":"0",
        "points":"0"
    } (...)
] (...)
```

Fig. 4. A fragment of the JSON structure of a new question.

3   Conclusions and Future Work

In this paper, we presented and discussed the integration of a set of CBR mechanisms in an E-learning system for reinforcing student knowledge assessment processes already implemented. We approached the main stages of CBR integration and explained how it was made, exposing the way it acts during an assessment session in conjunction with the previous implementation of the rule based reasoning mechanisms of the system. The CBR system developed allows for diversifying the process of generating assessment questions over time, session after session. This way, the system becomes more capable in understanding how it can relate the students' knowledge analyzing the questions system launched to students in a certain domain of knowledge. The quality of the questions increases as new cases are inserted in the system's database. Over time, as new questions are generated, we can achieve a very satisfactory question generation mechanisms, ensuring a sustained way for continuing a knowledge assessment process beyond the structures placed initially in the system's knowledge. However, this not correspond to the current state of the system. Despite the potential of the CBR integration carried out, the system stills remain a prototype, being a little more than a simple proof of concept.

Although we consider that the results obtained quite positive, we intend to improve them changing and extending the current CBR implementation in order to raise the sophistication of the definition of the questions' headers and bodies. For example, it will be useful to extend the abilities of the task that changes the sentences used in the questions to allow substituting other word grammatical categorizations. Furthermore, the introduction of new interest and similarity measures will be quite pertinent for improving the introduction of distractors in the question's body, ensuring the generation of more adequate questions taking into consideration the student's profile and the assessment requirements of the knowledge domain.

Acknowledgements. This work has been supported by FCT – Fundação para a Ciência e Tecnologia within the R&D Units Project Scope: UIDB/00319/2020.

References

1. Preethi, S.: A survey on artificial intelligence. Int. J. Intell. Comput. Technol. (IJICT) **3**(2), 39–42 (2020)
2. Moore, J., Dickson-Deane, C., Galyen, K.: E-learning, online learning, and distance learning environments: are they the same? Internet High. Educ. **14**(2), 129–135 (2011). ISSN 10967516
3. Aamodt, A., Plaza, E.: Case-based reasoning: foundational issues, methodological variations, and system approaches. AI Commun. **7**(1), 39–59 (1994)
4. Bartsch-Spörl, B., Lenz, M., Hübner, A.: Case-based reasoning – survey and future directions. In: Puppe, F. (ed.) XPS 1999. LNCS, vol. 1570, pp. 67–89. Springer, Heidelberg (1999). https://doi.org/10.1007/10703016_4
5. Sharma, M., Sharma, C.: A review on diverse applications of case-based reasoning. In: Sharma, H., Govindan, K., Poonia, R.C., Kumar, S., El-Medany, W.M. (eds.) Advances in Computing and Intelligent Systems. AIS, pp. 511–517. Springer, Singapore (2020). https://doi.org/10.1007/978-981-15-0222-4_48
6. Wang, S.C., Yang, H.L.: A recommender mechanism based on case-based reasoning. Expert Syst. Appl. **39**(4), 4335–4343 (2012)
7. Mamcenko, J., Kurilovasi, E., Krikun, I.: On application of case-based reasoning to personalise learning. Inform. Educ. **18**(2), 345–358 (2019). https://doi.org/10.15388/infedu.2019.16
8. Henriet, J.: Collaborative CBR-based agents in the preparation of varied training lessons. Int. J. Comput. Sci. Sport IACSS Univ. Vienna Braca **13**(2), 4–19 (2014)

9. Belo, O., Coelho, J., Fernandes, L.: An evolutionary software tool for evaluating students on undergraduate courses. In Proceedings of 12th annual International Conference of Education, Research and Innovation (ICERI 2019), Seville, Spain, vol. 1, pp 2711–2721 (2019)
10. Perner, P.: Case-based reasoning – methods, techniques, and applications. In: Nyström, I., Hernández Heredia, Y., Milián Núñez, V. (eds.) CIARP 2019. LNCS, vol. 11896, pp. 16–30. Springer, Cham (2019). https://doi.org/10.1007/978-3-030-33904-3_2
11. Khamparia, A., Pandey, B.: A novel method of case representation and retrieval in CBR for e-learning. Educ. Inf. Technol. **22**(1), 337–354 (2017)
12. Huang, M.J., Huang, H.S., Chen, M.Y.: Constructing a personalized e-learning system based on genetic algorithm and case based reasoning approach. Expert Syst. Appl. **33**, 551–564 (2007)
13. McSherry, D.: A case-based reasoning approach to automating the construction of multiple choice questions. In: Bichindaritz, I., Montani, S. (eds.) ICCBR 2010. LNCS (LNAI), vol. 6176, pp. 406–420. Springer, Heidelberg (2010). https://doi.org/10.1007/978-3-642-14274-1_30
14. McDermott, K., Agarwal, P., Antonio, L., Roediger, H., Mcdaniel, M.: Both multiple-choice and short-answer quizzes enhance later exam performance in middle and high school classes. J. Exp. Psychol. Appl. **20**, 3–21 (2013)
15. Honnibal M., Montani, I., spaCy · Industrial-strength Natural Language Processing in Python (2017)

Meta-Learning for Hyperparameters Tuning in CNNs for Chest Images

Jesús García-Ramírez[1] , Rodrigo Ramos Díaz[1] , Jimena Olveres[1,2] ,
and Boris Escalante-Ramírez[1,2(✉)]

[1] Facultad de Ingeniería, Universidad Nacional Autónoma de México,
Mexico City, Mexico
{jesus-garcia,jolveres}@cecav.unam.mx, ruyrdiaz@comunidad.unam.mx
[2] Centro de Estudios en Computación Avanzada,
Universidad Nacional Autónoma de México, Mexico City, Mexico
boris@cecav.unam.mx

Abstract. Hyperparameter tuning is a time-consuming task for deep learning models. Meta-learning offers a promising solution to reduce the time required for this task. In this work, we propose a meta-learning approach to simulate a set of experiments and select a hyperparameter configuration (HC) that achieves high accuracy using a deep model. Our formulation involves conducting a grid search over hyperparameters to train a convolutional neural network and get an overview of their space. Then, a meta-regressor was trained using the experiment data to predict accuracy as a function of hyperparameter sets. Subsequently, the trained meta-regressor was employed to simulate diverse HCs and assess the corresponding deep model performance. Our approach was tested across two different domains: COVID-19 detection using X-ray images, and lung detection in computer tomography volumes. Furthermore, we evaluated the proposed approach with two different architectures. Our results show that the proposed method can simulate a set of experiments using the meta-regressor, saving time and computing resources during hyperparameter tuning.

Keywords: Deep learning · Meta-Learning · Simulation · Hyperparameter tuning

1   Introduction

Long training times in deep models are an important limitation especially in the absence of specialized hardware. Ceron and Castro [3], mention an example of the computational cost of training the Rainbow agent [9] with a powerful Graphic Processing Unit (NVIDIA Tesla P100). Each Atari game takes 5 days to train with the mentioned hardware and it is necessary to report the performance within confidence bounds. Consequently, an average of five independent runs is reported. They provide empirical evidence that Rainbow requires approximately 1,425 days without taking into account hyperparameter tuning.

© The Author(s), under exclusive license to Springer Nature Switzerland AG 2023
P. García Bringas et al. (Eds.): HAIS 2023, LNAI 14001, pp. 73–83, 2023.
https://doi.org/10.1007/978-3-031-40725-3_7

Meta-learning is the process of distilling the experience of multiple learning episodes, often covering a distribution of related tasks, and using this experience to improve future learning performance [10]. Meta-learning has emerged as a promising approach to expedite time-consuming tasks such as hyperparameter tuning by using meta-data [8,14]. This technique leverages the knowledge gained from previous experiences to learn more efficiently. By using a reduced number of performance examples, a meta-regressor can accurately predict the performance of new configurations without having to train them all. This enables the simulation of new performances in a more efficient manner.

Based on the above, and different from those approaches mentioned in literature [1,7,14], our main contribution constitutes a meta-learning formulation that predicts the accuracy of a deep model based on a regressor trained with a limited number of hyperparameter sets. To demonstrate the effectiveness of our proposed approach, we conducted experiments using chest medical images that include X-ray and computer tomography. First, we trained deep models using a grid search strategy, resulting in a collection of training examples. We then employed a meta-regressor to learn from these examples and predict the performance of new hyperparameter configurations, thus enabling the identification of high-performing hyperparameter settings for deep model training.

The proposed method was evaluated with an interpretable convolutional neural network using Class-Specific Gate (CSG) [12]. CSG considers a matrix G that is used to train specific convolutional kernels for each class in the penultimate layer of a deep model. In the ideal case, each kernel belongs to a single class, however, in order to reduce the complexity of the implementation, a kernel might share at most two classes. During training, two paths are followed. In the first one, a standard training is carried out in which all convolutional kernels are considered for the backpropagation step. In the second path, some epochs considering the matrix G are performed. Authors argue that the obtained models are more interpretable for humans than the optimized with standard training.

Our experiments show that the proposed method accurately predicts how well different hyperparameter configurations will perform. By using this method, we can simulate new experiments and reduce the time needed for hyperparameter tuning when training deep models. We also tested our method on two different types of chest images to show that it works well in different scenarios.

This paper is organized as follows: in Sect. 2 we introduce background of meta-learning: the proposed formulation for hyperparameter tuning is presented in Sect. 3; the experimental results are introduced in Sect. 4; finally, in Sect. 5 we show the conclusions and future work.

2   Meta-Learning

Meta-learning is the process of distilling the experience of multiple learning experience - often covering a distribution of related tasks - and using this experience to improve future learning performance [10]. The framework is further developed by introducing a mechanism which allows the model to incorporate knowledge from multiple related tasks. This is achieved by using a combination of meta-learning techniques, such as model architecture search [6] and hyperparameter optimization [14]. At the end of the paper, we discuss how this framework can be applied to reduce the time spent on hyperparameter tuning for deep learning models.

In conventional machine learning, a training dataset contains pairs of input (x_i) and output (y_i) values, represented as $D = (x_1, y_1), \ldots, (x_n, y_n)$. The goal of training a neural network is to learn a function that can accurately predict output values from inputs. This function is typically represented as it is shown in Eq. 1, where θ is a set of parameters, such as weights in a neural network. The parameters are learned through an optimization process that minimizes the difference between the predicted outputs and the predicted outputs in the training dataset.

$$\hat{y} = f_\theta(x) \tag{1}$$

Meta-learning is a learning technique that aims to obtain knowledge that can be used to learn the parameters θ of a model [10]. This is typically achieved by solving an optimization problem in the form of Eq. 2, where $\mathcal{L}$ is a loss function that measures the error between the true labels and the predicted ones, and ω are assumptions about "how to learn", such as the hyperparameters of a neural network. In this scheme, the optimization problem is solved across a set of related learning tasks, such as classification or regression problems, in order to learn a set of parameters that are better suited for these tasks. The resulting meta-learned parameters can then be used to improve the performance of a model on new, unseen tasks.

$$\theta^* = \arg\min_\theta \mathcal{L}(D; \theta, \omega) \tag{2}$$

This study demonstrates the effectiveness of using a meta-regressor to approximate the accuracy of different hyperparameter configurations for training deep models. The meta-regressor, which plays the role of the ω in meta-learning, was trained using multiple episodes collected from training the model using different hyperparameter configurations (ω) following a grid search strategy. By learning from the collected episodes, the meta-regressor can accurately predict the performance of new hyperparameter configurations without having to perform an exhaustive grid search. The experimental results presented in this study show that the proposed method can achieve high accuracy in predicting the performance of different hyperparameter configurations.

3   Meta-Learning for Hyperparameter Tuning

This section outlines the proposed method for hyperparameter tuning using meta-learning. Specifically, we introduce the use of a meta-regressor to predict the performance of a hyperparameter configuration when used to train a deep model. The meta-regressor takes important hyperparameters for convolutional neural network training as input and outputs the predicted accuracy. This approach aims to improve the efficiency of the hyperparameter tuning task by reducing the number of configurations that need to be trained and evaluated.

The proposed formulation can be seen graphically in Fig. 1. First, we need some examples of the training performance. In order to obtain those samples, we ran experiments following a grid search strategy [13]. To reduce the training time we ran the experiments only for few epochs, hypothesizing that if the performance increases in few epochs it will increase even more in subsequent epochs [20].

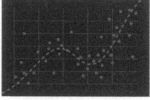

Lr	β_1	β_2	...	ϵ
0.0001	0.93	0.95	...	5e-07
...	...			
0.0009	0.95	0.95	...	9e-07

(a) Perform different experiments for few epochs with different hyperparameters.

(b) Use the results for build the regressor for predicting the performance of the hyperparameters

Lr	β_1	β_2	...	ϵ
0.0001	0.93	0.95	...	5e-07
...	...	...	...	...
0.0009	0.95	0.95	...	9e-07

(c) Simulate new experiments with the regressor with different hypeprparameters from the training.

	Covid	Non-Covid
Covid	53	3
Non-Covid	4	42

(d) Evaluate the best hyperparameters predicted by the regressor.

Fig. 1. Proposed method for hyperparameter tuning with meta-learning: (a)) Experimental results of few epochs using a grid search; (b) The obtained results are used to build a regressor for predicting the performance of the hyperparameters; (c) Simulation of new experiments with a regression model with new samples; (d) Evaluation of the best hyperparameters according to the results obtained in (c).

The results obtained from training deep models with different hyperparameter configurations were used to train the meta-regressor, as described in the background section. Specifically, some important the hyperparameters of the Adam optimizer [11] (learning rate, β_1, $beta_2$, ϵ) were used as features to train the meta-regressor for standard training. For CSG training, relevant hyperparameters related to interpretability were selected as features (see Table 1). The meta-regressor was trained using a set of episodes, each consisting of a combination of hyperparameters and their corresponding validation accuracy after a few epochs of training. Formally, the meta-regressor was trained to learn the mapping $\omega \rightarrow \mathcal{L}_{val}$, where ω represents the used hyperparameters and $\mathcal{L}_{val}$ represents the validation loss after a certain number of epochs.

To further evaluate the effectiveness of the proposed method, we conducted simulations of new experiments using the trained meta-regressor. We simulated experiments to explore if there was any hyperparameter configuration that outperformed the best result obtained in the previous grid search. Afterwards, we evaluated the performance of the selected hyperparameters configuration, identified by the meta-regressor, by training a deep model using the corresponding HC.

To clarify the objectives of the simulation, our aim is to observe whether there exists a hyperparameter configuration that performs better than the ones obtained through the grid search. By using the meta-regressor, we are able to simulate the performance of different hyperparameters without running the entire grid search, thereby reducing the time required for hyperparameter tuning. The method also allows us to obtain a hyperparameter configuration with good results in a shorter time compared to training the entire grid search. Furthermore, the proposed method can be easily adapted to different deep learning architectures and datasets, as long as a representative set of hyperparameter configurations is available for training the meta-regressor. Overall, the proposed method offers a practical and time-saving approach to hyperparameter tuning, which can lead to significant reductions in computational costs when conducting deep learning experiments.

4 Experimental Results

The aim of the experiments was to show that with a regression model, the experiments of hyperparameter tuning could be reduced simulating different HCs. In this section, we first describe the dataset. Then, we introduce the results obtained fitting the regression model. Finally, the results of the validation stage of the meta-regressor are presented.

4.1 Datasets Description

We used the updated kaggle X-ray dataset for COVID-19 detection. The number of images in the dataset are 21,165 images comprising four different classes: COVID-19, normal, pneumonia and lung opacity [4]. Additionally, we used 199 training volumes from the 2020 COVID-19 Lung CT Lesion Segmentation Challenge [18]. The volumes belong to chest computer tomography from patients with positive RT-PCR for SARS-CoV-2. In these experiments, we used a subset of 4,891 slices. Classes were balanced, so they were randomly sampled among images with and without lungs. In the present study, a random stratified selection approach was employed to partition both datasets into training (80%) and testing (20%) subsets, with 20% of the training subset reserved for validation purposes.

4.2 Results of the Meta-Regressor

As discussed in Sect. 3, in order to train the meta-regressor, it is necessary to gather examples of the system performance along with their corresponding sets of hyperparameters. To collect this data, we employed a grid search technique that systematically explores a range of values for the most significant hyperparameters of the learning method, examining its response to different hyperparameter configurations. This allowed us to assemble a comprehensive dataset encompassing a diverse set of hyperparameter combinations and their corresponding system performance measures, which was subsequently used to train the meta-regressor.

For the X-ray images, we followed a standard training procedure using the Adam optimizer [11]. The hyperparameters used to apply the grid search included the learning rate, β_1, β_2, and ϵ, this is because these hyperparameters are important during the optimization of the neural network weights. In this experiments, we used the VGG16 architecture [19], the agents was trained for five epochs to reduce the overall training time.

In the CSG training, we employed the hyperparameters listed in Table 1 for the grid search. These experiments used a computer tomography dataset to demonstrate the robustness of the proposed method. Since the tomography dataset contains more images than the X-ray dataset, we tested our method with a lighter architecture, specifically the VGG11 architecture. This also allowed us to validate our method with different neural network architectures. The agent was trained for 30 epochs.

Table 1. Hyperparameters used for the grid search in CSG training

Hyperparameter	Description
Learning rate (LR)	Learning rate for the optimizer
Mask Period (MP)	Number of epochs the period is alternated
Mask epoch min (MEM)	Epochs applying CSG training
Lr reg (L_REG)	Learning rate of the loss regularization path
λ reg (λ_REG)	Regularization coefficient

A computer with a Titan RTX graphic card, 128 GB of memory and a AMD thread tripper 3970 processor with 64 cores was used for experimentation. In order to show an empirical result of the training time during the hyperparameter tuning task, we ran the experiments of the grid search for the X-ray dataset, which took approximately 5 h (each epoch takes 30 s). In contrast, training with the computer tomography dataset took almost 10 days (each epoch takes near to 1 min).

We selected Random Forests (RF) [2] and Support Vector Regressor (SVR) [5] to build the regressor model due to their robustness to overfitting, and generalization capabilities. In the Random Forest (RF) model, we used a forest consisting of 100 decision, this empirically chosen value yielded the best performance across various practical applications [15]. In the case of the Support Vector Regression (SVR) model, multiple experiments were conducted using multiple kernels, including the radial basis function, linear, and polynomial kernels. The remaining parameters were set according to the default values recommended by the scikit-learn library [16].

During the grid search, the data collected was partitioned into a training set comprising 80% of the samples and a validation set comprising the remaining 20%. To ensure robustness and avoid potential bias from a single data split, we followed the methodology outlined in Raschka and Mirjalili work [17]. Specifically, we repeated the data splitting process one hundred times, each time using a different random seed. The results of this iterative selection process are summarized in Table 2, which presents the mean and standard deviation values obtained from these repetitions. Notably, the RF regressor exhibited superior performance in terms of mean squared error compared to the SVR. Consequently, we selected the RF model as the most promising candidate for validating new hyperparameter configurations. Finally, using the entire dataset, we constructed the meta-regressor.

Table 2. Results of the meta-regressor training. We show the results for both datasets, X-ray and Computer Tomography (CT). Random Forest regressor obtained the best performance with the lowest mean squared error (MSE).

Algorithm	X-ray	CT
RF	0.0122 ± 0.003	$3.96^{-5} \pm 3.34^{-5}$
SVR-RBF	0.0160 ± 0.002	0.0010 ± 0.0002
SVR-Poly	0.0159 ± 0.002	0.0010 ± 0.0003
SVR-Linear	0.0266 ± 0.004	0.0010 ± 0.0003

4.3   Validation with New Data

In this section, we present the outcomes of simulated experiments using the regression model. To validate the model's performance, we assessed various hyperparameters in conjunction with the regression model chosen in the preceding subsection (a Random Forest algorithm with 100 decision trees).

The simulations with the meta-learner were tested on a computer with less resources than the training computer described in the previous subsection. The computer has a core i7-6560 processor with 8 GB of memory. The experiments were run in a single core of the computer. The objective of employing a computer system with limited resources was to demonstrate the diminished duration required for hyperparameter tuning, as compared to a more robust computational platform.

We simulated 250,500 HCs for the X-ray dataset. Considering that each experiment with 5 epochs takes about 30 s in the computer with the Titan GPU for the X-ray dataset, if we trained the entire grid search it would take approximately 70.31 days, while the simulation of the experiments in the computer described in the above paragraph took 23.98 min. Although the simulation results for the top HC scores showed similar predicted accuracy, it is important to note that the validation of the HC space was performed using a range of percentiles rather than solely relying on the Top-HC. Table 3 presents some examples of the HC scores at different percentiles of the space.

Table 3. Best hyperparameter configurationS for the X-ray dataset with corresponding predicted accuracies of the regression model.

LR	β_1	β_2	ϵ	Predicted Accuracy	Real Accuracy
0.0001	0.82	0.70	$5x10^{-7}$	0.9580	0.9527
0.0001	0.82	0.89	$4x10^{-7}$	0.9509	0.9527
0.0001	0.62	0.90	$5x10^{-7}$	0.9450	0.9312
0.0001	0.59	0.52	$9x10^{-7}$	0.9400	0.9398

The next experiment aims to show the effects of increasing the number of epochs on the training of the agent. The learning curve of the best HC is depicted on Fig. 2. It can be seen that in the fifth epoch the predicted performance is similar to the real one (0.0053%). Then, we trained the model for 20 epochs and obtained 96.57% accuracy, which is an acceptable performance.

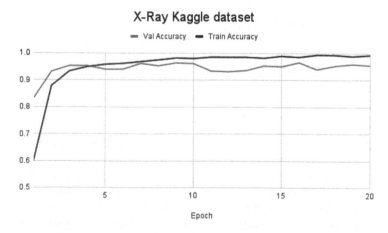

Fig. 2. Learning curve for the best HC. The accuracy at the fifth epoch is 95.27% and the highest accuracy was 96.57% training with 20 epochs.

Table 4 presents some of the HCs obtained for the computer tomography dataset. We initially used the first parameter configuration, expecting it to yield the best performance. However, the first and second HCs achieved similar performance. We also followed a similar strategy of the X-ray dataset to illustrate some parts of the hyperparameter space. Subsequently, we trained the agent with those hyperparameters, and obtained an accuracy of 98.87%, which was close to the predicted performance of 99.17%. Figure 3 shows the learning curve for this training. Despite the second HC yielding better performance, our approach accurately predicted the performance of the meta-regressor in general terms.

We simulated 108,864 HCs for this dataset, each experiment took approximately 30 min. Training the entire grid search would take about 54,432 days. However, with the regression model it took 15.66 min in the computer with limited resources, which is considerable less time than training all the HCs.

Table 4. Best hyperparameter configurations for the computer tomography dataset with corresponding predicted accuracies of the regression model.

LR	MP	MEM	L_REG	λ_REG	Predicted Accuracy	Real Accuracy
0.0006	5	5	0.007	0.004	0.9919	0.9887
0.0003	6	6	0.007	0.005	0.9896	0.9928
0.0003	4	2	0.003	0.005	0.9799	0.9856
0.0001	5	1	0.004	0.005	0.9699	0.9754

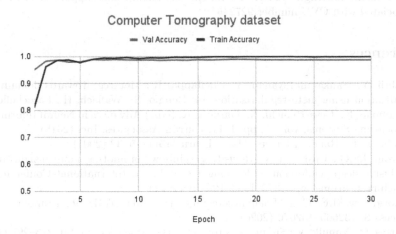

Fig. 3. Learning curve for the best HC. The best accuracy obtained after 30 epochs was 99.08%.

5 Conclusions and Future Work

Based on the clear findings presented in this paper, our proposed meta-learning approach exhibits promising potential in addressing the time-consuming nature of hyperparameter tuning tasks within deep learning models. We have demonstrated the robustness of our approach by involving X-ray images and a computer tomography dataset. Also, leveraging an interpretable convolutional neural network (CNN) and conducting experiments with CSG training and various architectural configurations.

By incorporating relevant hyperparameters as input during the training phase, our method effectively predicts the accuracy of deep models. This indicates its ability to provide valuable insights and inform decision-making regarding hyperparameter selection. However, it is important to discuss the primary limitation of our method, which lies in the requirement for some examples of the deep model performance to train the meta-regressor. This reliance on a sufficient number of performance examples may present challenges in scenarios where such data is limited or unavailable.

In the future, this technique could be extended to other types of deep learning models and datasets, potentially improving the efficiency of hyperparameter tuning across a range of applications. Also, we will apply our formulation to other performance evaluation functions such as F1 measure, precision, etc. Moreover, we wish to study the interpretability of the deep learning models and verify if it can be predicted with the proposed approach as well.

Acknowledgments. This work was supported by the Universidad Nacional Autónoma de México by means of PAPIIT grants TA101121 and IV100420. Rodrigo Ramos Díaz acknowledges CONACYT for the scholarship that supports his PhD studies associated with CVU number 927245.

References

1. Balaji, Y., Sankaranarayanan, S., Chellappa, R.: Metareg: Towards domain generalization using meta-regularization. In: Bengio, S., Wallach, H., Larochelle, H., Grauman, K., Cesa-Bianchi, N., Garnett, R. (eds.) Advances in Neural Information Processing Systems, vol. 31, pp. 1–11. Curran Associates, Inc. (2018)
2. Breiman, L.: Random forests. Mach. Learn. **45**(1), 5–32 (2001)
3. Ceron, J.S.O., Castro, P.S.: Revisiting rainbow: promoting more insightful and inclusive deep reinforcement learning research. In: International Conference on Machine Learning, pp. 1373–1383. PMLR (2021)
4. Chowdhury, M.E.: Can AI help in screening viral and COVID-19 pneumonia? IEEE Access **8**, 132665–132676 (2020)
5. Cortes, C., Vapnik, V.: Support-vector networks. Mach. Learn. **20**, 273–297 (1995)
6. Ding, Y., et al.: Learning to learn by jointly optimizing neural architecture and weights. In: Proceedings of the IEEE/CVF Conference on Computer Vision and Pattern Recognition (CVPR), pp. 129–138 (2022)

7. Franceschi, L., Frasconi, P., Salzo, S., Grazzi, R., Pontil, M.: Bilevel programming for hyperparameter optimization and meta-learning. In: Dy, J., Krause, A. (eds.) Proceedings of the 35th International Conference on Machine Learning. Proceedings of Machine Learning Research, vol. 80, pp. 1568–1577. PMLR (2018)
8. Garouani, M., Ahmad, A., Bouneffa, M., Hamlich, M., Bourguin, G., Lewandowski, A.: Using meta-learning for automated algorithms selection and configuration: an experimental framework for industrial big data. J. Big Data 9(1), 57 (2022)
9. Hessel, M., et al.: Rainbow: combining improvements in deep reinforcement learning. In: Proceedings of the AAAI Conference on Artificial Intelligence (2018)
10. Hospedales, T., Antoniou, A., Micaelli, P., Storkey, A.: Meta-learning in neural networks: a survey. IEEE Trans. Pattern Anal. Mach. Intell. 44(9), 5149–5169 (2021)
11. Kingma, D.P., Ba, J.: Adam: a method for stochastic optimization. arXiv preprint arXiv:1412.6980 (2014)
12. Liang, H., et al.: Training interpretable convolutional neural networks by differentiating class-specific filters. In: Vedaldi, A., Bischof, H., Brox, T., Frahm, J.-M. (eds.) ECCV 2020. LNCS, vol. 12347, pp. 622–638. Springer, Cham (2020). https://doi.org/10.1007/978-3-030-58536-5_37
13. Liashchynskyi, P., Liashchynskyi, P.: Grid search, random search, genetic algorithm: a big comparison for NAS. arXiv preprint arXiv:1912.06059 (2019)
14. Occorso, M., Sabbioni, L., Metelli, A.M., Restelli, M.: Trust region meta learning for policy optimization. In: ECMLPKDD Workshop on Meta-Knowledge Transfer, pp. 62–74. PMLR (2022)
15. Oshiro, T.M., Perez, P.S., Baranauskas, J.A.: How many trees in a random forest? In: Perner, P. (ed.) MLDM 2012. LNCS (LNAI), vol. 7376, pp. 154–168. Springer, Heidelberg (2012). https://doi.org/10.1007/978-3-642-31537-4_13
16. Pedregosa, F., et al.: Scikit-learn: machine learning in python. J. Mach. Learn. Res. 12, 2825–2830 (2011)
17. Raschka, S.: Model evaluation, model selection, and algorithm selection in machine learning. arXiv preprint arXiv:1811.12808 (2018)
18. Roth, H.R.: Rapid artificial intelligence solutions in a pandemic-the COVID-19-20 lung CT lesion segmentation challenge. Med. Image Anal. 82, 102605 (2022)
19. Simonyan, K., Zisserman, A.: Very deep convolutional networks for large-scale image recognition. In: Bengio, Y., LeCun, Y. (eds.) 3rd International Conference on Learning Representations, ICLR 2015, San Diego, CA, USA, 7–9 May 2015, Conference Track Proceedings (2015)
20. Xiao, X., Yan, M., Basodi, S., Ji, C., Pan, Y.: Efficient hyperparameter optimization in deep learning using a variable length genetic algorithm. arXiv preprint arXiv:2006.12703 (2020)

A Fuzzy Logic Ensemble Approach to Concept Drift Detection

Carlos del Campo[✉], Borja Sanz, Jon Díaz, and Enrique Onieva

DeustoTech, Faculty of Engineering, University of Deusto, Av. Universidades, 24, 48007 Bilbao, Spain
carlos.delcampo@opendeusto.es,
{borja.sanz,jon.diaz,enrique.onieva}@deusto.es

Abstract. Concept drift occurs when the statistical properties of a data distribution change over time, causing the performance of machine learning models trained on prior data to degrade. This is a prevalent issue in many real-world applications where the data distribution can shift due to factors such as user behaviour alterations, environmental changes, or modifications in the data-generating system. Detecting concept drift is crucial for developing robust and adaptive machine learning systems. However, identifying excessive drifts may lead to decreased model performance.

In this article, we present an ensemble method employing multiple concept drift detectors to detect concept drift. A fuzzy logic approach balances the outputs of the various drift detectors comprising the ensemble. The proposed framework can handle concept drift in regression problems. Experimental results demonstrate enhanced efficiency in detecting concept drifts under different conditions.

Keywords: Concept drift · Model adaptation · Drift detector · Ensemble learning · Fuzzy logic

1 Introduction

Data streams have significantly evolved, transitioning from early research on simple stochastic processes to today's highly complex and large-scale data streams. Previously, sensors primarily generated data streams, focusing on real-time processing and analysis. With the emergence of the internet and social media, data streams have diversified, encompassing text and multimedia data, and the volume of data has dramatically increased.

As a result, Effective handling of continuous data streams has become a priority across fields such as medicine [5], autonomous vehicle control [10], monitoring, control [6], and strategic planning [17], driven by global market trends. Changes in these data streams can impact trained model performance, underscoring the necessity for efficient concept drift handling. Despite many methods proposed for concept drift detection, their application is limited to specific drift types, with a lack of detectors for regression problems, and an overemphasis on classification models' error rate [11].

The transition from manual to automated concept drift detection and model adaptation has revolutionized the handling of continuous data, aimed at swift processing. Despite the automation advantages, unresolved challenges such as high-reliability issues persist in detections [16].

False alarms can trigger model retraining, increasing costs. Conversely, decreasing the sensitivity of a drift detector may result in a longer average detection delay. Thus, drift detectors must strike a balance between sensitivity and rigidity.

This article proposes a novel concept drift detection framework applicable to classification and regression use cases, combining multiple drift detectors to address these limitations. The proposed approach capitalizes on the strengths of different drift detection methods, identifying concept drift in various scenarios and employing fuzzy logic to balance the ensemble methods. The framework aims to minimize false alarms and average detection delay while maximizing the number of correctly detected drifts. The proposed method is evaluated using several benchmark datasets, simulating a stream and demonstrating its effectiveness in detecting concept drift under different conditions.

The novelty of our study lies in the application of a fuzzy system to determine the weights of individual drift detection models within an ensemble. This innovative approach enhances the ensemble's adaptability and performance in dynamic environments.

This paper is organized as follows. Section 2 presents a related literature review. Section 3 describes the architecture of the proposed framework and its integration with a model. Section 3.1 outlines the method for detecting concept drifts, and Sect. 3.2 details the employed fuzzy system. Subsequently, Sect. 4 presents the obtained experimental results. Finally, Sect. 5 offers conclusions and future work.

2 Literature Review

Anjin Liu et al. [12] proposed an innovative drift detection technique to convert the multivariate two-sample test problem into a goodness-of-fit test for multinomial distributions. They assume that a distribution change is more likely to occur in a closely located group of samples than in an arbitrary shape. To exploit this, they use EI-kMeans, a modified k-means algorithm that searches for optimal centroids to create partitions and employs the Chi-square test (X^2). Additionally, using a distance analysis approach, [8] utilizes centroids for concept drift detection, comparing data chunk centroids in a non-stationary stream.

Cioannis Mavromatis et al. [14] introduce a lightweight ensemble framework of concept drift detectors, comprising Adaptative Windowing (ADWIN), Page Hinkley, and Kolmogorov-Smirnov Windowing (KSWIN) detectors, enabling drift detection in time series without classification. A voting mechanism, in which each detector has equal weight, is employed to determine drift detection. As it is unlikely that a single sample would be classified as abnormal by multiple detectors, a sliding voting window is implemented. The work also differentiates natural and malicious drifts, with appropriate responses. Similarly, Joanna Komorniczak et al. [9] develop a Statistical Drift Detection Ensemble based on the statistical measures Drift Magnitude and Conditioned Marginal Covariate Drift, calculated using probability density distributions estimated through Kernel Density Estimation. Concept drift is identified by comparing the difference between these metrics and the averaged harmonic mean to a multiple of the harmonic mean's standard deviation.

Hang Yu et al. [19] suggest Active Drift Detection with Meta-Learning, a concept drift detector that can automatically pre-train. In the training phase, they develop a meta-detector after the meta-features based on the error rates of various concept drifts. Once it is trained, during the detection phase, the learned meta-detector is adjusted through stream-based active learning to suit the specific data stream better. This method not only provides concept drift detection but also provides information about the type of drift.

Cerqueira et al. [3] suggest a method to deal with concept drift detection based on a model compression approach. This approach involves replacing the loss of the predictive model, acting as the teacher, in the data stream with the mimicking loss of the student model, which is then used as input for traditional concept drift detection methods. The idea is to improve the accuracy of the detection process by using the student model's mimicking loss instead of the teacher's loss.

Amador Coelho et al. [1] introduce a novel drift detector called Quadtree-based Concept Drift Detector (QT), which utilizes a quadtree recursive space division structure to detect concept drift alarms. The QT detector conducts a geometric analysis of the spatial distribution of data in the streaming data without relying on statistical information about the data's distribution. Rather than using the classifier's output, the detector examines the data that led to classifier errors. In this way, the QT drift alarm is activated when sample data is assigned to a child hypercube previously occupied by the opposite class in the quadtree. The detector's sensitivity can be adjusted using a single parameter to control the detection threshold.

Bibinbe et al. [2] put forward a method to detect anomalies in time series extending Drag, a time series abnormal detection method to the data stream by using a similarity measure used in Matrix Profile, and clustering used in MILOF. Also, the method is designed to handle concept drifts in the data stream.

3   Proposed Framework

The flow in the framework is illustrated in Fig. 1. The data stream is directly fed into an ensemble comprising n KSWIN detectors, r ADWIN detectors, and t Page Hinkley detectors. The output generated by these detectors is aggregated into a matrix of shape $(W \times M)$, where W represents the time windows considered for analysing the output of the drift detectors and M denotes the total number

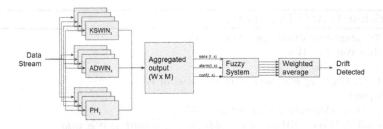

Fig. 1. Data flow in the proposed concept drift detector.

of detectors. This matrix is then used to calculate three indicators, which serve as input for the fuzzy system. The fuzzy system weighs the different detectors, assigning a value to each. The weighted average of the detector output, multiplied by the corresponding fuzzy output, is then calculated. A drift is detected if this weighted average exceeds a certain threshold (θ). If not, no changes in the data distribution are observed.

3.1 Ensemble

The methods included in the ensemble of drift detectors are a set of different parametrizations of well-known KSWIN, ADWIN and Page Hinkley methods. Next, details of those methods are presented.

KSWIN relies on the Kolmogorov-Smirnov test, measuring the absolute distance between two distributions within a sliding window. This window is partitioned into two sections: one containing prior data, and the other encompassing the most recent data. Drift detection is determined by the condition specified in Eq. 1, where r represents the size of incoming data, α denotes the probability for the KS-test [18] and $dist(R, W_k)$ refers to the distance measure between the reference distribution (R) and the sliding window distribution (W_k).

$$dist(R, W_k) > \sqrt{\frac{-\ln(\alpha)}{r}} \qquad (1)$$

ADWIN employs sliding windows of dynamic size, which are calculated online based on the observed changes within these windows. When no change is detected, the algorithm expands the window; conversely, if a change is observed, the window size is decreased. If two windows exhibit sufficient differences, the algorithm identifies concept drift and discards outdated tuples to reduce the window size [7]. The pseudocode of ADWIN is presented in Algorithm 1, where $\hat{\mu}$ represents the estimated mean of the partition.

The Page Hinkley Test, a sequential analysis technique, can serve as a concept drift detector. It calculates a cumulative sum (CUSUM) statistic, which quantifies the deviation of observed data from a reference or baseline value-typically the mean of the data series over a specific time frame [15]. The CUSUM statistic is computed by subtracting the baseline value from each observation and summing the resulting differences cumulatively. Equation 2 presents the expression

---

Algorithm 1: ADWIN algorithm

---

1 ADWIN: Adaptive Windowing Algorithm
2 Initialize Window Wa
3 **for** *each $t > 0$* **do**
4 | $Wa = Wa \cup x_t$ (i.e., add x_t to the head of Wa)
5 | **repeat**
6 | | Drop elements from the tail of Wa
7 | **until** $|\hat{\mu}Wa_0 - \hat{\mu}Wa_1| \geq \epsilon_c$ *holds for every split of Wa into* $Wa = Wa_0 \cdot Wa_1$
8 | ;
9 | Output $\hat{\mu}Wa$

---

for detecting an increase in the average, where δ denotes the minimal absolute value of the amplitude of the variation to being detected. x_i represents an individual data point in a sequence or set. U_n denotes the n-th term or element in the sequence of the cumulative sum.

$$U_n = \sum_{i=1}^{n}(x_i - m_0 - \frac{\delta_2}{2}), \; n \geq 1 \; avec \; U_0 = 0. \tag{2}$$

Then, $m_n = \min_{0 \leq k \leq n}(U_k), n \geq 1$ is calculated and if $U_n - m_0 \geq \lambda$ an alarm is triggered. In the shake of detecting a decrease in the average another test is performed calculating: $m_n = \max_{0 \leq k \leq n}(U_k), n \geq 1$. The alarm is then raised when: $M_n - T_n \geq \lambda$.

Begin by creating the ensemble using various instances of the three previously mentioned methods with distinct parameter configurations. Next, input the data into the drift detectors and structure historical alarm levels in a matrix with as many rows as timesteps and columns as detectors in the ensemble (denoted as *Aggregated output* in Fig. 1). Utilizing this matrix, calculate three indicators for each drift detector to provide inputs for the fuzzy system that determines the weights for balancing the final decision:

– $alarm(t, x)$ indicates whether detector x raised a flag for drift at timestep t. In this work, it is a binary variable with values of 0 or 1 based on the individual detector's output.
– $sens(t, x)$ signifies the sensitivity of detector x at step t. To compute this, a vector containing the last W alarms, denoted as win_t (Eq. 3), is used, and the alarm level raised by the individual detector is weighted based on its proximity to the current step t. The mathematical computation of this indicator can be found in Eq. 5.
– $coinc(t, x)$ represents the agreement of the individual detector's output with the rest of the ensemble within the time window win_t. To determine this, the distance to the outputs within the window is compared with the other detectors using Manhattan distance (Eq. 4). The mathematical computation of this indicator is provided in Eq. 6.

$$win_t = alarm(t, x) \ \forall \ x \in \{t - W...t\} \tag{3}$$

$$dist_t = \sum_{b=0}^{W} \mid win(b, i) - win(b, j) \mid \ \forall j \in \{0...M\} \tag{4}$$

$$sens(t, x) = \frac{\sum_{i=0}^{M} win(t, i) \cdot \{1...M\}}{\{1...M\} \cdot max(\frac{\sum_{i=0}^{M} win_t(i) \cdot \{1...M\}}{\{1...M\}})} \tag{5}$$

$$coinc(t, x) = \begin{cases} 1 - \frac{\frac{\sum_{x=0}^{M} dist_x}{(M-1) \cdot max(\frac{\sum_{x=0}^{M} dist_x}{M-1})}}{max(1 - \frac{\sum_{x=0}^{M} dist_x}{(M-1) \cdot max(\frac{\sum_{x=0}^{M} dist_x}{M-1})})} & \text{if } max(\frac{\sum_{x=0}^{M} dist_x}{M-1}) \neq 0 \\ 1 & \text{otherwise} \end{cases} \tag{6}$$

3.2 Fuzzy System

The fuzzy system is an essential component of this approach. It receives three inputs for each drift detector (x) to weigh their outputs:

- Coincidence $(coinc_x)$ assesses the agreement among individual detectors within the entire ensemble.
- Sensitivity $(sens_x)$ prevents overemphasizing methods that frequently raise drift alarms, thus reducing the importance of methods potentially producing a high number of false alarms.
- Alarm $(alarm_x)$ signifies the method's confidence in the detected drift.

Each antecedent has a range from 0 to 1 and includes two fuzzy sets: *high* and *low*. The "low" membership function is defined with values $a = 0$, $x = 0$, and $b = 1$, while the "high" membership function is set with values $a = 0$, $x = 1$, and $b = 1$, using the formula in Eq. 7. The resulting consequence is the confidence level computed by the fuzzy system.

$$\mu(x) = \begin{cases} 0, & x \leq a | x \geq c \\ \frac{x-a}{b-a}, & a \leq x \leq b \\ \frac{c-x}{c-b}, & b \leq x \leq c \end{cases} \tag{7}$$

The consequent presents seven different fuzzy sets, also using the Formula 7, in pursuance of better differentiation between the outputs. The membership function of the consequent is visualized in Fig. 2. Hence eight different fuzzy rules are created, embodied in Table 1. Both the consequent fuzzy sets and the fuzzy rules were selected based on their performance in an experiment conducted using dummy data, resulting in the best configuration.

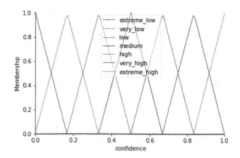

Fig. 2. Membership functions used in the output variable for the fuzzy system.

Table 1. Fuzzy Rules

	Alarm	Confidence	Sensitivity	Confidence
R_1	high	high	low	extreme high
R_2	high	high	high	high
R_3	high	low	low	very high
R_4	high	low	high	low
R_5	low	high	low	medium
R_6	low	high	high	low
R_7	low	low	high	extreme low
R_8	low	low	low	very low

4   Experimentation and Results

This section presents the experimental data in Subsect. 4.1. Additionally, the proposed configuration is elucidated in Subsect. 4.2. Lastly, the outcomes are deliberated in Subsect. 4.3.

4.1   Experimentation Data

This study employs widely used synthetic datasets for testing [13] to detect actual concept drifts and obtain accurate metrics as no real world datasets with registered concept drifts were found. The datasets encompass three distinct stream generation functions. First, the *sine* and *sea* generators rely on a series of classification functions. Second, the Random Tree (*rt*) generator functions through a sequence of tree random state functions. The generator's parameters, including maximum tree depth, minimum leaf depth, and fraction of leaves per level, are set to 6, 3, and 0.15, respectively. Each generator introduces two types of drift: abrupt and gradual, with two variations of the generators featuring reversed classification function orders.

Consequently, each stream generator yields four distinct datasets. In total, twelve different datasets are utilized, adhering to the naming structure in Eq. 8.

$$\{sea \mid sine \mid rt\}\text{-}\{abrupt \mid gradual\}\text{-}\{1 \mid 2\} \tag{8}$$

Each dataset contains 40,000 samples. For the abrupt datasets, concept drifts occur at time steps 10,000, 20,000, and 30,000, while in the gradual datasets, they occur at time steps 9,500, 20,000, and 30,500. The width of the drift in the gradual datasets remains constant at 1,000.

4.2 Configuration

In this research, the ensemble comprises 100 KSWIN instances, 51 ADWIN instances, and 100 Page Hinkley instances, following the parameterization specified in Table 2. The number of instances of each method is associated with the number of parameters it employs.

Table 2. Summary of the composition of the ensemble

KSWIN (100)	α	$\in \{0.05, 0.005, 0.0005, 0.00005, 0.000005\}$
	WS	$\in \{100, 200, 500, 1000\}$
	StS	$\in \{10, 20, 30, 40, 50\}$
ADWIN (51)	δ	$\in \{\frac{200 \cdot n}{1000000} \mid 0 \leq n \leq 50\} \cup \{0.0002\}$
Page Hinkley (100)	λ	$\in \{30, 50, 70\}$
	δ	$\in \{0.0005, 0.001, 0.005, 0.01, 0.05\}$
	α	$\in \{0.7, 0.9, 0.9999\}$

Five distinct metrics were chosen to evaluate the performance of the proposed framework:

- **True Positive Rate (TPR)** denotes the proportion of accurately detected drifts within an acceptable detection interval (ADI), in relation to the total number of detected drifts [4].
- **True Positives per Drift (TPD)** computes the ratio of detected drifts to the total number of drifts, considering only one drift per ADI.
- **Average Detection Delay (ADD)** quantifies the mean distance, based on instances, between actual and predicted concept drifts [4].
- **Drift Total (DT)** pertains to the overall number of drifts identified by a drift detector.
- **Drift Detection Ratio (DDR)** represents the ratio of predicted drifts to actual drifts.

It is noteworthy that a concept drift detector is capable of detecting multiple drifts within the interval of concept drift (ADI), which can result in an inflation of the true positive rate (TPR). Consequently, depending solely on TPR for evaluating the performance of a concept drift detector could lead to misleading outcomes. To mitigate this problem, researchers often use the True Positives per Drift (TPD) metric. In this investigation, both TPR and TPD were utilized, with the ADI set to 5% of the total dataset length for each metric.

4.3   Results

The results of the experiments are shown in Tables 3, 4 and 5, where only the deemed best detector for each detector type is illustrated.

Analyzing the results in Table 3, several conclusions arise. The Fuzzy method demonstrates consistent performance across datasets, achieving a perfect DD ratio (3/3) and a high TPR (1.00). While its ADD is higher than some competitors, it maintains an acceptable detection delay. Fuzzy's TPR and TPD values show its effectiveness in identifying drifts and minimizing false positives. Comparing Fuzzy to other methods, it outperforms KSWIN in TPR, TPD, DD, and DT, indicating superior accuracy in detecting concept drifts. KSWIN generates more false alarms, evidenced by its higher DT score. Fuzzy performs similarly to ADWIN and Page Hinkley in accuracy, with perfect TPR and DD scores. Despite higher ADD values than Page Hinkley, Fuzzy's overall performance remains competitive, signifying its potential as an effective concept drift detection method.

Examining the results from Table 4, Fuzzy holds a distinct advantage in detecting drifts across four datasets compared to other methods. Despite non-perfect TPR and TPD scores, Fuzzy significantly outperforms methods that often fail to detect drifts. The relevant comparison is with KSWIN. Fuzzy consistently detects more drifts than KSWIN, although KSWIN sometimes achieves better TPR and TPD scores. Fuzzy's balanced performance makes it a more reliable option.

Table 5 results show Fuzzy outperforming other methods in detecting drifts across gradual sea datasets, with superior detection accuracy and lower false alarm rates. Fuzzy detects nearly all drifts with the highest TPR, while other methods show lower TPR and higher DT. In abrupt datasets, the trend reverses: Fuzzy detects all drifts but has many false alarms. KSWIN misses one drift but has better TPR and DT. Page Hinkley's performance is comparable to Fuzzy, with fewer false alarms. Adwin fails to detect drifts across sea datasets.

The four methods-Fuzzy, ADWIN, KSWIN, and Page-Hinkley-exhibit varying performance in detecting concept drifts across tested datasets. Fuzzy consistently outperforms others in drift detection, with balanced TPR, TPD, and ADD metrics, making it reliable and effective across various datasets. ADWIN's performance is weaker, failing to detect drifts in most datasets. KSWIN shows inconsistent performance, detecting drifts in some cases but not in others, with less reliable detection capabilities than Fuzzy. PageHinkley exhibits mixed performance and is less dependable than Fuzzy due to inconsistency and variable

Table 3. Comparative results over *rt* datasets.

Dataset	Method	DD	TPR	TPD	ADD	DT
rt_abrupt_1	Fuzzy (0.1)	3/3	1.00	2.30	842.00	7
	ADWIN(0.0084)	3/3	1.00	1.00	821.33	3
	KSWIN(0.05, 200,40)	3/3	0.35	6.33	70.00	54
	PageHinkley(30, 0.05, 0.9999)	3/3	1.00	1.00	155.00	3
rt_gradual_1	Fuzzy (0.125)	3/3	1.00	1.00	1173.33	3
	ADWIN(0.0022)	3/3	1.00	1.00	1301.33	3
	KSWIN(0.005, 100, 30)	3/3	0.83	1.66	3374.67	6
	PageHinkley(50, 0.05, 0.9999)	3/3	1.00	1.00	543.67	3
rt_gradual_2	Fuzzy (0.15)	3/3	1.00	1.00	1066.67	3
	ADWIN(0.0098)	3/3	1.00	1.00	1056.00	3
	KSWIN(0.005, 500, 50)	3/3	0.57	1.33	4024.00	7
	PageHinkley(50, 0.05, 0.9999)	3/3	1.00	1.00	520.67	3
rt_abrupt_2	Fuzzy (0.175)	3/3	1.00	1.00	992.00	3
	ADWIN(0.007)	3/3	1.00	1.00	800.00	3
	KSWIN(0.0005, 500, 10)	3/3	0.75	1.00	118.67	4
	PageHinkley(30, 0.05, 0.9999)	3/3	1.00	1.00	131.67	3

Table 4. Comparative results over *sine* datasets.

Dataset	Method	DD	TPR	TPD	ADD	DT
sine_gradual_1	Fuzzy (0.008)	3/3	0.31	1.67	637.00	16
	ADWIN(0.0012)	0/3	0.00	0.00	0.00	0
	KSWIN(0.05, 100, 20)	1/3	1.00	0.33	4289.33	1
	PageHinkley(70, 0.05, 0.9999)	0/3	0.00	0.00	0.00	0
sine_gradual_2	Fuzzy (0.008)	2/3	0.45	1.67	1672.67	11
	ADWIN(0.0062)	0/3	0.00	0.00	0.00	0
	KSWIN(0.05, 500, 20)	2/3	1.00	1.00	2946.33	2
	PageHinkley(30, 0.05, 0.9999)	0/3	0.00	0.00	0.00	0
sine_abrupt_2	Fuzzy (0.008)	3/3	0.43	2.00	2185.33	14
	ADWIN(0.0054)	0/3	0.00	0.00	0.00	0
	KSWIN(0.05, 1000, 40)	2/3	1.00	0.67	620.67	2
	PageHinkley(70, 0.05, 0.9999)	0/3	0.00	0.00	0.00	0
sine_abrupt_2	Fuzzy (0.008)	3/3	0.42	1.67	4462.67	12
	ADWIN(0.0054)	0/3	0.00	0.00	0.00	0
	KSWIN(0.05, 500, 20)	1/3	1.00	0.33	11784	1
	PageHinkley(70, 0.05, 0.9999)	0/3	0.00	0.00	0.00	0

Table 5. Comparative results over *sea* datasets.

Dataset	Method	DD	TPR	TPD	ADD	DT
sea_gradual_1	Fuzzy (0.0175)	2/3	0.5	1.00	6023.33	6
	ADWIN(0.0054)	0/3	0.00	0.00	0.00	0
	KSWIN(0.05, 500, 10)	3/3	0.36	2.00	535.00	17
	PageHinkley(30, 0.005, 0.9999)	2/3	0.33	1.00	1370.33	9
sea_gradual_2	Fuzzy (0.015)	3/3	0.44	2.67	630.33	18
	ADWIN(0.0054)	0/3	0.00	0.00	0.00	0
	KSWIN(0.05, 1000, 40)	3/3	0.39	3.00	387.33	23
	PageHinkley(30, 0.001, 0.9999)	3/3	0.31	1.33	3071.33	13
sea_abrupto_1	Fuzzy (0.015)	3/3	0.36	3.00	1808.33	25
	ADWIN(0.0054)	0/3	0.00	0.00	0.00	0
	KSWIN(0.005, 500, 40)	2/3	0.67	0.67	4320.00	3
	PageHinkley(30, 0.001, 0.9999)	3/3	0.36	1.67	1915.33	14
sea_abrupto_2	Fuzzy (0.015)	3/3	0.23	2.00	1367.33	26
	ADWIN(0.0054)	0/3	0.00	0.00	0.00	0
	KSWIN(0.005, 1000, 50)	3/3	0.50	1.33	1186.00	8
	PageHinkley(30, 0.0005, 0.9999)	3/3	0.33	1.67	1587.33	15

TPR and TPD scores. Fuzzy emerges as the most effective and reliable choice among the methods for detecting concept drifts in tested datasets due to its generalization capabilities.

5   Conclusions and Future Works

This study introduces a novel drift detector framework designed to identify and adapt to concept drift in data streams. This framework combines base detectors to form an ensemble and employs a fuzzy system to take advantage of the diverse detectors within the ensemble. The proposed approach is versatile and can be applied to various tasks, including classification, time series analysis, and regression problems.

We assessed the performance of the proposed concept drift framework through experiments, which revealed effective generalization and accurate drift detection. However, the framework requires refinement, as it detects the same drift repeatedly and can generate false alarms. Future research will address these issues, enhance framework robustness, and incorporate a regressor and classifier for real-world application. While Fuzzy displays consistent, balanced results, the other three methods (ADWIN, KSWIN and PageHinkley) exhibit varying performance and less reliability due to inconsistent drift detection.

It is essential to note that these conclusions are drawn based on the specific datasets used in this study. Further research and testing on a wider range of datasets and under different conditions may provide additional insights into the performance of these methods. Nonetheless, the Fuzzy method's strong performance in this analysis highlights its potential as a robust and effective solution for detecting concept drifts in various applications.

References

1. Amador Coelho, R., Bambirra Torres, L.C., Leite de Castro, C.: Concept drift detection with quadtree-based spatial mapping of streaming data. Inf. Sci. **625**, 578–592 (2023). https://doi.org/10.1016/j.ins.2022.12.085, https://www.sciencedirect.com/science/article/pii/S0020025522015808
2. Bibinbe, A.M.S.N., Mahamadou, A.J., Mbouopda, M.F., Nguifo, E.M.: DragStream: an anomaly and concept drift detector in univariate data streams. In: 2022 IEEE International Conference on Data Mining Workshops (ICDMW), pp. 842–851 (2022). https://doi.org/10.1109/ICDMW58026.2022.00113
3. Cerqueira, V., Gomes, H.M., Bifet, A., Torgo, L.: STUDD: a student-teacher method for unsupervised concept drift detection. Mach. Learn. 1–28 (2022)
4. Choudhary, V., Gupta, B., Chatterjee, A., Paul, S., Banerjee, K., Agneeswaran, V.: Detecting concept drift in the presence of sparsity-a case study of automated change risk assessment system. arXiv preprint arXiv:2207.13287 (2022)
5. Desale, K.S., Shinde, S.V.: Addressing concept drifts using deep learning for heart disease prediction: a review. In: Gupta, D., Khanna, A., Kansal, V., Fortino, G., Hassanien, A.E. (eds.) Proceedings of Second Doctoral Symposium on Computational Intelligence. AISC, vol. 1374, pp. 157–167. Springer, Singapore (2022). https://doi.org/10.1007/978-981-16-3346-1_13
6. Green, D.H., Langham, A.W., Agustin, R.A., Quinn, D.W., Leeb, S.B.: Adaptation for automated drift detection in electromechanical machine monitoring. IEEE Trans. Neural Netw. Learn. Syst. 1–15(2022)
7. Grulich, P., Saitenmacher, R., Traub, J., BreSS, S., Rabl, T., Markl, V.: Scalable detection of concept drifts on data streams with parallel adaptive windowing (2018). https://doi.org/10.5441/002/edbt.2018.51
8. Klikowski, J.: Concept drift detector based on centroid distance analysis. In: 2022 International Joint Conference on Neural Networks (IJCNN), pp. 1–8 (2022). https://doi.org/10.1109/IJCNN55064.2022.9892399
9. Komorniczak, J., Zyblewski, P., Ksieniewicz, P.: Statistical drift detection ensemble for batch processing of data streams. Knowl. Based Syst. **252**, 109380 (2022). https://doi.org/10.1016/j.knosys.2022.109380, https://www.sciencedirect.com/science/article/pii/S095070512200692X
10. Lee, S., Park, S.H.: Concept drift modeling for robust autonomous vehicle control systems in time-varying traffic environments. Expert Syst. Appl. **190**, 116206 (2022)
11. Lima, M., Neto, M., Filho, T.S., de A. Fagundes, R.A.: Learning under concept drift for regression-a systematic literature review. IEEE Access **10**, 45410–45429 (2022). https://doi.org/10.1109/ACCESS.2022.3169785
12. Liu, A., Lu, J., Zhang, G.: Concept drift detection via equal intensity k-means space partitioning. IEEE Trans. Cybern. **51**(6), 3198–3211 (2021). https://doi.org/10.1109/TCYB.2020.2983962
13. López Lobo, J.: Synthetic datasets for concept drift detection purposes (2020). https://doi.org/10.7910/DVN/5OWRGB

14. Mavromatis, I., et al.: Le3d: A lightweight ensemble framework of data drift detectors for resource-constrained devices (2022). https://doi.org/10.48550/ARXIV. 2211.01840 , https://arxiv.org/abs/2211.01840
15. Mouss, H., Mouss, M., Mouss, K., Linda, S.: Test of page-hinckley, an approach for fault detection in an agro-alimentary production system, vol. 2, pp. 815–818 (2004). DOI: https://doi.org/10.1109/ASCC.2004.184970
16. Poenaru-Olaru, L., Cruz, L., van Deursen, A., Rellermeyer, J.S.: Are concept drift detectors reliable alarming systems? - a comparative study (2022). https://doi. org/10.48550/ARXIV.2211.13098, https://arxiv.org/abs/2211.13098
17. Sun, J., Li, H., Adeli, H.: Concept drift-oriented adaptive and dynamic support vector machine ensemble with time window in corporate financial risk prediction. IEEE Trans. Syst. Man, Cybern. Syst. 43(4), 801–813 (2013)
18. Togbe, M.U., Chabchoub, Y., Boly, A., Barry, M., Chiky, R., Bahri, M.: Anomalies detection using isolation in concept-drifting data streams. Computers 10(1), 13 (2021). https://doi.org/10.3390/computers10010013, https://www.mdpi.com/ 2073-431X/10/1/13
19. Yu, H., Zhang, Q., Liu, T., Lu, J., Wen, Y., Zhang, G.: Meta-add: a meta-learning based pre-trained model for concept drift active detection. Inf. Sci. 608, 996–1009 (2022). https://doi.org/10.1016/j.ins.2022.07.022, https://www. sciencedirect.com/science/article/pii/S0020025522007125

Multi-Task Gradient Boosting

Seyedsaman Emami[(✉)] [ID], Carlos Ruiz Pastor[ID],
and Gonzalo Martínez-Muñoz[ID]

Escuela Politécnica Superior, Universidad Autónoma de Madrid, Madrid, Spain
emami.seyedsaman@uam.es

Abstract. Gradient Boosting Machines (GBMs) have revealed outstanding proficiency in various machine learning applications, such as classification and regression. Gradient boosting builds a set of regression models in an iterative process, in which at each iteration, a regressor model is trained to reduce a given loss on a given objective. This paper proposes an extension of gradient boosting that can handle multi-task problems, that is, problems in which the tasks share the attribute space but not necessarily the data distribution. The objective of the proposed algorithm is to split the GB process into two phases, one in which the base models learn the multiple interconnected tasks simultaneously, and a second one, in which different models are built to optimize the loss function on each task. The performance of proposed model shows a better overall performance with respect to models that learn the tasks independently and all tasks together in several multi-task regression and classification problems.

Keywords: Gradient Boosting · Multi Task learning

1 Introduction

Gradient Boosting Machines (GBM) are a widespread class of machine learning algorithms that have acquired state-of-the-art results in applications, including regression [5,31] and classification [16,26,28] tasks. GBMs are based on combining the predictions of multiple weak learners in order to obtain a more precise outcome. The basic idea behind GBM is to iteratively train weak decision trees on the residual errors of the previous trees, with each new tree attempting to correct the errors of the previous ones [13]. In recent years, Gradient Boosting-based models have experienced significant advancements, resulting in increased training speed and accuracy by means of various techniques, such as XGBoost [9] which includes new regularization techniques, LightGBM [15] that introduced a novel subsampling technique and uses data histograms to reduce the training time of the decision trees drastically, and CatBoost [10] which proposes a novel approach for encoding categorical features and also includes a proposal to reduce the learning bias in the estimation of the residuals.

On some occasions, there are sets of problems that we solve with machine learning techniques can are very closely related. In these situations, instead of

P. García Bringas et al. (Eds.): HAIS 2023, LNAI 14001, pp. 97–107, 2023.
https://doi.org/10.1007/978-3-031-40725-3_9

creating a different model for each task, it could be sensible to create a model that learns the common information for all tasks, and tasks specific models that specialize in learning the task-specific information. Multitask Learning (MTL) is the area of ML that considers exploiting this relatedness between problems by developing techniques that couple the corresponding models together. One important approach [12] uses Support Vector Machines (SVM) as the base algorithm. The models for each task are defined as the combination of a common part, shared by all tasks, and a task-specific part. Another relevant strategy for neural networks consists in learning a shared data representation for all tasks, which is typically done by using shared hidden layers, and task-specific output neurons [6]. Some approaches for adapting boosting methods to MTL have also been proposed [7,14]. In [7], a boosting multi-task learning algorithm based on AdaBoost algorithm [21] is presented. This method applies an AdaBoost to iteratively optimize the common and task-specific parameters of the multi-task models applied to a multi-task web search ranking. In the approach presented in [14], boosted trees are combined with a deep neural network to produce near-optimal results in small tasks that are correlated to a large dataset. The deep model is trained with all common and task-specific data. Then, the output of the last hidden is used to train a task-specific gradient boosting model. Therefore, the values in the last hidden layer are considered as the inputs for boosting trees. Additionally, the authors in [18] have expanded upon the probabilistic methodology of XGBoost (XGBoostLSS) proposed by [20] to address load distribution prediction given the input vector. This improvement involves the training of two separate sets of decision tree regressors in XGBoostLSS, each trained on the mean and standard deviation of the Gaussian distribution, respectively. Building upon the foundation laid by [9], the authors of [8] introduced a novel approach called Task-wise Split Gradient Boosting Trees (TSGB). This method incorporates a task gain metric to assess the quality of tree splits for each task within a given dataset. Unlike traditional feature-wise splits, TSGB utilizes task-wise splits in the decision regressor trees, enabling the trees to be split based on the instances belonging to different task distributions. In the study conducted by [19], an extended version of TSGB was proposed to handle imbalanced datasets. This particular study focused on Multi-Task data encompassing various departments within a hospital setting. To address the issue of class imbalance, the authors employed the softmax function to normalize the input vector for all tasks. In the study conducted by [30], a novel tree structure was introduced to effectively address multi-task problems within the framework of [15]. This approach involved the utilization of a multi-output tree, where each task is associated with its computation of the Gradient and Hessian of the loss function, as opposed to having a single Gradient and Hessian for all tasks. By incorporating task-specific computations, the proposed tree structure enhances the modeling capabilities for multi-task scenarios.

In this paper, we propose a novel adaptation of gradient boosting [13] for multi-task learning to learn various tasks simultaneously. First, a set of models learn the common part for all tasks. Subsequent models are optimized to learn tasks-specific information not learned by the previous models.

The structure of this paper is organized as follows: The next section presents the proposed methodology; Sect. 3 includes an experimental comparison of the proposed with other state-of-the-art methods for MTL; the final section provides the conclusion of this work.

2   Methodology

This section describes the Gradient Boosting framework proposed by Friedman [13]. After this, a brief introduction to Multi-Task learning is given showing its connections with other learning algorithms. Lastly, the proposed Multi-Task learning - Gradient Boosting extension and its accompanying mathematical framework are given.

2.1   Gradient Boosting

Let us consider a dataset of N training instances, $\{x_i, y_i\}$, wherein x_i represents the input vector for the i-th example, and y_i corresponds to the output (which could either be a continuous value for regression or a label for classification). The objective is to learn a mapping function of inputs to outputs, $F(x)$, as an additive a collection of weak regression models (usually decision trees)

$$F(x) = \sum_{t=0}^{T} h_t(x), \tag{1}$$

where T represents the number of weak models to incorporate within the ensemble, and h_t is the t-th Decision Regressor Tree. In gradient boosting, the process of learning function $F(x)$ is done iteratively. At each boosting iteration, t, the ensemble is expanded stagewise by training a new weak model $h_t(x)$ while keeping previous models unchanged

$$F_t(x) = F_{t-1}(x) + h_t(x). \tag{2}$$

The training of $h_t(x)$ is determined by the minimization of a given loss function $\Psi(y_i, F(\mathbf{x}_i))$

$$h_t = \underset{h_t}{\operatorname{argmin}} \sum_{i=1}^{N} \Psi\left(y_i, F_{t-1}(x_i) + h_t(x_i)\right) \tag{3}$$

where the model h_0 is given by the constant value, c, that minimizes the training set loss

$$h_0 = \underset{c}{\operatorname{argmin}} \sum_{i=1}^{N} \Psi(y_i, c). \tag{4}$$

The optimization problem given in Eq: 3, is solved by training each model, h_t, on the steepest gradient descent in the N-data point space at F_{t-1}

$$u_{i,t} = -\frac{\partial \Psi\left(y_i, F(x_i)\right)}{\partial F(x_i)}\Bigg|_{F(x_i)=F_{t-1}(x_i)}. \tag{5}$$

These pseudo-residuals constitute a new dataset $\{x_i, u_{i,t}\}_{i=1}^N$, in which the h_t decision tree model is trained. In addition, a second optimization Newton step is generally carried out to update the output values of the decision tree leaves. This is done because the h_t decision tree regressor is generally trained to minimize the squared loss, which may be different from the objective loss Ψ. Thus, the precise numerical output value for the J terminal nodes of tree h_t is updated as

$$\gamma_{t,j} = \underset{\gamma}{\operatorname{argmin}} \sum_{x_i \in \mathbb{R}_j} \Psi\big(y_i, F_{t-1}(x_i) + \gamma\big). \tag{6}$$

where $\mathbb{R}_j$ if the region for the j-th tree leave of the tree defined as $h_t(x) = \sum_{j=1}^J \gamma_{t,j} \mathbb{I}(x \in \mathbb{R}_j)$.

In order to avoid overfitting during training, gradient boosting includes a regularization learning rate hyper-parameter, $\nu > 0$, such that the final raw output of the ensemble is given by

$$F(x) = h_0 + \sum_{t=1}^T \nu h_t(x). \tag{7}$$

2.2 Multi-Task Learning

Multi-task learning (MTL) aims at solving multiple problems jointly to improve the generalization performance of the system at a given task by leveraging cross-information from other tasks. The term has been widely used for a broad range of different task architectures. However, in this work, we consider the homogeneous multi-task setting. This setting considers τ supervised learning tasks with the same input space $\mathcal{X}$ and output space $\mathcal{Y}$, but with possibly different distributions $P^1(x, y), \ldots, P^\tau(x, y)$ in the joint space $\mathcal{X} \times \mathcal{Y}$. In this scenario, given a loss function Ψ, the goal is to select τ functions $H^r : \mathcal{X} \to \mathcal{Y}$ such that the expected risk

$$\sum_{r=1}^\tau \int_{\mathcal{X} \times \mathcal{Y}} \Psi(H^r(\mathbf{x}), y) P^r(\mathbf{x}, y)$$

is minimized. Most times, these distributions are unknown, and instead, we have a multi-task sample $D = \bigcup_{r=1}^\tau \{(\mathbf{x}_i^r, y_i^r) \sim P^r(\mathbf{x}, y), i = 1, \ldots, m^r\}$, where m^r is the number of instances in the r-th task. A popular strategy to solve this multi-task problem is to minimize a regularized empirical multi-task risk, which is defined as

$$\sum_{r=1}^\tau \frac{1}{m^r} \sum_{i=1}^{m^r} \Psi(H^r(x), y) + \Omega_r(H^r). \tag{8}$$

Here, $\Omega_r(H^r)$ are regularizers that penalize the complexity of functions H^r. From Eq. (8), it can be observed that the risk of each task can be minimized independently. This strategy is called independent-task learning (ITL). In ITL, no information is shared between tasks: each model H^r is trained using only the data instances of task r. Another straightforward strategy is to ignore the task information and to use a common function H for all tasks, i.e. $H^r(x) = H(x)$ for $r = 1, \ldots, \tau$; this approach is called common-task learning (CTL).

In between these two opposite approaches, we can define proper MTL strategies, which consider task-specific coupled models H^r that share information between tasks. In general, MTL strategies use a combination of common and task-independent parts

$$H^r(x) = f(x) + g^r(x), \tag{9}$$

where function f is common for all tasks and g^r are task-specific functions. For instance, in the work presented in [12], the authors consider a linear SVM framework, where the models for each task are defined as $h^r(x) = w \cdot x + v^r \cdot x + b^r$, where w is a common parameter for all tasks and, v^r and b^r are task-independent parameters biases respectively. This approach was later extended for the non-linear case [4],

$$H^r(x) = w \cdot \phi(x) + v^r \cdot \psi^r(x) + b^r, \tag{10}$$

where ϕ is a common transformation with an associated reproducing kernel, i.e. $k(x_1, x_2) = \phi(x_1) \cdot \phi(x_2)$; and analogously for each task-specific transformation $\psi^1, \ldots, \psi^\tau$. Other works that have adapted the common and specific tasks combination strategy include applications for: the LS-SVMs [29], ranking SVM [17], the twin SVM [22] or a convex formulation of this approach [24] adapted to neural networks [25].

Moreover, this combination strategy has been linked [4] with the Learning Using Privileged Information (LUPI) paradigm [27]. The main idea of LUPI is that it is possible to improve the learning process by providing privileged information about the instances. Specifically, the learning rate of the primary model, which is trained with the original data, can be improved by modeling the residuals of such a model using another model trained with privileged information. Although this seems like a futile trade-off, an advantage can be obtained when the second model is simpler than the primary one. This idea is connected to the combination-based MTL strategies, as the primary model can be interpreted as the common model and the residuals as the task-specific (10). Here, the original data can be defined by a non-linear transformation ϕ, while for the task-specific parts, simpler models can be applied, for example considering linear transformations ζ^r.

2.3   Multi Task - Gradient Boosting

In this work, we propose a novel method that extends gradient boosting to enable simultaneous learning of multi-task problems in both classification and regression contexts. In GB the final raw prediction (7) is given by a sum of the outputs of the estimators. In an MTL scenario with τ different problems, it seems natural to apply a combination-based strategy by defining a first block of T_c common estimators and a block of $T_s = T - T_c$ task-independent estimators that model the task-specific part

$$F_T^r(x) = h_0(x) + \sum_{t=1}^{T_c} \nu h_t(x) + \sum_{t=T_c+1}^{T} \nu h_t^r(x).$$

This approach follows Eq. (9), where the common part is defined as $f(x) = h_0(x) + \sum_{t=1}^{T_c} \nu h_t(x)$, ; while the task-specific parts are defined as $g_r(x) = \sum_{t=T_c+1}^{T} \nu h_t^r(x)$.

In our proposal, the optimization process work as follows. First, the base model h_0 is always common, so it takes into account the data from all tasks in order to compute Eq. 4. Then, the first T_c models, which are common to all tasks, are built as follows

$$h_t = \underset{h_t}{\arg\min} \sum_{r=1}^{\tau} \sum_{i=1}^{m_r} \Psi\left(y_i^r, F_{t-1}(x_i^r) + h_t(x_i^r)\right). \tag{11}$$

Finally, $T - T_c$ task-independent models are built by minimizing the error in each task as

$$h_t^r = \underset{h_t^r}{\arg\min} \sum_{i=1}^{m_r} \Psi\left(y_i^r, F_{t-1}^r(x_i^r) + h_t^r(x_i^r)\right). \tag{12}$$

After each iteration, the leaves of the trees should be updated with Eq. 6 using all data points for the trees that handle the common part and only with the task-specific instances for the latter trees.

3   Experiments and Results

To assess the performance of the proposed Multi Task-Gradient Boosting (mt-GB)[1], a comparison with state-of-the-art models was carried out in several regression and classification problems. The comparison includes Linear and Gaussian kernel Support Vector Machines (linear_SVM and (rbf_SVM)) [23]; Gradient Boosting (GB), XGBoost [9] and Multi-Layer Perceptron (MLP) [3]. For SVM, GB, and MLP the sklearn implementation was used. In our experiments, both *CTL* and *ITL* strategies were considered for each model, that is, using a common model for all tasks or using an independent model for each task. The prefixes ctl and itl were added when reporting the results for *CTL* and *ITL* approaches respectively. For example, a common multi-layer perceptron for all tasks is designated as ctl_MLP and if an independent multi-layer perceptron is built for each task then the term itl_MLP is used.

For the validation of the different algorithms, a 5-fold cross-validation procedure was used and the reported results are the average performance on the left-out folds except for the Adult dataset in which a single train-test partition was applied due to its size ($\approx$ 32000 instances). Moreover, data stratification by task is performed so that the proportions of instances of each task are kept approximately equal across folds. In the classification problems, the folds are

---

[1] github.com/GAA-UAM/MT_GB.

also stratified by class. All the tested algorithms require the selection of a set of hyperparameters. For this, an additional within-train grid search with a 5-fold cross-validation procedure was executed. Note that, in *CTL* approaches a single model is built and, thus, a single set of hyperparameters is selected for each training set; whether in *ITL* approaches one grid-search CV is carried out for each task since an independent model is created for each task. In Table 1 the considered hyperparameters of the grid search are shown. As it can be observed from the table, the hyperparameter grid for SVMs in the `Adult` dataset was reduced due to the high computational requirements for building SVM models. Any other hyperparameters of each model not shown in Table 1 are set to their default value in the corresponding implementation of each model.

Regarding the datasets, we shall consider the following three multi-task regression datasets:

- `school`[2]: This dataset consists on 15 362 examination records from 139 secondary schools. The problem consists of predicting the scores of students based on some attributes, and the prediction in each school defines a different task. This dataset has been widely used in *MTL* works, see [1,2,11,12].
- `computer`: This dataset contains the likelihood, as gathered in a survey of 180 users, of purchasing 20 different items. The predictions for each user define the tasks. This problem has been considered also in [1,2].
- `parkinson`[3]: this dataset contains multiple voice data instances, represented by 26 attributes, of patients in the early stages of Parkinson disease. Each task consists of predicting the UPDRS score, a measure of the movement, for each patient.

For classification, we consider three problems based on the following datasets:

- `landmine`[4]: This is a binary classification problem in which the goal is to decide whether a landmine is present or not in a given image. Detection of different types of landmines defines the different tasks. This dataset is rather imbalanced with 13916 and 904 instances for not mine and mine respectively.
- `adult`[5]: The goal is to predict whether the yearly salary of a particular person is greater than 50 K based on sociocultural data. We can define different tasks by dividing the population by either gender or race. In this study, we have considered both dividing the data by gender `ad_(G)` (2 tasks) and by race `ad_(R)` (5 tasks).

---

[2] https://home.ttic.edu/~argyriou/code/.
[3] https://archive.ics.uci.edu/ml/datasets/Parkinsons+Telemonitoring.
[4] https://andreric.github.io/files/datasets/LandmineData_19.mat.
[5] https://archive.ics.uci.edu/ml/datasets/adult.

Table 1. Hyperparameter values for the grid search of the analyzed models

Model	Grid	Values	Range
mt-GB	Learning rate	$10^{-\mu}$	$\mu \in [1,3]$
	Max depth	[2, 5, 10, 20]	
	Subsample	[0.5, 0.75, 1]	
	Common estimators (T_c)	[0, 5, 10, 20, 50]	
SVM	C	10^{μ}	$\mu \in [0,3]$
	Epsilon (Regression tasks)	$2^{-\mu}$	$\mu \in [0,3]$
	Gamma (Gaussian kernel)	$10^{-\mu/2}$	$\mu \in [0,3]$
SVM (Adult)	C	[100]	
	Gamma (Gaussian kernel)	[0.01, 0.05]	
MLP	L2	$10^{-\mu}$	$\mu \in [0,4]$
XGBoost and GB	Learning rate	[0.025, 0.05, 0.1, 0.5, 1]	
	Max depth	[2, 5, 10, 20]	
	Subsample	[0.5, 0.75, 1]	

4   Results

The average across folds results of the experiments are summarized in Tables 2 and 3 for regression and classification respectively for the proposed Multi Task-Gradient Boosting (mt-GB) and the different CTL and ITL tested models. For regression, the models were evaluated based on Mean Absolute Error (MAE) and Root Mean Squared Error (RMSE). In classification tasks, the average recall and accuracy are reported. In addition, Tables 2 and 3 report in between parenthesis, the rank of each method within each dataset. The best-performing model for each dataset (i.e. rank 1) is also highlighted with the gray background in the tables.

The regression results shown in Table 2 reveal that there are significant variations in the models' performance across datasets and metrics. However, the proposed mt-GB model is the most stable as it obtains the best average rank across problems and metrics. The proposed model obtains the best performance in **Parkinson** (using the metric MAE) and in **Computer** (RMSE); it is second in **Computer** (MAE) and no worse than fourth in the other problem and metric configurations. The second best method in terms of the number of best performances is ctl_GB, which obtains two best performances in **Computer** for both MAE and RMSE. However, the performance of ctl_GB in the other problems is not as good. In fact, after the proposed method, the models with the best average rank are itl_GB and itl_XGBoost. On the other hand, the performance of SVM and MLP-based models are sub-optimal in the tested datasets and metrics for both itl and ctl configurations. In fact, gradient boosting-based methods are in general the ones with the best overall performances.

For the classification problems shown in Table 3, the proposed mt_GB model achieves the highest recall score on the **Landmine** dataset, while ctl_XGBoost obtained the best recall in **ad_(R)** and **ad_(S)** datasets. In terms of accuracy, itl_GB outperformed all other models on the **ad_(G)** problem, while ctl_GB

Table 2. Average generalization performance of regression models using Mean Absolute Error (MAE) and Root Mean Square Error (RMSE) metrics, with rankings by dataset and metric (in parentheses), and mean ranks across three datasets and two metrics.

	MAE			RMSE			Mean rank
model	School	Computer	Parkinson	School	Computer	Parkinson	
mt_GB	8.107 (4)	1.615 (2)	0.011 (1)	10.208 (3)	2.033 (1)	0.047 (3)	2.34
ctl_rbf_SVM	8.101 (3)	2.136 (6)	4.004 (8)	10.337 (5)	2.601 (5)	6.078 (8)	5.84
ctl_linear_SVM	8.157 (6)	2.164 (7)	7.916 (10)	10.390 (6)	2.689 (9)	9.929 (10)	8.00
ctl_MLP	8.140 (5)	2.600 (11)	6.084 (9)	10.317 (4)	3.152 (11)	7.701 (9)	8.16
ctl_XGBoost	8.031 (2)	2.169 (8)	0.919 (6)	10.164 (2)	2.603 (7)	1.790 (7)	5.34
ctl_GB	8.027 (1)	2.177 (9)	0.765 (5)	10.163 (1)	2.601 (6)	1.774 (6)	4.67
itl_rbf_SVM	8.459 (9)	1.719 (4)	0.506 (4)	10.838 (9)	2.296 (4)	0.926 (4)	5.67
itl_linear_SVM	8.732 (10)	1.963 (5)	0.950 (7)	11.216 (10)	2.606 (8)	1.565 (5)	7.50
itl_MLP	10.515 (11)	2.300 (10)	13.900 (11)	13.689 (11)	2.955 (10)	18.576 (11)	10.67
itl_XGBoost	8.301 (8)	1.678 (3)	0.012 (3)	10.631 (8)	2.260 (3)	0.042 (1)	4.34
itl_GB	8.289 (7)	1.614 (1)	0.011 (2)	10.575 (7)	2.187 (2)	0.044 (2)	3.50

Table 3. Average generalization performance of regression models using recall and accuracy metrics, with rankings by dataset and metric (in parentheses), and mean ranks across three datasets and two metrics.

	Recall			Accuracy			Mean rank
model	ad_(G)	ad_(R)	landmine	ad_(G)	ad_(R)	landmine	
mt-GB	0.796 (3)	0.789 (4)	0.580 (1)	0.872 (2)	0.869 (4)	0.900 (9)	3.84
ctl_rbf_SVM	0.758 (9)	0.757 (10)	0.535 (10)	0.841 (10)	0.840 (9)	0.914 (5)	8.84
ctl_linear_SVM	0.757 (10)	0.763 (6)	0.502 (11)	0.850 (6)	0.853 (6)	0.936 (1)	6.67
ctl_MLP	0.776 (6)	0.760 (9)	0.570 (4)	0.843 (8)	0.834 (11)	0.928 (2)	6.67
ctl_XGBoost	0.797 (1)	0.799 (1)	0.559 (8)	0.871 (3)	0.872 (2)	0.905 (8)	3.84
ctl_GB	0.792 (4)	0.797 (2)	0.544 (9)	0.869 (5)	0.874 (1)	0.897 (10)	5.16
itl_rbf_SVM	0.753 (11)	0.755 (11)	0.574 (2)	0.836 (11)	0.837 (10)	0.917 (4)	8.16
itl_linear_SVM	0.759 (8)	0.760 (8)	0.563 (5)	0.847 (7)	0.849 (7)	0.912 (6)	6.84
itl_MLP	0.769 (7)	0.763 (7)	0.560 (7)	0.843 (9)	0.843 (8)	0.924 (3)	6.84
itl_XGBoost	0.792 (5)	0.788 (5)	0.571 (3)	0.870 (4)	0.869 (5)	0.911 (7)	4.84
itl_GB	0.797 (2)	0.792 (3)	0.560 (6)	0.874 (1)	0.870 (3)	0.873 (11)	4.84

achieved the highest accuracy on ad_(R). The results of accuracy for landmine need to be considered in combination with the recall results as the dataset is quite imbalanced, i.e. 93.9% for the majority class. In this context, the best accuracy result obtained by ctl_linear_SVM in landmine is not really a good performance since the recall for this model is very close to 0.5, which indicates that the output of the model is almost always the majority class.

5 Conclusion

A novel Multi Task-Gradient Boosting approach is presented that extends the traditional gradient boosting algorithm to handle multi-task problems for both classification and regression. The algorithm works in two phases. First, a set of models are fitted to all tasks that learn the common information shared between all tasks. Then, task-specific estimators are created to model task specificities not considered by the common models. The proposed algorithm is compared to independent and common task models showing a generalization performance better on average on the tested classification and regression multi-task problems.

Future work would involve exploring the extension of other well-known algorithms, such as XGBoost, to handle multi-task learning scenarios to further improve model performance and efficiency.

Acknowledgments. This work was supported by PID2019-106827GB-I00 / AEI / 10.13039/501100011033.

References

1. Argyriou, A., Evgeniou, T., Pontil, M.: Convex multi-task feature learning. Mach. Learn. **73**(3), 243–272 (2008)
2. Argyriou, A., Pontil, M., Ying, Y., Micchelli, C.: A spectral regularization framework for multi-task structure learning. In: Platt, J., Koller, D., Singer, Y., Roweis, S. (eds.) Advances in Neural Information Processing Systems, vol. 20. Curran Associates, Inc. (2007)
3. Bishop, C.M., et al.: Neural Networks for Pattern Recognition. Oxford University Press, Oxford (1995)
4. Cai, F., Cherkassky, V.: SVM+ regression and multi-task learning. In: International Joint Conference on Neural Networks, IJCNN 2009, Atlanta, Georgia, USA, 14–19 June 2009, pp. 418–424. IEEE Computer Society (2009)
5. Cai, J., Xu, K., Zhu, Y., Hu, F., Li, L.: Prediction and analysis of net ecosystem carbon exchange based on gradient boosting regression and random forest. Appl. Energy **262**, 114566 (2020)
6. Caruana, R.: Multitask learning. Mach. Learn. **28**, 41–75 (1997)
7. Chapelle, O., Shivaswamy, P.K., Vadrevu, S., Weinberger, K.Q., Zhang, Y., Tseng, B.L.: Boosted multi-task learning. Mach. Learn. **85**(1–2), 149–173 (2011)
8. Chen, M., et al.: Task-wise split gradient boosting trees for multi-center diabetes prediction. CoRR abs/2108.07107 (2021)
9. Chen, T., et al.: Xgboost: extreme gradient boosting. R package version 0.4-2 **1**(4), 1–4 (2015)
10. Dorogush, A.V., Ershov, V., Gulin, A.: Catboost: gradient boosting with categorical features support (2018)
11. Evgeniou, T., Micchelli, C.A., Pontil, M.: Learning multiple tasks with kernel methods. J. Mach. Learn. Res. **6**, 615–637 (2005)
12. Evgeniou, T., Pontil, M.: Regularized multi-task learning, pp. 109–117. KDD 2004, Association for Computing Machinery, New York, NY, USA (2004)
13. Friedman, J.H.: Greedy function approximation: a gradient boosting machine. Ann. Stat. **29**(5), 1189–1232 (2001)

14. Jiang, J., Wang, R., Wang, M., Gao, K., Nguyen, D.D., Wei, G.W.: Boosting tree-assisted multitask deep learning for small scientific datasets. J. Chem. Inf. Model. **60**(3), 1235–1244 (2020)
15. Ke, G., et al.: Lightgbm: a highly efficient gradient boosting decision tree. In: Guyon, I., Luxburg, U.V., Bengio, S., Wallach, H., Fergus, R., Vishwanathan, S., Garnett, R. (eds.) Advances in Neural Information Processing Systems, vol. 30. Curran Associates, Inc. (2017)
16. Lawrence, R., Bunn, A., Powell, S., Zambon, M.: Classification of remotely sensed imagery using stochastic gradient boosting as a refinement of classification tree analysis. Remote Sens. Environ. **90**(3), 331–336 (2004)
17. Liang, X., Zhu, L., Huang, D.: Multi-task ranking SVM for image cosegmentation. Neurocomputing **247**, 126–136 (2017)
18. Liu, H., Zhang, X., Sun, H., Shahidehpour, M.: Boosted multi-task learning for inter-district collaborative load forecasting. IEEE Trans. Smart Grid, 1–1 (2023)
19. Ma, H., Dong, Z., Chen, M., Sheng, W., Li, Y., Zhang, W., Zhang, S., Yu, Y.: A gradient boosting tree model for multi-department venous thromboembolism risk assessment with imbalanced data. J. Biomed. Inform. **134**, 104210 (2022)
20. März, A.: Xgboostlss - an extension of xgboost to probabilistic forecasting. CoRR abs/1907.03178 (2019)
21. Mason, L., Baxter, J., Bartlett, P., Frean, M.: Boosting algorithms as gradient descent. In: Advances in Neural Information Processing Systems, vol. 12 (1999)
22. Mei, B., Xu, Y.: Multi-task ν-twin support vector machines. Neural Comput. Appl. **32**(15), 11329–11342 (2020)
23. Platt, J., et al.: Probabilistic outputs for support vector machines and comparisons to regularized likelihood methods. Adv. Large Margin Classifiers **10**(3), 61–74 (1999)
24. Ruiz, C., Alaíz, C.M., Dorronsoro, J.R.: Convex formulation for multi-task L1-, L2-, and LS-SVMs. Neurocomputing **456**, 599–608 (2021)
25. Ruiz, C., Alaíz, C.M., Dorronsoro, J.R.: Convex MTL for neural networks. Logic J. IGPL (2022)
26. Sun, R., Wang, G., Zhang, W., Hsu, L.T., Ochieng, W.Y.: A gradient boosting decision tree based GPS signal reception classification algorithm. Appl. Soft Comput. **86**, 105942 (2020)
27. Vapnik, V., Izmailov, R.: Learning using privileged information: similarity control and knowledge transfer. J. Mach. Learn. Res. **16**, 2023–2049 (2015)
28. Wang, C., Deng, C., Wang, S.: Imbalance-xgboost: leveraging weighted and focal losses for binary label-imbalanced classification with xgboost. Pattern Recogn. Lett. **136**, 190–197 (2020)
29. Xu, S., An, X., Qiao, X., Zhu, L.: Multi-task least-squares support vector machines. Multim. Tools Appl. **71**(2), 699–715 (2014)
30. Ying, Z., Xu, Z., Li, Z., Wang, W., Meng, C.: MT-GBM: a multi-task gradient boosting machine with shared decision trees. CoRR abs/2201.06239 (2022)
31. Zhang, Y., Haghani, A.: A gradient boosting method to improve travel time prediction. Transp. Res. Part C: Emerg. Technol. **58**, 308–324 (2015)

Exploratory Study of Data Sampling Methods for Imbalanced Legal Text Classification

Daniela L. Freire[1]([✉]) [ID], Alex M. G. de Almeida[2] [ID], Márcio de S. Dias[3] [ID],
Adriano Rivolli[4] [ID], Fabíola S. F. Pereira[5] [ID], Giliard A. de Godoi[4] [ID],
and Andre C. P. L. F. de Carvalho[1] [ID]

[1] University of Sao Paulo, Sao Paulo, Brazil
{danielalfrere,andre}@icmc.usp.br
[2] Ourinhos College of Technology, Sao Paulo, Brazil
alex.marino@fatecourinhos.edu.br
[3] Federal University of Catalan, Catalão, Brazil
marciodias@ufcat.edu.br
[4] Federal Technological University of Paraná, Curitiba, Brazil
rivolli@utfpr.edu.br, giliardgodoi@alunos.utfpr.edu.br
[5] Federal University of Uberlândia, Uberlândia, Brazil
fabiola.pereira@ufu.br

Abstract. This article investigates the application of machine learning algorithms in the legal domain, focusing on text classification tasks and addressing the challenges posed by imbalanced class distributions. Given the very high number of ongoing legal cases in Brazil, the integration of machine learning tools in the workflow of courts has the potential to enhance justice efficiency and speed. However, the imbalanced nature of legal datasets presents a significant hurdle for traditional machine learning algorithms, which tend to prioritize the majority class and disregard minority classes. To mitigate this problem, researchers have developed imbalance learning techniques that either modify supervised learning or improve the dataset class distribution to improve predictive performance. Data sampling techniques, such as oversampling and undersampling, play a crucial role in balancing class distributions and enabling the training of accurate machine learning models. In this study, a real dataset comprising lawsuits from the Court of Justice of São Paulo, in the state of São Paulo, Brazil, is used to evaluate the effects of different imbalance learning techniques, including oversampling, undersampling, and combined methods, in predictive performance for a binary classification task. The experimental results provided valuable insights into the comparative performance of these techniques and their applicability in the legal domain.

Keywords: Machine learning · Text classification · Data sampling · Imbalanced data · Natural language processing

P. García Bringas et al. (Eds.): HAIS 2023, LNAI 14001, pp. 108–120, 2023.
https://doi.org/10.1007/978-3-031-40725-3_10

1 Introduction

Machine learning (ML) algorithms have been successfully used in the Justice Systems, particularly in Brazil, where the magnitude of ongoing legal proceedings necessitates attention. According to the National Council of Justice's annual report "Justice in Numbers" [15], in 2022, the number of active cases amounted to a staggering 77.23 million. By integrating tools into the workflow of courts that assist in the analysis, classification, and retrieval of legal documents, improvements in efficiency can be achieved. Automating legal text classification tasks is especially crucial considering the scarcity of human resources in the public sector and the escalating demand for legal processes. Text classification is a widely studied and applied Natural Language Processing (NLP) task that focuses on predicting categorical labels assigned to textual instances. These instances can encompass various textual units, ranging from individual phrases to entire documents, thereby introducing inherent complexity to the task at hand [4]. These tasks traditionally require substantial human resources and working hours, which could otherwise be directed toward more cognitively demanding endeavors. The Brazilian Justice System can expedite its operations by harnessing ML, enhancing overall speed and productivity.

Nonetheless, using ML algorithms frequently encounters challenges and potential biases when dealing with classification datasets characterized by imbalanced class distributions [13]. If appropriately addressed, such class imbalances can significantly maintain the accuracy of predictive models and impede their ability to provide reliable outputs for decision-making purposes. The performance of these techniques may need to improve or exhibit more optimistic results due to the inherent design of many machine learning algorithms, which assume that each class has the same number of observations in the classification data. Consequently, these algorithms may inadvertently prioritize the majority class, disregarding the significance of a limited number of examples to achieve satisfactory performance.

In order to deal with class imbalance, researchers have developed imbalance learning techniques capable of effectively processing and extracting valuable information from datasets exhibiting a severely skewed distribution. The primary objective of these techniques is to enable prediction algorithms to achieve a more realistic and accurate estimation of the outcome variable rather than disregarding the minority classes present in the data. By modifying the prediction algorithm or enhancing the dataset, these imbalance learning techniques aim to address the issue above [7].

Data sampling encompasses techniques that manipulate a training dataset intending to achieve a balanced or improved balance in the class distribution. Once the dataset is appropriately balanced, traditional machine learning algorithms can be directly trained on the transformed data without requiring modifications. This data preparation approach provides a means to effectively tackle the challenge of imbalanced classification, even when confronted with severely skewed class distributions [6]. Various data sampling methods exist; only some universal methods can be considered optimal for all classification problems and models. Like selecting a predictive model, meticulous experimentation is essential to identify the most suitable data sampling technique for each problem. Within the data sampling techniques applied to the training dataset, two primary methodologies are commonly employed: oversampling and undersampling. Oversampling methods involve the duplication of instances within the minority class or the synthesis of new instances based on existing examples from the minority class. Conversely, undersampling methods encompass deleting or selecting a subset of instances from the majority class.

In this literature review, various techniques for addressing imbalanced class datasets are discussed. The authors of [16] evaluate the performance of SMOTE-IPF, which combines SMOTE with IPF, and consistently find superior classification results in terms of accuracy, precision, recall, and F-measure. In [5], a two-step approach using DSMOTE and Rotation Forest is proposed to handle imbalanced hyperspectral data, where synthetic samples are generated to address class imbalance and classifier diversity is leveraged to improve accuracy. The authors of [1] explore oversampling techniques for multiclass imbalanced problems, highlighting the advantages, limitations, and the importance of appropriate method selection based on dataset characteristics and classification algorithms. Finally, [11] introduces OBGAN, a method utilizing GANs to generate synthetic samples near minority class boundaries, demonstrating enhanced classification accuracy for minority classes in imbalanced datasets through experimental results.

In this paper, we assess the effectiveness of imbalance learning techniques in the context of a real dataset comprising lawsuits from Court São Paulo (in Portuguese, Tribunal de Justiça de São Paulo or TJSP). The study explores the utilization of oversampling, undersampling, and combined methods to evaluate their respective capabilities in a binary classification task. Through a comprehensive analysis, this research aims to shed light on the comparative performance of these techniques within the given dataset. The remainder of this paper is organized as follows. Section 2 presents a background and a brief description of techniques and methodologies employed. The experimental study is discussed and reported in Sect. 3. Finally, Sect. 4 reports the main conclusions and points out future research directions.

2   Background

This section describes some of the more widely used and implemented oversampling and undersampling methods. Among the oversampling methods highlight: Random Oversampling (RO) [2], Synthetic Minority Oversampling Technique (SMOTE) [3], Borderline-SMOTE [8], and Adaptive Synthetic Sampling (ADASYN) [9]. Among the undersampling methods describe: Random Undersampling (RU), Near Miss Undersampling (NMU) [18], Tomek Links Undersampling (TLU) [10], and Edited Nearest Neighbors Rule (ENN).

2.1   Oversampling and Undersampling Methods

The most straightforward oversampling technique, known as Random Oversampling, involves randomly duplicating instances from the minority class within the training dataset. On the other hand, SMOTE stands as the most popular and successful oversampling method. SMOTE operates by identifying instances that exhibit proximity in the feature space. It accomplishes this by constructing a line between such instances and generating new synthetic samples. This approach facilitates the augmentation of the minority class with synthetic examples. To further enhance the performance of SMOTE, various extensions have been proposed. Borderline-SMOTE, for instance, selects instances from the minority class that a k-nearest neighbor classification model misclassifies. Only synthetic samples with a classification challenge are generated, focusing on the "difficult" instances. Another extension, Adaptive Synthetic Sampling, considers the density of examples within the minority class. It generates synthetic samples inversely proportional to the density, emphasizing regions of the feature space with low minority class density while generating fewer or no synthetic samples in high-density regions. These variations of the SMOTE method offer more refined and selective approaches for synthesizing minority class examples, contributing to improving the oversampling process.

The most straightforward oversampling technique, known as the Random One category of techniques, focuses on selecting a robust and representative subset of examples from the majority class. Near Miss methods utilize the k-nearest neighbors (KNN) algorithm to identify relevant examples from the majority class. NearMiss-1 selects instances from the majority class that exhibits the smallest average distance to the three nearest instances from the minority class. NearMiss-2, on the other hand, selects instances from the majority class with the smallest average distance to the three farthest instances from the minority class. NearMiss-3 involves selecting a specific number of majority class examples for each instance in the minority class that is closest in proximity. Another set of techniques aims to remove instances from the majority class. These approaches typically focus on identifying examples contributing to classification difficulties, thereby introducing ambiguity to the decision boundary. Tomek Links is one of the most well-known undersampling approaches for deletion. A Tomek Links refers to a pair of instances in the training dataset that is nearest neighbors and belongs to different classes. These links often involve misclassified examples found along the class boundary, and instances from the majority class are deleted accordingly. The Edited Nearest Neighbors (ENN) rule is another method for selecting deleted instances. This rule utilizes the k = 3 nearest neighbors to identify misclassified instances within the dataset, subsequently removing them. This method of resampling and classification was proposed by Dennis Wilson in 1972. The ENN procedure can be iterated multiple times on the same dataset, thereby refining the selection of instances from the majority class. This extension, initially referred to as "unlimited editing", is more commonly known as Repeatedly Edited Nearest Neighbors.

2.2   Text Vectorization

Machine learning algorithms are not capable of directly processing raw text data. Instead, textual information needs to be transformed into numerical representations, typically in the form of vectors. In natural language processing, a general approach to feature extraction from text involves the construction of a word corpus, wherein all the unique words present in the text are collected and organized. This corpus serves as a repository containing the entire text's vocabulary. Each word within this corpus is assigned a unique identifier or index. A numerical vector representation can be constructed by representing the text as a collection of word indices, capturing the essential information encoded within the text. These numerical representations enable machine learning algorithms to operate effectively on the transformed text data. Consequently, this process of converting raw text into a numerical representation facilitates the utilization of various machine-learning techniques, allowing for the analysis, modeling, and prediction of text-based data in natural language processing tasks.

One widely used algorithm for text vectorization is the Term Frequency-Inverse Document Frequency (TF-IDF) vectorizer, which combines the concepts of term frequency (TF) and document frequency (DF). Term frequency represents the number of occurrences of a specific term within a document, indicating the importance of the term in that document. It allows each text to be represented as a matrix, where the rows represent the number of documents and the columns represent the different terms found throughout all documents. On the other hand, document frequency refers to the number of documents having a specific term, which indicates the term's commonality [17].

Inverse Document Frequency (IDF) is a weight assigned to each term, aiming to reduce the weight for terms that appear in multiple documents. IDF can be calculated using the Eq. (1).

$$\text{IDF}_i = \log\left(\frac{N}{\text{DF}_i}\right) \tag{1}$$

IDF_i represents the IDF score for term i, DF_i is the number of documents having term i, and N is the total number of documents. The IDF score decreases as the document frequency of a term increases. If a term appears in all documents (DF_i equals N), its IDF score becomes zero, suggesting that it provides little informative value and can be considered a stopword.

The $TF-IDF$ score is computed by multiplying the term frequency matrix by its corresponding IDF score, as shown in the Eq. (2).

$$\text{TF-IDF}_{ij} = \text{TF}_{ij} \times \text{IDF}_i \tag{2}$$

$TF-IDF_{ij}$ represents the TF-IDF score for term i in document j, TF_{ij} is the term frequency for term i in document j, and IDF_i is the IDF score for term i.

TF-IDF vectorization remains a valuable technique for representing textual data as numerical vectors, facilitating the application of traditional machine learning algorithms in various NLP tasks.

3 Study Experimental

In this section, we address an experimental study with a real dataset comprising lawsuit decisions from Court São Paulo, labeled into two classes that specify is a lawsuit belongs to a set of lawsuits that approach the Right Consumer theme (class_1) or not (class_0) [12]. We seek to answer the following research question: *which data sampling technique results in the shortest error rate in lawsuit decisions classification task in the sought-after theme?*

3.1 Dataset and Data Preprocessing

The training set has 13,573 texts from lawsuit decisions, 2,088 of (class_1), and 11,482 not (class_0). The validation dset has 2,560 texts from lawsuit decisions, 584 of (class_1), and 1,976 not (class_0). Additionally, we have a production set with 350 lawsuit decisions, only two of them from (class_1). We use TF-IDF for text vectorization, limiting our vocabulary to 3,000 features, where each feature, or n-gram, represents a measurable piece of text that can be used for analysis. N-grams are contiguous sequences of words collected from a text sequence. We used n-grams with n from 1 to 5. The n in n-grams specify the size of several items to consider: unigram for $n = 1$, bigram for $n = 2$, trigram for $n = 3$, and so on.

3.2 Classification Approach

We use the Support Vector Machines (SVMs) algorithm for the classification task with Stochastic Gradient Descent (SGD). SGD is a simple and efficient approach to fitting linear classifiers under convex loss functions, which has been successfully applied to large-scale and sparse ML problems often encountered in text classification and natural language processing. We use the class SGDClassifier, from scikit-learn version 1.2.2 Python library [14], which implements a straightforward stochastic gradient descent learning routine that supports different loss functions and penalties for classification. After tuning the hyperparameters as can be seen in Table 1:

3.3 Procedure

We evaluate the classification accuracy using eight different methods:

- Method 1 - Unbalance. First, we create a classification model using the training set without any sampling technique, thus, the dataset is imbalanced.
- Method 2 - RU. We randomly chose 2,088 texts from lawsuit decisions from class_0, resulting in a training set with 4,176 texts, with the same amount of texts to each class.
- Method 3 - NMU. The training set had 2,262 texts, 174 texts from lawsuit decisions from class_0, and 2,088 from class_1.

- Method 4 - SMOTE. The training set had 22,964 texts, with the same amount of texts for each class.
- Method 5 - ADASYN. The training set had 23,688 texts, 11,482 texts from lawsuit decisions from class_0, and 12,206 from class_1.
- Method 6 - Random Oversampling. The training set had 22,964 texts, with the same amount of texts for each class.
- Method 7 - Borderline-SMOTE. The training set had 22,964 texts, with the same amount of texts for each class.
- Method 8 - Edited Nearest Neighbours. The training set had 3,159 texts, 1,071 texts from lawsuit decisions from class_0, and 2,088 from class_1.
- Method 9 - TLU. The training set had 11,570 texts, 11,482 texts from lawsuit decisions from class_0, and 2,088 from class_1.

We measure the performance using various metrics, such as balance accuracy, precision, recall, f1-score, geometric mean (g-mean), and kappa. We also calculate the error rate by dividing the error number of class i by the total errors of both classes, as shown in the Eq. (3).

$$.\%error_{class\_j} = \frac{error_{class\_j}}{\sum_{i=0}^{1} error_{class\_i}} \tag{3}$$

3.4 Results

The evaluated methods presented different behaviors. RU reduced the number of texts of class_0 by 36%, getting with the proportion 2:1 between class_0 and class_1. NMU did a drastic reduction in class_0 in 1.5%, getting with the proportion 1:12 between class_0 and class_1. SMOTE, Random Oversampling, and Borderline-SMOTE equally balanced both classes, getting the proportion 1:1 between class_0 and class_1. In the case of ADASYN, the balancing was almost equal between class_0 and class_1, getting the proportion about 1:1. Edited Nearest Neighbours reduced the number of texts of class_0 in 9%, getting with the proportion 1:2 between class_0 and class_1. TLU can not balance the training set. First, we report the metrics results in every method at Tables 2 and 3. After, we compare the available metrics for every method in Table 4. Finally, we compare the error rate for every method in each dataset: training, validation, and production, in Fig. 1, 2, and 3 respectively.

We can see in Tables 2 and 3 that all of the methods had good performance in classifying the train and validation dataset with an f1-score of about 97%. However, when focusing on each class separately, we noticed that some methods had low performance, like in the case of NMU, where the precision was 71%, and the f1-score was 83%. These low grades are likely due to the drastic reduction in the number of class_0 samples made by this method, which resulted in only 174 texts from class 0 against 2088 from class_1.

Table 4 shows that RU had the highest score in g-mean e kappa metrics, achieving 0.99%. The geometric mean combined "sensitivity" and "specificity" metrics into a single score that balances both concerns. Sensitivity refers to the

Table 1. SGD Classifier tuned parameters

Parameter	value	Parameter	Value
alpha	*0.0001*	n_iter_no_change	*5*
average	*False*	n_jobs	*-1*
class_weight	*None*	penalty	*'l2'*
early_stopping	*False*	power_t	*0.5*
epsilon	*0.1*	random_state	*123*
eta0	*0.001*	shuffle	*True*
fit_intercept	*True*	tol	0.001,
l1_ratio	*0.15*	validation_fraction	*0.1*
learning_rate	*'optimal'*	verbose	*0*
loss	*'hinge'*	warm_start	*False*
max_iter	*1000*		

Table 2. Performance comparison - Training set

		Supp.	Pre	Mavg	Wavg	Rec	Mavg	Wavg	F1	Mavg	Wavg	Acc
Unbalance	C 0	11482	1.00	0.99	1.00	1.00	1.00	1.00	1.00	1.00	1.00	1.00
	C 1	2088	0.99			1.00			0.99			
RU	C 0	2088	1.00	1.00	1.00	1.00	1.00	1.00	1.00	1.00	1.00	1.00
	C 1	2088	1.00			1.00			1.00			
NMU	C 0	174	0.99	1.00	1.00	0.99	1.00	1.00	0.99	1.00	1.00	1.00
	C 1	2088	1.00			1.00			1.00			
SMOTE	C 0	11482	1.00	1.00	1.00	1.00	1.00	1.00	1.00	1.00	1.00	1.00
	C 1	11482	1.00			1.00			0.99			
ADASYN	C 0	11482	1.00	1.00	1.00	1.00	1.00	1.00	1.00	1.00	1.00	1.00
	C 1	12206	1.00			1.00			1.00			
RO	C 0	11482	1.00	1.00	1.00	1.00	1.00	1.00	1.00	1.00	1.00	1.00
	C 1	11482	1.00			1.00			1.00			
Borderline	C 0	11482	1.00	1.00	1.00	1.00	1.00	1.00	1.00	1.00	1.00	1.00
	C 1	11482	1.00			1.00			1.00			
ENN	C 0	1071	1.00	1.00	1.00	1.00	1.00	1.00	1.00	1.00	1.00	1.00
	C 1	2088	1.00			1.00			1.00			
TLU	C 0	11482	1.00	0.99	1.00	1.00	0.99	1.00	1.00	0.99	1.00	1.00
	C 1	2088	0.98			0.99			0.99			

true positive rate and summarizes how well the positive class was predicted. Specificity complements sensitivity, or the true negative rate, and summarises how well the negative class was predicted. Cohen's kappa is calculated based on the confusion matrix. However, in contrast to calculating overall accuracy, Cohen's kappa considers imbalance in class distribution and can. Therefore, g-mean and kappa can be most suitable for unbalanced datasets.

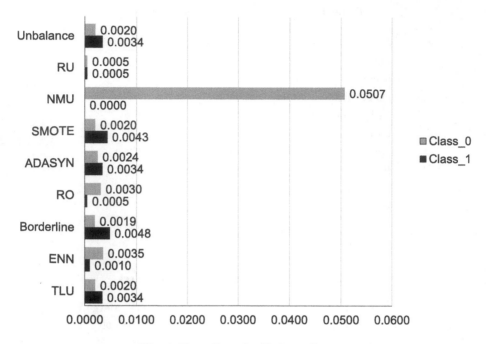

Fig. 1. Error Rate for Training Dataset

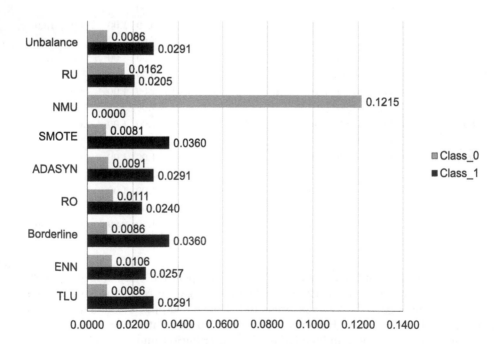

Fig. 2. Error Rate for Validation Dataset

Table 3. Performance comparison - Validation set

		Support	Prec	Mavg	Wavg	Rec	Mavg	Wavg	F1	Mavg	Wavg	Acc
Unbalance	C 0	1976	0.99	0.99	1.00	0.99	1.00	1.00	0.99	1.00	1.00	1.00
	C 1	584	0.97			0.97			0.97			
RU	C 0	1976	0.99	0.97	0.98	0.98	0.98	0.98	0.99	0.98	0.98	0.98
	C 1	584	0.95			0.98			0.96			
NMU	C 0	1976	1.00	0.85	0.93	0.88	0.94	0.91	0.94	0.88	0.91	0.91
	C 1	584	0.71			1.00			0.83			
SMOTE	C 0	1976	0.99	0.98	0.99	0.99	0.98	0.99	0.99	0.98	0.99	0.99
	C 1	584	0.97			0.96			0.97			
ADASYN	C 0	1976	0.99	0.98	0.99	0.99	0.98	0.99	0.99	0.98	0.99	0.99
	C 1	584	0.97			0.97			0.97			
RO	C 0	1976	0.99	0.98	0.99	0.99	0.98	0.99	0.99	0.98	0.99	0.99
	C 1	584	0.96			0.98			0.97			
Borderline	C 0	1976	0.99	0.98	0.99	0.99	0.98	0.99	0.99	0.98	0.99	0.99
	C 1	584	0.97			0.96			0.97			
ENN	C 0	1976	0.99	0.98	0.99	0.99	0.98	0.99	0.99	0.98	0.99	0.99
	C 1	584	0.96			0.97			0.97			
TLU	C 0	1976	0.99	0.98	0.99	0.99	0.98	0.99	0.99	0.99	0.98	0.99
	C 1	584	0.97			0.97			0.97			

Table 4. Metrics Comparison

Method	Balanced accuracy	Precision	Recall	F1-score	G-mean	Kappa
Unbalance	0.997	0.997	0.997	0.997	0.997	0.991
RU	0.999	0.999	0.999	0.999	0.999	0.999
NMU	0.996	0.999	0.999	0.999	0.996	0.993
SMOTE	0.997	0.997	0.997	0.997	0.997	0.995
ADASYN	0.997	0.997	0.997	0.997	0.997	0.994
RO	0.996	0.996	0.996	0.996	0.996	0.993
Borderline	0.997	0.997	0.997	0.997	0.997	0.995
ENN	0.981	0.986	0.985	0.985	0.981	0.960
TLU	0.981	0.986	0.986	0.986	0.981	0.962

According to the charts of Fig. 1, 2, and 3, considering the classification in the training dataset, all data sampling methods obtained good results in error rates, except the NMU, which had an error rate of 5% to class_0 due to the drastic reduction in data number in this class. In the data validation dataset, except for the NMU, the data sampling methods obtained error rates between 0.81% (SMOTE) and 1.62% (Randon Undersampling) for class_0 classification and class_1 classification of this dataset, the error rates varied from 2.05%(Randon Undersampling) to 3.60% (SMOTE and Borderline SMOTE). Regarding

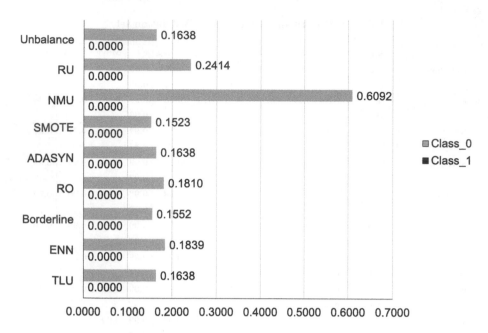

Fig. 3. Error Rate for Production Dataset

classification in the production dataset, all data sampling methods got right the class_1 of two lawsuit decisions, so the error rates to class_1 were 0% in all cases. Conversely, for class_0, the error rate using the classifier trained with the unbalanced dataset was 16.38%; the ADASYN and Tomek Links methods had the same error rate for class_0; only SMOTE and Borderline SMOTE achieved error rates lower than this, achieving 15%, and the other methods had error rates above 16.38%.

4 Conclusion

The issue of imbalanced class distributions in classification datasets can lead to the failure or misleading performance of machine learning algorithms. Many algorithms assume equal class observations, which can result in disregarding minority class examples. In this paper, data sampling methods were applied to address imbalance in a lawsuit decision text dataset. The selection of the most suitable data sampling technique for each project is crucial, as there is no universal optimal method. The SMOTE and Borderline SMOTE methods were found to be the most effective for predicting validation and production data in our dataset. Additionally, the choice of appropriate evaluation metrics is essential to accurately assess models with imbalanced class distributions. Metrics such as g-mean and kappa were selected to avoid misleading conclusions. This study contributes to advancing knowledge and innovation in the application of machine learning algorithms to justice system problems. Future work could involve exploring other data sampling methods, evaluating the performance on different justice system datasets, and investigating the impact of additional evaluation metrics.

Acknowledgment. The authors would like to express their sincere gratitude to the São Paulo Justice Court, Brazil, for their valuable financial and intellectual support in conducting this research. The support provided by all the individuals involved in this collaboration, with their insightful discussions, guidance, and expertise, contributed to this study's completion.

References

1. Abdi, L., Hashemi, S.: To combat multi-class imbalanced problems by means of over-sampling techniques. IEEE Trans. Knowl. Data Eng. **28**(1), 238–251 (2015)
2. Batista, G.E., Prati, R.C., Monard, M.C.: A study of the behavior of several methods for balancing machine learning training data. ACM SIGKDD Explor. Newsl. **6**(1), 20–29 (2004)
3. Chawla, N.V., Bowyer, K.W., Hall, L.O., Kegelmeyer, W.P.: Smote: synthetic minority over-sampling technique. J. Artif. Intell. Res. **16**, 321–357 (2002)
4. Coelho, G.M.C., et al.: Text classification in the Brazilian legal domain. In: International Conference on Enterprise Information Systems, pp. 355–363 (2022)
5. Feng, W., et al.: Dynamic synthetic minority over-sampling technique-based rotation forest for the classification of imbalanced hyperspectral data. IEEE J. Sel. Top. Appl. Earth Observ. Remote Sens. **12**(7), 2159–2169 (2019)
6. Fernández, A., García, S., Galar, M., Prati, R.C., Krawczyk, B., Herrera, F.: Learning from Imbalanced Data Sets, vol. 10. Springer, Heidelberg (2018). https://doi.org/10.1007/978-3-319-98074-4
7. Haixiang, G., Yijing, L., Shang, J., Mingyun, G., Yuanyue, H., Bing, G.: Learning from class-imbalanced data: review of methods and applications. Expert Syst. Appl. **73**, 220–239 (2017)
8. Han, H., Wang, W.-Y., Mao, B.-H.: Borderline-SMOTE: a new over-sampling method in imbalanced data sets learning. In: Huang, D.-S., Zhang, X.-P., Huang, G.-B. (eds.) ICIC 2005. LNCS, vol. 3644, pp. 878–887. Springer, Heidelberg (2005). https://doi.org/10.1007/11538059_91
9. He, H., Bai, Y., Garcia, E.A., Li, S.: ADASYN: adaptive synthetic sampling approach for imbalanced learning. In: IEEE International Joint Conference on Neural Network, pp. 1322–1328 (2008)
10. Ivan, T.: Two modifications of CNN. IEEE Trans. Syst. Man Commun. **6**, 769–772 (1976)
11. Jo, W., Kim, D.: OBGAN: minority oversampling near borderline with generative adversarial networks. Expert Syst. Appl. **197**, 116694 (2022)
12. de Justiça Secretaria de Jurisprudência, S.T.: Precedentes qualificados (2023)
13. Ma, Y., He, H.: Imbalanced Learning: Foundations, Algorithms, and Applications. Wiley, Hoboken (2013)
14. Pedregosa, F., et al.: Scikit-learn: machine learning in python. J. Mach. Learn. Res. **12**, 2825–2830 (2011)
15. de Justiça Departamento de Pesquisas Judiciárias, C.N.: Justiça em números 2022. Justiça em números 2022 (2022)
16. Sáez, J.A., Luengo, J., Stefanowski, J., Herrera, F.: Smote-ipf: Addressing the noisy and borderline examples problem in imbalanced classification by a re-sampling method with filtering. Inf. Sci. **291**, 184–203 (2015)

17. Salton, G., Buckley, C.: Term-weighting approaches in automatic text retrieval. Inf. Process. Manage. **24**(5), 513–523 (1988)
18. Yen, S.J., Lee, Y.S.: Under-sampling approaches for improving prediction of the minority class in an imbalanced dataset. In: Huang, D.S., Li, K., Irwin, G.W. (eds.) Intelligent Control and Automation. Lecture Notes in Control and Information Sciences, vol. 344, pp. 731–740. Springer, Cham (2006). https://doi.org/10.1007/978-3-540-37256-1_89

Exploring Delay Reduction on Edge Computing Architectures from a Heuristic Approach

Hilal Alawneh[1,2], Jose David Nuñez-Gonzalez[1,2(✉)], and Manuel Graña[2]

[1] Department of Applied Mathematics, University of the Basque Country
UPV/EHU, 20600 Eibar, Spain
hilal.alawneh.81@gmail.com
[2] Grupo de Inteligencia Computacional, University of the Basque Country
UPV/EHU, 20001 San Sebastian, Spain

Abstract. Edge computing is a new promising paradigm helps users to execute their tasks on edge network which is closer to them rather than cloud. It can reduce application response time especially for those are critical to time such as healthcare applications, real-time apps, game playing, or traffic systems. Edge User Allocation (EUA) problem is responsible for allocate user application into edge servers on the edge network as app vendors' needing. In this paper, we propose a heuristic called Nearest Edge Server with Highest Capacity (NESHC) to solve the EUA problem. We use a real-word dataset in our extensive experiments. The results show that NESHC can reduce elapsed CPU time and outperform baseline approach (Optimal) and two state-of-the-art approaches (ICSOC19 and TPDS20). The reduction of delay causes increasing of user allocated into edge servers and leveraging the overall utilization of edge network system.

1 Introduction

Recently, the sector of Information Technology (IT) has developed dramatically with about 50-billion Internet of Things (IoT) devices will be connected to the Internet in the coming years [14]. This development will lead to the production of complex and computation intensive IoT applications that generate a big data [2]. Some limitations such as power and computational capabilities (i.e., CPU and memory) have caused downside effects on the execution of such resource-demanding applications on the devices [18]. Cloud computing is a technology that can support this growth by allowing on-demand access to a massive pool of computation resources [5, 17]. However, the resources of cloud computing are centralized and far distance from IoT devices where the data generated and caused different problems regarding to applications that required critical conditions for execution such as reaching a high level of quality of services, low response time, ability to real-time interactive, and ensure a secure platform. Therefore, using only cloud platform to execute such applications leads to some issues like security problems, generating a high delay and latency, interrupting the seamless of real-time interaction and violation of the quality of services [15]. Edge and fog computing have been used to provide more secure platform, reduce delay and latency, enable interaction for real-time applications, and enhance the quality of services by providing a pool of computational and storage capabilities at the edge and fog level of networks where they are close to IoT devices [4,6].

Edge computing is a new paradigm extending the cloud computing can reduce the latency for end-to-end devices, provide real-time interaction for the latency-sensitive applications where the edge servers that are much closer to end-user than cloud servers [12]. The process of determining which edge servers will serve which users is called Edge User Allocation (EUA), which is a critical problem in edge computing paradigm [12]. In edge computing paradigm, the computing, networking, and storage resources are span closer to the edge of the network by the number of edge servers which are closer to the end-users [3]. Edge computing provides lower network latency than the conventional cloud computing paradigm. This paradigm also offers a capability by enabling computation and storage at the edge level of the network. This substantially reduces data transfer (and bandwidth consuming) between the end user and the cloud [16]. Edge computing is especially important for extensive streaming applications or critical systems that require real-time decision-making, such as autonomous traffic systems, healthcare, or online gaming.

The edge servers are limited resources which might not be able to serve all the users within its coverage. Thus, some of the users might also be allocated in other coverage of the edge servers, or be allocated to the cloud. In order to ensure the Quality of Services (QoS) from the standpoint of the app vendor, the optimization target in this case is to maximize the number of users allotted to edge servers. Also, it's important to reduce the number of edge servers needed to serve those users. By lowering the cost of the app vendor's hiring edge servers to serve their app users [10], and increasing the resource usage on edge servers [7], this will guarantee the cost effectiveness of the allocation. One of the main goals in the server consolidation problem in cloud computing is to reduce the number of required servers [1,9]. Edge user allocation (EUA) problem is the term used to describe the aforementioned issue [10,11,13], by allocating user's task to the required edge servers in efficient way. The EUA problem is NP-hardness which becomes hard to solve effectively in an expanding edge computing environment. In this paper, we propose a heuristic approach called Nearest Edge Server with Highest Capacity (NESHC) to solve the EUA problem and reduce the delay of application execution on the edge network. The main contributions of this paper include:

- Proposes NESHC heuristic to solve NP-hardness of the EUA problem.
- Solving the complexity of the EUA problem by finding the optimal solution for user's task allocation into edge servers.
- Reduces the delay of execution time-aware applications such as real-time application.

– On a real-world dataset, extensive evaluations are performed to show that the efficiency of the proposed approach. The outcomes demonstrate that our approach outperforms some of baseline and the state-of-the-art approaches.

The remainder of the paper is organized as follows. Section 2 presents our proposed heuristic approach. Section 3 shows the results of the work compared with baseline and state-of-the-art approaches. The conclusion and future work are presented in Sect. 4.

2   Proposed Method

Edge user allocation (EUA) is NP-hard problem aims to find the best edge server for users for allocation where a dense distribution of edge servers and limited computing resources make it extremely computationally expensive to solve optimally the edge user allocation (EUA) problem in a large-scale scenario [12]. In some cases, the optimal solution would be high expensive, for example, if there are only 512 users and 125 edge servers, finding an optimal solution takes up to 23 s. This is unacceptable for applications or services that require real-time or near-real-time decisions. In order to efficiently find an optimal solution for the EUA problem and reducing the delay of applications execution, we introduce a heuristic approach called Nearest Edge Server with Highest Capacity (NESHC). The main aim of our heuristics is to reduce the delay in finding an optimal solution for edge user allocation problems to allow real-time applications or time-critical applications to complete their tasks within a required period of time. In this paper, we re-use the definition of the EUA problem which proposed by the authors in [10]. They set three definitions to handle with the EUA problem:

– Definition 1. Classical Bin Packing (BP) Problem: All bins are homogeneous with a similar bin capacity and the size of an item is presented as a single aggregation measure.
– Definition 2. Variable Sized Bin Packing (VSBP) Problem: This is a more general variant of the classical BP problem, where a limited collection of bin sizes is allowed and the objective is to minimize the total size of bins used, which is slightly different from the objective of the classical BP problem.
– Definition 3. Vector Bin Packing (VBP) Problem: By contrast, the size of an item in the VBP problem is associated with a multi-dimensional vector. The objective remains similar, in which the sum of packed item size vectors must not exceed the bin capacity vector in each dimension, which is normalized to 1 without loss of generality. It is called as multi-capacity BP problem in some works.

For user tasks allocation, edge servers have differential remaining capacity and multi-dimensional resource requirements. As a result, the EUA problem can be represented as a hybrid of the VSBP and VBP problems, yielding a variable sized vector bin packing (VSVBP) problem. Our goal is to reduce the delay for the user allocation problem by finding the best edge server to allocate the user tasks and outperform both baseline and state-of-the-art approaches.

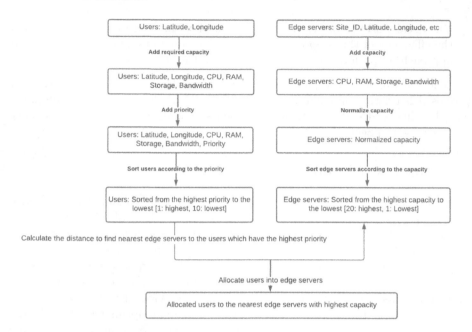

Fig. 1. The Flow Chart of the Heuristic Algorithm

As we can be seen in Fig. 1, our model considers the priority according to app vendor's needing and required capacity to serve user tasks and sorts users task in ascending manner from highest priority to lowest priority. After that, the capacity according to (CPU, RAM, Storage, and Bandwidth) for each edge servers will be randomly generated and sorted in descending order to find the highest capacity between all edge servers. The distance between the highest priority user task and the highest edge server capacity will be measured to find the nearest edge servers candidate to serve the user task in order to reduce overall delay and avoid sending user tasks to far distance edge servers or to the cloud.

Nearest Edge Server with Highest Capacity (NESHC)

In large-scale scenarios, finding an optimal solution will take very long time due to the problem's NP-hardness. In this section we propose a heuristic algorithm called Nearest Edge Server with Highest Capacity (NESHC) to solve the EUA problem. Suppose we have a set of users and a set of edge servers, we need to allocate user's task with highest priority to the nearest edge server with highest capacity. The edge servers will be sorted in descending order according to their capacity of CPU, RAM, Storage, and Bandwidth. Also, users will be sorted in ascending order according to their task's priority. The distance between users with highest priority and the edge servers with highest capacity will be calculated to find the nearest edge servers for users to be allocated. Given a set of edge servers S and a set of users U (lines 1–4), NESHC allocates an app vendor's users to edge servers. At the beginning all user tasks are unallocated. In line

5, the model sorts all edge servers according to their capacity of four vectors (CPU, RAM, Storage, and Bandwidth) in descending order to find the highest edge servers capacity where 1 is the lowest capacity and 20 is the highest capacity. The capacity will be normalized to be an integer number between 1 and 20. The model sorts all user tasks according to their priority generated by the app vendors in ascending order where 1 indicates to the highest priority and 10 indicates to the lowest priority (line 6). In line 7, the model calculates the distance between user u with highest priority and edge server s with highest capacity to find the nearest edge server s to the user u. In lines (8–15), NESHC allocates users which hold the highest priority to the nearest active edge server with the highest capacity, next to the nearest inactive edge server with the highest capacity. The process continue allocates all users from the highest priority to the lowest priority. Otherwise, if there are no free edge servers to serve user task, the user will be connected to the app vendor's cloud server to be allocated there line (16–18).

1. **initialization**
2. **a set of edge servers S and a set of users U**
3. **all users u_j , $\forall u_j \in U$, are unallocated**
4. **end initialization**
5. **sort edge server S in descending order according to their capacity of CPU, RAM, Storage, and Bandwidth, i.e. [20: highest, 1: lowest]**
6. **sort user u in ascending order of their priority, i.e. [1: highest, 10: lowest]**
7. **calculate the distance between user u with highest priority and edge server s with highest capacity to find the nearest edge server s to user u**
8. **for each user $u_j \in U$ do**
9. $S_{u_j} \triangleq$ **user u_j's nearest edge servers;**
10. $S_{u_j}^{active} \triangleq$ **user u_j's active nearest edge servers;**
11. **if $S_{u_j}^{active}! = \emptyset$ then**
12. **allocate user u_j to a nearest edge server $s_i \in S_{u_j}^{active}$ which has the highest capacity**
13. **else**
14. **allocate user u_j to a nearest edge server $s_i \in S_{u_j}$ which has the highest capacity**
15. **end if**
16. **if s_i cannot be decided then**
17. **allocate user u_j to the central cloud server**
18. **end if**
19. **end for**

3   Experiments and Results

All experiments are conducted on a Windows machine equipped with Intel Core i7-10510U processor (4 CPUs, 2.3 GHz) and 16 GB RAM. The software environment we utilized is Python 3.10.9 on windows 10 Pro. 64-bit. Python programming language is implemented using Python Jupyter Notebook[1], which can be freely downloaded from the Anaconda website[2]. The experiments are conducted on the publicly available EUA real-world dataset [3] [10], which contains the geographical locations of end-users and all cellular base stations in Australia.

We have conducted the experiments on a real-world dataset to evaluate the performance of our approaches against other baseline and state-of-the-art approaches. The five representative approaches, namely a Greedy baseline, a Random baseline, and three state-of-the-art approaches for solving the EUA problem:

- Greedy: This method allocates each user to the edge server with the largest available capacity, regardless of whether the server is active or not. Users are not allocated in any specific order.
- Random: This approach allocates each user to a random edge server available. Users are allocated in no specific order.
- ICSOC19 [11]: The proposed optimal approach will be used in our experimental evaluation. They proposed two approaches to tackled the EUA problem.
- TPDS20 [8]: The authors in this approach tackle the EUA problem by maximizing the number of allocated users while minimizing the overall system cost, which is determined using the expenses of required computing resources on edge servers. But TPDS20 does not provide dynamic QoS, users' QoS level are pre-specified at random.
- MCF [12]: Proposes an approach to solve the edge user allocation problem in large-scale scenarios. They aim to allocate the maximum number of users in minimum number of edge servers as possible.

We choose ICSOC19, TPDS20 and MCF as benchmark state-of-the-art approaches because they solved, the same problem which we handle in this paper, edge user allocation problem. Also, they used the same dataset EUA dataset that we use to conduct the experimental evaluation in this paper. In order to evaluate our proposed approach, we use the same experimental settings that handled in [12], which enable us to make a comparison between our proposed approach with aforementioned two baseline approaches and three state-of-the-art approaches. The simulation considers an urban area of $1.8km^2$ covered by 125 base stations, each station has one edge server. Each edge server covers a radius of 100–150m which is generated randomly. The results art taken by the average of repeated experiment 100 times to obtain 100 different user distributions. To evaluate the performance of our approach, we compare the CPU time taken to solve the EUA problem with results obtained by the six approaches (Optimal, Greedy, Random, ICSOC19, TPDS20 and MCF). The Optimal solution to a small-scale instance of the EUA problem can be found with an Integer Programming solver, e.g., Gurobi3 or IBM ILOG CPLEX4 [12]. The settings of the experiments are shown in Table 1.

---

[1] https://github.com/jupyter/.
[2] https://www.anaconda.com/.
[3] https://github.com/swinedge/eua-dataset.

Table 1. Experimental Settings [12]

	Users	Edge servers	Available resources (μ)
Set #1	100, ..., 1000	50%	35
Set #2	500	10%, ..., 100%	35
Set #3	500	50%	30, 35, ..., 75

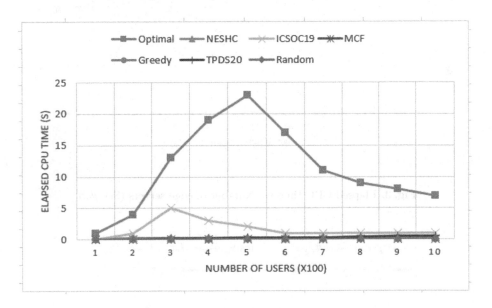

Fig. 2. Elapsed CPU time vs. Number of users (Set #1)

The results show that the NESHC approach can efficiently reduce over-all delay for users tasks and enable time-aware applications to execute their requests within required time constraint. Figure 2 shows the efficiency of NESHC to reduce the average CPU execution time taken to solve an instance of the EUA problem. The maximum elapsed CPU time in seconds to solve the EUA problem is 0.308 s for NESHC at 1000 users, while the required time to solve the EUA problem by Optimal and ICSOC19 is up to 23 s and 5 s, respectively. NESHC can solve the EUA problem in 0.183 s when there are 100 users needed to be allocated. The authors of MCF indicated that MCF, Greedy, TPDS20, and Random required only 1–2 milliseconds to solve the EUA problem [12] and this is very short time and unreasoning to solve the EUA problem by allocating efficiently 1000 users to 125 edge servers. In Fig. 3, it can be seen that the Optimal takes up to 48 s to solve the EUA problem when the percentage of number of servers is 80%. ICSOC19 also takes 8 s at 60% of number of servers. The maximum elapsed CPU time for our approach NESHC is 0.506 s at 50% of number of servers. Figure 4 illustrates that both Optimal and ICSOC19 takes up to 30 s and 9 s at 45 and 55 available server capacity, respectively, to solve the EUA

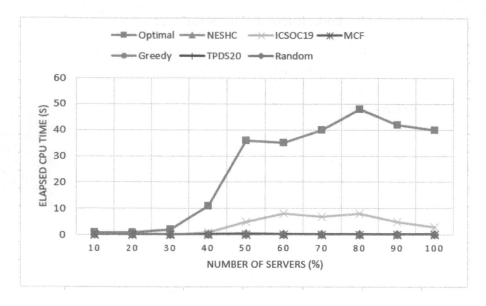

Fig. 3. Elapsed CPU time vs. Number of edge servers (Set #2)

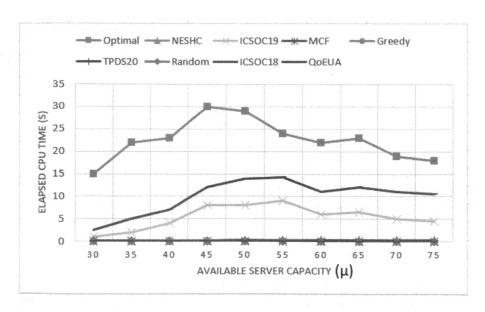

Fig. 4. Elapsed CPU time vs. Edge server capacity (Set #3)

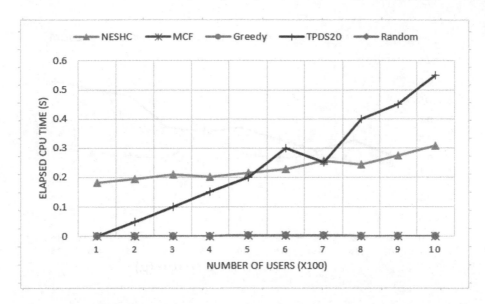

Fig. 5. Elapsed CPU time vs. Number of users (Set #1) without Optimal and ICSOC19

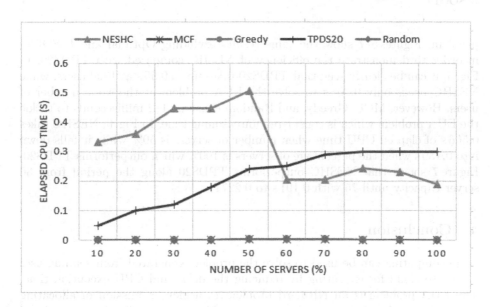

Fig. 6. Elapsed CPU time vs. Number of edge servers (Set #2) without Optimal and ICSOC19

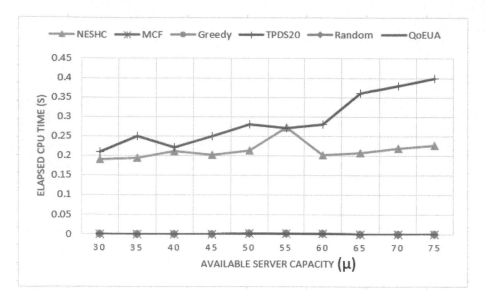

Fig. 7. Elapsed CPU time vs. Edge server capacity (Set #3) without Optimal and ICSOC19

problem. Figures 5–7 show the same results excluding Optimal and ICSOC19 in order to demonstrate the efficiency of NESHC compared with TPDS20. In Fig. 5, it can be clearly seen that TPDS20 takes up to 0.55 s at 1000 users, while NESHC needs only 0.308 s to solve the EUA problem at the same number of users. However, MCF, Greedy, and Random consume 1–2 milliseconds to tackle the EUA problem which is considered unreasoning time. In Fig. 6, NESHC takes 0.506 s of elapsed CPU time when number of servers is 50% while it falls down into 0.189 s when the percentage of servers is 100% which outperforms TPDS20. Figure 7 shows that NESHC outperforms TPDS20 along the period from 30 server capacity until 75 with 0.191 s to 0.227 s.

4   Conclusion

Edge computing can be used to solve the problem generated from sending user data into cloud for executing by reducing the delay and CPU execution time. The EUA problem is an NP-hard problem to achieve a mission of allocating efficiently users' tasks into some edge servers. Many user applications are critical to time such that healthcare applications which required a small amount of time to be served as well as real-time applications. Nearest Edge Server with Highest Capacity (NESHC) is a heuristic approach can efficiently solve the EUA problem and reducing the overall delay for user's tasks which be allocated into edge network. Delay reduction indirectly means that our system can increase the number of allocated users into edge servers in the edge network. Our experiments on a real-world dataset show that NESHC outperforms the baseline approach (Optimal) and state-of-the-art approaches (ICSOC19 and TPDS20) in elapsed CPU time required to allocate users into edge servers. In the future, the system could be modified to utilize Fog network which provides more extensive resources capabilities which meets users' needs.

Acknowledgment. Authors received research funds from 59 the Basque Government as the head of the Grupo de Inteligencia Computacional, Universidad del Pais Vasco, UPV/EHU, from 2007 until 2025. The current code for the grant is IT1689-22. Additionally, authors participate in Elkartek projects KK-2022/00051 and KK-2021/00070. The Spanish MCIN 5has also granted the authors a research project under code PID2020-116346GB-I00.

References

1. Ahmad, R.W., Gani, A., Hamid, S.H.A., Shiraz, M., Yousafzai, A., Xia, F.: A survey on virtual machine migration and server consolidation frameworks for cloud data centers. J. Netw. Comput. Appl. **52**, 11–25 (2015)
2. Almutairi, J., Aldossary, M.: A novel approach for IoT tasks offloading in edge-cloud environments. J. Cloud Comput. **10**(1), 1–19 (2021)
3. Bonomi, F., Milito, R., Zhu, J., Addepalli, S.: Fog computing and its role in the internet of things. In: Proceedings of the First Edition of the MCC Workshop on Mobile Cloud Computing, pp. 13–16 (2012)
4. Cong, P., Zhou, J., Li, L., Cao, K., Wei, T., Li, K.: A survey of hierarchical energy optimization for mobile edge computing: a perspective from end devices to the cloud. ACM Comput. Surv. (CSUR) **53**(2), 1–44 (2020)
5. Elgendy, I.A., Zhang, W.Z., Liu, C.Y., Hsu, C.H.: An efficient and secured framework for mobile cloud computing. IEEE Trans. Cloud Comput. **9**(1), 79–87 (2018)
6. Elgendy, I.A., Zhang, W., Tian, Y.C., Li, K.: Resource allocation and computation offloading with data security for mobile edge computing. Future Gener. Comput. Syst. **100**, 531–541 (2019)
7. Ferreto, T.C., Netto, M.A., Calheiros, R.N., De Rose, C.A.: Server consolidation with migration control for virtualized data centers. Future Gener. Comput. Syst. **27**(8), 1027–1034 (2011)
8. He, Q., et al.: A game-theoretical approach for user allocation in edge computing environment. IEEE Trans. Parallel Distrib. Syst. **31**(3), 515–529 (2019)
9. Jennings, B., Stadler, R.: Resource management in clouds: survey and research challenges. J. Netw. Syst. Manage. **23**, 567–619 (2015)
10. Lai, P., et al.: Optimal edge user allocation in edge computing with variable sized vector bin packing. In: Pahl, C., Vukovic, M., Yin, J., Yu, Q. (eds.) ICSOC 2018. LNCS, vol. 11236, pp. 230–245. Springer, Cham (2018). https://doi.org/10.1007/978-3-030-03596-9_15
11. Lai, P., et al.: Edge user allocation with dynamic quality of service. In: Yangui, S., Bouassida Rodriguez, I., Drira, K., Tari, Z. (eds.) ICSOC 2019. LNCS, vol. 11895, pp. 86–101. Springer, Cham (2019). https://doi.org/10.1007/978-3-030-33702-5_8
12. Lai, P., et al.: Cost-effective app user allocation in an edge computing environment. IEEE Trans. Cloud Comput. **10**(3), 1701–1713 (2020)

13. Peng, Q., et al.: Mobility-aware and migration-enabled online edge user allocation in mobile edge computing. In: 2019 IEEE International Conference on Web Services (ICWS), pp. 91–98. IEEE (2019)
14. Rababah, B., Alam, T., Eskicioglu, R.: The next generation internet of things architecture towards distributed intelligence: Reviews, applications, and research challenges. J. Telecommun. Electr. Comput. Eng. (JTEC) **12**(2) (2020)
15. Sahni, Y., Cao, J., Zhang, S., Yang, L.: Edge mesh: a new paradigm to enable distributed intelligence in internet of things. IEEE Access **5**, 16441–16458 (2017)
16. Satyanarayanan, M.: The emergence of edge computing. Computer **50**(1), 30–39 (2017)
17. Tyagi, H., Kumar, R.: Cloud computing for IoT. Internet Things (IoT) Concepts Appl., 25–41 (2020)
18. Yousefpour, A., et al.: All one needs to know about fog computing and related edge computing paradigms: a complete survey. J. Syst. Archit. **98**, 289–330 (2019)

Probability Density Function
for Clustering Validation

Pau Figuera[1(✉)], Alfredo Cuzzocrea[2], and Pablo García Bringas[1]

[1] D4K Group, University of Deusto, Bilbao, Spain
pau.figueras@opendeusto.es, pablo.garcia.bringas@deusto.es
[2] iDEA Lab, University of Calabria, Rende, Italy
alfredo.cuzzocrea@unical.it

Abstract. The choice of the number of clusters is a leading problem in Machine Learning. Validation methods provide solutions, with the drawback that inference is not possible. In this manuscript, we derive a distribution for the number of clusters for clustering validation. The starting point of our approach is the data transformation to the probabilistic space. Then, the dependence of the non-negative factorization to the dimensionality of the space span provides a sequence of the traces when the dimensionality varies. Its limit is a gamma. This result allows a non-excluding discussion when interpreting probabilities as credibility levels, and we open the door to inference for clustering validation.

Keywords: Nonnegative Matrix Factorization · Traces Sequence Limit · Probabilistic Clustering Validation · Clustering Credibility

1 Introduction

Clustering techniques constitute a series of algorithms with increasing applications in Machine Learning (ML), and perhaps one of the fields that experienced the most growth since from appearance of the classic k-means method [18]. A review reflecting this point of view of its growth is [14]. The fundamental idea is to group observations or items into similar groups. If groups are disjoint, it is hard clustering. If overlap between the data is allowed, it is soft clustering.

A common problem for all classification methods is determining the number of clusters. This problem, known as cluster validation, is controversial. Many existing methods seem to care about certain algorithms [1, p. 22]. Some authors have tried to establish the properties for good validation criteria. It is sensitivity versus the number of clusters [1, chap. 23] and [10].

A very extended validation criterion consists of constructing a loss function $\mathcal{L}$ that minimizes some norm between observations and a statistic representing the number of groups. The loss function optimization provides parameters for the best estimate.

P. García Bringas et al. (Eds.): HAIS 2023, LNAI 14001, pp. 133–144, 2023.
https://doi.org/10.1007/978-3-031-40725-3_12

Extended effective methods for validations are the Silhouette index and the gap statistic. The silhouette value measures how similar an object is to its cluster (cohesion) compared to other clusters (separation). It represents the separation distance between the resulting clusters [21]. The gap statistic compares the within-cluster dispersion to the expectation of a reference distribution [24].

Other constructions based on ideas of soft clustering are attributed to [12], who introduced an indicator function for observations based on kernelization using the null hypothesis as a classifier. The use of likelihood cross-validation to infer information on the number of model components is a work of [23]. A different approach uses the similarity between clusters evaluating similarity with the χ^2 statistic [20]. The work of [26] presents a purely algebraic approach, in which elements are clustered by collinearity. Also, as a consequence of the coronavirus pandemic, we detected an increasing interest in this area [17,22], and the review paper focused on bioinformatics of [25].

In this manuscript, we propose a validation method for the number of clusters. The objective is to build up a density, allowing the inference. First, we consider the data matrix in the probabilistic space. Then, identifying the non-negative factorization space span with clusters, we construct a sequence of the traces for different dimensions of the non-negative approximation. The limit of this sequence is a gamma. This result makes it possible to associate credibility, or probabilities in the Bayesian sense, with the choice of the number of clusters.

We structure this manuscript with a quick introduction of Non-negative matrix factorization (NMF) methods to obtain the probabilistic image of the data matrix in Sect. 3. In Sect. 4, we derive a statistic whose limit distribution follows a gamma probability density function (pdf). In Sect. 5 there are some examples.

2   Related Work

Clustered data sets support generative models when probabilistic classification is assumed. There are two concepts of probabilistic clustering: the first concept supposes that each entity belongs to each cluster with a different probability [8], while the second concept classifies the observations that most likely belong to each distribution [6]. Both approaches are based on determining the suitable mixtures or *components*; in number and parameter, $f(\mathbf{x}|\theta) = \sum \alpha_j g_j(\mathbf{x}|\theta_j)$ ($\mathbf{x}$ is the vector corresponding to an observed entity, g is a density with parameter θ, and α gives the mixing weights assigned to each density; the sum is performed on the overall set of mixtures), converting an unsupervised classification problem into a parameter estimation problem that assigns probabilities of membership to each item in each cluster. The credibility (likelihood) is the quality of classification, which is necessary to evaluate the posterior probability of the number of mixtures [23].

Several studies focused on this viewpoint of probabilistic clustering for validation issues are attributed to [12], who introduced an indicator function for observations based on kernelization and used the null hypothesis as a classifier.

In [23] is used likelihood cross-validation to infer information on the number of model components. Using a different approach, the similarity between clusters can be evaluated from the χ^2 statistic between probabilistic classifications [20].

By introducing an index and assuming that each cluster is generated by a parametric distribution, the minimum can be taken as the validation index [11]. More recent works include [19], which, in the scope of astronomical observations and under the hypothesis of normality and the existence of a correlation, presents an algorithm in which the posterior of the correlations follows a gamma *pdf*. The work of [26] presents a purely algebraic approach, in which elements are clustered by collinearity.

The probabilistic nature of the NMF allows its use for probabilistic type classifications. A survey on this point is [6]. The use of NMF techniques for clustering are introduced by [7]. These are probabilistic classifications and are equivalent to k-means introducing a Bayesian classifier. However, the derived properties have not been exploited for validation purposes as we do.

3   Data Matrix Probabilistic Image

Let us consider a data set consisting of m observations or items, each identified with the label or sub-index i, valued under n *iid* variables. There is no statistical hypothesis, but values are taken from the non-negative real set, each denoted by j. Here, the data can be handled by a matrix $\mathbf{X} \in \mathbb{R}_+^{m \times n}$. Additionally, $\mathbf{x}_i = (x_{i1}, \ldots, x_{in})$ is a row vector representing each item, and the column vectors $\mathbf{x}_j = (x_{j1}, \ldots, x_{jm})'$ are the values of $\mathbf{x}$ on the observational variable j. We also impose the condition of linear independence of the columns.

The transformation of $\mathbf{X}$ given by

$$[\mathbf{Y}]_{ij} = [\mathbf{X}]_{ij} \, \mathbf{D}_X \, \mathbf{M}_X \qquad (i = 1, \ldots, m \text{ and } j = 1, \ldots, n) \qquad (1)$$

with $\mathbf{D}_X$ and $\mathbf{M}_X$ as diagonal matrices of appropriate dimensions defined as

$$\mathbf{M}_X = \operatorname{diag} \left(\sum_j x_{ij} \right)^{-1} \qquad (2)$$

$$\mathbf{D}_X = \operatorname{diag} \left(m \right)^{-1} \qquad (3)$$

is invariant under changes in measurement scale, and $\sum_{ij} \mathbf{Y} = 1$.

One must pose the NMF on matrix $\mathbf{Y}$ to find matrices $\mathbf{W}$ and $\mathbf{H}$ such that the product

$$[\widehat{\mathbf{Y}}]_{ij} = [\mathbf{W}]_{ik} [\mathbf{H}]_{kj} \qquad (k = 1, \ldots, k) \qquad (4)$$

$$\approx [\mathbf{Y}]_{ij} \qquad (5)$$

minimizes some norm or divergence [4] while ensuring that $\sum_{ij} \mathbf{WH} = 1$.

The Kullback-Leibler (KL) divergence is [16]

$$D_{KL}([\mathbf{Y}]_{ij}\|[\mathbf{WH}]_{ij}) = \sum_{ij} [\mathbf{Y}]_{ij} \circledast \log \frac{[\mathbf{Y}]_{ij}}{[\mathbf{WH}]_{ij}} \tag{6}$$

The optimization process with Karush-Kuhn-Tucker (KKT) conditions provides the following solutions: [9]

$$[\mathbf{W}]_{ik} \leftarrow [\mathbf{W}]_{ik} \circledast \left(\frac{[\mathbf{Y}]_{ij}}{[\mathbf{WH}]_{ij}} [\mathbf{H}]'_{kj} \right) \tag{7}$$

$$[\mathbf{H}]_{kj} \leftarrow [\mathbf{H}]_{kj} \circledast \left([\mathbf{W}]'_{ik} \frac{[\mathbf{Y}]_{ij}}{[\mathbf{WH}]_{ij}} \right) \tag{8}$$

where $\circledast$ is the Hadamard or element-wise product and the matrix fraction is the quotient for equal sub-index entries.

To adjust the product (3) or the approximation (4), it is necessary, after selecting a value for k, to apply an iterative process, switching between (7) and (7) until the following condition is satisfied:

$$\left\| [\widehat{\mathbf{Y}}]_{ij} - [\mathbf{Y}]_{ij} \right\|_1 \le \epsilon \qquad (\epsilon > 0) \tag{9}$$

Here, $\|\cdot\|_1$ is the Hilbert or L_p ($p = 1$) norm (the sum of all involved entries, which should be not confused with the Hilbert-Schmidt norm, which is L_2 or the Gaussian norm), which is induced in a natural way from the sums of definition (6).

This optimization process, based on KL divergence as the objective function, is known as the *em* algorithm. In most cases, the results are entirely equal to Expectation maximization (EM) algorithm, which always converges [5]. However, the *em* algorithm results are asymptotes of EM [2] in the general case.

The NMF admits statistical interpretation when suitable normalization conditions are imposed. For the matrices involved in formula (4), one must introduce the constraint $\|\cdot\|_1 = 1$ for columns of $\mathbf{Y}$ and $\mathbf{W}$ and rows of $\mathbf{H}$. These well-known conditions are also called *probabilistic normalizations* [7].

In [7], it is demonstrated that probabilistic normalization leads to

$$[\mathbf{WH}]_{ij} = \frac{1}{k} [\widetilde{\mathbf{W}}]_{ik} [\widetilde{\mathbf{H}}]_{kj} \tag{10}$$

Here, the tilde symbol indicates that the matrices have been normalized. We identify

$$[\widetilde{\mathbf{W}}]_{ik'} \sim P(w_i \,|\, k') \tag{11}$$

$$[\widetilde{\mathbf{H}}]_{k'j} \sim P(h_j \,|\, k') \tag{12}$$

for a fixed k'.

Value k is also referred as the *model components*. In clustering applications, they are identified with [1, p. 22], and in the case of using these techniques in the information retrieval problem, with the latent variables [7].

4 Sequence of Traces

The trace

$$\text{tr}(\widehat{\mathbf{Y}}'\widehat{\mathbf{Y}}) = \sum_k \text{diag}([\mathbf{W}]_{ik}[\mathbf{H}]_{kj})'([\mathbf{W}]_{ik}[\mathbf{H}]_{kj}) \tag{13}$$

leads to a sequence with varying k in the NMF factorization space span.

$$\widetilde{z}_k = \left\{ \text{tr}\left([\mathbf{W}]_{i1}[\mathbf{H}]_{1j}\right)'([\mathbf{W}]_{i1}[\mathbf{H}]_{1j}), \text{tr}\left([\mathbf{W}]_{i2}[\mathbf{H}]_{2j}\right)'([\mathbf{W}]_{i2}[\mathbf{H}]_{2j}), \dots \right\} \tag{14}$$

$$= \left\{ \widetilde{z}_1, \widetilde{z}_2, \dots \right\} \tag{15}$$

Naming as z

$$z = \text{tr}\left([\mathbf{Y}]'_{ij}[\mathbf{Y}]_{ij}\right) \tag{16}$$

The quotient of (15) and (16)

$$z_k = \left\{ \frac{\widetilde{z}_k}{z} \right\}_k \tag{17}$$

is a decreasing sequence.

It is easy to see by imposing the same approximation condition for ϵ in formula (9) for all products of $\mathbf{WH}$ obtained with different values of k and introducing

$$\left\| [\mathbf{W}]_{ik}[\mathbf{H}]_{kj} \right\|_1 = \frac{1}{k} \left\| [\widetilde{\mathbf{W}}]_{ik}[\widetilde{\mathbf{H}}]_{kj} \right\|_1 \tag{18}$$

and the inequality

$$\frac{1}{k^2}\text{tr}\left([\widetilde{\mathbf{W}}]_{ik}[\widetilde{\mathbf{H}}]_{kj}\right)'([\widetilde{\mathbf{W}}]_{ik}[\widetilde{\mathbf{H}}]_{kj}) > \frac{1}{(k')^2}\text{tr}\left([\widetilde{\mathbf{W}}]_{ik'}[\widetilde{\mathbf{H}}]_{k'j}\right)'([\widetilde{\mathbf{W}}]_{ik'}[\widetilde{\mathbf{H}}]_{k'j}) \tag{19}$$

holds only if $k' > k$.

4.1 Traces Sequence Limit

From sequence (17), function

$$\varphi(z_k) = \left(\frac{z_k}{z}\right)^{-z} \tag{20}$$

is a one-to-one map of the KL divergence, preserving the decreasing behavior.

The change of variables

$$\frac{1}{\nu} = \frac{z_k - z}{z} \tag{21}$$

leads to

$$\varphi(\nu) = \frac{z}{\nu^2}\left(1 + \frac{1}{\nu}\right)^{-z} \qquad \left(\left|\frac{\partial z_k}{\partial \nu}\right| = \frac{z}{\nu^2}\right) \tag{22}$$

with variation domain $z/(z_1 - z) \le \nu < +\infty$, since $z_k \to z$ when k increases, as consequence of (9) for $k > \min(m, n)$.

Equation (22) is now

$$\varphi(\nu) = \frac{z}{1 - z}\frac{\partial}{\partial \nu}\left(1 + \frac{1}{\nu}\right)^{1-z} \tag{23}$$

Taking into account number e definition [13]

$$\left(1 + \frac{1}{\nu}\right)^{1-z} \xrightarrow[\nu \to \infty]{} \exp\left(\frac{1 - z}{\nu}\right) \tag{24}$$

and substituting (24) en (23),

$$\varphi(\nu) = c\frac{\partial}{\partial \nu}\exp\left(\frac{1 - z}{\nu}\right) \qquad \left(c = \frac{z}{1 - z}\right) \tag{25}$$

Introducing now the changes $x = 1/\nu$ and $\lambda = z - 1$, restricting values of λ to $0 < \lambda < 1$,

$$\varphi(x, \lambda) = c\frac{1}{x^2}\frac{\partial}{\partial x}e^{-\lambda x} \qquad \left(\left|\frac{\partial \nu}{\partial x}\right| = \frac{1}{x^2} \text{ and } \left|\frac{\partial z}{\partial \lambda}\right| = 1\right) \tag{26}$$

$$= c\frac{\partial}{\partial x}\frac{\partial^2}{\partial \lambda^2}e^{-\lambda x} \tag{27}$$

leads to equation

$$\frac{\partial^r}{\partial x^r}\frac{\partial^{p-2}}{\partial \lambda^{p-2}}\varphi(\lambda, x) = (-1)^{r+p}c\frac{\partial^r}{\partial x^r}\frac{\partial^p}{\partial \lambda^p}e^{-\lambda x} \quad (p > 2 \text{ and } r \ge 1) \tag{28}$$

4.2   Normalization of Traces Sequence Limit

Taking the derivatives in (28)

$$f(x, \lambda) = (-1)^{r+p}c\lambda^r x^p e^{-\lambda x} \tag{29}$$

and normalizing

$$f(x\lambda) = \frac{f(x, \alpha, \lambda)}{\displaystyle\int_0^{+\infty}\int_0^1 f(x, \alpha, \lambda)d\lambda\,dx} \tag{30}$$

$$= \frac{1}{\Gamma(p+1)}\lambda^r x^p e^{-\lambda x} \tag{31}$$

For $\alpha = r = p + 1$

$$f(x, \alpha, \lambda) = \frac{1}{\Gamma(\alpha)} \lambda^{\alpha} x^{\alpha-1} e^{-\lambda x} \tag{32}$$

is gamma *pdf* of parameters α and λ.

The Eq. (32) allows modeling the number of clusters with a gamma pdf. However, it only makes sense for values of $x \in \mathbb{Z}_+$, which can be achieved by introducing a base in (20). In this manuscript, we have followed the widespread criterion in statistics of omitting it.

4.3 Loss Function Equivalence

To relate the NMF with clustering techniques, one must identify the dimensionality of the decomposition of the space span with clusters, transforming the clustering problem into an estimation of k densities [6, p. 61]. So, credibility (probability) for the number of clusters are the integer values of the gamma support pdf. On the other hand, equation (32) models a cluster density for the case that x is restricted to the positive integers.

The equivalence of relation (20) with a loss function is evident if we consider the expansion of the divergence KL

$$D_{KL}(z_k \| z) = z \log z - z \log z_k \tag{33}$$
$$= H(z) - H(z_k | z) \tag{34}$$

where $D_{KL}(z_k \| z)$ can be assimilated to the mutual information $I(z | z_k)$ and $H(\cdot)$ are entropies.

In this case, the function (32) is a regular enough one-to-one map of a loss function of formula (33), or in Information terms (34). In this manuscript, we do not go beyond with the more rich Information Theory interpretation to make our exposition as simple as we can.

From this point on, the procedure we followed consisted in obtaining the limit distribution, and normalizing it to be consistent with probability postulates, instead of the usual procedure of parameters optimization.

5 Examples

Obtention of the pdf of Eq. (32) requires several parameters, shown in Algorithm 1. For better control, we divide the process into three procedures. The first objective (procedure I of Algorithm 1) is to determine the sequence of traces. So, we must add to the data the number of components k and the degree of approximation ϵ of (9). Value k is the number of model components, providing also a sequence of k terms. To alleviate the iterative process, we do not use the approximation criteria but 3 iterations to obtain matrices (7) and (8) with random initialization conditions. This process is repeated 25 times, taking the arithmetic mean of each term. Also, its necessary to determine the rank of matrix $\mathbf{Y'Y}$ of Eq. (4) and its trace. The sequences of traces must be keep in a matrix $\mathbf{Z}$.

Algorithm 1: Traces Sequence Limit Function.

Procedure 1

Input: Data Matrix: $\mathbf{X}$
            Parameters: k (components), q (re-estimations), ϵ (approximation)
Output: $\mathbf{Z}$ (traces), rk (rank), z (trace of $\mathbf{Y}'\mathbf{Y}$)
$\mathbf{Y} \leftarrow \mathbf{X}$;
$rk \leftarrow \mathbf{Y}$;
$z \leftarrow \mathbf{Y}$;
for $q \leftarrow 1$ **to** *re-estimations* **do**
$\quad$ **for** $k \leftarrow 1$ **to** *components* **do**
$\quad\quad$ Initialize $\mathbf{W}$ $\mathbf{H}$;
$\quad\quad$ **while** $\epsilon' \geq \epsilon$ **do**
$\quad\quad\quad$ compute $\mathbf{W}$ and $\mathbf{H}$;
$\quad\quad\quad$ $\epsilon' = \|\mathbf{WH} - \mathbf{Y}\|$;
$\quad\quad\quad$ $z_k = \mathrm{tr}(\mathbf{WH})'\mathbf{WH})$
$\quad$ $\mathbf{Z} \leftarrow z_k$

Procedure 2

Input: $\mathbf{Z}$, rk, z
Output: S_{mean} (traces), J (Basis transformation)

$J = \frac{z}{1-z}$
$J_z = J\sqrt{mn}$
support $= J_z (1,1,\dots)$
for $k \leftarrow 1$ **to** *components* **do**
$\quad$ $S_{mean} = \sum_i \mathbf{Z}_{ik}/m$;

Procedure 3

Input: S_{means}
Output: α,λ
$\alpha - 1 = \max S_{mean}$
$\lambda = 1 - 1/\alpha$

The second phase (procedure II) consists to pick the output procedure I as input (matrix containing the sequence of traces $\mathbf{Z}$, the trace of matrix $z = \mathbf{Y}'\mathbf{Y}$, and the rank of matrix $\mathbf{Y}$). Then, for each value of k an estimator of its expected value is computed. The goal is to express the estimation of the traces on the support $\mathbb{Z}_+$. It is achieved by

$$c_r = \frac{z}{1-z}\sqrt{mn_r} \tag{35}$$

where n_r is the number of linear independence variables. Multipliying each term of the sequence by (35) the dot lines of Fig. 2 are obtained.

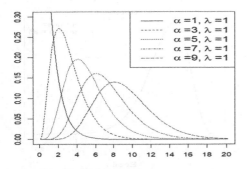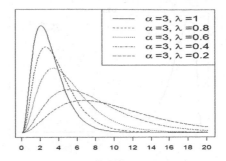

Fig. 1. Gamma pdf plots. Left panel shows the effect of parameter α with fixed lambda. Right panel fixes α and varies λ. Both figures shares the same axis scale.

Procedure III of the algorithm estimates the parameters of gamma pdf. It requires setting its maximum to the supremum of sequence (20). The maximum of relation (32) is $(\alpha - 1)/\lambda$. Since the expectation of a standard gamma distribution, obtained from (32) with the change of variables $t = \lambda x$ is α [3], equating both expressions,

$$\lambda = 1 - \frac{1}{\alpha} \tag{36}$$

Effect of parameters α and λ is shown in Fig. 1.

Results obtained for several selected data sets of the UCI repository (https://archive.ics.uci.edu/ml/datasets.php) are shown in Fig. 2.

Table 1. Results comparative. Categories are the number of different species given by the data set author. Silhouette and Gamma (the proposed validation criteria) columns are the number of clusters provided by these methods.

Data Set	Categories	Silhouette	Gamma
Iris	3	2	3
Glass	7	4	7
Seeds	3	2	2
Ecoli	6	3	5

To illustrate the behavior of our validation criteria, the results obtained are compared with the well-known Silhouette index. To obtain this index we have used the package *factoextra* R-package [15] taking as bootstrap parameter $B = 70$. Table 1 shows the result of the comparison. To do it the maximum of the pdf shown in the Fig. 1 with the values of the Silhouette index has been taken. It can be seen that our values are better for validation than those obtained with the classical indexes that we compare, if the number of categories that generates the data is taken as true values.

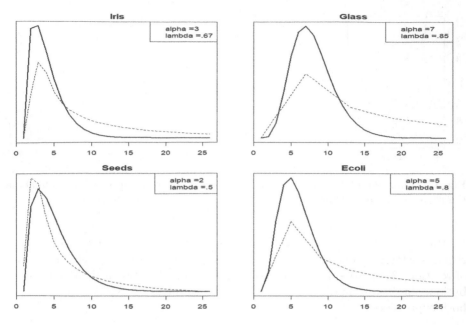

Fig. 2. Representation of the studied data sets. Gamma parameters are at the legend. Dashed lines correponds to formula (20) and continuous line are the corresponding gamma pdf.

An issue is that for a density, it is immediate to be able to the hypotheses test. For the sufficient statistic $\theta = \{\alpha, \lambda\}$, one can define acceptance regions $\mathcal{R}$ for value θ_0. The hypotheses test consists of regions

$$
\mathcal{R}(x) = \begin{cases} 1 & \text{if } \theta \leq \theta_0 \\ \dfrac{\displaystyle\int_{\theta \leq \theta_0} f(x; \alpha, \lambda)d\theta}{\displaystyle\int_{\mathcal{C}} f(x; \alpha, \lambda)d\theta} & \text{otherwise} \end{cases} \tag{37}
$$

where $\mathcal{C}$ is a compact set on which parameters take values.

6   Conclusion

The NMF lets to build a sequence of traces when the dimension of the space span takes values on $\mathbb{Z}_+$. The decreasing behavior of this sequence lets to construct a function of the traces. The limit distribution of the sequence of traces is a gamma pdf when normalizing. This result provides a validation criterion and opens the door to inference for the clustering validation problem. The existence of a pdf lets to construct confidence intervals or hypothesis test. Also, graphical results are easy to interpret, and special skills are not necessary to discourse on results. This can be used in advantage to discuss with the expert criteria with no excluding this kind of knowledge.

References

1. Aggarwal, C.C.: Clustering: Algorithms and Applications. CRC Press Taylor and Francis Group, Boca Raton (2014)
2. Amari, S.I.: Information geometry of the EM and em algorithms for neural networks. Neural Netw. **8**(9), 1379–1408 (1995)
3. Balakrishnan, N., Nevzorov, V.B.: A Primer on Statistical Distributions. Wiley, Hoboken (2004)
4. Chen, J.C.: The nonnegative rank factorizations of nonnegative matrices. Linear Algebra Appl. **62**, 207–217 (1984)
5. Dempster, A., Laird, N., Rubin, D.: Maximum likelihood from incomplete data via the EM algorithm. J. Royal Stat. Soc. **39**(1), 1–38 (1977)
6. Deng, H., Han, J.: Probabilistic models for clustering. In: Data Clustering, pp. 61–86. Chapman and Hall/CRC (2018)
7. Ding, C., Li, T., Peng, W.: On the equivalence between non-negative matrix factorization and probabilistic latent semantic indexing. Comput. Stat. Data Anal. **52**(8), 3913–3927 (2008)
8. Dougherty, E.R., Brun, M.: A probabilistic theory of clustering. Pattern Recogn. **37**(5), 917–925 (2004)
9. Figuera, P., García Bringas, P.: On the probabilistic latent semantic analysis generalization as the singular value decomposition probabilistic image. J. Stat. Theory Appl. **19**, 286–296 (2020). https://doi.org/10.2991/jsta.d.200605.001
10. Fränti, P., Sieranoja, S.: K-means properties on six clustering benchmark datasets. Appl. Intell. **48**(12), 4743–4759 (2018)
11. Fred, A.L., Jain, A.K.: Cluster validation using a probabilistic attributed graph. In: 2008 19th International Conference on Pattern Recognition, pp. 1–4. IEEE (2008)
12. Har-Even, M., Brailovsky, V.L.: Probabilistic validation approach for clustering. Pattern Recogn. Lett. **16**(11), 1189–1196 (1995)
13. Hyslop, J.M.: Infinite Series. Dover Publications, New York (2006)
14. Jain Anil, K.: Data clustering: 50 years beyond k-means. Pattern Recogn. Lett. **31**(8, SI), 651–666 (2010). https://doi.org/10.1016/j.patrec.2009.09.011. 19th International Conference on Pattern Recognition (ICPR 2008), Tampa, FL, DEC 08-11, 2008
15. Kassambara, A., Mundt, F.: factoextra: Extract and visualize the results of multivariate data analyses (2019). https://CRAN.R-project.org/package=factoextra. r package version 1.0.6
16. Kullback, S., Leibler, R.A.: On information and sufficiency. Ann. Math. Stat. **22**(1), 79–86 (1951)
17. Li, Y., Hu, P., Liu, Z., Peng, D., Zhou, J.T., Peng, X.: Contrastive clustering. In: Proceedings of the AAAI Conference on Artificial Intelligence, vol. 35, pp. 8547–8555 (2021)
18. MacQueen, J., et al.: Some methods for classification and analysis of multivariate observations. In: Proceedings of the fifth Berkeley Symposium on Mathematical Statistics and Probability, pp. 281–297 (1967)
19. Olivares, J., et al.: Kalkayotl: a cluster distance inference code. Astron. Astrophys. **644**, A7 (2020)
20. Pallis, G., Angelis, L., Vakali, A., Pokorny, J.: A probabilistic validation algorithm for web users' clusters. In: 2004 IEEE International Conference on Systems, Man and Cybernetics (IEEE Cat. No. 04CH37583), vol. 5, pp. 4129–4134. IEEE (2004)

21. Rousseeuw, P.J.: Silhouettes: a graphical aid to the interpretation and validation of cluster analysis. J. Comput. Appl. Math. **20**, 53–65 (1987)
22. Sinaga, K.P., Yang, M.S.: Unsupervised k-means clustering algorithm. IEEE Access **8**, 80716–80727 (2020)
23. Smyth, P.: Model selection for probabilistic clustering using cross-validated likelihood. Stat. Comput. **10**(1), 63–72 (2000)
24. Tibshirani, R., Walther, G., Hastie, T.: Estimating the number of clusters in a data set via the gap statistic. J. R. Stat. Soc. Ser. B (Stat. Methodol.) **63**(2), 411–423 (2001)
25. Ullmann, T., Hennig, C., Boulesteix, A.L.: Validation of cluster analysis results on validation data: a systematic framework. Wiley Interdisc. Rev. Data Min. Knowl. Discov. **12**, e1444 (2022)
26. Usefi, H.: Clustering, multicollinearity, and singular vectors. Comput. Stat. Data Anal. **173**, 107523 (2022)

Comprehensive Analysis of Different Techniques for Data Augmentation and Proposal of New Variants of BOSME and GAN

Asier Garmendia-Orbegozo[1]([✉]) [iD], Jose David Nuñez-Gonzalez[1] [iD],
Miguel Angel Anton Gonzalez[2] [iD], and Manuel Graña[3] [iD]

[1] Department of Applied Mathematics, University of the Basque Country
UPV/EHU, 20600 Eibar, Spain
asier.garmendiao@ehu.eus
[2] TECNALIA, Basque Research and Technology Alliance (BRTA), 20009 San
Sebastian, Spain
[3] Computation Intelligence Group, University of the Basque Country UPV/EHU,
20018 San Sebastian, Spain

Abstract. In many environments in which detection of minority class instances is critical, the available data intended for training Machine Learning models is poorly distributed. The data imbalance usually produces deterioration of the trained model by generalisation of instances belonging to minority class predicting as majority class instances. To avoid these, different techniques have been adopted in the literature and expand the original database such as Generative Adversarial Networks (GANs) or Bayesian network-based over-sampling method (BOSME). Starting from these two methods, in this work we propose three new variants of data augmentation to address data imbalance issue. We use traffic event data from three different areas of California divided in two subgroups attending their severity. Experiments show that top performance cases where reached after using our variants. The importance of data augmentation techniques as preprocessing tool has been proved as well, as a consequence of performance drop of systems in which original databases with imbalanced data where used.

Keywords: Data augmentation · Data imbalance · GANs

1 Introduction

Machine Learning (ML) and specially Deep Learning (DL) models have become one of the most effective and useful tool for prediction and inference in different environments such as biomedicine or smart cities. Although data availability is not a matter to be concerned, data imbalance could cause deterioration of performance of the models. No matter the size of the database if there are few

P. García Bringas et al. (Eds.): HAIS 2023, LNAI 14001, pp. 145–155, 2023.
https://doi.org/10.1007/978-3-031-40725-3_13

instances of one of the possibles classes to be determined, the algorithm might generalise by classifying almost all instances as part of the majority class.

In many cases it is of special interest the correct classification of the minority class. For instance, in a cancer diagnosis problem the cost of predicting wrongly a patient with cancer as a cancer-free case is critical. Generally, in databases the minority cases become from patient that suffer cancer, and if this imbalance is extreme, models should generalize by classifying almost all instances as part of majority class, obtaining a high accuracy yet. Other examples of such imbalances could be found in fraud commitment detection where fraudulent cases are less frequent by far.

In traffic event prediction different factors are responsible for causing traffic delays or accidents, and identification of them in real time is crucial for avoiding uncomfortable situations. In this area the instances belonging to traffic misfortunes are a minority in comparison to usual traffic sensor readings too.

To avoid these situations in which minority class instances could not be detected, training the models with as much instances from minority class as majority class instances should be the solution. Over-sampling is a suitable methodology to modify the class variable distribution at a data-level stage (preprocessing), before the learning process. By this way, the model obtains enough information from the minority class to detect these exceptions while performing in real scenarios.

In this work, starting from two different alternatives for expanding original data we proposed three novel ways for generating new instances. Each of them are evaluated in a large, real-world dataset consisting of traffic sensor observations and from the different metropolitan areas from the state of California over a period of three months.

The rest of the paper is organised as follows. Section 2 reviews some of the most representatives works published in the literature. Section 3 specifies the new alternatives proposed by this work. In Sect. 4 the materials and methodology applied in this work are presented. In Sect. 5 we conduct different experiments of classification tasks using data generated by all the alternatives proposed and the results are presented. In Sect. 6 discussion of these results and conclusions are made.

2   State of the Art

Different methodology has been applied to expand original databases to obtain a more generalised source of knowledge resulting on an optimized inference model. In [7] they propose the primitive GAN algorithm in which a generator and discriminator play an adversarial process in which they simultaneously train two models: a generative model that captures the data distribution, and a discriminative model that estimates the probability that a sample came from the training data rather than from the generator. The training procedure for the generator is to maximize the probability of the discriminator making a mistake. By this way, new instances are created with similar characteristics of the original data.

Cibersecurity systems usually face the problem of data imbalance. In [9] they proposed a Multi-task learning model with hybrid deep features (MEMBER) to address different challenges like class imbalance or attack sophistication. Based on a Convolutional Neural Network (CNN) with embedded spatial and channel attention mechanisms, MEMBER introduces two auxiliary tasks (i.e., an auto-encoder (AE) enhanced with a memory module and a distance-based prototype network) to improve the model generalization capability and reduce the performance degradation suffered in imbalanced databases. Continuing with intrusion detection area, a tabular data sampling method to solve the imbalanced learning task of intrusion detection, which balances the normal samples and attack samples was proposed in [6]. In [14] TGAN was presented, as a method for creating tabular data creating discrete and continuous variables like medical or educational records. In [15] they developed CTAB-GAN, a novel conditional table GAN architecture with the ability to model diverse data types, including a mix of continuous and categorical variables, solving data imbalance and long tail issues, i.e., certain variables having drastic frequency differences across large values. In [4] they proposed a method to train generative adversarial networks on multivariate feature vectors representing multiple categorical values.

Bayesian network-based over-sampling method (BOSME) was introduced in [12], which is a new over-sampling methodology based on Bayesian networks. What makes BOSME different is that it relies on a new approach, generating artificial instances of the minority class following the probability distribution of a Bayesian network that is learned from the original minority classes by likelihood maximization.

Some other researchers opted for treating multi-modal data in order to optimize the trained network's inference accuracy. In [13] they proposed an end-to-end framework named Event Adversarial Neural Network (EANN), which is able to obtain event- invariant features and thus benefit the detection of fake news on newly arrived events. In [8] they proposed an audio-visual Deep CNNs (AVDCNN) SE model, which incorporates audio and visual streams into an unified network model. For traffic event detection were also used other approaches that include data from multiple type and sources. In [2] they annotated social streams such as microblogs as a sequence of labelling problem. They presented a novel training data creation process for training sequence labelling models. This data creation process utilizes instance level domain knowledge. In [3] they proposed Restricted Switching Linear Dynamical System (RSLDS) to model normal speed and travel time dynamics and thereby characterize anomalous dynamics. They used the city traffic events extracted from text to explain those anomalous dynamics. In [10] they used human mobility and social media data. A detected anomaly was represented by a sub-graph of a road network where people's routing behaviors significantly differ from their original patterns. They then try to describe a detected anomaly by mining representative terms from the social media that people posted when the anomaly happened. In [5] they used Twitter posts and sensor data observations to detect traffic events using semi-supervised deep learning models such as Generative Adversarial Networks. They extend the multi-modal Generative adversarial Network model to a semi-supervised architecture to characterise traffic events.

3   Proposed Approach

As we mentioned in the introductory part in classification environments in which data imbalances can cause the performance deterioration of the machine learning model, it is of special interest to have a balanced class distribution. For this purpose, BOSME was proposed tackling this issue by generating synthetic data following the probability distribution of a Bayesian network. Moreover, in the majority of the cases GANs become the first option at extending databases and address imbalance learning tasks. In this work, we assess both option and propose three new variants that raise from both methodologies.

3.1   Variant 1: Feeding the Discriminator of GAN with Data Proceeding from BOSME

The idea of GAN is to maximize the capability of the generator of creating instances as equal as possible as original ones by trying to confuse the discriminator and this last trying to distinguish real data from synthetic data. Originally, discriminator is fed by data generated by the generator raised from normal distribution. If we substitute these data by data generated by BOSME which expand databases including synthetic data from the minority class, the capability of distinguishing real data of the discriminator might be enhanced. Following this idea, we propose this variant, in which first BOSME is applied to the original database and next, a modified version of GAN is applied, where the discriminator is fed by the synthetic data proceeding from BOSME.

3.2   Variant 2: Feeding the Discriminator of GAN with Data Proceeding from BOSME+data Proceeding from the Generator

As the continuation of the variant proposed above, we expand the data with which the discriminator of GAN is fed. We mixed two types of data, the data proceeding from the generator, which is raised from noise, and the synthetic data proceeding from BOSME. By this way, a more general vision of the synthetic data could obtain the discriminator improving its ability to distinguish fake data from real data.

In the previous variant, the data proceeding from BOSME only feeds the discriminator with data from the minority class which could cause some problems in certain environments. In contrast, with this last variant this issue is tackled. A simplistic graphic description is given in Fig. 1

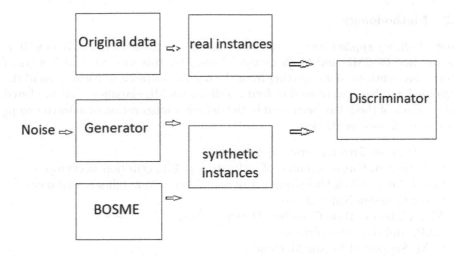

Fig. 1. Graphic diagram of Variant 2

3.3 Variant 3: Application of GAN with Minority Class Data

Finally, we opted for dividing the original data based on its class. The data that belong to minority class is used to feed GAN, and synthetic data is created following the GAN architecture. By this way, data imbalance issue is addressed and the resulting classification task should be enhanced.

4 Materials and Methods

4.1 Material and Environment

In this work we tested each of the variants proposed in the above section as well as the original GAN and BOSME methodology by expanding original data from a large, real-world dataset consisting of traffic sensor observations and from the different metropolitan areas from the state of California over a period of three months.

The Caltrans Performance Measurement System (PeMS) [1] provides large amount of traffic sensor data that has been widely used by the research communities. We collected traffic events within a three months period from 31st July 2013 to 31st October 2013, for three different metropolitan area of the state of California, i.e., Bay Area, North Central and Central Coast. We divided each traffic event depending their level of risk, i.e., hazard and control. In each case we identified the minority class to proceed with each variant proposed in this work.

The environment in which all testing and training procedure took place is the following. We used Machine Learning oriented sklearn [11] library of Python in a 64 bit Windows operating system running on Intel Core i5-2010U CPU at 1,6 GHz × 4.

4.2 Methodology

First of all, we applied each of the three variants proposed in Sect. 3 as well as the original BOSME and GAN methodologies. By this way, we had 5 ways of generating synthetic data starting from the original databases. Next, each of the expanded databases were used to feed 7 well-known ML classifiers that are listed below. Each of them has been used in the default configuration of sklearn except for the attributes mentioned.

- DT: Decision Tree (criterion = entropy)
- RF: Random Forest (number of estimators = 150, criterion = entropy)
- knn: k-Nearest Neighbors(number of neighbors = 3, weights = distance)
- GNB: Gaussian Naive Bayes
- AB: Adaboost (Base Classifier: Decision Tree)
- MLP: Multilayer Perceptron
- SVM: Supported Vector Machine

Different performance metrics were used for determining which of the aforementioned techniques for extending the original data fits best with traffic event prediction task. These are accuracy, recall, precision, F1 score and AUC (Area Under the ROC Curve). AUC is the area below the ROC curve, i.e., a graph showing the performance of a classification model at all classification thresholds. What is plotted in the curve is the FPR and TPR in the x and y axes, respectively, whose definitions are given in Eq. 4 and 5. The definitions of the rest of the metrics mentioned above are given in Eqs. 1 ,3 and 6, where TP, TN, FP, and FP stand for True Positives, True Negatives, False Positives, and False Negatives, respectively.

$$Accuracy(Acc) = \frac{TP + TN}{TP + TN + FP + FN} \tag{1}$$

$$Recall(Re) = \frac{TP}{TP + FN} \tag{2}$$

$$Precision(Pr) = \frac{TP}{TP + FP} \tag{3}$$

$$TruePositiveRate(TPR) = \frac{TP}{TP + FN} \tag{4}$$

$$FalsePositiveRate(FPR) = \frac{FP}{FP + TN} \tag{5}$$

$$F1 - score(F1) = \frac{2 * Pr * Re}{Pr + Re} \tag{6}$$

5   Experimental and Results

Each of the methodologies cited in this work were tested for data augmentation of original traffic event databases. For 10 different seeds a 10-fold cross validation were developed in each case to obtain all performance metrics. In each table, in the first column the metropolitan area of event detection and the data augmentation methodology applied are given, where BA, NC and CC stand for Bay Area, North Central and Central Coast respectively. Vx stand for x variant we proposed in Sect. 3, and Original means that the evaluation was done using the original database. The abbreviation of each classifier is given in Sect. 4.

As it could be observed in Table 1 in the majority of the cases the application of GAN or BOSME independently outperforms the variants we proposed in terms of accuracy. This metric is not very representative, because the original database also is useful. In fact, due to the class imbalance in these databases, the accuracy does not degrade, i.e., the few minority class instances could be wrongly classified even offering a good accuracy overall. Other metrics are needed to obtain more general conclusion, so we opted for attending Precision, Recall, F1-Score and AUC. As the most determining action is the correct classification of instances from the minority class, Recall is the most representative metric, since it determines how good is a classifier predicting a positive instance as positive, i.e., it defines a ratio between instances classified as positive ones and all positive

Table 1. Accuracies of different classifiers for different data augmentation techniques for different areas.

Area-Method	RF (%)	DT (%)	knn (%)	GNB (%)	AB (%)	MLP (%)	SVM (%)
BA-GAN	99.3225	99.3225	99.3225	88.1021	99.3225	97.3432	96.6745
BA-V1	97.1225	97.1572	96.8251	95.2354	45.4789	96.8561	97.0731
BA-V2	97.0996	97.1572	96.8605	95.2354	16.0777	97.0553	97.0731
BA-V3	99.3225	99.3225	99.2871	88.2349	99.3225	96.9801	96.7631
BA-BOSME	99.3225	99.3225	99.2915	94.6687	99.3225	96.0369	95.1868
BA-Original	97.3282	96.4740	97.2193	96.8827	96.9784	97.2423	97.4849
NC-GAN	98.9076	98.9076	98.9076	92.1753	98.9076	94.8792	94.8929
NC-V1	93.6228	93.6774	92.7625	89.526	50.2666	92.7489	93.2815
NC.V2	93.6091	93.6774	92.8444	89.526	92.4212	92.7489	93.2815
NC-V3	98.9076	98.9076	98.8529	91.4788	98.9076	94.729	94.8929
NC-BOSME	98.9076	98.9076	98.9076	92.4212	98.9076	93.1177	93.2407
NC-Original	94.4505	93.0577	94.5378	94.4424	93.6777	94.8301	94.8661
CC-GAN	99.6858	99.6858	99.6858	94.7013	99.686	96.1925	96.1535
CC-V1	99.6466	99.6858	96.7422	4.9455	99.6863	2.9438	96.1533
CC-V2	95.0855	95.1241	94.6209	90.8156	91.3716	94.5051	94.5051
CC-V3	99.686	99.6858	99.6858	94.7013	99.686	95.918	96.1535
CC-BOSME	99.6858	99.6858	99.6858	94.0726	99.6858	92.9348	93.5239
CC-Original	95.3254	92.7939	95.4468	95.6437	94.2579	95.6121	95.8008

instances. As shown in Table 2 in the Original database cases the performance metric drops significantly. Thus, it is necessary more instances from the minority lass for the proper training of each of the classifiers.

Other interesting metric to be observed is the AUC. One way of interpreting AUC is as the probability that the model ranks a random positive example more highly than a random negative example. In this case, the original database offers the worst performance given the moderate percentage of random negative instances due to the generalization as a consequence of data imbalance. Attending the rest of the variants mentioned and proposed within this work, we can not deduce which is the best given that in each area for some method some variants perform better than others and vice-versa for other methods. For instance, variant 2 suits best for Random Forest classifier, whereas for knn classifier is the worst option. The application of GAN and BOSME independently offers a regular performance between different classifiers. However, the highest percentage is obtained by the combination V3-AB in Bay Area, V1-AB in North Central and V2-AB in Central Coast, which means that our variants are the most adequate applying the best classifier. Table 3 shows all these measurements of the aforementioned metric.

Table 2. Recall of different classifiers for different data augmentation techniques for different areas.

Area-Method	RF (%)	DT (%)	knn (%)	GNB (%)	AB (%)	MLP (%)	SVM (%)
BA-GAN	99.3225	99.3225	99.3225	88.1021	99.3225	97.3432	96.6745
BA-V1	97.1225	97.1572	96.8251	95.2354	45.4789	96.8561	97.0731
BA-V2	97.0996	97.1572	96.8605	95.2354	16.0777	97.0553	97.0731
BA-V3	99.3225	99.3225	99.2871	88.2349	99.3225	96.9801	96.7631
BA-BOSME	99.3225	99.3225	99.2915	94.6687	99.3225	96.0369	95.1868
BA-Original	66.129	65.2011	63.9704	64.8414	66.21	56.6379	58.0993
NC-GAN	98.9076	98.9076	98.9076	92.1753	98.9076	94.8792	94.8929
NC-V1	93.6228	93.6774	92.7625	89.526	50.2666	92.7489	93.2815
NC.V2	93.6091	93.6774	92.8444	89.526	92.4212	92.7489	93.2815
NC-V3	98.9076	98.9076	98.8529	91.4788	98.9076	94.729	94.8929
NC-BOSME	98.9076	98.9076	98.9076	92.4212	98.9076	93.1177	93.2407
NC-Original	69.3718	68.9104	69.0945	66.1001	68.3082	64.2413	61.3296
CC-GAN	99.6858	99.6858	99.6858	94.7013	99.686	96.1925	96.1535
CC-V1	99.6466	99.6858	96.7422	4.9455	99.6863	2.9438	96.1533
CC-V2	95.0855	95.1241	94.6209	90.8156	91.3716	94.5051	94.5051
CC-V3	99.686	99.6858	99.6858	94.7013	99.686	95.918	96.1535
CC-BOSME	99.6858	99.6858	99.6858	94.0726	99.6858	92.9348	93.5239
CC-Original	67.337	65.3427	65.278	71.0973	66.0623	63.9602	65.1639

Table 3. AUC of different classifiers for different data augmentation techniques for different areas.

Area-Method	RF (%)	DT (%)	knn (%)	GNB (%)	AB (%)	MLP (%)	SVM (%)
BA-GAN	90.2775	89.871	90.5662	49.1252	91.5185	63.6251	58.9844
BA-V1	90.8908	89.871	71.726	65.9578	56.018	57.1239	58.1556
BA-V2	90.4126	89.871	72.8234	65.9578	71.1632	59.0527	58.1556
BA-V3	90.3776	89.871	85.553	49.1935	92.5633	62.1791	58.9629
BA-BOSME	90.6981	89.871	90.1002	66.1345	90.3663	65.4085	66.256
BA-Original	82.6257	68.4206	74.1477	71.2723	75.8556	80.7843	71.7135
NC-GAN	91.8614	91.4632	91.4632	68.8858	91.4632	60.176	62.4061
NC-V1	91.9706	91.4632	76.2103	68.8858	97.6291	67.3004	62.4061
NC-V2	91.8896	91.4632	76.568	68.8858	74.5844	67.3004	62.4061
NC-V3	91.9108	91.4632	91.9939	68.5141	92.5419	60.0394	62.4061
NC-BOSME	91.835	91.4632	91.4632	69.1838	93.9506	69.3278	68.0071
NC-Original	83.5906	70.2484	76.7554	74.5938	74.9902	81.4973	76.1547
CC-GAN	97.0206	97.0206	97.0206	72.4319	98.4706	66.0791	67.1447
CC-V1	97.1699	96.8562	71.374	71.8002	97.7436	63.1151	66.9084
CC-V2	96.5661	97.0206	71.6273	0.5	99.5428	69.3871	67.0409
CC-V3	97.2947	97.0206	97,0206	72.4319	97.8178	70.6532	67.1447
CC-BOSME	97.0206	97.0206	97.0206	75.007	97.0206	76.2153	74.9746
CC-Original	79.7884	65.2088	72.5906	82.3193	75.6649	77.5265	75.4132

6   Discussion and Conclusion

In this work we realised the importance of having a balanced data in classification tasks in order to avoid generalisation of the resulting training of the classifiers. In different environments an incorrect classification of an instance belonging to minority class could have a critical impact. Thus, a data preprocessing is needed to extend minority class instances and address this issue.

First, we looked through the accuracies of different classifiers after applying every data augmentation methodology described in previous sections. We saw that there was no evident difference between the application of different method for balancing data or starting from the original database training the classifiers. The low number belonging to the minority class was causing this, their incorrect classification not degrading severely.

However, if we look other metrics such Recall or AUC, we can figure out the importance of these data augmentation techniques. By this way, the classifiers have enough instances from both classes for training phase, and the problem of generalisation is tackled. In each metropolitan area used analysed in the experimental process the original data augmentation techniques perform more regularly than the variants proposed in this work. In fact, if we determine their goodness attending their overall performance metric within all the classifiers we can deduce that they outperform the variants we proposed. Nevertheless, the highest AUC values where obtained by one of the variants proposed in Sect. 3 for each metropolitan area.

For Bay Area, the highest AUC value was obtained after applying our third variant, i.e., the application of GAN for the minority class instances, and posterior use of Adaboost (Decision Tree as base classifier) as classifier.

For North Central area, our first approach gives the highest AUC value, i.e., the use of the new instances proceeding from BOSME and the instances proceeding from the generator as the entry for the discriminator, and the posterior use of GAN for the creation of new instances. Finally, Adaboost (Decision Tree as base classifier) was used as classifier.

In case of Central Coast, the second approach gives the best AUC value, i.e., the use of the new instances proceeding from BOSME as the entry for the discriminator, and the posterior use of GAN for the creation of new instances. Finally, Adaboost (Decision Tree as base classifier) was used as classifier.

To summarize, the power of the data augmentation techniques as preprocessing tool in data imbalance environments has been exceedingly demonstrated in this work. The adequateness of each variant proposed in this work depends on the characteristics and distribution of the original database, and the posterior machine learning model to be adopted for the classification task. For more complex models such as Adaboost or Random Forest where more than a single classifier are evaluated our variants outperform the original GAN and BOSME. Although, the highest values of AUCs are obtained by one of these variants in each metropolitan area the overall performance in more simple models is better for the simplest data augmentation methodologies. Depending the application or the limitations of the hardware to be deployed all the system, some options would be more adequate than others. For instance, if we have to adjust the models size or the training time is critic lighter models should be used and the original GAN and BOSME would be the option to adopt in these cases. In contrast, if there are no such restrictions, the possibility of finding the best classifier and the best variant for addressing data imbalance issue would be the best alternative. Following this line, finding an automatic way of finding the best combination of data augmentation and classification model would alleviate big part of finding the best alternative, improving system's time efficiency.

Acknowledgments. Authors received research funds from 59 the Basque Government as the head of the Grupo de Inteligencia Computacional, Universidad del Pais Vasco, UPV/EHU, from 2007 until 2025. The current code for the grant is IT1689-22. Additionally, authors participate in Elkartek projects KK-2022/00051 and KK-2021/00070. The Spanish MCIN 5has also granted the authors a research project under code PID2020-116346GB-I00.

References

1. Caltrans. performance measurement system (pems). Accessed 07 Mar 2023, http://pems.dot.ca.gov,

2. Anantharam, P., Barnaghi, P., Thirunarayan, K., Sheth, A.: Extracting city traffic events from social streams. ACM Trans. Intell. Syst. Technol. **6**, 1–27 (2015). https://doi.org/10.1145/2717317

3. Anantharam, P., Thirunarayan, K., Marupudi, S., Sheth, A., Banerjee, T.: Understanding city traffic dynamics utilizing sensor and textual observations, vol. 30 (2016)

4. Camino, R.D., Hammerschmidt, C.A., State, R.: Generating multi-categorical samples with generative adversarial networks. ArXiv abs/1807.01202 (2018)

5. Chen, Q., Wang, W., Huang, K., De, S., Coenen, F.: Multi-modal generative adversarial networks for traffic event detection in smart cities. Expert Syst. Appl. **177**, 114939 (2021). https://doi.org/10.1016/j.eswa.2021.114939, https://www.sciencedirect.com/science/article/pii/S0957417421003808

6. Ding, H., Chen, L., Dong, L., Fu, Z., Cui, X.: Imbalanced data classification: A KNN and generative adversarial networks-based hybrid approach for intrusion detection. Future Gener. Comput. Syst. **131**, 240–254 (2022). https://doi.org/10.1016/j.future.2022.01.026, https://www.sciencedirect.com/science/article/pii/S0167739X22000346

7. Goodfellow, I., et al.: Generative adversarial nets. In: Ghahramani, Z., Welling, M., Cortes, C., Lawrence, N., Weinberger, K. (eds.) Advances in Neural Information Processing Systems. Curran Associates Inc

8. Hou, J.C., Wang, S.S., Lai, Y.H., Tsao, Y., Chang, H.W., Wang, H.M.: Audio-visual speech enhancement using multimodal deep convolutional neural networks. IEEE Trans. Emerg. Top. Comput. Intell. **2**(2), 117–128 (2018). https://doi.org/10.1109/TETCI.2017.2784878

9. Lan, J., Liu, X., Li, B., Sun, J., Li, B., Zhao, J.: Member: a multi-task learning model with hybrid deep features for network intrusion detection. Comput. Secur. **123**, 102919 (2022). https://doi.org/10.1016/j.cose.2022.102919, https://www.sciencedirect.com/science/article/pii/S016740482200311X

10. Pan, B., Zheng, Y., Wilkie, D., Shahabi, C.: Crowd sensing of traffic anomalies based on human mobility and social media. IN: Proceedings of the 21st ACM SIGSPATIAL International Conference on Advances in Geographic Information Systems (2013)

11. Pedregosa, F., et al.: Scikit-learn: machine learning in python. J. Mach. Learn. Res. **12**, 2825–2830 (2012)

12. Rosario, D., Nuñez-Gonzalez, J.D.: Bayesian network-based over-sampling method (bosme) with application to indirect cost-sensitive learning. Sci. Rep. 12 (2022). https://doi.org/10.1038/s41598-022-12682-8, https://www.nature.com/articles/s41598-022-12682-8

13. Wang, Y., et al.: Eann: event adversarial neural networks for multi-modal fake news detection. In: Proceedings of the 24th ACM SIGKDD International Conference on Knowledge Discovery & Data Mining, pp. 849–857. KDD 2018, Association for Computing Machinery, New York, NY, USA (2018). https://doi.org/10.1145/3219819.3219903

14. Xu, L.: Synthesizing tabular data using generative adversarial networks (2018)

15. Zhao, Z., Kunar, A., van der Scheer, H., Birke, R., Chen, L.Y.: Ctab-gan: Effective table data synthesizing. ArXiv abs/2102.08369 (2021)

Multidimensional Models Supported by Document-Oriented Databases

Rosa Matias[1,2]([✉]) and Maria Beatriz Piedade[1,2]

[1] School of Technology and Management, Polytechnic of Leiria, 2411-901 Leiria, Portugal
{rosa.matias,beatriz.piedade}@ipleiria.pt
[2] Computer Science and Communication Research Center (CIIC), School of Technology and Management, Polytechnic of Leiria, 2411-901 Leiria, Portugal

Abstract. For decades the multidimensional model has been applied to development data warehouses. It usually consists of a fact table surrounded by dimensional tables. It aims to enhance the exploration of historical data and is supported mostly by relational databases. Meanwhile the evolution to Big Data is responsible for the proliferation of other types of databases namely document-oriented databases. They store the data in collections of documents such as JSON documents. In this context some efforts have been made to adapt the multidimensional model to document-oriented databases to take advantages of the exploration capabilities provided by it. The model adaptation efforts suggest: (i) a collection of documents only with fields representing both measures and dimensions; (ii) a collection of documents with fields representing measures and with subdocuments representing dimensions; (iii) collections for facts and collections for dimensions. In this work it is presented a study about the mentioned approaches. Three document-oriented data warehouses are developed using the same scenario. Nevertheless, each uses a different approach. Later, the same group of analytical queries is applied to them to identify the commands complexity and gather execution times. The results show that the first and second approaches outperforms the third. The second approach has a richer organization and requires less storage space regarding the first. A schema for a metamodel is presented to couple the multidimensional model to document data warehouses to eliminate the gap between them.

Keywords: Decision Support Systems · Multidimensional Model · NoSQL Databases

1 Introduction

The multidimensional model supports the ad-hoc formulations of analytical queries. It intends to provide an easy mechanism to explore and summarize the data to obtain insight and wisdom and tell reliable data stories. Meanwhile large amounts of data (volumes) characterized by diversity (variety), are produced daily, and consumed at high speeds (velocity) [1, 2]. As for the variety, the data is classified as structured, semi-structured and unstructured [3]. With volume, variety and velocity comes new storage needs and the proliferation of NoSQL (Not Only SQL) database systems. The variety of data

P. García Bringas et al. (Eds.): HAIS 2023, LNAI 14001, pp. 156–167, 2023.
https://doi.org/10.1007/978-3-031-40725-3_14

leads to studies where only structured data are considered, only semi-structured data are considered, only unstructured data are considered, or hybrid combinations and of them.

This work intends to apply concepts used in traditional multidimensional concepts to document-oriented databases. Namely the authors aim to promote analytic queries using document-oriented databases obtaining at the same time the benefits that the multidimensional model brings to the interactive data exploration of historical data [4, 5]. Three data models for document data warehouses are studied and implemented. The objective is to identify their advantages and disadvantages. As so the same scenario and group of analytical queries are applied to them.

There is the need to address the influence of both the database structure and the document structure in analytical queries performance [6]. In this work three specific models are investigated regarding analytical queries execution times and writing complexity. The queries are built using the aggregation pipeline mechanism of a wide-spread document-oriented database engine (MongoDB). As so, a query is resolved using a pipeline built through connected stages. A stage receives documents, process them, and sends the output to the next. The execution times are gathered for the whole query (pipeline) and for individual stages to identify the heaviest. In the last case the database optimizer is applied to gather execution times. Additionally, a metamodel is proposed aiming to adapt and assist analytical queries operations. There is the need to adjust document-oriented data warehouses to user graphic interfaces of Business Intelligence (BI) tools. OLAP is usually supported by relational database characterized by a strong schema definition opposed to the schemeless approach of document-oriented databases. Despite JSON documents are self-descriptive, it is hard to formulate analytical queries due to the lack of metadata that identifies explicitly concepts such as measure, dimensions, the respective attributes and how concepts are related.

The present document is divided as follows: first related work, then the scenario is presented, then the group of analytical queries are described, and their execution times shown. Later a schema for a metamodel is proposed to assist the execution of ad-hoc analytical queries promoting the exploration of data in document-oriented data warehouses modeled in agreement the studied approaches. Finally, discussions and conclusions.

2 Related Work

NoSQL databases have been gained attention since organizations start to produce high volumes of information consumed at a huge velocity. For instance, in platforms related to the Internet of Things (IoT), social networks, mobile apps or web applications with millions of users. In the classification of NoSQL databases there are document-oriented databases. They store the information in semi-structured format such as the Java Script Object Notation (JSON) format. As so, as opposed to the traditional relational model, instead of the tables there are the collections and instead records there are documents. Also, they have a schemeless approach [7, 8] in contrast with the rigid schemas of the relational model garnishing flexibility. Meanwhile the schemeless approach presents difficulties to model a data warehouse and to perform analytical queries (OLAP queries) [5, 9].

The multidimensional model supports the easy exploration of data. Consequently, the exploration of historical data using document-oriented data warehouses have been gained attention. Some authors highlight the importance of NoSQL data warehouses and the need to adapt NoSQL databases [10, 11], to the usual ad-hoc execution of analytical queries [4, 5]. A common question is how to represent the traditional multidimensional model using document-oriented databases. In studies done by Chevalier et al. [12] are proposed the following three models to simulate the dimensional model using document databases:

- Model MDD1: a single collection where each document keeps at the same level not only measures but also the associated dimensions.
- Model MDD2: a single collection with a main document that for measures and with subdocuments one for each dimension.
- Model MDD3: one collection for the facts linked to collections one for each dimension.

Each of those models is implemented in this work using document-oriented databases. The objective is to identify the advantages and the disadvantages between them and to help in the selection of an appropriate model in the development of a document-oriented data warehouse. Later, analytical queries are built to observe their behavior in each approach. Others have proposed to extract schemas from already existing document-oriented databases, by using, the MapReduce paradigm [5] or a schema-on-read approach to enable analytical queries, with the discover of hierarchies in the data using incremental detection of functional dependencies [8]. In this work, the data warehouse architects, with domain knowledge, are responsible to configure a schema to represent the dimensional model adapted to document-oriented databases. They can act in already under development or existing document-oriented databases. It is intended to simulate the dimensional model in document-oriented databases promoting the navigation properties of OLAP operations through the combination of fields simulating attributes and measures.

Others have proposed to analyze the structure of documents in document-oriented databases regarding analytical queries performance using attribute selectivity as a metric to improve query performance [6]. This work concerns the study of three models and the exploration of its specific queries regarding not only their overall execution time but also their specific stages estimate execution time. The models differ not only in the document structure (with or without subdocuments) but also in database structure (a single or multiple collections).

3   The Scenario

A MongoDB database system version 6.04 with a cluster implements the document-oriented data warehouses. This section characterizes the target scenario for the three modelling approaches. Subsequently it is presented the data preparation process. Then it is described the final properties of the collections.

3.1   The Target Scenario

The case study is related to an online product store and the source files are in CSV and JSON formats. The source files are accessible at the University of Helsinki [13]. They are also used in various studies. For instance, to study multimodal databases where structured and semi-structured data coexists [3, 14]. To develop benchmarks for multimodal databases [15, 16]. In this work the original scenario is utilized to study semi-structured data stored in a NoSQL document-oriented database. In the mentioned other studies, a data warehouse is built under a relational database engine, but it implements and populates a dimensional model with heterogeneous data types analyzing its behavior in the presence of analytical queries. The data type variety includes the capacity to manage data in various formats such as the graph format and the document format. The original environment was found interesting, since it may be easily transformed into each of three models under observation. Besides it is built for data analysis.

Figure 1 displays the original star schema that the three approaches simulate. The schema is concerning a conventional multidimensional model. There are a fact table surrounded by 3 dimensions tables. The fact table represents an order line with a measure (unit price). The axes of analysis are products, customers, and the date.

Table 1 describes the source files, their formats, and the total number of lines (instances). The *customers.csv* file has attributes about clients namely the client first name, last name, gender, and browser. The *products.csv* file has attributes about products, their brand, the vendor country, and the vendor industry. The *orders.json* has attributes about orders and the ordered products (order product line). The *orders.json* data is denormalized. All at all there are 142 257 orders with 497 000 order lines (Table 1).

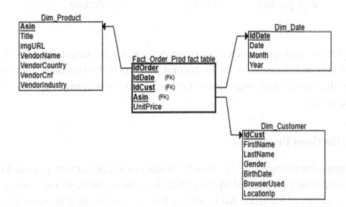

Fig. 1. The original multidimensional model that three approaches will simulate (adapted [3]).

On the MongoDB server three data warehouses are implemented. The ProjMDD1 data warehouse to simulate MDD1 approach. The ProjMDD2 data warehouse to simulate MDD2 approach. Finally, the ProjMDD3 data warehouse to simulate the MDD3 approach. Table 2 describes for each the respective collections and their granularity.

3.2 The Extract Transform and Load (ETL) Process

A project was developed and is responsible to extract, transform, and load the original files into the different document-oriented data warehouses. The project has a pipeline

Table 1. The original files, their format as well as the number of assigned instances.

File	Format	Instances
Date	csv	7 633
Customers	csv	9 949
Products	csv	10 116
Orders	json	142 257
Orders	json	497 000 (line orders)

Table 2. The properties of the three data warehouses and their collections.

DW	Collection	Granularity	Properties
ProjMDD1	lineorder	order line	A collection
ProjMDD2	order	order	A collection with subdocument
ProjMDD3	order	order	A collection with references
ProjMDD3	dim_date	date	A collection
ProjMDD3	dim_customer	customer	A collection
ProjMDD3	dim_product	product	A collection

with 3 subsystems each generates data in agreement to the target models. The project serializes the original datasets to JSON format and loads the returned data to the MongoDB Server. In this context, there are some transformation operations since the source file had some noise.

3.3   The Collections Properties

Table 3 describes the storage size of the collections in each document-oriented data warehouse. The collection represented by ProjMDD1 occupies more storage space regarding the other collections (55.2MB). All at all the lowest storage size is associated with the ProjMDD3.

Table 3. The properties of the three data warehouses and their collections.

DW	Collection	Storage size (MB)	Documents
ProjMDD1	lineorder	**55.2**	497 000
ProjMDD2	order	*44.6*	142 257
ProjMDD3	order	11.6	142 257
ProjMDD3	dim_date	0.152	7 633
ProjMDD3	dim_customer	0.606	9 949
ProjMDD3	dim_product	0.740	10 116

4 The Queries

Table 4 describes the analytical queries (Q01...Q05). The same queries were submitted to the different document-oriented data warehouses. The initial query (Q01) involves the product dimension and aggregates by both the country and the brand attributes (from the product dimension). The query Q02 represents a slice operation over Q01: only some seller countries are considered. Query Q03 only some seller countries are also considered and there are two different dimensions involved, namely the product (attribute brand) and customer (attribute gender). Query Q04 is an initial query and uses attributes from the date dimension, the product dimension, and the customer dimension. Query Q05 represent a drill-down over Q04 using the date hierarchy (year → month). All the queries consider only two years of analysis namely the years from 2021 to 2022.

Table 4. The semantic of the queries submitted to the different data warehouses.

Query	Group	Filter	Accumulator
Q01	Country Brand	--	SUM (unitprice)
Q02	Country Brand	For a small number of countries	SUM (unitprice)
Q03	Country Gender	For a small number of countries	SUM (unitprice)
Q04	Year Country Gender	--	SUM (unitprice)
Q05	Year Month Country Gender	--	SUM (unitprice) navigation using the date hierarchy (year → month)

The queries were built using the MongoDB aggregation pipeline mechanism. It is a process where several synchronous stages are carried out. Each state produces an output that is communicated to the next stage until a result is achieved. Table 5 describes the evolved stages.

Table 5. The aggregation pipeline and their stages.

Stage	Description
$match	To filter the data
$lookup	To join collections
$group	To summarize the data
$project	To select the fields to display

Despite the semantics of queries being the same for all projects, as there are 3 different models, each project needs specific queries. All at all for the three projects there are 15 different queries. Code 1 exemplifies the Q02 query for the MDD1 document-oriented data warehouse. There is a filter operation been done by the $match stage, a group by operation done by the $group stage and, finally, a project operation done by the $project stage.

```
[{$match:{
   VendedorCountry: "Italy",
   $expr:{$or: [{$eq: [{$year:  "$OrderDate"},2022]},
                {$eq: [{$year: "$OrdeDate"} , 2021]}]}}},
 {$group: {
   _id:["$VendedorCountry", "$Brand"],
   total-price: {$sum: "$UnitPrice"}}},
 {$project: {
   Country: {$arrayElemAt: ["$_id", 0]},
   Brand:{ $arrayElemAt: ["$_id", 1]},
   total-price: 1,_id: 0, }}]
```
                    Code 1 – A sample query: Q02 of the MDD1 project

5 The Performance

The queries with the same semantic were submitted to the three data warehouses. Each query was executed 10 times. The average execution times are described in Table 6.

The queries submitted to ProjMDD3 have significant different execution times regarding the other projects. Even though it occupies less storage space and is more in agreement with the multidimensional model. Document-oriented databases are not optimized to follow the same paradigm of common data warehouses where data is spread among some tables. In the translation between the multidimensional model and a model for document-oriented data warehouses the rule one table one collection is not advisable since join operations have performance drawbacks. As may be observed there are performance advantages in using only one document to store all the data.

Table 6. The execution time for the different queries at the different data warehouses (ms).

Proj/Query	Q01	Q02	Q03	Q04	Q05
MDD1	3268	708	1013	3085	3295
MDD2	632	506	552	686	754
MDD3	58077	73548	437579	2404308	31654640

The queries submitted to ProjMDD1 and ProjMDD2 have better response times. ProjMDD2 outperform the others not only in slice but also in aggregation (group) operations. On the other hand, ProjMDD2 also has a better organization than project ProjMDD1 since dimensions are stored as subdocuments. So, there are clear boundaries between facts and dimensions and between dimensions themselves. Also, ProjMDD2 needs less space (Table 3) to store the data than ProjMDD1. In ProjMDD1 the are 497 000 documents. In ProjMDD2 there are 142 257 documents and, in each order line is stored inside an array. Since the projects ProjMDD1 and ProjMDD2 are more similar they are studied concerning the estimate average execution times of each individual aggregation pipeline stages. The estimates execution times were collected using the values of execution plans produced by the document-oriented database optimizer. Table 7 presents the estimated number of documents before the group stage of all the 5 queries.

Table 7. The number of documents between stages for the data warehouses.

Project/Query	Q01	Q02	Q03	Q04	Q05
Before	155638	**25997**	**25997**	155638	155638
$group	64	9	3	141	388
$project	64	9	3	141	388
Final	64	9	3	141	388

Table 8. Presents the estimate execution times of the queries in ProjMDD1 and Table 9 the estimate execution times of the queries in ProjMDD2. Figure 2 the graphics projections. ProjMDD2 has more stages since each document has an array of order lines that must be decomposed (stage $unwind).

Table 8. The estimate execution times for different stages in ProjMDD1 (ms).

Stage	Q01	Q02	Q03	Q04	Q05
$match	2764	637	918	2422	2427
$group	*496*	**_68_**	**_90_**	*653*	*860*
$project	0	0	0	0	0

Table 9. The estimate execution times for different stages in ProjMDD2 (ms).

Stage	Q01	Q02	Q03	Q04	Q05
$match	273	247	314	262	257
$unwind	172	80	98	69	74
$match	--	70	126	--	--
$group	*203*	**54**	**51**	*296*	*341*
$project	0	0	0	0	0

The number of documents received by the $group stage influences the overall esti-mated execution time as well as the number of attributes. The $project stage is optimized in the context of the $group by stage and as so is presented the 0 value.

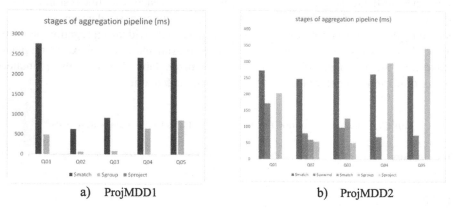

a)   ProjMDD1   b)   ProjMDD2

Fig. 2. The estimate execution times for the different stages ProjMDD1 (a)/ProjMDD2 (b)

6   The Meta Model Schema

The authors propose a metamodel to describe document data warehouses enabling and reenforcing data navigation (Fig. 3). It couples the concepts of the multidimensional world with the document-oriented databases paradigm and describes: (i) the type of document-oriented data warehouse (MDD1, MDD2, MDD3); (ii) the correspondence between the document fields and the measures; (iii) the default accumulator operators for measures; (iv) the correspondence between the subdocument fields and the dimensions attributes; (v) the correspondence between subdocuments fields and the dimensions hierarchies.

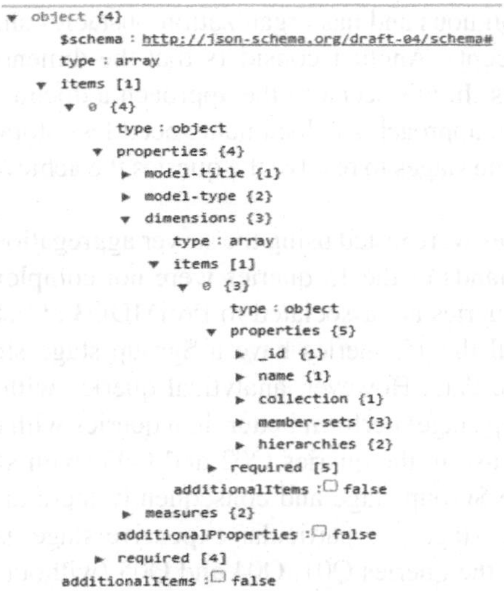

```
▼ object {4}
    $schema : http://json-schema.org/draft-04/schema#
    type : array
    ▼ items [1]
        ▼ 0 {4}
            type : object
            ▼ properties {4}
                ▶ model-title {1}
                ▶ model-type {2}
                ▼ dimensions {3}
                    type : array
                    ▼ items [1]
                        ▼ 0 {3}
                            type : object
                            ▼ properties {5}
                                ▶ _id {1}
                                ▶ name {1}
                                ▶ collection {1}
                                ▶ member-sets {3}
                                ▶ hierarchies {2}
                            ▶ required [5]
                            additionalItems :☐ false
                ▶ measures {2}
            additionalProperties :☐ false
        ▶ required [4]
    additionalItems :☐ false
```

Fig. 3. The Schema Model

7 Discussion

For many decades the dimension model has been applied. Its logical representation has a main fact table surrounded by auxiliar descriptive tables. The data analysts are accustomed with that model. In document-oriented databases there are collections instead of tables and documents instead of records.

Despite the huge denormalization the ProjMDD1 is the simplest document. Yet there is not a clear boundary between the fields representing measures and the fields representing the dimension attributes. Everything is mixed. The ProjMDD2 describes itself having clear boundaries between measures and dimensions and between dimensions themselves. ProjMDD3 is like the multidimensional model, i.e., a fact table surrounded by dimension tables. In it there is a collection surrounded by other collections.

In the adaptation of the dimensional model to document-oriented data warehouses the approach a main collection for facts surrounded by collections for dimensions has performance drawbacks as was observed in the execution times associated to ProjMDD3 (Table 6). In document databases join operations using collections are particularly expensive since they were designed and optimized to store high volumes of highly denormalized data and to guarantee schema flexibility to software developers [7] and so rapid changing requirements can easily be adapted. The data is usually stored inside a single collection. But that approach is not in agreement with the navigation properties of OLAP applications and does not promote data exploration through the combination of attributes and measures stored in different tables. With all the data in one collection and with a schemeless approach there is the need to specify metadata, namely, to specify and identify the fields representing the attributes of dimensions and the fields representing measures to promote their combination. Meanwhile there are two approaches to take into consideration. Both store all the data in one collection. But they have different structures. One just considers both facts and dimensions in fields at the same level which can be ambiguous and has organization obstacles since there is not a clear boundary between concepts. Another considers that the dimensions should be represented by subdocuments. In this scenario the approach a document all fields just need more storage space. The approach subdocuments need less storage. Although it needs more aggregation pipeline stages to resolve the queries the achieved execution times are better.

The analytical queries were tested using the server aggregation pipeline mechanism. All at all, the 15 commands of the 15 queries were not complex to write. In general, the most complicated queries are associated to ProjMDD3 affected by join operations between collections. All the 15 queries have a $group stage since analytical queries typically summarize the data. However, analytical queries with both a slice ($match stage) and group ($group stage) perform better than queries with only the $group stage. Essentially, that is because in the queries Q02 and Q03 (with slice) a filter operation is performed before the $group stage and consequently there are fewer documents to summarize. The $group stage is a particular expensive stage as may be observed in Table 8 and Table 9 for the queries Q01, Q04 and Q05 (without slice). In ProjMDD2, as the number of attributes in the $group increase it also increases the execution time (Table 9 and Q04 and Q05). As for the ProjMDD3 all the queries used the $lookup stage to join collections. The commands become more complex to write and with unsatisfactory execution times. The application of the dimensional model with collections for facts and collections for dimensions is impracticable to apply within document-oriented databases. As the number of collections start to grow the response execution time becomes useless.

To simulate the dimensional model through document-oriented databases, and to take advantages of its navigation capabilities the authors propose a JSON schema for a metamodel to establish a bridge between the multidimensional model and the document-oriented data warehouses. The JSON schema is used to describes the structure of a document-oriented data warehouse. Namely, it is used to describe concepts such as the model approach (one of three), the fields representing measures, the fields representing dimensions, and how the navigation hierarchies are organized.

8   Conclusions

It is straightforward to build document-oriented data warehouses supported by document-oriented databases because they are widespread. The present work intends to contribute to the identification of a model that can be applied in the development of a document-oriented data warehouse and on a schema that can represent it. As the scenario concerning the MDD2 approach has better execution times than all the others. Also, it has a clearer organization since it uses subdocuments to represent dimensions establishing clear boundaries between concepts. If a schema metamodel is used to describe how the collections are organized, then approaches like MDD1 and MDD2 can be easily adapted to OLAP analytical queries taking advantages of its navigation paradigm. Despise project MDD3 is more in agreement with the multidimensional model it is not recommend because it is not compatible with document-oriented data warehouses philosophy. In future work it is intended to observe the queries behavior in the different models, after optimization through indexes, optimization through query rewriting, materialized views, and in a distributed environment. Also, to analyze other document-oriented databases.

Acknowledgment. This work was financed by national funds through FCT – Fundação para a Ciência e a Tecnologia, I.P., under the project UIDB/04524/2020.

References

1. Berisha, B., Mëziu, E. Shabani, I.: Big data analytics in cloud computing: an overview. J. Cloud Comput. **11**(1) (2022). https://doi.org/10.1186/s13677-022-00301-w
2. Jemmali, R., Abdelhedi, F., Zurfluh, G. DLToDW: transferring relational and NoSQL databases from a Data Lake. SN Comput. Sci. **3**(5). https://doi.org/10.1007/s42979-022-012 87-7
3. Bimonte, S., Gallinucci, E, Marcel, P., Rizzi, S.: Data variety, come as you are in multi-model data warehouses. Inf. Syst. **104**, p. 101734 (2022). https://doi.org/10.1016/j.is.2021.101734
4. Rizzi, S.: OLAP and NoSQL: happily ever after. In: Chiusano, S., Cerquitelli, T., Wrembel, R. (eds.) ADBIS 2022. LNCS, vol. 13389, pp. 35–44. Springer, Cham (2022)https://doi.org/ 10.1007/978-3-031-15740-0_4
5. Bouaziz, S., Nabli, A., Gargouri, F.: Design a data warehouse schema from document-oriented database. Procedia Comput. Sci. **159**, 221–230 (2019). https://doi.org/10.1016/j.procs.2019. 09.177
6. Soransso, R.A.S.N., Cavalcanti, M.M.: Data modeling for analytical queries on document-oriented DBMS (2018). https://doi.org/10.1145/3167132.3167191
7. Sahatqija, K., et al. Comparison between relational and NOSQL databases. In: 2018 41st international convention on information and communication technology, electronics and microelectronics (MIPRO), pp. 0216-0221. IEEE (2018)
8. Atzeni, P., Bugiotti, F., Cabibbo, L., Torlone, R.: Data modeling in the NoSQL world. Comput. Stand. Interfaces **67**, 103149 (2020). https://doi.org/10.1016/j.csi.2016.10.003
9. Chouder, M.L., Rizzi, S., Chalal, R.: EXODuS: exploratory OLAP over document stores. Inf. Syst. **79**, 44–57 (2019). https://doi.org/10.1016/j.is.2017.11.004
10. Bicevska, Z., Oditis, I.: Towards NoSQL-based data warehouse solutions. Procedia Comput. Sci. **104**, 104–111 (2017)
11. Prakash, D.: NOSOLAP: moving from data warehouse requirements to NoSQL databases. In: ENASE, pp. 452–458 (2019)
12. Chevalier, M., El Malki, M., Kopliku, A., Teste, O., Tournier, R.: Implementation of multidimensional databases with document-oriented NoSQL. In: Madria, S., Hara, T. (eds.) DaWaK 2015. LNCS, vol. 9263, pp. 379–390. Springer, Cham (2015). https://doi.org/10.1007/978-3-319-22729-0_29
13. Unibench: Towards benchmarking multi-model DBMS: Unified Database Management Systems (UDBMS). University of Helsinki. https://www.helsinki.fi/en/researchgroups/ unified-database-management-systems-udbms/research/unibench-towards-benchmarking-multi-model-dbms. Accessed 1 Apr 2023
14. Bimonte, S., et al.: To each his own: accommodating data variety by a multimodel star schema. In: Proceedings of the 22nd International Workshop on Design, Optimization, Languages and Analytical Processing of Big Data co-located with EDBT/ICDT 2020 Joint Conference (EDBT/ICDT 2020) (2020)
15. Zhang, C., Lu, J., Xu, P., Chen, Y.: UniBench: a benchmark for multi-model database management systems. In: Nambiar, R., Poess, M. (eds.) TPCTC 2018. LNCS, vol. 11135, pp. 7–23. Springer, Cham (2019). https://doi.org/10.1007/978-3-030-11404-6_2
16. Zhang, C., Lu, J.: Holistic evaluation in multi-model databases benchmarking. Distrib. Parallel Databases **39**(1), 1–33 (2019). https://doi.org/10.1007/s10619-019-07279-6

Financial Distress Prediction in an Imbalanced Data Stream Environment

Rubens Marques Chaves[1]([⊠]) (iD), André Luis Debiaso Rossi[2] (iD), and Luís Paulo Faina Garcia[1]([⊠]) (iD)

[1] University of Brasília, Brasília, DF 70910-090, Brazil
rubens.chaves@bcb.gov.br, luis.garcia@unb.br
[2] São Paulo State University, Itapeva, SP 18409-010, Brazil
andre.rossi@unesp.br

Abstract. Corporate bankruptcy predictions are crucial to companies, investors, and authorities. However, most bankruptcy prediction studies have been based on stationary models, and they tend to ignore important challenges of financial distress like data non-stationarity, concept drift and data imbalance. This study proposes methods for dealing with these challenges and uses data collected from financial statements quarterly provided by companies to the Securities and Exchange Commission of Brazil (CVM). It is composed of information from 10 years (2011 to 2020), with 905 different corporations and 23,834 records with 82 indicators each. The sample majority have no financial difficulties, and only 651 companies have financial distress. The empirical experiment uses a sliding window, a history and a forgetting mechanism to avoid the degradation of the predictive model due to concept drift. The characteristics of the problem, especially the data imbalance, the performance of the models is measured through AUC, G_{mean}, and F_1-Score and achieved 0.95, 0.68, and 0.58, respectively.

Keywords: Machine Learning · Bankruptcy · Financial Distress · Data Stream · Data Imbalance · Concept Drift · Brazil · CVM

1 Introduction

Nowadays, markets and companies are tightly intertwined, with a huge amount of capital flowing among market players. About 23% of the capital assets and 48% of the liability of a financial institution come from other financial institutions [9] and allow better risk and capital allocation sharing among enterprises. On the other hand, it opens the way to systemic risk, as noticed during the subprime financial crisis in 2008, which had spread globally [11]. Consequently, bankruptcy or financial distress prediction (FDP) could avoid or deal with systemic risk and diminish its consequences [33]. Moreover, it is relevant because stakeholders and the corporate owner could take action before the occurrence of bankruptcy. For

P. García Bringas et al. (Eds.): HAIS 2023, LNAI 14001, pp. 168–179, 2023.
https://doi.org/10.1007/978-3-031-40725-3_15

instance, it could empower owners to address the financial state of the enterprise in order to avert a bankruptcy scenario [26].

The FDP using economic-financial indicators has been extensively researched since the late 1960s [22]. Altman (1968) [4] was the first relevant work about it and used a statistical tool called Multiple Discriminant Analysis (MDA) for bankruptcy prediction, which became very popular among finance professionals. Around the 1990s, scholars started to use Artificial Intelligence (AI) and Machine Learning (ML) methods for bankruptcy prediction or FDP [10,37]. In some reviews, Alaka *et al.* (2018) [2] and Shi & Li (2019) [32] have already verified that, on average, ML models have more accuracy than statistical models.

There is a gap in the studies about FDP since most of them deal with stationary data [4,5], whereas the indicators come through a data flow and are non-stationary [31,35]. They have temporal order and timestamp associated with it. Agrahari and Singh (2021) [1] state that any data sequence with a timestamp is known as a Data Stream (DS), so FDP should be treated as a data stream problem. Additionally, in real-world applications, FDP has to deal with imbalanced classes and concept drift over time.

This study integrates two fields that are typically developed separately, the FDP and the time dimension of the data, treating it in a data stream environment. The contributions of this study are (*i*) a benchmark of ML classifiers for FDP in a DS environment; (*ii*) a benchmark of methods for data imbalance from DS; (*iii*) an experiment using a real-world database from the CVM; (*iv*) a realist scenario evaluation; (*v*) an impact analysis about the prediction horizon increasing.

This paper is structured as follows: Sect. 2 presents concepts to understand FDP and ML in a DS environment. Section 3 brings the reviews, surveys, and relevant studies that were the starting point of this paper. Section 4 explains the strategies used to preprocess the data, deal with concept drift, train the classifiers, and metrics to measure the performance. Section 5 brings some data and charts to illustrate the selection of the best classifier. Finally, Sect. 6 presents the conclusion and future work possibilities.

2   Background

Financial distress refers to a situation in which an enterprise is unable to meet its financial obligations and debt repayments. In other words, it could be defined as an inability to pay debts or preferred dividends having consequences like overdrafts, liquidation for the interests of creditors, and it may lead to a statutory bankruptcy proceeding. [4]. Some symptoms include late or missed debt payments, declining credit scores, high levels of debt, and difficulty obtaining new credit [34].

J. Sun *et al.* (2014) [34] present financial distress from two different perspectives. From a theoretical perspective, it has degrees such as mild financial distress when an enterprise faces a temporary cash-flow difficulty, and it is severe when the business fails and starts statutory bankruptcy proceedings. Additionally, it is a dynamic changing process resulting from a continuous abnormality of business operation taking months, years, or even longer to happen [1]. The second is the empirical perspective when the enterprise faces difficulty paying debts on time and renegotiating debts with creditors.

Since the 90s, ML has been used to deal with bankruptcy prediction or financial distress identification [2,32]. In a supervised learning problem, the goal is to learn a mapping between the input vector X and the output vector Y, given that there is a training set D of input-output pairs (x_i, y_i). Indeed there is an unknown function $y = f(x)$ generating each y_i. Therefore, the model training has to find a hypothesis h that approximates the function f. When the output y_i is one of a finite set, the learning problem is called classification, and if it has only two classes, it is a binary classification [29]. For example, a dataset for FDP contains healthy (negative class) and non-healthy (positive class) enterprises. Thus, it is a binary classification problem.

Nowadays, data is becoming increasingly ubiquitous [15]. Researchers have responded to this trend by developing ML algorithms for DS commonly known as incremental learning, real-time data mining, *online* learning, or DS learning [15]. Each item has an associated timestamp, and predictive models must consider items temporal order in real-time [1,19]. When the timestamp t is considered to the supervised learning set of input-output pairs (x_i, y_i) in D, the problem is described as a set of tuples with timestamp mark $D^t = \{(x_1^t, y_1^t), (x_2^t, y_2^t), ..., (x_n^t, y_n^t)\}$. Where i is a natural number bounded by $1 \leq i \leq n$, and identifies a element of the data chunk at the moment t.

H. M. Gomes *et al.* (2019) [15] define concept drift as a change in the statistical properties of a DS over time, and highlight that it occurs when the distribution of target concepts in a DS changes, leading to a degradation in the models' results. In the Eq. 1, $P^t(x_i, y_i)$ is the probability of an element x_i receiving the label y_i at time t. However, over time, this probability may change. It is a common problem in DS environments, where data is constantly generated and updated, making it challenging to maintain the accuracy.

$$\exists x : P^t(x_i, y_i) \neq P^{t+1}(x_i, y_i) \tag{1}$$

In some datasets, the classes are not equally distributed, which means that at least one of them is in the minority concerning the others [13]. It biases the learning process towards the majority class and impairs the model generalization. There are two types of imbalance: intrinsic, when imbalance is something natural to the problem, for example, the financial situation of companies that are usually healthy, with a minority facing financial troubles; and extrinsic, which occurs when the imbalance results from a failure in the data collection [15].

Besides that, F. Shen *et al.* (2020) [31] have already noticed that some metrics used to evaluate ML models, such as accuracy, are not suitable for imbalanced data. It occurs when the metric uses more elements from the majority class distorting the result. Thus, it is necessary to use other set of metrics. For example, true positive rate (TPR), also known as sensitivity or recall [25], harmonic mean of precision and sensitivity when beta is equal 1 (F_1) [25], geometric mean of specificity and sensitivity (G_{mean}) [25], Area Under the Curve of Receiver Operating Characteristic (AUC-ROC) [25], and Area Under the Curve of Precision and Sensitivity (AUC-PS) [30].

3   Related Work

The recent interest in FDP can be justified by the evolution of ML methods which has opened new possibilities and has achieved better results [5,32]. On the other hand, the academy's interest in DS learning is more recent and dates from the 2000s. The data nature is changing, the technology is collecting data all the time, and the computational power is not increasing at the same rate [14]. Given the current industry needs, there are challenges to address before the application of DS learning in real-world problems [15]. For instance, the concept drift challenge pervades different domains where the predictions are ordered by time, like bankruptcy prediction, FDP, and others [1].

The initial studies about FDP identification date from 1968 [4]. Even though it is not a new research field, in recent years, there has been a growing interest in financial and business [24,32]. T. M. Alam *et al.* (2020) [3] highlight that predicting financial distress poses two significant challenges. Firstly, the combination of economic and financial indicators, which remains a difficult task despite the efforts of specialists. Secondly, it is necessary to address the problem of data imbalance since in real-world scenarios, the amount of healthy enterprises is much larger than those facing financial distress.

S. Wanget *et al.* (2018) [36] consider two problems inherent to DS: data imbalance and concept drift. Both are very present, usually together. The authors point out that although this combination of problems frequently exists in real situations, few studies address these issues, and propose: (*i*) a *framework* to handle these cases; (*ii*) some algorithms to minimize these problems jointly. In addition, the authors highlight the lack of studies to assess the effects of data imbalance on misconceptions.

J. Sun *et al.* (2019) [35] and F. Shen *et al.* (2020) [31] noticed that previous studies on FDP seldom consider the problem of concept drift and neglect how to predict the industry financial distress in a DS environment. Both used data from Chinese companies, the sliding window method and realized that the data imbalance problem is an obvious issue related to FDP. To address it they used SMOTEBoost and Adaptive Neighbor SMOTE-Recursive Ensemble Approach (ANS-REA), respectively. J. Sun *et al.* (2019) [35] verified the existence of concept drift in FDP and associated the use of the sliding window method as the reason for outperforming stationary models. To overcome the concept drift, F. Shen *et al.* (2020) [31] used a sliding window and a forgetting mechanism. Additionally, they suggested parameter optimization and different forgetting mechanism to improve accuracy. Despite 70 attributes usage, the authors proposed the addition of new financial and non-financial indicators in the model.

This study proposes a benchmark evaluation of some ML classifiers already used for FDP in a DS environment, like Logistic Regression (LR), Support Vector Machine (SVM), Random Forest (RF), Decision Tree (DT) [31,35], and adds

XGBoost and CatBoost commonly used in stationary environments [20, 22]. Another benchmark is about methods for data imbalance like SMOTE (Synthetic Minority Over-Sampling Technique) [8], and its variants like BorderlineSMOTE [16], ADASYN [18], SVMSMOTE [27], SMOTEENN [6] e SMOTE-Tomek [28] because its popularity [12]. The idea is to evaluate them through an experiment using a real-world database from the CVM and also evaluate the impact on the model's results after increasing the prediction horizon.

4   Methodology

This study has gathered data from the companies listed in the CVM[1]. The most important documents were: the asset balance sheet, balance sheet of liabilities, income statement, and cash flow statement. They were used to produce a dataset with 23,834 entries and 82 economic-financial indicators, organized into 40 quarters over ten years (2011 to 2020). The data is strongly imbalanced: 2.73% are data of companies in financial distress situation, while 97.27% are not.

The sequence of quarters $X^{t-h}, ..., X^{t-2}, X^{t-1}, X^t, X^{t+1}, X^{t+2}, ..., X^{t+k}$ is the DS where t is the present, $t - h$ is a past moment and $t + k$ are quarters not presented to the model yet. Each quarter X is a set of distinct data companies x with 82 attributes each. Companies in a past quarter (X^{t-h}) have a label (Y^{t-h}), which can be "financial distress" or "normal"; companies in the present quarter (X^t) or ahead $(X^{t+i}, i \in 1, ..., k)$ have no label and are the ones to be predicted by the model.

In this proposal, the model is trained with data from a sliding window and a subset of the historical data, as shown in Fig. 1. The *sliding window* is used to deal with concept drift and minimize its impact on the model performance. It comprises the eight most recent quarters of labeled data and its size is fixed a priori. The *history* data comprises data quarters older than those in the sliding window set and includes only instances of the minority class. These data are used to reduce the imbalanced problem, but passes through a forgetting mechanism to reduce the importance of old instances. It is an adaptation of exponential weighting scheme [23]: $f(h) = 1 - exp^{-\alpha h}$, where h is the distance to the oldest quarter of the sliding window set and α is a forgetting coefficient. The function $f(h)$ returns the proportion of elements to forget for a specific historical quarter h. The *prediction target*, also known as the test set, is the data quarter which will be predicted by the model using the financial indicators, which are already known at time t. The *prediction horizon* (k) specifies how many quarters in advance the prediction will be performed. In this work, we assume the values 2, 4, 8, 12, 16, 20, and 24 quarters.

In addition to using historical data containing only cases from the minority class, this study also applies oversampling techniques to increase the number of instances of companies in financial distress to mitigate the problem of data imbalance. The idea is to create synthetic samples to increase the minority class to 50% and 100% of the majority class to identify the best balancing rate (Rt) for

---

[1] https://dados.cvm.gov.br/.

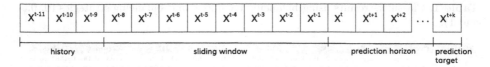

| history | sliding window | prediction horizon | prediction target |

Fig. 1. Sliding window after eleven quarter with three historic quarters and eight quarters for the window

each model using methods to balance the data (*i.e.* SMOTE, BorderlineSMOTE, ADASYN, SVMSMOTE, SMOTEENN, and SMOTETomek).

In the preprocessing phase, a set of instances of the minority class is oversampled before model training. Figure 2 illustrates the training set generation. In step 1, it selects all instances of the minority class from the sliding window mc and merge with instances from the history after the forgetting mechanism hmc'. Hence, it merges the selected set $hmc' + mc$ with the sliding window majority class Mc. Then, in step 2.1, it applies the oversampling technique. Step 2.2 minimizes the creation of synthetic instances by the under-sampling technique $(hmc' + mc)' + Mc'$.

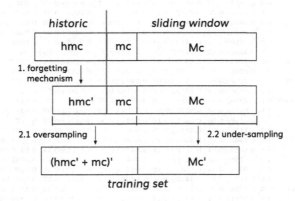

Fig. 2. Data preprocessing to generate the training set

After the sliding window has accumulated enough data, with eight quarters, the training process is conducted in rounds using the prepared training set. Because of the time dependence of the data, the nested cross-validation on time series [21] is more appropriate to train and validate the classification model (*i.e.* LR, SVM, RF, DT, XGBoost and CatBoost).

Mainly because of the imbalance condition of the dataset and the importance of correct classification of the minority samples, the metrics used to evaluate models performance were F_1-Score and G_{mean}. Other important metrics were the AUC-ROC to measure the overall accuracy [7,17] and the AUC-PS to complement the analysis [30].

Table 1. Classifiers results using balancing technique and balancing strategies (0, 0.5 and 1).

Metric	Preprocessing	Rt	LR	DT	SVC	RF	XGBoost	CatBoost
F$_1$-Score	-	-	0.0812±0.00	*0.3562±0.12*	0.0000±0.00	0.4133±0.03	0.4203±0.14	0.4581±0.14
	SMOTE	0.5	0.2019±0.03	0.3516±0.10	0.0013±0.00	0.3976±0.03	0.5132±0.12	0.5683±0.12
		1.0	0.2611±0.02	0.3138±0.12	0.0705±0.00	0.3640±0.03	0.5247±0.12	0.5665±0.13
	B.SMOTE	0.5	0.1912±0.02	0.3200±0.12	0.0019±0.00	0.3658±0.03	0.4649±0.13	0.5179±0.15
		1.0	0.2319±0.01	0.3231±0.12	0.0656±0.00	0.3442±0.03	0.4657±0.13	0.5124±0.15
	ADASYN	0.5	0.1730±0.01	0.3187±0.14	0.0038±0.00	0.3605±0.03	0.4729±0.14	0.5241±0.15
		1.0	0.2211±0.01	0.3143±0.13	0.0558±0.01	0.3301±0.04	0.4769±0.13	0.5165±0.16
	SVMSMOTE	0.5	0.1885±0.03	0.3614±0.10	0.0020±0.00	*0.4474±0.02*	*0.5302±0.12*	0.5743±0.13
		1.0	0.2524±0.02	0.3602±0.13	*0.0706±0.00*	0.4273±0.03	0.5273±0.12	0.5792±0.13
	SMOTEENN	0.5	0.1977±0.03	0.3517±0.11	0.0016±0.00	0.4108±0.03	0.5167±0.12	0.5719±0.13
		1.0	0.2649±0.01	0.3307±0.11	0.0671±0.00	0.3730±0.03	0.5288±0.12	**0.5812±0.12**
	SMOTETomek	0.5	0.1896±0.03	0.3521±0.11	0.0013±0.00	0.4030±0.03	0.5142±0.12	0.5621±0.12
		1.0	*0.2674±0.01*	0.3113±0.11	0.0705±0.00	0.3700±0.03	0.5216±0.12	0.5681±0.12
G$_{mean}$	-	-	0.2490±0.09	*0.5575±0.12*	0.0000±0.00	0.5124±0.11	0.5272±0.14	0.5518±0.14
	SMOTE	0.5	0.5429±0.06	0.5604±0.10	0.0038±0.01	0.5089±0.14	0.6614±0.12	0.6624±0.12
		1.0	0.6837±0.12	0.5190±0.13	*0.2334±0.06*	0.4838±0.14	0.6845±0.12	0.6722±0.13
	B.SMOTE	0.5	0.5226±0.04	0.5346±0.11	0.0057±0.01	0.4744±0.15	0.6008±0.13	0.6218±0.15
		1.0	0.6320±0.13	0.5298±0.12	0.2055±0.07	0.4572±0.15	0.6103±0.13	0.6236±0.15
	ADASYN	0.5	0.5147±0.03	0.5266±0.13	0.0111±0.01	0.4714±0.18	0.6171±0.14	0.6248±0.15
		1.0	0.6474±0.13	0.5193±0.13	0.1552±0.05	0.4448±0.18	0.6325±0.13	0.6275±0.16
	SVMSMOTE	0.5	0.5238±0.06	0.5698±0.11	0.0057±0.01	*0.5544±0.14*	0.6766±0.12	0.6698±0.13
		1.0	0.6843±0.12	0.5620±0.12	0.2316±0.06	0.5407±0.15	**0.6961±0.12**	*0.6882±0.13*
	SMOTEENN	0.5	0.5307±0.06	0.5596±0.11	0.0047±0.01	0.5218±0.14	0.6620±0.12	0.6668±0.13
		1.0	0.6842±0.12	0.5379±0.12	0.2284±0.06	0.4907±0.14	0.6908±0.12	0.6865±0.12
	SMOTETomek	0.5	0.5228±0.06	0.5575±0.10	0.0038±0.01	0.5137±0.14	0.6618±0.12	0.6593±0.12
		1.0	*0.6927±0.11*	0.5161±0.12	0.2321±0.06	0.4871±0.14	0.6834±0.12	0.6754±0.12
AUC-ROC	-	-	0.7525±0.01	0.6571±0.07	0.5106±0.03	0.9102±0.03	0.9405±0.02	0.9436±0.03
	SMOTE	0.5	0.8004±0.02	0.6590±0.06	0.6035±0.07	*0.9298±0.03*	0.9379±0.03	0.9484±0.02
		1.0	0.8304±0.03	0.6397±0.07	0.6461±0.01	0.9280±0.03	0.9395±0.03	0.9514±0.02
	B.SMOTE	0.5	0.7832±0.02	0.6448±0.06	0.6027±0.03	0.9223±0.03	0.9331±0.03	0.9471±0.03
		1.0	0.8073±0.02	0.6424±0.07	0.5932±0.03	0.9223±0.03	0.9304±0.03	0.9469±0.03
	ADASYN	0.5	0.7859±0.02	0.6440±0.08	0.6279±0.05	0.9265±0.03	0.9315±0.03	0.9469±0.03
		1.0	0.8145±0.02	0.6395±0.07	0.6051±0.02	0.9189±0.04	0.9310±0.03	0.9481±0.02
	SVMSMOTE	0.5	0.7950±0.03	0.6655±0.06	0.5943±0.07	0.9291±0.02	0.9364±0.03	0.9474±0.03
		1.0	0.8268±0.03	0.6620±0.07	*0.6520±0.01*	0.9251±0.03	0.9374±0.03	0.9479±0.03
	SMOTEENN	0.5	0.7990±0.02	0.6595±0.06	0.5962±0.08	0.9269±0.03	0.9404±0.03	0.9506±0.02
		1.0	0.8306±0.02	0.6483±0.07	0.6410±0.01	0.9287±0.03	*0.9424±0.03*	**0.9520±0.02**
	SMOTETomek	0.5	0.7959±0.03	*0.6586±0.06*	0.5986±0.07	0.9280±0.03	0.9384±0.03	0.9485±0.02
		1.0	*0.8314±0.02*	0.6370±0.07	0.6454±0.00	0.9276±0.03	0.9389±0.03	0.9513±0.02
AUC-PS	-	-	0.0768±0.00	0.3831±0.11	0.0349±0.00	0.5821±0.14	0.5677±0.14	0.6136±0.15
	SMOTE	0.5	0.1134±0.01	0.3745±0.09	0.0503±0.01	0.5733±0.13	0.5657±0.14	0.6352±0.14
		1.0	0.1363±0.01	0.3504±0.10	0.0646±0.00	0.5368±0.14	0.5768±0.13	0.6342±0.13
	B.SMOTE	0.5	0.1029±0.01	0.3454±0.11	0.0475±0.00	0.5725±0.14	0.5250±0.15	0.6067±0.15
		1.0	0.1195±0.01	0.3475±0.11	0.0617±0.02	0.5552±0.15	0.5131±0.15	0.5954±0.15
	ADASYN	0.5	0.0996±0.01	0.3432±0.13	0.0481±0.00	0.5522±0.16	0.5190±0.15	0.6039±0.16
		1.0	0.1175±0.01	0.3413±0.13	*0.0765±0.02*	0.5282±0.17	0.5083±0.14	0.5919±0.16
	SVMSMOTE	0.5	0.1078±0.02	0.3886±0.09	0.0473±0.01	*0.5872±0.14*	0.5724±0.14	0.6388±0.14
		1.0	0.1311±0.01	*0.3926±0.11*	0.0764±0.01	0.5631±0.14	0.5816±0.14	0.6360±0.14
	SMOTEENN	0.5	0.1134±0.02	0.3764±0.10	0.0494±0.01	0.5789±0.13	0.5719±0.14	**0.6414±0.13**
		1.0	0.1383±0.01	0.3621±0.09	0.0680±0.01	0.5438±0.13	*0.5822±0.14*	0.6386±0.13
	SMOTETomek	0.5	0.1096±0.02	0.3809±0.10	0.0498±0.01	0.5749±0.13	0.5691±0.14	0.6336±0.13
		1.0	*0.1386±0.01*	0.3437±0.10	0.0667±0.01	0.5438±0.13	0.5787±0.13	0.6335±0.13

5   Results

Firstly the classifiers' performances were evaluated after preprocessing approach using different balancing strategies rate ($Rt = \{0, 0.5, 1\}$) and different prediction horizon (2, 4, 8, 12, 16, 20, and 24 quarters), the average and the standard deviation of metrics (F$_1$-Score, G$_{mean}$, AUC-ROC and AUC-PS) were computed. In Table 1, the average best results of F$_1$-Score, G$_{mean}$, AUC-ROC and AUC-PS for the combination of classifier, preprocessing approach, and balancing strategies were presented. The italic values are the best results of a classifier among balancing techniques (in a column), and the bold number is the best result for a specific metric among all classifiers.

In Table 1 it is possible to observe that the best predictive performance (bold values) is related to the CatBoost for most of the metrics analysed. Additionally, the best balancing technique is the SMOTEENN with a balancing rate $Rt = 1$ because it presents the higher value for F_1 and AUC-ROC, while the values for G_{mean} and AUC-PS are very close. Hence, the CatBoost classifier and SMOTEENN with a balancing strategy of 100% are better.

Next analyses are about the impact of prediction horizon variation (2, 4, 8, 12, 16, 20 and 24) on the metrics F_1-Score, G_{mean}, AUC-ROC and AUC-PS, using the CatBoost classifier and SMOTEENN (100%) as balancing technique. In Fig. 3, the x-axis is the prediction horizon quarters and the y-axis is the average result of the metrics over time.

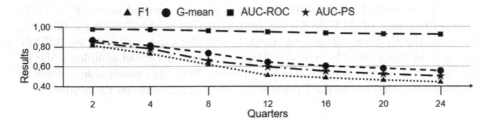

Fig. 3. The evaluation metrics F_1-Score, G_{mean}, AUC-ROC and AUC-PS after changing the precision horizon from 2 quarters to 24 quarters

Figure 3 shows that the prediction horizon and classifier performance measured by F_1-Score, G_{mean}, AUC-ROC, and AUC-PS are inversely proportional. It means that when the prediction horizon increases, the classifier performance decreases. Hence, the best classifier result is when the prediction horizon is smaller (*i.e.* 2 quarters). The AUC-ROC behavior differs from others because the strong data imbalance rate impacts it, and it should be analyzed together with AUC-PS [30].

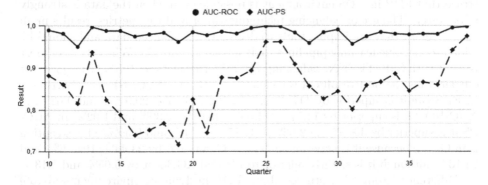

Fig. 4. Classifier AUC-ROC and AUC-PS evolution during training using prediction horizon of 2 quarters

The final analysis is about the CatBoost behavior over cross-validation on time series using the SMOTEENN with a balancing strategy of 100% and a prediction horizon of 2 quarters. Figure 4 shows a chart where the x-axis is the classifier result, and the y-axis is the quarter, a variation curve of AUC-ROC, a variation curve of AUC-PS. As time goes, the AUC-ROC remains always above 0.95 while AUC-PS get its worst value (0.7164) in the 19th quarter and increases until it reaches its best value (0.9760) in the 39th quarter. Thus, there is an increasing trend for the AUC-PS curve because of the accumulation of financial distress instances in history, which reduces the number of synthetic samples necessary to balance the data chunk. The valleys in the AUC-ROC and AUC-PS curves (quarters 12, 19, 28, and 31) may be interpreted as concept drifts.

On this study the best overall results were obtained using CatBoot and the balancing method of SMOTEENN. The results may be compared with F. Shen *et al.* [31] because they used a very similar methodology and forgetting coefficient set to "1", its best classifier is RF and the balancing method is the ANS-REA. The performance of AUC-ROC was better in this study (0.9519 vs. 0.9138), however, the F_1-Score (0,5811 vs. 0.8003) and the G_{mean} (0,6865 vs. 0.8783) was not. In this study the minority class represents 2.73% of samples while in the Shen's study the minority class represents 33%, this reasonable difference explains the difference in the F_1-Score and the G_{mean} between the studies.

6   Conclusion

This study investigates the FDP with strongly imbalanced data in a DS environment combining different classifiers, preprocessing data balancing techniques, and data selection to deal with concept drift. This approach is more suitable than those that deal with stationary data because enterprises' economic-financial indicators are susceptible to concept drift [35], and it can be the basis for building an autonomous FDP solution.

The empirical experiment uses data from 2011 to 2020, consisting of 651 financially distressed companies and 23,183 matching normal enterprises, all of which are listed on the Brazilian stock exchange from CVM. The results demonstrate that FDP in a DS environment is possible even when the data is strongly imbalanced. The use of balancing techniques improved the metrics' results in all cases. Hence, they are import tools to deal with imbalanced data and should be added to machine learning pipelines to deal with FDP in DS. When the CatBoost is used with SMOTEENN, balancing the minority class at 100% of majority, it outperforms the best results of the classifiers LR, DT, SVC, RF, and XGBoost. In F_1-Score it is superior by 117.35%, 63.17%, 723.23%, 29.91%, and 9.62%, in AUC-ROC it is superior by 14.51%, 44.55%, 46.01%, 2.39% and 1.02%, in AUC-PS it is superior by 360.75%, 62.66%, 734.77%, 8.75%, and 9.69%. The exception is in G_{mean} because it is superior to DT, SVC, and RF by 23.44%, 194.86%, and 24.13%, although it is slightly inferior to LR and XGBoost by 0.65% and 1.13%.

Differently, from other studies about FDP in dynamic environments [31, 35] that did not use AUC-PS, in this study it complemented the information from

AUC-ROC and helped to identify the moments of concept drift and the way the model recovered from a drift. It also showed that the sliding window, the history, and the forgetting mechanism are important to deal with the concept drift. Thus, it should be used more often when dealing with imbalanced data and data streams. Additionally, the prediction horizon should be increased with caution because it severe impacts the classifiers performance.

The experiment performed during this study may be improved with the use of a period larger than ten years because this could enlarge the history and fewer synthetic instances of the minority class will be necessary. The forgetting coefficient should also be adjusted to more accurate parameter optimization to improve the accuracy because, with the current value, the mechanism forgets most historic instances til the second quarter of the history. Different sliding window lengths could be tried or even an adaptive sliding window [23] could be used. Moreover, further research could be conducted on concept drift to identify different types of drift and adapt the models after detecting a drift [1]. For this purpose, the dataset used in this study is available on GitHub[2].

Acknowledgment. This study was financed in part by the Coordenação de Aperfeiçoamento de Pessoal de Nível Superior - Brasil (CAPES) - Finance Code 001.

References

1. Agrahari, S., Singh, A.K.: Concept drift detection in data stream mining: a literature review. J. King Saud Univ. Comput. Inf. Sci. (2021). https://doi.org/10.1016/j.jksuci.2021.11.006
2. Alaka, H.A., et al.: Systematic review of bankruptcy prediction models: towards a framework for tool selection. Expert Syst. Appl. **94**, 164–184 (2018). https://doi.org/10.1016/j.eswa.2017.10.040
3. Alam, T.M., et al.: Corporate bankruptcy prediction: an approach towards better corporate world. Comput. J. **64**(11), 1731–1746 (2020). https://doi.org/10.1093/comjnl/bxaa056
4. Altman, E.I.: Financial ratios, discriminant analysis and the prediction of corporate bankruptcy. J. Financ. **23**(4), 589–609 (1968). https://doi.org/10.1111/j.1540-6261.1968.tb00843.x
5. Barboza, F., Kimura, H., Altman, E.: Machine learning models and bankruptcy prediction. Expert Syst. Appl. **83**, 405–417 (2017). https://doi.org/10.1016/j.eswa.2017.04.006
6. Batista, G.E.A.P.A., Prati, R.C., Monard, M.C.: A study of the behavior of several methods for balancing machine learning training data. SIGKDD Explor. Newsl. **6**(1), 20–29 (2004). https://doi.org/10.1145/1007730.1007735
7. Bradley, A.P.: The use of the area under the ROC curve in the evaluation of machine learning algorithms. Pattern Recogn. **30**(7), 1145–1159 (1997). https://doi.org/10.1016/S0031-3203(96)00142-2
8. Chawla, N.V., Bowyer, K.W., Hall, L.O., Kegelmeyer, W.P.: SMOTE: synthetic minority over-sampling technique. J. Artif. Intell. Res. **16**(1), 321–357 (2002). https://doi.org/10.5555/1622407.1622416

---

[2] https://github.com/rubensmchaves/ml-fdp.

9. Duarte, F., Jones, C.: Empirical network contagion for U.S. financial institutions. FRB of NY Staff Report **1**(826) (2017)

10. Efrim Boritz, J., Kennedy, D.B.: Effectiveness of neural network types for prediction of business failure. Expert Syst. Appl. **9**(4), 503–512 (1995). https://doi.org/10.1016/0957-4174(95)00020-8. https://www.sciencedirect.com/science/article/pii/0957417495000208. Expert systems in accounting, auditing, and finance

11. Eichengreen, B., Mody, A., Nedeljkovic, M., Sarno, L.: How the subprime crisis went global: evidence from bank credit default swap spreads. J. Int. Money Financ. **31**(5), 1299–1318 (2012). https://doi.org/10.1016/j.jimonfin.2012.02.002

12. Fernández, A., García, S., Herrera, F., Chawla, N.V.: Smote for learning from imbalanced data: progress and challenges, marking the 15-year anniversary. J. Artif. Intell. Res. **61**(1), 863–905 (2018)

13. Fernández, A., García, S., Galar, M., Prati, R.C., Krawczyk, B., Herrera, F.: Learning from Imbalanced Data Sets. Springer, Cham (2018). https://doi.org/10.1007/978-3-319-98074-4

14. Gama, J.: A survey on learning from data streams: current and future trends. Progress Artif. Intell. **1**(1), 45–55 (2012). https://doi.org/10.1007/s13748-011-0002-6

15. Gomes, H.M., Read, J., Bifet, A., Barddal, J.P., Gama, J.: Machine learning for streaming data: state of the art, challenges, and opportunities. ACM SIGKDD Explor. Newsl. **21**(2), 6–22 (2019). https://doi.org/10.1145/3373464.3373470

16. Han, H., Wang, W.-Y., Mao, B.-H.: Borderline-SMOTE: a new over-sampling method in imbalanced data sets learning. In: Huang, D.-S., Zhang, X.-P., Huang, G.-B. (eds.) ICIC 2005. LNCS, vol. 3644, pp. 878–887. Springer, Heidelberg (2005). https://doi.org/10.1007/11538059_91

17. Hanley, J., Mcneil, B.: The meaning and use of the area under a receiver operating characteristic (ROC) curve. Radiology **143**, 29–36 (1982). https://doi.org/10.1148/radiology.143.1.7063747

18. He, H., Bai, Y., Garcia, E.A., Li, S.: ADASYN: adaptive synthetic sampling approach for imbalanced learning. In: 2008 IEEE International Joint Conference on Neural Networks (IEEE World Congress on Computational Intelligence), pp. 1322–1328 (2008). https://doi.org/10.1109/IJCNN.2008.4633969

19. He, H., Chen, S., Li, K., Xu, X.: Incremental learning from stream data. IEEE Trans. Neural Netw. **22**(12), 1901–1914 (2011). https://doi.org/10.1109/TNN.2011.2171713

20. Huang, Y.P., Yen, M.F.: A new perspective of performance comparison among machine learning algorithms for financial distress prediction. Appl. Soft Comput. **83**, 105663 (2019). https://doi.org/10.1016/j.asoc.2019.105663

21. Hyndman, R.J., Athanasopoulos, G.: Forecasting: Principles and Practice. OTexts (2021)

22. Jabeur, S.B., Gharib, C., Mefteh-Wali, S., Arfi, W.B.: CatBoost model and artificial intelligence techniques for corporate failure prediction. Technol. Forecast. Soc. Change **166**, 120658 (2021). https://doi.org/10.1016/j.techfore.2021.120658

23. Klinkenberg, R.: Learning drifting concepts: example selection vs. example weighting. Intell. Data Anal. **8**(3), 281–300 (2004). https://doi.org/10.5555/1293831.1293836

24. Kumbure, M.M., Lohrmann, C., Luukka, P., Porras, J.: Machine learning techniques and data for stock market forecasting: a literature review. Expert Syst. Appl. **197**, 116659 (2022). https://doi.org/10.1016/j.eswa.2022.116659

25. Li, Z., Huang, W., Xiong, Y., Ren, S., Zhu, T.: Incremental learning imbalanced data streams with concept drift: the dynamic updated ensemble algorithm. Knowl.-Based Syst. **195**, 105694 (2020). https://doi.org/10.1016/j.knosys.2020.105694
26. Lin, X., Zhang, Y., Wang, S., Ji, G.: A rule-based model for bankruptcy prediction based on an improved genetic ant colony algorithm. Math. Probl. Eng. 753251 (2013). https://doi.org/10.1155/2013/753251
27. Nguyen, H.M., Cooper, E.W., Kamei, K.: Borderline over-sampling for imbalanced data classification. Int. J. Knowl. Eng. Soft Data Paradigm **3**(1), 4–21 (2011). https://doi.org/10.1504/IJKESDP.2011.039875
28. Rana, C., Chitre, N., Poyekar, B., Bide, P.: Stroke prediction using Smote-Tomek and neural network. In: 2021 12th International Conference on Computing Communication and Networking Technologies (ICCCNT), pp. 1–5 (2021). https://doi.org/10.1109/ICCCNT51525.2021.9579763
29. Russell, S., Norvig, P.: Artificial Intelligence: A Modern Approach, 3rd edn. Prentice Hall, Hoboken (2010)
30. Saito, T., Rehmsmeier, M.: The precision-recall plot is more informative than the ROC plot when evaluating binary classifiers on imbalanced datasets. PLoS ONE **10**, 1–21 (2015). https://doi.org/10.1371/journal.pone.0118432
31. Shen, F., Liu, Y., Wang, R., Zhou, W.: A dynamic financial distress forecast model with multiple forecast results under unbalanced data environment. Knowl.-Based Syst. **192**, 105365 (2020). https://doi.org/10.1016/j.knosys.2019.105365
32. Shi, Y., Li, X.: A bibliometric study on intelligent techniques of bankruptcy prediction for corporate firms. Heliyon **5**(12), 12 (2019). https://doi.org/10.1016/j.heliyon.2019.e02997
33. Silva, T.C., da Silva Alexandre, M., Tabak, B.M.: Bank lending and systemic risk: a financial-real sector network approach with feedback. J. Financ. Stab. **38**, 98–118 (2017). https://doi.org/10.1016/j.jfs.2017.08.006
34. Sun, J., Li, H., Huang, Q.H., He, K.Y.: Predicting financial distress and corporate failure: a review from the state-of-the-art definitions, modeling, sampling, and featuring approaches. Knowl.-Based Syst. **57**, 41–56 (2014). https://doi.org/10.1016/j.knosys.2013.12.006
35. Sun, J., Zhou, M., Ai, W., Li, H.: Dynamic prediction of relative financial distress based on imbalanced data stream: from the view of one industry. Risk Manag. **21**(4), 215–242 (2019). https://doi.org/10.1057/s41283-018-0047-y
36. Wang, S., Minku, L.L., Yao, X.: A systematic study of online class imbalance learning with concept drift. IEEE Trans. Neural Netw. Learn. Syst. **29**(10), 4802–4821 (2018). https://doi.org/10.1109/TNNLS.2017.2771290
37. Wilson, R.L., Sharda, R.: Bankruptcy prediction using neural networks. Decis. Support Syst. **11**(5), 545–557 (1994). https://doi.org/10.1016/0167-9236(94)90024-8

Improving the Quality of Quantum Services Generation Process: Controlling Errors and Noise

Jaime Alvarado-Valiente[1][(✉)] [iD], Javier Romero-Álvarez[1] [iD], Danel Arias[2] [iD],
Erik B. Terres[2] [iD], Jose Garcia-Alonso[1] [iD], Enrique Moguel[3] [iD],
Pablo García Bringas[2] [iD], and Juan M. Murillo[3] [iD]

[1] Escuela Politécnica, Quercus Software Engineering Group,
University of Extremadura, Cáceres, Spain
{jaimeav,jromero,jgaralo}@unex.es
[2] University of Deusto, Bilbao, Spain
danel.arias@opendeusto.es, {e.terres,pablo.garcia.bringas}@deusto.es
[3] CénitS-COMPUTAEX, Cáceres, Spain
enrique@unex.es, director@cenits.es

Abstract. As the industry moves towards practical applications of quantum computing, it faces significant obstacles such as specific platform dependency and lack of mature tools. These obstacles make the creation of quantum applications a slow and complex process that requires specialized knowledge of quantum mechanics and computer science, which compromises the quality of quantum services. Therefore, the need to ensure an adequate level of quality in quantum software is fundamental. To address these challenges, this work proposes a process that enables developers to create high-quality quantum services in an automated and standardized way, using an extension of the OpenAPI specification. Furthermore, we analyze the challenges faced by NISQ devices, the most advanced quantum computers available today, due to errors and noise such as decoherence, gate errors, and readout errors. This process will make it possible to measure, at runtime, the stability and fidelity of the quantum circuits included in the generated quantum services.

Keywords: Quantum Computing · Quantum Services · Quantum Program Security · Quantum Code Analysis

1 Introduction

Quantum computing is a computational model that leverages the principles of quantum mechanics to manipulate and process information. This computing paradigm holds the potential to deliver high computational capacity, thereby allowing for the resolution of problems that have previously eluded classical computing, such as those that fall within the complexity class of BQP [1]. Therefore, the advent of quantum computing has garnered the attention of prominent technology companies like Amazon, IBM, or Google have invested extensively in

P. García Bringas et al. (Eds.): HAIS 2023, LNAI 14001, pp. 180–191, 2023.
https://doi.org/10.1007/978-3-031-40725-3_16

developing new quantum machines and providing them to users through their cloud platforms [2].

The utilization of quantum computers via cloud platforms, which are offered by different providers, has similarities with classical computing and service-oriented architectures. This entails that quantum computing may be employed within classical-quantum hybrid architectures, wherein both technologies contribute their resources in the form of services [3]. To create high-quality quantum services and hybrid architectures, developers require appropriate tools and techniques that enable them to attain the desired security standards [4]. It should be noted that the absence of adequate software engineering methods for quantum services presents various challenges, including the low abstraction level that developers must work with and the absence of integration, deployment, or quality and security control mechanisms for the software they develop [5].

Consequently, various solutions are emerging to bridge the divide between classical processes and quantum computing and tackle these problems [6]. However, quantum devices today face significant challenges due to the presence of errors and noise, which limits their scalability and usability. Therefore, controlling and improving the quality of new quantum systems is essential [7]. For example, Noisy Intermediate-Scale Quantum (NISQ) devices, which are the most advanced quantum computers available today [8], suffer from various types of noise and errors, such as decoherence, gate errors, and readout errors, among others. Thus, understanding the effects of noise and errors in NISQ devices is crucial for quantum software development [8]. When developing a quantum circuit, the results obtained in a NISQ backend may be misleading due to errors and noise. Therefore, it is crucial to evaluate the circuit's stability. Knowing how much the circuit deviates from the "perfect result" provides a direct measurement of its stability. As a result, two implementations with the same objective output but with a different sequence of operations may have different stability measurements.

Measuring the fidelity of a circuit involves comparing the distribution of results obtained in a real backend versus a simulated "perfect backend" (without noise or errors) after multiple executions of the circuit implementation. However, performing multiple executions is time and resource-intensive, as it requires repeated calls to services that offer real backends (which often have waiting queues, and can take minutes or even hours to execute). Additionally, executing in a simulator is generally slower as it must simulate the quantum characteristics. Thus, it is essential to know the stability of quantum circuits at runtime when developing a quantum program.

To this end, this paper proposes a tool for developers that combines an extension of the OpenAPI specification[1], along with a real-time measurement process of the quantum circuits to be executed. The OpenAPI extensions allow developers to define and generate quantum services in a similar and standardized way as classical services are defined. While the measurement process allows to

---

[1] https://www.openapis.org/.

check of the stability and evaluate the circuits included in the generated services at runtime.

To explain this, the organization of the paper is as follows: Sect. 2 provides an analysis of the background of the presented work and a discussion of the most relevant related work; Sect. 3 presents the proposal for the automatic generation and deployment of quantum services and the whole process of estimating and measuring the characteristics of the quantum circuits contained in those services; Sect. 4 includes the results of the measurements of the process; and finally Sect. 5 outlines some conclusions and presents the next steps to be carried out in the context of this research.

2   Background

NISQ computers represent a cutting-edge technology in the field of quantum computing, but their potential can be limited by environmental noise that can corrupt the qubit state. Such noise-induced decoherence is a fundamental issue that arises from the unavoidable interaction between qubits and their environment, which causes unpredictable and irreversible changes in the qubit state, leading to errors in measurement results. These errors pose challenges for addressing the quality and security requirements, which are crucial factors for the development of practical quantum applications [9].

In addition to decoherence, NISQ computers are also susceptible to operational errors, such as readout and gate errors. Readout errors arise when the measurement time exceeds the decoherence time of the qubits [10]. Gate errors, on the other hand, can result from various factors, including temperature fluctuations, electromagnetic interference, and environmental conditions [11]. Due to the limited number of qubits and short coherence times, the impact of gate errors can be significant and may impair the reliable execution of quantum algorithms.

To prevent malicious exploitation, quantum circuits must be secured against quantum errors that could be used by malicious agents to manipulate the correct state of a quantum circuit. It is therefore imperative for programmers to prioritize the development of quantum software with robustness that meets strict quality criteria. Any compromise in the security of quantum software can have severe consequences, particularly for sensitive applications such as cryptography or financial transactions, highlighting the criticality of ensuring error-free execution [12]. As a result, addressing quality and security requirements presents a significant challenge.

Therefore, the use of support tools during software design has proven to be an effective method for developers to improve the quality of their software. Despite this, there is a notable lack of such tools for quantum computing software, which presents a challenge for developers in this field. While support tools have been successful in enhancing the quality of classical computing software, their absence in the field of quantum computing adds an additional obstacle for developers tackling this complex issue [7].

Quantum simulations are currently the primary tool for approximating output noise in quantum circuits, but they have the main problem of a computationally intensive task. Obtaining the state vector of the output requires exponential memory with respect to the number of qubits, which can compromise the time of the simulation [13]. While certain circuits can be simulated in polynomial time, these are subject to specific constraints that do not apply to general-purpose analysis. For instance, stabilizer circuits can be efficiently simulated in classical systems, but they can only be written with CNOT, Hadamard, or Phase Gates [14]. This limitation presents a challenge in simulating general-purpose quantum circuits, which are the ones that will provide a quantum advantage over classical computers. Due to the exponentially increasing complexity of quantum circuits, it is not feasible to simulate larger circuits on classical systems. Thus, to estimate the error in quantum circuits in real-time, complete classical simulations are not a feasible solution.

In order to approximate quantum error, Aseguinolaza et al. [15] developed a highly accurate tool to approximate quantum error. Their algorithm utilizes a multiplicative noise rule to estimate noise, based on publicly available IBM computers noise models. They applied the algorithm to verify that the circuit fidelity aligns with the estimated error rate for various simple circuits, including the one-dimensional Ising model, quantum phase estimation, and the Grover algorithm.

The idea that simple mathematical algorithms make precise error rate estimations possible opens the door for more sophisticated error estimation algorithms for a broad range of general-purpose circuits. The development of these algorithms is essential to ensure that quantum software guarantees a minimum standard of quality and security. By limiting the execution of unsafe circuits, which have not passed the quality criteria, and by developing reliable and efficient error correction and error estimation methods, the quantum computing industry can mitigate the risks of quantum noise and ensure that the potential of this technology can be fully realized.

To ensure that quantum software meets strict quality and security requirements, a continuous integration and deployment process is essential. This process involves the use of OpenAPI for the generation of quantum services, facilitating their integration and use on different platforms and systems. By adapting these tools to work with quantum software [16], they can be combined with circuit measurements for the generation of quality services, which can help to detect potential errors and security issues in the code at an early stage.

3   Quantum Services Generation, Deployment and Error Measurement

The objective of this section is to provide an overview of the entire process of generating and deploying quantum services, along with a discussion of how to measure the quantum circuits that are part of these services.

3.1   OpenAPI Specification for Quantum Service Generation and Deployment

To achieve the continuous generation and deployment of quantum services, the OpenAPI specification has been utilized along with its code generator, which has been integrated into a workflow executed in the GitHub Actions tool[2].

The OpenAPI specification, also known as Swagger, is an industry-standard format used to describe RESTful APIs. It provides a machine-readable interface that enables automated documentation, client code generation, and testing of APIs. This specification, with the extension we have designed on it, enables the design of services including quantum properties.

With the new variables added, the developer can indicate which quantum circuit we want to encapsulate in the service—specifying the URL where it is available—, the quantum machine provider for which we want to generate it, the machine on which it will run, and the number of shots to launch—the latter two at runtime.

Once the developer has defined the services in the YAML specification, it goes through the OpenAPI code generator, which has also been modified to work with the new variables added to the specification. This generates circuit code ready for deployment and consumption. Once the code is ready, it is automatically deployed in a Docker container, and the user is given the URL where the API endpoints are available. This process is carried out once the developer makes a commit of the YAML in the GitHub repository, at which point the workflow execution is automatically triggered. The whole workflow can be seen in Fig. 1.

In addition, as explained below, an enhancement has been added to analyze the circuits included in the specification.

3.2   Controlling Errors and Noise Through Estimation and Measurement

In order to evaluate the quality of the circuits included in the services and to find possible problems and vulnerabilities, a parallel process has been included to the deployment part that is in charge of predicting and estimating these possible errors in real execution time, as shown in the steps 6 and 7 of the workflow described above in Fig. 1. This error estimation acts as a monitoring tool for the developer that serves as a crucial component in understanding and mitigating the effects of noise and errors in quantum devices. For this purpose, within the workflow, the files containing only the code corresponding to the circuits are generated. These files are stored in a different repository to be analyzed and to obtain a report with these error measurements.

Therefore, in our process to estimate errors, we first studied the causes of errors through backend calibration analysis. We then measured the error of various circuits in different real backends. With the information collected, we developed a naïve estimation technique. Additionally, we further improved the error

---

[2] https://github.com/features/actions.

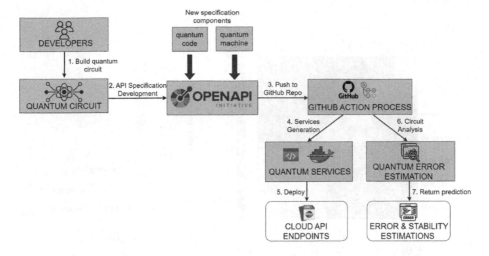

Fig. 1. Workflow for the generation and deployment of quantum services

estimation accuracy with machine learning approaches. In this section, we will dissect those steps with a further explanation.

We performed data analysis of all IBM Quantum backends, focusing on the error and stability of individual gates and qubits through the calibrations given by IBM Quantum. To investigate the error and stability of a quantum backend, we analyzed the calibration data provided by the backend. Our analysis includes examining error distributions, identifying the most impactful errors, and investigating correlations between the backends and other parameters.

Users can access this calibration data to gain insight into the behavior of the quantum backends. However, understanding the underlying complexities and their impact on the quantum circuit may require a deep level of knowledge which makes it challenging.

This calibration data includes various parameters that can help explain the noise and error susceptibility of the backend. The IBMQ backend calibration data includes parameters such as error probabilities and lengths of basic gates[3], readout errors, probabilities of measuring 1 and 0 in certain states[4], T1 and T2 relaxation times, and qubit frequency and anharmonicity. These parameters can help explain the noise and error susceptibility of the backend.

For instance, the error probability and length in nanoseconds of each basic gate can provide insights into how each gate contributes to the overall error of the backend. Similarly, the probability of error and length in nanoseconds of a readout can reveal the error in the measurement of the qubits. By analyzing T1 and T2 relaxation times in microseconds, the frequency of the qubits in GHz,

---

[3] The basic gates create the basis on which the rest of the gates that make up the circuit are composed.

[4] This consists on preparing a 0 state and measuring if a 1 is read and viceversa. Thus, these probabilities are related to the readout error.

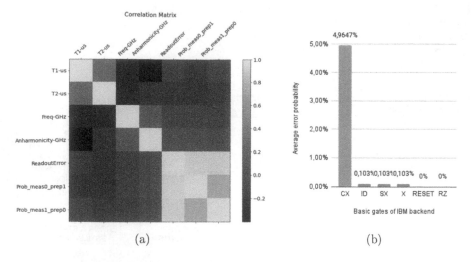

Fig. 2. (a) Correlation matrix of the different calibration metrics. The readout error is a combination of the probability of measuring 0 having prepared a 1 state and vice versa. (b) Average probability of error for the basic gates of IBM Quantum backends, based on the calibrations retrieved from IBM.

and the anharmonicity of the qubits in GHz can provide information about the coherence and stability of the qubits.

Based on our data analysis, we can draw several conclusions about the error and stability of the IBM Quantum backends:

1. Firstly, we found that there is no significant correlation between readout errors and gate errors. This means that these errors are independent of each other and improving one type of error may not necessarily lead to an improvement in the other. Therefore, these errors can be studied independently. The same happens with noise and stability calibrations, there is no significant correlation between these (see Fig. 2a).
2. Secondly, we identified CNOT (Controlled NOT) gates as the most error-prone gate across all backends. In fact, we found that there is a significant difference between the error rates of CNOT gates and the error rates of other gates (see Fig. 2b). This is an important finding as CNOT gates are widely used in quantum circuits, and improving their error rate could significantly improve the overall performance of the backends.
3. Finally, we found that while errors are backend-dependent, gate and readout errors are similar across all backends. Specifically, we found that the error rates are proportional when comparing different backends. This means that there is not a significant variation in error rates across backends, which is useful information for users to take into account when selecting a backend for their applications.

To estimate the error of a quantum circuit, we first developed a basic approach, which we refer to as the "naïve approach to quantum error estimation".

This approach consists of obtaining the error probabilities of the basic gates and readout error of the backend b in which the circuit c will be executed. Next, we determine the number of each basic gate g_i and the number of measurements m that comprise c. Finally, we compute the total error probability as the sum of the product of the number of each basic gate and its corresponding error probability, plus the product of the number of measurements and the measurement error probability, divided by the total number of operations in the circuit:

$$\frac{1}{N_{ops}} \left(\sum_i^{n_g} g_i \cdot err(g_i) + m \cdot err(m) \right) \tag{1}$$

where N_{ops} is the total number of operations in c, n_g is the total number of basic gates in c, g_i is the number of the i-th basic gate in c, $err(g_i)$ is the error probability of the i-th basic gate in b, m is the number of measurements in c, and $err(m)$ is the measurement error probability in b.

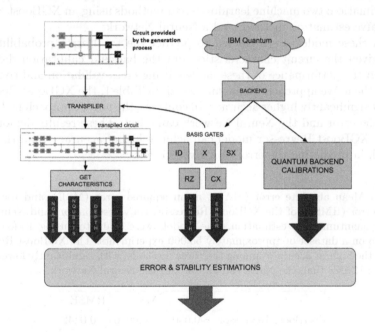

Fig. 3. Workflow of the quantum error estimation process for IBM Quantum backends

While the "naïve approach to quantum error estimation" is a simple and effective way to estimate the error of a quantum circuit, we also explored other alternatives. Such an approach involves using machine learning and AI techniques to model the error behavior of quantum devices. By analyzing large datasets of calibration data and experiment results, these models can learn to predict the error of a given circuit with higher accuracy than the naïve approach. To train such models, we first created a dataset by running approximately 140000 experiments, using various circuits of different sizes and complexities. We then used this dataset to train two different models: an XGBoost Regressor and a Neural Network. The accuracy of these estimators is discussed in Sect. 4.

Therefore, we define the process for our quantum error estimation for a circuit and a backend as the following as shown in Fig. 3. First, we retrieve the backend information from the IBM Quantum cloud service. This information includes the backend calibration data and the gate basis. We then transpile the circuit to the basic gates and extract the characteristics (number of gates of each type, depth, number of qubits, number of classical bits, etc.). After that, we process all the data and we pass it to the estimator.

4   Evaluation

As we introduced before, we explored three different approaches to quantum error estimation: two machine learning-based methods using an XGBoost Regressor, a naïve estimation method, and a Neural Network.

Both these models were trained to predict the total error probability of a circuit given the circuit characteristics and the backend calibration data. We evaluated the performance of these models using cross-validation and compared them to the naïve approach. As it can be seen in Table 1, the XGBoost Regressor achieved significantly higher accuracy. In contrast, the naïve approach had nearly double the error and the Neural Network came last. These results demonstrate that the XGBoost Regressor model can achieve higher accuracy than the naïve approach in predicting the error of a given circuit.

Table 1. Mean absolute error (MAE), mean squared error (MSE), and root mean squared error (RMSE) of the XGBoost Regressor, Naïve estimation, and Neural Network for quantum error estimation. The models were evaluated using 10-fold cross-validation on a dataset of approximately 55,000 experiments. The XGBoost Regressor achieved the highest accuracy among the three methods, with significantly lower MAE, MSE, and RMSE than the Naïve estimation and the Neural Network.

	MAE	MSE	RMSE
XGBoost Regressor	~0.0308	~0.0020	~0.0442
Naïve Estimation	~0.0629	~0.0120	~0.1096
Neural Network	~0.0868	~0.0112	~0.1052

To further evaluate the performance of the three error estimation methods, we executed the experiment on a set of specific circuits. For each circuit, we first used the estimators to predict the error probability and then ran the circuit on both a real quantum backend and a no-noise simulator. By comparing the results from the two runs, we calculated the actual error of the circuit. We

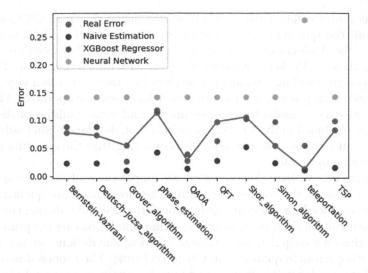

Fig. 4. Errors measured (in red) and errors estimated by the 3 different estimators in some popular and widely used quantum circuits. (Color figure online)

then compared the estimated error probability from each estimator to the actual error probability. This evaluation allowed us to assess the accuracy of the estimators in predicting the error probability of specific circuits. The results, shown in Fig. 4, demonstrate that the XGBoost Regressor model is the most accurate estimator, while the naïve method underestimates the error and the Neural Network performs unsatisfactorily. However, the tabular nature of the dataset may have contributed to the poor performance of the Neural Network, indicating the need for a more sophisticated preprocessing of the dataset. The underestimation of error by the naive method, on the other hand, is explained by the fact that it does not take into account other error-inciting factors such as decoherence, relaxation or other forms of noise.

5   Conclusions

Quantum computing is a promising computational paradigm that offers solutions to previously unsolvable problems. However, the current state of quantum computing raises concerns regarding security and quality due to existing methods of quantum software usage and the lack of abstraction. Prioritizing research and development in quantum computing is essential to address these challenges. This paper proposes a solution that consists of adopting classical service engineering techniques and methods to address challenges in the development and utilization of quantum services.

To achieve this, a standardized method has been proposed for defining quantum services, which utilizes the OpenAPI specification. The process involves generating source code for the quantum services using the OpenAPI Code Generator from the quantum circuit and OpenAPI specification. Additionally, to streamline the deployment of these services, a workflow has been created for deploying them in Docker containers using the GitHub Actions tool. This will help in managing and maintaining the services in a more organized way. To further enhance this process, a monitoring tool has been incorporated. This tool allows developers to assess the error estimates and vulnerabilities of the quantum circuits included in the services. With this tool, developers can easily detect and resolve any issues that may arise, thus ensuring that the quantum services are performing optimally.

Furthermore, we have demonstrated the importance of accurate quantum error estimation in the context of quantum services. Accurate quantum error estimation is crucial for achieving optimal performance and reducing the impact of noise on quantum circuits. Although quantum simulations are the primary tool for approximating output noise, complete classical simulations are not feasible for estimating errors in quantum circuits in real-time. The proposed monitoring tool can help developers easily detect and resolve errors, ensuring reliability and usefulness in practical applications. To achieve reliability and usefulness, accurate error estimation is necessary. While there is still much work to be done in mitigating the effects of noise and errors in quantum circuits, ongoing research in improving the quality of individual gates and measurements and creating standards for circuit design can help fully realize the potential of quantum computing in practical applications.

Acknowledgments. The authors would like to acknowledge the partial financial support by the Ministry of Science (QSERV project, PID2021-124045OB-C31 and PID2021-124054OB-C33) funded by MCIN/AEI /10.13039/50100011033 and by "ERDF A way of making Europe". Also, to the Basque Government (projects TRUSTIND - KK-2020/00054, and REMEDY - KK-2021/00091). It is also funded by the QSALUD project (EXP 00135977/MIG-20201059) in the lines of action of the Center for Technological Development and Innovation (CDTI); and by the Ministry of Economy and Digital Transformation of the Government of Spain through the call for the Quantum ENIA project - Quantum Spain Project, and by the European Union through the Recovery, Transformation and Resilience Plan - NextGenerationEU in the framework of the Agenda España Digital 2025.

References

1. Aaronson, S.: BQP and the polynomial hierarchy. In: Proceedings of the Annual ACM Symposium on Theory of Computing, pp. 141–150 (2009)
2. MacQuarrie, E.R., Simon, C., Simmons, S., Maine, E.: The emerging commercial landscape of quantum computing. Nat. Rev. Phys. **2**(11), 596–598 (2020)
3. Rojo, J., Valencia, D., Berrocal, J., Moguel, E., García-Alonso, J.M., Murillo, J.M.: Trials and tribulations of developing hybrid quantum-classical microservices systems. arXiv, vol. abs/2105.04421 (2021)
4. Moguel, E., Rojo, J., Valencia, D., Berrocal, J., Garcia-Alonso, J., Murillo, J.M.: Quantum service-oriented computing: current landscape and challenges. Softw. Qual. J. **30**(4), 983–1002 (2022)

5. Akbar, M.A., Khan, A.A., Mahmood, S., Rafi, S.: Quantum software engineering: a new genre of computing (2022). https://arxiv.org/abs/2211.13990v1
6. Garcia-Alonso, J.M., Rojo, J., Valencia, D., Moguel, E., Berrocal, J., Murillo, J.M.: Quantum software as a service through a quantum API gateway. IEEE Internet Comput. **26**, 34–41 (2021)
7. Piattini, M., Serrano, M., Perez-Castillo, R., Petersen, G., Hevia, J.L.: Toward a quantum software engineering. IT Prof. **23**(1), 62–66 (2021)
8. Endo, S., Cai, Z., Benjamin, S.C., Yuan, X.: Hybrid quantum-classical algorithms and quantum error mitigation. J. Phys. Soc. Jpn. **90**(3), 032001 (2021)
9. Schlosshauer, M.: Decoherence, the measurement problem, and interpretations of quantum mechanics. Rev. Mod. Phys. **76**(4), 1267–1305 (2005). http://arxiv.org/abs/quant-ph/0312059
10. Nachman, B., Urbanek, M., de Jong, W.A., Bauer, C.W.: Unfolding quantum computer readout noise. npj Quantum Inf. **6**(1), 1–7 (2020). https://www.nature.com/articles/s41534-020-00309-7
11. Georgopoulos, K., Emary, C., Zuliani, P.: Modelling and simulating the noisy behaviour of near-term quantum computers. Phys. Rev. A **104**(6), 062432 (2021). http://arxiv.org/abs/2101.02109. [quant-ph]
12. Arias, D., et al.: Let's do it right the first time: survey on security concerns in the way to quantum software engineering. Neurocomputing **538**, 126199 (2023). https://www.sciencedirect.com/science/article/pii/S0925231223003041
13. Isakov, S.V., et al.: Simulations of quantum circuits with approximate noise using qsim and Cirq (2021). http://arxiv.org/abs/2111.02396. [quant-ph]
14. Gidney, C.: Stim: a fast stabilizer circuit simulator. Quantum **5**, 497 (2021). http://arxiv.org/abs/2103.02202. [quant-ph]
15. Aseguinolaza, U., Sobrino, N., Sobrino, G., Jornet-Somoza, J., Borge, J.: Error estimation in IBM quantum computers (2023). http://arxiv.org/abs/2302.06870. [physics, physics:quant-ph]
16. Romero-Álvarez, J., Alvarado-Valiente, J., Moguel, E., García-Alonso, J., Murillo, J.M.: Using open API for the development of hybrid classical-quantum services. In: Troya, J., et al. (eds.) ICSOC 2022. LNCS, vol. 13821, pp. 364–368. Springer, Cham (2023). https://doi.org/10.1007/978-3-031-26507-5_34

Comparison of Deep Reinforcement Learning Path-Following System Based on Road Geometry and an Adaptive Cruise Control for Autonomous Vehicles

F. Barreno[1]([✉]), M. Santos[2], and M. Romana[3]

[1] Computer Science Faculty, Complutense University of Madrid, 28040 Madrid, Spain
febarren@ucm.es
[2] Institute of Knowledge Technology, Complutense University of Madrid, 28040 Madrid, Spain
msantos@ucm.es
[3] Civil Engineering School, Technical University of Madrid, 28040 Madrid, Spain
manuel.romana@upm.es

Abstract. This paper presents an intelligent path-following system implemented using deep reinforcement learning based road curvature influence. The vehicle dynamics features are obtained with a 3-DOF vehicle model. The intelligent system consists of a deep deterministic policy gradient (DDPG) agent to control the longitudinal speed and a deep Q-network (DQN) to control the lateral vehicle movement. The road curvature effect is considered through the perceived acceleration and the ideal angular velocity due to the road itself is used to train the model agents. The outputs of the intelligent system are acceleration and steering angle continuous values. The proposed model has been compared to an Adaptive Cruise Control (ACC) for longitudinal and lateral control, giving better results in terms of duration of the jerk peaks. On the order hand, ACC is less sensitive during road curvature changes. The results suggest this intelligent system can assist the driver and that the proposed intelligent vehicle control can be applied to autonomous driving to make it safer and more comfortable.

Keywords: Deep learning · ADAS system · reinforcement learning · driving · autonomous driving · road · industry 4.0

1 Introduction

Advanced Driver Assistance Systems (ADAS) help the driver control the vehicle and can assist in dangerous maneuvers, driver distraction or high-risk situations. The homologation of ADA systems and the gradual introduction of autonomous cars on the road will change the driving experience in different aspects, such as steering control, acceleration and braking, and general safety [1].

The way the driver perceives the different geometric characteristics of the road can lead to different driving behavior depending on the type and characteristics of the road [2–4]. Vehicle dynamics allows the recognition of certain features of the road

© The Author(s), under exclusive license to Springer Nature Switzerland AG 2023
P. García Bringas et al. (Eds.): HAIS 2023, LNAI 14001, pp. 192–203, 2023.
https://doi.org/10.1007/978-3-031-40725-3_17

geometry. These features can be derived from inertial information such as accelerometer and gyroscope readings, GPS data, and CAN bus data, which have proven useful in this field. These data can then be used to obtain certain driving characteristics and implicitly recognize how the road geometry is [5].

The objective of this work is to design an intelligent control system of a vehicle using the characteristics extracted from the geometry of the road during driving, and obtain the appropriate values of longitudinal acceleration and steering angle. A 3-DOF experimental model of vehicles has been used. The control system has been designed with deep reinforcement learning (DRL). The intelligent system here proposed for driving assistance focuses on characterizing the driving of the vehicle based on the effect of the curvature of the road, so that it incorporates the geometry of the road through certain characteristics related to it, as the longitudinal and lateral acceleration of the vehicle, perceived by the driver when taking the curves [6]. This contributes to a safer driving as an inappropriate speed in a bend could be unsafe for a given section of road.

This control system is applied in a car following scenario, where the control of the speed in order to maintain a safe distance is crucial [7]. The results obtained here are promising. The developed system could be integrated in all vehicles that have inertial vehicle information and can be used to increase road safety and reduce traffic accidents, reducing the driver load [8].

Driver models are critical elements of speed control systems [9]. In general, driver models have been developed using two approaches: rule-based and supervised learning [10, 11]. Lately, deep learning approaches with reinforcement learning have proven to be an effective solution to decision making problems in different fields [12]. Regarding vehicles, in [13], the authors use of Deep Q-Learning to control a simulated car. An optimal control is applied to the path-following for an autonomous underwater vehicle in [14]. A novel car-following control model combining machine learning and kinematics models for automated vehicles is proposed in [15]. In [16], a safe velocity control method for AV based on reinforcement learning considering the following vehicle is proposed. In [17], a model for human-like autonomous car following that applies deep reinforcement learning is presented. Most recently, a data-centric application of adaptive cruise control employing DRL has been proposed in [18]. Based on the DRL approach, it considers multiple objectives, including safety, passenger comfort and efficient use of road capacity. The main difference between this work and the ones cited lies in the consideration of the effect of some geometrical characteristics of the road, specifically the curvature of the road, while driving.

The rest of the paper is structured as follows. Section 2 presents the vehicle dynamics, which is the basis for the path following model. Section 3 describes the proposed intelligent deep reinforcement learning system that provides longitudinal and lateral control. Results are discussed in Sect. 4. Conclusions and future works end the paper.

2   Vehicle Dynamics Based on the Influence of Road Geometry

The vehicle is affected by forces that determine its dynamics during its movement. The geometry of the road is designed to allow vehicles to move with a certain degree of safety and comfort, but the vehicle is implicitly affected by the forces exerted on it due to the geometry of the road. A critical point in driving is turning in a curve; if a vehicle is travelling at too high a speed when cornering, the forces on vehicle produce unsafe and uncomfortable accelerations. The acceleration which is measured in the moving direction of the vehicle is the longitudinal acceleration, which is the acceleration parallel to the linear velocity. The acceleration measured in the rotational vehicle direction is the lateral acceleration. Acceleration due to the road is determined as follow [19]:

$$a_{road} = g(\rho + f_t) \tag{1}$$

where a_{road} (m/s^2), is the critical acceleration due to road geometry influence, g (m/s^2) is the acceleration of gravity, ρ (m) is the road cross slope and f_t is the maximum transversal friction mobilized coefficient. In order to maintain safety and comfort, this acceleration a_{road} is the limiting acceleration for a horizontal curve. Independently of the cross slope and the maximum mobilized coefficient of friction, a_{road} can be determined as follow [20]:

$$a_{road} = |\omega| \cdot v_l \tag{2}$$

where ω (rad/s) is the yaw rate and v_l (m/s) is the vehicle linear speed.

According to [19], the driver's perceived lateral acceleration due to unsafe driving behavior is:

$$a_p = |a_{lat}| - a_{road} \tag{3}$$

where a_p (m/s^2) is the driver perceived acceleration and a_{lat} (m/s^2) is the lateral acceleration. This acceleration corresponds to the "feeling" of driving due to the influence of the road geometry.

On this basis, it is possible to use the simplified Ackermann model of a vehicle [19], where the radius of curvature of the path, the wheelbase of the vehicle and the angle of the front wheel are the parameters used to define it. In fact, it has been found that when a vehicle is cornering, the speed of the vehicle is higher, so the centrifugal force of the vehicle on the road is also higher.

To describe the forces acting on the vehicle, the steering angle is defined as the angle between the front of the vehicle and the direction of the turning wheel:

$$\delta = tan^{-1}\left(W/R\right) \tag{4}$$

where δ (radians), is the steering angle, W is wheelbase (m) and R (m), is the radius of curvature.

The Ackermann yaw rate (AYR) is the theoretical ideal. This would be the yaw rate that would occur without lateral slippage of the tire. The AYR would be strictly a function of wheelbase, steering angle and speed and is defined as [21]:

$$AYR = \frac{v_l \cdot \tan(\delta)}{W} \tag{5}$$

where AYR (degree/s) is idealized yaw rate, v_l (m/s) is the linear velocity.

Understeer (*US*) is a phenomenon where the actual yaw of the vehicle is less than what it should theoretically be induced by the position of the front wheels. In this case, the front of the vehicle tends to run out the curve on the outside. This is mainly due to the inertia of the vehicle entering in a curve at too high a speed but can also be caused by poor quality of front tires or a slippery road surface. Considering AYR and the yaw rate, *US* is defined [19]:

$$US = \frac{AYR}{\omega} \tag{6}$$

where ω (degree/s) is the yaw rate. Understeer is present if US > 1.

Oversteer (*OS*) is the phenomenon of rear axle skidding that can occur in a vehicle when attempting to negotiate a curve or when it is already turning. This occurs when the rear of the vehicle tries to overtake the front. Then, if US < 1 it means oversteering.

The side slip or lateral deviation (e_1) is defined as the distance (m) between the center of gravity of the vehicle and the nearest point on the desired path, while the relative yaw angle (e_2) (rad) is the angle between the center line of the vehicle and the tangent to the desired path [19].

3 Path Following System Using Deep Reinforcement Learning

The deep reinforcement learning path following system here proposed is implemented considering the road curvature effect. The road geometry effect is obtained from measured features in the vehicle, taking into account longitudinal and lateral forces through longitudinal and lateral acceleration measurements, yaw and steering angle readings.

The characterization of the driving style when approaching a curve is based on the following consideration. If the current turning speed is too high, the lateral acceleration will be high, resulting in poor vehicle maneuverability. Indeed, the perceived lateral acceleration, which assesses the driver's sensation while driving, will be perceptible, therefore the road curvature effect is extracted indirectly through the vehicle dynamics using of the longitudinal and lateral acceleration, and yaw rate. On the order hand, if the turning speed is high, the understeer phenomena during the driving is presented, the steering angle must be kept in a certain range so as not to produce a skid of the rear of the vehicle, that is, producing oversteer or on the contrary, producing understeer when the current vehicle turn is less than 1, that theoretically should induce the position of the front wheels.

Thus, from the characteristics measured from the vehicle dynamics (Table 1) it is possible to obtain the acceleration perceived by the user and, in this way, the road curvature effect at each curve transition.

Deep reinforcement learning with the autonomous vehicle is applied using the Matlab/Simulink tool. The environment consists in a 3-DOF model for the ego vehicle and a simple longitudinal model for the lead vehicle. The aim of the training is to get the ego car to travel at a reference speed while maintaining a safe distance from the lead car by controlling the longitudinal acceleration, never exceeding the speed of the lead car and also keeping the ego car centered in its lane by controlling the steering angle of the vehicle. The longitudinal controller takes into account the interaction of the ego-vehicle

Table 1. Measured variables of DRL system.

Variables	Descriptions	Units
a_{long}	Longitudinal acceleration	m/s^2
a_{lat}	Lateral acceleration	m/s^2
a_p	Lateral perceived acceleration	m/s^2
ω	Yaw rate	rad/s
J_k	Longitudinal jerk	m/s^3
v_l	Vehicle linear speed	m/s
δ	Steering angle	rad/s
e_1	Lateral deviation	m
e_2	Yaw angle	rad

with ahead vehicles, while the lateral controller only takes into account the elements that affect the lateral movement of the ego-vehicle.

The interaction of ego car and lead car (vehicle ahead) is defined as follows. If the relative distance is less than the safety distance, vehicle follows the minimum of the ahead vehicle's speed and the set vref. In this way, the vehicle keeps a certain distance from the vehicle ahead. If the relative distance is greater than the safety distance, the vehicle follows the set vref. Variable road curvature for a more realistic approach is implemented. Figure 1 shows the proposed system and the environment.

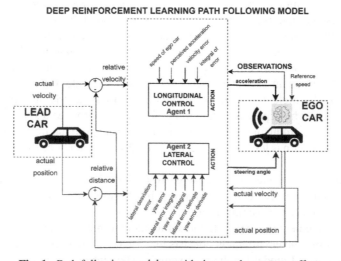

Fig. 1. Path following model considering road curvature effect.

In this paper, deep learning is used to train policies using the DDPG agent and the DQN agent, allowing them to interact with an environment in which the vehicle is moving. These policies are used to implement the longitudinal acceleration and steering angle control systems. The Simulink platform is used to evaluate the DDPG and DQN algorithms, test them with parameter settings, and monitor training progress.

The ECE cycle is an urban or interurban cycle, also known as a UDC. It is designed to represent driving conditions. It is characterized by low vehicle speed, low engine load and low exhaust temperature. The ECE cycle is chosen as the reference cycle to simulate the road test of light commercial vehicles. The standard ECE driving cycle consists of several phases characterized by acceleration, constant speed and deceleration [21]. For this work, two ECE profiles have been implemented to evaluate the performance of path following model proposed (Fig. 2).

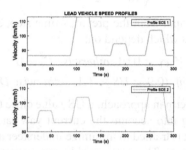

Fig. 2. ECE cycle used in this paper.

3.1 Vehicle Longitudinal Control Using DDPG Agent

The longitudinal control is a DDPG agent. The reward for observations and actions is estimated by the DDPG using a representation of the critical value function, and it selects the actions applying a representation of the actor's policy. The observations from the environment are the longitudinal measurements: the ego car longitudinal velocity, the velocity error e_v, that is, the difference between reference speed of ego car and ego car linear speed, its integral, lateral perceived acceleration and longitudinal jerk. The action signal consists of continuous acceleration values between -3 and 2 m/s^2. The reward r_t is obtained at every time t as follows (7):

$$r(t) = -\left(\frac{e_v^2}{100} + \frac{a_{(t-1)}^2}{10} + \frac{a_{p(t-1)}^2}{10} + \frac{j_{k(t-1)}^2}{10} \right) + C_t + D_t \tag{7}$$

where, e_v is error speed (between lead and ego car), $a_{(t-1)}$ is the longitudinal acceleration input from the previous time step, $a_{p(t-1)}$ is the lateral perceived acceleration, $j_{k(t-1)}$ is the longitudinal jerk to measure sudden changes in longitudinal acceleration, and C and D are constants which depend on:

$$C_t = 1 \; if \; e_v < 0.1, otherwise \; C_t = 0$$
$$D_t = 1 \; if \; a_p < 0.25, otherwise \; D_t = 0 \tag{8}$$

The configured hyperparameters of the DDPG agent for the longitudinal control are showed in Table 2, second column.

3.2   Vehicle Lateral Control Using DQN Agent

The lateral control system is a DQN agent. The reward for observations and actions is estimated by the DQN agent using a representation of the critical value function and chooses the actions applying a representation of the actor's policy. The environmental observations containing the lateral measurements are the lateral deviation e_1, relative yaw angle e_2, their derivatives and their integrals. The action signal consists of steering angle actions which take values from -0.5 to 0.5 (rad).

The reward r_t is obtained at every time t as follows (9):

$$r(t) = -\left(\frac{e_1^2}{10} + \frac{s_{t-1}^2}{2}\right) + 2(C_t + D_t) \tag{9}$$

where, s_{t-1} is the steering input from the previous time step, e_1 is the lateral deviation and C_t and D_t are constants which depend on:

$$C_t = 1 \; if \; e_1 < 0.01, \; otherwise \; C_t = 0$$
$$D_t = 1 \; if \; (0.9 < US < 1.1), \; otherwise \; D_t = 0 \tag{10}$$

On the basis of the Ackerman approach, a US value close to 1 will result in the yaw motion being stable, taking into account the current yaw rate and the geometric yaw rate. In this way, the system is trained to minimize understeer and oversteer, and to keep lateral deviation to a minimum. The configured hyperparameters of the DQN agent for lateral control are showed in Table 2, third column.

Table 2. Training DDPG and DQN agents hyperparameters and obtained reward.

	DDPG	DQN
Learning rate	0.001	0.001
Gradient threshold method	L2 norm	L2 norm
Minibatch size	64	64
Discount factor	0.99	0.99
Simulation duration	60 s	60s
Sample time	0.1 s	0.1s
Max. Episodes	2500	2500
Stop reward values	480	1200
Average reward	550.21	1204.65
Total number of steps	172	172

4   Results and Discussion

The road user's experience of the road, both in terms of comfort and safety, depends to a large extent on the road conditions. Thus, the geometry of a road has a significant impact on the safety or perception of driving.

In the simulation experiments, the speed obtained with the path following system is shown along with other road characteristics. The obtained speed considers the real conditions of the road geometry by means variable road curvature. The training time of DDPG and DQN agents is high, as for each experiment the simulations lasted more than one hour each. The characteristics of the computer used are IntelCore i7 1,2 GHz processor with 8 Gb RAM.

The following figures show the results obtained for different ECE profiles, vehicle longitudinal readings (Fig. 3 and Fig. 5) and vehicle lateral readings (Fig. 4 and Fig. 6). In each figure, the upper graph shows the ego vehicle speed (red), lead vehicle (orange) and v_{ref} of ego vehicle (blue) in km/h. The second graph shows the safe distance and relative distance between ego vehicle and vehicle ahead in meters. The third graph represents the instantaneous longitudinal acceleration (m/s^2); the fourth graph shows lateral perceived acceleration (m/s^2). Bottom graph shows the vehicle jerk (m/s^3). The jerk or jolt is the rate at which an object's acceleration changes with respect to time. Therefore, it is important to avoid sudden jerking of the vehicle to improve comfort.

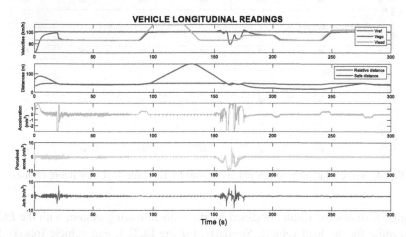

Fig. 3. Vehicle longitudinal readings obtained from ECE profile 1. (Color figure online)

Figure 3 represents the results obtained by the trajectory tracking system with the ECE 1 speed profile for the lead vehicle, taking into account the longitudinal movement of the vehicle. The first graph shows the speed of the ego vehicle (km/h), the reference speed v_{ref} to the ego vehicle and the speed of the lead vehicle. The ego vehicle increases its speed to reach the reference speed until it matches the speed of the lead vehicle if the speed is lower than v_{ref}. The 2nd graph shows the relative distance between the vehicles (m). The distance will increase if the speed of the vehicle in front is higher than that of the ego vehicle. Longitudinal acceleration (m/s^2) values and perceived lateral acceleration (m/s^2) are shown in the 3rd and 4th graphs, respectively. If the curvature of the road increases, the radius of curvature is smaller, therefore there are changes in longitudinal acceleration and jerk to reduce or increase the ego speed to adapt its speed to the curvature of the road. Changes in longitudinal acceleration are generally not abrupt, and if there are sudden changes, they occur on the section of the road where the curvature increases. In addition, the perceived lateral acceleration remains within the range of −0.5 to 0.5 m/s², which makes driving comfortable and pleasant [22]. As shown in the bottom graph, the jerk (m/s³) is close to zero except in the area where the curvature changes. The radius of curvature in this area is approximately 100 m.

Figure 4 shows the results obtained by the ECE 1 speed profile path following system considering the lateral readings of the vehicle obtained during the simulation. The upper graph shows the steering angle (rad/s) applied to ego vehicle to keep the vehicle centered on road. Second graph is showing yaw rate error (rad/s), that it is zero or practically zero. The 3rd graph represents the lateral deviation of ego vehicle (m). Bottom graph shows road curvature (m⁻¹). Typically, changes in these signals occur from the time the vehicle starts until it is moving smoothly and in the area where the radius of curvature is small.

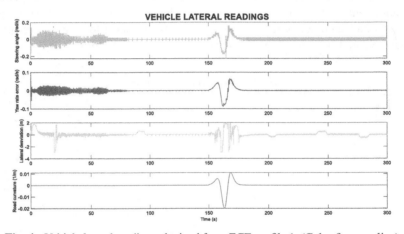

Fig. 4. Vehicle lateral readings obtained from ECE profile 1. (Color figure online)

Figure 5 shows the results obtained by the path following system with the ECE 2 speed profile for the lead vehicle. Similarly, for the ECE 1, ego vehicle follows lead vehicle easily, maintains the safety distance, adjusts it to reference speed and, if the lead vehicle's speed is lower, the ego vehicle adjusts it to the lead vehicle's speed. The most noticeable changes in acceleration and jerk are in the area of the road where the radius of curvature changes abruptly.

In addition, an adaptive longitudinal and lateral cruise control (ACC) has been implemented for comparison purposes. Figure 6 shows the results obtained by the path following system with the ECE 2 speed profile for the lead vehicle. The results are similar to the human-like DRL approach. Ego vehicle follows lead vehicle, maintains the safety distance, and the ego vehicle adjusts it to the lead vehicle speed. The jerk peaks duration is greater than with the DRL model. By contrast, under this approach the system is less sensitive to changes in curvature.

On the order hand, in [18] a DRL approach for safe and comfortable driving is proposed. The jerk values are around 10 m/s³ during accelerations and around 16–18 m/s³ in sharp decelerations in a traffic scenario. It does not consider the road curvature. In our work, there are occasional jerk spikes regardless of the sudden decelerations of the

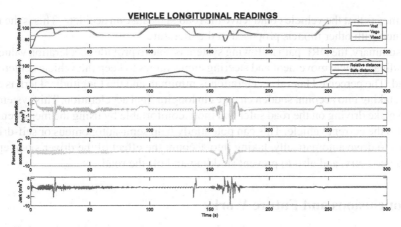

Fig. 5. Vehicle longitudinal readings obtained from ECE profile 2. (Color figure online)

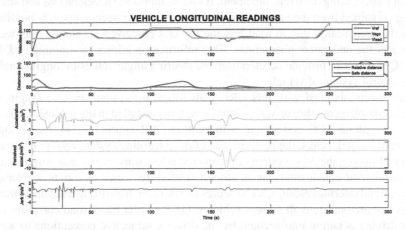

Fig. 6. Vehicle longitudinal adaptive cruise control. (Color figure online)

lead vehicle and the abrupt changes in the curvature of the road. Maximum jerk value during acceleration is 5 m/s³ and occasionally, 10 m/s³ in abrupt decelerations. The human-like perception approach can reduce the intensity and the duration of the jerk peaks (between 4 s and 5 s) when the speed of the leading vehicle decreases abruptly in the traffic scenario compared to [18].

This proves that taking into account human-like perception, it is possible to reduce the sensations that over-acceleration induces on the vehicle by the road geometry and excessive speed on turns (and hence, the centripetal force on the user). However, there may be a coasting speed (where there is no acceleration and therefore not inappropriate jerking or cornering) and the sensations due to the centripetal force cannot be avoided. So, the main way to get a comfortable driving is to avoid as much as possible this phenomenon, which is measured by the perceived acceleration, and also to avoid as much as possible the understeering and oversteering by not driving at an adequate speed, which means that the vehicle could leave the road and cause an accident. This is the main difference with other models proposed in the literature.

In summary, the DRL path following system is able to provide acceleration values for longitudinal vehicle movement and steering angle values to keep the vehicle centered on the road. The perceived lateral acceleration is minimal, and the longitudinal jerk is close to zero, taking into account sudden changes in longitudinal acceleration. This system can help to make driving on the road safer and more comfortable by using the measurements built into the current vehicle. This can potentially help semi-autonomous or self-driving vehicles to drive automatically, taking into account the effect of the driver's perception of road geometry, and also to prevent skidding and off the road.

5 Conclusions and Future Works

In this paper, an intelligent path following system has been designed considering road geometry effect using deep reinforcement. It uses as inputs the accelerations and steering readings obtained from the car sensors. Based on those measurements, it is possible to obtain the acceleration due to road and the driver's perceived acceleration as well as to consider the understeer phenomena. This information allows the training of DDPG and D-QN agents to provide acceleration and steering angle values to longitudinal and lateral control system of vehicle.

The results obtained with this DRL path following system are encouraging and useful to complement other driver assistance systems installed in the vehicle. It has been compared with an ACC system and with another DLR approach [18]. Regarding the duration of the jerk peaks, the performance of deep learning system based on geometry is better. However, the ACC system implemented is less sensitive to changing curvature.

A number of conclusions can be drawn. The system uses as inputs acceleration, gyroscope and steering readings, all measures can be taken from the inertial measurement sensors that are built into all current vehicles. On the order hand, road curvature effect during driving is taking into account by the driver's subjective perceptions to adopt a safe and comfortable driving behavior.

Future work could consider other factors that are beginning to be measured by intelligent sensors, such as drowsiness, distraction, fatigue, wheel/road interaction, weather, etc.

References

1. Paden, B., Cap, M., Yong, S.Z., et al.: A survey of motion planning and control techniques for self-driving urban vehicles. IEEE Trans. Control Syst. Technol. 1, 33–55 (2016)
2. Martín, S., Romana, M.G., Santos, M.: Fuzzy model of vehicle delay to determine the level of service of two-lane roads. Expert Syst. Appl. 54, 48–60 (2016)
3. Barreno, F., Romana, M.G., Santos, M.: Fuzzy expert system for road type identification and risk assessment of conventional two-lane roads. Expert. Syst. 39(9), e12837 (2022). https://doi.org/10.1111/exsy.12837
4. Wu, C., Yu, D., Doherty, A., Zhang, T., Kust, L., Luo, G.: An investigation of perceived vehicle speed from a driver's perspective. PLoS ONE 12(10), e0185347 (2017)

5. Barreno, F., Santos, M., Romana, M.: Abnormal driving behavior identification based on naturalistic driving data using LSTM recurrent neural networks. In: García Bringas, P., et al. SOCO 2022. Lecture Notes in Networks and Systems, vol. 531, pp. 435–443. Springer, Cham (2023). https://doi.org/10.1007/978-3-031-18050-7_42

6. Barreno, F., Santos, M., Romana, M.G.: A novel adaptive vehicle speed recommender fuzzy system for autonomous vehicles on conventional two-lane roads. Expert Syst. e13046 (2022). https://doi.org/10.1111/exsy.13046

7. Wang, J., Zhang, L., Zhang, D., Li, K.: An adaptive longitudinal driving assistance system based on driver characteristics. IEEE Trans. Intell. Transp. Syst. **14**, 1 (2013)

8. Zhu, M., Wang, X., Tarko, A., et al.: Modeling car-following behavior on urban expressways in Shanghai: a naturalistic driving study. Transp. Res. Part C: Emerg. Technol. **93**, 425–445 (2018)

9. Wang, X., Chen, M., Zhu, M., Tremont, P.: Development of a kinematic-based forward collision warning algorithm using an advanced driving simulator. IEEE Trans. Intell. Transp. Syst. **17**(9), 2583–2591 (2016)

10. Kuefler, A., Morton, J., Wheeler, T., Kochenderfer, M.: Imitating Driver Behavior with Generative Adversarial Networks. arXiv preprint arXiv:1701.06699 (2017)

11. Zhang, J., Wang, F.-Y., Wang, K., Lin, W.-H., Xu, X., Chen, C., et al.: Data-driven intelligent transportation systems: a survey. IEEE Trans. Intell. Transp. Syst. **12**(4), 1624–1639 (2011)

12. Li, Y.: Deep reinforcement learning: an overview. arXiv preprint arXiv:1701.07274 (2017)

13. Yu, A., Palefsky-Smith, R., Bedi, R.: Deep reinforcement learning for simulated autonomous vehicle control. Course Project Reports: Winter, 2016 (2016)

14. Wang, Z., Li, Y., Ma, C., Yan, X., Jiang, D.: Path-following optimal control of autonomous underwater vehicle based on deep reinforcement learning. Ocean Eng. **268**, 113407 (2023)

15. Yang, D., Zhu, L., Liu, Y., Wu, D., Ran, B.: A novel car-following control model combining machine learning and kinematics models for automated vehicles. IEEE Trans. Intell. Transp. Syst. **20**(6), 1991–2000 (2018)

16. Wang, Z., Huang, H., Tang, J., Meng, X., Hu, L.: Velocity control in car-following behavior with autonomous vehicles using reinforcement learning. Accid. Anal. Prev. **174**, 106729 (2022)

17. Zhu, M., Wang, X., Wang, Y.: Human-like autonomous car-following model with deep reinforcement learning. Transp. Res. Part C: Emerg. Technol. **97**, 348–368 (2018)

18. Selvaraj, D.C., Hegde, S., Amati, N., Deflorio, F., Chiasserini, C.F.: A deep reinforcement learning approach for efficient Safe and Comfortable Driving. Appl. Sci. **13**(9), 5272 (2023)

19. Rajamani, R.: Vehicle Dynamics and Control. Springer Science & Business Media, Berlin (2011). https://doi.org/10.1007/978-1-4614-1433-9

20. Barreno, F., Santos, M., Romana, M.: Fuzzy logic system for risk and energy efficiency estimation of driving maneuvers. In: Gude Prego, J.J., de la Puerta, J.G., García Bringas, P., Quintián, H., Corchado, E. (eds.) CISI. AISC, vol. 1400, pp. 94–104. Springer, Cham (2022). https://doi.org/10.1007/978-3-030-87872-6_10

21. Xie, C., Ogden, J.M., Quan, S., Chen, Q.: Optimal power management for fuel cell–battery full hybrid powertrain on a test station. Int. J. Electr. Power Energy Syst. **53**, 307–320 (2013)

22. De Winkel, K.N., Irmak, T., Happee, R., Shyrokau, B.: Standards for passenger comfort in automated vehicles: acceleration and jerk. Appl. Ergon. **106**, 103881 (2023)

Deep Learning

A New Hybrid CNN-LSTM for Wind Power Forecasting in Ethiopia

E. Tefera[1], M. Martínez-Ballesteros[2(✉)], A. Troncoso[3],
and F. Martínez-Álvarez[3]

[1] Department of Software Engineering, Addis Ababa Science and Technology
University, Addis Ababa, Ethiopia
ejigu.tefera@aastustudent.edu.et
[2] Department of Computer Science, University of Seville, 41012 Seville, Spain
mariamartinez@us.es
[3] Data Science and Big Data Lab, Pablo de Olavide University, 41013 Seville, Spain
{atrolor,fmaralv}@upo.es

Abstract. Renewable energies are currently experiencing promising
growth as an alternative solution to minimize the emission of pollutant
gases from the use of fossil fuels, which contribute to global warming.
To integrate these renewable energies safely with the grid system and
make the electric grid system more stable, it is vitally important to
accurately forecast the amount of wind power generated at specific wind
power generation sites and the timing of this generation. Deep learning
approaches have shown good forecasting performance for complex and
nonlinear problems, such as time series wind power data. However, further study is needed to optimize deep learning models by integrating
multiple models with hyperparameter optimization, to attain optimal
performance from these individual models. In this paper, we propose
a hybrid CNN-LSTM model for wind power forecasting in Ethiopia.
Bayesian optimization is applied to tune the hyperparameters of the individual learners, including 1D-CNN and LSTM models, before building
the hybrid CNN-LSTM model. The proposed model is tested on three
case study wind power datasets obtained from the Ethiopian Electric
Power Corporation. According to the MAE, RMSE, and MAPE evaluation metrics, the hybrid model performs significantly better than benchmark models, including ANN, RNN, BiLSTM, CNN, and LSTM models,
for all case study data.

Keywords: hybrid models · time series · renewable energies ·
forecasting

1 Introduction

Renewable energy has shown promising growth in recent years due to its sustainability, environmentally friendly nature, and abundant availability as a source of
electric energy [22]. Among various types of renewable energy, wind power has

© The Author(s), under exclusive license to Springer Nature Switzerland AG 2023
P. García Bringas et al. (Eds.): HAIS 2023, LNAI 14001, pp. 207–218, 2023.
https://doi.org/10.1007/978-3-031-40725-3_18

demonstrated remarkable growth as one of the most effective strategies to combat climate change and meet greenhouse gas emission targets in many countries. Governments and researchers strongly encourage the production and consumption of wind energy [22]. Accurately quantifying the amount of renewable energy production, particularly wind energy generation, is crucial for the safe integration of renewable energy into the grid system and to enhance efficient power grid operation [3]. However, wind power generation is inherently random, nonlinear, non-stationary, and highly intermittent, making its integration with the grid system challenging.

Despite significant renewable energy potential in Ethiopia, including hydroelectric, wind, and geothermal energy, current energy production is limited, and the energy supply falls short of rising energy consumption demands [24]. Furthermore, the absence of electric load estimation and modeling methods contributes to energy fluctuations and power interruptions that affect electric energy transmission and distribution systems [15]. As a result, energy outages and power interruptions affect all customer categories, increasing defensive expenditures due to unreliable and unstable energy supply. Therefore, accurate prediction of wind power generation can play a key role in improving the reliability and stability of the power system [7] and enable safe integration of produced wind power into the grid system [4].

Recently, deep learning has shown remarkable performance in various applications, including renewable energy forecasting, due to its ability to handle nonlinear, non-stationary, spatiotemporal data generated from energy systems. Recurrent Neural Networks (RNN), Convolutional Neural Networks (CNN), Deep Belief Networks (DBN), and Multilayer Perceptron (MLP) are among the well-known and widely used deep learning algorithms, with Long Short-Term Memory (LSTM) standing out in the context of time series forecasting [6].

To improve the accuracy of energy forecasting in the renewable energy sector, various artificial intelligence techniques have been applied. An example of this is the Bayesian optimization-based artificial neural network model developed in [19]. Additionally, the precision of short-term forecasting has been enhanced by utilizing hybrid deep learning models that integrate various neural network architectures. Several studies have shown that these hybrid models outperform single models in various applications [11,19], and [20], and have been successful in accurately predicting wind speed and evapotranspiration [7,27].

This paper aims to evaluate the effectiveness of a hybrid model of 1D-CNN and LSTM for forecasting wind power time series data in Ethiopia for the first time. The model leverages CNN's feature extraction capability from nonlinear wind power time series data and the potential of LSTM in learning high temporal time series data. The paper's contributions can be summarized as follows:

1. The optimal hyperparameters were determined using Bayesian optimization algorithm to obtain the optimal performance of the proposed model.
2. A CNN-LSTM hybrid model was developed for day-ahead wind power forecasting by using the effective feature extraction capabilities of 1D-CNN and forecast generalization of LSTM models

3. The effectiveness of a hybrid of CNN-LSTM model against base line models such as 1D-CNN, LSTM, ANN and BiLSTM is verified for wind power forecasting using the metrics of mean absolute error (MAE), root mean square error (RMSE), and mean absolute percentage error (MAPE).

2 Related Works

Industries and institutions can generate a considerable volume of data on their day-to-day operations by introducing sensor devices [18]. The energy sector, including renewable energy, is among the few that produces data on a timely basis regarding customer energy consumption, such as minute, hourly, and daily usage. Furthermore, wind farms' Supervisory Control and Data Acquisition (SCADA) systems collect data related to wind power at specified time intervals. This type of data is known as time-series data, representing a series of periodic measurements of a variable. Specifically, time series data generated from energy systems is nonlinear and non-stationary, exhibiting not only temporal correlation but also spatial patterns [8].

The energy sector, particularly in the field of renewable energy forecasting, has made significant advancements with the utilization of Artificial Intelligence (AI) methods such as machine learning and deep learning techniques [1,21]. These algorithms have been extensively used to forecast various weather parameters. Furthermore, a combination of different AI techniques has emerged as a preferred approach in recent times to develop models that perform better than individual models.

Several studies have shown that hybrid deep learning models outperform individual or single models [10]. To prove this, Goh et al. [5] investigated a hybrid of a convolutional neural network (1D-CNN) and a long short memory network (LSTM). They obtained an improvement of 16.73% for single-step prediction and 20.33% for 24-step load prediction. Additionally, [11] implemented a hybrid 1D-CNN and BiLSTM model to enhance wind speed prediction accuracy and address uncertainty modeling issues. Results indicated that the proposed hybrid approach achieved a 42% improvement over reference approaches. Another study by [9] proposed the combination of Ensemble Empirical Mode Decomposition (EEMD) and BiDLSTM system for accurate wind speed forecasting.

Furthermore, Wang et al. [25] proposed a 3-hour ahead average wind power prediction method based on a convolutional neural network. The authors in [26] introduced a deep learning approach based on a pooling long short-term memory (LSTM) based convolutional neural network to predict short- and medium-term electric consumption. Results revealed that the proposed method improved short- and medium-term load forecasting performance. Authors in [20] developed the CNN-LSTM-LightGBM-based short-term wind power prediction model by considering various environmental factors. Moreover, a hybrid deep learning model to accurately forecast the very short-term (5-min and 10-min) wind power generation of the Boco Rock wind farm in Australia was proposed by Hossain et al. [7]. However, the authors used the Harris Hawks Optimization algorithm to improve the proposed model.

Another hybrid model was introduced by J. Yin et al. [27] to forecast short-term (1–7-day lead time) evapotranspiration (ET0). The authors used a hybrid Bi-LSTM that combines BiLSTM and ANN using three meteorological data (maximum temperature, minimum temperature, and sunshine duration). The best forecast performance for short-term daily ET0 was found.

Lu et al. [14] proposed a hybrid model based on a convolutional neural network and long short-term memory network (CNN-LSTM) for short-term load forecasting (STLF). The authors noted that forecasting accuracy can be notably improved. T. Li et al. [13] introduced a hybrid CNN-LSTM model by integrating the convolution neural network (CNN) with the long short-term memory (LSTM) neural network to forecast the next 24-hour PM2.5 concentration in Beijing, China. Results indicated that the proposed multivariate CNN-LSTM model achieved the best results due to low error and shorter training time.

3   Methods

The section presents the main parts of the methodology carried out in the proposed hybrid deep learning model, the CNN-LSTM model, for wind power forecasting. The main features of the methodology are presented in Fig. 1.

In particular, a description of the selected deep learning algorithms, CNN and LSTM, used to build the hybrid model, data preprocessing, hyperparameter tuning, model training, and evaluation are described in this section. The study uses three wind power datasets generated from different wind farm sites as case study data. Each dataset is divided into training and test sets, while maintaining the order of the time series data. The first three years of data are used to build and fit the model, and the final one-year data is used to assess the model's performance. Hyperparameter tuning is performed on the training data using a k-fold cross-validation approach.

3.1   Deep Learning Models

Deep learning algorithms have emerged as one of the most widely used approaches in artificial intelligence in the last years. One of the key advantages of deep learning is its ability to automatically learn features and extract multi-level abstract representations from complex data sets, setting it apart from other machine learning models. In particular, deep learning models such as those discussed in Sect. 3.1 have demonstrated better performance in handling large and complex data, including image processing, pattern extraction, classification, and time series forecasting [12].

RNNs are a type of deep learning method that is particularly effective in handling large datasets containing temporal dependencies. RNNs can learn sequential data by recursively applying operations during the forward pass and using backpropagation through time for learning. As such, RNNs have been studied for many real-world applications that generate sequential and time series data, including speech synthesis, natural language processing, and image captioning

[17]. However, a challenge for RNNs is long-term dependency, which leads to the vanishing gradient problem as the gap between relevant information and the point where it is needed grows [17]. To address the limitations of RNNs, LSTM and Gated Recurrent Unit (GRU) techniques were introduced. These methods can retain information over long periods, allowing for processing complex and sequential data. LSTM is especially notable for its ability to handle time series forecasting. The main deep learning algorithms involved in the hybrid model CNN-LSTM, CNN and LSTM respectively, are briefly described in the following subsections.

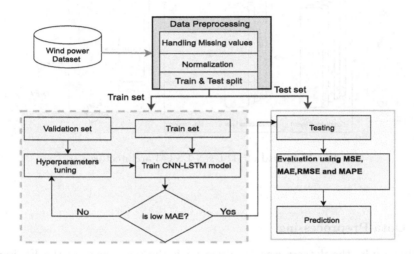

Fig. 1. General scheme of the methodology including CNN-LSTM hybrid model.

CNN. This type of deep learning algorithm mimics humans' visual perception processing systems. They have become the most widely used and extensively studied deep learning method for tasks such as computer vision, image segmentation, classification, and natural language processing, demonstrating remarkable performance [5]. Additionally, CNNs have recently gained attention from researchers as a solution for time series forecasting problems such as wind power and solar radiation [8].

LSTM. This type of deep learning algorithm was developed to solve the vanishing gradient problem in RNN by introducing an efficient memory cell that can handle long-term dependencies [2]. The memory cells in LSTM networks can retain the previous information for the next learning step. In addition to the cell unit, LSTM includes three gate structures: the input gate, forget gate, and output gate [16]. The main function of these gates in LSTM layers is to control the flow of data into and out of the cell state. The forget gate, which consists of sigmoid activation nodes, determines which previous states should be retained and which ones should be discarded [23].

This paper proposes a hybrid model that combines a one-dimensional convolutional neural network (1D-CNN) and LSTM, as shown in Fig. 2. The 1D-CNN is capable of extracting meaningful features from wind power time series data, and the LSTM network can leverage long-term dependencies among the extracted features to produce improved prediction results.

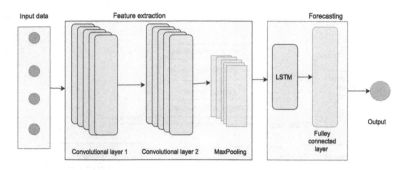

Fig. 2. Hybrid of 1D-CNN-LSTM architecture.

3.2   Data Preprocessing

For this study, the dataset was obtained with the permission of the Ethiopian Electric Power Corporation. The source dataset was collected from three groups of wind power generation plants managed by the corporation. For all groups of wind power data, the time resolution is the same ranging from 9 February 2019 to 25 July 2022, referred by Dataset 1, Dataset 2, and Dataset 3. The wind power plants from which data is generated is located just outside Adama Town in Oromia Regional State of Ethiopia, which is 95 km southeast of Addis Ababa, the capital city of Ethiopia. For further information, the dataset used to establish the findings of this paper is available at https://github.com/DataLabUPO/WindPower_HAIS23.

To improve the performance of the proposed model, we performed data preprocessing, which included handling missing values and removing duplicates. The dataset must be transformed into favorable range values for deep learning model training to effectively learn the input data. In this case, the dataset is scaled into (0,1), which will improve computation and model convergence speed. The min-max normalization method was used to transform the data into the range (0,1), as expressed by Eq. 1.

$$n = \frac{(X_0 - X_{min})}{X_{max} - X_{min}} \tag{1}$$

where n represents the normalized values of X, while X_0 represents the current value of the variable X. X_{min} and X_{max} refer to the minimum and maximum data points for the variable X in the input dataset.

3.3   Performance Evaluation

Different evaluation techniques, such as MAE (Eq. 2), RMSE (Eq. 3), MSE (Eq. 4), and MAPE (Eq. 5), have been used to determine the prediction performance of trained models.

$$MAE = \frac{1}{n} \sum_{i=1}^{n} |y - \hat{y}| \tag{2}$$

$$RMSE = \sqrt{\frac{1}{n} \sum_{i=1}^{n} \left(y - \hat{y}\right)^2} \tag{3}$$

$$MSE = \frac{1}{n} \sum_{i=1}^{n} \left(y - \hat{y}\right)^2 \tag{4}$$

$$MAPE = \frac{1}{n} \sum_{i=1}^{n} \frac{|y - \hat{y}|}{y} * 100 \tag{5}$$

where y and $\hat{y}$ represent the actual and predicted values, respectively. In addition, n represents the total number of observations used to train the model.

3.4   Analysis and Result Discussion

In order to develop the hybrid CNN-LSTM model for wind power forecasting, it is crucial to determine the optimal hyperparameters. In this study, we define the range and type of hyperparameters for each deep model including 1D-CNN and LSTM models within their respective hyperparameter spaces. The best combination of optimal hyperparameters was determined using the Bayesian optimization algorithm and some of the optimal values found for each model are not the same despite we define the same hyperparameter space and types such as learning_rate, activation function, etc. For example, hyperparameters space, parameter type, and optimal values searched for 1D-CNN and LSTM models are shown in Table 1.

After searching for the optimal parameters for each deep learning model, 1D-CNN and LSTM models were defined in intercorrelated sequence layers. In the first learning phase, the extraction of time series features was achieved using the 1D-CNN convolution layer. Learning the temporal correlation of the time series

Table 1. Hyperparameters used for the proposed hybrid CNN-LSTM model.

Model	Parameter name	Types/Range values	Optimal value selected
1D-CNN	Number of filters	$[32, 64, 128, 256]$	64
	Kernel_size	$[2, 3, 4, 5]$	3
	Dropout_rate	$[0.1, 0.2, 0.4, 0.5]$	0.1
	Activation function	$[relu, tanh, Linear]$	relu
	pool_type	$[MaxPooling1D, AveragePooling1D]$	MaxPooling1D
	n_neurons_at_dense_layer	$[20, 30, 40, 50]$	40
	Epoch	$[32, 64, 128, 260]$	64
	Batch_size	$[20, 30, 40, 50]$	40
	Learning_rate	$[0.0001, 0.001, 0.01, 0.1]$	0.001
	Optimizer	$[RMSProp, Adam, Adadalta]$	Adam
LSTM	Activation function	$[relu, tanh, Linear]$	tanh
	Dropout_rate	$[0.1, 0.2, 0.4, 0.5]$	0.1
	n_neurons_at_hidden_layer	$[20, 30, 40, 50]$	40
	Optimizer	$[RMSProp, Adam, Adadalta]$	RMSProp
	Epoch	$[32, 64, 128, 260]$	64
	Batch_size	$[20, 30, 40, 50]$	40
	Learning_rate	$[0.0001, 0.001, 0.01, 0.1]$	0.01

Table 2. Forecasting performance of deep learning models using MAE, RMSE, and MAPE metrics on training and test data.

Dataset	Model	Training			Testing		
		MAE	RMSE	MAPE (%)	MAE	RMSE	MAPE (%)
Dataset 1	ANN	0.4791	0.5453	4.531	0.5462	0.6167	2.6550
	RNN	0.0679	0.0914	1.3477	0.0818	0.1031	1.1363
	1D-CNN	0.0596	0.0774	1.3740	0.0679	0.0853	1.1737
	LSTM	0.0586	0.0792	1.2552	0.0671	0.0845	1.2552
	BiLSTM	0.0589	0.0791	1.1188	0.0655	0.0835	1.0726
	CNN-LSTM	0.0507	0.0685	1.1262	0.0634	0.0809	1.1409
Dataset 2	ANN	0.1899	0.2361	1.9730	0.1998	0.2396	1.7481
	RNN	0.0967	0.1216	1.5542	0.1051	0.1247	1.8984
	1D-CNN	0.0663	0.0900	1.0412	0.0761	0.0970	1.1553
	LSTM	0.0681	0.0922	1.0427	0.0690	0.0883	1.1358
	BiLSTM	0.0683	0.0925	1.1188	0.0693	0.0889	1.1302
	CNN-LSTM	0.0572	0.0771	1.0850	0.0678	0.0882	1.0482
Dataset 3	ANN	0.2639	0.3390	2.3053	0.1349	0.1708	1.6200
	RNN	0.1161	0.1526	1.4745	0.1135	0.1416	1.4356
	1D-CNN	0.1026	0.1336	1.3590	0.1048	0.1327	1.1482
	LSTM	0.1098	0.1434	1.4502	0.1057	0.1311	1.2454
	BiLSTM	0.1106	0.1406	1.2073	0.1006	0.1284	1.1405
	CNN-LSTM	0.0874	0.1133	1.2107	0.0991	0.1264	1.1003

data was performed in the second learning phase. Finally, the fully connected layer produced the predicted output, as defined in the last layer.

Table 2 presents the results of a day ahead wind power prediction using the hybrid deep learning model that combines 1D-CNN and LSTM models for the three wind power datasets. Using optimal hyperparameter configurations, the proposed CNN-LSTM model was compared against four individual deep learning models, including simple RNN, LSTM, 1D-CNN, and BiLSTM. Based on the evaluation results of MAE, RMSE, and MAPE presented in Table 2, it can be observed that the shallow ANN exhibited the worst performance with the highest MAE and RMSE error values of 0.4791 and 0.5451, respectively, on the training data for all three cases. Similarly, the ANN performed poorly on the test data with the largest MAE and RMSE error values of 0.5461 and 0.6167, respectively, followed by the inferior performance of the RNN models on both the training and test data compared to the rest of the deep learning models (LSTM, BiLSTM, 1D-CNN) and CNN-LSTM, as summarized in Table 2. More importantly, based on the MAE and RMSE evaluation metrics, the CNN-LSTM model exhibits the lowest error on both the training and test data for all case study datasets used in this paper. From this, we can conclude that the combination of CNN-LSTM enhanced by the hyperparameter tuning approach outperforms the single optimized deep learning models and achieves excellent performance for the non-linear and highly intermittent wind power forecasting problems.

Additionally, Fig. 3 displays the average MSE error values of all models on the three wind power datasets analyzed in this study. The results indicate that the ANN model had significantly larger error values for the MSE metric compared to the other deep learning models. The results demonstrate the capability of deep learning models in learning the nonlinear and complex wind power data as compared to the shallow ANN architecture. On the other hand, the hybridizing of deep learning LSTM and 1D-CNN models with the use of an automatic hyperparameter optimization approach yields the lowest MSE error and exhibits improved forecasting performance. Furthermore, the CNN-LSTM model exhibited the best performance on the test data, with the smallest MSE error, as depicted in Fig. 4, while the shallow ANN was the poorest model, followed by the RNN model, for all three wind power datasets analyzed.

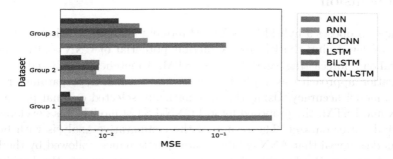

Fig. 3. MSE error on the training set for different models on three datasets.

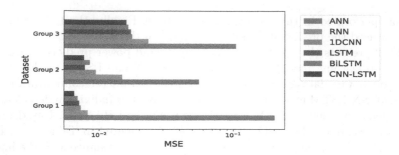

Fig. 4. MSE error on the test set for different models on three datasets.

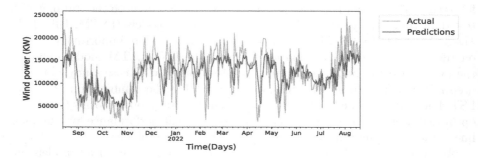

Fig. 5. Actual and predicted values for CNN-LSTM model in Dataset 1.

Figure 5 shows the predicted curve and the actual test data for Dataset 1 of daily wind power generation obtained by the CNN-LSTM model. It can be observed that the actual observation and the model output follow the same curve and the gap between the two curves is very small. Therefore, it can be concluded that the CNN-LSTM model fits the actual curve accurately. In other words, the model performed well and did not demonstrate either overestimation or underestimation on the test data.

4   Conclusion

This paper proposes a hybrid CNN-LSTM model for improved wind power forecasting by leveraging the feature extraction potential of CNN and the better temporal data forecasting capabilities of LSTM. A metaheuristic-based Bayesian optimization approach was applied to select the optimal hyperparameters that improve model accuracy. Using the automatically selected optimal parameters of CNN and LSTM, the proposed hybrid CNN-LSTM models was developed for each wind power dataset. The results of the comparative analysis with benchmark models reveal that ANN exhibits lower performance, followed by the RNN models. However, the hybrid CNN-LSTM model outperforms the benchmark methods for daily wind power forecasting. Specifically, the performance of the hybrid models are verified for each dataset compared to the single model and found significant improvements in terms of lower MAE, RMSE, and MAPE values for the three wind power datasets when using the CNN-LSTM model.

Acknowledgements. The authors would like to thank the Spanish Ministry of Science and Innovation and the Junta de Andalucía for their support within the projects PID2020-117954RB and TED2021-131311B, PYC20 RE 078 USE, PY20-00870 and UPO-138516, respectively.

References

1. Bedi, J., Toshniwal, D.: Deep learning framework to forecast electricity demand. Appl. Energy **238**, 1312–1326 (2019)
2. Bouktif, S., Fiaz, A., Ouni, A., Serhani, M.A.: Optimal deep learning LSTM model for electric load forecasting using feature selection and genetic algorithm: comparison with machine learning approaches. Energies **11**(7), 1636 (2018)
3. Buturache, A.N., Stancu, S., et al.: Wind energy prediction using machine learning. Low Carbon Econ. **12**(01), 1 (2021)
4. Duan, J., Wang, P., Ma, W., Fang, S., Hou, Z.: A novel hybrid model based on nonlinear weighted combination for short-term wind power forecasting. Int. J. Electr. Power Energy Syst. **134**, 107452 (2022)
5. Goh, H.H., et al.: Multi-convolution feature extraction and recurrent neural network dependent model for short-term load forecasting. IEEE Access **9**, 118528–118540 (2021)
6. Habtemariam, E.T., Kekeba, K., Martínez-Ballesteros, M., Martínez-Álvarez, F.: A Bayesian optimization-based LSTM model for wind power forecasting in the Adama district, Ethiopia. Energies **16**(5) (2023)
7. Hossain, M.A., Chakrabortty, R.K., Elsawah, S., Gray, E.M., Ryan, M.J.: Predicting wind power generation using hybrid deep learning with optimization. IEEE Trans. Appl. Supercond. **31**(8), 1–5 (2021)
8. Hadjout, D., Torres, J.F., Troncoso, A., Sebaa, A., Martínez-Álvarez, F.: Electricity consumption forecasting based on ensemble deep learning with application to the Algerian market. Energy **243**, 123060 (2022). https://doi.org/10.1016/j.energy.2021.123060
9. Jaseena, K., Kovoor, B.C.: EEMD-based Wind Speed Forecasting system using Bidirectional LSTM networks. In: 2021 International Conference on Computer Communication and Informatics (ICCCI), pp. 1–9. IEEE (2021)
10. Khochare, J., Rathod, J., Joshi, C., Laveti, R.N.: A short-term wind forecasting framework using ensemble learning for Indian weather stations. In: 2020 IEEE International Conference for Innovation in Technology (INOCON), pp. 1–7. IEEE (2020)
11. Kosana, V., Teeparthi, K., Madasthu, S.: Hybrid convolutional Bi-LSTM autoencoder framework for short-term wind speed prediction. Neural Comput. Appl. (2022)
12. Kumari, P., Toshniwal, D.: Deep learning models for solar irradiance forecasting: a comprehensive review. J. Clean. Prod. **318**, 128566 (2021)
13. Li, T., Hua, M., Wu, X.: A hybrid CNN-LSTM model for forecasting particulate matter (PM2.5). IEEE Access **8**, 26933–26940 (2020)

14. Lu, J., Zhang, Q., Yang, Z., Tu, M.: A hybrid model based on convolutional neural network and long short-term memory for short-term load forecasting. In: 2019 IEEE Power & Energy Society General Meeting (PESGM), pp. 1–5. IEEE (2019)
15. Meles, T.H.: Impact of power outages on households in developing countries: evidence from Ethiopia. Energy Econ. **91**, 104882 (2020)
16. Ozer, I., Efe, S.B., Ozbay, H.: A combined deep learning application for short term load forecasting. Alex. Eng. J. **60**(4), 3807–3818 (2021)
17. Paramasivan, S.K.: Deep learning based recurrent neural networks to enhance the performance of wind energy forecasting: a review. Rev. d'Intelligence Artif. **35**(1), 1–10 (2021)
18. Pérez-Chacón, R., Luna-Romera, J.M., Troncoso, A., Martínez-Álvarez, F., Riquelme, J.C.: Big data analytics for discovering electricity consumption patterns in smart cities. Energies **11**(3), 683 (2018)
19. Rahaman, H., Bashar, T.R., Munem, M., Hasib, M.H.H., Mahmud, H., Alif, A.N.: Bayesian optimization based ANN model for short term wind speed forecasting in newfoundland, Canada. In: 2020 IEEE Electric Power and Energy Conference (EPEC), pp. 1–5. IEEE (2020)
20. Ren, J., Yu, Z., Gao, G., Yu, G., Yu, J.: A CNN-LSTM-LightGBM based short-term wind power prediction method based on attention mechanism. Energy Rep. **8**, 437–443 (2022)
21. Torres, J.F., Hadjout, D., Sebaa, A., Martínez-Álvarez, F., Troncoso, A.: Deep learning for time series forecasting: a survey. Big Data **9**(1), 3–21 (2021). https://doi.org/10.1089/big.2020.0159
22. Shahid, F., Zameer, A., Muneeb, M.: A novel genetic LSTM model for wind power forecast. Energy **223**, 120069 (2021)
23. Tian, C., Ma, J., Zhang, C., Zhan, P.: A deep neural network model for short-term load forecast based on long short-term memory network and convolutional neural network. Energies **11**(12), 3493 (2018)
24. Tiruye, G.A., Besha, A.T., Mekonnen, Y.S., Benti, N.E., Gebreslase, G.A., Tufa, R.A.: Opportunities and challenges of renewable energy production in Ethiopia. Sustainability **13**(18), 10381 (2021)
25. Wang, H.K., Song, K., Cheng, Y.: A hybrid forecasting model based on CNN and informer for short-term wind power. Front. Energy Res. **9**, 1041 (2022)
26. Yang, Y., Haq, E.U., Jia, Y.: A novel deep learning approach for short and medium-term electrical load forecasting based on pooling LSTM-CNN model. In: 2020 IEEE/IAS Industrial and Commercial Power System Asia (I&CPS Asia), pp. 26–34. IEEE (2020)
27. Jiménez-Navarro, M.J., Martínez-Ballesteros, M., Brito, I.S., Martínez-Álvarez, F., Asencio-Cortés, G.: A bioinspired ensemble approach for multi-horizon reference evapotranspiration forecasting in Portugal. In: Proceedings of the ACM/SIGAPP Symposium on Applied Computing, pp. 441–448 (2023). https://doi.org/10.1145/3555776.3578634

Companion Classification Losses for Regression Problems

Aitor Sánchez-Ferrera[1]([✉])[iD] and Jose R. Dorronsoro[2,3][iD]

[1] Intelligent Systems Group, Department of Computer Science and Artificial Intelligence, University of the Basque Country UPV/EHU, Leioa, Spain
aitor.sanchezf@ehu.eus
[2] Department of Computer Engineering, Universidad Autónoma de Madrid, Madrid, Spain
[3] Inst. Ing. Conocimiento, Universidad Autónoma de Madrid, Madrid, Spain

Abstract. By their very nature, regression problems can be transformed into classification problems by discretizing their target variable. Within this perspective, in this work we investigate the possibility of improving the performance of deep machine learning models in regression scenarios through a training strategy that combines different classification and regression objectives. In particular, we train deep neural networks using the mean squared error along with categorical cross-entropy and the novel Fisher loss as companion losses. Finally, we will compare experimentally the results of these companion loss methods with the ones obtained using the standard mean squared loss.

Keywords: deep neural networks · companion losses · mean squared error · categorical crossentropy · Fisher loss · representation learning

1 Introduction

Learning the underlying structure of data is crucial to achieve good results in regression and classification tasks using machine learning methods. In this context, several studies have been conducted in the field of *representation learning*, which aims to learn good representations of data to enhance the performance of deep learning methods as supervised predictors [2]. Moreover, the advent of modern and flexible DNN environments such as Keras [6] and its Tensorflow [1] backend or PyTorch [14] has enabled the design of more complex architectures that facilitate the undertaking of supervised tasks. In this sense, the capability of creating DNNs with diverse architectures has led researchers to experiment with models which are trained by learning different tasks in parallel while they use a shared data representation. The assumption behind this methodology is close to the standard one in multitask learning, i.e., that what is learned for each task can help learning others [3].

Building upon this notion, [9] proposed the application of companion losses to improve the performance of classification models. In particular, they proved

P. García Bringas et al. (Eds.): HAIS 2023, LNAI 14001, pp. 219–230, 2023.
https://doi.org/10.1007/978-3-031-40725-3_19

that the use of training objectives that combined different classification losses (categorical cross-entropy, the Hinge loss, and a novel Fisher loss) can be beneficial in tackling classification problems. Encouraged by these promising results, [10] used companion losses to train DNN models to tackle tasks related to ordinal regression, where the class labels contain ranking information about the underlying samples [7]. In this case, they considered the cross-entropy loss, the mean-squared error, and the Fisher loss. Note that the mean-squared error is a loss function related to regression problems, so this last paper mixes classification and regression losses in its experiments. Nevertheless, there are other works that propose multi-task learning mixing classification and regression objectives in artificial neural networks. For instance, [5] combined the cross-entropy and the mean squared error for age prediction. In addition, a deep multi-task multi-channel learning framework for disease classification and clinical score regression was proposed by [12]. Finally, [13] trained their models to perform regression and classification jointly to model Alzheimer's disease diagnosis. Besides these works, other contributions extend the combination of classification and regression training objectives to random forests. Concretely, some contributions proposed to train random forests by means of a joint objective function of classification and regression for computer vision tasks, such as multi-object segmentation [11], object detection [16] and pose estimation [15].

This work follows this line of research to improve the performance of deep learning models in regression. Specifically, we propose to combine the mean-squared error with the categorical cross-entropy and the novel Fisher loss to reduce the errors of the predictions of DNNs in regression scenarios. However, unlike in the related works we have mentioned earlier, the regression datasets we consider in our experimentation only consist of a single target variable. Thus, we will have to discretize our original regression datasets into classification problems to train our models jointly for both classification and regression. More precisely, our contributions here are:

- The proposal of deep neural networks for regression that combine classification and regression losses during their training.
- A series of experiments comparing the performance of our companion models against those using only the mean-squared error during its training.
- A statistical analysis of the results obtained by the models used in the experiments.

The remaining of this paper is structured as follows. In Sect. 2 we provide an overview of the losses we consider for our companion models and present the formulation of the combined objectives. Section 3 describes the details of the experiments performed and, finally, Sect. 4 presents the conclusions of this work and the lines of research for further development of this methodology.

2   Companion Losses for Regression

We work with DNN architectures that have a sample x as input and whose output is denoted by $F(x, \mathcal{W})$, where $\mathcal{W}$ represents the parameters of the model, i.e., the set of weight matrices and bias vectors. We denote the ground truth target values as y, which are continuous in regression problems and categorical in classification problems. Moreover, the output of the last hidden layer of the networks is computed as $z = \Phi(x, \widetilde{W})$, where $\widetilde{W}$ are the weights and biases of the model up to the last hidden layer. Thus, the output of regression networks using a linear activation function is computed as $\hat{y} = Wz + B$, where W and B are the weights and bias, respectively, of the output layer. Given this, a neural network used to solve regression problems can be trained using the mean squared error loss function by minimizing

$$\ell_{mse}(\mathcal{W}) = \frac{1}{2N} \sum_{n=1}^{N} (y^n - W\Phi(x^n, \widetilde{W}) - B)^2, \tag{1}$$

where N is the total number of patterns in the training set.

In classification DNNs, unlike in regression networks, the output layer generally uses the Softmax activation function, which converts the output into a probability distribution over K possible classes. This enforces the output values to verify that $\sum_k F_k(x; \mathcal{W}) = 1$ and we assume that $P(k|x) \approx F_k(x; \mathcal{W})$. Then, we can train a DNN for classification tasks using the categorical cross-entropy, that is, minimizing the negative log likelihood:

$$\ell_{ce}(\mathcal{W}) = - \sum_{n=1}^{N} \sum_{k=0}^{K-1} y_k^n \log F_k(x^n; \mathcal{W}), \tag{2}$$

where K is the number of classes considered in the classification problem and y is a one-hot encoded vector containing the ground truth classes of the patterns in the training set. Once the model is trained, the class of an instance is determined according to $\arg\max_k F_k(x; \mathcal{W}^*)$, where $\mathcal{W}^*$ is the set of optimal weights.

Finally, we also consider a novel Fisher loss for DNNs. In the linear case, if we denote the between-class and total covariance matrices of the sample patterns as S_B and S_T respectively, together with their respective counterparts s_B and s_T for the projections $z = Ax$, the Fisher criterion maximizes the trace criterion $g(A) = \text{trace}(s_T^{-1} s_B) = \text{trace}((A^T S_T A)^{-1}(A^T S_B A))$. According to [18], this can be achieved by solving the following least squares problem

$$\min \frac{1}{2} ||y^f - XW - \mathbf{1}_N B||^2, \tag{3}$$

where W is a $d \times K$ matrix of weights, d is the dimension of the inputs, B is a $1 \times K$ bias vector and $\mathbf{1}_N$ is an all-ones vector. In addition, y^f is the Fisher target matrix, where we have $y_{nk}^f = \frac{N - N_k}{N \sqrt{N_k}}$ when the n-th row is associated with a pattern x^n corresponding to class k, and $y_{nm}^f = -\frac{\sqrt{N_m}}{N}$ for $m \neq k$, where N_k is the number of instances belonging to class k. Building on this, [8] proposed to extend the use of the Fisher loss to deep neural networks by formulating it as

$$\ell_f(y_f, \hat{y}_f) = \frac{1}{2} ||y^f - \Phi(X; \widetilde{W})W - \mathbf{1}_N B||^2, \tag{4}$$

where $\hat{y}_f$ denotes the output of the network. In this way, the Fisher loss forces the last hidden layer of the model to produce a projection of data that maximizes the Fisher criterion and, hence, concentrates the patterns belonging to the same class while pushing aside the ones from different classes.

As mentioned earlier, the goal of this work is to investigate whether the use of companion classification losses improves the performance of DNN in regression scenarios. Therefore, we will train our models using the mean squared error as the main loss of our training procedure, while using the categorical cross-entropy and the Fisher loss as auxiliary losses. As an example, following the formulation suggested in [9,10], a model that combines the mean squared error and the Fisher loss requires multiple outputs and targets to minimize the following companion loss:

$$\ell(y, y_f, \hat{y}, \hat{y}_f) = \ell_{mse}(y, \hat{y}) + \lambda \ell_f(y_f, \hat{y}_f), \tag{5}$$

where $\hat{y}$ and $\hat{y}_f$ are the predictions for minimizing the MSE and the Fisher loss, respectively, and λ is a hyperparameter that must be appropriately chosen and represents the weight of the Fisher companion loss in the general training objective of the model. Note that the Fisher loss in this case is only used to learn a good representation of data that may improve the performance of the DNN in regression problems, i.e., minimizing the scoring function of the model when solving a regression problem. Finally, and although our companion models will have several output values, we will consider only as the predictions of the model the single outputs corresponding to the mean squared error predictor.

3   Experimental Results

In this section we describe the design of the proposed models, report the datasets we will use and the strategies to transform them into classification problems, present the proposed experimental methodology, and describe the results along with a final brief discussion in this regard.

3.1   Models Proposed

We will consider three different models based on different combinations of the loss functions described in Sect. 2. Specifically, the configurations of the models proposed are the following:

- mse: the model uses a single linear output and the mean squared error loss function. The predictions are equal to the unique output of the model.
- mse_ce: the model uses two different outputs. The first one is linear and it is used to minimize the mean squared error loss, while the second one corresponds to the result of the softmax activation function and it minimizes the categorical cross-entropy loss. The predictions are again equal to the linear output.

Table 1. Training and (when available) test patterns and number of features.

	n. patterns train	n. patterns test	dimension
abalone	4177	–	8
bodyfat	252	–	14
cadata	20640	–	8
cpusmall	8192	–	12
housing	506	–	13
mg	1385	–	6
mpg	392	–	7
sotavento	17544	8760	200
space_ga	3107	–	6

Table 2. Discretization method used for the discretization of the original regression problems and number of classes considered.

	discretization method	n. classes considered
abalone	automatic	$K = 2, K = 3, K = 4, K = 5$
bodyfat	automatic	$K = 2, K = 3, K = 4, K = 5$
cadata	automatic	$K = 2, K = 3, K = 4, K = 5$
cpusmall	automatic	$K = 2, K = 3, K = 4, K = 5$
housing	manual	$K = 4, K = 5$
mg	automatic	$K = 2, K = 3, K = 4, K = 5$
mpg	automatic	$K = 2, K = 3, K = 4, K = 5$
sotavento	manual	$K = 3, K = 4$
space_ga	automatic	$K = 2, K = 3, K = 4, K = 5$

– mse_fisher: the model uses two linear outputs, the first one to minimize the mean squared error and the second one corresponding to the minimization of the Fisher loss. The predictions are once more equal to the first output of the model.

3.2   Datasets and Their Discretizations

We will be using nine different datasets, concretely abalone, bodyfat, cadata, cpusmall, housing, mg, mpg, sotavento and space_ga. All have been taken from the LIBSVM data repository [4], except for Sotavento, which was provided by the UAM–ADIC Chair for Data Science and Machine Learning. Table 1 shows the statistics of the datasets, including their training and, when available, test sample sizes and dimensions.

As described before, we will use the categorical cross-entropy and the Fisher loss as companion losses in our proposed companion models. Since these two functions correspond to classification contexts, we need to transform the original regression problems into classification ones. In our case, we will perform this transformation by discretizing the target variables of our datasets. The goal of this procedure is to group the instances into different classes based on their target values. Note that we can define multiple classification problems from the same regression problem, depending on the number of artificial classes we want to consider. Thus, the resulting number of classes K of the generated classification problems can be considered a hyperparameter that must be adjusted during the experimentation phase of this paper.

1. The manual definition of the classes according to the context of the target and,
2. The automatic definition of the classes according to a statistical criterion.

In the first method, the classes of the instances are set by analyzing the information (e.g., range and context) of the target variables. This has been the procedure to discretize the housing and sotavento datasets. More precisely, the target values in the housing dataset describe house prices and these are delimited withing the range $[5, 50]$, so we have considered two discretizations based on using $K = 4$ and $K = 5$ classes and establishing the following categories:

- Categories when $K = 4$: "very low" ($[5, 20)$), "low" ($[20, 30)$), "high" ($[30, 40)$), and "very high" ($[40, 50]$).
- Categories when $K = 5$: "very low" ($[5, 10)$), "low" ($[10, 20)$), "normal" ($[20, 30)$), "high" ($[30, 40)$) and "very high" ($[40, 50]$).

Similarly, the target values in sotavento represent the production of the electriticy generated by the Sotavento wind farm normalized to the range $[0, 1]$. Thus, in this case we have considered two discretizations based on $K = 3$ and $K = 4$ classes establishing the following categories:

- Categories when $K = 3$: "low" ($[0, 0.3)$), "normal" ($[0.3, 0.6)$) and "high" ($[0.6, 1]$).
- Categories when $K = 4$: "very low" ($[0, 0.2)$), "low" ($[0.2, 0.4)$), "normal" ($[0.4, 0.6)$) and "high" ($[0.6, 1]$).

In the second method, we set the classes of the instances by dividing their ranges according to the percentiles of the target variables. It is clear that the manual approach to transform the original regression problems into classification problems is more expensive, since special knowledge about the problem must be used. Table 2 describes the method used for each transformation and the number of classes considered in the generated classification problems.

3.3 Experimental Methodology

The models considered for the experimentation include an L_2 regularization term that involves the use of an α hyperparameter whose optimal value must be found. Moreover, the models that use multiple losses have an additional hyperparameter λ that represents the weight of the companion losses in their training objectives.

Finally, as stated in Sect. 3.2, we propose different discretizations of the original regression problems for each of the considered datasets, which entails another additional hyperparameter K representing the number of classes of the generated classification problems in the case of the companion models.

All in all, we have up to three hyperparameters to fix in our experiments, which are adjusted using a 5-fold cross-validation (CV) grid search. In particular, the α values will be of the form 10^k, with k in the range $-5 \leq k \leq 2$. Similarly, we consider λ values within the range $[0, 1]$, as we restrict the companion losses not to have a higher weight than the main mean-squared error loss. Thus, to find the optimal λ, we will examine values of the form $0.05 * k$, with k now in the range $0 \leq k \leq 20$. Finally, we find the optimal K among the discretizations presented in Table 2. In this way, we will find the optimal values α^*, λ^* and K^* for each of the hyperparameters of the models considered.

With respect to the evaluation of the models, we will test their performance by the following procedure:

1. We generate 5-fold cross-validated predictions estimates five times for each of the input data points using different seeds from the ones we use during hyperparametrization.
2. We compute the averages of these five predictions.
3. We finally compute the mean absolute error between these average predictions and the ground truth values of each problem

Remember that in the Sotavento dataset we have different data samples for training and test, namely, the years 2016 and 2017 for train and validation, and 2018 for test. In that case, we will use a 2-fold CV grid search procedure jointly on data from 2016 and 2017 to find the optimal α^*, λ^* and K^* hyperparameters. Once set these optimal values, we will fit the models five times in the training set using different seeds for weight initialization and minibatch handling, generate their predictions per each data point in the test set and compute the mean absolute error among their averages and the ground truth values.

3.4   Results and Discussion

We analyze now the results for each of the datasets considered. Note that we define three different architectures for our artificial neural networks based on the use of one/two (based on the complexity of the problem, one for cadata, cpusmall, housing, mg, mpg, and space_ga, while two for abalone, bodyfat, and sotavento), three and five hidden layers. Tables 3, 4 and 5 show the MAE of the predictions of the optimal models for the one/two, three and five hidden-layer architectures, respectively. The last column of each table contains the p-values obtained by the Wilcoxon signed rank test [17] when comparing the absolute errors of the mse model and the ones generated by the companion model that obtained the lowest errors among the mse_ce and mse_fisher models. Finally, smaller values are highlighted in boldface when the absolute error distributions of the mse and the best companion model are statistically different at the $p = 0.10$ level or below.

Table 3. Mean absolute errors and p values for mse, mse_ce and mse_fisher models with one-two (depending on the dataset) hidden layers.

	mse	mse_ce	mse_fisher	p-value
abalone	**1.458**	1.463	1.466	**0.05**
bodyfat ($\times 10^2$)	0.107	0.107	0.107	1.00
cadata ($/10^4$)	**3.507**	3.519	3.525	**0.05**
cpusmall	2.023	2.023	2.044	1.00
housing	2.065	2.065	2.061	0.80
mg ($\times 10^2$)	8.981	**8.911**	8.996	**0.03**
mpg	1.869	1.891	1.870	0.80
sotavento ($\times 10^2$)	6.616	6.678	**6.541**	**0.00**
Space_ga ($\times 10^2$)	7.442	7.442	7.462	1.00

Table 4. Mean absolute errors and p values for mse, mse_ce and mse_fisher models with three hidden layers.

	mse	mse_ce	mse_fisher	p-value
abalone	1.463	1.466	1.460	0.69
bodyfat ($\times 10^2$)	0.113	0.113	0.133	1.00
cadata ($/10^4$)	3.343	3.354	**3.239**	**0.00**
cpusmall	2.025	2.025	2.029	1.00
housing	2.085	2.056	**1.978**	**0.01**
mg ($\times 10^2$)	9.197	9.100	9.120	0.40
mpg	1.899	1.899	1.908	1.00
sotavento ($\times 10^2$)	6.698	**6.639**	6.842	**0.00**
space_ga ($\times 10^2$)	7.044	7.107	7.117	0.40

Table 5. Mean absolute errors and p values for mse, mse_ce and mse_fisher models with five hidden layers.

	mse	mse_ce	mse_fisher	p-value
abalone	1.462	1.467	1.457	0.18
bodyfat ($\times 10^2$)	0.122	0.122	0.120	0.59
cadata ($/10^4$)	3.264	**3.165**	3.225	**0.00**
cpusmall	2.017	2.017	2.050	1.00
housing	2.080	2.080	**1.970**	**0.06**
mg ($\times 10^2$)	9.281	**9.155**	9.172	**0.07**
mpg	1.916	1.957	1.986	0.21
sotavento ($\times 10^2$)	6.786	**6.528**	6.761	**0.00**
space_ga ($\times 10^2$)	**6.978**	7.169	7.149	**0.02**

Among the models with one and two hidden layers, we can reject the null hypotheses at level $p = 0.05$ level in favor of the mse network when comparing it to our companion models in the abalone and cadata datasets. However, our companion models outperform the mean-squared error-based model in the mg (in the case of mse_ce) and sotavento (in the case of mse_fisher) regression problems. Regarding the errors given by the models that use three hidden layers, with a 1% significance level, the mse_fisher is better than the mse when tackling the cadata and housing problems. Moreover, the mse_ce outperforms the sotavento problem with a 0% significance. Finally, when using five hidden layers, mse produces lower errors in the space_ga dataset with a 2% significance, while the mse_ce network outperforms the cadata and sotavento problems with p values below 0.005. Furthermore, we can reject the null hypothesis in favor for the mse_fisher and mse_ce models against the mse in housing and mg, respectively, but now with a 10% significance. Model differences do not appear to be significative in all other cases not mentioned above.

Note that there are some cases where the errors generated by the mse model and our companion networks are exactly the same. This is because the CV procedure found $\lambda = 0$ as the optimal hyperparameter value in our companion models. As a result, since λ represents the weight of the companion loss of our combined models, when $\lambda = 0$ we obtain models that perform exactly the same as the mse network. An example of this can be seen in Table 3, where the three models get the same errors for the bodyfat problem. Finally, notice that the mse model can still produce lower errors than a companion model even when the training CV procedure sets $\lambda > 0$, since the latter may have a lower generalization ability. All in all, the models trained using only the mean-squared error perform similar to the companion models when using few hidden layers. Nevertheless, the use of deeper architectures led to a slightly better performance of the networks that combine regression and classification objectives to address regression problems.

Finally, for a more concise discussion, Table 6 depicts a brief summary of the experiments that we have carried out in this work. Specifically, to make an objective comparison among the models considered, we have gathered the results of the experiments in which the mse achieved its lowest errors; in other words, we will consider the best mse architectures against the competing mse_ce and mse_fisher models with the same architecture, giving thus a slight edge to the mean squared error based models. In this regard, the mse network outperforms the companion models rejecting the null hypothesis of the Wilcoxon signed rank test in two out of nine experiments. Conversely, the mse_ce model shows a better performance in three. Finally, in the remaining four experiments the null hypotheses cannot be rejected since $p > 0.10$, so we conclude that the corresponding models give similar results.

Table 6. Mean absolute errors and p values for `mse`, `mse_ce` and `mse_fisher` models using the optimal architecture for the `mse` network. Smaller values in bold face when absolute error distributions of the mse and the best companion model are statistically different.

	n_hidden_layers	mse	mse_ce	mse_fisher	p-value
abalone	2	**1.458**	1.463	1.466	**0.05**
bodyfat ($\times 10^2$)	2	0.107	0.107	0.107	1.00
cadata ($/10^4$)	5	3.264	**3.165**	3.225	**0.00**
cpusmall	5	2.017	2.017	2.05	1.00
housing	2	2.065	2.065	2.061	0.80
mg ($\times 10^2$)	1	8.981	**8.911**	8.996	**0.03**
mpg	1	1.869	1.891	1.870	0.80
sotavento ($\times 10^2$)	5	6.786	**6.528**	6.761	**0.00**
space_ga ($\times 10^2$)	5	**6.987**	7.169	7.149	**0.02**

4   Conclusions and Further Work

In this work we have proposed the use of classification losses (i.e., the categorical cross-entropy and the novel Fisher loss) as companion objectives for neural networks to tackle regression problems. Our motivation for this is that previous studies showed that the combination of classification and regression training objectives improved the performance of machine learning models in different tasks in the field of supervised learning.

Overall, we have carried out 27 experiments (taking into account that we have used three losses for each of the datasets considered) in which we have compared the performance of neural networks trained using only the mean-squared error against models that use companion classification losses during their training. In a brief summary, the `mse` model outperformed in three out of 27 experiments, while the companion models got better results in nine out of 27. Finally, in the rest of experiments the results were similar, as the error distributions were not significantly different. This allows us to conclude that using companion classification losses for regression problems may be useful depending on the problems that we want to tackle. Also, we have applied manual (in the case of `housing` and `sotavento` datasets) and automatic methods (in the remaining problems) for discretizing regression problems in order to employ our companion models. In this regard, the results show that both strategies can be useful for implementing the use of companion losses in deep neural networks.

As lines for future work, we propose to extend this methodology to other companion classification losses. In this work we have only considered the categorical cross-entropy and the Fisher loss. However, there are other functions, such as the Hinge loss, that may lead to an improvement of the representations learned for regression problems. Additionally, it would also be interesting to explore the design of a criterion to find optimal discretizations that improve our companion models. Another point of interest would be to extend the search space of the λ hyperparameter, which represents the weight of the companion losses in the general training objective of our models. In this work we have limited its values within the range $[0, 1]$, but we think that letting this hyperparameter to take values bigger than 1 may be benefitial for our companion models, since there were some experiments in which the optimal λ value was found to be $\lambda = 1.0$, hinting that possibly better results could be obtained using larger λ ranges.

Apart from that, we point out that in this work we have used the mean absolute error between the regression targets and outputs as the scoring function in order to choose the optimal hyperparameters of our models; in other words, when choosing these optimal hyperparameters we have not considered the performance of the classification component of our companion models. This suggests that, alternatively, it would be valuable to try to use other scorings that mix a regression criterion with a measure that takes into account the classification performance of our companion models, as this may lead to better results. We are currently pursuing these lines of work as well as other related venues in order to improve the use of companion models for regression.

Acknowledgments. The authors acknowledge financial support from the European Regional Development Fund and the Spanish State Research Agency of the Ministry of Economy, Industry, and Competitiveness under the project PID2019-106827GB-I00. They also thank the support of the UAM–ADIC Chair for Data Science and Machine Learning and gratefully acknowledge the use of the facilities of Centro de Computación Científica (CCC) at UAM. They finally acknowledge the financial support of the Department of Education of the Basque Government under the grant PRE-2022-1-0103.

References

1. Abadi, M., et al.: TensorFlow: large-scale machine learning on heterogeneous systems (2015). https://www.tensorflow.org/, software available from tensorflow.org
2. Bengio, Y., Courville, A., Vincent, P.: Representation learning: a review and new perspectives. IEEE Trans. Pattern Anal. Mach. Intell. **35**(8), 1798–1828 (2013)
3. Caruana, R.: Multitask learning. Mach. Learn. **28**, 41–75 (1997)
4. Chang, C.C., Lin, C.J.: LIBSVM: a library for support vector machines. ACM Trans. Intell. Syst. Technol. (TIST) **2**(3), 1–27 (2011)
5. Chen, J., Cheng, L., Yang, X., Liang, J., Quan, B., Li, S.: Joint learning with both classification and regression models for age prediction. In: Journal of Physics: Conference Series, vol. 1168, p. 032016. IOP Publishing (2019)
6. Chollet, F., et al.: Keras (2015). https://github.com/fchollet/keras
7. Christensen, R.H.B.: ordinal-regression models for ordinal data. R Packag. Version **28**, 2015 (2015)
8. Diaz-Vico, D., Dorronsoro, J.R.: Deep least squares fisher discriminant analysis. IEEE Trans. Neural Netw. Learn. Syst. **31**(8), 2752–2763 (2019)
9. Díaz-Vico, D., Fernández, A., Dorronsoro, J.R.: Companion losses for deep neural networks. In: Sanjurjo González, H., Pastor López, I., García Bringas, P., Quintián, H., Corchado, E. (eds.) HAIS 2021. LNCS (LNAI), vol. 12886, pp. 538–549. Springer, Cham (2021). https://doi.org/10.1007/978-3-030-86271-8_45

10. Díaz-Vico, D., Fernández, A., Dorronsoro, J.R.: Companion losses for ordinal regression. In: Garcia Bringas, P., et al. (eds.) Hybrid Artificial Intelligent Systems. HAIS 2022. LNCS, vol. 13469, pp. 211–222. Springer, Cham (2022). https://doi.org/10.1007/978-3-031-15471-3_19

11. Glocker, B., Pauly, O., Konukoglu, E., Criminisi, A.: Joint classification-regression forests for spatially structured multi-object segmentation. In: Fitzgibbon, A., Lazebnik, S., Perona, P., Sato, Y., Schmid, C. (eds.) ECCV 2012. LNCS, vol. 7575, pp. 870–881. Springer, Heidelberg (2012). https://doi.org/10.1007/978-3-642-33765-9_62

12. Liu, M., Zhang, J., Adeli, E., Shen, D.: Deep multi-task multi-channel learning for joint classification and regression of brain status. In: Descoteaux, M., Maier-Hein, L., Franz, A., Jannin, P., Collins, D.L., Duchesne, S. (eds.) MICCAI 2017. LNCS, vol. 10435, pp. 3–11. Springer, Cham (2017). https://doi.org/10.1007/978-3-319-66179-7_1

13. Liu, M., Zhang, J., Adeli, E., Shen, D.: Joint classification and regression via deep multi-task multi-channel learning for Alzheimer's disease diagnosis. IEEE Trans. Biomed. Eng. **66**(5), 1195–1206 (2018)

14. Paszke, A., et al.: Automatic differentiation in pytorch. In: Advances in Neural Information Processing Systems, vol. 32, pp. 8024–8035. Curran Associates, Inc. (2019)

15. Schulter, S., Leistner, C., Wohlhart, P., Roth, P.M., Bischof, H.: Alternating regression forests for object detection and pose estimation. In: Proceedings of the IEEE International Conference on Computer Vision (ICCV), December 2013

16. Schulter, S., Leistner, C., Wohlhart, P., Roth, P.M., Bischof, H.: Accurate object detection with joint classification-regression random forests. In: Proceedings of the IEEE Conference on Computer Vision and Pattern Recognition (CVPR), June 2014

17. Wilcoxon, F.: Individual comparisons by ranking methods. Biom. Bull. **1**(6), 80–83 (1945). https://www.jstor.org/stable/3001968

18. Zhang, Z., Dai, G., Xu, C., Jordan, M.I.: Regularized discriminant analysis, ridge regression and beyond. J. Mach. Learn. Res. **11**, 2199–2228 (2010)

Analysis of Transformer Model Applications

M. I. Cabrera-Bermejo[1]([✉]) [iD], M. J. Del Jesus[1] [iD], A. J. Rivera[1] [iD],
D. Elizondo[2] [iD], F. Charte[1] [iD], and M. D. Pérez-Godoy[1] [iD]

[1] Universidad de Jaén, Campus Las Lagunillas s/n, Jaén, Spain
{mbermejo,mjjesus,arivera,fcharte,lperez}@ujaen.es
[2] De Montfort University, Gateway House, Leicester, UK
elizondo@dmu.ac.uk

Abstract. Since the emergence of the Transformer, many variations of
the original architecture have been created. Revisions and taxonomies
have appeared that group these models from different points of view.
However, no review studies the tasks faced according to the type of
data used. In this paper, the modifications applied to Transformers to
work with different input data (text, image, video, etc.) and to solve
disparate problems are analysed. Building on the foundations of existing
taxonomies, this work proposes a new one that relates input data types
to applications. The study shows open challenges and can serve as a
guideline for the development of Transformer networks for specific applications with different types of data by observing development trends.

Keywords: Neural Networks · Transformers · Applications · Survey

1 Introduction

Transformer [59] was introduced in 2017 as a sequence-to-sequence network
based only on attention mechanisms, removing recurrence and convolutions. Its
use has spread, and numerous models have been developed that strictly follow
the original architecture, make minor modifications to it or severally change it.
They initially emerged as networks to carry out machine translation with text
sequences. However, currently there are models that solve different tasks with
any input data. This has resulted in the emergence of studies and taxonomies
that categorize Transformers from different points of view. Nevertheless, there
is no review of these at application level or according to the type of data used.

In this paper a survey of Transformers, according to applications and the
type of data these networks work with, is carried out. This aims to provide

---

The research carried out in this study is part of the project "ToSmartEADs: Towards
intelligent, explainable and precise extraction of knowledge in complex problems of
Data Science" financed by the Ministry of Science, Innovation and Universities with
code PID2019-107793GB-I00/AEI/10.13039/501100011033.

insights into common modifications for the use of different types of data and their respective applications. Not all AI model users are Transformer experts, so choosing the right one for the task at hand is not always easy. This is where this paper would be helpful. In addition, knowing the most frequently used architecture and components in each type of application (with their possibilities and limitations) can help in the development of new proposals to address research challenges in the area.

The module-level and architecture-level taxonomy proposed in [42] is used to group the modifications and components used. This makes possible to observe the adaptations applied in architectures that work with a particular data type or achieving a certain goal.

This paper is organized as follows: Sect. 2 introduces the original Transformer [59] and the taxonomy at the module and architecture level [42]. Section 3 describes the methodology followed and our review from the point of view of the applications and data types used in Transformer networks. Finally, Sect. 4 contains our conclusions.

2   Background

The Transformer [59] is composed of encoders and decoders with a similar structure: Multi-Head Attention (MHA) and Feed Forward Networks (FFN) as main elements, with residual connections and normalization after them. Positional encoding is included at the bottom of encoder and decoder stacks to add information about the position of the tokens in the sequence. Moreover, the decoder contains a Masked MHA to prevent positions from attending to subsequent positions and a MHA over the output of the encoder stack.

Transformer networks have become one of the most widely used and powerful architectures, with many variations and modifications to the original definition emerging. Taxonomies and studies are beginning to appear that group all Transformers models from different points of view. Given that, our aim is to present a review of Transformers applications based on the type of data these networks work with, we analyse them considering the module-level and architecture-level categorizations presented in [42].

To perform the module-level taxonomies, vanilla Transformer is divided into four different modules: Attention, Positional Encoding (PE), Normalization and FFN. The most extensively studied is the attention-level categorization with the improvements on attention mechanism divided into Sparse attention (Sparse), Linearized attention, Query Prototype, Memory Compression (MC), Low-Rank self-attention, attention With Prior and Improved Multi-Head Mechanism. The positional information is encoded as Absolute Sinusoidal Position Encodings (Absolute) in [59]. This is the first of the classes within PE of [42], along with Relative Position Representations (Relative), Implicit Representations and Other Representations (Other). With regard to the classification of the normalization, a distinction is made between those works in which the placement of these layers is modified (Placement), those that substitutes the normalization formula

(Substitutes) and those that removes it (Removed). The last module to categorize is FFN. Three categories are grouped: those studies that explore different Activation Functions (AF), those that replace FFN with similar structures with many more parameters, and those that remove these layers (Removed). In the taxonomy of Attention and FFN we have included two additional classes: Original and Other, as many models use original components or major modifications that do not fit into the other classes.

The architecture-level taxonomy proposed in [42] studies Transformers that modify the original one beyond the modules, making higher-level modifications. It differentiates those studies that adapt the Transformer to be lightweight (Lightweight) in terms of model size, memory, computation time or Floating Point Operations Per Second. Architectures that strengthen cross-block connectivity are grouped in a separate category. Another class includes those that adapt computation time conditioned to inputs. Finally, there are the Transformers with Divide-and-Conquer Strategies, among which are the recurrent (Recurrent), where a cache memory is maintained to incorporate the history information, and the hierarchical (Hierarchical), which decomposes inputs hierarchically into elements of finer granularity. In addition, several studies have explored alternative architectures for Transformer (Alternative). In the Normalization and Architecture, the Original class has also been included, as many models use the one proposed by Vaswani [59].

3 Analysis of Transformer Model Applications

This section reviews the different applications that have been addressed with Transformers. To this end, first the review methodology is presented and then the different categories that have been defined.

3.1 Methodology

This review of Transformers applications based on the type of data analyse proposals with a significant contribution between 2017 and 2023. For this purpose, we have gathered relevant articles related to Transformer networks from different leading bibliographic databases such as Scopus, Google Scholar, Elsevier, Springer, IEEE, ACM or arXiv. The documents were analysed taking into account the publication site (journal, congress, conference, or other), the authors, the year of publication, the database where they were published, the number of citations, the task solved and the contribution made.

Subsequently, and given the limited number of pages present in a conference article, the most relevant ones were selected given the characteristics above for inclusion in this study. These are categorized according to the type of data used and the application to be performed. Furthermore, every element of these models is classified according to module-level and architecture taxonomies described in [42].

In the following subsections, tables have been included following the same structure to contain all the information in a more visual way. These tables include a column for the target application of the model (the acronyms used in this column are described at the beginning of each subsection). Then, a column is included for each Transformer module: Attention, PE, Normalization (Norm) and FFN. Finally, a column is included for the Architecture (Arch) and a column for the Reference (Ref) of the corresponding paper. In addition, in cases where the type of data used may change slightly (such as multimodal), a first column has been included detailing the type of data used. The categories used in the modules and the architecture are described in Sect. 2.

3.2   Text

Transformers emerged as an architecture for handling text data, with a focus on machine translation, and most Transformer networks work with text data as input. All these are shown in this category (Table 1) describing the jobs they perform, among which we found: *Translation, Generation* and *Prediction*. In addition, there are those that solve multiple with a single architecture (*Multitask*).

Table 1. Taxonomy of Textual Data Processing Transformers

Application	Attention	PE	Norm	FFN	Arch	Ref
Translation	Original	Absolute	Original	Original	Lightweight	[41]
Translation	Original	Absolute	Original	Original	Lightweight	[18]
Translation	Original	Absolute	Original	Original	Lightweight	[61]
Translation	Original	Absolute	Original	Original	Lightweight	[60]
Translation	Original	Absolute	Original	Original	Original	[4]
Multitask	Original	Absolute	Original	Original	Lightweight	[35]
Multitask	Original	Absolute	Original	Original	Original	[14]
Multitask	Original	Absolute	Original	Original	Original	[46]
Multitask	Linearized	Relative	Original	Original	Lightweight	[51]
Generation	Original	Absolute	Original	Original	Original	[65]
Generation	Original	Absolute	Original	Original	Original	[62]
Generation	Original	Absolute	Placement	Original	Original	[66]
Generation	Sparse	Absolute	Substitutes	Original	Original	[52]
Prediction	Other	Absolute	Original	Original	Original	[1]
Prediction	Original	Absolute	Original	Original	Original	[49]
Prediction	Sparse	Relative	Original	Original	Original	[64]

Most of the models that make machine translation try to improve on the vanilla Transformer. The one that is developed in [41] compresses the decoder sublayers into one for a higher degree of parallelism. In the case of [60], they propose to produce multiple successive words in parallel at each time step, keeping the autoregressive property and improving translation speed. One of the most popular works can be found in [18], where the architecture avoids this autoregressive property and produces its outputs in parallel. Furthermore, as a proposed improvement to the previous one in quality of decoder hidden representations is [61]. In contrast to the above that seek to improve the original, [4] proposes the incorporation of small adaptive layers to adapt the machine translation.

Many Transformer architectures are designed to face multiple tasks with text, an example is BERT [14], it has been used as a backbone for many studies like in

[35, 46], which make minor modifications. In the former, memory consumption is reduced, while in the latter, clinical domain knowledge is integrated. Another multitasking model is presented in [51], modifying the attention to be linear and using relative PE to improve the efficiency of the vanilla transformer.

With regard to the text generation task, the study in [66] shows a network that generates answers to questions with the incorporation of convolutions in the Vaswani encoder. The proposed in [52] learns dynamic patterns of sparse attention for language modelling (understanding this as a text generation task). Another example is the proposal in [62] of a generative dialogue system combining transfer learning and Transformers. In [65], they revisited triple extraction as a sequence generation job (which jointly extracts entities and relations).

About prediction task, in [49] an adaptation of BERT for rare diseases diagnosis is proposed. The proposal in [64] modifies the original architecture to perform Named Entity Recognition, using sparse attention and relative PE. The model described in [1] performs relation and event extraction tasks to test their multilingual transferability (understanding these as prediction), modifying attention and extracting syntactic distances.

As can be seen in the Table 1, most models that work with text use the original Transformer. In some studies minor modifications are made, especially with sparse attention, changes in normalization or the use of relative PE. Furthermore, most of those that perform machine translation use lightweight architectures, trying to improve the original, whose goal was sequences translation.

3.3 Image and Video

Table 2 lists all architectures included in this category based on Transformers for solving various tasks such as *Object Detection* (OD), *Image Generation, Image Captioning* and *Classification*. Also, there is a multitasking model (*Multitask*).

For object detection, the proposal in [2] applies feature extraction before the Transformer encoder and a classifier after it. In the same way, [6] presents DETR (DEtection TRansformer) that uses a Transformer encoder-decoder with little changes, with a Convolutional Neural Network (CNN) ahead and a FFN following it. Based on the latter, the model defined in [73] improves DETR with a deformable attention module. Finally, [58] faces place recognition and address as an OD task. It extracts lines for input images and uses a Transformer for line clustering. After that, they apply other Transformer for cluster description.

The model described in [33], that builds a GAN completely free of convolutions using only pure Transformer-based architecture with many changes and a grid self-attention, is included on image generation. In addition, [48] uses sparse attention and the Vaswani's Transformer for generate images. One of the mentioned in text generation ([52]) is also carrying out image generation.

With respect to image captioning, in [44] both grid and region features are used to achieve complementary information of them inside the same image. In [11] they incorporate a priori knowledge in the attention with memory vectors and a meshed connectivity between encoding and decoding modules. The proposal in [31] introduces region and global features into the attention.

Table 2. Taxonomy of Image and Video Data Processing Transformers

Data	Application	Attention	PE	Norm	FFN	Arch	Ref
Image	OD	Sparse	Absolute	Original	Original	Original	[73]
Image	OD	Original	Absolute	Substitutes	AF (Leaky ReLU)	Original	[58]
Image	OD	Original	Absolute	Original	Original	Original	[2]
Image	OD	Original	Absolute	Original	Original	Original	[6]
Image	Generation	Other	Relative	Substitutes	AF (GELU)	Original	[33]
Image	Generation	Sparse	Absolute	Original	Original	Original	[48]
Image	Captioning	Original	Absolute	Original	Original	Original	[31]
Image	Captioning	Original	Abs/Rel	Original	Original	Original	[44]
Image	Captioning	Other	Absolute	Original	Original	Original	[11]
Image	Classification	Original	Absolute	Placement	AF (GELU)	Hierarchical	[16]
Image	Classification	Original	Other	Placement	AF (GELU)	Original	[23]
Image	Classification	Original	Absolute	Placement	Original	Original	[69]
Image	Classification	Other	Absolute	Placement	AF (GELU)	Hierarchical	[5]
Image	Classification	Other	Absolute	Placement	AF (GELU)	Hierarchical	[30]
Image	Classification	Original	Absolute	Original	Original	Original	[8]
Image	Multitask	Other	Absolute	Placement	AF (GELU)	Hierarchical	[43]
Video	Classification	Original	Absolute	Placement	AF (GELU)	Original	[68]
Video	Classification	Original	Absolute	Placement	Original	Original	[3]

We distinguish those works that perform classification. With images: [16] proposes a model with a Transformer encoder that previously patches the original input image and applies a linear projection; [69] uses a set of reduction and normal cells containing Transformers; and [8] uses a hybrid architecture between CNN and Transformer for image matching. There are also models that perform image segmentation as classification [5,23,30]. In [23], they treat volumetric images using Transformers, while the last two make use of hierarchical frame-level Swin Transformer [43] to create two different models. Concerning classification with video, [68] apply pre-processing and the Token Shift Transformer that include the Token Shift Module. Also, [3] uses a Transformer whose attention factorizes the spatial and temporal dimensions of the input video.

Finally, in [43] they propose a general-purpose backbone for computer vision and run experiments in image classification, object recognition and semantic segmentation. This architecture has a shifted window based self-attention and minor changes with respect to the original Transformer.

For image and video processing on Transformers, Table 2 shows that attention, normalization and FFN are the most modified elements. In the case of the FFN, the use of the GELU function as an activation function stands out. So many modifications on the original are needed to adapt these networks to the use of pixels from an image and frames from a video instead of text sequences.

3.4   Audio

Transformers using audio spectrograms as input and/or output data accomplish various applications such as *Speech Enhancement* (SE), *Speech Recognition* (SR), *Text-to-Speech* (TTS), *Speech Separation* (SS) and *Generation* (Table 3).

Table 3. Taxonomy of Audio Processing Transformers

Application	Attention	PE	Norm	FFN	Arch	Ref
Generation	MC	Relative	Original	Original	Lightweight	[27]
SS	Original	Absolute	Placement	Original	Recurrent	[55]
TTS	Original	Absolute	Original	Original	Original	[38]
TTS	Other	Absolute	Placement	Original	Lightweight	[29]
TTS	Original	Removed	Original	AF (non-linear)	Original	[70]
SR	Original	Other	Original	Original	Original	[47]
SR	Original	Relative	Placement	AF (swish)	Original	[20]
SR	Other	Absolute	Placement	Original	Original	[15]
SR	Original	Relative	Original	AF (non-linear)	Original	[10]
SE	Original	Removed	Original	Removed	Alternative	[67]
SE	Other	Removed	Original	Original	Alternative	[34]
SE	Original	Removed	Original	Other	Original	[13]
SE	Other	Removed	Placement	AF (GELU)	Lightweight	[32]

Speech recognition is one of the most studied tasks when working with audio. Three similar proposals are found in [15,20,47], which apply preprocessing to data before the Transformer. Conformer [20] stands out by including CNN before the FFN. A different approach is [10], which faces speech recognition in real time with a Transducer network whose encoder contains a modified Conformer.

Text-to-speech is solved in [29] by using Locality-Sensitive Hashing Attention and Reversible Residual Network to reduce the memory used. Local LSTM before attention to encode PE locally, directly and differently to original Transformer is used in [70]. In [38] the vanilla Transformer is adapted to the specific task by applying pre- and post-processing to the data.

In speech Enhancement, the proposal in [67] replaces FFN with 1D CNN and uses local LSTM as in [70] to remove original PE. In [34] they use self-attention with Gaussian-weighted and Short-Time Fourier Transform. The architecture defined in [13] combines Intra and Inter Transformers, as well as other elements, eliminates positional encoding and modifies FFN to use GRU, ReLU and linear transformations. There is also a model [32] that reduces the computational cost for this task by taking consecutive frames and treating them as a local window that computes attention by using hierarchical frame-level Swin Transformer [43] layers with an attention mechanism adapted to these frame windows.

In [55] they use a structure with two recurrently connected embedded Transformers for speech separation. An architecture that reduces the intermediate memory requirement by modifying attention and PE is described in [27]. It allows the generation of one-minute musical compositions.

Table 3 shows that PE is the most modified element in Transformers that use audio as input data, since the model must be adapted to work with spectrograms. The most common is use relative PE or remove it. We also find modifications in the placement of normalization, in the FFN activation function and, as the most notable change, the use of adapted attention to work with audio signals.

3.5 Tabular

All proposals analysed use structured or tabular data to perform the same overall task, *Prediction*, but in different domains (Table 4).

Table 4. Taxonomy of Structured Data Processing Transformers

Application	Attention	PE	Norm	FFN	Arch	Ref
Prediction	Sparse	Absolute	Removed	Original	Original	[40]
Prediction	Original	Absolute	Original	Original	Original	[53]
Prediction	Other	Removed	Placement	Original	Original	[45]
Prediction	Original	Absolute	Original	Original	Original	[7]
Prediction	Sparse	Absolute	Original	Original	Lightweight	[71]
Prediction	Original	Other	Original	Other	Original	[36]
Prediction	Original	Absolute	Original	Original	Original	[25]
Prediction	Original	Relative	Original	Original	Original	[63]

Two of these works perform molecular prediction [7,45]. One of them run experiments on a large collection of datasets that represent typical tasks in molecule modelling, grouped like prediction: regression, binary classification, multiclass classification, etc. The other one performs molecular property prediction. In [63] a model that performs property prediction with polymers is defined.

Other works [40,53,71] carry out times series prediction, including elements for capturing temporal information. The study in [53] performs this job in medical field by adding dense interpolation and masked self-attention mechanism. Informer [71] is a lightweight Transformer for Long Sequence Time-Series Forecasting that uses its own sparse attention. In [40] a graph Transformer that captures spatial and time dependent data with graph structure for forecasting and prediction by applying sparsity to the whole architecture is defined.

Within prediction, some models make classification. The proposal in [36] suggests a new architecture with Gaussian range encoding and two-tower structure that captures time and channel stream for Human Activity Recognition. In [25] they create a Prior-Data Fitted Network with Transformers to perform supervised classification for small datasets in less than a second.

For Transformers working with tabular data, changes in attention to adapt it to this type of data are the most common, as shown in Table 4. However, modifications to the other elements are also made in some cases.

3.6 Multimodal

Most of the proposals working with several types of data (Table 5) consider linguistic and visual data. In addition, multitasking is one of the most studied applications of multimodal data.

Table 5. Taxonomy of Multimodal Data Processing Transformers

Data	Application	Attention	PE	Norm	FFN	Arch	Ref
Text-Image	Multitask	Original	Absolute	Original	Original	Original	[37]
Text-Image	Multitask	Original	Absolute	Original	Original	Original	[17]
Text-Image	Multitask	Original	Absolute	Original	Original	Original	[57]
Text-Image	Multitask	Original	Abs/Rel	Original	Original	Original	[50]
Text-Image	Multitask	Original	Absolute	Original	Original	Original	[39]
Text-Image	Multitask	Original	Absolute	Original	Original	Original	[54]
Text-Image	Multitask	Original	Absolute	Original	Original	Original	[12]
Text-Image	Classification	Original	Absolute	Original	Original	Original	[72]
Text-Image	Classification	Original	Other	Original	Original	Original	[24]
Text-Image	Generation	Original	Absolute	Original	Original	Original	[26]
Text-Image	Generation	Original	Absolute	Original	Original	Original	[19]
Text-Video	VC	Original	Absolute	Original	Original	Original	[28]
Text-Video	Multitask	Original	Absolute	Original	Original	Original	[56]
Text-Audio	Multitask	Original	Absolute	Original	Original	Original	[21]
Text-Audio	Classification	Sparse	Absolute	Original	Original	Original	[9]
Text-Image-Audio	Classification	Original	Absolute	Original	Original	Original	[22]

Most studies that use a stream of linguistic and visual data use text and images. In many studies like [17,37,39,50,54,57], models are multitasking. Most of them slightly modify a BERT architecture [14], except for [39] which employs Vaswani's original Transformer [59]. In [12] they introduce a new task of Edited Media Understanding that consists in answering questions on image manipulation by multitasking, with classification and generation of responses. Other works carry out only one task, like in [19,26] where they generate responses to questions asked about images and the text of the images. Other case is [24] that performs different types of classification on user interfaces. Classification is carried out in [72] for the skin lesion diagnosis using self-attention and guided-attention.

There are also articles dealing with linguistic and visual data flows through text and video: using a BERT Large [56] for multitasking or two stream encoder, cross-modal attention and a text only decoder for Video Captioning (VC) [28].

The processing of audio and text signals together incorporates the study described in [21], whose model conducts Machine Translation and Speech Translation with a shared semantic memory network between encoder and decoder of the original Transformer. In [9] a model for emotion recognition using cascaded cross-attention block to fuse text and audio modalities is proposed.

A Transformer that works with language, acoustic, and vision features is defined in [22], encoding all features separately and using a bimodal cross-attention layer to exchange multimodal information for predicting whether the input is humorous or not.

The most common in architectures dealing with multimodal data is to work with different Transformers for the different types of data, and then to unify them or pre-process the data in order to feed them together into one Transformer. As shown in Table 5, except some modifications made to the PE, vanilla Transformer is widely used.

4 Conclusion

In this survey, we review Transformers solving different tasks and group them according to the type of data used as input. Most of the existing works use text sequences to resolve multiple tasks, but Transformers are increasingly being applied to image, video, audio, multimodal or tabular data processing, with structured data being the least studied.

This review shows that text-based models typically use the original architecture or BERT [14] without changes. Many improve the vanilla Transformer in memory, computation time, etc. Those working with visual data such as image or video commonly modify the attention to adapt to working with pixels (spatial information) or with frames (spatio-temporal information). Furthermore, these also modify normalization and often use GELU as an activation function in FFN. For those working with spectrograms and audio signals, it is most usual to change the PE to encode the time and frequency information of this type of data and the attention to attend to it. In addition, they also make changes to the normalization and the FFN activation function. Transformers working with tabular data mostly transform the attention to deal with this data. A unified semantic space is used to work with multimodal data. Some of these models apply one Transformer for each data type and unify the outputs into another. Other works unify input data first and feed it into a Transformer. Except for certain modifications, the vanilla Transformer or BERT is commonly used.

References

1. Ahmad, W.U., et al.: Gate: graph attention transformer encoder for cross-lingual relation and event extraction. In: Proceedings of the AAAI, vol. 35, no. 14, pp. 12462–12470 (2021)
2. Alamri, F., et al.: Transformer-encoder detector module: Using context to improve robustness to adversarial attacks on object detection. In: Proceedings of the ICPR, pp. 9577–9584 (2021)
3. Arnab, A., et al.: ViViT: a video vision transformer. In: Proceedings of the ICCV, pp. 6836–6846 (2021)
4. Bapna, A., Firat, O.: Simple, scalable adaptation for neural machine translation. In: Proceedings of the EMNLP IJCNLP, pp. 1538–1548 (2019)
5. Cao, H., et al.: Swin-Unet: unet-like pure transformer for medical image segmentation. In: Karlinsky, L., Michaeli, T., Nishino, K. (eds.) Computer Vision – ECCV 2022 Workshops. ECCV 2022. LNCS, vol. 13803, pp. 205–218. Springer, Cham (2023). https://doi.org/10.1007/978-3-031-25066-8_9
6. Carion, N., Massa, F., Synnaeve, G., Usunier, N., Kirillov, A., Zagoruyko, S.: End-to-end object detection with transformers. In: Vedaldi, A., Bischof, H., Brox, T., Frahm, J.-M. (eds.) ECCV 2020. LNCS, vol. 12346, pp. 213–229. Springer, Cham (2020). https://doi.org/10.1007/978-3-030-58452-8_13
7. Chen, B., et al.: Path-augmented graph transformer network. arXiv:1905.12712 (2019)
8. Chen, J., et al.: Shape-former: bridging CNN and transformer via ShapeConv for multimodal image matching. Inf. Fusion 91, 445–457 (2023)

9. Chen, W., et al.: Key-sparse transformer for multimodal speech emotion recognition. In: Proceedings of the ICASSP, pp. 6897–6901 (2022)

10. Chen, X., et al.: Developing real-time streaming transformer transducer for speech recognition on large-scale dataset. In: Proceedings of the IEEE ICASSP, pp. 5904–5908 (2021)

11. Cornia, M., et al.: Meshed-memory transformer for image captioning. In: Proceedings of the CVPR, pp. 10575–10584 (2020)

12. Da, J., et al.: Edited media understanding frames: reasoning about the intent and implications of visual misinformation. In: Proceedings of the ACL IJCNLP, pp. 2026–2039 (2020)

13. Dang, F., et al.: DPT-FSNet: dual-path transformer based full-band and sub-band fusion network for speech enhancement. In: Proceedings of the ICASSP, pp. 6857–6861 (2022)

14. Devlin, J., et al.: BERT: pre-training of deep bidirectional transformers for language understanding. In: Proceedings of the NAACL, pp. 4171–4186 (2019)

15. Dong, L., et al.: Speech-transformer: a no-recurrence sequence-to-sequence model for speech recognition. In: Proceedings of the IEEE ICASSP, pp. 5884–5888 (2018)

16. Dosovitskiy, A., et al.: An image is worth 16×16 words: transformers for image recognition at scale. arXiv:2010.11929 (2020)

17. Gao, D., et al.: FashionBERT: text and image matching with adaptive loss for cross-modal retrieval. In: Proceedings of the ACM SIGIR, pp. 2251–2260 (2020)

18. Gu, J., et al.: Non-autoregressive neural machine translation. In: Proceedings of the ICLR (2018)

19. Gui, L., et al.: KAT: a knowledge augmented transformer for vision-and-language. In: Proceedings of the NAACL, pp. 956–968 (2022)

20. Gulati, A., et al.: Conformer: convolution-augmented transformer for speech recognition. In: Proceedings of the Interspeech, pp. 5036–5040 (2020)

21. Han, C., et al.: Learning shared semantic space for speech-to-text translation. In: Proceedings of the ACL IJCNLP, pp. 2214–2225 (2021)

22. Hasan, M.K., et al.: Humor knowledge enriched transformer for understanding multimodal humor. In: Proceedings of the AAAI, vol. 14B, pp. 12972–12980 (2021)

23. Hatamizadeh, A., et al.: UNETR: transformers for 3D medical image segmentation. In: Proceedings of the IEEE/CVF WACV, pp. 1748–1758 (2022)

24. He, Z., et al.: ActionBert: leveraging user actions for semantic understanding of user interfaces. In: Proceedings of the AAAI, vol. 7, pp. 5931–5938 (2021)

25. Hollmann, N., et al.: TabPFN: a transformer that solves small tabular classification problems in a second. arXiv:2207.01848 (2022)

26. Hu, R., et al.: Iterative answer prediction with pointer-augmented multimodal transformers for Text-VQA. In: Proceedings of the CVPR, pp. 9989–9999 (2020)

27. Huang, C.Z.A., et al.: Music transformer. arXiv:1809.04281 (2018)

28. Huang, G., et al.: Multimodal pretraining for dense video captioning. In: Proceedings of the AACL, pp. 470–490 (2020)

29. Ihm, H.R., et al.: Reformer-TTS: neural speech synthesis with reformer network. In: Proceedings of the Interspeech, pp. 2012–2016 (2020)

30. Iqbal, A., Sharif, M.: BTS-ST: Swin transformer network for segmentation and classification of multimodality breast cancer images. KBS **267**, 110393 (2023)

31. Ji, J., et al.: Improving image captioning by leveraging intra- and inter-layer global representation in transformer network. In: Proceedings of the AAAI, vol. 35, no. 2, pp. 1655–1663 (2021)

32. Jiang, W., et al.: Low complexity speech enhancement network based on frame-level swin transformer. Electronics **12**(6) (2023)

33. Jiang, Y., et al.: TransGAN: two pure transformers can make one strong GAN, and that can scale up. In: Proceedings of the NIPS, vol. 34, pp. 14745–14758 (2021)
34. Kim, J., et al.: T-GSA: transformer with gaussian-weighted self-attention for speech enhancement. In: Proceedings of the IEEE ICASSP, pp. 6649–6653 (2020)
35. Lan, Z., et al.: Albert: a lite bert for self-supervised learning of language representations. In: Proceedings of the ICLR, pp. 344–350 (2020)
36. Li, B., et al.: Two-stream convolution augmented transformer for human activity recognition. In: Proceedings of the AAAI, vol. 35, no. 1, pp. 286–293 (2021)
37. Li, L.H., et al.: VisualBERT: a simple and performant baseline for vision and language. arXiv:1908.03557 (2019)
38. Li, N., et al.: Neural speech synthesis with transformer network. In: Proceedings of the AAAI, vol. 33, pp. 6706–6713 (2019)
39. Li, W., et al.: UNIMO: towards unified-modal understanding and generation via cross-modal contrastive learning. In: Proceedings of the ACL IJCNLP, pp. 2592–2607 (2021)
40. Li, Y., Moura, J.M.F.: Forecaster: a graph transformer for forecasting spatial and time-dependent data. Front. Artif. Intell. Appl. **325**, 1293–1300 (2020)
41. Li, Y., et al.: An efficient transformer decoder with compressed sub-layers. In: Proceedings of the AAAI, vol. 35, no. 15, pp. 13315–13323 (2021)
42. Lin, T., et al.: A survey of transformers. AI Open **3**, 111–132 (2022)
43. Liu, Z., et al.: Swin transformer: hierarchical vision transformer using shifted windows. In: Proceedings of the ICCV, pp. 10012–10022 (2021)
44. Luo, Y., et al.: Dual-level collaborative transformer for image captioning. In: Proceedings of the AAAI, vol. 35, no. 3, pp. 2286–2293 (2021)
45. Maziarka, L., et al.: Molecule attention transformer. arXiv:2002.08264 (2020)
46. Michalopoulos, G., et al.: UmlsBERT: clinical domain knowledge augmentation of contextual embeddings using the unified medical language system metathesaurus. In: Proceedings of the NAACL, pp. 1744–1753 (2021)
47. Mohamed, A., et al.: Transformers with convolutional context for asr. arXiv:1904.11660 (2019)
48. Parmar, N., et al.: Image transformer. In: Proceedings of the ICML, vol. 80, pp. 4055–4064 (2018)
49. Prakash, P., et al.: RareBERT: transformer architecture for rare disease patient identification using administrative claims. In: Proceedings of the AAAI, vol. 35, no. 1, pp. 453–460 (2021)
50. Qi, D., et al.: ImageBERT: cross-modal pre-training with large-scale weak-supervised image-text data. arXiv:2001.07966 (2020)
51. Qin, Z., et al.: cosFormer: rethinking softmax in attention. arXiv:2202.08791 (2022)
52. Roy, A., et al.: Efficient content-based sparse attention with routing transformers. TACL **9**, 53–68 (2021)
53. Song, H., et al.: Attend and diagnose: clinical time series analysis using attention models. In: Proceedings of the AAAI, pp. 4091–4098 (2018)
54. Su, W., et al.: VL-BERT: pre-training of generic visual-linguistic representations. arXiv:1908.08530 (2019)
55. Subakan, C., et al.: Attention is all you need in speech separation. In: Proceedings of the IEEE ICASSP, pp. 21–25 (2021)
56. Sun, C., et al.: VideoBERT: a joint model for video and language representation learning. In: Proceedings of the ICCV, pp. 7463–7472 (2019)
57. Sun, L., et al.: RpBERT: a text-image relation propagation-based BERT model for multimodal NER. In: Proceedings of the AAAI, vol. 15, pp. 13860–13868 (2021)

58. Taubner, F., et al.: LCD - line clustering and description for place recognition. In: Proceedings of the 3DV, pp. 908–917 (2020)

59. Vaswani, A., et al.: Attention is all you need. In: Proceedings of the NIPS, vol. 30, pp. 5999–6009 (2017)

60. Wang, C., et al.: Semi-autoregressive neural machine translation. In: Proceedings of the EMNLP, pp. 479–488 (2018)

61. Wang, Y., et al.: Non-autoregressive machine translation with auxiliary regularization. In: Proceedings of the AAAI, pp. 5377–5384 (2019)

62. Wolf, T., et al.: TransferTransfo: a transfer learning approach for neural network based conversational agents. arXiv:1901.08149 (2019)

63. Xu, C., et al.: Transpolymer: a transformer-based language model for polymer property predictions. NPJ Comput. Mater. **9**, 1–14 (2023)

64. Yan, H., et al.: Tener: adapting transformer encoder for named entity recognition. arXiv:1911.04474 (2019)

65. Ye, H., et al.: Contrastive triple extraction with generative transformer. In: Proceedings of the AAAI, vol. 35, no. 16, pp. 14257–14265 (2021)

66. Yu, A.W., et al.: Fast and accurate reading comprehension by combining self-attention and convolution. In: Proceedings of the ICLR (2018)

67. Yu, W., et al.: Setransformer: speech enhancement transformer. Cogn. Comput. **14**, 1152–1158 (2022)

68. Zhang, H., et al.: Token shift transformer for video classification. In: Proceedings of the ACM MM, pp. 917–925 (2021)

69. Zhang, Q., et al.: ViTAEv2: vision transformer advanced by exploring inductive bias for image recognition and beyond. IJCV **131**, 1141–1162 (2023)

70. Zheng, Y., et al.: Improving end-to-end speech synthesis with local recurrent neural network enhanced transformer. In: Proceedings of the IEEE ICASSP, pp. 6734–6738 (2020)

71. Zhou, H., et al.: Informer: beyond efficient transformer for long sequence time-series forecasting. In: Proceedings of the AAAI, vol. 35, pp. 11106–11115 (2021)

72. Zhou, L., Luo, Y.: Deep features fusion with mutual attention transformer for skin lesion diagnosis. In: Proceedings of the ICIP, pp. 3797–3801 (2021)

73. Zhu, X., et al.: Deformable DETR: deformable transformers for end-to-end object detection. In: Proceedings of the ICLR, pp. 1–16 (2021)

Real-Time Workflow Scheduling in Cloud with Recursive Neural Network and List Scheduling

Vahab Samandi$^{(\boxtimes)}$, Peter Tiňo , and Rami Bahsoon

School of Computer Science, University of Birmingham, Birmingham B15 2TT, UK
{vxs899,P.Tino,r.bahsoon}@cs.bham.ac.uk

Abstract. This paper investigates the problem of dynamic workflow scheduling in cloud computing. In a real-time scenario, the only available information is input data size, and the other task execution requirements, such as execution time, memory consumption, and output data size, must be estimated. In this study, we ask whether a more accurate estimation of task execution requirements can be obtained if workflow structure is taken into account explicitly and whether such estimations can result in more efficient task resource allocations and better computing resource utilization. We compare the estimation accuracy of a graph learning neural network, e.g., Recursive Neural Network (RecNN), with two standard prediction models (that do not consider the workflow structure), e.g., a *linear* and *non-linear* regression. We used two types of scientific workflows, Montage and LIGO, to train the prediction models. The execution time (makespan) comparison of the newly generated workflows with the original set of workflows shows that *the RecNN* model estimates the task information more accurately than linear and non-linear regression models, and the makespan of the workflow generated by the estimated values by *RecNN* is closer to the makespan of the original workflows. To the best of our knowledge, we are the first to consider the overall workflow topological structure in real-time workflow scheduling scenarios. The result shows that explicitly considering the workflow structure through structure learning models such as *RecNN* can considerably improve workflow scheduling in the cloud.

Keywords: Scientific workflow · Dynamic workflow scheduling · Recursive neural network · Graph learning

1 Introduction

Distributed systems, e.g., grid, cluster, and cloud computing, tend to aggregate heterogeneous computing resources and power to provide elastic computing at scale. Cloud computing technology provides computing as a utility, similar to traditional public utility services, such as electricity, gas, and water. Utility computing is a business service model that delivers computing power on-demand,

P. García Bringas et al. (Eds.): HAIS 2023, LNAI 14001, pp. 244–255, 2023.
https://doi.org/10.1007/978-3-031-40725-3_21

where end users and corporate pay for the services to the providers similar to how they pay for public utility services ("pay-as-you-go") and offer processing power and storage, including software, in the form of services. Clouds, as an example, consist of a large pool of computing resources such as physical infrastructure, platform development, and software services in an entirely virtualized model, which is easily usable and accessible by consumers worldwide [15]. Complex applications such as scientific workflows consist of a large number of interactive tasks that use or create large-scale datasets. These workflows are used in diverse scientific domains, such as bioinformatics, astronomy, climate science, etc., and require a large amount of processing power that is beyond the ability of a single machine [7]. On the other hand, they can be executed on parallel machines to obtain the shortest possible execution time. With the emergence of the grid and cloud computing technologies, the computing power needed for processing these large parallel applications is provided. Workflow applications are commonly represented in the form of a directed acyclic graph (DAG). Nodes represent computational tasks with a particular amount of computational workload, and edges represent precedence constraints (data dependency), i.e., the direction of data flow from one task to another. Workflow scheduling is defined as mapping tasks into the processing units for execution, considering the precedence constraints among tasks [8]. Static scheduling algorithms presume precise workflow execution requirements such as task runtime, data transmission time, and memory usage. On the other hand, dynamic scheduling algorithms are designed to tackle the unavailability and lack of accurate information for scheduling workflows. In practice, it is not usually possible to know task execution requirements in advance, and one can estimate them using the *mean* of the historically observed workflow execution requirements for that workflow type, which is, in most cases, inadequate. Structured domains such as DAGs are usually categorized by complex patterns of processes and information flow with variable size and complexity. The discovery, recognition, and classification of these patterns is a challenging problem in applications that exhibit scale, dependencies, and unclear patterns of interactions and information flow among its constituent components. Learning these patterns can have a variety of uses. Most learning models deal with organized data according to relatively poor structures and classify static information like arrays and sequences. They are unable to organize and classify structured information with different sizes efficiently. For example, for scheduling scientific workflows in a dynamic environment, we need a learning model capable of learning graphs to estimate the scheduling target parameters. A recursive neural network (RecNN) [12] is a graph learning model and a generalized form of recurrent neural network (RNN). But the structure of the recursive network is a deep graph rather than an RNN chain-like structure. Sperduti and Starita [22] defined a generalized recursive neuron that formalizes and extends several standard networks such as real-time recurrent networks, neural trees, simple recurrent networks, and backpropagation through time networks to structures. Frasconi et al. [16,17] used the recursive neural network in natural language processing. They proposed Recursive Neural Tensor Network (RNTN) to capture the compositional effects with higher accuracy.

The performance of dynamic workflow scheduling has been widely studied in the literature, including hybrid modeling and simulation-based [19] and analytical [4] techniques. A comprehensive taxonomy of dynamic scheduling strategies is introduced by Sonmez et al. [21] concerning workflow information (task execution time and size of output files) and resource information (resource status, processing power, and inter-cluster link speed). Brevik et al. [11] introduced a binomial method batch predictor (BMBP) that predicts the time a job would wait in a queue before its execution is initiated by observing the historical data obtained from the previous waiting time. Nurmi et al. in [6] implemented BMBP in an online service system that made BMBP an interesting technique used in workflow scheduling for resource selection in [5]. Xiaojin Ma et al. [23] proposed a real-time multiple workflow scheduling with cost minimization under deadline constraints. After the current task is completed, the algorithm tunes the task parameters after the current task completes the execution. Rodriguez and Buyya [14] proposed dynamic scheduling for multi-tenant scientific workflow. They introduced workflow as a service (WaaS) using and modeling containers for scheduling and resource provisioning.

In this work, we systematically study to what degree it pays off to consider the full workflow structure (expressed as DAG) when predicting features necessary for online scheduling algorithms (such as memory usage or task runtime) purely based on the input data size. The DAG structures are accounted for by RecNN models. To the best of our knowledge, this is the first study of this kind. The workflow structure has been recently considered through a graph convolution network in a priority allocation model [2]. However, this approach assumes that the crucial information of task execution time (runtime) is known in advance, whereas, in the real-time scenarios we are interested in, this information is not available. On the other hand, existing approaches that solely use input data size to predict other task features without accounting for workflow structure, e.g., [9,10], have their own intricate model constructions. In this first pilot study, we do not apply those models as this would confound our study. Asking whether including workflow structure when predicting task features is beneficial makes sense if the other aspects of predictive model construction remain fixed. This is why we resort to using single hidden layer non-linear neural network models whose input is either (i) the original feature (input data size) on its own (no workflow structure considered), or (ii) there is an additional structure code provided by the RecNN. In addition, we study two simplified versions of the predictor type of (i), where only linear modelling or simple summary mean output is allowed.

The remaining part of this paper is organized as follows: Sect. 2 explains some preliminary concepts on directed acyclic graphs (DAGs) and briefly explains a recursive neural network. Then, we describe and analyze the characteristics of two real scientific workflows used in this work. In Sect. 3, we discuss the experiment and training of the learning models. In Sect. 4, we discuss the estimation process and model performance comparison, and in Sect. 5, we discuss a conclusion and future works.

2   Preliminaries

Graphs: a directed graph G consists of a set of vertices V_G, and a set of directed edges, E_G: $(v_i, v_j) \in E_G$ denotes a link from vertex $v_i \in V_G$ to $v_j \in V_G$.

A graph G' is defined as a subgraph of a graph G, if $V_{G'} \subseteq V_G$, and $E_{G'} \subseteq E_G$. For a vertex $v \in V_G$ of graph G, the sets of its parents and children, $Pa(v)$ and $Ch(v)$, are defined as $Pa(v) = \{w \in V_G | (w, v) \in E_G\}$ and $Ch(v) = \{w \in V_G | (v, w) \in E_G\}$, respectively. The number of input and output edges of v is then $in\_deg(v) = |Pa(v)|$ and $out\_deg(v) = |Ch(v)|$, respectively.

We assume a consistent ordering on parents and children of vertices. Let $Ch(v)_i \in V_G$ and $Pa(v)_j \in V_G$ denote the ith child and j^{th} parent of v, respectively. The *max_degree* of a graph G is $max_{v \in V_G}\{out\_deg(v), in\_deg(v)\}$. $|V| = n$ is the number of nodes in a graph.

This work considers finite vertex directed acyclic graphs (DAGs). The maximum out-degree of a graph vertices among all graphs in a domain D is called the *max_degree* of the domain D.

2.1   Recursive Neural Network

The recursive neural network is an extension of a recurrent neural network from linearly ordered data to graph structures. For a vertex $v \in V_G$ the output $y_j(v)$ of the j-th state unit is computed as

$$y_j(v) = f\left(\sum_{i=1}^{N_L} w_{ij}\, l_i(v) + \sum_{k=1}^{out\_deg(v)} \sum_q v_{kjq}\, y_q(Ch(v)_k)\right) \quad (1)$$

The output of the neuron for a vertex v is computed recursively on the output computed for all the vertices pointed by it[1]. We assume that the number of recursive connections of a recursive neuron should be equal to the *max degree* of the domain D, even if not all of them will be used for computing the output of a vertex v with $out\_deg(v) < max\_degree$.

To understand how recursive neurons work, let us consider a single recursive neuron s and a single graph G. The number of recursive connections for a recursive neuron must be the same as the *max_degree* of the domain. $o(v)$ is the computed output for a sub-graph X at vertex v, i.e., the output of s computed for vertex v. In other words, the structure of a graph is encoded by a generalized neuron by replicating the same recursive neuron and connecting these copies according to the graph structure; the obtained outputs are used for the approximation or classification by a feedforward network (See Fig. 1). When considering a structured domain D, the number of recursive connections of s must be equal to the *max_degree* of the domain.

---

[1] The number of recursive connections of a recursive neuron should be equal to the *max_degree* of the domain D, even if not all of them will be used for computing the output of a vertex v with $out\_deg(v) < max\_degree$.

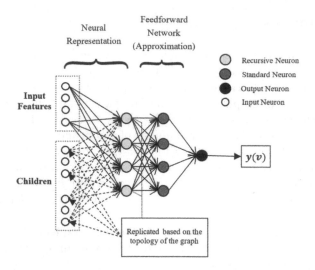

Fig. 1. An architecture of recursive neural network: the neural representation is used to encode the graph structure, and then it uses a feedforward network for the approximation.

In our previous work [20], we proposed a bottom-up top-down recursive neural network model (BUTD RecNN). BUTD RecNN model can be trained using available input information from both directions (Bottom-up and Top-down) of the directed acyclic graph, which includes two opposite directions networks for graph encoding. However, in this work, we used a regular recursive neural network that is explained in the previous section because in the dynamic environment, the only available parameter for a task scheduling algorithm is the input data size, and the remaining task resource parameters, such as runtime, memory usage, and output data size, are unavailable and required for task scheduling should be estimated.

2.2   Scientific Workflows

Applications that are chosen for this work include Montage [13] and LIGO [1]. Figure 2 represents a simplified version of these workflows. NASA developed Montage as a portable software toolkit that allows for making a mosaic of astronomical images. The input files are in the Flexible Image Transport System (FITS) format workflow from astronomical sources. The size of the workflow varies based on the number of images required to build the mosaic. The different size of the input parameter of the workflow is specified as a *degree*. Montage workflow is I/O- and data-intensive workflow. The Laser Interferometer Gravitational-Wave Observatory (LIGO) workflow is used to discover and detect a gravitational wave regarding the structures of exotic objects such as black holes, the nonlinear dynamics, and the nature of gravity from the astrophysics origin. It is mostly considered a CPU-intensive workflow with high memory con-

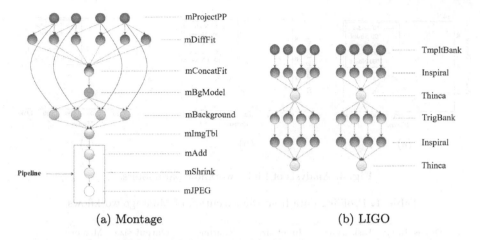

(a) Montage   (b) LIGO

Fig. 2. Example of scientific workflows

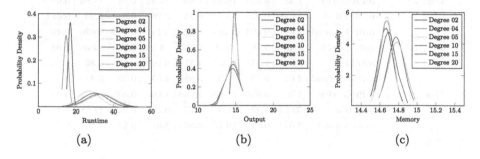

(a)   (b)   (c)

Fig. 3. Analysis of Montage workflow parameters.

sumption. These are the standard workflows that are used for the evaluation of our proposed work.

A sensitivity analysis of the input parameters on the behavior of tasks shows that the change in the size of the input data affects the structure, size, and overall execution time (makespan) of the workflows. The input data size is the only parameter available in a dynamic situation. Figure 3 shows the probability density function (PDF) of the Montage workflow task parameters, such as runtime, output data size, and memory usage for different sizes of workflows. Diagrams show that higher-degree input sizes of the Montage workflows have greater average values and standard deviations for runtime. However, the probability density functions of the memory usage and output data size parameters for different sizes of workflows are almost the same. For LIGO workflows, a change in the input data size also affects the size and structure of the workflow but only slightly affects the task parameters, i.e., the probability density functions of the LIGO task parameters are nearly the same for different sizes of workflows (see Fig. 4). The LIGO Inspiral tasks read a large amount of data but produce a small amount.

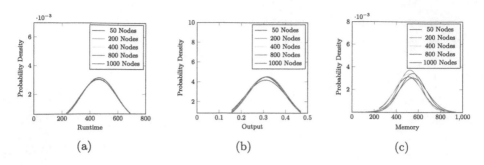

Fig. 4. Analysis of LIGO workflow parameters.

Table 1. Profiling data from the execution of Montage workflows

Degree Input	Task Type	Input size		Runtime		Output size		Memory	
		Mean	STD	Mean	STD	Mean	STD	Mean	STD
Deg. 2	mProjectPP	1.48	0.035	16.86	1.10	14.89	0.35	14.66	0.07
	mDiffFit	33.18	0.055	0.14	0.15	0.26	0.004	2.90	0.037
	mBackground	2.07	0.004	0.25	0.32	4.14	0.008	69.20	0.10
Deg. 10	mProjectPP	1.45	0.10	30.10	6.70	14.53	1.00	14.69	0.08
	mDiffFit	32.40	1.67	2.42	4.41	0.26	0.02	9.30	0.76
	mBackground	2.03	0.13	5.29	5.98	4.05	0.26	6.42	0.46
Deg. 20	mProjectPP	1.46	0.085	33.61	10.50	14.66	0.84	14.77	0.09
	mDiffFit	32.64	1.43	2.39	4.77	0.26	0.02	11.88	0.62
	mBackground	2.06	0.11	10.13	6.50	4.08	0.22	7.86	0.75

Table 1 provides the task characteristics data extracted from the Montage workflow execution. The mProject tasks spent the majority of the runtime. That is because mProject tasks perform most of the input/output data transmission. In general, Montage consists of high data-intensity tasks. Therefore, they spend the majority of the runtime on the input/output operations. The mDiffFit tasks, on the other hand, have a shorter runtime, but they also perform a large amount of input/output operations. mBackground tasks require less runtime and input/output operations. Table 1 shows that higher-degree Montage workflows have higher mean and standard deviation values for all measurements. Therefore, estimating the target parameters based on the *mean* is more error-prone. The task characteristics data of the LIGO workflow execution is provided in Table 2. The most computationally intensive task of the LIGO workflow, which consumes almost 92% of the total runtime, is Inspiral. Inspiral also performs about 90% of the input/output operations. TmpltBank is the second most computationally intensive task. They read a high amount of data. Thinca and TrigBank have low runtime and input/output operations.

Table 2. Profiling data from the execution of LIGO workflows

No of Nodes	Task Type	Input size		Runtime		Output size		Memory	
		Mean	STD	Mean	STD	Mean	STD	Mean	STD
50 Nodes	TmpltBank	101.27	0.059	18.13	0.43	0.09	0.00	89.12	0.37
	Inspiral	723.55	8.12	464.84	126.74	0.30	0.09	701.12	112.95
	Thinca	0.30	0.095	5.38	0.22	0.03	0.01	1.87	1.05
	TrigBank	0.03	0.01	5.12	0.31	0.01	0.00	1.88	0.15
400 Nodes	TmpltBank	101.27	0.062	18.12	0.40	0.09	0.00	93.11	0.60
	Inspiral	723.66	8.13	460.07	130.46	0.31	.089	711.73	134.43
	Thinca	0.31	0.089	5.35	0.23	0.030	0.00	2.00	0.73
	TrigBank	0.03	0.01	5.11	0.32	0.01	0.00	1.99	0.22
1000 Nodes	TmpltBank	101.27	0.065	18.13	0.41	0.09	0.00	95.12	0.72
	Inspiral	723.67	8.12	460.9	132.17	0.31	0.88	730.38	146.56
	Thinca	0.31	0.88	5.36	0.24	0.03	0.00	2.05	0.94
	TrigBank	0.029	0.01	5.1	0.32	0.01	0.00	2.13	0.28

3   Experiments

We prepared training and testing datasets by characterizing the two types of workflows used in this work. We used a set of 5,000 Montage and a set of 5,000 LIGO workflows datasets. We first profile these workflows, collecting information such as memory usage, task runtime, input data size, and output data size for each task. The input data size is the input feature to the RecNN model and the memory usage, task runtime, and output data size are the output targets to be predicted. We employed three prediction models in this experiment. One is a regular recursive neural network which is a graph learning model capable of explicitly accounting for the workflow structure. The other two are linear and non-linear (simple feedforward neural network) regression models. We also consider a baseline model that estimates the target features as the *mean* values of the training targets.

The out-out-sample model performance was evaluated through 5-fold cross-validation. The model selection was performed by 5-fold cross-validation on the training folds (nested cross-validation). The recursive network used in this experiment has a single hidden layer with fifteen recursive neurons. Each parent output of the recursive neuron is given to a non-linear regression model with two hidden layers to compute the final output. The non-linear regression model we chose for the Montage workflow has two hidden layers, including fifteen neurons in each layer and, the non-linear regression model for the LIGO workflow has two hidden layers, including six neurons in each layer.

We generated workflows using the estimated values by the learning models for the task parameters. We then executed these newly generated workflows on the CloudSim using the HNF [3] list scheduling algorithm. To compare the performance of the prediction models, we compared the makespan of the newly created workflows with the original workflows by executing them on the CloudSim [18].

Our implementation extends some of the existing classes of the CloudSim. A simulation environment for all experiments consists of one Datacenter, one Host, and five VMs. Each Processing unit has a speed of 1,000 million instructions per second (MIPS), 4 GB RAM, 10 Gbps bandwidth, and a storage capacity of 1 TB. We applied the same CloudSim configurations for the scheduling algorithms we used in this experiment to produce consistent results.

4   Target Features Estimation

One way to estimate the workflow task parameters is to use the *mean* values of previous executions of similar tasks. In the case of dynamic workflow schedul-ing, we only have the input data size, and the other task scheduling require-ments should be estimated. It isn't easy to generate estimates that are simple to compute and have good accuracy. A better estimation would result in effi-cient resource allocation of tasks and better resource utilization. Based on the data given in Table 1, tasks such as mDiffFit have a high standard deviation. Therefore, estimations based on the mean result in significant estimation errors. Most input/output operations and memory usage have small standard deviation values. Therefore target parameters estimation can be easily estimated by mean. However, the values of the runtime standard deviation in most cases are very high to have an accurate estimation using the mean.

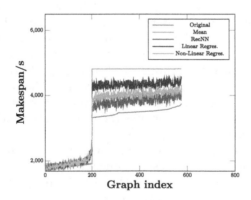

Fig. 5. Comparison of the makespan of the Montage workflows

The other way to estimate the target parameters is to use standard linear or non-linear prediction models. But these models are also not suitable to be used for structured patterns as they are not capable of capturing the relevant information about graph structures. In this work, we used a recursive network, which is a graph learning model, to estimate the target parameters. We then compared the estimation accuracy of the RecNN model with the estimation accuracy of linear and non-linear prediction models and, finally, with the mean value. We generated workflows using the estimated values by the learning models for the task parameters. We then executed these newly generated workflows on the CloudSim using a list scheduling algorithm. However, the main aim of this work is not to check and evaluate the performance of the scheduling algorithm but rather the accuracy of the prediction models in estimating the target parameters that can be subsequently used in our hybrid scheduling approach by an appropriate scheduling algorithm (in our case - HNF list scheduling).

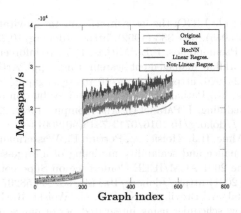

Fig. 6. Makespan comparison of the LIGO workflows

The mean cross-validated makespan values for the different predictors used in our study are presented in Fig. 5 and Fig. 6 for Montage and LIGO workflow types, respectively. The best (lowest) makespans are obviously obtained for (usually unrealistic) situations when the task scheduling requirements required by the scheduling algorithms are known (the line labeled as *Original*). Also, as expected, the worst performance is obtained by the simple mean predictor. The order of performance for the other predictors (best-to-worst) is: RecNN → nonlinear regression → linear regression. This shows that the relationship between the input data size and the task scheduling requirements to be predicted is nonlinear. Most importantly, it is beneficial to consider the workflow structure when making such predictions.

5   Conclusion

Task scheduling in a distributed system is an NP-hard problem. In a real-time situation where it is not possible to know task execution requirements in advance, the task parameters are required to be estimated. A good prediction model that can accurately estimate the target parameters can help in an efficient task scheduling into the resources and minimizing the total execution time of the workflow. We used a recursive neural network (RecNN), which is a graph learning model, and a linear and non-linear regression model to estimate the task parameters. We then evaluated their estimation accuracy. The RecNN model outperforms compared to the linear and non-linear prediction models. Because RecNN is capable of learning structural patterns, whereas the other two models do not provide efficient learning for structures with different sizes, and they are only suitable for static information and sequences. In the future, we aim to generalize this method for more types of workflows.

References

1. Abramovici, A., et al.: LIGO: the laser interferometer gravitational-wave observatory. Science **256**(5055), 325–333 (1992). https://doi.org/10.2307/2877074
2. Kintsakis, A.M., Psomopoulos, F.E., Mitkas, P.A.: Reinforcement learning based scheduling in a workflow management system. Eng. Appl. Artif. Intell. **81**, 94–106 (2019). ISSN 0952–1976, https://doi.org/10.1016/j.engappai.2019.02.013
3. Shirazi, B., Wang, M., Pathak, G.: Analysis and evaluation of heuristic methods for static task scheduling. J. Parallel Distrib. Comput. 10(3), 222–232 (1990). ISSN 0743–7315, https://doi.org/10.1016/0743-7315(90)90014-G
4. Kerbyson, D.J., Alme, H.J., Hoisie, A., Petrini, F., Wasserman, H.J., Gittings, M.: Predictive performance and scalability modeling of a large-scale application. In: Proceedings of the 2001 ACM/IEEE Conference on Supercomputing. New York, NY, USA, p. 37 (2001) https://doi.org/10.1145/582034.582071
5. Nurmi, D., Mandal, A., Brevik, J., Koelbel, C., Wolski, R., Kennedy, K.: Evaluation of a workflow scheduler using integrated performance modelling and batch queue wait time prediction. In: Proceedings of the 2006 ACM/IEEE Conference on Supercomputing, SC 2006, Tampa, FL, USA, p. 29 (2006). https://doi.org/10.1109/SC.2006.29
6. Nurmi, D.C., Brevik, J., Wolski, R.: QBETS: queue bounds estimation from time series. In: Proceedings of the 2007 ACM SIGMETRICS International Conference on Measurement and Modeling of Computer Systems (SIGMETRICS 2007). New York, NY, USA, pp. 379–380 (2007). https://doi.org/10.1145/1254882.1254939
7. Deelman, E., et al.: The future of scientific workflows. Int. J. High Perform. Comput. Appl. **32**(1), 159–175 (2018). https://doi.org/10.1177/1094342017704893
8. Deelman, E., et al.: Pegasus, a workflow management system for science automation, Future Gener. Comput. Syst. **46**, 17–35 (2015). ISSN 0167–739X, https://doi.org/10.1016/j.future.2014.10.008
9. Da Silva, R.F., Juve, G., Rynge, M., Deelman, E., Livny, M.: Online task resource consumption prediction for scientific workflows. Parallel Process. Lett. **25**(03), 1541003 (2015). https://doi.org/10.1142/S0129626415410030
10. Lee, H., Cho, S., Jang, Y., Lee, J., Woo, H.: A global DAG task scheduler using deep reinforcement learning and graph convolution network. IEEE Access **9**, 158548–158561 (2021). https://doi.org/10.1109/ACCESS.2021.3130407
11. Brevik, J., Nurmi, D., Wolski, R.: Predicting bounds on queuing delay for batch-scheduled parallel machines. In: Proceedings of the eleventh ACM SIGPLAN Symposium on Principles and Practice of Parallel Programming (PPoPP 2006), New York, NY, USA, pp. 110–118 (2006). https://doi.org/10.1145/1122971.1122989
12. Pollack, J.B.: Recursive distributed representations. Artif. Intell. **46**(1–2), 77–105 (1990). ISSN 0004–3702, https://doi.org/10.1016/0004-3702(90)90005-K
13. Jacob, J.C., et al.: Montage: a grid portal and software toolkit for science-grade astronomical image mosaicking. Int. J. Comput. Sci. Eng. 4(2), 73–87 (2009). https://doi.org/10.1504/IJCSE.2009.026999

14. Rodriguez, M.A., Buyya, R.: Scheduling dynamic workloads in multi-tenant scientific workflow as a service platforms. Future Gener. Comput. Syst. **79**, 739–750 (2018). Part 2, ISSN 0167–739X, https://doi.org/10.1016/j.future.2017.05.009
15. Buyya, R., Broberg, J., Goscinski, A.M.: Cloud Computing: Principles and Paradigms. Wiley, Hoboken (2011). ISBN: 978-0-470-88799-8
16. Socher, R., et al.: Recursive deep models for semantic compositionality over a sentiment treebank. In: Proceedings of the 2013 Conference on Empirical Methods in Natural Language Processing, pp. 1631–1642, Seattle, Washington, USA (2013)
17. Socher, R., Huang, E., Pennin, J., Manning, C.D., Ng, A.: Dynamic pooling and unfolding recursive autoencoders for paraphrase detection. In: Proceedings of the 24th International Conference on Neural Information Processing Systems (NIPS 2011), Red Hook, NY, USA, pp. 801–809 (2011). https://doi.org/10.5555/2986459.2986549
18. Calheiros, R.N., Ranjan, R., Beloglazov, A., De Rose, C.A., Buyya, R.: CloudSim: a toolkit for modeling and simulation of cloud computing environments and evaluation of resource provisioning algorithms. Softw. Pract. Exper. **41**(1), 23–50 (2011). https://doi.org/10.1002/spe.995
19. Pllana, S., Fahringer, T.: Performance prophet: a performance modeling and prediction tool for parallel and distributed programs. In: 2005 International Conference on Parallel Processing Workshops (ICPPW 2005), Oslo, Norway, 2005, pp. 509–516 (2005). https://doi.org/10.1109/ICPPW.2005.72
20. Samandi, V., Tiňo, P., Bahsoon, R.: Duplication scheduling with bottom-up top-down recursive neural network. In: Yin, H., Camacho, D., Tino, P. (eds.) Intelligent Data Engineering and Automated Learning - IDEAL 2022, IDEAL 2022. Lecture Notes in Computer Science, vol. 13756, pp. 170–178. Springer, Cham (2022). https://doi.org/10.1007/978-3-031-21753-1_17
21. Sonmez, O., Yigitbasi, N., Abrishami, S., Iosup, A., Epema, D.: Performance analysis of dynamic workflow scheduling in multicluster grids. In: Proceedings of the 19th ACM International Symposium on High Performance Distributed Computing, ACM, pp. 49–60 (2010). https://doi.org/10.1145/1851476.1851483
22. Sperduti, A., Starita, A.: Supervised neural networks for the classification of structures. IEEE Trans. Neural Netw. **8**(3), 714–735 (1997). https://doi.org/10.1109/72.572108
23. Ma, X., Xu, H., Gao, H., Bian, M.: Real-time multiple-workflow scheduling in cloud environments. IEEE Trans. Netw. Serv. Manage. **18**(4), 4002–4018 (2021). https://doi.org/10.1109/TNSM.2021.3125395

Robust Losses in Deep Regression

Adrián Rubio[1] and Jose R. Dorronsoro[1,2][(✉)] [iD]

[1] Department of Computer Engineering, Universidad Autónoma de Madrid, Madrid,
Spain
jose.dorronsoro@uam.es
[2] Inst. Ing. del Conocimiento, Universidad Autónoma de Madrid, Madrid, Spain

Abstract. What is the noise distribution of a given regression problem
is not known in advance and, given that the assumption on which noise
is present is reflected on the loss to be used, a consequence is that neither
the loss choice should be fixed beforehand. In this work we will address
this issue examining seven regression losses, some of them proposed in
the field of robust linear regression, over twelve problems. While in our
experiments some losses appear as better suited for most of the problems,
we feel more appropriate to conclude that the choice of a "best loss" is
problem dependent and perhaps should be handled similarly to what is
done in hyperparameter selection.

Keywords: Deep Neural Networks · Robust Regression · MSE ·
MAE · Huber loss · log cosh loss · Cauchy loss

1 Introduction

Mean squared error (MSE) [4] has been historically the canonical loss for linear regression and, by extension, for neural network models. However, while
mathematically easy to handle and widely studied and used, the MSE has also
well known disadvantages, particularly its lack of robustness when facing outliers [12]. A natural alternative in this case is the mean absolute error (MAE),
closely related to the MSE as it yields the target median as the best constant
regression model, just as the MSE yields the target mean. The well known Huber
loss [12], together with some variants, has long been proposed as another robust
alternative intermediate between MSE and MAE, but the advent of the advanced
front ends for deep networks, such as Keras [8], PyTorch [16] or Mxnet [23], has
made quite easy to enlarge not only network architectures but, also, the range of
possible regression losses that can be defined an used. Examples of these taken
from Keras are, besides the MSE, the MAE, Huber and Log Cosh losses. To
these one can add other losses such as the Cauchy, pseudo Huber or ϵ-insensitive
loss, this one customarily used in Support Vector Regression.

The rationales for any such choice are varied. For instance, the ϵ-insensitive
loss generalizes the MAE, penalizing errors only when their absolute error is
bigger than ϵ; it reduces to the MAE when $\epsilon = 0$. On the other hand, the MSE,

© The Author(s), under exclusive license to Springer Nature Switzerland AG 2023
P. García Bringas et al. (Eds.): HAIS 2023, LNAI 14001, pp. 256–268, 2023.
https://doi.org/10.1007/978-3-031-40725-3_22

MAE, Log Cosh or Cauchy losses are usually derived by assuming a certain noise distribution n for the general regression target model $y = \phi(x) + n$, where ϕ is the true (but, of course, unknown) regression function. This leads to the obvious question of which distribution would be better suited to a given regression problem. Seen from the previous noise density assumption, it is clear that, even allowing for the key role that the central limit theorem gives to Gaussian noise, there should be no a priori preferred noise model for a given problem. The goal of this work is thus to study whether this agnostic noise assumption may held for general regression problems.

Some of the previous losses present some mathematical difficulties, particularly the lack of derivatives everywhere. This has resulted in a focus on their use on linear regression problems whose simple structure allows the application of particular techniques such as linear programming or iteratively reweighted least squares. However, the advent of modern neural networks has led to the wide use of non differentiable activation functions, particularly ReLUs. While their non differentiability is akin to that of the previous losses, these networks are routinely trained by methods such as gradient descent or its advanced variants.

This suggests to study the previous regression losses in a neural network setting where we can benefit from both the expressiveness of the powerful non linear models these networks produce together with the robustness that these losses may provide. We will consider such an approach here, considering a series of classical regression problems taken mostly from the LIBSVM repository [7] and working with the above mentioned losses to determine which one is better suited to each of them, taking statistical significance into account. More precisely, our main contributions here are

- The proposal of deep neural regression models that use robust losses.
- An empirical study of the performance of these models over twelve regression problems, study that includes a significance analysis of the experimental results.
- Some first conclusions on the suitability of these losses in regression problems.

The rest of the paper is organized as follows. In Sect. 2 we describe in some detail and motivate the regression losses to be considered and in Sect. 3 we will present our experimental set up and results, and discuss them. Finally, Sect. 4 offers some our main conclusions and pointers to possible further work.

2   General Regression Losses

Given a sample $S = \{(x^p, y^p)\}$ and a regression model $f(x^p; w)$, recall that the mean squared error, MSE, is defined as

$$mse(w|S) = \frac{1}{N} \sum_p (y^p - f(x^p; w))^2.$$

MSE has long been the standard loss in regression problems and there are many reasons for that, the most important probably being its mathematical simplicity that yields, among other advantages, a rather straight forward analytic solution in the linear case. But despite these advantages, MSE regression also has well known drawbacks, particularly the detrimental effect of high value target outliers that cause the square loss to amplify their negative effect on the MSE estimation.

To counter this, many ideas have been proposed in the field of robust estimation. A first example is to replace the mean squared error with the mean absolute error, MAE, with the loss being now

$$mae(w|S) = \frac{1}{N} \sum_p |y^p - f(x^p; w)|.$$

This is an example of the more general M-estimators introduced by Peter Huber [12], where the loss has the general form

$$L_\rho(w|S) = \frac{1}{N} \sum_p \rho(y^p - f(x^p; w)),$$

for an appropriate ρ, which is generally taken as a function which increases less rapidly than the square. Besides MSE (with $\rho(z) = z^2$) and MAE (with $\rho(z) = |z|$), possibly the best known M estimator is the Huber loss, associated with the function

$$\rho(z, \delta) = \begin{cases} \frac{1}{2} z^2 & \text{if } |z| < \delta, \\ \delta \left(|z| - \frac{\delta}{2} \right) & \text{if } |z| \geq \delta. \end{cases}$$

A differentiable variant, the pseudo Huber loss, defined as

$$\rho(z, \delta) = \delta \left(\sqrt{1 + \frac{z^2}{\delta^2}} - 1 \right)$$

is also widely used.

The M in the name M-estimator refers to "maximum likelihood type" and the MSE, MAE and Huber losses can actually be derived from a maximum likelihood estimate, MLE, of the sample's noise; in fact, recall that the basic assumption in regression is that the targets y are related to the "true" regression function ϕ through $y = \phi(x) + n$, where n denotes zero mean noise with density p. Then given an i.i.d. sample $\{(x^p, y^p)\}$, if we want to approximate the targets y^p with a model $f(x^p; w)$ parametrized by a weight set w, a natural way to estimate the optimal weights w^* is by maximizing the sample's likelihood

$$\mathcal{L}(w|S) = \prod_1^N p(y^p - f(x^p; w)).$$

Usually, one actually estimates w^* by minimizing the minus log likelihood, i.e.,

$$w^* = \arg\min -\sum_1^N \log p(y^p - f(x^p; w)).$$

Then, the three losses are the result of such an MLE approach where we associate the MSE with the Gaussian density $p(z) \propto e^{-z^2}$, the MAE with the Laplace density $p(z) \propto e^{-|z|}$ and the Huber loss with

$$p(z, \delta) \propto \begin{cases} e^{-\frac{1}{2}z^2} & \text{if } |z| < \delta, \\ e^{\delta(|z| - \frac{\delta}{2})} & \text{if } |z| \geq \delta; \end{cases}$$

in other words, the local MSE, MAE or Huber losses $\ell(y, f(x; w))$ are just minus the logarithm of the corresponding density.

Seen from this light, it appears that the use of one of these three losses is well justified if we believe that the noise follows its associated density. But this is something which is not guaranteed beforehand and that may be very well not the case in concrete problems. Thus, it may be of interest to consider other densities in addition to the above ones. Examples are the inverse cosh density [18]

$$p(z) = \frac{1}{\pi \cosh(z)},$$

and the Cauchy density centered at 0 [13]

$$p(z, \sigma) = \frac{1}{\pi \sigma \left(1 + \frac{z^2}{\sigma^2}\right)}.$$

It is easy to check that their corresponding losses are the log cosh loss

$$\text{lcosh}(w|S) = \sum_1^N \log \cosh(y^p - f(x^p; w)),$$

and the Cauchy loss

$$\text{cauchy}(w|S) = \sum_1^N \log \left(1 + \frac{(y^p - f(x^p; w))^2}{\sigma^2}\right).$$

It must be observed that the ρ term $\log \left(1 + \frac{(z^2)}{\sigma^2}\right)$ in the Cauchy loss is locally convex near its minimum at 0 but not for large values of z. Another important loss in machine learning is the ϵ-insensitive loss

$$\text{eps}(w|S) = \sum_1^N [|y^p - f(x^p; w)| - \epsilon]_+,$$

where $[z]_+ = \max\{0, z\}$; the ρ function is now $\rho(z, \epsilon) = [|z| - \epsilon]_+$. This loss coincides with the MAE when $\epsilon = 0$ and its associated density $p(z, \epsilon) \propto e^{-[|z| - \epsilon]_+}$ is sometimes called Vapnik's density [1].

As mentioned above, some of the previous losses have the drawback of not being differentiable. For linear models this has led to different algorithmic approaches to solve their minimum problem, such as linear programming [2] in the case of both the MAE and the ϵ-insensitive losses. An alternative in this case is the standard, Lagrangian based, dual formulation, which allows a powerful, kernel based non linear extension [20]. Other approaches frequently used in M-estimation are iterative re-weighting algorithms [9] or the Newton-Raphson method [15].

These methods have been mostly applied in a linear setting; in contrast with the large literature on linear robust regression, the study of robust non linear regression seems to have received somewhat less attention, following essentially two different approaches. The first one has been centered on kernel based regression, where versions of iterative weighting schemes [5] or loss functions adapted to their use in Lagrangian duality [1] or in NORMA learning [17] have been proposed, or particular kernels are used [6,22]; a study on the robustness of SVMs is [14].

Another way to achieve non linear robust regression is through deep learning. For instance, in [3] convolutional networks built using the MAE and Tukey's biweight losses are proposed for regression problems in computer vision. In [11] deep models built upon the Huber loss and Least Trimmed Squares (a technique to detect and remove outliers while building regression models) are proposed for robust signal processing and in [19] theoretical results are given for deep regression with the Huber, Cauchy and Tukey's biweight losses. Finally, in [10] deep networks trained with the ϵ-insensitive loss are considered.

In any case, we can notice that the non-differentiabilities of the losses listed above are quite mild, taking place at one or at most two points. In fact, and as mentioned above, they are quite similar to the non differentiability of the ReLU activation function, which is nowadays routinely used in neural networks. Moreover, all of them can be defined so that the automatic differentiation capabilities of modern deep neural network backends allow its easy used as the losses of deep models; as a matter of fact, the MSE, MAE, Huber and log cosh losses are already included among the regression losses of Keras.

This makes quite natural the consideration of these losses in neural network models, which is just the approach we will follow here looking, in a given problem, for the loss that may best reflect the target noise on that problem. We will consider next for this goal deep models built using the MSE, MAE, ϵ-insensitive, Huber, pseudo Huber, log cosh and Cauchy losses.

3   Experimental Results

In this chapter we will describe the datasets we will use, the experimental methodology followed and the results obtained using the seven losses mentioned above.

3.1   Models and Data

We will consider 12 regression problems. Three, `cal-housing`, `winequality-red`, `winequality-white` come from the Kaggle repository, another eight, `abalone`, `cadata`, `cpusmall`, `bodyfat`, `housing`, `mg`, `mpg`,

Table 1. Data sizes and dimensions.

	size	dimension
abalone	4177	8
cadata	20640	8
cal-housing	5000	8
concrete	1030	8
cpusmall	8192	12
bodyfat	252	14
housing	506	13
mg	1385	6
mpg	392	7
space-ga	3107	6
winequality-red	1599	11
winequality-white	4898	11

`space-ga`, are taken from the regression datasets on LIBSVM's repository, and the `concrete` dataset from the UCI repository. Sample sizes and dimensions are given in Table 1; we have dropped the string variable `ocean-proximity` in the `cal-housing` dataset and used only its first 5,000 patterns.

We will consider seven regression losses discussed before, namely, MSE, MAE, ϵ-insensitive, Huber, pseudo-Huber, log cosh and Cauchy, with the acronyms `mse`, `mae`, `eps-ins`, `huber`, `ps-huber`, `l-cosh` and `cauchy`, respectively. In order to avoid potential overflows with the log cosh loss, we have also scaled the targets in `cadata` and `cal-housing` to the range $[0, 1]$. We have used the native Keras implementation of MSE, MAE, Huber and log cosh, and our own implementation of the others losses on the Tensorflow backend.

Table 2. Ranges of the hyperparameters considered.

	models	ranges
α	all	`[10.**k for k in range(-6, 2)]`
δ	huber, ps-huber	`[1., 1.2, 1.4, 1.6, 1.8, 2.]`
ϵ	eps-ins	`[0.] + [2**k for k in range(-7, -1)]`
σ	cauchy	`[0.1, 0.2, 0.5, 1.]`

3.2   Methodology

In all cases we consider a fully connected multilayer perceptron with a single hidden layer and 100 neurons. Batch size was 200 for all datasets and we used the Adam optimizer, with its parameters left at their default values. All models require a regularization hyperparameter α; moreover the Huber, pseudo Huber, ϵ-insensitive and Cauchy require an extra hyperparameter; we will denote it as δ for the Huber and pseudo Huber losses, ϵ for the ϵ-insensitive one and σ for Cauchy loss.

Since the datasets do not have separate train and test splits, we have used the entire datasets for both hyperparameter estimation and model testing. To keep both processes reasonably separate, we have proceeded as follows. We first found the optimal hyperparameters by cross validation (CV) with a grid search over five folds with a fixed seed for both random folding definition using scikit-learn's KFold class, and random initialization and minibatch handling in Keras. The hyperparameter ranges are given in Table 2. Notice that we consider an $\epsilon = 0$ value among the hyperparameters explored by the ϵ-insensitive loss; recall that when $\epsilon = 0$, this loss coincides with the MAE. For each loss considered, we have used this same loss to compute the corresponding CV scores; that is, when using, say, the Cauchy loss, its selected α and σ hyperparameters are those for which their Cauchy loss is smallest.

Table 3. Optimal model hyperparameters.

problem	param	mse	mae (ϵ)	eps-ins (δ)	huber	ps-huber (δ)	l-cosh	cauchy (σ)
abalone	α	0.0001	0.001	0.001	0.0001	0.0001	0.0001	0.01
	(ϵ, δ, σ)	-	-	0.00781	1.4	1.2	-	0.2
bodyfat	α	0.001	0.01	0.01	0.001	0.001	0.001	0.01
	(ϵ, δ, σ)	-	-	0.00781	1.8	1.8	-	0.2
cadata	α	0.00001	0.00001	0.00001	0.00001	0.0	0.00001	0.0001
	(ϵ, δ, σ)	-	-	0.0	1.4	1.4	-	0.1
cal-housing	α	0.0001	0.001	0.001	0.0001	0.0001	0.0001	0.0001
	(ϵ, δ, σ)	-	-	0.00781	1.6	1.0	-	1.0
concrete	α	0.0001	0.00001	0.0001	0.00001	0.00001	0.00001	0.0001
	(ϵ, δ, σ)	-	-	0.01562	1.2	1.4	-	0.1
cpusmall	α	0.0001	0.001	0.001	0.00001	0.00001	0.00001	0.001
	(ϵ, δ, σ)	-	-	0.0	1.4	1.0	-	0.2
housing	α	0.001	0.01	0.001	0.0001	0.0001	0.0001	0.001
	(ϵ, δ, σ)	-	-	0.01562	1.6	1.8	-	1.0
mg	α	0.0001	0.001	0.001	0.0001	0.0001	0.0001	0.001
	(ϵ, δ, σ)	-	-	0.00781	1.6	1.2	-	0.5
mpg	α	0.001	0.01	0.01	0.0001	0.0001	0.001	0.01
	(ϵ, δ, σ)	-	-	0.00781	1.8	1.6	-	0.2
space-ga	α	0.00001	0.0001	0.0001	0.00001	0.00001	0.00001	0.0001
	(ϵ, δ, σ)	-	-	0.00781	2.0	1.4	-	0.5
winequality-red	α	0.001	0.01	0.001	0.001	0.001	0.001	0.001
	(ϵ, δ, σ)	-	-	0.01562	1.6	1.2	-	1.0
space-ga	α	0.001	0.001	0.001	0.0001	0.0001	0.0001	0.01
	(ϵ, δ, σ)	-	-	0.01562	1.0	1.2	-	0.2

The final optimal hyperparameters appear in Table 3. Notice that the ϵ value is 0 for the `cadata` and `cpusmall`; thus, in these problems the MAE and ϵ-insensitive models are essentially the same, up to small numerical changes. Once they are obtained, we applied five times the `cross_val_predict` procedure in scikit-learn to the models associated with each different loss, each time using again a different but fixed seed for the 5 folds we used as well as for Keras initialization and minibatches. We recall that `cross_val_predict` fits cyclically the model on four of the five folds and predicts on the remaining one. The final model predictions are just the means of these five individual CV predictions.

Table 4. Medians of the absolute errors of each model.

	mse	mae	eps-ins	huber	ps-huber	l-cosh	cauchy
abalone	1.040	0.982	0.975	1.030	1.026	1.030	1.046
cadata	4.559	4.016	3.990	4.577	4.509	4.592	4.471
cal-housing	3.964	3.528	3.477	4.016	3.966	4.104	3.890
concrete	2.001	1.792	1.746	1.799	1.851	1.828	1.775
cpusmall	1.525	1.331	1.325	1.410	1.424	1.422	1.455
bodyfat	0.693	0.289	0.306	0.827	0.835	0.727	0.690
housing	1.430	1.466	1.401	1.432	1.433	1.429	1.414
mg	6.959	6.428	6.478	6.767	6.813	6.810	6.726
mpg	1.324	1.292	1.317	1.387	1.355	1.351	1.320
space-ga	5.168	5.157	5.219	5.250	5.279	5.217	5.259
winequality-red	0.360	0.359	0.310	0.378	0.377	0.371	0.367
winequality-white	0.439	0.365	0.370	0.404	0.407	0.413	0.415

Table 5. Median based model ranks across all problems.

	mse	mae	eps-ins	huber	ps-huber	l-cosh	cauchy
abalone	6.0	2.0	1.0	5.0	3.0	4.0	7.0
cadata	5.0	2.0	1.0	6.0	4.0	7.0	3.0
cal-housing	4.0	2.0	1.0	6.0	5.0	7.0	3.0
concrete	7.0	3.0	1.0	4.0	6.0	5.0	2.0
cpusmall	7.0	2.0	1.0	3.0	5.0	4.0	6.0
bodyfat	4.0	1.0	2.0	6.0	7.0	5.0	3.0
housing	4.0	7.0	1.0	5.0	6.0	3.0	2.0
mg	7.0	1.0	2.0	4.0	6.0	5.0	3.0
mpg	4.0	1.0	2.0	7.0	6.0	5.0	3.0
space-ga	2.0	1.0	4.0	5.0	7.0	3.0	6.0
winequality-red	3.0	2.0	1.0	7.0	6.0	5.0	4.0
winequality-white	7.0	1.0	2.0	3.0	4.0	5.0	6.0
mean	5.0	2.1	1.6	5.1	5.4	4.8	4.0

3.3   Results

Given that we work with seven different losses and, also, seven different scores when choosing optimal hyperparameteres, it is not clear beforehand how to select a neutral score to rank and compare the performance of each loss model. On the other hand, whatever the ranking score used, we also have to check whether the resulting rankings are statistically significant, which entails working with each error distribution.

Under this idea, we are going to use the median of the absolute error distributions of each model to rank them. Obviously, this is an arbitrary choice and notice that these medians shouldn't be too far away from the mean of the absolute errors, i.e., from the MAE score and, hence, being favorable to the MAE based models. On the other hand, it is also quite natural, as it considers the direct deviations between predictions and targets, something that other scores such as, say, the log cosh or Cauchy ones, only do in a more indirect way.

In any case, these median values for each problem and loss are given in Table 4, while the relative model rankings for each problem are in Table 5; its last row contains mean rank values across all problems. We point out that, in order to compensate for different target scales, we have multiplied by 100 the MAE scores in the `cadata, cal-housing, mg` and `space-ga`, and by 1,000 those in `bodyfat`. As it can be seen, the MAE loss performs quite well under this score, but the ϵ-insensitive loss performs even better. MAE losses get the second best mean rank, followed by a relatively distant Cauchy loss; the worst rank is that of the pseudo Huber loss, followed by those of the Huber and MSE losses.

In any case, a smaller median is only an indirect indication of a model being better than another and, moreover, this median difference may not be statistically significant. To measure this, we have applied the following procedure. For each problem, we sort first the different loss models by the increasing median values of their absolute error distribution; then we compute the p-values derived from a Wilcoxon signed rank test between the absolute errors of the loss with the smallest mean on a given problem (which with an abuse of language we will term as the best) and those of the other losses. We compensate for multiple comparisons by applying a Bonferroni-Dunn correction, where we multiply the test's p-values by the number of loss models being compared against the best one, namely, six in our case. (Equivalently, we are demanding a significance level six times smaller than that of a single comparison.) We accompany these p-values with another indirect comparison of model performance, namely, the proportion for a given problem of samples for which the absolute errors of the best model are smaller than those of the loss model they are being compared with.

The corresponding model names sorted by the error medians, the p-values and the proportions appear in Table 6. As it can be seen, we can split the problems into three groups. Problems `abalone, bodyfat, cadata, cal-housing`, `winequality-red` and `winequality-white` make the first one, where the p-values when comparing the best loss model (i.e., that with the smallest median) with the others (except the second best) show the absolute errors to be statis-

Table 6. For each problem, models are sorted by increasing medians; p-values and proportions are with respect the best model in each case.

problem loss-pv-prop		best	1	2	3	4	5	6
abalone	loss	eps-ins	mae	ps-huber	l-cosh	huber	mse	cauchy
	pvalue	-	1.0	0.0	0.0	0.0	0.0	0.0
	prop	-	50.32	53.41	53.51	53.6	53.58	53.51
bodyfat	loss	mae	eps-ins	cauchy	mse	l-cosh	huber	ps-huber
	pvalue	-	0.1282	0.0	0.0	0.0	0.0	0.0
	prop	-	56.35	72.62	73.81	73.81	75.4	79.37
cadata	loss	eps-ins	mae	cauchy	ps-huber	mse	huber	l-cosh
	pvalue	-	1.0	0.0	0.0	0.0	0.0	0.0
	prop	-	49.76	54.71	55.09	56.12	56.02	56.47
cal-housing	loss	eps-ins	mae	cauchy	mse	ps-huber	huber	l-cosh
	pvalue	-	0.1372	0.0	0.0	0.0	0.0	0.0
	prop	-	50.96	54.28	55.1	56.96	57.3	57.42
concrete	loss	eps-ins	cauchy	mae	huber	l-cosh	ps-huber	mse
	pvalue	-	1.0	0.7706	0.3609	0.1275	0.1715	0.0
	prop	-	52.14	52.91	52.82	52.82	52.23	57.38
cpusmall	loss	eps-ins	mae	huber	l-cosh	ps-huber	cauchy	mse
	pvalue	-	0.0868	1.0	0.8576	1.0	0.2104	0.0
	prop	-	48.35	50.46	51.38	50.35	50.84	54.58
housing	loss	eps-ins	cauchy	l-cosh	mse	huber	ps-huber	mae
	pvalue	-	1.0	1.0	1.0	0.7929	1.0	0.1438
	prop	-	51.58	51.78	51.78	52.37	49.6	51.78
mg	loss	mae	eps-ins	cauchy	huber	l-cosh	ps-huber	mse
	pvalue	-	0.3885	1.0	1.0	1.0	1.0	0.9516
	prop	-	48.66	50.32	50.25	48.81	49.31	49.03
mpg	loss	mae	eps-ins	cauchy	mse	l-cosh	ps-huber	huber
	pvalue	-	1.0	1.0	0.1864	0.0251	0.4798	0.0397
	prop	-	51.28	54.85	56.38	55.1	52.04	53.83
space-ga	loss	mae	mse	l-cosh	eps-ins	huber	cauchy	ps-huber
	pvalue	-	1.0	1.0	1.0	0.5256	0.6464	0.0116
	prop	-	50.89	51.11	51.11	50.95	50.76	52.66
winequality-red	loss	eps-ins	mae	mse	cauchy	l-cosh	ps-huber	huber
	pvalue	-	0.3002	0.0	0.0	0.0	0.0	0.0
	prop	-	49.09	56.35	55.78	57.47	57.41	57.41
winequality-white	loss	mae	eps-ins	huber	ps-huber	l-cosh	cauchy	mse
	pvalue	-	0.2911	0.0	0.0	0.0	0.0	0.0
	prop	-	51.1	54.08	55.19	54.7	57.17	57.92

tically significant well below the 0.05 level. In all these problems the best or second best models are either those of the ϵ-insensitive or the MAE loss. The small p-values are generally accompanied by proportions clearly above 50%.

Problems `concrete`, `cpusmall`, `mpg` and `space-ga` make a second group, where now the difference between the best model and the others is not statistically significant except for the model with the largest median. Here again the best or second best models are either those of the ϵ-insensitive or the MAE loss, except for `concrete` (where the Cauchy loss is second) and `space-ga` (where the MSE is second). MSE is the worst loss for `concrete` and `cpusmall`, Huber for `mpg` and the pseudo Huber for `space-ga`. Finally, no significant differences among all loss models appear for problems `housing` and `mg`.

4   Conclusions and Further Work

Given the basic assumption on (homoscedastic) regression of the targets being of the form $y = \Phi(x) + n$, with ϕ the "true" regression function and n some zero mean noise, it is clear that a concrete choice of the noise distribution should be very important to obtain a good model. The mean squared error (MSE), long used as the standard regression loss, is based on the assumption of the noise being Gaussian, but its lack of robustness led to the study, mostly in a linear setting, of alternative, more robust losses and, hence, of alternative noise distributions. In fact, even without any robustness consideration, it is clear that individual regression problems should have their own, specific noise distributions which, in turn, should be reflected on the loss to be minimized for model training. In other words, there is no an priori universal loss, and deciding which one is better suited to a given problem should be an important issue.

We have pursued these ideas in this work, where we have considered seven different losses and have studied them over twelve regression problems using neural network models. Our results point to a better performance of the MAE and ϵ insensitive losses, with the caveat that our definition of "best" models is based on the median of the model's absolute errors, which shouldn't be too far from their mean, i.e., from their MAE or ϵ insensitive loss. In fact, in all problems the error distributions of these two losses (often the best and second best) are not significantly different. However, the best error distribution is different from those of all models but the second best in six problems and also from the distribution of the worst model in another four problems; moreover, it turns out that the MSE error distribution is significantly different from the best one in eight problems.

The main conclusion we can draw from the preceding is that there is no an a priori best loss that can be safely applied to any regression problem; on the other hand, it may be safely said that each concrete problem will have an associated "best" loss. Moreover, and in the same vein, the usual assumption of regression noise to be Gaussian does not seem to be universally warranted and each problem is likely to have its own noise distribution.

In any case, we point out that ours is a preliminary study, as more problems should be considered, as well as other neural architectures. Similarly, other losses should also be considered; in fact the by now classical theory of robust linear regression has also studied losses such as Tukey's biweight loss, trimmed means or the Hampel loss [21], or the logistic loss [14]. A further possibility would be, for a given model, to combine somehow the predictions of those losses that yield the best individual results according to our experimental setting. Besides a straight average, a way of doing so would be to combine some of them in a stacked model that mixes the outputs of individual loss models in a single joint output. Another alternative is to define companion losses where the final model is trained not on a single loss but on a new one which is the direct combination of the best ones in a given problem. We are currently exploring these possibilities.

Acknowledgements. The authors acknowledge financial support from the European Regional Development Fund and the Spanish State Research Agency of the Ministry of Economy, Industry, and Competitiveness under the project PID2019-106827GB-I00. They also thank the support of the UAM–ADIC Chair for Data Science and Machine Learning and gratefully acknowledge the use of the facilities of Centro de Computación Científica (CCC) at UAM.

References

1. Anand, P., Rastogi, R., Chandra, S.: A class of new support vector regression models. Appl. Soft Comput. **94**, 106446 (2020)
2. Barrodale, I., Roberts, F.D.K.: An improved algorithm for discrete l1 linear approximation. SIAM J. Numer. Anal. **10**(5), 839–848 (1973)
3. Belagiannis, V., Rupprecht, C., Carneiro, G., Navab, N.: Robust optimization for deep regression, pp. 2830–2838 (2015)
4. Bishop, C.M.: Pattern Recognition Machine Learning. Information Science and Statistics, Springer, New York (2006)
5. Brabanter, K.D., Brabanter, J.D., Suykens, J.A.K., Vandewalle, J., Moor, B.D.: Robustness of kernel based regression: influence and weight functions. In: The 2012 International Joint Conference on Neural Networks (IJCNN), Brisbane, Australia, 10–15 June 2012, pp. 1–8. IEEE (2012)
6. De Carvalho, F.D.A., Neto, E.D.A.L., Ferreira, M.R.: A robust regression method based on exponential-type kernel functions. Neurocomputing **234**, 58–74 (2017)
7. Chang, C.C.C., Lin, C.J.: LIBSVM data: classification, regression, and multi-label. https://www.csie.ntu.edu.tw/~cjlin/libsvmtools/datasets/
8. Chollet, F., et al.: Keras (2015). https://github.com/fchollet/keras
9. Daubechies, I., Devore, R., Fornasier, M., Güntürk, C.: Iteratively reweighted least squares minimization for sparse recovery. Commun. Pure Appl. Math. **63**(1), 1–38 (2010)
10. Diaz-Vico, D., Prada, J., Omari, A., Dorronsoro, J.: Deep support vector neural networks. Integr. Comput.-Aided Eng. **27**(4), 389–402 (2020)
11. Diskin, T., Draskovic, G., Pascal, F., Wiesel, A.: Deep robust regression. In: 2017 IEEE 7th International Workshop on Computational Advances in Multi-Sensor Adaptive Processing, CAMSAP 2017, pp. 1–5. IEEE (2017)
12. Huber, P.J.: Robust Statistics. Wiley Series in Probability and Statistics, Wiley, Hoboken (1981)
13. Liu, T., Tao, D.: On the robustness and generalization of Cauchy regression. In: 2014 4th IEEE International Conference on Information Science and Technology, pp. 100–105 (2014)
14. Messem, A.V., Christmann, A.: A review on consistency and robustness properties of support vector machines for heavy-tailed distributions. Adv. Data Anal. Classif. **4**(2–3), 199–220 (2010)
15. Ortega, J., Rheinboldt, W.: Iterative Solution of Nonlinear Equations in Several Variables. Classics in Applied Mathematics, Society for Industrial and Applied Mathematics (1970)

16. Paszke, A., et al.: Automatic differentiation in pytorch. In: Advances in Neural Information Processing Systems vol. 32, pp. 8024–8035. Curran Associates, Inc. (2019)
17. Prada, J., Dorronsoro, J.R.: General noise support vector regression with non-constant uncertainty intervals for solar radiation prediction. J. Modern Power Syst. Clean Energy **6**(2), 268–280 (2018)
18. Saleh, R.A., Saleh, A.K.M.E.: Statistical properties of the log-cosh loss function used in machine learning. arXiv (2022)
19. Shen, G., Jiao, Y., Lin, Y., Huang, J.: Robust nonparametric regression with deep neural networks (2021)
20. Smola, A.J., Schölkopf, B.: A tutorial on support vector regression. Stat. Comput. **14**(3), 199–222 (2004)
21. Venables, W.N., Ripley, B.D.: Modern Applied Statistics with S, 4th edn. Springer, Cham (2002). Statistics and Computing
22. Yang, L., Ren, Z., Wang, Y., Dong, H.: A robust regression framework with laplace kernel-induced loss. Neural Comput. **29**(11), 3014–3039 (2017)
23. Zhang, A., Lipton, Z.C., Li, M., Smola, A.J.: Dive into deep learning. CoRR abs/2106.11342 (2021)

Structure Learning in Deep Multi-Task Models

Carlos Ruiz[1(✉)], Carlos M. Alaíz[1], and José R. Dorronsoro[1,2]

[1] Dept. Computer Engineering, Universidad Autónoma de Madrid, Madrid, Spain
carlosruizpastor@protonmail.com
[2] Inst. Ing. Conocimiento, Universidad Autónoma de Madrid, Madrid, Spain

Abstract. Multi-Task Learning (MTL) aims at improving the learning process by solving different tasks simultaneously. Two general approaches for neural MTL are hard and soft information sharing during training. Here we propose two new approaches to neural MTL. The first one uses a common model to enforce a soft sharing learning of the tasks considered. The second one adds a graph Laplacian term to a hard sharing neural model with the goal of detecting existing but a priori unknown task relations. We will test both tasks on real and synthetic datasets and show that either one can improve on other MTL neural models.

1 Introduction

Multi-Task Learning (MTL) solves simultaneously several related problems with the aim of improving the overall learning process [1]. However, it is necessary to define the overall MTL procedure so that model learning for one task can benefit from the learning of others and the techniques to achieve this can vary depending on the underlying learning algorithms. In particular, the Multi-Task (MT) adaptations for deep Neural Networks (NNs), which have been successful in many fields such as image recognition, text processing or generative tasks, can be roughly divided in two main groups: hard and soft sharing approaches [8]. In hard sharing technique all tasks share the first layers of the network, layers which are followed by task-specific layers [3]. It is thus an approach with a hard coupling of the task models, something which may be more adequate for clearly defined and more or less strongly related tasks. On the other hand, soft sharing techniques, such as those in [9,10], employ different strategies to share information between task models, such as learnable weights connecting some layers of task-specific networks, or regularization schemes used to enforce a coupling between task-specific weights [15]. Here, the connection between tasks is indirect and typically learnable, which results in more flexible models that can adapt well to groups of tasks that are loosely related.

The authors acknowledge support from the European Regional Development Fund and the Spanish State Research Agency of the Ministry of Economy, Industry, and Competitiveness under the project PID2019-106827GB-I00. They also thank the UAM–ADIC Chair for Data Science and Machine Learning and gratefully acknowledge the use of the facilities of Centro de Computación Científica (CCC) at UAM.

P. García Bringas et al. (Eds.): HAIS 2023, LNAI 14001, pp. 269–280, 2023.
https://doi.org/10.1007/978-3-031-40725-3_23

Anyway, besides the recurring problem of the lack of interpretability of NNs, in the MTL case we can add the importance of finding an interpretation of the relation between tasks. In this work we propose two approaches to adaptive, neural MTL models which combine hard and soft sharing techniques and lend themselves to offer an interpretation of task interdependency. More precisely, we first present a model based on the convex combinations of a common and task-specific networks, where the common model can be interpreted as a way to soft share task information and for which the combination parameters are learnable. Second, we define a graph-based technique where we add to a hard sharing network a graph structure to capture the pairwise task relations, structure that is also to be learned. Thus, our contributions here are:

- A convex combination-based model for soft sharing neural MTL.
- A graph-based model for hard sharing neural MTL.
- The testing our proposals over four image problems and three synthetic ones.

The rest of the paper is structured as follows. In Sect. 2 we briefly review the hard and soft sharing neural MTL paradigms. In Sect. 3 we present our two model proposals and in Sect. 4 we describe our experiments. Finally, in Sect. 5 we discuss our results and give pointers to future work.

2   Multi-Task Learning with Neural Networks

We first describe the concrete MTL setting we will consider here. Formally, we consider T problems with shared input $\mathcal{X}$ and output $\mathcal{Y}$ spaces, where there exist possibly different joint distributions $P_r(x, y)$ on $\mathcal{X} \times \mathcal{Y}$ for $r = 1, \ldots, T$. Given a loss function ℓ, for each problem we suppose that there exists a relation between the input and output spaces $h_r^* : \mathcal{X} \to \mathcal{Y}$ that minimizes the MT expected risk

$$\sum_{r=1}^{T} \int_{\mathcal{X} \times \mathcal{Y}} \ell(h_r(x), y) dP_r(x, y),$$

and the problem of approximating each function h_r is considered a task. However, the distributions P_r are not known, and instead we sample m_r instances for each task $r = 1, \ldots, T$, to obtain the MT dataset $\{(x_i^r, y_i^r) \sim P_r(x, y), i = 1, \ldots, m_r\}$. Given a hypothesis space $\mathcal{H}$, that is, the set of model functions that we consider, the goal is now to find the functions h_r^* that minimize the empirical regularized risk

$$h_1^*, \ldots, h_T^* = \arg\min_{h_1, \ldots, h_T} \sum_{r=1}^{T} \frac{1}{m_r} \sum_{i=1}^{m_r} \ell(h_r(\boldsymbol{x}_i^r), y_i^r) + \Omega(h_1, \ldots, h_T). \quad (1)$$

Here, the first term is the empirical average of the loss and $\Omega(h_1, \ldots, h_T)$ is a regularization term that penalizes the complexity of the models $h_1, \ldots, h_T$.

Observe that in (1) when the regularizer Ω can be decoupled as sum of task-specific regularizers, we get the trivial approach of minimizing separately the empirical risk for each task; we will call this Independent Task Learning (ITL).

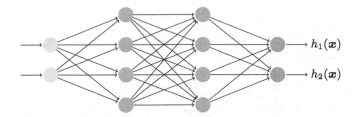

Fig. 1. Hard sharing NN for two tasks. The input neurons are shown in yellow, the hidden ones in cyan and the output ones in magenta.

The opposite approximation is to model all tasks with a single common model h, i.e. $h_1 = \ldots = h_T = h$; we will call this Common Task Learning (CTL). Between these two options, we can find proper MT approaches, which consider task-specific models h_r that, nevertheless, are somehow coupled together, so the learning of one task affects the learning of others. As proposed in [8], we can group the neural MT approaches into the **hard** and **soft** sharing strategies, which we describe next.

2.1 Hard Sharing Multi-Task Learning

This strategy was presented in [3], where the author proposes to use an NN with shared hidden layers for all tasks, plus task-specific output layers. Figure 1 shows an MTL network following this approach. In [3], and as depicted in Fig. 1, we call f the shared component of the neural network, and we have $h_r(\cdot) = w_r \cdot f(\cdot) + b_r$. This can be extended to model the task-specific parts with multiple layers. In that case, we would define networks with an initial number of shared hidden layers, which learn the shared representation, and add after them another set of task-specific layers, which model the task-specific functions. This strategy seems better suited for strongly related tasks, where we assume that there exists a common representation that is useful for all tasks. At the same time, it considers a homogenous interdependency between all tasks and does not give any insight on the underlying task structure. Notice that, when comparing such an MT network with one which learns a common model for all tasks, the hard sharing approach does not much increase the complexity of the model, as when sharing all the hidden layers, we only multiply by T the number of weights in the output layer. Moreover, this complexity is also lower than that of using an independent network for each task. These characteristics make this technique a good candidate for problems where either the tasks are easy to learn or all tasks have a strong interdependency.

2.2 Soft Sharing Multi-Task Learning

In contrast to the hard sharing approach, in the soft sharing strategies the goal is not to learn a shared representation but to use task-specific networks that

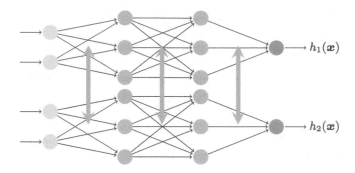

Fig. 2. Soft sharing NN for two tasks. The green thick arrows represent the soft connection between the parameters.

are connected in a more loose manner, as shown in Fig. 2. Along this line, in [7] the authors propose a strategy named "cross-stitch" networks which uses one network for each task, but these networks are connected using a linear combination of the outputs of every layer, including the hidden ones. In this model, these connections between networks are also learnable parameters. The "sluice networks" [9] extend this with learnable skip-layer connections.

The soft sharing approaches might work better with loosely related tasks: each one is modeled by an independent network with its own weights, and the information transfer between tasks is indirect, so it can deal with different types of task dependencies and infer them from data. In contrast to the hard sharing technique, these approaches significantly increase the complexity of our models. First, task-specific networks are considered, so the cost is at least equal to that of using independent networks for each task; also, a number of trainable parameters to determine the soft sharing scheme, e.g. cross-stitch units, are included. Furthermore, some hyperparameters have to be typically added to balance the learning of the task-specific networks weights and that of the task-relation parameters. Even with these caveats, the soft sharing approaches should work better for problems with weak, heterogeneously related tasks.

3   Adaptive Mixed Multi-Task Neural Networks

Both the hard and soft sharing MTL approaches for neural networks have their strengths and weaknesses. As stressed before, the first ones are more prone to work well with strongly related tasks, while the second ones are better suited to weakly connected ones. In this section, we present our two proposals, which combine elements from both hard and soft sharing: the Adaptive Convex and Adaptive Graph Multi-Task Neural Networks.

3.1   Adaptive Convex Multi-Task Neural Network

Our first proposal is based on the work presented in [13], where, inspired by previous works with Support Vector Machines (SVMs) [11], a convex multi-task

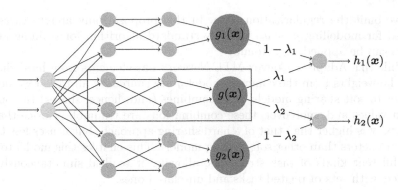

Fig. 3. Adaptive Convex MTL NN for two tasks. The common network is framed in a box. The grey circles represent the intermediate functions that will be combined for the final output: $g_1(\boldsymbol{x})$, $g_2(\boldsymbol{x})$ and $g(\boldsymbol{x})$. (Color figure online)

neural model is proposed. The idea is to apply a convex combination between a common network, shared by all tasks, and task-independent networks. In this proposal, the formal definition of the predictive model for the r-th task is

$$h_r(\boldsymbol{x}_i^r; \lambda_r, \Psi, \Psi_r) = \lambda_r g(x_i^r; \Psi) + (1 - \lambda_r)g_r(x_i^r; \Psi_r), \ \lambda_r \in [0,1], \qquad (2)$$

where $g(x_i^r; \Psi)$ models a common network, with parameters Ψ for all tasks, $g_r(x_i^r; \Psi_r)$ are the task-specific networks with parameters Ψ_r; λ_r are the combination parameters. Observe here that the λ_r values are included as parameters of the general model h_r.

In Fig. 3 we show an example of an Adaptive Convex MTL network for a problem with two tasks. The original formulation of [13] used a single common combination hyperparameter λ that had to be selected using, for example, a cross validation (CV) procedure. However, as it can be observed in this figure, it is natural to include the combination parameters as learnable weights of the network. Also, since there is no need to apply costly procedures like CV, we can consider, as illustrated in (2), several task-specific combination parameters λ_r.

Therefore, in this work we present a formulation with learnable combination values λ_r; however, these cannot be directly introduced as parameters of the general network h_r because they are constrained as $\lambda_r \in [0,1]$. Since introducing constraints in NNs parameters is not natural, we instead consider unconstrained scalar parameters p_r that are passed through a sigmoid function, i.e. $\lambda_r = \sigma(p_r)$. Therefore, to learn these parameters, alongside those of common and task-specific networks, we proceed as follows. Given an MT dataset, as presented in Sect. 2, the Adaptive Convex MTL Network, with parameters Ψ, Ψ_r and λ_r for $r = 1, \ldots, T$, is trained solving the following problem:

$$\min_{\psi, \psi_r, p_r} \sum_{r=1}^{T} \sum_{i=1}^{m} \ell(\sigma(p_r)g(x_i^r; \Psi) + (1 - \sigma(p_r))g_r(x_i^r; \Psi_r), y_i^r); \qquad (3)$$

here we omit the regularization term. In this proposal, any architectures can be used for modelling g or g_r, and any standard algorithm for training neural models can be applied, e.g. Adam.

While this Adaptive Convex MTL Network has elements from hard sharing (e.g.. the weights from the common model g are shared by all tasks) we believe it closer to soft sharing models, as it combines (and, hence, shares) the output neuron values and, moreover, these combinations are trainable. Notice that its complexity is higher than that of a hard sharing approach, but it uses less trainable parameters than other soft sharing models. This enables this model to deal with different kinds of task structures, allowing it to deal simultaneously, for instance, with sets of related tasks and unrelated ones.

3.2   Adaptive Graph Multi-Task Neural Network

Our second proposal is also inspired by previous work on MTL with SVMs [4,12], where the parameters for each task are coupled together using a graph-based regularization. For this approach, consider a graph where each node represents a task, and the edge weights in the adjacency matrix indicate task relations. Therefore, if we have two strongly connected tasks, t_1 and t_2, the weight $A_{1,2}$ should be large, and it should be small if these tasks are weakly related. The graph-based regularization is applied as follows. Given a linear model for each task, $h_r(x) = w_r \cdot x + b_r$, the following term is added to the loss function:

$$\sum_{r=1}^{T} \sum_{s=1}^{T} A_{rs} \|w_r - w_s\|^2. \tag{4}$$

This regularization penalizes the distances between task parameters, putting a larger weight on those tasks that should be closer according to A.

Furthermore, this idea is not limited to linear models; in [4,12] it is used with kernel models, i.e. $h_r(x) = w_r \cdot \phi(x) + b_r$, where ϕ is an implicit kernel transformation, and since $w_r, r = 1, \ldots, T$, are all elements of the same space, we can compute the pairwise distances of (4). Following the same idea, we propose to use models defined as $h_r(x) = w_r \cdot f(x; \Theta) + b_r$ where f is now a learnable transformation of the original data, modeled by the hidden layers of the neural network, as done in the hard sharing approach. In Fig. 4 we present an example of a multi-task network that follows this graph-based approach.

It is clear that a good choice of the matrix A is crucial for an effective regularization in (4). In some cases, it may be possible to select A using expert knowledge, but this is not the usual situation. In [12] a method to learn such a matrix from the data is proposed where, for better interpretability and standardization, A is a row-stochastic matrix. That is, all the entries A_{rs} must be non-negative and $\sum_s A_{rs} = 1$. However, notice that a row-stochastic matrix that trivially minimizes (4) is the identity matrix, which is not interesting. To avoid this solution, in [12] the entropy of each row of A is also maximized.

In this work, we propose to learn this matrix A with a neural approach. The stochastic property involves some constraints and, similarly to our other, pre-

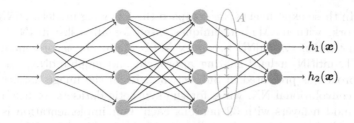

Fig. 4. Adaptive Graph MTL NN for two tasks. The green arrows and oval represent the soft connection between weights induced by the graph regularization. (Color figure online)

vious proposal, we consider scalar unconstrained values p_{rs}, for $r, s = 1, \ldots, T$; with these parameters we define the matrix A entries using the softmax function

$$A_{rs} = \text{soft}(\boldsymbol{p}_r, s) = \frac{\exp(p_{rs})}{\sum_{t=1}^{T} \exp(p_{rt})},$$

with $\boldsymbol{p}_r = (p_{r1}, \ldots, p_{rT})^{\mathsf{T}}$. In this approximation the network is trained to solve the problem

$$\min_{w_r, b_r, \Theta, p_{rs}} \sum_{r=1}^{T} \sum_{i=1}^{m} \ell(w_r \cdot f(x; \Theta) + b_r, y_i^r) + \nu \sum_{r=1}^{T} \sum_{t=1}^{T} \text{soft}(\boldsymbol{p}_r, s) \, \|w_r - w_s\|^2$$

$$- \mu \sum_{r=1}^{T} \sum_{s=1}^{T} \text{soft}(\boldsymbol{p}_r, s) \log(\text{soft}(\boldsymbol{p}_r, s)) \tag{5}$$

where we omit standard L_2 regularization weights and ν and μ are hyperparameters to balance the weight of each term of the loss functions, i.e., the loss value, the graph regularization and the matrix entropy, in this order.

This graph-based MTL model is essentially a hard sharing network where we have added a trainable graph regularization as a soft sharing technique. Since the hidden layers are shared, this is a model that assumes that all tasks can benefit from a common representation. At the same time, the last layer with the adaptive regularization can help to find and exploit more specific task structure; in particular, it can enforce or dismiss pairwise relations between tasks. In this approach, the increase on the number of parameters is moderate, since we only add T^2 parameters; however, two new hyperparameters ν and μ are included in the model definition. In summary, we add complexity to the hard sharing approach with the goal of finding the task structure, a better interpretation, and possibly better predictions.

4   Experimental Results

To test our proposals we consider two experiments: a first group of image classification problems, and a second one of regression problems using synthetic datasets. In these experiments, we compare the following models: ctlNN, a common network, with no MTL techniques, used for all tasks; itlNN, task independent networks; cvx-mtlNN a convex MTL approach, as presented in Subsect. 3.1; hs-mtlNN, a hard sharing approach; and graph-mtlNN, an adaptive graph approach as presented in Subsect. 3.2. In all the image datasets we use the same convolutional NN, while for the synthetic datasets we use a network with two hidden layers with 32 neurons each. Our implementation is publicly available[1]. All the models considered are trained using the AdamW method, and we select the weight decay hyperparameter α in a CV grid search, where the grid is $\left\{10^{-2}, 10^{-1}, 10^{0}\right\}$ for the image problems and $\left\{10^{-5}, 10^{-4}, 10^{-3}, 10^{-2}\right\}$ for the synthetic ones.

4.1   Image Problems

We consider four MT image problems based on transformations of the MNIST [6] and fashion-MNIST [14] datasets. The **variations** datasets are generated with the transformations given in [2], which define three tasks: standard, random and images. In the **rotated** datasets we define six tasks by applying [5] rotations of 0, 15, 30, 45, 60 and 75 degrees, respectively. Problems var-MNIST and rot-MNIST are generated applying the variations and rotated transformations, respectively, to MNIST; and analogously for var-FMNIST and rot-FMNIST with respect to fashion-MNIST. See Fig. 5 for examples of the images generated.

All four MT datasets contain 28×28 grey-scale images, with 60 000 patterns for training and 10 000 for test, with 10 balanced classes in both sets. Moreover, each task is roughly uniformly distributed, with about the same number of instances per task, in both the train and test sets. We refer the reader to [13] for more details about the generation of these MT image datasets.

The architecture of all models in these experiments is a convolutional NN proposed in Pytorch tutorial[2]. Also, we use the training set for a CV grid search of the weight decay hyperparameter α, where the f1 score with macro average is used as the validation metric. Once we have the optimal α, we train five independent models and obtain five test scores. Table 1 shows the average and standard deviations for the macro f1 test scores; model rankings for each problem are also given. Although the common approach seems too rigid to learn all tasks, the independent approach gets good results, with a second ranking overall. We observe that our cvx-mtlNN proposal, which can balance the influence of the common and independent approaches, gets the best results in all problems. Also, graph-mtlNN, which is more restrictive, ties with the hard sharing model in the overall ranking for third place.

4.2   Synthetic Problems

We also test our proposals on problems with an underlying task structure which, however, is not reflected on the train dataset; the goal here is to check if that

---

[1] https://github.com/carlosruizp/convexMTLPyTorch.
[2] www.pytorch.org/tutorials/intermediate/spatial_transformer_tutorial.html.

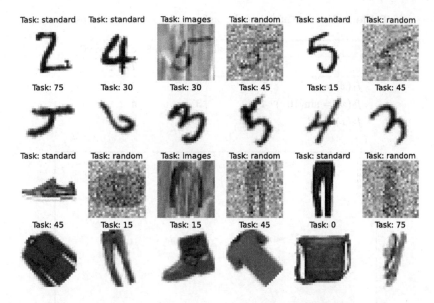

Fig. 5. Images of the four classification problems used. Each image has a title indicating the corresponding task. The rows correspond to `var-MNIST`, `rot-MNIST`, `var-FMNIST` and `rot-FMNIST` (from top to bottom).

Table 1. Image datasets results in terms of macro f1 score. The rankings for each problem are given in parentheses. The last column is the average of the rankings.

	var-mnist	rot-mnist	var-fmnist	rot-fmnist	rank
itlNN	0.9034 ± 0.0056 (5)	0.9524 ± 0.0018 (2)	0.6711 ± 0.0072 (5)	0.8152 ± 0.0046 (2)	3.50
ctlNN	0.9252 ± 0.0010 (4)	0.9366 ± 0.0023 (5)	0.7258 ± 0.0068 (2)	0.7643 ± 0.0028 (5)	4.00
cvx-mtlNN	0.9371 ± 0.0017 (1)	0.9695 ± 0.0013 (1)	0.7509 ± 0.0066 (1)	0.8351 ± 0.0040 (1)	1.00
hs-mtlNN	0.9259 ± 0.0065 (3)	0.9504 ± 0.0018 (3)	0.7168 ± 0.0051 (4)	0.7847 ± 0.0065 (3)	3.25
graph-mtlNN	0.9307 ± 0.0024 (2)	0.9475 ± 0.0019 (4)	0.7205 ± 0.0079 (3)	0.7794 ± 0.0053 (4)	3.25

hidden structure can be discovered. For this we consider three synthetic one-dimensional MTL regression problems denoted as `clustersA`, `clustersB` and `clustersC`. In all we follow the same generation procedure. First, we set three "real" tasks t_1, t_2 and t_3, defined by the functions $f_1(x) = x^2$, $f_2(x) = \sin(10x)$ and $f_3(x) = x^3$. Then, we subdivide each real task t_i in a number T_i of "virtual" tasks; this results in a total of $T = \sum_i T_i$ tasks which are given to the models. We label these new tasks as i_j, where $i = 1, 2, 3$ represents the real task, and $j = 1, \ldots, T_i$, is the label of the j-th virtual task associated with the real task i. In Table 2 we give for each real task the number of virtual tasks in each of the three synthetic problems considered. For example, for `clustersA`, we have $T_1 = 1, T_2 = 4, T_3 = 1$, i.e., there are 4 task labels that actually have the same underlying task because all are defined using the same function $f_2(x) = \sin(10x)$. For each task label i_j, we sample uniformly 50 points $x_k \in (-2, 2)$, $k = 1, \ldots, 50$,

Table 2. Number of "virtual" tasks in the synthetic datasets.

	clustersA		clustersB		clustersC	
	T_r	T	T_r	T	T_r	T
$f_1(x) = x^2$	1	6	2	7	4	13
$f_2(x) = \sin(10x)$	4		3		4	
$f_3(x) = x^3$	1		2		5	

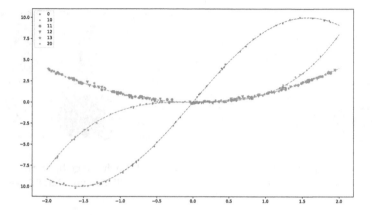

Fig. 6. Synthetic problem clustersA.

and then we use the corresponding function to compute the values $f_i(x_k)$; finally, the target values are defined as $y_k = f_i(x_k) + \epsilon_k$, where $\epsilon_k \sim N(0, 0.1)$. Figure 6 illustrates the resulting dataset for clustersA.

For the synthetic experiments, we consider a nested CV procedure, with 5 internal and 5 external task-stratified folds. The inner folds are used for hyper-parameter selection, with the mean squared error as validation metric, while the outer folds are used to compute the test scores on five different test sets. Table 3 shows the average test mean squared errors and the corresponding standard deviations. The common model is clearly the worst, as expected, since a single model obviously cannot be expected to fit all tasks; also, while the independent models get much better scores, it still has an overall fourth ranking. The reason for this is that while joining all virtual tasks would result in a single independent problem easy to learn, learning each virtual task separately is a harder problem. The convex combination cvx-mtlNN results in a better model but both hard sharing models perform better in these synthetic problems. Here our graph-mtlNN proposal has a slight advantage over hs-mtlNN, obtaining the best score in clustersA and clustersB, and the second best after hs-mtlNN in clustersC. Moreover, Fig. 7 shows the resulting adjacency matrices learned in each problem by the graph-based approach. Here, we can see that the task structure is more clearly detected in the first two problems, but less so in clustersC. In any case, our graph-mtlNN model clearly sheds light on the underlying task structure.

Table 3. Test mean squared error for synthetic datasets. The rankings for each problem are given in parentheses. The last column is the average of the rankings.

	clustersA		clustersB		clustersC		rank
itlNN	0.0730 ± 0.0872	(4)	0.0777 ± 0.0770	(4)	0.0512 ± 0.0164	(4)	4.00
ctlNN	10.2223 ± 1.9515	(5)	13.5414 ± 2.4692	(5)	11.7223 ± 1.4112	(5)	5.00
cvx-mtlNN	0.0351 ± 0.0205	(3)	0.0542 ± 0.0398	(3)	0.0431 ± 0.0098	(3)	3.00
hs-mtlNN	0.0280 ± 0.0161	(2)	0.0269 ± 0.0118	(2)	0.0172 ± 0.0017	(1)	1.33
graph-mtlNN	0.0183 ± 0.0057	(1)	0.0240 ± 0.0088	(1)	0.0195 ± 0.0019	(2)	1.00

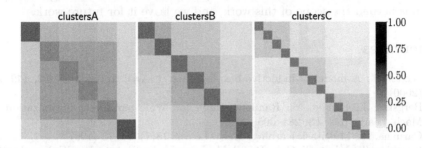

Fig. 7. Synthetic adjacency matrices learned by graph-mtlNN models.

5   Discussion and Conclusions

The Multi-Task Learning (MTL) techniques used with neural networks can be divided in hard and soft sharing approaches. In this work we have presented two proposals that combine these approaches. The first one is defined by a convex combination of a common and task-specific networks, for which the combination parameters are also learnable weights, which is closer to the soft sharing techniques. This design can deal with problems where no strong task relations are expected, but it assumes that all tasks can share the same common information. Our second model follows a hard sharing approach where the hidden layers are shared among all tasks, and where the task-specific output layers not only build task specific models but are also used to detect the task structure. Here, the tasks are conceptually placed in a graph and a regularization term is added to the network's overall penalty to capture pairwise task relationships, measured by the adjacency matrix weights that are learned during training. This approach is better suited for strongly related tasks, where learning the task structure can be useful, but it can also be too restrictive for loose task relations.

We conducted two types of experiments to test our proposals, including a pure hard sharing approach for comparison. The first set of experiments focused on four image-based multi-task problems without expected task relationships. The second set involved three multi-task synthetic problems where task relationships were present but unknown, requiring MTL models to identify them. The convex combination proposal excels in image experiments due to its flexibility, yielding superior results. Conversely, in synthetic problems, the graph-based proposal consistently outperforms other models by effectively detecting the underlying task structure. In any case, one of our proposals surpass the hard sharing approach in both situations.

This contribution marks an initial exploration of these ideas in neural MTL, and further developments are underway. We highlight the potential of combining our proposed MTL techniques, such as applying a convex combination to the output layers of hard sharing networks. Additionally, extending graph regularization beyond output weights to specific subnetworks with shared architectures is another avenue worth exploring. Moreover, although we compare our proposals with a hard sharing network, the comparison with other soft sharing techniques remains beyond the scope of this work, and we leave it for future work.

References

1. Baxter, J.: A model of inductive bias learning. J. Artif. Intell. Res. **12**, 149–198 (2000)
2. Bergstra, J., Bengio, Y.: Random search for hyper-parameter optimization. J. Mach. Learn. Res. **13**, 281–305 (2012)
3. Caruana, R.: Multitask learning. Mach. Learn. **28**(1), 41–75 (1997)
4. Evgeniou, T., Micchelli, C.A., Pontil, M.: Learning multiple tasks with kernel methods. J. Mach. Learn. Res. **6**, 615–637 (2005)
5. Ghifary, M., Kleijn, W.B., Zhang, M., Balduzzi, D.: Domain generalization for object recognition with multi-task autoencoders. In: IEEE International Conference on Computer Vision, ICCV, pp. 2551–2559. IEEE Computer Society (2015)
6. LeCun, Y., Bottou, L., Bengio, Y., Haffner, P.: Gradient-based learning applied to document recognition. Proc. IEEE **86**(11), 2278–2324 (1998)
7. Misra, I., Shrivastava, A., Gupta, A., Hebert, M.: Cross-stitch networks for multi-task learning. In: 2016 IEEE Conference on Computer Vision and Pattern Recognition, CVPR 2016, pp. 3994–4003. IEEE Computer Society (2016)
8. Ruder, S.: An overview of multi-task learning in deep neural networks. CoRR abs/1706.05098 (2017)
9. Ruder, S., Bingel, J., Augenstein, I., Søgaard, A.: Sluice networks: Learning what to share between loosely related tasks. CoRR abs/1705.08142 (2017)
10. Ruder, S., Bingel, J., Augenstein, I., Søgaard, A.: Latent multi-task architecture learning. In: The Thirty-Third AAAI Conference on Artificial Intelligence, AAAI 2019, pp. 4822–4829. AAAI Press (2019)
11. Ruiz, C., Alaíz, C.M., Dorronsoro, J.R.: Convex formulation for multi-task L1-, L2-, and LS-SVMs. Neurocomputing **456**, 599–608 (2021)
12. Ruiz, C., Alaíz, C.M., Dorronsoro, J.R.: Adaptive graph Laplacian MTL L1, L2 and LS-SVMs. Log. J. IGPL (accepted)
13. Ruiz, C., Alaíz, C.M., Dorronsoro, J.R.: Convex multi-task learning with neural networks. In: Garcia Bringas, P., et al. (eds.) HAIS 2022. Lecture Notes in Computer Science, vol. 13469, pp. 223–235. Springer, Cham (2022). https://doi.org/10.1007/978-3-031-15471-3_20
14. Xiao, H., Rasul, K., Vollgraf, R.: Fashion-MNIST: a novel image dataset for benchmarking machine learning algorithms (2017)
15. Yang, Y., Hospedales, T.M.: Deep multi-task representation learning: a tensor factorisation approach. In: 5th International Conference on Learning Representations, ICLR 2017, Toulon, France, 24–26 April 2017, Conference Track Proceedings. OpenReview.net (2017)

Validating by Deep Learning an Efficient Method for Genomic Sequence Analysis: Genomic Spectrograms

Ana Guerrero-Tamayo[1]([✉]) [iD], Borja Sanz Urquijo[1] [iD], Concepción Casado[2] [iD],
María-Dolores Moragues Tosantos[3] [iD], Isabel Olivares[2] [iD],
and Iker Pastor-López[1] [iD]

[1] Faculty of Engineering, University of Deusto, Avenida de las Universidades, 24, 48007 Bilbao, Biscay, Spain
ana.guerrero@deusto.es
[2] National Microbiology Center (NMC) - Instituto de Salud Carlos III (ISCIII), Ctra. de Pozuelo, 28, Majadahonda, 28222 Madrid, Spain
[3] Faculty of Medicine and Nursing, University of the Basque Country UPV/EHU, Barrio Sarriena s/n, 48940 Leioa, Biscay, Spain

Abstract. Traditionally, comparative and simultaneous analysis of multiple genomic sequences is performed using multiple sequence alignment algorithms. However, these algorithms are computationally complex, limiting the number of sequences that can be analyzed or requiring the comparison of only fragments, leading to a loss of information. Moreover, it is necessary to implement manual adjustments letter by letter after the alignment. Spectrograms offer a way to represent genomic sequences that enables comparison without relying on these traditional methods. Genomic spectrograms are alignment-free, thereby reducing sequence handling and processing time. Several studies have used this representation, and it appears promising. In this study, we validate this representation using a pre-trained Convolutional Neural Network (Inception V3) and transfer learning with a well-documented dataset of HIV-1 sequences to classify recombinant and non-recombinant sequences. As HIV-1 is a small organism, we can work with all fully sequenced genomes and validate the approach. In addition, we processed all HIV-1 complete genomes, not just fragments, handling a total of 134.54 million DNA nucleotides. This way, we did not lose any microbiological information. Sensitivity for classification is 96.33% in the best tested configuration and a validation accuracy over 87.81% in all tested configurations. AUC and Confusion Matrix demonstrate balanced accuracy rates. Our research provides further endorsement to the studies conducted to date and encourages the application of this representation method to genomic research.

Keywords: Genome · Spectrogram · Deep Learning · Convolutional Neural Network · Transfer Learning

University of Deusto - Research Training Grants Program.

1 Introduction

In recent years, advances in sequencing technologies have revolutionized the field of genomics, allowing for the rapid and cost-effective generation of vast amounts of genomic data [15,21]. These technologies have a significant impact on the field of metagenomics, which involves the study of genetic material extracted directly from environmental samples [4]. Metagenomics provides a new perspective on the diversity and functions of microbial communities, revealing previously unknown species and metabolic pathways [20,32,34].

However, the state of the art is not enough to face the current challenges, like the interpretation of the complete human genome [7] or the sequencing of almost 2 million SARS-CoV2 sequences [5]. With the increasing amount of sequencing data, new challenges emerge in the field of bioinformatics, particularly in the area of multiple sequence alignment [33]. Assembling and aligning large and complex genomes, as well as metagenomic datasets, is a computationally intensive task that requires sophisticated algorithms and high-performance computing resources. Moreover, these datasets often contain errors and variations that make it challenging to achieve accurate alignments.

Multiple alignment techniques and algorithms are statistical approximations that require complex expert manual adjustments [12]. In general, the most common multiple sequence alignment algorithms, such as ClustalW or MUSCLE, tend to have a time complexity on the order of $\mathcal{O}(N^2 L)$, where N is the number of sequences and L is the average sequence length. That is, the execution time will increase quadratically with N and L. This means that a multiple sequence alignment of 40 sequences with an average length of one million nucleotides can take hours or even days to complete.

Working with genomic spectrograms is alignment-free. Therefore, it is not necessary to compare all the sequences letter by letter and to make manual adjustments based on expert knowledge. Compared with alignment-dependent processes, processing time and computational requirements should be minimal.

Our objective was to validate the utility of spectrograms in the field of microbiology. Spectrograms offer advantages such as converting viral sequences into images, addressing issues like multiple sequence alignment. To accomplish this, we verified that the classification of complete HIV-1 genomic spectrograms into recombinant and non-recombinant forms using a pretrained CNN (Inception V3) aligned with microbiological evidence.

2 Background

The Fast Fourier Transform (FFT) is a computational algorithm that efficiently calculates the Discrete Fourier Transform (DFT) of a sequence. This is, the Fourier coefficients of a time-domain signal. It is widely used in signal processing, data analysis, and other related fields to analyze and manipulate signals in the frequency domain. By recursively breaking down the DFT into smaller subproblems, the FFT algorithm utilizes a divide-and-conquer approach that can efficiently compute the DFT using simple operations. This results in a significant acceleration in computing time compared to direct computation of the DFT, particularly for larger input sizes.

$$X_k = \sum_{n=0}^{N-1} x_n \cdot e^{-\frac{2\pi i}{N}kn} \qquad (1)$$

Spectrograms represent the time evolution of the Fast Fourier Transform. Common applications of spectrograms in various fields are in:

- Acoustics: Spectrograms are widely used in acoustics to analyze and visualize sound signals, such as speech, music, and animal vocalizations [23]. They can reveal important information about the frequency content, timing, and intensity of sounds, which can be used for various purposes, such as speech recognition, music analysis, and bioacoustics research [11,16].
- Signal processing: Spectrograms are used in signal processing to analyze and manipulate various types of signals, such as vibration signals [18], electromagnetic signals [10], and radar signals [14]. They can help identify patterns, anomalies, and other characteristics of signals that are difficult to detect in the time domain.
- Medical imaging: Spectrograms are used in medical imaging to analyze and visualize physiological signals, such as electrocardiograms (ECGs) [19] and electroencephalograms (EEGs). They can help diagnose and monitor various medical conditions, such as obstructive sleep apnea [22] or autism spectrum disorders [31].
- Astrophysics: Spectrograms are used in astrophysics to analyze and classify gravitational waves from core-collapse supernova [28].
- Seismology: Spectrograms are used in seismology to analyze and visualize seismic signals, such as avalanches [30] or seismic events [8]. They can provide information about the location, magnitude, and source of seismic events, which can help seismologists monitor and predict seismic activity.

Its successful application in such diverse fields suggests that this type of representation could be applied to new fields such as genomics. There is a growing trend in research to apply genomic spectrograms, which are closely linked with machine learning and deep learning techniques [2,9,24]. But most of them focus mainly on incomplete genome, fragments of coding regions. Usually, the size of the sequences does not allow working with complete genomes due to computational limitations. This can lead to loss of biological information contained in non-coding regions or other auxiliary elements. Validating this representation system using the complete genome of a given organism can provide additional support to the studies carried out and to future studies in this line.

3   Materials and Methods

All experiments ran in this equipment:

- Processing Unit: Intel(R) Xeon(R) Gold 5220R CPU @ 2.20 GHz.
- Installed RAM: 256 GB usable.
- Operative System: Windows 10 Education. Version: 21H1.
- GPU: NVIDIA RTX A6000. Total memory: 179451 MB. VRAM: 48571 MB.

3.1   Case of Study

The genome is the complete set of genetic instructions encoded in the DNA (deoxyribonucleic acid) of an organism. It contains all the information necessary for the development, function, and reproduction of an individual. The genome is composed of genes, which are specific sequences of DNA that encode for proteins or RNA (ribonucleic acid) molecules, as well as non-coding regions that regulate gene expression and other cellular processes. The genome is organized into chromosomes, which are long, linear or circular structures made up of DNA and associated proteins. Nucleotides are the building blocks of DNA and RNA, which are the two types of nucleic acids found in living organisms. Each nucleotide consists of a nitrogenous base, a sugar molecule, and a phosphate group. There are four types of nitrogenous bases found in DNA: adenine (A), thymine (T), guanine (G), and cytosine (C). In RNA, thymine is replaced by uracil (U) [6]. Depending on the type and complexity of the organism, the length of its genome can be extremely extensive, making it difficult to handle and compare. The entire human genome is composed of approximately 3 billion DNA nucleotides. The genome of the long-tailed lizard Anolis carolinensis, which is a species commonly used in research, has approximately 1.8 billion DNA nucleotides. The genome of Saccharomyces cerevisiae, which is a fungus commonly used in research and food production, has approximately 12 million DNA nucleotides. The bacterium Salmonella enterica subsp. Enterica Serovar Typhimurium strain, which is a common cause of food poisoning, has a circular genome approximately 4.9 million nucleotides in length [1]. The DNA of all these organisms is too long for a graphic representation of their complete genome. However, the genome size of viruses, which are the smallest "quasi-living" organisms, is much smaller and presents with a more simple structure.

Consequently, we focused on working with virus genomes, which are the most tractable due to their compact size and simple structure. Within this group, we selected Human Immunodeficiency Virus Type 1 (HIV-1) as our primary model organism. Its genome is small, even compared to other viruses. It consists of approximately 9.8 thousands of nucleotides in length. In contrast, the SARS-CoV2 genome is approximately 30 thousands of nucleotides, roughly three times the size of the HIV-1 genome. As a result, HIV-1 is computationally manageable.

Since the 1980s, the human immunodeficiency virus (HIV) has caused a global health crisis by triggering the AIDS pandemic, which attacks the immune system and leaves individuals vulnerable to various infections and cancers. Despite progress in understanding, preventing, and treating HIV/AIDS, it remains a significant public health challenge. In 2021, it was estimated that around 38 million people worldwide were living with HIV/AIDS, with sub-Saharan Africa being the region most affected. However, interventions like antiretroviral therapy (ART) and pre-exposure prophylaxis (PrEP) have considerably improved the prognosis for those living with HIV/AIDS [3]. Nevertheless, ongoing efforts are necessary to address the pandemic and guarantee fair access to prevention, testing, and treatment services. The severity of this global health crisis led to a high number of complete sequenced samples (13554 complete genomes until 2020).

HIV-1 is known for its high mutation rate, which enables it to evade the host immune system and develop resistance to antiretroviral drugs. However, another important mechanism that contributes to the genetic diversity of HIV-1 is recombination. Recombination occurs when two genetically distinct viruses infect the same cell and exchange genetic material during the replication process.

In the case of HIV-1, recombination can occur between two different subtypes of the virus, which are prevalent in different regions of the world. This can result in the emergence of new recombinant forms that have unique genetic characteristics and may have different clinical outcomes compared to the parental viruses. Recombination can also occur within the same subtype, leading to the generation of diverse viral variants that can further evolve and adapt to their environment. The high level of genetic diversity of HIV-1 poses significant challenges to the development of effective vaccines and antiretroviral therapies. Understanding the mechanisms of HIV-1 recombination and the genetic factors that contribute to viral diversity is crucial for developing new approaches to combat the global HIV/AIDS epidemic [26].

The importance of genetic recombination in HIV-1 results in the existence of many recombinant sequences perfectly classified as such. So, we have a case study with a sufficient and adequate dataset to validate the experiment through Deep Learning, being the handling of information computationally affordable.

3.2 HIV-1 Sequence Labelling

Our first step was downloading HIV-1 all complete sequences from Los Alamos National Laboratory HIV Database [17]. This compendium is divided into two categories:

- Pure Groups. M, N, O, and P. Group M is the most widespread in the world and is divided into nine subtypes: A, B, C, D, F, G, H, J, and K. Those four pure groups are called non-recombinants.
- Circulating Recombinant Forms (CRF). Those are called recombinant sequences.

Following this criterion, we labelled each sequence as non-recombinant (pure groups) or recombinant (CRF sequences).

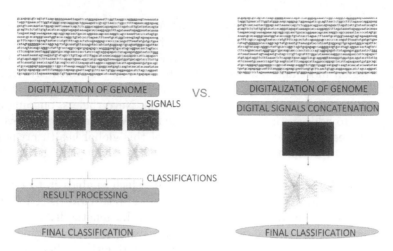

Fig. 1. Comparison of Procedures

3.3   Spectrogram Generation

The first step is to digitize the genome, decomposing it into 4 digital signals (one per nucleotide). At each position of the genome, the signal for a particular nucleotide type is activated only if that nucleotide is present at that position, while the signals corresponding to the other three nucleotides remain deactivated.

We aim to accelerate experimentation by simultaneously working with the spectrograms of individual nucleotides, rather than employing four parallel networks for each nucleotide. To achieve this, we concatenate the spectrograms of each nucleotide into a single image (Fig. 1).

It should be noted that this system could be only viable for analyzing small to medium genomes. For more complex organisms, a separate network would be required for each nucleotide.

Figure 2 presents the image resulting of concatenating the spectrograms of each of the 4 nucleotides into a single image. The x-axis denotes the nucleotide position, while the y-axis represents the frequency range from 0 to 0.5 Hz. Due to the concatenation of the four spectrograms, the length of the figure is four times the sequence length. The z-axis corresponds to the spectrogram calculation.

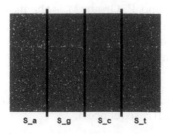

Fig. 2. Spectrogram Scheme

We generated the spectrograms using Python, Scipy library. In order to avoid biases and bad practices during the Convolutional Neural Network (CNN) training, we omitted axes, margins and any other elements that may distort the operation of the network.

3.4 Dataset Setup and Adjustments

Considering the total number of samples available in both categories, the dataset is structured as shown in Table 1.

Table 1. HIV-1 Dataset Structure

Dataset	Recombinant	Non-Recombinant	TOTAL
Train (83.13%)	1903 (16.89%)	9364 (83.11%)	11267
Validation (14.66%)	338 (17.01%)	1649 (82.99%)	1987
Test (2.21%)	150 (50.00%)	150 (50.00%)	300
	2391 (17.64%)	**11163 (82.36%)**	**13554**

The 82.36% of the sequenced HIV-1 virus are non-recombinant. Recombinant HIV-1 viruses are the 17.64% of the total sequenced. The train and validation folders are aligned with these percentages. As depicted, the weighting of the test dataset (50%/50%) intentionally differs from that of the training and validation datasets (17%/83%) in order to detect any under-fitting biases during the training stages.

Initial testing revealed that traditional data augmentation on datasets notably compromised the performance, likely due to the modification of the biological significance of the sequence. Using this technique would be detrimental, particularly if rotations are produced. This is because the precise orientation of the image determines its biological significance. As a result, we refrained from utilizing this approach.

3.5 Validation Method

Inception is a deep convolutional neural network (CNN) developed for the first time by Google researchers at 2014. Its novel Inception module allows the network to learn spatial and channel-wise features efficiently. This Inception module combines multiple filter sizes (1×1, 3×3, 5×5) and pooling operations within a single layer. And it reduces the number of parameters and computational cost through the use of 1×1 convolutions (bottleneck layers). Inception V3 is formed by symmetric and asymmetric building blocks, which include convolutions, average pooling, max pooling, concatenations, dropouts, and fully connected layers. Batch normalization is applied to activation inputs. Loss is calculated using softmax.Its architecture consists of:

- Convolutional and pooling layers.
- Inception modules (multiple, each with 1×1, 3×3, 5×5 convolutions, and pooling).
- Auxiliary classifiers (x2, used during training for intermediate supervision).
- Global average pooling. It reduces spatial dimensions to 1×1.
- Output layer: 1000 neurons (softmax, for ImageNet's 1000 classes).

Figure 3 shows a detailed scheme of Inception V3 architecture (extracted from Inception V3 Advanced Guide by Google [13]):

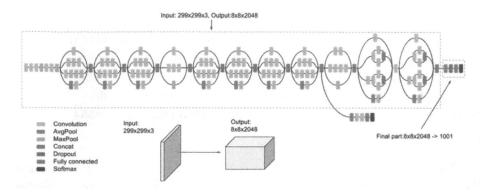

Fig. 3. Inception V3 Architecture

Inception v3 achieves higher accuracy on image recognition tasks compared to its predecessor, Inception v2 [27, 29]. This is due to a better use of batch normalization and improved training techniques. Inception v3 uses efficient training with smaller models and techniques to reduce overfitting (e.g., dropout, weight decay). It outperforms other pretrained networks (VGG, ResNet, GoogLeNet) by capturing local and global features with multiple filter layers of different sizes.

Transfer learning uses a pre-trained model to start training a new model for a related task. It reuses learned feature maps to detect general visual features. This helps the new model learn specific features faster, with less data and time. Transfer learning is useful with limited training data, as it leverages knowledge from pre-trained models trained on large datasets. To apply transfer learning, we replaced the last fully connected layer and the classification layer. This approach has been successfully applied in many computer vision applications, including object detection, segmentation, and recognition. In addition, it is widely used in complex image typologies, such as X-ray images [25] or diabetic retinopathy detection [35], achieving consistent positive results.

We did all the experimentation using MATLAB2021b App Deep Learning Designer.

3.6 Performance Measurement

We did all the performance measurement using MATLAB2021b.

To measure and evaluate the performance of each CNN in the different preset configurations, the following parameters were considered: validation accuracy, training time, confusion matrix and test accuracy.

4 Results

To evaluate the performance of our model, we conducted a test bench with various hyperparameter configurations by empirical validation, as shown in the Table 2. Our purposes were to find the optimal combination of hyperparameters that would result in the best performance of the model and to test the robustness of the model.

Table 2. Inception V3 Results

Hyperparameters	Val. Acc.	Training Time	Confusion Matrix	AUC	Test Acc.
Learning Rate: 0.0001 Batchsize: 52 Epochs: 10	0.8938	00:48:28	143 (95%) − 7 (5%) 43 (29%) − 107 (71%)	0.9226	0.8333
Learning Rate: 0.0100 Batchsize: 52 Epochs: 10	**0.9260**	**00:49:07**	**149 (99%) − 1 (1%) 13 (9%) − 137 (91%)**	**0.9863**	**0.9533**
Learning Rate: 0.0001 Batchsize: 52 Epochs: 30	0.8908	02:08:18	145 (97%) − 5 (3%) 38 (25%) − 112 (75%)	0.9499	0.8567
Learning Rate: 0.0100 Batchsize: 52 Epochs: 30	**0.9482**	**02:28:01**	**146 (97%) − 4 (3%) 7 (5%) − 143 (95%)**	**0.9943**	**0.9633**
Learning Rate: 0.0001 Batchsize: 128 Epochs: 10	0.8868	00:33:54	145 (97%) − 5 (3%) 54 (36%) − 96 (64%)	0.8729	0.8033
Learning Rate: 0.0100 Batchsize: 128 Epochs: 10	0.9321	00:34:54	147 (98%) − 3 (2%) 21 (14%) − 129 (86%)	0.9850	0.9200
Learning Rate: 0.0001 Batchsize: 128 Epochs: 30	0.8782	01:42:06	141 (94%) − 9 (6%) 48 (32%) − 102 (68%)	0.9075	0.8100
Learning Rate: 0.0100 Batchsize: 128 Epochs: 30	**0.9351**	**01:49:35**	**147 (98%) − 3 (2%) 14 (9%) - 136 (91%)**	**0.9867**	**0.9433**

The optimal configurations, defined as those that achieve the best and most balanced results, are highlighted in bold in Table 2. Among them, the configuration with 10 Epochs stands out, as it significantly reduces the training time compared to other configurations, while maintaining a high hit rate without suffering excessive penalties. Despite the varying dataset weighting, all configurations achieved an accuracy rate exceeding 87%. However, the accuracy significantly deteriorated in the recombinant sequences category for Learning Rate = 0.0001. The validation of this representation model should not only be the measurement of the absolute accuracy level. We also need balanced hit rates in both categories of the virus. Consequently, the best configuration is for Learning Rate = 0.0100, Batchsize = 52 and Epochs = 30.

Furthermore, the computation times are manageable, especially when compared to the computation times handled by other bio programs. We are working simultaneously with 13554 complete HIV-1 sequences and obtaining results with a Test Accuracy of 0.9633 in the optimal configuration, with an Average Hit Rate of 0.9450 in the configurations corresponding to Learning Rate = 0.0100.

5   Conclusions

Our research demonstrates that utilizing genomic spectrograms is a valid approach for representing and managing genomic sequences. The alignment-free nature of this representation method allowed us to save time by avoiding multiple sequence alignment and manual adjustments. The use of a pre-trained CNN (Inception V3) with transfer learning achieved high accuracy rates for classifying recombinant and non-recombinant HIV-1 sequences. The AUC and Confusion Matrix analysis revealed that the accuracy was balanced, indicating that genomic spectrograms provide a reliable representation of genomic sequences. We were able to validate this representation model by using whole genomes instead of just fragments. As a result, we processed the complete information without any loss of data. Overall, our findings suggest that genomic spectrograms are an efficient and practical alternative to multiple sequence alignment for analyzing large-scale genomic data.

It is highly interesting to develop biological algorithms specifically designed for the analysis of genomic sequences represented through spectrograms. Developing algorithms tailored to this approach could lead to further advancements in genomic research and analysis. By taking advantage of the alignment-free nature of this representation method, we can reduce the computational complexity of traditional alignment-based approaches and potentially uncover novel biological insights. Overall, our study highlights the potential benefits of developing specialized algorithms for analyzing genomic sequences represented through spectrograms.

Our next steps will involve repeating the experiment with other viruses and different viral characteristics, such as specific organ involvement, mortality, morbidity, antiviral resistance, etc. Additionally, we will analyze the feasibility of these concatenated spectrograms in larger organisms, such as bacteria.

References

1. Archive, E.E.N.: ENA (2023). https://www.ebi.ac.uk/ena/browser/. Accessed 12 May 2023
2. Bonidia, R.P., et al.: Feature extraction approaches for biological sequences: a comparative study of mathematical features. Brief. Bioinform. **22**(5), bbab011 (2021)
3. Celum, C., Baeten, J.M.: Antiretroviral-based HIV-1 prevention: antiretroviral treatment and pre-exposure prophylaxis. Antivir. Ther. **17**(8), 1483–1493 (2012)
4. Chiu, C.Y., Miller, S.A.: Clinical metagenomics. Nat. Rev. Genet. **20**(6), 341–355 (2019)
5. Collaboration, I.I.N.S.D.: SARS-CoV2 database (2023). https://covid19.sfb.uit.no/. Accessed 23 May 2023
6. Corona, D.Y.: Brock. Biología de los microorganismos. Pearson, London (2015)
7. Cortés-Ciriano, I., Gulhan, D.C., Lee, J.J.K., Melloni, G.E., Park, P.J.: Computational analysis of cancer genome sequencing data. Nat. Rev. Genet. **23**(5), 298–314 (2022)
8. Curilem, M., et al.: Discriminating seismic events of the Llaima volcano (Chile) based on spectrogram cross-correlations. J. Volcanol. Geoth. Res. **367**, 63–78 (2018)
9. Dimitrova, N., Cheung, Y.H., Zhang, M.: Analysis and visualization of DNA spectrograms: open possibilities for the genome research. In: Proceedings of the 14th ACM International Conference on Multimedia, pp. 1017–1024 (2006)
10. Dong, X., et al.: Detection and identification of vehicles based on their unintended electromagnetic emissions. IEEE Trans. Electromagn. Compat. **48**(4), 752–759 (2006)
11. Elemans, C.P., Heeck, K., Muller, M.: Spectrogram analysis of animal sound production. Bioacoustics **18**(2), 183–212 (2008)
12. Gaschen, B., et al.: Diversity considerations in HIV-1 vaccine selection. Science **296**(5577), 2354–2360 (2002)
13. Google: Inception v3 advanced guide (2023). https://cloud.google.com/docs/inception-v3-advanced. Accessed 05 June 2023
14. Harmanny, R., De Wit, J., Cabic, G.P.: Radar micro-doppler feature extraction using the spectrogram and the cepstrogram. In: 2014 11th European Radar Conference, pp. 165–168. IEEE (2014)
15. Hu, T., Chitnis, N., Monos, D., Dinh, A.: Next-generation sequencing technologies: an overview. Hum. Immunol. **82**(11), 801–811 (2021)
16. Jothimani, S., Premalatha, K.: MFF-SAug: multi feature fusion with spectrogram augmentation of speech emotion recognition using convolution neural network. Chaos Solitons Fractals **162**, 112512 (2022)
17. Laboratory, L.A.N.: The HIV database (2023). https://www.hiv.lanl.gov/. Accessed 09 June 2023
18. Leonard, F., Lanteigne, J., Lalonde, S., Turcotte, Y.: Free-vibration behaviour of a cracked cantilever beam and crack detection. Mech. Syst. Signal Process. **15**(3), 529–548 (2001)
19. Li, H., Boulanger, P.: Structural anomalies detection from electrocardiogram (ECG) with spectrogram and handcrafted features. Sensors **22**(7), 2467 (2022)
20. Lu, Z.X., Wang, X.R., Lian, X.L., Liao, X.P., Liu, Y.H., Sun, J.: Advances in the discovery of novel antibiotic-resistant genes based on functional metagenomics. Biotechnol. Bull. **38**(9), 17 (2022)

21. McCombie, W.R., McPherson, J.D., Mardis, E.R.: Next-generation sequencing technologies. Cold Spring Harb. Perspect. Med. **9**(11), a036798 (2019)
22. McNames, J., Fraser, A.: Obstructive sleep apnea classification based on spectrogram patterns in the electrocardiogram. In: Computers in Cardiology 2000, vol. 27 (Cat. 00CH37163), pp. 749–752. IEEE (2000)
23. Miyamoto, S., Nose, T., Hiroshiba, K., Odagiri, Y., Ito, A.: Two-stage sequence-to-sequence neural voice conversion with low-to-high definition spectrogram mapping. In: Pan, J.-S., Ito, A., Tsai, P.-W., Jain, L.C. (eds.) IIH-MSP 2018. SIST, vol. 110, pp. 132–139. Springer, Cham (2019). https://doi.org/10.1007/978-3-030-03748-2_16
24. Morales, J.A., et al.: Deep learning for the classification of genomic signals. Math. Probl. Eng. **2020**, 1–9 (2020)
25. Mujahid, M., Rustam, F., Álvarez, R., Luis Vidal Mazón, J., Díez, I.D.L.T., Ashraf, I.: Pneumonia classification from X-ray images with inception-v3 and convolutional neural network. Diagnostics **12**(5), 1280 (2022)
26. Nájera, R., Delgado, E., Pérez-Alvarez, L., Thomson, M.M.: Genetic recombination and its role in the development of the HIV-1 pandemic. AIDS **16**, S3–S16 (2002)
27. Nguyen, T.-T., Huynh, K.-T.: Spliced image forgery detection based on the combination of image pre-processing and inception V3. In: Dang, T.K., Küng, J., Chung, T.M., Takizawa, M. (eds.) FDSE 2021. LNCS, vol. 13076, pp. 308–322. Springer, Cham (2021). https://doi.org/10.1007/978-3-030-91387-8_20
28. Roma, V., Powell, J., Heng, I.S., Frey, R.: Astrophysics with core-collapse supernova gravitational wave signals in the next generation of gravitational wave detectors. Phys. Rev. D **99**(6), 063018 (2019)
29. Saini, M., Susan, S.: Data augmentation of minority class with transfer learning for classification of imbalanced breast cancer dataset using inception-V3. In: Morales, A., Fierrez, J., Sánchez, J.S., Ribeiro, B. (eds.) IbPRIA 2019, Part I. LNCS, vol. 11867, pp. 409–420. Springer, Cham (2019). https://doi.org/10.1007/978-3-030-31332-6_36
30. Suriñach, E., Flores-Márquez, E.L., Roig-Lafon, P., Furdada, G., Tapia, M.: Estimation of avalanche development and frontal velocities based on the spectrogram of the seismic signals generated at the vallée de la sionne test site. Geosciences **10**(3), 113 (2020)
31. Tawhid, M.N.A., Siuly, S., Wang, H., Whittaker, F., Wang, K., Zhang, Y.: A spectrogram image based intelligent technique for automatic detection of autism spectrum disorder from EEG. PLoS One **16**(6), e0253094 (2021)
32. Tong, L., et al.: Discovery of RNA and DNA viruses using next-generation sequencing: metagenomics. CVR Genom. (2023)
33. Wang, T., et al.: The human pangenome project: a global resource to map genomic diversity. Nature **604**(7906), 437–446 (2022)
34. Wani, A.K., et al.: Discovering untapped microbial communities through metagenomics for microplastic remediation: recent advances, challenges, and way forward. Environ. Sci. Pollut. Res. 1–24 (2023)
35. Yadav, S., Awasthi, P.: Diabetic retinopathy detection using deep learning and inception-v3 model. Int. Res. J. Mod. Eng. Technol. Sci. **4**, 1731–1735 (2022)

Sentiment Analysis for Vietnamese – Based Hybrid Deep Learning Models

Cach N. Dang[1](✉) ⓘ, María N. Moreno-García[2] ⓘ, Fernando De la Prieta[3] ⓘ,
Kien V. Nguyen[1,4] ⓘ, and Vuong M. Ngo[5] ⓘ

[1] Science and Technology Application for Sustainable Development (STASD) Research Group,
Ho Chi Minh City University of Transport (UTH), Ho Chi Minh 70000, Vietnam
cach@ut.edu.vn
[2] Data Mining (MIDA) Research Group, University of Salamanca, 37007 Salamanca, Spain
mmg@usal.es
[3] Biotechnology, Intelligent Systems and Educational Technology (BISITE) Research Group,
University of Salamanca, 37007 Salamanca, Spain
fer@usal.es
[4] Ho Chi Minh University of Banking, Ho Chi Minh 70000, Vietnam
kiennv_htttql@hub.edu.vn
[5] Ho Chi Minh City Open University, Ho Chi Minh City, Vietnam
vuong.nm@ou.edu.vn

Abstract. Sentiment analysis of public opinion expressed in social networks has
been developed into various applications, especially in English. Hybrid approaches
are potential models for reducing sentiment errors on increasingly complex training data. This paper aims to test some hybrid deep learning models' reliability
in some domains' Vietnamese language. Our research questions are to determine
whether it is possible to produce hybrid models that outperform the Vietnamese
language. Hybrid deep sentiment-analysis learning models are built and tested
on reviews and feedback of the Vietnamese language. The hybrid models outperformed the accuracy of Vietnamese sentiment analysis on Vietnamese datasets.
It contributes to the growing body of research on Vietnamese NLP, providing
insights and directions for future studies in this area.

Keywords: Hybrid Deep Learning Models · Sentiment Analysis · Machine
Learning

1 Introduction

Sentiment analysis, commonly called opinion mining, is a branch of natural language
processing (NLP) that focuses on locating and obtaining subjective data from text. Due
to its many uses, such as sentiment categorization, opinion summarizing, customer feedback analysis, and social media monitoring, sentiment analysis has recently attracted a
lot of attention. As a result, sentiment analysis has become an increasingly effective
tool for businesses, researchers, and legislators to understand public opinion and customer preferences better as more individuals worldwide share their ideas and feelings
on various internet platforms.

P. García Bringas et al. (Eds.): HAIS 2023, LNAI 14001, pp. 293–303, 2023.
https://doi.org/10.1007/978-3-031-40725-3_25

In recent years, deep learning approaches have been significant sentiment analysis tasks for numerous languages, including English [1], Spanish [2], Thai [3], Persian [4], Chinese [5], Arabic [6], and Hindi [7]. These techniques have been shown to outperform traditional machine learning methods by automatically learning hierarchical representations of text data, capturing features, and addressing the challenges posed by the inherent complexity of natural languages.

However, more research needs to be done on sentiment analysis in Vietnamese, an Austroasiatic language spoken by nearly 100 million people. Vietnamese presents difficulties for NLP tasks because of its distinctive language features, which include a complicated system of diacritical marks, tonal variances, and generally free word order. Vietnamese is also regarded as a low-resource language in NLP, with few annotated datasets and pre-trained models readily available.

This study proposes a hybrid deep learning model for Vietnamese sentiment analysis that incorporates Convolutional Neural Networks (CNN), Long Short-Term Memory networks (LSTM), and Support Vector Machines (SVM) to close this gap. The following are the work's main contributions:

1. We present a hybrid deep learning model that effectively captures Vietnamese text features by combining CNN, LSTM, and SVM.
2. We comprehensively compare our proposed model with several baseline models, including traditional machine learning techniques and standalone deep learning models, demonstrating the superiority of our approach on benchmark Vietnamese sentiment analysis datasets.
3. Our work contributes to the growing body of research on Vietnamese NLP, providing insights and directions for future studies in this area.

The rest of the paper is organized as follows: Sect. 2 discusses related work in Vietnamese sentiment analysis, highlighting the limitations of existing approaches. Section 3 describes the proposed hybrid deep learning model in detail, including the CNN layer, LSTM layer, and attention mechanism. Section 4 presents the experimental setup and results, comparing our model with baseline models on benchmark datasets. Finally, Sect. 5 concludes the paper and discusses future directions for research.

2   Related Work

Previous studies on Vietnamese sentiment analysis have primarily focused on traditional machine learning techniques, such as Naïve Bayes [8], SVM [9], and Decision Trees [10]. Unfortunately, these models rely on handcrafted features, such as bag-of-words (BoW), term frequency-inverse document frequency (TF-IDF), and n-grams, which limit their generalizability and performance. Some studies also proposed rule-based techniques for Vietnamese sentiment analysis [11] or presented a lexicon-based method for sentiment analysis of Facebook comments in the Vietnamese language [12]. The authors in [12] proposed a lexicon-based method for sentiment analysis by building a Vietnamese emotional dictionary (VED), including five sub-dictionaries: noun, verb, adjective, and adverb. In addition, the authors in [13], and [14] used NLP, entity relationships, and named entity ontology to recognize customer opinions and detect opinion spam in reviews of Vietnam e-commerce websites.

With the success of deep learning in various NLP tasks, researchers started exploring deep learning techniques for Vietnamese sentiment analysis. Vu et al. applied LSTM to Vietnamese sentiment analysis [15]. They presented variants of LSTM for Sentiment Analysis on Vietnamese students' Feedback Corpus that LSTM could effectively outperform traditional machine learning models. Nguyen et al. [16] also applied LSTM to span detection for Vietnamese aspect–based sentiment analysis.

CNN and LSTM are also investigated for Vietnamese sentiment analysis. Vo et al. [17] provide a novel and efficient way for integrating the advantages of CNN and LSTM in Vietnamese text. However, their work did not incorporate an attention mechanism, which has been shown to improve performance in other languages.

Recent studies have started to explore transfer learning and pre-trained language models for Vietnamese sentiment analysis. Nguyen et al. [18] proposed BERT fine-tuning method for Sentiment Analysis of Vietnamese on reviews about food and restaurant on Foody and product reviews on various e-commerce sites. Similarly, Truong et al. [19] used a pre-trained PhoBERT model for Vietnamese sentiment analysis, demonstrating promising results.

Despite these developments, research on Vietnamese sentiment analysis primarily focuses on single deep learning architectures, and the possibility of combining different architectures has yet to be investigated. To fill this gap, we present a hybrid deep learning model that combines CNN, LSTM, and SVM to extract Vietnamese text features.

3   Proposed Model

The proposed hybrid deep learning model consists of three main components: a word embedding layer, a CNN layer, and an LSTM layer with an attention mechanism, as proposed in the research [20] and using the research [21], but these models are applied to English languages. In this paper, we apply two models on Vietnamese language. We start by using a pre-trained BERT model to create the feature vector. Then, we used the CNN and LSTM models in the following stages: BERT -> CNN -> LSTM or BERT -> LSTM -> CNN. In the model's final stage, we use an SVM instead ReLU (rectified linear activation function) function because of its efficiency in word processing, especially in high dimensional contexts, such as natural language processing. The architecture of hybrid deep learning models is shown in the Fig. 1. Moreover, the details of these model connections, the connection process, and the data-processing flow are indicated in Table 1 and Table 2.

3.1   Word Embedding Layer

The first step in our model is to convert the input text into a sequence of word embeddings. Word embeddings are continuous vector representations that capture semantic relationships between words. In this study, we use a pre-trained BERT model for Vietnamese. A pre-trained BERT model is used in this study. After adjusting the parameters, the BERT model is used as a feature extractor to generate input data for the proposal of hybrid models. The Vietnamese datasets are fed into the BERT model to create the feature vectors. These embeddings are used as the input to the subsequent layers of the hybrid models.

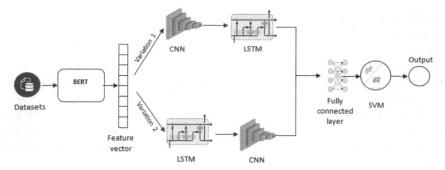

Fig. 1. Architecture of hybrid deep learning models for sentiment analysis.

Table 1. A Hybrid CNN-LSTM Model.

Layer (type)	Output Shape	Parameter #
BERT (base-uncased)	(None, 768, 1)	110,000,000
conv1d (Conv1D)	(None, 768, 512)	2,048
conv1d_1 (Conv1D)	(None, 768, 256)	393,472
conv1d_2 (Conv1D)	(None, 768, 128)	98,432
lstm_1 (LSTM)	(None, 500)	1,258,000
dense_1 (Dense)	(None, 50)	25,050
dense_2 (Dense)	(None, 2)	102
Total parameters: 111,777,104		
Trainable parameters: 111,777,104		
Non-trainable parameters: 0		

3.2   CNN Layer

CNN is a deep neural network design that is usually made up of convolutional and pooling or subsampling layers that feed into a fully connected classification layer [22]. The CNN layer is designed to capture local features in the input text. It consists of multiple filters with varying sizes, which are applied to the word embeddings to capture different n-grams in the Vietnamese text. Each filter is followed by a rectified linear unit (ReLU) activation function to introduce non-linearity into the model. After applying the filters, we use max pooling to reduce the dimensionality of the feature maps and retain the most important features. The output of the CNN layer is a set of high-level feature representations that capture local semantic information in the input text.

A single convolutional (1D CNN) is employed in this study. The first layer of the hybrid model is the CNN, which receives the vector produced by word embedding. It has three convolution layers consisting of 512, 256, and 128 filters, respectively, with a kernel size = 3, which is used to reduce the output's complexity and prevent the overfitting of the data.

Table 2. A Hybrid LSTM-CNN Model.

Layer (type)	Output Shape	Parameter #
BERT (base-uncased)	(None, 768, 1)	110,000,000
lstm_1 (LSTM)	(None, 768, 500)	1,004,000
conv1d_1 (Conv1D)	(None, 768, 512)	768,512
conv1d_2 (Conv1D)	(None, 768, 256)	393,472
conv1d_3 (Conv1D)	(None, 768, 128)	98,432
flatten (Flatten)	(None, 98304)	0
dense_2 (Dense)	(None, 50)	4,915,250
dense_3 (Dense)	(None, 2)	102
Total parameters: 117,179,768		
Trainable parameters: 117,179,768		
Non-trainable parameters: 0		

3.3 LSTM Layer with Attention Mechanism

The second layer of the hybrid model is the LSTM [23], which produces a matrix fed into the classifier. The LSTM layer captures the input text's long-range dependencies and global features. We employ LSTM cells, which process the input text in both forward and backward directions, allowing the model to effectively learn the context and relationships between words in a sentence. The output of the LSTM layer with attention mechanism is a weighted sum of the LSTM hidden states, which serves as a context vector that captures the global semantic information in the input text.

3.4 Fully Connected Layer and Output

The context vector generated by the LSTM layer with attention mechanism is passed through a fully connected (dense) layer with a ReLU activation function. This layer further processes the high-level features extracted by the CNN and LSTM layers, enabling the model to learn more complex relationships in the data.

Finally, the output of the fully connected layer with 128 nodes is fed into a SVM activation function to produce the final sentiment classification probabilities. The model is trained using categorical cross-entropy loss, and the sentiment label with the highest probability is selected as the final prediction.

4 Experimental Results

We implement our model using the Pytorch [24] and train it on Google Colab Pro with GPU Tesla P100-PCIE-16GB or GPU Tesla V100-SXM2-16GB [25]. The model is prepared using the Adam optimizer with a learning rate of 0.00005 and a batch size of 64. We use a dropout rate of 0.5 to prevent overfitting. The hyperparameters for the CNN and LSTM are selected through a grid search. Then, we compare our proposed model with several baseline single models, including SVM; deep neural networks (DNN) [26]; CNN; and LSTM. To evaluate the performance of the models, we use accuracy, precision, recall, F1-score, and AUC as the evaluation metrics.

4.1 Dataset and Preprocessing

We evaluate our proposed hybrid deep learning model on two benchmark Vietnamese sentiment analysis datasets:

1. USAL-UTH dataset collected by us: The USAL-UTH dataset consists of 10,000 Vietnamese customer comments collected from Shopee[1] e-commerce system. The reviews are labeled as positive or negative based on the rating, Negative with a 1–2 start, Positive with a five start.
2. UIT-VSFC dataset [27]: The UIT-VSFC dataset contains 16,000 Vietnamese students' feedback, with three classes: positive, neutral, and negative.

Figure 2 shows word cloud comments and feedback from the datasets described in Sect. 4.1. We perform tokenization, stop word removal, and diacritic normalization during preprocessing of the raw text. We then pad the sequences to a fixed length and convert them into the word embedding representations using PhoBERT [28] model for Vietnamese.

(a)   (b)

Fig. 2. Word cloud of the combined dataset: (**a**) USL-UTH dataset in the first panel; (**b**) UIT-SVFC in the second panel.

4.2 Results and Discussion

The experimental results show that our proposed hybrid deep learning model achieves state-of-the-art performance on the USAL-UTH and UIT-VSFC datasets. Furthermore,

---

[1] https://shopee.vn/.

the model outperforms the baseline models in terms of accuracy, precision, recall, F1-score, and AUC, as shown in Tables 3 and 4, and illustrated in Figs. 3 and 4.

Table 3. The metrics comparison for the models with two classes (positive and negative) on UIT-SVFC dataset.

Models	Accuracy	Recall	Precision	F-Score	AUC
SVM	92.24	81.62	78.85	77.99	87.22
DNN	93.56	84.74	79.86	81.80	88.03
CNN	93.49	84.56	80.00	81.85	88.09
LSTM	93.42	82.93	80.74	81.69	88.49
LSTM-CNN	93.53	83.47	80.72	81.92	88.50
CNN-LSTM	93.52	83.82	80.61	82.01	88.43

Table 4. The metrics comparison for the models with two classes (positive and negative) on USAL-UTH dataset.

Models	Accuracy	Recall	Precision	F-Score	AUC
SVM	93.33	94.54	92.57	93.52	93.35
DNN	93.35	93.38	93.90	93.63	93.36
CNN	93.56	94.06	93.58	93.81	93.56
LSTM	93.38	93.89	93.37	93.62	93.38
LSTM-CNN	93.21	94.17	92.73	93.42	93.21
CNN-LSTM	93.94	95.12	93.17	94.12	93.95

For the USAL-UTH dataset, our model achieves an accuracy of 93.94%, an improvement of 0.59% over the standalone DNN model and 0.61% over the standalone SVM model. On the UIT-VSFC dataset, our model attains an accuracy of 93.53%, outperforming the standalone SVM model by 1.29%, respectively. In comparing sentiment analysis models applied on USAL-UTH and UIT-VSFC datasets, the combined CNN-LSTM are high value in all metrics (see Fig. 5).

These results demonstrate the effectiveness of our proposed hybrid deep learning model in capturing features of Vietnamese text. The combination of CNN, LSTM, and SVM allows the model to learn complex relationships between words and their contexts, leading to superior performance in sentiment analysis tasks.

The performance gap between our model and traditional machine learning techniques is even larger, highlighting the advantages of deep learning approaches in sentiment analysis for Vietnamese.

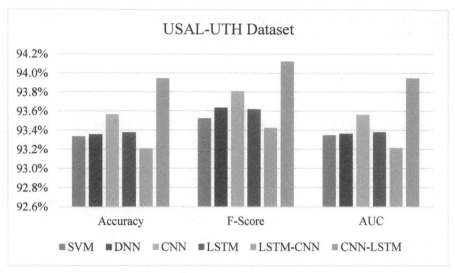

Fig. 3. Accuracy, F_Score, and AUC values of the models with BERT for Shopee customer comments dataset.

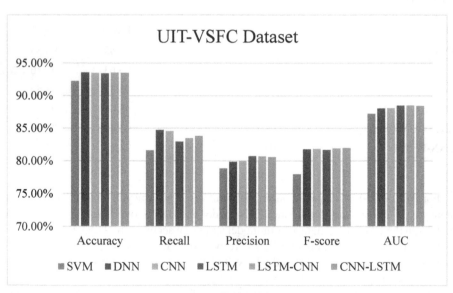

Fig. 4. Accuracy, F_Score, and AUC values of the models with BERT for Students Feedback dataset.

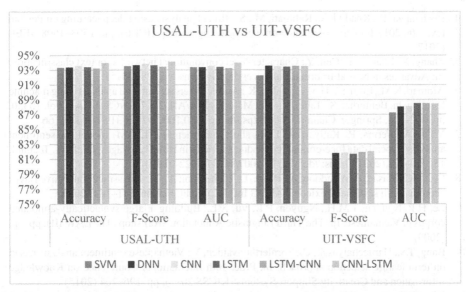

Fig. 5. Comparing Accuracy, F_Score, and AUC values with BERT on USAL-UTH and UIT-VSFC datasets.

5 Conclusion and Future Work

In this paper, we proposed a hybrid deep learning model for sentiment analysis in Vietnamese that combines CNN, LSTM, and SVM. Our model effectively captures features of Vietnamese text and outperforms on benchmark Vietnamese sentiment analysis datasets. This work contributes to the growing body of research on Vietnamese NLP and provides insights for future studies in this area.

Despite the promising results, there is stillroom for improvement and further exploration. Potential future work directions include exploring other deep learning architectures; Incorporating pre-trained language models; Leveraging transfer learning and domain adaptation; Expanding to other NLP tasks; Developing large-scale annotated datasets. By addressing these challenges and exploring these future directions, we believe our work can pave the way for more advanced and effective NLP models for Vietnamese and other low-resource languages.

References

1. Chen, Y.: Convolutional neural network for sentence classification. University of Waterloo (2015)
2. Paredes-Valverde, M.A., Colomo-Palacios, R., Salas-Zárate, M.d.P., Valencia-García, R.: Sentiment analysis in Spanish for improvement of products and services: a deep learning approach. Sci. Program. **2017**, 1–6 (2017)
3. Vateekul, P., Koomsubha, T.: A study of sentiment analysis using deep learning techniques on Thai Twitter data. In: 2016 13th International Joint Conference on Computer Science and Software Engineering (JCSSE), pp. 1–6. IEEE (2016)

4. Roshanfekr, B., Khadivi, S., Rahmati, M.: Sentiment analysis using deep learning on Persian texts. In: 2017 Iranian Conference on electrical engineering (ICEE), pp. 1503–1508. IEEE (2017)

5. Zhang, X., Zhao, J., LeCun, Y.: Character-level convolutional networks for text classification. In: Advances in Neural Information Processing Systems, vol. 28 (2015)

6. Alomari, K.M., ElSherif, H.M., Shaalan, K.: Arabic tweets sentimental analysis using machine learning. In: Benferhat, S., Tabia, K., Ali, M. (eds.) IEA/AIE 2017. LNCS (LNAI), vol. 10350, pp. 602–610. Springer, Cham (2017). https://doi.org/10.1007/978-3-319-60042-0_66

7. Yadav, V., Verma, P., Katiyar, V.: Long short term memory (LSTM) model for sentiment analysis in social data for e-commerce products reviews in Hindi languages. Int. J. Inf. Technol. **15**, 759–772 (2023). https://doi.org/10.1007/s41870-022-01010-y

8. Le, C.-C., Prasad, P., Alsadoon, A., Pham, L., Elchouemi, A.: Text classification: Naive Bayes classifier with sentiment lexicon. IAENG Int. J. Comput. Sci. **46**, 141–148 (2019)

9. Le, H.P., Nguyen, T.M.H., Nguyen, P.T., Vu, X.L.: Building a large syntactically-annotated corpus of Vietnamese. In: The Third Linguistic Annotation Workshop (The LAW III), pp. 6p. (2009)

10. Bang, T.S., Haruechaiyasak, C., Sornlertlamvanich, V.: Vietnamese sentiment analysis based on term feature selection approach. In: Proc. 10th International Conference on Knowledge Information and Creativity Support Systems (KICSS 2015), pp. 196–204 (2015)

11. Kieu, B.T., Pham, S.B.: Sentiment analysis for Vietnamese. In: 2010 Second International Conference on Knowledge and Systems Engineering, pp. 152–157. IEEE (2010)

12. Trinh, S., Nguyen, L., Vo, M., Do, P.: Lexicon-based sentiment analysis of Facebook comments in Vietnamese language. In: Król, D., Madeyski, L., Nguyen, N.T. (eds.) Recent developments in intelligent information and database systems. SCI, vol. 642, pp. 263–276. Springer, Cham (2016). https://doi.org/10.1007/978-3-319-31277-4_23

13. Nguyen, P., Le, L., Ngo, V., Nguyen, P.: Using entity relations for opinion mining of Vietnamese comments. arXiv preprint arXiv:1905.06647 (2019)

14. Nguyen, L., Pham, N., Ngo, V.M.: Opinion spam recognition method for online reviews using ontological features. arXiv preprint arXiv:1807.11024 (2018)

15. Nguyen, V.D., Van Nguyen, K., Nguyen, N.L.-T.: Variants of long short-term memory for sentiment analysis on Vietnamese students' feedback corpus. In: 2018 10th International Conference on Knowledge and Systems Engineering (KSE), pp. 306–311. IEEE (2018)

16. Nguyen, K.T.-T., Huynh, S.K., Phan, L.L., Pham, P.H., Nguyen, D.-V., Van Nguyen, K.: Span detection for aspect-based sentiment analysis in Vietnamese. arXiv preprint arXiv:2110.07833 (2021)

17. Vo, Q.-H., Nguyen, H.-T., Le, B., Nguyen, M.-L.: Multi-channel LSTM-CNN model for Vietnamese sentiment analysis. In: 2017 9th International Conference on Knowledge and Systems Engineering (KSE), pp. 24–29. IEEE (2017)

18. Nguyen, Q.T., Nguyen, T.L., Luong, N.H., Ngo, Q.H.: Fine-tuning BERT for sentiment analysis of Vietnamese reviews. In: 2020 7th NAFOSTED Conference on Information and Computer Science (NICS), pp. 302–307. IEEE (2020)

19. Truong, T.-L., Le, H.-L., Le-Dang, T.-P.: Sentiment analysis implementing BERT-based pre-trained language model for Vietnamese. In: 2020 7th NAFOSTED Conference on Information and Computer Science (NICS), pp. 362–367. IEEE (2020)

20. Dang, C.N., Moreno-García, M.N., De la Prieta, F.: Hybrid deep learning models for sentiment analysis. Complexity **2021**, 1–16 (2021)

21. Dang, C.N., Moreno-García, M.N., De la Prieta, F.: Using hybrid deep learning models of sentiment analysis and item genres in recommender systems for streaming services. Electronics **10**, 2459 (2021)

22. Yamashita, R., Nishio, M., Do, R.K.G., Togashi, K.: Convolutional neural networks: an overview and application in radiology. Insights Imaging **9**(4), 611–629 (2018). https://doi.org/10.1007/s13244-018-0639-9

23. Hochreiter, S., Schmidhuber, J.: LSTM can solve hard long time lag problems. In: Advances in Neural Information Processing Systems, vol. 9 (1996)

24. https://pytorch.org/

25. https://colab.research.google.com/notebooks/pro.ipynb

26. Aggarwal, C.C.: Neural Networks and Deep Learning, vol. 10, p. 3. Springer, Heidelberg (2018). https://doi.org/10.1007/978-3-319-94463-0

27. Van Nguyen, K., Nguyen, V.D., Nguyen, P.X., Truong, T.T., Nguyen, N.L.-T.: UIT-VSFC: Vietnamese students' feedback corpus for sentiment analysis. In: 2018 10th International Conference on Knowledge and Systems Engineering (KSE), pp. 19–24. IEEE (2018)

28. Nguyen, D.Q., Nguyen, A.T.: PhoBERT: pre-trained language models for Vietnamese. arXiv preprint arXiv:2003.00744 (2020)

Optimizing LIME Explanations Using REVEL Metrics

Ivan Sevillano-Garcia$^{(\boxtimes)}$, Julian Luengo, and Francisco Herrera

Department of Computer Science and Artificial Intelligence, Andalusian Research Institute in Data Science and Computational Intelligence (DaSCI), University of Granada, 18071 Granada, Spain
isevillano@ugr.es

Abstract. Explainable artificial intelligence (XAI) has emerged as a crucial topic in the field of machine learning to provide insights into the reasoning performed by artificial intelligence (AI) systems. However, the lack of a clear definition of explanation and a standard methodology for evaluating the quality of explanations has made it challenging to develop effective XAI systems. One commonly used approach is Local Linear Explanations, but the evaluation of their quality is still unclear due to theoretical inconsistencies. This issue is even more challenging in image recognition, where visual explanations often detect edges rather than providing clear explanations for decisions. To address this issue, several metrics that quantitatively measure different aspects of explanation quality in a robust and mathematically consistent manner has been proposed. On this work, we apply the REVEL framework approach, which standardizes the concept of explanation and allows for the comparison of different explanations and the absolute evaluation of individual explanations. We provide a guide of the REVEL framework to perform an optimization process that aims to improve the explainability of machine learning models. We apply the proposed five metrics on the CIFAR 10 benchmark and demonstrate their descriptive, analytical and optimization power. Our work contributes to the development of XAI systems that provide reliable and interpretable explanations for AI reasoning.

Keywords: Explainable artificial intelligence · Local Linear Explanations · Evaluation metrics

1 Introduction

Artificial intelligence (AI) has become an essential technology in today's world, with applications ranging from image recognition to natural language processing thanks to the development of Deep Learning [6]. However, as AI systems become more complex, the need for understanding their inner workings has grown. This has led to the emergence of the field of explainable artificial intelligence (XAI), which aims to provide interpretable and understandable explanations for the made by AI systems [2]. The ability to understand the reasoning of AI systems is crucial for ensuring their reliability, accountability, and transparency.

XAI has become a crucial topic in the field of machine learning because it provides insights into the reasoning performed by AI systems. However, developing effective XAI systems is challenging due to the lack of a clear and formal mathematical definition of what constitute an explanation and a standard methodology for evaluating the quality of explanations [7]. This has led to inconsistencies in the evaluation of XAI systems, particularly in image recognition tasks where visual explanations can be vague and hard to interpret [4]. One commonly used approach to provide explanations in XAI systems is Local Linear Explanations (LLE), which provides a linear approximation of the model's decision boundary around the point of interest. A widely used method to obtain LLE explanations is Local Interpretable Model-Agnostic Explanations (LIME) [8], a popular method for explaining the decisions made by AI models. The method has been shown to be effective in explaining image recognition decisions. However, LIME has parameters to optimize manually, including the sigma parameter to control the neighborhood size, that could have a significant impact on the quality of the generated explanations.

To evaluate the quality of the explanations and thus be able to choose one over the other, the framework REVEL (Robust Evaluation VEctorized Local-linear-explanation) [9] is proposed. In the work where REVEL is proposed, different previous methodologies and their strengths and weaknesses are discussed in order to develop five metrics and a robust methodology of evaluation of LLE explanations.

In this work, the evaluative capability of the REVEL framework is used to optimize the LIME sigma parameter in order to obtain higher quality explanations. For this purpose, we propose a methodology where the five metrics of the REVEL framework are applied on different explanation configurations of the sigma parameter and a study on the impact in order to establish a criterion for choosing a specific sigma value is conducted.

The experimental study is performed on the CIFAR10 dataset as a benchmark to determine the optimal value of the LIME sigma parameter, which controls the size of the LIME neighborhood. For this purpose, we choose a range of values of the same parameter and we make a comparison between them to establish quality criteria on which to decide. We also provide visual examples of the explanations generated by LIME for different values of sigma to demonstrate the impact of the parameter on the quality of the generated explanations.

This work is structured as follows: Section 2 describes the most important points we need to know in order to perform the study, which are the characteristics of LIME to generate explanations on the one hand, and the requirements and metrics used in the REVEL framework to evaluate them on the other hand. Section 3 describes the objective and methodology we followed to conduct the study. Section 4 details the characteristics of the experiment such as the description of the dataset, parameters we will set and the range of the sigma parameter we want to optimize. In addition, the results obtained by LIME under the REVEL framework are collected and analyzed. Section 5 shows the differences between two explanations with different configurations are shown visually. Finally, Sect. 6 provides the conclusions of the work.

2   Related Works

In this section we describe the key concepts on the literature that we will need for the development of the methodology. Those concepts are the LIME method to generate explanations and the REVEL Framework to evaluate those explanations.

2.1   Generating Explanations: LIME Method

There has been an increasing interest in developing XAI systems to provide explanations for the reasoning of AI models. One popular approach is Local Interpretable Model-Agnostic Explanations (LIME) [8], which generates local surrogate models to approximate the behavior of the black-box model in the vicinity of a given input. LIME has been shown to be effective in various applications, including image recognition, text classification, and recommender systems.

The sigma parameter in LIME controls the width of the kernel used to generate the local surrogate models. A smaller value of sigma results in a more localized and detailed explanation, whereas a larger value of sigma results in a more global and less detailed explanation. The choice of the sigma value is crucial because it can greatly affect the quality of the explanation. If the sigma value is too small, the explanation may be too specific to the given input and not generalizable to other inputs. On the other hand, if the sigma value is too large, the explanation may be too general and not informative enough.

Therefore, finding the optimal value of sigma is crucial to generate accurate and informative explanations. However, determining the optimal value of sigma can be challenging because it depends on the specific characteristics of the input data and the black-box model.

Formally, sigma controls the weight given to each neighbor based on its distance from the original example, using the following formula:

$$w(x') = e^{-d(x,x')\sigma^2},\tag{1}$$

where $d(x_i, x)$ is the Euclidean distance between the original example x and the neighbour x'.

2.2   Evaluating Explanations: REVEL Framework

As evaluating the XAI explanation proposal can be difficult, several proposal has been developed to achieve this task. The proposal of [3] is based on desirable qualitative aspects for an explanation without including ways to measure them. A quantitative way of achieving an analysis of explanations is made by [1], where the LEAF framework is proposed, designed for the evaluation and comparison of explanations. In [9] an analysis of LEAF is made, highlighting its advantages and inconsistencies. It also proposes REVEL, a framework that fixes the inconsistencies of LEAF and adds a new metric not considered as such in LEAF.

The REVEL Framework includes five different metrics that can be used to evaluate explanation proposals: Local Fidelity, Local Concordance, Prescriptivity, Conciseness, and Robustness. A description of which aspect each metric measure and how to measure them with the REVEL Framework is summarized in Table 1. For a more detailed description of how the metrics are calculated, we recommend reading the article where the REVEL metrics are proposed.

Table 1. Summary of the metrics developed by REVEL and the qualitative aspect they measure

Name	What is evaluated	How REVEL evaluate this aspect
Local Concordance	How similar is the LLE to the original black-box model on the original example	Regularized distance between output vectors of black-box and explanation
Local Fidelity	How similar is the LLE to the original black-box model on a neighborhood of original example	Mean of regularized distances of output vectors of black-box and explanation over the neighbourhood
Prescriptivity	How similar is the LLE to the original black-box model on the closest neighbour that changes the class of the original example	Regularized distance between output vectors of black-box and explanation on this neighbour
Conciseness	How brief and direct is the explanation	Mean of the absolute feature importance of the model
Robustness	How much two explanations generated by the same LLE generator differ	Expectation of cosine similarity between importance matrixes

3   Optimizing LIME Explanations

In this section, we present our approach to optimize the sigma parameter of LIME explanations by leveraging the REVEL Framework and its metrics. Our goal is to enhance the explainability of machine learning models by finding the optimal value of the sigma parameter in LIME, which significantly influences the quality and interpretability of the generated explanations. By applying the REVEL metrics, the different LIME explanations produced with varying sigma values can quantitatively evaluate and the most effective explanation for a given task can be identified. Through this optimization process, we aim to provide reliable and interpretable explanations that enhance our understanding of AI reasoning.

We initially produce a variety of LIME explanations using various sigma parameter values to start the optimization process. This enables us to identify a range of explanation quality, from extremely localized and specific to more broad explanations. The performance of each set of explanations is then assessed using the REVEL metrics, taking into account the Local Fidelity, Local Concordance, Prescriptivity, Conciseness, and Robustness criteria for explanation quality. We can learn more about how different sigma values affect the overall quality of the explanations by studying the results, and also determine which sigma value produces the most appealing and useful explanations. The optimization process enables us to improve the explainability of machine learning models and enhance the transparency of AI systems in various domains.

Below we describe some of the criteria that should be taken into account when choosing one configuration over another for each metric:

- A high **Local Concordance** metric is necessary, since it indicates that the explanation given fits well with the example to be explained.
- A high **Local Fidelity** metric is also necessary, since it indicates that the explanation given fits well with the neighbourhood of example to be explained. We should not notice much difference between this metric and the local concordance as it would indicate that the neighborhood chosen does not represent well the locality of the example to be explained.
- It is desirable a good **Prescriptivity** metric. This is because this metric contemplates the generalization of the explanation to a point far enough away to change class. It is not expected to obtain a high score, but it is useful to compare between explanations. In addition, by comparing with the Local Concordance and ocal Fidelity metrics, it gives an idea of the score it should have at most.
- The **Conciseness** metric is an indication of how many features have been discarded by the explanation, being recommended that neither too many nor too few are eliminated.
- The **Robustness** metric must be as high as possible since in ensures it is obtained an explanation as close as possible to each other. This metric is important in stochastic methods, such as LIME and SHAP methods, which use a reduced random list of neighbors to generate explanations, generating a different explanation each time.

With these criteria, we will be able to choose the sigma value with the best behaviour on the experimental study. However, the final selection of the explanation must depend on the results of the experimental study and the different metrics relation. That is why the decision to choose one configuration over the other must be made with the full understanding of the metrics proposed.

4   Experimental Study: REVEL Metrics Case of Study

In this section, the experimental setup used to optimize the explanations offered by LIME based on its sigma parameter is defined. Then, the results generated by this experimental setup are analyzed.

4.1   Experimental Setup

We used the CIFAR 10 dataset [5] in our experiments. The default model used is efficientnetb2 [11], trained for 100 epochs with a learning rate of 1e-05 using the SGD optimizer with L2 regularization. This model achieved an accuracy of 95.2% on the test set. We selected the same 100 examples from the test set to apply the measures.

To generate the neighbors for LIME, we used the method of hiding squares of size $\left(\dfrac{N}{8}, \dfrac{N}{8}\right)$ from the original image. Each square is considered a feature, and hiding a square means changing it to gray in the original image. We generated examples that are more likely to influence the creation of LIME explanation, as in [10].

For each example and each value of sigma, we generated 10 different LIME explanations with 1000 neighbours.

4.2   Results and Analysis

In this section we present the results of our experimentation, which consists of evaluating the LLE generated by LIME with different sigma values (2, 4, 6, 8, 10, 12, 14, 16, 18 and 20) using the REVEL metrics: Local Concordance, Local Fidelity, Prescriptivity, Conciseness and Robustness. We start by showing the descriptive median and interquartile range statistics of the metrics for all sigma values in Table 2.

Table 2. Median and interquartile range of each of the LIME configuration over each metric of REVEL

Sigma	Local_Concordance	Local_Fidelity	Prescriptivity	Robustness	Conciseness
2	**99.38% ± 2.08**	**99.24% ± 2.34**	76.32% ± 27.81	**98.05% ± 1.13**	73.45% ± 8.82
4	98.84% ± 4.17	98.25% ± 4.35	81.29% ± 18.71	97.32% ± 1.16	75.19% ± 10.65
6	98.78% ± 5.80	98.19% ± 5.72	83.95% ± 18.32	96.51% ± 1.40	75.57% ± 9.95
8	98.27% ± 6.57	98.45% ± 5.87	84.14% ± 11.58	95.84% ± 1.54	75.79% ± 8.47
10	98.51% ± 9.78	97.80% ± 8.22	82.99% ± 14.22	95.52% ± 1.86	76.18% ± 9.19
12	94.09% ± 15.96	94.14% ± 12.51	83.59% ± 14.54	94.06% ± 2.44	75.80% ± 9.37
14	96.30% ± 14.73	95.67% ± 11.53	85.22% ± 13.92	93.67% ± 2.33	**76.55% ± 7.67**
16	94.65% ± 21.82	93.77% ± 16.83	85.20% ± 13.38	93.15% ± 2.84	75.26% ± 8.67
18	90.09% ± 30.01	92.10% ± 20.50	**86.36% ± 13.20**	92.36% ± 2.35	75.93% ± 9.61
20	92.23% ± 20.92	92.72% ± 16.18	84.77% ± 11.95	91.99% ± 3.20	76.45% ± 9.68

The previous table provides a comprehensive summary of the evaluation results obtained for the proposed LIME configuration with different values of the sigma parameter. We can say that, as sigma increases, the Local Concordance, the Local Fidelity and the Robusstness metrics decrease, while prescriptivity increases. It is not clear if Conciseness metric has any impact over the sigma

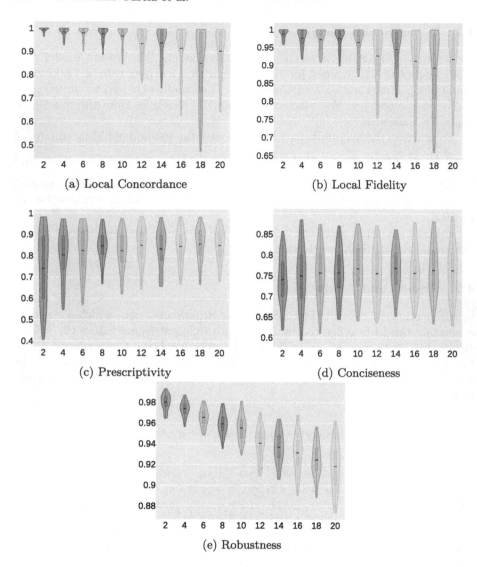

Fig. 1. Violin plots for each metric (y axis) over different sigma values (x axis).

parameter. However, due to the variability of the results and the need to further analyze their distribution, we complement the table with violin plots in Fig. 1.

Local Concordance and Local Fidelity metrics decrease with increasing sigma, the prescriptivity metric tends to increase, reaching similar values for these three metrics. Indeed, the reason for this behavior is that the sigma parameter in LIME controls how important nearby neighbors are. The larger the value, the more it considers distant neighbors, so the close neighborhood loses slightly in importance. However, this behavior seems to increase the predictive capacity of the Prescriptivity metric.

Regarding the conciseness metric, we have not reached clear conclusions as they all seem to have the same measure.

We can observe that as we increase the sigma, the less robust the explanation. The explanation for this is that as the sigma increases, the more distant neighborhood becomes more important and more distant neighbors are generated. This causes the variability to increase.

Finally, with the partial conclusions of each metric, general conclusions can be drawn for the choice of sigma. Based on our experiments, we observe that the optimal value of sigma for generating high-quality LLEs is the one that strikes a balance between local fidelity, local concordance, and prescriptivity metrics. Specifically, our results indicate that sigma values of 14, 16 or 18 produce the best balance, that is, they achieve good results in the Prescriptivity metric without the Local Concordance, Local fidelity and Robustness measures decreasing too much. We can also notice that increasing the sigma value more causes the Local Concordance, Local Fidelity and Robustness measures to decrease, while the improvement in Prescriptivity is slight. Thus, to obtain more robust explanations and best quality explanations, we recommend using a sigma value of 14.

5   Explanation Visualization: Impact of the Sigma Parameter

To further illustrate the impact of the sigma parameter on the LIME explanations, we propose visualizations of two explanations, one with sigma set to the optimized value of 14 and another with sigma set to 2. The visualizations aim to show the differences in the explanations generated by LIME with different sigma values.

In the visualization, we highlight important positive features for each class in green, irrelevant features in yellow, and important negative features in red.

The first visualization corresponds to the optimized sigma value of 12. In this case, the LIME explanation highlights the most important features for the classification of the image. As shown in Fig. 2, the regions with the highest contribution to the classification are the most of the cat region.

In contrast, when we set sigma to 2, the LIME explanation changes significantly. As shown in Fig. 3, the most important region for the classification is now smaller, centered in less regions. This change in the explanation is expected, given that a smaller sigma value means that LIME gives more importance to the local features of the image.

These visualizations demonstrate the importance of selecting an appropriate sigma value for the LIME explanations. The optimization process we proposed helps to find a suitable value for the specific problem. Additionally, the visualizations highlight the potential impact of sigma on the generated explanations, and how small changes in its value can lead to significant differences in the highlighted features.

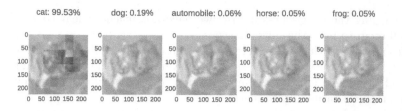

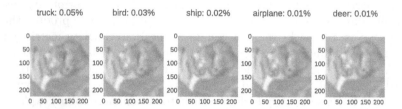

Fig. 2. Visualization of the explanation with sigma = 14

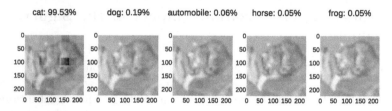

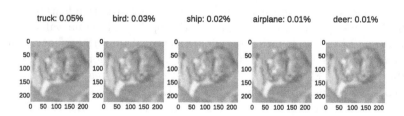

Fig. 3. Visualization of the explanation with sigma = 2

6   Conclusion

Our work analyse a practical usage of REVEL Framework. This framework proposed several metrics which aim to provide a better understanding of the quality of the LIME explanations by evaluating how well they reflect the model behavior. In fact, thanks to this analysis we optimize the sigma parameter of LIME, which determines the explanation that this method provides.

We also show that these metrics provide complementary information, with local concordance and local fidelity being highly correlated and prescriptivity capturing a different aspect of the explanations. Also, Robustness is a metric to take into account. We can't say nothing about the Conciseness metric, at least on this experimental setup.

Our proposed analysis is an useful approach for researchers and practitioners who use LIME to have a better understanding of the model interpretation and explanation. By providing a more comprehensive evaluation of LIME explanations, these metrics can help to identify weaknesses and areas for improvement in the generated explanations.

Acknowledgements. This work was supported by the Spanish Ministry of Science and Technology under project PID2020-119478GB-I00 financed by MCIN/AEI/10.13039/501100011033. This work was also partially supported by the Contract UGR-AM OTRI-6717 and the Contract UGR-AM OTRI-5987. and projects P18-FR-4961 by Proyectos I+D+i Junta de Andalucia 2018. The hardware used in this work is supported by the projects with reference EQC2018-005084-P granted by Spain's Ministry of Science and Innovation and European Regional Development Fund (ERDF) and the project with reference SOMM17/6110/UGR granted by the Andalusian "Consejería de Conocimiento, Investigación y Universidades" and European Regional Development Fund (ERDF).

References

1. Amparore, E., Perotti, A., Bajardi, P.: To trust or not to trust an explanation: using leaf to evaluate local linear XAI methods. PeerJ Comput. Sci. **7**, e479 (2021)
2. Arrieta, A.B., et al.: Explainable artificial intelligence (XAI): concepts, taxonomies, opportunities and challenges toward responsible AI. Inf. Fusion **58**, 82–115 (2020)
3. Confalonieri, R., Coba, L., Wagner, B., Besold, T.R.: A historical perspective of explainable artificial intelligence. Wiley Interdisc. Rev. Data Min. Knowl. Discov. **11**(1), e1391 (2021)
4. Doshi-Velez, F., Kim, B.: Towards a rigorous science of interpretable machine learning. arXiv preprint arXiv:1702.08608 (2017)
5. Krizhevsky, A., Nair, V., Hinton, G.: Cifar-10, **5**(4), 1 (2010). (canadian institute for advanced research), http://www.cs.toronto.edu/kriz/cifar.html
6. LeCun, Y., Bengio, Y., Hinton, G.: Deep learning. Nature **521**(7553), 436–444 (2015)
7. Miller, T.: " but why?" understanding explainable artificial intelligence. XRDS: crossroads. ACM Mag. Students **25**(3), 20–25 (2019)
8. Ribeiro, M.T., Singh, S., Guestrin, C.: "why should i trust you?": explaining the predictions of any classifier, pp. 1135–1144. KDD 2016, Association for Computing Machinery, New York, NY, USA (2016). https://doi.org/10.1145/2939672.2939778
9. Sevillano-García, I., Luengo, J., Herrera, F.: Revel framework to measure local linear explanations for black-box models: deep learning image classification case study. Int. J. Intell. Syst. (2023). https://doi.org/10.48550/ARXIV.2211.06154, https://arxiv.org/abs/2211.06154
10. Slack, D., Hilgard, A., Singh, S., Lakkaraju, H.: Reliable post hoc explanations: Modeling uncertainty in explainability. In: Ranzato, M., Beygelzimer, A., Dauphin, Y., Liang, P., Vaughan, J.W. (eds.) Advances in Neural Information Processing Systems, vol. 34, pp. 9391–9404. Curran Associates, Inc. (2021)
11. Tan, M., Le, Q.: Efficientnet: Rethinking model scaling for convolutional neural networks. In: International Conference on Machine Learning, pp. 6105–6114 (2019)

Assessing the Impact of Noise on Quantum Neural Networks: An Experimental Analysis

Erik Terres Escudero$^{(\boxtimes)}$, Danel Arias Alamo$^{(\boxtimes)}$, Oier Mentxaka Gómez ,
and Pablo García Bringas

Deusto University, Bilbao, Spain
{e.terres,pablo.garcia.bringas}@deusto.es,
{danel.arias,oiermentxaka}@opendeusto.es

Abstract. In the race towards quantum computing, the potential benefits of quantum neural networks (QNNs) have become increasingly apparent. However, Noisy Intermediate-Scale Quantum (NISQ) processors are prone to errors, which poses a significant challenge for the execution of complex algorithms or quantum machine learning. To ensure the quality and security of QNNs, it is crucial to explore the impact of noise on their performance. This paper provides a comprehensive analysis of the impact of noise on QNNs, examining the Mottonen state preparation algorithm under various noise models and studying the degradation of quantum states as they pass through multiple layers of QNNs. Additionally, the paper evaluates the effect of noise on the performance of pre-trained QNNs and highlights the challenges posed by noise models in quantum computing. The findings of this study have significant implications for the development of quantum software, emphasizing the importance of prioritizing stability and noise-correction measures when developing QNNs to ensure reliable and trustworthy results. This paper contributes to the growing body of literature on quantum computing and quantum machine learning, providing new insights into the impact of noise on QNNs and paving the way towards the development of more robust and efficient quantum algorithms.

Keywords: Quantum Computing · Quantum Neural Networks · Quantum Machine Learning · Noisy Intermediate-Scale Quantum

1 Introduction

In recent years, quantum computing has made remarkable progress, and its potential advantages over classical computing have become increasingly apparent. Quantum neural networks (QNNs) are a promising approach to quantum artificial intelligence that leverage the unique properties of quantum systems to achieve exponential memory capacity, scalability, and faster learning. Several researchers have proposed QNNs as a possible alternative to classical neural networks, highlighting their potential benefits [1–3].

P. García Bringas et al. (Eds.): HAIS 2023, LNAI 14001, pp. 314–325, 2023.
https://doi.org/10.1007/978-3-031-40725-3_27

Noisy Intermediate-Scale Quantum (NISQ) processors have made quantum systems with hundreds of qubits available, which is a significant milestone for quantum computing. However, the results generated by these systems are still noisy and prone to errors, which poses a challenge for the execution of complex algorithms or quantum machine learning. The combination of the inherent instability of neural networks with the inconsistency and error-proneness of quantum computing creates a challenging landscape for researchers to navigate. Nevertheless, these challenges present a unique opportunity for researchers to explore new methods and techniques to address the limitations of both quantum computing and neural networks.

Ensuring the quality and security of quantum neural networks is a crucial step in guaranteeing that production-ready industry models perform as intended, requiring high accuracy and robustness against noisy data. Potential quantum errors could be exploited by malicious agents to manipulate the output of the network, leading to inaccurate predictions or faulty decisions. To safeguard against such attacks, quantum software development must adopt a rigorous approach with strict quality criteria and error-free execution [4].

Our work provides a comprehensive analysis of the impact of noise on quantum neural networks. We examine the Mottonen state preparation algorithm [5] under various noise models and study the degradation of quantum states as they pass through multiple layers of quantum neural networks. Additionally, we evaluate the effect of noise on the performance of quantum neural networks and highlight the challenges posed by noise models in quantum computing.

The structure of this paper is organized as follows. In Sect. 2, we review the existing literature and highlight the key contributions of prior research in this area. In Sect. 3, we describe our experimental approach and methodology for analyzing the effects of noise on quantum neural networks. In Sect. 4, we present the empirical findings of our analysis. In Sect. 5, we discuss the implications of our findings and their significance. Finally, in Sect. 6, we draw conclusions and suggest future research directions in this field.

1.1 Quantum Neural Networks

Quantum computing leverage qubits, which grants it with unique properties such as superposition and entanglement. In order to operate, quantum computers make use of quantum gates (e.g. rotation R_x, and CNOT/C_x). Even if these properties make Quantum computing powerful, the current state of the art in quantum computers are NISQ (Noisy Intermediate-Scale Quantum) which suffer from various types of noise and errors that make them less reliable if not correctly used. To mitigate this, researchers are working on different physical improvements or algorithms, such as Quantum error correction algorithms.

Quantum neural networks are a special type of neural network which leverage the power of these quantum properties to learn complex data models and solve problems. To implement such networks, Variational Quantum Circuits (VQC) are constructed by a series of gates with trainable parameters which can be tuned.

These circuits approximate classical learning by emulating the internal structure of classical neural networks using a construction of CNOT and Rotation Gates. This layer structure, known as a strongly entangled layer, is similar to a classical layer. CNOT connections represent synapse connections, while rotations on the layer represent weighted sum transformations [6].

While more complex network structures, such as quantum activation functions or quantum recurrent networks, have been proposed, their high implementation complexity makes them impractical for this work. Therefore, we will rely on standard rotation/entangled layered networks [7–9].

1.2 The Challenges on Measuring Error on Quantum Neural Networks

The challenges surrounding quantum neural networks are multifaceted, stemming from both the early state of quantum computing and the complexity of neural networks. One key challenge is the inherent error proneness of quantum hardware, which limits the viability of deep QNNs. Due to the current noise in quantum computers, the circuits on the hardware can only have limited depth, restricting the size and complexity of QNNs that can be developed. Developing deeper QNNs demands multiple layers of quantum gates, which increases the impact of errors.

Another significant challenge is the lack of a clear theoretical framework for QNNs. This makes it difficult to understand and quantify the errors in these systems and develop effective error correction techniques. Furthermore, the development of such techniques is also challenging due to the complex interplay between the quantum hardware and the neural network algorithms. Therefore, addressing these challenges is necessary to enable the development of robust QNNs that can effectively solve complex problems.

2   Related Work

Quantum Variational Circuits are a type of parametrized quantum circuit that use a hybrid learning methodology for training quantum neural networks [10]. Quantum data is processed by the circuit, while the output and the training is done by classical training optimization techniques, such as backpropagation. This approach makes them a powerful tool for solving a wide range of problems in fields such as supervised classification [7,11,12] and reinforcement learning [13,14].

Two primary techniques are commonly utilized for initializing data into the circuit, namely Angle Embedding and Amplitude Embedding. Whilte angle-based states make use of fewer gates, their information storage capacity scales linearly with the number of qubits, which makes them unsuitable for handling high-dimensional data. On the other hand, amplitude embedding techniques, such as Mottonen state preparation algorithm, enable exponentially greater data dimensionality at the expense of an exponentially larger number of required gates [5].

Despite the potential benefits of quantum neural networks, the presence of noise in NISQ computers can reduce their learning capacity by causing barren plateaus, which result in a vanishing gradient and limit the learning capabilities of these systems [15]. Although several Quantum Error Correction techniques exist, they do not guarantee error-free execution of quantum circuits [16]. However, recent research suggests that the presence of some low level of noise may help avoid saddle points and ensure the model's convergence [17]. In order to achieve quantum advantage, it is essential to ensure that quantum computers are robust against environmental noise and gate errors [18].

3 Methodology

The present study aims to tackle three fundamental challenges in QNNs: (1) how environmental noise and gate error affects the state of a quantum system as it passes through a quantum neural network, (2) how resilient amplitude state preparation algorithms are to noise, and (3) how noise impacts the performance of pre-trained quantum neural networks.

To evaluate the impact of noise on the quantum state under increasing layers, we will prepare uniformly initialized quantum neural networks and run several executions with random weights to evaluate the degradation of the state. We will analyze the rate of degradation with respect to two baselines: the resultant state of a noise-free evaluation on the same circuit and the expected convergence state of the system under high noise.

Regarding the second problem, we will evaluate the resilience of amplitude state preparation algorithms to noise by analyzing the effect of different noise models on the prepared state. We will provide visual information of the resultant state and a later comparison of the effect under quantum neural networks.

For the third problem, we will first train multiple quantum neural networks in a noise-free environment and then evaluate their performance under various noisy models provided by IBM Quantum. We will use the MNIST dataset as a benchmark and measure the degradation in performance caused by the noise. To better understand the impact of noise on classification performance, we will conduct experiments with different class splits and analyze how the space of the classification is affected by the noise perturbation.

To avoid any bias in the results, we will use multiple noise models with different specifications to evaluate the impact of noise on QNNs. This will allow us to examine how different noise models affect QNNs in unique ways, ensuring that the results are not influenced by a single noise model.

Overall, our approach involves training and testing quantum neural networks under different noisy conditions, using appropriate metrics to evaluate performance, and comparing the results to identify the impact of noise on the quantum neural network.

3.1   Experimental Setup

To provide accurate results on the quantum simulations, real quantum machine specifications will be used. Specifically, we will make use of the AER simulator, which mimics the execution of the quantum circuits on actual devices, providing reliable and precise results. In order to minimize bias and ensure the quality of the work, we have selected four distinct quantum systems to extract their specifications for the simulator: IBM Cairo, IBMQ Guadalupe, IBM Hanoi, and IBMQ Mumbai. These simulators were chosen based on their compatibility with our research requirements, ensuring a minimum of 8 qubits and the capability to sample from a variety of quantum models.

We chose the MNIST dataset to test the impact of noise on trained quantum machine learning models' inference capacity. We will test all models for 2 (0–1), 4 (0–3), and 10 (0–9) classes to investigate whether the number of classes affects the error rate. Given that the input dimension is 784, we will use amplitude encoding because angle embeddings are not feasible. To reduce redundancy and address memory restrictions, we will reduce the data to 14×14 (196) dimensions through max pooling (2×2 kernels) with strides (2×2). We will then project the 196 dimensions to the 256 states of an 8 qubits system, setting the extra states to zero.

We will use Pennylane as the main quantum machine learning library and Qiskit as a backend for quantum circuit simulation. The circuits will have 8 qubits, and the networks will follow a standard structure. We will prepare the initial state with a Mottonen state preparation circuit followed by a sequential chain of strongly entangled layers. In total, we will prepare 5 different networks, with 1, 3, 5, 7 and 9 layers respectively. Measurements will be given as the average state of each qubit at the end of the circuit. To account for a variable number of classes and since the quantum circuits contain 8 qubits, we will connect the output of the quantum network to a classical dense classification layer.

To train the quantum neural networks, we will utilize the Pennylane lightning plugin with Tensorflow as the interface, following a supervised learning approach. The 5 networks will be trained on the MNIST dataset, split into three categories: 0–1, 0–3, and 0–9, for 1, 2, and 4 epochs, respectively. We will use the Adam optimizer with a learning rate of 0.01 and a categorical cross-entropy loss function. The adjoint optimization algorithm will be employed as the backprop-agation algorithm, as it is both fast and reliable. The training will use 600 shots on the quantum circuit and a batch size of 16 to reduce the statistical noise in the measurement outcomes.

4   Results

The experimental result reveals that noise in IBM quantum systems causes latent states to converge towards a uniform distribution, rendering the system unable to distinguish between real states and the uniform states. As depicted in Fig. 1, the degradation rate of the system follows an exponential decay. The rate of degra-dation of the state strongly varies with the chosen noise model chosen, with IBM Hanoi and IBMQ Mumbai allowing for deeper networks without impactful degradation, taking up to 50 steps to fully converge towards a uniform distribu-tion, while IBM Guadalupe takes up to 10 layers and IBM Cairo takes up to 5 layers.

Although intrinsic noise per-turbs the state of quantum sys-tems, the overall distribution of the data appears to remain. As shown in Fig. 2, for example, on IBM Hanoi or IBMQ Mumbai at layer 15, while a clear uniform floor has been formed, the highest states of the distribution still retain their order and relative magnitude with the original state. However, as the depth increases, the mag-nitude of conservation of the real

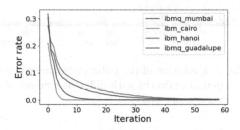

Fig. 1. χ^2 distance with respect to a uniform distribution per iteration, up to 60 iterations for the 4 specified backends.

state decreases until the distribution is equal to the uniform distribution.

It is worth noting that IBM noise models are updated regularly, and their specifications are updated online daily. During the development of the paper, the noise models cycled between lower and higher noise models, with some unable to hold the distribution under even one layer. Therefore, it is essential to ensure that the model's specifications meet certain robustness criteria before using noisy models in production, especially as no alert is triggered when the noise models are updated.

Our analysis of Amplitude Embedding algorithms revealed that high noise errors in gates or readout resulted in a faulty distribution of the state, causing specific pixels of the image to have sharper values than their neighbors. Figure 3 provides a clear example of this behavior in IBM Cairo, where a faulty CNOT with an error rate of 1, acting between qubits 0 and 1, creates a sharp pixel in the background. This pixel absorbs half of the distribution of the state, maintaining the shape of the zero in the background but completely altering the distribution of the data.

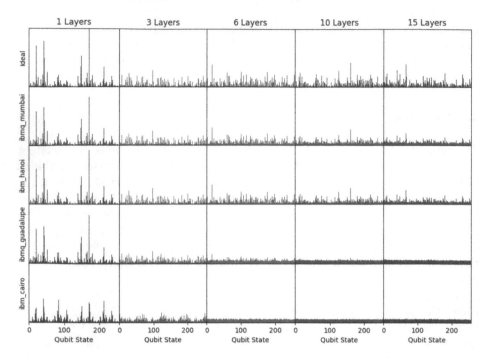

Fig. 2. Evolution of the qubit state under the 4 specified noise models in several quantum neural networks with different amount of random weighted layers (1, 3, 6, 10 and 15 layers respectively) .

In contrast, IBM Hanoi, IBMQ Guadalupe, and IBMQ Mumbai were able to prepare the state in a way that was still visible. Although IBMQ Guadalupe added a higher degree of background noise, the most important pixels were still present in the image. Among the three, IBMQ Mumbai was the most precise noise model in preparing quantum states by providing an evenly distribute state through the expected pixels while keeping a moderate background noise. Yet, as it can be seen in Fig. 1, the background noise in IBMQ Mumbai is stronger than IBM Hanoi's, degrading the state of the circuit faster. IBM Hanoi, while not having the best distribution over the pixels, contains the most robust noise distribution over the different backends.

As the data is encoded through binary CNOT gates, most of the noise in the images can be clearly attributed to binary location. This trend is visible in the results obtained from IBMQ Guadalupe and IBM Hanoi, where a trace of high intensity pixels can be seen on the even pixels on the right side of the images. It is important to note that this noise distribution behaves differently from classical noise, which is uniformly distributed throughout the image. The noise in quantum data follows a clear trend to focus on states which are divisible by different powers of two. This characteristic of quantum noise should be taken into account when dealing with data preparation or noise correction in future algorithms.

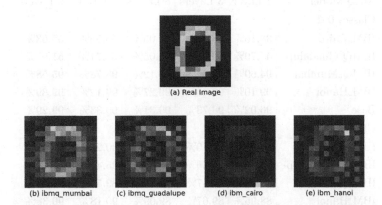

(a) Real Image

(b) ibmq_mumbai   (c) ibmq_guadalupe   (d) ibm_cairo   (e) ibm_hanoi

Fig. 3. Mottonen State Preparation on the specified noise models from different quantum computers: (a) Real image, (b) IBMQ Mumbai noise model effect, (c) IBMQ Guadalupe noise model effect, (d) IBM Cairo noise model effect, (e) IBM Hanoi noise model effect.

The results presented in Table 1 clearly demonstrate the impact of noise levels on model accuracy. In particular, the noise levels in IBM Cairo are significant enough to severely limit the model's learning ability, as evidenced by the deformed pixel shown in the state preparation process. This shift in the data leads to a significant decrease in accuracy, as expected.

While IBMQ Guadalupe is a less noisy model compared to IBM Cairo, it still struggles to maintain accuracy beyond a one-layer neural network and quickly degrades towards a random model. On the other hand, IBM Hanoi and IBMQ Mumbai, which are the least noisy models, are able to maintain performance over different numbers of layers, but still suffer a noticeable accuracy loss.

Our analysis showed that certain noise models had a greater impact on QNNs trained with different numbers of layers. This can be attributed to the fact that noise models affect specific gates, readouts, or connections with varying degrees of strength. As a result, different weight sets trained on the same data may be impacted differently by the same noise model, resulting in varying levels of performance degradation.

Additionally, we observed a significant decrease in accuracy when increasing the number of classes on the network. For instance, IBMQ Mumbai, which was able to accurately solve the 2 and 4 classes split, struggled when dealing with 10 classes, failing to reach 50% accuracy in any number of layers. Similarly, IBM Hanoi, which performed better initially, also suffered significantly, with only one model achieving 70% accuracy.

Table 1. Accuracy of the pre-trained QNNs for the specified noise models and number of layers.

Noise Model	1 Layer	3 Layers	5 Layers	7 Layers	9 Layers
Classes 0–1					
IBM_Cairo	38.16%	36.53%	38.05%	55.56%	55.63%
IBMQ_Guadalupe	47.79%	50.31%	38.05%	55.71%	61.95%
IBMQ_Mumbai	94.69%	97.34%	99.12%	98.78%	95.58%
IBM_Hanoi	99.10%	99.43%	99.27%	99.12%	99.89%
Base	96.02%	98.73%	99.31%	99.33%	99.29%
Classes 0–3					
IBM_Cairo	26.43%	19.10%	26.5%	30.23%	26.49%
IBMQ_Guadalupe	39.13%	24.56%	23.64%	25.45%	28.12%
IBMQ_Mumbai	80.67%	55.47%	89.71%	89.53%	78.29%
IBM_Hanoi	88.95%	89.67%	89.09%	90.18%	90.38%
Base	84.23%	92.79%	93.86%	94.56%	94.74%
All Clases					
IBM_Cairo	9.83%	10.22%	10.57%	9.70%	11.62%
IBMQ_Guadalupe	25.74%	17.04%	10.57%	21.08%	13.12 %
IBMQ_Mumbai	44.87%	29.03%	17.02%	37.56%	29.52%
IBM_Hanoi	54.22%	69.51%	70.46%	68.16%	52.47 %
Base	59.46%	70.45%	72.74%	78.22%	79.43%

5   Discussion

In this study, we aimed to investigate the impact of noise on quantum neural networks in IBM quantum systems. Our findings suggest that the presence of noise in quantum systems causes latent states to converge towards a uniform distribution, making it difficult to distinguish between real states and uniform states. The rate of degradation of the state strongly depends on the chosen noise model, with IBM Hanoi and IBMQ Mumbai being the least noisy models, while IBMQ Guadalupe and IBM Cairo experience a more significant loss of accuracy. However, on initial layers, the distribution of the data appears to retain certain structure, allowing for classical post-processing of the output. Nevertheless, these results highlight the need for noise-robust systems to build deep QNNs reliably.

The analysis on the effect of Amplitude Embedding in different quantum computing environments showed that high noise errors in gates or readout resulted in a faulty distribution of the state, causing specific pixels of the image to have sharper values than their neighbors. This effect can be attributed to the high dependency of the Mottonen State preparation on CNOT gates, with are one of the most error-prone gates. The exponential need of CNOT gates implies a high probability of degradation on noisy quantum systems. Notably, since CNOT gates are binary gates, the error trace observed on the image exhibited a clear binary aspect, where sets of powers of 2 manifested high noise values.

This trend is visible in the results obtained from IBMQ Guadalupe and IBM Hanoi, where a trace of high-intensity pixels can be seen on the even pixels on the right side of the images. This characteristic of quantum noise should be taken into account when dealing with data preparation or noise correction in future algorithms.

The results presented in this study clearly demonstrate the significant impact of noise levels on the accuracy of QNNs. Models with cleaner state preparation achieved better accuracies, and the accuracy of the models was directly related to their ability to retain the distribution of their data from the uniform distribution. These findings highlight the importance of having circuit quality measures in place to assess the stability of QNNs under ongoing noise circumstances. As seen in the table, circuits trained with similar expected accuracy can yield vastly different results when subjected to noise.

The impact of increasing the number of classes on the performance of QNNs is significant. This is due to the nature of QNNs as mathematical functions that map data spaces. As the number of classes increases, the distance between different class spaces decreases, making it easier for any perturbation in the data caused by intrinsic noise to move the latent data from one class to another. Therefore, if the goal is to develop deeper and more complex QNNs, it is crucial to reduce noise to a level where perturbations have even lower thresholds of action. Otherwise, accumulated noise perturbations will inevitably distort the output, leading to incorrect classifications.

Given the high cost of training quantum neural networks on actual quantum computers, the training in this study was conducted on simulators. However, training on a noise-robust quantum computer could reveal valuable insights into the capacity and limitations of QNNs in real-world environments. Therefore, an important future direction would be to extend these results to real quantum computers. Another potential line of research would involve conducting an ablation study on the different noise factors that make up a general noise model in quantum computing, such as T1, T2, and gate errors. Such an analysis could help identify which noise factors are most significant and require the most attention in developing robust QNNs.

6   Conclusion

In this investigation, the effect of noise in IBM quantum systems on deep quantum neural networks has been studied. The results indicate that noise in quantum systems causes qubit states to converge exponentially towards a uniform distribution, rendering the system unable to operate with the state. The rate of degradation of the state depends on the chosen noise model, highlighting the need for noise-robust systems to develop deep quantum neural networks reliably. Nonetheless, the fundamental structure of the quantum state remains intact for several layers, indicating the feasibility of developing noise reduction techniques on the quantum output.

The study demonstrated the influence of noise on quantum state preparation, highlighting that noise-tolerant models resulted in improved image representation in the quantum state. Notably, the observed noise in quantum systems differed from classical systems, as it exhibited a pattern aligned with multiples of powers of 2, potentially due to interactions between various CNOT gates and connectivity structures. This unique characteristic of quantum noise should be taken into account in future algorithms for noise correction or data preparation.

The current state of quantum hardware limits the depth of circuits that can be used, making it challenging to build deep QNNs. Different noise models affect QNNs with varying degrees of strength, which can impact their performance differently. Furthermore, increasing the number of classes in a dataset leads to a decrease in accuracy due to the geometrical nature of QNNs as mathematical functions that map data spaces. These findings underscore the importance of developing circuit quality measures to assess the stability of QNNs under noise and the need for future work to explore training on actual quantum hardware.

Acknowledgements. The authors would like to acknowledge the partial financial support by Ministry of Science (project QSERV-UD, PID2021-124054OB-C33), and also to the Basque Government (projects TRUSTIND - KK-2020/00054, and REMEDY - KK-2021/00091). Additionally, the authors wish to acknowledge the selfless support from IBM, who generously provided their quantum computing equipment for the project. Finally, it is important to also express gratitude for the support and drive that the regional government of Bizkaia is providing in all matters related to the development of quantum technologies as a driving force for progress of the Society of this historic territory.

References

1. Ezhov, A.A., Ventura, D.: Quantum neural networks. In: Kasabov, N. (ed.) Future Directions for Intelligent Systems and Information Sciences. Studies in Fuzziness and Soft Computing, vol. 45, pp. 213–235. Physica Verlag, Heidelberg (2000). https://doi.org/10.1007/978-3-7908-1856-7_11
2. Gupta, S., Zia, R.: Quantum neural networks. J. Comput. Syst. Sci. **63**(3), 355–383 (2001). https://www.sciencedirect.com/science/article/pii/S0022000001917696
3. Schuld, M., Sinayskiy, I., Petruccione, F.: The quest for a quantum neural network. Quantum Inf. Process. **13**(11), 2567–2586 (2014). https://doi.org/10.1007/s11128-014-0809-8
4. Arias, D., et al.: Let's do it right the first time: Survey on security concerns in the way to quantum software engineering. Neurocomputing **538**, 126199 (2023). https://www.sciencedirect.com/science/article/pii/S0925231223003041
5. Mottonen, M., Vartiainen, J.J., Bergholm, V., Salomaa, M.M.: Transformation of quantum states using uniformly controlled rotations (2004). arXiv:quant-ph/0407010, http://arxiv.org/abs/quant-ph/0407010
6. Schuld, M., Bocharov, A., Svore, K.M., Wiebe, N.: Circuit-centric quantum classifiers. Phys. Rev. A **101**(3) (2020). https://doi.org/10.1103/physreva.101.032308
7. Henderson, M., Shakya, S., Pradhan, S., Cook, T.: Quanvolutional Neural networks: powering image recognition with quantum circuits. arXiv:1904.04767 [quant-ph] (2019)

8. Maronese, M., Destri, C., Prati, E.: Quantum activation functions for quantum neural networks. arXiv:2201.03700 [quant-ph] (2022)
9. Bausch, J.: Recurrent quantum neural networks. arXiv:2006.14619 [quant-ph, stat] (2020)
10. Cerezo, M., et al.: Variational quantum algorithms. Nat. Rev. Phys. **3**(9), 625–644 (2021). arXiv:2012.09265 [quant-ph, stat]
11. Rebentrost, P., Mohseni, M., Lloyd, S.: Quantum support vector machine for big data classification. Phys. Rev. Lett. **113**(13), 130503 (2014). arXiv:1307.0471 [quant-ph]
12. Hur, T., Kim, L., Park, D.K.: Quantum convolutional neural network for classical data classification. Quantum Mach. Intell. **4**(1), 3 (2022). https://doi.org/10.1007/s42484-021-00061-x
13. Lockwood, O., Si, M.: Reinforcement learning with quantum variational circuits. arXiv:2008.07524 [quant-ph, stat] (2020).
14. Lockwood, O.: Playing Atari with hybrid quantum-classical reinforcement learning. In: NeurIPS (2021)
15. Wang, S. et al.: Noise-induced barren plateaus in variational quantum algorithms. Nat. Commun. **12**(1), 6961 (2021). https://www.nature.com/articles/s41467-021-27045-6
16. Roffe, J.: Quantum error correction: an introductory guide. Contemp. Phys. **60**(3), 226–245 (2019). arXiv:1907.11157 [quant-ph].
17. Liu, J., Wilde, F., Mele, A.A., Jiang, L., Eisert, J.: Noise can be helpful for variational quantum algorithms. arXiv:2210.06723 [quant-ph] (2022)
18. Huang, H.-Y., et al.: Quantum advantage in learning from experiments. Science **376**(6598), 1182–1186 (2022). arXiv:2112.00778 [quant-ph]

Varroa Mite Detection Using Deep Learning Techniques

Jose Divasón[1(✉)], Francisco Javier Martinez-de-Pison[1], Ana Romero[1], Pilar Santolaria[2], and Jesús L. Yániz[2]

[1] University of La Rioja, Logroño, Spain
{jose.divason,fjmartin,ana.romero}@unirioja.es
[2] University of Zaragoza, Zaragoza, Spain
{psantola,jyaniz}@unizar.es

Abstract. The varroa mite is a major problem for beekeeping today because it threatens the survival of hives. This paper develops deep learning methods for detecting varroa in images to monitor the level of infestation of the hives in order to use treatments against varroa in time and save the bees. The ultimate goal is its implementation by beekeepers. Therefore, the deep learning models are trained on pictures taken by smartphone cameras covering the entire board where both pupae and varroas are placed. This makes the object detection task a challenge, since it becomes a small object detection problem. This paper shows the experiments that have been developed to solve this challenge, such as the use of super resolution techniques, as well as the difficulties encountered.

Keywords: varroa mites · beekeping · small object detection

1 Introduction

Varroa destructor, commonly known as varroa mites, are a parasitic species that feed on the bodily fluids of honey bees. These mites (see Fig. 1) are considered one of the most significant threats to honey bee health, as they weaken and damage the bees' immune systems, making them more susceptible to disease and other stressors. In addition to causing direct harm to individual bees (both pupae and adults), varroa mites also transmit various viruses that can further weaken colonies and lead to their collapse [27]. In fact, *varroosis* is currently the most damaging disease in beekeeping worldwide. In the European Union it is endemic, being the only beekeeping disease that requires systematic treatment of bee colonies in order to keep parasitization rates below harmful thresholds.

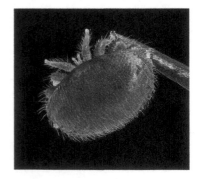

Fig. 1. A varroa destructor

P. García Bringas et al. (Eds.): HAIS 2023, LNAI 14001, pp. 326–337, 2023.
https://doi.org/10.1007/978-3-031-40725-3_28

(a) Sticky board method   (b) Sugar shake method   (c) Pupae method

Fig. 2. Cropped images of the three methods.

Given the crucial role that honey bees play in pollination and the global food supply, the development of effective and efficient detection methods for varroa mites is therefore critical to the survival of honey bees and the industries that rely on their pollination services. One promising avenue for varroa detection is through the use of deep learning techniques applied to images of honey bees. By training neural networks to recognize the unique characteristics of varroa mites, researchers and beekeepers could quickly and accurately identify infested colonies and take appropriate action to treat and manage the infestation. The development of such methods has the potential to improve the way beekeepers monitor and protect their hives, ultimately helping to protect the future of honey bees and the vital ecosystems they support. Different methods have been proposed to count varroa mites in hives [10,21]. Three of them are explained below, which can be combined with artificial vision algorithms (see Fig. 2).

- Bottom board and sticky board: it consists of placing on the bottom of the hive a board and a white card on it with a sticky substance to which the mites that fall on it stick.
- Sugar shake or alcohol wash: invasive methods that require washing the bees with powdered sugar, if they are to be kept alive, or with alcohol or liquid soap, sacrificing them. This permits a large part of the varroa mites to be removed from bees, which can be counted on the container in which they remain.
- Bee breeding counting: a hive frame is extracted during the breeding period; then, varroa mites and pupae are counted.

This work is mainly based on the last method. The main advantage of this method is that, in addition to being very reliable, the varroa infestation rate during the breeding season can be known and thus can be treated earlier. The models will also be analyzed with a few images of the sticky board method. Regarding the image analyses concerning the three approaches, all methods share one fact: large images are captured, but very small objects have to be detected.

The article is structured as follows. Section 2 presents related papers in two important areas for this work: the small object detection task and the use of

AI for varroa mite detection. Section 3 shows the dataset creation, the metrics and deep learning techniques used in this work. Experiments and results are discussed in Sect. 4. Finally, conclusions are shown in Sect. 5.

2 Related Work

2.1 Object Detection and Small Object Detection

Object detection is a fundamental problem in computer vision that deals with identifying and localizing objects of interest in a digital image. Deep learning techniques, particularly convolutional neural networks (CNNs), have revolutionized this field and achieved state-of-the-art results in recent years [17,23,34]. Small Object Detection (SOD) is a particular instance of object detection that is focused on detecting small-size (or tiny) objects. This issue is particularly relevant in fields such as biology (where small objects like cells are relatively small compared to the input image), satellite images [19], drone scenes [11,31] and more [13,30,32]. Many more challenges appear in small object detection tasks compared to object detection [6].

For instance, *noisy feature problems* could appear since small objects usually have low resolution, and this often causes neuronal networks to have problems learning good representations from their blurred shapes. In addition, due to the typical structure of object detectors (a backbone combined with a detection head), there is usually an *information loss*: the feature extractor component usually reduces the size of the feature maps and tends

Fig. 3. One image with a varroa mite on a adult bee, taken from [3].

to learn high-dimensional features. This is particularly critical with small objects, because they are inevitably seen as very few pixels within the network. In fact, the standard Faster R-CNN architecture has an effective stride of 16 i.e., a 16 × 16 object is seen as a single pixel by the region proposal network (RPN).

Different approaches have been investigated to try to alleviate these problems [5,6]. For instance, one of the main techniques is the use of specific data-augmentation strategies [33]; indeed, some authors copy instances of the small objects and paste them in different positions of the image with one or several random transformations [4,14]. Moreover, another powerful technique is the use of super-resolution [7,28] to partly reconstruct the blurry appearance of small objects and even the introduction of Generative Adversarial Networks (GANs) to generate new visually similar data to feed the algorithms.

2.2 Varroa Mite Detection and Deep Learning

There are some works related to adult honey bees detection, monitorization [15,29], tracking the movement of pollens [24] and others [1,2,20] with deep learning. However, less research has been done for varroa mite detection

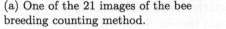

(a) One of the 21 images of the bee breeding counting method.   (b) One of the 5 images of the bottom board method.

Fig. 4. Two images from the dataset.

and counting. Probably, the most similar work to us is the one by Bilil *et al.* [3], in which YOLOv5 and Single Shot Detector (SSD) are used to detect and distinguish between the healthy and the infected bees. Concretely, the starting point is an existing dataset [25] that is modified by including other public images to define six classes: healthy bee, the bee with pollen, drone, queen, varroa mite infected bee and varroa mite. The images have a high resolution and are restricted to adult bees, see [3, Figure 2] and Fig. 3. In contrast, our interest relies on varroa mite detection on pupae and working with photos that can be taken easily with a mobile device by the beekeeper. An initial attempt on pupae and varroa mite detection was developed in a master thesis [12]. The results were not fully satisfactory, mainly due to poorly adjusted bounding boxes.

In recent years there have also been mobile applications that use AI to count varroa[1]. However, either the results are not good or they are commercial apps where the models are not publicly available. In addition, none of them is suitable for varroa mite detection on pupae.

3   Methods

3.1   Dataset Creation

The dataset contained 21 images with a resolution of 4032 × 3024 pixels and captured by a smartphone camera. The capture method was the third one presented in the introduction, during the months of February to June 2022, and with different lighting conditions. The images contained both pupae and varroa mites from different hives, being the number of varroa mites highly variable in each image (ranging from 2 to 187). A total of 732 varroa mites were identified by experts from these images. Figure 4a is one of such images and Fig. 2c a 512 × 512 pixels crop.

---

[1] For instance, https://beemapping.com, www.beescanning.com and https://apisfero.org.

In addition, 5 images of the board method (first method described in intro-duction) were also available, and obtained under the same conditions as above. These images contained varroa mites (a total of 460), but no pupae appeared. However, they also contained many other noisy artifacts like dust, dirt and soil. Figure 4b is one of such images and Fig. 2a a 512 × 512 pixels crop.

3.2   Metrics

The Intersection over Union (IoU) is a measure of overlap between two bounding boxes, defined as the ratio of the area of overlap between the two bounding boxes to the area of their union. If the IoU between the predicted bounding box and the ground truth bounding box is above a certain threshold, the predicted bounding box is considered a true positive.

The Average Precision (AP) measures the quality of the detection output by computing the area under the precision-recall curve. Obviously, AP is dependent on the IoU threshold used to determine whether a predicted bounding box is a true positive or a false positive. The mean average precision (mAP) is the average of AP of all classes. The mAP score is usually calculated ranging different IoU, i.e., mAP corresponds to mAP@[0.5,0.95,0.05] that is the average AP for IoU from 0.5 to 0.95 with a step size of 0.05. Similarly, mAP50 represents the mAP computed at a fixed IoU threshold of 0.5.

Analogously, the mean average recall (mAR) is the recall averaged over dif-ferent IoU. This work used both metrics for evaluating the models, based on the `torchmetrics` Python package.

3.3   Deep Learning Methods

Current state-of-the-art approaches are based on CNN object detectors. There are two main families of detectors: one-stage methods (such as the YOLO fam-ily [22], SSD [18] and EfficientDet [26]) and two-stage methods (the R-CNN family [8,9,23]).

In two-stage detections, one part of the network (the RPN) generates candi-date object proposals (the candidate bounding boxes), and the other part ana-lyzes them, ranks their likelihood to be a true positive, and classifies and locates the objects inside. One-stage detectors, on the other hand, directly predict the class and location of objects without the need for a separate proposal generation stage. It is kwown that one-stage detectors are generally faster and more flexible but may sacrifice some accuracy. Two-stage detectors are more accurate, par-ticularly for small objects. However, they are slower and require more training data. Thus, since the varroa mites are a small object detection challenge (with low resolution), it made more sense to use a Faster R-CNN approach.

We also tried several state-of-the-art neuronal networks as different back-bones (the part of a neural network that is responsible for feature extraction) for the Faster R-CNN, such as ResNet50 FPN, EfficientNet B0 to B7, MobileNetV3 Large FPN, and so on.

(a) A too broad bounding box.   (b) A wrong varroa mite prediction.

Fig. 5. Training with wide bounding boxes.

Due to the low resolution of the images, the small objects and the difficulty to distinguish sometimes varroa mites from soil or other artifacts, we tried
super-resolution techniques to improve the quality of the images (see Fig. 9).
Specifically, we used Enhanced Deep Residual Networks [16], to multiply by 2,
3 and 4 the resolution of the input images.

4   Experiments and Results

Experiments were performed on a computing server with two NVIDIA RTX
3090 GPUs. As a metric we used mAP50, i.e., detection was considered successful when the IoU was at least 50%. We chosen this metric over mAP, because
beekeepers are interested in the number of varroa mites, rather than in a perfect
fit of the bounding boxes. The images of the dataset were split by 80–20%, but
also ensuring that a similar proportion of varroa mites was maintained between
both sets.

A baseline approach with the default Faster R-CNN configuration and parameters achieved a mAP score of 0.1543. Thus, models did not learn well with the
initial experiments. Analyzing why this was happening, we detected that the
bounding boxes created by the experts were too large. We concluded that the
detection of small objects was very sensitive to the quality of the bounding boxes,
not only because a small variation of a few pixels greatly affected the metric,
but also because too large a bounding box caused the neural networks to learn
from the background and not from the desired object.

Thus, bounding boxes had to be manually tuned and adjusted properly.
Figure 5a shows an example of a too broad bounding box, which makes neuronal network to learn from the contour of the pupae and the shades, instead

of learning from the varroa mite. Figure 5b shows precisely a wrong prediction caused by underadjusted bounding boxes.

Multiple tests were performed to find out the best model. The main decisions and parameters that showed the best performance are the following:

1. As varroa mites tend to be reddish, we performed a preprocessing of the images that proved to improve the quality of the detection, specifically we decreased the intensity of the blue and green channels of each image to an 80%, with no modifications on the red channel. This improved the detection results.
2. The learning rate was set to 0.01, but *ReduceLRonPlateau* technique was used to reduce the value a factor of 0.75 when the metric stopped improving during 10 consecutive epochs, see Fig. 6. Stochastic gradient descent (SGD) was used for optimizing the objective function. The maximum number of epochs was 300.
3. We performed data augmentation in each batch. The techniques that worked best were random 224×224 crop (ensuring a balance between the number of crops with and without varroa mites), rotation, horizontal flip, vertical flip, a soft random brightness (limited to 0.05) and random contrast (limited of 0.05).
4. The best backbone was *Resnet50-FPN*, where the anchor generator parameter was set to 35. Some pre-trained weights were tested (such as those ones based on the COCO dataset), but the best results were obtained with no pre-trained weights.

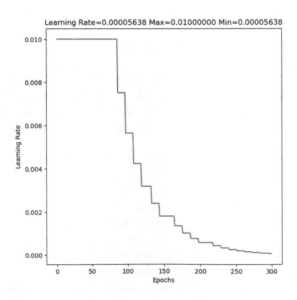

Fig. 6. Reduce Learning Rate on Plateau strategy for the best model.

Figure 7 shows both the mAP and mAR evolution during the training of the best model. The final mAP50 score was 0.7368 and mAR10 was 0.4452.

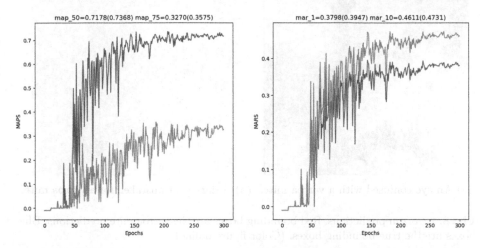

Fig. 7. Evolution of the mAP (left plot) and mAR (right plot) validation values during the training of the best model. Blue curves represent mAP50 and mAR1, wheras orange curves represent mAP75 and mAR10. (Color figure online)

Although the metrics show a decent performance, a detailed analysis of the predictions shows that the model makes some blatant errors. In fact, the validation images contains a total of 192 varroa mites, of which the model is able to detect 163. The model fails with artifacts and pupae eyes, indeed there are 96 false positives. If one distinguish the validation images between those with and without pupae, 91 of 95 varroa mites are detected when no pupae appears (with 18 false positives), and 72 of 97 varroa mites are detected when pupae appears, but with 78 false positives. This means that recall is not good enough. Figure 8a shows an example of errors in the prediction, where a pupae eye is mistaken for a varroa mite. Figure 8b shows another error, where a ground stain is mistaken for another varroa mite. These examples show that the problem is truly difficult. In fact, depending on the positions of the pupae, the experts themselves find it difficult to distinguish between eyes or varroa mites, being the main problem the resolution of the images. Although the images have been taken with good resolution smartphone cameras (12 Mpx), the level of detail of small objects is rather low and this causes that there is not enough gradient for the neural network to learn the features.

Trying to overcome this problem, some super-resolution techniques (explained in Sect. 3.3) were performed. Figure 9 shows an example of a varroa mite before and after the application of the super-resolution method. As can be seen, visually the image quality seems to have improved quite a bit. The varroa mite has a much more defined contour, however it can be appreciated that the neuronal network behind the super resolution has *invented* some parts of the varroa mite. Similar behavior was observed in other elements: dark spots, dust, dirt and soil.

(a) An eye confused with a varroa mite.   (b) A dark spot mistaken for a varroa mite.

Fig. 8. Errors in predictions. Red bounding boxes are the varroa mite predictions. Blue boxes are the true bounding boxes. (Color figure online)

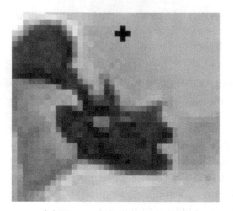

(a) Crop of an input image.   (b) Crop after applying super-resolution.

Fig. 9. Before and after super-resolution techniques.

None of the super-resolution techniques ($\times 2$, $\times 3$, $\times 4$) were able to improve the results. Indeed, results were even slightly worse. Super resolution does not improve images enough for the network to learn to distinguish correctly the varroa mites. In fact, visually varroa mites are very similar to some spots and pupae eyes (even if super resolution is applied), being also quite difficult for humans to distinguish among them.

5   Conclusions and Further Work

This paper presents an approach to varroa mite detection by means of artificial intelligence techniques, from pictures captured with smartphones. The approach is based on deep learning, since the use of more standard computer vision or machine learning techniques, despite being less computationally expensive, would be much more sensitive to changes in light and cameras, obtaining worse results.

The similarity between the eyes of bee pupae and varroa mites, in addition to the low resolution of the input dataset, pose a challenge of small object detection. Different techniques have been employed, including super resolution, to alleviate these problems, obtaining decent results. As future work, to further improve the system and avoid false positives (for instance, when varroa mites are mistaken for dark spots), beekeeping experts are currentling compiling a new dataset by taking closer images, so that each board is divided into several photos (thus, the resolution improves). A crop of these new images is shown in Fig. 10b, where it is easier to distinguish the varroa mite from the spots than in Fig. 10a.

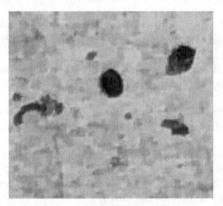
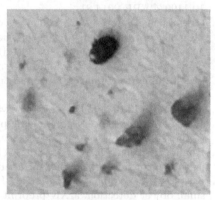

(a) Crop of an image of the original dataset. It is difficult to distinguish the varroa mite from the soil and spots.

(b) Crop of an image of the new dataset. The resolution is much better and makes it easier to distinguish varroa mites.

Fig. 10. Comparison between old and new images.

Acknowledgments. This work is supported by grants PID2020-112673RB-I00, PID2020-116641GB-I00 and PID2021-123219OB-I00 funded by MCIN/AEI/ 10.13039/ 501100011033, and the DGA-FSE (grant A07-17R).

References

1. Alves, T.S., et al.: Automatic detection and classification of honey bee comb cells using deep learning. Comput. Electr. Agric. **170**, 105244 (2020)
2. Bilik, S., et al.: Machine learning and computer vision techniques in bee monitoring applications. arXiv preprint arXiv:2208.00085 (2022)
3. Bilik, S.: Visual diagnosis of the varroa destructor parasitic mite in honeybees using object detector techniques. Sensors **21**(8), 2764 (2021). https://doi.org/10. 3390/s21082764

4. Chen, C., et al.: RRNet: a hybrid detector for object detection in drone-captured images. In: Proceedings of the IEEE/CVF International Conference on Computer Vision Workshops (2019)
5. Chen, G., et al.: A survey of the four pillars for small object detection: multi-scale representation, contextual information, super-resolution, and region proposal. IEEE Trans. Syst. Man Cybern.: Syst. **52**(2), 936–953 (2022). https://doi.org/10.1109/TSMC.2020.3005231
6. Cheng, G., Yuan, X., Yao, X., Yan, K., Zeng, Q., Han, J.: Towards large-scale small object detection: survey and benchmarks. arXiv preprint arXiv:2207.14096 (2022)
7. Deng, C., Wang, M., Liu, L., Liu, Y., Jiang, Y.: Extended feature pyramid network for small object detection. IEEE Trans. Multimed. **24**, 1968–1979 (2021)
8. Girshick, R.: Fast R-CNN. In: Proceedings of the IEEE International Conference on Computer Vision, pp. 1440–1448 (2015)
9. Girshick, R., Donahue, J., Darrell, T., Malik, J.: Rich feature hierarchies for accurate object detection and semantic segmentation. In: 2014 IEEE Conference on Computer Vision and Pattern Recognition, pp. 580–587 (2014). https://doi.org/10.1109/CVPR.2014.81
10. Gregorc, A., Sampson, B.: Diagnosis of varroa mite (varroa destructor) and sustainable control in honey bee (Apis mellifera) colonies-a review. Diversity **11**(12), 243 (2019). https://doi.org/10.3390/d11120243
11. Gupta, H., Verma, O.P.: Monitoring and surveillance of urban road traffic using low altitude drone images: a deep learning approach. Multimed. Tools Appl., 1–21 (2022)
12. Higuera Pinillos, N.: Detección de varroa y pupas de abejas mediante procesamiento de imágenes y aprendizaje profundo, Master Thesis, Universidad de La Rioja (2022)
13. Huang, H., Tang, X., Wen, F., Jin, X.: Small object detection method with shallow feature fusion network for chip surface defect detection. Sci. Rep. **12**(1), 3914 (2022)
14. Kisantal, M., Wojna, Z., Murawski, J., Naruniec, J., Cho, K.: Augmentation for small object detection. arXiv preprint arXiv:1902.07296 (2019)
15. Kulyukin, V., Mukherjee, S.: On video analysis of omnidirectional bee traffic: counting bee motions with motion detection and image classification. Appl. Sci. **9**(18), 3743 (2019)
16. Lim, B., Son, S., Kim, H., Nah, S., Mu Lee, K.: Enhanced deep residual networks for single image super-resolution. In: Proceedings of the IEEE Conference on Computer Vision and Pattern Recognition Workshops, pp. 136–144 (2017)
17. Lin, T.Y., Dollár, P., Girshick, R., He, K., Hariharan, B., Belongie, S.: Feature pyramid networks for object detection. In: Proceedings of the IEEE Conference on Computer Vision and Pattern Recognition, pp. 2117–2125 (2017)
18. Liu, W.: SSD: single shot MultiBox detector. In: Leibe, B., Matas, J., Sebe, N., Welling, M. (eds.) ECCV 2016, Part I. LNCS, vol. 9905, pp. 21–37. Springer, Cham (2016). https://doi.org/10.1007/978-3-319-46448-0_2
19. McAllister, E., Payo, A., Novellino, A., Dolphin, T., Medina-Lopez, E.: Multispectral satellite imagery and machine learning for the extraction of shoreline indicators. Coast. Eng. **174**, 104102 (2022)
20. Ngo, T.N., Rustia, D.J.A., Yang, E.C., Lin, T.T.: Automated monitoring and analyses of honey bee pollen foraging behavior using a deep learning-based imaging system. Comput. Electron. Agric. **187**, 106239 (2021)
21. Pietropaoli, M., et al.: Evaluation of two commonly used field tests to assess varroa destructor infestation on honey bee (Apis mellifera) colonies. Appl. Sci. **11**(10), 4458 (2021). https://doi.org/10.3390/app11104458

22. Redmon, J., Divvala, S., Girshick, R., Farhadi, A.: You only look once: unified, real-time object detection. In: Proceedings of the IEEE Conference on Computer Vision and Pattern Recognition, pp. 779–788 (2016)

23. Ren, S., He, K., Girshick, R., Sun, J.: Faster R-CNN: towards real-time object detection with region proposal networks. In: Advances in Neural Information Processing Systems, vol. 28 (2015)

24. Rodriguez, I.F., Megret, R., Acuna, E., Agosto-Rivera, J.L., Giray, T.: Recognition of pollen-bearing bees from video using convolutional neural network. In: 2018 IEEE Winter Conference on Applications of Computer Vision (WACV), pp. 314–322. IEEE (2018)

25. Schurischuster S., Kampel, M.: Varroa dataset (2020). https://zenodo.org/record/4085044

26. Tan, M., Pang, R., Le, Q.V.: Efficientdet: scalable and efficient object detection. In: Proceedings of the IEEE/CVF Conference on Computer Vision and Pattern Recognition, pp. 10781–10790 (2020)

27. Vilarem, C., Piou, V., Vogelweith, F., Vétillard, A.: Varroa destructor from the laboratory to the field: control, biocontrol and IPM perspectives-a review. Insects **12**(9), 800 (2021). https://doi.org/10.3390/insects12090800

28. Wang, Z., Chen, J., Hoi, S.C.: Deep learning for image super-resolution: a survey. IEEE Trans. Pattern Anal. Mach. Intell. **43**(10), 3365–3387 (2020)

29. Yang, C.R.: The use of video to detect and measure pollen on bees entering a hive. Ph.D. thesis, Auckland University of Technology (2018)

30. Yu, X., Gong, Y., Jiang, N., Ye, Q., Han, Z.: Scale match for tiny person detection. In: Proceedings of the IEEE/CVF Winter Conference on Applications of Computer Vision, pp. 1257–1265 (2020)

31. Zhu, P., et al.: Detection and tracking meet drones challenge. IEEE Trans. Pattern Anal. Mach. Intell. **44**(11), 7380–7399 (2021)

32. Zhu, Z., Liang, D., Zhang, S., Huang, X., Li, B., Hu, S.: Traffic-sign detection and classification in the wild. In: Proceedings of the IEEE Conference on Computer Vision and Pattern Recognition, pp. 2110–2118 (2016)

33. Zoph, B., Cubuk, E.D., Ghiasi, G., Lin, T.-Y., Shlens, J., Le, Q.V.: Learning data augmentation strategies for object detection. In: Vedaldi, A., Bischof, H., Brox, T., Frahm, J.-M. (eds.) ECCV 2020, Part XXVII. LNCS, vol. 12372, pp. 566–583. Springer, Cham (2020). https://doi.org/10.1007/978-3-030-58583-9_34

34. Zou, Z., Chen, K., Shi, Z., Guo, Y., Ye, J.: Object detection in 20 years: a survey. Proc. IEEE (2023)

Evolutionary Computation
and Optimization

Enhancing Evolutionary Optimization Performance Under Byzantine Fault Conditions

Carlos Cotta[1,2]([envelope]) [ID]

[1] Department of Lenguajes y Ciencias de la Computación, ETSI Informática,
Campus de Teatinos, Universidad de Málaga, 29071 Málaga, Spain
ccottap@lcc.uma.es
[2] ITIS Software, Universidad de Málaga, Málaga, Spain

Abstract. We evaluate the performance of panmictic evolutionary algorithms (EAs) in Byzantine environments, where fitness values are unreliable due to the potential presence of malicious agents. We investigate the impact of this phenomenon on the performance of the algorithm considering two different models of malicious behavior of different severity, taking the unreliability rate of the environment as a control parameter. We observe how there can be a significant toll in the quality of the results as the prevalence of cheating behavior increases, even for simple functions. Subsequently, we endow the EA with mechanisms based on redundant computation to cope with this issue, and examine their effectiveness. Our findings indicate that while a mechanism based on statistical averaging can be an effective approach under a relatively benign fault model, more hostile environments are better tackled via an approach based on majority voting.

Keywords: Evolutionary algorithms · Byzantine faults · Panmixia · Resilience

1 Introduction

Emerging computational environments such as peer-to-peer networks and volunteer computing (VC) platforms [10,11] have become promising ecosystems for running computationally intensive tasks. This is for example the case of evolutionary algorithms (EAs) [7,21]. Needless to say, when deploying any complex computing task on this kind of environments numerous challenges arise due to the dynamic nature and irregularity of the resulting computational landscape [1], thus highlighting the need for algorithmic resilience. Fortunately, EAs are

This work is supported by Spanish Ministry of Science and Innovation under project Bio4Res (PID2021-125184NB-I00 – http://bio4res.lcc.uma.es) and by Universidad de Málaga, Campus de Excelencia Internacional Andalucía Tech.

P. García Bringas et al. (Eds.): HAIS 2023, LNAI 14001, pp. 341–351, 2023.
https://doi.org/10.1007/978-3-031-40725-3_29

not just inherently resilient [5] but also flexible enough to incorporate mechanisms to cope with perturbations caused by the volatility or heterogeneity of the environment [15, 16].

This work is primarily concerned with another source of disruption not related to the irregularities of the computational substrate but to logical failures of malicious nature [19]. Specifically, we consider *cheating faults*, a kind of Byzantine failure whereby one or more contributors of computational resources do not provide trustworthy results but do however purposefully alter the computation by submitting wrong results. This can be done with the mere purpose of feigning an activity (for instance, in order to obtain any rewards associated with the participation in the VC platform) or even with the malicious aim of damaging the computation itself. Previous research has shown that these faults can have an impact on EAs which will depend on the precise components of the algorithm targeted or affected by such faults [13]. Distributed EAs can retain global asymptotic convergence under some conditions [20] (see also [12]), and EAs with fine-grained spatial structure can withstand certain mild types of Byzantine faults [14]. More hostile faults seem to quickly degrade the performance of EAs on some problems though [3], when the evaluation of fitness is targeted by malicious agents.

Our analysis in this work aims to examine this performance drop more qualitatively, and to study some countermeasures to cope with these faults. To this end, we will start by providing a description of the algorithmic setting in which Byzantine faults can take place (Sect. 2). Then, two types of Byzantine faults of different severity are considered, as described in Sect. 2.1, and two strategies for coping with these are provided in Sect. 2.2, making use of redundant computation in order to handle the uncertainty in fitness values associated to such faults. Subsequently, we report the experimental results attained when using either of these strategies in Sect. 3. We close the paper with an outlook of these results and an outline of future work in Sect. 4.

2   Algorithmic Setting

Let us consider an EA with a panmictic population aiming to optimize a certain objective function $f(\cdot)$, which we shall term the *true fitness* function. In order to evaluate this function for the individuals in the population, the EA relies on a number of *helpers*. For instance, this is consistent with the use of master-slave models [2], whereby individuals are distributed among a collection of computational nodes that provide this fitness evaluation service. These helpers may vary dynamically and are not directly traceable by the EA, e.g., imagine they are behind some cloud or VC service layer, and hence the EA as a client has no control −nor even knowledge− on where the computation is done (i.e., it cannot pinpoint the particular source of each fitness value computed either). Now, the issue under study here arises when some of these helpers are *cheaters*, which provide wrong results. As a crucial consideration, notice that in the scenario considered here fitness evaluation is never uncheatable, that is, there is no trusted helper which could be eventually used to check whether a particular fitness result is correct or not. Therefore, any coping mechanism has to work under the assumption that invocations to the objective function might be always subject to failure.

2.1 Modelling Byzantine Faults

As a starting point, we focus a very simple model whereby fitness evaluation requests get an erroneous result with some probability ρ (c.f. [19,20]). We shall denote this wrong result $\hat{f}^t(\cdot)$ as the *unreliable fitness*, where the superscript t represents the current time and is used to denote the fact that cheaters do not necessarily return the same wrong result if the very same solution is submitted for evaluation at different times. Obviously, it is impossible to know beforehand whether the value obtained after an evaluation request is its actual true fitness or an incorrect value, as mentioned before.

In order to quantitatively represent the cheating behavior we are going to consider two simple models of malicious computation:

(i) randomizer, whereby cheaters return a value which is uncorrelated with the true fitness, e.g., a random value within the range of the function (this behavior would correspond to nodes which want to merely feign an activity); in this work, we have considered cheaters that return a previously observed fitness value (randomly selected, and thus lacking any logical relation with the solution submitted for evaluation).

(ii) inverter, whereby cheaters return a value which is inversely correlated with the true fitness (as it would happen if there were computational actors which wanted to inflict damage on the optimization process). In this work, we have considered the following inverter function:

$$\hat{f}^t(x) = f^t_{\max} - (f(x) - f^t_{\min}), \tag{1}$$

where $f^t_{\max}$ and $f^t_{\min}$ are respectively the maximum and minimum fitness observed so far.

2.2 Strategies for Handling Byzantine Faults

In order to tackle this kind of faults in an optimization setting, some inspiration can be drawn from noisy environments [9,17]. However, it must be noted that the unreliable fitness does not gravitate in this case around some underlying true fitness (as it is commonly assumed in many scenarios with uncertainty or noisy fitness functions). For this reason, the phenomenon tackled here has a fundamentally different nature. To scrutinize this issue, we are going to consider mechanisms to handle unreliable fitness based on redundant computation: firstly, each new solution will be re-evaluated k times for some $k > 1$; Let $\mathcal{F}^t(x) = [\hat{f}^t_1(x), \ldots, \hat{f}^t_k(x)]$ be the sequence of so obtained unreliable fitness values. Subsequently, we will try to extract an approximation $\tilde{f}^t(x)$ of the true

Table 1. Results (mean deviation from the optimum) of the EA with no unreliability handler. In all tables, symbols next to numerical values indicate statistical significance – check the main text of Sect. 3 (p. 5) for details.

	inverter			
ρ	ONEMAX	TRAP	MMDP	LEADING-ONES
0.00	0.00 ± 0.00★	5.02 ± 0.52★	0.00 ± 0.00★	0.00 ± 0.00★
0.05	0.00 ± 0.00★	5.24 ± 0.45★	0.00 ± 0.00★	2.80 ± 0.69●●
0.10	0.00 ± 0.00★	5.04 ± 0.41★	0.00 ± 0.00★	10.94 ± 1.00●●
0.15	0.00 ± 0.00★	3.76 ± 0.36○★	0.00 ± 0.00★	18.88 ± 0.80●●
0.20	0.00 ± 0.00★	4.64 ± 0.39★	0.00 ± 0.00★	26.32 ± 0.90●●
0.25	0.00 ± 0.00★	6.02 ± 0.35●★	0.00 ± 0.00★	36.94 ± 0.58●●
0.30	0.00 ± 0.00★	6.98 ± 0.33●★	0.71 ± 0.21●●	45.12 ± 0.61●●
0.35	0.00 ± 0.00★	8.48 ± 0.28●★	6.40 ± 0.73●●	53.02 ± 0.71●●
0.40	0.00 ± 0.00★	10.46 ± 0.27●★	13.86 ± 1.01●●	64.74 ± 0.42●●
0.45	1.22 ± 0.85	10.88 ± 0.26●★	17.01 ± 1.08●	75.64 ± 0.40●●
0.50	16.80 ± 2.41●	19.60 ± 1.94●★	20.64 ± 1.27●★	83.08 ± 0.39●★
	randomizer			
ρ	ONEMAX	TRAP	MMDP	LEADING-ONES
0.00	0.00 ± 0.00★	5.02 ± 0.52★	0.00 ± 0.00★	0.00 ± 0.00★
0.05	0.00 ± 0.00★	5.36 ± 0.60★	0.00 ± 0.00★	0.60 ± 0.34●●
0.10	0.00 ± 0.00★	4.78 ± 0.53★	0.00 ± 0.00★	1.42 ± 0.48●●
0.15	0.00 ± 0.00★	4.98 ± 0.51★	0.00 ± 0.00★	1.70 ± 0.57●●
0.20	0.00 ± 0.00★	3.58 ± 0.34●★	0.00 ± 0.00★	2.60 ± 0.64●●
0.25	0.00 ± 0.00★	2.88 ± 0.32●★	0.00 ± 0.00★	8.18 ± 1.19●●
0.30	0.00 ± 0.00★	1.54 ± 0.18●★	0.00 ± 0.00★	13.18 ± 1.34●●
0.35	0.00 ± 0.00★	1.22 ± 0.19●★	0.13 ± 0.07○○	15.88 ± 1.16●●
0.40	0.00 ± 0.00★	1.38 ± 0.12●★	1.30 ± 0.17●●	19.64 ± 1.06●●
0.45	0.00 ± 0.00★	2.14 ± 0.18●★	2.62 ± 0.28●●	22.76 ± 1.52●●
0.50	0.00 ± 0.00★	3.26 ± 0.17●★	4.31 ± 0.30●●	28.94 ± 1.33●●

fitness (ideally, an perfect estimation thereof) from these k fitness values by using some appropriate function. To this end, we have considered two possibilities here:

(i) average$k$, namely the average of the k fitness values, i.e.,

$$\tilde{f}^t(x) = \frac{1}{k} \sum_{i=1}^{k} \hat{f}_i^t(x). \tag{2}$$

(ii) majority$k$ (cf. [4]), namely keeping the most repeated value (or an average of the most repeated values if there was a tie). More precisely, let $\sigma : \mathbb{R} \times \mathbb{R}^k \to \{0, \dots k\}$ be defined such that $\sigma(f, \mathcal{F})$ is the number of occurrences of value

Table 2. Results (mean deviation from the optimum) of the EA with majority3.

	inverter			
ρ	ONEMAX	TRAP	MMDP	LEADING-ONES
0.00	$0.00 \pm 0.00\star$	$9.46 \pm 0.34\bullet\bullet$	$0.00 \pm 0.00\star$	$0.00 \pm 0.00\star$
0.05	$0.00 \pm 0.00\star$	$9.62 \pm 0.47\bullet\bullet$	$0.00 \pm 0.00\star$	$0.32 \pm 0.21\circ\circ$
0.10	$0.00 \pm 0.00\star$	$9.66 \pm 0.50\bullet\bullet$	$0.00 \pm 0.00\star$	$2.26 \pm 0.62\bullet\bullet$
0.15	$0.00 \pm 0.00\star$	$9.48 \pm 0.39\bullet\bullet$	$0.00 \pm 0.00\star$	$6.22 \pm 0.91\bullet\bullet$
0.20	$0.00 \pm 0.00\star$	$10.08 \pm 0.46\bullet\bullet$	$0.00 \pm 0.00\star$	$12.98 \pm 1.04\bullet\star$
0.25	$0.00 \pm 0.00\star$	$9.90 \pm 0.41\bullet\bullet$	0.08 ± 0.06	$23.12 \pm 0.92\bullet$
0.30	$0.00 \pm 0.00\star$	$9.96 \pm 0.42\bullet\bullet$	$0.17 \pm 0.08\bullet\star$	$33.28 \pm 0.86\bullet\star$
0.35	$0.00 \pm 0.00\star$	$10.40 \pm 0.35\bullet\bullet$	$0.89 \pm 0.17\bullet\star$	$44.20 \pm 0.61\bullet\star$
0.40	$0.00 \pm 0.00\star$	$12.44 \pm 0.33\bullet\bullet$	$5.34 \pm 0.58\bullet\star$	$57.44 \pm 0.63\bullet$
0.45	$0.00 \pm 0.00\star$	$12.96 \pm 0.35\bullet\bullet$	$14.77 \pm 0.70\bullet\star$	$72.78 \pm 0.48\bullet\star$
0.50	$16.52 \pm 2.37\bullet\star$	$22.30 \pm 1.81\bullet\bullet$	$22.67 \pm 1.05\bullet\circ$	$84.76 \pm 0.35\bullet\bullet$
	randomizer			
ρ	ONEMAX	TRAP	MMDP	LEADING-ONES
0.00	$0.00 \pm 0.00\star$	$9.46 \pm 0.34\bullet\bullet$	$0.00 \pm 0.00\star$	$0.00 \pm 0.00\star$
0.05	$0.00 \pm 0.00\star$	$10.16 \pm 0.45\bullet\bullet$	$0.00 \pm 0.00\star$	$0.00 \pm 0.00\star$
0.10	$0.00 \pm 0.00\star$	$8.82 \pm 0.41\bullet\bullet$	$0.00 \pm 0.00\star$	0.20 ± 0.20
0.15	$0.00 \pm 0.00\star$	$9.60 \pm 0.49\bullet\bullet$	$0.00 \pm 0.00\star$	0.12 ± 0.12
0.20	$0.00 \pm 0.00\star$	$9.34 \pm 0.48\bullet\bullet$	$0.00 \pm 0.00\star$	0.60 ± 0.44
0.25	$0.00 \pm 0.00\star$	$9.04 \pm 0.39\bullet\bullet$	$0.00 \pm 0.00\star$	$0.50 \pm 0.25\bullet\bullet$
0.30	$0.00 \pm 0.00\star$	$9.82 \pm 0.39\bullet\bullet$	$0.00 \pm 0.00\star$	$1.52 \pm 0.56\bullet\bullet$
0.35	$0.00 \pm 0.00\star$	$9.46 \pm 0.52\bullet\bullet$	$0.00 \pm 0.00\star$	$2.12 \pm 0.70\bullet\bullet$
0.40	$0.00 \pm 0.00\star$	$8.86 \pm 0.42\bullet\bullet$	0.04 ± 0.04	$6.20 \pm 1.25\bullet\bullet$
0.45	$0.00 \pm 0.00\star$	$8.84 \pm 0.39\bullet\bullet$	$0.13 \pm 0.07\circ\star$	$9.22 \pm 1.22\bullet\bullet$
0.50	$0.00 \pm 0.00\star$	$9.92 \pm 0.34\bullet\bullet$	$1.61 \pm 0.22\bullet\bullet$	$17.20 \pm 1.53\bullet\bullet$

f in vector $\mathcal{F}$, and let $\sigma^*(x,t) = \max\{\sigma(f, \mathcal{F}^t(x)) \mid f \in \mathcal{F}^t(x)\}$. Now, we consider

$$\tilde{f}^t(x) = \frac{1}{|\mathcal{F}'|} \sum_{f \in F'} f \tag{3}$$

where $\mathcal{F}' = \{f \in \mathcal{F}^t(x) \mid \sigma(f, \mathcal{F}^t(x)) = \sigma^*(x,t)\}$.

3   Experimental Results

The experiments have been conducted with an EA that uses binary tournament selection, single-point crossover ($p_X = .9$), bit-flip mutation (p_M equivalent to a mutation rate $1/\ell$ per bit, where ℓ is the number of bits), and elitist generational

Table 3. Results (mean deviation from the optimum) of the EA with average3.

	inverter			
ρ	ONEMAX	TRAP	MMDP	LEADING-ONES
0.00	0.00 ± 0.00⋆	9.46 ± 0.34••	0.00 ± 0.00⋆	0.00 ± 0.00⋆
0.05	0.00 ± 0.00⋆	9.30 ± 0.37••	0.00 ± 0.00⋆	0.00 ± 0.00⋆
0.10	0.00 ± 0.00⋆	9.02 ± 0.41••	0.04 ± 0.04	0.14 ± 0.11⋆
0.15	0.00 ± 0.00⋆	9.04 ± 0.33••	0.13 ± 0.07∘∘	3.00 ± 0.77•⋆
0.20	0.00 ± 0.00⋆	10.50 ± 0.32••	0.41 ± 0.14••	15.16 ± 1.50•
0.25	0.00 ± 0.00⋆	10.78 ± 0.35••	1.23 ± 0.18••	22.82 ± 1.08•⋆
0.30	0.00 ± 0.00⋆	11.56 ± 0.35••	2.70 ± 0.25••	36.00 ± 0.94••
0.35	0.00 ± 0.00⋆	12.24 ± 0.33••	4.37 ± 0.31••	47.62 ± 0.68••
0.40	0.00 ± 0.00⋆	12.92 ± 0.34••	9.56 ± 0.37••	56.88 ± 0.57•⋆
0.45	0.00 ± 0.00⋆	13.62 ± 0.32••	17.17 ± 0.69••	73.30 ± 0.40•
0.50	19.10 ± 2.33••	28.26 ± 1.95••	26.17 ± 0.80••	85.26 ± 0.30••
	randomizer			
ρ	ONEMAX	TRAP	MMDP	LEADING-ONES
0.00	0.00 ± 0.00⋆	9.46 ± 0.34••	0.00 ± 0.00⋆	0.00 ± 0.00⋆
0.05	0.00 ± 0.00⋆	9.52 ± 0.51••	0.00 ± 0.00⋆	0.00 ± 0.00⋆
0.10	0.00 ± 0.00⋆	9.50 ± 0.47••	0.00 ± 0.00⋆	0.00 ± 0.00⋆
0.15	0.00 ± 0.00⋆	9.46 ± 0.51••	0.00 ± 0.00⋆	0.00 ± 0.00⋆
0.20	0.00 ± 0.00⋆	8.74 ± 0.42••	0.00 ± 0.00⋆	0.00 ± 0.00⋆
0.25	0.00 ± 0.00⋆	9.54 ± 0.42••	0.00 ± 0.00⋆	0.00 ± 0.00⋆
0.30	0.00 ± 0.00⋆	10.02 ± 0.37••	0.00 ± 0.00⋆	0.00 ± 0.00⋆
0.35	0.00 ± 0.00⋆	10.06 ± 0.36••	0.00 ± 0.00⋆	0.00 ± 0.00⋆
0.40	0.00 ± 0.00⋆	10.48 ± 0.41••	0.00 ± 0.00⋆	0.00 ± 0.00⋆
0.45	0.00 ± 0.00⋆	10.62 ± 0.38••	0.17 ± 0.08•	0.00 ± 0.00⋆
0.50	0.00 ± 0.00⋆	11.12 ± 0.35••	0.21 ± 0.09•⋆	0.02 ± 0.02⋆

replacement. The population size is $\mu = 100$ individuals, and the total number of fitness evaluations is 10^6 (including redundant computations). The unreliability rate ρ ranges from 0 to 0.5 in steps of 0.05 (the results for $\rho = 0$ can be used for gauging the basal performance of the EA). We consider a *raw* EA that uses no unreliability handling mechanism in addition to the majority$k$ and average$k$ handlers. For the latter two, the value $k = 3$ is considered. Four objective functions are used in the experiments, namely ONEMAX (using $\ell = 100$ bits), Deb's 4-bit fully deceptive function [6] (TRAP, using 25 blocks of 4 bits), Goldberg et al.'s Massively Multimodal Deceptive Problem [8] (MMDP, using 17 blocks of 6 bits), and Rudolph's LEADING-ONES [18] (using $\ell = 100$ bits). We perform 50 runs for each handler and problem.

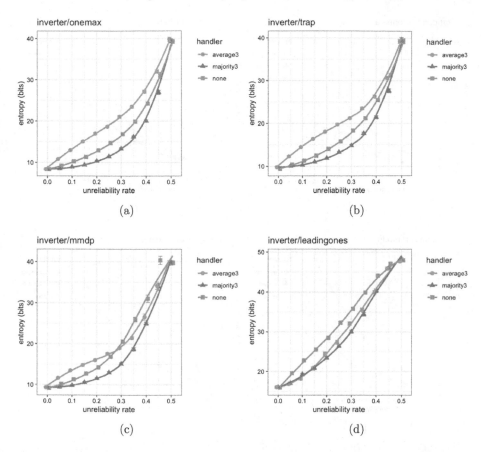

Fig. 1. Minimum population entropy as a function of the unreliability rate for the inverter model. The data points are the average of 50 runs, the error bars span the standard error of the mean, and the solid lines are visual guides. (a) ONEMAX(b) TRAP(c) MMDP(d) LEADING-ONES.

Table 1, 2 and 3 show the numerical results attained. Each entry in these tables indicates the mean relative error (percentage distance from the optimum) and the standard error of the mean, measured from the best true fitness of any solution generated during each run. In addition, two symbols indicate the statistical significance (according to a Wilcoxon test) of the difference with respect to the base case (no handler, $\rho = 0$) and to the best result for all three scenarios (using average$k$, majority$k$, or no handler) and the same ρ and cheating model (entry marked with $\star$) respectively. In either case, • and ∘ indicate significance at $\alpha = .05$ and $\alpha = 0.1$ respectively, and absence of a symbol indicates no statistical significance of the corresponding difference. Analyzing firstly the results corresponding to the raw EA (Table 1) it is evident that in general the unreliability of the environment has a clear toll on the performance of the EA, whose results markedly degrade for increasing values of ρ. There is an interesting anomaly for

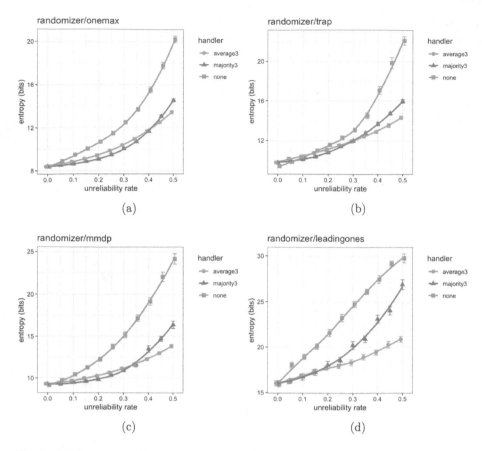

Fig. 2. Minimum population entropy as a function of the unreliability rate for the randomizer model. The data points are the average of 50 runs, the error bars span the standard error of the mean, and the solid lines are visual guides. (a) ONEMAX(b) TRAP(c) MMDP(d) LEADING-ONES.

the TRAP function, in which moderate values of ρ provide a subtle improvement in the results. Clearly, the slightly misleading fitness information seems to be carrying the EA out of some of the deceptive local optima. On a more general note, it is clear that the randomizer model provides a milder disturbance than the inverter model across all problems. This is consistent with the lower population diversity attained during the run (compare the curves labelled as none in Fig. 1 and Fig. 2 for each problem, which indicate a more more focused search for the latter model).

Focusing on this inverter model, observe now the results of majority3 and average3 (Tables 2 and 3 respectively). The majority3 handler provides a clear improvement for this harder unreliability model. The ONEMAX problem is quite simple and therefore the EA seems to be less sensitive to ρ, but still this handler matches the best results and improves these for the largest value of ρ. The result for the TRAP function are slightly worse due to the previously mentioned anomaly, which the majority3 actually ameliorates. This can be also seen in Fig. 1, in which the lowest diversity of the population is depicted for the inverter model. Note how the majority3 handler manages to reach a lower entropy, which indicates greater convergence of the population. Unfortunately, for the TRAP function this implies falling into suboptimal regions. Note also in Table 3 that for low values of ρ the average3 handler is actually more competitive in the LEADING-ONES function. The reason for this may be found in the nature of this particular objective function: the worst values (typically those of random solutions in the initial population) are close to 0, and therefore tend to be out-weighted when averaged with high true fitness values, therefore providing valuable information to be exploited by the EA.

Finally, the randomizer model seems to provide a less challenging scenario, and this is where the average3 handler seems to excel. The results for the ONE-MAX and the LEADING-ONES functions are markedly superior, and this can be basically attributed to the same reason mentioned before with regard to the structure of fitness values and the possibility for high true fitness values to drag the average upwards, supplying guidance to the EA. This is also true for the MMDP function in which the signal-to-noise ratio is lower but the diversity balance seems to fit well to the EA. Indeed, it can be observed in Fig. 2 that the search is much more focused under this failure model, as reflected by the smaller population entropy attained by the EA.

4   Conclusions

The presence of cheaters can have a noticeable impact in the performance of panmictic EAs, even for simple objective functions. As the unreliability of the environment increases, the performance of the EA (as measured by the average fitness attained after a fixed number of invocations to the fitness function) drops in general. We have considered two mechanisms to cope with this issue on the basis of performing redundant computations. A handler based on averaging (reminiscent of the approaches commonly used in noisy environments) can work well in a relatively benign scenario in which cheaters provide random yet unbiased values. We hypothesize the reason lies in the possibility of marginally exploiting some fitness gradient information via the aggregate average. However, dealing with malevolent agents that actively try to provide fitness information manipulated to direct the algorithm in the opposite direction is better dealt with using a handler based on majority voting (defaulting to the average if no majority is obtained), which imposes a more strict criterion for assigning fitness, and relies of the observation that for unreliability rates less than 0.5 (and therefore non-pathological) the chances of obtaining a majority vote for the real fitness is higher than the opposite. Further research is required to optimize the computational tradeoffs involved in these mechanisms. We are currently working along this line, as well as towards the development of more sophisticated handling mechanisms and their deployment in more complex scenarios.

Acknowledgments. The author thanks Daan van den Berg (VU Amsterdam) for interesting discussions arising from a previous work [3].

References

1. Camacho, D., et al.: From ephemeral computing to deep bioinspired algorithms: new trends and applications. Futur. Gener. Comput. Syst. **88**, 735–746 (2018)
2. Cantú-Paz, E.: Master-slave parallel genetic algorithms. In: Efficient and Accurate Parallel Genetic Algorithms. Genetic Algorithms and Evolutionary Computation, vol. 1, pp. 33–48. Springer, Boston (2001). https://doi.org/10.1007/978-1-4615-4369-5_3
3. Cotta, C.: On the performance of evolutionary algorithms with unreliable fitness information. In: Mora, A.M. (ed.) EvoStar 2023 Late Breaking Abstracts. Czech Republic, Brno (2023)
4. Cotta, C.: Tackling adversarial faults in panmictic evolutionary algorithms. In: Genetic and Evolutionary Computation Conference Companion (GECCO 2023 Companion), p. 2. ACM Press, New York, NY (2023). In press
5. Cotta, C., Olague, G.: Resilient bioinspired algorithms: a computer system design perspective. In: Jiménez Laredo, J.L., Hidalgo, J.I., Babaagba, K.O. (eds.) EvoApplications 2022. LNCS, vol. 13224, pp. 619–631. Springer, Cham (2022). https://doi.org/10.1007/978-3-031-02462-7_39
6. Deb, K., Goldberg, D.: Analyzing deception in trap functions. In: Whitley, L. (ed.) Second Workshop on Foundations of Genetic Algorithms, pp. 93–108. Morgan Kaufmann Publishers, Vail (1993)
7. Vega, F.F.: Evolutionary algorithms: perspectives on the evolution of parallel models. In: Novais, P., Camacho, D., Analide, C., El Fallah Seghrouchni, A., Badica, C. (eds.) Intelligent Distributed Computing IX. SCI, vol. 616, pp. 13–22. Springer, Cham (2016). https://doi.org/10.1007/978-3-319-25017-5_2
8. Goldberg, D., Deb, K., Horn, J.: Massive multimodality, deception and genetic algorithms. In: Männer, R., Manderick, B. (eds.) Parallel Problem Solving from Nature - PPSN II, pp. 37–48. Elsevier Science Inc., New York (1992)
9. Jin, Y., Branke, J.: Evolutionary optimization in uncertain environments - a survey. IEEE Trans. Evol. Comput. **9**(3), 303–317 (2005)
10. Lavoie, E., Hendren, L.: Personal volunteer computing. In: Proceedings of the 16th ACM International Conference on Computing Frontiers, pp. 240–246. ACM, New York (2019)
11. Mengistu, T.M., Che, D.: Survey and taxonomy of volunteer computing. ACM Computing Surveys **52**(3), 1–35 (2019)
12. Muszynski, J.: Cheating-tolerance of parallel and distributed evolutionary algorithms in desktop grids and volunteer computing systems. Ph.D. thesis, University of Luxembourg (2015)
13. Muszyński, J., Varrette, S., Bouvry, P., Seredyński, F., Khan, S.U.: Convergence analysis of evolutionary algorithms in the presence of crash-faults and cheaters. Comput. Math. Appl. **64**(12), 3805–3819 (2012)
14. Muszyński, J., Varrette, S., Dorronsoro, B., Bouvry, P.: Distributed cellular evolutionary algorithms in a byzantine environment. In: 2015 IEEE International Parallel and Distributed Processing Symposium Workshop, pp. 307–313. IEEE Press, Hyderabad, India (2015)
15. Nogueras, R., Cotta, C.: Self-healing strategies for memetic algorithms in unstable and ephemeral computational environments. Nat. Comput. **16**(2), 189–200 (2017)

16. Nogueras, R., Cotta, C.: Analyzing self-⋆ island-based memetic algorithms in heterogeneous unstable environments. Int. J. High Perform. Comput. Appl. **32**(5), 676–692 (2018)
17. Rakshit, P., Konar, A., Das, S.: Noisy evolutionary optimization algorithms - a comprehensive survey. Swarm Evol. Comput. **33**, 18–45 (2017)
18. Rudolph, G.: Convergence properties of evolutionary algorithms. Verlag Dr. Kovač (1997)
19. Sarmenta, L.F.: Sabotage-tolerance mechanisms for volunteer computing systems. Futur. Gener. Comput. Syst. **18**(4), 561–572 (2002)
20. Varrette, S., Tantar, E., Bouvry, P.: On the resilience of [distributed] EAs against cheaters in global computing platforms. In: 25th IEEE International Symposium on Parallel and Distributed Processing Workshop Proceedings, pp. 409–417. IEEE, Anchorage AK (2011)
21. Xiong, N., Molina, D., Ortiz, M.L., Herrera, F.: A walk into metaheuristics for engineering optimization: principles, methods and recent trends. Int. J. Comput. Intell. Syst. **8**, 606–636 (2015)

A Hybrid Based Genetic Algorithm for Solving the Clustered Generalized Traveling Salesman Problem

Ovidiu Cosma[iD], Petrică C. Pop[(✉)][iD], and Laura Cosma[iD]

Technical University of Cluj-Napoca, North University Center of Baia Mare,
Dr. V. Babes 62A, 430083 Baia Mare, Romania
{ovidiu.cosma,petrica.pop}@mi.utcluj.ro

Abstract. We study the clustered generalized traveling salesman problem (CGTSP), which is an extension of the generalized traveling salesman problem (GTSP), which in turn generalizes the well-known traveling salesman problem (TSP). The investigated problem was motivated by several practical applications such as modern logistics, data clustering, internet networks, etc., and it is defined on a graph, whose set of vertices are split up into clusters, and the clusters are further partitioned into sub-clusters of vertices. The aim of the CGTSP is to look for a minimum length tour that visits exactly one vertex from each sub-cluster with the main constraint that all the sub-clusters belonging to each given cluster are visited contiguously. In this paper, we describe a hybrid algorithm for solving the CGTSP that integrates the Dijkstra's shortest path algorithm and a TSP solver within a genetic algorithm. Finally, we present a new set of instances for CGTSP derived from the GTSP_LIB [8] and some preliminary computational results are stated on a set of 40 instances to asses the efficiency of our designed hybrid based genetic algorithm.

Keywords: Hybrid algorithms · genetic algorithms · generalized traveling salesman problem · clustered generalized traveling salesman problem

1 Introduction

The clustered generalized traveling salesman problem (CGTSP) is an extension of the generalized traveling salesman problem (GTSP), which in turn generalizes the well-known traveling salesman problem (TSP). The CGTSP is defined on a graph, whose whole set of vertices is divided into a predefined number of vertex sets, called clusters, which in turn are split up into a number of sub-clusters, and it looks for a Hamiltonian tour with the following properties: it visits exactly one vertex from each sub-cluster and all the sub-clusters belonging to each given cluster are visited contiguously and minimizes the cost of the tour.

The existing literature concerning the CGTSP is scarce: the problem was introduced by Sepehri et al. [22] motivated by a practical application for optimal

© The Author(s), under exclusive license to Springer Nature Switzerland AG 2023
P. García Bringas et al. (Eds.): HAIS 2023, LNAI 14001, pp. 352–362, 2023.
https://doi.org/10.1007/978-3-031-40725-3_30

routing of dangerous substances in warehousing operations. The same authors proposed a mixed integer programming formulation of the problem containing a polynomial number of constraints and variables. Foumani et al. [10] described another interesting application of the CGTSP in optimizing the robotic auto- mated storage and retrieval system and presented a solution approach based on Cross-Entropy (CE) method. They tested their approach on two sets of instances, each one containing 42 instances, and compared it against the solutions obtained by solving the model proposed by Sepehri et al. [22]. Baniasadi et al. [2] described some applications of the CGTSP in modern logistics and presented a solution approach based on transforming the problem into a classical TSP.

The CGTSP is closely related to the generalized traveling salesman problem (GTSP), the clustered traveling salesman problem (CTSP) and classical travel- ing salesman problem (TSP), and it belongs to the class of generalized network design problems. This class of combinatorial optimization problems extends in a natural way the classical network design problems and their main feature is that the vertices of the original graph are split up into a predefined number of clusters, and the feasibility restrictions are expressed with regard to the clusters rather to individual vertices of the graph. For more information regarding the class of generalized network design problems and some intensively investigated problems, we refer to [3–9,11,13–21,23].

The scope of this paper is to present a new solution approach for CGTSP, in which we combine a genetic algorithm with Dijkstra's shortest path algorithm and a TSP Solver.

The present paper is structured as follows: the second section presents the definition of the CGTSP, Sect. 3 describes our developed hybrid novel solution approach. In Sect. 4, we provide a set of new instances for CGTSP derived from the GTSP_LIB [8] and some preliminary computational results achieved by our developed hybrid based genetic algorithm on a set of 40 instances, and finally in Sect. 5, we present some concluding remarks and we mention some future research directions.

2   Problem Statement

Let us consider $G = (V, E)$ an undirected complete graph with the set of vertices denoted by V and the set of edges denoted by E.

The entire set of vertices V is partitioned into k nonempty subsets of vertices denoted by $C_1, ..., C_k$ and which will be called *clusters*. Therefore, the following conditions are fulfilled:

1. $V = C_1 \cup C_2 \cup ... \cup C_k$
2. $C_l \cap C_p = \emptyset$ for all $l, p \in \{1, ..., k\}$ and $l \neq p$.

Further, the vertices from each cluster are partitioned into a number of sub- clusters.

We identify two kinds of edges in our graph: edges which link vertices belonging to sub-clusters from the same cluster, and edges which link vertices belonging to sub-clusters from different clusters.

In addition, the cost function $c : E \rightarrow R_+$ associates to every edge $e = (u, v) \in E$ a positive value denoted by $c_e = c(u, v)$, value which is called the cost of the edge.

The *clustered generalized traveling salesman problem* looks for a minimum cost tour H satisfying the following properties:

1. H visits exactly one vertex from each sub-cluster;
2. All the sub-clusters belonging to each given cluster are visited consecutively before moving to a new cluster.

In Fig. 1, we displayed an illustration of the CGTSP and two feasible solutions of the problem in the case of a graph G containing 18 vertices which are partitioned into three clusters C_1, C_2, C_3. Further, the vertices from each cluster are partition into a number of sub-clusters, i.e. $C_1 = V_1 \cup V_2$, $C_2 = V_3 \cup V_4 \cup V_5$ and $C_3 = V_6 \cup V_7$.

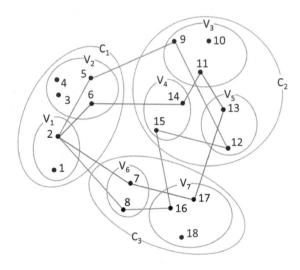

Fig. 1. Illustration of the CGTSP and two feasible solutions of the problem

Obviously, the CGTSP is NP-hard optimization problem because it includes the classical TSP as a special case when all the clusters are singletons.

3   The Proposed Hybrid Algorithm

To address the Clustered Generalized Traveling Salesman Problem (CGTSP), we develop a hybrid solution approach that integrates a genetic algorithm (GA) with Dijkstra's shortest path algorithm (ShPA) and a TSP Solver (TSPSol).

The chromosome data structure comprises two essential components, namely the Sub-Cluster visiting Order (sco) and the Vertices visiting Order (vo), which dictate the sequence in which sub-clusters and vertices should be traversed. The initial element of the sco is the starting sub-cluster denoted as $[v_s]$ and the first element of vo is the starting vertex, denoted as v_s. By following the vo, a feasible solution of the CGTSP may be obtained.

The chromosomes associated with the two feasible solutions of the CGTSP depicted in Fig. 1, denoted as cr_1 and cr_2, are:

$$cr_1 : \begin{cases} sco = [1,2,3,5,4,7,6] \\ vo = [2,5,9,12,15,16,8] \end{cases} \qquad cr_2 : \begin{cases} sco = [1,2,4,3,5,7,6] \\ vo = [2,6,14,11,13,17,7] \end{cases}$$

The source sub-cluster is determined to be C_1, as it possesses the smallest number of vertices.

Typically, random chromosomes yield suboptimal solutions for the CGTSP. When solely relying on the genetic algorithm for their evolution, the process can become quite sluggish. We developed a Chromosome Enhancement Algorithm (CEA) with the aim of accelerating chromosome evolution and enhancing their quality. This algorithm incorporates both the ShPA and a TSPSol. It can change the sco and the vo elements, excepting the first ones, that represent the starting sub-cluster and the starting vertex respectively. The CEA is integrated into the proposed GA for CGTSP solving.

3.1   The Chromosome Enhancement Algorithm

Algorithm 1 (CEA) illustrates the chromosome enhancement operation. In the beginning of the CEA loop, in step 3, the TSPSol algorithm is executed on a copy G' of a subgraph of G that only includes the vertices in the vo and all the edges between them, with the aim of enhancing the solution of the CGTSP. To enforce the sub-cluster visiting constraints, the costs of edges linking vertices from different clusters are increased by $n \times c_{max}$, where c_{max} is the cost of the most expensive edge in G, and n is the number of sub-clusters. The TSPSol tries to improve the sco while keeping the vertices from vo. Eventually, the cost of the solution, the sco and the vo are updated based on the outcome.

Subsequently, a subgraph G'' is established from the original graph G. This is accomplished by converting the source sub-cluster SC_s into a single vertex (v_s), appending a copy of the source sub-cluster to G'' and the sco, and eliminating all edges that do not link adjacent sub-clusters in the sco. Next, the ShPA is applied to identify the shortest path from v_s in the starting sub-cluster to its copy in the last sub-cluster, while visiting all other sub-clusters along the way (step 11). As the Euclidean instances adhere to the triangle inequality, only a single vertex from each sub-cluster needs to be visited, and the solution obtained from the ShPA is also a viable solution for the CGTSP. The ShPA find the best CGTSP possible solution, without changing the sco.

Assuming that the Sub-Cluster visiting Order (*sco*) already contains the optimal sub-cluster visiting sequence, the application of the ShPA will yield the optimal solution for the CGTSP. However, in most cases, this assumption does not hold, and the ShPA produces a set of potentially useful vertices. These vertices are then utilized in the next iteration of the loop, where the TSP solver is employed to refine and adjust the *sco*.

The two steps described earlier are iterated in the CEA while they continue to produce improvements in the CGTSP solution. The CEA terminates at the first step that does not enhance the solution of the CGTSP.

The CEA's loop concludes within a limited number of iterations. The TSPSol optimization executed in step 3 cannot deteriorate the solution since it operates on a graph G' that encompasses all the vertices in the solution. In the worst case, the solution stands unaltered. Similarly, the ShPA optimization executed in step 11 enhances the solution or, in the worst case, leaves it unaltered. This is because the solution's path is a subgraph of G'', and ShPA can only enhance or leave it unchanged. Since both steps enhance the solution, the procedure will conclude after a finite number of steps. Typically, in small instances, the loop concludes after one or two iterations. In the most complex cases, we observed a maximum of five iterations.

Algorithm 1. Chromosome Enhancement Algorithm

---

input: chromosome $c\{sco, vo\}$
1:   $z \leftarrow \infty$
2: **do**
3:     Determine vo' by running the TSPSol on G'
4:     **if** $cost(vo') < z$ **then**
5:         $z \leftarrow cost(vo')$
6:         $vo \leftarrow vo'$
7:         update sco
8:     **else**
9:         STOP
10:    **end if**
11:    Determine vo' by running the ShPA on G''
12:    **if** $cost(vo') < z$ **then**
13:        $z \leftarrow cost(vo')$
14:        $vo \leftarrow vo'$
15:    **else**
16:        STOP
17:    **end if**
18: **while** *true*

Initial Population. To begin the GA, the initial population is constructed as follows: a sub-cluster with the least number of nodes is selected as the starting sub-cluster. Next, an equal number of random chromosomes are created for each possible v_s, with their *vo* randomly initialized to include at least one node from each sub-cluster. Finally, all initial population chromosomes are improved using CEA.

Crossover. The crossover operator generates two offspring chromosomes, denoted by o_1 and o_2, by combining two parent chromosomes, p_1 and p_2. Each offspring chromosome inherits its v_s from a different parent. To initialize the *sco* of the offspring chromosomes, the first sub-cluster is randomly selected, and subsequent sub-clusters are alternately selected from p_1 and p_2. They are added either at the beginning or at the end of the *sco* list, aiming to respect the adjacencies present in the parent chromosomes and avoiding duplicates. When verifying sub-clusters adjacency, the first and last elements of *sco* are considered adjacent. If a solution cannot be found using this method, the alternation of parents can be ignored. If this method does not yield a solution, then the next sub-cluster is randomly chosen from the remaining options.

Whenever a sub-cluster is added to *sco*, the corresponding node is also added to *vo*. Once all sub-clusters have been added, *sco* and *vo* are rotated so that the starting sub-cluster and starting vertex are in the first position. Finally, the two offspring chromosomes undergo further processing by CEA.

Mutation. The mutation operator produces a modified version of a chromosome through the following process: randomly select a cluster cl and for each sub-cluster within cl, replace the corresponding vertex from *vo* with another randomly chosen vertex from the same sub-cluster.

Selection. The selection used in our hybrid approach based on genetic algorithms is obtained by hybridizing elitist and random selection methods.

Parameter Adjustment. Through experimentation, the GA parameters have been fine-tuned to the following: the initial population is constructed by adding 3 times the value of ps chromosomes, where ps was set to 50. The completion of each new generation occurs either when a total of $noff = 2.5 \times ps \times |Cs|$ offspring, excluding duplicates, have been generated, or when $5 \times ps \times |Cs|$ crossover operations have been carried out. In our selection strategy the first parent is randomly selected from the top 20% of chromosomes belonging to the current population, while the second parent is randomly selected from the entire population. Let $sizecp$ represent the current population size. At the conclusion of every generation, the mutation operator is applied to a quantity of $0.3 \times ps \times |Cs|$ chromosomes. The input for the mutation operation is randomly selected from the first $min(noff, sizecp)$ chromosomes. The GA terminates when no progress has been made over the previous 10 consecutive generations. If the last generation fails to improve the solution, the current population size is increased by 50%. However, if the solution was improved in the last generation, the current population size is reduced by 25%, but this reduction is limited to prevent the population size from falling below the ps chromosome limit.

4 Preliminary Computational Results

The GA was coded in Java, utilizing the Concorde TSPSol [1] and the ShPA algorithms from the Lemon optimization library [12]. Each instance was subjected to 15 independent runs on a computer equipped with an Intel(R) Core i3-8100 CPU @ 3.6 GHz and 8 GB RAM.

Since the instances used in [2,10] could not be obtained from the authors, we generated a new set of test instances based on the euclidean instances in the GTSP_Lib [8]. The clusters in these instances will be sub-clusters in the new instances generated for CGTSP. To distribute the sub-clusters into clusters, we uniformly divided the area covered by the instance nodes into ro rows and co columns, forming $ro \times co$ rectangular regions. Each cluster in the new generated instances is composed of all the sub-clusters whose centers are located in the same region. The center of a sub-cluster is the center of the smallest rectangle that includes all its nodes. The generated instances are available at: http:// cosma.cunbm.utcluj.ro/CGSTP/instances.html.

An example of a generated instance for CGTSP is shown in Fig. 2. Sub-clusters are indicated with blue rectangles, and their centers are marked with a small red cross. Regions are drawn in magenta. The number of the sub-clusters and the number of the clusters they belong to are written in red above each sub-cluster. This example corresponds to instance 50pcb442 in the GTSP_Lib. The new CGTSP instance was generated with $ro = 4$ and $co = 4$.

In Table 1, we present the outcomes achieved by our hybrid based genetic algorithm approach. The table comprises of the following components: the first seven columns provide information about our generated instances: nc for the number of clusters, n for the number of sub-clusters, N for the number of vertices, and ro and co to indicate the instance's generation process. The next four columns report the results achieved by the proposed GA: $BestS$ denotes the best solution obtained, $AvgS$ represents the average of the solutions found in the 15 runs for each instance, and $AvgT$ represents the average execution time required by the developed application to produce the solution. Specifically, $AvgT$ indicates the average duration needed by the application to initiate the construction of the generation in which the best solution is first discovered. If $AvgT = 0$, it implies that the best solution was present in the initial population each time. The value of $AvgT$ is in seconds. Gap reflects the difference between $BestS$ and $AvgS$ and it is calculated using the formula:

$$Gap = \frac{AvgS - BestS}{BestS} \times 100.$$

The "=" symbol is used to indicate a value that is identical to the best solution for the corresponding instance.

Analyzing the results presented in Table 1, we may notice that our developed hybrid based genetic algorithm found the best solution in each run for 31 out of 40 instances that were tested. For the remaining 9 instances, the Gap lies within 0.002% and 0.359% in the case of the instance 100i1000 − 410. The average

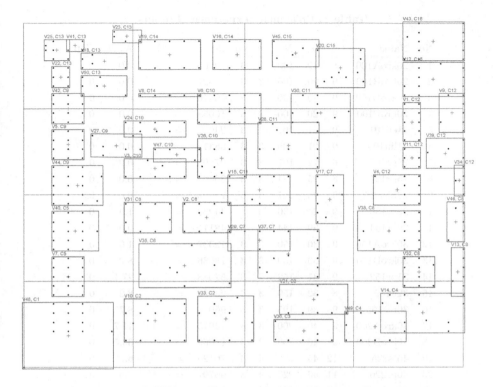

Fig. 2. An instance generated for CGTSP

running times for the first 30 instances are up to 86 s, and the highest average running tine is 3721.8 s in the case of instance 210pr1002.

5   Conclusions and Further Research Directions

The scope of this paper was to present a new approach for solving the clustered generalized traveling salesman problem (CGTSP), namely a hybrid based genetic algorithm. Our hybrid solution approach integrates the Dijkstra's shortest path algorithm and a TSP solver within a genetic algorithm, resulting a powerful and efficient novel solution approach for solving the CGTSP.

Since the instances used by Baniasadi et al. [2] and Foumani et al. [10] could not been obtained from the literature, we generated novel instances for CGTSP, which are available at: http://cosma.cunbm.utcluj.ro/CGSTP/instances.html. The preliminary computational results on a set consisting of 40 instances prove that our proposed hybrid based genetic algorithm delivers good quality solutions within reasonable computational times.

It is our scope to continue our research on the CGTSP and to look into some other methods to improve our developed solution approach, such as local search strategies. It is our intention to assess the generality and scalability of our designed hybrid based genetic algorithm by testing it on larger instances.

Table 1. Preliminary experimental results

No.	Name	nc	n	N	ro	co	BestS	AvgS	AvgT	Gap
1	20kroA100	8	20	100	3	3	10405	=	0.0	0
2	20kroB100	9	20	100	3	3	11327	=	0.0	0
3	20kroD100	9	20	100	3	3	10516	=	0.0	0
4	20kroE100	9	20	100	3	3	10051	=	0.0	0
5	21eil101	9	21	101	3	3	249	=	0.0	0
6	21lin105	9	21	105	3	3	8841	=	0.0	0
7	22pr107	6	22	107	3	3	27898	=	0.9	0
8	25pr124	8	25	124	3	3	36605	=	0.0	0
9	26bier127	9	26	127	3	3	78205	=	0.0	0
10	28pr136	9	28	136	3	3	44239	=	1.9	0
11	29pr144	9	29	144	3	3	48111	=	0.0	0
12	30kroA150	9	30	150	3	3	12337	=	1.0	0
13	30kroB150	9	30	150	3	3	13036	=	8.2	0
14	31pr152	9	31	152	3	3	52088	=	27.1	0
15	32u159	8	32	159	3	3	23793	=	8.2	0
16	39rat195	9	39	195	3	3	960	=	8.7	0
17	40kroA200	9	40	200	3	3	14615	=	11.7	0
18	40kroB200	9	40	200	3	3	14809	=	33.5	0
19	45ts225	12	45	225	4	3	70125	=	6.2	0
20	46pr226	11	46	226	4	3	66797	=	0.0	0
21	50pcb442	16	50	442	4	4	14732	14733.73	63.9	0.012
22	50rat783	16	50	783	4	4	1879	=	29.7	0
23	50pr1002	16	50	1002	4	4	56804	56820.13	35.9	0.028
24	50vm1084	15	50	1084	4	4	63396	=	65.3	0
25	50pcb1173	16	50	1173	4	4	10255	=	50.8	0
26	53gil262	12	53	262	4	3	1088	=	66.8	0
27	53pr264	8	53	264	4	3	30192	=	85.6	0
28	56a280	12	56	280	4	3	1197	=	74.7	0
29	60pr299	15	60	299	4	4	25369	=	24.7	0
30	64lin318	16	64	318	4	4	21999	=	74.2	0
31	88pr439	20	88	439	5	4	65478	=	182.7	0
32	89pcb442	20	89	442	5	4	22679	22719.72	398.1	0.180
33	100rat783	20	100	783	5	4	2694	2696.80	544.4	0.104
34	100i1000-410	20	100	1000	5	4	5754	5774.63	1724.7	0.359
35	100pr1002	20	100	1002	5	4	83552	83573.00	862.1	0.025
36	100vm1084	20	100	1084	5	4	88330	88332.13	554.4	0.002
37	100pcb1173	20	100	1173	5	4	14514	=	594.5	0
38	115rat575	25	115	575	5	5	2615	2615.17	356.4	0.006
39	157rat783	25	157	783	5	5	3624	3632.57	2540.5	0.236
40	201pr1002	36	201	1002	6	6	125930	=	3721.8	0

Acknowledgments. This work was supported by the project COSO that received funding from Romania's National Recovery and Resilience Plan PNRR-III-C9-2022-I8, under grant agreement 760070.

References

1. Applegate, D., Bixby, R., Chvatal, V., Cook, W.: Concorde tsp solver. http://www.tsp.gatech.edu/concorde/index.html
2. Baniasadi, P., Foumani, M., Smith-Miles, K., Ejov, V.: A transformation technique for the clustered generalized traveling salesman problem with applications to logistics. Eur. J. Oper. Res. **285**(2), 444–457 (2020)
3. Cosma, O., Pop, P.C., Pop Sitar, C.: A two-level based genetic algorithm for solving the soft-clustered vehicle routing problem. Carpathian J. Math. **38**(1), 117–128 (2022)
4. Cosma, O., Pop, P.C., Zelina, I.: An effective genetic algorithm for solving the clustered shortest-path tree problem. IEEE Access **9**, 15570–15591 (2021)
5. Cosma, O., Pop, P.C., Zelina, I.: A novel genetic algorithm for solving the clustered shortest-path tree problem. Carpathian J. Math. **36**(3), 401–414 (2020)
6. Demange, M., Monnot, J., Pop, P.C., Ries, B.: On the complexity of the selective graph coloring problem in some special classes of graphs. Theor. Comput. Sci. **540–541**, 82–102 (2014)
7. Feremans, C., Labbe, M., Laporte, G.: Generalized network design problems. Eur. J. Oper. Res. **148**(1), 1–13 (2003)
8. Fidanova, S., Pop, P.C.: An improved hybrid ant-local search for the partition graph coloring problem. J. Comput. Appl. Math. **293**, 55–61 (2016)
9. Fischetti, M., Salazar-Gonzales, J.J., Toth, P.: A branch-and-cut algorithm for the symmetric generalized traveling salesman problem. Oper. Res. **45**(3), 378–394 (1997)
10. Foumani, M., Moeini, A., Haythorpe, M., Smith-Miles, K.: A cross-entropy method for optimising robotic automated storage and retrieval systems. Int. J. Prod. Res. **56**(19), 6450–6472 (2018)
11. Ghiani, G., Improta, G.: An efficient transformation of the generalized vehicle routing problem. Eur. J. Oper. Res. **122**, 11–17 (2000)
12. The LEMON library. http: https://lemon.cs.elte.hu/trac/lemon
13. Matei, O. Pop, P.C.: An efficient genetic algorithm for solving the generalized traveling salesman problem. In Proceedings of 6th IEEE International Conference on Intelligent Computer Communication and Processing, pp. 87–92 (2010)
14. Petrovan, A., Pop, P.C., Sabo, C., Zelina, I.: Novel two-level hybrid genetic algorithms based on different Cayley-type encodings for solving the clustered shortest-path tree problem. Expert Syst. Appl. **215**, 119372 (2023)
15. Pop, P.C.: The generalized minimum spanning tree problem: an overview of formulations, solution procedures and latest advances. Eur. J. Oper. Res. **283**(1), 1–15 (2020)
16. Pop, P.C., Matei, O., Sabo, C., Petrovan, A.: A two-level solution approach for solving the generalized minimum spanning tree problem. Eur. J. Oper. Res. **265**(2), 478–487 (2018)
17. Pop, P.C., Fuksz, L., Horvat Marc, A., Sabo, C.: A novel two-level optimization approach for clustered vehicle routing problem. Comput. Ind. Eng. **115**, 304–318 (2018)

18. Pop, P.C.: Generalized Network Design Problems. Modeling and Optimization. De Gruyter Series in Discrete Mathematics and Applications, Germany (2012)
19. Pop, P.C., Matei, O., Sabo, C.: A new approach for solving the generalized traveling salesman problem. In: Blesa, M.J., Blum, C., Raidl, G., Roli, A., Sampels, M. (eds.) HM 2010. LNCS, vol. 6373, pp. 62–72. Springer, Heidelberg (2010). https://doi.org/10.1007/978-3-642-16054-7_5
20. Pop, P.C.: New integer programming formulations of the generalized traveling salesman problem. Am. J. Appl. Sci. 4(11), 932–937 (2007)
21. Schmidt, J., Irnich, S.: New neighborhoods and an iterated local search algorithm for the generalized traveling salesman problem. EURO J. Comput. Optim. 10, 100029 (2022)
22. Sepehri, M.M., Motlagh, S.M.H., Ignatius, J.: A model for optimal routing of dangerous substances in warehousing operations via K-nested GTSP. Int. J. Nonlinear Sci. Num. Simul. 11(9), 701–704 (2010)
23. Smith, S.L., Imeson, F.: GLNS: an effective large neighborhood search heuristic for the generalized traveling salesman problem. Comput. Oper. Res. 87, 1–19 (2017)

Feature Ranking for Feature Sorting and Feature Selection with Optimisation

Paola Santana-Morales[1], Gretel Alonso[1], Isabela Ortigosa de Araujo[1],
Jessica Coto-Palacio[2], Raquel Beltran-Barba[1], Luís Correia[3],
and Antonio J. Tallón-Ballesteros[4(✉)]

[1] University of Huelva, Huelva, Spain
{paola.morales,isabela.ortigosa}@alu.uhu.es,
gretel.alonsograveran@estudiante.unia.es
[2] International University of Andalusia, Huelva, Spain
jessica.cotopalacio@estudiante.unia.es
[3] LASIGE, Faculdade de Ciências, Universidade de Lisboa, Lisbon, Portugal
luis.correia@ciencias.ulisboa.pt
[4] Department of Electronic, Computer Systems and Automation Engineering,
University of Huelva, Huelva, Spain
antonio.tallon.diesia@zimbra.uhu.es

Abstract. This paper introduces a framework called $FR4(FS)^2+$ which stands for Feature Ranking for Feature Sorting and Feature Selection with Optimisation. It is a tandem combining feature sorting which obtains a feature ranking and then only a certain percentage of the promising features are kept in order to be submitted to a further feature subset selection. The test-bed comprises three NIPS 2003 challenges which are still open in the sense that there is not currently a final approach to face these challenges successfully. Experimental results show that the approach is competitive and can be further exploited.

Keywords: Data mining · Feature Sorting · Feature Selection · Correlation-based Feature Selection (CFS) · CoNsistency-based feature Selection (CNS)

1 Introduction

Attribute selection [11], in the field of Data Mining [1], consists of obtaining a subset of attributes sufficiently representative of the original problem. This issue is a crucial element in the pre-processing stage of large data sets with many attributes, to apply machine learning techniques [7], a problem that has been widely discussed from different perspectives in the field of feature engineering. Failure to perform this process of selecting relevant features can result in inefficient modelling, longer runtime, reduced interpretability and model performance, and low generalisability.

The above problems can be compensated by removing irrelevant attributes for a specific task, combining attributes and removing redundant or correlated attributes. On the one hand, there is no best technique for all cases and, on the other hand, a single attribute selection technique may not be sufficient to identify all relevant attributes, but the above solutions constitute a flexible and iterative process, which may vary depending on the prediction or classification task, the type of data and the learning algorithm used.

Obtaining more robust, reliable, less biased models, improved performance, better knowledge of the data set, reduction of redundancies and validation of relevant features, are advantages derived from the combination of different attribute selection techniques [9]. This paper proposes a new two step approach combining different techniques for feature selection.

This document is structured in 6 parts. After this introduction, theoretical elements and the state of the art on attribute selection will be discussed (Sect. 2). This is followed by a description of our proposed feature selection method (Sect. 3) and then the experiments that were performed on the different data sets (Sect. 4). Finally, we analyse the results obtained from the training and evaluation of the algorithms used (Sect. 5), and we draw conclusions on the impact of the proposed combination of feature selection techniques (Sect. 6).

2   Feature-Based Data Selection

Feature selection is a process of selecting a subset of important features from a larger data set in order to predict or explain new information [2]. Feature selection methods can be classified into two categories: feature subset selection and feature ranking. The first aims to find the smallest data set that can still provide accurate results while the latter involves ranking features based on a specific evaluation measure to determine which attributes are most relevant [5].

There are several types of feature selection methods widely used, including filters, embedded feature selection, semi-wrappers and wrappers [16]. Filters evaluate each feature's relevancy individually or in a subset based on an internal measure, such as correlation or statistical analysis. Embedded feature selection includes selecting the best features and eliminates the least relevant for the learning process in an integrated way. Semi-wrappers evaluate the effectiveness of a feature set using a supervised machine learning approach that differs from the target algorithm, whereas in the wrapper method the same algorithm and its hyper-parameters is used to compute the quality of the data set and to predict new data [8]. The main drawback of this method is overfitting. Once the most relevant features have been selected, the K-nearest neighbour algorithm can be used to classify new data on the subset of selected features. Figure 1 shows a taxonomy from the types of Feature selection methods: filter [14], embedded feature selection, semi-wrappers [16] and wrappers [8].

3   Proposal

This paper is an extension of a previous proposal published in a paper entitled *Feature ranking for feature sorting and feature selection: FR4(FS)$^{2+}$* [15]. It aims

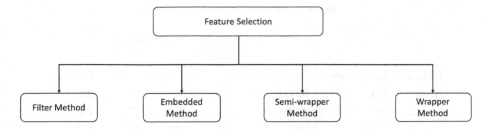

Fig. 1. Taxonomy of Feature Selection Methods

to go further by optimising the solution achieved using a search procedure within feature subset selection based on Best First, which is a well-known Artificial Intelligence-based greedy meta-heuristic, in order to obtain more interpretable, accurate and efficient models. The optimisation step is addressed with techniques that evaluate the feature subsets of the original data sets independently of the classification algorithm, using feature filtering. The proposed approach may be considered a hybrid procedure given that it mixes feature ranking and feature subset selection. Specifically, additional feature selection techniques will be applied to data sets that have been reduced according to methods that are based on information theory, and that propose as relevant features those that generate a high information gain (InfoGain) or a high gain ratio (GainRatio) and that, therefore, reduce the uncertainty in the class; the size of the selected subset is constrained to a 90% of the attributes with a positive incidence as in [15]. This time the data set will be reduced again, using CFS (Correlation-based Feature Selection) and CNS (CoNsistency-based feature Selection) feature selection techniques. CNS uses the concept of consistency to reduce the dimensionality of the input data and maximise the accuracy of the model by exploring all possible combinations of attributes; it looks for feature subset with a similar consistency to those with the full feature set. CFS is based on the correlation between attributes and the class of the training data, maximising relevance to the class and minimising redundancy between attributes. The performance of the resulting models is evaluated on test sets, preventing biases from being introduced in the selection process and ensuring that informed decisions are made.

4   Experimentation

The experimental work of this paper has been carried out using the visual tool Weka [6] (*Waikato Environment for Knowledge Analysis*), particularly version 3.8. We apply attribute selection based on feature ranking and then feature subset selection to three data sets, which are shown in Table 1.

Classification methods are strategies used to predict the response variable of a database. In the project we have used three of these methods: J48, JRip and IBk. J48 classifier is an implementation of the C4.5 algorithm proposed by Quinlan [13]. It is a classifier that induces decision trees [12] to classify data.

Table 1. Description of data sets

| | | | Distribution of Instances | | | |
| | | | Train | | Test | |
Data set	No. Instances	No. Features	Class 1	Class 2	Class 1	Class 2
Arcene	200	10000	66	84	22	28
Dexter	600	20000	225	225	75	75
Gissete	7000	5000	2625	2625	875	875
Average	2600.0	11667.7	-	-	-	-

On the other hand, JRip classifier is the *RIPPER* algorithm based on reduced incremental pruning to reduce the error. Finally, the IBk classifier is the k-nearest neighbour classifier [10].

To evaluate the effectiveness of results on the different configurations we will use three metrics: Accuracy, Cohen's kappa and confusion matrix. The first of these, Accuracy, represents the percentage of observations that are correctly classified. Likewise, in the confusion matrix, each column represents the number of predictions in each class, while each row represents the instances in the actual class. Thus, the diagonal of the matrix will consist of the instances that have been correctly predicted. Cohen's kappa coefficient measures the degree of agreement based on comparing the observed agreement in a data set. Jacob Cohen [3] first introduced this metric as a measure of agreement between observers of psychological behaviour, it was intended to measure the level of agreement or disagreement between two people observing the same phenomenon.

As mentioned above, the main idea of this paper is to aggregate the application of the CFS and CNS Feature Selection methods. Table 2 shows the number of attributes selected in each of the scenarios.

Run time is a performance measure that we use to indicate how long a classification algorithm will take to train on a certain dataset [4]. Table 3 shows the execution time of each scenario when applying the C4.5, *1*-NN and RIPPER classifiers. In addition, in the last two columns of this table, the runtime average and standard deviation have been added.

5   Results and Analysis

Table 4 shows the test results obtained by comparing the seven scenarios described in the previous section, for the three data sets. We observe that applying a second attribute selection method after applying Gain Ratio for the Arcene data set, according to the metrics used, only improves the result when the classifier is *1*-NN. On the other hand, it is more convenient to use Info Gain + CFS when the algorithm being used is C4.5, in other cases it does not improve the performance.

For the Dexter data set (refer to Table 4), the use of CFS or CNS after using Gain Ratio improves the results of the C4.5 and *1*-NN classifiers. For

Table 2. Number of selected attributes from each dataset after applying Feature Selection methods

Data set	Scenario	No. Selected Attributes
Arcene	GainRatio	2218
	GainRatio + CFS	82
	GainRatio + CNS	10
	InfoGain	2218
	InfoGain + CFS	79
	InfoGain + CNS	7
Dexter	GainRatio	228
	GainRatio + CFS	44
	GainRatio + CNS	26
	InfoGain	228
	InfoGain + CFS	46
	InfoGain + CNS	28
Gissete	GainRatio	1480
	GainRatio + CFS	72
	GainRatio + CNS	22
	InfoGain	1480
	InfoGain + CFS	70
	InfoGain + CNS	21

example, as reflected by the confusion matrix of the C4.5 algorithm, Gain Ratio + CNS increases in 2 the true positives and in 4 the true negatives, compared to the confusion matrix where only Gain Ratio is used. In the case of the 1-NN algorithm, Gain Ratio + CFS finds 7 true positives more, keeping the true negatives equal to the original Gain Ratio. With Info Gain it is more convenient to apply CNS when the classifier is C4.5 and CFS when it is 1-NN, although with CNS the results reported in literature are also improved. The existing results are not improved when the classifier is RIPPER.

For the Gisette data set, as Table 4 reports, there is no improvement in the results compared to applying a single attribute selection method. If Gain Ratio + CNS is applied in combination with the C4.5 classifier, according to the confusion matrix, it would be able to properly classify 3 more samples than if CNS is not applied, but it would not be able to improve the performance of Info Gain. On the other hand, a slight improvement is perceived in the RIPPER algorithm when Info Gain + CNS is applied, since this combination is able to properly classify one more sample, although it should be noted that the Gain Ratio results are not improved.

In summary, applying two attribute selection methods presents dissimilar behavior for each database and in some cases, it is able to improve the results reported in literature. For this dataset, in general it is not convenient to apply

Table 3. Execution time (in seconds) from each dataset after applying Feature Selection methods

Data set	Scenario	Execution time (seconds)			Average	Standard Deviation
		C4.5	1NN	RIPPER		
Arcene	GainRatio	0.54	0.01	0.9	0.48	0.54
	GainRatio + CFS	0.04	0.00	0.09	0.04	0.05
	GainRatio + CNS	0.03	0.00	0.07	0.03	0.04
	InfoGain	0.43	0.02	0.54	0.33	0.27
	InfoGain + CFS	0.07	0.00	0.08	0.05	0.04
	InfoGain + CNS	0.01	0.00	0.01	0.01	0.01
Dexter	GainRatio	1.11	0.00	1.04	0.72	0.62
	GainRatio + CFS	0.15	0.00	0.38	0.18	0.19
	GainRatio + CNS	0.06	0.00	0.11	0.06	0.06
	InfoGain	0.47	0.00	0.86	0.44	0.43
	InfoGain + CFS	0.15	0.00	0.71	0.29	0.37
	InfoGain + CNS	0.11	0.00	0.30	0.14	0.15
Gissete	GainRatio	28.61	0.00	74.10	34.24	37.37
	GainRatio + CFS	1.13	0.00	3.87	1.67	1.99
	GainRatio + CNS	0.52	0.00	1.40	0.64	0.71
	InfoGain	28.50	0.00	107.54	45.35	55.71
	InfoGain + CFS	0.84	0.00	2.46	1.10	1.25
	InfoGain + CNS	0.18	0.00	1.00	0.39	0.53

CFS or CNS when using the RIPPER algorithm, since the existing results will not be improved.

For Arcene (see Table 4), the combination of the application Gain Ratio + CNS and then the 1-NN classifier improves the existing results. This is not the case for the Dexter data set, where applying Info Gain and then RIPPER is still the best option. However, there are improvements in the other algorithms for this database. Finally, for the Gisette data set, the best option is still to choose Gain Ratio and then RIPPER as classifier, although there are minimal improvements in the other algorithms.

Table 5 below shows the mean and standard deviation for each scenario, for each classifier. In the case of the C4.5 classifier, the average and standard deviation is slightly higher in both Accuracy and Cohen's Kappa metrics when the datasets are in the last two scenarios, i.e. being subjected to data reduction using the InfoGain technique and after having applied the CFS and CNS attribute selection techniques. In particular, the best results are obtained in the InfoGain + CFS scenario.

Unlike the C4.5 classifier, the 1-NN classifier obtains a better mean for the first two optimised scenarios: GainRatio, GainRatio + CFS and GainRatio +

Table 4. Test Results

Data set	Scenario	Accuracy			Cohen's kappa			Confusion matrix		
		C4.5	1NN	RIPPER	C4.5	1NN	RIPPER	C4.5	1NN	RIPPER
Arcene	FULL	82.00	80.00	68.00	0.6200	0.5900	0.3200	14 8 / 1 27	16 6 / 4 24	10 12 / 4 24
	GainRatio	76.00	76.00	76.00	0.5130	0.4983	0.5277	16 6 / 6 22	13 9 / 3 25	17 5 / 7 21
	GainRatio + CFS	74.00	82.00	70.00	0.4698	0.6256	0.3822	15 7 / 6 22	15 7 / 2 26	13 9 / 6 22
	GainRatio + CNS	68.00	86.00	66.00	0.3377	0.7117	0.2998	12 10 / 6 22	17 5 / 2 26	12 10 / 7 21
	InfoGain	76.00	80.00	72.00	0.5130	0.5819	0.4205	16 6 / 6 22	14 8 / 2 26	13 9 / 5 23
	InfoGain + CFS	84.00	80.00	68.00	0.6656	0.5819	0.3311	15 7 / 1 27	14 8 / 2 26	11 11 / 5 23
	InfoGain + CNS	70.00	76.00	70.00	0.3822	0.5082	0.3822	13 9 / 6 22	15 7 / 5 23	13 9 / 6 22
Dexter	FULL	90.00	62.67	86.67	0.8000	0.2500	0.7300	66 9 / 6 69	43 32 / 24 51	62 13 / 7 68
	GainRatio	85.33	82.67	87.33	0.7067	0.6533	0.7467	64 11 / 11 64	60 15 / 11 64	64 11 / 8 67
	GainRatio + CFS	88.00	87.33	82.00	0.7600	0.7467	0.6400	66 9 / 9 66	67 8 / 11 64	60 15 / 12 63
	GainRatio + CNS	89.33	83.33	85.33	0.7867	0.6667	0.7067	66 9 / 7 68	62 13 / 12 63	63 12 / 10 65
	InfoGain	88.00	80.00	90.00	0.7600	0.6000	0.8000	64 11 / 7 68	50 25 / 5 70	66 9 / 6 69
	InfoGain + CFS	86.67	83.33	84.67	0.7333	0.6667	0.6933	65 10 / 10 65	67 8 / 17 58	62 13 / 10 65
	InfoGain + CNS	88.67	82.67	84.00	0.7733	0.6533	0.6800	65 10 / 7 68	64 11 / 15 60	60 15 / 9 66
Gisette	FULL	93.60	95.31	94.80	0.9000	0.9100	0.9000	812 63 / 49 826	818 57 / 25 850	843 32 / 59 816
	GainRatio	94.29	96.97	94.74	0.8857	0.9394	0.8949	824 51 / 49 826	842 33 / 20 855	825 50 / 42 833
	GainRatio + CFS	94.40	94.34	93.31	0.8880	0.8869	0.8663	810 65 / 33 842	828 47 / 52 823	822 53 / 64 811
	GainRatio + CNS	94.46	94.11	94.51	0.8891	0.8823	0.8903	833 42 / 55 820	828 47 / 56 819	824 51 / 45 830
	InfoGain	94.69	96.69	94.51	0.8937	0.9337	0.8903	831 44 / 49 826	837 38 / 20 855	841 34 / 62 813
	InfoGain + CFS	94.40	94.40	93.09	0.8880	0.8880	0.8617	808 67 / 31 844	827 48 / 50 825	819 56 / 65 810
	InfoGain + CNS	94.69	94.29	94.57	0.8937	0.8857	0.8914	827 48 / 45 830	816 59 / 41 834	831 44 / 51 824

CNS. However, the standard deviation is slightly higher for the last two scenarios. The same behaviour occurs in the RIPPER classifier.

Table 5. Average and Standard Deviation of each experimental scenario

Scenario	Average ± SD					
	C4.5		1NN		RIPPER	
	Accuracy	Cohen's kappa	Accuracy	Cohen's kappa	Accuracy	Cohen's kappa
GainRatio	85.21 ± 9.14	0.7018 ± 0.1864	85.21 ± 10.72	0.6970 ± 0.2238	86.06 ± 9.44	0.7231 ± 0.1847
GainRatio + CFS	85.47 ± 10.43	0.7059 ± 0.2143	87.89 ± 6.19	0.7531 ± 0.1308	81.77 ± 11.66	0.6295 ± 0.2422
GainRatio + CNS	83.93 ± 14.03	0.6712 ± 0.2933	87.81 ± 5.62	0.7536 ± 0.1137	81.95 ± 14.55	0.6323 ± 0.3022
InfoGain	86.23 ± 9.47	0.7222 ± 0.1931	85.56 ± 9.63	0.7052 ± 0.1981	85.50 ± 11.91	0.7036 ± 0.2493
InfoGain + CFS	88.36 ± 5.40	0.7623 ± 0.1140	85.91 ± 7.54	0.7122 ± 0.1580	81.92 ± 12.77	0.6287 ± 0.2711
InfoGain + CNS	84.45 ± 12.87	0.6831 ± 0.2674	84.32 ± 9.25	0.6824 ± 0.1904	82.86 ± 12.33	0.6512 ± 0.2558

6   Conclusions

This paper developed a new approach to feature selection under the hybrid paradigm of feature ranking and feature subset selection for supervised machine learning problems in order to optimise the rearrangement of the initial feature space according to the ranking achieved by a couple of feature selection procedures by only keeping a percentage (ninety in this contribution) of the potentially beneficial attributes under the hypothesis that positive weights may have a positive effect in the classification model and may be able to endow a machine learning algorithm to distinguish instances from different classes. The novelty of the paper relies on the application of an optimisation step based on feature subset selection with CFS and CNS, independently. The experimentation included a test-bench of three binary data sets concerning complex problems from NIPS 2003 challenges. The main conclusion may be summarised in these statements. For GainRatio, the optimiser CNS is a good choice, in general terms. For Info-Gain, there is not a clear winner between the optimisation conducted CFS and CNS although given that CNS tends to retain a lower number of attributes, the first option may follow CNS as the optimisation path. Another good point falls in the fact that CFS and CNS as optimisers after any fast feature ranking procedure (InfoGain and GainRatio) may avoid wasting a huge amount computing time which may be consumed by the direct running of CFS and CNS starting for the raw scenario.

References

1. Azevedo, A.: Data mining and knowledge discovery in databases. In: Advanced Methodologies and Technologies in Network Architecture, Mobile Computing, and Data Analytics, pp. 502–514. IGI Global (2019)

2. Cantú-Paz, E., Newsam, S., Kamath, C.: Feature selection in scientific applications. In: Proceedings of the Tenth ACM SIGKDD International Conference on Knowledge Discovery and Data Mining, pp. 788–793 (2004)
3. Cohen, J.: A coefficient of agreement for nominal scales. Educ. Psychol. Measur. **20**(1), 37–46 (1960)
4. Doan, T., Kalita, J.: Predicting run time of classification algorithms using meta-learning. Int. J. Mach. Learn. Cybern. **8**, 1929–1943 (2017)
5. Guyon, I., Elisseeff, A.: An introduction to variable and feature selection. J. Mach. Learn. Res. **3**(Mar), 1157–1182 (2003)
6. Hall, M., Frank, E., Holmes, G., Pfahringer, B., Reutemann, P., Witten, I.H.: The WEKA data mining software: an update. ACM SIGKDD Explor. Newsl **11**(1), 10–18 (2009)
7. Kohavi, R.: Glossary of terms. Spec. Issue Appl. Mach. Learn. Knowl. Discov. Process. Mach. Learn. **30**(2/3), 271–274 (1998)
8. Kohavi, R., John, G.H.: Wrappers for feature subset selection. Artif. Intell. **97**(1–2), 273–324 (1997)
9. Kuhn, M., et al.: Applied Predictive Modeling, vol. 26. Springer, Cham (2013)
10. Larose, D.T., Larose, C.D.: k-nearest neighbor algorithm (2014)
11. Majeed, N.M., Ramo, F.M.: A comparison between the performance of features selection techniques: survey study. Technium. **6**, 56–65 (2023)
12. Pandey, P., Prabhakar, R.: An analysis of machine learning techniques (J48 & AdaBoost)-for classification. In: 2016 1st India International Conference on Information Processing (IICIP), pp. 1–6. IEEE (2016)
13. Salzberg, S.L.: C4.5: Programs for machine learning by j. ross quinlan. morgan kaufmann publishers, inc., 1993. Machine Learn. **16**, 235–240 (1994). Kluwer Academic Publishers
14. Sánchez-Maroño, N., Alonso-Betanzos, A., Tombilla-Sanromán, M.: Filter methods for feature selection – a comparative study. In: Yin, H., Tino, P., Corchado, E., Byrne, W., Yao, X. (eds.) IDEAL 2007. LNCS, vol. 4881, pp. 178–187. Springer, Heidelberg (2007). https://doi.org/10.1007/978-3-540-77226-2_19
15. Santana-Morales, P., Merchán, A.F., Márquez-Rodríguez, A., Tallón-Ballesteros, A.J.: Feature ranking for feature sorting and feature selection: Fr4 (fs) 2. In: Bio-inspired Systems and Applications: from Robotics to Ambient Intelligence: 9th International Work-Conference on the Interplay Between Natural and Artificial Computation, IWINAC 2022, Puerto de la Cruz, Tenerife, Spain, 31 May–3 June 2022, Proceedings, Part II, pp. 545–550. Springer, Cham (2022). https://doi.org/10.1007/978-3-031-06527-9_54
16. Tallón-Ballesteros, A.J., Riquelme, J.C., Ruiz, R.: Semi-wrapper feature subset selector for feed-forward neural networks: applications to binary and multi-class classification problems. Neurocomputing **353**, 28–44 (2019)

Efficient Simulation of Pollutant Dispersion Using Machine Learning

Guido F. M. G. Carvalho[1,2]([✉]) [iD], Douglas F. Corrêa[1,2] [iD], David A. Pelta[2] [iD],
Diego C. Knupp[1] [iD], and Antônio J. Silva Neto[1] [iD]

[1] Universidade do Estado do Rio de Janeiro, Nova Friburgo, Brazil
{guido.fraga,douglas.correa,diegoknupp,ajsneto}@iprj.uerj.br
[2] Department of Computer Science and AI, Universidad de Granada, Granada, Spain
dpelta@ugr.es

Abstract. An efficient and accurate system capable of predicting con-
taminant source location is important for environmental monitoring and
security systems. However, one of the main challenges in developing such
a system is the high computational cost associated with modeling the
physical aspects of atmospheric dispersion. The present work addresses
this issue by proposing a faster solution that uses a Multi Layer Perceptron (MLP) Neural Network to predict sensor readings based on
the source location coordinates. The MLP is trained using synthetic
data generated by solving the advection diffusion equation numerically,
and collected at predetermined sensor locations and time. The proposed
method generates accurate predictions in a fraction of the time required
for the conventional method. This approach can help in detecting and
identifying contaminants quickly and efficiently, and it has potential
applications in environmental monitoring and security systems, making
it an important tool for protecting public health and safety.

Keywords: Pollution Dispersion · Advection-Diffusion Equation ·
Finite Difference Method · Multi Layer Perceptron Neural Network ·
Environmental Monitoring

1 Introduction

Identifying the sources of pollutant distribution is an important task in environmental monitoring, pollution control, and public health in general. The ability
to precisely identify the sources of contaminants and implement effective mitigation measures in a timely manner can significantly improve the efforts of
environmental monitoring and pollution control.

A common approach to model the dispersion of pollutants in the atmosphere
is to use the advection diffusion equation. This equation describes the transport
of a substance by a fluid flow and the simultaneous diffusion of the substance into
the fluid, such as air [9]. However, solving this equation can be challenging due
to the computational expense and time-consuming nature of solving its partial

P. García Bringas et al. (Eds.): HAIS 2023, LNAI 14001, pp. 372–383, 2023.
https://doi.org/10.1007/978-3-031-40725-3_32

differential equation. Traditionally, unconditionally stable techniques such as the implicit approach of the Finite Difference Method (FDM) have been used to solve this problem [3,8].

Such methods consists of discretizing the studied domain into a grid of nodes, and calculating the solution at each point. As each node corresponds to an unknown concentration value that needs to be determined, the number of equations that need to be solved increases rapidly as the size of the mesh or the number of nodes increases. For example, for a simple mesh of 50×50 nodes, the method would have to solve a 2500×2500 system of equations for each time step. This involves a significant amount of computation and memory usage, and the time required to solve such a large system increases substantially as the number of equations increases. As the mesh becomes more complex or the number of nodes increases, the computational cost of solving the system of equations can become prohibitively expensive. Therefore, more efficient algorithms may be necessary to solve these types of problems accurately and efficiently.

To solve this issue, a Multi Layer Perceptron Neural Network will be trained to predict sensor readings based on the source location coordinates (i.e. the direct problem) in a more computationally efficient manner. The network will take the source location coordinates as input and generate a set of predicted sensor readings, with each output corresponding to the reading of a sensor positioned at a specific known location.

Synthetic data will be generated by solving the bidimensional advection-diffusion equation, with appropriate parameters and boundaries. The generated data will be collected at specific positions, simulating sensors, after a set amount of time has passed. This data will then be used to train the model.

The model described in this work will serve as the foundation for a larger project aimed at accurately predicting the location of contaminants from observed concentrations, in real-time. This project aligns with several of the United Nations Sustainable Development Goals, including Climate Action, Industry, Innovation and Infrastructure, and Life on Land.

Once trained, the neural network can efficiently predict sensor readings for any source location within the studied domain. The aim of this work is to solve the direct problem using this neural network model, significantly reducing the computational cost associated with solving the advection diffusion equation. This reduction in computational burden enables real-time or near real-time solutions to inverse problems, specifically the identification of source coordinates, based on readings from a set of sensors. Inverse problems refer to the process of determining the input parameters of a system based on the output measurements. This approach holds potential for various applications, including applications in environmental monitoring, security systems, industrial safety, and agriculture [6].

The paper is organized as follows: The second section presents the Problem Definition, which is divided into two subsections: Physical Problem and Numerical Solution, describing the mathematical model and numerical method used to solve the problem. The third section discusses the Neural Network aspect of the work, also divided into two subsections: Generating Training Data and Model

Architecture and Configuration. This section explains how data was generated using the numerical solution and the configuration parameters of the trained NN models. In the Results section, the performances of models with different architectures are compared, and the best one is selected. Finally, the Conclusion section summarizes the main contributions of the paper and proposes future research directions.

Identifying the sources of pollutant distribution is an important task in environmental monitoring, pollution control, and public health in general. The ability to precisely identify the sources of contaminants and implement effective mitigation measures in a timely manner can significantly improve the efforts of environmental monitoring and pollution control.

A common approach to model the dispersion of pollutants in the atmosphere is to use the advection diffusion equation. This equation describes the transport of a substance by a fluid flow and the simultaneous diffusion of the substance into the fluid, such as air [9]. However, solving this equation can be challenging due to the computational expense and time-consuming nature of solving its partial differential equation. Traditionally, unconditionally stable techniques such as the implicit approach of the Finite Difference Method (FDM) have been used to solve this problem [3, 8].

Such methods consists of discretizing the studied domain into a grid of nodes, and calculating the solution at each point. As each node corresponds to an unknown concentration value that needs to be determined, the number of equations that need to be solved increases rapidly as the size of the mesh or the number of nodes increases. For example, for a simple mesh of 50×50 nodes, the method would have to solve a 2500×2500 system of equations for each time step. This involves a significant amount of computation and memory usage, and the time required to solve such a large system increases substantially as the number of equations increases. As the mesh becomes more complex or the number of nodes increases, the computational cost of solving the system of equations can become prohibitively expensive. Therefore, more efficient algorithms may be necessary to solve these types of problems accurately and efficiently.

To solve this issue, a Multi Layer Perceptron Neural Network will be trained to predict sensor readings based on the source location coordinates (i.e. the direct problem) in a more computationally efficient manner. The network will take the source location coordinates as input and generate a set of predicted sensor readings, with each output corresponding to the reading of a sensor positioned at a specific known location.

Synthetic data will be generated by solving the bidimensional advection-diffusion equation, with appropriate parameters and boundaries. The generated data will be collected at specific positions, simulating sensors, after a set amount of time has passed. This data will then be used to train the model.

The model described in this work will serve as the foundation for a larger project aimed at accurately predicting the location of contaminants from observed concentrations, in real-time. This project aligns with several of the United Nations Sustainable Development Goals, including Climate Action, Industry, Innovation and Infrastructure, and Life on Land.

Once trained, the neural network can efficiently predict sensor readings for any source location within the studied domain. The aim of this work is to solve the direct problem using this neural network model, significantly reducing the computational cost associated with solving the advection diffusion equation. This reduction in computational burden enables real-time or near real-time solutions to inverse problems, specifically the identification of source coordinates, based on readings from a set of sensors. Inverse problems refer to the process of determining the unknown input parameters of a system based on the output measurements. This approach holds potential for various applications, including applications in environmental monitoring, security systems, industrial safety, and agriculture [6].

The paper is organized as follows: The second section presents the Problem Definition, which is divided into two subsections: Physical Problem and Numerical Solution, describing the mathematical model and numerical method used to solve the problem. The third section discusses the Neural Network aspect of the work, also divided into two subsections: Generating Training Data and Model Architecture and Configuration. This section explains how data was generated using the numerical solution and the configuration parameters of the trained NN models. In the Results section, the performances of models with different architectures are compared, and the best one is selected. Finally, the Conclusion section summarizes the main contributions of the paper and proposes future research directions.

2   Problem Definition

In this section, the physical problem studied in this work will be presented, as well as the approach used to solve it numerically.

2.1   Physical Problem

The bidimensional advection diffusion problem is a mathematical model that describes the evolution of a substance that is transported by a fluid in two dimensions. This problem arises in many physical systems such as the dispersion of pollutants in the atmosphere or the diffusion of chemicals in porous media. The model involves two main mechanisms: advection, which represents the transport of the substance by the fluid, and diffusion, which represents the spreading of the substance due to its concentration gradient [4,7]. The mathematical equation that governs this process is the two-dimensional advection-diffusion equation, which can be written in terms of the substance concentration $c(x, y, t)$ as:

$$\frac{\partial c}{\partial t} + \mathbf{v} \cdot \nabla c = D \nabla^2 c \tag{1}$$

where $\mathbf{v}$ is the velocity vector of the fluid, D is the diffusion coefficient, and ∇ is the gradient operator. This equation describes how the concentration of the substance changes over time due to advection and diffusion effects. The solution of this equation can provide insights into the behavior of the substance and help predict its spatial and temporal distribution in the system.

The boundary conditions used in this study are second type contour conditions, where the derivative of the solution with respect to the normal direction is set to zero at the boundaries of the domain $[0, L_x] \times [0, L_y]$. This means that there is no flux of the substance across the boundary, which is a physically reasonable assumption for many practical problems.

Mathematically, these conditions can be expressed as:

$$\frac{\partial c}{\partial x}(0, y, t) = \frac{\partial c}{\partial x}(L_x, y, t) = 0 \quad \text{for } 0 \leq y \leq L_y, \, t \geq 0 \tag{2}$$

$$\frac{\partial c}{\partial y}(x, 0, t) = \frac{\partial c}{\partial y}(x, L_y, t) = 0 \quad \text{for } 0 \leq x \leq L_x, \, t \geq 0 \tag{3}$$

As for the initial condition, a bell curve was used to model the initial concentration of a substance that is released from a point source. Specifically, the Gaussian formula was applied:

$$c(x, y, 0) = Q_0 \exp\left(-\frac{(x - x_0)^2}{2\sigma_x^2} - \frac{(y - y_0)^2}{2\sigma_y^2}\right) \tag{4}$$

where Q_0 is the amplitude of the bell curve, (x_0, y_0) is the center of the curve (source location), and σ_x and σ_y control the width of the curve in the x and y directions, respectively. An ideal scenario for modeling the release of a substance from a point source would be achieved by setting σ_x and σ_y to zero. This would result in an initial concentration that is localized at a single point. However, this scenario presents a challenge when it comes to the numerical solution. Even with a fine grid resolution, the solution might become unstable due to numerical errors caused by the singularity at the point source. This can lead to nonphysical oscillations in the solution, which would not accurately represent the physical behavior of the system. By using a Gaussian bell curve with small values of σ_x and σ_y, it is possible to obtain a more accurate solution. Figures 1 and 2 show a representation of a initial condition with $Q_0 = 100$, $x_0 = y_0 = 1$ and $\sigma_x = \sigma_y = 0.03$.

By specifying these boundary and initial conditions, the bidimensional advection diffusion problem can be fully defined and numerical methods such as FDM can be applied to obtain the solution for the substance concentration as it evolves over time by specifying appropriate boundary and initial conditions.

In this work, the physical parameters used were the velocity vector $\mathbf{v} = (1, 0)$, a diffusion coefficient of $D = 0.01$, and a domain size of $L_x = L_y = 2$.

2.2   Numerical Solution

The Finite Difference Method is a popular numerical technique for solving partial differential equations like the bidimensional advection diffusion problem [5]. One

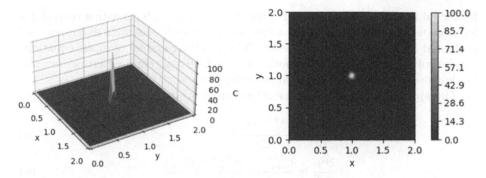

Fig. 1. Initial condition curve.

Fig. 2. Contour plot of the initial condition curve.

usual approach is to use an implicit formulation, where the solution at the next time step is expressed in terms of the solution at the current time step. This allows for greater numerical stability and accuracy, but also requires the solution of a system of linear equations at each time step [8].

To apply the FDM to the advection-diffusion equation, the domain is discretized into a grid of N_x equally spaced points in the x direction and N_y equally spaced points in the y direction, with grid spacings $\Delta x = \frac{L_x}{N_x-1}$ and $\Delta y = \frac{L_y}{N_y-1}$, respectively. This creates a total of $(N_x - 2)(N_y - 2)$ interior grid points, where the concentration values will be computed. The boundary grid points are treated separately, using the appropriate boundary conditions. Figure 3 shows an example of a discretized mesh with $N_x = N_y = 10$.

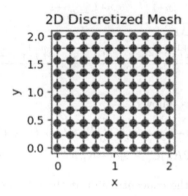

Fig. 3. Example of discretized mesh.

The initial concentration distribution is then set on the interior grid points at time $t = 0$, and the finite difference equations are iteratively solved at each time step to evolve the concentration distribution in time. The derivative approximations for the implicit method are obtained by replacing the time derivative with a forward difference, the spatial derivatives of the diffusion term with a central difference and the derivatives of the advection term with backward differences, all evaluated at an advanced time instant. The resulting system of linear equations can be solved using matrix methods such as Gaussian elimination or iterative methods such as the Jacobi or Gauss-Seidel method.

The approximations for the derivatives used are as follows:

$$\frac{\partial c}{\partial t} \approx \frac{c_{i,j}^{n+1} - c_{i,j}^{n}}{\Delta t} \tag{5}$$

$$\frac{\partial^2 c}{\partial x^2} \approx \frac{c_{i+1,j}^{n+1} - 2c_{i,j}^{n+1} + c_{i-1,j}^{n+1}}{\Delta x^2} \tag{6}$$

$$\frac{\partial^2 c}{\partial y^2} \approx \frac{c_{i,j+1}^{n+1} - 2c_{i,j}^{n+1} + c_{i,j-1}^{n+1}}{\Delta y^2} \tag{7}$$

$$\frac{\partial c}{\partial x} \approx \frac{c_{i,j}^{n+1} - c_{i-1,j}^{n+1}}{\Delta x} \tag{8}$$

$$\frac{\partial c}{\partial y} \approx \frac{c_{i,j}^{n+1} - c_{i,j-1}^{n+1}}{\Delta y} \tag{9}$$

where the indexes $i = 0, 1, \ldots, N_x - 1$ and $j = 0, 1, \ldots, N_y - 1$ are used to represent the discrete position of a point on the grid on the x and y directions, respectively. The index n is used to represent the discrete time level of the solution, with $n = 0$ corresponding to the initial time and each subsequent value of n representing a later time step in the solution. Therefore, $c_{i,j}^{n}$ represents the concentration value at grid point (i, j) at time step $n\Delta t$.

Using Eqs. (5) to (9) on Eq. (1), arrives at the following equation:

$$\frac{c_{i,j}^{n+1} - c_{i,j}^{n}}{\Delta t} + u\frac{c_{i,j}^{n+1} - c_{i-1,j}^{n+1}}{\Delta x} + v\frac{c_{i,j}^{n+1} - c_{i,j-1}^{n+1}}{\Delta y}$$
$$= D\left(\frac{c_{i+1,j}^{n+1} - 2c_{i,j}^{n+1} + c_{i-1,j}^{n+1}}{\Delta x^2} + \frac{c_{i,j+1}^{n+1} - 2c_{i,j}^{n+1} + c_{i,j-1}^{n+1}}{\Delta y^2}\right) \tag{10}$$

that can be rearranged as follows

$$(-U_x - K_x)C_{i-1,j}^{n+1} + (-U_y - K_y)C_{i,j-1}^{n+1} + (1 + U_x + U_y + 2K_x +$$
$$+ 2K_y)C_{i,j}^{n+1} + (-K_y)C_{i,j+1}^{n+1} + (-K_x)C_{i+1,j}^{n+1} = C_{i,j}^{n} \tag{11}$$

This equation describes the concentration at the interior grid points of the discretized domain, where U_x, U_y, K_x and K_y represent coefficients obtained from the discretization of the partial derivatives of the advection and diffusion terms, respectively. They are given by:

$$U_x = \frac{u\Delta t}{\Delta x} \tag{12}$$

$$U_y = \frac{v\Delta t}{\Delta y} \tag{13}$$

$$K_x = \frac{D\Delta t}{\Delta x^2} \tag{14}$$

$$K_y = \frac{D\Delta t}{\Delta y^2} \tag{15}$$

3 Neural Network

Neural networks consist of a large number of interconnected processing nodes or "neurons" that can process and transmit information. Each neuron takes input from other neurons and applies a mathematical function to generate an output, which is then passed on to other neurons in the network. By adjusting the weights and biases of the connections between neurons, neural networks can learn to recognize complex patterns and make predictions based on input data.

One popular type of neural network is the Multilayer Perceptron (MLP) network. MLP networks consist of multiple layers of interconnected neurons, with each layer processing information from the previous layer. The first layer of neurons takes input data and passes it on to the next layer. This process continues through each subsequent layer until the final output layer produces a prediction or classification based on the input data. The MLP structure was chosen because it is a simple and effective model for solving regression problems, such as the one presented.

During the training phase, the MLP neural network is presented with a set of input-output pairs, and the training process is repeated for a defined number of iterations, or epochs. The input layer receives the data, and the output layer generates a prediction based on the learned patterns. In this specific problem, the input layer consists of source coordinates, and the output layer consists of the concentration observed in a set of 12 sensors. The network adjusts itself to minimize the difference between the predicted sensor readings and the actual sensor readings for each input during each epoch. This iterative process continues until the network is able to accurately predict the sensor readings for new, unseen source locations [1].

3.1 Generating Training Data

To train the neural network model, a dataset will be generated by solving the bidimensional advection diffusion problem for different source locations within the domain and collecting data at a set of predetermined sensor locations, at a specific time instant.

The source locations will be defined by varying the values of x_0 and y_0 in the Gaussian formula given by Eq. (4). For each source location, the advection diffusion problem will be solved for one step advanced in time, rendering the data collected at a time instant $t_1 = \Delta t$. For this work, the time step was set to $\Delta t = 0.1$. This simulated time is consistent for all datasets generated.

The sensor locations in this study will be arranged in a semi-ellipse shape inside the domain. This arrangement has been chosen to optimize sensor coverage. The source location will vary within the region in front of the sensors, allowing for more precise measurements in areas of interest. This approach generates a comprehensive range of scenarios that can be used to train the model.

A numerical grid with $N_x = N_y = 80$ grid points was used to discretize the domain and solve the advection-diffusion equation. The time step was set to $\Delta t = 0.1$, and 12 sensors were positioned on the domain as shown on Fig. 4.

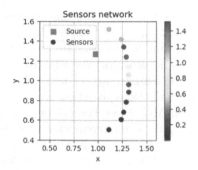

Fig. 4. Source location.

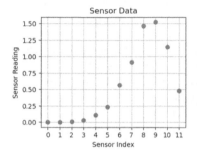

Fig. 5. Observed values of each sensor.

Figures 4 and 5 illustrate the simulation results for a single source location. These figures represent only one example of the 800 cases that were simulated. This dataset was divided in three categories, 300 cases were used for training, 250 for validation, and 250 for testing.

3.2   Model Architecture and Configuration

The determination of the number of hidden layers and neurons within each layer are determined based on the complexity of the problem and the amount of available data. In this specific problem, the input layer comprises two neurons representing the source coordinates x_0 and y_0, while the output layer consists of 12 neurons representing sensor data. A higher number of hidden layers and neurons can capture more complex relationships but can also lead to overfitting.

The activation function used in this MLP model was Sigmoid, which is a widely used activation function in neural networks [2]. The optimizer used is Adam, a popular stochastic gradient descent optimization algorithm that adapts the learning rate for each weight based on the first and second moments of the gradients. This optimizer helps the model converge faster and more accurately. The loss function employed in this model is Mean Squared Error (MSE), a commonly used loss function that measures the average squared difference between the predicted and actual values. MSE is suitable for regression problems and helps the model learn how to minimize the difference between predicted and actual values, and is calculated using the following equation:

$$MSE(y, \hat{y}) = \frac{1}{n} \sum_{i=1}^{n} (y_i - \hat{y}_i)^2 \tag{16}$$

where y is the actual value, $\hat{y}$ is the prediction, and n is the number of samples.

After conducting tests to determine the optimal number of epochs for the model, it was found that 1000 epochs was a suitable number for our problem. The number of epochs chosen depends on the convergence rate and the model's performance on the validation dataset. In this case, the number of epochs was selected through a process of trial and error, with the goal of finding the optimal balance between avoiding overfitting or underfitting and ensuring the model can generalize well on new data.

Model configuration is highly problem-dependent, and different problems may require different choices. In future work, further experimentation and optimization could be pursued to fine-tune the model architecture and configuration, considering specific characteristics of the problem domain.

4   Results

Once the models were trained, they were used to predict sensor readings for previously unseen source coordinates that had never been introduced to the model (i.e., test dataset). The MSE values for the output of each Neural Network Model and dataset are presented in Table 1. These values were calculated by using results from all simulations for each configuration and dataset.

Table 1. Results obtained for different MLP configurations

# of Hidden Layers	Nodes per Layer	MSE ($\times 10^{-3}$)		
		Training	Validation	Test
2	24	4.856	4.927	5.201
	32	4.358	4.427	5.339
	48	3.790	3.714	4.506
3	24	3.120	3.323	3.921
	32	2.959	2.850	**3.850**
	48	2.842	2.847	4.364
5	24	2.563	2.791	4.481
	32	1.842	2.012	4.240
	48	1.613	1.923	4.402

Based on Table 1, the optimal model has 3 hidden layers with 32 nodes, with a test error of 3.850×10^{-3}. Using more than 3 hidden layers may lead to overfitting, as evidenced by the 5 hidden layers' significant increase in test error. Therefore, the 3 hidden layers with 32 nodes per layer strike a good balance between model complexity and generalization, making it the best option.

In terms of computational efficiency, the proposed model was capable of generating predictions for all 800 cases in less than a minute on a computer with a CPU clocked at 3.5 GHz and 16 GB of RAM. It's important to note that this time is based on multiple runs to ensure accuracy and applies to the generation of 800 different cases. In comparison, the conventional method, as discussed in Sect. 2.2, took about 27 min to generate predictions for the same 800 cases. The significant difference in the generation time of these two methods highlights the potential advantage of the proposed model in terms of computational efficiency.

The results obtained from the selected neural network are shown in Fig. 6, which displays the case with the median MSE value obtained from the test dataset. It is worth noting that the predicted values show an expected variability when compared to the actual values. This observed variance falls within the range commonly observed in experimental data in real-world scenarios, where uncertainty is an inherent feature.

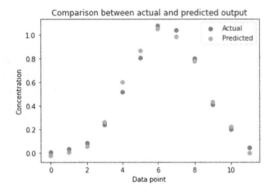

Fig. 6. Comparison between NN Prediction and exact data.

5   Conclusion

The study presented a method to solve the advection-diffusion equation using a Multilayer Perceptron Neural Network trained to predict sensor readings based on source location coordinates. The method provides a fast and efficient alternative to the conventional Finite Difference Method, which can become computationally expensive for large systems. The neural network was trained on a dataset generated by solving the advection diffusion problem for different source locations and collecting data at predetermined sensor locations.

The chosen neural network configuration was found to be with 3 hidden layers with 32 nodes each. The proposed model can generate data about 27 times faster than traditional methods.

Apart from the trained model, another significant aspect that can be derived from this study is the dataset generated in Sect. 3.1. These data sets hold considerable value as they can readily facilitate the training of various model types and contribute to addressing related issues within this research domain in future endeavors, eliminating the necessity of re-solving the numerical problem.

Future work could include the implementation of the proposed model in the solution to the inverse problem of pollutant source identification; further exploration of other types of neural networks and the incorporation of additional features such as a tridimensional domain, and different wind directions and speed. Additionally, applying the method to real experimental data could validate its effectiveness and performance. Overall, this study provides a promising approach to pollutant source identification and environmental monitoring using neural networks.

Acknowledgements. The authors acknowledge the financial support provided by Coordenação de Aperfeiçoamento de Pessoal de Nível Superior (CAPES, Finance Code 001), Conselho Nacional de Desenvolvimento Científico e Tecnológico (CNPq), Fundação Carlos Chagas Filho de Amparo à Pesquisa do Estado do Rio de Janeiro (FAPERJ), CAPES PrInt, process number 88887.716424/2022-00.

D. Pelta acknowledges support from projects PID2020-112754GB-I00, MCIN /AEI/10.13039/501100011033 and FEDER/Junta de Andalucía-Consejería de Transformación Económica, Industria, Conocimiento y Universidades/Proyecto (BTIC-640-UGR20).

References

1. Bishop, C.M.: Neural networks and their applications. Rev. Sci. Instrum. **65**(6), 1803–1832 (1994)
2. Dombi, J., Jónás, T.: The generalized sigmoid function and its connection with logical operators. Int. J. of Approx. Reason. **143**, 121–138 (2022)
3. Liu, F., Zhuang, P., Anh, V., Turner, I.: Stability and convergence of the difference methods for the space-time fractional advection-diffusion equation. App. Math. Comp. **191**, 12–20 (2007)
4. Moreira, D., Vilhena, M., Buske, D.: The state-of-art of the GILTT method to simulate pollutant dispersion in the atmosphere. Atmosph. Res. **92**(1), 1–17 (2009)
5. Noye, B., Tan, H.: Finite difference methods for solving the two-dimensional advection-diffusion equation. Int. J. Numer. Meth. Fluids **9**(1), 75–98 (1989)
6. Piazza, S., Blokker, E.M., Freni, G., Puleo, V.: Impact of diffusion and dispersion of contaminants in water distribution networks modelling and monitoring. Water Supply (2020)
7. Prieto, F.U., Muñoz, J.J.B., Corvinos, L.G.: Application of the generalized finite difference method to solve the advection-diffusion equation. J. Comp. App. Math. **235**, 1849–1855 (2011)
8. Silva Neto, A.J., Becceneri, J.C.: Técnicas de inteligência computacional inspiradas na natureza-aplicação em problemas inversos em transferência radiativa. Soc. Brasileira de Mat. Aplicada e Comput. (SBMAC) **41**, 122 (2009)
9. Stockie, J.M.: The mathematics of atmospheric dispersion modeling. SIAM Rev. **53**, 349–372 (2011)

Hybrid Intelligent Parsimony Search in Small High-Dimensional Datasets

Jose Divasón⬤, Alpha Pernia-Espinoza⬤, Ana Romero⬤,
and Francisco Javier Martinez-de-Pison$^{(\boxtimes)}$⬤

University of La Rioja, Logroño, Spain
{jose.divason,alpha.pernia,ana.romero,fjmartin}@unirioja.es

Abstract. The search for machine learning models that generalize well with small high-dimensional datasets is a current challenge. This paper shows a specific hybrid methodology for this kind of problems combining HYB-PARSIMONY and Bayesian Optimization. The methodology proposes to use HYB-PARSIMONY with different random seeds and select those features that had the highest mean probability. Subsequently, with these features, a hyperparameter adjustment is performed with Bayesian Optimization. The results show that the methodology substantially improves the degree of generalization and parsimony of the obtained models compared to previous methods.

Keywords: HYB-PARSIMONY · small high-dimensional datasets · parsimonious modeling · auto machine learning · PSO-PARSIMONY · GA-PARSIMONY

1 Introduction

Obtaining models that generalize well with small high-dimensional datasets (SHDD) is not an easy task. The curse of dimensionality coupled with the low number of instances causes many machine learning algorithms to have trouble describing the underlying structure of the data. A common way to deal with such problems is to use robust validation methods and algorithms that perform well with high-dimensional datasets, such as trees and neural networks. One of the AutoML libraries that gives the best results in this kind of problems on tabular data is `Autogluon` [8], which constructs an ensemble with artificial neural networks and tree-based algorithms such LightGBM [10], XGBoost [2], CatBoost [6], RandomForest, and so on.

However, complex ensemble models that make use of advanced methods may contain biases that are difficult to detect. This is why companies are increasingly demanding explainable models with a small number of input variables, even if their accuracy is not as good as with ensemble models. Thus, a linear model or a decision tree with a few rules can be more useful in many decision-making processes. Even a black box model that has been created with a reduced selection of the original features can be more easily analyzed with current techniques such as ELI5 and SHAP [12].

P. García Bringas et al. (Eds.): HAIS 2023, LNAI 14001, pp. 384–396, 2023.
https://doi.org/10.1007/978-3-031-40725-3_33

This paper is structured as follows. The related work is discussed in Sect. 2. Subsequently, in Sect. 3, an analysis of the existing HYB-PARSIMONY [4] method with high dimensions is performed with the ultimate goal of obtaining two linear models that allow to roughly predict the most appropriate number of iterations and the expected F_{beta} score in the search for the required features. Finally, Sect. 4 presents a new hybrid methodology combining HYB-PARSIMONY with Bayesian Optimization (BO) for the search of accurate low complexity (parsimonious) models on small size (hundreds or few thousands of instances) and high dimensionality (tens or hundreds of features) datasets.

2   Related Work

Hyperparameter optimization (HO) and feature selection (FS) are important techniques in machine learning, because they can improve the accuracy of predictive models. However, determining the right hyperparameters and the most relevant subset of features can be a complex problem, especially when dealing with high-dimensional datasets.

Current approaches to solving combinatorial problems in machine learning often draw inspiration from nature, particularly from biological systems such as animal herding, bacterial growth, and other natural phenomena. These methods usually involve a population of simple individuals that interact both locally and globally with each other according to simple rules. For example, one such meta-heuristic approach is the Grey Wolf Optimizer (GWO), which was proposed by Mirjalili et al. [15] and was inspired by the behavior of grey wolves. The Salp Swarm Algorithm, also proposed by Mirjalili et al. in [14], was inspired by the swarming behavior of salps when navigating and foraging in oceans. Other techniques inspired by animals include bats [18], glowworm [13], and bee colony [9] optimization.

Particle Swarm Optimization (PSO) is one of the most commonly used optimization technique. Originally proposed by Kennedy and Eberhart [11], PSO has been the subject of much research, with numerous improvements proposed in terms of topology, parameter selection, and other technical modifications. For example, there are hybridizations of PSO with other meta-heuristic methods, such as the improved binary particle swarm optimization proposed by Chuang et al. [3], which uses the 'catfish effect' to introduce new particles into the search space if the best solution does not improve in a certain number of consecutive iterations.

Despite the success of these approaches, there are challenges associated with using meta-heuristic methods to solve combinatorial problems in machine learning. For example, GA-PARSIMONY was proposed in [16,17] to search for parsimonious solutions with genetic algorithms (GA) by performing HO and FS, and was successfully applied in many fields [1,7]. However, in this kind of problems where each solution has a high computational cost, it is not possible to evaluate a large number of individuals in each iteration. This makes GA not as efficient as other optimization techniques where hundreds or thousands of individuals are evaluated. As a continuation of this methodology, the authors used PSO combined with a parsimony criterion to find parsimonious and accurate machine learning models. The main novelty in the PSO-PARSIMONY methodology [5] was that it included a strategy in which the best position of each particle was computed considering not only the goodness-of-fit but also the principle of parsimony. The comparison between both methods was performed on 13 public datasets, and the results showed that PSO always improved accuracy over GA, but GA found solutions approximately 10% less complex on datasets with a low number of features.

3   The HYB-PARSIMONY Method with High-Dimensional Datasets

To combine the strengths of GA-PARSIMONY and PSO-PARSIMONY, the algorithm HYB-PARSIMONY was proposed in [4] by Divasón et al. as a hybrid combination that incorporates GA operations (selection, crossover and mutation) and PSO optimization[1]. The methodology improved the search of parsimonious ML models against the other methodologies.

In HYB-PARSIMONY, the following equation was proposed to calculate the percentage of particles to be substituted by GA crossover in each iteration t:

$$pcrossover = max(0.80 \cdot e^{(-\Gamma \cdot t)}, 0.10) \tag{1}$$

Figure 1 shows thirteen curves obtained with different Γ values. In the first iterations, the hybrid method performs the substitution by crossing a high percentage of particles. As the optimization process progresses, the number of substituted particles is reduced exponentially until it ends up fixed at a percentage of 10%. Thus, the hybrid method begins by facilitating the search for parsimonious models using GA-based mechanisms and ends up using more PSO optimization.

3.1   Performance of Feature Selection in High-Dimensional Datasets

To analyze the behavior of the hybrid method in high-dimensional datasets as a function of Γ, and with different dimensions and populations, a methodology was implemented with the following experiment's parameters:

- *method*: HYB vs previous methods (PSO or GA).
- *nruns*: number of runs with different random seeds. Value: 10.
- Γ (only for the hybrid method). Values: 0.005, 0.007, 0.010, 0.015, 0.020, 0.030, 0.050, 0.080, 0.130, 0.210, 0.350, 0.560, 1.100, 1.170.
- *P*: population size. Values: $[5, 5 + 1 \cdot 5, 5 + 2 \cdot 5, ..., 40]$.
- $\#feats$: dimension of the hypothetical data set. Values: 50, 150, 250, 350.

---

[1] HYB-PARSIMONY is available for Python at https://github.com/jodivaso/HYBparsimony.

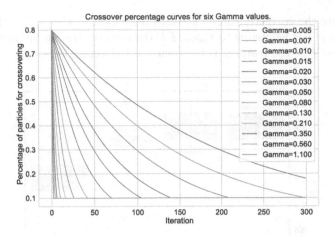

Fig. 1. Example of thirteen curves created with different Γ values to establish the percentage of individuals to be replaced by crossover in each iteration.

- i_{dim}: intrinsic dimension that refers to the features, F_{selec}, with relevant information present in a dataset. That is, the number of input features of the hypothetical model that explains an hypothetical target. Values: $5, 5 + 1 \cdot 20$, $5 + 2 \cdot 20$, ..., $\lfloor 0.90 \cdot \#feats \rfloor$.
- β: value which balances the weight between recall and precision in the F_{beta} score used to evaluate each individual (see below). Values: $[0.20, 0.20 + 1 \cdot 0.06$, $0.20 + 2 \cdot 0.06$, ..., $1.68]$.

For each combination of experiment's parameters, F_{selec} were randomly selected according to i_{dim}. In particular, F_{selec} corresponded to i_{dim} random feature positions selected within the range $[0, \#feats - 1]$.

To evaluate each solution, F_{beta} score was used. Based on the $F1$ score, F_{beta} is the weighted harmonic mean of precision and recall where β determines the weight between recall and precision in the combined score. $\beta < 1$ gives more weight to precision, while $\beta > 1$ favors recall. F_{beta} is equal to $F1$ score with $\beta = 1.0$ and to precision with $\beta = 0.0$.

It is defined as:

$$F_{beta} = \frac{(1 + \beta^2)(precision \cdot recall)}{\beta^2 \cdot precision + recall} \tag{2}$$

and:

$$precision = \frac{TP}{TP + FP} \tag{3}$$

$$recall = \frac{TP}{TP + FN} \tag{4}$$

where TP are the correctly chosen features belonging to F_{selec}, TN the features not chosen and not belonging to F_{selec}, FP the features chosen but not belonging to F_{selec}, and FN the features not chosen but belonging to F_{selec}.

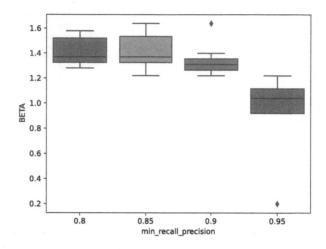

Fig. 2. Distribution of the best β that successfully met the objectives of overcoming a minimum precision and recall defined by thr_{pr} (values = 0.80, 0.85, 0.90, 0.95).

Each combination of [$method$ with Γ, P, $\#feats$, i_{dim} and β] was run 10 times with different randoms seeds, a maximum number of iterations of $T = 300$, $tol = 10^{-9}$, and an early stopping of 35.

All experiments[2] were implemented in 2 separately 40-core composed, respectively, of Intel(R) Xeon(R) CPU E5-2650 v3 @ 2.30 GHz with 128 GB of RAM memory, and Intel(R) Xeon(R) CPU E5-2630 v4 @ 2.20 GHz with 192 GB of RAM memory.

Figure 2 shows the number of experiments that successfully met the objectives of overcoming a minimum precision and recall defined by a threshold, thr_{pr}, and by each β and P values. The distribution of the best β is presented for each experiment and thr_{pr}. At low thr_{pr} values, the median of the best β for each combination of [$method$, Γ, P, $\#feats$, i_{dim}] is about 1.3. This indicates that precision tends to be prioritized over recall. Only at $thr_{pr} = 0.95$ it is observed that the median of the best β is close to 1.0, so the relationship between precision and recall is balanced when the level of demand is very high.

Figure 3 shows respectively the mean of the last iteration ($last_{iter}$) and the average of F_{beta} with $\beta = 1.34$ and for each method and P. GA and HYB with low Γ converge, on average, faster than PSO and HYB with high Γ values, as they reach twice the number of final iterations. With respect to F_{beta}, the highest

---

[2] The total number of experiments was 115170, resulting from all combinations.

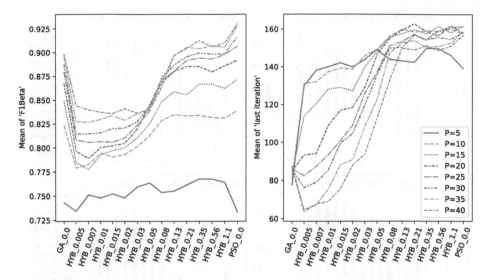

Fig. 3. Mean of the F_{beta} (left) and last iteration ($last_{iter}$) (right) achieved with $\beta = 1.34$ and for each method and P.

averages are obtained with PSO and HYB with Γ values greater than 0.08, but GA has similar performance to HYB_0.08.

However, these results are average values that may be different, for each method, depending on $\#feats$ and i_{dim}. Figure 4 shows the distribution of F_{beta} for each method with $\#feats = 150$, $\beta = 1.34$ and four different i_{dim} values: 5, 45, 85 and 125. At very low values of i_{dim}, GA is competitive with the hybrid and PSO methods. However, as the intrinsic dimension is closer to the real dimension of the dataset, PSO and hybrid models with high Γ obtain better accuracy. The problem is that for a particular dataset the intrinsic dimension of the data will be unknown, so it will be necessary to realize an estimation of i_{dim} in order to select an appropriate method.

In order to have a quick estimate of the hybrid model for F_{beta} and $last_{iter}$, linear *Ridge* models were trained with the previously obtained dataset but eliminating instances corresponding to GA and PSO, and selecting only those cases with a β within the range $[0.92, 1.64]$ where the methodology was most successful. Equations 5 and 6 correspond to the best Ridge models selected with a 10-fold cross-validation RMSE error of 0.0815 and 57.36 with values of the *alpha* Ridge's hyperparameter equal to 4.0 and 2.0, respectively.

$$\hat{F_{beta}} = -0.0462 \cdot \Gamma - 0.0027 \cdot P + 0.0012 \cdot \#feats - 0.0011 \cdot i_{dim} - 0.0108 \cdot \beta - 0.88 \quad (5)$$

$$\hat{last_{iter}} = 28.391 \cdot \Gamma - 0.8883 \cdot P + 0.2963 \cdot \#feats - 0.38 \cdot i_{dim} + 36.517 \cdot \beta + 72.71 \quad (6)$$

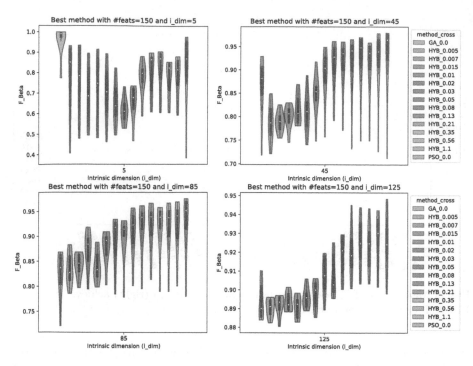

Fig. 4. Violin plot of F_{beta} with $\beta = 1.34$, $\#feats = 150$ and for each method and four different i_{dim} values. The order of the violin plots in the legend (from top to bottom) corresponds to their position when viewed from left to right.

Using these two models, it was possible to approximately predict the values of F_{beta} and $last_{iter}$ for a data set dimension, $\#feats$, and a fixed value of P. Figure 5 shows the box plots for F_{beta} and $last_{iter}$ obtained from a simulation performed with multiple combinations of the input values for four high-dimensional data sets: *ailerons* ($\#feats = 40$), *crime* ($\#feats = 127$), *blog* ($\#feats = 276$) and *slice* ($\#feats = 378$). Each simulation was performed by fixing $P = 15$ and for each $\#ncols$, with $\Gamma \in [0.0, 0.0 + 0.1, ..., 1.1]$, $i_{dim} \in [0.10 \cdot \#feats, 0.10 \cdot \#feats + 5, ..., \#feats]$, and $\beta \in [0.92, 0.92 + 0.1, ..., 1.64]$. The graphs show the expected reduction that can be obtained in $last_{iter}$ vs. F_{beta} depending on the Γ used. However, estimates will be approximate and may vary greatly depending on the dataset (type and size[3]) and the machine learning algorithm used for modeling the problem.

4   Strategy for Working with SHDD

Creating accurate models with SHDD is a current challenge. If the dataset has hundreds or a few thousand instances, and the dimension is high (several tens or

---

[3] As can be seen in Fig. 5.

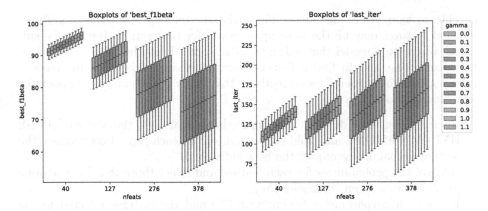

Fig. 5. Box plots of F_{beta} (left) and $last_{iter}$ (right) for $\Gamma \in [0.0, 0.0 + 0.1, ..., 1.1]$ and four $\#feats$ values obtained by simulation with $P = 15$, and different i_{dim} and β values. The order of the boxplots in the legend (from top to bottom) corresponds to their position when viewed from left to right for each $\#feats$.

Table 1. Results for 7 datasets obtained with BO (J) versus HYB-PARSIMONY with $thr_{fs} = 0.50$ followed by BO.

Dataset				BO	HYB-PARSIMONY and BO		
name	$train_{size}$	$test_{size}$	$\#feats$	J_{BO}	$last_{iter}$	$J0.5$	$Fs0.5$
slice	2000	23000	378	**.1414**	165.8 (42.4)	.1449 (.0022)	148.0 (3.74)
blog	2000	50397	276	.8216	178.6 (45.6)	**.8154 (.0170)**	67.0 (17.42)
crime	1107	1108	127	**.6373**	199.0 (0.0)	.6379 (.0076)	28.8 (4.32)
ailerons	2000	11750	40	.3984	131.2 (17.9)	**.3982 (.0016)**	13.2 (2.05)
bank	2000	6192	32	.6745	160.0 (32.1)	**.6726 (.0023)**	15.6 (1.52)
puma	2000	6192	32	.8762	106.2 (16.3)	**.2006 (.0250)**	3.6 (0.89)
pol	2000	13000	26	.3165	148.0 (32.2)	**.2413 (.0034)**	7.2 (0.45)

hundreds of features), the search for models that correctly generalize the problem will face two fundamental problems: the curse of dimensionality and an excessive over-fitting in the optimization process.

Although there are algorithms, such as trees and neural networks, that may be less affected by the curse of dimensionality, in these cases it is highly recommended to use feature selection or dimensional reduction. In addition, the regularization included in machine learning algorithms helps penalize models that are too complex and with high probability of overfitting. The proposed hybrid methodology greatly facilitates both aspects since it seeks to reduce as much as possible the number of features of the selected model, as well as its internal complexity.

However, HYB-PARSIMONY is such an intensive search method that when working with SHDD the method may find parsimonious solutions that are too specific to that set of instances. Thus, the chosen hyperparameters and the selected features may be the most appropriate for that sample but not be sufficient to create a model that will generalize correctly in the future. To reduce this over-fitting and to find a feature selection that can be used to create a robust model that generalizes correctly in this kind of problems, we propose the following methodology:

1. Repeat n runs with different random seeds the search for the best model with HYB-PARSIMONY and hold-out validation. In each repetition, extract the feature probability vector of the best individual.
2. Average the probabilities for each feature and select those that have a value greater than a given threshold, thr_{fs}.
3. Performs hyperparameter tuning with BO and the features selected in the previous point.
4. Repeat points 2 and 3 with different thr_{fs}.
5. Select the model that obtains the best error J with another test dataset.

Table 2. Proposed methodology with different thr_{fs} vs. BO with all features (J_{BO}).

dataset	J_{BO}	$J0.2$	$Fs0.2$	$J0.3$	$Fs0.3$	$J0.4$	$Fs0.4$	$J0.5$	$Fs0.5$	$J0.6$	$Fs0.6$	$J0.7$	$Fs0.7$
slice	.1414	.1392	346.4	.1374	294.2	**.1370**	**228.2**	.1449	148.0	.1583	85.8	.2267	40.2
blog	.8216	.8265	247.0	.8288	196.8	.8234	128.8	**.8154**	**67.0**	1.014	29.4	.9462	10.8
crime	.6373	**.6367**	**108.8**	.6371	85.0	.6386	56.4	.6379	28.8	.6461	12.8	.7867	3.8
ailerons	.3984	.3986	33.2	.3994	25.4	.3993	17.8	**.3982**	**13.2**	.4338	9.8	.5043	5.6
bank	.6745	.6729	29.4	.6756	24.6	.6744	20.4	**.6726**	**15.6**	.6791	11.4	.6889	9.0
puma	.8762	.3030	12.2	.2308	7.6	.2096	4.6	**.2006**	**3.6**	.2007	3.6	.2230	2.8
pol	.3165	.2736	13.2	.2584	10.4	.2461	8.2	.2413	7.2	.2413	7.2	**.2387**	6.4

Table 1 shows the results with 7 high-dimensional datasets of using the described methodology versus using BO with all features ($\#feats$). In these experiments, 2000 rows were selected for training/validation (except crime where half of them were used) and the rest were utilized as a test dataset to verify the degree of generalization of the models. J_{BO} corresponds to the testing RMSE error obtained from a model that used all the input features and whose hyperparameters were adjusted by BO. The last three columns corresponds to the new proposal. First, 25 runs of HYB-PARSIMONY were performed with $\Gamma = 0.50$, $nruns = 200$, $P = 15$, $early\_stopping = 35$, hold-out validation with a 20%, and $KernelRidge$ as ML algorithm. Finally, $ReRank$ was set to 0.001 which corresponds to the maximum difference between the J of two models to be considered equal. A high value of this parameter facilitates the search for parsimony in HYB-PARSIMONY because between two models with a similar J the less complex model is selected. Next, hyperparameter tuning with BO was done of a $KernelRidge$ algorithm with the features whose probabilities were greater o equal than 0.50 ($thr_{fs} = 0.50$). Columns in table indicate: the last iteration ($last_{iter}$) of HYB-PARSIMONY, RMSE ($J0.5$) and the number of features used

($Fs0.5$) in the final model. The results correspond to the average values and the standard deviation (in parentheses) of 5 runs of the whole methodology with different random seeds.

Table 3. HYB-PARSIMONY *vs.* PSO-PARSIMONY.

dataset	HYB-PARSIMONY				PSO-PARSIMONY			
	$last_{iter}$	thr_{fs}	J	Fs	$last_{iter}$	thr_{fs}	J	Fs
slice	**165.8**	.4	**.1370 (.003)**	**228.2 (6.0)**	182.8	.5	.1372 (.002)	239.0 (6.9)
blog	**178.6**	.5	**.8154 (.017)**	**67.0 (17.4)**	191.6	.0	.8215 (.000)	276.0 (0.0)
crime	199.0	.2	**.6367 (.002)**	**108.8 (1.3)**	**175.4**	.1	.6371 (.000)	124.8 (1.3)
ailerons	**131.2**	.5	**.3982 (.002)**	**13.2 (2.1)**	154.8	.5	.3984 (.002)	16.0 (3.5)
bank	160.0	.5	.6725 (.002)	**15.6 (1.5)**	**149.8**	.5	**.6724 (.002)**	16.8 (1.6)
puma	106.2	.5	.2006 (.025)	**3.6 (0.9)**	**104.4**	.4	**.1894 (.000)**	4.0 (0.0)
pol	148.0	.7	.2387 (.004)	6.4 (0.6)	**127.2**	.7	**.2374 (.003)**	**6.2 (0.5)**

As can be observed in Table 1, the proposed methodology obtained more accurate models in 5 of the 7 datasets, in addition to the fact that in the remaining ones the differences between J_{BO} and $J0.5$ were not excessive. However, the most outstanding results were observed in the significant reduction of the number of average features. For example, in slice the number of features was reduced to 39.1%, in blog to 24.2%, in crime to 22.7%, in ailerons to 33%, in puma to 11.3%, or in pol to 27.7%. In conclusion, the methodology helped to find more accurate models with a significant reduction of features. However, these results could be improved by using different thr_{fs} as shown in Table 2.

Table 3 shows a comparative analysis of the HYB-PARSIMONY methodology versus the previous method, PSO-PARSIMONY. The results show that the new methodology improved J in the four higher dimensionality datasets in conjunction with a considerable reduction in the number of features. However, PSO-PARSIMONY obtained better J in bank, puma and pol, but with worse parsimony in the first two.

Finally, Table 4 shows a comparison of the proposed methodology versus the use of the sklearn-genetic-opt library for feature selection using 10 runs with different random seeds. With this package the procedure consisted of three steps: perform the hyperparameter adjustment with GA, select with GA the best features and finally perform again the hyperparameter tuning with GA but using only the selected variables. It can be clearly observed that the new methodology obtained better results with statistical significance in all datasets (p-value < 0.05 in Wilcoxon–Mann–Whitney test), although in some cases the feature reduction was lower.

Table 4. HYB-PARSIMONY *vs.* SKLEARN-GENETICS-OPT.

dataset	J_{hyb}	J_{gen}	p-value	Fs_{hyb}	Fs_{gen}	p-value
slice	**0.131430**	0.142033	0.000330	**183.3**	202.4	0.000489
blog	**0.823028**	0.841876	0.002827	275.8	**143.6**	0.000085
crime	**0.630145**	0.633698	0.011330	70.7	**67.7**	0.148308
ailerons	**0.398032**	0.398548	0.025748	40.0	**22.9**	0.000062
bank	**0.672656**	0.676080	0.021134	24.7	**19.8**	0.000143
puma	**0.189436**	0.258673	0.000183	**4.0**	11.0	0.000048
pol	**0.236990**	0.276652	0.000183	**6.0**	15.7	0.000058

5   Conclusions

GA-PARSIMONY, PSO-PARSIMONY and HYB-PARSIMONY are methodologies that have been developed for the search of accurate but low complexity ML models. However, an intensive search with these methods in SHDD can lead to overfitted models.

The proposed methodology is based on repeating HYB-PARSIMONY with different random seeds and by using hold-out validation. In this way, at each run the search for the best model is validated with a different part of the dataset. Averaging the feature probability vectors allows one to make a more robust selection of the final features. Once these are selected, with different thresholds, BO is used to fit the hyperparameters of the model.

Results demonstrated that it is possible to obtain more accurate models with a significant reduction in the number of features against other methodologies.

Acknowledgement. The work is supported by grant PID2020-116641GB-I00 and the European Regional Development Fund under Project PID2021-123219OB-I00 funded by MCIN/AEI/ 10.13039 501100011033 FEDER, UE. We are also greatly indebted to Banco Santander for the REGI2020/41 and REGI2022/60 fellowships.

References

1. Antonanzas-Torres, F., Urraca, R., Antonanzas, J., Fernandez-Ceniceros, J., Martinez-de Pison, F.J.: Generation of daily global solar irradiation with support vector machines for regression. Energy Convers. Manage. **96**, 277–286 (2015). https://doi.org/10.1016/j.enconman.2015.02.086
2. Chen, T., Guestrin, C.: XGBoost: a scalable tree boosting system. In: Proceedings of the 22nd ACM SIGKDD International Conference on Knowledge Discovery and Data Mining, KDD 2016, pp. 785–794. ACM, New York (2016). https://doi.org/ 10.1145/2939672.2939785

3. Chuang, L.Y., Tsai, S.W., Yang, C.H.: Improved binary particle swarm optimization using catfish effect for feature selection. Expert Syst. Appl. **38**(10), 12699–12707 (2011). https://doi.org/10.1016/j.eswa.2011.04.057

4. Divasón, J., Pernia-Espinoza, A., Martinez-de Pison, F.J.: New hybrid methodology based on particle swarm optimization with genetic algorithms to improve the search of parsimonious models in high-dimensional databases. In: García Bringas, P., et al. (eds.) HAIS 2022. LNCS, vol. 13469, pp. 335–347. Springer, Cham (2022). https://doi.org/10.1007/978-3-031-15471-3_29

5. Divasón, J., Fernandez-Ceniceros, J., Sanz-Garcia, A., Pernia-Espinoza, A., Martinez-de Pison, F.J.: PSO-PARSIMONY: a method for finding parsimonious and accurate machine learning models with particle swarm optimization. Application for predicting force-displacement curves in T-stub steel connections. Neurocomputing **548**, 126414 (2023). https://doi.org/10.1016/j.neucom.2023.126414

6. Dorogush, A.V., Ershov, V., Gulin, A.: CatBoost: gradient boosting with categorical features support (2018)

7. Dulce-Chamorro, E., de Pison, F.J.M.: An advanced methodology to enhance energy efficiency in a hospital cooling-water system. J. Build. Eng. **43**, 102839 (2021). https://doi.org/10.1016/j.jobe.2021.102839

8. Erickson, N., et al.: AutoGluon-tabular: robust and accurate AutoML for structured data. arXiv preprint arXiv:2003.06505 (2020)

9. Karaboga, D., Basturk, B.: Artificial bee colony (ABC) optimization algorithm for solving constrained optimization problems. In: Melin, P., Castillo, O., Aguilar, L.T., Kacprzyk, J., Pedrycz, W. (eds.) IFSA 2007. LNCS (LNAI), vol. 4529, pp. 789–798. Springer, Heidelberg (2007). https://doi.org/10.1007/978-3-540-72950-1_77

10. Ke, G., et al.: LightGBM: a highly efficient gradient boosting decision tree. Adv. Neural. Inf. Process. Syst. **30**, 3146–3154 (2017)

11. Kennedy, J., Eberhart, R.: Particle swarm optimization. In: Proceedings of ICNN 1995 - International Conference on Neural Networks, vol. 4, pp. 1942–1948 (1995). https://doi.org/10.1109/ICNN.1995.488968

12. Lundberg, S.M., Lee, S.I.: A unified approach to interpreting model predictions. In: Proceedings of the 31st International Conference on Neural Information Processing Systems, NIPS 2017, pp. 4768–4777. Curran Associates Inc., Red Hook (2017)

13. Marinaki, M., Marinakis, Y.: A glowworm swarm optimization algorithm for the vehicle routing problem with stochastic demands. Expert Syst. Appl. **46**, 145–163 (2016). https://doi.org/10.1016/j.eswa.2015.10.012

14. Mirjalili, S., Gandomi, A.H., Mirjalili, S.Z., Saremi, S., Faris, H., Mirjalili, S.M.: Salp swarm algorithm: a bio-inspired optimizer for engineering design problems. Adv. Eng. Softw. **114**, 163–191 (2017). https://doi.org/10.1016/j.advengsoft.2017.07.002

15. Mirjalili, S., Mirjalili, S.M., Lewis, A.: Grey wolf optimizer. Adv. Eng. Softw. **69**, 46–61 (2014). https://doi.org/10.1016/j.advengsoft.2013.12.007

16. Martinez-de Pison, F.J., Ferreiro, J., Fraile, E., Pernia-Espinoza, A.: A comparative study of six model complexity metrics to search for parsimonious models with GAparsimony R Package. Neurocomputing **452**, 317–332 (2021). https://doi.org/10.1016/j.neucom.2020.02.135

17. Martinez-de Pison, F.J., Gonzalez-Sendino, R., Aldama, A., Ferreiro-Cabello, J., Fraile-Garcia, E.: Hybrid methodology based on Bayesian optimization and GA-parsimony to search for parsimony models by combining hyperparameter optimization and feature selection. Neurocomputing **354**, 20–26 (2019). https://doi.org/10.1016/j.neucom.2018.05.136
18. Yang, X.S.: A new metaheuristic bat-inspired algorithm. In: González, J.R., Pelta, D.A., Cruz, C., Terrazas, G., Krasnogor, N. (eds.) Nature Inspired Cooperative Strategies for Optimization (NICSO 2010). Studies in Computational Intelligence, vol. 284, pp. 65–74. Springer, Heidelberg (2010). https://doi.org/10.1007/978-3-642-12538-6_6

An Integer Linear Programming Model for Team Formation in the Classroom with Constraints

Gonzalo Candel[1], Victor Sánchez-Anguix[2]([✉]) [iD], Juan M. Alberola[3] [iD],
Vicente Julián[3,4] [iD], and Vicent Botti[3,4] [iD]

[1] Universitat Politècnica de València, Camino de Vera, s/n, 46022 Valencia, Spain
goncanpe@inf.upv.es
[2] Instituto Tecnológico de Informática, Grupo de Sistemas de Optimización
Aplicada, Ciudad Politécnica de la Innovación, Edificio 8g, Universitat Politècnica de
València, Camino de Vera s/n, 46022 Valencia, Spain
vicsana1@upv.es
[3] Valencian Research Institute for Artificial Intelligence (VRAIN),
Universitat Politècnica de València, Camino de Vera, s/n, 46022 Valencia, Spain
{jalberola,vjulian,vbotti}@upv.es
[4] ValgrAI (Valencian Graduate School and Research Network of Articial Intelligence),
Universitat Politècnica de València, Camino de Vera, s/n, 46022 Valencia, Spain

Abstract. Teamwork is essential in many industries to tackle complex projects. Thus, the development of teamwork skills is crucial in higher education. In the classroom, the formation of teams must be fostered throughout all phases to promote the development of these skills. Several criteria for forming teams in the classroom have been proposed, including Belbin's role taxonomy or Myers-Briggs type indicator. However, finding optimal teams or partitions of members into teams is a highly combinatorial problem that requires of optimization techniques. This paper presents an integer linear programming model for team formation in the classroom that includes constraints requested by lecturers and allows for the incorporation of different team evaluation heuristics. We study the performance and the scalability of the model using different solvers, conditions, and problem instance types.

Keywords: Teamwork · integer linear programming · team evaluation heuristics · team formation · optimization

1 Introduction

Increasingly, teamwork prevails in industries to address complex projects that can consume many resources and require extensive planning and management. In these scenarios, large-scale projects that cannot be carried out individually often have to be tackled, requiring the participation of individuals working together. Therefore, the demand for skills related to teamwork such as communication, task allocation, leadership, and conflict resolution, is constant.

© The Author(s), under exclusive license to Springer Nature Switzerland AG 2023
P. García Bringas et al. (Eds.): HAIS 2023, LNAI 14001, pp. 397–408, 2023.
https://doi.org/10.1007/978-3-031-40725-3_34

In this sense, it is crucial that competencies related to teamwork can be developed in higher education degrees. In fact, the importance of future professionals relies on their technical and soft skills, among which teamwork is included [22]. Teamwork requires skills related to the ability to communicate to express and defend ideas in front of a group of peers, leadership, or efficient time management, among many others [15].

To promote the personal development of team members in a classroom, teams must be structured in a way that allows for a satisfactory experience. In the literature, several approaches for forming teams in the classroom have been proposed, ranging from simple ones such as grouping students according to their average grade, or the time they have available for work, to more complex approaches based on personality and behavior such as the Belbin's role taxonomy [5], the Myers-Briggs type indicator [17] (MBTI) or the Big five inventory [13].

The problem of finding optimal teams or partitions of members into teams is known as the team formation problem. Finding an optimal partition of students into teams is a highly combinatorial problem that is both difficult to be solved manually and using algorithms [14]. In fact, many variants of the team formation problem are NP-hard problems [14]. Thus, the use of optimization techniques is necessary to tackle this problem appropriately. Typically, the team formation problem relies on a function that is capable of estimating team performance prior to carrying out the task at hand. This function can be named as the team evaluation heuristic, as it approximates the performance of the team by relying on different criteria.

In the literature, several authors have proposed the use of heuristic and metaheuristic algorithms to tackle the team formation problem in the classroom. For instance, Yannibelli et al. [29] proposed a genetic algorithm based on crowding to group students based on Belbin's role taxonomy. In another study, Andrejczuk et al. [3] proposed an anytime heuristic to tackle large instances of team formation based on personality traits, congeniality, and competences. The authors in [4, 26] propose a genetic algorithm for dividing students into teams based again on Belbin's role taxonomy. The article [11] proposes a multi-objective genetic algorithm that aims to foster homogeneity across groups and heterogeneity within groups.

While heuristics and metaheuristics are necessary to tackle larger instances, they may not be advisable for conducting experiments to compare the effectiveness of several team evaluation heuristics in the classroom. As mentioned, team evaluation heuristics are functions that estimate team performance based on several criteria. Due to the small number of teams that one may form in the classroom, one should reduce variability in the study to make the most of available data. Heuristics and metaheuristics may introduce noise into the study due to their approximate nature, and exact methods such as mathematical programming may be preferred. Ideally, exact methods should be as scalable as possible to ensure their use in large classrooms.

Algorithms for integer linear programming (ILP) are well-suited for obtaining optimal solutions to complex problems due to their ability to handle discrete decision variables [12]. These types of algorithms have been successfully applied to various similar optimization problems, such as resource allocation [28], matching of students to supervisors [24], task assignment to agents based on their capabilities [8], project allocation to individuals according to their skills [7,23], or grouping of students for peer assessment [27]. These algorithms allow us to obtain optimal solutions to problems, making them suitable for situations where one wants to conduct experiments to compare several team evaluation heuristics.

In this work, we propose a linear integer programming model for team formation. The model allows for the incorporation of various constraints (e.g., team size, members who should be placed together or not, etc.) that commonly arise in a classroom setting. In addition to this, the model is generic and it can incorporate several team evaluation heuristics. In this article, we study the performance of the model under two team evaluation heuristics: one based on Belbin's role taxonomy [5] and another based on Myer-Briggs Type Indicator [17]. We focus on these two criteria as they have been widely employed in the literature [2–4,9,26]. We present experiments to compare the performance and scalability of implementations of this model under different non-commercial solvers.

The rest of the paper is organized as follows. Section 2 briefly formalizes the team formation problem in the classroom and introduces two team evaluation heuristics employed in this study for creating problem instances. Then, Sect. 3 presents the mathematical model for team formation. Section 4 provides the evaluation of the model by comparing different solvers. Finally, Sect. 5 highlights some concluding remarks and draws some future work lines.

2   Team Formation Problem in the Classroom

The team formation problem in the classroom typically aims to partition a set of students into disjoint teams. Let us briefly formalize the problem.

Given a set of students $S = \{s_1, \ldots, s_p\}$, we aim to form teams whose sizes are in the set $\mathcal{L} = \{l_1, \ldots, l_r\}$.

We define $N \subset S \times S$ as the set of pairs of students who should not be in the same team for pedagogical issues. Similarly, we define $C \subset S \times S$ as the set of pairs of students who should be in the same team. We define $T = \{t_1, \ldots, t_q\}$ as the set of feasible teams. A team t_i will be feasible if and only if $l \in \mathcal{L}$ and it is satisfied that $\forall s_j, s_k \in t_i, (s_j, s_k) \notin N$.

The goal of team formation problems in the classroom is finding a partition of students into teams that is optimal. Typically, the optimality of a team is linked to its performance. However, exactly knowing a team's performance prior to the execution of their tasks is not possible. Therefore, team formation problems typically employ a heuristic to estimate or serve as a proxy function for team performance (i.e., the team evaluation heuristic). One of the common heuristics found in the literature is using team heterogeneity as an approximation to future team performance. Heuristics based on the Belbin taxonomy and the Myer-Briggs indicator have been a common approach due to their foundations on management and psychology theories. In this article, we will employ two team evaluation heuristics based on both studies to analyze the performance of our ILP model.

2.1 Belbin Team Evaluation Heuristic

Belbin's role taxonomy defines one of the most important theories regarding successful team dynamics [5]. In this theory, Belbin identifies eight behavioral patterns that are required for a successful team. He called these behavioral patterns as roles. A team member could play different roles within the team as a result of the emergence of different behaviors at different times. That is, there is no limitation on the number of roles that may be played by an individual. Belbin stated that a good balance in the distribution of roles within a team showed more satisfactory team-level results than teams with overrepresented or lacking roles. To obtain the predominant roles of each member, the Belbin Self-Perception Inventory is used [16]. This inventory calculates a numerical score for each of the roles for each team member.

The heuristic defined for this theory considers that a team member has a predominant role when they obtain a *high* or *very high* score associated with this role, according to the salience level defined by Partington and Harris [18].

If $b_{j,k}$ is the score obtained by student s_j in role k, and β_k is the threshold for which it is considered *high*, then we say that the team acquires a positive score in role k if any of the members surpass or equalize threshold β_k. We formalize this score as $f_k(t_i)$. The total score of the team $f(t_i)$ is the sum of the scores obtained for each of the roles normalized by the maximum to be achieved. Formally, both are defined as follows:

$$f_k(t_i) = \begin{cases} 1 & \text{if } \exists s_j \in t_i, b_{j,k} \geq \beta_k \\ 0 & \text{otherwise} \end{cases} \qquad (1)$$

$$f(t_i) = \frac{1}{8} \times \sum_{k=1}^{8} f_k(t_i)$$

2.2 MBTI Team Evaluation Heuristic

The Myers-Briggs Type Indicator (MBTI) is an instrument that focuses on identifying an individual's personality in four different dimensions [17]. Each of these dimensions is formed by 2 traits that are opposite to each other, and whose combination defines 16 different personalities. The MBTI inventory allows to obtain a score for each of these four dimensions, determining the personality trait assigned to an specific team member in these dimensions.

The heuristic used is a normalized version of the one presented by Pieterse et al. [21]. In this heuristic, we will assume that k is one of the four dimensions (introversion-extraversion, sensation-intuition, thinking-feeling, judging-perceiving) and k_1 and k_2 are the traits in that dimension (e.g., introversion and extraversion for the introversion-extraversion dimension). In addition, $\gamma_k(s_j, k_l)$ is a function that returns 1 if student s_j shows the trait k_l in dimension k. The heuristic applied to a specific dimension and team will return 0 if all members show the same personality trait; 1 if at least one member presents a different trait compared to the other members; and 2 otherwise. The final score of a team is represented as the sum of the scores obtained for each dimension normalized by the maximum score to be achieved:

$$
f_k(t_i) = \begin{cases} 0 & \text{if } \exists k_l, \sum_{s_j \in t_i} \gamma_k(s_j, k_l) = |t_i| \\ 1 & \text{if } \exists k_l, \sum_{s_j \in t_i} \gamma_k(s_j, k_l) = 1 \\ 2 & \text{otherwise} \end{cases} \tag{2}
$$

$$
f(t_i) = \frac{1}{8} \times \sum_{k=1}^{4} f_k(t_i)
$$

3   Integer Linear Programming Model

In this section, we describe the formulation of the ILP model that seeks to maximize the sum of scores of teams formed in the classroom. Apart from constraints that ensure that students are partitioned into disjoint teams, the model is based on some common constraints that lecturers and teachers want to employ when forming teams in the classroom:

- Constraints to put two or several students together in the same team.
- Constraints to avoid two or several students being placed into the same team.
- Constraints to control the size of the teams.
- Constraints to control the number of teams formed for each team size.

The model assumes that all feasible teams $t_i \in T$ have been generated, as it creates a binary decision variable for each of the teams that can be formed in the classroom. In addition to this, and due to the fact that decision variables represent the choice of specific teams, the model can incorporate any team evaluation heuristic into the objective function. Let $\mathcal{L} = \{l_1, \dots, l_r\}$ define the set of allowed team sizes for the team formation. The ILP model is defined as follows:

$$
\max \sum_{t_i \in T} f(t_i) \times \delta_i \tag{3a}
$$

s.t.

$$
\sum_{t_i \in T, s_j \in t_i} \delta_i = 1 \qquad \forall s_j \in S \tag{3b}
$$

$$
\sum_{t_i \in T, s_j, s_k \in t_i} \delta_i = 1 \qquad \forall (s_j, s_k) \in C \tag{3c}
$$

$$
m_l \leq \sum_{t_i \in T, |t_i| = l} \delta_i \leq M_l \qquad \forall l \in \mathcal{L} \tag{3d}
$$

where, on the one hand, δ_i is a binary decision variable that indicates whether feasible team t_i is chosen or not for the solution. Specifically, its value will be 1 when the team participates in the team structure and 0 otherwise. On the other hand, constraint 3b ensures that a student is assigned to precisely one team, ensuring the partition into disjoint teams. Next, constraint 3c ensures that students that should go in the same team are assigned to the same team. Finally, constraint 3d limits allowed team sizes, and the number of teams for each allowed team size with lower and upper bounds m_l and M_l respectively. Finally, as shown in 3a, $f(.)$ is a function that numerically estimates the performance or quality of a team. For instance, it could represent any of the team evaluation heuristics presented in Sect. 2. With respect to the constraint that precludes students from being placed on the same team, this can be easily implemented without any formal constraint by not generating decision variables that represent teams with incompatible members.

4   Experiments

In this section, we show the different experiments that we conducted to study the scalability of the proposed model under different non-commercial solvers and conditions. The main goal of the experiments is to assess the scalability of the ILP model under different conditions. First, we introduce the solvers that will be employed in the experiments, then we describe the problem instances used in the evaluation, and, finally, we describe the results obtained in the experiments.

4.1   Solvers

The solvers that will be employed in the study are non-commercial solvers. The reason behind this is that team formation problems in the classroom are common in educational settings and, therefore, many educational institutions may not have access to commercial solvers. The solvers employed in the experiments are:

- SCIP [6] is one of the fastest academic solvers for mixed integer programming and mixed integer nonlinear programming.
- COIN-OR Branch and Cut (CBC) [10] is an open-source solver that allows solving linear programming and mixed integer programming problems, and is a variant of the branch and bound technique, which among its operations includes adding cutting planes to search for the solution more efficiently.
- CP-SAT [20] is a solver designed to solve integer programming problems that consists of a Lazy Clause Generation solver over a SAT solver. Lazy Clause Generation is a search technique in Constraint Programming (CP) that adds explanation and learning to a propagation-based solver, which is responsible for narrowing down the range taken by the decision variables.

The implementation of the mathematical model has been carried out using the Google ORTools library [20]. First, we are interested in verifying that all solvers find the same solution for the same problem. Second, we aim to validate the scalability of the solvers as the problem size increases. Finally, we want to test if the team evaluation heuristic influences the execution time.

Table 1. Average execution time and percentage of instances solved optimally by each solver for each combination of classroom size (20, 30, 60), team size (3 to 5) and team evaluation heuristic (Belbin and MBTI)

Sizes		Belbin						MBTI					
		CBC		CP-SAT		SCIP		CBC		CP-SAT		SCIP	
Classroom	Team	Time	%	Time	%	Time	%	Time	%	Time	%	Time	%
20	4	0.11	100	2.82	100	0.77	100	0.12	100	2.97	100	0.59	100
	5	0.49	100	4.84	100	3.34	100	0.53	100	5.01	100	3.30	100
30	3	0.08	100	1.71	100	0.77	100	0.08	100	1.79	100	0.74	100
	5	15.93	100	65.52	100	185.00	100	17.55	100	63.10	100	194.01	100
60	3	1.07	100	15.10	100	11.30	100	1.04	20	15.37	20	14.19	20
	4	92.79	100	443.16	100	2081.971	100	103.22	20	491.34	20	1987.56	20
	5	-	0	-	0	-	0	-	0	-	0	-	0

4.2 Problem Instances

To compare the performance of different solvers, several problem instances have been created. For this, an original dataset was used containing a total of 260 anonymous students from the Tourism degree at the Polytechnic University of Valencia. The dataset includes the results of their Belbin and MBTI tests.

Next, we generated synthetic classrooms by sampling this dataset. This allowed us to create different problem instances with characteristics similar to those that would be found in real classrooms. These instances have been used to carry out experiments and evaluate different solutions under a variety of conditions.

Specifically, the tests have been performed on 30 randomly generated instances for 3 different classroom sizes: 20, 30, and 60 students. Thus, the performance of the different solvers will be observed on a total of 120 different instances in terms of execution time and the solution values obtained. Each of the 120 generated instances can be solved with different constraints regarding the team size. However, it was defined that the possible teams to be formed will have a minimum of 3 students and a maximum number of 5. In particular, experiments have been carried out by just allowing team sizes of 3, 4, and 5 students.

4.3 Results

The experiments were carried out on a machine with 4 cores and 8 GB of RAM. Each type of solver has been executed a total of 5 times on each instance to capture statistical differences in the execution time of the different solvers.

The methodology used to obtain the fastest solver follows a multiproblem analysis methodology, which is common in the field of optimization with metaheuristics [19]. More specifically, we have carried out an analysis for each family of problems. In this context, a family of problems combines classroom size, allowed team size, and team evaluation heuristic. First, we obtain the average execution time that each solver has taken to solve each prospective instance. Each family of problems consists of 30 instances. Therefore, for each subproblem and solver we obtain 30 measures (i.e., the average execution time of the solver for each of the 30 instances). Then, we employ a non-parametric test to compare the execution time of the three solvers for each of the subproblems. More specifically, we employ the Friedman test. The Friedman test is the extension for more than two populations of the Wilcoxon signed-rank test, and it either assumes that the distributions are identical (null hypothesis) or at least two solver execution times are different from each other. The Wilcoxon signed-rank test with corrected p-values is employed in case of rejecting the null hypothesis to detect pairs of execution times that are different from each other.

Table 1 shows the experiments' results. The table shows the average execution time, the percentage of problem instances solved optimally for each solver, and a combination of classroom size, team size, and team evaluation heuristic. For each family of problems, we have underlined the statistically better results than the rest using the methodology described above.

First, it is important to emphasize that the solutions obtained by different solvers are the same for a given problem instance and the same combination of classroom size, team size, and team evaluation heuristic. Therefore, we consider that all solvers have achieved the optimal solution whenever the problem could be solved.

As observed, CBC is generally the fastest solver of the three solvers for the instances that we tested. In fact, the results suggest that CBC is orders of magnitude faster than SCIP and CP-SAT. The difference between CBC and the other two solvers is also statistically significant, as suggested by the Friedman and Wilcoxon signed-ranked posthoc tests. Of course, the fact that CBC is faster applies only to the type of problems and the model employed in the experiments. Other solvers may provide better results for other types of problems or models. A fact that seems to stem from the experiments is the necessity to test a model for the team formation problem with different solvers, as there seem to be significant and large differences among different solvers.

As the reader may have observed, the number of decision variables in the proposed model directly depends on the number of teams that can be formed. If no other constraint is provided, this depends on the classroom size and the number of allowed team sizes. We carried out some additional experiments with extra team sizes to analyze how the computation time of the model grows with the number of decision variables. The results of this experiment can be found in Fig. 1. More specifically, the figure shows the average computation time for CBC and the 95% confidence interval for instances with a varying number of decision variables. Please, note that the number of decision variables in the figure is expressed in thousands. The figure shows that the model's execution time seems to grow exponentially with the number of decision variables. This is an expected behavior, as many team formation problem variants are NP-hard problems [14]. In the results, some solvers could not solve some of the larger instances, as it stems from the percentage of instances solved in Table 1. In fact, the problems

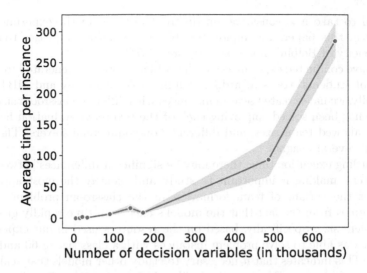

Fig. 1. Average computation time per instance for CBC and 95% confidence interval depending on the number of decision variables

with 60 students and teams of size 5 could not be solved by any of the solvers, given the computational resources available.

This exponential behavior may make it challenging to solve larger problem instances in a reasonable time with common hardware. For instance, instances with 80 to 100 students, which may be found in some Spanish university classrooms. This limitation is in line with this type of models, as mentioned by other authors [1,25]. That opens the room to study alternative ILP formulations that can scale better for larger instances.

Another insight provided by the experiments is related to the two types of team evaluation heuristics employed. While the execution time seems similar for both heuristics in smaller instances, some instances for MBTI seem harder to solve for large instances. For instance, only 20% of the problem instances could be solved optimally with the given resources for 60 students and team sizes of 3 and 4 students, respectively. This result may indicate that the distribution of traits in students may influence the resolution time of models. Thus, the distribution of traits may also influence the scalability of the model and the most appropriate solver for solving the problem.

5   Conclusions

In this paper, we have proposed an integer linear programming model for solving the team formation problem in the classroom. The model incorporates several common constraints in the classroom: disjoint teams, allowed team sizes, students that should be paired together, and students that should be placed in different teams. The objective function of the problem is general, and it can be extended to take into consideration different criteria. In the experiments carried out in this paper, we employ two team evaluation heuristics that foster heterogeneity of Belbin's role taxonomy and MBTI.

We have conducted experiments with problem instances generated from a real dataset of students' traits regarding Belbin's role taxonomy and MBTI. More specifically, we have created several instances with different classroom sizes. Each instance has been solved employing each of the two team evaluation heuristics, different allowed team sizes, and different non-commercial solvers. The results point out several insights.

Regarding execution time, there may be significant differences between available solvers, making it important to study and identify the most appropriate solver for the variant of team formation in the classroom problem. Another insight comes from the fact that the model's execution time rapidly grows with the problem size. Specifically, based on the resources used in our experiments, no solver was able to solve problem instances with a class size of 60 and a team size of 5. This indicates that it necessary to study other models that scale better with larger instances. Exact methods like the one proposed in this paper are necessary as they obtain the optimal solution, allowing us to compare various team evaluation heuristics. Thus, it is necessary to study alternative formulations that scale better with the size of the problem for specific team formation in the classroom problems. This is especially the case for large classroom sizes like the ones found in many Spanish universities.

The experiments also suggest that despite the fact that both team evaluation heuristics aim for heterogeneity, the distribution of traits among students may influence the hardness of the problem instance. Therefore, different solvers and models may perform differently under different team evaluation heuristics that foster diversity. In future work, we also plan to propose several integer linear problems for team formation in the classroom problem and study their appropriateness for different problem types.

Acknowledgement. This work was partially supported with grant DIGITAL-2022 CLOUD-AI-02 funded by the European Comission and grant PID2021-123673OB-C31 funded by MCIN/AEI/10.13039/501100011033 and by "ERDF A way of making Europe".

References

1. Aguiar, A., Pinheiro, P.R., Coelho, A.L.V., Nepomuceno, N., Neto, Á., Cunha, R.P.P.: Scalability analysis of a novel integer programming model to deal with energy consumption in heterogeneous wireless sensor networks. In: Le Thi, H.A., Bouvry, P., Pham Dinh, T. (eds.) MCO 2008. CCIS, vol. 14, pp. 11–20. Springer, Heidelberg (2008). https://doi.org/10.1007/978-3-540-87477-5_2
2. Alberola, J.M., Del Val, E., Sanchez-Anguix, V., Palomares, A., Teruel, M.D.: An artificial intelligence tool for heterogeneous team formation in the classroom. Knowl.-Based Syst. **101**, 1–14 (2016)

3. Andrejczuk, E., Bistaffa, F., Blum, C., Rodríguez-Aguilar, J.A., Sierra, C.: Synergistic team composition: a computational approach to foster diversity in teams. Knowl.-Based Syst. **182**, 104799 (2019)
4. Aranzabal, A., Epelde, E., Artetxe, M.: Team formation on the basis of Belbin's roles to enhance students' performance in project based learning. Educ. Chem. Eng. **38**, 22–37 (2022)
5. Belbin, R.M.: Team Roles at Work. Routledge (2012)
6. Bestuzheva, K., et al.: The SCIP optimization suite 8.0. arXiv preprint arXiv:2112.08872 (2021)
7. Campêlo, M., Figueiredo, T.F.: Integer programming approaches to the multiple team formation problem. Comput. Oper. Res. **133**, 105354 (2021)
8. Crawford, C., Rahaman, Z., Sen, S.: Evaluating the efficiency of robust team formation algorithms. In: Osman, N., Sierra, C. (eds.) AAMAS 2016. LNCS (LNAI), vol. 10002, pp. 14–29. Springer, Cham (2016). https://doi.org/10.1007/978-3-319-46882-2_2
9. Farhangian, M., Purvis, M., Purvis, M., Savarimuthu, B.T.R.: Modeling team formation in self-assembling software development teams. In: Proceedings of the 2016 International Conference on Autonomous Agents & Multiagent Systems, pp. 1319–1320 (2016)
10. Forrest, J., Lougee-Heimer, R.: CBC user guide. In: Emerging Theory, Methods, and Applications, pp. 257–277. INFORMS (2005)
11. Garshasbi, S., Mohammadi, Y., Graf, S., Garshasbi, S., Shen, J.: Optimal learning group formation: a multi-objective heuristic search strategy for enhancing intergroup homogeneity and intra-group heterogeneity. Expert Syst. Appl. **118**, 506–521 (2019)
12. Genova, K., Guliashki, V.: Linear integer programming methods and approaches - a survey. J. Cybern. Inf. Technol. **11**(1), 3–25 (2011)
13. John, O.P., Donahue, E.M., Kentle, R.L.: The Big Five Inventory – Versions 4a and 5. University of California, Berkeley/Institute of Personality and Social Research, Berkeley (1991)
14. Juárez, J., Santos, C., Brizuela, C.A.: A comprehensive review and a taxonomy proposal of team formation problems. ACM Comput. Surv. (CSUR) **54**(7), 1–33 (2021)
15. Mellon, C.: What are the benefits of group work? (2015)
16. Meredith, B.R.: Management teams: why they succeed or fail. Hum. Resour. Manage. Int. Digest (2010)
17. Myers, I.B.: The Myers-Briggs type indicator: manual (1962)
18. Partington, D., Harris, H.: Team role balance and team performance: an empirical study. J. Manage. Dev. **18**, 694–705 (1999)
19. Peres, F., Castelli, M.: Combinatorial optimization problems and metaheuristics: review, challenges, design, and development. Appl. Sci. **11**(14), 6449 (2021)
20. Perron, L.: Operations research and constraint programming at Google. In: Lee, J. (ed.) CP 2011. LNCS, vol. 6876, pp. 2–2. Springer, Heidelberg (2011). https://doi.org/10.1007/978-3-642-23786-7_2
21. Pieterse, V., Kourie, D.G., Sonnekus, I.P.: Software engineering team diversity and performance. In: 2006 Annual Conference of the South African Institute of Computer Scientists and Information Technologists on IT Research in Developing Countries, pp. 180–186 (2006)
22. Prada, E.D., Mareque, M., Pino-Juste, M.: Teamwork skills in higher education: is university training contributing to their mastery? Psicol.: Reflexão e Crítica **35**(5), 1–13 (2022)

23. Ramchurn, S.D., Polukarov, M., Farinelli, A., Jennings, N., Trong, C.: Coalition formation with spatial and temporal constraints (2010)
24. Sanchez-Anguix, V., Chalumuri, R., Aydoğan, R., Julian, V.: A near pareto optimal approach to student-supervisor allocation with two sided preferences and workload balance. Appl. Soft Comput. **76**, 1–15 (2019)
25. Tarplee, K.M., Friese, R., Maciejewski, A.A., Siegel, H.J.: Scalable linear programming based resource allocation for makespan minimization in heterogeneous computing systems. J. Parallel Distrib. Comput. **84**, 76–86 (2015)
26. Ugarte, N., Aranzabal, A., Arruarte, A., Larrañaga, M.: Using the behavioural tendency of students in a team environment for team formation. In: 2022 IEEE Frontiers in Education Conference (FIE), pp. 1–9. IEEE (2022)
27. Uto, M., Nguyen, D.T., Ueno, M.: Group optimization to maximize peer assessment accuracy using item response theory and integer programming. IEEE Trans. Learn. Technol. **13**(1), 91–106 (2019)
28. Vecina, M.Á., et al.: A decision support tool for the static allocation of emergency vehicles to stations. In: García Bringas, P., et al. (eds.) HAIS 2022. LNCS, vol. 13469, pp. 141–152. Springer, Cham (2022). https://doi.org/10.1007/978-3-031-15471-3_13
29. Yannibelli, V., Amandi, A.: A deterministic crowding evolutionary algorithm to form learning teams in a collaborative learning context. Expert Syst. Appl. **39**(10), 8584–8592 (2012)

Improved Evolutionary Approach for Tuning Topic Models with Additive Regularization

Maria Khodorchenko$^{(\boxtimes)}$ (ID), Nikolay Butakov (ID), and Denis Nasonov (ID)

ITMO University, 49 Kronverksky pr., St Petersburg 197101, Russia
mariyaxod@yandex.ru

Abstract. The paper addresses a problem of tuning topic models with additive regularization by introducing a novel hybrid evolutionary approach that combines Genetic and Nelder-Mead algorithms to generate domain-specific topic models with better quality. Introducing Nelder-Mead into the Genetic Algorithm pursues the goal of enhancing exploitation capabilities of the resulting hybrid algorithm with improved local search. The conducted experimental study performed on several datasets on Russian and English languages shows noticeable increase in quality of the obtained topic models. Moreover, the experiments demonstrate that the proposed modification also improves the convergence dynamics of the tuning procedure, leading to a stable increases in quality from generation to generation.

Keywords: Topic modeling · Evolutionary algorithms · Genetic algorithm · Nelder-Mead optimization · Hyperparameter optimization · ARTM

1 Introduction

Data volumes are increasing every year, and the need for their rapid processing for the development of intelligent business products is growing. One of the types of data used includes texts that are generated in a substantial volume and are quite easy to collect. However, their processing is hampered by the lack of explicit labeling and, often, unstructured, which makes it natural to apply unsupervised methods. Topic modeling is a family of NLP methods, mainly unsupervised, related to text representations learning through latent variables, called topics, which can be directly interpreted by humans. Topic modelling is often used for exploratory analysis, text categorization tasks and as a part of dimensionality reduction and feature engineering steps to prepare data to be used by other machine learning models.

From scientific and technical literature, it is possible to identify the following several main approaches to topic modelling: statistical models (for instance, NMF [1] or LSI [2]); non-neural Bayesian models (for instance, LDA [3] or PLSA

[4]); neural topic models (for instance, [5] or BERTopic [6]); Semi-bayesian models (for instance, BigARTM [7]).

Despite the existence of numerous methods and modifications for solving mathematical modeling problems, there remains a need for their correct choice for a specific text corpus with its static characteristics. Often it requires fine-grained controlling on how the model is trained and incorporating certain restrictions on the training process in the form of regularizers. Regularizers influence characteristics of words-to-topics and topics-to-documents distributions, and thus may greatly affect the quality of the resulting models. It should be noted that Latent Dirichlet Allocation model (LDA) is the most well-known method in the field, having the widest acceptance. But it has a major drawback. Any adaptation of LDA to a specific dataset requiring special regularizers demands to update the whole training algorithm [8] and creating special modifications of LDA. There are plenty of such modifications that are not unified with some single framework.

Up to now, the most flexible and universal approach to topic modeling is an additive regularization (ARTM), which allows configuring the desired characteristics by setting appropriate regularizers and their hyperparameters. The tuned model is able to repeat the behavior of such well-known models as latent Dirichlet placement (LDA) and probabilistic latent semantic analysis (PLSA), and also provides the highest quality, comparable to neural models, being significantly cheaper to train in terms of computational resources. It should be emphasized that ARTM based models has gained more attention and wider acceptance in recent times due to their flexibility.

However, the task of selecting hyperparameters of models with additive regularization is accompanied by the following difficulties: 1) a variety of configurable hyperparameters due to the flexibility of ARTM, which requires the involvement of a highly qualified specialist for manual configuration of models; 2) the absence of an effective (strongly correlated with human) quality assessment, taking into account both local (at the level of the received distributions and individual documents) and global (at the level of topics) characteristics customized models, which is especially important for ARTM and neural models; 3) the lack of a developed apparatus for optimizing ART models, including in connection with the problem (2); 4) significant training time for models on large text corpora, which is unacceptable in conditions with limited resources or limited available time.

Existing solutions for training and optimizing models with additive regularization have high flexibility and performance. However, their practical use is associated with the need for a competent selection of a set of suitable regularizers [9], their hyperparameters, and the order of their application, which, among other things, may be unique for a particular text corpora. This activity slows down the process of model development and requires sufficient qualifications from the user. In [10,11] authors proposed an approach based on growing a training strategy with metaheuristic like Genetic Algorithm from the family of evolutionary algorithms (that are commonly used in cases of difficult objective function landscapes [12,13]), and surrogate models trained on-the-fly to tackle down aforementioned problems.

Though there is a room for improvement in terms of quality enhancement. One of the development directions is integration of algorithms that may enhance local area exploitation capabilities of the metaheuristic for fine-grained tuning of hyperparameters to yield better quality of the resulting models. Nelder-Mead algorithm in its term is known to tackle functions that may not have derivatives [14] and is considered to be a good technique for solving real-world problems [15]. In this paper, we propose a hybrid metaheuristic algorithm based on existing Genetic Algorithm for ARTM training strategy optimization and Nelder-Mead algorithm that improves exploitation in local areas of the search space. These modifications further extends findings on this topic.

Our contributions in this work can be summarized as follows: 1) proposing a novel hybrid approach based on Genetic Algorithm and Nelder-Mead algorithm for the problem of hyperparameter tuning of ARTM-based topic models; 2) an experimental study of the proposed approach that allows to estimate its efficiency and applicability.

The rest of the paper is organized as follows. Section 2 presents a review of related works for the domain of topic models hyperparameter tuning. Section 3 contains a description of the newly proposed approach based on a hybrid metaheuristic. Section 4 describes the experimental setup and study conducted to prove the efficiency of the proposed method. Section 5 summarizes the proposed approach and conducted experiments into a conclusion and future works.

2   Related Work

When working with flexible topic models that have hyperparameters, there is a need to carefully configure them as a solution that is able to provide acceptable quality often highly depends on the characteristics of the data itself.

The baseline approach here is manual tuning. Though, manual tuning is fraught with such problems as the need of basic understanding of regularizers and significant amount of time to conduct the experiments [7]. More over, models like ARTM may require multistage training [9,16] where each stage spins different set of regularizers or different parameters values for them to obtain better quality of the resulting topic model.

There are various software solutions for automatic optimization of thematic models of various families. Genism [17] implements "classical methods" of thematic modeling, such as LDA, and the ability to configure their parameters. The OCTIS library [18] provides the ability to configure a number of thematic models, including neural ones, using Bayesian optimization, which provides a fairly efficient and fast operation. The disadvantages include the lack of special-specific optimization algorithms for different families of models. Step towards the automatic tuning is done with TopicNet [9] - an instrument to build training recipes, i.e. pipelines for model tuning. Topic Net works specifically with a family of models with additive regularization by means of a greedy adjustment algorithm. Though the library provides initial preconfigured pipelines to optimize topic models full exploiting of the library still requires a lot of configuration efforts to construct a feasible pipeline for a specific dataset.

The authors of this work proposed their own approach [10,11] to tackle the problem of hyperparameter tuning. Based on metaheuristics like Genetic Algorithm (GA) [19], Particle Swarm Optimization (PSO) [20], Bayesian Optimization (BO) [21] this approach differs from others due to it optimizes not just a set of hyper parameters, but also the order in which regularizers with these parameters should be applied to the model in separate sequential stages of topic model training and how long each such stage should last. Such an approach allows to gain better quality for the model. There is also a modification of this approach [11] based on surrogate computations that allows to significantly reduce time of optimization while keeping quality on approximately the same level. Despite improved quality provided by this solution there is still room for improvement by extending used metaheuristics.

At the same time, automatic adjustment is complicated by the lack of uniform quality measurement metrics. Recent studies have been devoted to improving this situation [10,22–25] and proposed new metrics which better corresponds to human evaluation including metrics learning approach based on AutoML techniques [23]. Though the problem of metrics is far from resolving up to know.

3   Problem Statement

At first, let us formally define the topic modelling task for models based on additive regularization [7]. As it was already mentioned earlier, the goal is to identify semantic structure of some text or document corpora. To achieve that, topic modelling assumes building of two matrices, namely distribution over latent topics for documents $p(t|d)$ and distribution over words for topics $p(w|t)$, in a such way that the combination of these matrices would give us another matrix as close as possible to observable from the corpora the words over documents matrix.

In general, the problem of topic modeling is considered incorrectly posed, because it can be reduced to the problem of stochastic matrix decomposition, defined in Eq. (1).

$$M = \Phi \cdot \Theta, \tag{1}$$

where M - document-term matrix of size $n \times m$, Φ and Θ - full rank stochastic matrices of size $n \times k$ and $n \times m$ respectively.

In case of additive regularization, we are looking for maximization of the log-likelihood with the addition of regularizers weighted sum to produce some solution for the task of matrix factorization Eq. (2). Such a solution would consist if two matrices Φ (probabilities of terms in the topic) and Θ (probabilities of topics in the document) which should satisfy our objective.

$$argmax_{\Phi,\Theta} \sum_{d \in D} \sum_{w \in W} n_{dw} ln \sum_{t \in T} \phi_{wt}\theta_{td} + R(\Phi,\Theta), \tag{2}$$

where D - a set of documents in the corpora, n_{dw} - number of times word w appears in document d, R is the weighted sum of regularizers.

There are many kinds of regularizers that can be applied to restrain Φ and Θ to find eventually a better solution. For instance, Decorrelator Phi and Smooth/Sparse Theta are the ones used often. The former tries to decorrelate columns in the Φ matrix (e.g. force topics to be more different in words they consist of). Application of this regularizer may improve the interpretability of topics.

The latter tries to smooth or to sparse subsets of topics that can be found in particular documents. Thus it influence and allow controlling a number of significant topics in the topics mixture the model should assign individual documents. It may be important and require different settings. For instance, when one deals with a long documents consisting of discussions of different aspects of a complex mechanism like a car, he or she may wish to increase smoothness due to naturally high number of possible topics per document. In contrary, when one deals with a corpora of short messages or comments from a social network it is more naturally to assume only one or maximum two main topics per document [22].

Both of these regularizers have their own parameters to be tuned (we classify them as hyperparameters of the whole model too). The list of other supported regularizers can be found at BigARTM documentation[1].

To tune hyper parameters of topic models, one needs to have some metrics which can somehow express quality of the model. From a human perspective, it can be ease of topics interpretation, presence of out-of-meaning words in a topic, correct representation of particular texts with mixtures provided by the model. However, such metrics require human assessment which in many cases may be too expensive or even impossible to substantially cover various parts of the hyperparameters' search space. To overcome this problem many different metrics correlating to a some degree with human assessment have been proposed. For example, the coherence C [26] of topic t is calculated as shown in Eq. (3).

$$C_t = \frac{2}{k(k-1)} \sum_{i=1}^{k-1} \sum_{j=i+1}^{k} \left[log \frac{p(w_i, w_j)}{p(w_i)p(w_j)} \right]_+, \tag{3}$$

where k is number of tokens in the topic, w_i and w_j are tokens from the topic, $p(w_i, w_j)$ - joint probability of tokens w_i and w_j in a corpora (co-occurrences).

The coherence is one of the most widespread metrics for quality estimation up to the present moment [23]. In recent studies, its modification has been proposed in [11] to improve its correlation with human assessment and have the form of Eq. (4).

$$Fitness = mean(C_i) + \min(C_i), \forall i = \overline{1, K}, \tag{4}$$

where K is a number of topics. Hereafter we denote this metric as "Fitness", similarly to the notation used in the theory of evolutionary algorithms.

---

[1] https://bigartm.readthedocs.io/en/stable/tutorials/regularizers_descr.html.

Following the approach described in [10,11] we represent in the same way a set of hyper parameters to be optimized. The important difference here as it was mentioned in Sect. 2 is that the approach assumes representing the whole training procedure consisting of: common model's parameters like the numbers of main and background topics; a sequence of few stages denoting different sets of regularizers to be applied and how long each stage will last; parameters of regularizers in each stage. We will call this representation a learning strategy hereafter. An example of a learning strategy is presented on Fig. 1.

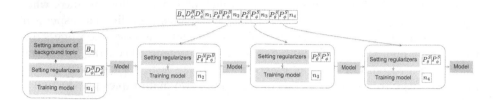

Fig. 1. An example of a learning strategy for multistage training of a topic model: each stage has a separate set of regularizers with its own parameters values and different number of iterations of training.

Thus the goal of a topic modeling hyperparameters optimization algorithm is to find a learning strategy that will maximize the fitness according to Eq. (4).

4 Hybrid Genetic Algorithm with Nelder-Mead Optimization for Topic Models with Additive Regularization

The original algorithm shows good results when working with limited number of fitness evaluations. One of its main features is in efficient exploration of the search field defined by the bounds. Still, it is possible to improve the convergence and speed up computations.

We propose a hybrid algorithm with Nelder-Mead optimization to stabilize the training procedure and improve convergence, as it helps to search for better solution in the vicinity of the initial point in a small amount of iterations.

The overall scheme of the approach is provided on the Fig. 2. After population initialization with a set of hyperparameters (search bounds are provided in Sect. 5.2) original crossover and mutation are performed which can dramatically change the population to ensure exploration abilities of the algorithm. To provide local improvements of the mutated population Nelder-Mead optimization is performed for several iterations on a 30% sample of points obtained after mutation procedure. The resulting individual is compared by fitness function with the initial point and in case of higher values the new individual replaces the initial in population.

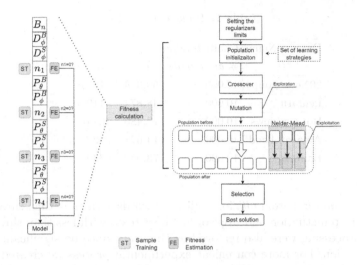

Fig. 2. Proposed approach scheme.

Fitness calculation procedure includes topic model training (see Fig. 1) and measuring the resulting model score. In general the training is done using all the available input data. Full training of the model according to predefined learning strategy can take from seconds to minutes and, thus, the whole optimization may take significant time and computational resources. To reduce the workload we propose to train on a random sample of data at each training iteration as defined by "ST" on the image.

On the early training stages, it is possible to get overregularized models, which result in the lack of topics or inability of coherence computating. In such cases, the resulting fitness is zeroed and, thus, the training can be aborted earlier which is done by comparing estimated fitness on each of the training stages with 0.

5 Experimental Study

5.1 Datasets Description

For experimental study we selected several datasets in russian and english languages: 20 Newsgroups dataset [27] - newsfeeds on 20 different topics, though some of them are close to each other, like "baseball" and "hockey"; Lentaru [28] - news collected from russian website lenta.ru for 20 years (from 1999 to 2019); Amazon food [29] - reviews on food made by Amazon users; Hotel Reviews [30] - collection of reviews from visitors of 1000 hotels; Banners [31] - dataset with web-pages and short advertisement banner text that lead to the web-page.

Each of the datasets was preprocessed according to a common pipeline. Steps included text cleaning, such as removal of non-related to text HTML artifacts, tokenization, lemmatization (*Mystem* from *pymystem3* for russian language and

Table 1. Table Type Styles

Dataset Name	Characteristic		
	# documents	Voc size	Avg text len
20Newsgroups	10,000	59,974	117.8
Lentaru	10,000	48,874	119.5
Hotel-reviews	10,000	13,480	22.6
Amazon Food	10,000	14,678	32.5
Banners	10,000	73,062	330

WordNetLemmatizer from *nltk* for english) of words with more than three letters, filtering out punctuation and stopwords. Short texts with less than three tokens after preprocessing were also removed as they introduce no significant statistical information. For more convenient experimental process we created random samples of 10,000 documents (where applicable) for further usage. The information on datasets is summarized in Table 1 - they differ in terms of statistical characteristics and, thus, provide variability for the experimental study.

The resulting data was converted to vowpal wabbit format demanded by the topic model. Co-occurrence dictionaries for the datasets used to calculate coherence scores, were created with window size parameter set to 10.

5.2 Hyperparameters

All experiments were conducted on blade servers with the following parameters: 2 × Intel(R) Xeon(R) Gold 5215 CPU @ 2.50 GHz, 256 Gb RAM, 8 Tb HDD.

We defined a set of hyperparameters, which form a learning strategy to iteratively train and improve the model, according to [10]. Still, to avoid obtaining models with too high sparsity, the search field regularizer bounds of parameters values for the main topics were extended to allow smoothness in case of strong decorrelation. The admissible upper bound of iterations number was set to 30 (Table 2).

Table 2. Search field bounds

Regularizers	Description	Bounds	Variable type
D_ϕ^S, D_ϕ^B	Decorrelators	$[0, 1e5]$	Float
n_1, n_2, n_3, n_4	Number of iterations	$[0, 30]$	Integer
B_N	Number of background topics	$[0, 5]$	Integer
P_ϕ^S, P_θ^S	Sparsing/Smoothing of main topics	$[-1e3, 1e3]$	Float
P_ϕ^B, P_θ^B	Smoothing of background topics	$[0, 1e2]$	Float

All the hyperparameters of the genetic algorithm (adaptive mutation, crossover type and probability, etc.) were set as indicated for the original algorithm.

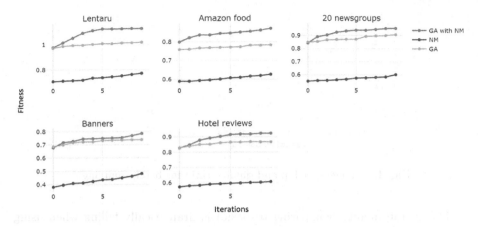

Fig. 3. Experimental results of topic model tuning with different algorithms. X-axis shows the generations of original Genetic algorithm.

5.3   Algorithm Effectiveness

We compared the basic version of genetic algorithm, Nelder-Mead optimization and the proposed hybrid approach. To have a valid comparison of the approaches, we matched the number of fitness estimations with the original genetic algorithm. The amount of generations (of original genetic algorithm) was set to 10 as the base GA shows convergence at this stage. Amount of specific topics for each of the datasets was also set to 10.

From the average results provided on Fig. 3 can be seen that pure Nelder-Mead algorithm (indicated as "NM") has a slow convergence as it is good at exploring local areas but has difficulties with obtaining new solutions in case of significant search area.

Genetic algorithm ("GA") comparing to it's hybrid version with Nelder-Mead ("GA wit NM") reveals worse convergence dynamic and tend to have explicit periods with small changes in fitness. The proposed version gains result up to 11% better, which indicates improvement in solution search.

5.4   Speeding Up Computations

To identify the difference between training using all batches and sampling procedure, we measured the dynamics of quality ratio changing (ratio between version with sampling and basic approach) with the amount of sampled data used for training.

Figure 4 shows average results of training the model with the sampling technique. It can be seen that sampling initialization on each of the training stages consume significant amount of time, which leads to the absence of speedup when utilizing more than 50% of data.

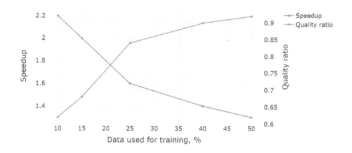

Fig. 4. Average speedup and quality ratio for batch sampling.

The overall quality (comparing to basic) is dramatically falling when using less than 25% of data, so the proposed "safe" area for this training mode is in usage of 40% of data with 0.9 ratio and 1.4 speedup.

6   Conclusion

This paper proposes a novel hybrid genetic algorithm with Nelder-Mead optimization to tune topic models with additive regularization. The modifications followed the goal of improving convergence by integrating the mechanism of extensive local search after the mutation step, which balance the exploration and exploitation abilities of the algorithm.

Experimental results show that the new algorithm demonstrates a stable quality improvement, up to 11%, which reveals effectiveness of the proposed hybrid algorithm. We also investigated ways of speeding up computations with a sampling approach that demonstrates an ability to gain 1.4 acceleration with 10% quality loss.

The future work is directed towards the further optimization procedure speedup. In the defined frame, several improvements will be explored - conducting the sensitivity analysis of the hyperparameters to dynamically change the search area bounds, surrogate model improvement and utilization of the previously calculated individuals. All these modifications are aimed to increase the algorithm effectiveness and provide a simple and low fidelity topic modeling tool for practitioners.

Acknowledgements. This research is financially supported by the Russian Science Foundation, Agreement 17-71-30029, with co-financing of Bank Saint Petersburg.

References

1. Shi, T., Kang, K., Choo, J., Reddy, C.K.: Short-text topic modeling via nonnegative matrix factorization enriched with local word-context correlations. In: Proceedings of the 2018 World Wide Web Conference, WWW 2018, Republic and Canton of Geneva, CHE, pp. 1105–1114. International World Wide Web Conferences Steering Committee (2018)

2. Wang, Q., Xu, J., Li, H., Craswell, N.: Regularized latent semantic indexing: a new approach to large-scale topic modeling. ACM Trans. Inf. Syst. **31**, 5:1–5:44 (2013)
3. Blei, D.M., Ng, A.Y., Jordan, M.I.: Latent dirichlet allocation. J. Mach. Learn. Res. **3**, 993–1022 (2003)
4. Hofmann, T.: Probabilistic latent semantic indexing. In: Proceedings of the 22nd Annual International ACM SIGIR Conference on Research and Development in Information Retrieval, SIGIR 1999, pp. 50–57. Association for Computing Machinery, New York (1999)
5. Rezaee, M., Ferraro, F.: A discrete variational recurrent topic model without the reparametrization trick. In: Proceedings of the 34th International Conference on Neural Information Processing Systems, NIPS 2020, Red Hook, NY, USA. Curran Associates Inc. (2020)
6. Grootendorst, M.: BERTopic: neural topic modeling with a class-based TF-IDF procedure. arXiv preprint arXiv:2203.05794 (2022)
7. Vorontsov, K., Frei, O., Apishev, M., Romov, P., Dudarenko, M.: BigARTM: open source library for regularized multimodal topic modeling of large collections. In: Khachay, M.Y., Konstantinova, N., Panchenko, A., Ignatov, D.I., Labunets, V.G. (eds.) AIST 2015. CCIS, vol. 542, pp. 370–381. Springer, Cham (2015). https://doi.org/10.1007/978-3-319-26123-2_36
8. Rieger, J., Jentsch, C., Rahnenführer, J.: RollingLDA: an update algorithm of Latent Dirichlet Allocation to construct consistent time series from textual data. In: Findings of the Association for Computational Linguistics: EMNLP 2021, Punta Cana, Dominican Republic, November 2021, pp. 2337–2347. Association for Computational Linguistics (2021)
9. Bulatov, V., et al.: TopicNet: making additive regularisation for topic modelling accessible. In: LREC (2020)
10. Khodorchenko, M., Teryoshkin, S., Sokhin, T., Butakov, N.: Optimization of learning strategies for ARTM-based topic models. In: de la Cal, E.A., Villar Flecha, J.R., Quintián, H., Corchado, E. (eds.) HAIS 2020. LNCS (LNAI), vol. 12344, pp. 284–296. Springer, Cham (2020). https://doi.org/10.1007/978-3-030-61705-9_24
11. Khodorchenko, M., Butakov, N., Sokhin, T., Teryoshkin, S.: Surrogate-based optimization of learning strategies for additively regularized topic models. Log. J. IGPL **31**(2), 287–299 (2023)
12. Pavlenko, A., Chivilikhin, D., Semenov, A.: Asynchronous evolutionary algorithm for finding backdoors in Boolean satisfiability. In: 2022 IEEE Congress on Evolutionary Computation (CEC), pp. 1–8. IEEE (2022)
13. Butakov, N., Nasonov, D.: Co-evolutional genetic algorithm for workflow scheduling in heterogeneous distributed environment. In: 2014 IEEE 8th International Conference on Application of Information and Communication Technologies (AICT), pp. 1–5. IEEE (2014)
14. Singer, S., Nelder, J.: Nelder-Mead algorithm. Scholarpedia **4**(7), 2928 (2009)
15. Takenaga, S., Ozaki, Y., Onishi, M.: Practical initialization of the Nelder-Mead method for computationally expensive optimization problems. Optim. Lett. **17**(2), 283–297 (2023). https://doi.org/10.1007/s11590-022-01953-y
16. Vorontsov, K., Frei, O., Apishev, M., Romov, P., Suvorova, M., Yanina, A.: Non-Bayesian additive regularization for multimodal topic modeling of large collections. In: Proceedings of the 2015 Workshop on Topic Models: Post-Processing and Applications, pp. 29–37 (2015)
17. Řehůřek, R., Sojka, P.: Software framework for topic modelling with large corpora (2010)

18. Terragni, S., Fersini, E., Galuzzi, B.G., Tropeano, P., Candelieri, A.: OCTIS: comparing and optimizing topic models is simple! In: Proceedings of the 16th Conference of the European Chapter of the Association for Computational Linguistics: System Demonstrations, pp. 263–270 (2021)
19. Katoch, S., Chauhan, S.S., Kumar, V.: A review on genetic algorithm: past, present, and future. Multimed. Tools Appl. **80**, 8091–8126 (2021). https://doi.org/10.1007/s11042-020-10139-6
20. Kennedy, J., Eberhart, R.: Particle swarm optimization. In: Proceedings of ICNN 1995-International Conference on Neural Networks, vol. 4, pp. 1942–1948. IEEE (1995)
21. Pelikan, M., Goldberg, D.E., Cantú-Paz, E., et al.: BOA: the Bayesian optimization algorithm. In: Proceedings of the Genetic and Evolutionary Computation Conference, GECCO-1999, vol. 1, pp. 525–532. Citeseer (1999)
22. Khodorchenko, M., Butakov, N.: Developing an approach for lifestyle identification based on explicit and implicit features from social media. Procedia Comput. Sci. **136**, 236–245 (2018). 7th International Young Scientists Conference on Computational Science, YSC 2018, Heraklion, Greece, 02–06 July 2018
23. Khodorchenko, M., Butakov, N., Nasonov, D.: Towards better evaluation of topic model quality. In: 2022 32nd Conference of Open Innovations Association (FRUCT), pp. 128–134. IEEE (2022)
24. Lund, J., et al.: Automatic evaluation of local topic quality. arXiv preprint arXiv:1905.13126 (2019)
25. Doogan, C., Buntine, W.: Topic model or topic twaddle? Re-evaluating semantic interpretability measures. In: Proceedings of the 2021 Conference of the North American Chapter of the Association for Computational Linguistics: Human Language Technologies, pp. 3824–3848. Association for Computational Linguistics (2021)
26. Newman, D., Lau, J.H., Grieser, K., Baldwin, T.: Automatic evaluation of topic coherence. In: Human Language Technologies: The 2010 Annual Conference of the North American Chapter of the ACL, California, pp. 100–108. ACL (2010)
27. Lang, K.: NewsWeeder: learning to filter netnews. In: Proceedings of the Twelfth International Conference on Machine Learning, pp. 331–339 (1995)
28. Yutkin, D.: Corpus of Russian news articles collected from lenta.ru (2018)
29. McAuley, J.J., Leskovec, J.: From amateurs to connoisseurs: modeling the evolution of user expertise through online reviews. In: Proceedings of the 22nd International Conference on World Wide Web, WWW 2013, pp. 897–908. Association for Computing Machinery, New York (2013)
30. Datafiniti's Business Database: Datafiniti's hotel reviews
31. Nevezhin, E., Butakov, N., Khodorchenko, M., Petrov, M., Nasonov, D.A.: Topic-driven ensemble for online advertising generation. In: COLING (2020)

Time of Arrival Error Characterization for Precise Indoor Localization of Autonomous Ground Vehicles

Rubén Álvarez⬢, Rubén Ferrero-Guillén⬢, Paula Verde(✉)⬢,
Alberto Martínez-Gutiérrez⬢, Javier Díez-González⬢, and Hilde Perez⬢

Department of Mechanical, Computer and Aerospace Engineering,
Universidad de León, 24071 León, Spain
`paula.verde@unileon.es`

Abstract. Autonomous Ground Vehicles (AGVs) are supposing a revolution to automate the internal transportation of modern factories following the paradigms of Industry 4.0 and Smart Manufacturing. However, the optimal integration of these mobile robots into high-precision industrial tasks requires the definition of a stable and robust localization system attaining centimeter accuracy. For this purpose, we propose in this paper the optimal deployment of a Time of Arrival (TOA) Ultra Wideband architecture that reduces the localization errors by minimizing the signal path and by granting robustness against multipath effects through the short duration of the emitted pulses which is critical for industrial saturated environments. To attain competitive localization results, we characterize the error bounds of the TOA architecture considering noise, clock, and multipath uncertainties which represents a novelty in the literature of the localization field. This characterization is later used to guide a genetic algorithm to optimally allocate the sensor distribution of the TOA architecture in space to minimise the localization errors in the scenario analyzed in this paper. Results present mean errors up to 21 cm which enables successfully addressing AGVs precision industrial tasks.

Keywords: Autonomous-Vehicle · Local Positioning Systems ·
Genetic Algorithms · Cramèr-Rao Bound

1 Introduction

Automatic Guided Vehicles (AGVs) are in charge of the internal transportation of modern factories within the Industry 4.0 paradigm [1]. Their efficient use implies the definition of a collaborative framework that organizes trajectories, goals, and loads of these mobile industrial robots in order to meet the global necessities of the industrial plant without producing bottlenecks [24].

This work was partially supported by the Spanish Research Agency (AEI) under grant number PID2019-108277GB-C21/AEI/10.13039/501100011033 and the University of León.

However, AGVs still present some technological challenges in order to take full advantage of the benefits of these vehicles: the integration into industrial internet platforms [31], the optimized navigation of AGVs fleets [25], or achieving the precise localization of these vehicles to address complex industrial tasks in collaboration with other digital industrial devices [34].

In this sense, the localization of AGVs in industrial indoor scenarios cannot be addressed through Global Navigation Satellite Systems (GNSS) since their signals are significantly degraded when traversing building walls. Moreover, other effects such as multipath interference further mitigate the GNSS localization signals, rendering these systems unable to attain competitive localization results for AGVs' precision navigation.

Consequently, most autonomous mobile robots (AMRs) make use of visual procedures or the mapping of the operating environment through Light Detection And Ranging (LIDAR) technology [19] to navigate in indoor environments. Nevertheless, although AMRs can attain satisfactory localization results to allow their navigation in indoor spaces, the collaboration of AGVs with other industrial devices in order to address complex industrial tasks still requires a more precise localization system.

For this purpose, we propose in this paper the deployment of an ad-hoc Ultra Wideband (UWB) sensor network to improve the localization accuracy of AGVs in industrial scenarios. UWB technology grants robustness against multipath effects through the short duration of the emitted pulses which is critical for industrial saturated environments [8], and also reduces the Non-Line-of-Sight (NLOS) effects through the high frequency of the localization signal [28].

In addition, the consideration of an ad-hoc network with the free capacity to locate the sensor distribution further reduces the localization uncertainties of the positioning system [10]. This entails addressing the Node Location Problem (NLP) [15], which has been classified as NP-Hard both in coverage and localization accuracy [26].

Due to the computational complexity of the NLP, a metaheuristic solution is recommended to address this problem [6,30]. These optimizations usually make use of the Cramér-Rao Bounds (CRB) as the fitness indicator of the performance of each analyzed sensor arrangement during the optimization process [11].

This is due to the principles of the CRB which define the lower achievable error of a sensor distribution in a particular target location at study [21]. Therefore, the CRB is an indicator of the maximal performance of a localization system that can guide the necessary NLP optimization to reach competitive localization results in ad-hoc localization networks.

Thus, we propose in this paper the characterization of the CRB for a UWB Time of Arrival (TOA) localization architecture based on noise, clock, and multipath uncertainties. This characterization represents a novelty in the literature to the authors' knowledge since a complete characterization of the ranging and clock errors of a UWB TOA architecture including altogether these three error sources has not been previously presented in any research contribution.

Subsequently, the proposed CRB characterization will guide a Genetic Algorithm (GA) optimization for addressing the NLP in order to optimally locate the architecture sensors of the proposed localization system to provide an accurate and stable target positioning calculation to enable the precision navigation of AGVs in indoor industrial environments.

The remainder of the paper is organized as follows: Sect. 2 presents the CRB characterization of the TOA architecture considering noise, clock, and multipath uncertainties; Sect. 3 describes the GA proposed to address the NLP of this paper; Sect. 4 shows and analyzes the results of the localization system and Sect. 5 concludes the paper.

2   CRB Characterization of a UWB TOA Indoor Architecture

CRB defines the minimum variance of an unbiased estimator of a deterministic unknown parameter. When it is applied to the Target Sensor (TS) coordinates in a localization system, it determines the minimum error bound achievable by any algorithm used to determine the target location [5].

Recently, a matrix form of the Fisher Information Matrix (FIM) (i.e., the inverse of the CRB) was defined in a generic form to introduce the required error characterization to determine the lower achievable error in a particular TS location given a particular localization architecture [21]:

$$
\begin{aligned}
FIM_{mn} = &\left(\frac{\delta h(TS)}{\delta TS_m}\right)^T R^{-1}(TS)\left(\frac{\delta h(TS)}{\delta TS_n}\right) \\
&+\tfrac{1}{2}tr\left\{R^{-1}(TS)\left(\frac{\delta R(TS)}{\delta TS_m}\right)R^{-1}(TS)\left(\frac{\delta R(TS)}{\delta TS_n}\right)\right\}
\end{aligned}
\tag{1}
$$

where m and n represent the TS coordinates analyzed for element (FIM_{mn}) of the FIM, $h(TS)$ is the vector defining the spatial propagation of the localization signal in the architecture analyzed and $R(TS)$ is the covariance matrix of the system.

This FIM characterization allows the direct definition of the minimum error bound of the architecture at study (i.e., the Root Mean Squared Error (RMSE)) through the computation of the following equation [14]:

$$
RMSE(AGV_i) = \sqrt{trace(FIM)^{-1}}
\tag{2}
$$

where, particularizing for this paper, $RMSE\ (AGV_i)$ represents the RMSE in a particular AGV location studied.

This methodology defines the error bounds of a particular architecture given a defined sensor arrangement through the characterization of the h vector and the R matrix. In the next subsection, we detail this characterization for the UWB TOA architecture considered in this paper for the indoor navigation of AGVs.

2.1   UWB TOA Error Characterization

The TOA localization architecture is based on the measurement of the total time-of-flight of the localization signal from an emitter to a receiver [33]. Each architecture receiver generates a sphere of potential locations for the target being required at least four nodes to completely define the mathematical problem without ambiguities [12].

But, although the architecture sensors can receive the localization signal, the signal received might suffer enough degradation for rendering it unable to be properly used to determine the target location. Thus, the localization signal accumulates uncertainties during transmission from the emitter to the receiver. These uncertainties are mainly due to noise [2] and multipath [29] effects in indoor spaces.

In addition, uncertainties during the time measurement process must also be considered for building a robust error characterization [3].

Therefore, we present in this paper the most complete definition of the localization error of the TOA architecture in indoor environments through the consideration of the predominant error sources (i.e., noise, multipath, and clock uncertainties). This model is the first in the literature that considers these three error sources together to the authors' knowledge, thus, representing a novelty for the localization community.

In addition, this error characterization is built under the demonstration of the independence of the three error sources as introduced in [3,32]. This independence allows us to model different error characterizations for each error source and finally compute the global error of the architecture through the sum of the modeled errors.

Particularizing for the TOA architecture of this paper, noise uncertainties are defined through a Log-Normal path loss model [2] that considers the Line Of Sight (LOS) and NLOS signals paths through a ray tracing algorithm presented in [4] as follows:

$$
\sigma^2_{TOA(noise)_i} = \frac{c^2}{B^2 \left(\frac{P_T}{P_N} \right)} PL(d_0) \left[\left(\frac{d_{i_{LOS}}}{d_0} \right)_{CSi} + \left(\frac{d_{i_{NLOS}}}{d_0} \right)^{\frac{n_{NLOS}}{n_{LOS}}}_{CSi} \right]^{n_{LOS}} \tag{3}
$$

where c is the speed of the radioelectric waves; B is the signal bandwidth; P_T is the power of transmission; P_N is the mean noise power obtained through the Johnson Nyquist equation; $PL(d_0)$ is the path loss in the reference distance d_0 which has been defined as $1\,\mathrm{m}$ in UWB indoor environments [17]; $d_{i_{LOS}}$ and $d_{i_{NLOS}}$ are the LOS/NLOS distances covered by the positioning signal from the TS to the TOA architecture sensor i respectively, and n_{LOS} and n_{NLOS} represent the LOS/NLOS path loss exponents of the Log-Normal model proposed respectively.

The clock error characterization considers the truncation, the clock drift, and the initial-time offset uncertainties affecting the time measurement process as introduced in [3]:

$$\sigma^2_{TOA(clock)_i} = \frac{1}{n_s} \sum_{k=1}^{n_s} \{|T_i - f_{TR}\left[(T_i + U_i - U_0 \quad + T_0(\eta_i - \eta_0) + T_i\eta_i)\right]|c^2\}$$

(4)

where n_s represents the number of Monte Carlo simulations performed to determine the expected clock error variance; T_i is the ideal time-of-flight from TS to architecture sensor i; f_{TR} is the truncation of the time measurement determined by the architecture clocks characteristics; U_i and U_0 are the ideal time-lapse from the last synchronization process of the architecture sensor i and TS clocks respectively; T_0 is the ideal time-lapse between the last synchronization process of the architecture clocks and the emission of the positioning signal and η_i and η_0 are the clock drifts of the architecture sensor i and the TS respectively.

As for the multipath error, we make use of the well-known statistical model by Saleh and Valenzuela [29]:

$$\sigma^2_{TOA(multipath)_i} = \bar{G}_i log(1 + d_i)$$

(5)

$$\bar{G}_i = G(d_0) \left[\left(\frac{d_{i_{LOS}}}{d_0}\right) + \left(\frac{d_{i_{NLOS}}}{d_0}\right)^{\frac{n_{NLOS}}{n_{LOS}}} \right]^{-n_{LOS}}$$

(6)

$$G(d_0) = \left(\frac{G_T G_R \lambda_0^2}{16\pi^2 d_0^2}\right)$$

(7)

where $\bar{G}_i$ is the multipath power gain of the localization signal from the TS to the architecture sensor i; d_i is the distance from TS to architecture sensor i; $G(d_0)$ is the average multipath power gain at the reference distance d_0 also 1 m in the Saleh-Valenzuela model [29]; G_T and G_R are the gains of the transmitting and receiving antennas and λ_0 is the wavelength of the localization signal.

The combination of the noise, clock and multipath uncertainties described constitutes the definition of the error characterization of this paper. The consideration of independent error sources allows the constitution of the final error expression introduced in the R matrix of the FIM model of Eq. 1:

$$\sigma^2_{TOA_i} = \sigma^2_{TOA(noise)_i} + \sigma^2_{TOA(clock)_i} + \sigma^2_{TOA(multipath)_i}$$

(8)

In order to complete the required information to build the FIM matrix, the characterization of the h vector is needed. This characterization is based on the signal path of the TOA architecture as follows:

$$h_{TOA_i} = \|TS - CS_i\|$$
$$i = 1, ..., N_{CS}$$

(9)

All these equations presented in this Section represent the fundamentals to define the error characterization of the optimization of the sensor location of the UWB TOA architecture proposed for indoor AGV navigation. The particularities of the optimization of this paper are described in the following Sect. 3.

3   Genetic Algorithm Optimization

The definition of the CRB of Sect. 2 enables the definition of the minimum localization error given a particular sensor distribution in space. However, the attainment of competitive localization results in indoor spaces requires an optimal definition of the sensor arrangement. This is defined as the NLP and is addressed in the literature considering the CRB as the fitness function [13,16].

The high complexity of the NLP recommends the implementation of meta-heuristic techniques for attaining an acceptable solution within a polynomial time (e.g., such as simulated annealing, differential evolution, bat algorithm [20]). In this context, GA stand out as a consequence of their balance between exploration, intensification, and overall robustness for different optimization problems [14].

Through the codification of a population of individuals, where each individual represents a valid solution to the problem at hand, GA achieve an acceptable solution by introducing selection pressure into the population. In this context, different genetic operators interact with the population, sorting, crossing, and mutating the population until a sufficient solution is reached [10].

In order to implement a GA optimization for the NLP, two main aspects must be discussed, the fitness evaluation and the population codification. The codification of the population is generally performed in binary code (i.e., genotype), so that it can be efficiently translated into the real variables of the problem (i.e., phenotype). This translation should minimise the generation of individuals that represent invalid solutions.

In our case study, we aim to deploy a sensor distribution over an indoor scenario, for which we have devised the codification represented in Fig. 1.

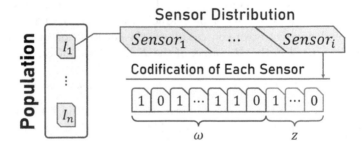

Fig. 1. Codification of each individual of the population for the proposed GA optimization of the NLP for indoor scenarios.

Given the particularities of the scenario, nodes are to be located in the scenario walls, so they do not interfere with machinery access or use in the industrial plant [27]. Therefore, any individual that entails at least a single node out of the scenario walls will be considered invalid.

Such a scenario would result in the generation of an overwhelming number of invalid individuals, which would render the GA optimization futile. In this context, we have devised the codification for this problem depicted in Fig. 1.

The proposed codification translates the genotype of an individual, which entails the different sensor coordinates, into the 3D location of each sensor while guaranteeing the correct placement of the sensors over a continuous space of solutions. This is achieved through the consideration of two variables of each gene (i.e., each sensor location), the ω and z coordinates. While z represents the actual vertical location of the sensor, ω traverses through the different scenario walls as depicted in Fig. 2. Consequently, the x and y Cartesian coordinates can be attained from ω.

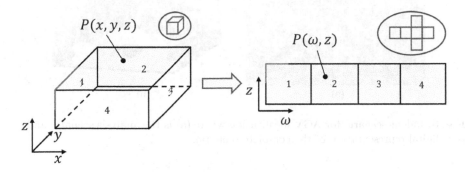

Fig. 2. Conversion between the (ω, z) and the (x, y, z) 3D Cartesian coordinates for indoor scenarios.

Consequently, the proposed codification results are practical for performing sensor distribution optimizations over indoor scenarios, such as the one presented in this paper, which we will describe in the following Section.

On the other hand, once established the codification, a fitness evaluation is required for determining how well each individual performs (i.e., fitness value). In our proposal, we attain the performance of each possible sensor distribution through the evaluation of the CRB, based on Eqs. 1–9.

In this context, from Eq. 2, a RMSE is achieved for each possible location of interest for performing localization, given a single sensor distribution. Considering the error distribution of all target points of interest, the following fitness value is proposed for quantifying the performance of each individual:

$$ff_{CRB} = \frac{1}{n_{TLE}} \sum_{k=1}^{n_{TLE}} \left(1 - \frac{RMSE(AGV)_k}{RMSE_{ref}}\right) \tag{10}$$

where n_{TLE} is the number of points that constitute the Target Location Environment (i.e., all the possible target locations), and $RMSE_{ref}$ is a reference value representing the maximum achievable RMSE error for the scenario of study, so that the actual fitness function, ff_{CRB}, is bounded to the $[0, 1]$ interval.

4   Results

4.1   Scenario of Study

In order to evaluate the performance of our optimization proposal, we have modeled an indoor scenario that resembles an industrial environment, depicted in Fig. 3. This scenario contains different machines and elements destined for industrial processes, which represent an Obstacle Area (OA) for the AGV navigation and for the localization signals.

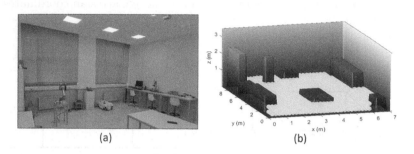

Fig. 3. Indoor scenario for AGV localization where (a) is the analysis scenario and (b) is a digital representation of the complete scenario.

AGVs can roam freely over the available space, which renders the environment ground as the Target Location Environment (TLE). Therefore, sensors destined for localizing the AGV are to be located over the scenario wall, thus forming the Node Location Environment (NLE).

From this scenario, the devised GA performs the sensor distribution optimization. Table 1 includes the main parameters regarding the simulation characteristics. All simulations were executed in the M programming software, through an Intel® i9 3.2 GHz CPU with 32 GB of RAM.

Thus, Fig. 3 and Table 1 establish a common framework in which to evaluate the different sensor configurations achieved by the GA.

4.2   Optimization Results

This section presents an analysis of the results of the optimization obtained by the GA for the scenario described above. The TOA architecture is highly dependent on the synchronism between its nodes, which leads the optimization into reducing both the signal paths and the clock measurements for all the AGV navigation regions without compromising any area. The simulations have promoted the use of 5 and 6 sensors to achieve competitive coverage in the totality of the evaluated points.

Table 2 presents a summary of the main performance results for the different configurations of the proposed architecture attained during multiple executions of the proposed methodology.

Table 1. Configuration of the localization network and hyperparameters of the GA optimization for the proposed analysis.

(a) UWB TOA Parameters [7,22].

Parameter	Value
Frequency	3.9 GHz
Transmitted BW	≥ 500 MHz
Power Transmitted	-10.4 dBm
Antenna Gain	3 dBi
Sensitivity	-100 dBm
Clock Frequency	1 GHz
Frequency-drift	U{0, 8} ppm
Initial-time Offset	U{5.5, 6} ns
Time from Sync	1 μs
Time-frequency product	1

(b) GA Hyperparameters, adjusted as in [18].

Hyperparameter	Value
Population	100
Selection Operator	Tournament 2
Crossover Operator	Multi-point
Mutation Operator	3%
Elitism Operator	13%
Stop Criteria	120 Generations or Convergence
TLE Points	1904
NLE Points	16384
Number of combination	$1.18 \cdot 10^{21} / 1.93 \cdot 10^{25}$

Table 2. Statistical results for the RMSE in centimeters for the optimizations performed by the GA algorithm.

	Mean (cm)	Median (cm)	σ (cm)^2	RMSE ≤ X	N° of points
5 sensors	23.60	23.20	3.04	X = 20 cm	7.72%
				X = 25 cm	75.05%
				X = 30 cm	96.43%
6 sensors	21.48	21.28	2.19	X = 20 cm	25.47%
				X = 25 cm	93.28%
				X = 30 cm	99.79%

As shown in Table 2, the 6-sensor configuration is superior in terms of mean error and error stability. In this sense, the 5-sensor architecture increases the target positioning calculation uncertainty by 9.86% and the mean error deviation by 38.81%, which recommends the deployment of the 6-sensor configuration since it does not suppose a significant increase in the system complexity that can justify the difference of the results achieved. In this way, a greater homogeneity is obtained in the uncertainty calculation of the localization error, which favors the performance of precision tasks of the AGVs in the scenario analyzed.

In addition, the errors obtained in investigations with scenarios of similar dimensions [9,23], are on the same order of magnitude as those observed in our research. This fact reinforces the reliability and applicability of TOA architectures in indoor scenarios.

Finally, Fig. 4 shows the evaluation of the accuracy achieved by the chosen architecture. For this purpose, each of the discretized target location points considered during the GA optimization is evaluated in terms of RMSE.

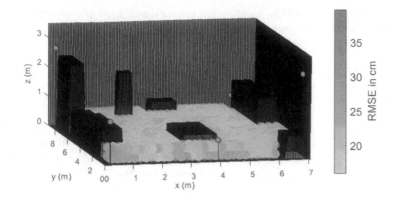

Fig. 4. Accuracy analysis for 6-sensors in terms of CRB in centimeters.

Therefore, the final optimized positioning network verifies the capability of the TOA architecture as a competitive system for AGVs' precision navigation in indoor environments.

5   Conclusions

The design and deployment of a robust and accurate localization system represents a crucial step for AGV integration in the industrial plant, especially when performing high-precision tasks.

Vision-based localization has been widely proposed for self-localization in the field of robotics. However, their viability can become compromised for dynamic industrial scenarios with variable light conditions. In this context, we propose a TOA LPS based on UWB for localizing AGVs in a scenario that mimics industrial conditions.

In this paper, we devise a novel methodology for optimally deploying TOA LPS, which is particularised for indoor scenarios. For this purpose, we propose a new characterization model of the localization uncertainties of a TOA architecture, which considers for the first time in the literature the combined effect of noise degradation, clock imperfect measurements, and multipath interference.

We have implemented the proposed model over a realistic scenario, attaining a localization architecture that achieves competitive accuracy results for AGV navigation.

References

1. Ali, M., Khan, W.U.: Implementation issues of AGVs in flexible manufacturing system: a review. Glob. J. Flex. Syst. Manag. **11**(1), 55–61 (2010). https://doi.org/10.1007/BF03396578

2. Álvarez, R., Díez-González, J., Alonso, E., Fernández-Robles, L., Castejón-Limas, M., Perez, H.: Accuracy analysis in sensor networks for asynchronous positioning methods. Sensors **19**(13), 3024 (2019)
3. Álvarez, R., Díez-González, J., Sánchez-González, L., Perez, H., et al.: Combined noise and clock CRLB error model for the optimization of node location in time positioning systems. IEEE Access **8**, 31910–31919 (2020)
4. Alvarez, R., Diez-Gonzalez, J., Strisciuglio, N., Perez, H.: Multi-objective optimization for asynchronous positioning systems based on a complete characterization of ranging errors in 3D complex environments. IEEE Access **8**, 43046–43056 (2020)
5. Álvarez, R., Díez-Gonzalez, J., Verde, P., Ferrero-Guillén, R., Perez, H.: Combined sensor selection and node location optimization for reducing the localization uncertainties in wireless sensor networks. Ad Hoc Netw. **139**, 103036 (2023)
6. Aydemir, S.B., Kutlu Onay, F.: Marine predator algorithm with elite strategies for engineering design problems. Concurr. Comput. Pract. Exp. **35**(7), e7612 (2023)
7. Barral, V., Suárez-Casal, P., Escudero, C., García-Naya, J.A.: Assessment of UWB ranging bias in multipath environments. In: Proceedings of the International Conference on Indoor Positioning and Indoor Navigation (IPIN), Alcala de Henares, Spain, pp. 4–7 (2016)
8. Bottigliero, S., Milanesio, D., Saccani, M., Maggiora, R.: A low-cost indoor real-time locating system based on TDOA estimation of UWB pulse sequences. IEEE Trans. Instrum. Meas. **70**, 1–11 (2021)
9. Chugunov, A., Petukhov, N., Kulikov, R.: ToA positioning algorithm for TDoA system architecture. In: 2020 International Russian Automation Conference (RusAutoCon), pp. 871–876 (2020)
10. Díez-González, J., Álvarez, R., González-Bárcena, D., Sánchez-González, L., Castejón-Limas, M., Perez, H.: Genetic algorithm approach to the 3D node localization in TDOA systems. Sensors **19**(18), 3880 (2019)
11. Díez-Gonzalez, J., Álvarez, R., Perez, H.: Optimized cost-effective node deployments in asynchronous time local positioning systems. IEEE Access **8**, 154671–154682 (2020)
12. Díez-González, J., Álvarez, R., Sánchez-González, L., Fernández-Robles, L., Pérez, H., Castejón-Limas, M.: 3D Tdoa problem solution with four receiving nodes. Sensors **19**(13), 2892 (2019)
13. Díez-González, J., Álvarez, R., Verde, P., Ferrero-Guillén, R., Martínez-Gutiérrez, A., Perez, H.: Optimal node distribution in wireless sensor networks considering sensor selection. In: Sanjurjo González, H., Pastor López, I., García Bringas, P., Quintián, H., Corchado, E. (eds.) SOCO 2021. AISC, vol. 1401, pp. 512–522. Springer, Cham (2022). https://doi.org/10.1007/978-3-030-87869-6_49
14. Díez-González, J., Álvarez, R., Verde, P., Ferrero-Guillén, R., Perez, H.: Analysis of reliable deployment of TDOA local positioning architectures. Neurocomputing **484**, 149–160 (2022)
15. Díez-González, J., Verde, P., Ferrero-Guillén, R., Álvarez, R., Pérez, H.: Hybrid memetic algorithm for the node location problem in local positioning systems. Sensors **20**(19), 5475 (2020)
16. Domingo-Perez, F., Lazaro-Galilea, J.L., Bravo, I., Gardel, A., Rodriguez, D.: Optimization of the coverage and accuracy of an indoor positioning system with a variable number of sensors. Sensors **16**(6), 934 (2016)
17. Elmezughi, M.K., Afullo, T.J.: An efficient approach of improving path loss models for future mobile networks in enclosed indoor environments. IEEE Access **9**, 110332–110345 (2021)

18. Ferrero-Guillén, R., Díez-González, J., Álvarez, R., Pérez, H.: Analysis of the genetic algorithm operators for the node location problem in local positioning systems. In: de la Cal, E.A., Villar Flecha, J.R., Quintián, H., Corchado, E. (eds.) HAIS 2020. LNCS (LNAI), vol. 12344, pp. 273–283. Springer, Cham (2020). https://doi.org/10.1007/978-3-030-61705-9_23

19. Gellert, A., Sarbu, D., Precup, S.A., Matei, A., Circa, D., Zamfirescu, C.B.: Estimation of missing lidar data for accurate AGV localization. IEEE Access **10**, 68416–68428 (2022)

20. Goyal, S., Patterh, M.S.: Modified bat algorithm for localization of wireless sensor network. Wireless Pers. Commun. **86**(2), 657–670 (2016). https://doi.org/10.1007/s11277-015-2950-9

21. Kaune, R., Hörst, J., Koch, W.: Accuracy analysis for TDOA localization in sensor networks. In: 14th International Conference on Information Fusion, pp. 1–8. IEEE (2011)

22. Krška, J., Navrátil, V.: Utilization of carrier-frequency offset measurements in UWB TDoA positioning with receiving tag. Sensors **23**(5) (2023). https://www.mdpi.com/1424-8220/23/5/2595

23. Lopes, S.I., Vieira, J.M.N., Albuquerque, D.: High accuracy 3D indoor positioning using broadband ultrasonic signals. In: 2012 IEEE 11th International Conference on Trust, Security and Privacy in Computing and Communications, pp. 2008–2014 (2012). https://doi.org/10.1109/TrustCom.2012.172

24. Martínez-Gutiérrez, A., Díez-González, J., Ferrero-Guillén, R., Verde, P., Álvarez, R., Perez, H.: Digital twin for automatic transportation in industry 4.0. Sensors **21**(10), 3344 (2021)

25. Martínez Gutiérrez, A., Díez González, J., Verde, P., Ferrero Guillén, R., Pérez, H.: Análisis de algoritmos de navegación para una flota de robots móviles mediante gemelos digitales (2022)

26. Nguyen, N.T., Liu, B.H.: The mobile sensor deployment problem and the target coverage problem in mobile wireless sensor networks are NP-hard. IEEE Syst. J. **13**(2), 1312–1315 (2018)

27. Pan, H., Qi, X., Liu, M., Liu, L.: Indoor scenario-based UWB anchor placement optimization method for indoor localization. Expert Syst. Appl. **205**, 117723 (2022)

28. Rahayu, Y., Rahman, T.A., Ngah, R., Hall, P.: Ultra wideband technology and its applications. In: 2008 5th IFIP International Conference on Wireless and Optical Communications Networks (WOCN 2008), pp. 1–5. IEEE (2008)

29. Saleh, A.A., Valenzuela, R.: A statistical model for indoor multipath propagation. IEEE J. Sel. Areas Commun. **5**(2), 128–137 (1987)

30. Verde, P., Díez-González, J., Ferrero-Guillén, R., Martínez-Gutiérrez, A., Perez, H.: Memetic chains for improving the local wireless sensor networks localization in urban scenarios. Sensors **21**(7), 2458 (2021)

31. Wan, J., Tang, S., Hua, Q., Li, D., Liu, C., Lloret, J.: Context-aware cloud robotics for material handling in cognitive industrial Internet of Things. IEEE Internet Things J. **5**(4), 2272–2281 (2017)

32. Wang, M., Chen, Z., Zhou, Z., Fu, J., Qiu, H.: Analysis of the applicability of dilution of precision in the base station configuration optimization of ultrawideband indoor TDOA positioning system. IEEE Access **8**, 225076–225087 (2020)

33. Wang, W., Zhang, Y., Tian, L.: TOA-based NLOS error mitigation algorithm for 3D indoor localization. China Commun. **17**(1), 63–72 (2020)

34. Witrisal, K., et al.: Localization and tracking. In: Oestges, C., Quitin, F. (eds.) Inclusive Radio Communications for 5G and Beyond, pp. 253–293. Academic Press (2021)

Feature Selection Based on a Decision Tree Genetic Algorithm

Mihai-Alexandru Suciu[✉] and Rodica Ioana Lung

Centre for the Study of Complexity, Babeş-Bolyai University, Cluj-Napoca, Romania
mihai-suciu@ubbcluj.ro, rodica.lung@econ.ubbcluj.ro
http://csc.centre.ubbcluj.ro/

Abstract. The feature selection problem has become a key undertaking within machine learning. For classification problems, it is known to reduce the computational complexity of parameter estimation, but also it adds an important contribution to the explainability aspects of the results. In this paper, a genetic algorithm for feature selection is proposed. The importance, as well as the effectiveness of features selected by each individual, is evaluated by using decision trees. The feature importance indicated by the decision tree is used during selection and recombination. The tree inducted by the best individual in the population is used for classification. Numerical experiments illustrate the behavior of the approach.

Keywords: genetic algorithms · decision trees · feature selection

1 Introduction

Exploring different feature selection mechanisms represents a key step in the process of understanding the behavior of classification models in the presence of redundant or incomplete information while also largely contributing to the model's explainability. As the need for feature selection methods is obvious in the context of big data, from the explainability and attention to detail point of view it can also add value when used in smaller contexts. Ideally, it may provide insight into the contribution of each feature, or group of features, to the overall results and reduce the computational complexity while increasing the explainability.

Evolutionary computation models for feature selection are abundant [2, 3, 12, 16, 18]. Genetic algorithms (GAs) have been the first natural choice, since the binary representation fits within this problem naturally. Many examples of genetic algorithms are mentioned in [18] with applications in various fields. In particular, the combination with decision trees has been appealing from the beginning [1], with many subsequent variants following, expanding to random forests [6] or multiobjective optimization [17]. Another approach uses GAs to

P. García Bringas et al. (Eds.): HAIS 2023, LNAI 14001, pp. 433–444, 2023.
https://doi.org/10.1007/978-3-031-40725-3_37

generate robust parsimonious support vector regression models and feature selection. PSO methods are also used for feature selection, in [3] particle swarm optimization is used to search for accurate models, hypermarameter tuning, and feature selection.

Features selected by using GAs have been used in many practical applications, such as network intrusion detection [13], chemistry [6]. The performance of a decision tree and a naive Bayes method using a genetic algorithm-generated feature set is analyzed in [10]. A complex method combining feature and instances selection is presented in [14].

The complexity of the problem of selecting or identifying important features has led to the development of several mainstream approaches: filter methods, in which features are assigned a value measuring their importance [8], wrapper methods that select feature sets evaluated based on the performance of the classification model fitted based on them [7], and embedded methods, that perform feature selection while building the model, such as decision trees and random forests.

In spite of the large existing body of work, challenges are still multiple and there is room for exploring the behavior of search heuristics for this problem. In real datasets, features are seldom really independent. However, they may contribute in a different way to explaining a particular characteristic. Reducing the data set is always a unpredictable procedure that has to be performed carefully in order to ensure that no important information is lost.

In this paper, a genetic algorithm (GA) wrapper method hybridized with an embedded mechanism is proposed. The wrapper and embedded mechanism use decision trees that provide the GA population with fitness values as well as with feature importances that are used during the recombination and selection process.

2   fsGA-DT: Feature Selection Using a Genetic Algorithm and Decision Trees

The binary classification problem addressed here consists in finding a rule that assigns classes, or labels, to data, based on information provided by a training set in which classes are known. Let $X \subset \mathbb{R}^{n \times d}$ be a data set with n instances and d attributes (or features) and $Y \subset \{0, 1\}^n$ their corresponding labels. The feature selection problem consists of finding the subset of attributes that best explain the data, i.e. that provide a good solution to the classification problem. Minimizing the size of this set is also desirable.

Decision trees [15] are classification and regression models that split the data space into regions as pure as possible, that is, containing most instances in the same class. The tree representation is suitable for this type of rule, as the data is split recursively, usually in a top-down approach starting with the entire data set at the root node. There are many flavors of decision trees, depending on the way the split is performed, the types of hyperplanes used, termination criteria, etc. Axis parallel DTs chose at each node level the best feature to define the hyperplane and split data based on some criterion indicating the strength of the split. Feature importances are then assigned based on their contribution to the tree. A standard way to compute feature importances in trees is by considering the total reduction of the criterion when using that feature (normalized) [9].

fsGA-DT evolves a population of individuals that encode feature sets and uses information provided by decision trees to guide the search. Communication between the GA population and DTs is two-way: information flows from GA to the DT in the form of feature sets and from DT to the GA in the form of performance evaluation and feature importances to be used during the evolution process. Figure 1 illustrates the communication stages within fsGA-DT and Algorithm 1 presents its outline. The details of each phase are explained in what follows.

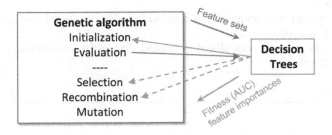

Fig. 1. Communication between GA and DTs. Initialization is performed based on information offered by DTs exclusively. During evaluation feature sets are send to DTs and evaluated, receiving a fitness value and feature importances that are used during selection and recombination.

Encoding. fsGA-DT uses binary encoding. An individual x is represented as a bitstring of size d, where a value of 1 indicates that the corresponding feature is selected and 0 that it is not. For individual x we denote by $FS(x) = \{j_1, \ldots, j_k\}$, $FS(x) \subset \{1, 2, \ldots, d\}$ the set of features that are selected based on it.

Evaluation. An individual x is evaluated by inducting a decision tree on the set $FS(x)$ of features selected by it. The dataset used to select the features is randomly split into a training set containing 70% of instances and a validation set of 30% of instances and the DT is evaluated using the validation set. The AUC (area under the curve [5]) is used as a performance indicator. AUC takes values between 0 and 1 and measures the robustness of the classification with respect to probability thresholds. It can be used to compare results, with the higher value considered the better.

Feature Importance During Evaluation. DT are embedded methods for feature selection. During the tree induction, a decision is made at each node level regarding the feature used to split node data. Based on the structure of the tree, an importance measure is assigned to each feature in the data set. These value are

---

Algorithm 1. fsGA-DT outline

1: **Input:** X, y;
2: **Parameters:** population size p_{size}, maximum number of generations, crossover probability, mutation rate μ, mutation probability, maximum dept of DT, the flavor of DT used for evaluation.
3: **Output:** best individual, Ψ_{best}, over all generations;
4: Initialize population P (using the feature importance of DTs);
5: Set best individual Ψ_{best} at random from P;
6: Evaluate Ψ_{best} using 10 DTs and average AUC values.
7: **for** a number of generations **do**
8:     Evaluate P by computing $FS(x), fs(x)$ for each $x \in P$;
9:     Identify x_{best} in P. Evaluate x_{xbest} using 10 DTs and average AUC values.
10:     Replace Ψ_{best} with x_{best} if better;
11:     Select p_{size} individuals from P using tournament selection (Sect. 2, paragraph Selection);
12:     Apply feature recombination on selected individuals (Sect. 2, paragraph Feature based Crossover);
13:     bitflip mutation on each offspring created through recombination
14:     $P \leftarrow$ offsprings;
15: **end for**
16: **Return:** Ψ_{best}

---

normalized, belong to $[0, 1]$, and are passed to individuals in the population during the evaluation phase. Thus, each individual x is assigned a vector containing the feature importance $fs(x) \in \mathbb{R}^d$. $fs(x)$ will have positive values adding to 1 for features assigned nodes in the evaluating DT and 0 for the other positions.

Initialization. In order to start the search with a population of good solutions, the initialization reverses the evaluation process: a number of decision trees equal to the population size are grown, and individuals in the initial population are created from each tree by setting to 1 all features that have a positive feature importance in the tree. The trees used in this stage are inducted until all leaves are pure, in order to get an overview of potentially useful features from the beginning of the search.

Best Individuals. Each iteration the best individual in the population is re-evaluated by averaging results reported by 10 decision trees in order to reduce the variability in AUC values. fsGA-DT preserves the best individual over all iterations, evaluated in this manner.

Selection. Tournament selection is used based on the fitness value. However, if two individuals have the same fitness (AUC), the one having the mean value of positive feature importance higher is selected. One motivation behind this scheme is to drive the search toward a smaller number of features, as for each individual, the sum of $fs(x)$ adds to 1, and a higher mean indicates a smaller number of values. Another one is to enhance diversity, as for some problems, many distinct settings may yield the same AUC values but with different feature importance values. The goal is to preserve features with higher importance and also use importance values fs during variation.

Feature Based Crossover. The crossover operator creates two offspring o_1 and o_2 from two parents x_1 and x_2 using the following approach: for each feature (bit), the value from x_1 or x_2 with the highest feature importance is copied in o_1 ans it is also copied in o_2 but with a probability equal to the crossover probability p_{cross}. Other features in o_2 are set at random, with a probability of 0.5.

Mutation. fsGA-DT uses bitflip mutation and it is applied with mutation rate on o_1 and o_2 by flipping each bit with a bitflip probability.

Selection for Survival. To enhance diversity, offsprings replace all parents, while the best individual over the entire search, denoted with Ψ_{best}, is preserved separately.

Output and Performance Evaluation. The algorithm outputs the best individual Ψ_{best}. The features indicated by it are used to train a DT and then a test set is used to evaluate the performance of the DT on the features provided by fsGA-DT. From the best individual, features with importances higher than the mean of the individual are selected and used for predictions.

3   Numerical Experiments

Numerical experiments are performed to test the performance of fsGA-DT. We performed experiments on synthetically generated data sets with varying degrees of difficulty and real-world data sets. All data sets represent a binary classification problem. We compare the results obtained by fsGA-DT against a Decision Tree classifier, as the baseline embedded feature selection method.

Data. The difficulty of synthetic data sets is controlled by varying the values of the parameters used to generate them: the number of instances in the data set, the number of attributes, the overlap between data instances of different classes, the number of random attributes added to the generated data set in order to increase the difficulty. In order to ensure reproducibility, we use the make_classification function from the scikit-learn[1] Python library [9]. All combinations of the following parameters for the make_classification function are used: the number of instances (250, 500, 1000), the number of features (50, 100, 150), the number of classes (2), the class separator (0.1, 1), the weight of each class (0.5), and the seed (500). Each combination generates a different data set.

---

[1] version 1.1.1.

The real-world data sets on which we perform experiments are the Connectionist Bench (Sonar, Mines vs. Rocks) data set (R_1) which has 208 instances and 60 attributes; the Parkinson's Disease Classification data set (R_2), which has 756 instances and 754 attributes, and the Musk data set (version 1) (R_3) which has 476 instances and 168 attributes. The data sets are taken from the UCI Machine Learning Repository [4].

Performance Evaluation. To evaluate the performance of each classifier on each test problem, we split the data into train and test instances. Training data consists of 70% of the data instances of the test problem (chosen randomly), and the remaining 30% of data compose the test data. We train the models on the train data and report the AUC (area under the ROC curve) [5,11] for the test data. The AUC can be interpreted as the probability of ranking positive selected samples higher than negative selected samples.

100 independent runs are performed on each data set with different random splits between training and test sets. Data sets are then grouped based on a parameter of the data set (number of instances, number of attributes, overlap), and parameters of the genetic algorithm (size of the population, number of generations, mutation probability for each bit) and ECDF (empirical cumulative distribution function) plots are produced to illustrate the distribution of AUC values reported by the two methods. The plots show the proportion of elements that are less than or equal to a specific point from the plot; when comparing multiple curves on the same plot, the rightmost one indicates a smaller probability of taking smaller values and can be considered better.

Parameter Settings. The parameters used for by fsGA-DT are population size $(50, 100)$, the number of generations $(200, 300)$, crossover probability (0.7), mutation probability (0.2), bit flip mutation probability $(0.03, 0.05)$, and tournament size $(3, 5)$). For the Decision Tree, the split criterion is the *Gini* index, and the maximum depth of the tree is 5. The feature importances computed by the `sklearn.tree.DecisionTreeClassifier` class computed as the normalized total reduction of the criterion brought by that feature is used.

Numerical Results. Figure 2 presents ECDF plots on the synthetic data sets for different parameters and their values and Figs. 3, 4, and 5 present ECDF plots for the real world data sets. Tables 1 and 2 present significance results for a ttest comparing AUC values reported by both methods for the 100 independent runs. The tested null hypothesis is that mean AUC reported by fsGA-DT is smaller than that reported by DT; rejecting it indicates that we can state that differences in results are significant, and fsGA-DT output can be considered better than that of DT. We find that for most settings, the differences in results are significant. The most 'successes' are registered for $d_3 = 1000$ instances and $p_2 = 1$ overlapping parameters. Results reported for the real-world data sets are similar.

Table 1. Statistical comparisons between results obtained by fsGA-DT and DT on the synthetic data sets for different parameter values of the genetic algorithm. The synthetic data sets parameters are: number of instances in the data set (d_1 - 250, d_2 - 500, and d_3 - 1000 data instances), number of attributes (p_1 : 50, 100, 150), classes overlap (p_2 : 0.1, 1). The parameters for the genetic algorithm part of fsGA-DT are: population size (p_3 : 50, 100), number of generations (p_2 : 200, 300, and bit flip mutation probability (p_5 : 0.03, 0.05). A ($\triangle$) symbol indicates that fsGA-DT reports statistically better results, a ($\times$) symbol indicates that the DT approach obtains statistically better results, and a ($-$) symbol indicates no significant difference between results, according to a t-test comparing results on the test sets over the 100 runs.

p_1	p_2	p_3	p_4	p_5	d_1	d_2	d_3	p_1	p_2	p_3	p_4	p_5	d_1	d_2	d_3
50	0.1	50	200	0.03	×	−	△	100	1.0	50	200	0.03	−	△	△
50	0.1	50	200	0.05	△	△	△	100	1.0	50	200	0.05	△	△	△
50	0.1	50	300	0.03	−	△	△	100	1.0	50	300	0.03	△	△	△
50	0.1	50	300	0.05	△	−	△	100	1.0	50	300	0.05	△	△	△
50	0.1	100	200	0.03	−	△	△	100	1.0	100	200	0.03	△	△	△
50	0.1	100	200	0.05	△	−	△	100	1.0	100	200	0.05	△	△	△
50	0.1	100	300	0.03	−	△	△	100	1.0	100	300	0.03	−	△	△
50	0.1	100	300	0.05	△	△	△	100	1.0	100	300	0.05	△	△	−
50	1.0	50	200	0.03	△	△	△	150	0.1	50	200	0.03	−	−	△
50	1.0	50	200	0.05	△	△	△	150	0.1	50	200	0.05	△	△	△
50	1.0	50	300	0.03	△	△	△	150	0.1	50	300	0.03	−	×	×
50	1.0	50	300	0.05	△	△	△	150	0.1	50	300	0.05	△	−	−
50	1.0	100	200	0.03	△	△	△	150	0.1	100	200	0.03	−	−	△
50	1.0	100	200	0.05	△	△	△	150	0.1	100	200	0.05	−	−	△
50	1.0	100	300	0.03	△	△	△	150	0.1	100	300	0.03	−	−	△
50	1.0	100	300	0.05	△	△	△	150	0.1	100	300	0.05	−	×	−
100	0.1	50	200	0.03	×	−	−	150	1.0	50	200	0.03	△	△	△
100	0.1	50	200	0.05	−	−	−	150	1.0	50	200	0.05	△	△	−
100	0.1	50	300	0.03	−	−	△	150	1.0	50	300	0.03	−	△	−
100	0.1	50	300	0.05	×	−	△	150	1.0	50	300	0.05	△	−	−
100	0.1	100	200	0.03	−	△	×	150	1.0	100	200	0.03	−	△	△
100	0.1	100	200	0.05	−	−	−	150	1.0	100	200	0.05	△	△	△
100	0.1	100	300	0.03	×	−	△	150	1.0	100	300	0.03	×	△	−
100	0.1	100	300	0.05	−	△	−	150	1.0	100	300	0.05	−	−	△

Table 2. Same as above: statistical comparisons between results obtained by fsGA-DT and DT on the real world data sets (R_1, R_2, and R_3) for different parameter values of the genetic algorithm: population size (p_1 : 50, 100), number of generations (p_2 : 200, 300, and bit flip mutation probability (p_3 : 0.03, 0.05).

p_1	p_2	p_3	R_1	R_2	R_3
50	200	0.03	–	×	–
50	200	0.05	△	×	△
50	300	0.03	△	–	△
50	300	0.05	–	△	△
100	200	0.03	△	–	–
100	200	0.05	–	–	–
100	300	0.03	△	△	–
100	300	0.05	△	–	△

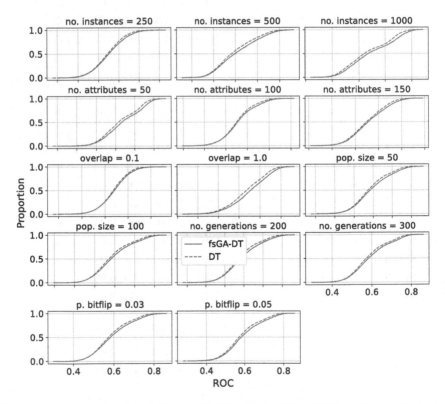

Fig. 2. ECDF plots for the results obtained by fsGA-DT and DT on the synthetic data sets for different parameters. Results are reported for the test data on 100 independent runs. Any point on the curve indicates the percentage (derived from probability) of results with an AUC value lower than the corresponding value on the x axis: thus a the curve on the most right-side, or lower, represents less values lower than the one on the left (above) and can be considered better.

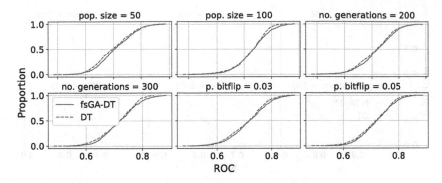

Fig. 3. ECDF plots for the results reported over 100 independent runs by fsGA-DT and DT on the real-world data set R_1. Same as Fig. 2: a point on the curve indicates the percentage (derived from probability) of results with an AUC value lower than the corresponding value on the x axis: thus a the curve on the most right-side, or lower, represents less values lower than the one on the left (above) and can be considered better.

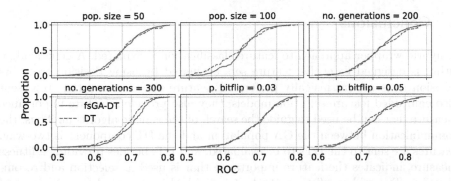

Fig. 4. ECDF plots for the results reported over 100 independent runs by fsGA-DT and DT on the real-world data set R_2. Same as Fig. 2: a point on the curve indicates the percentage (derived from probability) of results with an AUC value lower than the corresponding value on the x axis: thus a the curve on the most right-side, or lower, represents less values lower than the one on the left (above) and can be considered better.

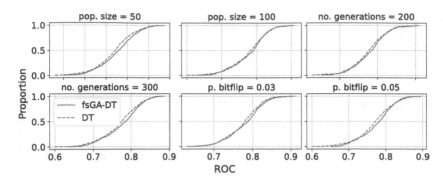

Fig. 5. ECDF plots for the results reported over 100 independent runs by fsGA-DT and DT on the real-world data set R_3. Same as Fig. 2: a point on the curve indicates the percentage (derived from probability) of results with an AUC value lower than the corresponding value on the x axis: thus a the curve on the most right-side, or lower, represents less values lower than the one on the left (above) and can be considered better.

4 Conclusions

A hybrid wrapper approach to feature classification is explored. A genetic algorithm is designed to evolve feature sets evaluated by using decision trees. As decision trees are intrinsically performing feature selection and thus represent also embedded feature selection models, they also provide a feature importance measure that can be used to guide the search of the genetic algorithm. Thus, the communication between the GA population and the DT component is two-way: features are sent to the DTs to be evaluated, and DT, besides providing a fitness measure, indicates the feature importance that is used in selection and recombination. To avoid overfitting, the best individual is evaluated by using several trees grown on randomly split data into train and validation sets.

While there are many approaches based on genetic algorithms to feature selection, results show that there is still room to explore different communication mechanisms and new genetic operators that use specific information from classifiers during evolution. The method presented here can be used as a starting point to explore other options by first validating it by comparisons with other feature selection approaches and by performing extensive numerical experiments in order to identify its strengths and weaknesses on different scenarios.

The feature selection problem is a complex one, and every small step towards improving upon existing methods may add value and add to the understanding of the problem.

Acknowledgements. This work was supported by a grant of the Ministry of Research, Innovation and Digitization, CNCS - UEFISCDI, project number PN-III-P1-1.1-TE-2021-1374, within PNCDI III.

References

1. Bala, J., Huang, J., Vafaie, H., Dejong, K., Wechsler, H.: Hybrid learning using genetic algorithms and decision trees for pattern classification. In: Proceedings of the 14th International Joint Conference on Artificial Intelligence, IJCAI 1995, vol. 1, pp. 719–724. Morgan Kaufmann Publishers Inc., San Francisco (1995)
2. Cai, J., Luo, J., Wang, S., Yang, S.: Feature selection in machine learning: a new perspective. Neurocomputing **300**, 70–79 (2018). https://doi.org/10. 1016/j.neucom.2017.11.077, https://www.sciencedirect.com/science/article/pii/ S0925231218302911
3. Ceniceros, J.F., Sanz-Garcia, A., Pernia-Espinoza, A., Martinez-de-Pison, F.J.: PSO-PARSIMONY: a new methodology for searching for accurate and parsimonious models with particle swarm optimization. Application for predicting the force-displacement curve in T-stub steel connections. In: Sanjurjo González, H., Pastor López, I., García Bringas, P., Quintián, H., Corchado, E. (eds.) HAIS 2021. LNCS (LNAI), vol. 12886, pp. 15–26. Springer, Cham (2021). https://doi.org/10. 1007/978-3-030-86271-8_2
4. Dua, D., Graff, C.: UCI machine learning repository (2017). http://archive.ics.uci. edu/ml
5. Fawcett, T.: An introduction to ROC analysis. Pattern Recognit. Lett. **27**(8), 861–874 (2006). https://doi.org/10.1016/j.patrec.2005.10.010. rOC Analysis in Pattern Recognition
6. Hansen, L., Lee, E.A., Hestir, K., Williams, L.T., Farrelly, D.: Controlling feature selection in random forests of decision trees using a genetic algorithm: classification of class I MHC peptides. Combin. Chem. High Throughput Screen. **12**(5), 514–519 (2009). https://doi.org/10.2174/138620709788488984
7. Kohavi, R., John, G.H.: Wrappers for feature subset selection. Artif. Intell. **97**(1), 273–324 (1997). https://doi.org/10.1016/S0004-3702(97)00043-X, https://www. sciencedirect.com/science/article/pii/S000437029700043X
8. Lazar, C., et al.: A survey on filter techniques for feature selection in gene expression microarray analysis. IEEE/ACM Trans. Comput. Biol. Bioinf. **9**(4), 1106–1119 (2012). https://doi.org/10.1109/TCBB.2012.33
9. Pedregosa, F., et al.: Scikit-learn: machine learning in Python. J. Mach. Learn. Res. **12**, 2825–2830 (2011)
10. Rahmadani, S., Dongoran, A., Zarlis, M., Zakarias: Comparison of naive bayes and decision tree on feature selection using genetic algorithm for classification problem. J. Phys.: Conf. Ser. **978**(1), 012087 (2018). https://doi.org/10.1088/1742-6596/ 978/1/012087, https://dx.doi.org/10.1088/1742-6596/978/1/012087
11. Rosset, S.: Model selection via the AUC. In: Proceedings of the Twenty-First International Conference on Machine Learning, ICML 2004, p. 89. Association for Computing Machinery, New York (2004). https://doi.org/10.1145/1015330.1015400
12. Sanz-Garcia, A., Fernandez-Ceniceros, J., Antonanzas-Torres, F., Pernia-Espinoza, A., de Pison, F.M.: Ga-parsimony: A GA-SVR approach with feature selection and parameter optimization to obtain parsimonious solutions for predicting temperature settings in a continuous annealing furnace. Appl. Soft Comput. **35**, 13–28 (2015). https://doi.org/10.1016/j.asoc.2015.06.012, https://www.sciencedirect. com/science/article/pii/S1568494615003610

13. Stein, G., Chen, B., Wu, A.S., Hua, K.A.: Decision tree classifier for network intrusion detection with GA-based feature selection. In: Proceedings of the 43rd Annual Southeast Regional Conference, vol. 2, pp. 136–141. ACM-SE 43, Association for Computing Machinery, New York (2005). https://doi.org/10.1145/1167253.1167288

14. Theodoridis, P.K., Gkikas, D.C.: Optimal feature selection for decision trees induction using a genetic algorithm wrapper - a model approach. In: Kavoura, A., Kefallonitis, E., Theodoridis, P. (eds.) Strategic Innovative Marketing and Tourism. SPBE, pp. 583–591. Springer, Cham (2020). https://doi.org/10.1007/978-3-030-36126-6_65

15. Utgoff, P.E.: Incremental induction of decision trees. Mach. Learn. **4**(2), 161–186 (1989). https://doi.org/10.1023/A:1022699900025

16. Vafaie, H., De Jong, K.: Genetic algorithms as a tool for feature selection in machine learning. In: Proceedings Fourth International Conference on Tools with Artificial Intelligence TAI 1992, pp. 200–203 (1992). https://doi.org/10.1109/TAI.1992.246402

17. Xue, B., Cervante, L., Shang, L., Browne, W.N., Zhang, M.: Multi-objective evolutionary algorithms for filter based feature selection in classification. Int. J. Artif. Intelli. Tools **22**(04), 1350024 (2013). https://doi.org/10.1142/S0218213013500243

18. Xue, B., Zhang, M., Browne, W.N., Yao, X.: A survey on evolutionary computation approaches to feature selection. IEEE Trans. Evol. Comput. **20**(4), 606–626 (2016). https://doi.org/10.1109/TEVC.2015.2504420

Exact and Heuristic Lexicographic Methods for the Fuzzy Traveling Salesman Problem

Boris Pérez-Cañedo[1,2]([✉]) [iD], Pavel Novoa-Hernández[3] [iD], David A. Pelta[3] [iD], and José Luis Verdegay[3] [iD]

[1] Grupo de Investigación en Modelos de Decisión y Optimización, Departamento de Ciencias de la Computación e Inteligencia Artificial, Universidad de Granada, 18014 Granada, Spain
[2] Department of Mathematics, University of Cienfuegos, 55100 Cienfuegos, Cuba
bpcanedo@gmail.com
[3] Departamento de Ciencias de la Computación e Inteligencia Artificial, Universidad de Granada, 18014 Granada, Spain
{pavelnovoa,dpelta,verdegay}@ugr.es

Abstract. The traveling salesman problem is notorious not only for its significance in theoretical computer science but also for the vast number of real-world problems it is involved in. In this paper, we propose a branch and bound method and a 2-opt method for solving traveling salesman problems, in situations where pairwise distances, costs, or travel times between cities are not known precisely and are modeled with triangular fuzzy numbers. A lexicographic criterion is used for ranking such fuzzy numbers. This approach is shown to produce intuitively better results than those obtained by using linear ranking functions. Computer codes are provided for reproducibility and practical applications. This research also provides a starting point for the extension to the fuzzy environment of other methods for solving classical (non-fuzzy) traveling salesman problems.

Keywords: fuzzy traveling salesman problem · fuzzy linear assignment · fuzzy linear programming · branch and bound · 2-opt heuristic · lexicographic method

1 Introduction

The traveling salesman problem (TSP) is a well-known combinatorial optimization problem notorious for the difficulty of its solution and wide range of practical applications. In today's economic, environmental, and health contexts, the TSP and related routing problems are particularly useful and necessary for modeling a number of practical situations in regard to, e.g., sustainable transportation and tourism, and, in general, the achievement of the Sustainable Development Goals (SDGs) [7,17,19].

P. García Bringas et al. (Eds.): HAIS 2023, LNAI 14001, pp. 445–456, 2023.
https://doi.org/10.1007/978-3-031-40725-3_38

Transportation is a key component of tourism supply chains; efficient and effective management of these supply chains largely depend on it [1]. Undoubtedly, it is in these contexts where models and algorithms of mathematical programming and soft computing (including those of the TSP and related routing problems) are called to play a fundamental role in the recovery of both sectors [19]. Researchers have worked on TSP applications that aim to find solutions to routing problems in the transportation and tourism sectors taking into consideration the SDGs and, in some cases, the current health context. For example, Emre and Umut [7] used a multi-objective TSP to determine the safest and shortest transportation routes for medical waste vehicles during the COVID-19 pandemic in a district of Istanbul. Păcurar et al. [12] solved a TSP in the context of the COVID-19 pandemic to produce tourist routes that avoid overcrowding and ensure that social distancing measures are respected.

A common assumption for solving TSPs is that the pairwise distances, costs, or travel times between the points are known precisely. This is rarely fulfilled in practice due to, e.g., traffic or weather conditions. Therefore, decision-makers are often faced with imperfect information, and decisions may need to be made based on experts' subjective judgments about the possible values of the problem parameters. Fuzzy set theory [20] provides a well-founded mathematical framework for the treatment of such judgments and has been successfully applied to optimization for more than 50 years. The TSP with fuzzy numbers as pairwise distances, costs, or travel times (hereafter FTSP) fits the general fuzzy integer linear programming (FILP) model with imprecise costs proposed in [9], where, among other approaches, it was suggested to use linear ranking functions to transform FILP problems into conventional (non-fuzzy) ones. Several works report using linear ranking functions, e.g. the Center of Gravity method or Yager's index, for solving TSPs in fuzzy environments. Botzheim et al. [4] used a eugenic bacterial memetic algorithm to solve an FTSP in which the distances between cities were modeled with triangular fuzzy numbers (TFNs). The authors used the Center of Gravity method to rank fuzzy numbers. Yager's ranking index was used in [11] to solve fuzzy linear assignment problems (FLAPs) and FTSPs with LR-type fuzzy numbers. Kuchta [10] proposed a fuzzy generalized TSP (see [16] for an introduction) with travel times represented by TFN, in which cities are not treated as single points but as networks with their own points to visit. Changdar et al. [6] developed an algorithm that combines an ant colony algorithm with a genetic algorithm to solve a solid multiple TSP, in which costs for traveling between cities using different conveyances are fuzzy-rough variables compared according to a linear ranking function.

In [14], however, it was shown that using linear ranking functions to solve fuzzy linear programming problems does not always guarantee solutions with unique optimal objective values, i.e. there may exist other solutions that produce intuitively better values. Consequently, a lexicographic method was proposed to solve FLAPs in [13], and in the review paper [15] computer codes were provided.

The linear assignment problem (LAP) is known to constitute a relaxed version of the classical TSP, in which the subtour elimination constraints are removed

[2,17]. So, existing methods for solving FLAPs, such as those proposed in [3,11,13] could also be used, along with classical branch and bound schemes [2,17], to solve FTSPs. Following this idea, in this paper, we propose two lexicographic methods for solving the FTSP and compare them with their counterparts based on linear ranking functions. Specifically,

- A branch and bound method is developed for the FTSP; it uses the FLAP for lower bound calculations and lexicographic ranking criteria for comparing fuzzy numbers,
- The 2-opt heuristic for solving non-fuzzy TSPs is extended to the fuzzy case using lexicographic ranking criteria,
- Computer codes for solving FTSPs are developed in the Python programming language.[1]

In addition to the previous contributions, our aim is to demonstrate, from a methodological point of view, the advantages of using lexicographic ranking criteria for solving the FTSP, and how such criteria can be used to extend to the fuzzy case existing models and algorithms for solving conventional (non-fuzzy) TSPs. Furthermore, by focusing our attention not only on the theoretical dimension of the problem but also on developing computer codes for its solution, this research is a starting point for the design of future automated decision-making systems that effectively handle fuzzy uncertainty in routing problems raised in the framework of the SDGs. The rest of this paper is organized as follows. The basic definitions and a mathematical model for the FTSP are presented in Sect. 2. The main contributions are introduced in Sect. 3. An example is given in Sect. 4 for illustration purposes. Lastly, concluding remarks are presented in Sect. 5.

2   Fuzzy Model for the Traveling Salesman Problem

This section presents the fundamental definitions used throughout the paper and ends with a formulation of the FTSP. We use a common parametric representation of TFNs given by $\tilde{a} = (\underline{a}, a, \overline{a})$, with $[\underline{a}, \overline{a}]$ and a as the supporting interval and the peak value, respectively. Basic definitions and arithmetic operations with these fuzzy numbers can be found in [20] and [8].

2.1   Preliminaries

Definition 1. *For an arbitrary TFN $\tilde{a} = (\underline{a}, a, \overline{a})$, let $f_k(\tilde{a}) := w_{k1}\underline{a} + w_{k2}a + w_{k3}\overline{a}$ ($k = 1, 2, 3$) be three linear functions of the parameters of $\tilde{a}$ with each w_{kr} chosen so that the matrix $[w_{kr}]$ is non-singular. Furthermore, let $\leq_{lex}$ denote the lexicographic order relation on $\Re^3$. Given two TFNs $\tilde{a}$ and $\tilde{b}$, then:*

1. $\tilde{a} \prec \tilde{b}$ if and only if $\left(f_k(\tilde{a}) \right)_{k=1,2,3} <_{lex} \left(f_k(\tilde{b}) \right)_{k=1,2,3}$;

---

[1] Download available from GitHub https://github.com/bpcanedo/ftsp.git.

2. $\tilde{a} \preccurlyeq \tilde{b}$ if and only if $\left(f_k(\tilde{a})\right)_{k=1,2,3} <_{lex} \left(f_k(\tilde{b})\right)_{k=1,2,3}$ or $\left(f_k(\tilde{a})\right)_{k=1,2,3} = \left(f_k(\tilde{b})\right)_{k=1,2,3}$.

Theorem 1. *Let $\tilde{a}$ and $\tilde{b}$ be arbitrary TFNs, and let f_1, f_2 and f_3 be given as in Definition 1. Then, $\tilde{a} = \tilde{b}$ if and only if $\left(f_k(\tilde{a})\right)_{k=1,2,3} = \left(f_k(\tilde{b})\right)_{k=1,2,3}$.*

The proof follows from the non-singularity of matrix $[w_{kr}]$, as stated in Definition 1.

2.2   Problem Formulation

Suppose a salesman leaves a city (call it 1) and needs to visit other cities, indexed by $(2, 3, \ldots, n)$, exactly once, and then return to city 1. The cost of traveling from city i to city j is uncertain and is modeled with a non-negative TFN denoted by $\tilde{c}_{ij}$. The aim is to determine a sequence (tour) in which the cities are visited that minimizes the total cost of the tour. This problem can be formulated as the following mixed-integer fuzzy linear programming problem.

$$\min \ \tilde{z}(x) = \sum_{i=1}^{n} \sum_{j=1}^{n} \tilde{c}_{ij} \times x_{ij} \tag{1}$$

$$\text{s.t.} \sum_{j=1}^{n} x_{ij} = 1 \quad (i = 1, 2, \ldots, n), \tag{2}$$

$$\sum_{i=1}^{n} x_{ij} = 1 \quad (j = 1, 2, \ldots, n), \tag{3}$$

$$u_i - u_j + n x_{ij} \leq n - 1 \quad (i, j = 2, \ldots, n \text{ and } i \neq j), \tag{4}$$

where the x_{ij} $(i, j = 1, 2, \ldots, n)$ are binary variables (with $x_{ij} = 1$ if the salesman travels from city i to city j, and $x_{ij} = 0$ otherwise) and the u_i $(i = 2, 3, \ldots, n)$ are non-negative real variables. The objective function (1) states that a tour of minimum cost is desired. Constraints (2) and (3) guarantee that each city is visited only once. Lastly, constraints (4) are the Miller-Tucker-Zemlin subtour elimination constraints.

3   Proposed Methods

In this section, we propose an exact method and a heuristic method to solve the FTSP. They constitute fuzzy extensions of known methods for solving non-fuzzy TSPs. Furthermore, instead of using linear ranking functions as in previous works [4, 6, 10, 11], we use a lexicographic criterion; hence, the following definition of an optimal solution for the FTSP:

Definition 2. *A solution x^* that satisfies the relations (2) to (4) (i.e. feasible) is said to be optimal for the FTSP if, according to Definition 1, there is no feasible x such that $\tilde{z}(x) \prec \tilde{z}(x^*)$, i.e. $\left(f_k(\tilde{z}(x))\right)_{k=1,2,3} <_{lex} \left(f_k(\tilde{z}(x^*))\right)_{k=1,2,3}$.*

3.1   Branch and Bound Method

The branch and bound method for the FTSP that will be presented shortly is based on the one described in [2] for the conventional TSP. The authors described the LAP relaxation of the TSP and some associated branching rules. We will follow this approach and use the FLAP as a relaxation of the FTSP. The lexicographic method in [13] will be used to solve each FLAP (see Appendix A). The steps of the proposed branch and bound method are as follows:

Step 1. Relax the FTSP by removing the subtour elimination constraints (4), i.e. transform the problem into an FLAP.

Step 2. Solve the FLAP obtained in Step 1 by using the lexicographic method [13]—see Appendix A. If the solution contains no subtours, then an optimal solution has been found; stop. Otherwise, store the problem in a list of *live* problems.

Step 3. While the list of *live* problems is not empty and a maximum number of iterations has not been reached, perform Steps 3.1 and 3.2.

> **Step 3.1.** Select one problem from the list and branch on it, i.e. create as many subproblems as the number of distinct cities a subtour in its corresponding solution has (each subproblem is created by assigning a large constant $\tilde{M}$ to the entry of the cost matrix corresponding to two consecutive cities in the subtour).
>
> **Example:** Let us suppose that a solution to a 4-city problem is $x_{14} = 1$, $x_{41} = 1$, $x_{23} = 1$, $x_{32} = 1$. This solution contains the subtours 1-4-1 and 2-3-2; therefore, it is not feasible for the FTSP. To prevent subtour 1-4-1 from recurring in solutions to subsequent subproblems, let $\tilde{c}_{14} = \tilde{M}$ for the first subproblem and $\tilde{c}_{41} = \tilde{M}$ for the second one.
>
> **Step 3.2.** Solve the subproblems (FLAPs) created in the previous step by using the lexicographic method [13]. Discard those subproblems whose solutions have objective function values that do not improve the best-found value. Those that improved, if feasible (i.e. contain no subtours), replace the best solution found so far. If they are not feasible, then store them in the list of *live* problems.

Step 4. Return the best solution.

Remark 1. To avoid transforming each FLAP into a lexicographic linear assignment problem (LLAP) repeatedly, and thus to improve efficiency in steps 2 and 3.2, initially each element $\tilde{c}_{ij}$ in the cost matrix of the FTSP is transformed into the tuple $\left(f_k\left(\tilde{c}_{ij}\right)\right)_{k=1,2,3}$ by using Definition 1, and the resulting matrix is used thereafter. Furthermore, the current implementation uses *depth first search* in Step 3.1 as the subproblem selection strategy and a strengthened branching rule (rule no. 3 in [2]).

3.2   2-opt Heuristic Method

The 2-opt heuristic is a simple yet powerful local search heuristic for the TSP. Given an initial tour, it repeatedly replaces two non-adjacent arcs with two others such that the resulting tour has a lower cost [18]. For example, let us consider the following tour in a 7-city FTSP $T = (1, 3, 2, 5, 4, 6, 7, 1)$. The non-adjacent arcs could be $(3, 2)$ and $(6, 7)$. 2-opts replaces these arcs with $(3, 6)$ and $(2, 7)$, and reverses the subpath $(2, 5, 4, 6)$; thus it produces a new tour $\bar{T} = (1, 3, 6, 4, 5, 2, 7, 1)$. The new tour is accepted if, according to Definition 1, $\mathrm{Cost}(\bar{T}) \prec \mathrm{Cost}(T)$. The evaluation of the cost function is easier if the problem is symmetric, in which case $\bar{T}$ is accepted if $\tilde{c}_{36} \oplus \tilde{c}_{27} \prec \tilde{c}_{32} \oplus \tilde{c}_{67}$. In general, given two non-adjacent arcs (v_i, v_{i+}) and (v_j, v_{j+}) in the current tour $T = (1, \ldots, v_i, v_{i+}, \ldots, v_j, v_{j+}, \ldots, 1)$, 2-opt replaces these arcs with (v_i, v_j) and (v_{i+}, v_{j+}) and reverses the subpath $(v_{i+}, \ldots, v_j)$; thus a new tour $\bar{T}_{ij} = (1, \ldots, v_i, v_j, \ldots, v_{i+}, v_{j+}, \ldots, 1)$ is obtained, which replaces T if $\mathrm{Cost}(\bar{T}) \prec \mathrm{Cost}(T)$. The procedure continues until no further improvements are possible.

4 Illustrative Example and Comparison with Linear Ranking Function-Based Approach

In this section, we present a toy example to illustrate the proposed methods. All calculations were carried out using the developed codes and the Kuhn-Munkres algorithm for solving LAPs provided in module Munkres 1.1.4 (see https://software.clapper.org/munkres/), with Python 3.8.3 on a computer with an Intel® Core™ i3-4005U @ 1.70GHz × 4 and 4GB RAM running Ubuntu 20.04.3 LTS.

We consider a 9-city FTSP that models a situation in which a tourist wishes to visit nine points of interest (POIs) in a city, but travel costs (in terms of the time taken to go from one POI to another) cannot be determined exactly and are estimated using TFNs.[2]

In Table 1, we present optimal and approximate solutions to this problem obtained by using the proposed lexicographic methods and the linear ranking function-based approach. We use Yager's index $f_1(\tilde{a}) = (\underline{a} + 2a + \overline{a})/4$ as the first comparison index, which is an extensively used in the literature for comparing fuzzy numbers, and the peak value and length of the supporting interval of $\tilde{a}$ as the second and third comparison indexes, respectively.

Table 1. Results obtained with the proposed approach and the existing one.

	Branch and Bound Method		2-opt Method with 100 restarts	
	Tour	Objective value	Tour	Objective value
Lexicographic criterion	$(1, 4, 8, 7, 3, 2, 5, 6, 9, 1)$	$(777.0, 989.0, 1265.0)$	$(1, 8, 7, 5, 4, 3, 2, 6, 9, 1)$	$(781.5, 1001.0, 1236.5)$
Linear ranking function	$(1, 8, 7, 5, 4, 3, 2, 6, 9, 1)$	$(781.5, 1001.0, 1236.5)$	$(1, 8, 7, 5, 4, 3, 2, 6, 9, 1)$	$(781.5, 1001.0, 1236.5)$

Figure 1 depicts the fuzzy costs of the tours obtained via branch and bound. It is noticeable that using a lexicographic criterion instead of a single linear ranking function produces an intuitively better solution to the FTSP.

---

[2] The cost matrix is available at https://github.com/bpcanedo/ftsp.git.

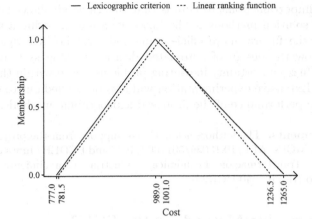

Fig. 1. Fuzzy costs of the tours.

Furthermore, we see from Table 1 that the same results were obtained by 2-opt regardless of the criterion used. Because 2-opt is a heuristic method, there is no guarantee that it will succeed in finding optimal solutions. However, the experimental results shown in Fig. 2 from Appendix B indicate that it is less likely that the ranking function-based approach will reach the optimal solution of the FTSP or outperform the lexicographic approach. The same happens if we permute the comparison indices, although very similar (but still in favor of the lexicographic approach) results are observed in this example if the peak value is used as the first comparison index. Nevertheless, this superiority of the lexicographic approach is achieved at the expense of increased execution time.[3]

The results presented are preliminary, and a more complete characterization of the performance of the lexicographic 2-opt method would require further experimentation with matrices of different sizes. We leave this for future work together with applying the proposed method for case studies analysis in the tourism sector within the SDGs framework.

5   Concluding Remarks

In this paper, we proposed a lexicographic branch and bound method and a lexicographic 2-opt heuristic method to solve FTSPs. The results showed that the lexicographic approach produces intuitively better results than those obtained using a linear ranking function-based approach. Computer codes were provided for reproducibility and practical applications. Since the TSP is an NP-hard problem in the general setting, the proposed methods are expected to face the same limitations as the classical ones when solving large instances of the problem.

---

[3] Computer codes to replicate these results are available at https://github.com/bpcanedo/ftsp.git.

However, an important point to note is that this research shows how to extend existing TSP solution methods to the fuzzy environment using a lexicographic approach. In the future, more efficient methods will be investigated to solve FTSPs to allow the design of automated decision-making systems that effectively handle fuzzy uncertainty in routing problems raised within the framework of the SDGs. Extensive experimentation will also be carried out to obtain information on the performance of the proposed lexicographic methods.

Acknowledgements. The authors acknowledge support from the projects PID2020-112754GB-I00, MCIN/AEI /10.13039/501100011033 and FEDER/Junta de Andalucía-Consejería de Transformación Económica, Industria, Conocimiento y Universidades/Proyecto (B-TIC-640-UGR20).

A   Lexicographic Method for the FLAP

The FLAP can be formulated as the fuzzy integer linear programming problem

$$\min \sum_{i=1}^{n}\sum_{j=1}^{n} \tilde{c}_{ij} \times x_{ij} \tag{5}$$

$$\text{s.t. constraints (2) and (3),}$$

where the x_{ij} $(i,j = 1,2,\ldots,n)$ are binary variables. Definition 1 was used in [13] to transform problem (5) into LLAP (6).

$$\operatorname*{lexmin} \sum_{i=1}^{n}\sum_{j=1}^{n} c_{ij}x_{ij} \tag{6}$$

$$\text{s.t. constraints (2) and (3),}$$

where $c_{ij} = \Big(f_1\left(\tilde{c}_{ij}\right), f_2\left(\tilde{c}_{ij}\right), f_3\left(\tilde{c}_{ij}\right)\Big)$ $(i,j = 1,2,\ldots,n)$.

Theorem 2. *An optimal solution to LLAP* (6) *is optimal for FLAP* (5).

Proof. See [13].

Burkard et al.'s [5] general algebraic framework can be used to efficiently solve LLAP (6). In their framework, it is assumed that the LAP cost coefficients are elements of a totally ordered commutative semigroup $\left(H, *, \leq \right)$, with internal composition $*$ and total order relation $\leq$, which fulfills the following properties:

1. $\forall x,y,z \in H,\ x \leq y \implies x*z \leq y*z$ (i.e. $\leq$ is compatible with $*$),
2. $\forall x,y \in H$ with $x \leq y\ \exists z \in H$ such that $x*z = y$.

The authors developed a method, similar to the Hungarian method, to find optimal assignments by using the concept of an admissible transformation, i.e. a transformation that does not alter the relative order of the assignments. The following theorem describes admissible transformations for algebraic assignment problems (see [5]).

Theorem 3. *Let $I, J \subseteq \{1, 2, \dots, n\}$, $m = |I| + |J| - n \geq 1$, and $c = \min\{c_{ij} : i \in I, j \in J\}$. Then the transformation of matrix C into matrix $\bar{C}$, $T : C \mapsto \bar{C}$, defined by*

$$\bar{c}_{ij} * c = c_{ij} \quad i \in I, j \in J,$$
$$\bar{c}_{ij} = c_{ij} * c \quad i \notin I, j \notin J,$$
$$\bar{c}_{ij} = c_{ij} \quad otherwise,$$

is admissible with $z_T = c * c * \cdots * c$, where the expression in the right-hand side contains m factors.

It can be shown that $\left(\mathbb{R}^3, +, \leq_{\text{lex}}\right)$ is a totally ordered commutative semigroup that meets the properties mentioned above. Consequently, LLAP (6) can be solved with the following method proposed in [5], using $+$ and $\leq_{\text{lex}}$ in place of $*$ and $\leq$, respectively.

Step 1. Perform row reductions in matrix C, i.e. perform admissible transformations as in Theorem 3 with $I = \{k\}$, $J = \{1, 2, \dots, n\}$. Start with $k = 1$ and let $z := z_T$ be the corresponding index. Continue with $k = 2, \dots, n$ and update $z := z * z_T$. Afterward, all elements in the transformed matrix are non-negative with respect to z, i.e. $z \leq \bar{c}_{ij} * z$.

Step 2. Perform column reductions, i.e. perform admissible transformations with $I = \{1, 2, \dots, n\}$, $J = \{k\}$, for $k = 1, 2, \dots, n$. Afterward, every row and column in the transformed cost matrix contains at least one 0-element. All other elements remain non-negative with respect to z.

Step 3. Determine a maximum matching in the following bipartite graph $G = (V; W; E)$, where V contains the row indices of the transformed cost matrix, W the column indices, and $(i, j) \in E$, if and only if $\bar{c}_{ij} * z = z$.

Step 4. If the maximum matching is perfect, then stop: The optimal solution is given by this matching and z is the optimal value of the objective function. Otherwise, go to Step 5.

Step 5. Determine a minimum cover of the transformed cost coefficients with a value of 0. This cover produces the new index sets I and J. I contains the indices of the uncovered rows and J contains the indices of the uncovered columns.

Step 6. Perform an admissible transformation determined by the new index sets I and J as in Theorem 3, update $z := z * z_T$, and go to Step 3.

B   Preliminary Experimental Results

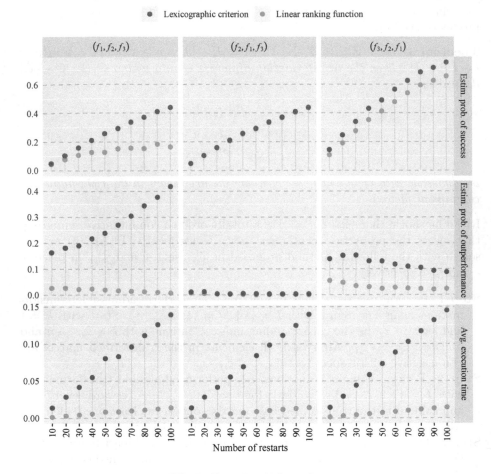

Fig. 2. Experimental results.

References

1. Aćimović, S., Mijušković, V.M., Todorović, I., Spasenić, A.T.: The role and impor- tance of transport within the tourism supply chain. In: Karanovic, G., Poly- chronidou, P., Karasavvoglou, A., Maskarin Ribaric, H. (eds.) Tourism Manage- ment and Sustainable Development. CE, pp. 93–106. Springer, Cham (2021). https://doi.org/10.1007/978-3-030-74632-2_7
2. Balas, E., Toth, P.: Branch and bound methods. In: Lawler, E.L., Lenstra, J.K., Rinnooy Kan, A.H.G., Shmoys, D.B. (eds.) The Traveling Salesman Problem: A Guided Tour of Combinatorial Optimization, pp. 361–401. Wiley, Chichester (1985)

3. Baykasoğlu, A., Subulan, K., Karaslan, F.S.: A new fuzzy linear assignment method for multi-attribute decision making with an application to spare parts inventory classification. Appl. Soft Comput. **42**, 1–17 (2016). https://doi.org/10.1016/j.asoc.2016.01.031

4. Botzheim, J., Földesi, P., Kóczy, L.T.: Solution for fuzzy road transport traveling salesman problem using eugenic bacterial memetic algorithm. In: IFSA/EUSFLAT Conference, pp. 1667–1672 (2009)

5. Burkard, R.E., Hahn, W., Zimmermann, U.: An algebraic approach to assignment problems. Math. Program. **12**, 318–327 (1977). https://doi.org/10.1007/BF01593800

6. Changdar, C., Pal, R.K., Mahapatra, G.S.: A genetic ant colony optimization based algorithm for solid multiple travelling salesmen problem in fuzzy rough environment. Soft. Comput. **21**(16), 4661–4675 (2016). https://doi.org/10.1007/s00500-016-2075-4

7. Eren, E., Rıfat Tuzkaya, U.: Safe distance-based vehicle routing problem: medical waste collection case study in COVID-19 pandemic. Comput. Industr. Eng. **157**, 107328 (2021). https://doi.org/10.1016/j.cie.2021.107328

8. Hanss, M.: Applied Fuzzy Arithmetic. Springer, Heidelberg (2005). https://doi.org/10.1007/b138914

9. Herrera, F., Verdegay, J.: Three models of fuzzy integer linear programming. Eur. J. Oper. Res. **83**(3), 581–593 (1995). https://doi.org/10.1016/0377-2217(93)E0338-X

10. Kuchta, D.: Fuzzy stage dependent travelling salesman problem with networks as nodes. In: Borzemski, L., Grzech, A., Świątek, J., Wilimowska, Z. (eds.) ISAT 2015, Part I. AISC, vol. 429, pp. 89–100. Springer, Cham (2016). https://doi.org/10.1007/978-3-319-28555-9_8

11. Kumar, A., Gupta, A.: Methods for solving fuzzy assignment problems and fuzzy travelling salesman problems with different membership functions. Fuzzy Inf. Eng. **3**(1), 3–21 (2011). https://doi.org/10.1007/s12543-011-0062-0

12. Păcurar, C.M., Albu, R.G., Păcurar, V.D.: Tourist route optimization in the context of COVID-19 pandemic. Sustainability **13**(10), 5492 (2021). https://doi.org/10.3390/su13105492

13. Pérez-Cañedo, B., Concepción-Morales, E.R.: A lexicographic approach to fuzzy linear assignment problems with different types of fuzzy numbers. Internat. J. Uncertain. Fuzziness Knowl.-Based Syst. **28**(03), 421–441 (2020). https://doi.org/10.1142/S0218488520500178

14. Pérez-Cañedo, B., Concepción-Morales, E.R.: A method to find the unique optimal fuzzy value of fully fuzzy linear programming problems with inequality constraints having unrestricted L-R fuzzy parameters and decision variables. Expert Syst. Appl. **123**, 256–269 (2019). https://doi.org/10.1016/j.eswa.2019.01.041

15. Pérez-Cañedo, B., Verdegay, J.L., Concepción-Morales, E.R., Rosete, A.: Lexicographic methods for fuzzy linear programming. Mathematics **8**(9) (2020). https://doi.org/10.3390/math8091540

16. Pop, P.C.: The generalized traveling salesman problem (GTSP). In: Generalized Network Design Problems, pp. 60–99. De Gruyter (2012). https://doi.org/10.1515/9783110267686.60

17. Punnen, A.P.: The traveling salesman problem: applications, formulations and variations. In: Gutin, G., Punnen, A.P. (eds.) The Traveling Salesman Problem and Its Variations. Combinatorial Optimization, vol. 12, pp. 1–28. Springer, Boston (2007). https://doi.org/10.1007/0-306-48213-4_1

18. Rego, C., Glover, F.: Local search and metaheuristics. In: Gutin, G., Punnen, A.P. (eds.) The Traveling Salesman Problem and Its Variations. Combinatorial Optimization, vol. 12, pp. 309–368. Springer, Boston (2007). https://doi.org/10.1007/0-306-48213-4_8
19. Verdegay, J.L., Brito, J., Cruz, C. (eds.): Computational Intelligence Methodologies Applied to Sustainable Development Goals. Studies in Computational Intelligence, Springer, Cham (2022). https://doi.org/10.1007/978-3-030-97344-5
20. Zadeh, L.: Fuzzy sets. Inf. Control 8(3), 338–353 (1965). https://doi.org/10.1016/S0019-9958(65)90241-X

A Novel Genetic Algorithm
with Specialized Genetic Operators
for Clustering

Hermes Robles-Berumen[1] , Amelia Zafra[2]([envelope]) , and Sebastián Ventura[2]

[1] Department of Electrical Engineering and Earth Science,
Autonomous University of Zacatecas, Jardín Juárez 147 Centro,
98000 Zacatecas, Mexico
hermes@uaz.edu.mx

[2] Department of Computer Science and Numerical Analysis, Andalusian Research
Institute in Data Science and Computational Intelligence (DaSCI),
University of Cordoba, Campus Universitario de Rabanales, 14071 Córdoba, Spain
{azafra,sventura}@uco.es

Abstract. Clustering is an unsupervised learning task that groups objects in a multi-dimensional space based on similarity criteria. The goal is to make groups that contain objects that are similar to each other and different from other groups. This work proposes a novelty genetic algorithm to solve the clustering problem based on partitions and estimate automatically the number of clusters. The proposal, GASGO (Genetic Algorithm with Specialized Genetic Operators), includes a representation based on codebooks and the use of specialized and improvement mutation and crossover operators that achieve a high performance to solve clustering problems. The experimental study evaluates 10 clustering validation indexes, 46 data sets, and 8 previous proposals of GAs for clustering considered the state of the art in the area. Results show that GASGO improves the performance for all CVIs compared to the previous proposals.

Keywords: Genetic Algorithms · Clustering · Machine Learning

1 Introduction

Clustering or cluster analysis is a data mining task classified as an unsupervised exploratory analysis technique [10]. It attempts to group a set of patterns (represented in a multidimensional space) into groups or clusters based on similarity criteria. Intuitively, patterns within a cluster are more similar to each other than patterns belonging to other clusters. The clustering problem can be posed as an optimization problem that tries to find the most appropriate grouping of the data by optimizing some objective related to the properties of the groups, such as compactness (similar objects are within the same group) or the separation (different objects are in different groups). These properties are known as the goodness of the clustering solution and are measured using Clustering Validation Indexes (CVIs) [1].

P. García Bringas et al. (Eds.): HAIS 2023, LNAI 14001, pp. 457–468, 2023.
https://doi.org/10.1007/978-3-031-40725-3_39

Clustering has been applied to a wide variety of problems in many different fields. Despite its great importance and the enormous research efforts devoted to designing new clustering algorithms, there is still a need to develop new proposals that efficiently solve the problem in different fields [8].

Our work is focused on solving partitional clustering using Genetic Algorithms (GAs). GAs are presented as efficient and robust optimization and search techniques in large and complex search spaces, achieving optimal or very close to optimal solutions. In the last few years, evolutionary computing algorithms have been widely applied to clustering problems, due to their capacity to adapt to different problems with very few changes, and to manage constraints in an efficient way. Thus, different proposals employing different encodings, operators, and evaluation functions have been developed. This paper proposes a new proposal that uses a codebook-based encoding to reduce computational complexity and the application of specialized crossover and mutation genetic operators that achieve a robust algorithm for clustering. Our proposal offers good performance in different scenarios and estimates correctly the number of clusters. The main contribution of this work can be summarized in the following points:

- It presents a new proposal based on GA that carries out grouping task and automatically estimates the optimal number of groups.
- It uses a codebooks-based representation. This solution encoding is combined with crossover and mutation operators designed for clustering problem that allow a more efficient search and, as a consequence, finds better clusters.
- An extensive experimental study is carried out that considers both the optimization on the estimation of the number of clusters and on CVIs. Concretely, it is considered 8 algorithms, 48 data sets and 10 CVIs.
- The source code of our proposed is included at LEAC library [18] with the rest of previous proposals. In addition, information of experiments are publicly available in the LEAC repository to support future comparison.

The rest of the paper is organized as follows, Sect. 2 discusses the state-of-the-art of clustering with GAs in the literature. In Sect. 3, we present our proposal based on GA for clustering. In Sect. 4, we present our experimental results and compare those results with the state-of-the-art. Finally, in Sect. 5, we conclude the paper and focus on possible extensions of the present work.

2   Clustering Techniques Based on Genetic Algorithms

GAs have been used widely for solving clustering tasks due to their capability to solve optimization problems. Several research efforts in developing GA-based clustering algorithms have been reported in the literature. In this work, the study is focused on GAs that predict both the number of clusters and the grouping task using one objective. Following, the main features with respect to encoding, genetic operators and fitness function are described.

One of the first proposals is VGA (A Variable-string-length Genetic Algorithm) [5]. It uses a coding based on centroids with numeric values with represent the centroids of each group. It uses traditional genetic operators (one-point crossover and uniform mutation). It uses a step of Kmeans algorithm as a local search operator. The fitness function is I index (a CVI proposed by authors). Then, GCUK (Genetic Clustering for Unknown K) [6] was proposed. It uses a coding based on centroids with numeric values with represent the centroids of each group. It uses traditional genetic operators (one-point crossover and uniform mutation). It uses a step of Kmeans algorithm as a local search operator and the fitness is the Davies-Bouldin index.

Later, Hruschka et al. [14] propose CGA (Clustering Genetic Algorithm). It uses coding based on labels with integer numbers that represent the cluster to which each instance belongs. It uses specialized genetic operators, crossover by a combination of groups, and mutation based on the splitting and merging of groups. The fitness function is the Silhouette function. Afterward, Hruschka et al. developed a new proposal, EAC (Evolutionary Algorithm for Clustering) [13]. It uses coding based on labels with integer numbers that represent the cluster to belong to each instance. It uses Kmeans algorithm as a search local operator that replaces the crossover operator and a specialized mutation operator based on split and merger groups. It uses a simplified silhouette index as the fitness function. An evolution of EAC to be faster is proposed by Alves et al. [3,17]. It is called FEAC (Fast Evolutionary Algorithm for Clustering). It is similar to EAC, but linearly normalizes the fitness function of each group to achieve a more efficient proposal. Two proposals are developed with two different fitness functions: rand index and simplified silhouette.

More recently, it is developed GGA (Grouping Genetic Algorithm) [2]. It uses coding based on labels with integer numbers that represent the cluster to which each instance belongs. It uses a specialized crossover operator to combine groups and a mutation operator specialized for splitting and merging groups. For evolution, they propose an island model that allows parallelling the procedure. It uses a local search called optimum for the neighbor. It used the Davies-Bouldin index as the fitness function. Finally, TGCA (Two-Stage Genetic Clustering Algorithm) [12] is proposed by He et al. It uses two phases. First, it focuses on the search for the best number of clusters and then deals to find the globally optimal cluster centers. It uses a coding based on centroids with a numeric value that represents the centroids of each cluster. It uses traditional crossover and mutation operators (one-point crossover, min-max mutation and generation of new individuals). It uses Kmeans as a local search operator and the fitness function is the VRC index.

3   Proposed Model

This section describes the algorithm GASGO (Genetic Algorithm with Specific Genetic Operators). The general process of the algorithm is described in Fig. 1 and its main features are described in the following sections. The parent selector is a roulette selection, the stopping criterion is the number of generations and population update applies elitism keeping the best solutions of the previous population.

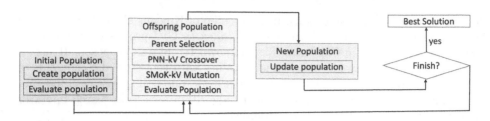

Fig. 1. The main steps of GASGO.

3.1   Individual Representation

Individuals are coded using codebooks that have proven their efficiency working with GA [9]. A codebook is equivalent to the combination of encodings based on centroids and label-based to determine explicitly the membership of all vectors. Our representation is adapted to work with variable-size solutions due to that the number of clusters is unknown and the algorithm must obtain the optimal value for each data set. In addition, it is used an array of instance indexes, similar to a linked list, to facilitate certain operations, like adding or removing instances to a group, when the genetic operators are applied.

The individual chromosome (solution) represented by χ is $[\{\mu_j\}|\{C_j\}]$.

$$[\{\mu_j\}|\{C_j\}] = [[\mu_1, \mu_2, ..., \mu_{k_v}]|[\alpha_1, \alpha_2, ..., \alpha_n]]$$

where $\{\mu_j\}$ is the jth centroid, $\{C_j\}$ is the group of instances associated to each centroid $j : j \in \{1, ..., k\}$ and α_i is the group label to which instance, x_i, belongs.

3.2   Initialization of the Population

In the first generation, a random population representing different search space solutions is created at the initial stage. This random sampling is carried out in two steps:

- Initialization of number of groups. It is generated random values of k to establish the number of initial groups of each chromosome, this number will be between $\in [2, \sqrt{n}]$ being n the number of instances in the dataset.
- Initialization of centroids. It is selected random instances to be the initial centroids of each solution.

3.3   Genetic Operators

GASGO uses both crossover and mutation operator that have been adapted to obtain a high performance for solving clustering task and work with the specific individual encoding.

Crossover Operator. The crossover operator is based on Pairwise Nearest Neighbor (PNN) method [9]. In our proposal, the properties of PNN method are studied and customized to be used to find the optimal number of groups.

This extended crossover from CBGA algorithm [9] and that we have called PNN-kV (Pairwise Nearest Neighbor for k Variable) is described in Fig. 2. It receives two codebook chromosomes and generates one new codebook chromosome. The novelty is that the codebook of each parent represents a different number of clusters, k and k', respectively and the new offspring will have a different also value, k''. In this operator, the offspring obtains new centroids combining the centroids of each parent. Each cluster is generated based on partitions of the two parents and each instance is included in the group with the shorter distance. Then, empty clusters are removed and centroids are updated with the new groups. The last step applies PNN-kV method, but previously, the value of k'' is randomly selected from an interval $[k''_{min}, k''_{max}]$ where $k''_{min} = min(k, k') - (max(k, k') - min(k, k')) \cdot 0.5$ and $k''_{max} = max(k, k') + (max(k, k') - min(k, k')) \cdot 0.5$. Moreover, a restriction limits the minimum value of k'' to 2 and the maximum value to $\sqrt{n}$. The procedure that merges the clusters is based on [9].

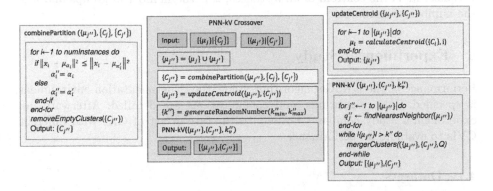

Fig. 2. The Crossover operator

Mutation Operator. The mutation operator allows exploring different numbers of groups splitting groups, merging groups or keeping groups with a new distribution. It has been called SMoK-kV mutation (Split, Merged or Kept groups for k variable). This operator receives one codebook chromosome and generates one new codebook chromosome. First, the Mühlenbein procedure improved [11] determines the number of clusters k' for the new individual.

$$k' = k \pm (k_{\max} - k_{\min}) \cdot \gamma \qquad (1)$$

where $\gamma = \sum_{i=a+1}^{b} \alpha_i 2^{-i}$, $a = \xi_1 \times \frac{\text{Current generation}}{\text{Max generations}}$, $b = a + \xi_2$, $\alpha_i \in \{0, 1\}$ is randomly generated with $P(\alpha_i = 1) = \frac{i-a}{2 \times \xi_2}$. The parameters ξ_1 y ξ_2 are defined by user, $k_{\max} = \sqrt{n}$, $k_{\min} = 2$, the signed $\pm$ is selected with 0.5 probability. It is included the restriction that k' is limited to $[k_{\min}, k_{\max}]$.

Obtained k', there are three possibilities: if $(k' < k)$ then, it is necessary to reduce the number of groups. This method uses an inversely proportional roulette to the average radius of the groups. If $(k' > k)$ then, it is necessary to add new clusters. This method uses a proportional roulette to the average radius of the groups. Finally, if $(k' = k)$ then, it is necessary to change the distribution of the groups maintaining the number of clusters. This method selects one group and its centroid is removed. Then, Kmeans method is applied with $k' - 1$ and a centroid is selected and split. In the case that $k = 2$, an instance is randomly selected and it is used as a new centroid.

3.4   Fitness Function

The fitness function uses Variance Ratio Criterion (VRC). This index measures the internal cohesion of the group and the isolation from external groups.

$\text{VRC} = \frac{SS_B}{SS_W} \cdot \frac{(n-k)}{(k-1)}$ where $SS_B = \sum_{j=i}^{k} |C_j| \|\mu_j - M\|^2$ is the overall variance between groups and $SS_W = \sum_{j=1}^{k} \sum_{x_i \in C_j} \|x_i - \mu_j\|^2$ is the overall within-group variance, M is the centroid of all instances, k is the number of groups and n is the number of instances.

4   Experimental Study

Performance of the GASGO algorithm. First, the experimentation environment is specified: data, algorithms, and configurations are detailed. Afterward, an experimental study compares GASGO with state of art of GAs with different CVIs to evaluate its performance.

4.1   Datasets

Data sets include both synthetic and real data that cover a wide range of properties. The 46 algorithms have different numbers of instances, classes, and attributes. Table 1 shows the most important characteristic of each data set, such as the number of instances, attributes, and classes. Although clustering does not use the number of classes, it is selected data sets with this information to evaluate measures that require this information.

Data sets have been converted. Thus, nominal attributes with v values are transformed to v binary attributes, numerical attributes have been normalized using the Z_5 method [16], and missing values are eliminated. Information after adaptions is shown in Table 1. In addition, data sets used with transformations commented are available at Github en LEAC.

Table 1. Data sets description

Synthetic dataset				Real dataset			
Name	Attributes	Instances	Classes	Name	Attributes	Instances	Classes
A1	2	3000	20	Appendicitis	7	106	2
A2	2	5250	35	Banana	2	5300	2
A3	2	7500	50	Cleveland	13	303(297)	5
Aggregation	2	788	7	Dermatology	34	366(358)	6
Compound	2	399	6	Ecoli	7	336	8
D31	2	3100	31	Hepatitis	19	155(80)	2
Dim2	2	1351	9	Leaves plant	64	1600	100
Dim32	32	1024	16	Magic	10	19020	2
Dim128	128	1024	16	Mammographic	5	961(830)	2
Flame	2	240	2	Marketing	13	8993(6876)	9
G2-8-20	8	2048	2	Optdigits	64	5620	10
G2-8-80	8	2048	2	Page blocks	10	5473	5
G2-128-20	128	2048	2	Phoneme	5	5404	2
G2-128-80	128	2048	2	Pima	8	768	2
Jain	2	373	2	Saheart	9(9)	462	2
Path-based	2	300	3	Segment	19	2310	7
R15	2	600	15	Spambase	57	4601	2
S1	2	5000	15	Spect heart	22	267	2
S2	2	5000	15	Thyroid	21	7200	3
S3	2	5000	15	Vowel	13	990	11
S4	2	5000	15	Wdbc	30	569	2
Spiral	2	312	3	Wisconsin	9	699(683)	2
Unbalance	2	6500	8	Yeast	8	1484	10

4.2 Clustering Validation Indexes

CVIs are used to evaluate the performance of clustering algorithms. This study considers 10 relevant measures to analyze the algorithms [4]. Concretely, six internal indexes and three external indexes are used. Internal indexes evaluate clustering in terms of structural characteristics of groups formed. External indices evaluate clustering based on a predefined structure, which is imposed on the data set and reflects the known grouping of the data set.

Three internal indexes that assess the *Compactness* property in the groups are used:

- Sum of euclidean distances (SED) = $\sum_{C_j} \sum_{x_i \in C_j} \|x_i - \mu_j\|$ where μ_j is the centroid of j-th group C_j.
- Sum of square error (SSE) = $\sum_{C_j} \sum_{x_i \in C_j} (x_i - \mu_j)^T (x_i - \mu_j)$ $= \sum_{C_j} \sum_{x_i \in C_j} \|x_i - \mu_j\|^2$ where μ_j is the centroid of j-th group C_j.
- Distortion Distance (DD) = $\sum_{C_j} \sum_{x_i \in C_j} \|x_i - \mu_j\|^2/(n \cdot d)$ where n and d are the number of instances and the number of features, respectively.

Four internal indexes that assess both the *Compactness* and *Separation* properties of the groups are used:

- Davies-Bouldin index (DB) = $\frac{1}{k} \sum_j^k R_{C_j,qt}$ where $R_{C_j,qt} = \max_{j,j \neq j'} \{(S_{C_j,q} + S_{C'_j,q})/\|\mu_j - \mu'_j\|_t\}$, $\|\|_t$ is the Minkowski distance and $S_{C_j,q} = \left(\frac{1}{|C_j|} \sum_{x_i \in C_j} \{\|x_i - \mu_j\|_2^q\}\right)^{1/q}$ is the dispersion inside of C_j.

- Xie-Beni index (XB) $= \frac{\sum_{j=1}^{k} \sum_{x_i}^{n} u_{ji}^2 \|x_i - \mu_j\|^2}{n \cdot (d_{min})^2}$, where $d_{min} = \min_{j,j'=1, j \neq j'}^{k}$ $\|\mu_j - \mu_{j'}\|$.
- Silhouette index (S) $= \sum_i^n s(x_i)/n$. Given $x_i \in C_j$, $s(x_i) = (b(x_i) - a(x_i))/ \max\{a(x_i), b(x_i)\}$, where $a(x_i) = \sum_{x_{i'} \in C_j} D(x_i, x_{i'})/|C_j|$ and $b(x_i) = \min \{D(x_i, x_{i''}) \mid x_{i''} \in C_{j''} \text{ y } C_j \neq C_{j''}\}$.
- Dunn index (SD) $= \min_{1 \leq j \leq k} \left\{ \min_{1 \leq j' \leq k, j' \neq j} \left\{ \frac{\delta(C_j, C_{j'})}{\max_{1 \leq j'' \leq k} \{\Delta(C_{j''})\}} \right\} \right\}$, where $\delta(C_j, C_{j'})$ $= \min\{D(x_i, x_{i'}) \mid x_i \in C_j, x_{i'} \in C_{j'}\}$ and $\Delta(C_{j''}) = \max\{D(x_i, x_{i''}) \mid x_i, x_{i''} \in C_{j''}\}$ is the diameter of $C_{j''}$.

Finally, three external measures are considered. For these measures, it is necessary to know the real classes considered in the dataset. For all measures is considered a, patterns belonging to the same group and the same class and the same group; b, patterns belonging to the same class and different groups; c, patterns belonging to different classes but the same group and d, patterns belonging to different classes and different groups.

- Rand index $(\Omega) = \frac{a+d}{a+b+c+d}$
- Jaccard index (J) $= \frac{a}{a+b+c}$
- Recall $= \frac{a}{a+b}$

4.3 Algorithms

This study includes 8 GAs considered the state of the art that solve the clustering problem and estimate the number of clusters. They are presented in Sect. 2. All proposals included GASGO algorithm are included in the library LEAC [18]. It is an open library available in LEAC github.

The configuration parameters of different algorithms are described in Table 2. These values correspond to the default configuration values by the authors of each algorithm and it used the same parameters for all datasets.

Table 2. Configuration parameters of GAs

GA	Number Generations	Population Size	Crossover Probability	Mutation Probability
GGA [2]	100	4×20	$P_c(j)$ [12]	$P_m(j)$ [12]
CGA [14]	200	20	*	*
EAC [13]	500	20	*	*
FEAC [3,17]	500	20	*	*
VGA [5]	1000	50	0.8	0.05
GCUK [6]	100	50	0.8	0.001
TGCA [12]	200	60	$P_s(i)$ [12]	$P_m(i)$ [12]
GASGO	300	50	p_c (Eq. (2))	p_m (Eq. (3))

*It does not employ crossover and mutation probabilities. After the selection process, these operators are applied in some selected genotypes.

In our proposal the probability of crossover and mutation are adaptive based on [7]:

$$p_c = \begin{cases} k_1 \times \frac{\mathcal{F}_{\max} - \mathcal{F}'}{\mathcal{F}_{\max} - \bar{\mathcal{F}}} & \text{si } \mathcal{F}' > \bar{\mathcal{F}} \\ k_3 & \text{if } \mathcal{F}' \leq \bar{\mathcal{F}} \end{cases} \qquad (2)$$

$$p_m = \begin{cases} k_2 \times \frac{\mathcal{F}_{\max} - \mathcal{F}(\chi_\iota)}{\mathcal{F}_{\max} - \bar{\mathcal{F}}} & \text{if } \mathcal{F}(\chi_\iota) > \bar{\mathcal{F}} \\ k_3 & \text{if } \mathcal{F}(\chi_\iota) \leq \bar{\mathcal{F}} \end{cases} \qquad (3)$$

where k_1 y k_3 are 1, k_2 and k_4 are 0.5, $\mathcal{F}'$ is the best value of fitness of the individuals to crossover and $\mathcal{F}_{\max}$ is the maximum value of fitness of the current population and $\bar{\mathcal{F}}$ is the average value of the current population.

For the experimental study was used cross-validation 10-fold. Due to the randomness of the models, 20 runs were performed for each partition and the mean values of the test are shown in the results.

4.4   Study of Clustering Validations Indexes

This study evaluates the performance of GASGO algorithm on 10 CVIs considering both internal and external measures. For this study, it is compared our proposal with the previous proposals considered the state of the art of GAs with k variable described in Sect. 2.

To perform this comparison, we performed a statistical study to determine if there are significant differences in the results of the CVIs comparing all data sets and all proposals. It is used a non-parametric test, Friedman's test [15]. A Friedman's test is carried out for each performance metric by algorithms across all datasets. For each measure, Friedman's test gives a ranking value that is assigned to each algorithm. The algorithm with the best value for one dataset receives a rank of 1, the following a rank of 2, and so on. Finally, we computed the average rank for each algorithm. The lower the mean rank, the better results of the algorithm for the metric in more datasets. Table 3 shows the ranking values for each algorithm and measure. It can be seen that our proposal obtains one of the lowest values in most of the measures. It indicates that it obtains the best values compared to the rest of the algorithms. To obtain generalized results involving all the studied metrics, we have followed a meta-ranking study. To this end, we have applied Friedman's test on the average ranks of each algorithm considering all measures. The last row of Table 3 contains the ranking values for this analysis. It is worth highlighting that our proposals obtains the lowest average rank value.

Friedman's test results are shown in Table 4. They indicate significant differences between algorithms with a 99% of confidence. The results of subsequently Shaffer's post-test are graphically represented in Fig. 3. GASGO achieves the best performance obtaining the lowest ranking value with a wide difference between the second and third proposals. Another interesting observation is that

Table 3. Ranking values for algorithm and CVI for all data sets

Measure	GASGO	CGA	EAC	FEAC$_{RI}$	FEAC$_{SS}$	GCUK	GGA	TGCA	VGA
S. Euclidean Distances (SED)	4.2174	7.1848	5.9348	3.8370	5.0217	3.4130	5.2283	4.6630	5.5000
S. Square Error (SSE)	4.0543	6.9783	6.0109	4.1304	5.0870	3.3043	5.1957	4.6957	5.5435
Distortion Distance (DD)	3.8587	6.9022	5.9891	4.1413	4.9457	3.3804	5.3370	4.8152	5.6304
Silhouette index (S)	3.6739	3.5435	4.8043	6.2826	4.5652	5.1196	3.5870	6.4239	7.0000
Davies–Bouldin index (DB)	3.9674	4.4239	3.8587	6.7283	3.4022	4.1957	4.9674	7.3261	6.1304
Xie Beni index (XB)	3.6957	3.4674	4.7065	6.8370	4.2935	3.8587	4.3587	7.4022	6.3804
Dunn's index (D)	3.6413	4.0326	5.0435	6.2935	4.9565	4.9022	4.3043	5.6304	6.1957
Rand index (Ω)	3.9239	5.4348	5.2065	2.5761	5.0109	5.2826	5.0870	6.2717	6.2065
Jaccard index(J)	3.9130	4.7174	5.1848	3.4674	5.1522	6.0543	4.5326	6.2717	5.7065
Recall	4.6333	2.7667	4.1778	5.2778	4.5444	6.6667	4.4667	6.3000	6.1667
Ranking	**2.500**	4.800	5.600	4.800	4.100	4.300	4.400	7.100	7.400

Table 4. Results of Friedman test (CVIs)

Statistical Test	df	p-value
Friedman's chi-squared = 24.693	df = 8	= 0.001752
Iman Davenport's correction of Friedman's rank Corrected Friedman's chi-squared = 4.0183	df1 = 8 df2 = 72	= 0.000548

both VGA and TGCA obtain significantly worse results than the other proposals.

In conclusion, GASGO has obtained the best values both in the internal measurements of compactness and separation and in the external measurements. TGCA, which is another algorithm that uses the same fitness function that GASGO, obtains significantly worse results in this study. This shows the importance of properly combining all the components of a GA to achieve high performance in the search process and obtain the best partitions.

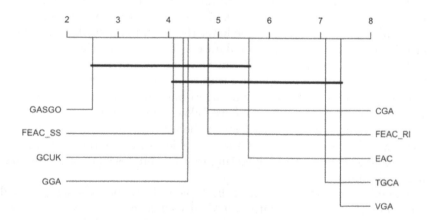

Fig. 3. Critical distance of Shaffer's post-test for CVIs ($\alpha = 0.01$)

5   Conclusions

This paper introduces Genetic Algorithm with Specialized Genetic Operators (GASGO), a GA for solving partitional clustering. GASGO encodes solutions using codebooks that have proven their efficiency working with GA. This representation together with specialized genetic operators achieves a robust algorithm that carries out an efficient search process to solve clustering problems. Genetic operators combine methods such as the PNN method, the Mühlenbein procedure and the Kmeans method and include the estimation of the number of clusters in all phases. Furthermore, representation and operators are optimized so that GASGO obtains a high performance.

An exhaustive experimental study assessed the performance of GASGO against 8 representatives GAs, 46 data sets and 10 CVIs. Results have shown that GASGO obtains the best results considering all CVIs and data sets.

Future work can focus on several aspects. Exhaustive studies on computational time and estimation of the number of clusters should be carried out to show that GASGO is competitive in both parameters. The evaluation of these measures is very relevant in current studies. Moreover, other clustering approaches, more data sets and CVIs considering different properties should be analyzed to draw relevant conclusions.

Acknowledgements. This research was supported in part by grant PID2020-115832GB-I00 funded by MICIN/AEI/10.13039/501100011033 and by the ProyExcel-0069 project of University, Research and Innovation Department of the Andalusian Board and the European Regional Development Fund.

References

1. Abdalameer, A.K., Alswaitti, M., Alsudani, A.A., Isa, N.A.M.: A new validity clustering index-based on finding new centroid positions using the mean of clustered data to determine the optimum number of clusters. Expert Syst. Appl. **191**, 116329 (2022)
2. Agustín-Blas, L.E., Salcedo-Sanz, S., Jiménez-Fernández, S., Carro-Calvo, L., Del Ser, J., Portilla-Figueras, J.A.: A new grouping genetic algorithm for clustering problems. Expert Syst. Appl. **39**(10), 9695–9703 (2012)
3. Alves, V.S., Campello, R.J.G.B., Hruschka, E.R.: Towards a fast evolutionary algorithm for clustering. In: IEEE International Conference on Evolutionary Computation, Vancouver, BC, Canada, 16–21 July, pp. 1776–1783 (2006)
4. Arbelaitz, O., Gurrutxaga, I., Muguerza, J., Pérez, J.M., Perona, I.: An extensive comparative study of cluster validity indices. Pattern Recogn. **46**(1), 243–256 (2013)
5. Bandyopadhyay, S., Maulik, U.: Nonparametric genetic clustering: comparison of validity indices. Trans. Syst. Man Cybern. Part C **31**(1), 120–125 (2001)
6. Bandyopadhyay, S., Maulik, U.: Genetic clustering for automatic evolution of clusters and application to image classification. Pattern Recogn. **35**(6), 1197–1208 (2002)
7. Chang, D.X., Zhang, X.D., Zheng, C.W.: A genetic algorithm with gene rearrangement for k-means clustering. Pattern Recogn. **42**(7), 1210–1222 (2009)

8. Ezugwu, A.E., et al.: A comprehensive survey of clustering algorithms: state-of-the-art machine learning applications, taxonomy, challenges, and future research prospects. Eng. Appl. Artif. Intell. **110**, 104743 (2022)
9. Fränti, P.: Genetic algorithm with deterministic crossover for vector quantization. Pattern Recogn. Lett. **21**(1), 61–68 (2000)
10. Gan, G., Ma, C., Wu, J.: Data Clustering: Theory, Algorithms, and Applications. SIAM (2020)
11. Haghrah, A., Nazari-Heris, M., Mohammadi-Ivatloo, B.: Solving combined heat and power economic dispatch problem using real coded genetic algorithm with improved mühlenbein mutation. Appl. Therm. Eng. **99**, 465–475 (2016)
12. He, H., Tan, Y.: A two-stage genetic algorithm for automatic clustering. Neurocomputing **81**, 49–59 (2012)
13. Hruschka, E.R., Campello, R.J.G.B., de Castro, L.N.: Evolving clusters in gene-expression data. Inf. Sci. **176**(13), 1898–1927 (2006)
14. Hruschka, E.R., Ebecken, N.F.F.: A genetic algorithm for cluster analysis. Intell. Data Anal. **7**(1), 15–25 (2003)
15. Kvam, P., Vidakovic, B., Kim, S.: Nonparametric Statistics with Applications to Science and Engineering with R, vol. 1. Wiley, Hoboken (2022)
16. Milligan, G., Cooper, M.: A study of standardization of variables in cluster analysis. J. Classif. **5**, 181–204 (1988)
17. Naldi, M.C., Campello, R.J., Hruschka, E.R., de Carvalho, A.C.: Efficiency issues of evolutionary k-means. Appl. Soft Comput. **11**, 1938–1952 (2011)
18. Robles-Berumen, H., Zafra, A., Fardoun, H.M., Ventura, S.: LEAC: an efficient library for clustering with evolutionary algorithms. Knowl. Based. Syst. **179**, 117–119 (2019)

The Analysis of Hybrid Brain Storm Optimisation Approaches in Feature Selection

Dragan Simić[1]([⊠]) [iD], Zorana Banković[2], José R. Villar[3] [iD], José Luis Calvo-Rolle[4] [iD], Svetislav D. Simić[1] [iD], and Svetlana Simić[5] [iD]

[1] Faculty of Technical Sciences, University of Novi Sad, Trg Dositeja Obradovića 6, 21000 Novi Sad, Serbia
dsimic@eunet.rs, {dsimic,simicsvetislav}@uns.ac.rs
[2] Frontiers Media SA, Paseo de Castellana 77, Madrid, Spain
[3] University of Oviedo, Campus de Llamaquique, 33005 Oviedo, Spain
villarjose@uniovi.es
[4] Department of Industrial Engineering, University of A Coruña, 15405 Ferrol-A Coruña, Spain
jlcalvo@udc.es
[5] Faculty of Medicine, University of Novi Sad, Hajduk Veljkova 1–9, 21000 Novi Sad, Serbia
svetlana.simic@mf.uns.ac.rs

Abstract. The volume of data available has risen significantly in recent years due to advancements in data gathering techniques in different fields. The collected data in many domains are typically of high dimensionality, making it impossible to select an optimum range of features. There are many existing research papers that discuss feature selection process used by metaheuristic algorithm. One of them is brain storm optimisation (BSO) algorithm, which is relatively new swarm intelligence algorithm that mimics the brainstorming process in which a group of people solve a problem together. The aim of this paper is to present and analyse hybrid BSO algorithm solutions combined with other metaheuristic algorithms in feature selection process. The hybrid BSO algorithm overcomes the lack of exploitation in the original BSO algorithm; and simultaneously, the obtained statistical results prove the efficiency and robustness over other state-of-the-art approaches.

Keywords: Brain storm optimisation algorithm · feature selection · metaheuristic · classification · clustering

1 Introduction

In recent times, data include raw material from all information. This data and information in turn provide knowledge through modelling, data mining, analysis, interpretation, and visualisation. The volume of data available has risen significantly in recent years due to advancements in data gathering techniques in different fields, resulting in increased processing time and space complexity. The collected data in many domains are typically of high dimensionality, making it impossible to select an optimum range of features and exclude unnecessary ones [1]. Inappropriate features in the dataset lead to a poor recognition rate and a large drop in their analysis and outcomes.

© The Author(s), under exclusive license to Springer Nature Switzerland AG 2023
P. García Bringas et al. (Eds.): HAIS 2023, LNAI 14001, pp. 469–480, 2023.
https://doi.org/10.1007/978-3-031-40725-3_40

Feature selection (FS) refers to techniques for selecting a subset of input features that are most relevant to the target variable being predicted. By removing unnecessary and outdated features, FS reduces the dimensionality and improves the quality of the resulting attribute vector [2]. FS has been used for various purposes, including: gene prediction [3], speech recognition [4], classification and diagnosis of breast cancer and diabetes [5, 6], etc.

A metaheuristic algorithm is a search procedure designed to find a good solution to an optimisation problem for complex problems. It is imperative to find a near-optimal solution based on imperfect or incomplete information in this real-world of limited resources; it takes computational power and time. Researchers now face a hurdle in the implementation and high-precision suggestion of modern metaheuristics for real-world applications. As a result, several researchers are working to solve FS challenges by using hybrid metaheuristics. By merging and coordinating the exploration and exploitation processes, hybridisation aims to identify compatible alternatives to ensure the best possible output of the applied optimisation methods. A typical strategy for addressing such issues is to combine the advantages of various independent architectures through the hybridisation of metaheuristic methods [7, 8]. Contrary to these ideas, features can be selected at random, but it does not guarantee an improvement of accuracy.

In 2011, a metaheuristic-based algorithm called brain storm optimisation (BSO) algorithm was developed [9]. The algorithm is motivated by the brainstorming process of humans. Brainstorming is a creative way of solving a specific problem by a group of people. In the brainstorming process, several people share their ideas with each other related to the problem that should be solved, where any idea is acceptable and criticism is not allowed. In the end, from all suggested ideas, the best possible solution is selected. Similarly, in the BSO algorithm, initially random solutions are generated; as in any other swarm intelligence algorithm, each solution is analogous to an idea in the brainstorming process. At every iteration the idea is modified; in other words, the solution's position is updated according to the previous knowledge. The solutions are diverged into several clusters. One individual or more individuals are selected to generate new solutions by some genetic operators.

Numerous research papers develop and apply the classic BSO algorithm. Some multi-objective optimisation problems (MOPs) based on BSO algorithms are proposed. In these multi-objective BSO algorithms, population is updated by new solutions after the solutions are clustered, which may decrease the speed of convergence [10, 11]. Therefore, BSO is not only an optimisation method but it could also be viewed as a framework for solving other real-word problems.

The aim of this paper is to analyse some implementations of BSO algorithm and other metaheuristics-based algorithms to solve feature selection. The authors would like to compare other researches which are based on hybrid BSO solutions in feature selection. The authors have experience in various approaches, such as: (i) first, feature selection [12, 13]; and (ii) second, research in BSO [14], and (iii) finally, research in clustering methods [15–18].

The rest of the paper is organized in the following way: Sect. 2 provides an overview of the basic idea on: (i) feature selection process; and (ii) brain storm algorithm. Modelling and applications of the bio-inspired hybrid systems combining BSO algorithm and metaheuristics-based algorithm for solving feature selection process are presented in Sect. 3. Section 4 provides conclusions and some directions for future research.

2 Feature Selection and Brain Storm Optimisation Algorithm

Feature selection techniques can be applicable to any area where there is a chance of facing the dimensionality problem. However, at the beginning, it is interesting to precisely define the term *feature selection* relative to *feature extraction*. It can sound the same but some differences exist.

Feature selection is a type of data pre-processing task that consists of removing irrelevant and redundant features in order to improve the predictive performance of data clustering and/or classifying methods. The dataset with the full set of features is the input to the feature selection method, which will select a subset of features. Irrelevant features can be defined as features that are not correlated with the class variable, and removing such features will not be harmful for the predictive performance. Redundant features can be defined as those features which are strongly correlated with other features, so that removing those redundant features should also not be harmful for the predictive performance [19].

On the same way, a feature of a given parameter set refers to an attribute described by one or more elements of the original pattern vector. In an application to imaging, the elements are each pixel, and a feature may be selected as a subset of the pixel intensity values. More commonly, a feature describes some combinations of the original pixels.

The precise meanings of a pre-processing operation and a *feature extraction* process overlap, but in general a feature extraction operation involves the reduction in dimensionality of the pattern vector. The primary reason for such a transformation is to provide a set of measurements with more discriminatory information and less redundancy. The classifier/cluster tool depends on the information from a feature extraction device, and thus cannot normally provide that information without a completely designed feature extractor. This enigma remains the primary reason for the difficulty in evaluating competing feature extraction methods. These techniques can be effective, though they increase the complexity of the process. Many common mathematical parameters are used as feature measurements. A set of *n-space* Euclidean distance measurements is a very common example. In other situations where the identity of the patterns is known, transformation matrices for minimising intra-set pattern entropy or intra-set pattern dispersion and functional approximation methods are commonly used.

Feature extraction involves reducing the number of resources required to describe a large set of data. When performing analysis of complex data, one of the major problems stems from the number of variables involved. Analysis with a large number of variables generally requires a large amount of memory and computation power. It may also cause a classification algorithm to overfit to training samples and generalise poorly to new samples. Feature extraction is a general term for methods of constructing combinations of variables to tackle these problems, while still describing the data with sufficient accuracy. Many machine learning (ML) practitioners believe that properly optimized feature extraction is the key to effective model construction [20].

One of the well-known methods for lowering the number of features used for classification is principal component analysis (PCA). The PCA method transforms the original feature set to a new space where the obtained features are orthogonal and named principal components. The maximal variation in the original dataset is represented by the first principal component. The problem with the PCA method is that it does not preserve the original features which are sometimes necessary. Therefore, in order to preserve features, numerous methods based on metaheuristics were proposed, and that will be the focus of this research.

2.1 Feature Selection

Feature selection is important, as irrelevant and redundant input variables can distract or mislead learning algorithms, possibly resulting in lower predictive performance. Additionally, it is desirable to develop models using only the data that is required to make a prediction.

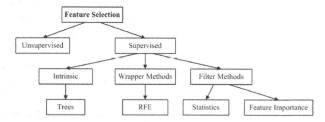

Fig. 1. Overview of feature selection techniques (Adapted from [21])

Feature selection methodologies may generally group into the following: (*I*) supervised – that use the target variable; and (*II*) unsupervised – that do not use the target variable. Additionally, the supervised feature selection techniques fall into three general classes: (*i*) intrinsic (or implicit) methods – that automatically select features as part of fitting the model; (*ii*) filter methods – those that score each input feature and allow a subset to be selected; and (*iii*) wrapper methods – those that explicitly choose features that result in the best performing model.

The applied feature selection methods depend on data types. The general overview of feature selection techniques is presented in Fig. 1 [21]. A *wrapper method* such as the popular *Recursive Feature Elimination* (RFE) method can be used, since it is agnostic to the input variable type. When a mixture of input variable data types is present, different *Filter methods* can be used. *Statistical methods*, such as correlation, are popular for scoring input features. The features can then be ranked by their scores and a subset with the largest score can be used as input to a model. The choice of statistical measures depends on the data type of the input variables. The broader field of scoring the *Relative Importance* of input features is referred to as feature importance and there are numerous model-based techniques whose outputs can be used to aid in interpreting the model, interpreting the dataset, or in selecting features for modelling.

The basic feature selection process can be determined in four steps (aspects) shown in Fig. 2.: (i) Generating process: Generate the candidate feature subset; (ii) Evaluation criteria: Evaluate the characteristics of the subset; (iii) Stop criterion: Decide when to

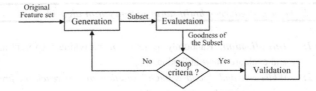

Fig. 2. The process diagram of feature selection (Adapted from [21])

stop; and (iv) Verification and Validation results: Verify that the expected results are achieved [21].

2.2 Brain Storm Optimisation

Brain storm optimisation (BSO) is relatively new swarm intelligence algorithm. It is inspired by collective behaviour of human beings. It has attracted a number of researchers and has good performance in its applications for complex problems.

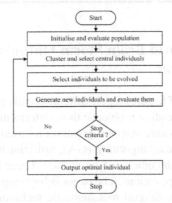

Fig. 3. The execution workflow of brain storm optimisation algorithms (Adapted from [22])

Brainstorming is a process of collecting new ideas about a specific problem from a group of people without any prejudicing or ordering. Then, these ideas are evaluated and filtered one by one to select the best idea. The general description of BSO flowchart is displayed in Fig. 3 [22].

The basic steps of BSO are summarised by the pseudo code revealed in Algorithm 1. In a BSO algorithm, the solutions are separated into several clusters. The best solution of the population will be kept if the new generated solution at the same index is not better. New individual can be generated based on one or two individuals in clusters. The exploitation ability is enhanced when the new individual is close to the best solution found till that moment. The exploration ability is enhanced when the new individual is randomly generated, or generated by individuals in two clusters.

Algorithm 1 *The basic procedure of brain storm optimisation algorithm*

Begin

Step 1:	***Initialisation.*** Randomly generate **n** individuals (potential solutions), and evaluate the **n** individuals;
Step 2:	**While** *not find "good enough" solution or not reach the pre-determined maximum number of iterations* **do**
Step 3:	***Solution clustering/classification*** *operation: Diverge **n** individuals into **m** groups by a clustering/classification algorithm;*
Step 4:	***New solution generation*** *operation: Select solution(s) from one or two group(s) randomly to generate new individual (solution);*
Step 5:	***Solution selection*** *operation: Compare the newly generated individual (solution) and the existing individual (solution) with the same individual index; the better one is kept and recorded as the new individual;*
Step 6:	*Evaluate the **n** individuals (solutions);*
Step 6:	**end While**
Step 7:	*Post-process the results and visualisation;*

End.

---

3   Modelling the Hybrid Brain Storm Optimisation Algorithms for Feature Selection

Finding the optimal subset of features for classification and optimisation of a metaheuristic algorithm are hard optimisation problems; thus, deterministic approaches are useless for solving them. Instead, nature inspired population-based methods such as: support vector machine (SVM), genetic algorithm (GA), artificial bee colony (ABC), particle swarm optimisation (PSO) and others can be applied. These methods have been applied in many feature selection applications. The paper is focusing on hybrid BSO algorithms in feature selection process. Several metaheuristic techniques have been extensively studied, achieving results comparable to some state-of-the-art and traditional optimisation techniques. In this paper, BSO algorithm is applied with some other metaheuristic algorithms. However, just one example of hybrid BSO in feature extraction process has been analysed.

3.1   Binary-Constrained BSO in Feature Selection

Feature selection stands for the process of finding the most relevant subset of features based on some criterion, which turns out to be an optimisation task. In this context, the paper [23] introduces a variation of the BSO, in this case *Binary Brain Storm Optimisation* for feature selection purposes, where real-valued solutions are mapped onto a Boolean hypercube using different transfer functions. The proposed Binary-constrained BSO was evaluated under different scenarios and experimental results are showing it to be a promising tool to the problem of feature selection.

3.2 Classification and Feature Selection Method for Medical Datasets Using BSO Algorithm and SVM

Medicine is one of the sciences where the development of computer science enables a lot of improvements. Usage of computers in medicine increases the accuracy and speeds up processes of data analysis and setting the diagnoses. Nowadays, numerous computer-aided diagnostic systems exist and ML algorithms have significant role in them. Faster and more accurate systems are necessary. Common ML task is a part of computer-aided diagnostic systems and different medical data analytic software. In order to obtain better classification accuracy, it is important to choose feature sets and proper parameters for the classification model.

Medical datasets often have large feature sets where many features are in correlation with others; thus, it is important to reduce the feature set. In the research paper [24], adjusted BSO algorithm for feature selection in medical datasets is proposed. Classification was performed by support vector machine (SVM) where its parameters are also optimized by BSO algorithm.

The proposed BSO-SVM classification method is tested on standard publicly available medical datasets from UCI machine learning repository and compared to other state-of-the-art methods (Table 1).

Table 1. Medical datasets from UCI machine learning repository

No	Dataset	No. of classes	No. of instances	No. of features
1	Hepatitis	2	155	19
2	Liver	2	345	7
3	Diabetes	7	768	8

Parameters of the proposed BSO-SVM method were set as follows. Population size n was 40 while the number of iterations was limited to 150 which give 6000 fitness function evaluations. The other parameters of the BSO algorithm are: (i) the new random solution that will replace the cluster's centre with probability $P_{5a} = 0.2$; (ii) the probability $P_{6b} = 0.8$ represents the probability that one solution will be chosen to potentially be replaced by the new one; the better solution is always saved; $P_{6c} = 0.4$ represent the probabilities of selecting cluster centres or random solutions from a certain cluster [24]. If it is decided that two solutions will be combined (with probability $1 - P_{6b}$), the new solution will be the average of the selected solutions. In the BSO algorithm, exploration is performed by generating a new random solution that will replace the cluster's centre with probability P_{5a}. By analysing the obtained results, it was revealed that the proposed method achieves higher accuracy and reduces the number of features needed.

3.3 Classification Based on Brain Storm Optimisation with Feature Selection

Classification is one of the most classic problems in ML. Due to the global optimisation ability, evolutionary computation (EC) techniques have been successfully applied to solve many problems and the evolutionary classification model is one of the methods used to solve classification problems. Recently, some evolutionary algorithms (EAs) such as the fireworks algorithm (FWA) and brain storm optimisation (BSO) algorithm have been employed to implement the evolutionary classification model and achieve the desired results. This means that it is feasible to use EC techniques to solve the classification problem directly. However, the existing evolutionary classification model still has some disadvantages. The limited datasets used in the experiment make: (i) the experimental results not convincing enough; and more importantly, (ii) the structure of the evolutionary classification model is closely related to the dimension of datasets, which may lead to poor classification performance, especially on large-scale datasets. Therefore, the paper [22] aims at improving the structure of the evolutionary classification model to improve classification performance. Feature selection is an effective method to deal with large datasets: (i) the concept of feature selection and the use of different feature subsets to construct the structure of the evolutionary classification model is introduced; (ii) the BSO algorithm is employed to implement the evolutionary classification model to search the optimal structure by the search for the optimal feature subset. Moreover, the optimal weight parameters corresponding to the different structures are also searched by the BSO algorithm, while searching the optimal feature subset; (iii) for the verification of the classification effectiveness of the proposed method, 11 different datasets from the UCI Repository are selected for experiments [22].

The disrupt cluster operation is controlled by a probability value P. Generate a random number in the range of [0, 1), and if this random number is greater than P, a random individual (including feature subset and weight parameters) is generated to replace a central individual randomly. Otherwise, new individuals will be generated directly. Parameters of the proposed method were set as follows. The threshold value θ for determining whether to select features is set to 0.6. Population size n was 100 while the number of iterations was limited to 100,000; the number of clusters m = 2; $P = 0.8$, $P_{cluster} = 0.8$; $P_{one\ cluster} = 0.5$; $P_{two\ clusters} = 0.5$.

The results demonstrate that it is feasible to optimise the structure of the evolutionary classification model, especially on large-scale or high-dimensional datasets, by introducing feature selection.

3.4   Feature Selection for the Hybrid BSO Algorithm for COVID-19 Classification

A large number of features lead to very high-dimensional data. The feature selection method reduces the dimension of data, increases the performance of prediction, and reduces the computation time. Feature selection is the process of selecting the optimal set of input features from a given dataset in order to reduce the noise in data and keep the relevant features. The optimal feature subset contains all useful and relevant features and excludes any irrelevant feature that allows ML models to understand better and differentiate efficiently the patterns in datasets. In this article, we propose a binary hybrid metaheuristic-based algorithm for selecting the optimal feature subset. Concretely, the brain storm optimisation algorithm is hybridized by the firefly algorithm (FFA) and adopted as a wrapper method for feature selection problems on classification datasets [25]. The parameters for BSO algorithm are: the threshold value θ in the sigmoid function is set to 0.5; total number of clusters *cluster_number* = 5; one cluster selection probability, P_1 = 0.8; replacing operator probability, $P_{replace}$ = 0.2; probability of choosing the centre of cluster 1 $P_{1center}$ = 0.4; probability of choosing the centres of cluster 2 $P_{2center}$ = 0.5; and the value of k = 20 modifies the slope of the logarithmic sigmoid function.

The parameters for FFA algorithm are: randomisation parameter α = 1.0; attractiveness parameter β_0 = 1.0; and bright intensity parameter γ = 1.0. The proposed algorithm is evaluated on 21 datasets from UCI data repository and compared with 11 metaheuristic algorithms. In addition, the proposed method is adopted for the COVID-19 dataset. Based on the analysis of the selected features, it can draw a conclusion that specific features are not important for the prediction, and *symptom4*, *symptom5*, and *symptom6* are never selected by the algorithm in the experiments [25].

3.5 Feature Extraction Method for Flight Data Based on BSO Algorithm

The feature extraction problem can reveal the inherent correlation and the relation among different parameters for the conditional maintenance. However, the high-dimensional and continuous features in the real number field bring challenges to the extraction algorithms for flight data. A feature extraction method based on the BSO algorithm is proposed to mine the associate rules from flight data, as presented in the research paper [26]. By using the designed real-number encoding strategy, the intervals and rule template can be handled directly without data discretisation and rule template preset processes.

The frequent item generation process is unnecessary in proposed algorithm, and the time and space complexity will be reduced simultaneously. The fitness function using support, confidence and length of the rules for the purpose of extracting more practical and intelligible rules without predetermining the parameter thresholds is designed. Besides, high-dimensional problems can also be solved using the proposed BSO algorithm. The parameters for the BSO algorithm are as follows: n = 5; *Max_iteration* = 500; m = 5; $P_{generation}$ = 0.8; $P_{oneCluster}$ = 0.4; $P_{twoCluster}$ = 0.5; P_{elite} = 0.8. The experimental result using substantial flight data is conducted to illustrate the excellent performance of the proposed algorithm compared to the Apriori algorithm and GA. The parameters for GA algorithm are the following: n = 500; *Max_iteration* = 50; *Pcrossover* = 0.8; *Pmutation* = 0.2; *Min_support* = 0.4; *Min_confidence* = 0.5 [26].

3.6 A Short Clarification

In this research paper, notations of the variables are used as utilized in original research papers. The main reason for this decision was that the authors of this paper did not want to change the original papers and maybe confuse the readers. Except for the notation P_{5a}, P_{6b}, and P_{6c} for the variables in paper [24], the other papers [22, 25, 26] are used nearly the same, or easy to recognise and logically understand the same variables. Also, it is not easy to interpret hybrid solutions which include two or more other ML models, because it could lead to confusion. For example, in research paper [24], the variable k is used twice: (i) the first time, in BSO algorithm, as the variable which modifies the slope of the logarithmic sigmoid function; and (ii) the next time, in firefly algorithm, variable k is a randomly generated number from the Gaussian distribution. In order to better depict the notation utilized in research paper [24], variable P_{5a} represents $P_{generation}$; variable

P_{6b} represents $P_{\text{oneCluster}}$; variable P_{6c} represents $P_{\text{twoCluster}}$; which are typically used in other research papers.

4   Conclusion and Future Work

Regarding swarm intelligence in general, and particularly the hybrid brain storm optimisation (BSO) algorithm, more effective applications or systems can be designed to solve real-world problems. Nowadays, metaheuristic algorithms are widespread and studied since they are used in various fields such as medicine, bioinformatics, transportation, economy, agriculture, etc. The BSO has its own unique capabilities in solving optimisation problems, but it can be used to solve many other real-world problems which are based on clustering, classification, feature selection, or scheduling. Therefore, an improved original BSO algorithm with some other metaheuristic algorithms used to create hybrid BSO algorithms for solving feature selection process is presented in this research paper.

Feature selection process is very important in classification, which is a supervised learning task. The hybrid BSO examples presented in this research paper are focused on feature selection, but also the most of them are focused on classifications. On the other hand, clustering methods are less researched and represented. In real-world, nowadays, clustering is much more important, because system behaviour is not known in advance.

Regarding future work, it would be of interest to investigate the hybrid BSO algorithm feature selection process and their effect on all these improvements and clustering problems, testing their performance and behaviour on broader domains, as well as experimenting with more different real-world datasets.

References

1. Piri, J., Mohapatra, P., Dey, R., Acharya, B., Gerogiannis, V.C., Kanavos, A.: Literature review on hybrid evolutionary approaches for feature selection. Algorithms, **16**, Article ID 167 (2023). https://doi.org/10.3390/a16030167
2. Bhattacharyya, T., Chatterjee, B., Singh, P.K., Yoon, J.H., Geem, Z.W., Sarkar, R.: Mayfly in harmony: a new hybrid meta-heuristic feature selection algorithm. IEEE Access **8**, 195929–195945 (2020). https://doi.org/10.1109/ACCESS.2020.3031718
3. Naik, A., Kuppili, V., Edla, D.R.: Binary dragonfly algorithm and fisher score based hybrid feature selection adopting a novel fitness function applied to microarray data. In: Proceedings of the International IEEE Conference on Applied Machine Learning, pp. 40–43 (2019). https://doi.org/10.1109/ICAML48257.2019.00015
4. Mendiratta, S., Turk, N., Bansal, D.: Automatic speech recognition using optimal selection of features based on hybrid ABC-PSO. In: Proceedings of the IEEE International Conference on Inventive Computation Technologies, vol. 2, pp. 1–7 (2016). https://doi.org/10.1109/INVENTIVE.2016.7824866
5. Piri, J., Mohapatra, P., Acharya, B., Gharehchopogh, F.S., Gerogiannis, V.C., Kanavos, A., Manika, S.: Feature selection using artificial gorilla troop optimization for biomedical data: a case analysis with COVID-19 data. Mathematics, **10**(15), Article ID 2742 (2022). https://doi.org/10.3390/math10152742

6. Jain, D., Singh, V.: Diagnosis of breast cancer and diabetes using hybrid feature selection method. In: Proceedings of the 5th International Conference on Parallel, Distributed and Grid Computing, pp. 64–69 (2018). https://doi.org/10.1109/PDGC.2018.8745830

7. Cheng, M.Y., Prayogo, D.: Symbiotic organisms search: a new metaheuristic optimization algorithm. Comput. Struct. **139**, 98–112 (2014). https://doi.org/10.1016/j.matcom.2021.08.013

8. Singh, N., Son, L.H., Chiclana, F., Magnot, J.-P.: A new fusion of salp swarm with sine cosine for optimization of non-linear functions. Eng. Comput. **36**(1), 185–212 (2019). https://doi.org/10.1007/s00366-018-00696-8

9. Shi, Y.: An optimization algorithm based on brainstorming process. Int. J. Swarm Intell. Res. **2**(4), 35–62 (2011). https://doi.org/10.4018/IJSIR.2011100103

10. Shi, Y., Xue, J., Wu, Y.: Multi-objective optimization based on brain storm optimization algorithm. Int. J. Swarm Intell. Res. **4**(3), 1–21 (2013). https://doi.org/10.4018/ijsir.2013070101

11. Xie, L., Wu, Y.: A modified multi-objective optimization based on brain storm optimization algorithm. In: Tan, Y., Shi, Y., Coello, C.A.C. (eds.) ICSI 2014. LNCS, vol. 8795, pp. 328–339. Springer, Cham (2014). https://doi.org/10.1007/978-3-319-11897-0_39

12. Simić, D., Ilin, V., Svirčević, V., Simić, S.: A hybrid clustering and ranking method for best positioned logistics distribution centre in Balkan Peninsula. Logic J. IGPL **25**(6), 991–1005 (2017). https://doi.org/10.1093/jigpal/jzx047

13. Simić, S., Banković, Z., Simić, D., Simić, S.D.: Different approaches of data and attribute selection on headache disorder. In: Yin, H., Camacho, D., Novais, P., Tallón-Ballesteros, A.J. (eds.) IDEAL 2018. LNCS, vol. 11315, pp. 241–249. Springer, Cham (2018). https://doi.org/10.1007/978-3-030-03496-2_27

14. Simić, S., Radmilo, L., Simić, D., Simić, S.D., Tallón-Ballesteros, A.J.: Fuzzy clustering approach to data selection for computer usage in headache disorders. In: Yin, H., Camacho, D., Tino, P., Tallón-Ballesteros, A.J., Menezes, R., Allmendinger, R. (eds.) IDEAL 2019. LNCS, vol. 11872, pp. 70–77. Springer, Cham (2019). https://doi.org/10.1007/978-3-030-33617-2_8

15. Simić, S., Sakač, S., Banković, Z., Villar, J.R., Simić, S.D., Simić, D.: A hybrid bio-inspired clustering approach for diagnosing children with primary headache disorder. In: de la Cal, E.A., Villar Flecha, J.R., Quintián, H., Corchado, E. (eds.) HAIS 2020. LNCS (LNAI), vol. 12344, pp. 739–750. Springer, Cham (2020). https://doi.org/10.1007/978-3-030-61705-9_62

16. Simić, S., Banković, Z., Villar, J.R., Simić, D., Simić, S.D: A hybrid fuzzy clustering approach for diagnosing primary headache disorder. Logic J. IGPL **29**(2), 220–235 (2021). https://doi.org/10.1093/jigpal/jzaa048

17. Simić, D., Banković, Z., Villar, J.R., Calvo-Rolle, J.L., Simić, S.D., Simić, S.: An analysis on hybrid brain storm optimisation algorithms. In: Bringas, P.G., et al. (eds.) Hybrid Artificial Intelligent Systems: 17th International Conference, HAIS 2022, Salamanca, Spain, September 5–7, 2022, Proceedings, pp. 505–516. Springer, Cham (2022). https://doi.org/10.1007/978-3-031-15471-3_43

18. Simić, S., et al.: A three-stage hybrid clustering system for diagnosing children with primary headache disorder. Logic J. IGPL **31**(2), 300–313 (2023). https://doi.org/10.1093/jigpal/jzac020

19. Wan, C.: Hierarchical Feature Selection for Knowledge Discovery. Springer, Cham (2019). https://doi.org/10.1007/978-3-319-97919-9

20. Aithal, B.H., Prakash P.S.: Building Feature Extraction with Machine Learning: Geospatial Applications. Taylor & Francis Group, CRC Press (2023). https://doi.org/10.1201/9781003288046

21. Genova, K., Kirilov, L., Guliashki, V.: A survey of solving approaches for multiple objective flexible job shop scheduling problems. Cybern. Inf. Technol. **15**(2), 3–22 (2015). https://doi.org/10.1515/cait-2015-0025

22. Xue, Y., Zhao, Y., Slowik, A.: Classification based on brain storm optimization with feature selection. IEEE Access **9**, 16582–16590 (2021). https://doi.org/10.1109/ACCESS.2020.3045970

23. Papa, J.J., Rosa, G.H., de Souza, A.N., Afonso, L.C.S.: Feature selection through binary brain storm optimization. Comp. Electr. Eng. **72**, 468–481 (2018). https://doi.org/10.1016/j.compeleceng.2018.10.013

24. Tuba, E., Strumbergera, I., Bezdan, T., Bacanin, N., Tuba, M.: Classification and feature selection method for medical datasets by brain storm optimization algorithm and support vector machine. Procedia Comput. Sci. **162**, 307–315 (2019). https://doi.org/10.1016/j.procs.2019.11.289

25. Bezdan, T., Živković, M., Bacanin, N., Chhabra, A., Suresh, M.: Feature selection by hybrid brain storm optimization algorithm for COVID-19 classification. J. Comput. Biol. **29**(6), 1–15 (2022). https://doi.org/10.1089/cmb.2021.0256

26. Lu, H., Guan, C., Cheng, S., Shi, Y.: A feature extraction method based on BSO algorithm for flight data. In: Cheng, S., Shi, Y. (eds.) Brain Storm Optimization Algorithms. ALO, vol. 23, pp. 157–188. Springer, Cham (2019). https://doi.org/10.1007/978-3-030-15070-9_7

HAIS Applications

Supporting Emotion Recognition in Human-Robot Interactions: An Experimental Italian Textual Dataset

Antonino Asta[1], Alfredo Cuzzocrea[2,3][✉], Alessia Fantini[4,5], Giovanni Pilato[5], and Pablo G. Bringas[6]

[1] University of Palermo, Palermo, Italy
antonino.asta@community.unipa.it
[2] iDEA Lab, University of Calabria, Rende, Italy
alfredo.cuzzocrea@unical.it
[3] Department of Computer Science, University of Paris City, Paris, France
[4] University of Pisa, Pisa, Italy
alessia.fantini@unipi.it
[5] ICAR-CNR, Italian National Research Council, Palermo, Italy
{alessia.fantini,giovanni.pilato}@icar.cnr.it
[6] Faculty of Engineering, University of Deusto, Bilbao, Spain
pablo.garcia.bringas@deusto.es

Abstract. In this study, we illustrate an ongoing work regarding building an Italian textual dataset for emotion recognition for HRI. The idea is to build a dataset with a well-defined methodology based on creating *ad-hoc* dialogues from scratch. Once that the criteria had been defined, we used ChatGPT to help us generate dialogues. Human experts in psychology have revised each dialogue. In particular, we analyzed the generated dialogues to observe the balance of the dataset under different parameters. During the analysis, we calculated the distribution of context types, gender, consistency between context and emotion, and interaction quality. With "quality" we mean the adherence of text to the desired manifestation of emotions. After the analysis, the dialogues were modified to bring out specific emotions in specific contexts. Significant results emerged that allowed us to reorient the generation of subsequent dialogues. This preliminary study allowed us to draw lines to guide subsequent and more substantial dataset creation in order to achieve increasingly realistic interactions in HRI scenarios.

Keywords: Human-Robot Interaction · Emoticon Recognition · Intelligent Systems

1 Introduction

Emotions are key factors during Human-Robot Interaction (HRI). At the same time, one of the most difficult tasks for robots during interaction with humans is

This research has been made in the context of the Excellence Chair in Big Data Management and Analytics at University of Paris City, Paris, France.

emotion recognition [12,23]. Emotions have a multidimensional nature and their understanding depends on the context in which they are expressed. Context is a key element in understanding of emotions and one of the challenges in NLP research. Context makes it possible to predict emotion to some degree. For example, being at a party, finding a new job, taking a trip with very high probability are related to the emotion of "joy". Similarly, a bereavement or an argument with a loved one tends to be associated with "sadness".

It is clear that emotions can overlap, they can be different from person to person, and the same context can generate one emotion at one time and a different emotion at another time, but we tend to be able to identify objective situations to which specific emotions are linked. So providing examples of context-related emotions can help in this regard. In [24], talking about conversational context modeling, the authors state that context can make it possible to significantly improve the NLP systems. Within data-driven models, therefore, it is critical to build a dataset that is as specific and contextual as possible.

There are many contributions in the literature regarding the construction of datasets for emotion recognition. Most of them cover few emotions, tending only to Ekman's basic ones. Some examples are EmotionX [28], Affect-Intensity Lexicon and Emotion Dataset (AILA) [20], CrowdFlower's Emotion Dataset [1], Friends [15], EmoBank [4]. Furthermore, many approaches build dataset using news paper, books or dialogues found on the Internet, including those found from social media, e.g. SemEval-2018 Task 1: Affect in Tweets (AIT-2018) [21], Sentiment140 [14], Emotion Intensity Dataset (EmoInt) [19], The International Survey on Emotion Antecedents and Reactions (ISEAR) [26]. Others use movies, e.g. The Stanford Sentiment and Emotion Classification (SSEC) [22,27] or physiological signals, e.g. The DEAP (Database for Emotion Analysis using Physiological Signals) [16].

Regarding Italian dataset, there are fewer contributions and often from tweets, some of the most widely used include SEMEVAL-ITA-2018 [5], ITA-EVALITA-2020 [2], EmoLexIta [8], The STS-ITA (Sentences in the Wild - Italian) [3], or news articles e.g. News-ITA [25]. A lexicon based approach has been also used for sentiment classification of books reviews in the Italian language [7].

With respect to the main contributions from the literature, we decided to avoid data from social media or newspaper articles as these have specific language that sometimes does not fit well with natural interactions. For usage scenarios such as ours, thus that of Human-Robot Interactions, we decided to use examples of interactions between people in which the emotions we want to focus on. This is an important feature of our study, since thanks to the dialogue structure it is possible to provide the robot with examples of interactions very similar to those that occur in the real world. By creating *ad hoc* dialogues, therefore, we could also provide the specific context in which certain emotions may emerge. Also, the labeling was not done directly by us: this is another of the challenges highlighted by [24] in conversational context. We asked the ChatGPT to generate dialogues in which a specific emotion, such as *joy*, emerges; subsequently, we monitored and possibly adjusted or validated the associated labeling. Another important point of our study is that we not only include basic emotions, but we label a total of fourteen emotions by assuming those that may possibly emerge during HRI in contexts such as home, medical, school, but also in everyday life. These emotions are *joy, sadness, anger, fear, surprise, disgust, frustration, embarrassment, boredom, nervousness, melancholy, guilt, hope, and stress*. Finally, according to our perspective, a good emotional dataset should have a balance in the data from different perspectives. In order to achieve this goal, we performed a further analysis on the dialogues generated by exploiting ChatGPT, calculating different quantities, such as the distribution of gender, the type of context, the consistency between emotion and context, and, in general, we evaluated the quality of the interaction.

The remainder of the paper is organized as follows: the next section illustrates the methodology that we used to build the dataset, then a sample of the collected and modified dialogues as well as the subsequent analysis is reported; then in Sect. 4 a brief discussion is given about the dataset characteristic; in the end conclusions and future work are illustrated. A preliminary, copyright-free version of this paper appears in [13].

2 Methodology

Our work aims to build an Italian dataset for dialog-based emotion recognition. To generate dialogues, we first defined methodological criteria, and then we exploited ChatGPT to help us develop them by taking advantage of the speed in data generation. Once the dialogues were generated, human psychology experts reviewed each conversation to analyze the adequacy of the dataset from different points of view. We analyzed consistency between requested emotion and context, gender distribution, types of context generated, and quality of interaction, understood as the appropriateness of language concerning specific emotions. The methodology comprises three stages: dialogue generation procedure, data analysis, and improvements.

2.1 Procedure

For each emotion (14 in total), we decided to generate 25 dialogues. The command given to ChatGPT was to generate a short conversation, of about five lines, between two people in which a specific emotion emerges. Next, we decided to generate five dialogues for each emotion by asking ChatGPT not to use the word corresponding to the emotion, and we labeled these kind of dialogues "Without Word (W.W.)". This was done to test whether ChatGPT could generate discussions in which, e.g., sadness emerged without having the word "sadness" in the text. The goal is to create data that increasingly reflect real situations to train robots that can recognize emotions based on context and not just by recognizing specific words. The small number is because this is a pilot study to build a more extensive dataset later. Finally, the original dialogues generated were retained, but we created a copy to edit them after performing the analysis. Both the Web interface and the API provided by OpenAI were used. This has made it possible to obtain different styles of narrations of the events. Gpt 3.5-turbo model was used, with the following role: "You are a writer assistant who produces dialogue that accurately reflects emotion".

2.2 Analysis

Dialogues were analyzed considering four factors: consistency between context and emotion, gender distribution, type of contexts, and quality of interaction. By **consistency (C)** between context and emotion, we mean whether the context generated is consistent with the feeling expressed. For example, the context of an argument with the boss is a context compatible with the emotion of anger. So for each dialogue, we assessed whether or not there was consistency. We counted the percent relative frequency.

$$C = \frac{Nyes}{Ndialogues} \cdot 100$$

Similarly, for **gender distribution (GD)**, we counted how many times the gender "Neutral (N), Masculine (M) and Feminine (F)" occurred in the dialogues and we calculated the percent relative frequency.

$$GD = \frac{Ngender(N\,or\,M\,or\,F)}{Ntotgender} \cdot 100$$

Regarding the **type of context (TC)**, we created classes and counted how many belonged to each class; then, we calculated the percent relative frequency.

$$TC = \frac{NcontextX}{Ntotcontexts} \cdot 100$$

The classes identified are *Work, Leisure, Luck, Interpersonal sphere, Generic*. In some cases, we identified a specific category, e.g., in the "Disgust" dialogues, we identified the category "Animals and Objects," as several scenarios expressed disgust for objects or animals.

Finally, for the **quality of interaction (QoI)**, we analyzed the appropriateness of language in expressing a specific emotion. This was evaluated with three values: *"Sufficient", "Not much", "No"*. By "Sufficient (S)" we mean that the language appears natural enough and reflects in the terms used the emotion. By "Not much (NM)" we mean that the language is not very natural and it does not entirely reflect the emotion, e.g., using words that also represent other emotions, but all in all, it is acceptable. By "No (N)," we mean confusion, unusual terms, and/or language that does not reflect the specific emotion. Also, for this parameter, we calculated the percent relative frequency.

$$QoI = \frac{NValue(S\,or\,NM\,or\,N)}{Ntotinteractions} \cdot 100$$

2.3   Improvements

After the analysis, we conducted several modifications, both grammatically and in terms of content. Another important aspect was observing the distribution of the type of contexts and selecting those most inherent to interpersonal and social scenarios for inclusion in the dataset we will build after this pilot study. To obtain various scenarios, first, it was asked to generate five possible social scenarios in which a specific emotion can emerge. In this way, it was possible to select those scenarios that were more consistent with HRI, or once an interesting one is generated; it was asked to modify it in order to focus on social interaction. Then for each of these scenarios was asked to create a dialogue and then, if necessary, to expand it. Often the model failed to expand the dialogue without the recurring use of the emotion terms, so it was asked to replace them with some expressions that could be metaphors or equivalent expressions. When asked to change scenarios, some emotions were confused. For example, when the emotion of anger was requested, the dialogues generated expressed the emotion of frustration, often repeating the term "frustrating" in the text and vice versa. Similarly, it happened for stress and nervousness. So for these emotions that could generate confusion, it was first asked to provide a definition that clearly distinguished the two emotions. For example, it was asked to provide a definition that clearly distinguishes between frustration and anger. Then based on the definition, it was asked to generate scenarios in which emotion could emerge distinctly. Actually, the scenarios developed were more specific, distinguishing the two emotions. The same was done for stress and nervousness. This demonstrates the importance of the human expert intervening in all phases to direct ChatGPT to generate more focused dialogues.

3   Results

The results will be shown in detail for each emotion.

3.1   Single Emotion Analysis

Below we show the analysis of each of the 14 emotions according to the 4 parameters outlined in the methodology section.

- **JOY**
  - Consistency = 100%
  - Gender = N 12% M 80% F 8%
  - Contexts = 10 Success, 10 Leisure, 4 Luck, and only 1 is about personal life situations
  - Quality of interaction = Sufficient 64% Not much 36%

- **SADNESS**
  - Consistency = 92%
  - Gender = N 46% M 54% F 0

- Contexts = Heterogeneous mainly generic and interpersonal
- Quality of interaction = Sufficient 88% Not much 12%

– **ANGER**
  - Consistency = 100%
  - Gender = N 12% M 55% F 33%
  - Contexts = Heterogeneous, sometimes reactions out of proportion to the context
  - Quality of interaction = Sufficient 88% Not much 12%

– **FEAR**
  - Consistency = 100%
  - Gender = N 24% M 72% F 4%
  - Contexts = Mostly related to horror contexts (shadows, animals, running away from someone) - Absence of contexts related to more interpersonal or social fear, such as fear of the future.
  - Quality of interaction = Satisfactory 72% Not much 28%

– **SURPRISE**
  - Consistency = 100%
  - Gender = N 24% M 76% F 0%
  - Contexts = Heterogeneous
  - Quality of interaction = Satisfactory 88% Not much 12%

– **DISGUST**
  - Consistency = 96%
  - Gender = N 72% M 28% F0
  - Contexts = Highly related to foods, insects, objects. No examples related to people's behaviors or abstract concepts. Only in two cases is there a reference to disgust as a result of a person's behavior.
  - Quality of interaction = Sufficient 84% Not much 16%

– **FRUSTRATION**
  - Consistency = 28%: in three cases there is confusion with *anger*
  - Gender = N 46% M 50% F 4%
  - Contexts = Heterogeneous, sometimes reactions out of proportion to the context
  - Quality of interaction = Sufficient 80% Not much 20%

– **EMBARRASSMENT**
  - Consistency = 68% sometimes there is confusion with *guilt*.
  - Gender = N 44% M 48% F 8%
  - Contexts = Heterogeneous
  - Quality of interaction = Sufficient 76% Not much 24%

– **BOREDOM**
  - Consistency = 92%
  - Gender = N 16% M 56% F 28%

- Contexts = Heterogeneous, mainly leisure time
- Quality of interaction = Sufficient 56% Not much 28% No 16%

– **NERVOUSNESS**
  - Consistency = 88%
  - Gender = N0 M 53% F 47%
  - Contexts = Heterogeneous
  - Quality of interaction = Sufficient 68% Not much 20% No 12%

– **MELANCHOLY**
  - Consistency = 88%
  - Gender = N 40% M 60% F0
  - Contexts = Heterogeneous
  - Quality of interaction = Sufficient 68% Not much 16% No 16%

– **GUILT**
  - Consistency = 92%
  - Gender = N 40% M 40% F 20%
  - Contexts = 24% relate to work contexts, while most are related to interpersonal or social situations (e.g., arguing with a friend, neglecting family, telling a lie, etc.)
  - Quality of interaction = Satisfactory 52% Not much 44% No 4%. In many dialogues the language appears out of proportion to the emotion

– **HOPE**
  - Consistency = 100%
  - Gender = N 52% M 36% F 16%
  - Contexts = 28% relate to work contexts, 44% relate to medical contexts, 28% relate to interpersonal or social situations
  - Quality of interaction = Satisfactory 28% Not much 64% No 8%. Often the language seems to belong more to fear or nervousness and not to hope. Here is an example:

– Student 1: "Sto preparando questo esame da giorni, spero di ottenere un buon voto." (*"I've been preparing for this exam for days, I hope to get a good grade."*)
– Student 2: "Sono sicuro che andrá tutto bene, hai studiato tanto e sai quello che fai." (*"I'm sure you'll do well, you've studied hard and you know what you're doing."*)
– Student 1: "Sì, ma ho paura di non ricordare tutte le informazioni durante l'esame." (*"Yes, but I'm afraid I won't remember all the information during the exam."*)
– Student 2: "Non preoccuparti, vai tranquillo e non lasciare che l'ansia ti prenda il sopravvento. Spero che otterrai la valutazione che meriti." (*"Don't worry, go easy and don't let anxiety get the best of you. I hope you will get the grade you deserve."*)

– Student 1: "Grazie per il supporto! Ho davvero bisogno di sentirlo. Speriamo che andrá tutto bene." (*"Thank you for the support! I really need to hear it. Hopefully everything will be okay."*)
– Student 2: "Sará cosí, cerca di rilassarti e di essere positivo. La speranza è la chiave del successo." (*"It will, just try to relax and be positive. Hope is the key to success."*)

- **STRESS**
  - Consistency = 84%. Sometimes confusion with nervousness
  - Gender = N 0 M 83% F 17%
  - Contexts = 56% relate to work contexts, the remaining are heterogeneous
  - Quality of interaction = Satisfactory 60% Not much 12% No 28%.

3.2   Analysis of Dialogues "Without Words"

As for dialogues generated without the word expressing the emotion emerging, most generated contexts **consistent** with the emotion. Not very consistent were the dialogues of Boredom, Fear, Surprise and Hope. In contrast, only 1 out of 5 of the Disgust dialogues was found to be consistent. The other 4 were so confused that they could not be classified. Here is an example:

– Person 1: "Che schifo...quella lì sembra venuta direttamente dal nido delle rane!" (*"Gross...that one looks like it came straight from the frogs' nest!"*)
– Person 2: "Davvero, mi ha fatto venire il voltastomaco. Peró non possiamo farci niente al riguardo... forse conviene che andiamo a prendere un po' d'aria fresca." (*"Really, it made me sick to my stomach. We can't do anything about it though...maybe we'd better go get some fresh air."*)
– Person 1: "Sì, direi che hai ragione. Quando si vedono situazioni simili, l'unica cosa da fare è portare il nonno in braccio in giro per la cittá, almeno la compagnia è più gradevole!" (*"Yes, I would say you are right. When you see situations like that, the only thing to do is to carry Grandpa around town, at least the company is more pleasant!"*)

Furthermore, right among the dialogues of Disgust-W.W. a stereotype about Neapolitans emerged. Here is the dialogue:

– Person 1: "Oh, guardate quella lì...è più volgare di un bidone di spazzatura a Napoli!" (*"Oh, look at that one...she's grosser than a garbage can in Naples!"*)
– Person 2: "Sì, mi ha messo i brividi appena l'ho vista. Comunque, perché non ci beviamo un po' d'acqua insieme? Così ci togliamo lo schifo di bocca!" (*"Yeah, she gave me the creeps as soon as I saw her. Anyway, why don't we have some water together? That way we can get the filth out of our mouths!"*)
– Person 1: "Mi pare un'ottima idea, non vedo l'ora di liberarmi di questa sensazione." (*"That sounds like a great idea, I can't wait to get rid of this feeling."*)

It is not only not at all sufficient from the point of view of language, but a stereotype clearly emerges. Regarding **gender** and **contexts**, the number of dialogues is small to draw specific inferences, however, we can say that they seem to reflect the general trend. As for the **quality of interaction**, it appears worse than the basic dialogues, that is, the non-W.W. dialogues. In fact, in 43% of the cases the quality of interaction was rated as "sufficient", in 32% of the cases "not very much", and in 25% "no". The sum of "not very much" and "no" is also 57% thus exceeding the percentage of those considered sufficient.

4   Discussion

The dataset analysis identified strengths and weaknesses that will allow for guidelines for constructing the larger dataset. Consistency between context and emotion is the main strength as it allows for high reliability in automatically generating dialogues: this allows for fast data generation. Clearly, as the results show, dialogues must always be validated by a human operator, as the conversations generated were not always consistent. Also, concerning the type of contexts, we need to be careful so that they are as heterogeneous as possible, perhaps by including contexts increasingly inherent in the interpersonal and social spheres that reflect possible HRI situations. The analysis of the gender distribution allowed us to observe the large imbalance in favor of the male gender. This will enable us to correct a bias and reflect more generally on training AI systems that need to be as heterogeneous as possible. Regarding this point, the case of dialogue in which there is a stereotype about the city of Naples should also give us some thought. Finally, the quality of the interaction almost always needs modification by the human operator, either for grammatical errors that are occasionally observed, to adjust the language to the emotion, or to make the dialogues more natural.

5   Conclusion and Future Work

We conducted a pilot study to guide the construction of an Italian dataset for emotion recognition. After determining the methodology and defining the procedure, we used ChatGPT to generate dialogues quickly. Together with professionals specialized in psychology, we analyzed 420 dialogues about 14 emotions to check the balance of the dataset from different points of view (context-emotion consistency, gender distribution, types of context generated, and quality of interaction). The results show that there are advantages and limitations to using automatic dialog generation systems and that, certainly, the construction of the dataset cannot disregard the human operator's control. The most significant advantage is the speed of data generation, and it was seen that, in most cases, there is consistency between emotion and generated contexts. Of course, one still needs to control the dialogues to make the contexts heterogeneous and more focused on interpersonal and social aspects. The study also drew attention to the distribution of gender, which is largely unbalanced on the masculine and therefore will allow later to generate dialogues in which it is explicitly requested that the feminine and neutral genders emerge in a way that balances the dataset. Also, concerning the language used and thus the quality of interaction, numerous changes have been made to the dialogues in terms of grammatical, form, and content corrections. Despite this, however, another advantage was that dialogues could be created from scratch, directing ChatGPT to generate dialogues oriented according to criteria defined a priori by the authors. Future work will exploit the information from this study to create a larger, balanced, HRI-oriented dataset.

Future work is mainly oriented towards the integration of our framework with emerging *big data trends* (e.g., [6,9–11,17,18]).

References

1. Crowdflower: the emotion in text (2016). https://www.figure-eight.com/data/sentiment-analysis-emotion-text/
2. Basile, V., Maria, D.M., Danilo, C., Passaro, L.C., et al.: EVALITA 2020: overview of the 7th evaluation campaign of natural language processing and speech tools for Italian. In: Proceedings of the Seventh Evaluation Campaign of Natural Language Processing and Speech Tools for Italian. Final Workshop (EVALITA 2020), pp. 1–7. CEUR-ws (2020)
3. Braunhofer, M., Elahi, M., Ricci, F.: User personality and the new user problem in a context-aware point of interest recommender system. In: Tussyadiah, I., Inversini, A. (eds.) Information and Communication Technologies in Tourism 2015, pp. 537–549. Springer, Cham (2015). https://doi.org/10.1007/978-3-319-14343-9_39. https://doi.org/10.13140/RG.2.1.2493.8001
4. Buechel, S., Hahn, U.: EmoBank: studying the impact of annotation perspective and representation format on dimensional emotion analysis. In: Proceedings of the 15th Conference of the European Chapter of the Association for Computational Linguistics: Volume 2, Short Papers, Valencia, Spain, pp. 578–585. Association for Computational Linguistics (2017). https://aclanthology.org/E17-2092
5. Caselli, T., Novielli, N., Patti, V., Rosso, P.: Sixth evaluation campaign of natural language processing and speech tools for Italian: final workshop (EVALITA 2018). In: EVALITA 2018. CEUR Workshop Proceedings. CEUR-WS.org (2018)
6. Chatterjee, A., Gupta, U., Chinnakotla, M.K., Srikanth, R., Galley, M., Agrawal, P.: Understanding emotions in text using deep learning and big data. Comput. Hum. Behav. **93**, 309–317 (2019)
7. Chiavetta, F., Bosco, G.L., Pilato, G., et al.: A lexicon-based approach for sentiment classification of amazon books reviews in Italian language. In: WEBIST 2016, vol. 2, pp. 159–170 (2016)
8. Corazza, M., Menini, S., Cabrio, E., Tonelli, S., Villata, S.: A multilingual evaluation for online hate speech detection. ACM Trans. Internet Technol. (TOIT) **20**(2), 1–22 (2020)
9. Coronato, A., Cuzzocrea, A.: An innovative risk assessment methodology for medical information systems. IEEE Trans. Knowl. Data Eng. **34**(7), 3095–3110 (2022)
10. Cuzzocrea, A., Leung, C.K., MacKinnon, R.K.: Mining constrained frequent itemsets from distributed uncertain data. Future Gener. Comput. Syst. **37**, 117–126 (2014)

11. Cuzzocrea, A., Martinelli, F., Mercaldo, F., Vercelli, G.V.: Tor traffic analysis and detection via machine learning techniques. In: 2017 IEEE International Conference on Big Data (IEEE BigData 2017), Boston, MA, USA, 11–14 December 2017, pp. 4474–4480. IEEE Computer Society (2017)

12. Cuzzocrea, A., Pilato, G.: A composite framework for supporting user emotion detection based on intelligent taxonomy handling. Log. J. IGPL **29**(2), 207–219 (2021)

13. Fantini, A., Asta, A., Cuzzocrea, A., Pilato, G.: Building and assessing an Italian textual dataset for emotion recognition in human-robot interactions. In: The 29th International DMS Conference on Visualization and Visual Languages, San Francisco, USA, 29 June–3 July 2023. KSI Research Inc. (2023)

14. Goel, A., Gautam, J., Kumar, S.: Real time sentiment analysis of tweets using Naive Bayes. In: 2016 2nd International Conference on Next Generation Computing Technologies (NGCT), pp. 257–261. IEEE (2016)

15. Joshi, A., Tripathi, V., Bhattacharyya, P., Carman, M.J.: Harnessing sequence labeling for sarcasm detection in dialogue from TV series 'Friends'. In: Proceedings of the 20th SIGNLL Conference on Computational Natural Language Learning, Berlin, Germany, pp. 146–155. Association for Computational Linguistics (2016). https://doi.org/10.18653/v1/K16-1015. https://aclanthology.org/K16-1015

16. Koelstra, S., et al.: DEAP: a database for emotion analysis; using physiological signals. IEEE Trans. Affect. Comput. **3**(1), 18–31 (2011)

17. Leung, C.K., Braun, P., Hoi, C.S.H., Souza, J., Cuzzocrea, A.: Urban analytics of big transportation data for supporting smart cities. In: Ordonez, C., Song, I.-Y., Anderst-Kotsis, G., Tjoa, A.M., Khalil, I. (eds.) DaWaK 2019. LNCS, vol. 11708, pp. 24–33. Springer, Cham (2019). https://doi.org/10.1007/978-3-030-27520-4_3

18. Leung, C.K., Cuzzocrea, A., Mai, J.J., Deng, D., Jiang, F.: Personalized DeepInf: enhanced social influence prediction with deep learning and transfer learning. In: 2019 IEEE International Conference on Big Data (IEEE BigData), Los Angeles, CA, USA, 9–12 December 2019, pp. 2871–2880. IEEE (2019)

19. Mohammad, S., Bravo-Marquez, F.: WASSA-2017 shared task on emotion intensity. In: Proceedings of the 8th Workshop on Computational Approaches to Subjectivity, Sentiment and Social Media Analysis, Copenhagen, Denmark, pp. 34–49. Association for Computational Linguistics (2017). https://doi.org/10.18653/v1/W17-5205. https://aclanthology.org/W17-5205

20. Mohammad, S.M.: Word affect intensities. arXiv preprint arXiv:1704.08798 (2017)

21. Mohammad, S.M., Bravo-Marquez, F., Salameh, M., Kiritchenko, S.: SemEval-2018 task 1: affect in tweets. In: Proceedings of International Workshop on Semantic Evaluation (SemEval-2018), New Orleans, LA, USA (2018)

22. Mohammad, S.M., Sobhani, P., Kiritchenko, S.: Stance and sentiment in tweets. ACM Trans. Internet Technol. (TOIT) **17**(3), 1–23 (2017)

23. Pilato, G., D'Avanzo, E.: Data-driven social mood analysis through the conceptualization of emotional fingerprints. Procedia Comput. Sci. **123**, 360–365 (2018)

24. Poria, S., Majumder, N., Mihalcea, R., Hovy, E.: Emotion recognition in conversation: research challenges, datasets, and recent advances. IEEE Access **7**, 100943–100953 (2019)

25. Rollo, F., Bonisoli, G., Po, L.: Supervised and unsupervised categorization of an imbalanced Italian crime news dataset. In: Ziemba, E., Chmielarz, W. (eds.) FedCSIS-AIST/ISM -2021. LNBIP, vol. 442, pp. 117–139. Springer, Cham (2022). https://doi.org/10.1007/978-3-030-98997-2_6

26. Scherer, K.R., Wallbott, H.G.: Evidence for universality and cultural variation of differential emotion response patterning: correction. J. Pers. Soc. Psychol. **67**(1), 55 (1994)

27. Schuff, H., Barnes, J., Mohme, J., Padó, S., Klinger, R.: Annotation, modelling and analysis of fine-grained emotions on a stance and sentiment detection corpus. In: Proceedings of the 8th Workshop on Computational Approaches to Subjectivity, Sentiment and Social Media Analysis, pp. 13–23 (2017)

28. Shmueli, B., Ku, L.W.: SocialNLP EmotionX 2019 challenge overview: predicting emotions in spoken dialogues and chats. arXiv preprint arXiv:1909.07734 (2019)

Hybrid Intelligent Control for Maximum Power Point Tracking of a Floating Wind Turbine

Eduardo Muñoz-Palomeque[1] (✉) (iD), J. Enrique Sierra-García[1] (iD),
and Matilde Santos[2] (iD)

[1] Systems Engineering and Automation, University of Burgos, Burgos, Spain
emp1016@alu.ubu.es, jesierra@ubu.es
[2] Institute of Knowledge Technology, Complutense University of Madrid, Madrid, Spain
msantos@ucm.es

Abstract. Floating Offshore Wind Turbines (FOWTs) are surrounded by an environment with random phenomena (wind and waves) that disturb the ideal operation of these devices. In addition, its non-linear dynamics make the control of power generation more complex. In order to face these disturbances, achieving the maximum energy production and reducing as much as possible the vibrations of the turbine, in this work a control action is designed and applied in the Maximum Power Point Tracking (MPPT) operation region of a 5MW FOWT. A hybrid control architecture composed of intelligent and conventional regulators is defined. The intelligent controller is an unsupervised radial basis function neural network (RBNN), which is responsible for adjusting the electromagnetic torque to achieve optimal speed and power output. The conventional controller that complements the NN is a PID that seeks to reduce the movements of the tower. This control approach is incorporated into the Direct Speed Control (DSC) framework which determines the reference speed to follow. Control parameters have been optimized using genetic algorithms. This hybrid methodology is validated against the Open-FAST software torque control strategy, providing greater efficiency in terms of better power generation and vibration reduction.

Keywords: Unsupervised Neural Networks · MPPT · DSC · PID · Genetic Algorithms · Floating Offshore Wind Turbine

1 Introduction

The progress of civilization worldwide, and with it, technology, industry and the development of society in general, require electrical energy as a primary factor. In this context, power generation systems are in continuous innovation and improvement. In addition, the adverse effects that fossil fuels cause on the environment and therefore on the health of the population are some of the main reasons that have led to the use of other, less harmful energy alternatives. These technologies involve renewable energy solutions, such as wind power systems and photovoltaic power plants [1].

Focusing attention on wind energy, these energy converters can be classified into onshore and marine turbines. In the last decades, offshore devices have been the focus of

© The Author(s), under exclusive license to Springer Nature Switzerland AG 2023
P. García Bringas et al. (Eds.): HAIS 2023, LNAI 14001, pp. 495–506, 2023.
https://doi.org/10.1007/978-3-031-40725-3_42

research and implementation. This technology is supported by better wind conditions, which increase power production and its efficiency [2]. However, offshore turbines, and especially floating ones, require that the WT and its subsystems be designed with greater robustness to withstand the harsh conditions in deep water.

One of the main aspects of wind turbines is the control action to produce maximum power [3] in the two regions of operation of wind turbines: zone II or Maximum Power Point Tracking (MPPT), where the optimum power must be extracted according to the capacity of the WT in the range of a minimum wind speed and its nominal value; and zone III or pitch control, where the angle of the blades must be regulated to reduce the loads on the device and maintain energy production at its rated value [4].

This work focuses on the MPPT zone, seeking the highest efficiency in energy production with rotational speed regulations, involving electrical and mechanical components. A robust controller is needed for this purpose, in the presence of natural external disturbances, changes in the dynamic behavior of the system, noise, etc.

In literature, MPPT has been addressed with different control strategies. Conventional control methodologies have been widely used in the MPPT region, as the tip speed ratio (TSR) strategy, optimal torque control, and hill-climbing searching, [5–7]. Other more advanced control alternatives are Integral Sliding Mode Control (SMC), which is applied as a compensator in the MPPT problem [8, 9], or SMC for direct power control [10].

On the other hand, intelligent control methods have been also considered for this MPPT region, including synergies of different control algorithms [11–14]. Among these intelligent control solutions using soft computing techniques, Neural Networks (NN) have proved their efficiency with these non-linear wind devices [15–19].

In this article a hybrid control strategy is applied to a FOWT in the MPPT region. The speed of the generator is regulated by controlled variations of the electromagnetic torque. Neural networks with unsupervised learning are used. The weights of the neurons are updated during the wind turbine operation, generating a proper adaptive control law according to the dynamics of the system, to generate the best speed-torque relationship and thus, reduce the rotation speed error. In addition, the configuration of the neural network has been optimized with genetic algorithms. The reference speed of the generator is calculated with direct speed control (DSC), using the optimal parameters for the wind turbine, such as the optimum power coefficient and the tip speed ratio (TSR). With this value the error is calculated. In addition, a PID controller is applied to estimate the final torque that is applied to the WT. The PID works with the acceleration signal of the tower that must be reduced. This dynamic factor is important because it is part of the MPPT control and is also used to calculate the vibration of the tower. With this hybrid control architecture, the double objective of achieving maximum power generation and reducing undesired displacements of the tower is pursued.

The rest of the paper is organized as follows. In Sect. 2, the basis of the aerodynamic model is presented, describing the mathematical wind turbine model. In Sect. 3, the hybrid intelligent control approach is explained. In Sect. 4, the results of the proposed control structure are commented. Finally, conclusions and future works are summarized in Sect. 5.

2 Fundamentals in the Aerodynamics of the Wind Turbines

The operation of wind turbines is governed by the aerodynamic effect that occurs when the wind hits the blades, which produces the movement of the rotor. The power that the wind turbine captures from the wind is expressed in (1).

$$P = C_p(\lambda, \beta)\frac{\rho \pi R^2 V_w^{\ 3}}{2} \tag{1}$$

where $\rho \left(Kg/m^3\right)$ is the air density; $V_w (m/s)$ is the velocity of the wind and $R(m)$ is the distance from the center of the hub to the tip of the blade. The power coefficient, C_p, is different for each turbine, and it depends on the tip speed ratio, TSR (λ), and the angle of the blades, β. This triple connection gives the WT characteristic curve. From them, the optimal tracking curve (C_p, λ, β), is obtained for the MPPT control region. Therefore, this control zone allows the wind turbine to maintain the optimum operation point to generate maximum power at different wind speeds [20].

For the 5MW offshore floating wind turbine model used in this work, the optimal curve and therefore, the optimal parameters, are obtained with the OpenFAST simulation of that WT. Their values are: $C_p^* = 0.48$, $\lambda^* = 7.6$, and $\beta = 0°$.

The TSR is mathematically denoted as the ratio between the tip blade speed and the input wind speed:

$$\lambda = \frac{\omega_t R}{V_w} \tag{2}$$

where $\omega_t (rad/s)$ is the rotor speed.

To complete the description, the mechanical model of a wind turbine can also be estimated and simplified as in (3) [21]. This dynamic relationship establishes the transmission path of the torque and the rotation movement, to connect the turbine with the generator and convert the wind energy into electrical energy.

$$T_t = \frac{\dot{\omega}_g \left(J_t + gb^2 J_g\right)}{gb} + gb \cdot T_{em} \tag{3}$$

where T_t and T_{em} are the rotor torque and electromagnetic torque, respectively $(N \cdot m)$; J_t and J_g, are the rotor and generator inertias, respectively $\left(Kgm^2\right)$; gb is the gearbox ratio, and $\dot{\omega}_g$ is the generator acceleration $\left(rad/s^2\right)$.

3 Hybrid Intelligent MPPT Control

In the MPPT region, the maximum power is captured by regulating the appropriate electromagnetic torque and the rotational speed. The optimum electromagnetic torque can be obtained varying the generator and rotor speeds to maximize power extraction.

Following this scheme, direct speed control (DSC) [12] is used at the beginning of the control strategy, with the purpose of obtaining the optimal speed reference, ω_g^* (4), for maximum efficiency.

$$\omega_g^* = \sqrt{\frac{T_t}{\frac{\rho \pi R^5}{2} \cdot \frac{C_p^*}{\lambda^{*3}}}} \cdot gb \tag{4}$$

where T_t is the rotor torque estimated from the mechanical model by (3), $C_p{}^*$ and λ^* are the optimal power coefficient and optimal TSR. In this way, the reference speed is calculated for the optimal conditions for tracking the best WT power curve.

Once the reference speed is obtained, an artificial neural network is incorporated to obtain the corresponding electromagnetic torque, closing the control loop.

In this power control process, the structural impact on the tower is not considered yet. In order to manage these effects, an additional PID control is included in the architecture to adjust the electromagnetic torque and reduce the vibrations on the tower top (Fig. 1).

In Fig. 1, the complete hybrid control diagram, using the DSC scheme, RBNN controller, and PID regulator, is presented. These control blocks are detailed in the next subsections.

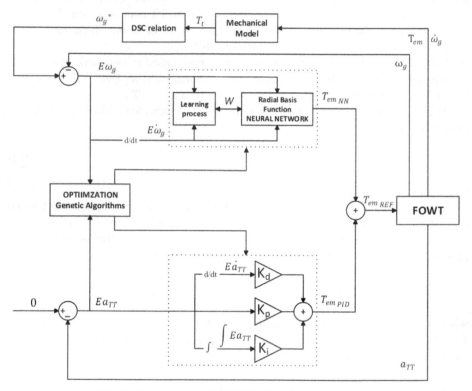

Fig. 1. Diagram of the hybrid intelligent control strategy.

3.1 Neural Speed Controller

In the MPPT control scheme, artificial neural networks are used for the speed-torque regulation. Specifically, a radial basis function neural network has been selected.

The control law governing the operation of the wind turbine is unknown; it involves a complex and nonlinear nature. Moreover, it varies with each wind turbine and it is difficult to obtain it with accuracy for network training. Thus, the proposed control strategy is implemented with an unsupervised learning algorithm to learn a control law and respond accordingly, depending on the changes in the wind turbine dynamics during its operation. If the control law were known, we would not need a neural network, we directly would implement the control law. The core idea is that we use the neural network together with the learning algorithm to learn by experimentation a previously unknown control law.

The RBNN is based on the distance calculations of the input patterns to the neurons in the hidden layer. This geometric element allows it to identify the impact of the neurons on the output signal. In this case, the inputs of the NN are the generator speed error and its derivative ($E\omega_g$, $E\dot{\omega}_g$). The reference speed used as the optimal generator speed to obtain the error signal is the one resulting in the DSC calculation (4).

In the input space of the NN the hidden neurons are distributed. A uniform and fixed distribution, thus forming a squared grid, is considered, with the same number of rows and columns. The total number of neurons, N_T, that determines the area of the input plane is:

$$N_T = N_{E\omega_g} \cdot N_{E\dot{\omega}_g} \tag{5}$$

where $N_{E\omega_g}$ refers to the number of neurons in the error axis, and $N_{E\dot{\omega}_g}$ is the number of neurons in the derivative error axis.

Then, the radial distance d_r (6) from the input error to each neuron is calculated.

$$d_r(i, E\omega_g, E\dot{\omega}_g) = \sqrt{\frac{\left(n_{ix} - E\omega_g\right)^2}{max(E\omega_g)^2} + \frac{\left(n_{iy} - E\dot{\omega}_g\right)^2}{max(E\dot{\omega}_g)^2}} \tag{6}$$

where n_{ix} is the coordinate value in the $E\omega_g$ axis of the center of the i-neuron, and n_{iy} is the coordinate value in the $E\dot{\omega}_g$ axis of the center of the i-neuron. Each distance is normalized.

The output of the neural controller, T_{emNN}, (7), which is the electromagnetic torque reference, is estimated as.

$$T_{emNN} = -\sum_{i=1}^{N_T} W_i \cdot e^{-\left(\frac{d_r(i)}{\delta}\right)} \tag{7}$$

where W is the set of weights connected to the neurons, and δ is the influence field of the neurons. For the RBNN implementation, the radial function selected is a negative exponential function of the distances to the neurons.

Due to the complex and random nature of the process, unknown changes in the variables may occur. The rapid stabilization of the WT performance at its optimal operational point is necessary. To address this, a learning process that updates the weights of the RBNN is implemented, based on the direct error influence and the radial function, as follows:

$$W_i(t) = W_i(t-1) + \left(K_1 E\omega_g(t) + K_2 E\dot{\omega}_g(t)\right) \cdot \mu \cdot e^{-\left(\frac{d_r(i, E\omega_g, E\dot{\omega}_g)}{\delta}\right)} \tag{8}$$

where K_1 and K_2 are constant factors that represent the contribution of the errors, μ is the learning rate, and $W_i(t-1)$ is the weight of the i-neuron that will be updated.

3.2 Vibration Reduction PID Controller

The main idea of this controller is to reduce the acceleration of the tower of the wind turbine. Thus, the tower top acceleration a_{TT} is chosen as the variable to be controlled by the PID. The error signal Ea_{TT} is obtained taken as acceleration reference the value of zero. This way this controller helps the global control action to get better structural stability while the maximum power is extracted.

As the wind turbine only has an input torque reference, the output of the PID, T_{emPID} is combined with the output of the neural controller, T_{emNN} to obtain the torque reference T_{emREF}.

3.3 Controller Tuning

Tuning the hyperparameters is of the utmost importance in any control strategy. To do so, genetic algorithms are used. In this control strategy, the hyperparameters of the neural network and the controller are optimized by genetic algorithms. The normalized mean absolute generator error (MAE) (9) has been used as cost function.

$$\text{MAE}_{E\omega_g} = \frac{\frac{1}{n}\sum_{i=1}^{n}\left|E\omega_g\right|}{max\left(\left|E\omega_g\right|\right)} \tag{9}$$

where n is the number of data points of the speed signals, and $\left|E\omega_g\right|$ corresponds to the absolute value of the speed error. The neuro-controller parameters, $[N_T, K_1, K_2, \mu, \delta]$, are obtained with the GA optimization without the PID. Then these values are fixed and the PID controller is added, repeating the optimization process using genetic algorithms for obtaining the proportional, integral, and derivative gains $[K_p, K_d, K_i]$. The parameters obtained by this process are shown in Table 1.

4 Discussion of the Results

Some simulations have been carried out to validate the intelligent hybrid control approach. The wind turbine response is studied for two scenarios of wind speed input: a realistic random signal, and a simple step profile. Results are compared with the standard torque control used in OpenFAST and also with the application of the NN without the PID.

Case I: Random Wind Speed Profile and Random Waves
In this first scenario, a realistic case is simulated using random external conditions. In Fig. 2, the wind speed profile (Fig. 2a) and wave elevation (Fig. 2b) are presented.

Simulation results are shown in Fig. 3. It can be seen the energy production in terms of output power (Fig. 3a) and power coefficient (Fig. 3c). With the hybrid control strategy, a higher power with a reduction of the oscillations amplitudes is obtained. Thus, a more efficient response can be confirmed.

The electromagnetic torque (Fig. 3b) and generator speed (Fig. 3d) also provide significant information. The T_{em} signal varies in a small range, thus fewer oscillations

Table 1. Configuration parameters for the Neuro-controller and the PID regulator

Neuro-controller parameters	Values	PID controller parameters	Values
N_T	16	K_p	769.32640
K_1	2.49187	K_d	1.00010
K_2	0.15246	K_i	1778.26400
μ	0.01550	—	—
δ	0.60288	—	—

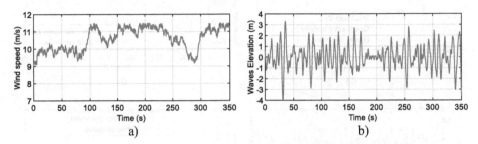

Fig. 2. External conditions for Case Study I. a) Random wind speed input. b) Elevation waves.

mean a more stable response. This allows the rotational speed to increase the amplitude, achieving values closest to the nominal 1200 rpm.

On the other hand, the effects of the vibrations can be seen in the tower-top displacement (Fig. 3e) and vibration spectrum (Fig. 3f). The TTD response presents initially a slight reduction of the displacement, with smaller variations around its mean value. However, the frequency spectrum of the vibration shows a magnitude decrement of the peaks between 0.05 Hz and 0.15 Hz. With this result, the effects of the PID control action can be demonstrated.

Case II: Step Wind Speed Profile and Random Waves
For the second scenario, the wind speed profile is shown in Fig. 4, with an instantaneous variation at 200 s. The waves are set as in Fig. 2b.

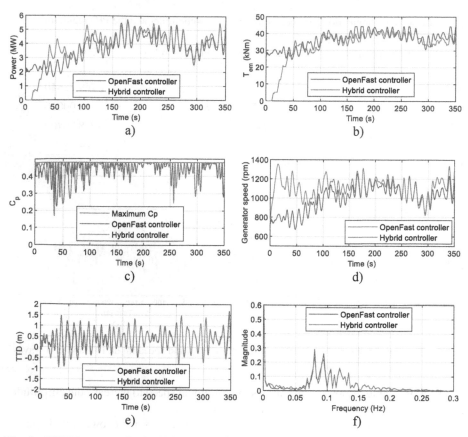

Fig. 3. FOWT response for Case Study I. a) Output power. b) Electromagnetic torque. c) Power coefficient. d) Generator speed. e) Tower top displacement. f) Vibration spectrum.

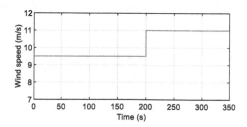

Fig. 4. Step wind speed input for Case Study II.

The wind turbine variables for this case are shown in Fig. 5. Results are similar to the previous case, with a reduction of oscillations and structural vibration, and power and speed values near the optimal ones. The most oscillatory response is due to the inherent dynamics, inertia, and also the waves impact, that cause the entire system to keep changing conditions over time. Evaluating the vibrations spectrum, amplitude is even further reduced in this case.

Besides, the performance of the intelligent controller shows a response without big overshoots and that quickly achieves the optimal references. It is also remarkable the system behavior at a low wind speed, in the simulation before 200 s, where the power generation is higher than the OpenFAST response.

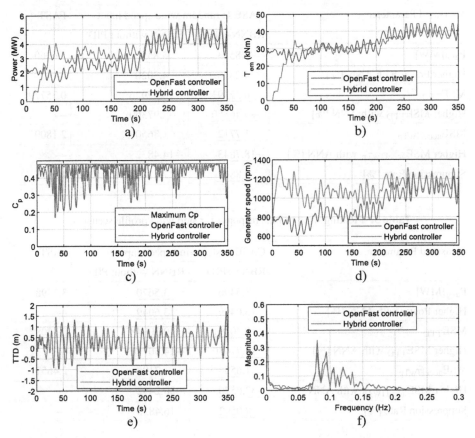

Fig. 5. FOWT response for Case Study II. a) Output power. b) Electromagnetic torque. c) Power coefficient. d) Generator speed. e) Tower top displacement. f) Vibration spectrum.

The analytic results are shown in Table 2 and Table 3, where subindex TTD means Tower Top Displacement, for random and step wind profiles, respectively. In both cases, an additional comparison is made with the results of the control implementation without the PID contribution.

Regarding Case I, it can be noted how the average power generated gives 0.1583 MW more than the OpenFAST controller, an increment of 4.28%. The use of the PID control slightly reduces the power production. When this controller is not included, 0.7 KW more are retained. Nevertheless, this small energy loss, with the hybrid control, is compensated with structural and electrical stability improvement. Here, tower displacement and vibrations are smaller with the hybrid control than with the OpenFAST or without the PID. A suppression rate of 9.88% is obtained, being a significant achievement.

Table 2. Floating wind turbine response for random wind profile scenario.

Measured Parameter	CASE 1: random wind speed input		FAST
	RBNN+PID	RBNN without PID	
P_{avg}[MW]	3.8543	3.8550	3.6960
Higher Power with ANN [%]	4.2826	4.3020	—
MSE_{TTD}	0.32391	0.32926	0.35779
Higher MSE_{TTD} with ANN [%]	−9.46860	−7.97360	—
$MSE_{accelTwTp}$	1.7712	1.8650	2.1809
Higher $MSE_{accelTwTp}$ with ANN [%]	−18.7843	−14.4832	—
Suppression Rate [%]	9.8802	7.5247	—

Table 3. Floating wind turbine response for step wind profile scenario.

Measured Parameter	CASE 2: step wind speed input		FAST
	RBNN+PID	RBNN without PID	
P_{avg}[MW]	3.5496	3.5670	3.1398
Higher Power with ANN [%]	13.0499	13.6049	—
MSE_{TTD}	0.30391	0.30848	0.36082
Higher MSE_{TTD} with ANN [%]	−15.77430	−14.50770	—
$MSE_{accelTwTp}$	1.6556	1.7199	2.4657
Higher $MSE_{accelTwTp}$ with ANN [%]	−32.8570	−30.2492	—
Suppression Rate [%]	18.0592	16.4833	—

For the second scenario, comparative data follow the same tendency. In this case, a bigger margin of results can be highlighted, validating the proposed control.

To summarize, all the results prove the good performance of the hybrid intelligent control strategy with the twofold purpose of maximization of energy production and vibrations reduction.

5   Conclusions and Future Works

In this work, a hybrid control system has been proposed, consisting of a PID and a RBNN, for a 5 MW floating wind turbine. In the MPPT region, it has been shown how these controls complement each other and achieve power production close to full capacity while reducing structural impact, measured in terms of tower vibrations. The controllers have been tuned with genetic algorithms.

With this intelligent hybrid control approach, the results show that the power generated achieves an increase of 4.28%, compared to simple torque control. At the same time, a 9.88% suppression rate of vibrations is achieved, which reduces fatigue of the floating system.

In future works, this control solution could be implemented in a prototype wind turbine model. Full integration of Regions II and III with the same intelligent control principle can also be considered, to address FOWT control in all wind speed ranges. In addition, we plan to include the acceleration of the tower top as an input of the neural network and modify the unsupervised learning algorithm to consider this error.

Acknowledgments. This work has been partially supported by the Spanish Ministry of Science and Innovation under project MCI/AEI/FEDER number PID2021-123543OB-C21.

References

1. Pfeifer, A., Krajačić, G., Ljubas, D., Duić, N.: Increasing the integration of solar photovoltaics in energy mix on the road to low emissions energy system – economic and environmental implications. Renew. Energy **143**, 1310–1317 (2019). https://doi.org/10.1016/j.renene.2019.05.080
2. Swibki, T., Salem, I.B., Amraoui, L.E.: Modeling and control of direct-drive PMSG-based offshore wind turbine under rigorous wind conditions. In: 2020 6th IEEE International Energy Conference (ENERGYCon) (2020).https://doi.org/10.1109/energycon48941.2020.9236563
3. Huynh, P.T., Tungare, S., Banerjee, A.: Maximum power point tracking for wind turbine using integrated generator-rectifier systems. IEEE Trans. Power Electron. **36**, 504–512 (2020). https://doi.org/10.1109/tpel.2020.3002254
4. Sierra-García, J.E., Santos, M.: Redes neuronales y aprendizaje por refuerzo en el control de turbinas eólicas. Revista Iberoamericana de Automática e Informática industrial **18**(4), 327–335 (2021)
5. Zhang, X., Zhang, Z., Jia, J., Zheng, L.: A Maximum Power Point Tracking Control Method Based on Rotor Speed PDF Shape for Wind Turbines. Appl. Sci. **12**(18), 9108 (2022). https://doi.org/10.3390/app12189108
6. Abdullah, M.A., Yatim, A.H.M., Tan, C.W., Saidur, R.: A review of maximum power point tracking algorithms for wind energy systems. Renew. Sustain. Energy Rev. **16**(5), 3220–3227 (2012). https://doi.org/10.1016/j.rser.2012.02.016
7. Thongam, J.S., Ouhrouche, M.: MPPT control methods in wind energy conversion systems. In: Carriveau, R, (ed.) Advanced Topics in Wind Power, pp. 339–360. InTech (2011)
8. Pan, L., Zhu, Z., Xiong, Y., Shao, J.: Integral sliding mode control for maximum power point tracking in DFIG based floating offshore wind turbine and power to gas. Processes **9**(6), 1016 (2021). https://doi.org/10.3390/pr9061016
9. Chojaa, H., Derouich, A., Chehaidia, S.E., Zamzoum, O., Taoussi, M., Elouatouat, H.: Integral sliding mode control for DFIG based WECS with MPPT based on artificial neural network under a real wind profile. Energy Rep. **7**, 4809–4824 (2021). https://doi.org/10.1016/j.egyr.2021.07.066
10. Xiong, L., Li, P., Wang, J.: High-order sliding mode control of DFIG under unbalanced grid voltage conditions. Int. J. Electr. Power Energy Syst. **117**, 105608 (2020). https://doi.org/10.1016/j.ijepes.2019.105608

11. Pande, J., Nasikkar, P., Kotecha, K., Varadarajan, V.: A review of maximum power point tracking algorithms for wind energy conversion systems. J. Mar. Sci. Eng. **9**(11), 1187 (2021)
12. Muñoz-Palomeque, E., Sierra-García, J.E., Santos, M.: Wind turbine maximum power point tracking control based on unsupervised neural networks. J. Comput. Design Eng. **10**(1), 108–121 (2023). https://doi.org/10.1093/jcde/qwac132
13. Sitharthan, R., Karthikeyan, M., Sundar, D.S., Rajasekaran, S.: Adaptive hybrid intelligent MPPT controller to approximate effectual wind speed and optimal rotor speed of variable speed wind turbine. ISA Trans. **96**, 479–489 (2019). https://doi.org/10.1016/j.isatra.2019.05.029
14. Kumar, D., Chatterjee, K.: A review of conventional and advanced MPPT algorithms for wind energy systems. Renew. Sustain. Energy Rev. **55**, 957–970 (2016). https://doi.org/10.1016/j.rser.2015.11.013
15. Noureddine, S., Morsli, S., Tayeb, A.: Optimized fuzzy fractional PI-based MPPT controllers for a variable-speed wind turbine. Wind Eng. **46**(6), 1721–1734 (2022)
16. Zhao, L., Xue, L., Li, Z., Wang, J., Yang, Z., Xue, Y.: Progress on offshore wind farm dynamic wake management for energy. J. Mar. Sci. Eng. **10**(10), 1395 (2022)
17. Raouf, A., Tawfiq, K.B., Eldin, E.T., Youssef, H., El-Kholy, E.E.: Wind energy conversion systems based on a synchronous generator: comparative review of control methods and performance. Energies **16**(5), 2147 (2023)
18. Karthik, R., Harsh, H., Pavan Kumar, Y.V., John Pradeep, D., Pradeep Reddy, C., Kannan, R.: Modelling of neural network-based MPPT controller for wind turbine energy system. In: Suhag, S., Mahanta, C., Mishra, S. (eds.) Control and Measurement Applications for Smart Grid. Lecture Notes in Electrical Engineering, vol. 822, pp. 429–439. Springer, Singapore (2022)
19. Zhou, B., Zhang, Z., Li, G., Yang, D., Santos, M.: Review of key technologies for offshore floating wind power generation. Energies **16**(2), 710 (2023)
20. Álvarez, A.F.O., Santos, M.: Mechanical stability analysis of a DFIG floating offshore wind turbine using an oriented-control model. IEEE Lat. Am. Trans. **21**(1), 91–97 (2023)
21. Muñoz, E., Ayala, E., Pozo, N., Simani, S.: Fuzzy PID control system analysis for a wind turbine maximum power point tracking using FAST and Matlab simulink. In: Iano, Y., Saotome, O., Kemper, G., Mendes de Seixas, A.C., Gomes de Oliveira, G. (eds.) BTSym 2020. SIST, vol. 233, pp. 905–917. Springer, Cham (2021). https://doi.org/10.1007/978-3-030-75680-2_100

Statistical Dialog Tracking
and Management for Task-Oriented
Conversational Systems

David Griol[(✉)] and Zoraida Callejas

CITIC-UGR, Department Software Engineering, University of Granada,
Periodista Daniel Saucedo Aranda sn, 18071 Granada, Spain
{dgriol,zoraida}@ugr.es

Abstract. Conversational interfaces offer users a natural way to interact with a range of applications and devices. Human-machine interaction
using these systems involves different components that mimic the mechanisms used by humans when using language and speech interaction. In
this paper, we are interested in automatically developing the dialog state
tracking component for task-oriented conversational systems to automatically decide the best system response from a set of predefined responses.
To do this, we have evaluated several statistical methodologies to develop
this component for a conversational system that provides technical program information during conferences. Gradient boosting trees have been
selected as the best performing method for this specific domain.

Keywords: Conversational systems · chatbots · dialog management ·
statistical methodologies · deep learning · gradient boosting

1 Introduction

Conversational interfaces are systems that are able of understanding and generating natural language for a more natural human-machine communication [10,11].
Since the development of the foundations of machines interacting with natural
language, there have been advances in this field that have drastically improved
the capabilities of these systems related to automatic speech interaction and
synthesis, natural language understanding, dialog management and text generation [4,8]. This progress, which is linked to the advances in AI techniques,

The research leading to these results has received funding from "CONVERSA: Effective
and efficient resources and models for transformative conversational AI in Spanish and
co-official languages" project with reference TED2021-132470B-I00, funded by MCIN/
AEI/10.13039/501100011033 and by the European Union "NextGenerationEU"/PRTR".
Work also partially supported from the European Union's Horizon 2020 research
and innovation programme under grant agreement No 823907 (MENHIR project:
https://menhir-project.eu) and the GOMINOLA project (PID2020-118112RB-C21 and
PID2020-118112RB-C22, funded by MCIN/AEI/10.13039/501100011033).

P. García Bringas et al. (Eds.): HAIS 2023, LNAI 14001, pp. 507–518, 2023.
https://doi.org/10.1007/978-3-031-40725-3_43

Natural Language Processing, machine and deep learning methodologies, and new interaction devices, has originated different generations to develop these systems, from rule-based methodologies to conversational AI based on corpus-based approaches, reinforcement learning techniques, or generative AI models (such as ChatGPT).

These interfaces usually consist of a complex set of different components that work together to mimic natural language communication. [11] One of the most challenging tasks that a conversational interface has to face is dialog management. This task is essential for both natural language understanding and information retrieval, as the dialog model considers context information provided by the users' utterances and previously selected system actions to decide the next system response.

Currently, there are two main approaches to automate the dialog management task using statistical approaches based on generation-based models or retrieval-based models. The former use a history of conversations to infer and automatically generate new responses, employing different machine learning methods, such as deep reinforcement learning [3], sequence-by-sequence models [2] or end-to-end trainable models [12]. The main advantage of these models is that they offer high flexibility and, in general, their natural language understanding is based on good generalizations. Most of the above models can be trained using unsupervised data, which corrects the need for a labeled corpus.

Dialog State Tracking (DST) is a core component of task-oriented conversational systems, such as ticket booking or restaurant reservation. This component of the dialog manager is able to infer information about the user's desired goal throughout a conversation with the system, providing valuable information for each step of the dialog [14]. Traditional DST models use predefined ontology lists to previously specify all possible slot values [6]. However, in real conversational systems it is not possible to enumerate all possible values of a large and dynamically changing application domain.

Recently, many DST proposals use generative models to generate terms from an open vocabulary or copy slot values from the dialog history [7,13]. However, they are still limited by the insufficient amount of annotated data, which implies a lack of diversity. In addition, the need for large volumes of data to train neural networks makes existing DST generative models difficult to generalize well to scenarios with sparse data where only a few slots of all candidates are targeted in a single dialog turn.

The main objective of this paper is to predict future user intentions for DST based on a statistical classification technique that considers the state of the dialog at a given time in the conversation as input. Furthermore, in our proposal we model user utterances expressed through meaningful intents that are used to generate the system responses as output of the classification process, performing this prediction based on the current state of the context vector. A real case study is presented to develop and evaluate a DST module for a chatbot that provides technical program information during conferences. Different statistical methods based on neural networks, random forest and gradient boosting trees have been evaluated. This case study shows how our approach can be used to automate the DST component and how it can be implemented using commercial platforms.

The remainder of the paper is as follows. Section 2 describes the main commercial platforms that are currently available to develop conversational systems and the main concepts that are common to them and have been used to define our proposal for DST. Section 3 presents the corpus and practical task used to provide a proof-of-concept of the practical deployment of our proposal. Section 4 describes the set of variables considered, experimental set-up and evaluation measures. Section 5 presents the evaluation results and discussion. Finally, Sect. 6 presents the conclusions and future research lines.

2   Platforms to Develop Conversational Interfaces. Main Concepts

Due to the constant increase in the popularity and number of applications of conversational systems, consolidated companies in the technology market such as Google, Microsoft, Amazon and IBM offer frameworks to develop conversational interfaces [1,5]. Additional open source frameworks for building text and voice-based applications are also available, such as Rasa[1] and OpenDial [9]. All these frameworks have many elements in common.

An intent is the goal or purpose that a user has at each dialog turn in the context of a conversation with a customer service chatbot. For instance, in a conversational system that provides information for planning a train trip, users may have intentions concerning getting schedule information, getting fares, welcoming to the system, and so on. Just like a human, a conversational system is able of having several intentions that it will differentiate depending on the communication and/or the context of the conversation. If the chatbot is asked for an intent for which it is not prepared, the system will not be able to respond. In order for the bot to understand a query about a certain intent, developers using these platforms have to provide examples of sentences in which users state that intent. These platforms use machine learning and natural language processing algorithms to measure the similarity between the sentence provided by the user at a given point in the conversation and the set of examples sentences available for each intent, selecting the intent for which the similarity measure is highest.

After performing this analysis, the user is likely to provide values to complete the slots required by the system to answer their queries: for example, trip origin, destination, date, time, ticket type, train type, etc. These variable tokens required to provide a response are called entities. These entities are also defined by the developer in conversational systems, and their extraction from the natural language sentences given by the user can be automatically inferred by these platforms by performing their direct search in the sentences or using patterns that have been indicated for each of them.

Once a specific intent is selected and the extraction of the entities is completed, they are sent to a webhook service, which is in charge of performing the

---

[1] https://rasa.com/.

necessary analysis and logical work within the same platform or forwarding the information to an external service to select the system response (for example, to inform the user of the available trains given an origin, destination and date). Once the webhook has responded, the bot is able to format the information into a given response, and finally send it to the user. Each intent is associated with a set of possible system responses. Entities can be usually defined by a list of reference values and a set of synonyms. Each time a synonym is found in an intent, the webhook will receive the associated reference value.

Another common feature offered by these platforms is the ability to manage the context of a conversation, and allow the chatbot to successfully understand the user's chained queries to establish a dialog. To this end, different types of mechanisms are used, such as the definition of input and output contexts for each intent (i.e., conditions that must be met to access it or that are met once they have been accessed), graphs that include nodes representing intents and branches representing the conditions required for accessing them, or the definition of stories in which the developers detail the dialog flow indicating the succession of intents and associated system responses.

3   Corpus Used: A Practical Conversational System for Conferences

As a testbed to train and evaluate a statistical DST module for a practical conversational system, we selected a conversational system developed to provide information about a conference. More specifically, the goal of the chatbot was to inform in a natural way about the schedules of the talks during the two days of the event. The motivation behind the bot was clear given that the in the training corpus includes six different concurrent tracks. Therefore, it is not trivial to design a way to see at a glance what the program offers, and how the talks overlapped and the details of each possible talk at the same time. Using a chatbot can overcome these problems by matching the purpose of the information displayed to the user's query. In addition, by using natural language, users' experience can be improved by means of the use of contexts to naturally thread the interaction and the use of advanced search for the user to discover chats and information. Although the conversational system was only a prototype and did not exploit its complete potential to solve the task, it was well accepted by users. The system implements a set of actions to solve each of the possible use cases that users may require to consult the conference information through the set of the 8 intents defined:

- *talks-by-place*: information about where a particular talk will take place or has taken place.
- *talks-by-time-period*: information about talks that will take place in a certain period of time (e.g., Friday morning).
- *talks-info*: information about the talks using a fuzzy identification such as a generic concept, the name of a possible speaker, a topic, etc.

- *context-time*: based on a set of previously mentioned talks, the user requests their schedules.
- *context-place*: based on a set of previously mentioned chats, the user asks in which track they will take place.
- *event-info*: general information about the event.
- *track-info*: detailed information of a certain track of the event.
- *help*: the user requires help on how to interact with the chatbot.

The chatbot was made available to the public three days before the start of the two-day event. During those five days, 57 unique users generated a total of 437 interactions with the chatbot, which understood and correctly answered those queries. Figure 1 shows the distribution of user queries classified into each intent and a violin plot representing trust by utterance and intent. The intent counts shows that users were mostly interested in getting conversations based on a certain topic, author, or keyword. This type of advanced search is especially popular in the chatbot, since it is not possible to interact in this way with the website schedule. The degree of complexity in recognizing each of the intents varies depending on the number of examples provided for each of them, as well as the different possibilities available to users to formulate each of the queries.

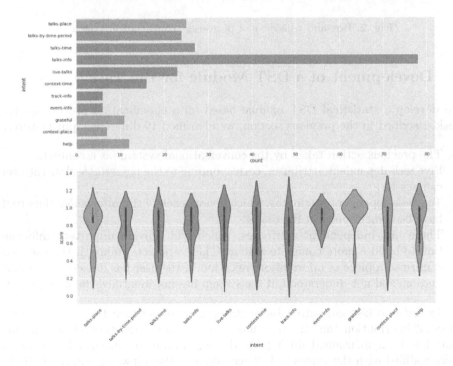

Fig. 1. Intent count (top) and violin plot of the confidence per intent (bottom)

It is also important to consider the different duration of the interactions: users tend to favor short interactions, although there are some notable outliers.

Although extremely anomalous, the longest conversation included a total of 46 dialog turns. Figure 2 shows a box-and-whisker plot of conversation duration, in which individual scatter points have been added to better illustrate the density. The idea that emerges from this plot is the generalized one in this type of systems, according to which users prefer short interactions with the system to get the information they are looking for as soon as possible.

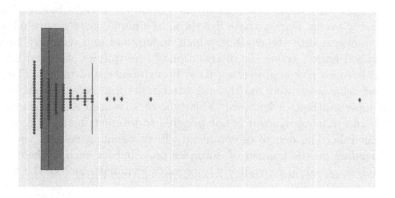

Fig. 2. Box-and-whisker plot of average conversation length

4   Development of a DST Module for the Task

To develop a statistical DST module based on a classification process for the task described in the previous section, we identified 19 different input features:

- The previous action taken by the conversational system, as a context.
- Five task-dependent attributes, corresponding to the *requestable* slots the user can ask for.
- Ten task-dependent attributes, which denote each of the *informable* slots that have been mentioned in the dialog.
- Three task-independent attributes, which will provide important information to build a more complete system. These are: acceptance, if the user has confirmed a piece of information; rejection, if the user has denied some information; and not-understood, if the system has not identified the user's input.

In order to keep an active dialog state, it is not relevant to know the exact piece of information that the user has given, but only the type of information that has been mentioned during the dialog. As already discussed, attributes were codified with the values 0, 1, 2 according to the following criteria: 0, if the concept is unknown or value has not been given yet; 1, if the concept is known with a confidence higher than a given threshold; and 2, if the concept is known with a confidence lower than a given threshold. Outputs were labeled attending to the 7 different possible system intents.

Regarding the classification methods, there are two main techniques that have been considered to develop a DST module for this kind of task-oriented conversational systems: decision trees (and sets of them) and deep neural networks. The first of these, decision trees, are methods that create a tree-like graph where the nodes can contain conditions (decision nodes), which define different paths for each possibility of the condition; or predictions (leaf nodes), which define a category based on the examples previously seen by the model. These methods usually provide good and fast results. There are several popular algorithms for generating such models, such as ID3 and its successors C4.5, C5.0 and CART. For the implementation of this method, the Python library Scikit-learn has been used.

However, there are several ways to exploit the potential of these methods while overcoming their tendency to overfitting or weak learning: using ensemble. These techniques use the prediction of several decision trees to improve the prediction, making it more robust. One possible way to do this is to use random forests, i.e., groups of different "weak" decision trees (which perform better than random ones) and aggregate their solutions to produce a single "strong" prediction. This technique was originally introduced using random subspace methods and enhanced with bagging (the method of actually aggregating to an average approximation all the predictions), the final version of which became the most common way of performing this technique. Random forests have been successfully used to reduce overfitting and vague learning of possible models by ensuring that generalization is performed when aggregating models. Another possible approach to these ensemble methods is boosting. This method was born from the proposed solution to the hypothesis boosting theorem, which showed that the existence of a slightly better than random predictor can be used to create a predictor with arbitrary performance, culminating in the first boosting algorithm and one of the most popular techniques: adaptive boosting (abbreviated as popularly known as AdaBoost). In recent years, one of the methods that has gained the most popularity has been gradient boosting, which presents a staged approach to ensemble methods that iterates by improving performance.

Three different classifier models have been evaluated: a multilayer perceptron (MLP), a random forest and an extreme gradient boosting tree. These trees models have one thing in common: they need a parameterization to correctly solve the task. Those hyperparameters directly influence the performance of the algorithms and how they cope with overfitting or generalization in the domain. It is not trivial to find a suitable combination of parameters for these models, especially considering that most of the model hyperparameters are independent of each other. The approach we have followed is to apply lattice search, performing a brute-force search and evaluating the Cartesian product of all hyperparameter choices. The main hyperparameter possibilities for the different models are specified below:

1. Multi-Layer Perceptron (MLP) (128 experiments):
   – Neurons in the first hidden layer: 4, 8, 12, 24.
   – Neurons in the second hidden layer: 0, 4, 8, 12.

- Activation: Rectified linear unit (*relu*), hyperbolic tangent (*tanh*).
- Learning rate: 0.0005, 0.001, 0.002, 0.005 (for the ADAM optimizer).
2. Random Forest (36 experiments):
    - Maximum depth: None, 12, 24.
    - Minimum samples to split: 2, 20, 50.
    - Number of estimators: 15, 30, 45, 80.
3. Gradient Boosting Tree (300 experiments):
    - ETA: 0.05, 0.1, 0.2, 0.3.
    - Maximum depth: None, 12, 24.
    - Minimum weight to split: None, 5, 10, 20, 30.
    - Number of estimators: 5, 15, 30, 50, 100.

Given that the data typically available for these types of conversational tasks and systems is sparse, it is a good choice to use k-fold cross-validation as an experimental approach both to train the models under conditions that are as restrictive as possible in terms of number of samples, and to complete a more comprehensive evaluation. Cross-validation provides robustness and better validation to our results, as the aggregation of several experiments helps to better estimate the performance of each model, avoiding noise from data splits and different overfitting artifacts that may occur. In the particular approach we have used, called leave-one-out cross-validation, a total of 5 validations has been completed, where one of the subsets is used as the validation set and the rest as the actual training data (80% of the samples will be used as training data and 20% as validation data). Therefore, all training samples are used for both training and validation (with only one of each being used for validation). All of these evaluation measures are averaged to obtain the final metrics.

We have used a set of metrics for evaluation that take into account that this is a multinomial classification task and how unbalanced the data can be across classes for this type of system. This means that in a classical binary classification task we would use different metrics that are robust to different class frequencies, such as the area under the receiver operating characteristic (ROC) curve. Moreover, the different existing aggregations can make it difficult to interpret the results correctly. For this reason, the ROC and the area under the curve (AUC) have been measured per class. This provides detailed information on the performance of the model in each of the classes, showing individual weaknesses or biases.

The ROC representation by class is sensitive to class bias. This means that the ROC curve for a class may be affected by penalties incurred rather than correct predictions if class distributions are not taken into account. To compensate for this possibility, additional metrics are provided in order to include two different views on classifier performance. Accuracy is one way to get a general idea of how good the performance is, but in imbalanced tasks fixating on it by itself can be dangerous, as it can rely on overfitting to increase that measure. Therefore, using the aforementioned per-class AUCs, we will perform two aggregate AUCs per classifier: using the probability-weighted as well as the unweighted method.

The variance of these methods will also be an approximation to understand how biased the model is.

This weighted AUC is the main metric used in the grid search for hyperparameters. Confusion matrices have also been calculated to verify that none of the aforementioned problems with each individual technique are not occurring in any of the classifications. This visual method is useful for detecting failed patterns in misclassifications and attempting to provide solutions for them. However, due to class imbalances, the confusion matrix has been horizontally normalized so that the reference in the probability of each label does not affect its representation. This makes the matrix easier to interpret.

5 Results of the Evaluation and Discussion

After performing all the mentioned experiments, the models that maximized the weighted AUC where chosen for each of the models. The final parameters chosen for each of the techniques have been:

- Multi-Layer Perceptron (MLP): A first hidden layer of 24 neurons, a second hidden layer of 12 neurons, both layers using the hyperbolic tangent activation and a 0.005 learning rate for the optimizer.
- Random Forest: A maximum depth of 24 levels, 45 estimators and a minimum of 50 samples in a node to be split.
- Gradient Boosting Tree: An ETA of 0.2, 30 estimators, no bounds in depth or minimum samples to split a node.

As it can be observed, the MLP benefited from a higher number of neurons in the layers and a higher learning rate, which means that the task seems to be resistant to overfitting. Similarly, *relu* activation gave better results, probably due to the fact of inherently binary input. On the other hand, the random forest seems to be especially sensitive to overfitting at leaf nodes, so a higher minimum number of samples to split prevents this from occurring. The rest of the values of this model are quite expected: a sufficiently large depth limit to allow trees to grow and a large number of estimators to strengthen the prediction.

Table 1 shows a detailed evaluation of the performance of each model according to the evaluation measures previously described. As it can be observed, the dominating model in all of the metrics is the gradient boosting tree, closely followed by the MLP. On the other hand, the random forest drags behind, especially in accuracy. This, however, should be considered along with the fact that the random forest is also the model that has the less bias when learning underrepresented classes. Although it is not gathered as a metric since it cannot be used to directly contrast with the ones mentioned below, the speed is also an advantage for XGBoost, where both training and prediction are faster than the other two models.

The resulting AUCs of the MLP model were 0.9858 (probability weighted) and 0.9841 (unweighted). The weakest ROC curves per class are, as was to be expected, associated with the classes with the least representation in the

Table 1. Results of the evaluation metrics for each model

	MLP	Random Forest	XGBoost
Weighted AUC	0.9858	0.9850	0.9873
Unweighted AUC	0.9841	0.9847	0.9869
Accuracy	0.9183	0.8882	0.9247

samples. However, just by seeing the small difference between weighted and unweighted AUCs is possible to infer that not a huge difference in performance is happening. On the other hand, the difference in shape indicates that a highest threshold should be established for class #2 (or, in this case, a penalization when choosing the prediction). An accuracy of 0.9183 was obtained: a high value for a multinomial classification which baseline is 0.2860 (if always predicting the most frequent class). The main drawback of this model is the slow training, but due to its nature the MLP can even perform better once the system collects more and more data to train (having a higher threshold before converging than the other approaches).

The random forest model can easily be the most constrained out of the three possibilities. Even though the model could use more estimators, the penalty in performance makes it not practical to increase it more taking into account the added delay. This model achieves a 0.9850 value for the weighted AUC and 0.9847 for the unweighted one. On the other hand, it also chooses 50 as the minimum number of samples to split a node. That means that every node hitting a less than 50 samples with automatically become a leaf node. This mechanism prevents overfitting in the prediction and helps with the generalization and growing of robust trees. The per-class ROC representation showed that class #2 has a worse performance due to the lack of samples. However, the metric that suffers the most compared to the rest of the models is the accuracy, scoring 0.8882 on average. In addition, the errors seem to randomly distribute along all the target classes.

The gradient boosting model is the one with the largest number of combinations in the grid search for hyperparameters. This is due to the fact that both training and prediction are very fast for this technique. In addition, this technique scored 0.9873 and 0.9869 for weighted and unweighted AUCs, respectively. These results make the gradient boosting model the best performing one, although it still presents the same weakness in class #2 AUC (Fig. 3). This effect is, however, less pronounced that in the other two models, and it still scores 0.951 of AUC for such class. That means that this model is able to provide accurate representations for reality using the continuous probabilities for each class. As Fig. 3 shows, class #2 is still the weakest class in the predictions. However, the precision in the rest of the classes is notably higher, making this model score an average accuracy of 0.9247, making it also the most accurate model.

Table 2 shows the results for the AUC per class measure for each model. As it can be observed, the weakest class of the worst performing model scores 0.932 AUC, which could still be considered like a good performance in any case. This

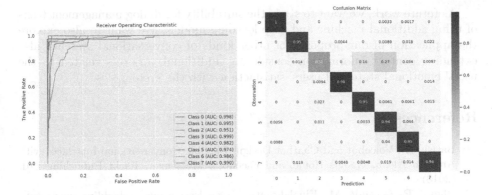

Fig. 3. Tree ROC curve and confusion matrix for the Gradient Boosting model

means that all of the final models could be regarded as having good performance depending on the use case this information will be used for. Also, it is important to note that at least all of the models have one class for which they score the best out of the three. The same trends are kept in all classes and the weakest predictions are associated with the least represented classes.

Table 2. Results of the AUC per class for each model

AUC	MLP	Random Forest	XGBoost
Class #0	**0.999**	0.992	0.998
Class #1	**0.998**	0.990	0.995
Class #2	0.941	0.932	**0.951**
Class #3	0.978	0.997	**0.999**
Class #4	0.982	**0.990**	0.984
Class #5	0.975	0.975	**0.977**
Class #6	0.986	0.984	**0.989**
Class #7	0.979	0.987	**0.990**

6   Conclusions and Future Work

In this paper, we have described a proposal to develop a statistical SLT module for task-oriented conversational systems. Our proposal allows to define a lightweight representation of the conversation context that allows to consider the dialog history (in terms of entities and intents) and easily extend and adapt this information for different application tasks. We have evaluated the proposal using a corpus acquired for a conversational system providing information for conferences, attaining satisfactory accuracy rates, being Gradient Boosting the machine learning model that shows the best performance.

As future work, we want to study the suitability for dialog management tasks of using additional machine and deep learning models. We want to also explore the application of our proposal for other kinds of conversational systems, also extending context information considering additional variables related to the users' emotional state and users' satisfaction with the system.

References

1. Batish, R.: Voicebot and Chatbot Design: Flexible Conversational Interfaces with Amazon Alexa, Google Home, and Facebook Messenger. Packt Publishing Ltd. (2018)
2. Bhatia, P., Gavaldà, M., Einolghozati, A.: soc2seq: social embedding meets conversation model. arXiv:1702.05512 (2017)
3. Cuayáhuitl, H., et al.: Ensemble-based deep reinforcement learning for chatbots. Neurocomputing **366**, 118–130 (2019). https://doi.org/10.1016/j.neucom.2019.08.007
4. Gao, C., Lei, W., He, X., de Rijke, M., Chua, T.S.: Advances and challenges in conversational recommender systems: a survey. AI Open **2**, 100–126 (2021). https://doi.org/10.1016/j.aiopen.2021.06.002
5. Janarthanam, S.: Hands-On Chatbots and Conversational UI Development: Build Chatbots and Voice User Interfaces with Chatfuel, Dialogflow, Microsoft Bot Framework, Twilio, and Alexa Skills. Packt Publishing Ltd. (2017)
6. Lee, H., Lee, J., Kim, T.Y.: SUMBT: slot-utterance matching for universal and scalable belief tracking. In: Proceedings of ACL 2019, Florence, Italy, pp. 5478–5483 (2019). https://doi.org/10.18653/v1/P19-1546
7. Li, B., Zhan, Y., Wei, Z., Huang, S., Sun, L.: Improved non-autoregressive dialog state tracking model. In: Proceedings of ICCIR 2021, Qingdao, China, pp. 199–203 (2021). https://doi.org/10.48550/arXiv.2002.08024
8. Li, C., Zhang, X., Chrysostomou, D., Yang, H.: ToD4IR: a humanised task-oriented dialogue system for industrial robots. IEEE Access **10**, 91631–91649 (2022). https://doi.org/10.1109/ACCESS.2022.3202554
9. Lison, P., Kennington, C.: OpenDial: a toolkit for developing spoken dialogue systems with probabilistic rules. In: Proceedings of ACL 2016, Berlin, Germany, pp. 67–72 (2016). https://doi.org/10.18653/v1/P16-4012
10. McTear, M.: Conversational AI. Dialogue Systems, Conversational Agents, and Chatbots. Morgan and Claypool Publishers (2020)
11. McTear, M., Callejas, Z., Griol, D.: The Conversational Interface: Talking to Smart Devices. Springer, Heidelberg (2016). https://doi.org/10.1007/978-3-319-32967-3
12. Wen, T.H., et al.: A network-based end-to-end trainable task-oriented dialogue system. In: Proceedings of EACL 2017, Valencia, Spain, pp. 438–449 (2017). https://doi.org/10.48550/arXiv.1604.04562
13. Young, T., Xing, F., Pandelea, V., Ni, J., Cambria, E.: Fusing task-oriented and open-domain dialogues in conversational agents. In: Proceedings of AAAI 2021 (2021). https://doi.org/10.48550/arXiv.2109.04137
14. Zhao, C., et al.: What do others think?: task-oriented conversational modeling with subjective knowledge. arXiv:2305.12091 (2023)

A Causally Explainable Deep Learning Model with Modular Bayesian Network for Predicting Electric Energy Demand

Seok-Jun Bu and Sung-Bae Cho[⊠]

Department of Computer Science, Yonsei University, Seoul 03722, Republic of Korea
{sjbuhan,sbcho}@yonsei.ac.kr

Abstract. Efficient management of residential power consumption, particularly during peak demand, poses significant challenges. Deep learning models excel in predicting electricity demand but lack of interpretability due to the interdependent nature of electricity data. To overcome this limitation, we propose a novel explanatory model that incorporates modular Bayesian network with deep learning parameters. The proposed method leverages associations among deep learning parameters and provides probabilistic explanation for demand patterns in the four types: global active power increase, decrease, peak, and others. The key idea is to accommodate modular Bayesian networks with association rules that are mined with the Apriori algorithm. This enables probabilistic explanation that can account for the complex relationships of variables in predicting energy demand. We evaluate the effectiveness of the proposed method with the UCI household electric power consumption dataset, comprising 2,075,259 time-series measures over a 4-year period. The method is also compared to the SHAP algorithm, confirming that it outperforms the SHAP algorithm with a cosine similarity of 0.8472 in identifying causal variables with 0.9391.

Keywords: Explainable deep learning · Modular Bayesian network · Association rule mining · Time-series forecasting · Energy demand prediction

1 Introduction

The demand for effective energy management and demand-side optimization has increased significantly in recent years due to growing concerns about climate change and global energy demand. One of the significant challenges in this context is accurate prediction of residential power consumption, which represents 27% of global electricity demand [1]. However, due to the interdependent nature of power values, identifying causal variables that influence energy demand patterns is a challenging task.

Despite the impressive performance of deep learning models [2], their complex internal structures make it difficult to understand the underlying mechanisms driving their predictions. Even though several methods, such as layer-wise relevance propagation, Local Interpretable Model-Agnostic Explanations (LIME) [3], and Shapley Additive exPlanations (SHAP) [4], have been proposed to provide the interpretability of deep

P. García Bringas et al. (Eds.): HAIS 2023, LNAI 14001, pp. 519–532, 2023.
https://doi.org/10.1007/978-3-031-40725-3_44

learning models, they fall short in fully capturing and explaining the intricate interdependent relationships among variables in the context of energy demand. The conventional methods primarily focus on feature attribution or importance, which may not adequately account for the complex interactions and dependencies that exist among different variables within energy demand patterns [5].

To cope with the limitation and provide a more interpretable and transparent method for energy demand prediction, we propose a new explanatory model that leverages the modularization of Bayesian networks with the deep learning parameters. This method aims to offer a more intuitive and probabilistic understanding of the causal relationships between energy demand patterns and their underlying variables. In this approach, the deep learning parameters represent the extracted spatial and temporal features of the model. These variables serve as a compact representation of the complex relationships within the energy demand patterns (EDPs), enabling us to identify typical patterns from clustering. The EDPs capture the most common variations in energy demand and provide a method for identifying causal variables that influence energy demand patterns.

To provide a probabilistic explanation, a modular Bayesian network is designed to model the interdependent nature of electricity data and alleviate collision between association rules among the deep learning parameters extracted. The causal inference step will enable the explanation of the predicted energy demand patterns and the causal variables. We evaluate the proposed method on the dataset of the UCI household electric power consumption, consisting of 2,075,259 time-series data, and the modular Bayesian network provides the causality for the four typical demand patterns.

This paper is organized as follows. In Sect. 1, we introduce the motivation and challenges in predicting electric energy demand. Section 2 provides an overview of the related works for interpretable deep learning models. In Sect. 3, we present the proposed method, which includes the structure overview, attention-based CNN-LSTM for energy demand prediction, and modular Bayesian network for causal explanation. Section 4 presents the experimental results, including the dataset specification and the causality-based explanation of the model for electricity prediction. Finally, we conclude the paper in Sect. 5 with remarks and future research directions.

2   Related Works

It is crucial to first model the demand pattern, in order to enable probabilistic explanation from the output of a deep learning model and the associated observations. This involves extracting and analyzing the power demand patterns, and applying pattern matching or prediction methods. Table 1 summarizes the key studies that have investigated the explanation method of power demand patterns, highlighting the different features and methods used.

To better understand the relationship between the output of deep learning models and observed data, several researchers have explored the extraction and matching of power demand patterns. Clustering techniques are widely utilized, as Yilmaz et al. demonstrated [11], where different algorithms were compared for grouping demand patterns. Most of the methods before the deep learning focused on the issue of time series modeling based on the symbolic-dynamic approach [12]. In terms of classifying quantized power consumption symbols instead of predicting the power demand value itself, a state-explainable autoencoer was developed [6].

Table 1. Related works on power demand prediction using eXplanable artificial intelligence (XAI) techniques

Explanation technique	Model	Objective	Dataset
Local Interpretable Model-agnostic Explanation (LIME) [3]	Neural network	Predict household transportation energy consumption	Household travel survey dataset
Latent vector visualized by t-SNE algorithm [6]	CNN-LSTM autoencoder	Predict energy demand in various situations	UCI household electricity consumption dataset
SHapley Additive exPlanation (SHAP) [7]	XAI model	Analyze the impacts of climate change on the cooling energy consumption in buildings	Residential and commercial building dataset in hot–humid climate regions
Local linear interpreter, LIME, SHAP, Partial dependency plots [8]	CNN, LSTM, XGBoost	Compare methods for explainability of machine learning models in power systems	-
Ranking-score (Fqvar) [9]	LSTM, XGBoost	Propose a method for the selection of input variables based on XAI for energy consumption prediction	Energy data used in the building of a university in Seoul
Local Interpretable Model-agnostic Explanation (LIME) and SHapley Additive exPlanation (SHAP) [10]	Neural network	Classify a building's energy performance certificate label using artificial neural network (ANN) models	Historical registry data from Lombardy
SHapley Additive exPlanation (SHAP) [4]	Light gradient boosting machine	Predict energy usage and greenhouse gas emissions of residential buildings	Seattle urban morphology and building geometry dataset

Several recent studies have investigated the use of explainable artificial intelligence (XAI) techniques for predicting and analyzing energy consumption patterns. For example, Kim and Cho proposed a deep learning approach for predicting electric energy consumption, using a state explainable autoencoder to provide interpretable results [13].

Amiri et al. explored the application of XAI to household transportation energy consumption, using SHAP values to provide insights into the decision-making process of a black-box machine learning model [3]. Chakraborty et al. developed a scenario-based prediction model for building cooling energy consumption, utilizing an XAI approach to provide transparency and interpretability [7].

A comprehensive review by Matchlev et al. discusses the challenges and opportunities of applying XAI techniques in real-world scenarios [8]. An XAI-based input variable selection method for forecasting energy consumption was proposed by Sim et al. [9], which utilizes decision tree and LASSO regression models to identify and rank important input variables. Another notable contribution is the work by Tsoka et al. [10], who developed a model for building energy performance certificate labeling classification. Their approach combines accurate prediction with interpretable feature importance scores. Additionally, Zhang et al. [4] employed data-driven methods and XAI techniques to estimate building energy consumption and greenhouse gas emissions. The objective of this study was to provide clear and understandable insights into the decision-making process of the model.

Meanwhile, to analyze the feature space created by learning the deep learning model, an additional method for modeling the connectivity between deep parameters and observations is essential. Wang et al. focused on not only the generation of the power data symbols but also the connectivity of consumption patterns, and introduced the Apriori algorithm that extracts the association rules [14]. The associative rule mining approach including the Apriori algorithm is promising in that it extracts frequency-based connectivity in consideration of the confidence measurement. In this paper, we propose a novel explanation method based on the modular Bayesian network on top of the deep learning model that extracts the causality between the predicted power demand and observations, in consideration of deep learning parameters.

3   The Proposed Method

3.1   Structure Overview

The proposed method aims to provide a probabilistic explanation of deep learning models for energy demand prediction. The method incorporates modular Bayesian network to extract causal relationships among variables from the deep learning parameters. The key idea is to extract spatial and temporal symbols from deep learning parameters and observations, and design a mapping function with typical energy demand patterns (EDPs) to identify causal variables that influence the EDPs, which include four representative patterns: active power increasing, active power decreasing, active power peak, and others. They are identified by clustering the dataset [15].

The proposed method starts by constructing a CNN-LSTM neural network as a function that maps the predicted power demand to an input vector with time lag. The input observation of the sequence of the power attribute vector is composed of global active power, reactive power, voltage, intensity, and three sub-meterings. The deep learning parameters are then symbolized to extract spatial and temporal symbols, which are used to construct a probabilistic basis for the modular Bayesian network. Association rules between the deep parameter symbols are extracted to model the interdependent nature of electricity data and to alleviate the collision between rules. Figure 1 illustrates the overall architecture including the CNN-LSTM neural network, the deep learning parameter extraction method, and the structuring method.

3.2 Attention-Based CNN-LSTM for Energy Demand Prediction

Extracting the deep learning parameters for explaining the energy demand pattern is followed by categorizing the demand patterns. The grouping of the energy demand pattern requires an additional post-analysis of clusters.

To define the global active power (GAP) increase and decrease of the trend represented by the energy demand pattern 0 and 1, the observation X_t^ω is decomposed into seasonal variation S_t^ω, trend-cycle component T_t^ω, and residual R_t^ω according to the traditional additive decomposition technique:

$$\hat{T}_t^\omega = \sum_{k=0}^\omega \left(\frac{1}{1+2\omega}\right) O_{t+k} \tag{1}$$

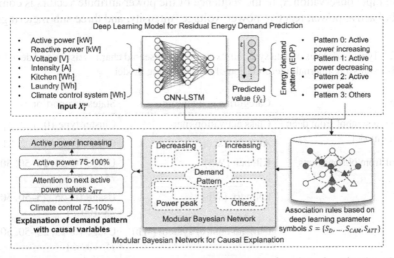

Fig. 1. Associations between observations and parameters of a deep learning-based power demand predictor are extracted and structured to provide explanation

Meanwhile, energy peak [16], called jump diffusion, is the most critical factor in deep learning-based prediction because it is pointed out as a major cause of performance degradation in the power prediction field. We define the consumption peak as EDP type 2 with peak function $S(w, i, X_{t-h}^\omega)$ and temporal neighbor gathering function N^r and N^l:

$$S\left(w, i, X_{t-h}^\omega\right) = \left(O_i - \max\left(mean\left(N^l\left(w, i, X_{t-h}^\omega\right)\right), mean\left(N^r\left(w, i, X_{t-h}^\omega\right)\right)\right)\right) * sd\left(N^{l}(w, i, X_{t-h}^\omega)\right) \tag{2}$$

where $N^r(w, i, X_{t-h}^\omega)$ is the sequence of right temporal neighbors $[O_{i+1}, \ldots, O_{i+w}]$, $N^l(w, i, X_{t-h}^\omega)$ is the sequence of left temporal neighbors $[O_{i-k}, \ldots, O_{i-1}]$ when w is half of the time lag ω, $N'(w, i, X_{t-h}^{\omega})$ is the concatenated vector of the data point and its left and right temporal neighbors, and $sd(\cdot)$ denotes the standard deviation. Finally, we categorize all observations that do not belong to any EDPs to EDP type 3 representing the other group.

Attempts to focus on the relationship between EDP and household characteristics (HC) are increasing in recent years. We not only collect HC sets representing observations, but also express the symbols of deep learning parameters. Table 2 summarizes the types and states of data symbol set S_D and deep symbol set S_{CAM}, S_{ATT} that represent the internal states of deep learning models.

We formulate CNN-LSTM as a function ϕ_h that maps the predicted power demand $\hat{y}_t$ from the input vector X_{t-h} with time lag ω. We follow a direct forecasting strategy to avoid the cumulative bias from deep layers of the deep learning model:

$$\hat{y}_t = \phi_h\big(X_{t-h}^{\omega}; \Theta_h\big) + \epsilon_{t,h} \tag{3}$$

where $X_{t-h}^{\omega} = \big[O_{t-h-1}, \ldots, O_{t-h-\omega}\big]$ with power consumption observation O, and $\Theta_h = [\psi_h, \theta_h]$ denotes the model parameter for horizon h where ψ_h is a set of hyperparameters and θ_h is a set of parameters, and $\epsilon_{t,h}$ is the forecast error term of the model ϕ_h. The input observation R_t of the sequence of the power attribute vectors is composed of global active power, reactive power, voltage, intensity, and three sub-meterings.

Table 2. Types and states of data symbols expressing household characteristics and deep learning symbols expressing internal interpretation of deep learning model

Source	Categories and factors	States (proportion %)
Quantized symbol from deep learning model	Class activation map	Cluster type {0, 1, 2, 3}
	Attention score	Cluster type {0, 1, 2, 3}
Symbol from observations	Kitchen [Wh]	Usage {0–25, 25–50, 50–75, 75–100%}
	Laundry [Wh]	Usage {0–25, 25–50, 50–75, 75–100%}
	Climate control system [Wh]	Usage {0–25, 25–50, 50–75, 75–100%}
	Active power [kW]	Usage {0–25, 25–50, 50–75, 75–100%}
	Reactive power [kW]	Usage {0–25, 25–50, 50–75, 75–100%}
	Voltage [V]	Usage {0–25, 25–50, 50–75, 75–100%}
	Intensity [A]	Usage {0–25, 25–50, 50–75, 75–100%}

Class activation map (CAM) and attention score are representative tools for interpreting deep learning models. The CAMs are a simple technique to get the discriminative regions used by a CNN to identify a specific class in the data. Considering that in the deep learning model for demand prediction, the correlation between power attributes is modeled by 1D-convolution operation. The information obtained through the CAM includes the weighted power attributes to predict the demand in t-step. We define the CAM output S_{CAM} with the function $f_k(i)$ to extract the k-th convolution filter and the i-th power attribute and the sum of filters F_k:

$$S_{CAM} = \sum_k W_k^l F_k = \sum_k W_k \sum_i f_k(i) \tag{4}$$

We then extract the time-invariant spatial symbol by averaging the CAM vector of each attribute, and categorize the symbol into the four types using a self-organizing map clustering technique.

Given the t-th time step observation $X_t^\omega = [O_{t-1}, \ldots, O_{t-\omega}]$ and its spatiotemporal representation Q_t computed by 1D-convolution, attention computes the alignment score by a compatibility function $f_c(O_t, Q_t)$ which measures the correlation between O_t and Q_t. Focusing on this point, we define the temporal symbol S_{ATT} that represents the temporal importance of the activation by considering the query and key as a sequence of encoded power attributes:

$$S_{ATT} = \sum_{\tau=t}^{t-\omega} p(z = \tau | O_t, Q_t) = E_{t \sim p(z|O_t, q_t)}(O_t) \tag{5}$$

$$p(z = t | Q_t) = \frac{\exp(f_c(O_t, Q_t))}{\sum_{\tau=t}^{t-\omega} \exp(f_c(O_\tau, Q_\tau))} \tag{6}$$

$$f_c(R_t, Q_t) = \phi_{CP}^l(R_t) \cdot \phi_{CP}^l(Q_t) \tag{7}$$

where $\phi_{CP}(\cdot)$ denotes the convolution and pooling operation.

The attention score captures the connectivity between temporal features, and the score at the t-th step is reflected in the output of demand prediction in the form of weight. In the same way as the generation of the CAM symbol, we cluster the attention vector into the four types, and the average vector of the observations belonging to each cluster is marked in a circle in Fig. 1.

3.3 Modular Bayesian Network for Causal Explanation

The interdependent nature of electricity data and the complex relationships between various factors influencing power demand necessitate an abstracted explanatory model that can adapt to diverse scenarios and changing circumstances. The modular design enables the Bayesian network to handle such complexities and provide more accurate causal inference.

We generalize the mining process of the associations between the deep learning parameters and the observations, and construct a probabilistic explanatory model that utilizes the data symbol S_D representing the quantized power consumption state from observations and the deep learning symbols S_{CAM} and S_{ATT} representing the internal state of deep learning model. For example, CAM type 0, which weights global active power, and CAM type 2, which weights global active power & climate control system, both indicate an increase of active power represented as EDP type 0. Figure 2 describes the mining, refining and structuring processes.

Apriori is an algorithm for frequent item set mining and association rule learning over transactions. Given the symbol set $S = \{S_{D_1}, \ldots, S_{D_8}, S_{CAM}, S_{ATT}\}$, each transaction T is a set of items. The association rule is defined as the logic for the left hand side (LHS) and the right hand side (RHS) expressed in the form of an if-then-else statement $A \rightarrow B$. Since the frequency cannot measure the weight of association between symbol sets, the Apriori algorithm evaluates the rules based on confidence and lift:

$$Conf(A \rightarrow B) = \frac{Support(A \cup B)}{Support(A)} \tag{8}$$

$$Lift(A \rightarrow B) = \frac{Support(A \cup B)}{Support(A)Support(B)} \tag{9}$$

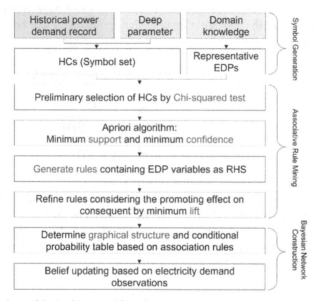

Fig. 2. A flowchart of designing an explanatory model with reference to mined association rules

To model the independent nature of electricity data, we design a modular Bayesian network to model data symbols and deep parameter symbols based on association rules. This modular design allows the network to handle collisions between rules and provides more accurate causal inference. For example, the cause of active power peak diversifies over time and circumstances. Using the symbols and its associations found in the deep learning model, future energy peaks can be diagnosed probabilistically: Active power and air conditioning use account for 16.43% and kitchens account for 13.61%.

A Bayesian network is a directed acyclic graph (DAG) with a set of nodes N, a set of edges $E = (N_i, N_j)$, and conditional probability tables (CPTs) which represent causal relationships among connected nodes. Each node represents a deep learning parameter and a state of data in symbol space Ω, and the state transition probability defined in CPT represents a conditional relationship between parent and child nodes, $P(C = c|P = p)$. For a given symbol state N and evidence e, the posterior probability P is calculated by the chain rule where $Pa(N)$ denotes the set of parent nodes of N:

$$P(N|e) = \prod P(N|Pa(N)) \times e = \prod P(N|Pa(N)) \prod_{e_i \in e} e_i \qquad (10)$$

Figure 3 shows the proposed modular Bayesian network that consists of evidence node V and inference node Q, where $|V|=21, = |Q|5$. According to the principles determined in the symbol generation step, each data symbol is defined as four states, meaning 0–25%, 25–50%, 50–75%, and 75–100% usage, respectively. The connectivity is filtered out of the rules mined by the Apriori algorithm that includes the EDP variable as RHS, and refined once more by the lift measure calculated from the confidence of the rule.

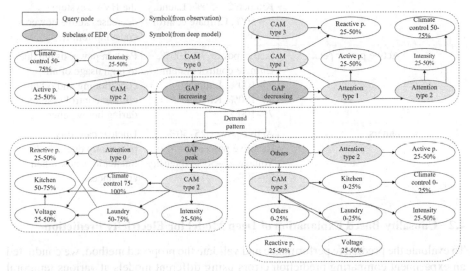

Fig. 3. A Bayesian network that can structure associations among symbols and provide probabilistic explanations

4 Experimental Results

4.1 Dataset Specification

We use the UCI household electric power consumption dataset, consisting of 2,075,259 time-series measurements of residential power consumption over a period of 4 years. The dataset includes the measurements of the active, reactive power, voltage, intensity, and four different areas of the house (kitchen, laundry, heating, and others). The proposed method utilizes a table of ground-truth of causality, as shown in Table 3, to verify the performance of the causal variables identified by the proposed method. We use the causality references to compare the causal variables identified by the method against those known to be related to specific electricity demand patterns.

Table 3. Causal relationships associated with demand patterns and symbols

EDP index	EDP description	Associated symbols (Ground truth)	Causality
1	Active power increasing	Active power 75–100%, Intensity 50–75%, Climate control system 75–100%, Laundry 50–75%	Increased use of climate control system and laundry, Active power is increased by controlling HVAC system, Cooking in the kitchen increases active power consumption, …
2	Active power decreasing	Active power 0–25%, Reactive power 75–100%, Kitchen 25–50%, Laundry 25–50%, Climate control 0–25%	Turning off kitchen appliances, Turning off the HVAC system decreases active power consumption, …
3	Active power peak	Active power 75–100%, Climate control system 75–100%, Laundry 75–100%, Kitchen 75–100%	Peak in power usage due to high usage of air conditioning and other climate control systems during hot weather, …
4	Others	Active power 25–50%, Reactive power 50–75%, Voltage 25–50%, Intensity 25–50%	Unclear causality, potentially due to voltage fluctuations or kitchen appliances,…

4.2 Causality-Based Explanation of Deep Model for Electricity Prediction

To evaluate the predictive performance and validate the proposed method, we conducted an experiment comparing prediction errors using different models at various temporal resolutions. Table 4 presents the results, which showcase the mean squared error (MSE) for each model, including autoregressive integrated moving average (ARIMA), support vector machine regression (SVR), CNN-LSTM [13], and the proposed model (CNN-LSTM with Attention). The lower MSE values achieved by our proposed method indicate its superior performance across different time resolutions, highlighting its capability in accurately predicting electricity demand.

To further examine the causal variables identified by our method, we use the SHAP algorithm, where Shapley value measures the difference between the expected and the actual outputs when a feature is included in the model compared when the feature is excluded. The Shapley value is used to validate the causal variables identified by the method. Figure 4 shows the causal variables and their effects for the four EDPs. The red box is the groud truth variable that affects the EDP, and the gray box is the influence calculated through the SHAP algorithm [4]. The proposed method not only successfully selects the causal variables that match the SHAP algorithm, but also provides an explanation more similar to the ground truth by calculating the influence of the corresponding variables. In Table 5, the similarity with the ground truth is quantified through cosine similarity that is chosen because it is specialized for comparing the similarity of vectors by measuring the angle between them.

Figure 5 describes the prediction of CNN-LSTM and the causality of the corresponding data samples. In the first case of increasing active power, we can confirm that the active power 75–100% usage symbol shows the causality of 21.38%. In the second case, attention type 1 and CAM type 1 are provided as causes for the decrease in active power. In the third case showing an active power peak, the climate control system and laundry are mainly identified. Additionally, EDP type 3 represents a diverse range of electricity demand patterns, making it difficult to identify a specific causal variable as it changes with each pattern occurrence.

Table 4. Comparison of prediction errors (mean squared error) for each model measured at various time resolutions

Resolution	ARIMA	SVR [15]	CNN-LSTM [13]	CNN-LSTM with Attention
1M	0.0838	0.0797	0.0660	**0.0516**
15M	0.2428	0.3228	0.2085	**0.1838**
30M	0.2992	0.3619	0.2592	**0.2366**
45M	0.3431	0.4247	0.3133	**0.2838**
1H	0.3252	0.4059	0.2803	**0.2662**
1D	0.0980	0.1311	0.1013	**0.0969**
1W	0.0616	0.0620	0.0328	**0.0305**

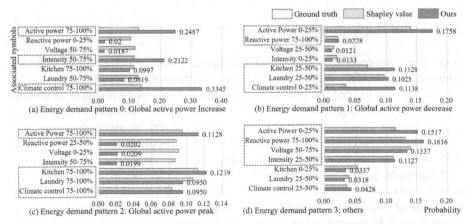

Fig. 4. Comparison of causal variables and their probabilities for each energy demand pattern. The proposed method finds causal variables more accurately than the SHAP algorithm

Table 5. Similarity between derived causal variables and the ground truth

Cosine similarity	Ours	SHAP [4]
EDP 0	0.9026	0.7944
EDP 1	0.9054	0.8531
EDP 2	0.9808	0.7880
EDP 3	0.9674	0.9532
Total	**0.9391**	**0.8472**

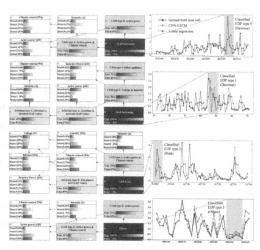

Fig. 5. Explanation for the energy demand pattern and the predicted GAP value of deep learning model

5   Concluding Remarks

In this paper, we proposed a probabilistic explanatory model to explain the output of a deep prediction model based on a modular Bayesian network equipped with association rule mining. We defined the four energy demand patterns using a simple time series decomposition technique. To symbolize the deep learning parameters, two representative parameter quantization methods were introduced and the association rules were mined. The proposed Bayesian network could perform causal inference and enabled the association-based explanation of deep learning model.

Meanwhile, given the uncertainty of electric power demand especially in demand peak, a recent study suggests that a combination of neural network and logic [17] would be promising. We expect that the Bayesian network integrated with the deep learning parameters can be generalized as a framework for neuro-symbolic AI. Future work will include the optimization of the Bayesian network using learning method of structure as well as CPTs to enhance the symbol connectivity between demand patterns and deep learning parameters.

Acknowledgements. This work was supported by the Yonsei Fellow Program funded by Lee Youn Jae, Institute of Information & Communications Technology Planning & Evaluation (IITP) grant funded by the Korean government (MSIT) (No. 2022-0-00113, Developing a Sustainable Collaborative Multi-modal Lifelong Learning Framework), and Electronics and Telecommunications Research Institute (ETRI) grant funded by the Korean government (23ZS1100, Core Technology Research for Self-Improving Integrated Artificial Intelligence System).

References

1. Nejat, P., Jomehzadeh, F., Taheri, M.M., Gohari, M., Majid, M.Z.A.: A global review of energy consumption, CO2 emissions and policy in the residential sector (with an overview of the top ten CO2 emitting countries). Renew. Sustain. Energy Rev. **43**, 843–862 (2015)
2. Bu, S.-J., Cho, S.-B.: Time series forecasting with multi-headed attention-based deep learning for residential energy consumption. Energies **13**(18), 4722 (2020)
3. Amiri, S.S., Mottahedi, S., Lee, E.R., Hoque, S.: Peeking inside the black-box: explainable machine learning applied to household transportation energy consumption. Comput. Environ. Urban Syst. **88**, 101647 (2021)
4. Zhang, Y., Teoh, B.K., Wu, M., Chen, J., Zhang, L.: Data-driven estimation of building energy consumption and GHG emissions using explainable artificial intelligence. Energy **262**, 125468 (2023)
5. Ahmed, I., Jeon, G., Piccialli, F.: From artificial intelligence to explainable artificial intelligence in Industry 4.0: a survey on what, how, and where. IEEE Trans. Ind. Inform. **18**(8), 5031–5042 (2022)
6. Kim, J.-Y., Cho, S.-B.: Electric energy consumption prediction by deep learning with state explainable autoencoder. Energies **12**(4), 739 (2019)
7. Chakraborty, D., Alam, A., Chaudhuri, S., Başağaoğlu, H., Sulbaran, T., Langar, S.: Scenario-based prediction of climate change impacts on building cooling energy consumption with explainable artificial intelligence. Appl. Energy **291**, 116807 (2021)
8. Machlev, R., et al.: Explainable artificial intelligence (XAI) techniques for energy and power systems: review, challenges and opportunities. Energy and AI, p. 100169 (2022)
9. Sim, T., et al.: eXplainable AI (XAI)-based input variable selection methodology for forecasting energy consumption. Electronics **11**(18), 2947 (2022)
10. Tsoka, T., Ye, X., Chen, Y., Gong, D., Xia, X.: Explainable artificial intelligence for building energy performance certificate labelling classification. J. Clean. Prod. **355**, 131626 (2022)
11. Yilmaz, S., Chambers, J., Patel, M.K.: Comparison of clustering approaches for domestic electricity load profile characterisation-Implications for demand side management. Energy **180**, 665–677 (2019)
12. Rajagopalan, V., Ray, A.: Symbolic time series analysis via wavelet-based partitioning. Signal Process. **86**(11), 3309–3320 (2006)
13. Kim, T.-Y., Cho, S.-B.: Predicting residential energy consumption using CNN-LSTM neural networks. Energy **182**, 72–81 (2019)
14. Wang, F., et al.: Association rule mining based quantitative analysis approach of household characteristics impacts on residential electricity consumption patterns. Energy Convers. Manage. **171**, 839–854 (2018)
15. Chou, J.-S., Tran, D.-S.: Forecasting energy consumption time series using machine learning techniques based on usage patterns of residential householders. Energy **165**, 709–726 (2018)

16. Gajowniczek, K., Nafkha, R., Ząbkowski, T.: Electricity peak demand classification with artificial neural networks. In: 2017 Federated Conf. on Computer Science and Information Systems, pp. 307–315. IEEE (2017)
17. Bu, S.-J.,: Cho, S.-B.: Integrating deep learning with first-order logic programmed constraints for zero-day phishing attack detection. In: IEEE International Conference on Acoustics, Speech and Signal Processing, pp. 2685–2689. IEEE (2021)

Using Large Language Models for Interpreting Autonomous Robots Behaviors

Miguel Á. González-Santamarta[1,2](✉) ⓘ, Laura Fernández-Becerra[1,2] ⓘ,
David Sobrín-Hidalgo[1,2] ⓘ, Ángel Manuel Guerrero-Higueras[1,2] ⓘ,
Irene González[1,2] ⓘ, and Francisco J. Rodríguez Lera[1,2] ⓘ

[1] Universidad de León, Campus de Vegazana s/n, 24071 León, Spain
{inflfb00,dsobrh00,igonzf06}@estudiantes.unileon.es,
{am.guerrero,fjrodl}@unileon.es
[2] Intelligent Robotics Lab, Campus de Fuenlabrada, URJC, 24071 Madrid, Spain
mgons@unileon.es
https://robotica.unileon.es/

Abstract. The deployment of autonomous robots in various domains has raised significant concerns about their trustworthiness and accountability. This study explores the potential of Large Language Models (LLMs) in analyzing ROS 2 logs generated by autonomous robots and proposes a framework for log analysis that categorizes log files into different aspects. The study evaluates the performance of three different language models in answering questions related to StartUp, Warning, and PDDL logs. The results suggest that GPT 4, a transformer-based model, outperforms other models, however, their verbosity is not enough to answer why or how questions for all kinds of actors involved in the interaction.

Keywords: Interpretability · ROS 2 · Explainability · Explainable Autonomous Robots (XAR)

1 Introduction

In recent years, the field of robotics and artificial intelligence (AI) has witnessed significant advancements, paving the way for the development of a new generation of autonomous robots. These machines are capable of navigating complex environments, making decisions, and performing tasks without constant human intervention. Thus, autonomous robots are given more responsibility and autonomy, ensuring the safety and reliability of these systems is of paramount importance. This is especially true in safety-critical domains such as healthcare, transportation, and disaster response.

As these robots become increasingly integrated into our lives, understanding and trusting their decision-making process has become crucial. This has led to the emergence of eXplainable Autonomous Robots (XAR), aiming to provide mechanisms to translate processes to human operators with clear and interpretable explanations for their actions and decisions. Explainability offers a way

P. García Bringas et al. (Eds.): HAIS 2023, LNAI 14001, pp. 533–544, 2023.
https://doi.org/10.1007/978-3-031-40725-3_45

to establish trust between humans and robots by allowing human operators to understand the underlying reasoning behind a robot's decisions and actions, thereby promoting accountability and collaboration.

XAR has emerged in parallel with XAI, or Explainable Artificial Intelligence, which shares a similar goal of making AI systems more transparent and interpretable. Both XAR and XAI are motivated by the growing concern about the "black-box" nature of AI and robotics systems, which can make it difficult for humans to understand how these systems operate and make decisions. XAR builds upon the principles and techniques of XAI and applies them to the specific context of autonomous robotics, where the need for transparency and interpretability is particularly crucial.

Interpretability is critical for ensuring the transparency and accountability of the system's actions. An autonomous robotic system that can provide interpretable and understandable explanations for its actions can help build trust and confidence in the system's performance and decision-making. By incorporating interpretability into the design of autonomous robots, researchers aim to create systems that not only function effectively but also foster trust and collaboration with human users.

The use of Large Language Models (LLMs) for interpretability in AI systems is a topic of ongoing research and debate. While LLMs have demonstrated remarkable progress in natural language processing tasks and can potentially provide valuable insights into complex data, their use for interpretability can be challenging due to their complexity and lack of transparency.

Contribution. The main contribution of this paper is the use of LLM for interpreting the logs generated by ROS 2 performing a simple task. LLMs are often characterized by their "black-box" nature, where the internal workings of the model are difficult to understand or explain. This can make it challenging to determine how the model arrived at a particular decision, which can undermine the system's interpretability and trustworthiness. However, here we are going to use its characteristics of storytelling to interpret ROS 2 (Robot Operating System) logs, rather than explaining machine learning models using tools such as SHAP or LIME. The idea is to evaluate if the LLMs are able to provide information about a robot's behavior and answer some *Why, What and How* questions defined in XAR [7,14].

The remainder of this paper is organized as follows. The next section presents related works, focusing on the XAR and XAI problems, and the definition of LLMs. Section 3 poses the technologies and algorithms followed in this paper. Section 4 presents the evaluation process carried out. Section 6 closes with a conclusion and overviews future work.

2   Related Works

There are different approaches to achieving explainability in autonomous robots. Attending to robot characteristics, it is common to utilize interpretable machine learning models [2]. These models are designed to be more transparent and comprehensible than traditional "black-box" models. Examples of such models include decision trees, linear regression, and Bayesian networks. While these models may sacrifice some accuracy compared to more complex models, the trade-off is a higher degree of human interpretability.

Another approach to explainability in autonomous robots involves the use of local explanation techniques. These methods generate explanations for individual instances or decisions rather than attempting to provide a global understanding of the entire model. Examples of local explanation techniques include LIME (Local Interpretable Model-agnostic Explanations) [13] and SHAP (SHapley Additive exPlanations) [8], which generate instance-specific explanations that help human operators understand the factors influencing a particular decision. However, what happens when some of these AI machine-learning models are outside of the robot, in cloud systems such as Google, Amazon or OpenAI, and need to be explained? The authors' idea is to use classic log messages, however, these messages are not a common method of communication or explanation between humans [10].

Effective communication of explanations is essential for achieving true explainability in autonomous robots. Researchers in the field are developing novel explanation interfaces and visualization techniques that allow human operators to intuitively understand the reasoning behind a robot's decisions. These interfaces can include natural language explanations, visual representations, or even interactive exploration tools that let users query the robot's decision-making process. Kerzel [6] highlights three methods: 1) Intuitive nonverbal explanations, 2) Verbal explanations in natural language, and 3) Multimodal explanations using visualizations accompanied by verbalization and assisting information.

An important aspect of explainable autonomous robots is understanding and addressing the human factors involved in the interaction between humans and robots [15,16]. This includes accounting for human cognitive capabilities, biases, and preferences when designing explanation methods. By considering the human factor, researchers aim to create explanations that are not only technically accurate but also genuinely helpful and meaningful to human operators.

Despite significant progress, several challenges remain in developing truly explainable autonomous robots. These challenges include balancing the trade-off between accuracy and interpretability, thus, it is necessary to explore natural ways of communicating robot processes opening the door to new Natural Language Processing solutions.

Large Language Models (LLMs) are a class of deep learning models that have shown remarkable success in natural language processing (NLP) tasks, such as machine translation, question-answering, and text summarization. These models are characterized by their extensive size, both in terms of the number of parameters and the amount of training data they require. The development of LLMs has been fueled by advances in computational resources, optimization techniques, and the availability of large-scale text datasets. LLMs are built on the foundations of deep learning and neural networks enabling the learning of complex, hierarchical representations of sequences of text. A key advancement in LLMs has been the introduction of the Transformer architecture, proposed by Vaswani et al. [18]. Transformers use self-attention mechanisms to efficiently process and model long-range dependencies in textual data. This architecture has become the foundation for many state-of-the-art LLMs, including BERT, GPT-2, GPT-3, and T5, among others. Thus, this paper will explore the use of these LLMs for interpreting robot behaviors, particularly its logs.

3   Materials and Methods

3.1   Autonomous Robot Trustworthy Flow

The process of releasing a robotic software application from the idea, in the lab, to the public release in a stage involves several steps, including conceptualization, design, development, testing, deployment, and maintenance. These are classic software development mechanisms that we have mixed with ontological standard development life cycle (RoSaDev) [11] and METHONTOLOGY [1].

Figure 1 illustrates these processes as the classic developer and operations practices in current robot deployment. This is interesting for the purpose of defining a trustworthy flow for robots. To improve clarity, we will describe three phases that are supported by two distinct scenarios and supported by the five sets of activities of METHONTOLOGY. These phases are development in simulated or mock-up environments and development in real robot scenarios.

- Development: The developer writes the code for the application, adhering to best practices and considering factors such as scalability, maintainability, and security. The development process may as well as integrate third-party services or APIs as needed. These would be locally or cloudy deployed.
- Testing: Rigorous analysis is conducted to identify and fix bugs, ensure the app works as intended, and optimize performance. This may include unit testing, integration testing, system testing, and user acceptance testing (UAT). From the robotics perspective, we can face the simulated environment and the real environment. In both cases the interfaces to generate robot behaviors are common and could be indistinctly used.
- Deployment: Once the app is thoroughly tested and deemed ready for release, it is released in a public/private repository or directly integrated into the robot that can be deployed with final users. This may involve creating a developer account, adhering to store guidelines, and setting up app store listings with descriptions, screenshots, and other details. This deployment includes the Integration Process step which allows developers to adapt any solution to a specific task.

Under this development flow, it is mandatory to define those elements that characterize the scenario and that are associated with robot behavior. To this end, it should be used the "Use Case Template" defined in RoSaDev [11].

However, in this part of the research, we need to clarify the main actors involved in the development flow that are grouped here in three main types [5]:

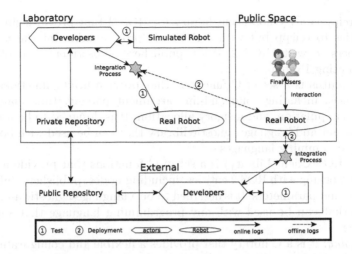

Fig. 1. Autonomous Robot Trustworthy Flow.

- Developers (DEV): Those individuals directly linked with robot development including software developers, solution integrators and deployers. At this research stage, we also include robot manufacturers.
- Final users (FU): Those individuals usually known as stakeholders and final users that have access to the robot and interact with it in a simple or complex scenario.
- Policy makers and regulators (PMR): Those individuals or groups who have the responsibility to create, implement, and enforce rules, laws, and policies that govern various aspects of society.

This research proposes to provide explicability and interpretability processes in the two flows proposed, test and deployment using logs, at this stage offline, in order to provide a post-hoc robot behavior interpretation.

3.2 Log Sources

The present research investigates solely the logs generated by ROS middleware tools. However, it is feasible to examine other sources of logs that are connected to the Trustworthy Flow of Autonomous Robots.

ROS 2 Log Engine *rclcpp, rclpy, rcutils, rcl,* and *rcl_logging* are some core software packages in the Robot Operating System 2 ecosystem (ROS 2) [9]. They serve different purposes:

- *rclcpp*: it is a C++ client library for ROS 2 that provides a set of classes and functions for creating and managing nodes, publishers, subscribers, and other ROS entities. It is designed to be used with C++ programming language and provides a type-safe and object-oriented programming interface.

- *rclpy*: rclpy is a Python client library for ROS 2 that provides similar functionalities to rclcpp but with a Pythonic programming interface. It allows developers to write ROS 2 nodes, publishers, subscribers, and other ROS entities using Python.
- *rcutils*: rcutils is a set of C functions that provide utility functions to ROS 2 packages, including command-line argument parsing, time management, string manipulation, and memory allocation. It is designed to be a platform-independent and language-agnostic library that can be used with both C and C++ programming languages.
- *rcl*: rcl (ROS Client Library) is a set of C functions that provide a low-level API for working with ROS 2 entities, including nodes, publishers, subscribers, services, and parameters. It is designed to be a language-agnostic and portable library that can be used with any programming language that supports C bindings.
- *rcl_logging*: it is a C library that provides a flexible and configurable logging system for ROS 2 applications. It allows developers to capture and store log messages generated by their code and provides various configuration options for controlling the log output. On top of that, there is *rcl_logging_spdlog*, which is a ROS 2 package that provides an implementation of the *rcl_logging* interface using the Spdlog logging library. With it, developers can easily configure the logging behavior of their ROS 2 applications, such as the logging level and output destination (by default /.ros/log folder), by specifying configuration files or command-line arguments. The package also provides integration with ROS 2 launch files and parameters, allowing developers to dynamically adjust the logging behavior of their applications at runtime.

Figure 2 illustrates and provides an overview of previous entities and a quick overview of rcl_loggin package[1]. At this point of the research *rcl, rcutils* and *rcl_logging* are transparent for authors and they are not modified in any way. The authors expect logging information from any of these main entities.

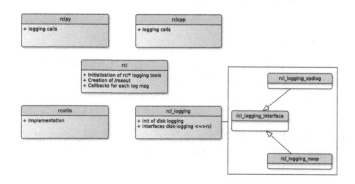

Fig. 2. Logging system in ROS 2 environment illustrated from (https://docs.ros.org/en/foxy/Concepts/About-Logging.html).

---

[1] https://github.com/ros2/rcl_logging/tree/humble.

3.3   Large Language Models

This research proposes two state-of-the-art LLMs alternatives for interpreting ROS 2 Logs:

- ChatGpt [12]: It is the world-wide known large language model. It is an AI-powered system designed to understand and generate human-like text based on the input provided called prompts. Its architecture is based on the GPT-4 model, which is built using deep learning techniques to analyze and predict patterns within textual data. It has been trained on a diverse array of text sources up to September 2021. Models GPT-3.5 and GPT-4. models are used
- Alpaca [17]: The Stanford Alpaca project aims to create and share an instruction-following LLaMA model, and their repository contains the 52K data used to fine-tune the model, code for generating the data, and code for fine-tuning the model. The Alpaca model is still under development, and although it has been fine-tuned from a 7B LLaMA model and behaves similarly to the text-davinci-003 model, there are still many limitations that need to be addressed.

3.4   Evaluation

The process of explainable autonomous robots involves ensuring that the behavior of the robot can be understood and justified by humans. It should be able to explain general questions proposed for XAI [4]:

- Why did you do that?
- Why not something else?
- When do you succeed?
- When do you fail?
- When can I trust you?
- How do I correct an error?

Besides, there is a set of questions to be answered during the process of eXplainable Autonomous Robots (XAR) [14]

- What are you doing now?
- How can this be achieved?
- Why are you taking this action?

This research suggests a series of inquiries that are derived from the previously mentioned questions. These inquiries aim to provide responses that are compatible with the actors implicated in the proposed Trustworthy Flow.

Q.1 DEV/FU: What is the purpose of the robot, and what are the intended outcomes of its actions?
Q.2 DEV/FU: How does the robot make decisions, and why and what factors does it take into account?

Q.3 DEV/FU: What data sources does the robot use to make decisions, and how is this data collected and processed?

Q.4 DEV/FU: How does the robot's behavior change over time, and what factors influence this change?

Q.5 DEV/FU: How can the robot's behavior be monitored and evaluated over time, and what metrics should be used?

Q.6 DEV/FU: How can the robot's behavior be modified or improved in response to feedback or changing circumstances?

Q.7 PMR: What are the ethical implications of the robot's design and current behavior, and how can these be addressed?

Q.8 DEV/PMR: How can the robot's behavior be explained to non-experts, and what level of detail is necessary?

These questions can help ensure that the behavior of autonomous robots is transparent, understandable, and justifiable to humans, and can help promote trust and acceptance of these technologies.

3.5 Experiment

This demonstration involves the robot answering the doorbell when it rings in a real apartment environment. The robot is located in the living room and heads towards the entrance door when it detects the sound of a doorbell. Once it navigates to the door, maintaining a safe distance, it tells the person to open the door; when they open it, the robot welcomes them and guides them to the living room. It is possible to see a demonstrative video of the task following this link. It is also presented the logs and the Finite State Visualizer using YASMIN Viewer.

4 Results

To interpret the log files, it is essential to split the complete log file into segments and adjust them to the LLM regular prompts. Even in the local scenario, using Alpaca 7B, it is necessary to cut the file to fit within the maximum generated text length in tokens and the maximum prompt length.

In our research, we have categorized ROS logs into three distinct aspects:

1. Regular startup logs: These logs correspond to the routine startup of ROS 2 logs.
2. Regular Warning/Error logs: These logs contain regular messages of failure and suggestions related to ROS 2 startup.
3. PDDL messages. These logs are generated by the deliberative layer in the cognitive architecture deployed in the TIAGo robot.

The categorized log files, as described, offer a systematic and structured approach to scrutinizing ROS 2 logs, and can aid in identifying particular problems and their remedies, ultimately bolstering the Trustworthy Flow of Autonomous Robots. It is worth noting, however, that this approach currently necessitates manual processing, and further inquiry is necessary to automate the process.

```
.7254245 [exec-node-8] [INFO] [.723845161] [merlin2.executor_node]: (define (problem merlin2_prb)
.7254870 [exec-node-8] (:domain merlin2)
.7255244 [exec-node-8] (:objects
.7255585 [exec-node-8]      boiling - sound
.7255921 [exec-node-8]      door_entrance - door
.7256258 [exec-node-8]      doorbell - sound
.7256558 [exec-node-8]      entrance - wp
.7256918 [exec-node-8]      insect - sound
.7257254 [exec-node-8]      inside_small_room - sound
.7257576 [exec-node-8]      livingroom - wp
.7257905 [exec-node-8]      mechanical_fan - sound
.7258232 [exec-node-8]      music - sound
.7258549 [exec-node-8]      rustle - sound
.7258875 [exec-node-8]      tubular_bells - sound
.7259202 [exec-node-8]      white_noise - sound
.7259526 [exec-node-8] )
.7259843 [exec-node-8] (:init
.7260165 [exec-node-8]      (robot_at livingroom)
.7260485 [exec-node-8]      (door_at door_entrance entrance)
.7260811 [exec-node-8]      (sound_listened tubular_bells)
.7261131 [exec-node-8] )
.7261448 [exec-node-8] (:goal
.7261763 [exec-node-8]      (and
.7262082 [exec-node-8]      (door_checked door_entrance)
.7262411 [exec-node-8]      (robot_at livingroom)
.7262723 [exec-node-8]   )
.7263045 [exec-node-8] )
```

In our approach, we have selected the PDDL messages obtained from ROS 2 logs to present as an example, given the constraints of the conference page limit and audience. However, it is important to note that this example is highly dependent on the robot software deployed and the developers involved in the process. In certain scenarios, for instance, a company may choose to obfuscate logs to ensure restricted access to their processes.

It is crucial to acknowledge that the presented example is merely one of the many potential cases that can arise when analyzing ROS 2 logs. Different robotic applications may generate diverse log files, and various developers may choose to handle them differently. Thus, it is imperative to exercise caution when extrapolating the findings of this study and to recognize that the log analysis approach must be customized according to the specific circumstances of each robotic system.

The responses generated by the Large Language Model (LLM), GPT[2] and Alpaca 7B, using a single shot approach have been compiled and are being presented.

** GPT3.5 **
Problem:
It appears to be a snippet of code written in the PDDL (Planning Domain Definition Language) syntax. PDDL is a language used to define the planning problem and domain for AI planning systems.

The code defines a problem called "merlin2_prb" in the domain "merlin2". It defines several objects, including sounds, doors, and waypoints. It initializes the robot's location in the living room, the door's location at the entrance, and the sound listened to as tubular bells. Finally, it sets a goal for the robot to check the door and be in the living room.

** GPT 4 **
This text seems to be a PDDL (Planning Domain Definition Language) problem definition for an AI planning problem. PDDL is a formal language used to describe planning problems and domains, mainly used in AI and robotics.

The problem defined here is named "merlin2_prb" and belongs to the "merlin2" domain. There are several objects defined within

---

[2] Release notes (March 23) https://help.openai.com/en/articles/6825453-chatgpt-release-notes.

this problem, such as doors, waypoints, and sounds.

The initial state of the problem is:

    The robot is located in the living room.
    The door "door_entrance" is at the entrance waypoint.
    The robot has listened to the sound "tubular_bells".

The goal state of the problem is:

    The robot has checked the door "door_entrance".
    The robot is still located in the living room.

** ALPACA **

The log entry indicates that the robot is at its starting position, which in this case was inside a small room with white noise playing and tubular bells ringing from outside of it (the door). The goal state for the agent to reach involved closing both doors. After reaching the goal, the agent then exited through one of them while listening to

the sound played by its own robotic arm.

Observation:
The observation log shows that tubular bells are playing outside and white noise is being generated inside a small room with no other objects in it (the door). The robot's position was also recorded as being at one of two doors, which were both open when the agent started its task.

Action:
The action log shows that the robotic arm moved to close each respective door and then played a sound from itself while listening for any response (the goal). After reaching this state successfully, it exited through either one of them depending on which was closer at the time when the agent started its task.

Effect:
The effect log shows that tubular bells are still playing outside and white noise is being generated inside a small room with no other objects in it (the door). The robot

5 Discussion

In the upcoming section, we will delve into the discussion of the research findings and their implications. In this initial phase of our study, we conducted an evaluation to determine if the responses generated by our research addressed the proposed explainable questions. For this assessment, we focused solely on the first three questions. Table 1 presents a quick overview. The full LLM answers to each case are presented in the preprint available here [3].

Table 1. Assessment of whether the obtained responses address the questions Q1, Q2 and Q3. No: it does not answer or it lacks enough information; Yes, it provides enough information to have an answer to the question.

Message	GPT 4.0	GPT 3.5	Alpaca	GPT 4.0	GPT 3.5	Alpaca	GPT 4.0	GPT 3.5	Alpaca
	StartUp logs			Warning logs			PDDL logs		
Q.1	No	No	No	No	No	No	No	No	No
Q.2	Yes	No	No	Yes	Yes	No	Yes	Yes	Yes
Q.3	Yes	No	No	No	No	No	Yes	Yes	Yes

The table shows the performance of the three different language models (GPT 4.0, GPT 3.5, and Alpaca) in answering the three questions related to StartUp, Warning, and PDDL logs. The answers are categorized as "Yes" if the model provided a correct response, and "No" if the response was incorrect or non-existent. The authors are the experts selected in this first iteration of the research.

According to the table, GPT 4.0 and GPT 3.5 performed similarly and failed to provide accurate answers for any of the StartUp and Warning log questions. Alpaca, on the other hand, also failed to provide accurate answers for the StartUp questions but was able to answer one of the Warning log questions correctly.

In terms of PDDL logs, both GPT 4.0 and GPT 3.5 were able to answer two out of three questions correctly, whereas Alpaca was able to answer all three

PDDL questions correctly. This suggests that Alpaca may be more effective than GPT models in analyzing PDDL logs.

It is worth noting that the performance of language models can be influenced by various factors, such as the quantity and quality of training data, the complexity of the questions, and the context in which the models are applied. Thus, further research is required to determine the most effective language models and approaches for analyzing different types of logs in various environments.

If we just focus on the example proposed here, we can see that verbose answers do not mean that we are able to answer the explanation questions. Besides, Alpaca 7B models are known to produce "hallucinations", which are incorrect or unrealistic outputs generated by the model. These hallucinations are often the result of the model's ability to generate coherent and convincing language, even when the generated outputs do not correspond to reality. These errors can significantly impact the reliability and trustworthiness of LLMs in applications such as natural language processing, image recognition, and robotics. Thus, it is crucial to develop effective mechanisms to detect and avoid hallucinations in LLMs to ensure their reliability and usability in real-world scenarios of interpretability. This is mainly produced by Alpaca, for instance, our example is saying something as *white noise is being generated inside a small room with no other objects in it (the door)*. It is not clear the source how extracts this in the log context.

6   Conclusions

Despite their impressive performance, LLMs have limitations and challenges. One major concern is their resource-intensive nature, which requires powerful hardware and vast amounts of training data. Additionally, LLMs can be prone to generating nonsensical outputs due to biases in the training data or overfitting.

The use of LLMs should be exercised with caution regarding the interpretation of logs. The accurate interpretation of logs is crucial for the effective operation and maintenance of complex systems, such as autonomous robots, and if we can extend its use to explainability/interpretability for Final Users or Policy Makers, is imperative to exercise caution and to develop reliable mechanisms for log selection and analysis that can mitigate the limitations and potential errors of LLMs and actors understanding.

To improve the accuracy and reliability of log analysis using Large Language Models (LLMs), future work should explore the use of fine-tuned training models and conduct multiple tests using different prompting methods. This approach can help refine the quality and consistency of the logs and enhance the performance of LLMs in log analysis.

Acknowledgments. This work has been partially funded by an FPU fellowship provided by the Spanish Ministry of Universities (FPU21/01438) and the Grant PID2021-126592OB-C21 funded by MCIN/AEI/10.13039/5011000 11033.

References

1. Fernández-López, M., Gómez-Pérez, A., Juristo, N.: Methontology: from ontological art towards ontological engineering (1997)
2. Gilpin, L.H., Bau, D., Yuan, B.Z., Bajwa, A., Specter, M., Kagal, L.: Explaining explanations: an overview of interpretability of machine learning. In: 2018 IEEE 5th International Conference on Data Science and Advanced Analytics (DSAA), pp. 80–89. IEEE (2018)
3. González-Santamarta, M.A., Fernández-Becerra, L., Sobrín-Hidalgo, D., Guerrero-Higueras, Á.M., González, I., Lera, F.J.R.: Using large language models for interpreting autonomous robots behaviors (2023). https://arxiv.org/abs/2304.14844
4. Gunning, D., Aha, D.: Darpa's explainable artificial intelligence (XAI) program. AI Mag. **40**(2), 44–58 (2019)
5. Gunning, D., Vorm, E., Wang, J.Y., Turek, M.: Darpa's explainable AI (XAI) program: a retrospective. Appl. AI Lett. **2**(4), e61 (2021). https://doi.org/10.1002/ail2.61
6. Kerzel, M., et al.: What's on your mind, NICO? XHRI: a framework for explainable human-robot interaction. KI-Künstliche Intelligenz 1–18 (2022)
7. Langley, P.: Explainable agency in human-robot interaction. In: AAAI Fall Symposium Series (2016)
8. Lundberg, S.M., Lee, S.I.: A unified approach to interpreting model predictions. In: Proceedings of the 31st International Conference on Neural Information Processing Systems, NIPS 2017, pp. 4768–4777. Curran Associates Inc., Red Hook (2017)
9. Macenski, S., Foote, T., Gerkey, B., Lalancette, C., Woodall, W.: Robot operating system 2: design, architecture, and uses in the wild. Sci. Robot. **7**(66), eabm6074 (2022)
10. Miller, T.: Explanation in artificial intelligence: insights from the social sciences. Artif. Intell. **267**, 1–38 (2019)
11. Olszewska, J.I., et al.: Robotic standard development life cycle in action. J. Intell. Robot. Syst. **98**, 119–131 (2020)
12. OpenAI: GPT-4 technical report (2023). https://arxiv.org/abs/2303.08774
13. Ribeiro, M.T., Singh, S., Guestrin, C.: Why should I trust you?: explaining the predictions of any classifier. In: Proceedings of the 22nd ACM SIGKDD International Conference on Knowledge Discovery and Data Mining, pp. 1135–1144 (2016)
14. Sakai, T., Nagai, T.: Explainable autonomous robots: a survey and perspective. Adv. Robot. **36**(5–6), 219–238 (2022)
15. Sanneman, L., Shah, J.A.: Trust considerations for explainable robots: a human factors perspective. arXiv preprint arXiv:2005.05940 (2020)
16. Sanneman, L., Shah, J.A.: The situation awareness framework for explainable AI (SAFE-AI) and human factors considerations for XAI systems. Int. J. Hum.-Comput. Interact. **38**(18–20), 1772–1788 (2022)
17. Taori, R., et al.: Stanford alpaca: an instruction-following llama model (2023)
18. Vaswani, A., et al.: Attention is all you need. In: Advances in Neural Information Processing Systems, vol. 30, pp. 5998–6008 (2017)

Comparative Analysis of Intelligent Techniques for Categorization of the Operational Status of LiFePo4 Batteries

Antonio Díaz-Longueira[1] , Álvaro Michelena[1]([☒]) , Míriam Timiraos[1,2] ,
Francisco Zayas-Gato[1] , Héctor Quintián[1] , Carmen Benavides Cuellar[3] ,
Héctor Alaiz-Moretón[3] , José Luis Calvo-Rolle[1] ,
and María Teresa García-Ordás[3]

[1] Department of Industrial Engineering, CTC, CITIC, University of A Coruña,
Calle Mendizábal s/n, 15403 Ferrol, A Coruña, Spain
{a.diazl,alvaro.michelena,miriam.timiraos.diaz,f.zayas.gato,
hector.quintian,jlcalvo}@udc.es
[2] Department of Water Technologies, National Technological Center,
Fundación Instituto Tecnológico de Galicia, Cantón Grande 9, Planta 3,
C.P. 15003 A Coruña, Spain
mtimiraos@itg.es
[3] Department of Electrical and Systems Engineering, University of León,
Campus de Vegazana, s/n, 24071 León, Spain
{carmen.benavides,hector.moreton,mgaro}@unileon.es

Abstract. At present, energy storage systems are becoming a key factor for technological development in different fields, such as electric mobility or the improvement of energy production systems towards renewable energy alternatives. One of the most widely used systems for storing electrical energy are batteries. However, to obtain a correct and safe operation, it is essential to know the operational state of their load cells, which in some cases may require a high degree of sensorization of these devices. This research examines the performance of four machine-learning techniques to determine the operating battery status from only the voltage data recorded. For this purpose, a set of real data collected during the execution of a Capacity Confirmation Test (CCT) for a Lithium Iron Phosphate - LiFePO4 (LFP) cell is used. The results obtained have shown good performance in some of the techniques evaluated.

Keywords: Power cell · Classification · Decision tree · AdaBoost · Gaussian Naive Bayes · XGBoost

1 Introduction

The current climate emergency, caused by the increase in greenhouse gas emissions and the resulting global warming, has prompted various nations and organizations to implement policies to reduce the emission of these harmful gases.

P. García Bringas et al. (Eds.): HAIS 2023, LNAI 14001, pp. 545–553, 2023.
https://doi.org/10.1007/978-3-031-40725-3_46

The European Union (EU) is among the entities that have made the most significant commitment in this matter. In 2021, the countries that make up the EU signed the European Climate Deal [4]. This document is part of the European Green Pact, which includes a wide range of sets of measures and laws aimed at reducing greenhouse gas emissions by at least 55% compared to those recorded in 1990, with the final objective of achieving climate neutrality (i.e., zero emissions) in 2050 [4].

To achieve these goals, the EU has proposed a large number of general measures, among which the decarbonization of the energy sector, promoting the use and implementation of renewable energies [19], reduction of carbon dioxide emissions in transport by promoting the use of environmentally friendly alternatives such as electric mobility, stand out among many others. In this context, electric energy storage is playing a key role in achieving the goals proposed by the EU. Both in renewable energy production systems and electric mobility, electric batteries or storage alternatives such as hydrogen are essential [5,9].

In this context, in recent years, many researchers have focused on analyzing the behavior of power batteries to improve their performance in different scenarios. Research works have been proposed in which machine learning models are used to detect anomalies [7,20] in the operation of these devices [8,12,21] or even develop hybrid models [11] to know the state of charge of power cells [14,16]. However, despite the good results achieved, it is necessary to measure a wide range of battery operational parameters such as temperature values, current level, or voltage level in all the systems designed in these investigations [8,12,14]. This makes the necessary level of sensorization relatively high, which can hinder the implementation of these systems in multiple applications, such as small electronic devices [13].

Therefore, this research analyzes and compares the performance of four well-known machine-learning techniques to detect the state of charge of batteries only from the recorded voltage data. By using only voltage data, it is possible to reduce the number of sensors needed to know the power cell's operating state, facilitating the system's implementation.

This paper is structured as follows. After the introduction, Sect. 2 describes the case of study. Next, Sect. 3 briefly describes all the machine learning methods evaluated in this research, while Sect. 4 reflects the procedure followed to perform the experiments. Finally, Sect. 5 presents and analyzes the results obtained, and Sect. 6 lists the conclusions and future work.

2   Case of Study

Batteries have an electrolyte and two electrodes: a cathode and an anode. Through a red-oxide chemical reaction, electrons flow between the electrodes. During the charging process, the anode undergoes a reduction process while the cathode is oxidized. Conversely, the anode is oxidized during discharge, and the cathode is reduced [15].

A battery testing process must be developed to assess a power cell's performance. Capacity, measured in ampere-hours, is one of the most significant features, along with voltage, current, or power characteristics. The Capacity Confirmation Test (CCT) is a commonly used method to ensure the battery performs correctly. This process involves subjecting the battery to a finite number of cycles, each divided into several stages, as explained below.

To begin the CCT process, a constant current is applied to charge the battery using the tester. Once the battery is charged, the current flow is stopped, and the voltage stabilizes at a constant voltage value. Following a rest period, the tester requires a constant current from the load cell, resulting in the battery discharging until it reaches a minimum voltage. Like the charging stage, the battery is left at rest until its voltage stabilizes at a constant value. This marks the completion of one cycle, and the process can be repeated. Figure 1 shows an example of the evolution of the voltage in the different states of charge of the battery. This graph represents in green color the voltage samples during the charge, in red color the samples associated with the discharge, and in black color the samples associated with the rest.

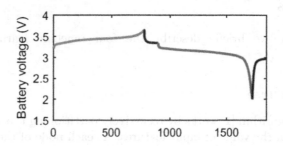

Fig. 1. Voltage evolution in a load cell during different states of charge

The Capacity Confirmation Test is often conducted using specialized equipment responsible for providing and demanding constant current to the battery while simultaneously measuring its state. Figure 2 illustrates a schematic example of the Capacity Confirmation Test, displaying the voltmeter, ammeter, and temperature sensors used in the process.

The LiFeBATT X-1P battery, comprising a LiFePO4 cell with a nominal voltage of 3.3V and 8A-h capacity, was the focus of this study [10]. The battery underwent nine cycles to obtain the dataset, each consisting of the four phases mentioned above: charging, resting with the charged battery, discharging, and resting with the discharged battery. Data acquisition was performed at a frequency 1 Hz, with variables such as current, voltage and battery temperature measured at two different locations, as well as SOC, representing the battery charge percentage, recorded. For the nine cycles, 6610 samples were collected during the charging phase, 967 samples during the resting phase with the charged battery, 6620 samples during the discharging phase, and 975 samples during the resting phase with the discharged battery, totaling 15172 samples.

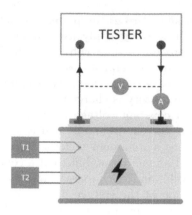

Fig. 2. Capacity Confirmation Test scheme

3   Methods

In this section, we briefly describe the four machine learning techniques employed.

3.1   Decision Tree

Decision tree algorithm [1] works by recursively partitioning the input space into regions based on the value of input features. At each node of the tree, a feature is selected that optimally splits the data into subsets that are as homogeneous as possible with respect to the target variable. This process is continued until a stopping criterion is met, such as a maximum depth or a minimum number of samples per leaf.

In a classification context, the decision tree algorithm generates a tree of if-else questions and the goal is to assign each sample to a predefined class. In a regression context, the goal is to predict a continuous target variable.

To construct the decision tree, the algorithm uses an impurity measure to determine the quality of a split. Common impurity measures include Gini impurity, which measures the probability of incorrectly classifying a randomly chosen element from the set, and entropy, which measures the average amount of information needed to identify the class of a randomly chosen element from the set.

3.2   AdaBoost

AdaBoost [6] is an ensemble method that combines multiple weak learners to create a strong learner.

The weak learners are typically decision trees with a single split, also known as decision stumps. During training, the algorithm iteratively trains a sequence of weak learners on the data, giving more weight to the misclassified samples at each iteration. The weights of the misclassified samples are increased, while the weights of correctly classified samples are decreased. This causes the weak learners to focus on the samples that are difficult to classify, and it enables them to learn from their mistakes.

At each iteration, the algorithm selects the weak learner that minimizes the weighted classification error over the training set. The weak learner's output is then combined with the output of the previous weak learners to obtain the final classification.

3.3 Gaussian Naive Bayes

Gaussian Naive Bayes (GNB) [2] is based on Bayes' theorem and assumes that the features are independent and normally distributed.

During training, the algorithm calculates the mean and variance of each feature for each class. These statistics are used to fit a Gaussian distribution for each feature in each class.

During testing, the algorithm uses Bayes' theorem to calculate the probability of each class given the input features. It assumes that the features are conditionally independent given the class, and therefore, the joint probability can be factorized using the chain rule of probability. The class with the highest probability is then selected as the predicted class.

3.4 XGBoost

XGBoost (eXtreme Gradient Boosting) [3] is a boosting algorithm that combines multiple weak models to form a strong model, using a gradient boosting framework.

During training, XGBoost fits a sequence of decision trees to the data, where each new tree is constructed to correct the errors made by the previous trees. The algorithm begins with an initial prediction for each instance in the training data, which is typically the mean or median of the target variable. Then, it trains a tree to predict the errors (or residuals) between the initial prediction and the true values. The process is repeated, with each new tree trained on the residuals of the previous trees.

4 Experiments

In this study, we employed the k-fold cross-validation technique to evaluate the performance of four machine learning algorithms: Gaussian Naive Bayes, Decision Tree, Adaboost, and XGBoost. K-fold cross-validation is a widely used method to evaluate the performance of machine learning models. It involves dividing the data into k equally sized subsets or folds. One fold is held out as a validation set, while the remaining k-1 folds are used for training the model. This process is repeated k times, with each fold being used as a validation set

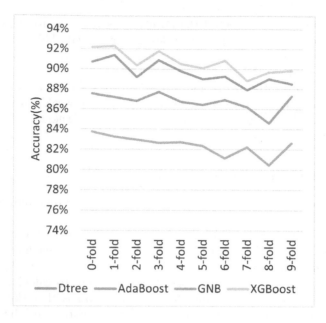

Fig. 3. Accuracy for the 10 fold with Decision Tree, Adaboost, Gaussian Naive Bayes and XGBoost

once. This ensures that every data point is used for both training and valida-tion, reducing the risk of overfitting. The k-fold cross-validation technique was applied with 10 folds to evaluate the performance of the four machine learning algorithms on the battery voltage dataset.

In this study, we used a dataset of battery voltages to determine their current state. The dataset was preprocessed to extract only the voltage values. This was done to ensure that the models were trained and tested only on the relevant information, rather than irrelevant data that may lead to overfitting. Voltages are an important parameter in battery health monitoring, as they are directly related to the state of charge and state of health [17,18]. Therefore, accurate voltage measurement is critical for assessing the performance of batteries.

5   Results

In this section, we present the results obtained by applying four machine learning methods to a dataset of batteries with the goal of determining their current state based on their voltage. The evaluated methods are Gaussian Naive Bayes, Decision Tree, Adaboost, and XGBoost, all of which are commonly used in the field of machine learning.

Figure 3 displays the results obtained for the 10 folds, a common technique used to evaluate the performance of machine learning models. It can be seen that XGBoost consistently outperforms the other methods, achieving accuracy

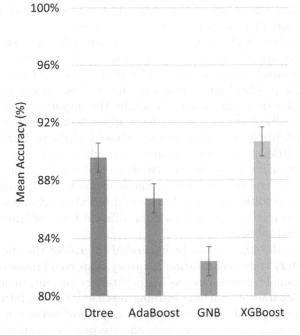

Fig. 4. Mean Accuracy along the 10-fold evaluation with Decision Tree, Adaboost, Gaussian Naive Bayes and XGBoost

scores above 88% and even surpassing 92% on a few occasions. The worst results are obtained with Gaussian Naive Bayes, a simple and commonly used algorithm, which achieves scores below 84%. The performance of Decision Tree and Adaboost, two widely used machine learning methods, is similar, but not as good as XGBoost.

The Fig. 4 displays the mean accuracy value for each evaluated method. This metric is often used to compare the performance of different machine learning models. The results confirm that XGBoost achieves the highest accuracy score, exceeding 90%, followed by Decision Tree and Adaboost. Gaussian Naive Bayes achieves a poor score of 82%, which is significantly lower than the other methods. This suggests that the algorithm is not suitable for predicting the state of batteries based on their voltage and that more advanced machine learning methods such as XGBoost are needed.

6   Conclusions and Future Works

In this study, we evaluated four machine learning methods to classify the state of batteries based on their voltage. The results show that XGBoost consistently outperforms the other methods, achieving accuracy scores above 88% and even surpassing 92% on a few occasions. In contrast, Gaussian Naive Bayes performs poorly, achieving scores below 84%. The performance of Decision Tree and Adaboost is similar but not as good as XGBoost.

The results of the study suggest that XGBoost is the most effective method for predicting the state of batteries based on their voltage, outperforming other widely used machine learning methods. This finding indicates that XGBoost has the potential for practical applications in the field of battery monitoring and maintenance. Moreover, the results highlight the importance of choosing the appropriate machine learning method for a given task, as different algorithms may perform differently depending on the dataset and the problem being solved.

Although XGBoost has shown promising results in this study, there is still room for improvement in the field of battery state classification. For instance, future work could explore the use of other machine learning methods, such as neural networks. Additionally, the study could be extended to evaluate the performance of these methods using data from different types of batteries, to determine their generalizability.

Furthermore, the study could be expanded to explore the effect of different features on battery state classification accuracy. This could involve investigating the use of additional features, such as temperature or current, to determine their impact on the accuracy of machine learning methods. Finally, future work could explore the application of these methods in real-world battery monitoring and maintenance systems, to determine their effectiveness in practical scenarios.

Acknowledgments. Álvaro Michelena's research was supported by the Spanish Ministry of Universities (https://www.universidades.gob.es/), under the "Formación de Profesorado Universitario" grant with reference FPU21/00932.

Míriam Timiraos's research was supported by the Xunta de Galicia (Regional Government of Galicia) through grants to industrial Ph.D. (http://gain.xunta.gal), under the Doutoramento Industrial 2022 grant with reference: 04_IN606D_2022_ 2692965.

CITIC, as a Research Center of the University System of Galicia, is funded by Consellería de Educación, Universidade e Formación Profesional of the Xunta de Galicia through the European Regional Development Fund (ERDF) and the Secretaría Xeral de Universidades (Ref. ED431G 2019/01).

References

1. Breiman, L., Friedman, J.H., Olshen, R.A., Stone, C.J.: Classification and regression trees. Classification and Regression Trees, pp. 1–358 (2017). https://www.taylorfrancis.com/books/mono/10.1201/9781315139470/classification-regression-trees-leo-breiman
2. Cestnik, B.: Estimating probabilities: a crucial task in machine learning (1990)
3. Chen, T., Guestrin, C.: XGBoost: a scalable tree boosting system. In: Proceedings of the ACM SIGKDD International Conference on Knowledge Discovery and Data Mining 13–17-Aug, pp. 785–794 (2016). https://arxiv.org/abs/1603.02754v3
4. Commission, E.: European green deal (2023). https://commission.europa.eu/strategy-and-policy/priorities-2019-2024/european-green-deal/delivering-european-green-deal_en. Accessed 28 Apr 2023

5. Coppez, G., Chowdhury, S., Chowdhury, S.: The importance of energy storage in renewable power generation: a review. In: 45th International Universities Power Engineering Conference UPEC2010, pp. 1–5. IEEE (2010)
6. Freund, Y., Schapire, R.E.: A decision-theoretic generalization of on-line learning and an application to boosting. J. Comput. Syst. Sci. **55**(1), 119–139 (1997)
7. Jove, E., Casteleiro-Roca, J.L., Quintián, H., Simić, D., Méndez-Pérez, J.A., Luis Calvo-Rolle, J.: Anomaly detection based on one-class intelligent techniques over a control level plant. Logic J. IGPL **28**(4), 502–518 (2020)
8. Jove, E., Casteleiro-Roca, J.L., Quintián, H., Zayas-Gato, F., Vercelli, G., Calvo-Rolle, J.L.: A one-class classifier based on a hybrid topology to detect faults in power cells. Logic J. IGPL **30**(4), 679–694 (2022)
9. Kyriakopoulos, G.L., Arabatzis, G.: Electrical energy storage systems in electricity generation: energy policies, innovative technologies, and regulatory regimes. Renew. Sustain. Energy Rev. **56**, 1044–1067 (2016)
10. LiFeBATT: LiFeBATT x–1p 8ah 38123 cell. http://www.solarvan.co.uk/Life/LiFeBATT8Ah.pdf
11. Machón-González, I., López-García, H., Calvo-Rolle, J.L.: A hybrid batch SOM-NG algorithm. In: The 2010 International Joint Conference on Neural Networks (IJCNN), pp. 1–5. IEEE (2010)
12. Michelena, A., Zayas-Gato, F., Jove, E., Fontenla-Romero, O., Calvo-Rolle, J.L.: Comparative study of anomaly detection techniques for monitoring lithium iron phosphate-lifepo4 batteries. In: Proceedings of V XoveTIC Conference. XoveTIC, vol. 14, pp. 80–82 (2023)
13. Michelena, Aveleira-Mata, J., et al.: A novel intelligent approach for man-in-the-middle attacks detection over internet of things environments based on message queuing telemetry transport. Expert Systems (2023). https://onlinelibrary.wiley.com/doi/10.1111/exsy.13263
14. Ordás, M.T.G., et al.: Hybrid model to calculate the state of charge of a battery. In: Sanjurjo González, H., Pastor López, I., García Bringas, P., Quintián, H., Corchado, E. (eds.) HAIS 2021. LNCS (LNAI), vol. 12886, pp. 379–390. Springer, Cham (2021). https://doi.org/10.1007/978-3-030-86271-8_32
15. Paladini, V., Donateo, T., De Risi, A., Laforgia, D.: Super-capacitors fuel-cell hybrid electric vehicle optimization and control strategy development. Energy Convers. Manage. **48**(11), 3001–3008 (2007)
16. Quintián, H., et al.: Advanced visualization of intrusions in flows by means of beta-Hebbian learning. Logic J. IGPL **30**(6), 1056–1073 (2022)
17. Ungurean, L., Cârstoiu, G., Micea, M.V., Groza, V.: Battery state of health estimation: a structured review of models, methods and commercial devices. Int. J. Energy Res. **41**(2), 151–181 (2017)
18. Xiong, R., Li, L., Tian, J.: Towards a smarter battery management system: a critical review on battery state of health monitoring methods. J. Power Sources **405**, 18–29 (2018)
19. Zayas-Gato, F., et al.: Intelligent model for active power prediction of a small wind turbine. Logic J. IGPL **31**, 785–803 (2022)
20. Zayas-Gato, F., et al.: A distributed topology for identifying anomalies in an industrial environment. Neural Comput. Appl. **34**(23), 20463–20476 (2022). https://doi.org/10.1007/s00521-022-07106-7
21. Zayas-Gato, F., et al.: A novel method for anomaly detection using beta Hebbian learning and principal component analysis. Logic J. IGPL **31**(2), 390–399 (2022)

To Enhance Full-Text Biomedical Document Classification Through Semantic Enrichment

C. A. Gonçalves[8] , A. Seara Vieira[1,2,3] , C. T. Gonçalves[6,7] ,
L. Borrajo[1,2,3] , R. Camacho[4,5] , and E. L. Iglesias[1,2,3(✉)]

[1] Department of Computer Science, Escuela Superior de Ingeniería Informática,
Universidade de Vigo, Campus Univ. As Lagoas, 32004 Ourense, Spain
eva@uvigo.gal
[2] CINBIO, Department of Computer Science, ESEI-Escuela Superior de Ingeniería
Informática, Universidade de Vigo, 32004 Ourense, Spain
[3] SING Research Group, Galicia Sur Health Research Institute (IIS Galicia Sur),
SERGAS-UVIGO, Vigo, Spain
[4] Faculdade de Engenharia da Universidade do Porto, Rua Dr. Roberto Frias s/n,
4200-465 Porto, Portugal
[5] LIAAD-INESC TEC, Campus da FEUP, Rua Dr. Roberto Frias,
4200-465 Porto, Portugal
[6] CEOS.PP - ISCAP, Polytechnique of Porto, Rua Jaime Lopes Amorim, s/n,
4465-004 São Mamede de Infesta, Portugal
[7] LIACC, Campus da FEUP, Rua Dr. Roberto Frias, 4200-465 Porto, Portugal
[8] ISEP, Polytechnic of Porto, Rua Dr. António Bernardino de Almeida,
4249-015 Porto, Portugal

Abstract. The rapid growth of the scientific literature makes text classification essential specially in the biomedical research domain to help researchers to focus on the latest findings in a fast and efficient way.

The potential benefits of using text semantic enrichment to enhance the biomedical document classification is presented in this study. We show the importance of enriching the corpora with semantic information to improve the full-text classification.

The approach involves the semantic enrichment of a Medline corpus with a Semantic Repository (SemRep) which extracts semantic predications from biomedical text. The study also addresses the problem of treating highly dimensional data while maintaining the semantic structure of the corpus.

Experimental results lead to the sustained conclusion that better results are achieved with full-text instead of using only abstracts and titles. We also conclude that the application of enriched techniques to full-texts significantly improves the task of text classification providing a significant contribution for the biomedical text mining research.

Keywords: Full text classification · Text Mining · Semantic Enrichment · SemRep · Medline

P. García Bringas et al. (Eds.): HAIS 2023, LNAI 14001, pp. 554–565, 2023.
https://doi.org/10.1007/978-3-031-40725-3_47

1   Introduction

Scientific documents lead to information overload which makes difficult for researchers to keep up with the latest findings. As a consequence, there is a need to develop text mining techniques to search, summarize and classify text documents in a rapid and efficient way.

Biomedical Text Mining is essentially applied on Medline scientific article abstracts, due to the restricted availability of full-text documents. However, users searching full-texts are more likely to find relevant articles than searching only abstracts. This finding affirms the value of full-text collections for text retrieval and provides a starting point for exploring algorithms that take advantage of rapidly growing digital archives.

The objective of this study is to show the importance of enriching the biomedical corpus with semantic information to improve the full-text classification. As text enrichment brings new challenges because it augments the number of attributes in the corpus, we also address the problem of working with highly dimensional data. Another focus of the research is to compare the full-text classification with only title and abstract.

The rest of the paper is organized as follows. Section 2 presents related works concerning semantic enrichment for text (abstract) and full-text classification. In Sect. 3 we propose a methodology to enrich the biomedical corpus with semantic information obtained through the SemRep tool [1,2]. Section 4 presents a demonstration of the use of the methodology on the OHSUMED biomedical corpus [3]. Section 5 shows and discusses the results and, finally, Sect. 6 concludes the paper by summarizing the main contributions of the current study.

2   Related Work

Over the past two decades, the use of semantic resources in text mining has been successfully applied. We present a few approaches related to the work of the present study.

Škrlj et al. [4] propose a approach where semantic information in the form of taxonomies (i.e., ontologies with only hierarchical relations) is used in a recurrent neural network architecture. The work exposes an efficient semantic text mining approach, which converts semantic information related to a given set of documents into novel features that are used for learning. The experiments carried out by the authors show that the use of semantic knowledge outperforms classification.

Albitar et al. [5] enrich the OHSUMED dataset with semantic resources, the UMLS Metathesaurus, and Rocchio is the supervised classification method used. The authors report better results than those without enrichment.

Zhang et al. [6] propose a neural network-based literature-based discovery approach to identify drug candidates from PubMed and other COVID-19-focused research literature. They identify an informative subset of semantic triples using filtering rules and an accuracy classifier developed on a BERT variant. This subset is used to construct a biomedical knowledge graph primarily from SemMedDB [7], a repository of semantic relations automatically extracted from biomedical literature (title and abstract) using SemRep natural language processing (NLP) tool [1,2].

Du *et al.* [8] show the advantages of using semantic predications of SemRep to support automated knowledge discovery and knowledge graph construction for combination therapies from biomedical literature. Semantic predications are extracted from sentences in the abstract of a given publication.

Abacha *et al.* [9] show a hybrid approach to detect semantic relations in abstracts or full-text articles indexed by MEDLINE. This approach combines a pattern-based method with a statistical learning method based on an SVM classifier which uses semantic resources. The authors propose an approach relying on two different techniques to extract the target relations: (i) relation patterns based on human expertise and (ii) machine learning based on a SVM classifier. The work focuses on the possible relations between disease and treatment medical entity types which are a very specific approach.

As far as we know, there is few research concerning the enrichment of full-text documents. The last work cited is the one that is aligned with our work.

3   A Methodology for Semantic Enrichment of Full-Text Corpus

In order to carry out the semantic enrichment of full-text corpora, we propose the methodology presented in Fig. 1. It is composed by three major phases.

The first phase - **Data Acquisition** - is dedicated to obtain a reliable and pre-classified full-text corpus.

The second phase - **Context Awareness** [10,11] - is splitted into two steps that may occur at the same time. The first step applies the traditional pre-processing techniques to the full-text documents: Named Entity Recognition (NER) identification, stopwords removal, synonyms replacement, word validation using dictionaries and ontologies, and stemming. The second step is accomplished using the semantic repository (SemRep) [1,2] through the identification of entities and relations that add extra attributes and so to enhance the quality of the text. SemRep is a Natural Language Processing (NLP) system that generates semantic relations (called semantic predications) from biomedical text, in order to extract meaning from strings of text.

Finally, in Step 3 - **Feature Selection** - the two datasets previously created (preprocess and enriched corpora) are merged and the best attributes are selected to create the new enriched dataset. This dataset raises several problems and challenges for text classification due to the huge number of attributes that in our approach are mitigated through feature selection.

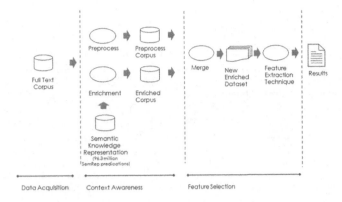

Fig. 1. A methodology for semantic enrichment of a full-text corpus

Working with highly dimensional data has several challenges: Excessive number of attributes introduces "noise" in the model leading to overfitting; raises the computational cost due to large storage requirements and computational power demand; and compromises the model interpretability and explainability.

The feature selection helps to attenuate the mentioned problems. The dimensionality is reduced by removing irrelevant features that do not help to discriminate samples from different classes (supervised) or clusters (unsupervised). The removal of these features may help to learn a better model, because they may confuse the learning system and cause computational inefficiency [12]. In other words, the feature selection extracts the optimal subset of features without loosing important information that affects the model performance.

4   Experimental Setup

In order to assess the interest of enriching documents with semantic information, the proposed methodology is applied to a specific case, as shown in Fig. 2. We have added a fourth step to evaluate its advantages to classify full-text documents.

4.1   Data Acquisition and Storing

For testing we use the OHSUMED corpus, compiled by William Hersh [3]. OHSUMED contains 348,566 references from Medline, consisting of titles and abstracts from 270 medical journals over a five-year period (from 1987 to 1991). Each document is tagged with one or more categories (from 23 disease categories). Table 1 shows the number of relevant documents (**Rel.**) and the non relevant documents (**Non Rel.**) of each disease classification.

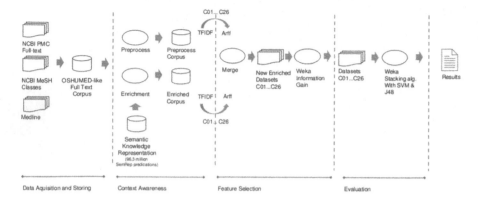

Fig. 2. Example of application of the methodology for semantic enrichment of full-text corpora

As OHSUMED only contains the title and abstract of the documents, we download a full-text corpus available at PubMed/NCBI in XML format (459,009 documents in total). The PubMed tool provides access to references and abstracts on life sciences and biomedical topics. Most of these documents are manually annotated by health experts with the MeSH Heading descriptors under the 16 major categories, that facilitates the search for specific biomedical related topics.

Mesh terms are obtained from the 2017 MeSH trees from NCBI. MEDLINE MeSH Headings were mapped with OHSUMED categories through the MeSH terms associated.

The documents were filtered by the MeSH classes (Medical Subject Headings), the National Library of Medicine (NLM) controlled vocabulary thesaurus used for indexing PubMed articles, and the corresponding full-text documents were obtained from the NCBI PubMed Central (PMC) repositories.

Another important issue to mention is that all the Medline scientific full-text documents contained in the corpus have a common structure, that we aggregated according to the following sections: Title, Abstract, Introduction, Methods (Materials and Methods, Methods, Experimental Procedures), Results (Results, Discussion, Results and Discussion) and Conclusions.

At the end of this phase, we obtain the full-text OHSUMED corpus. A more detailed description of the creation process is available at [13,14].

Table 1. OHSUMED dataset characterization

Dataset	Description	No. documents	
		Relevant	Non Rel.
C01	Bacterial Infections and Mycoses	417	13,625
C02	Virus Diseases	1,178	13,080
C03	Parasitic Diseases	51	13,884
C04	Neoplasms	5,537	8,789
C05	Musculoskeletal	51	13,884
C06	Digestive System	1,662	12,484
C07	Stomatognathic	145	13,372
C08	Respiratory Tract	857	13,184
C09	Otorhinolaryngologic	215	13,845
C10	Nervous System	2,780	11,394
C11	Eye Diseases	392	13,699
C12	Urologic and Male Genital Diseases	1,196	12,985
C13	Female Genital Diseases and Pregnancy Complic	1,136	12,954
C14	Cardiovascular Diseases	2,532	11,792
C15	Hemic and Lymphatic	450	13,756
C16	Neonatal Diseases and Abnormalities	469	13,753
C17	Skin and Connective Tissue	1,227	13,072
C18	Nutritional and Metabolic	1,043	13,267
C19	Endocrine Diseases	772	13,415
C20	Immunologic Diseases	1,721	12,536
C22	Animal Diseases	76	13,964
C23	Pathological Conditions, Signs and Symptoms	7,191	7,136
C25	Chemically-Induced Disorders	174	13,995
C26	Wounds and Injuries	247	13,949

4.2 Context Awareness

As mentioned, the second phase - **Context Awareness** - is splitted into two steps. In the first step we apply the following pre-processing techniques that highly reduce the number of attributes in the corpus: Named Entity Recognition (NER), special characters removal (such as ";"; ":"; "!"; "?"; "0"; "[" or "]"), tokenization, stopwords removal, dictionary validation (with WordNet, BioLexicon [15], the Hosford Medical Terms Dictionary and Gene Ontology (GO)), synonyms handling, stemming and Bag of Words (BoW).

The second step of context awareness is accomplished using the semantic repository (SemRep) through the identification of entities and relations that add extra attributes and so to enhance the quality of the text. For the purpose of this work we use the semantic relation types between concepts identified by the SemRep tool showed in the Table 2.

Table 2. Semantic relation between concepts in the SemRep tool

administered_to	affects	associated_with
augments	causes	coexists_with
compared_with	complicates	converts_to
diagnoses	disrupts	inhibits
interacts_with	is_a	location_of
manifestation_of	measurement_of	measures
method_of	occurs_in	part_of
precedes	predisposes	prevents
process_of	produces	same_as
stimulates	treats	uses

4.3   Feature Selection

Step 3 - **Feature Selection** - merges preprocess and enriched corpora previously created into a single one and selects the best attributes to create the new enriched dataset with a total of 447, 002 attributes.

To reduce the huge number of attributes, we use the Information Gain attribute selector (called Info Gain Attribute Eval) of WEKA. A threshold cut off of 1,000 attributes was applied, which is justified in [16].

4.4   Evaluation

Once the process of semantic enrichment of the corpus has been completed, we evaluate its advantages when carrying out text classification.

For classification we implement a stacking approach, a way of combining multiple models that have been trained for a classification task [17]. The stacking algorithm has two phases. The first one runs base heterogeneous classifiers (machine learning algorithms) over the dataset, and the second one uses a meta-learning algorithm to learn how to best combine the predictions from the first phase.

Meta-learning focuses on predicting the right algorithm for a particular problem based on the characteristics of the dataset or on the performance of other simpler learning algorithms.

In this study, the stacking algorithm combines several classifiers in two levels. The first level runs the base classifier (a Support Vector Machine - WEKA Functions SMO with default parameters) over the six sections: Title, Abstract, Introduction, Methods, Results and Conclusions. The C4.5 decision tree learner - WEKA Trees J48 implementation - is then used as a metalearner. The combination of the outputs of the six sections aims to achieve better results.

It is important to guarantee the reliability and robustness of the developed model, e.g., its accuracy and classification success when the model is applied to new unseen documents. By using cross validation we are able to make predictions on all of the data. A 10-fold cross validation is used by the stacking algorithm.

The metric used for the evaluation is the Kappa value, a statistical measure that determines the agreement between different classifiers.

This measure takes into account the possibility of casual successes, and can take values between −1 and 1, indicating the negative values that there is no agreement, and the values between 0 and 1 the level of existing agreement. Between 0.01 and 0.20 is a slight agreement, between 0.21 and 0.40 fair agreement, 0.41 and 0.60 moderate agreement, 0.61 and 0.80 substantial agreement, and between 0.81 and 1.0 perfect agreement. Given these values, the larger the agreement, the more reliable the results of the classifiers.

The WEKA tool uses the Corrected Resample T-Test as a statistical significance of a pair-wise comparison of schemes. According to the study, this approach performs better than the standard T-Test, and this technique is used as default by the WEKA tool used on this study.

5   Results and Discussion

For a better understanding of the work, we discuss the results divided in two comparative studies.

The first study presents a comparison between a dataset composed by titles and abstracts and a full-text dataset.

The dataset composed by titles and abstracts has less terms because the title includes a few discriminative terms describing the article and the abstract is a very succinct text presenting a general overview of the paper.

The full-text dataset contains much more information because, besides the title and the abstract, it contains the rest of the document that is composed by four general sections: Introduction, Methods (Materials and Methods, Methods, Experimental Procedures), Results (Results, Discussion, Results and Discussion) and Conclusions.

The results (shown in Fig. 3) are obtained using the enriched corpus to create the datasets (TA and full-text) and the stacking algorithm to classify.

From Fig. 3, we can conclude that full-text documents benefit more from semantic enrichment than those with only the title and abstract. The results achieved are better in 18 of the 26 datasets. Only in four of the datasets (C03, C05, C07 and C22) title and abstract achieve better results, and in two of the datasets is neither better or worse (C25 and C26).

Considering only results with a Kappa statistic greater than 61% (with at least a substantial agreement) we obtained eleven results that are better using the full-text dataset, shown in Fig. 4. In it, we can see the percentage increment obtained when using the full-text dataset. The increment varies from 53.5% of C11 and 357.9% of C10. Thus, we can say that using terms from others sections in addition to those of the title and abstract has an high positive impact on the classification process.

The second study presents a comparison between pre-processed full-text versus full-text enrichment with the SemRep tool. The Kappa results obtained are presented in Table 3. It shows the results using only the pre-processing techniques and applying the enrichment process through the methodology presented at Fig. 2.

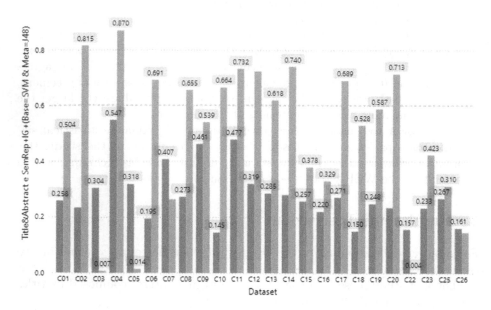

Fig. 3. Comparing Enriched Title-Abstract vs Enriched Full-Text

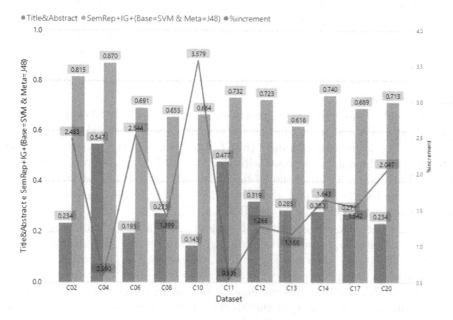

Fig. 4. Comparing Enriched TA vs Enriched Full-Text with Kappa greater than 61%

Table 3. Kappa results comparison between the Pre-Processing versus Enrichment. The (+) represents the best result. Results with the highest statistical significance are shown in **bold**

Dataset	Pre-proc Full-text	Enriched Full-text	Dataset	Pre-proc Full-text	Enriched Full-text
C01	0,295	0,504(+)	C13	0,383	**0,618**(+)
C02	0,638	**0,815**(+)	C14	0,519	**0,740**(+)
C03	0,241(+)	0,007	C15	0,068	0,378(+)
C04	0,792	**0,870**(+)	C16	0,007	0,329(+)
C05	0,007	0,014	C17	0,432	**0,689**(+)
C06	0,383	**0,691**(+)	C18	0,239	0,528(+)
C07	0,093	0,264(+)	C19	0,266	0,587(+)
C08	0,320	**0,655**(+)	C20	0,509	**0,713**(+)
C09	0,270	0,539(+)	C22	0,007(+)	0,004
C10	0,519	**0,664**(+)	C23	0,451(+)	0,423
C11	0,568	**0,732**(+)	C25	0,133	0,310(+)
C12	0,501	**0,723**(+)	C26	0,032	0,146(+)

From Table 3 it can be concluded that the best results are obtained when the enrichment is applied to all sections. On eleven results they are even greater than 61%.

Only considering the Kappa results greater than 61% (see Fig. 5), we can compare the percentage increase when applying the semantic enrichment technique. The increment varies from $9,8\%$ (C04 results) to $104,6\%$ (C08 results). The average increment is of $47,9\%$ when comparing only the pre-processing datasets.

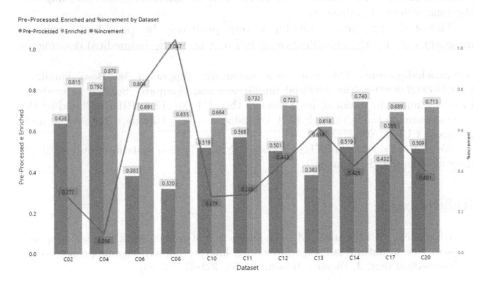

Fig. 5. Comparing Results Pre-Processed vs Enrichment with Kappa greater than 61%

An interesting insight from this study is the substantial agreement 0.61–0.80 achieved by eleven of the datasets (see Fig. 5). We can also point out that datasets C02 and C04 achieve an almost perfect agreement (0.81–0.99).

6   Conclusions

The research presented in this paper highlights the importance of using text semantic enrichment to enhance the Medline full-text document classification. The approach involves the semantic enrichment of an OHSUMED corpus with full text using the Semantic Repository (SemRep) which extracts semantic predications from biomedical text.

SemRep predications identify relationships between entities in MEDLINE documents. SemRep can to combine and link knowledge from several sources and discover connections which might otherwise go unnoticed.

Semantic enrichment led to an expected substantial growth in the number of terms, which raises the problem of highly dimensional data maintaining the semantic structure of the corpus. This fact requires the application of feature selection in order to reduce the number of terms to a value that does not compromise the accuracy obtained by the algorithms.

This work was accomplished recurring to the WEKA tool, and using a stacking algorithm, a Support Vector Machine algorithm as baseline and a C4.5 implementation as the meta learner.

The results achieved support the conclusion that the best results are obtained with full text instead of using only titles and abstracts, despite having applied the same techniques to data sets with only titles and abstracts.

Another sustained conclusion by these results is that the application of semantic enrichment techniques to the full text documents significantly improves the task of text classification.

The study presented contributes very positively by providing significant improvements for the classification of full text scientific biomedical documents.

Acknowledgement. This work was financially supported by Base Funding - UIDB/00027/2020 of the Artificial Intelligence and Computer Science Laboratory - LIACC - funded by national funds through the FCT/MCTES (PIDDAC) and by Portuguese national funds through FCT - Fundação para a Ciência e Tecnologia, under the project UIDB/05422/2020.

We acknowledge the SoftCPS - Software Cyber-Physical Systems Group (ISEP) for their assistance and resources.

References

1. Rindflesch, T.C., Fiszman, M.: The interaction of domain knowledge and linguistic structure in natural language processing: interpreting hypernymic propositions in biomedical text. J. Biomed. Inform. **36**(6), 462–477 (2003)

2. Rindflesch, T.C., Fiszman, M., Libbus, B.: Semantic interpretation for the biomedical research literature. In: Chen, H., Fuller, S.S., Friedman, C., Hersh, W. (eds.) Medical Informatics Integrated Series in Information Systems. ISIS, vol. 8, pp. 399–422. Springer, Boston (2005). https://doi.org/10.1007/0-387-25739-X_14

3. Hersh, W., Buckley, C., Leone, T.J., Hickam, D.: OHSUMED: an interactive retrieval evaluation and new large test collection for research. In: Croft, B.W., van Rijsbergen, C.J. (eds.) SIGIR 1994, pp. 192–201. Springer, London (1994). https://doi.org/10.1007/978-1-4471-2099-5_20

4. Škrlj, B., Kralj, J., Lavrač, N., Pollak, S.: Towards robust text classification with semantics-aware recurrent neural architecture. Mach. Learn. Knowl. Extr. 1(2), 575–589 (2019)

5. Albitar, S., Espinasse, B., Fournier, S.: Semantic enrichments in text supervised classification: application to medical domain. In: The Twenty-Seventh International Flairs Conference, pp. 425–430 (2014)

6. Zhang, R., Hristovski, D., Schutte, D., Kastrin, A., Fiszman, M., Kilicoglu, H.: Drug repurposing for COVID-19 via knowledge graph completion. J. Biomed. Inform. 115, 103696 (2021)

7. Kilicoglu, H., Shin, D., Fiszman, M., Rosemblat, G., Rindflesch, T.C.: SemMedDB: a PubMed-scale repository of biomedical semantic predications. Bioinformatics 28(23), 3158–3160 (2012)

8. Du, J., Li, X.: A knowledge graph of combined drug therapies using semantic predications from biomedical literature: algorithm development. JMIR Med. Inform. 8(4), e18323 (2020)

9. Ben Abacha, A., Zweigenbaum, P.: A hybrid approach for the extraction of semantic relations from MEDLINE abstracts. In: Gelbukh, A. (ed.) CICLing 2011. LNCS, vol. 6609, pp. 139–150. Springer, Heidelberg (2011). https://doi.org/10.1007/978-3-642-19437-5_11

10. Avram, A., Matei, O., Pintea, C.-M., Pop, P.: Context quality impact in context-aware data mining for predicting soil moisture. Cybern. Syst. 51(7), 668–684 (2020)

11. Avram, A., Matei, O., Pintea, C.-M., Pop, P.C.: Influence of context availability and soundness in predicting soil moisture using the context-aware data mining approach. Logic J. IGPL 31, 762–774 (2023)

12. Sammut, C., Webb, G.I. (eds.): Encyclopedia of Machine Learning and Data Mining, 2nd edn. Springer, New York (2017). https://doi.org/10.1007/978-1-4899-7687-1

13. Gonçalves, C., Iglesias, E.L., Borrajo, L., Camacho, R., Vieira, A.S., Gonçalves, C.T.: LearnSec: a framework for full text analysis. In: de Cos Juez, F., et al. (eds.) HAIS 2018. LNCS, vol. 10870, pp. 502–513. Springer, Cham (2018). https://doi.org/10.1007/978-3-319-92639-1_42

14. Gonçalves, C.A.O., Camacho, R., Gonçalves, C.T., Seara Vieira, A., Borrajo Diz, L., Iglesias, E.L.: Classification of full text biomedical documents: sections importance assessment. Appl. Sci. 11(6), 2674 (2021)

15. Rebholz-Schuhmann, D., et al.: BioLexicon: towards a reference terminological resource in the biomedical domain. In: Proceedings of the of the 16th Annual International Conference on Intelligent Systems for Molecular Biology (ISMB 2008) (2008)

16. Forman, G., et al.: An extensive empirical study of feature selection metrics for text classification. J. Mach. Learn. Res. 3, 1289–1305 (2003)

17. Wolpert, D.H.: Stacked generalization. Neural Netw. 5(2), 241–259 (1992)

Predicting Innovative Cities Using Spatio-Temporal Activity Patterns

Ricardo Muñoz-Cancino[1], Sebastián A. Ríos[2], and Manuel Graña[1]([⊠])

[1] Computational Intelligence Group, University of Basque Country,
20018 San Sebastián, Spain
manuel.grana@ehu.eus
[2] Business Intelligence Research Center (CEINE), Industrial Engineering
Department, University of Chile, Beauchef 851, 8370456 Santiago, Chile

Abstract. Understanding cities' complexity is essential for correctly developing public policies and urban management. Only some studies have attempted to relate the activity carried out by city inhabitants with the macro characteristics of a city, mainly its capacity to innovate. In this study, we seek to find those features that allow us to distinguish between an innovative city from those still on the way to becoming one. To carry out this analysis, we have the activity patterns decomposition obtained through geo-tagged social media digital traces and their respective innovation index for more than 100 cities worldwide. The results show that it is possible to predict the city's innovative category from their activity patterns. Our model achieves an AUC = 0.71 and a KS = 0.42. This result is significant because it allows us to establish a relationship between the activities carried out by people in the city and their innovation index, a characteristic given for the capacity and development of cultural assets, infrastructure, and the quality of markets.

Keywords: Smart Cities · Spatiotemporal Patterns · Geo-tagged digital traces · Dynamic Topic Model

1 Introduction

Cities are complex systems characterized by various social, economic, political, and environmental factors. Innovation is critical to address challenges such as urbanization, social equality, and climate change, which is why it is crucial in urban planning and policy-making. The ability of a city to encourage innovation is crucial in attracting investment, retaining talent, and enhancing the life quality for its citizens. There are various measures to quantify each city's innovation potential and establish comparison rankings between them. To define these indexes, researchers and practitioners utilize various factors, including a city's research and development capabilities, cultural assets, available infrastructure, and even the quality of markets and how connected they are to the world. In this article, we want to study how the activity carried out by the inhabitants of the city measured through digital traces correlates with innovation indicators. In particular, we will use the activity description based on a decomposition in spatiotemporal city activity patterns and study its ability to predict whether a city will be innovative.

The main findings of our work are:

- It is possible to use the activity pattern decomposition of a city to predict if it will be innovative.
- Defining an indetermination zone and excluding it to train the models allows us to improve the power of discrimination.
- Although it is possible to generate synthetic data from the activity pattern decomposition, it does not improve the performance indicators of the models.
- Random forest, trained without indeterminates, generates the best results and achieves an AUC = 0.71, KS = 0.42, and Precision = 70%.
- We present the features that most influence the probability of being innovative and analyze how they influence the probability.

Our study is structured as follows. Section 2 briefly presents previous work on city innovation, topic modeling, and synthetic data generators. Then, in Sect. 3, we present the proposed methodology and the experimental setup to determine the probability of a city being innovative. Then, in Sect. 4, we show the results of the experiments carried out, and finally, in Sect. 5, we present the conclusions of our work and propose lines of future work.

2   Related Work

In this section, we present previous work related to our study. In Sect. 2.1, we show the importance of innovation within the context of public policy. Then, in Sect. 2.2, we introduce topic models using digital traces. Finally, Sect. 2.3 shows the state-of-the-art models for generating synthetic data.

2.1   City Innovation and Public Policies

Innovative cities attract more investment and new businesses, leading to economic prosperity for their inhabitants. Also, innovative cities usually see increased employment opportunities, not only in the number of jobs available but also in the quality and specialization of these jobs [2,9]. City innovation rankings assess and compare innovation levels across different cities and provide valuable information for policymakers to develop public policies that help improve weak aspects [5]. In addition, city innovation rankings can also help recognize best practices and successful strategies from other cities to adapt and implement in other contexts. By examining the factors used in these rankings, policymakers can gain insights into which areas of innovation their city may be lacking and learn from other cities' experiences in addressing similar issues.

2.2 Topic Modeling Using Digital Traces

Topic Modeling is a technique widely used to uncover latent patterns in a collection of documents. Latent Dirichlet Allocation is one of the most popular methods where it is assumed that each document in a corpus is generated from a mixture of latent topics. Furthermore, each topic is assumed to be a probability distribution over the words [4]. Dynamic topic modeling extends this model family considering the data's temporal evolution. It is designed to capture the evolution of topics over time and how the distribution of documents also changes over time. Both LDA and DTM have been adapted to discover activity patterns from digital traces collected in cities. For example, LDA has been applied to discover activity patterns from phone calls and credit card purchase georeferences, while DTM has been applied using geo-tagged social media activity.

2.3 Generative Models and Synthetic Data Generation

Generative models aim to learn the distribution of real-world data and generate consistent samples from it. Statistical methods like Gaussian Mixtures Models and Bayesian Networks were commonly used for this, but deep learning models have recently gained popularity. These models generate synthetic data, which can be helpful when obtaining real data is expensive or sensitive [13]. Below we describe some of the most popular methods for generating synthetic data. A Gaussian copula captures the dependence structure between variables. This method uses a copula function to model the joint distribution of several random variables, even if they have different marginal distributions. Generative adversarial networks (GANs) are models where a generator network produces synthetic data to imitate real data while a discriminator network distinguishes between real and synthetic samples [6]. CTGAN [15] extends these models and introduces a sampling process according to log frequency, and kernel density estimation is used to handle multimodal distributions. Autoencoders are unsupervised models that can be used for low-dimensional representation and synthetic data generation. Variational Autoencoder interprets the latent space produced by the encoder as a probability distribution modeling the training samples as independent random variables [10]. TVAE is an adaptation for tabular data that uses the same pre-processing as CTGAN and the evidence lower bound loss (ELBO) [14].

3 Methodology and Experimental Design

3.1 Dataset

The study analyzes city activity patterns from a social media dataset with around 32 million geo-tagged urban activities collected from various platforms over 17 years. The dataset covers 127 cities worldwide and is available for seven 3-year time slices from 2005 to 2021. Each city is characterized by a $k \times s$ matrix, where $k = 3$ represents the number of city activity patterns and $s = 7$ represents the number of time slices. Our previous research [11] provides a detailed description of the social media platforms included in this dataset and a comprehensive analysis of the geo-tagged digital traces. The study also utilizes the Innovation Cities Index [1], an annual quantitative index that ranks the most innovative cities globally based on cultural assets, human infrastructure, and networked markets. The definition of city/town, their location, and respective centers were obtained from the World Cities Database provided by Simplemaps [12]. This index [1] highlights Tokyo, Boston, New York, Sydney, and Singapore as the most innovative cities. In contrast, the last places are occupied by Zaporizhzhia (Ukraine), Douala (Cameroon), Madurai (India), La Paz (Bolivia), and Khartoum (Sudan).

From the activity pattern decomposition, nine features are generated. The first three features correspond to the average of each activity pattern over time. Then a ratio is generated between the average of each activity pattern in the first two time slices against the average of the last two. Finally, a coefficient of variation is generated for each activity pattern that consists of the average of each one divided by its standard deviation. These features will be used to predict whether or not the city is innovative.

3.2 Target

The city within the top 50 positions in the City Innovation Ranking will be classified as innovative. Otherwise, we will classify the city on the way to being innovative or non-innovative. For the indeterminate exercise, an indeterminate city is between places 50 and 135 in the innovation ranking. The city innovation ranking ranges between 1 and 500. This non-indeterminate approach to training classification models is widely used in credit risk to enhance the performance of models to predict creditworthiness.

3.3 Synthetic Data Generation for City Data Augmentation

A step before modeling that will allow us to deal with the small number of samples in the problem is to train a data synthesizer. In this way, increasing the number of training records while maintaining the characteristics that describe a city is possible. To do this, we compared the performance of a set of state-of-the-art synthetic data generators, Gaussian Copula, CopulaGAN, CTGAN, and TVAE (See Sect. 2.3). Despite needing to be more rigorous with the hyperparameters selection of these models, we work with two architectures in the case of CTGAN and TVAE. Gaussian Copula and CopulaGAN are trained both using the default configuration. Arch A is the default configuration in both cases. At the same time, Arch B is a setup for the generator with two linear residual layers and the discriminator with two linear layers, both of size (512, 512) for the CTGAN and TVAE Arch B, set hidden layers of (256, 256, 256) for both the encoder and the decoder.

3.4   Innovation Ranking Assessment

This study aims to determine the probability of a city being innovative. For this, we have proposed the methodology detailed in Fig. 1. The diagram begins with the search for information in the real world. The detail of this stage up to the transformation and aggregation can be seen in our previous investigation. These stages were included to give context to our problem. Once the data is available, the activity pattern decomposition for each city and its respective innovation ranking. We generated three large data sets from this information. The first dataset corresponds to the original data set containing the 127 study cities. The second dataset is the augmented dataset obtained from the data synthesizer, and the third dataset is the original dataset, excluding those cities whose ranking is between positions 50 and 135. This filter is applied only to the training set and seeks to maximize the discrimination capacity of the algorithms.

Once the three sets of data described above are available, multiple models are trained under the following schematization. The data set is split into training and test datasets, several algorithms are trained, and the performance metrics on the test set are stored. This procedure is performed N times with each dataset using different training and test partitions. In the case of training with the synthetic dataset, the evaluation on the test set is always on real data. Finally, all the resulting metrics are consolidated, the model's performance is compared using statistical tests, and the results of the best model are analyzed.

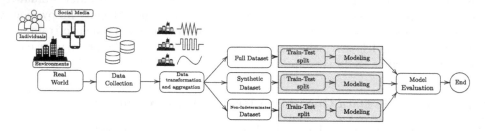

Fig. 1. Proposed methodology for innovative city assessment

3.5   Evaluation Metrics

This section presents a set of metrics to evaluate the performance of synthetic data generators and classification models used in innovation ranking assessment. The metrics include AUC, Kolmogorov-Smirnov statistic (KS), Accuracy, Precision, Recall, and F-measure. The AUC is a performance measure representing the area under the curve of a plot between the true positive rate and the false positive rate. It provides an overall measure of performance that considers all possible thresholds for classifying a sample as innovative or non-innovative. F-measure is the harmonic mean of precision and recall [3,7] and is helpful for dichotomous outputs. KS statistic measures the distance between two cumulative distributions [8] and is used to assess discriminatory power in innovation ranking assessment and similarity in synthetic data generation. KSTest, used in Synthetic data generators, is defined as 1-D, where D is the KS statistic, and higher values indicate better synthetic data generation.

3.6   Experimental Setup

In this study, we set $N = 100$, which consists of training 100 models with each data set. Logistic Regression (LR), Decision Tree (DT), Random Forest (RF), and Light Gradient Boosting (LGB) are the algorithms used. For the models trained with the full dataset and the non-indeterminate dataset, an exhaustive search for hyper-parameters is performed using grid search for the LGB model, varying the number of estimators (20, 40), the learning rate (0.01,0.05,01) and the minimum child samples (2%, 4%). In the case of the synthetic dataset, 20,000 samples are extracted, and RF and LGB hyper-parameters are optimized using grid search. For both models, the number of estimates is varied (100,200, 500), and for LGB, the learning rate is varied (0.05.01), and the minimum child samples (2%, 4%), and for RF, the maximum deep is varied (2,4,8). Finally, a non-parametric test (Wilcoxon Test) is used to compare the models.

4   Results

In this section, we present the results of our methodology. We start comparing the synthesizers. Then, we analyze the city innovation prediction performance. Finally, we show the most important features and how they contribute to the innovation probability.

4.1   Synthetic Data Generation Performance

Table 1 shows the results of applying different algorithms to generate synthetic data. KSTest-mean corresponds to the average KSTest over the ten features, the target plus the nine predictors. It is observed that Gaussian Copula is the one that generates the best results. For this reason, we will use this model to generate synthetic data that help us predict if a city is innovative or not.

Table 1. Synthetic data generators performance

Synthesizer	Arch	KSTest-mean
Gaussian Copula	A	0.870
Copula GAN	A	0.582
CTGAN	A	0.669
	B	0.712
TVAE	A	0.811
	B	0.856

4.2   Predicting Innovative Cities

This section compares classification models used to predict whether a city will be in the top 50 of the innovation ranking based on its decomposition activity pattern. Table 2 represents the results after 100 runs. The Model column shows the algorithm used, Training Data is the dataset used, and Model id presents an identifier we will use later to refer to each model. The rest of the columns correspond to the metrics used for this classification problem. Each table cell displays the average and standard deviation of the respective metric. The model that obtained the highest performance for the respective metric is shown in bold. When a column has more than one value in bold, it is because there are no statistically significant differences between both models with a confidence level of 99%.

Table 2. City innovation classification results

Model	Training Data	Model id	AUC	KS	Accuracy	Recall	Precision	F-measure
Logistic Regression	Real Data	LR_r	0.61 ± 0.09	0.35 ± 0.11	0.66 ± 0.07	0.04 ± 0.07	0.12 ± 0.22	0.05 ± 0.09
	Real Data Ind	LR_i	0.63 ± 0.09	0.37 ± 0.12	0.63 ± 0.07	0.18 ± 0.15	0.29 ± 0.19	0.20 ± 0.14
Decision Tree	Real Data	DT_r	0.59 ± 0.07	0.19 ± 0.12	0.64 ± 0.06	0.46 ± 0.15	0.42 ± 0.12	0.42 ± 0.10
	Real Data Ind	DT_i	0.60 ± 0.08	0.22 ± 0.14	0.62 ± 0.07	**0.54 ± 0.14**	0.42 ± 0.12	0.46 ± 0.10
Light Gradient Boosting	Real Data	LGB_r	0.69 ± 0.08	**0.42 ± 0.12**	**0.70 ± 0.06**	0.37 ± 0.21	**0.46 ± 0.24**	0.39 ± 0.19
	Real Data Ind	LGB_i	0.69 ± 0.07	**0.42 ± 0.11**	0.68 ± 0.06	**0.50 ± 0.21**	0.46 ± 0.18	**0.45 ± 0.16**
	Synthetic Data	LGB_s	0.59 ± 0.08	0.31 ± 0.08	**0.71 ± 0.07**	0.07 ± 0.07	0.48 ± 0.13	0.13 ± 0.11
Random Forest	Real Data	RF_r	0.69 ± 0.08	0.40 ± 0.11	**0.70 ± 0.06**	0.35 ± 0.16	**0.53 ± 0.18**	0.40 ± 0.13
	Real Data Ind	RF_i	**0.71 ± 0.08**	**0.42 ± 0.11**	**0.70 ± 0.06**	**0.51 ± 0.16**	**0.52 ± 0.15**	**0.50 ± 0.11**
	Synthetic Data	RF_s	0.60 ± 0.08	0.32 ± 0.09	0.70 ± 0.07	0.07 ± 0.07	0.49 ± 0.42	0.12 ± 0.11

As shown in the table, the RF_i model is the one that achieves the best results in all the metrics used in the study. This model corresponds to the one trained on a sample excluding the cities in the indeterminacy zone, positions between 50 and 135 in the city innovation ranking, but which were evaluated on test samples considering all the cities. This approach not only manages to obtain the best results when training a model with random forest but also increases the discrimination power of several further models, which is a helpful strategy to address this type of problem. Regarding the use of synthetic data to increase the training sample. The augmented dataset achieves the highest accuracy when training the LGB_s model. However, no significant increases are observed in the rest of the metrics, so it did not turn out to be the most effective strategy to predict whether a city is innovative or not.

The best model, RF_i achieves an AUC of 0.71. This result is 3.3% higher than traditional training (RF_r), achieving the next best results. Table 3 shows the comparison between all the implemented models. Each cell shows the percentage increase $\frac{AUC_{row} - AUC_{column}}{AUC_{column}}$. The table shows only statistically significant differences using a Wilcoxon test with a confidence level of 99%. If the null hypothesis of equality of means cannot be rejected, this result is replaced with *. This comparison was made for all the metrics, and based on it, the models that achieved the best results in each metric were determined, as shown in Table 2.

Table 3. Model comparison based on AUC results

AUC	LR_r	LR_i	DT_r	DT_i	LGB_r	LGB_i	LGB_s	RF_r	RF_i	RF_s
LR_r	*	−2.5%	*	*	−10.6%	−11.4%	4.7%	−11.4%	−14.2%	*
LR_i	2.5%	*	6.7%	*	−8.3%	−9.1%	7.4%	−9.2%	−12.1%	4.6%
DT_r	*	−6.3%	*	*	−14.1%	−14.9%	*	−14.9%	−17.6%	*
DT_i	*	*	*	*	−11.9%	−12.7%	*	−12.7%	−15.5%	*
LGB_r	11.9%	9.1%	16.4%	13.5%	*	*	17.1%	*	−4.1%	14.2%
LGB_i	12.9%	10.1%	17.5%	14.5%	*	*	18.2%	*	−3.2%	15.2%
LGB_s	−4.5%	−6.9%	*	*	−14.6%	−15.4%	*	−15.4%	−18.1%	−2.5%
RF_r	12.9%	10.1%	17.5%	14.6%	*	*	18.2%	*	−3.2%	15.2%
RF_i	16.6%	13.7%	21.4%	18.3%	4.2%	3.3%	22.1%	3.3%	*	19.0%
RF_s	*	−4.4%	*	*	−12.4%	−13.2%	2.6%	−13.2%	−16.0%	*

4.3 Main Features to Predict Innovative Cities

In this section, we analyze the most important attributes to determine whether a city is innovative. The attributes used come from the city activity pattern decomposition and correspond to aggregations of this information. In order to obtain the importance of these features, SHAP values were used on the test sets. Specifically, we use the average of the absolute values of the SHAP values. These SHAP values were stored during the 100 runs and averaged to obtain the final results. Table 4 shows an average importance value. The feature that contributes the most to determining whether a city is innovative corresponds to the coefficient of variation of activity pattern 1, followed by the growth ratio of activity pattern 2. Figure 2 is presented to understand how these affect attributes in the probability of being innovative. This Figure contains the average absolute SHAP values for the test samples during the 100 training runs.

Table 4. Feature Importance

Feature Name	Importance
Activity Pattern_1_cv	25.6%
Activity Pattern_2_R	14.2%
Activity Pattern_1_R	13.6%
Activity Pattern_0_mean	10.1%
Activity Pattern_2_mean	9.6%
Activity Pattern_0_R	7.8%
Activity Pattern_2_cv	7.3%
Activity Pattern_1_mean	6.3%
Activity Pattern_0_cv	5.6%

Figure 2(e) shows the SHAP values for the most important feature, the coefficient of variation of activity pattern 1 (AP 1). An inflection point close to 2 is observed, where values less than this threshold decrease the probability of a city being innovative. In comparison, higher values increase it up to a coefficient of variation close to 4. However, higher values positively affect the probability and do so with constant effects. The second most important variable, the growth rate on activity pattern 2, has a similar behavior. Those cities whose AP 2 significance has decreased over time also decrease their probability of being innovative, while those that have increased their participation also increase their probability of being innovative. An opposite effect is observed in the same ratio for AP 1, whose decrease increases the probability of being innovative.

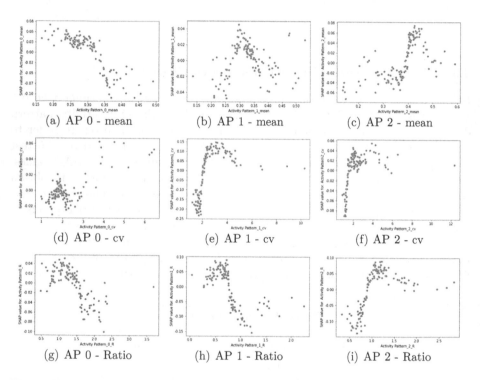

Fig. 2. Feature Importance Analysis using SHAP Values. Each subfigure shows the predictor along with their corresponding SHAP Values.

5   Conclusions and Future Work

In this study, we associate characteristics of a city obtained from the activity of its inhabitants with structural characteristics such as a city's ability to innovate. To meet this objective, we use the activity pattern decomposition of each city and its respective innovation ranking. Our proposal models this challenge as a classification problem. For the training, three approaches are used: working with the complete data set, increasing the information with synthetic data, and removing indeterminates. The results show that training without indeterminates achieves the best results when training a random forest model, achieving better results on all the proposed metrics. This model performs well in determining if a city will be innovative, with an AUC of 0.71 and a KS of 0.42. Additionally, we present the features that most influence this probability and how they affect it. As future work, it is expected to increase the number of cities in the study, complement the description of each one, and improve their description based on activity patterns.

Acknowledgements. This work would not have been accomplished without the financial support of CONICYT-PFCHA/DOCTORADO BECAS CHILE/2019-21190345. The last author received research funds from the Basque Government as the head of the Grupo de Inteligencia Computacional, Universidad del Pais Vasco, UPV/EHU, from 2007 until 2025. The current code for the grant is IT1689-22. Additionally, the author participates in Elkartek projects KK-2022/00051 and KK-2021/00070. The Spanish MCIN has also granted the author a research project under code PID2020-116346GB-I00.

References

1. 2thinknow Innovation Cities Index 2021: Innovation Cities Index 2021: Top 100 World's Most Innovative Cities (2021). https://innovation-cities.com/worlds-most-innovative-cities-2021-top-100/25477/. Accessed 23 Oct 232021
2. Acs, Z.J.: Innovation and the growth of cities. In: Innovation and the Growth of Cities. Edward Elgar Publishing, Cheltenham (2002)
3. Carrillo-de Albornoz, J., Aker, A., Kurtic, E., Plaza, L.: Beyond opinion classification: extracting facts, opinions and experiences from health forums. PLoS ONE **14**(1), e0209961 (2019)
4. Blei, D.M., Ng, A.Y., Jordan, M.I.: Latent dirichlet allocation. J. Mach. Learn. Res. **3**, 993–1022 (2003). https://doi.org/10.1162/jmlr.2003.3.4-5.993
5. Chen, Y., Li, W., Yi, P.: Evaluation of city innovation capability using the TOPSIS-based order relation method: The case of Liaoning province, China. Technol. Soc. **63**, 101330 (2020)
6. Goodfellow, I., Bengio, Y., Courville, A.: Deep Learning. MIT Press, Cambridge (2016)
7. Ho, P.S., Mo, G.J., Chan-Hee, J.: Receiver operating characteristic (ROC) curve: practical review for radiologists. KJR **5**(1), 11–18 (2004)
8. Hodges, J.: The significance probability of the Smirnov two-sample test. Ark. Mat. **3**(5), 469–486 (1958)
9. Johnson, B.: Cities, systems of innovation and economic development. Innovation **10**(2–3), 146–155 (2008)
10. Kingma, D.P., Welling, M.: Auto-encoding variational Bayes. arXiv preprint arXiv:1312.6114 (2013)
11. Muñoz-Cancino, R.: On the use of multi-sensor digital traces to discover spatio-temporal human behavioral pattens. Ph.D. thesis, University of Basque Country (2023)
12. Simple Maps: Basic World Cities Database (2021). https://simplemaps.com/data/world-cities. Accessed 3 Sept 2021

13. Torres, D.G.: Generation of synthetic data with generative adversarial networks. Ph.D. thesis, Ph. D. Thesis, Royal Institute of Technology, Stockholm, Sweden (2018)
14. Xu, L., Skoularidou, M., Cuesta-Infante, A., Veeramachaneni, K.: Modeling tabular data using conditional GAN. CoRR abs/1907.00503 (2019)
15. Xu, L., et al.: Synthesizing tabular data using conditional GAN. Ph.D. thesis, Massachusetts Institute of Technology (2020)

Daily Accumulative Photovoltaic Energy Prediction Using Hybrid Intelligent Model

Antonio Díaz-Longueira[1] , Míriam Timiraos[1,2]([✉]) ,
Juan Albino Méndez Pérez[3] , José-Luis Casteleiro-Roca[1] ,
and Esteban Jove[1]

[1] CTC, Department of Industrial Engineering, CITIC, University of A Coruña,
EPEF, Calle Mendizábal s/n, Campus de Esteiro, 15403 Ferrol, A Coruña, Spain
{a.diazl,miriam.timiraos.diaz,jose.luis.casteleiro,esteban.jove}@udc.es
[2] Fundación Instituto Tecnológico de Galicia, Department of Water Technologies,
National Technological Center, Cantón Grande 9, Planta 3, 15003 A Coruña, Spain
mtimiraos@itg.es
[3] Department of Computer Science and System Engineering, University of La
Laguna, Avda. Astrof. Francisco Sánchez s/n, 38200 S/C de Tenerife, Spain
jamendez@ull.edu.es

Abstract. Nowadays, there is an increase in the use of renewable energies to fight against climatic change. One of the most popular energy is
solar one, which could have two different produced energies: thermal and
electrical. The case study used in this research is an installation located
in the University of A Coruña, in Ferrol, and it is a photovoltaic array
with five rows of 12 solar panels each one, with a total peak power of 12,9
kW. The installation is correctly oriented to the South, with an inclina-
tion of 35° to achieve the theoretical performance of 99,82%. The model
created in this research predicts the accumulated daily energy produced
by the installation base on the solar hours predicted by the meteorological service. The other inputs of the model are the real solar hours
and the energy produced the day before the prediction. A hybrid model
is created by dividing the dataset with a clustering technique to create
groups. Then, each cluster trains a regression algorithm to increase the
global prediction performance. K-Means are used to create the clusters
and Artificial Neural Networks, Support Vector Machines for Regression and Polynomial Regression are used to create the local models for
clusters.

Keywords: Solar energy · Photovoltaic panels · Clustering · Artificial
neural networks · Support vector machines for regression · Polynomial
regression

1 Introduction

Nowadays, renewable energies are one of the most important pillars in the energy
mix. One of the easiest to install energy anyplace is solar energy in both topolo-

P. García Bringas et al. (Eds.): HAIS 2023, LNAI 14001, pp. 577–588, 2023.
https://doi.org/10.1007/978-3-031-40725-3_49

gies: thermal or photovoltaic [14]. This fact is why there is a lot of recent research about predicting the energy that an installation can produce [3,32,33]. If the building with the solar installation has a building management system (BMS) to improve energy efficiency, the prediction of the energy production could help the BMS to decide the main source of the energy that the building uses each time [25,35].

Artificial intelligent techniques show better performance than the traditional regression algorithms in the field of this research [7,8]. Moreover, when these techniques are combined with a hybrid model, the prediction improves its performance; there are several previous types of research like [2,6,19] that predict the temperature of a thermal solar panel outlet, or [16,18,27] that uses a different model depending on the dataset characteristics.

This research uses three different algorithms to create local models that predict the energy produced by photovoltaic solar installations. Artificial neural networks, support vector machines, and polynomial regression are chosen as regressions techniques because they are well known and their performance in this field was demonstrated in previous works [11,20,26]. The algorithm used to create the clusters that divide the dataset is the K-means algorithm. This is a very fast and simple technique that divides the dataset into the number of clusters that the user selects based on the Euclidean distance between the samples.

The rest of the paper is structured as follows: after this introduction, Sect. 2 describes briefly the installation under study, and Meteogalicia is present as a website to pick the meteorological variables. Then, the model approach is shown in Sect. 3, as the model created is a hybrid one, the procedure to train this type of model is described. Section 4 presents the research results and, as the hybrid model is composed of different training parts, this section is divided into several subsections. The research finishes with the conclusions and future works in Sect. 5.

2   Case Study

The installation of the case study is located in Ferrol, A Coruña, is represented in Fig. 1. There are a total of 60 solar panels, connected in 5 arrays of 6 panels in series and 2 in parallel. The nominal power is 12 kW, with a peak power of 12,9 kW; the daily mean global radiation (at the installation) is 3555 Wh/m^{2}day.

There was made a study of some meteorological variables to study the viability of the installation. Table 1 shows these variables; the mean external temperature is measured in Celsius degrees, the mean steam pressure is measured in Hectopascals, and the relative humidity in percentage.

Meteogalicia

As this research only takes the account the data from the inverter in the installation, and the accumulated energy produced during the day, the authors used

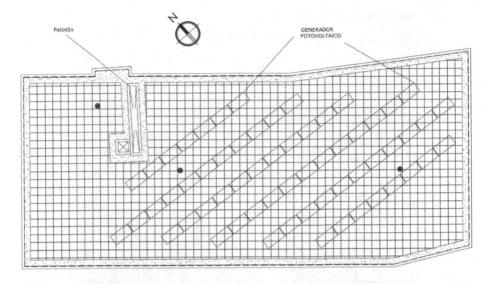

Fig. 1. Layout of the panels in the installation.

Table 1. Meteorological variables

	Jan	Feb.	Mar.	Apr.	May	Jun.	Jul.	Aug.	Sep.	Oct.	Nov.	Dec.
Temperature °C	9.6	8.8	11.7	12.3	14.4	17.8	18.9	19.3	18	15.4	11.9	9.9
Pressure (HPa)	1014	923	1104	1126	1321	1612	1783	1839	1755	1466	1196	1044
Humidity %	85	81	81	79	80	79	82	82	85	84	86	86

meteorological data from Meteogalicia. This is the meteorological service of Galicia and has a lot of meteorological stations that log some variables in several locations. In Fig. 2 it can be seen the locations of the meteorological stations, with the used one selected (CIS Ferrol).

It is decided to use these meteorological variables as not all photovoltaic installations have a weather station to log variables in the specific location of the installation. Moreover, the meteorological variable used is the sun hours during the days; the main aim of this research is the study of energy prediction using the minimum weather variables [1].

3   Model Approach

A model was created in this research with the aim to predict the evolution of daily energy produced by solar photovoltaic installation. Figure 3 represent a simplified data-flow diagram of the model.

The model developed in this research is a hybrid intelligent model that has internally several local models to increase the performance of the prediction.

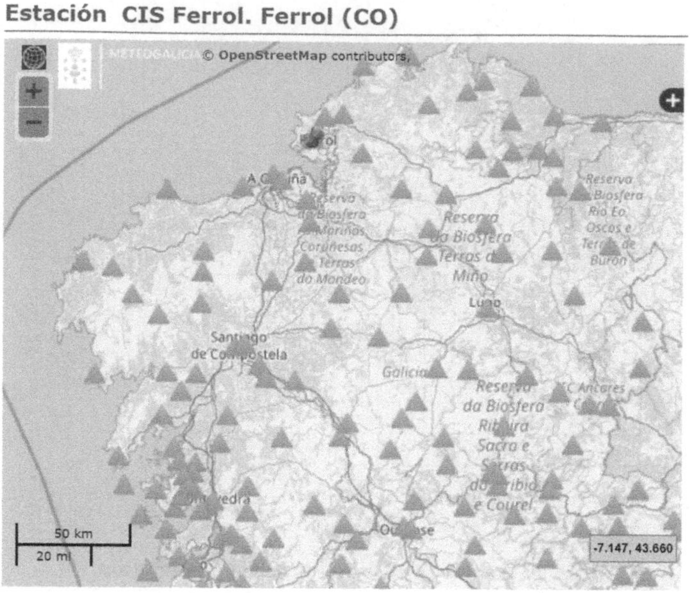

Estación CIS Ferrol. Ferrol (CO)

Fig. 2. Meteogalicia meteorological stations distributions.

Figure 4 represent the internal diagram of this hybrid model, where it is possible to see that the local model used depends on the specific inputs.

Figure 5 shows the simplified flowchart to create a hybrid intelligent model like the one described in this research. The whole steps are the following:

1. Firstly, with the aim to perform a validation of the final model, it was necessary to create a sub dataset to isolate some of the samples of the training process (*validation dataset*).
2. In the clustering phase, the rest of the dataset was divided several times to create different configurations of hybrid models. There were created 2 clusters, to create a hybrid model with two local models; then, the dataset was divided 3 times, to create three clusters to train three local models; and so on until the maximum number of clusters.
3. After the creation of the clusters, some of the samples for each cluster were isolated from the next step to allow the hybrid topology test. It is recommended that the selections be performed with a dataset that didn't use in the regression phase and that this dataset has samples from all the clusters (*hybrid test dataset*).
4. In the regression phase, the local models were created taking into account all the regression algorithms that will be used, and all the possible variations in each algorithm.
5. Once all the local models were created, it is necessary to choose the best one taking into account the prediction error for each cluster and each algorithm. It must be taken into account that in this research a K-fold cross validation

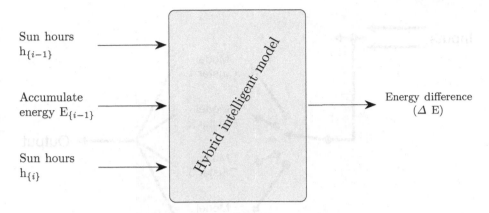

Fig. 3. Simplified data-flow diagram to predict the difference in the Energy produced.

was used, which implies that each algorithm was trained K times of each cluster.

6. As there was used cross validation, once the best regression algorithm was selected, it must be train another local model for each cluster, using all the samples available.
7. In the best hybrid topology selection phase, the *hybrid test dataset* is used to check the results obtained in each hybrid topology. The best topology will be the one with less prediction error.
8. Once the best topology is chosen, the *validation dataset* was used to calculate the error of the final model.

The algorithm used in this research is very typical in artificial intelligence, and for this reason, the author avoids the explanation of the algorithms. To create the clusters it was uses the K-means algorithm [15, 17, 22–24, 29]. To create the local models, Artificial Neural Networks [5, 9, 10, 12, 21], Support Vector Machines [28, 30] and Polynomial Regression [4, 13, 31, 34] was used.

In the results sections, it is explained the specific configuration for each regression algorithm.

Data Processing

The dataset used in this research has a sample time of one day, as the measured is the accumulated energy during the day. The meteorological variables were chosen with the same sample time; the total sun hours. The model uses the sun hours and the energy from the previous day, and the predicted sun hours for the day to predict the energy produced. The initial dataset has 1859 samples, from isolated 93 samples to create the *validation dataset*, the 5% of the initial dataset. Then, the clusters were created, and, again, 5% of the samples from each cluster was isolated to create the *hybrid test dataset*, which has 882 samples.

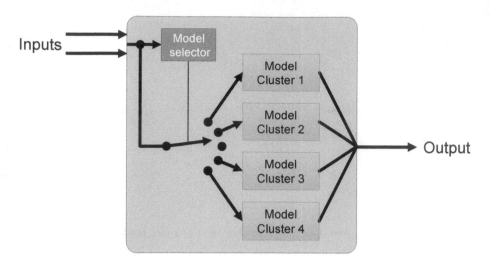

Fig. 4. Internal configuration of the hybrid intelligent model.

4   Results

The results of this research are divided into four different subsections. First of all, there is presented the clustering results to create the model and then, the local model results are shown.

4.1   Clustering Results

Table 2 shows the number of samples for each cluster when the dataset is divided using K-Means. There were created 9 different hybrid topologies, dividing the dataset several times to create from 2 to 9 clusters, and also it is taking into account the global model using all dataset (without creating any cluster).

4.2   Local Regression Models

A total of 18 regression algorithms were tested for each cluster. 15 neural networks, with a feedforward configuration, one hidden layer with tan-sigmoid as the activation function for the neurons in this layer, and a linear function in the neuron of the output layer. The number of neurons in the hidden layer was varied from 1 to 15. It is also training a support vector machine for Regression, but in this research, the algorithm used was the least squared modification for SVM. Moreover, the polynomial regression algorithm is trained for the clusters data; first and second degree is chosen in this case as different algorithms to test.

Table 3 shows the MSE (Mean Squared Error) as a performance measurement of the regression algorithm. It must be taken into account that the data was normalized prior to the training phase, and the values of the MSE in the table are in 10^{-3} range (it is also indicated in the caption of the table). The MSE values

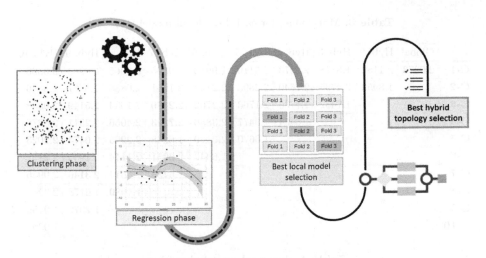

Fig. 5. Flowchart to create a hybrid intelligent model.

Table 2. Number of samples for each cluster

	Global	Hyb. 2	Hyb. 3	Hyb. 4	Hyb. 5	Hyb. 6	Hyb. 7	Hyb. 8	Hyb. 9	Hyb. 10
C-1	1678	794	480	345	291	169	158	131	123	94
C-2		884	566	351	293	232	193	146	126	120
C-3			632	457	310	286	218	204	154	130
C-4				525	357	305	236	212	174	144
C-5					426	319	246	216	178	163
C-6						368	275	240	179	171
C-7							351	253	184	173
C-8								277	237	200
C-9									321	210
C-10										273

are obtained using K-fold cross validation, which is a validation technique that uses all the available data to calculate the performance of the algorithm. K-fold cross validation divides the data 10 times (in this research specific case) and uses each group as a test set (and the rest of the groups as a train set). This validation technique requires that each algorithm was trained k times, 10 times in this research until all the groups were used as test sets.

Table 4 indicates the best regression technique and its configuration for each local model. The "ANN*" means an artificial neural network with * neurons in the hidden layer, "LS-SVR" means least square support vector machines for regression, and "Poly*" means polynomial regression of * degree.

Table 3. MSE values for each best local model $(\cdot 10^{-3})$

	Global	Hyb. 2	Hyb. 3	Hyb. 4	Hyb. 5	Hyb. 6	Hyb. 7	Hyb. 8	Hyb. 9	Hyb. 10
C-1	2.0073	2.1182	1.8178	2.2273	2.5110	1.9913	1.9525	3.2065	3.4983	3.5393
C-2		1.8953	2.4795	2.7640	2.2893	2.2144	2.1951	2.0888	2.0667	1.8846
C-3			1.7482	1.7735	2.1763	2.2702	2.2430	2.1684	2.5119	2.0538
C-4				1.6464	1.9477	2.3886	2.7243	2.4056	2.2511	2.8276
C-5					1.6670	2.0120	1.6268	2.2905	2.0474	2.2023
C-6						1.6942	2.3951	2.1114	2.1954	2.2161
C-7							1.5433	1.5614	2.3146	2.0955
C-8								1.1989	1.6178	2.2263
C-9									1.2072	1.9150
C-10										1.0394

Table 4. Best local model algorithm

	Global	Hyb. 2	Hyb. 3	Hyb. 4	Hyb. 5	Hyb. 6	Hyb. 7	Hyb. 8	Hyb. 9	Hyb. 10
C-1	LS-SVR	ANN03	ANN07	Poly1	Poly1	LS-SVR	ANN01	ANN01	Poly1	ANN01
C-2		ANN03	ANN04	Poly1	ANN01	ANN01	Poly1	ANN01	ANN01	LS-SVR
C-3			ANN07	ANN04	ANN02	ANN01	Poly1	Poly1	Poly1	ANN01
C-4				ANN02	ANN04	Poly1	Poly1	LS-SVR	ANN01	Poly1
C-5					Poly1	Poly1	ANN03	ANN01	ANN02	ANN01
C-6						ANN01	ANN01	LS-SVR	LS-SVR	ANN01
C-7							ANN03	LS-SVR	ANN01	Poly1
C-8								LS-SVR	LS-SVR	ANN02
C-9									ANN03	LS-SVR
C-10										ANN05

4.3 Hybrid Model Results

To check what is the of the internal topology, including the global model and the nine hybrid topologies, is the best for the final model, a new dataset that was isolated from the training of the local models is used to calculate the performance of each topology. As it is explained before, the data was normalized, and the values shown for the MSE are in the range of 10^{-3}.

Table 5. MSE values for each hybrid configuration $(\cdot 10^{-3})$

Global	Hyb. 2	Hyb. 3	Hyb. 4	Hyb. 5	Hyb. 6	Hyb. 7	Hyb. 8	Hyb. 9	Hyb. 10
2.0218	2.0857	122.2522	1.7638	1.7134	1.8923	1.7144	1.8281	1.7031	**1.6638**

In Tables 5 and 6 the best regression algorithms for each final local model are shown. The training of the final model requires that the final local models must the trained again one more time. As K-fold cross validation is used to calculate the performance of the local models, the previous regression models didn't use all the available data for each cluster. When the final topology is defined, new models are created using all the data for the final cluster's topology.

Table 6. Algorithm for each local model inside the hybrid topology

Cluster 1	Cluster 2	Cluster 3	Cluster 4	Cluster 5	Cluster 6	Cluster 7	Cluster 8	Cluster 9	Cluster 10
ANN01	LS-SVR	ANN01	Poly1	ANN01	ANN01	Poly1	ANN02	LS-SVR	ANN05

4.4   Validation Results

Once the hybrid model was created, a validation test was performed to calculate the accuracy of the model using another different dataset. Table 7 shows the performance metrics for the final hybrid model. In this table, the MSE, the MAE (Mean Absolute Error) and the NMSE (Normalized MSE) are calculated with raw data and with normalized data.

Table 7. Performance metrics for the best hybrid configuration

	MSE	MAE	NMSE
Hybrid configuration with 10 local models	$3.9565 \cdot 10^{7}$	$4.4041 \cdot 10^{3}$	0.1026
(with normalized values)	$1.8099 \cdot 10^{-3}$	$2.9787 \cdot 10^{-2}$	

Figure 6 shows the error plots for the validation dataset for each model. The upper plots are in real values, and the lower plots are created with normalized values.

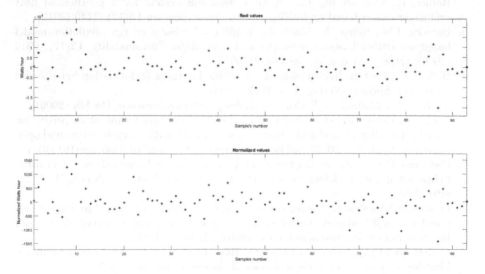

Fig. 6. Error plot (upper with real values, lower with normalized values)

5   Conclusions and Future Work

The main conclusion of this research is that it is possible to use simple meteo-rological data to predict the electrical energy produced in a solar installation. It is necessary to clarify that the meteorological data used in this research is from the autonomous meteorological agency of Galicia then, these data are not from the specific location of the solar installation.

Despite that the MAE in the model validation is 4404, the energy is measured in Wh. That means an error lower than 4.5 kWh, which is a good prediction taking into account that is the energy produced during the day.

In future work, a new model will be created, increasing the sample time of the data (for example, energy produced in 5 o 10 min), and meteorological data from the location of the solar installation. The authors think that with these new variables, the performance of the model could increase sufficiently to use the hybrid model in real installations connected to the grid, using the output of the model as an input of the building management system to be more efficient in the use of energy.

Acknowledgement. Míriam Timiraos's research was supported by the "Xunta de Galicia" (Regional Government of Galicia) through grants to industrial PhD (http://gain.xunta.gal/), under the "Doutoramento Industrial 2022" grant with reference: 04_IN606D_2022_2692965.

References

1. Meteogalicia.   observation.   meteorological   network   (2021).   https://www.meteogalicia.gal. Accessed 16 Apr 2023
2. Aláiz-Moretón, H., Castejón-Limas, M., Casteleiro-Roca, J.L., Jove, E., Fernández Robles, L., Calvo-Rolle, J.L.: A fault detection system for a geothermal heat exchanger sensor based on intelligent techniques. Sensors **19**(12), 2740 (2019)
3. Barrera, J.M., Reina, A., Maté, A., Trujillo, J.C.: Solar energy prediction model based on artificial neural networks and open data. Sustainability **12**(17), 6915 (2020). https://doi.org/10.3390/su12176915
4. Bishop, C.: Pattern Recognition and Machine Learning (Information Science and Statistics). Springer-Verlag, New York (2006)
5. del Brío, B., Molina, A.: Redes neuronales y sistemas borrosos. Ra-Ma (2006)
6. Casteleiro-Roca, J.L., et al.: Solar thermal collector output temperature prediction by hybrid intelligent model for smartgrid and smartbuildings applications and optimization. Appl. Sci. **10**(13), 4644 (2020). https://doi.org/10.3390/app10134644
7. Casteleiro-Roca, J.L., et al.: Short-term energy demand forecast in hotels using hybrid intelligent modeling. Sensors **19**(11), 2485 (2019). https://doi.org/10.3390/s19112485
8. Fernandez-Serantes, L., Casteleiro-Roca, J., Calvo-Rolle, J.: Hybrid intelligent system for a half-bridge converter control and soft switching ensurement. Revista Iberoamericana de Automática e Informática industrial (2022)
9. Galipienso, M., Quevedo, M., Pardo, O., Ruiz, F., Ortega, M.: Inteligencia artificial. Modelos, técnicas y áreas de aplicación. Editorial Paraninfo (2003)

10. González, J., Hernando, V.: Redes neuronales artificiales: fundamentos, modelos y aplicaciones. RA-MA (2000)
11. Gonzalez-Cava, J.M., et al.: Machine learning techniques for computer-based decision systems in the operating theatre: application to analgesia delivery. Logic J. IGPL **29**(2), 236–250 (2020). https://doi.org/10.1093/jigpal/jzaa049
12. Harston, A.M.C., Pap, R.: Handbook of Neural Computing Applications. Elsevier, Amsterdam (2014)
13. Heiberger, R., Neuwirth, E.: Polynomial regression. In: R Through Excel, pp. 269–284. Use R, Springer, New York (2009). https://doi.org/10.1007/978-1-4419-0052-4_11
14. Joselin Herbert, G., Iniyan, S., Sreevalsan, E., Rajapandian, S.: A review of wind energy technologies. Renew. Sustain. Energy Rev. **11**(6), 1117–1145 (2007). https://doi.org/10.1016/j.rser.2005.08.004
15. Jove, E., et al.: Attempts prediction by missing data imputation in engineering degree. In: Pérez García, H., Alfonso-Cendón, J., Sánchez González, L., Quintián, H., Corchado, E. (eds.) SOCO/CISIS/ICEUTE -2017. AISC, vol. 649, pp. 167–176. Springer, Cham (2018). https://doi.org/10.1007/978-3-319-67180-2_16
16. Jove, E., Casteleiro-Roca, J.L., Quintiá, H., Méndez-Pérez, J.A., Calvo-Rolle, J.L.: Anomaly detection based on intelligent techniques over a bicomponent production plant used on wind generator blades manufacturing. Revista Iberoamericana de Automática e Informática industrial **17**(1), 84–93 (2020). https://doi.org/10.4995/riai.2019.11055
17. Jove, E., Casteleiro-Roca, J.L., Quintián, H., Méndez-Pérez, J.A., Calvo-Rolle, J.L.: Virtual sensor for fault detection, isolation and data recovery for bicomponent mixing machine monitoring, vol. 30, pp. 671–687. Vilnius University Institute of Mathematics and Informatics (2019)
18. Jove, E., Casteleiro-Roca, J.L., Quintián, H., Simić, D., Méndez-Pérez, J.A., Luis Calvo-Rolle, J.: Anomaly detection based on one-class intelligent techniques over a control level plant. Logic J. IGPL **28**(4), 502–518 (2020)
19. Jove, E., et al.: Hybrid intelligent model to predict the remifentanil infusion rate in patients under general anesthesia. Logic J. IGPL **29**(2), 193–206 (2020). https://doi.org/10.1093/jigpal/jzaa046
20. Khandakar, A., et al.: Machine learning based photovoltaics (PV) power prediction using different environmental parameters of Qatar. Energies 12(14), 2782 (2019). https://doi.org/10.3390/en12142782
21. López, R., Fernández, J.: Las Redes Neuronales Artificiales. Netbiblo (2008)
22. MacQueen, J.: Some methods for classification and analysis of multivariate observations, pp. 281–297 (1967)
23. Moody, J., Darken, C.: Fast Learning in Networks of Locally-Tuned Processing Units, vol. 1 (1989). https://doi.org/10.1162/neco.1989.1.2.281
24. Orallo, J., Quintana, M., Ramírez, C.: Introducción a la minería de datos (2004)
25. Porras, S., Jove, E., Baruque, B., Calvo-Rolle, J.L.: A comparative analysis of intelligent techniques to predict energy generated by a small wind turbine from atmospheric variables. Logic J. IGPL (2022). https://doi.org/10.1093/jigpal/jzac031
26. Rahul, S.G., Kavitha, P., Dhivyasri, G.: Prediction of electricity load using artificial neural network for technology tower block of vit university. Int. J. Appl. Eng. Res. **12**(84), 7717–7723 (2017)
27. Simić, S., Banković, Z., Villar, J.R., Simić, D., Simić, S.D.: A hybrid fuzzy clustering approach for diagnosing primary headache disorder. Logic J. IGPL **29**(2), 220–235 (2020). https://doi.org/10.1093/jigpal/jzaa048

28. Steinwart, I., Christmann, A.: Support Vector Machines. Springer, Heidelberg (2008)
29. Viñuela, P., León, I.: Redes de neuronas artificiales: un enfoque práctico. Pearson Educación - Prentice Hall, Upper Saddle River (2004)
30. Wang, L., Wu, J.: Neural network ensemble model using PPR and LS-SVR for stock et forecasting (2012). https://doi.org/10.1007/978-3-642-24728-6_1
31. Wu, X.: Optimal designs for segmented polynomial regression models and web-based implementation of optimal design software. State University of New York at Stony Brook, Stony Brook (2007)
32. Wu, Z., Li, Q., Xia, X.: Multi-timescale forecast of solar irradiance based on multi-task learning and echo state network approaches. IEEE Trans. Ind. Inf. **17**(1), 300–310 (2021). https://doi.org/10.1109/TII.2020.2987096
33. Zayas-Gato, F., et al.: Intelligent model for active power prediction of a small wind turbine. Logic J. IGPL (2022). https://doi.org/10.1093/jigpal/jzac040
34. Zhang, Z., Chan, S.: On kernel selection of multivariate local polynomial modelling and its application to image smoothing and reconstruction. J. Signal Process. Syst. **64**(3), 361–374 (2011). https://doi.org/10.1007/s11265-010-0495-4
35. Zidan, A., El-Saadany, E.F.: Distribution system reconfiguration for energy loss reduction considering the variability of load and local renewable generation. Energy **59**, 698–707 (2013). https://doi.org/10.1016/j.energy.2013.06.061

Comparison of Geospatial Trajectory Clustering and Feature Trajectory Clustering for Public Transportation Trip Data

Hector Cogollos Adrian[1]([✉])[iD], Bruno Baruque Zanon[1][iD],
Santiago Porras Alfonso[2][iD], and Petr Dolezel[3][iD]

[1] Grupo de Inteligencia Computacional Aplicada (GICAP),
Departamento de Digitalización, Escuela Politécnica Superior,
Universidad de Burgos, Av. Cantabria s/n, 09006 Burgos, Spain
hcogollos@ubu.es
[2] Metaheurísticos (GRINUBUMET), Departamento de Economía Aplicada,
Facultad de Ciencias Económicas y Empresariales, Universidad de Burgos,
Pza. de la Infanta Dł. Elena, s/n, 09001 Burgos, Spain
[3] Faculty of Electrical Engineering and Informatics, University of Pardubice,
Studentska 95, 532 10 Pardubice, Czech Republic

Abstract. One of the techniques for the analysis of travel patterns on a public transport network is the clustering of the users movements, in order to identify movement patterns. This paper analyses and compares two different methodologies for public transport trajectory clustering: feature clustering and geospatial trajectory clustering. The results of clustering trip features, such as origin, destination, or distance, are compared against the clustering of travelled trajectories by their geospatial characteristics. Algorithms based on density and hierarchical clustering are compared for both methodologies. In geospatial clustering, different metrics to measure distances between trajectories are included in the comparison. Results are evaluated by analysing their quality through the silhouette coefficient and graphical representations of the clusters on the map. The results show that geospatial trajectory clustering offers better quality than feature trajectory clustering. Also, in the case of long and complete trajectories, density clustering using edit distance with real penalty distance outperforms other combinations.

Keywords: HDBSCAN · Agglomerative Clustering · Dynamic Time Warping distance · Edit distance with Real Penalty

1 Introduction

An increasing interest in promoting less polluting means of transportation, such as public transportation, has been apparent in recent years for most developed countries citizens. This change has been encouraged by institutions like the

P. García Bringas et al. (Eds.): HAIS 2023, LNAI 14001, pp. 589–599, 2023.
https://doi.org/10.1007/978-3-031-40725-3_50

United Nations through the Sustainable Development Goals or the European Union through the European Green Deal. To incentivize the use of public transportation, the understanding of the users behaviours and habits is considered of capital importance, so the services can adapt better to their needs [3,15].

In order to identify patterns that are relevant for a significant number of users, a massive number of trips must be analysed. To cope with this amount of data, a straightforward approach is to cluster their registered movements in an automated way and then analyse the characteristics of those clusters.

Two different methodologies for clustering public transport data are considered in this study. The first methodology focuses on extracting a certain number of features from each trip, in order to perform clustering according to those features, while the second methodology uses ordered sequences of GPS coordinates to measure similarity between trips in order to cluster them.

These methodologies can be found applied to real cases individually with ad-hoc adjustments to the data being analyzed. But there is no comparison in the literature when it comes to evaluating which clustering methodology has a better performance on the same data set, which is why the objective of this work is to determine which methodology offers more reliable results in a peer to peer comparison. To compare both methodologies two different hierarchical clustering algorithms have been chosen: HDBSCAN and Agglomerative clustering. Both algorithms have been applied using the Dynamic Time Warping (DTW) and Edit distance with Real Penalty (ERP) distance measures. The results have been quantified using the Silhouette coefficient as cluster evaluation technique, and verified using maps with a graphical representations of the clusters. As a test bench for the comparative, a public dataset containing the GPS traces of the trips registered by the users of the transport system of the city of Montreal, Canada; has been used. These trips are labelled by the purpose of the trip, enabling segmented analysis of users movements. The paper is structured following this outline: after this introduction, a brief review of the literature is addressed in Sect. 2. Then, the methodological proposal is detailed in Sect. 3. The dataset employed and this preprocessing is described in Sect. 4, followed by the experiments and results in Sect. 5. Finally, the last Section exposes the conclusions and future works.

2   Related Work

Trajectory clustering is a complex problem that has various practical applications such as surveillance security, abnormal behaviour detection, crowd behaviour analysis, or traffic control among others [6].

This work focuses on clustering GPS traces of public transport users. To perform this analysis, it is primarily recommended to carry out a statistical analysis of the data set, such as is proposed in [1] to obtain a detailed description of the data set. Additional statistics can also be obtained, such as common stop sub-sequences or probable destinations from an origin stop.

One of the biggest drawbacks that arise when grouping trajectories is the characteristic nature of the data, since they are composed of GPS locations and timestamps rather than independent variables on an abstract euclidean space. Two potential solutions have been proposed in the majority of cases found in literature. The first one, involves extracting variables or features from each trajectory, such as length, starting and ending point, etc. In Aaron et al. [8] spatial and usage habit features are extracted from user trajectories. Additionally, Yunzhe et al. [10] employs users trajectories data to determine different users characteristics such as place of residence or conveyance. The second one, is to apply clustering techniques using distance measures similar to those used in time series analysis, as in Li He et al. [9]. Two reviews can be highlighted in the literature regarding trajectory clustering. The first one, is about clustering of spatio-temporal data, which includes trajectory clustering [2]. The second review analyses the distance metrics in the literature used to perform trajectory clustering [5]. In this study, Dynamic Time Warping (DTW) and Edit distance with Real Penalty (ERP), are employed.

3   Methodological Proposal

The aim of this study is to determine which methodology has a better performance, feature or geospatial trajectory clustering. This section introduces the concept of trajectory, as well as the clustering algorithms and distances used, and defines the metrics employed to determine the result of the comparison.

For feature clustering, the features selected are: origin and destination coordinates, number of points on the trajectory and the distance travelled. For trajectory clustering, the distance measures between trajectories DTW and ERP are tested. Finally, numerical quality results of the clusters are analysed using the silhouette coefficient as a metric. The best results are plotted on a map to verify their coherence.

3.1   Trajectory Definition

A trajectory is defined as a sequence of geolocated points and corresponding timestamps, which are arranged in chronological order to indicate the subject's movement [2]. The focus of this study is on routes, where each GPS coordinate represents a point on the trajectory. In Eq. 1, it can be observed how a trajectory is constructed, where P is formed by latitude, longitude, and a timestamp.

$$T = (P_0, P_1, ..., P_i) \tag{1}$$

3.2   Clustering Algorithms

HDBSCAN and Agglomerative Clustering are employed in this work because they allow the use of different distance metrics than the conventional distances such as Euclidean, Manhattan, etc. This is important because trajectories cannot be measured with these distances, as they are a sequence of spatial locations. Therefore, DTW and ERP distance measures are used.

HDBSCAN is an extension of DBSCAN that implements a hierarchical algorithm to establish the maximum distance between neighbours, taking into account the stability of the clusters [11]. DBSCAN is a density-based clustering algorithm that uses the maximum distance between neighbours to determine which instances belong to the same cluster and which ones do not. This algorithm does not assign a cluster to all instances, but some may be classified as noise if they do not have neighbours.

Agglomerative Clustering is a hierarchical clustering algorithm [13], which means that it constructs a tree that has all instances in a single cluster at the root and each instance in a different cluster at the leaves. In this study, an ascending construction has been used, so it starts from the leaves and joins instances until the desired number of clusters is obtained.

3.3   Distance Measures

Specific distance measures are needed for trajectory clustering. This is because distances like Euclidean or Manhattan measure distances between independent variables. However, when working with trajectories, there is a sequence of stops that can also have a variable length. To calculate these distances, measures that compare these sequences to each other are used, such as DTW and ERP. For this study, an adapted version for trajectories which measures distances in two dimensions instead of one [5] is used.

DTW is a distance measure that, originally, allows comparing two time series by looking for the optimal alignment between them [4]. From this alignment, it measures the distances that exist between them.

ERP is based on edit distance on real sequence (EDR) [7]. This measure calculates the distance between two time series by calculating the number of modifications that would have to be made so that the two signals are equal with a certain tolerance. ERP, in turn, calculates the actual distance necessary to equalize the two series. In case the series do not have the same distance, a reference point is used. It is important to establish an adequate reference point. For this study, the Montreal city geographical centre is used as a reference pint.

3.4   Results Evaluation

The silhouette coefficient [14] has been selected as evaluation metric. It allows to use both DTW and ERP to calculate the quality of the clusters. In Eq. 2, it can be observed how the silhouette coefficient of an instance (i) is calculated. In the formula, a represents the average distance with the other instances in this cluster, while b represents the minimum distance of the instance with another cluster, which is the closest cluster to the instance being evaluated. To obtain the silhouette coefficient of the clustering, the average of the silhouette coefficient of all instances must be obtained.

$$s(i) = \frac{b - a}{max(a, b)} \tag{2}$$

The representation of the clusters on the maps is drawn using the most central trajectory of the cluster. This trajectory is the one that has the lowest average distance with the rest of the trajectories of the cluster. This is done due to the impossibility of calculating the average of a trajectory and the need to obtain a trajectory that can represent the cluster.

4   Dataset Description and Preprocessing

4.1   Description

This study uses the open dataset from the city of Montreal [12] to perform the comparison of algorithms of the two methodologies. This dataset was obtained through a mobile application that records users' trips and inquires about the purpose of the trip at the end of the route. For privacy reasons, the start, and end of the route have been removed in the dataset. Instead, the route begins and ends at the nearest intersection to the start and end of the route. Additionally, this dataset includes only filtered routes, and inconsistent routes have been removed.

4.2   Preprocessing

The Montreal dataset consists of 185,285 trajectories, out of which 12,935 belong to public transportation and has been selected for the study. Next, a filtering of the data has been carried out, discarding the trajectories with no defined purpose, which are only 5. To optimize calculations, the number of stops per trajectory have been reduced by only keeping those points that are the closest to a public transportation stop. For this purpose, the distance to the nearest stop of each point is calculated, and then points that are more than 20 m away from a stop are discarded. Also, if there are multiple consecutive points close to the same stop, the farthest ones are discarded. After this, trajectories that do not pass through at least two stops are discarded, resulting in 6,567 trajectories.

The dataset has been divided into subsets according to their purpose to make the experiment more robust. This results in different datasets that belong to different population segments with different characteristics. Table 1 shows a statistical description of each of these subsets, including the number of trajectories in each subset, the average number of stops, and the average distance travelled.

5   Experiments and Results

In this section, the results obtained in the experiments are presented and analysed. Two exploring grids of experiments have been designed. The first one, which is used for feature clustering, is a combination of each of the clustering algorithms with each of the subsets. The second one, which is used for trajectory clustering, is a combination of all clustering algorithms with all distance metrics

Table 1. Number of trajectories, average number of stops of the trajectories and average distance travelled by the trajectories for each of the purposes.

Purpose	Num. Trajectories	Avg. Stops	Avg. Distance (m)
Back home	2646	8.18	6382
Work	2101	8.16	6429
Leisure	602	7.83	5333
Education	469	7.9	7268
Shopping	323	8.17	4220
Gastronomic	160	6.83	5738
Other	97	8.27	6622
Health	96	8.28	5689
Picking up a person	73	8.03	5327

and all subsets of data. Next, the results are compared, and finally, some of the best results are represented on a map for visual inspection.

To understand the results, it is important to take into account the algorithm configuration, specifically the number of clusters used. The configuration used for Agglomerative Clustering has been determined using the Elbow method. This value has been calculated using a range of 2 to 20 clusters. On the other hand, for HDBSCAN, this number can vary, although the minimum number of instances per cluster is set to 5 by default. In order to understand the results of HDBSCAN, Table 2 shows the number of clusters created for feature clustering and trajectory clustering.

Table 2. Number of clusters used in HDBSCAN and Agglomerative Clustering for feature clustering, ERP trajectory clustering and DTW trajectory clustering.

Purpose	HDBSCAN			Agglomerative		
	Features	ERP	DTW	Features	ERP	DTW
Back home	2	23	43	8	5	9
Work	3	23	3	8	5	10
Leisure	2	18	4	8	7	10
Education	5	17	3	8	6	7
Shopping	3	14	2	6	7	8
Gastronomic	2	10	2	6	6	8
Other	2	9	0	9	7	7
Health	0	9	0	6	6	4
Picking up a person	0	6	0	8	5	4

After clustering the features using both algorithms and obtaining the Silhouette Coefficients as shown in Table 3, the results are evident. The results achieved through Agglomerative Clustering are stable but relatively low. On the other hand, HDBSCAN exhibits peaks where it produces significantly better results, while in other cases, it fails to create any clusters at all. It is apparent that forming clusters for smaller datasets is considerably more challenging, and if clusters are formed, they tend to be of inferior quality compared to those obtained through Agglomerative Clustering.

Table 3. Silhouette coefficient obtained in the clustering of features

Purpose	Agglomerative	HDBSCAN
Back home	0.16	**0.40**
Work	0.21	**0.33**
Leisure	0.20	**0.23**
Education	**0.20**	−0.19
Shopping	**0.18**	−0.10
Gastronomic	**0.22**	−0.01
Other	**0.26**	−0.11
Health	**0.21**	−
Picking up a person	**0.24**	−

The Silhouette Coefficient results obtained from geospatial trajectory clustering are presented in Table 4. It can be observed that the optimal algorithm combination, in the case of this dataset, is HDBSCAN with ERP. Conversely, the worst performing algorithm combination is HDBSCAN with DTW, which exhibits notably poor results and, in some instances, can not form clusters. Additionally, Agglomerative Clustering performs well with ERP. It is noteworthy that HDBSCAN is optimized for each dataset individually, while Agglomerative Clustering requires optimization of the number of clusters for each dataset. In this study, Agglomerative Clustering uses the same configuration for all datasets. Nonetheless, the results are consistently stable for all purposes.

Based on the results obtained from both methodology, it can be concluded that better clusters are obtained in the experiments with geospatial trajectory clustering. Particularly, the results obtained in geospatial trajectory clustering with ERP are significantly better than those obtained in feature clustering. To verify that the results are coherent, some of the experiments that yielded better results are visually analysed.

The maps represent the central trajectory of each obtained cluster; that is, the trajectory with the shortest distance to the rest of the trajectories in the cluster. Each is represented by a circle that indicates the start of the trajectory and a line marking the completed path. In Fig. 1, the results of HDBSCAN trajectory clustering and Agglomerative Clustering for the purpose of 'going to

Table 4. Silhouette coefficient obtained in the clustering of geospatial trajectories

Purpose	Agglo. ERP	Agglo. DTW	HDBSCAN ERP	HDBSCAN DTW
Back home	0.62	0.22	**0.99**	−0.46
Work	0.62	0.27	**0.99**	0.43
Leisure	0.58	0.17	**0.97**	−0.26
Education	0.60	0.36	**0.97**	−0.25
Shopping	0.55	0.23	**0.92**	−0.04
Gastronomic	0.60	0.24	**0.84**	0.08
Other	0.55	0.30	**0.78**	–
Health	0.57	0.41	**0.78**	–
Picking up a person	**0.63**	0.30	**0.63**	–

work' are shown. It can be observed that HDBSCAN has many more clusters, and they cover a greater variety of trips, while Agglomerative Clustering has fewer and closer clusters. This explains the better results of HDBSCAN due to its greater adaptability.

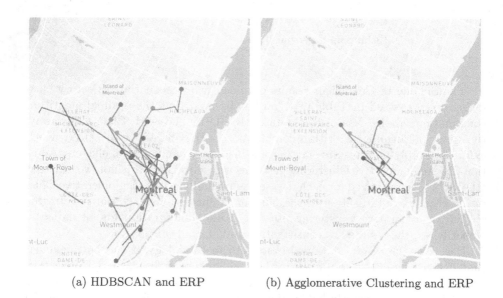

(a) HDBSCAN and ERP   (b) Agglomerative Clustering and ERP

Fig. 1. Representation of the trajectories for clusters that aim to go to work

When analysing one of the intermediate values in Table 4, such as gastronomic trips (Fig. 2), it is noteworthy that agglomerative clustering results in more dispersed clusters. However, HDBSCAN has achieved a better representation of the more dispersed clusters. Lastly, when comparing agglomerative clustering with HDBSCAN, agglomerative clustering does not account for clusters that move from the northwest to the southeast, which could be a heavily trafficked area.

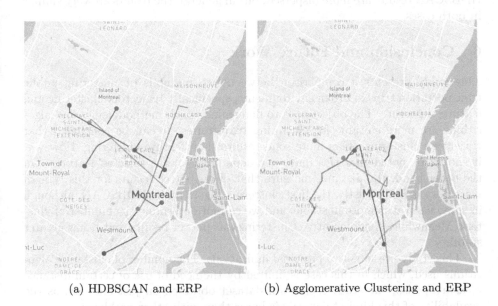

(a) HDBSCAN and ERP   (b) Agglomerative Clustering and ERP

Fig. 2. Representation of trajectories for clusters of people moving for gastronomic purposes

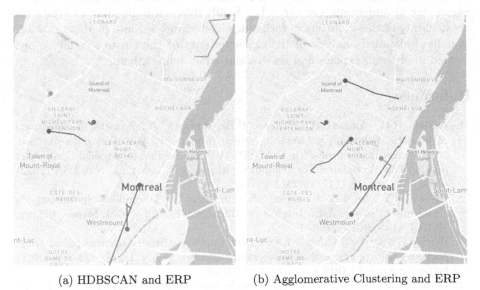

(a) HDBSCAN and ERP   (b) Agglomerative Clustering and ERP

Fig. 3. Representation of the trajectories for clusters whose purpose is to go and pick up a person

In Fig. 3, a comparison of HDBSCAN and Agglomerative Clustering is shown, which have very similar silhouette coefficient results. It can be observed that in this case, the difference in the number of clusters is only 1. On the other hand, HDBSCAN results are more dispersed, but in general, the results are very similar in both cases.

6   Conclusion and Future Work

This study presents a comparison between two methods of clustering public transportation trips in urban environments, specifically trajectory clustering and feature clustering. The objective is to determine which methodologies and algorithms are more suitable for clustering trajectories. It can be concluded that trajectory clustering offers more solid results than feature clustering. However, it should be noted that this may vary depending on the selected features. On the other hand, the distance measure that offers better results for this type of trajectory is ERP. Lastly, the best clustering algorithm is HDBSCAN, although in some cases it is more unstable, and we cannot determine the number of clusters. Meanwhile, Agglomerative Clustering has poorer results, but it has greater stability.

This study presents two principal limitations. The number of clustering algorithms used, which in this case is limited by the need of use of certain distance measures. Also, the study includes a dataset obtained on just one city, as the availability of this kind of datasets is lower than with other problems.

Based on these results, several lines of future work can be studied. On the one hand, the algorithm configurations can be studied deeply, emphasizing the parameter optimization. On the other hand, it remains pending of study the applicability of these clusters in tasks such as demand or route prediction. Additionally, a detailed analysis of the characteristics of the clusters could be performed in order to explain and understand what defines them.

References

1. Adrián, H.C., Alfonso, S.P., Zanón, B.B., Raffaetà, A., Zanatta, F.: Discovery of tourists' movement patterns in Venice from public transport data. In: SAC 2022: Proceedings of the 37th ACM/SIGAPP Symposium on Applied Computing, pp. 564–568. Association for Computing Machinery, New York, NY, USA (2022). https://doi.org/10.1145/3477314.3507355
2. Ansari, M.Y., Ahmad, A., Khan, S.S., Bhushan, G., Mainuddin: Spatiotemporal clustering: a review. Artif. Intell. Rev. **53**(4), 2381–2423 (2020). https://doi.org/10.1007/s10462-019-09736-1
3. Beirão, G., Sarsfield Cabral, J.A.: Understanding attitudes towards public transport and private car: a qualitative study. Transp. Policy **14**(6), 478–489 (2007). https://doi.org/10.1016/j.tranpol.2007.04.009
4. Berndt, D.J., Clifford, J.: Using dynamic time warping to find patterns in time series. In: AAAIWS 1994: Proceedings of the 3rd International Conference on Knowledge Discovery and Data Mining, pp. 359–370. AAAI Press (1994). https://doi.org/10.5555/3000850.3000887

5. Besse, P., Guillouet, B., Loubes, J.M., François, R.: Review and perspective for distance based trajectory clustering. ArXiv e-prints (2015). https://doi.org/10. 48550/arXiv.1508.04904
6. Bian, J., Tian, D., Tang, Y., Tao, D.: A survey on trajectory clustering analysis. ArXiv e-prints (2018). https://doi.org/10.48550/arXiv.1802.06971
7. Chen, L., Ng, R.: On the marriage of LP-norms and edit distance. In: VLDB 2004: Proceedings of the Thirtieth International Conference on Very Large Data Bases, vol. 30, pp. 792–803. VLDB Endowment (2004). https://doi.org/10.5555/1316689. 1316758
8. Gutiérrez, A., Domènech, A., Zaragozí, B., Miravet, D.: Profiling tourists' use of public transport through smart travel card data. J. Transp. Geogr. **88**, 102820 (2020). https://doi.org/10.1016/j.jtrangeo.2020.102820
9. He, L., Trépanier, M., Agard, B.: Space–time classification of public transit smart card users' activity locations from smart card data. Public Transport **13**(3), 579–595 (2021). https://doi.org/10.1007/s12469-021-00274-0
10. Liu, Y., Cheng, T.: Understanding public transit patterns with open geodemographics to facilitate public transport planning. Transportmetrica A: Transp. Sci. **16**(1), 76–103 (2020). https://doi.org/10.1080/23249935.2018.1493549
11. McInnes, L., Healy, J., Astels, S.: HDBSCAN: hierarchical density based clustering. J. Open Source Softw. 2(11), 205 (2017). https://doi.org/10.21105/joss.00205
12. de Montréal, V.: Déplacements MTL Trajet - Site web des données ouvertes de la Ville de Montréal (2023). https://donnees.montreal.ca/dataset/mtl-trajet
13. Müllner, D.: Modern hierarchical, agglomerative clustering algorithms. ArXiv e-prints (2011). https://doi.org/10.48550/arXiv.1109.2378
14. Rousseeuw, P.J.: Silhouettes: a graphical aid to the interpretation and validation of cluster analysis. J. Comput. Appl. Math. **20**, 53–65 (1987). https://doi.org/10. 1016/0377-0427(87)90125-7
15. Tsafarakis, S., Gkorezis, P., Nalmpantis, D., Genitsaris, E., Andronikidis, A., Altsitsiadis, E.: Investigating the preferences of individuals on public transport innovations using the maximum difference scaling method. Eur. Transp. Res. Rev. **11**(1), 1–12 (2019). https://doi.org/10.1186/s12544-018-0340-6

Image and Speech Signal Processing

Adapting YOLOv8 as a Vision-Based Animal Detection System to Facilitate Herding

Virginia Riego del Castillo[iD], Juan Felipe García Sierra[iD],
and Lidia Sánchez-González[✉][iD]

Departamento de Ingenierías Mecánica, Informática y Aeroespacial,
Universidad de León, 24071 León, Spain
{vriec,jfgars,lidia.sanchez}@unileon.es

Abstract. In this work, the YOLOv8 model is adapted to a specific problem in order to increase its performance. Thus, a vision-based system is developed to provide perceptual information to a robot to detect animals in the environment and to be able to perform herding tasks. For this purpose, a dataset is created by selecting animal images from the public AP10K dataset, as well as sheep images acquired by a camera attached to a 4-legged robot. Three different configurations of YOLOv8 are considered: nano, medium and extra-large, trained on the COCO dataset. Its fine-tuning with the animal image dataset shows an improvement in performance achieved not only from the point of view of the robot, but also from the point of view of a drone or a person. The best results are obtained with the YOLOv8 medium configuration when it is trained with the dataset that includes images of the robot's view.

Keywords: Precision Livestock Farming · Computer vision · 4-legged robot · Animal detection

1 Introduction

Agriculture is undergoing the same transformation as other fields due to the use of new technologies to streamline and facilitate their daily routines. There are many applications involving improved animal welfare as well as increased economic benefit. Some examples are provided in the existing reviews of Precision Livestock Farming (PLF) [1,9,11,14,15]. Thus, different sensors are used to identify and monitor livestock, usually attached to the animal as GPS collars [5] which sometimes injures the animals. Other approaches obtain information without contact. This is the case of Unmanned Aerial Vehicles (UAVs), which provide visual information on livestock, allowing them to be monitored and optimising production, from detecting diseases to analysing behaviour or feeding [10,13].

Taking advantage of the substantial improvements that have occurred in computer vision for detection, classification and segmentation of instances in images, application fields emerge that can benefit from these advances. This is the case

P. García Bringas et al. (Eds.): HAIS 2023, LNAI 14001, pp. 603–610, 2023.
https://doi.org/10.1007/978-3-031-40725-3_51

of PLF, where image processing techniques have been successfully applied. Some examples are livestock counting [8,12], weight estimation [3] or behaviour identification [18]. The images are usually taken by drones [12], although there are also works that analyse satellite images [16]. In addition, new methods are being developed that employ robots to assist sheep herding, avoiding predatory species [2,4,5].

Although existing models such as YOLOv8 [6] have outperformed the results provided by previous architectures, they still require tuning for particular problems, in particular when the images are taken from a different viewpoint or the animals present certain particular characteristics.

In this paper, we present the procedure to fit a pre-trained model based on YOLOv8 to optimise animal identification in order to be useful to automate herding tasks. This vision system can be deployed on a 4-legged robot to provide visual information and allow understanding of what the robot perceives through its cameras. As we consider more species than in previous work, it is more efficient in understanding its environment and acting accordingly [4].

In Sect. 2 we present the dataset that we have considered in this work to do the experiments and evaluate the model. Section 3 explains the procedure to adapt the existing model to this particular problem. The experiments and results obtained are presented in Sect. 4. Finally, Sect. 5 gathers the achieved conclusions.

2   Data Acquisition

As the aim is to provide a robot with intelligence to move the herd, the first aspect to analyse is how the animals behave when interacting with a robot. As the robot makes loud noises and is unfamiliar to the animals, it is interesting to study how they react to the proximity of a robot. For this purpose, videos were recorded in a closed enclosure with only two sheep.

The original videos acquired were trimmed to the same length of 10 s, which corresponds to 300 frames. The videos were captured from three different points of view: an aerial view obtained from a manually operated drone, an external view recorded by a person with a mobile phone and a ground view acquired by the camera attached to a 4-legged robot. Figure 1 shows samples of each view. A dataset of sheep images has been created by extracting the frames from the videos acquired with the robot's view and annotating them with the existing sheep.

To increase the number of samples and their variability, animal images have been added from a public dataset, the Animal Pose Estimation in the Wild Benchmark, known as AP-10K [17]. From the existing classes, we have filtered out those that can be found in the Iberian Peninsula, specifically in grazing areas.

It should be noted that the species of the experiment (sheep) can have a wide variety of coat colours. In particular, the captured videos show sheep with black fur, while most of the datasets show sheep with mainly light-coloured fur. Some examples of these differences can be seen in Fig. 2.

Fig. 1. Samples of the images acquired from different viewpoints: drone view (first column), human view (second column) and robot view (third column).

Fig. 2. Samples of sheep images from the AP-10K dataset (first row) and images acquired from the robot view (second row).

3   Adaptation of the Model for Animal Identification

YOLOv8 [6] is one of the most widely used state-of-the-art models in computer vision. One of the main reasons is its high performance and flexibility. Another reason is that it can solve multiple computer vision tasks such object detection, tracking, instance segmentation, image classification and pose estimation. In our case, we have focused on the object detection task because it allow us to detect how many animals are in the robot's surroundings and of which species. In the future, more complex tasks can be introduced to the robot to obtain more information about the environment, such as tracking to follow the animals and determine their trajectories or pose estimation from keypoints to know if the animals are feeding, resting or moving.

YOLOv8 has five different configurations, so the higher the number of parameters in the model, the better the results, but the higher the number of inferences per image. The configurations from lowest to highest number of parameters are: nano (YOLOv8n), small (YOLOv8s), medium (YOLOv8m), large (YOLOv8l) and extra-large (YOLOv8x). We have chosen three of them for the experiment: the fastest (YOLOv8n), the most accurate but also slowest (YOLOv8x) and the medium one, not so accurate but quiet fast (YOLOv8m). We have used pre-trained models with the COCO dataset [7]. The developers recommend the SGD optimiser with a learning rate of 10^{-2} and an input image size of 640×640 pixels. All models have been trained for 50 epochs with a batch size of 2 images due to the computational resources available (Intel(R) Core(TM) i7-9750H, 16GB RAM & NVIDIA GeForce RTX 2060).

The first approach consisted of training the YOLO models with the dataset generated from AP-10K [17], choosing those images with detections of the following species: cow, sheep, dog, fox, wolf, horse, cat and pig. The images were randomly divided considering the 70% of the images for training and 30% for validation, with detections of each species. The results show an mAP_{50} (mean average precision with a threshold of 0.5) of 0.91 in the training set and 0.75 in the validation set for the YOLOv8x model.

The second approach was to identify the two sheep on the farm from the robot's point of view (which is the desired final grazing system). In this case, the AP-10K dataset was augmented with images acquired by the camera attached to the 4-legged robot. As in the previous case, the dataset was divided into 70% for training and 30% for validation. The YOLOv8x model achieves an mAP_{50} of 0.91 in the training set and 0.76 in the validation set. As can be seen in the Table 1 the results of each approach are very similar. This table shows information about the model considered, the dataset used for training the model (AP-10K only or AP-10K together with the images acquired from the robot viewpoint) and the different metrics considered for both the training and validation sets.

Table 1. Results obtained for both the training set and the validation set by the models trained only with the AP-10K dataset and adding the images acquired by the robot view.

Dataset	Model	Millions of Parameters	Training Set				Validation Set			
			Precision	Recall	mAP50	mAP50:95	Precision	Recall	mAP50	mAP50:95
	YOLOv8n	3.010	0.9145	0.9139	0.9625	0.7995	0.8324	0.7742	0.8536	0.6374
AP-10K	YOLOv8m	25.860	0.9658	0.9616	0.9856	0.8821	0.8735	0.8290	0.9015	0.7047
	YOLOv8x	68.160	0.9824	0.9734	0.9912	0.9151	0.9115	0.8766	0.9370	0.7451
AP-10K	YOLOv8n	3.010	0.9397	0.9233	0.9706	0.7982	0.8355	0.7942	0.8659	0.6485
+	YOLOv8m	25.860	0.9703	0.9710	0.9892	0.8883	0.8933	0.8638	0.9249	0.7231
Sheep	YOLOv8x	68.160	0.9861	0.9767	0.9918	0.9102	0.9058	0.8677	0.9376	0.7583

Figure 3 shows the number of samples considered for training and testing for each category, distinguishing between the images from the AP-10K dataset and images captured by the camera attached to the robot.

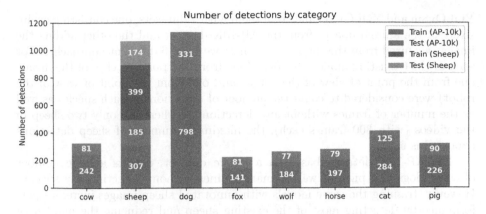

Fig. 3. Number of detections per category in the AP-10K dataset and the acquired images (Sheep) divided into training and test sets.

4   Experimental Results and Discussion

As mentioned in the previous section, all YOLOv8 models seem to perform well on both data sets. Figure 4 shows the relationship between the number of parameters in each experiment and the results obtained for the metrics considered (precision, recall, mAP_{50}, $mAP_{50:95}$). The results are similar using the public AP-10K dataset or by adding to this dataset the images taken by the camera attached to the 4-legged robot, which were manually annotated (denoted AP-10K + Sheep). The latter dataset provides the robot's point of view to be useful in herding tasks.

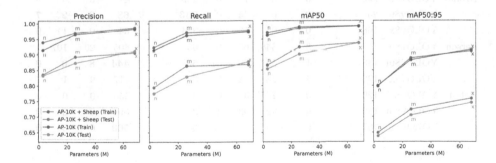

Fig. 4. Results obtained by the different models (YOLOv8n, YOLOv8m and YOLOv8x) for the considered metrics compared with the number of parameters in millions.

After that, a real validation of the models was carried out using the videos acquired by the drone, the person and the robot which were explained in detail in Sect. 2. We consider 3 configurations of the YOLOv8 models (YOLOv8n,

YOLOv8m and YOLOv8x) and train them with 2 datasets, one consisting exclusively of the animal images from the AP-10K dataset and the other adding the images acquired from the robot view. Thus, we have 6 different approaches. For each of the 6 existing models, 3 videos (one from the point of view of the drone, one from the point of view of the person and one from the point of view of the robot) were considered to count the number of detections of each species as well as the number of frames without any detection. As there are only two sheep in the videos (with 300 frames each), the maximum number of sheep detections expected is 600.

The AP-10K dataset, based on a public dataset, detects a large number of cows, dogs and pigs, as well as many frames without detecting any species. However, training the same models with annotated sheep images increases performance by detecting most of the existing sheep and reducing the number of undetected frames. Table 2 gathers the number of detections for each video. As already mentioned, the YOLOv8 architectures obtain better performances with a larger model, but in our case the medium configuration (YOLOvm) obtains the best results in all three views (drone, person and robot). We want to improve the detection efficiency from the robot's point of view, as this is our desired herding system, and that is the reason why we annotate the images from that point of view.

Table 2. Number of detections per category of the different models for videos taken from each point of view (Drone, Person and Robot), including the number of frames without detection of any kind..

		AP-10K					AP-10K + Sheep				
		No detection	Sheep	Cow	Dog	Pig	No detection	Sheep	Cow	Dog	Pig
Drone	YOLOv8n	299	0	0	1	0	259	41	0	5	0
	YOLOv8m	256	0	0	44	0	**233**	**68**	0	**2**	**7**
	YOLOv8x	168	0	0	133	0	244	64	0	14	0
Person	YOLOv8n	75	3	348	65	0	63	405	20	107	1
	YOLOv8m	133	1	59	90	31	**58**	**444**	8	0	0
	YOLOv8x	128	8	24	98	92	63	417	9	1	7
Robot	YOLOv8n	120	0	247	3	0	3	555	0	0	0
	YOLOv8m	180	0	32	93	4	**3**	**563**	0	0	0
	YOLOv8x	162	0	3	97	46	5	**563**	0	0	0

5   Conclusions

This work uses the existing YOLOv8 model for detecting animals in images to develop a vision-based system that can be deployed on a 4-legged robot to assist in herding tasks. Although YOLOv8 models are trained on the COCO dataset, additional training is performed on two different datasets of animals to fine tune them. The first consists of animal images from the AP-10K public dataset. The second adds images acquired by a camera attached to a 4-legged robot, which are manually annotated to provide information about the sheep in the video frames. Three different configurations of YOLOv8 are considered: the nano one, the medium and the extra-large. These three models are trained again with the two datasets created, increasing the initial performance of the YOLOv8 models. To validate the results, a validation is carried out with videos taken by a person, by a drone and by the 4-legged robot. The best results are provided by the YOLOv8m model trained with images from the AP10k dataset together with those acquired from the robot's point of view, demonstrating the optimisation achieved when the YOLOv8 model is adapted to the problem under consideration.

Acknowledgements. We gratefully acknowledge the financial support of Grant TED2021-132356B-I00 funded by MCIN/AEI/10.13039/501100011033 and by the "European Union NextGenerationEU/PRTR". Virginia Riego would like to thank Universidad de León for its funding support for her doctoral studies.

References

1. Aquilani, C., Confessore, A., Bozzi, R., Sirtori, F., Pugliese, C.: Review: precision livestock farming technologies in pasture-based livestock systems. Animal **16**(1), 100429 (2022). https://doi.org/10.1016/j.animal.2021.100429
2. Brown, J., Qiao, Y., Clark, C., Lomax, S., Rafique, K., Sukkarieh, S.: Automated aerial animal detection when spatial resolution conditions are varied. Comput. Electron. Agric. **193**, 106689 (2022). https://doi.org/10.1016/j.compag.2022.106689
3. Riego del Castillo, V., Sánchez-González, L., Fernández-Robles, L., Castejón-Limas, M., Rebollar, R.: Estimation of lamb weight using transfer learning and regression. In: García Bringas, P., et al. (eds.) 17th International Conference on Soft Computing Models in Industrial and Environmental Applications (SOCO 2022). SOCO 2022. LNCS, vol. 531, pp. 23–30. Springer, Cham (2023). https://doi.org/10.1007/978-3-031-18050-7_3
4. Riego del Castillo, V., Sánchez-González, L., Campazas-Vega, A., Strisciuglio, N.: Vision-based module for herding with a sheepdog robot. Sensors **22**(14), 5321 (2022). https://doi.org/10.3390/s22145321
5. Herlin, A., Brunberg, E., Hultgren, J., Högberg, N., Rydberg, A., Skarin, A.: Animal welfare implications of digital tools for monitoring and management of cattle and sheep on pasture. Animals **11**(3), 829 (2021). https://doi.org/10.3390/ani11030829
6. Jocher, G., Ayush, C., Qiu, J.: Ultralytics Yolov8. https://docs.ultralytics.com/
7. Lin, T.-Y., et al.: Microsoft COCO: common objects in context. In: Fleet, D., Pajdla, T., Schiele, B., Tuytelaars, T. (eds.) ECCV 2014. LNCS, vol. 8693, pp. 740–755. Springer, Cham (2014). https://doi.org/10.1007/978-3-319-10602-1_48
8. Meena, S.D., Agilandeeswari, L.: Smart animal detection and counting framework for monitoring livestock in an autonomous unmanned ground vehicle using restricted supervised learning and image fusion. Neural Process. Lett. **53**(2), 1253–1285 (2021). https://doi.org/10.1007/s11063-021-10439-4

9. Odintsov Vaintrub, M., Levit, H., Chincarini, M., Fusaro, I., Giammarco, M., Vignola, G.: Review: precision livestock farming, automats and new technologies: possible applications in extensive dairy sheep farming. Animal **15**(3), 100143 (2021). https://doi.org/10.1016/j.animal.2020.100143

10. Porto, S., Arcidiacono, C., Giummarra, A., Anguzza, U., Cascone, G.: Localisation and identification performances of a real-time location system based on ultra wide band technology for monitoring and tracking dairy cow behaviour in a semi-open free-stall barn. Comput. Electron. Agric. **108**, 221–229 (2014). https://doi.org/10.1016/j.compag.2014.08.001

11. Rejeb, A., Abdollahi, A., Rejeb, K., Treiblmaier, H.: Drones in agriculture: a review and bibliometric analysis. Comput. Electron. Agric. **198**, 107017 (2022). https://doi.org/10.1016/j.compag.2022.107017

12. Rivas, A., Chamoso, P., González-Briones, A., Corchado, J.M.: Detection of cattle using drones and convolutional neural networks. Sensors **18**(7), 2048 (2018). https://doi.org/10.3390/s18072048

13. Spedener, M., Tofastrud, M., Devineau, O., Zimmermann, B.: Microhabitat selection of free-ranging beef cattle in south-boreal forest. Appl. Anim. Behav. Sci. **213**, 33–39 (2019). https://doi.org/10.1016/j.applanim.2019.02.006

14. Stygar, A.H., et al.: A systematic review on commercially available and validated sensor technologies for welfare assessment of dairy cattle. Front. Vet. Sci. **8**, 634338 (2021). https://doi.org/10.3389/fvets.2021.634338

15. Tedeschi, L.O., Greenwood, P.L., Halachmi, I.: Advancements in sensor technology and decision support intelligent tools to assist smart livestock farming. J. Animal Sci. **99**(2), skab038 (2021). https://doi.org/10.1093/jas/skab038

16. Wang, D., Shao, Q., Yue, H.: Surveying wild animals from satellites, manned aircraft and unmanned aerial systems (UASS): a review. Remote Sens. **11**(11), 1308 (2019)

17. Yu, H., Xu, Y., Zhang, J., Zhao, W., Guan, Z., Tao, D.: AP-10K: a benchmark for animal pose estimation in the wild. In: Thirty-fifth Conference on Neural Information Processing Systems Datasets and Benchmarks Track (Round 2) (2021)

18. Zhu, W.X., Guo, Y.Z., Jiao, P.P., Ma, C.H., Chen, C.: Recognition and drinking behaviour analysis of individual pigs based on machine vision. Livestock Sci. **205**, 129–136 (2017). https://doi.org/10.1016/j.livsci.2017.09.003

Image Classification Understanding with Model Inspector Tool

Flávio A. O. Santos[1]([✉])(ID), Maynara Donato de Souza[1](ID), Pedro Oliveira[3](ID),
Leonardo Nogueira Matos[2](ID), Paulo Novais[3](ID), and Cleber Zanchettin[1](ID)

[1] Centro de Informática, Universidade Federal de Pernambuco,
Recife, Pernambuco, Brazil
`{faos,mds3,cz}@cin.ufpe.br`
[2] Departamento de computação, Universidade Federal de Sergipe,
Aracaju, Sergipe, Brazil
`leonardo@dcomp.ufs.br`
[3] University of Minho, Braga, Portugal
`pedro.jose.oliveira@algoritmi.uminho.pt, pjon@di.uminho.pt`

Abstract. This paper proposes a novel method called U Analysis for interpreting the behavior of image classification models. The method allows the evaluation of the interdependence between patches of information in an image and their impact on the model's classification performance. In addition, the paper introduces the Model Inspector tool that allows users to manipulate various visual features of an input image to understand better the model's robustness to different types of information. This work aims to provide a more comprehensive framework for model interpretation and help researchers and practitioners better understand the strengths and weaknesses of deep learning models in image classification. We perform experiments with CIFAR-10 and STL-10 datasets using the ResNet architecture. The findings show that ResNet model trained with CIFAR-10 and STL-10 presents counter-intuitive feature interdependence, which is seen as a weakness. This work can contribute to developing even more advanced tools for analyzing and understanding deep learning models.

Keywords: Interpretability · Trustworthy models · Image classification

1 Introduction

As deep learning models become more popular, they become more present in our lives in different applications. This is no different for image classification models; they are important for applications of several domains, for example,

---

P. Oliveira—Supported by the doctoral Grant PRT/BD/154311/2022 financed by the Portuguese Foundation for Science and Technology (FCT), and with funds from European Union, under MIT Portugal Program.

P. García Bringas et al. (Eds.): HAIS 2023, LNAI 14001, pp. 611–622, 2023.
https://doi.org/10.1007/978-3-031-40725-3_52

classifying medical images such as MRI [15] and classifying images in e-commerce to automatically tag products [11]. Despite their success, image classification models also have failures. For example, they are vulnerable to artificial and natural Adversarial attacks [20], biased to background information [21], and sometimes makes wrong prediction when we rotate the object in the scene [3]. This list of failures shows that we still need tools to harnessing and interpret the image classification model's behavior to understand its decision.

With the increase in model complexity and the resulting lack of transparency in the decision-making process, model interpretability methods have become increasingly important. The model transparency and interpretability usually are associated with the degree to which a human can understand the cause of a decision. When making predictions with a neural network, the data input is fed through many layers of multiplication with the learned weights and through non-linear transformations. A single prediction can involve millions of mathematical operations, thus being difficult for us humans to follow the exact mapping from data input to prediction. We would have to consider millions of weights that interact in a complex way to understand a prediction by a neural network. We need specific interpretability methods to interpret the behavior and predictions of neural networks.

In recent years, several methods have been proposed to interpret deep learning model outputs [16–19]. Given an input x, model f, and target category y, these interpretability methods build an attribution map a with the same size as x, where a_i means how much important the feature x_i for $f(x)_y$. There are some libraries developed with Python that we can use to instantiate these methods and interpret models developed in Pytorch or TensorFlow, for example Captum[1], Innvestigate [2], and TensorFlow Interpretability[2]. These libraries have an easy-to-use interface where we can instantiate the interpretability methods to produce the attribution maps to our inputs. Still, we need to codify all input interactions that we want to infer the impact of feature changes in model output or attribution maps, thus being a challenge to beginner or even intermediate users to debug its models.

In this paper, we propose a new method called U Analysis, which allows us to evaluate the importance of different patches in an image and understand the impact of removing them on the model's classification performance. We also introduce a Model Inspector tool that allows users to manipulate various visual features of an input image to understand better the model's sensitivity to different types of information. Our goal is to provide a more comprehensive framework for model interpretation and help researchers and practitioners better understand the strengths and weaknesses of deep learning models in image classification. This work is structured as follows. Section 2 discusses the proposed U Analysis, and Sect. 3 presents the Model inspector tool. The Sect. 4 presents and discuss the experiments made with U Analysis, and we conclude the work in Sect. 5.

---

[1] https://captum.ai/.

[2] https://tf-explain.readthedocs.io/en/latest/.

2   Related Works

In the recent years, the scientific community has proposed several interpretability methods [16–19]. These methods tries to decompose the model output strength into the input space, attributing a importance weight for each input pixel. Although these methods represents a path towards black-box model understanding, there is still concerns about its usefulness to infer how each input region (grid of features) impacts the model decisions [1]. Instead of attribute a degree of importance for each input feature, other methods proposes to infer the input feature importance by manipulating the input image and verify its impact on model output. [6] proposes the deletion and preservation games, where the first is to search for the smallest deletion mask (M_d) that when applied to the input image the model will change its prediction, on the other hand, the preservation game search for the smallest preservation mask (M_p) that when represents the sufficient input region to the model classify the input image correctly. [22] proposes the Occlusion approach to verify if some input image patch is important to model prediction by occluding it with a constant signal, such as grey patch.

The related works discussed so for focus on interpretability or model understanding methods that aim to attribute importance weights to individual input pixels, or infer the input region importance for model prediction. On the other hand, the method proposed in this work, called U Analysis (UA), addresses the co-dependence of input image patches for accurate model prediction. UA focuses on identifying groups of patches that need to co-exist to the model make accurate predictions. It systematically verifies the significance of these co-dependent patches by systematically manipulating the input image and observing the impact on the model's output. This method differs from the related works by explicitly finding the co-dependence among image patches rather than assigning importance weights to individual features or patches, instead it uses these weights as input to perform the analysis.

3   U Analysis

Different methods were proposed to visualize features and concepts learned by the neural network models, which have a performance that is less 'interpretative' and usually qualitatively evaluated. These methods compute how much each input feature contributes to the model output/prediction, but they do not explain the input features' interdependence nor the order of importance. In this work, we propose the U Analysis (UA), a systematic method to verify the co-dependence of input image patches for model prediction, a group of patches that must co-exist for the model to predict accurately.

The Algorithm 1 presents the U Analysis steps with a Python-based syntax. Given an input image x, model f, and attribution map I, the UA method first computes the importance of each x's patch of dimension $W \times W$ by summing up all attribution weight of each respective feature. Next, it sorts the x's patches by importance. It cumulatively replaces each one of the input images by noise,

---

Algorithm 1: U Analysis.

Input: Given a trained deep learning model f, input image x, target, interpretability vector I, window size w, order type *order*, and noise type n

$region\_weights \leftarrow get\_region\_importance(I, w)$;
$region\_sorted \leftarrow sort\_region(region\_weights, order)$;
$gen\_batch \leftarrow remove_regions(x, region\_sorted, noise)$;
$pred\_batch \leftarrow f(gen\_batch)$;
$y\_batch\_pred \leftarrow pred\_batch.argmax(1)$;
$pos\_pred\_correct \leftarrow where(y\_batch\_pred == target)$;
$u\_triples \leftarrow []$;
for $i = 0$ **to** $len(y\_pred\_correct) - 1$ **do**
    $idx\_left = pos\_pred\_correct[i]$;
    $idx\_right = pos\_pred\_correct[i + 1]$;
    if $(idx\_right - idx\_left)$ *is larger than one* **then**
        $middle\_idx \leftarrow choice\_between(idx\_left, idx\_right)$;
        $u\_triples.append((idx\_left, idx\_middle, idx\_right))$;

return $u\_triples$

---

creating new x_i images, where the x_i images are equal to x, except that does not have the information about the first i patches (i.e. *gen_batch* variable). Thus, assuming that the input image has N patches, the x_N image does not have any information (i.e., only noise such as zeros, ones, or Gaussian noise). Figure 1 shows a sample of the UA processing.

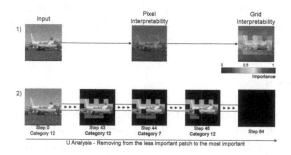

Fig. 1. U Analysis pipeline. The UA has two main steps, 1) given a input image it compute the model inference and interpretability, then it process the grid level interpretability. 2) Given the grid level interpretability, it sorts each image patch according to its importance and removes patch-by-patch from the input image from the less important to the most one.

After constructing the sequence of new images, it is possible to see that all the information from image x_i is present in $x_{j<i}$. Thus, if we have a case where $left < middle < right$ and $f(x_{left}) = y$, $f(x_{middle})! = y$, and $f(x_{right}) = y$, it means that the information contained in x_{left} and x_{right} is sufficient for the model to infer correctly. However, the patches in x_{middle} but not in x_{right} create negative strength for y when they coexist with the other patches. We call this counter-intuitive case as U-occurrence.

4 Model Inspector

Image comprises different types of visual information, such as shape, color, texture, patterns, and objects. Each type of information may impact the model classification decision in different ways, for example, a model may be biased to texture, color, or shape [3,9,14,23]. Thus, tweaking these types of information in the input image and evaluating the model with the newly image can help assess the classification model's robustness regarding different versions of the same signal, thus producing a local analysis of the model. Interpretability methods also can be used to debug image classification models. They produce how important is each input image pixel for model decision and attribution map to visualize. Thus the pixel importance can be used to compute metrics such as Top-K erasing and RFS [13]

Beyond these types of visual information, an image can be composed of two main spatial regions: foreground and background. The foreground is the image's main focus, which includes the subjects or objects of interest. On the other hand, the background is all the information that is not in the foreground. Usually, in image classification tasks, we want to classify the information that is in foreground, thus, it can be considered the signal while the background is the context. Background robustness is the ability of an image classification model to classify a signal even when it is on a different background. [21] showed that image classification models may be biased to background information and make a wrong prediction even when the foreground is present in the image but have a not common background. Thus, it is important to evaluate if the signal information is enough for the model to classify the image accurately or if the model is biased to background information.

The discussion presented so far shows we need a pipeline to evaluate the image classification model weakness. Therefore, we propose the image classification Model Inspector tool[3] whose goal is to allow users to evaluate image classification robustness against different types of transformations. It is composed of three different modules which the user can evaluate the image classification against different image processing functions, interpretability maps, and signal vs. noise sensitivity. The Model inspector is developed as a Web App which the user can load models from Pytorch or Timm[4] library and interact with its input-output results. In the following, we will present each Model inspector's module in detail.

---

[3] https://github.com/faos/image-classifier-model-inspector.
[4] https://timm.fast.ai/.

4.1   Image Processing

The image processing module comprises several image transformation functions that add noise to the input image. The user can apply these transformations in the input image and visualize the model output difference with the original image, thus getting insights about the model robustness related to the transformation. The module implements three types of noise: Gaussian noise, Shot noise, and Impulse noise. Although we may add them intentionally, they can be naturally caused by phenomena such as random variations in light, sensor noise in the camera, interference in the transmission process, or bit errors. These noise functions can also be found in [8], where the authors created ImageNet [5] variations with them to evaluate the robustness of several image classification architectures on the ImageNet [5] dataset.

Gaussian, Shot, and Impulse noise are transformations that change the image color of texture. However, in addition to them, the image processing module also has spatial transformations (e.g., Patch Shuffle, Horizontal Shuffle, Vertical Shuffle) that deform the shape of the objects in the image, but it keeps the texture and color information, so it is helpful to infer whether the object's shape is important to the model predictions. Patch shuffle transformation splits the input image in disjoint squared patches with size $W \times W$, shuffles them, and creates a new image. On the other hand, horizontal shuffle creates disjoint horizontal patches with height H and size equal to the input image, shuffle them, and create a new image. The vertical shuffle is similar to the horizontal, the difference is that the patches are vertical, so their size is equal to the image height, and the width is W. Figure 2 presents the pipeline of this module and an example of each analysis function.

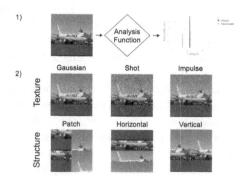

Fig. 2. Image processing pipeline. The part 1) show the main pipeline of the image processing; Given a input image, the user should select which function it will use to process the image and compare the model inference with the original image inference. The part 2) shows the functions available in model inspector, they are grouped by two types, texture and structure.

4.2   Interpretability

The interpretability module is composed of two main components: (1) interpretability methods and (2) U Analysis. In the first component, we implement a wrapper for the Captum library so the user can select the interpretability method and visualize its outputs. The second component implements the U Analysis discussed before, where the user can choose the noise method and window size. Besides, if the analysis finds counter-intuitive samples, it will show them. It is important to highlight that the attribution map used in the U Analysis is the output of the first component.

4.3   Signal

The signal module allows the users to interact with the input by selecting which region of the input image they consider the signal. The users may select the signal with three formats: rectangle, circle, and polygon. After selecting the signal, the module computes the signal-to-noise and background texture analyses. The signal-to-noise analysis calculates the importance of the signal region and compares it with the context to verify which region is more important to the model. The background texture analysis allows the user to apply all the image transformations from the first module to the image background only, thus verifying if the model decision is impacted by background texture changes while keeping the signal information. The noise analysis proposed in [13] inspired the background texture analysis. Figure 3 presents the signal pipeline.

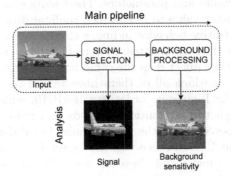

Fig. 3. Signal analysis pipeline. This module allows the user to select the signal of the input image using different formats, for example polygon, rectangle, and circle. After select the signal, it can add transformation to the image background to verify the model sensitivity to background changes while keeps the original signal. The main pipeline is composed of three steps, 1) select the input image, 2) select the signal information, and 3) apply the background processing functions. The signal selection and background processing has a output to compare the model inference using only each information.

5   Experiments and Results

5.1   U Analysis

This section presents the experiments and results achieved with the U Analysis. First, we describe the datasets and architecture used and then present the percentage of U occurrence found. To perform the experiments, we used the CIFAR-10 [10] and Self-Taught Learning 10 (STL-10) [4] datasets. The CIFAR-10 dataset is composed of 60,000 32×32 color images grouped into ten classes and has 50,000 images for training and 10000 for testing. It is a well-balanced dataset. Thus, each class has 5,000 training and 1,000 testing images. On the other hand, STL-10 has the same classes as CIFAR-10 (i.e., airplane, automobile, bird, cat, deer, dog, frog, horse, ship, and truck) but has 13,000 96×96 color images, where 5,000 are for training and 8,000 for testing. We train a ResNet-18 [7] instance for each dataset using Stochastic gradient descent (SGD) with a learning rate $1e - 2$. Each network was trained by 50 epochs, and we chose the model with best accuracy on test set to perform the U Analysis.

The U analysis has several hyperparameters. For example, we can use different interpretability methods to compute the contribution of each input pixel to the model output, the order in which we sort the patch can be random, increasing, or decreasing, and we can replace the original patch information with several types of noise, and the patch's size (noise window size) itself is a parameter. To perform the U Analysis with the ResNet-18, we use 10 different interpretability methods, 3 sorting types, 6 noise types, and 5 different patch sizes, resulting in 900 runs for each dataset. Figure 4 presents the results achieved by the U analysis with all datasets and parameters. The results group the U occurrence for each hyperparameter value to infer which configuration is more susceptible to finding counter-intuitive behavior in image classification.

The findings show that all the attribution methods used have almost the same U occurrence. Thus they affect it in the same way. This conclusion is similar to the sorting method, in which all of them have almost the same U occurrence percentage, except the Increasing order in CIFAR-10, which is slightly higher than others. Although the attribution methods and noise window order have close U occurrence percentages, the type of noise has different values for each parameter value. The U occurrence was the lowest for both datasets when we used the image region mean and Gaussian noise. We argue that this behavior can be due to different reasons. For example, while the Gaussian noise does not represent information regarding the dataset, thus is easy for the model ignores it, the image region mean is a statistic of the patch that was removed, thus it still has information about the original patch.

The results show that the noise window size is the most important hyperparameter, with a patch size of 10% the parameter value with the most U occurrence in all scenarios. This result indicates that tiny patches instead of bigger ones may impact the ResNet-18, as the 33% presents a low U occurrence. In addition, the ResNet-18 may correlate the features of lower patches instead of bigger ones.

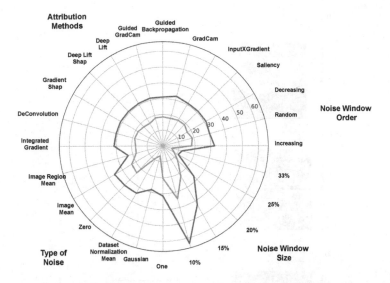

Fig. 4. U analysis results. The graph shows the results grouped by each parameter type (i.e. Attribution methods, type of noise, noise window size, and noise window order) and value. Besides, each curve represent the results for each dataset. The blue curve represents the results obtained from the CIFAR-10 dataset while the orange is with STL-10.

5.2   Model Inspector Demonstration

This section analyzes the model inspector tool and shows how the user can use it to infer insights about image classifier models. This analysis uses a ResNet-18 architecture trained with FGVC Aircraft [12] dataset to classify the aircraft manufacturer. Figure 5 presents the outputs obtained from the model inspector and has three crops extracted.

Part 1 shows the Image processing module applying the Gaussian transformation on the input image, while part 2 is the Patch shuffle transformation. Part 3 shows a sample of the signal module when we select the aircraft as the signal and apply the Gaussian noise into the background. All three parts have a barplot on the right to compare the ResNet output when we input the original image and the respective transformed image. Part 1 shows that when we insert Gaussian noise in the input image, the model changes its prediction, thus being sensitive to Gaussian noise. Part 2 also shows that when we destroy the spatial information with patch shuffle, the model also changes its prediction, which means that the signal structure is important for the prediction. Finally, part 3 shows that when we insert noise only in the background, the model does not change its prediction. Thus, joining these results with part 1, we can conclude that the model is sensitive to change in the signal only as it keeps its decision when we keep the original signal.

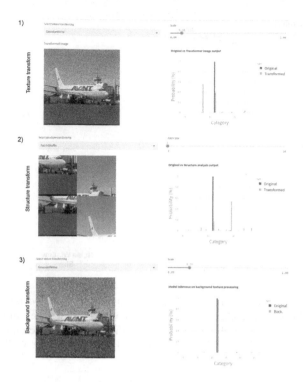

Fig. 5. Model inspector demonstration. Parts 1 and 2 show the outputs of the Image processing module for texture and structure transformation, respectively. While part 3 shows the result of the signal background texture transformation. On the left side, all parts have a selectbox so the user can select the transformation, and on the right side, there is a slider so the user can select the parameter value for the transformation.

6   Conclusion

In this paper, we presented U Analysis, a novel method for visualizing and interpreting the behavior of image classification models. UA allows us to understand the importance of patches in an image and their interactions, which can be used to understand how models make inferences and identify their weaknesses. Furthermore, we proposed a tool, Model Inspector, that allows users to interact with the input image and analyze the robustness of image classification models by changing visual information, such as texture, color, and shape.

Our experiments with UA show that the U-occurrence phenomenon can occur in some cases thus showing the image classification models has counter-intuitive feature interaction. We also showed that Model Inspector can be used to evaluate the robustness of image classification models to different versions of an image, and to detect biases in the model's decision-making process.

In summary, UA and Model Inspector are powerful tools for understanding and interpreting image classification models and can be used to improve their performance and identify their weaknesses. Our work may help further research in the field of model interpretability and lead to the development of even more advanced tools for analyzing and understanding deep learning models.

Acknowledgements. This work has been supported by FCT – Fundação para a Ciência e Tecnologia within the R&D Units Project Scope: UIDB/00319/2020.

References

1. Adebayo, J., Muelly, M., Abelson, H., Kim, B.: Post hoc explanations may be ineffective for detecting unknown spurious correlation. In: International Conference on Learning Representations (2022)
2. Alber, M., et al.: iNNvestigate neural networks! J. Mach. Learn. Res. **20**(93), 1–8 (2019). http://jmlr.org/papers/v20/18-540.html
3. Alcorn, M.A., et al.: Strike (with) a pose: neural networks are easily fooled by strange poses of familiar objects. In: Proceedings of the IEEE/CVF Conference on Computer Vision and Pattern Recognition (CVPR) (2019)
4. Coates, A., Ng, A., Lee, H.: An analysis of single-layer networks in unsupervised feature learning. In: Proceedings of the Fourteenth International Conference on Artificial Intelligence and Statistics, pp. 215–223. JMLR Workshop and Conference Proceedings (2011)
5. Deng, J., Dong, W., Socher, R., Li, L.J., Li, K., Fei-Fei, L.: ImageNet: a large-scale hierarchical image database. In: 2009 IEEE Conference on Computer Vision and Pattern Recognition, pp. 248–255. IEEE (2009)
6. Fong, R.C., Vedaldi, A.: Interpretable explanations of black boxes by meaningful perturbation. In: Proceedings of the IEEE International Conference on Computer Vision, pp. 3429–3437 (2017)
7. He, K., Zhang, X., Ren, S., Sun, J.: Deep residual learning for image recognition. In: Proceedings of the IEEE Conference on Computer Vision and Pattern Recognition, pp. 770–778 (2016)
8. Hendrycks, D., Dietterich, T.G.: Benchmarking neural network robustness to common corruptions and perturbations. In: 7th International Conference on Learning Representations, ICLR 2019, New Orleans, LA, USA, 6–9 May 2019. OpenReview.net (2019). https://openreview.net/forum?id=HJz6tiCqYm
9. Hendrycks, D., Zhao, K., Basart, S., Steinhardt, J., Song, D.: Natural adversarial examples. In: Proceedings of the IEEE/CVF Conference on Computer Vision and Pattern Recognition, pp. 15262–15271 (2021)
10. Krizhevsky, A., Hinton, G., et al.: Learning multiple layers of features from tiny images (2009)
11. Liu, S., Li, L., Song, J., Yang, Y., Zeng, X.: Multimodal pre-training with self-distillation for product understanding in e-commerce. In: Proceedings of the Sixteenth ACM International Conference on Web Search and Data Mining, pp. 1039–1047 (2023)
12. Maji, S., Kannala, J., Rahtu, E., Blaschko, M., Vedaldi, A.: Fine-grained visual classification of aircraft. Technical report (2013)
13. Moayeri, M., Pope, P., Balaji, Y., Feizi, S.: A comprehensive study of image classification model sensitivity to foregrounds, backgrounds, and visual attributes. In: IEEE/CVF Conference on Computer Vision and Pattern Recognition, CVPR 2022, New Orleans, LA, USA, 18–24 June 2022, pp. 19065–19075. IEEE (2022). https://doi.org/10.1109/CVPR52688.2022.01850

14. Nguyen, A., Yosinski, J., Clune, J.: Deep neural networks are easily fooled: high confidence predictions for unrecognizable images. In: 2015 IEEE Conference on Computer Vision and Pattern Recognition (CVPR), pp. 427–436 (2015). https://doi.org/10.1109/CVPR.2015.7298640

15. Saurav, S., Sharma, A., Saini, R., Singh, S.: An attention-guided convolutional neural network for automated classification of brain tumor from MRI. Neural Comput. Appl. **35**(3), 2541–2560 (2023)

16. Selvaraju, R.R., Cogswell, M., Das, A., Vedantam, R., Parikh, D., Batra, D.: Grad-CAM: visual explanations from deep networks via gradient-based localization. In: Proceedings of the IEEE International Conference on Computer Vision, pp. 618–626 (2017)

17. Simonyan, K., Vedaldi, A., Zisserman, A.: Deep inside convolutional networks: visualising image classification models and saliency maps. In: Bengio, Y., LeCun, Y. (eds.) 2nd International Conference on Learning Representations, ICLR 2014, Banff, AB, Canada, 14–16 April 2014, Workshop Track Proceedings (2014). http://arxiv.org/abs/1312.6034

18. Sudhakar, M., Sattarzadeh, S., Plataniotis, K.N., Jang, J., Jeong, Y., Kim, H.: Ada-SISE: adaptive semantic input sampling for efficient explanation of convolutional neural networks. In: IEEE International Conference on Acoustics, Speech and Signal Processing (2021)

19. Sundararajan, M., Taly, A., Yan, Q.: Axiomatic attribution for deep networks. In: Precup, D., Teh, Y.W. (eds.) Proceedings of the 34th International Conference on Machine Learning, ICML 2017, Sydney, NSW, Australia, 6–11 August 2017. Proceedings of Machine Learning Research, vol. 70, pp. 3319–3328. PMLR (2017). http://proceedings.mlr.press/v70/sundararajan17a.html

20. Wong, E., Rice, L., Kolter, J.Z.: Fast is better than free: revisiting adversarial training. In: 8th International Conference on Learning Representations, ICLR 2020, Addis Ababa, Ethiopia, 26–30 April 2020. OpenReview.net (2020). https://openreview.net/forum?id=BJx040EFvH

21. Xiao, K.Y., Engstrom, L., Ilyas, A., Madry, A.: Noise or signal: the role of image backgrounds in object recognition. In: International Conference on Learning Representations (2020)

22. Zeiler, M.D., Fergus, R.: Visualizing and understanding convolutional networks. In: Fleet, D., Pajdla, T., Schiele, B., Tuytelaars, T. (eds.) ECCV 2014. LNCS, vol. 8689, pp. 818–833. Springer, Cham (2014). https://doi.org/10.1007/978-3-319-10590-1_53

23. Zhang, T., Zhu, Z.: Interpreting adversarially trained convolutional neural networks. In: Chaudhuri, K., Salakhutdinov, R. (eds.) Proceedings of the 36th International Conference on Machine Learning, ICML 2019, Long Beach, California, USA, 9–15 June 2019. Proceedings of Machine Learning Research, vol. 97, pp. 7502–7511. PMLR (2019). http://proceedings.mlr.press/v97/zhang19s.html

Study on Synthetic Video Generation of Embryo Development

Pedro Celard[1,2,3](✉) ⓘ, Adrián Seara Vieira[1,2,3] ⓘ,
José Manuel Sorribes-Fdez[1,2,3] ⓘ, Rubén Romero[1,2,3] ⓘ,
Eva Lorenzo Iglesias[1,2,3] ⓘ, and Lourdes Borrajo Diz[1,2,3] ⓘ

[1] Computer Science Department, Universidade de Vigo, Escuela Superior de Ingeniería Informática, Campus Univ. As Lagoas, 32004 Ourense, Spain
pedro.celard.perez@uvigo.gal
[2] Department of Computer Science, CINBIO, Universidade de Vigo, ESEI-Escuela Superior de Ingeniería Informática, 32004 Ourense, Spain
[3] SING Research Group, Galicia Sur Health Research Institute (IIS Galicia Sur), SERGAS-UVIGO, Vigo, Spain

Abstract. Biomedical imaging is commonly used to obtain a correct diagnosis of the patient condition, but in certain treatments, namely in vitro fertilization for infertile couples, it is particularly important to monitor the development over time of the primary object of the study, such as the embryo. Currently, many computer vision architectures and models focus on the analysis, classification, or semantic segmentation of static images, neglecting the essential developing nature of certain cases. However, image generation architectures based on Generative Adversarial Networks and Autoencoders have evolved to adapt to video generation, which can be adjusted to the analysis of the image-to-image development of a particular medical study. This paper analyzes different synthetic image generation models, including the Temporal-GAN-v2 and a Video Diffusion Model, applied to time-lapse pictures of embryo fertilization and culture. The aim of this study is to verify the performance of each model using objective quantitative measures such as Fréchet Inception Distance (FID) and Fréchet Video Distance (FVD), and to evaluate the generation of image sequences for specific embryo stages.

Keywords: machine learning · deep neural networks · biomedical image analysis · prediction of clinical outcomes · embryo development

1 Introduction

Image generation models continue to evolve and produce higher quality results, allowing computer vision to be applied to new use cases in a wide range of areas within biomedicine [3]. One of the main applications of generative models is the creation of synthetic images. Mendes *et al.* [13] take lung segmentation maps as a guide to generate Computed Tomography (CT) images that can be used as training datasets. They use the Pix2Pix and conditional GAN models (CGANs)

© The Author(s), under exclusive license to Springer Nature Switzerland AG 2023
P. García Bringas et al. (Eds.): HAIS 2023, LNAI 14001, pp. 623–634, 2023.
https://doi.org/10.1007/978-3-031-40725-3_53

to transform a segmented image of the labels into a realistic CT scanner image. The quality of the generated images has been validated by experts in the field who evaluate their quality and realism. Al-Shargabi *et al.* [1] employ a custom CGAN to generate new chest X-ray images from COVID-19. The authors conclude that using new synthetic images in training helps several deep learning-based classification models to obtain better results. Dumagpi and Jeong [6] also generate synthetic X-ray images using a Deep Convolutional GAN. They conclude that the use of new images in combination with other image enhancement techniques reduces the false-positive rate by almost 20%, while the true-positive rate remains stable. In the field of embryo imaging, Dirvanauskas *et al.* [5] propose a GAN-based model to generate single images of early embryos. The authors are able to produce high-quality static images that can be used for data augmentation and training of other classification and semantic segmentation models.

The ability to generate not just a static image, but a sequence of images as a video, further increases the applicability of these models. There are currently two main branches of models, those based on Generative Adversarial Networks (GANs), and those based on diffusion models. In this paper we study two of the most popular video generation architectures applied to the analysis of fertilization image sequences and embryo culture for In Vitro Fertilization (IVF). IVF is one of the most widely used treatments for infertile couples. It consists of controlled ovarian hyperstimulation followed by egg retrieval, fertilization, and embryo culture for 2–6 days under controlled environmental conditions. Finally, embryos developed correctly and identified as having a good implantation potential are subjected to intrauterine transfer [7]. Continuous monitoring of the development through the different embryonic stages is essential for a correct assessment of embryo quality, and the application of computer vision techniques together with Convolutional Neural Networks (CNNs) may bring great benefits to these procedures.

Advances in computing power have favored the emergence of new architectures that make use of more sophisticated convolution operations, thus being able to generate video instead of static images. Nevertheless, these architectures have not been efficiently exploited in the biomedical field, being mostly used for the analysis of 3D models of areas such as the head, chest, and embryos [19]. In this paper we propose to study the application of video generation models to the generation of image sequences representing the biological development over time of embryos for IVF. A comparison is made between models with completely different architectures to identify the one that is best suited to this task. Such an artificial intelligence tool could be useful for forecasting, predicting responses to different treatments, identifying abnormal developments, and other tasks.

The article is structured as follows. Section 2 outlines the main image generation models studied in this work, the evaluation process and metrics, and the studied dataset. Section 3 describes and analyzes the obtained results. Finally, Sect. 4 concludes the paper.

2   Materials and Methods

2.1   Generative Models

Many authors use convolutional networks to address the problem of image generation, with GAN being one of the most widely used architectures. Many variants of the first GAN proposed by Goodfellow *et al.* [8] have emerged in recent years, achieving excellent results for the generation of static images [5]. Despite the good results of these works, new architectures are emerging to achieve even better image quality and variability. Gaussian diffusion models [18] have attracted the attention of many authors due to their ability to generate synthetic examples in different domains, both in conditional and unconditional cases [12,15].

Given the great ability of these architectures to generate static images, it is reasonable that the next step is to generate a sequence of these images related to each other, thus obtaining a video. This is not a simple transition, since learning how to generate one of the frames at the same time as it is directly related to the previous and next frames requires a large amount of computation and GPU memory. In addition, the resources required to train the model increase exponentially with the size of the images, making it difficult to generate high-resolution video. In this paper we study the capability of two video generation models to create new examples of image sequences showing the culture of fertilized eggs. These models are the Temporal GAN v2 proposed by Saito *et al.* [16], and the Video Diffusion Model proposed by Ho *et al.* [11].

2.2   Temporal GAN

The Temporal Generative Adversarial Network (version 2), also known as TGAN v2 [16], is capable of learning to generate high-resolution video with low computational cost. It consists of subgenerators and several discriminators, which help to learn the distribution of video frames at different image resolutions.

As shown in Fig. 1, the TGANv2 consists of a Convolutional Long Short Term Memory (CLSTM) which receives a noise vector z converted into a feature map with the same size of the images using a fully connected layer (FC). Then, it returns a new vector for each time frame (t) that will compose the video. At $t = 0$, the CLSTM only receives the z vector as input, but at $t \geq 1$ it also gets a feature map derived from the first iteration, thus establishing a relationship between them. This is followed by an upsampling block that doubles the size of the input feature map, after which the image is rendered at a given resolution. This process is repeated three more times, with a subsampling block in between each time, reducing the number of frames to avoid uncontrolled growth of the convolution operations. The output of the training stage is 4 videos of the same example in different resolutions. However, only the result of the last upsampling block is taken into account during inference.

For each upsampling block, a convolutional network (3D Resnet) analyzes whether the video received as input is real or not. To do this, it performs several 3-dimensional convolutional operations to analyze the images in height and

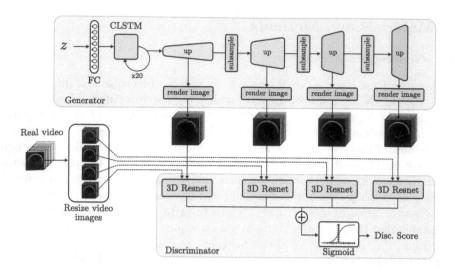

Fig. 1. Simplified Temporal GAN v2 architecture based on [16].

width, as well as checking the relationship between the different frames. Each 3D Resnet output is summed and passed through a sigmoid function, yielding a final discrimination score that takes into account the analysis of the different videos at different resolutions. As a GAN, each 3D Resnet acts as a discriminator, alternately receiving real examples that are resized to fit the input size of the network.

2.3   Video Diffusion Model

Image generative diffusion models are based on the transformation of the input x (real image) using a Gaussian noise addition process guided by an hyperparameter λ_t. The result of this transformation, represented as z_t, is both the output of the Gaussian process and the input to a convolutional network that attempts to learn how to remove the noise from z in order to obtain an estimate of the original image [11]. To generate video instead of static images, Ho *et al.* [11] propose to use a 3D U-Net as a "denoising" network. The traditional 2D U-Net [14] is widely used for image-to-image generation tasks. It consists of sequential downsampling convolutional blocks followed by a directly proportional number of upsampling blocks. The output of each downsampling block is concatenated to its corresponding upsampling block through a skip connection. The authors are inspired by the work of Özgün *et al.* [4], transforming 2D convolutions into 3D convolutions, and incorporating spatial and temporal attention blocks [2] to improve the video quality and temporal consistency. The complete architecture is shown in a simplified way in Fig. 2.

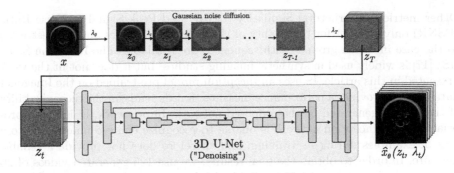

Fig. 2. Simplified Video Diffusion Model based on [11].

2.4   Experiments

Since video generation models require a large amount of data to capture their distribution, the lack of datasets is a problem for the study of video generation models. For this reason, Gomez *et al.* [7] created a public time-lapse dataset of the culture of embryos that have undergone IVF. It consists of 704 videos in different focal planes, for a total of 2.4 million images with a resolution of 500×500. The collection includes expert annotations for each stage of the embryo: polar body appearance, pronuclei appearance and disappearance, blastomere division from 2-cell stage to 9 (and more) cell stage, compaction, blastocyst formation, and expansion and hatching. Due to technical limitations, only one focal plane is used for training and 20 evenly spaced frames are extracted from each video (some with more than 500 frames).

The TGANv2 and VDM models are trained to generate videos consisting of 20 frames of different image sizes. Both models generate 32×32, 64×64, and 128×128 images, while only the TGANv2 could be trained to generate 256×256 images. This situation is caused by the high memory consumption of the VDM model training when it is expected to use high resolution images, making it impossible to run on currently available equipment. To train these models, the standard parameterizations recommended in the original works and 100,000 training steps are used. Both TGANv2 discriminator and VDM use an Adam optimizer with a learning rate of 1e–4, while the TGANv2 generator uses a learning rate of 5e–5. Furthermore, the TGANv2 uses a zero-centered gradient penalty, and the VDM uses 200 timesteps in the noise inclusion process and an L1 loss function. Source code available at https://github.com/pedrocelard/embrgen.

To analyze the performance of the two models we use the standard Fréchet Inception Distance (FID) [10] and Fréchet Video Distance (FVD) [20] metrics. Both metrics compare the distribution of fake images to the distribution of real images. In the case of FID the frames are compared as individual images, while FVD treats each video as a whole. Learning generative models of video is a much harder task than synthesizing static images, as the model must capture the temporal dynamics of a scene, in addition to the visual presentation of objects [20].

Other metrics as Structural Similarity (SSIM) and Peak Signal to Noise Ratio (PSNR) only account for the quality of the individual images and are restricted to the case in which ground-truth sequences are available. The Inception Score (IS) [17] is widely used in synthetic imaging studies, but it does not fit the work presented in this article. IS uses an Inception model pre-trained on the Imagenet dataset, and provides a performance measure that depends on the recognizability of the images generated by the proposed network. In our work, IS is not appropriate, as the Inception network is unable to recognize embryo images due to a lack of examples during its training, and therefore does not provide a reliable measure. In order to obtain the final results, we use 125 generated videos of 20 frames each, for a total of 2,500 individual images.

In addition, a classification model is used to check if the sequence of stages which the embryo goes through is correct. The generated fake sequences are classified frame by frame by a ResNet18 [9] trained on the real dataset. It is able to distinguish the real embryo images according to their stage. When classifying real sequences, the ResNet18 achieves an accuracy of 0.96, making it an excellent tool for classifying fake images and checking that the stage sequence is correct.

3   Results and Discussion

3.1   Standard Metrics

To analyze the video generation performance of the two models, we generate 20-frame image sequences of different sizes. The FID metric is then calculated to check the quality of the generated images separately, and the FVD to analyze the sequence as a whole. In Table 1 we present the quality scores for the generated videos, and the number of parameters of the generative model.

Table 1. FID and FVD results of video generation.

Model	Size	FID	FVD	Parameters
TGANv2	32×32	95.29	2534.91	5.63 M
	64×64	94.08	2099.61	6.42 M
	128×128	109.85	1713.31	9.58 M
	256×256	158.89	781.15	22.21 M
VDM	32×32	56.71	2116.20	35,7 M
	64×64	119.96	2511.15	35,7 M
	128×128	146.15	2499.69	35,7 M

With regard to the FID, the best results are obtained when working with a resolution of 32×32, and the VDM model is able to achieve better results than the TGANv2 at this resolution. However, caution should be exercised when analyzing these results before drawing conclusions that may be inaccurate, as very small image sizes are used to calculate the FID. The small number of pixels eliminates details that are essential for a correct analysis of the embryos, such as the cell division that determines the stage of the embryo, which is almost impossible to see at this resolution. For this reason, it would be advisable to work with images with a higher number of pixels even if a low FID result is obtained. When working with images larger than 64×64, the TGANv2 model is able to achieve a slightly better FID than with the smaller resolution, and also outperforms the VDM, a situation that is repeated with 128×128 images. Unfortunately, a comparison with 256×256 images is not possible, since, as mentioned above, there are memory limitations that do not allow the VDM to be trained with such a high resolution. Nevertheless, the results of the TGANv2 model are included to allow a comparison between different runs of the model.

When analyzing the FVD, the situation is quite different. TGANv2 achieves better results the larger the images are, even achieving an improvement from 1713.31 to 781.15 when going from 128×128 to 256×256 images. These results are much better than those of the VDM, proving that the videos generated by TGANv2 are very similar to real videos. As can be seen in Sect. 3.2, the quality of the videos generated by the VDM is visually good, but a large number of generated videos do not contain embryos, they are just a white circle, a circumstance that negatively affects the FVD result.

Finally, the number of model parameters is analyzed. The VDM has a constant number of parameters regardless of the image size. This situation is due to the use of the U-Net, as it is a convolutional architecture, the number of parameters is independent of the input, since the filter sizes are fixed. On the contrary, the TGANv2 parameters grow with the image size, even doubling in number when going from 128×128 images to 256×256 images. However, this is still much less than VDM in all its variants.

In conclusion, taking into account the FID and FVD results obtained, TGAN v2 is the best alternative for the generation of fertilization and embryo culture image sequences. The FVD is far superior to that of VDM, and in both 64×64 and 128×128 images the FID is also better. This conclusion is supported by the number of parameters and memory usage during training, allowing TGANv2 to generate higher resolution images with a much smaller number of parameters. However, visual analysis is extremely important when working with embryos, as morphological details and the characteristics of each stage of the embryo are of great importance. Therefore, the following sections provide a visual analysis of the generated images and their stages.

3.2   Visual Analysis

When generating image sequences of embryo development, it is important to remember that the embryo passes through different sequential stages. In this work we generate 20 frames for each video, thus obtaining a complete sequence of embryo development, from the second polar body detached stage (tPB2) to the hatched blastocyst stage (tHB) [7]. Figure 3 shows sequences of 10 equally spaced frames extracted from the videos generated by the two models at different image resolutions. It can be seen that as the image size increases, the level of detail becomes greater, making it possible to see how the number of cells increases throughout the video.

Fig. 3. 10-frame sequences extracted from 20-frame fake videos at various image sizes, including 32, 64 and 128 height and width for both models and 256 for the TGANv2.

Both models are able to generate realistic image sequences while preserving the developing nature of the real embryos in the dataset. However, when using generative models, one of the most important aspects is their ability to generate fake examples with high diversity. In Fig. 4, frames of 16 randomly selected examples generated by the models can be observed. It shows how the first frame generated by TGANv2 contains cytoplasms with irregular shapes, in contrast to VDM where they have a much more consistent circular shape. This situation is repeated in the last frame, where the VDM model most faithfully represents the expanded blastocyst. Finally, although both models produce a large variability in the videos they generate, VDM produces more examples of empty sequences, in which no embryo is observed.

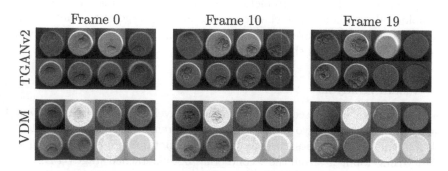

Fig. 4. Extracted frames from generated videos.

3.3 Embryo Development Stages

In order to test the ability of the models to generate fake images representing each stage of the embryo, a ResNet18 is trained with the real dataset. Then, it is used to classify each generated image to determine the stage of the embryo. The first frames should show the initial phases (tPB2, tPNa and tPNf), while the intermediate images will show the phases of cell proliferation (from t2 to t9+) and, at the end, the stages of blastulation (tM, tSB, tB, tEB and tHB) and the removal of the embryo for implantation (empty). Figure 5 shows the results obtained with the videos generated by TGANv2 and VDM using 128×128 frames. Below the solid line are the phases from tPB2 to tPNF, between the solid and dashed lines are the phases from t2 to t9+, between the dashed and dotted lines are the phases from tM to tHB, and finally above the dotted line is the empty stage.

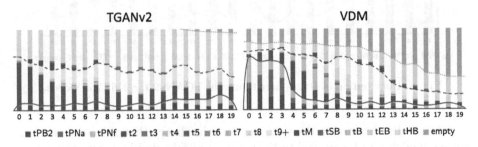

Fig. 5. Distribution of stages over frames in TGANv2 and VDM for 128×128 videos.

TGANv2 struggles to generate details at this resolution, so many images are classified as tEB, a stage where the blastocyst expands and the differentiation between cells is lost. Despite this, it can be observed how many other images are classified as t2 in the initial stages, while in the middle and final zone, those classified as t7, t8 and t9+ increase, mimicking the real dataset distribution. On the other hand, the VDM gives a much more realistic distribution. A large number of the first frames are classified as early stages (tPB2-tPNf), followed by the initiation of cell multiplication (t2–t4) and ending with stages t7–t9+. There are far fewer cases where the classifier assigns a tEB class in frames where it should not be found. However, as mentioned above, there are a large number of videos with empty frames in the first and middle frames, which should only occur in the last frames when the embryo is retrieved for implantation.

Finally, Fig. 6 shows the results obtained using TGANv2 to generate videos with a resolution of 256×256. In the first frames, there is a predominance of early stages and the appearance of 2 cells, while in the middle stages the number of cells increases and the initial stages decrease significantly. It can be seen that as the video progresses, the number of images classified as t2 to t4 decreases and those classified as t7–t9+ increase. In addition, images without embryos appear after the middle stages, and there is a large increase in the final frames, which closely mimics real cases. However, it can be seen that in some cases the stages of compaction completion and blastulation initiation (tM and tSB) are assigned prematurely. This situation is caused by the generation of multiple cells with low detail, resulting in images that appear to belong to a much more advanced stage than they really are.

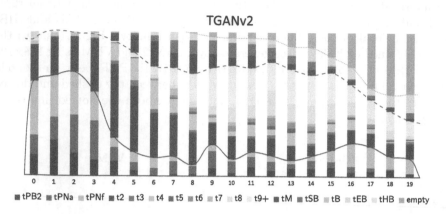

Fig. 6. Distribution of stages over frames in TGANv2 for 256×256 videos.

The results obtained in this work support the theory that video-oriented generative models can be applied to the creation of fake development sequences of embryo culture. Both analyzed models are able to generate high quality videos and faithfully represent the development of the embryo. The TGANv2 model is able to generate higher resolution images with far fewer parameters and memory usage than the VDM model, while the VDM model is able to better reproduce the embryo morphology at the expense of very high computational cost. The comparison of high resolution images is limited by the memory consumption of the VDM during training, which made it impossible to run. This limitation shows the urgent need to develop new video generation models capable of producing high resolution images with low computational cost. These results should be taken into account when considering video processing and generation using generative convolutional models. Future research should focus on improving models to create a more realistic embryo morphology, capable of generating details such as the polar bodies that mark the viability of the egg for fertilization or more differentiated blastomeres during the fragmentation phases.

4   Conclusion

In this work we study two generative models aimed at general-purpose video generation by applying them to the creation of fake videos of embryo culture for in vitro fertilization. These models may be useful for predicting the outcome of the fertilization process in early stages, identifying abnormal developments, and other tasks. After examining the results of FID and FVD, as well as the number of parameters required for each model, it is concluded that TGANv2 is able to generate videos that more closely resemble the distribution of real videos. Furthermore, the TGANv2 model achieves a better result when the separately generated images are taken into account by increasing the size of these images. This situation is repeated when the stages generated in each frame are analyzed by a ResNet18 classifier. The most realistic distribution is obtained with TGANv2 and a size of 256×256, although the process can still be improved to avoid generating images with phases that can be confusing due to their low detail. Nevertheless, visual analysis of the generated videos shows that the VDM model is able to generate the embryo morphology more faithfully.

For future work, an analysis of internal parameters of each model will be carried out in order to improve the results during image generation. In addition, the architecture of the models will be modified to generate the video according to a first initial image, from which to start the prediction of the development of the embryo. On top of this, more models and a larger number of data should be taken into account, so that this type of study can be used not only to generate embryonic development, but also to generate the evolution of any disease or medical condition analyzed by means of photographs, magnetic resonance imaging, computerized tomography, etc.

Acknowledgements. Pedro Celard is supported by a predoctoral fellowship from the Xunta de Galicia (ED481A 2021/286). This work has been partially supported by the Conselleria de Cultura, Educación e Universidade (Xunta de Galicia) under the scope of funding ED431C 2022/03-GRC Competitive Reference Group, and by the Ministerio de Ciencia e Innovación under the State Programmes for Knowledge Generation and Scientific and Technological Strengthening of the R&D&i System (PID2020-113673RB-I00).

References

1. Al-Shargabi, A.A., Alshobaili, J.F., Alabdulatif, A., Alrobah, N.: COVID-CGAN: efficient deep learning approach for Covid-19 detection based on CXR images using conditional GANs. Appl. Sci. **11**(16), 1174 (2021)
2. Bertasius, G., Wang, H., Torresani, L.: Is space-time attention all you need for video understanding? In: Proceedings of the 38th International Conference on Machine Learning, ICML 2021, 18–24 July 2021, Virtual Event. Proceedings of Machine Learning Research, vol. 139, pp. 813–824. PMLR (2021)
3. Celard, P., Iglesias, E.L., Sorribes-Fdez, J.M., Romero, R., Vieira, A.S., Borrajo, L.: A survey on deep learning applied to medical images: from simple artificial neural networks to generative models. Neural Comput. Appl. **35**(3), 2291–2323 (2023)
4. Çiçek, Ö., Abdulkadir, A., Lienkamp, S.S., Brox, T., Ronneberger, O.: 3D U-Net: learning dense volumetric segmentation from sparse annotation. In: Ourselin, S., Joskowicz, L., Sabuncu, M.R., Unal, G., Wells, W. (eds.) MICCAI 2016. LNCS, vol. 9901, pp. 424–432. Springer, Cham (2016). https://doi.org/10.1007/978-3-319-46723-8_49

5. Dirvanauskas, D., Maskeliūnas, R., Raudonis, V., Damaševičius, R., Scherer, R.: Hemigen: human embryo image generator based on generative adversarial networks. Sensors **19**(16), 3578 (2019)

6. Dumagpi, J.K., Jeong, Y.J.: Evaluating gan-based image augmentation for threat detection in large-scale xray security images. Appl. Sci. **11**(1), 36 (2021)

7. Gomez, T., et al.: A time-lapse embryo dataset for morphokinetic parameter prediction. Data Brief **42**, 108258 (2022)

8. Goodfellow, I., et al.: Generative adversarial nets. In: Advances in Neural Information Processing Systems, vol. 27. Curran Associates, Inc. (2014)

9. He, K., Zhang, X., Ren, S., Sun, J.: Deep residual learning for image recognition. In: 2016 IEEE Conference on Computer Vision and Pattern Recognition (CVPR), pp. 770–778 (2016)

10. Heusel, M., Ramsauer, H., Unterthiner, T., Nessler, B., Hochreiter, S.: Gans trained by a two time-scale update rule converge to a local nash equilibrium. In: Proceedings of the 31st International Conference on Neural Information Processing Systems, NIPS 2017, pp. 6629–6640. Curran Associates Inc., Red Hook (2017)

11. Ho, J., Salimans, T., Gritsenko, A., Chan, W., Norouzi, M., Fleet, D.J.: Video diffusion models (2022)

12. Kingma, D., Salimans, T., Poole, B., Ho, J.: Variational diffusion models. In: Advances in Neural Information Processing Systems, vol. 34, pp. 21696–21707. Curran Associates, Inc. (2021)

13. Mendes, J., et al.: Lung CT image synthesis using gans. Expert Syst. Appl. **215**, 119350 (2023)

14. Ronneberger, O., Fischer, P., Brox, T.: U-Net: convolutional networks for biomedical image segmentation. In: Navab, N., Hornegger, J., Wells, W.M., Frangi, A.F. (eds.) MICCAI 2015. LNCS, vol. 9351, pp. 234–241. Springer, Cham (2015). https://doi.org/10.1007/978-3-319-24574-4_28

15. Saharia, C., Ho, J., Chan, W., Salimans, T., Fleet, D.J., Norouzi, M.: Image superresolution via iterative refinement. IEEE Trans. Pattern Anal. Mach. Intell. **45**, 1–14 (2022)

16. Saito, M., Saito, S., Koyama, M., Kobayashi, S.: Train sparsely, generate densely: memory-efficient unsupervised training of high-resolution temporal GAN. Int. J. Comput. Vision **128**(10), 2586–2606 (2020)

17. Salimans, T., et al.: Improved techniques for training gans. In: Advances in Neural Information Processing Systems, vol. 29. Curran Associates, Inc. (2016)

18. Sohl-Dickstein, J., Weiss, E., Maheswaranathan, N., Ganguli, S.: Deep unsupervised learning using nonequilibrium thermodynamics. In: Proceedings of the 32nd International Conference on Machine Learning, vol. 37, pp. 2256–2265. PMLR, Lille (2015)

19. Tokuoka, Y., et al.: 3D convolutional neural networks-based segmentation to acquire quantitative criteria of the nucleus during mouse embryogenesis. npj Syst. Biol. Appl. **6**(1), 32 (2020)

20. Unterthiner, T., van Steenkiste, S., Kurach, K., Marinier, R., Michalski, M., Gelly, S.: Towards accurate generative models of video: a new metric & challenges (2018)

Image Reconstruction Using Cellular Automata and Neural Networks

Mihai-Adrian Loghin$^{(\boxtimes)}$ and Anca-Mirela Andreica

Babes-Bolyai University, Str. Mihail Kogălniceanu Street 1, Cluj-Napoca, Romania
mihai.loghin@stud.ubbcluj.ro, anca.andreica@ubbcluj.ro
https://www.cs.ubbcluj.ro/en/

Abstract. Combining cellular automata (CA) with convolutional neural networks (CNN) has been overtime an important topic of scientific interest in the field of computer vision. This has been due to the high number of common aspects between the two models, such as extracting information and making decision based on pixel neighbourhoods. While there are many recent papers on the subject, they are mainly focusing on the visual aspects of the problem and ignore the use of numerical evaluations for the obtained results. In this articles we present a numerical evaluation of a neural cellular automaton (NCA) with the task of reconstructing images. For this evaluation we employed several image quality metrics and the use of multiple training algorithms for the presented model. As such, we determined that cellular automata could be used as a method of restoring images, starting from a damaged state of the image, with a high accuracy. We also concluded that the algorithm presents certain weaknesses when it comes to images with very few details in them, where almost the entirety of the image is predominated by one colour.

Keywords: Cellular automata · Convolutional neural networks · Neural cellular automat · Image reconstruction

1 Introduction

A cellular automaton (CA) in its most basic form can be defined as grid in which each cell has a value and those values can change over time based on a set of rules that involves the neighboring cells and their values. Most of the time the grid has a rectangular form and the most popular way of defining the neighborhood of a cell is by using a Moore neighborhood [8,9]. In most cases all the cells get updated at the same time, but for our case we are using stochastic cellular automata where each cell has a chance to get an updated value or not [5]. For a long time, cellular automata have been used in multiple fields, from simulations to biology and our case, image processing. Our article focuses on image reconstruction using a hybrid between cellular automata and

---

Supported by the Romanian Ministry of Education and Research.

P. García Bringas et al. (Eds.): HAIS 2023, LNAI 14001, pp. 635–646, 2023.
https://doi.org/10.1007/978-3-031-40725-3_54

convolutional neural networks, that in some articles is called Neural Cellular Automata (NCA) [6].

While we are on the topic of image processing, we think that it is important to also define convolutional neural networks (CNN). This particular type of neural network has been created with the purpose of simulating the human eye by deconstructing the image in such a way that only the most important details remain. A CNN is formed by using only convolutional layers, those being layers in which a filter, defined by a matrix, is applied over the image with purpose of amplifying certain details from the image [2]. CNNs have been used for both image classification and image creation.

The main purpose of the proposed model is to reconstruct a target image starting from an initial state, that we will call a seed image. A seed image can be anything from an damaged version of the target image to a single dot on a white canvas. We consider that this approach for image reconstruction could be useful for reconstructing old paintings, discovering hidden patters in images or encoding images when saving them.

After the initial image is run a number of times through the model, the image will slowly transform into the target image it was trained for. Compared to other studies on the subject, that only focused on a visual analysis, we focus on offering a more in-depth analysis based on different training functions and evaluate the models on three levels of consistency and under multiple quality measures. As such, we consider our work to be one that validates the usage of the proposed model under multiple conditions.

2   State of the Art

To better emphasise our contribution, we will go over other attempts for NCA and image reconstruction. This will include the various other hybrids and how they have been experimented with.

There have been other attempts in the past to create cellular automata hybrids, including using neural networks. There have been other articles like [11] that have shown how this combination can be used for reconstructing the rules for one dimensional cellular automata. Another example would be article [3] that uses a model closer in design to the one used our article, that is used for reconstructing the rules for the Conway's Game of Life. Still, those models were not properly evaluated in our opinion. We also consider that there is a lot more ground to be covered than recreating a few subjective rules.

The idea behind article [11] is to find the rules of a CA based on its history. The history of the CA is defined by all the iterations of the CA until a stop point and for this stopping point, the neural network tries to find which set of rules has been used to get to that point. The article concludes that three levels of learning are possible.

In article [3] the main idea is to show how a CA can be represented as a convolutional neural network. For this purpose, the authors of the article trained a CNN by showing it videos of arbitrary CAs as training data. The article concludes that CAs with rules tht are more complex rules worse results compared CAs that have simpler rules.

Reconstructing images specifically can be found in article [6]. In our article we use modified version of the model used in the referenced article having even the first layer be trainable. The referenced article also has one specific issue, it does not present any, qualitative or quantitative, analysis of the results beyond showing the visual results. While it might be enough for an article to only show the visual results, this is only the case for when a subject is first brought to light. To obtain a better understanding of how the model can be improved, a more in-depth analysis of the results is needed.

The reason why we think this field is one worth studying is due to the fact that there have recently been many improvements done to the model mentioned before. For example, article [7] uses a modified version of the model that is capable of creating entirely new images, as a combination of two images the model was trained for. The above articles still lack a proper qualitative analysis of the model. We want to focus on further evaluating the quality of the results given by the model.

3 Proposed Model

The main idea behind the model is to be able to reconstruct an image by using a hybrid between cellular automata and convolutional neural networks.

Fig. 1. Moore neighborhood.

For the purposes of this paper, we only need to use a two dimensional cellular automat, defined with a Moore neighborhood. This means that for the update of each individual cell we will only look at the cells right next to it, like in (Fig. 1).

But now a question arises, how do we make this into a neural network? The answer is simple, we use a neural network composed of only convolutional layers. We are doing this because convolutional layers can have a similar property to cellular automata defined with a Moore neighborhood, depending on the sizes of the filter that is run over the image. In the case of a 3×3 filter the information that is transmitted from one layer of the network to the next is practically the same as if we used an update rule over the cells of a cellular automaton, in this case each cell being defined by a pixel. Looking at Fig. 2, the explanation becomes easier to understand.

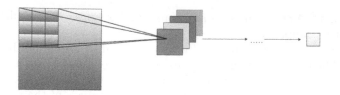

Fig. 2. A step in an NCA.

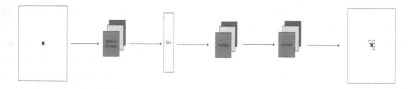

Fig. 3. The design of our model.

In the case of the model presented in this paper we take inspiration from other models in articles such as [3,6,7]. For this we use a neural network with three layers, all of which are convolutional layers. The model that can be seen in Fig. 3 is sequential and starts with a depthwise convolution continuing through a ReLU activation function to last two convolutional layers. For the first two layers of the model we use a 3×3 Glorot uniform filter [4] and the last layer uses a 1×1 Glorot uniform filter for the purposes of making sure each and every cell is updated.

3.1   Training Methods

Without being trained the model will not give any notable results. So in this section we will lay out the different ways we can train our model.

For training we have decided to use two different training algorithms that are similar in many ways, but in the end give out very different results. The aforementioned algorithms have a few common aspects, like:

1. both start from a batch of images, where at least one will be a seed image (since this is the main starting point)
2. the algorithms will use an L2 loss function where each and every of the images in the initial batch, after being run through the model for n times, will be compared to the target image
3. both algorithms will use an Adam optimizer with a learning rate of 0.001

The first training algorithm can also be found in other articles such as [6]. This algorithm can be described as follows:

1. we initialize a list of 255 seed images
2. we chose eight random images from the list initialized at step 1 and add them to the batch for this training step

3. we will replace the image at the index 0 from the batch with a seed image, so that the model will always be trained to reproduce an image starting from a seed image
4. training the biases by making the images go through n iterations of the CA and comparing the results with the target image, with an L2 loss function
5. now we replace the eight images taken from the list initialized at step 1 with the images resulted from step 4
6. we go back to step 2 but now with the new list for m training epochs

The main advantage of this algorithm is that the automaton learns how to recover from a bad state more easily and in a lot of cases it can improve the reconstruction after the initial n iterations that it was trained to reproduce the image in.

When it comes to the second training algorithm, we took a far simpler approach that might just look like a simplified version of the first training algorithm. The algorithm is in many ways similar to one of the mentioned training algorithms in article [6], but with some key differences like the way we choose the extra number of iterations. This algorithm will only use seed images in the batches initialized at each training epoch, hence we also reduced the size of the batch to half of its size in the first algorithm. The steps for this algorithm are:

1. we initialize a batch of four seed images
2. each of the four images will go through a n iterations of the CA and a loss will be calculated based on a L2 loss function that compares the difference between the resulted images and the target image
3. after the initial n iterations, the images will go through an extra number of n/2 iterations and a new loss will be calculated by comparing the results obtained at step 2 to the results obtained after the extra n/2 iterations
4. the losses obtained from the steps 2 and 3 are added together to form the loss based on which the biases are trained
5. we repeat steps 1 to 4 for m training epochs

This algorithm will producing more faithful reconstructions of the image, since it is focused only on reproducing the image starting from a seed image and maintaining it for few extra iterations.

4   Methods for Evaluating Our Results

When it comes to the analysis of the final results, we used different quality measures for image similarity. Those were used by comparing the original image to the one created by the automaton. The mentioned measures include: root mean square error (RMSE) [1], structural similarity index (SSIM) [10] and feature-based similarity index (FSIM) [12]. In this section of the article, we will be giving a short definition, including the formula, for every measure mentioned before in the hopes of giving a better understanding as to why we chose them.

We think it is worth mentioning that many other measures were tested before choosing the three mentioned above. While it might be a popular choice to choose Peak Signal-to-Noise Ratio as a measure, we didn't feel it is relevant enough for the experiments that we are doing.

4.1   RMSE

This is the most well known out of all of the three measures metioned before. This measure is defined by the following formula:

$$RMSE(x, y) = \sqrt{\frac{1}{m * n} \sum_{i=0,j=0}^{n-1,m-1} (y_{i,j} - x_{i,j})^2}, \tag{1}$$

where n and m represent the sizes of the pictures x and y. The ideal result for this formula is 0 [1].

4.2   SSIM

The main idea behind this measure is that the human eye observes multiple aspects of the image at a time. So rather than just being a difference between the values of the pixels of an image, this approach is more about the difference in the aspects of an image. The formula for this measure is:

$$SSIM(x, y) = [l(x, y)]^\alpha * [c(x, y)]^\beta * [s(x, y)]^\gamma, \tag{2}$$

where α, β and γ give the importance of each function, having a value between zero and one. The definitions for the individual functions can be found in the original article [10]. The ideal value for this measure is 1, but even a value such as 9.99 would represent a perfect or almost perfect reacreation of the original image.

4.3   FSIM

This measure can be considered a follow up to the previous one. Having an ideal result of 1. This measure, like the previous one, focuses on defining the similarity between the images as the similarity between the different aspect of the images, havin the following formula:

$$FSIM(x, y) = \frac{\sum_{p \in \Omega} S_L(p) * PC_m(p)}{\sum p \in \Omega PC_m(p)}, \tag{3}$$

where Ω represents all the possible values for x and y and the functions $PC_m(p)$ și $S_L(p)$ can be found in the original article [12].

5   Results Analysis

For each of the training algorithms we calculated how faithful the reconstruction is by comparing it to the target image using a variety of image similarity measures, such as: root mean square error (RMSE) [1], structural similarity index (SSIM) [10] and feature-based similarity index (FSIM) [12]. Also, for each of the algorithms we used a number of 6000 epochs and 100 CA iterations(in the case of the second algorithm fifty extra iterations). In the end we calculated the accuracy of the model by training it on 20 different images, as it can be seen in the Table 1 and Table 2. All the images were taken from https://github.com/googlefonts/noto-emoji/tree/main/png/128, last accessed on the tenth of May 2021. The results will be analyzed in three steps:

1. halfway through to the expected number of iterations for the image to be reconstructed
2. at the number of iterations at which the image is expected to be reconstruted almost perfectly
3. halfway over the expected number of iterations for the image to be reconstructed

The final results for the accuracy of the model can be observed in Table 3 and Table 4 . We will start by analyzing the results for the second training algorithm, then we will go and analyze the results of the first training algorithm and in the end we will take a look at a very particular case in which the model took a lot longer to do well.

We decided that it would be more relevant if we tested the model on a moderate amount of images and show the individual results at the different times steps for the cellular automaton that resulted after fitting the model to an image. This decision was made because the model is supposed to recreate an image at a time, not multiple images. In the end we show the final results for both of the training algorithms.

When it comes to the second training algorithm, we can see that the image is being reconstructed really well in the first 100 iterations, but results start becoming worse as it goes further to 150 iterations. Luckily, due to the fact that the algorithm also ensured during the training process that the image will try to maintain its form after the initial 100 iterations, the loss of information is really low.

For the first algorithm we can observe that while the results are still good, they are not as good as the results obtained by the second algorithm. Well, this is only when it comes to the first 100 iterations. When it gets further from the expected number of iterations in which we thought the best reproduction will happen, something strange happens. The results start improving, although the model was never explicitly trained to maintain or even improve the results after 100 iterations. We find this to be very interesting and a reason to look further

Table 1. Particular results for the first training algorithm for each individual image.

Image	Loss	CA iterations	RMSE	SSIM	FSIM
u1f31c.png	0.000526679	50	4.37E–05	0.9999831910	0.8218714
		100	4.97E–06	0.9999998390	0.984062081
		150	5.09E–06	0.9999998470	0.983026365
u1f35c.png	0.000468411	50	6.03E–05	0.9999741330	0.61855821
		100	6.35E–06	0.9999998730	0.996056556
		150	6.29E–06	0.9999998380	0.995776891
u1f3ee.png	0.000115519	50	2.24E–05	0.9999986390	0.900665835
		100	3.59E–06	0.9999999610	0.998485743
		150	3.34E–06	0.9999999680	0.998369375
u1f3ef.png	0.000171082	50	2.89E–05	0.9999974820	0.897671501
		100	6.56E–06	0.9999998910	0.997394437
		150	4.04E–06	0.9999999460	0.998889393
u1f3f0.png	2.87E–05	50	2.60E–05	0.9999979090	0.894949181
		100	2.36E–06	0.9999999870	0.999499914
		150	1.65E–06	0.9999999930	0.999609316
u1f3f3.png	4.48E–05	50	1.63E–05	0.9999987170	0.778295158
		100	1.99E–06	0.9999999850	0.994872321
		150	1.90E–06	0.9999999880	0.994861272
u1f3f3_200d_1f308.png	0.000127061	50	9.87E–05	0.9999114050	0.673190748
		100	4.53E–06	0.9999999590	0.998200514
		150	4.73E–06	0.9999999390	0.998257763
u1f3f3_200d_26a7.png	0.000737072	50	4.28E–05	0.9999882780	0.716604132
		100	4.99E–06	0.9999999220	0.986983667
		150	4.89E–06	0.9999999220	0.981098729
u1f3f4.png	0.001243538	50	6.11E–05	0.9999629130	0.814989408
		100	5.68E–06	0.9999998730	0.997139696
		150	5.32E–06	0.9999998940	0.997238241
u1f3f4_200d_2620.png	1.78E–05	50	7.40E–05	0.9999574060	0.715770099
		100	2.37E–06	0.9999999770	0.999452523
		150	2.18E–06	0.9999999780	0.999489427
u1f3f5.png	0.000130589	50	2.82E–05	0.9999983008	0.896477942
		100	6.90E–06	0.9999999253	0.993192146
		150	6.34E–06	0.9999999302	0.994673738
u1f3f7.png	0.000736489	50	6.14E–05	0.9999621167	0.670356924
		100	5.23E–06	0.9999999187	0.987850129
		150	5.91E–06	0.9999999059	0.985429576

into how the training algorithm can make the results obtained by the model far better.

For the particular case mentioned before, the one in which both algorithms struggled in giving better results, we are talking about an image representing a

Table 2. Particular results for the second training algorithm for each individual image.

Image	Loss	CA iterations	RMSE	SSIM	FSIM
u1f35c.png	8.46E–05	50	5.18E–05	0.9999848462	0.659076058
		100	2.53E–06	0.9999999865	0.999090351
		150	4.40E–06	0.9999999669	0.996930825
u1f35c.png	8.46E–05	50	5.18E–05	0.9999848462	0.659076058
		100	2.53E–06	0.9999999865	0.999090351
		150	4.40E–06	0.9999999669	0.996930825
u1f3ee.png	0.00013028	50	0.000117536	0.9998433747	0.499117839
		100	2.91E–06	0.9999999790	0.998865777
		150	3.77E–06	0.9999999683	0.997996457
u1f3ef.png	4.21E–05	50	4.26E–05	0.9999919303	0.817840158
		100	2.04E–06	0.9999999762	0.999684709
		150	3.77E–06	0.9999999331	0.999008884
u1f3f0.png	6.43E–05	50	3.61E–05	0.9999926017	0.825505113
		100	2.63E–06	0.9999999609	0.999478585
		150	3.81E–06	0.9999999438	0.998706076
u1f3f3.png	2.90E–05	50	1.75E–05	0.9999984652	0.596367148
		100	1.06E–06	0.9999999971	0.999123661
		150	1.76E–06	0.9999999922	0.99753384
u1f3f3_200d_1f308.png	6.98E–05	50	6.30E–05	0.9999666493	0.834216084
		100	2.28E–06	0.9999999796	0.999416942
		150	3.29E–06	0.9999999689	0.998848613
u1f3f3_200d_26a7.png	6.27E–05	50	5.49E–05	0.9999742248	0.615309255
		100	2.01E–06	0.9999999927	0.997501022
		150	3.19E–06	0.9999999777	0.993469405
u1f3f4.png	1.77E–05	50	8.31E–05	0.9999231770	0.73124869
		100	1.30E–06	0.9999999883	0.999721464
		150	1.89E–06	0.9999999796	0.999553854
u1f3f4_200d_2620.png	2.36E–05	50	7.22E–05	0.9999577202	0.726523932
		100	1.26E–06	0.9999999955	0.999727204
		150	1.94E–06	0.9999999890	0.999624125
u1f3f5.png	7.87E–05	50	9.08E–05	0.9999258210	0.517189422
		100	2.48E–06	0.9999999832	0.998489201
		150	3.09E–06	0.9999999780	0.997754043
u1f3f7.png	2.19E–05	50	5.34E–05	0.9999727346	0.706179227
		100	1.28E–06	0.9999999942	0.99933303
		150	2.04E–06	0.9999999867	0.997176772

red Chinese lamp, u1f3ee.png. The algorithms struggled in training the model to reconstruct this particular image and only on very rare occasions did the training go well. This could be due to a variety of factors such as:

Table 3. Results for the first training algorithm.

Method	Loss	CA iterations	RMSE	SSIM	FSIM
Average	3.29E–04	50	4.79E–05	9.9997723E–01	7.55E–01
		100	4.89E–06	9.9999991E–01	9.94E–01
		150	4.69E–06	9.9999990E–01	9.93E–01
ASD	3.27E–04	50	2.36E–05	2.68E–05	9.59E–02
		100	2.12E–06	9.75E–08	7.35E–03
		150	2.13E–06	1.27E–07	8.64E–03

Table 4. Results for the second training algorithm.

Method	Loss	CA iterations	RMSE	SSIM	FSIM
Average	4.95E–05	50	5.24E–05	9.9997173E–01	7.17E–01
		100	1.84E–06	9.9999999E–01	9.99E–01
		150	2.93E–06	9.9999997E–01	9.98E–01
ASD	2.97E–05	50	2.44E–05	3.7019004E–05	1.01E–01
		100	6.01E–07	9.8551512E–09	5.25E–04
		150	9.22E–07	1.7834214E–08	1.44E–03

- the color palette of the image, although it is fairly simple consisting only of shades of red and black. The simplicity might be the main reason behind the struggles when it comes to training the model. Although one might think that an image with larger color palette would be harder to reconstruct, this was never the case in any of the experiments.
- a more obvious problem could be that the initial results in the beginning of the training, for both algorithms, were really bad. But through repeated experiments with the same parameters, we can conclude that this is not the main cause for the bad results, especially when it comes to the second algorithm (Figs. 4 and 5).

Fig. 4. One of the results obtained by the first training alogorithm.

Fig. 5. One of the results obtained by the second training alogorithm.

6   Conclusion

In the previous section we have presented and discussed the results obtained by two versions of our proposed model. Due to a lack of good comparisons for our model, we focused on a standalone and more in-depth analysis. The analysis went over how the model performs after being trained using two training functions and how consistent the results remained at different numbers of iterations for the results NCA.

We observed that the model is capable of recreating a target image almost perfectly, with no visual indications of a mistake. Based on the results for the three measures of quality that we used, we conclude that the best results were obtained for the second training algorithm. While the difference between the results might seem small at first, it is also observable that the most consistent results were obtained for the second training algorithm as well.

With this, we can conclude that the proposed model, with the second training function, is a valid candidate for image reconstruction. As mentioned in the introduction, we consider that the results further confirm that the model could be useful in the future for regenerating destroyed images or for encoding images to be saved in a safer way.

7   Future Work

The results presented in this article can be further explored by modifying either the training algorithms or model.

In other studies such as [7] the model was modified in such a way that it can create new images by taking as input two images the model was trained for. By modifying the model we can also end up getting to video creation and recreation.

The training algorithms could also be modified so that the model could be trained to reconstruct multiple images, but not starting from a seed image since that would be to much of an ambiguous starting point.

Acknowledgements. This work was supported by a grant of the Romanian Ministry of Education and Research, CCCDI - UEFISCDI, project number PN-III-P2-2.1-PED-2019-2607, within PNCDI III.

References

1. Chai, T., Draxler, R.: Root mean square error (RMSE) or mean absolute error (MAE)? Geosci. Model Dev. **7**, 1247–1250 (2014). https://doi.org/10.5194/gmdd-7-1525-2014
2. Geron, A.: Hands-on Machine Learning with Scikit-Learn and TensorFlow: Concepts, Tools, and Techniques to Build Intelligent Systems. O'Reilly Media, Sebastopol (2017)
3. Gilpin, W.: Cellular automata as convolutional neural networks. Phys. Rev. E **100**(3), 032402 (2019). https://doi.org/10.1103/physreve.100.032402
4. Glorot, X., Bengio, Y.: Understanding the difficulty of training deep feedforward neural networks. In: Teh, Y.W., Titterington, M. (eds.) Proceedings of the Thirteenth International Conference on Artificial Intelligence and Statistics. Proceedings of Machine Learning Research, vol. 9, pp. 249–256. PMLR, Chia Laguna Resort, Sardinia (2010). https://proceedings.mlr.press/v9/glorot10a.html
5. LOUIS, P.Y., Nardi, F.R.: Probabilistic Cellular Automata. Springer, Heidelberg (2018). https://doi.org/10.1007/978-3-319-65558-1. https://hal.archives-ouvertes.fr/hal-01724251
6. Mordvintsev, A., Randazzo, E., Niklasson, E., Levin, M.: Growing neural cellular automata. Distill **5**, e23 (2020). https://doi.org/10.23915/distill.00023. https://distill.pub/2020/growing-ca
7. Ruiz, A.H., Vilalta, A., Moreno-Noguer, F.: Neural cellular automata manifold (2021)
8. Shiffman, D., Fry, S., Marsh, Z.: The Nature of Code (2012). https://books.google.ro/books?id=hoK6lgEACAAJ
9. Toffoli, T., Margolus, N.: Cellular Automata Machines: A New Environment for Modeling. MIT Press series in scientific computation, Cambridge (1987). https://books.google.ro/books?id=HBlJzrBKUTEC
10. Wang, Z., Simoncelli, E., Bovik, A.: Multiscale structural similarity for image quality assessment. In: The Thrity-Seventh Asilomar Conference on Signals, Systems Computers, vol. 2, pp. 1398–1402 (2003). https://doi.org/10.1109/ACSSC.2003.1292216
11. Wulff, N., Hertz, J.A.: Learning cellular automaton dynamics with neural networks. In: Hanson, S., Cowan, J., Giles, C. (eds.) Advances in Neural Information Processing Systems, vol. 5, pp. 631–638. Morgan-Kaufmann (1993). https://proceedings.neurips.cc/paper/1992/file/d6c651ddcd97183b2e40bc464231c962-Paper.pdf
12. Zhang, L., Zhang, L., Mou, X., Zhang, D.: FSIM: a feature similarity index for image quality assessment. IEEE Trans. Image Process. **20**(8), 2378–2386 (2011). https://doi.org/10.1109/TIP.2011.2109730

Agents and Multiagents

Monte-Carlo Tree Search for Multi-agent Pathfinding: Preliminary Results

Yelisey Pitanov[1], Alexey Skrynnik[2,3]($\boxtimes$), Anton Andreychuk[2], Konstantin Yakovlev[2,3], and Aleksandr Panov[2,3]

[1] Moscow Institute of Physics and Technology, Moscow, Russia
[2] AIRI, Moscow, Russia
tviskaron@gmail.com
[3] Federal Research Center "Computer Science and Control" of the Russian Academy of Sciences, Moscow, Russia

Abstract. In this work we study a well-known and challenging problem of Multi-agent Pathfinding, when a set of agents is confined to a graph, each agent is assigned a unique start and goal vertices and the task is to find a set of collision-free paths (one for each agent) such that each agent reaches its respective goal. We investigate how to utilize Monte-Carlo Tree Search (MCTS) to solve the problem. Although MCTS was shown to demonstrate superior performance in a wide range of problems like playing antagonistic games (e.g. Go, Chess etc.), discovering faster matrix multiplication algorithms etc., its application to the problem at hand was not well studied before. To this end we introduce an original variant of MCTS, tailored to multi-agent pathfinding. The crux of our approach is how the reward, that guides MCTS, is computed. Specifically, we use individual paths to assist the agents with the goal-reaching behavior, while leaving them freedom to get off the track if it is needed to avoid collisions. We also use a dedicated decomposition technique to reduce the branching factor of the tree search procedure. Empirically we show that the suggested method outperforms the baseline planning algorithm that invokes heuristic search, e.g. A*, at each re-planning step.

Keywords: Multi-agent Pathfinding · Monte-Carlo Tree Search · Planning

1 Introduction

Pathfinding problems naturally arise in various applications, like autonomous vehicles, household robotics [10], etc. Moreover, in a variety of settings the simultaneous operation of a group of robots is desirable. Thus, multi-agent pathfinding (MAPF) [18] problem arises. Indeed, numerous approaches to this problem are known, both learnable and non-learnable ones, see [20] for an overview.

In this work we would like to investigate how the machinery of Monte-Carlo Tree Search (MCTS) [3] can be applied to MAPF. The reason is two-fold. First,

P. García Bringas et al. (Eds.): HAIS 2023, LNAI 14001, pp. 649–660, 2023.
https://doi.org/10.1007/978-3-031-40725-3_55

MCTS, which can be seen as a hybrid approach that integrates planning and learning, has already been successfully applied to various problems with hard combinatorial structure, often outperforming the state-of-the-art competitors. Thus, it is tempting to study how well MAPF problem can be handled by MCTS. The second reason is that if the performance of MCTS is promising than it opens the door to incorporating various deep learning techniques that can further increase its efficiency (similarly to how deep learning was utilized to boost MCTS in playing board games like Go, reaching super-human performance [13]). In this work we focus on the first part, i.e. how can MCTS be adapted to MAPF and how well it can perform compared to standard search-based approaches.

To this end we introduce an original variant of MCTS that utilizes two key ingredients. The first ingredient is the specific reward-shaping and reward propagating mechanisms that are tailored to MAPF setting. Second, is how the branching factor of the search tree is reduced by decomposing the joint actions into a sequential combination of the individual agent's actions. As confirmed by the numerous experiments, the resultant algorithm is able to successfully solve complex MAPF instances and outperforms a baseline search-based solver.

2   Background

Multi-agent pathfinding in its classical variant [18] assumes that the set of K agents is confined to a graph $G = (V, E)$, where n start and goal vertices are distinguished. The time is discretized and at each time step an agent can wait in its current vertex or move to an adjacent one. The sequence of such actions is called a plan. Two plans for distinct agents are conflict-free if the agents following them never swap vertices at the same time step and never occupy the same vertex at the same time step (i.e. no *edge* and *vertex* collisions are allowed). The task is to find a set of plans $Plans = \{plan_1, plan_2, ..., plan_n\}$, one for each agent, s.t. all agents reach their goals and each pair of plans is conflict-free. Typically, in MAPF one wants to minimize one of the following cost objectives: $SOC = \sum_{i=1}^{n} cost(plan_i)$ or $makespan = \max_i cost(plan_i)$, where $cost(plan_i)$ is the cost of the individual plan, i.e. the number of time steps it took the agent i to reach its goal.

In this work we are interested in the formulation of MAPF problem as the sequential decision making problem, when at each time step the actions for the agents are decided (based on some action-selection policy), then these actions are executed, and then the cycle repeats until all the agents reach their goals or some predefined threshold on the number of time steps is met. Such framing of the problem is well formalized by Multi-agent Markov Decision Process (MAMDP) [9], which we describe next.

Multi-agent Markov Decision Process (MAMDP) can formally be represented as $\langle S, U, T, r, n, \gamma \rangle$. Here n is the number of agents and $\mathbf{U} = U_1 \times U_2 \times ... \times U_n$ is the joint action that is formed by combining the individual actions of all agents. S is the set of the environment states. In our case each state $s \in S$ encompasses the information on the locations of all agents. $T(s'|s, \mathbf{u}) : S \times \mathbf{U} \times S \to [0, 1]$ is the transition function. It defines the probability of transitioning to state s' when the joint action $\mathbf{u} \in \mathbf{U}$ is executed at state s. $r : S \times \mathbf{U} \to \mathbb{R}$ – is the reward function shared between all agents. This function specifies what reward (scalar value) the agents will get if they execute a specific action $\mathbf{u}$ at the specific environment state s. $\gamma \in [0, 1]$ is the discounting factor.

The task is to construct a policy π that specifies which actions an agent should take in different states of the environment to maximize the expected return G over an episode with length K, as defined by Eq. 1:

$$G_t = \sum_{k=0}^{K-t-1} \gamma^k r_{t+k+1} \text{ s. t. } s_t \in S, \tag{1}$$

where r_{t+k+1} is the reward received at time step $t + k + 1$, and s_t represents the state of the environment at time step t. Generally, the policy might be stochastic, i.e. it might map the states to the distribution of actions: $\pi : S \times \mathbf{U} \to [0, 1]$. Given the policy the exact (joint) action is sampled from the distribution at each time step.

Various approaches to obtain π for MAPF can be suggested. For example, one can invoke a complete/optimal MAPF solver at each time step and pick the first joint action from the MAPF solution. Another approach may be to invoke n egoistic single agent searches and to construct a joint action by combining the first actions comprising the n single-agents paths that do not take the other agents into account. In this work we will use such an approach as a baseline to compare with. One more direction to look at might be relying on reinforcement learning (RL) [19] to learn the policy. This, however, might be tricky in the multi-agent setting and non-trivial modifications of the learning-based algorithms are likely to be needed [11]. In this work we, would like, to explore another approach, i.e. to adapt Monte-Carlo Tree Search to multi-agent pathfinding due to the high efficiency of such type of search when it comes to the combinatorial problems with high branching factor.

Monte-Carlo Tree Search (MCTS) is a powerful search paradigm that is well-suited for the sequential decision making problems. Paired with the state-of-the-art machine learning techniques MCTS has recently achieved super-human performance in various board- and video-games, see [13,21] for example. As MCTS relies on the notion of reward it can also be attributed to as a model-based reinforcement learning method, that utilizes the reward(s) to learn to pick the promising actions.

In a nutshell MCTS picks an action given a state of the environment based on extensive simulating of how the environment would change and what rewards would be obtained if different (random) actions are sequentially executed. Indeed, it is not possible to simulate all possible sequences of actions in a limited time. To this end MCTS builds a tree (of a limited width anf depth) that contains the most promising candidates of the actions to be taken (partial plans). The nodes in that tree correspond to environment states and edges – to the actions. The root of the tree is the current state, i.e. the one for which we need to pick an action.

Particularly, MCTS is composed of the four steps that are executed iteratively and are intended to simultaneously build and explore the search tree: selection, expansion, simulation, and backpropagation. Selection is aimed at descending the constructed so far search tree. Conceptually, this can be seen as the process of picking the most promising partial plan to consider. To balance between the exploration (i.e. picking the parts of the search tree that were not considered before) and the exploitation (i.e. picking the partial plans that are characterized by the highest rewards) MCTS relies on assessing the nodes using the upper-confidence bounds techniques (which were initially suggested in the context of the multi-armed bandit problems [1]). Specifically, Upper Confidence Bound for search Trees (UCT) [7] is commonly used. When the tree is descended and the leaf node is picked, the latter is expanded by selecting an un-probed action and adding a new node to the tree. The added node is evaluated by simulating actions using a random policy and the resulting reward is backpropagated through the tree in a special fashion. The process is repeated until the time budget is reached. When it happens the action corresponding to the most visited outgoing edge of the root node is chosen to be executed. For more details on MCTS we refer the reader to an overview paper by Browne et al. [3]. In this work we will present our adaptation of MCTS for the multi-agent pathfinding in the next sections.

3   Problem Statement

Consider n homogeneous agents, navigating in the environment which is represented as a 4-connected grid, composed of the free and blocked cells (the latter correspond to the static obstacles of the environment). The timeline is discretized and at each time step an agent can wait at the current cell or move to one of the adjacent cells if it is not blocked. When two agents wish to move to the same free cell only one of them (random one) succeeds, while the other stay where it was. Thus the state transitions are stochastic.

Initially the agents are located at the unique start cells and for each agent a unique goal cell is specified. When an agent reaches the goal it is removed from the grid. This assumption is not uncommon in MAPF as it is reasonable for various practical applications. For example, think of the robots in the warehouse that need to go to the charging stations. Typically, these charging stations are located at the perimeter of the working area, thus a robot that reaches a charging station may be considered to leave the workspace.

The task is to define a policy that will map environment states to joint actions. Here the environment state is the grid plus the positions of all agents on it. Joint action is a combination of the individual actions of the distinct agents. Moreover, we assume that a limit of K_{max} time steps is given and the episode ends when this number of time steps passes (no matter where the agents are by this time).

To measure how well the policy copes with the problem at hand we use the following metrics, which we compute at the end of the episode:

- *Cooperative Success Rate (CSR)* is a boolean metric, i.e. it might be 0 or 1, that indicates whether all the agents manage to reach their goals;
- *Individual Success Rate (ISR)* is the fraction of agents that managed to reach their goal before the episode ends.
- *Episode Length (EL)* is the number of steps taken by the agents to complete the task. If not all agents reach their goals, EL is assigned the value of K_{max}.

When comparing different policies the one is better that provides higher CSR/ISR and lower EL. Please note that we do not aim to obtain an optimal policy in this work.

4   Related Work

Initially, MCTS algorithms demonstrated their effectiveness in antagonistic games with full information, such as chess or Go [13]. Modern versions of MCTS use deep neural networks to approximate state values instead of simulation. These approaches have also proven effective in single-agent settings where modifications enable agents to learn a model of the environment, allowing them to play Atari games [12,21]. MCTS is not tailored only to games, but is used in robotics [2,4], theorem proving [8] and even can be applied to find an efficient way to multiply matrices [5]. All these examples do, however, belong to the single-agent domain.

Despite the interest in using MCTS for multi-agent settings, a few works have applied it to MAPF. In [22] the authors propose a multi-agent MCTS for Anonymous MAPF in a grid-world environment. Their environment has a dense reward signal (the agent who reached any goal on the map received a reward and ended the episode), and there were no obstacles present, which simplifies collision avoidance. The authors build a separate tree for each agent using a classical algorithm. They then apply the best actions (forming a plan) from the trees jointly in simulator, to receive true scores of the solution and update the trees on that difference. This approach performs well even with a large number of agents. A recent paper [16] proposed a more sophisticated approach for multi-agent planning that combines RL and MCTS. The authors suggested a two-part scheme that includes a goal achievement module and a conflict resolution module. The latter was trained using MCTS. The construction of the search tree for each of the agents was also performed independently, and actions for other agents were selected using the currently trained policy. In contrast to this approaches, we propose a method which plans over a tree for the whole population of agents in the environment and modifies the reward function to guide the agents towards their goals.

5   Method

The straightforward adaptation of MCTS to the considered MAPF problem might be as follows. The nodes in the tree represent the states which are the positions of the agents on a grid, the edges correspond to joint actions. Thus, the branching factor of the tree is $|A|^n$, where $|A|$ is the number of possible individual actions and n is the number of agents. For large numbers of agents this leads to great computational overhead. To this end, we suggest to decompose the joint action into the individual ones in the tree, as described in the next sections.

The next problem which arises when one wants to adapt MCTS for MAPF is how to compute the reward at the end of the simulation phase, i.e. after the phase when the agents take random actions. Typically, MCTS is applied to antagonistic games where the outcome is either win (reward equals 1), loss (reward equals 0) or draw (reward equals 1/2). Thus, one may come with the following reward for our case: $R = n_{finished}/n$, where $n_{finished}$ is the number of agents that reached their goals. However, such a reward is extremely sparse, i.e. in numerous simulation rollouts the reward will be zero or very close to zero (as it is very hard to reach the goal by randomly moving on a grid for a limited number of steps). Thus it will be very hard to focus the search on promising parts of the tree. To this end we introduce an auxiliary intrinsic reward for every agent based on how often it reaches the cells lying on the shortest (individual) path to its goal. Intuitively, such reward shaping forces the agents to demonstrate the goal-reaching behavior while leaving them the freedom to step off the path when needed, e.g. when some agents need to give way to the other agents.

In the next sections we will elaborate more on how our variant of MCTS is designed.

5.1 Subgoal Based Reward Function

MCTS is effective in antagonistic games because they typically have a limited number of moves and a definite outcome (loss, win, draw). In MAPF, however, episodes may last longer and often the randomly-moving agents do not reach their goals. In such simulations, the agents may not receive a positive reward signal to guide the search.

We propose a technique that addresses this issue by encouraging subgoal achievement through intrinsic rewards, using a classic planning algorithm such as A*. The planning algorithm is used to find a path, ignoring other agents. The chosen subgoal is placed a short distance from the agent, for example, two steps away. The reward function is presented in Eq. 2:

$$r_t = \sum_{i=0}^{n-1} \frac{r_t^{a_i}}{n}, \qquad r_t^{a_i} = \begin{cases} r_{target}, & \text{if the agent } a_i \text{ reached the target,} \\ r_{subgoal}, & \text{if the agent } a_i \text{ reached the subgoal,} \\ 0, & \text{otherwise.} \end{cases} \qquad (2)$$

Achieving the subgoal yields a small positive reward (denoted by $r^s \in R$) that is less than the global target reward (denoted by $r^g \in R$) such that $r^s \ll r^g$. The reward comes from the environment for all agents when performing an joint action. This reward is divided by the number of agents in the environment to ensure consistency with the UCT exploration bonus. If the agent moves too far from the subgoal, the subgoal position is recalculated.

5.2   Multi-agent MCTS

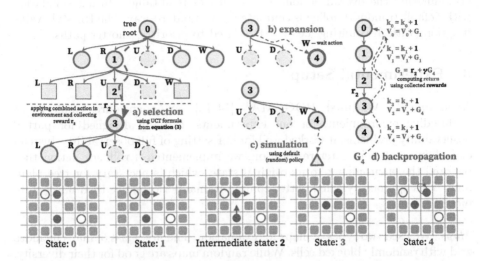

Fig. 1. The MAMCTS approach adapts MCTS for multi-agent tasks by treating action selection points for each agent as separate nodes in the tree, thereby reducing the branching factor. The figure shows all four phases of MCTS: a) selection; b) expansion; c) simulation; and d) backpropagation for multi-agent settings. Actions leading to the vertices shown with dotted lines are not considered during the selection phase. Filled circles represent agents, while empty circles represent their corresponding targets.

Naive application of MCTS to MAPF assumes generating $|A|^n$ child nodes for a search state (leave in the tree), where $|A|$ is the number of individual actions and n is the number of agents. Indeed, this is impractical. To reduce the branching factor we suggest a decomposition approach outlined in Fig. 1 (we note that this resembles the method suggested in [17]). We treat action selection points for each agent as separate nodes in the tree. Actions accumulated in this way are applied at the moment when the last agent selects their action (these nodes are represented as squares in the figure). Thus, the state of the environment is determined by the current positions of the agents and the accumulated actions of other agents. If the accumulated actions are insufficient to perform a joint action to start simulation, the default policy selects the remaining action. Additionally, the tree restricts the choice of actions that lead to static obstacles.

Node selection is performed using the UCT exploration bonus $UCT = \frac{V_j}{k_j} + C_p\sqrt{\frac{2*ln(k)}{k_j}}$, like in classical MCTS, but now for each separate node. In this equation, V_j is the total accumulated return of the j-th child node, C_p is the exploration coefficient, k is the number of visits to the parent node, and k_j is the number of visits to the child node.

The sequential approach to action selection also changes the calculation of the return G (see Eq. 1), now the discounting occurs only once between the execution of joint actions in the environment (between the square vertices in the figure). The vertices are updated using the same reward function value after accumulating the overall action. The return G is obtained during simulation with default (random) policy is computed in a standard way. The RL-style value function (with discounting, i.e. $\gamma < 1$) is used to prioritize shorter paths.

6   Experimental Setup

Environment. We used POGEMA[1] [14,15], an open-source multi-agent pathfinding environment, for our experiments. Initially designed for partial observability problems, it worked well for our setting of full observability. Instead of pickling states for later restoration, we implemented a rollback action that restored the environment to its original state, which is necessary for tree planning. This approach yielded better computational performance than naive state pickling.

Maps. We used two types of maps for evaluation. The first class of maps includes grid with randomly blocked cells. While random maps are good for their diversity, they do not pose complex challenges to the algorithm because narrow passages that require cooperative behavior rarely appear on the map. To demonstrate the potential of cooperative behavior, we used an approach proposed in [16] and created a set of challenging maps sorted by the intersection of individual paths of 16 agents. We used 2000 seeds when selecting maps and chose the 100 most challenging ones with sizes 16×16. These maps typically have only one central passage, forcing agents to act jointly. We report the example of a such cooperative map in Fig. 2(a). To generate them, we used an approach embedded in the POGEMA environment, with an obstacle density of 0.3. We also conducted post-processing on this set by filling empty components with obstacles that were smaller than five cells.

Secondly, we used maze maps generated with the LABMAZE package[2], that contains patterns of mazes and rooms with multiple entrances. These maps include many narrow passages and by design are more challenging than the random maps. Thus, we did not specifically select difficult seeds for this set. We believe that the "difficulty" of these maps is approximately the same as that of cooperative random maps. We used a size of 15×15 when generating the maps (since the LABMAZE package only supports odd sizes). The example of the generated map is presented in Fig. 2(b). The parameters used for generating the labmaze set of maps were: max_rooms: 30, has_doors: True, room_min_size: 5, room_max_size: 5, simplify: False, min_component_size: 4, retry_count: 1000, extra_connection_probability: 0.0.

---

[1] https://github.com/AIRI-Institute/pogema.
[2] https://github.com/deepmind/labmaze.

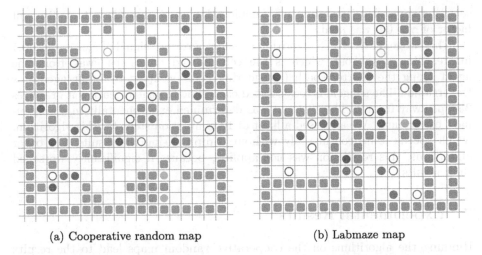

(a) Cooperative random map   (b) Labmaze map

Fig. 2. Examples of maps used during training: (a) Cooperative random maps, which were selected according to their difficulty. (b) Maze maps generated with the LABMAZE package. Agents are represented by filled circles and their targets are represented by empty circles. Each agent has its own target.

Algorithms. We were comparing four algorithms: Joint MCTS, MAMCTS, Subgoal MAMCTS, and modified A* [6]. Joint MCTS is a naive variant of MCTS, where action selection in the tree occurs in a joint action space of all agents. The second approach is MAMCTS, where the action space is reduced and only one agent is considered at each step of tree node expansion. The third variant is Subgoal MAMCTS, which uses a modified reward function that includes a signal for achieving subgoals (as described in Sect. 5). The A* algorithm was originally used for heuristic path planning in single-agent tasks. The algorithm constructs a plan on the full map, considering other agents as obstacles. The first action from the algorithm's plan is selected as the action in the environment. Preliminary experiments have shown that this straightforward approach works well for tasks with a small number of agents and maps without narrow passages. However, if agents need to interact, for instance, one agent has to let another pass, then the algorithm encounters significant issues. To overcome these issues, we introduced a heuristic – if the last two actions of the algorithm do not lead to the target, the agent chooses a random action instead.

During testing, all MCTS-based approaches received a reward of $r_{target} = +1$ for each agent achieving the goal (notably, the A* approach doesn't exploit this information). The episode of interaction with the environment lasted for 64 steps. The random priority approach was used as a conflict resolution system. If multiple agents attempted to move to the same cell at the same time step, one agent was randomly selected to occupy the cell, while the others remained in their original positions. When constructing the tree, it was forbidden to choose actions that lead to static obstacles. During execution MCTS algorithms performed 1000 selection-expansion iterations, using exploration coefficient $C_p = 1$. A discount factor of $\gamma = 0.9$ was used.

The Subgoal MAMCTS algorithm provides a reward signal of $r_{subgoal} = +0.1$ for reaching a subgoal, which is the cell located two steps away from the agent along the shortest path (considering cells occupied by other agents as traversable). The subgoal is recalculated each time the agent reaches it or moves 2 steps away from it. This distance was determined experimentally in a preliminary experiment. We also used a limit of 10 simulation steps for this algorithm, which speeds it up considerably without compromising the results. For other algorithms, this restriction was not applied, because it significantly worsened their results.

7   Experimental Results

Running the algorithms on the cooperative random maps lead to the results presented in Table 1. Here, for each algorithm, the averaged values of the metrics introduced in Sect. 3 are provided. First, it is worth noting that MAMCTS outperforms Joint MCTS. The action space of the Joint MCTS algorithm is too large, since exponentially dependent on the number of agents in the environment. Planning just one step ahead in the tree requires calculating results for 5^n possible nodes, significantly slowing down the search process. The difference is especially noticeable on maps with a large number of agents. The reward signal when an agent reaches the finish line is also quite rare, as can be seen by comparing the results of the MAMCTS and Subgoal MAMCTS algorithms. An additional reward signal solves the problem of long-term planning.

Table 1. The performance of different algorithms was compared on 100 cooperative random maps of size 16×16.

Agents	Joint MCTS			MAMCTS			Subgoal MAMCTS			A*		
	ISR	CSR	Ep. len.	ISR	CSR	Ep. len.	ISR	CSR	Ep. len.	ISR	CSR	Ep. len.
4	0.31	0.04	49.37	0.43	0.0	41.31	**1.0**	**1.0**	**18.8**	0.84	0.75	24.73
8	0.29	0.0	50.83	0.48	0.0	40.08	**0.99**	**0.93**	**21.7**	0.66	0.39	32.3
16	0.24	0.0	53.3	0.4	0.0	44.47	**0.9**	**0.21**	**30.14**	0.4	0.0	44.21

The modification of the A* algorithm performs well and outperforms all tree search algorithms except for Subgoal MAMCTS. The difference is especially noticeable on maps with 4 and 8 agents. Conflicts rarely occur in such cases, and the algorithm is sufficient even with random actions to resolve them.

The comparison of algorithms on maze maps largely repeats the results of the previous experiment. The results a reported in Table 2. The Subgoal MAMCTS approach remains the leader among the considered algorithms, followed by a modified A* algorithm in second place. It is also noteworthy that this set of maps turned out to be slightly easier than cooperative random maps.

Additionally, we compared the computational efficiency of the algorithms. I.e. we computed how long did it take for an algorithm to choose the actions for 16 agents (on average across all types of maps). On average, Joint MCTS needs 12.1 seconds to decide actions, MAMCTS takes 12.7 seconds, and Subgoal MAMCTS takes 4.2 seconds due to the limited number of steps in the simulation. As expected, the A* algorithm performs the best, taking only 0.02 seconds to choose actions.

Table 2. Testing results of algorithms on 100 labmaze maps of size 15×15. The Subgoal MAMCTS algorithm showed the best results.

Agents	Joint MCTS			MAMCTS			Subgoal MAMCTS			A*		
	ISR	CSR	Ep. len.	ISR	CSR	Ep. len.	ISR	CSR	Ep. len.	ISR	CSR	Ep. len.
4	0.39	0.0	48.25	0.54	0.0	37.74	**1.0**	**1.0**	**17.17**	0.9	0.79	22.41
8	0.32	0.0	50.82	0.55	0.0	39.16	**0.98**	**0.89**	**20.18**	0.83	0.54	26.42
16	0.22	0.0	54.19	0.5	0.0	42.02	**0.94**	**0.46**	**25.64**	0.58	0.07	38.62

In conclusion, it can be inferred that the proposed algorithm, Subgoal MAM-CTS, showed better results compared to all other algorithms. Reducing the branching factor by dividing the action space among agents, as well as adding an additional reward signal that guides the agent towards the target, were key factors in the success of this algorithm. On the downside, our current implementation of Subgoal MCTS is evidently slower compared to the search-based baseline.

8 Conclusion

In this study, we applied MCTS to the multi-agent pathfinding problem and proposed techniques to enhance its performance. Our MAMCTS outperforms vanilla MCTS and simple planning algorithms on various map variants, particularly in scenarios with high agent density. Although MAMCTS may not be as fast as individual pathfinding policies based on A* search, it proves efficient given sufficient computational resources and time. In the future, we plan to incorporate neural networks to accelerate the algorithm by approximating the policy and value function. Additionally, applying MCTS to the multi-agent problem opens up possibilities for solving more complex environments with changing map topology and agents possessing extra actions.

References

1. Auer, P., Cesa-Bianchi, N., Fischer, P.: Finite-time analysis of the multiarmed bandit problem. Mach. Learn. **47**, 235–256 (2002)
2. Best, G., Cliff, O.M., Patten, T., Mettu, R.R., Fitch, R.: Dec-MCTS: decentralized planning for multi-robot active perception. Int. J. Robot. Res. **38**(2–3), 316–337 (2019)

3. Browne, C.B., et al.: A survey of Monte Carlo tree search methods. IEEE Trans. Comput. Intell. AI Games **4**(1), 1–43 (2012)
4. Dam, T., Chalvatzaki, G., Peters, J., Pajarinen, J.: Monte-Carlo robot path planning. IEEE Robot. Autom. Lett. **7**(4), 11213–11220 (2022)
5. Fawzi, A., et al.: Discovering faster matrix multiplication algorithms with reinforcement learning. Nature **610**(7930), 47–53 (2022)
6. Ju, C., Luo, Q., Yan, X.: Path planning using an improved A-star algorithm. In: 2020 11th International Conference on Prognostics and System Health Management (PHM-2020 Jinan), pp. 23–26. IEEE (2020)
7. Kocsis, L., Szepesvári, C.: Bandit based Monte-Carlo planning. In: Fürnkranz, J., Scheffer, T., Spiliopoulou, M. (eds.) ECML 2006. LNCS (LNAI), vol. 4212, pp. 282–293. Springer, Heidelberg (2006). https://doi.org/10.1007/11871842_29
8. Lample, G., et al.: Hypertree proof search for neural theorem proving. In: Advances in Neural Information Processing Systems, vol. 35, pp. 26337–26349 (2022)
9. Nawaz, F., Ornik, M.: Multi-agent multi-target path planning in Markov decision processes. arXiv preprint arXiv:2205.15841 (2022)
10. Noh, D., Lee, W., Kim, H.R., Cho, I.S., Shim, I.B., Baek, S.: Adaptive coverage path planning policy for a cleaning robot with deep reinforcement learning. In: 2022 IEEE International Conference on Consumer Electronics (ICCE), pp. 1–6. IEEE (2022)
11. Rashid, T., Samvelyan, M., De Witt, C.S., Farquhar, G., Foerster, J., Whiteson, S.: Monotonic value function factorisation for deep multi-agent reinforcement learning. J. Mach. Learn. Res. **21**(1), 7234–7284 (2020)
12. Schrittwieser, J., et al.: Mastering atari, go, chess and shogi by planning with a learned model. Nature **588**(7839), 604–609 (2020)
13. Silver, D., et al.: Mastering the game of go without human knowledge. Nature **550**(7676), 354–359 (2017)
14. Skrynnik, A., Andreychuk, A., Yakovlev, K., Panov, A.: Pathfinding in stochastic environments: learning vs planning. PeerJ Comput. Sci. **8**, e1056 (2022). https://doi.org/10.7717/peerj-cs.1056. https://peerj.com/articles/cs-1056
15. Skrynnik, A., Andreychuk, A., Yakovlev, K., Panov, A.I.: POGEMA: partially observable grid environment for multiple agents. arXiv preprint arXiv:2206.10944 (2022)
16. Skrynnik, A., Yakovleva, A., Davydov, V., Yakovlev, K., Panov, A.I.: Hybrid policy learning for multi-agent pathfinding. IEEE Access **9**, 126034–126047 (2021)
17. Standley, T.: Finding optimal solutions to cooperative pathfinding problems. In: Proceedings of the AAAI Conference on Artificial Intelligence, vol. 24, pp. 173–178 (2010)
18. Stern, R., et al.: Multi-agent pathfinding: definitions, variants, and benchmarks. In: Proceedings of the International Symposium on Combinatorial Search, vol. 10, pp. 151–158 (2019)
19. Sutton, R.S., Barto, A.G.: Reinforcement Learning: An Introduction. MIT Press, Cambridge (2018)
20. Yakovlev, K., Andreychuk, A., Skrynnik, A., Panov, A.: Planning and learning in multi-agent path finding. Doklady Math. **106**, S79–S84 (2023). https://doi.org/10.1134/S1064562422060229
21. Ye, W., Liu, S., Kurutach, T., Abbeel, P., Gao, Y.: Mastering atari games with limited data. In: Advances in Neural Information Processing Systems, vol. 34 (2021)
22. Zerbel, N., Yliniemi, L.: Multiagent Monte Carlo tree search. In: Proceedings of the 18th International Conference on Autonomous Agents and MultiAgent Systems, pp. 2309–2311 (2019)

The Problem of Concept Learning and Goals of Reasoning in Large Language Models

Anfisa A. Chuganskaya[1] , Alexey K. Kovalev[1,2]([✉]) , and Aleksandr Panov[1]

[1] Federal Research Center "Computer Science and Control"
of the Russian Academy of Sciences, Moscow, Russia
{kovalev,panov}@airi.net
[2] AIRI, Moscow, Russia

Abstract. Modern large language models (LLMs) show good performance in the zero-shot or few-shot learning. This ability ability is a significant result even on tasks for which the models have not been trained is in part due to the fact that by learning from textual internet-scale data, such models build a semblance of a model of the world. However, the question of whether the entities on which that the model operates are concepts in the psychological sense remains open. Relying on conceptual reasoning schemes allows to increase the safety of models in solving complex problems. To address this question, we propose to use standard psychodiagnostic techniques to assess the quality of conceptual thinking of models. We test this hypothesis, by conducting experiments on a dataset adapted for LLMs from the psychological techniques of Kettel and Rubinstein and comparing the effectiveness of each of them. In this paper, we have shown that it is possible to distinguish several types of model errors in incorrect answers to standard tasks on conceptual thinking and to evaluate the type according to the classifications of distortions of conceptual thinking adopted in cultural and historical approaches in psychology. This makes it possible to use the tool of psychodiagnostic techniques not only to evaluate the effectiveness of models, but also to develop training procedures based on such tasks.

Keywords: Concept learning · Large language models · Psychology of thinking · Purpose of the activity · Sign-based world model

1 Introduction

Building a world model is one of the key tasks that cognitive agents, which generate their behavior in the external environment, have to implement. To solve this task, it is first necessary to choose an appropriate way to represent knowledge about the environment [6,15], as well as about the capabilities of the agent itself in that environment, which would allow effective implementation of methods for planning behavior and predicting the consequences of actions. Second, the agent's world model should be formed and updated through a learning process using sensor-mediated information from the external environment [12]. One

© The Author(s), under exclusive license to Springer Nature Switzerland AG 2023
P. García Bringas et al. (Eds.): HAIS 2023, LNAI 14001, pp. 661–672, 2023.
https://doi.org/10.1007/978-3-031-40725-3_56

of the key challenges in integrating knowledge representation and world model learning methods is the binding of symbols [11], which are used in the behavior planning task to describe actions and their outcomes.

The concept of a Sign-Based World Model [19,20] suggests formalizing the notion of a sign [13,23], which mediates some object or process of the real environment in the agent's world model and possesses a component structure used to solve the symbol binding problem. In this case, the name of the sign is a part of some language system, which itself is not only a tool and regulation for organizing the communication of agents, but also a source of conventional knowledge about the external environment and about the agents themselves. The implementation of the model of the cognitive agent's world on the basis of the theory of the Sign-Based World Model helps to create the so-called systems of embodied artificial intelligence, which declare the importance and necessity of considering the specifics of the agent's interaction with the environment for the generation and implementation of an effective action plan [21].

The main components of a sign, in addition to the name, are significance, meaning, and image. An image is a set of attributes necessary to distinguish the mediated entity from the rest in the current situation. The formation of an image can take place in a self-supervised mode and is realized by modern neural network encoders [37], including object encoders [17]. A significance is a set of rules agreed upon in a group of agents for the interaction and use of objects mediated by the agent. The significance of a sign is, in fact, part of the very language system in which the name of the sign is included. In this work, we propose to test the possibility of using modern neural network language models as a system of significances [3], as a variant of the technical solution to the problem of word bifunctionality. Finally, meaning is a realization of significances in a specific situation and can be modeled by a learning policy and a value function.

The modeling of the language system for the full implementation and operation of the sign components has so far been a key problem in the construction of cognitive agents with the Sign-Based World Model. However, the recent emergence of large (more than a hundred billion trainable parameters) pre-trained neural network language models [9,28] allows us to consider them as an approximation of the language system. The use of a huge amount of textual data collected from all kinds of sources in various domains, including the everyday life of real native speakers, when training such models suggests some approximation to the concept of universal common knowledge (common sense). Such models can be used not only to generate answers in natural language, but more generally to generate any sequence of tokens in response to a query. Moreover, depending on the problem to be solved, the choice of such tokens can be quite large: from a set of actions to a set of image patches. Thus, pre-trained Large Language Models (LLMs) can be considered as a general-purpose expert system, in which information and knowledge realized in a language system can be obtained by a specially formed query (prompt).

We consider the LLMs to be an approximation of significance for the implementation of the Sign-Based World Model of the cognitive agent. However, the question of whether the entities on which LLMs operate are concepts in the psychological sense remains open. Relying on conceptual reasoning schemes allows to increase the safety of models in solving complex problems. To address this question, we propose to use standard psychodiagnostic techniques to assess the quality of conceptual thinking of models. We test this hypothesis, by conducting experiments on a dataset adapted for LLMs from the psychological techniques of Kettel and Rubinstein and comparing the effectiveness of each of them. We have shown that it is possible to distinguish several types of model errors in incorrect answers to standard tasks on conceptual thinking and to evaluate the type according to the classifications of distortions of conceptual thinking adopted in cultural and historical approaches in psychology. This makes it possible to use the tool of psychodiagnostic techniques not only to evaluate the effectiveness of models, but also to develop training procedures based on such tasks.

Our contribution is as follows:

1. We propose to use standard psychodiagnostic techniques to assess the quality of conceptual thinking of LLMs.
2. Experimental results show that it is possible to use the tool of psychodiagnostic techniques not only to evaluate the formation of true concepts in LLMs.

2   Psychological Approaches to Thinking and Speech

Many authors [7,35] are faced with the need to consider psychological approaches to explain the formation of skills and the use of language to build internal (query formation stage) and external communication of an agent to achieve a goal when performing actions. Thus, the authors of the SayCan system [1] note that there are difficulties in adapting two tasks — on the one hand, working with language models for building reasoning and compiling action descriptions based on instructions for a robotic agent, which leads to high-level reasoning about complex tasks and diversity plan for the implementation of activities that are difficult for an agent with a limited set of skills, taking into account the characteristics of a particular implementation environment. Relying on conceptual reasoning schemes allows to increase the safety of models in solving complex problems.

Psychological concepts from the cultural-historical psychology of Lev Vygotsky [30] and the research of Jean Piaget [22] can be considered as methodological tools to explain the connection between the formation of concepts and their use in the context of the study of speech. This allows for a multidimensional view of the proposed models of embodied cognitive agents. The issue of using thinking models to develop and validate models has been developed using the Theory of Mind (ToM) methodology [8]. In recent years, much attention has been paid to the use of psychological models of thinking and reasoning, focusing not on the use of formal concepts and reasoning, but on the performance of communicative functions and solving everyday problems. In the work of Tomer Ullman [29], the aim was to consider the processes of thinking based on solving everyday attribution problems. In the experiments it was necessary to successfully predict where the object is located in a situation of different verbal designations of boxes with its placement (popcorn and chocolate). The reasoning model was based on the ToM proposed by Daniel Dennett. ToM is based on the assumption of the secrecy of mental processes and the need to determine the causes of behavior in a situation of false expectations. As Dennett notes, this approach is important for determining the causes of behavior, but it is not always suitable for solving direct rational tasks, which also include formal problems of reasoning based on concepts and generalizations.

Alternative theories are presented by a broader consideration of the range of tasks that are solved through the mutual development of speech and thinking (as proposed in the works of Piaget and Vygotsky). Vygotsky noted the importance of the connection between thinking and speech, as well as the need to consider the meaning of the word in meaningful unity. From the point of view of psycholinguistics [23], the word (name) performs two functions: indicative, indicating correlation with objects in the object field, and signicative, associated with understanding the meaning and functional meaning. In the process of human development, the meaning of the word is expanded, supplemented by experience and the definition of additional, significant features due to communication in a social environment. Vygotsky believed that the generalization of the meaning of the word is, in fact, is the process of concept formation. It was important for psychologists to determine the functional meaning of verbal signs and the process of concept formation itself. The nature of the strategy for solving this task allowed Vygotsky to formulate a sequence of stages (steps) of generalization of the meanings of the word into a concept and to identify the stages of transition from the subject relationship of the word with the object world to the disclosure of the signicative function.

Vygotsky identifies three stages in the formation of rational concepts:

1. **Syncrets** — the word (name) denotes objects that are similar in some subjective characteristics and logically belong to different classes.
2. **Complexes** — they do not reveal the full extent of the relationship of signs in a group denoted by one a word. In this case, the word is not a concept but the name of several objects, a word-"nickname".
3. **True concepts** — at this stage, two tasks are solved: the transition from the reflection of reality in its situational visual images to the reflection in concepts, rules, and the transition from the simple reproduction of representations to mental actions, i.e. to solving problems, formulating and testing hypotheses.

The development of conceptual thinking, the close relationship between the stages of thinking and speech were noted by the French psychologist Jean Piaget, who had common and debatable positions with Lev Vygotsky on the sociocultural principles of the development of the human psyche. Piaget distinguished the stages of the development of intelligence and supported the line of development of thinking from actions (operations) to the formation of verbal and logical connections [22].

In order to build systems that use not only the component of the word base as a set of symbols, but also take into account the multilevel nature of knowledge, we can consider the Sign-Based World Model (SBWM) proposed in the works of Gennady Osipov. It identifies three levels of worldviews based on different components of the sign and experience: rational, based on formal knowledge and generalizations, everyday, based on scenario knowledge, and mythological, based on emotions and personal meanings.

3   Methodology and Experimental Setup

In our work, we investigate how modern LLMs cope with solving problems in the area of SBWM and building true concepts. To do this, we propose to use standard psychodiagnostic techniques to assess the quality of conceptual thinking of models and compare the effectiveness of each of model. For the experimental material, we use basic techniques for studying true concepts and identifying essential features from standard psychodiagnostic techniques. Similar experimental methods using psychodiagnostic tasks were carried out in modern works to evaluate the effectiveness of GPT models. M. Kosinsky examines the use of classical volume theory problems to test the effectiveness of several language models [14]. It shows the improvement of modern models in solving problems to identify false beliefs, which is largely due to the nature of the tasks themselves, which are based on everyday tasks and do not require a transition to the level of abstract concepts. Indirectly, this was encountered during the subsequent generation of B. L. Bounefuff, G. Checki, K. R. Gossips, who have noted the problem that chatbots can be potentially harmful by demonstrating manipulative, ingratiating and narcissistic behavior [16]. The use of ready-made psychological tools to evaluate the effectiveness of each of the models allows you to build a new version of expert verification of the results of model answers based on correlation with ready-made answers and types of errors in tasks. In this study, we focused on conceptual tasks that combine the process of working with language models and reasoning.

We developed a methodology for conducting the study, which consisted of several steps:

1. The selection of a psychological indicator to evaluate the success of the activity (e.g., the correlation of the use of a word and the level of generalization and the gradation of this feature).
2. The selection of psychological techniques that are used in the diagnosis of these signs (e.g., the study of expressions or classification in solving problems of verbal-logical thinking).
3. The compilation of a dataset of questions based on tasks of psychological techniques (e.g., translation of tasks into a dialog form for LLMs).
4. Conducting experiments with n-iterations of presenting tasks for each of the LLMs (e.g., presenting a question from the dataset ten times to assess the model's performance on the task and the percentage of success).

5. Qualitative or quantitative assessment of the success in solving problems related to a particular psychological phenomenon

In our experiments, we evaluated the models in the zero-shot mode, but for further experiments, it is possible to use the few-shot mode or fine-tuning.

A similar scheme using psychological techniques as the basis for a dataset was proposed in the work of Kosinski, who took 40 classic false belief tasks widely used to test ToM in humans [14] and showed the effectiveness of solving belief recognition problems in everyday situations for different versions of the GPT family models (GPT-3 [3], GPT-3.5, GPT-4 [18]).

3.1   Dataset

For our experiment aimed at studying the use of LLMs for solving problems based on the use of true concepts and reasoning processes, taking into account the purpose of the task, we used two valid psychological methods that distinguish the parameters of concept formation, generalization and preservation of the purpose of reasoning.

The intelligence test tasks are taken from the Scale B of the 16-PF Cattell test [4]. The methodology of this questionnaire is based on a lexical hypothesis. The tasks from the test have been transformed into a dialog form of questions and presented in English since the considered LLMs are trained on the corpus of the English language to conduct the dialog. Such linguistic tasks with concepts are focused, on the one hand, on checking the correctness of the answer and the principle of explanation of the conclusion, on the other hand, it is a test of the use of meaningfully similar concepts for explanations based on LLM, and the acceptance of the reasoning task based on the focus of the cognitive task, which includes the allocation of the target component of the answer to the question not as a set of words, but as a process of reasoning with the definition of these conditions and tasks for solutions.

The second class of methods, which formed the basis for the compilation of questions, was taken on the basis of combining words by classes based on the allocation of essential features of concepts. We take Rubinstein's test of "identifying essential features" [25]. The tasks were also translated into English and presented in the form of questions. The methodology of this test reveals the logic of judgments, as well as the ability to maintain the direction and stability of the method of reasoning when solving a long series of similar tasks. Such a class of techniques is considered in clinical psychology.

According to the methodology of the study, we compiled a database of questions based on two methods: the Scale B 16 PF the Cattell questionnaire (9 questions related to concepts and their meanings were taken) and Rubinstein's methodology of "Identifying essential features" [25] (5 questions were taken). The small number of tasks is due to the complexity of automatically matching the model responses with the questionnaire responses. Automating the verification process and increasing the number of tasks is an important direction for further research.

Examples of questions and their modifications for the Scale B 16 PF the Cattell questionnaire and Rubinstein's methodology of "Identifying essential features" are shown in Figs. 1 and 2, respectively.

Initial question	Modification
Which of these words does not fit the other two: 1. candle 2. moon 3. lamp	Which of the words candle, moon, lamp do not fit the other two?
The word "Shovel" refers to the word "dig" as the word "knife" refers to the word: 1. sharp 2. cutting 3. sharpening	What do people do with a knife to cook food: cut, sharpen, kitchen?

Fig. 1. Examples from the Scale B 16 PF the Cattell questionnaire and their modification to query LLMs.

Initial question	Modification
Choose two words from the list that are most related in meaning to the word "Garden": plants, gardener, dog, fence, land.	From the words plants, gardener, dog, fence, land, which two words are closest in meaning to the word "Garden"?
Choose two words from the list that are most related in meaning to the word "Reading": eyes, book, glasses, text, word.	From the words eyes, book, glasses, text, word, which two words are closest in meaning to the word "Reading"?

Fig. 2. Examples from Rubinstein's methodology of "Identifying essential features' and their modification to query LLMs.

3.2 Large Language Models

Most modern research on LLMs [14, 27, 29, 32, 36] focuses on models with a large number of parameters such as GPT-3 [3], FLAN [33], PaLM [5], ChatGPT[1], and others. This is partly because such models are the most advanced representatives of LLMs, and partly because some properties, e.g. Chain of Thought [34], start to have a significant impact only when a large number of parameters are used. However, such models are either not available at all or have limited access. The study of LLMs with fewer parameters is an important scientific and practical topic, since they are mostly in the public domain.

---

[1] https://openai.com/blog/chatgpt.

In order to study the building true conceptsLLMs, we have selected the following models of the GPT family with an increasing number of parameters: **GPT-J 6B** [31] **(GPT-J)**, **GPT-NeoX-20B** [2] **(NeoX)**, and **Bloom 176B** [26] **(Bloom)**.

GPT-J 6B is a GPT-2-like [24] language model with 6 billion parameters trained on the Pile [10] dataset. GPT-NeoX-20B is a GPT-3-like [3] language model with 20 billion parameters also trained on the Pile [10] dataset. Bloom is a GPT-3-like [3] language model with 176 billion parameters trained on 46 different languages and 13 programming languages. For all models, we used implementations from the Hugging Face[2]. To form a relevant number of answers, there were 10 presentations of each of the 14 questions for each model.

We also ran an exploratory experiment on the ChatGPT model, asking each question three times. The model produces stable answers, allowing us to reduce the number of queries to three instead of 10.

3.3 Experimental Setup

To study the formation of a real concept in LLMs, we followed the following experimental setup. All models were tested in the zero-shot mode, i.e., only the modified task in the form of a question in English was used as the model input without any additional prompt. To test the robustness of the model, each of the 14 tasks was presented to the model 10 times and the model's responses were recorded. The standard Haginface API was used to access the model. The assessment of the model's responses was done manually by an expert psychologist according to the responses presented in the corresponding methodology. This approach was chosen due to the complexity of automating the evaluation process.

4 Results and Discussion

The responses of the models did not lead to correct decisions and had a number of distortions. All the answers could be classified into several categories:

– **A** — Reliance on minor signs, latent features.
– **B** — The lack of the goal of solving the problem in finding the right answer.
– **C** — Correct description of the meanings of the words from the question and the absence of generalizations based on significant features of concepts.
– **D** — Inclusion of an emotional component.
– **I** — Transfer of the task to another structure, i.e., housing and communal services as a communicative interaction.
– **F** — Incoherent texts.

These categories are similar in content to the types of thinking disorders that are diagnosed in clinical psychology (violation of thinking in the form of reduction or distortion of generalizations, of the dynamic and motivational components).

---

[2] https://huggingface.co.

In order to analyze LLMs, they allow to identify the type of error and to outline ways to solve it.

It is possible to give the types of responses that are obtained on the studied models.

Category A — NeoX: *"Fish" and "Mud" have nothing to do with any of the other words. Every single one of the adjectives are from vastly different types of metaphors. There is no defining connection between any of the words. This reductionist view does not preserve art:*

Category B — Bloom: *What would be the meaning and point it would make in the sentence?*
Any here fit both words a few and most?
What would be the meaning and point of such a sentence?
A: The best alternatives would be having none or at most one-couple of as options. Thus a sentence for an alternative is: "At most 1 in 3 students filled in the survey."
The problem here is more "in the world that English is solving for" such as not having any molecules or atoms available to visualize, or perhaps only being able to use a rough estimate based on a limited prior sample, or even that the problem itself may be underspecified, if there may hypothetically be some new observation missing that would add as many as 10–20% of new data points if that was the case.

Category C — GPT-J: *I have been trying to think of the most correct word for each of the three words without looking at the full paragraph.*
A: Candle moon lamp, because they appear to be in sequence or at least in the same place at the start.

Category D — Bloom: *is a trick question, created to trap fallible people with character test diagnosis, and we have been trying to answer it ever since the man first thought he was a specimen in a jar.*

Category I — NeoX: *What do people do with a knife to cook food: cut, sharpen, kitchen? Whatever it is, a man named Mike Chapman has survived knives, more than I can count on both hands over this past year, and interviews with him brought me to a conclusion. So I'll start by saying a brief prayer for the young lady as you read this. She will give you a better idea on what I'm writing about. Let me introduce myself, though. Indianapolis Indiana USA found me one Saturday night and asked why I was looking into a specific knife black market seemingly outside of my areas of interest and area code, ha ha.*

For the GPT-J model, the most frequent responses were constructed according to the type of pseudo-concept formation, where the main error was not retaining the target component of the reasoning. The field of answers on the use of the linguistic field of concepts corresponds to the topic, which shows the correctness of the solution within the framework of the LLM. However, the answer turns out to be incorrect, because the purpose of the reasoning task is not retained — not to attract additional knowledge, to narrow it down to the ones set in the question, and the chosen criteria of the celestial bodies (sun and moon) are not selected on essential signs, but only illustrate the example of pseudo-understanding. The criterion is explained in the context of searching for a generalizing word, which is also supported in the context of using only words, but without setting the target task of choosing a word. This replaces the purpose of the answer and leads to incorrect answers. It is justified in its conclusion, but it is based on secondary features, not on the meaning of the concept, which also interprets such a conclusion on the level of pseudo-concepts.

For Bloom, the most common responses are communicative in nature and descriptions based on latent features from distant conceptual classes. Most NeoX responses contain meaningless or emotionally saturated text. Thus, GPT-J was found to be the closest to the solution, providing answers to each of the trials. It has a bias toward pseudo-concepts based on latent features.

To test the effectiveness of evaluating work with concepts and thinking tasks, we set up an exploratory experiment with the most prominent representative of LLMs — ChatGPT. We received a sufficient number of correct answers describing the criteria of conceptuality. For example, one of the answers was as follows:

> The word "think" doesn't apply to the other two words, "see" and "hear." "Think" refers to the mental process of using one's mind to form thoughts, reason, or make judgments. It is an internal cognitive activity that does not necessarily involve the external senses of sight or hearing.

This makes it possible to evaluate the effectiveness of the method of a multidisciplinary approach using sign support as a criterion for working with LLM.

In the future, it is possible to extend the analysis by estimating the percentage of correct answers or types of answers for each model, and to switch to few-shot learning or fine-tuning to include the goal component in the reasoning model.

5   Conclusion

The models gave answers containing the same classes of answer distortions as in the answers to the questions of the Cattell's Scale B methodology. One of the solutions to the problem of developing the architecture of agents for solving more complex tasks is proposed on the basis of cultural-historical and activity approaches in the theory of SBWM, when building a model of the world of an intelligent agent, it is proposed to take into account the conceptual level by considering the categories of meaning and meaning. SBWM suggests studying the components of the sign structure, taking into account the mediation of objective reality and the linguistic component of the meaning of the word. This provides methodological opportunities for the development of models that take into account both functions of the word (name), and thus allow you to give instructions in natural language. Methodologically significant is the development of an internal plan of purposeful actions of agents, because the formation of a two-dimensional thinking that directly takes into account this information and its second plan, meanings.

In this paper, we used standard psychodiagnostic techniques to assess the formation of real concepts in LLMs. The results show that the considered models do not cope with the tasks from psychological questionnaires and, as mentioned above, give answers containing the same classes of answer distortions as in the answers to the questions of the Cattell's Scale B methodology. Thus, the methodological tools of psychological concepts based on the theory of cultural and historical psychology to show model limitations in the use of available LLMs.

As further research, we can highlight the expansion of the data set and types of questionnaires, the automation of the evaluation of the model responses, which will allow a thorough quantitative analysis. In our work, we used only the zero-shot mode to test the model without using examples. However, testing in few-shot mode or with additional fine-tuning of models on labeled data is also an important area of research.

References

1. Ahn, M., et al.: Do as i can, not as i say: grounding language in robotic affordances. arXiv:2204.01691 (2022)
2. Black, S., et al.: GPT-NeoX-20B: an open-source autoregressive language model. In: Proceedings of the ACL Workshop on Challenges & Perspectives in Creating Large Language Models (2022)
3. Brown, T., et al.: Language models are few-shot learners. Adv. Neural Inf. Process. Syst. **33**, 1877–1901 (2020)
4. Catell, R.: Handbook for the sixteen personality factor questionnaire (16 pf). clinical, educational, industrial, and research psychology, for use with all forms of the test by Cattell, Raymond (1970)
5. Chowdhery, A., et al.: PaLM: scaling language modeling with pathways. arXiv:2204.02311 (2022)
6. Chudova, N.: Some pertinent problems of modeling goal-setting in sign-based world models: a psychologist's perspective. Sci. Tech. Inf. Process. **48**, 423–429 (2021)
7. Colas, C., Karch, T., Moulin-Frier, C., Oudeyer, P.Y.: Vygotskian autotelic artificial intelligence: language and culture internalization for human-like AI. arXiv:2206.01134 (2022)
8. Dennett, D.C.: Beliefs about beliefs. Behav. Brain Sci. **1**(4), 568–570 (1978). https://doi.org/10.1017/S0140525X00076664
9. Devlin, J., Chang, M.W., Lee, K., Toutanova, K.: Bert: pre-training of deep bidirectional transformers for language understanding. arXiv:1810.04805 (2018)
10. Gao, L., et al.: The pile: an 800 GB dataset of diverse text for language modeling. arXiv:2101.00027 (2020)
11. Garcez, A.D., Lamb, L.C.: Neurosymbolic AI: the 3rd wave. Artif. Intell. Rev. 1–20 (2023). https://doi.org/10.1007/s10462-023-10448-w
12. Greff, K., Van Steenkiste, S., Schmidhuber, J.: On the binding problem in artificial neural networks. arXiv:2012.05208 (2020)
13. Gudwin, R., Queiroz, J. (eds.): Semiotics and Intelligent Systems Development. IGI Global (2007). https://doi.org/10.4018/978-1-59904-063-9
14. Kosinski, M.: Theory of mind may have spontaneously emerged in large language models. arXiv:2302.02083 (2023)

15. Lieto, A.: A computational framework for concept representation in cognitive systems and architectures: concepts as heterogeneous proxytypes. Procedia Comput. Sci. **41**, 6–14. Elsevier Masson SAS (2014)

16. Lin, B., Bouneffouf, D., Cecchi, G., Varshney, K.R.: Towards healthy AI: large language models need therapists too. arXiv:2304.00416 (2023)

17. Locatello, F., et al.: Object-centric learning with slot attention. Adv. Neural Inf. Process. Syst. **33**, 11525–11538 (2020)

18. OpenAI: Gpt-4 Technical report (2023)

19. Osipov, G.S., Panov, A.I., Chudova, N.V.: Behavior control as a function of consciousness. II. Synthesis of a behavior plan. J. Comput. Syst. Sci. Int. **54**(6), 882–896 (2015)

20. Osipov, G.S., Panov, A.I.: Relationships and operations in a sign-based world model of the actor. Sci. Tech. Inf. Process. **45**(5), 317–330 (2018)

21. Panov, A.I.: Goal setting and behavior planning for cognitive agents. Sci. Tech. Inf. Process. **46**(6), 404–415 (2019)

22. Piaget, J.: Les mécanismes perceptifs. Presses universitaires de France, Paris (1961). [in french]

23. Pospelov, D.A., Osipov, G.S.: Knowledge in semiotic models. In: Proceedings of the Second Workshop on Applied Semiotics, Seventh International Conference on Artificial Intelligence and Information-Control Systems of Robots (AIICSR'97), pp. 1–12. Bratislava (1997)

24. Radford, A., Wu, J., Child, R., Luan, D., Amodei, D., Sutskever, I.: Language models are unsupervised multitask learners. OpenAI blog (2019)

25. Rubinstein, S.: Experimental Methods of Pathopsychology and the Experience of their Application in the Clinic. Meditsina Publishing House, Moscow (1970). [in Russian]

26. Scao, T.L., et al.: Bloom: a 176b-parameter open-access multilingual language model. arXiv:2211.05100 (2022)

27. Shakarian, P., Koyyalamudi, A., Ngu, N., Mareedu, L.: An independent evaluation of ChatGPT on mathematical word problems (MWP). arXiv:2302.13814 (2023)

28. Thoppilan, R., et al.: LaMDA: language models for dialog applications. arXiv:2201.08239 (2022)

29. Ullman, T.: Large language models fail on trivial alterations to theory-of-mind tasks. arXiv:2302.08399 (2023)

30. Vygotsky, L.: Thinking and Speaking. The M.I.T Press, Cambridge (1962)

31. Wang, B., Komatsuzaki, A.: GPT-J-6B: a 6 billion parameter autoregressive language model, May 2021. https://github.com/kingoflolz/mesh-transformer-jax

32. Wang, J., et al.: On the robustness of ChatGPT: an adversarial and out-of-distribution perspective. arXiv:2302.12095 (2023)

33. Wei, J., et al.: Finetuned language models are zero-shot learners. arXiv:2109.01652 (2021)

34. Wei, J., et al.: Chain of thought prompting elicits reasoning in large language models. arXiv:2201.11903 (2022)

35. Zeng, A., et al.: Socratic models: composing zero-shot multimodal reasoning with language. arXiv:2204.00598 (2022)

36. Zhong, Q., Ding, L., Liu, J., Du, B., Tao, D.: Can ChatGPT understand too? A comparative study on ChatGPT and fine-tuned BERT. arXiv:2302.10198 (2023)

37. Zhu, Y., Min, M.R., Kadav, A., Graf, H.P.: S3VAE: self-supervised sequential VAE for representation disentanglement and data generation. In: Proceedings of the IEEE/CVF Conference on Computer Vision and Pattern Recognition, pp. 6538–6547 (2020)

Multi-agent System for Multimodal Machine Learning Object Detection

Eduardo Coelho[1] , Nuno Pimenta[1] , Hugo Peixoto[1] , Dalila Durães[1] ,
Pedro Melo-Pinto[2] , Victor Alves[1(✉)] , Lourenço Bandeira[3],
José Machado[1] , and Paulo Novais[1]

[1] ALGORITMI Research Centre/LASI, University of Minho, Braga, Portugal
{pg47164,a88322}@alunos.uminho.pt,
{hpeixoto,dad,valves,jmac,pjon}@di.uminho.pt
[2] CITAB, University of Trás-os-Montes and Alto Douro, Vila Real, Portugal
pmelo@utad.pt
[3] Schréder Hyperion, Carcavelos, Portugal
lourenco.bandeira@schreder.com

Abstract. Multi-agent systems have shown great promise in addressing complex problems that traditional single-agent approaches are not
be able to handle. In this article, we propose a multi-agent system for the
conception of a multimodal machine learning problem on edge devices.
Our architecture leverages docker containers to encapsulate knowledge in
the form of models and processes, enabling easy management of the system. Communication between agents is facilitated by Message Queuing
Telemetry Transport, a lightweight messaging protocol ideal for Internet of Things and edge computing environments. Additionally, we highlight the significance of object detection in our proposed system, which
is a crucial component of many multimodal machine learning tasks, by
enabling the identification and localization of objects within diverse data
modalities. In this manuscript an overall architecture description is performed, discussing the role of each agent and the communication protocol between them. The proposed system offers a general approach to
multimodal machine learning problems on edge devices, demonstrating
the advantages of multi-agent systems in handling complex and dynamic
environments.

Keywords: Multi-Agent System · Multimodality · Multimodal
Machine Learning · Object Detection

1 Introduction

The field of computer vision has extensively studied object detection, especially in safety-critical operations such as vehicle detection and tracking, but
researchers are now exploring the use of cross-modality features in conjunction

We thank Schréder Hyperion Company for the cooperation of this work.

with visual information, making it a relatively new area of research. This app-roach has been investigated in various research fields related to visual modal-ities, including video recognition, multimedia comprehension, image and video captioning, and person identification, however, combining multiple modalities poses certain difficulties, such as ensuring diversity among them or acquiring multi-domain sensor data in a synchronized manner [1, 2].

In multi-sensor data fusion, information from several sources is dynamically combined to produce an accurate and insightful picture of the targeted entities. In essence, this method transforms the unprocessed data gathered from many sources into a logical and consistent collection of assessments. The capacity to gain insights that would not be possible with a single sensor in isolation is this approach's main benefit [2].

As a matter of fact, just as humans rely on visual perception to navigate the driving environment, similarly autonomous vehicles depend on visual data in the form of images and videos [1]. Nevertheless, in unfavorable driving conditions, object detection is hindered, and visual data alone may not be sufficient to detect the presence of other vehicles. Consequently, additional modalities may be of value to improve safety-critical operations such as vehicle detection and tracking.

With the advent of the Internet of Things (IoT), the ordinary world becomes surrounded by an increasing number of distinct sensors that generate data from various modalities [3], such as radar, image, infra-red, seismic, and acoustic, among others. Each modality captures the environmental state from a different perspective. For instance, radar signals are immune to adverse weather condi-tions, such as changes in lighting, rain, and fog, but can be hindered by clut-ter and multi-path effects, making it difficult to determine target size. Seismic and acoustic signals can detect objects without a direct line-of-sight, but they also struggle with determining object size. Non-image modalities are less sus-ceptible to non-line-of-sight conditions, while images perform better in tracking and determining object dimensions [1]. So, the complementarity of these vari-ous modalities in object detection may prepare computer vision algorithms more capable and less error-prone in tasks where a small increase in detection accuracy may be fundamental.

In this article, we propose a multi-agent system for deploying a multimodal machine learning problem on edge devices, using docker containers to contain knowledge in the form of models and processes. The proposed system aims to address this conception of machine learning models while handling the complex-ity of multimodal data.

A single agent system would not be sufficient to handle all the tasks required, such as data collection, feature extraction, model training, and inference. This would lead to performance bottlenecks, a remarkable lack of scalability, and limited adaptability to different and dynamic environments. In contrast, the proposed multi-agent system allows for seamless coordination and collaboration between agents, each responsible for specific tasks. For example, some agents can collect data from sensors, while others can perform data feature extraction, model training, and/or inference.

2   Related Work

Object detection has been a challenging topic in computer vision research for several decades. Object detection aims to identify whether there are any object representations from specified categories in an image and, if so, to report the spatial location and extent of each object occurrence, for instance, via a bounding box [4]. Several are the techniques and methodologies for implementing unimodal object detection, but each modality depicts the status of the environment from a different angle [1] and computer vision algorithms may be favored in their detection accuracy if more modalities are adjoined.

Regarding multimodal data usage for object detection, some works implement the cooperation between different modalities in order to achieve higher object detection performance. For example, Chernov et al. [5] and Gang et al. [6] employ vision and acoustic data, where the former identified faults on the surface of welds that occur after the metal pipe welding operations, demonstrating the effectiveness of the suggested technology and also minimizing the number of required observations, and the latter used multimodal fusion at the feature level for solid-waste sorting, reporting that the feature-based fusion strategy outperformed the decision-based methodology. When compared to single modality utilization, both studies proved the accuracy enhancement of multimodal data employment.

In contrast, other modalities' cooperation may be studied, such as the Light Detection And Ranging (LiDAR) - camera, where approaches can be very distinct [3,7,8]. In particular, Guo et al. [7] handle bird's eye view of LiDAR point cloud and RGB image, retrieving their features and then fusing them with a deep multi-scale fusion method that combines region features for each input. Alternatively, Xu et al. [3] employ data from 2D pictures and 3D point clouds to detect barriers accurately in 3D in autonomous driving scenarios. The developed framework exploits 2D and 3D segmentation approaches to retrieve semantic information, which is then adaptively fused with an attention-based semantic fusion component and fed to a 3D detector. Furthermore, Gao et al. [8] refer a multi-scale feature merger module that divides the feature representation of multi-modal information utilizing multi-scale convolution and determines the weight of each modal feature channel. Addressing the problem of fusing image and point cloud due to the difference in data structure, they implement the idea of multi-scale convolution and selection kernel.

Many of the studies involving multisensory object detection are directed to autonomous driving problematics, but other fields of application exist, such as healthcare [9] or emotion analysis [10]. Furthermore, more than two modalities can be combined, although the system's complexity tends to increase, as more care must be employed.

In this sense, Roy et al. [1] developed a fusion-based non-image and image inference pipeline to surpass autonomous driving vehicle's visual sensors inability in non-line-of-sight situations. The researchers identified distinct vehicles using seismic, acoustic, radar, and image modalities, and their innovation lies in presenting and experimenting with different fusion approaches that can intelligently determine the most relevant sensors on a case-by-case basis. Results presented show interesting improvements compared to single modality approaches. Similarly, in the work of Mirzaei et al. [2] is introduced a multisensory data fusion approach via acoustics, infrared camera, and marine radar into an avian monitoring system, illustrating the habits of birds and bats in a proposed wind farm construction location. Single-sensor data is processed independently to identify and track targets and acquire their attributes, which are subsequently employed in the fusion process. For the integration of the infrared camera with the radar, a first stage (feature level) fusion occurs, followed by a second stage (decision level) fusion between the infrared camera, radar and acoustics.

3   Multi-agent System

Figure 1 represents the general multi-agent system and how agents interact from data acquisition until the sensor processing combination, in order to obtain relevant conclusions. System's agents are encapsulated as docker containers to represent models and processes that occur at the different stages. Moreover, a docker container is a self-contained and lightweight software package that encompasses all the essential elements required to run an application, such as code, runtime, system tools, system libraries, and configurations. By isolating software from its environment, containers ensure that applications function consistently, regardless of variations between development and staging environments [11].

Starting from the top, the schematic represents just a few of the possible sensory sources that can capture data from the environment, as sensors may be of several other types, for instance: location sensors (e.g. GPS, active badges), pressure sensors (e.g. barometer, pressure gauges), wearable sensors (e.g. accelerometers, gyroscopes, magnetometers), vital sign processing devices (heart rate, temperature), motion sensors (e.g. radar gun, speedometer, mercury switches, tachometer), among many others [12]. These are the primary source of information, and this data is perceived by sensory specific agents (represented in blue), whose responsibility is pre-processing such information, either through validation, standardization, format conversion or others. Then, they redirect data to agents with a specific know-how about that sensory data.

Next, such knowledge base agents (represented in dark blue) act in receiving the processed data and transforming it in knowledge capable of being valuable to a following information merging step. At this transformation stage, data may encompass actions from if-then-else rules or simple characteristics analysis all the way through complex machine learning or deep learning methodologies. It is important that these agents may operate under continuous training conditions by retaining information from the other processing agents that can be useful to enhance their own capabilities, learning to generate more robust judgements [6].

After individual data examination, a knowledge merging agent (represented in green) should proceed in order to correctly join the processed information from all data sources and return a plausible final result. Actions conducted may include an initial data alignment step (through timestamp information, for instance) or consecutive fusion levels between more similar modalities.

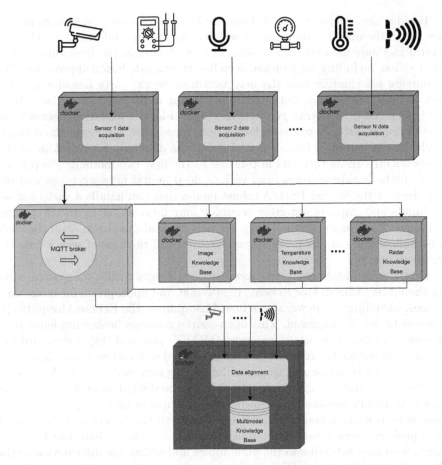

Fig. 1. The overall multi-agent system scheme, from data acquisition to the multimodal knowledge base.

More specifically, the process of multi-sensor data fusion involves the automatic integration of information from different sources to create a comprehensive and useful description of the desired targets. This technique converts raw data obtained from multiple sources into a cohesive set of inferences and its primary advantage is the ability to obtain information that may not be available from a single sensor [2]. Generally, fusion frameworks are based on feature-based and decision-based fusion principles. Feature-based fusion relies on a deep learning approach that automatically assigns higher weights to more relevant modalities during training. In contrast, decision-based fusion involves setting specific rules to prioritize more relevant modalities over others [1].

Just for stating some examples, fusion techniques may range from simple concatenation to more complex algorithms, such as low rank multimodal fusion [1]. The complexity of the intended approach depends on the nature of the problem in hands.

Besides this decision-level and feature-level resolution, researchers are also faced with the question on when (at which stage) to fuse information. There are several methods for multi-modal detection of objects in the literature on computer vision, including early fusion, deep fusion, and late fusion approaches. Prior to putting information into the detection framework, early fusion approaches seek to integrate the raw sensor data, producing a distinct sort of data. To get the best results, this strategy often needs pixel-level correlation between each type of sensor data. In contrast, late fusion approaches aggregate the detection results at the bounding box level after doing the detection for each kind of data independently. In its turn and in contrast to the first two methods, deep fusion-based methods take features from various deep neural network types and then fuse them at the feature level. A robust model that can handle a variety of sensor inputs and improve detection accuracy may be made using the deep fusion technique. Each fusion methodology has benefits and drawbacks, and the choice of technique relies on the particular application and the kind of sensor data that are accessible [3].

Lastly, to maintain communication between agents within the system, a broker should be utilized. Due to being lightweight and appropriate for usage on all devices, including low power single board computers, the Eclipse Mosquitto [13] message broker is suggested. This open-source message broker implements the Message Queuing Telemetry Transport (MQTT) protocol [14], a standard messaging protocol for the Internet of Things (IoT) developed as a very lightweight publish/subscribe messaging transport for linking remote devices with a minimal code footprint and low network bandwidth, thus making it suitable for low power sensors or mobile devices. By following the principle of message publication and topic subscription, numerous clients can link with the broker and subscribe to their preferred topics to either publish or read messages. There can be several clients who may subscribe to the same topics and utilize the information as they please. Essentially, the MQTT broker acts as a universal and uncomplicated interface for all connections [13].

4   Discussion

Upon analyzing the pertinent literature, including the aforementioned related works, it becomes readily apparent that there is a significant similarity between the aforementioned architecture and the general architectural design pursued by the latter. Typically, the majority of studies related to multimodal machine learning object detection involve a process flow that initiates with data acquisition, progresses to information extraction, and culminates with some form of fusion. The overall objective of the study is not important, as this process flow suits autonomous driving problems [1,3,7,8], avian monitoring [2] or even material surface inspection [5].

At the first stage, approaches on data retrieval and its pre-processing are generally similar and simple, with data maps [7], semantic information [3] or, more commonly, feature extraction [1,5]. These behaviors are included among actions performed by sensory specific agents represented in Fig. 1.

Then, this pre-processed information may cross through unimodal machine learning mechanisms in order to retrieve deeper and more conclusive information about the data, which corresponds to practices that can be performed by the previously denominated knowledge base agents.

Finally, the multimodal merging typically arises and it is at this step that researchers are more free to be creative and analyze which approach may be more suitable, as problems may advance through several possible and different approaches. Some perform fusion with all (or almost all) modalities at once [1], others resort to several consecutive fusion levels between modalities that are more analogous [2,5] and it also possible to project own alternatives that seem more suitable [3,7,8].

For the purpose of presenting a possible practical application scenario to the aforementioned system, the work of Roy et al. [1] may be used as a suitable example. As Fig. 2 depicts, a problem related to multi-modality sensing and data fusion for vehicle detection is presented, combining visual data from cameras and non-visual data from seismic, radar and acoustic sensors. In order to recognize multi-vehicle structures, the system employs a two-stage detection technique that first identifies individual cars in each modality individually. Through tests utilizing actual data, the authors illustrate how the suggested system works better than single-modality detection techniques.

Examining Fig. 2, it is believed that an easy association can be established with Fig. 1, as its distinct types of agents are reflected in the example study. Firstly, the multi-domain sensing and preprocessed data tasks represented in the image are closely related to functions inherent to the sensory specific agents. In both cases, raw data is captured from the sensor and preprocessed accordingly to requirements further imposed by knowledge base agents. These last agents see their action be represented by the unimodal networks developed by the authors. In this sense, knowledge networks specialized in each of the sensory sources are developed in the interest of extracting the most information about each modality. Evidently, the input of each network is provided by the sensory specific agents and the output is prepared with the goal of best-suiting the entrance in the fusion network. As for these fusion networks, they undoubtedly illustrate one of the possible approaches delineated for the knowledge merging agent, the last component of Fig. 1. In this example, the authors opted to merge non-image modalities in the first place, inputting the resulting prediction together with image data in a last fusion network, reaching a final vehicle prediction and tracking outcome.

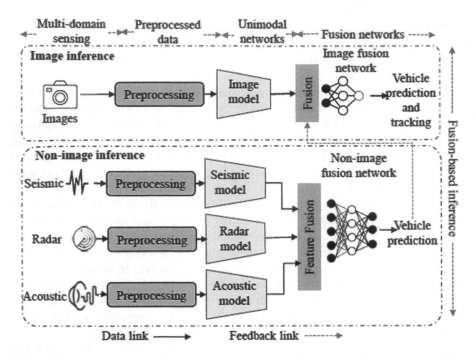

Fig. 2. Illustrative scheme of a practical approach to the proposed architecture. Taken from [1].

5   Conclusion

This article presents in detail the overall architecture of a multi-agent system for multimodality use, highlighting the role of each agent and the communication protocol that may be established between them. This system offers a general approach to multimodal machine learning problems on edge devices for object detection scenarios, illustrating the advantages of multi-agent systems in handling complex and dynamic sensory environments.

It demonstrates a similar process flow that other multimodal machine learning object detection studies may follow, highlighting the importance of data acquisition, pre-processing, and fusion for addressing complex problems. By adopting a comparable architecture, researchers can effectively utilize the knowledge base of previous studies to achieve their objectives while also incorporating their own creative solutions.

The complexity of multimodal data in machine learning issues presents obstacles that cannot be effectively handled by a single-agent system. These concerns are addressed by the suggested multi-agent system. Each agent in the proposed system is in charge of a particular assignment, allowing for effortless coordination and collaboration between them. This promotes scalability and flexibility in response to changing circumstances. The administration and communication inside the system are made easier by the usage of MQTT and Docker containers. Health care, autonomous driving, and emotion analysis are just a few of the areas in which the suggested technology might be used.

As future work, the presented multi-agent system is intended to be tested in practice against different arbitrary object detection scenarios, with different sensory sources and different interactions among agents.

Acknowledgements. This work has been supported by FCT (Fundação para a Ciência e Tecnologia) within the R&D Units Project Scope: UIDB/00319/2020.

References

1. Roy, D., Li, Y., Jian, T., Tian, P., Roy Chowdhury, K., Ioannidis, S.: Multimodality sensing and data fusion for multi-vehicle detection. IEEE Trans. Multimedia **25**, 2280–2295 (2022)
2. Mirzaei, G., Jamali, M.M., Ross, J., Gorsevski, P.V., Bingman, V.P.: Data fusion of acoustics, infrared, and marine radar for avian study. IEEE Sens. J. **15**(11), 6625–6632 (2015)
3. Xu, S., et al.: FusionPainting: multimodal fusion with adaptive attention for 3D object detection. In: 2021 IEEE International Intelligent Transportation Systems Conference (ITSC). IEEE (2021)
4. Liu, L., Ouyang, W., Wang, X., et al.: Deep learning for generic object detection: a survey. Int. J. Comput. Vis. **128**, 261–318 (2020)
5. Chernov, A.V.: Integrated video and acoustic emission data fusion for intelligent decision making in material surface inspection system. Sensors **22**, 8554 (2022)
6. Lu, G., Wang, Y., Xu, H., et al.: Deep multimodal learning for municipal solid waste sorting. Sci. China Technol. Sci. **65**, 324–335 (2022)
7. Guo, R., Li, D., Han, Y.: Deep multi-scale and multi-modal fusion for 3D object detection. Pattern Recogn. Lett. **151**, 236–242 (2021). ISSN 0167–8655
8. Gao, X., Zhang, G., Xiong, Y.: Multi-scale multi-modal fusion for object detection in autonomous driving based on selective kernel. Measurement **194**, 111001 (2022). ISSN 0263–2241
9. Cui, C., et al.: Deep multi-modal fusion of image and non-image data in disease diagnosis and prognosis: a review. Prog. Biomed. Eng. **5**, 022001 (2022)
10. Pandeya, Y.R., Lee, J.: Deep learning-based late fusion of multimodal information for emotion classification of music video. Multimed. Tools Appl. **80**, 2887–2905 (2021)
11. Use containers to Build, Share and Run your applications. https://www.docker.com/resources/what-container/. Accessed 24 Apr 2023
12. Bibri, S.E.: The IoT for smart sustainable cities of the future: an analytical framework for sensor-based big data applications for environmental sustainability. Sustain. Cities Soc. **38**, pp. 230–253 (2018). ISSN 2210–6707
13. Eclipse Mosquitto^{TM} An open source MQTT broker. https://mosquitto.org/. Accessed 18 Apr 2023
14. MQTT: The Standard for IoT Messaging. https://mqtt.org/. Accessed 18 Apr 2023

Biomedical Applicatons

Convolutional Neural Networks for Diabetic Retinopathy Grading from iPhone Fundus Images

Samuel Lozano-Juárez[1]⊙, Nuria Velasco-Pérez[1]⊙, Ian Roberts[2]⊙,
Jerónimo Bernal[2]⊙, Nuño Basurto[1]⊙, Daniel Urda[1](✉)⊙,
and Álvaro Herrero[1]⊙

[1] Grupo de Inteligencia Computacional Aplicada (GICAP),
Departamento de Digitalización, Escuela Politécnica Superior,
Universidad de Burgos, Av. Cantabria s/n, 09006 Burgos, Spain
{sljuarez,nuriavp,nbasurto,durda,ahcosio}@ubu.es
[2] Departamento de Ciencias de la Salud, Facultad de Ciencias de la Salud,
Universidad de Burgos, Paseo Comendadores, s/n, 09001 Burgos, Spain
jejavier@ubu.es

Abstract. Diabetic eye diseases is a major issue in Europe and the
prevalence of visual impairment and blindness caused by Diabetic
Retinopathy (DR) has significantly increased in the last decades. Efficient screening and early diagnose of DR by family physicians would
help to reduce costs in health systems and shorten waiting lists, thus
decreasing patients' emotional stress. In this sense, the use of portable
image devices (e.g., a mobile phone with a specific fundus image capturing device attach to it) combined with AI-based systems arise as a
powerful tool to address this problem. This paper develops 2 well-known
pre-trained Convolutional Neural Networks and fine-tune them on a local
Spanish cohort and 3 more publicly available fundus image dataset for
DR grading. The models trained were evaluated on fundus images captured using an iPhone mobile within the local Spanish cohort. The results
of the analysis showed how in one of the settings tested, one of the models was able to surpass human-level performance achieving an AUC of
0.679 in comparison to an AUC of 0.667 achieved by ophthalmologists
when diagnosing the grade of DR on the same iPhone fundus images,
although further work and improvements need to take place in order to
consider it for a realistic deployment in the daily clinical practice.

Keywords: Diabetic retinopathy · fundus image · deep learning ·
Convolutional Neural Networks · transfer learning · fine-tuning ·
smartphone · screening

1 Introduction and Previous Works

Although the proportion of people with diabetes developing proliferative Diabetic Retinopathy (DR) and severe visual loss has been declining between 1980

P. García Bringas et al. (Eds.): HAIS 2023, LNAI 14001, pp. 685–697, 2023.
https://doi.org/10.1007/978-3-031-40725-3_58

and 2008 in populations with improved diabetes control, the crude prevalence of visual impairment and blindness caused by DR increased substantially between 1990 and 2015 [7]. It has been estimated that the number of people with diabetes affected by any diabetic eye disease in Europe will increase from 6.4 million in 2019 to 8.6 million in 2050 [18].

Diabetic retinopathy can be effectively screened for and identified early in the disease course. Thus, some countries such as UK and USA have implemented national DR screening programs. Other organizations have developed guidelines for DR screening, referral, and follow-up. Screening for DR is necessary to detect referable cases. With effective treatments, the progression of DR can be slowed and vision preserved. The International Diabetes Federation estimates that there are 463 million adults aged 20 to 79 years with diabetes mellitus worldwide [14], and this number is projected to increase to 642 million by 2040 [21]. It is understood that there are not enough ophthalmologists to examine such a large amount of patients.

Therefore, telemedicine-based on digital retinal images in the primary care setting, electronically stored and sent to an ophthalmologist for analysis, is being increasingly used for DR screening [26]. Besides, these telemedicine pathways reduce, for certain cases, the long waiting lists to which patients may be subjected before being assessed by specialists, with the consequent emotional stress. Dispite those developments, a substantial proportion of patients with diabetes remain unscreened. For instance, 40% of patients with diabetes mellitus in the United States, or 38% in Canada, are not annually screened for diabetic retinopathy [3,22]. The use of portable imaging devices [5] and automated computer systems based on Artificial Intelligence (AI) are changing screening strategies and are improving the cost-effectiveness of screening. It was estimated that maximizing the cost-effectiveness of DR screening would save $1 billion over 20 years, compared with routine annual screening in type 1 diabetes in the USA [9].

In this sense, a significant increase in the number of publications related to the application of AI in the field of medicine has been observed in the last years with an increase of 84.6% between 2008 and 2018 [27]. This is partly attributed to the overall increase in the scope of this systems [24] covering various clinical fields such as radiography [1], or cardiology [15]. Additionally, the use of AI in diagnosis or surgery has also increased [28]. An example of AI's diagnostic capabilities is demonstrated in the detection of fractures [17], where, thanks to creating a large dataset, a Risk Prediction Model was developed able to detect heterogeneity in the data and the type of fractures that had occurred, and achieving a sensitivity of 91%. Within the AI field, Deep Learning (DL) aims to implement optimal neural network-based models for a specific problem based on a large amount of data. DL has also been widely used in medicine in recent years [23] replacing the use of classic neural networks. Specifically, in computer vision-related tasks, where the goal is to classify or identify a desired element using input images, some DL models have already been developed to reach human-level performance rates, provided that sufficient input information is available [6]. This kind of DL model has been applied to the problem of DR grading [11] with significant advances and achieving results above 90% on widely used metrics such as the AUC.

This paper presents the use of DL techniques for the classification of DR. The novelty of this study is linked to the image acquisition process and the images used to train DL models and make predictions in new unseen images. For this purpose, the use of a mobile phone camera was employed, specifically an iPhone, in contrast to previous works where images obtained through an Optical Coherence Tomography (OCT) are typically used. This work aims at reducing the costs associated with the use of an OCT and establishing an early diagnosis, thereby saving waiting time for patients. Convolutional neural networks (CNNs), particularly ResNet models which have been widely used in various clinical fields [8], are developed and fine-tuned in this work using transfer learning, which provides a foundation for experimentation. These CNNs models are trained using several DR-related datasets, allowing for more efficient training and expecting to improve the performance of these networks for this specific problem.

Overall, the main goals and contributions of this paper are next summarized:

- Explore and employ existing fundus image cohorts together with our local Spanish cohort in order to develop DL-based classification models.
- Use transfer learning to develop highly accurate models based on well-known pre-trained convolutional neural network architectures.
- Develop training optimization strategies to help models achieve higher accuracy.
- Obtain a final model which outperforms clinicians when grading diabetic retinopathy from iPhone fundus images.

The rest of the paper is organized as follows. Section 2 describes both the local Spanish cohort and other fundus image cohorts publicly available that have been used in this work to train and validate the developed models. The methods and experimental design used in this work are covered in Sect. 3. Next, the results obtained in the analysis carried out are included in Sect. 4. Finally, Sect. 5 shows some conclusions derived from this work and points out some future work in this research line.

2   Datasets

This section describes the main characteristics of the local Spanish cohort used in this work both to train DL-based models and as a reference to test the performance of the models that are going to be developed. Besides, some other publicly available fundus image cohorts are also described and jointly employed with this local Spanish one to increase the size of the dataset used to train the models.

2.1   Local Spanish Cohort

A set of patients attending the diabetes and ophthalmology sections of the "Hospital Universitario de Burgos", in Spain, were included to participate voluntarily in this study after signing an informed consent. The inclusion criteria considered

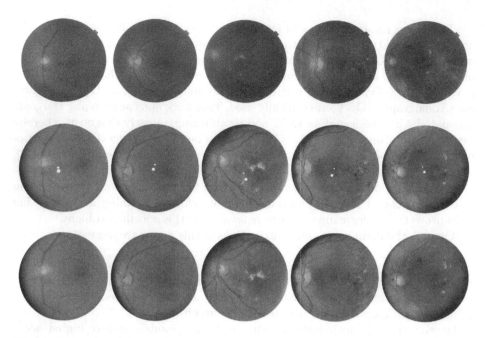

Fig. 1. Overview of fundus images of the same left eye obtained using an OCT (first row), an iPhone (second row) and an inpainted version of the iPhone ones removing the artificial white noise (third row). Columns correspond to the different DR grading (from no DR or grade 0, to proliferative DR or grade 4).

>18 years diabetic patients with no contraindication for pharmacological mydriasis, and no known allergy to tropicamide or phenylephrine eye drops. For each patient, two ophthalmologists independently diagnosed the grade of DR (from no DR or grade 0 to proliferative DR or grade 4) based on images obtained by an OCT and an iPhone 11 Pro mobile phone. The former is DRI OCT Triton which provides a true color fundus image (in white light, with 24-bit color), a photography angle 45°, equivalent to 30° (digital zoom), and a photographable pupil diameter of 2.5 mm or more, being the gold standard for this cohort in this study. The latter is a high-quality mobile phone to which a universal fundus image-capturing device named Ret-iN CaM[1] is attached.

Initially, 176 and 171 fundus images obtained through an OCT and the iPhone mobile, respectively, were available in this cohort. Since images were also labeled according to the quality of the image, in this study only good or very good (i.e., $quality = 4$ or $quality = 5$) were employed to develop DL-based methods to address the problem under study. Consequently, the number of fundus images available in this cohort is reduced to 113 OCT images and 99 iPhone images. For the latter, these images correspond to patients who are also evaluated using fundus images obtained through an OCT, i.e., the 113 OCT images

---

[1] Available at: https://apps.apple.com/es/app/ret-in-cam/id1509765945.

will include the equivalent fundus images for those patients evaluated using an iPhone. For each patient, the following labels are available:

- OCT-based diagnosis: DR grading by the two ophthalmologists and, in case of mismatch, the worst diagnosis. This is the gold standard, i.e., it is the reference of how good experts can do it nowadays using high-quality OCT fundus images.
- iPhone-based diagnosis: identical labelling procedure to the previous one, although in this case, it corresponds to the baseline in this work which could indicate the experts-level performance on grading DR based on iPhone fundus images.

2.2 Other Fundus Image Cohorts

Due to the low number of images that are available in the local Spanish cohort described in the previous section, and taking into account that ML-/DL-based models typically require hundreds or thousands of samples to develop models that perform accurately in new unseen data, other public and well-known fundus image cohorts have been explored and used in this work to train the proposed models. These cohorts and their main characteristics are next described:

- Kaggle dataset[2]. It is a collection of 32926 high-resolution color fundus images of the retina used for detecting DR. It includes images from both diabetic and non-diabetic patients, with varying degrees of severity of diabetic retinopathy. The dataset is labeled with categorical labels indicating the presence and severity of diabetic retinopathy, ranging from no diabetic retinopathy (grade 0) to proliferative diabetic retinopathy (grade 4). This dataset is commonly used for developing and evaluating ML algorithms for automated detection of diabetic retinopathy, which can aid in early diagnosis and treatment of this sight-threatening condition [25].
- DeepDRiD[3]. It is a collection of 2000 retinal images specifically curated for the task of diabetic retinopathy detection obtained from diabetic patients using different imaging modalities and devices. Accordingly, to the Kaggle dataset, DeepDRiD is labeled with categorical labels ranging from absence of diabetic retinopathy (grade 0) to proliferative stages (grade 4). In addition to the retinal images, the DeepDRiD dataset also includes other relevant information such as patient demographics, image acquisition details, and annotations for retinal lesions. This dataset is also widely used in research for developing and evaluating ML algorithms for automated detection and grading of diabetic retinopathy, with the goal of improving early detection and management of this vision-threatening complication in diabetics patients [19].

---

[2] Available at: https://www.kaggle.com/competitions/diabetic-retinopathy-detectio n/overview.
[3] Available at: https://github.com/deepdrdoc/DeepDRiD.

- Zenodo dataset[4]. It is a collection of 1437 color fundus images collected by the Department of Ophthalmology of the Hospital de Clínicas in Paraguay. Images were acquired through the Visucam 500 camera of the Zeiss brand and labeled by expert ophtalmologists into seven different categories. These labels were mapped to the ones used in our local Spanish cohort and to the ones present in the Kaggle and DeepDRiD datasets as follows: category 1 (no DR signs) is mapped to grade 0; category 2 (mild or early non-proliferative DR) is mapped to grade 1; category 3 (moderate non-proliferative DR) is mapped to grade 2; categories 4 and 5 (severe and very severe non-proliferative DR) are mapped to grade 3; and categories 6 and 7 (proliferative and advanced proliferative DR) are mapped to grade 4. Similarly to the previous datasets, this one is also employed in research to develop and evaluate ML algorithms aiming at accurately predicting DR from fundus images [20].

Finally, Table 1 summarizes the size of each dataset used in this work to develop ML-/DL-based solutions, as well as the class distribution both individually within each dataset and overall considering all datasets together, which clearly depicts a highly imbalanced classification problem.

Table 1. Datasets considered in this work with their corresponding total number of images and class distribution.

Dataset	Grade 0 (No DR)	Grade 1 (Mild)	Grade 2 (Moderate)	Grade 3 (Severe)	Grade 4 (Proliferative DR)	Total
OCT	25	20	58	4	6	113
iPhone	22	13	48	8	8	99
Kaggle	23610	2443	5292	873	708	32926
DeepDRiD	914	222	398	354	112	2000
Zenodo	711	6	110	349	261	1437
Total	25282	2704	5906	1588	1095	36575
%	69.12	7.39	16.15	4.34	3.00	

3   Methods and Experimentation

This section describes the DL methods and techniques used in this work to develop an accurate model for diabetic retinopathy grading from fundus images obtained through an iPhone mobile. Furthermore, details concerning the experimental design are also provided within this section.

---

[4] Available at: https://zenodo.org/record/4891308#.ZEaOEHZByUn.

3.1   Methods

Convolutional neural networks (CNNs) [10] have emerged as a powerful tool for object detection and image analysis-related tasks. With the availability of larger datasets, the performance of CNNs has significantly improved, enabling the development of automatic, non-assisted systems with lots of applications in different fields. In the field of medical imaging, where technical limitations of images can pose challenges for clinicians expertise, CNNs have become a promising tool in assisting with early-stage screening and diagnostics [2]. The goal of this study is to leverage the power of deep learning models, particularly CNNs architectures, and transfer learning techniques [16] to aid clinicians in the detection and classification of diabetic retinopathy from fundus images obtained with an iPhone mobile.

For this purpose, the analysis carried out in this work focuses on the local Spanish cohort described in Sect. 2.1, where the gold standard is the diagnostic of DR given by clinicians using OCT images. In this scenario, authors propose to analyze the benefits of fine-tuning two well-known pre-trained CNNs architectures on images of all datasets described in Sect. 2 for DR grading the 99 iPhone fundus images and compare their performance against a baseline diagnostic. Next, the baseline and CNNs methods employed in this work are described.

- Baseline. It corresponds to clinicians diagnostic of DR from fundus images captured by an iPhone mobile, which could be assumed as the human-level performance that we would like to reach, or ideally surpass, by using DL-based methods in this complex classification task.
- ResNet50V2. It belongs to the family of ResNet (Residual Network) models and its CNN architecture is based on residual blocks, which allow for the training of very deep neural networks. It consists of 50 layers, including convolutional, pooling, and fully connected layers. The key innovation of ResNet50V2 is the use of skip connections or "identity mapping" that allow the network to learn residual functions, which represent the difference between the input and output of a given layer. These residual functions are then added back to the original input, effectively "skipping" over a layer, and passed through activation functions to introduce non-linearity. This helps to mitigate the vanishing gradient problem and allows for more efficient and accurate training of deep neural networks [13]. ResNet50V2 is pre-trained on large image datasets, such as ImageNet, which enables it to capture general features from images and perform well on a wide range of computer vision tasks, such as image classification, object detection, and image segmentation.
- ResNet152. It is a highly advanced and deep CNN architecture that builds upon the ResNet50V2 model and consists of 152 layers. Due to the higher number of layers and parameters, this CNN architecture has a higher capacity than the previous one in order to learn more intricate patterns and representations from data. This increased capacity can enable the model to capture finer details and nuances in images, which can be particularly beneficial in tasks that demand fine-grained discrimination [12]. Similarly to its predeces-

sor, ResNet152 is also pre-trained on large image datasets and is available for fine-tuning and specialization in specific image-based tasks.

The baseline in this work does not require any kind of model implementation, since labels assigned by clinicians to the 99 iPhone images are already available in the local Spanish cohort, and similar labels are also present for the gold standard (i.e., using OCT images). Therefore, a performance metric can easily be computed to assess human performance in the task of DR grading from fundus images captured using an iPhone mobile. On the other hand, transfer learning is used in this work to train the two CNN architectures considered in the analysis, thus a pre-trained architecture is loaded as a starting point and further trained through fine-tuning using all images described in Sect. 2. For this purpose, the Keras deep learning API [4] has been used which easily allows to train and test different CNN architectures.

3.2 Experimentation

Some relevant aspects of the experimental design used in this work are next described:

– Image preprocessing. Original input images are resized and normalized according to the characteristics of the input images required by each ResNet CNN model considered in this study. In this sense, original images of size 1649×1248 pixels are resized and normalized using the built-in Keras pre-processing functions associated with each ResNet model, which ensures that the input size matches the one required by the network, as well as assures that pixels within each image are normalized according to the image distribution of the dataset used to pre-train these models (typically the ImageNet dataset). Furthermore, fundus images obtained using an iPhone mobile within the local Spanish cohort were preprocessed by an in-painting technique in order to remove some artificial white noise produced by the flashlight of the camera. The applied in-painting technique consists of a multi-step process. First, the mask corresponding to the points of light of the flash was generated. For this purpose, the HoughCircles function of the OpenCV package[5] was applied to the image previously converted to black and white and blurred. Of all the circles detected by this function, only those whose radius was no greater than 1/53 of the width of the image and which were located in the centre of the image were selected for the mask. Once the mask was obtained, a biharmonic in-painting was performed using the function included in the inpaint module of the Scikit-image collection[6].
– Training optimization. Due to the imbalance of the classes distribution (i.e., number of images available per grade of DR) and the different sizes of the

---

[5] Available at: https://docs.opencv.org/4.x/dd/d1a/group__imgproc__feature.html#ga47849c3be0d0406ad3ca45db65a25d2d.
[6] Available at: https://scikit-image.org/docs/stable/api/skimage.restoration.html#skimage.restoration.inpaint_biharmonic.

datasets considered to train the DL methods proposed, authors implemented a strategy that ensures that each batch of images used to adjust the parameters of the models is balanced both in the class and the dataset it belongs to. Thus, on each batch, the network would equally see the same amount of images corresponding to different grades of DR and different cohorts, with the hope of avoiding possible over-fitting issues which may turn out in models learning the over-represented class within the data. During the training process, hyper-parameters were set to the following values: the Adam optimizer was used with a learning rate of 0.001 and the categorical cross-entropy function was the loss function employed to optimize the loss/accuracy. Besides, batches of 80 images were used to train the DL models through a maximum number of 200 epochs, with an early-stopping strategy which stops the training process if there is no improvement of the accuracy over a validation set after 10 epochs.

- Evaluation strategy. This work trains and evaluates both CNN architectures described in the previous section by using a 5-fold stratified cross-validation strategy in which all images of the datasets included in Sect. 2 (i.e., 36575 fundus images) are split into 5 disjoint folds of equal sizes, ensuring that both classes and image dataset origin distributions are kept within each fold. This strategy trains both CNN architectures in 4 out of the 5 folds (known as the training set) and evaluates the trained model on the left out fold (known as the testing set). In particular, trained models are evaluated on images of the testing set which were captured using an iPhone mobile, ignoring the remaining ones that are out of interest in this study. To guarantee the randomness of the images employed to train and evaluate the models and avoid a possible bias-motivated by this selection, this procedure is repeated 5 times by rotating the folds used to form the training and testing sets.
- Performance metric. This work utilizes the Area Under the receiver operating characteristic Curve (AUC) to evaluate the goodness of the proposed methods, which is a quantitative measure suitable for imbalanced classification problems that compare the evolution of the true positive rate versus the false positive rate for different values of the classifying threshold. Then, an AUC value close to 0.5 would depict a random classifier while an AUC value close to 1 would reflect a very good one.

4 Results

This section presents and analyzes the results obtained by the DL models considered in this work, the ResNet50v2 and ResNet152 networks, under different settings which accounts for image pre-processing and batch balancing, thus resulting in four possible combinations: none of these two, only one, the other (previously unselected), and lastly, both at the same time. This information is presented in Table 2, where the selected settings for that particular execution are marked with a "X" and with a "-" otherwise.

To provide a reference for the objective to be improved in our experimentation, a "Baseline" column has been added. This value remains the same for any

Table 2. Average AUC performance results of the models tested for the different settings.

Balanced batch	In-painting	Baseline	ResNet50V2	ResNet152
-	-	0.667	0.608	0.632
-	X	0.667	0.610	0.665
X	-	0.667	0.666	0.639
X	X	0.667	0.679	0.645

combination of the adjustments as it is the human-level performance achieved by the ophthalmologists when grading DR using iPhone fundus images in comparison to the gold standard, as mentioned in Sects. 2.1 and 3.1.

The values obtained in the executions where no type of adjustment is used yield fairly low results in both ResNet models, remaining at best three-tenths below the Baseline, with ResNet152 achieving better results. In the first execution with one setting, shown in the table, only in-painting was used, where again ResNet152 reaches quite high values but in this case practically the same as the Baseline, although ResNet50v2 shows a slight and inconsequential improvement. In the third adjustment, a clear performance change can be observed between both DL models. There is a substantial improvement in ResNet50v2, where the value practically reaches the Baseline, while there is a decrease in the AUC value for ResNet152, indicating that this setting primarily benefits the former.

Lastly, the last setting made, which combines both techniques, yields a very good value for the first network, although the second one does not achieve the values of the second adjustment, clearly indicating that Batch Balancing performs worse. The value achieved by ResNet50v2 is not just a slight improvement but surpasses the baseline by more than a tenth.

Regarding the executions, ResNet152 clearly achieves more stable values throughout all executions, where Batch Balancing penalizes the network's performance, and in-painting achieves very good values. On the other hand, metrics have been increasing throughout the settings forResNet50v2, with the use of Batch Balancing standing out very clearly, achieving values superior to the established baseline.

Finally, Fig. 2 shows the confusion matrix of the best-performing model in all the settings analyzed (i.e., ResNet50v2 achieving an AUC of 0.679). It displays the five classes, ranging from grades 0 to 4, and shows the network's tendency to classify the majority class, i.e., grade 2. The classification of grade 2 is quite good, while the classification for grades 0, 1, and 4 is somewhat residual. On the other hand, the network is unable to perform a good classification of grade 3, establishing no well-classified values for it. Although the results of this best-performing network are promising compared to how expert clinicians are diagnosing these same patients using iPhone fundus images, the current model needs further improvement to be deployed in the daily clinical practice in healthcare

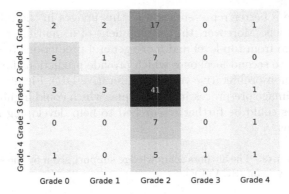

Fig. 2. Confusion matrix showing the true and predicted labels of the CNN with better performance (ResNet50V2 using a balanced batch and in-painted iPhone images).

centers. To this end, it is essential to collect many more fundus images of the local Spanish cohort, both OCT and iPhone ones.

5   Conclusions

This paper has presented a DL-based approach to address the problem of DR grading based on fundus images. In contrast to other previous approaches, this work has implemented a DL approach that predicts the grade of DR, using images obtained through an iPhone mobile rather than through an OCT. In this sense, this approach builds upon the telemedicine pathway. The performance of 2 CNNs has been compared to a baseline procedure that corresponds to the human-level performance where ophthalmologists have individually diagnosed the grade of DR within the same images.

The analysis carried out in this work has shown how DL-based approaches can outperform a human-based diagnosis, although further work and improvements need to take place in order to consider it for a realistic deployment in the daily clinical practice. Particularly, the results showed the benefits of using the batch balancing strategy together with the in-painted version of the iPhone images where the flashlight noise is removed, allowing to get a CNN model (ResNet50V2) that achieved an AUC of 0.679 (human-level performance: AUC of 0.667 over the same set of images).

Although positive outcomes have been obtained, there is still much more work that could be done to obtain better and more accurate predictors. In this sense, other mobile devices based on the Android system could be explored to analyze whether Android-based devices provide higher-quality images for the same task due to the existing differences in hardware (camera features) and software (image capturing and processing) with iPhone devices. In parallel, more fundus images captured using an OCT or mobile devices in the local Spanish cohort should be collected, in combination to the application of data augmentation techniques, in order to have a better representation of this images in the full dataset used to train the models. Moreover, the development of a multilayer solution could be explored to go from top-level and more general predictions (e.g., presence or absence of DR), to second-level ones which provide predictions for more detailed outcomes (e.g., non-proliferative versus proliferative DR). Finally, implementing some advanced image pre-processing techniques which could highlight important details in images could be further researched to help developing more powerful AI-based systems.

Acknowledgements. The authors acknowledge support given by the supercomputing center in Castilla y León (SCAYLE).

References

1. Akudjedu, T.N., Torre, S., Khine, R., Katsifarakis, D., Newman, D., Malamate-niou, C.: Knowledge, perceptions, and expectations of artificial intelligence in radiography practice: a global radiography workforce survey. J. Med. Imaging Radiat. Sci. **54**(1), 104–116 (2023)
2. Anwar, S.M., Majid, M., Qayyum, A., Awais, M., Alnowami, M., Khan, M.K.: Medical image analysis using convolutional neural networks: a review. J. Med. Syst. **42**, 1–13 (2018)
3. Boucher, M.C., et al.: Teleophthalmology screening for diabetic retinopathy through mobile imaging units within Canada. Can. J. Ophthalmol. **43**(6), 658–668 (2008)
4. Chollet, F., et al.: Keras (2015). https://keras.io
5. Constable, I., Yogesan, K., Eikelboom, R., Barry, C., Cuypers, M.: Fred hollows lecture: digital screening for eye disease. Clin. Exp. Ophthalmol. **28**(3), 129–132 (2000)
6. Esteva, A., et al.: Deep learning-enabled medical computer vision. NPJ Digit. Med. **4**(1), 1–9 (2021)
7. Flaxman, S.R., et al.: Global causes of blindness and distance vision impairment 1990–2020: a systematic review and meta-analysis. Lancet Glob. Health **5**(12), e1221–e1234 (2017)
8. Gonçalves, C.B., Souza, J.R., Fernandes, H.: CNN architecture optimization using bio-inspired algorithms for breast cancer detection in infrared images. Comput. Biol. Med. **142**, 105205 (2022)
9. Group, D.R.: Frequency of evidence-based screening for retinopathy in type 1 diabetes. N. Engl. J. Med. **376**(16), 1507–1516 (2017)
10. Gu, J., et al.: Recent advances in convolutional neural networks. Pattern Recognit. **77**, 354–377 (2018)
11. Gulshan, V., et al.: Development and validation of a deep learning algorithm for detection of diabetic retinopathy in retinal fundus photographs. JAMA **316**, 2402–2410 (2016)
12. He, K., Zhang, X., Ren, S., Sun, J.: Deep residual learning for image recognition. In: Proceedings of the IEEE Conference on Computer Vision and Pattern Recognition, pp. 770–778 (2016)
13. He, K., Zhang, X., Ren, S., Sun, J.: Identity mappings in deep residual networks. CoRR abs/1603.05027 (2016)

14. International Diabetes Federation: IDF diabetes atlas 2019 (2019). https://www.diabetesatlas.org/en/. Accessed 2 Mar 2020
15. Karatzia, L., Aung, N., Aksentijevic, D.: Artificial intelligence in cardiology: hope for the future and power for the present. Front. Cardiovasc. Med. **9** (2022)
16. Krishna, S.T., Kalluri, H.K.: Deep learning and transfer learning approaches for image classification. Int. J. Recent Technol. Eng. (IJRTE) **7**(5S4), 427–432 (2019)
17. Kuo, R.Y., et al.: Artificial intelligence in fracture detection: a systematic review and meta-analysis. Radiology **304**(1), 50–62 (2022). pMID: 35348381
18. Li, J.Q., et al.: Prevalence, incidence and future projection of diabetic eye disease in Europe: a systematic review and meta-analysis. Eur. J. Epidemiol. **35**, 11–23 (2020)
19. Liu, H., Teng, L., Fan, L., Sun, Y., Li, H.: A new ultra-wide-field fundus dataset to diabetic retinopathy grading using hybrid preprocessing methods. Comput. Biol. Med. **157**, 106750 (2023)
20. Mujeeb Rahman, K., Nasor, M., Imran, A.: Automatic screening of diabetic retinopathy using fundus images and machine learning algorithms. Diagnostics **12**(9), 2262 (2022)
21. Ogurtsova, K., et al.: IDF diabetes atlas: global estimates for the prevalence of diabetes for 2015 and 2040. Diabetes Res. Clin. Pract. **128**, 40–50 (2017)
22. of Ophthalmology, A.A.: Diabetic retinopathy ppp - updated 2017. https://www.aao.org/preferred-practice-pattern/diabetic-retinopathy-ppp-updated-2017. Accessed 22 Jan 2020
23. Piccialli, F., Somma, V.D., Giampaolo, F., Cuomo, S., Fortino, G.: A survey on deep learning in medicine: why, how and when? Inf. Fusion **66**, 111–137 (2021)
24. Pranav, R., Emma, C., Oishi, B., J., T.E.: AI in health and medicine. Nat. Med. **28**, 31–38 (2022)
25. Qin, X., Chen, D., Zhan, Y., Yin, D.: Classification of diabetic retinopathy based on improved deep forest model. Biomed. Signal Process. Control **79**, 104020 (2023)
26. Shi, L., Wu, H., Dong, J., Jiang, K., Lu, X., Shi, J.: Telemedicine for detecting diabetic retinopathy: a systematic review and meta-analysis. Br. J. Ophthalmol. **99**(6), 823–831 (2015)
27. Tran, B.X., et al.: Global evolution of research in artificial intelligence in health and medicine: a bibliometric study. J. Clin. Med. **8**(3), 360 (2019)
28. Yiming, Z., Ying, W., Jonathan, L.: Applications of explainable artificial intelligence in diagnosis and surgery. Diagnostics **12**, 237 (2022)

Risk Factors and Survival After Premature Hospital Readmission in Frail Subjects with Delirium

Guillermo Cano-Escalera[1,2], Manuel Grana[1,2]([✉]), and Ariadna Besga[3,4]

[1] Department of Computer Science and Artificial Intelligence,
Faculty of Computer Science, University of the Basque Country (UPV/EHU),
Paseo Manuel de Lardizabal, 1, 20018 Donostia-San Sebastian, Spain
[2] Computational Intelligence Group, University of the Basque Country (UPV/EHU),
Donostia-San Sebastian, Spain
ccpgrrom@ei.ehu.eus
[3] Department of Psychiatry, Hospital Universitario de Araba, Vitoria, Spain
[4] Biomedical Research Centre in Mental Health Network (CIBERSAM) G10,
Madrid, Spain

Abstract. In this study we assess the mortality risk after 6 months, 1 year, and 2 years of follow-up in a sample of frail patients diagnosed with delirium who had been readmitted to hospital before 30 days after discharge (premature readmission). We compute Kaplan Meier estimates of survival probability functions at the selected censoring times for the premature readmission cohort versus the non-premature readmission cohort. Addtionally, we compute Independent Samples T-Test, Logistic Regression, Random Forest and Boosting Classification to indetify significant risk factors for premature hospital readmission. We find that premature hospital readmission is associated with increased mortality at 6 months, 1 year, and 2 years. The study identifies as high risk factor for premature hospital readmission the following ones: suffering congestive heart failure (CHF), diabetes, the use of anti-arrhythmic and antidepressant drugs as well as variables that are indicators of frailty such as older age, low weight, male sex, polypharmacy, lack of balance, weight loss measured through calf circumference, and high dependency to perform activities of daily living are indicative of higher risk of premature hospital readmission.

Keywords: Frailty · Delirium · Premature hospital readmision · Survival

1 Introduction

Premature hospital readmission is the hospital readmission before 30 days have elapsed since the hospital discharge. It is a strong indicator of quality of attention and performance of the health care system [2–5]. The aims of this paper are twofold. Fistluy, to identify risk factors of premature readmission in a cohort of patients recruited at the Hospital Universitario de Alava. Those patients were diagnosed with delirium and some degree of frailty. Secondly, to assess their mortality risk after 6 months, 1 year and 2 years of follow-up. Due to its high prevalence and harmful effects, systematic identification of cases is key to good clinical practice, prevention and appropriate treatment of delirium and frailty. Delirium and frailty have been related in some studies but there is little evidence to demonstrate the relationship between frailty, delirium and short-term hospital readmissions.

Frailty is a medical condition characterized by the reduction of homeostatic reserves, exposing the individual to higher vulnerability to stressors and risk of negative health-related outcomes. Over the past decades, a progressive aging of the population has been observed. This demographic phenomenon is substantially responsible for the growing prevalence of frailty in our societies. Frailty is a clinical condition characterized by an excessive vulnerability of the individual to endogenous and exogenous stressors that generates a high risk of developing negative health-related events [38].

Delirium, aka acute confusional syndrome (ACS), is a neurocognitive disorder of complex aetiology, often under-diagnosed, that affects the cognitive functionality of the subject [42], being the second more prevalent psychiatric syndrome in the hospital setting [36]. The causes of delirium are multifactorial and include patient vulnerability factors such as dementia or cognitive impairment, medical comorbidity, malnutrition and potentially modifiable precipitating factors such as infections, dehydration, polypharmacy and surgery [19]. The prevalence of delirium at the end of life approaches 85% in palliative care settings [27].

In this paper, we deal with a cohort of frail patients suffering delirium at the time of hospital admission or during hospital stay. We aim to assess the insceased risk of death for those patients in the cohort that have a premature hospital readmission by means of survival analysis. Also, we consider the risk factors in this cohort leading to premature hospital admission. Risk factors are identified by means of logistric regresssion and by means of variable importance in random forest classification experiments.

2   Materials and Methods

2.1   Study Design and Subjects

Recruitment process [8] is as follows: The patients were admitted to the services of internal medicine and neurology at the University Hospital of Alava (UHA). Delirium was assessed by the Confusion Assessment Method (CAM) [26] at hospital admission in subjects with suspected delirium, while frailty was assessed by means of the Fried's frailty index (FFI) [18] during the hospital stay. Patient recruitment was implemented in the period from September 2017 to September 2018. Mortality follow-up until January 2021 was performed by querying the institutional EHR. Non-survivors were defined as all persons known to have died during the two-year follow-up period [9]. Following open science practices, the anonymized dataset has been preliminarily published in the Zenodo public repository [23]. In this paper we consider a cohort of 148 patients who were considered frail and who were diagnosed with delirium either at admittance of during their hospital stay.

To assess the functional status of the patient, the following tests were applied: Short Physical Performance Battery (SPPB), Fried's frailty index (FFI), and Barthel's index score (BIS) [33] that measures performance in activities of daily living. The SPPB [24] includes 3 tests: balance test, walking speed over 4 m, and sitting and stand up five times. FFI [18] defines frailty phenotype characterized by involuntary weight loss, fatigue, muscular weakness, slow march, and decay of physical activity.

Nutritional status was also assessed using the Mini Nutritional Assessment— Short Form (MNA-SF)—as a mean to identify older subjects at risk of malnutrition before the apparition of severe changes in weight or serum or protein concentrations [29,49]. The Pfeiffer's Brief Screening Test for Dementia (PBSTD) [15,37] was applied for mental condition assessment.

Experienced members of the research team (AB, GC) accessed the electronic health records (EHR) to extract sociodemographic data, survival data, clinical data such as comorbidities, and pharmacological information. Altogether, more than 300 variables were recorded for each patient.

2.2 Statistical Methods

The Jasp package (https://jasp-stats.org) has been used for variable selection and machine learning algorithm application. Selection of statistically significant variables ($p < 0.05$) in this cohort regarding premature hospital admission was carried out first by univariate Independent Samples T-Test. Over the selected variables, a further significant variable ($p < 0.05$) selection was carried out applying multivariate Logistic Regression predicting the premature hospital readmittance. Random Forest and Boosting Classification classification experiments predicting the premature hospital readmittance with ten repetitions of hold-out cross-validation were also performed. Variable relevance ranking was assessed from the out-of-bag accuracy estimation in each repetition. After the 10 repetitions, variables are ranked by the number of times that a variable appears among the top ten relevant variables.

For survival analysis, we used Rstudio 1.2 and R 3.6.3 (www.r-project.org, accessed on 1 March 2022) with packages HSAUR2, Survival, and Survminer. We computed the Kaplan-Meier estimate of the survival function and its variance [6,16,40] at 6 months, 1 year and 2 years censoring date.

3   Results

Figure 1 compares the survival probability Kaplan–Meier estimates of the premature readmission cohort versus the non-premature readmission cohort at 6

Table 1. Significant variables ($p < 0.05$) found by Independent Samples t-Test. CHF = Congestive heart failure

Variable	t	df	p
Barthel	2.001	144	0.047
CHF	−2.217	146	0.028
Arrhythmia	−2.518	146	0.013
Digoxin	−2.295	146	0.023
Ophthalmus	−2.444	146	0.016

Note: Student's t-test.

Table 2. Significant variables ($p < 0.05$) identified by multivariate Logistic Regression. CHF = Congestive heart failure

	Estimate	Standard Error	Standardized	Odds Ratio	z	Wald Statistic	df	p	95% CI
Barthel	−0.453	0.287	0.636	−1.581	1.581	2.500	1	0.114	(−1.015,0.109)
CHF	0.937	0.431	2.552	2.172	2.172	4.716	1	0.030	(0.091,1.782)
Arrhythmia	0.689	0.559	1.991	1.232	1.232	1.517	1	0.218	(−0.407,1.784)
Digoxin	0.679	0.750	1.972	0.906	0.906	0.820	1	0.365	(−0.791,2.149)
Ophthalmus	1.211	0.540	3.357	2.243	2.243	5.032	1	0.025	(0.153,2.269)

Note: CI—Confidence Interval.
AUC: 0.732

Table 3. Classification performance results averaged over 10 repetitions of hold-out validation: average (standard deviation)

	Test Accuracy	F1 Score
Random Forest	0,808 (0,045)	0,737 (0,064)
Boosting Classification	0,813 (0,084)	0,805 (0,090)

Table 4. Variable importance identified by Random Forest and Boosting Classification measured as the number of times (NT) that the variable appears in the 10 top in the validation and testing repetitions

Random Forest		Boosting Classification	
Variable	NT	Variable	NT
Age	6	Congestiveheartfailure	8
Anticoagulated	5	Arrhythmics	5
Arrhythmics	5	Age	4
Arrhythmia	4	Antidepressant	4
Congestiveheartfailure	4	Arrhythmia	4
Diabetes	4	MNACalfcircumference	4
Drugs	4	SPPBBalance	4
Gender	4		

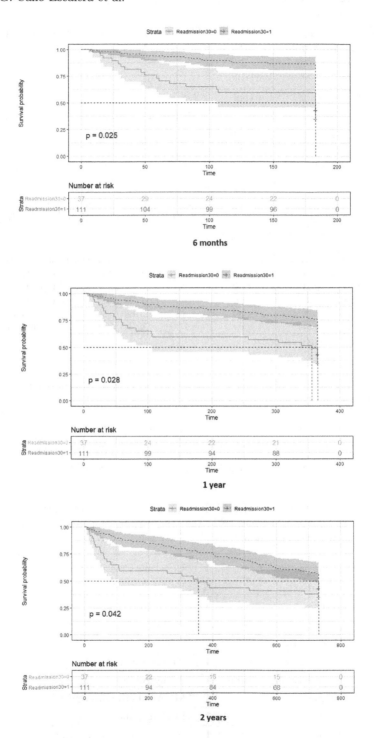

Fig. 1. Kaplan Meier survival curves for patients re-admitted to hospital after 30 days. Data is censored after 6 months.

months, 1 year and 2 years censoring times. Increased mortality in the premature readmission was statistically significant ($p < 0.05$) at the three censoring times.

Due to the large number of variables, applying multivariate Logistic Regression over all of them was unfeasible. Therefore, we first carried out a variable selection based on Independent Samples Univariate T-Test. Table 1 reports the significant results of these tests. We selected significant variables ($p < 0.05$) to carry out a multivariate Logistic Regression discriminating premature readmissions subjects versus non-premature readmission subjects. Significant variables are reported in Table 2.

Significant variables identified by Independent Samples T-Test were Barthel ($p < 0.047$), Congestive heart failure (CHF) ($p < 0.028$), Arrhythmia ($p < 0.013$), and use of Digoxin ($p < 0.023$), and Ophthalmus ($p < 0.016$). Significant variables identified by multivariate Logistic Regression were CHF ($p < 0.030$), and use of Ophthalmus ($p < 0.025$).

Non linear multivariate discrimination was tested applying Random Forest and Boosting Classification as implemented in Jasp. Classification performance measures over ten repetitions of hold-out validation are presented in Table 3. The accuracy was above 0.8 in both classifiers. Random Forest achieved a lower F1 score (0.73) compared with Boosting Classification (0.80). Variable importance in these models was estimated by out-of-bag accuracy estimation. The repeated appearance of a variable in the subset of the ten most important variables accross the validation process was taken as the measure of variable importance in Table 4. Relevant variables identified by Random Forest were Age, Anticoagulated, Arrhythmics, Arrhythmia, Congestive heart failure, Diabetes, number of Drugs and Gender. Relevant variables identified by Boosting Classification were CHF, Arrhythmics, Age, Antidepressant, Arrhythmia, MNA's Calf circumference and SPPB's Balance.

4 Discussion

In a global context of population aging, there is a growing interest in improving the quality of care for the elderly to avoid premature readmissions and at the same time to have optimal management of healthcare resources [19]. Therefore, the identification of risk factors for frail patients with delirium is becoming increasingly important to prevent their premature readmission.

Systematic reviews [10,31] have found that frailty in older people [12] is a strong predictor of mortality. Increase in the frailty index was associated with increased mortality while decrease has no effect on mortality [43–45]. There are also studies showing that the development of delirium is associated with increased mortality [34]. Our study found that frail subjects with delirium who had suffered premature readmission had lower survival rates at 6 months, 1 year and 2 years.

Our results of the application of Independent Samples T-Test and Logistic Regression as well as Random Forest and Boosting Classification to identify variables with higher risk of premature readmission versus non-premature readmission patients show that the risk factors for presenting readmission are associated with reduced physical capacity, such as a high age, male sex, weight loss measured through calf circumference, polypharmacy and lack of balance.

The loss of thickness of calf circumference demonstrated in the MNA and SPPB balance tests coincides with studies [20,47,52] that indicate that weakness, the loss of balance and limited capacity to perform routine physical activities often indicate the onset of frailty. This in turn is associated with frailty leading to increased hospital readmission and mortality [17,30,39]. Regarding pharmacology in the elderly patient, when multiple diseases coexist, a high number of drugs tends to be prescribed, with the risk of suffering adverse drug reactions and drug interactions associated with increased risk of mortality that increases with age as a direct consequence of the physiological changes of aging [22]. Polypharmacy presents a risk for mortality in elderly subjects [11,14]. Our results show that this polypharmacy has a direct impact on premature hospital readmission.

CHF is considered a geriatric syndrome in the same way as dementia, delirum, and frailty [13], is a leading cause of morbidity and mortality worldwide, contributes to a substantial deterioration of quality of life for patients [48]. The presence of frailty in chronic CHF is associated with an increased hazard for death and hospitalization [53]. In addition social frailty increases both heart failure rehospitalization and mortality [28]. In our study, both in the analysis by Independent Samples T-Test, Logistic Regression, and Machine Learning, the occurrence of CHF appears as a relevant variable for premature hospital readmission. CHF is considered the end-common pathway of a diverse number of disease states, including congenital heart disease, ischemia, arrhythmia, and external factors. Patients with heart failure are often medically complex, with multiple comorbidities and a long list of medications [21]. An anti-arrhythmic drugs, digoxin, appear in our results as a risk factor for premature readmission in frail subjects with delirium.

Although in the last 2 decades, digoxin use patterns have decreased, it is still widely prescribed [1]. Digoxin, used to help the heart function better and control heart rate, is one of the drugs with the greatest impact on premature readmission in the study. Further research on this drug impact is therefore needed.

Depression is common in medically vulnerable populations, including older adults and those with chronic medical illnesses such as cardiovascular disease. Some antidepressants have cardiovascular side-effects that may add to rather than reduce the risk for cardiac events [7]. Antidepressants are another drugs that are relevants for premature admission as the bibliography shows [41] and our data.

Another major disease with serious health consequences is diabetes. One study [46] found that people with diabetes had higher 30-day readmission rates and longer hospital stays.

According to a study [25], anticoagulation status did not significantly influence readmission outcomes in frail subjects, whereas our results are significant for premature readmission. Similar results were found among patients treated with oral anticoagulants (OAC) after percutaneous coronary intervention (PCI) who were found to be independent predictors of 30-day readmission. Also, during rehospitalization, compared to patients not on OACs, patients on OACs suffered a higher unadjusted rate of mortality and a longer length of stay [50].

Another variable that appears repeatedly in the statistics applied are the ophthalmic drugs used for the treatment of different eye conditions. It is well known that several ocular affections imply hospital readmission, such as diabetic retinopathy [51], and even greater association with mortality in frail subjects, such as glaucoma [32] or macular degeneration [35].

5   Conclusions and Future Work

In this study we assess the mortality risk after 6 months, 1 year and 2 years of follow-up of frail patients with delirium who had been readmitted to hospital in a period of less than 30 days after discharge. We find that premature hospital readmission is associated with increased mortality at 6 months, 1 year and 2 years by comparing Kaplan Meier mortality curves.

The study also confirms that congestive heart failure (CHF) and diabetes appears as a high risk factor for hospital readmission in frail patients with delirium. In addition, the use of some drugs such as anti-arrhythmic drugs, and especially digoxin, antidepressant, anticoagulated and drugs for ocular pathologies is associated with a higher risk of readmission.

It is worth noting that the results show that variables related to greater frailty such as older age, loss of thickness of calf circumference demonstrated in the MNA, polypharmacy, and lack of balance are also indicative of higher risk of premature hospital readmission in the group analysed in this study, which points to the need for approaches aimed at alleviating these detrimental states in their treatment.

References

1. Angraal, S., et al.: Digoxin use and associated adverse events among older adults. Am. J. Med. **132**(10), 1191–1198 (2019)
2. Artetxe, A., Ayerdi, B., Graña, M., Rios, S.: Using anticipative hybrid extreme rotation forest to predict emergency service readmission risk. J. Comput. Sci. **20**, 154–161 (2017)
3. Artetxe, A., Beristain, A., Graña, M.: Predictive models for hospital readmission risk: a systematic review of methods. Comput. Methods Programs Biomed. **164**, 49–64 (2018)
4. Artetxe, A., Beristain, A., Graña, M., Besga, A.: Predicting 30-day emergency readmission risk. In: Graña, M., López-Guede, J.M., Etxaniz, O., Herrero, Á., Quintián, H., Corchado, E. (eds.) SOCO/CISIS/ICEUTE -2016. AISC, vol. 527, pp. 3–12. Springer, Cham (2017). https://doi.org/10.1007/978-3-319-47364-2_1
5. Artetxe, A., Graña, M., Beristain, A., Ríos, S.: Balanced training of a hybrid ensemble method for imbalanced datasets: a case of emergency department readmission prediction. Neural Comput. Appl. **32**, 5735–5744 (2020)

6. Barakat, A., Mittal, A., Ricketts, D., Rogers, B.A.: Understanding survival analysis: actuarial life tables and the Kaplan-Meier plot. Br. J. Hosp. Med. **80**(11), 642–646 (2019)
7. Behlke, L.M., Lenze, E.J., Carney, R.M.: The cardiovascular effects of newer antidepressants in older adults and those with or at high risk for cardiovascular diseases. CNS Drugs **34**(11), 1133–1147 (2020)
8. Cano-Escalera, G., Graña, M., Irazusta, J., Labayen, I., Besga, A.: Risk factors for prediction of delirium at hospital admittance. Expert. Syst. **39**(4), e12698 (2021)
9. Cano-Escalera, G., Graña, M., Irazusta, J., Labayen, I., Besga, A.: Survival of frail elderly with delirium. Int. J. Environ. Res. Public Health **19**(4), 2247 (2022)
10. Chang, S.-F., Lin, P.-L.: Frail phenotype and mortality prediction: a systematic review and meta-analysis of prospective cohort studies. Int. J. Nurs. Stud. **52**(8), 1362–1374 (2015)
11. Chang, T.I., et al.: Polypharmacy, hospitalization, and mortality risk: a nationwide cohort study. Sci. Rep. **10**(1), 18964 (2020)
12. Clegg, A., Young, J., Iliffe, S., Rikkert, M.O., Rockwood, K.: Frailty in elderly people. Lancet **381**(9868), 752–762 (2013)
13. Dharmarajan, K., Rich, M.W.: Epidemiology, pathophysiology, and prognosis of heart failure in older adults. Heart Fail. Clin. **13**(3), 417–426 (2017)
14. Dovjak, P.: Polypharmacy in elderly people. Wien. Med. Wochenschr. **172**(5–6), 109–113 (2022)
15. Erkinjuntti, T., Sulkava, R., Wikström, J., Autio, L.: Short portable mental status questionnaire as a screening test for dementia and delirium among the elderly. J. Am. Geriatr. Soc. **35**(5), 412–416 (1987)
16. Everitt, B.S., Hothorn, T.: A Handbook of Statistical Analyses Using R. CRC Press, Boca Raton (2010)
17. Faye, A.S., et al.: Increasing prevalence of frailty and its association with readmission and mortality among hospitalized patients with IBD. Dig. Dis. Sci. **66**(12), 4178–4190 (2021)
18. Fried, L.P., et al.: Frailty in older adults: evidence for a phenotype. J. Gerontol. A Biol. Sci. Med. Sci. **56**(3), M146-56 (2001)
19. Friedrich, M.-E., et al.: Predictors of hospital readmission for patients diagnosed with delirium: An electronic health record data analysis. Acta Psychiatr. Scand. **147**(5), 506–515 (2022)
20. Gary, R.: Evaluation of frailty in older adults with cardiovascular disease: incorporating physical performance measures. J. Cardiovasc. Nurs. **27**(2), 120–131 (2012)
21. Goldgrab, D., Balakumaran, K., Kim, M.J., Tabtabai, S.R.: Updates in heart failure 30-day readmission prevention. Heart Fail. Rev. **24**(2), 177–187 (2018)
22. Gómez, C., Vega-Quiroga, S., Bermejo-Pareja, F., Medrano, M.J., Louis, E.D., Benito-León, J.: Polypharmacy in the elderly: a marker of increased risk of mortality in a population-based prospective study (NEDICES). Gerontology **61**(4), 301–309 (2015)
23. Graña, M., Besga, A.: Fragility and delirium data from UHA. zenodo.org (2021)
24. Guralnik, J.M., et al.: A short physical performance battery assessing lower extremity function: association with self-reported disability and prediction of mortality and nursing home admission. J. Gerontol. **49**(2), M85–M94 (1994)
25. Hall, C., et al.: Impact of frailty and anticoagulation status on readmission and mortality rates following falls in patients over 80. Baylor Univ. Med. Center Proc. **32**(2), 181–186 (2019)

26. Inouye, S.K., van Dyck, C.H., Alessi, C.A., Balkin, S., et al.: Clarifying confusion: the confusion assessment method. Ann. Intern. Med. **113**(12), 941–948 (1990). PMID: 2240918
27. Inouye, S.K., Westendorp, R.G., Saczynski, J.S.: Delirium in elderly people. Lancet **383**(9920), 911–922 (2014)
28. Jujo, K., et al.: Impact of social frailty in hospitalized elderly patients with heart failure: A FRAGILE-HF registry subanalysis. J. Am. Heart Assoc. **10**(17), e019954 (2021)
29. Kaiser, M.J., et al.: Validation of the mini nutritional assessment short-form (MNA-SF): a practical tool for identification of nutritional status. JNHA - J. Nutr. Health Aging **13**(9), 782 (2009)
30. Keeney, T., Jette, D.U., Cabral, H., Jette, A.M.: Frailty and function in heart failure: predictors of 30-day hospital readmission? J. Geriatr. Phys. Therapy **44**(2), 101–107 (2019)
31. Kim, D.J., Massa, M.S., Potter, C.M., Clarke, R., Bennett, D.A.: Systematic review of the utility of the frailty index and frailty phenotype to predict all-cause mortality in older people. Syst. Rev. **11**(1), 187 (2022)
32. Kühn, T., et al.: Glaucoma and mortality risk: findings from a prospective population-based study. Sci. Rep. **11**(1), 11771 (2021)
33. Mahoney, F.I., Barthel, D.W.: Functional evaluation: the Barthel index. Md. State Med. J. **14**, 61–65 (1965)
34. Maldonado, J.R.: Acute brain failure. Crit. Care Clin. **33**(3), 461–519 (2017)
35. McGuinness, M.B., Karahalios, A., Finger, R.P., Guymer, R.H., Simpson, J.A.: Age-related macular degeneration and mortality: a systematic review and meta-analysis. Ophthalmic Epidemiol. **24**(3), 141–152 (2017)
36. Ohl, I.C.B., et al.: Evaluation of delirium in aged patients assisted at emergency hospital service. Rev. Bras. Enferm. **72**(suppl 2), 153–160 (2019)
37. Pfeiffer, E.: A short portable mental status questionnaire for the assessment of organic brain deficit in elderly patients. J. Am. Geriatr. Soc. **23**(10), 433–441 (1975)
38. Proietti, M., Cesari, M.: Frailty: what is it? In: Veronese, N. (ed.) Frailty and Cardiovascular Diseases. AEMB, vol. 1216, pp. 1–7. Springer, Cham (2020). https://doi.org/10.1007/978-3-030-33330-0_1
39. Qian, A.S., Nguyen, N.H., Elia, J., Ohno-Machado, L., Sandborn, W.J., Singh, S.: Frailty is independently associated with mortality and readmission in hospitalized patients with inflammatory bowel diseases. Clin. Gastroenterol. Hepatol. **19**(10), 2054–2063 (2021)
40. Rich, J.T., et al.: A practical guide to understanding Kaplan-Meier curves. Otolaryngol.-Head Neck Surg. **143**(3), 331–336 (2010)
41. Samuel, S.V., Viggeswarpu, S., Wilson, B.P., Ganesan, M.P.: Readmission rates and predictors of avoidable readmissions in older adults in a tertiary care centre. J. Fam. Med. Primary Care **11**(9), 5246 (2022)
42. Setters, B., Solberg, L.M.: Delirium. Prim. Care **44**(3), 541–559 (2017)
43. Shi, S.M., Olivieri-Mui, B., McCarthy, E.P., Kim, D.H.: Changes in a frailty index and association with mortality. J. Am. Geriatr. Soc. **69**(4), 1057–1062 (2021)
44. Stolz, E., Hoogendijk, E.O., Mayerl, H., Freidl, W.: Frailty changes predict mortality in 4 longitudinal studies of aging. J. Gerontol. A Biol. Sci. Med. Sci. **76**(9), 1619–1626 (2021)
45. Stolz, E., Mayerl, H., Hoogendijk, E.O: Frailty in the oldest old: is the current level or the rate of change more predictive of mortality? Age Ageing **51**(2), afac020 (2022)

46. Tang, L., Li, K., Wu, C.J.: Thirty-day readmission, length of stay and self-management behaviour among patients with acute coronary syndrome and type 2 diabetes mellitus: a scoping review. J. Clin. Nurs. **29**(3–4), 320–329 (2019)
47. Topinková, E.: Aging, disability and frailty. Ann. Nutr. Metab. **52**(Suppl 1), 6–11 (2008)
48. Uchmanowicz, I., et al.: Frailty and the risk of all-cause mortality and hospitalization in chronic heart failure: a meta-analysis. ESC Heart Fail. **7**(6), 3427–3437 (2020)
49. Vellas, B., et al.: The mini nutritional assessment (MNA) and its use in grading the nutritional state of elderly patients. Nutrition **15**(2), 116–122 (1999)
50. Vidula, M.K., et al.: Causes and predictors of early readmission after percutaneous coronary intervention among patients discharged on oral anticoagulant therapy. PLoS ONE **13**(10), e0205457 (2018)
51. Xiao, Yu., et al.: Causes and risk factors of repeated hospitalization among patients with diabetic retinopathy. J. Diab. Res. **2022**, 1–7 (2022)
52. Xue, Q.L., Bandeen-Roche, K., Varadhan, R., Zhou, J., Fried, L.P.: Initial manifestations of frailty criteria and the development of frailty phenotype in the women's health and aging study ii. J. Gerontol. A Biol. Sci. Med. Sci. **63**(9), 984–990 (2008)
53. Yang, X., et al.: Impact of frailty on mortality and hospitalization in chronic heart failure: a systematic review and meta-analysis. J. Am. Heart Assoc. **7**(23), e008251 (2018)

Generalizing an Improved GrowCut Algorithm for Mammography Lesion Detection

Cristiana Moroz-Dubenco$^{(\boxtimes)}$ (iD), Laura Diosan (iD), and Anca Andreica (iD)

Department of Computer Science, Babeş-Bolyai University, Mihail Kogălniceanu 1, 400084 Cluj-Napoca, Romania
cristiana.moroz@ubbcluj.ro

Abstract. In the past five years, 7.8 million women were diagnosed with breast cancer. Breast cancer is curable if it is discovered in early stages. Therefore, mammography screening is essential. But, since interpretation can prove difficult, various automated interpretation systems have been proposed so far. A crucial step of the interpretation process is segmentation: identifying the region of interest. In this paper we aim to evaluate an improved version of the GrowCut algorithm - which reduces both the human intervention and the computational time, while preserving a high level of accuracy, and analyzes three possibilities of avoiding the need for initial background seeds: (1) automatically generating seeds inside the breast, (2) using the mammogram's black pixels and (3) not using background seeds - on a different, much larger dataset than the one initially used for experiments, in order to analyze the impact of a dataset's particularities and the influence of different seed types on the segmentation results, and to validate the initial conclusions. However, the experimental results presented in this paper do not only validate the premises, but also demonstrate that the improved version is a generic algorithm which can be used on any dataset with different types of background seeds.

Keywords: Mammogram Segmentation · Cellular Automaton · GrowCut · Mass Detection

1 Introduction

According to the World Health Organization, 2.3 million women were diagnosed with breast cancer in 2020, while another 7.8 million women were diagnosed in the past five years [10]. Breast cancer can be cured if the disease is identified in an early stage. According to the Centers for Disease Control and Prevention, a malignant tumor can be observed in a mammogram up to three years before it can be felt [2]. Therefore, it is recommended that mammographies are performed at regular intervals.

However, mammography interpretation is not only difficult, but also time-consuming, thus leading to an imminent need for an automated interpretation

P. García Bringas et al. (Eds.): HAIS 2023, LNAI 14001, pp. 709–720, 2023.
https://doi.org/10.1007/978-3-031-40725-3_60

system. There are many different methods that have been proposed in literature so far, but most of them follow the same steps, as presented in [4,6,7] and [14], to name just a few: *pre-processing, segmentation* and *classification*. In this paper we are focusing on mammogram segmentation. Accurate segmentation is an essential step in mammogram interpretation, as the shape of a mass is one of the factors to differentiate between benign and malignant masses [1]. Not only can tumors differ in size or shape, in localization or density, but a breast can contain other abnormalities as well, such as fibroadenoma or cysts, which can be mistaken by tumors. Moreover, the contour of a mass, especially when talking about malignant masses, is not always well-defined. If we take into consideration the possibility of having low contrast images, low image quality, high noise levels or poor illumination [13], we can state that mammography segmentation can prove to be a difficult task.

Different methods have been proposed so far, but, because the purpose of an interpretation system is to serve as a second opinion, recent research concentrates on unsupervised techniques. The GrowCut algorithm [17] is a semi-supervised segmentation method which requires initial seeds for the objects to be segmented, provided by a human expert, and iterates over the image until every pixel is assigned to a class. As most of the seed-based techniques, GrowCut relies directly on the accuracy of the initial seeds, thus being dependent on the human expert. In our previous work [12], we developed an improved version of the original GrowCut algorithm, which reduces both the human intervention and the computational time, while preserving a high accuracy score. The proposed approach analyzes three possibilities of avoiding the need for initial background seeds selection: (1) automatically generating initial seeds inside the breast, (2) using the mammogram's black pixels as initial seeds and (3) not using initial background seeds; introduces a threshold value in order to limit the change of a pixel's label based on the certainty that it belongs to a particular class; and decreases computational time by limiting the algorithm to a fixed number of iterations. The experiments were conducted on the 119 images that contain a mass from the mini-MIAS database [15].

In this study we evaluate the improved GrowCut algorithm on the mini-DDSM database [11]. The dataset contains a total of 9684 mammographies, from which we select those containing malignant abnormalities to conduct the experiments on. By testing our previously proposed method on a different dataset, we aim to: (1) study the impact of a dataset's characteristics on the segmentation results by analyzing the structural differences between the two datasets; (2) analyze the influence of different seed types on the segmentation performance; (3) validate the initial conclusion - that is, our improved version yields much better results when using initial background seeds outside the breast and when not using initial background seeds at all - and prove that the algorithm is generic, generating satisfactory results regardless of the particularities of a dataset.

2 Related Work

The classical GrowCut algorithm was introduced in [17]. The approach implies performing multi-label segmentation by using a Cellular Automaton, considering the pixels to be the cells and the image to be the space of cells. Starting with a number of user-labeled pixels, the algorithm aims to assign each pixel of an image to a class. A pixel p is characterized by a triplet composed of the label of the respective pixel (l_p), the certainty that it belongs to the class labeled with l_p, called the "strength" of the pixel (θ_p), and its feature vector (C_p). The initial state of the automaton is defined based on the user-labeled pixels - that is, the initial seeds are given the label provided by the user and a "strength" of 1, while the other pixels have the initial state $(l_p = 0, \theta_p = 0, C_p = I_p)$, where I_p is the intensity of p. The algorithm iterates over the image and updates the cells' labels and "strengths" with a function based on their neighbors' intensities. This process is repeated until the automaton converges to a stable state, meaning that no cell is updated during an iteration.

The authors of [3] propose an improved version of the original GrowCut algorithm, called semi-supervised GrowCut (SSGC), which involves automatic seed generation by using a multi-layer threshold approach combined with morphological operators. Multi-layer threshold is performed on the mammography in order to identify concentric regions, and only the layers with concentric regions are kept, thus obtaining a pre-segmentation of the tumor region. For the selection of the initial seeds, dilation is applied on the pre-segmented region, resulting in a background region mask, whose points are mapped to background seeds, while the points close to the centroid of the internal region are mapped to foreground seeds. After generating the initial seeds, the GrowCut algorithm is applied. SSGC obtains good results, but it is not as accurate as the original algorithm. However, it has the advantage of not needing human intervention.

[1] proposes an automatic detection and segmentation technique for mammograms based on a modified transition rule, named maximal strength updation (MCSU), in cellular automaton-based segmentation. The proposed technique is composed of two steps: first, a rough region of interest is obtained by a histogram-based thresholding and the initial seeds are selected based on the sum average feature from the segmented area; and secondly, a cellular automaton is used for refining the segmentation, with a modified update rule, which compares the current cell only with the neighbor with maximum "strength", thus reducing the computational time and leading to a faster convergence of the automaton. The method is evaluated on 70 abnormal mammograms from mini-MIAS [15] and compared with Snake-based active contour segmentation, Watershed segmentation, Improved levelset segmentation, Vector-valued levelset segmentation, Region growing segmentation and Cellular Automaton-based mass segmentation, concluding that the proposed method is significantly superior to all the other methods in terms of sensitivity, precision, area overlap measure, relative error, accuracy and computation time.

3   Proposed Method

In our previous work [12], we developed an approach based on the GrowCut algorithm [17] for mammography segmentation, called Threshold-based Grow-Cut (TbGC), which intends to reduce the human intervention and the computational time, while preserving a high level of accuracy.

Keeping in mind that unprocessed mammographies contain both the breast and a background, the problem of initial background seeds selection becomes more complicated, as the human expert needs to decide whether to choose the seeds inside the breast, where they could overlap glandular or connective tissue, which have the same properties as tumors, or outside of it, where they can lead, for dense breasts, to the entire breast being segmented as an abnormality. Moreover, the performance tests presented in [17] were conducted on 256×256 images, while medical images are usually larger, thus increasing the computational time.

TbGC tries to solve these problems of the original technique. In order to reduce the need for human intervention and to solve the problem of choosing initial background seeds, three variants are proposed: (1) generating the initial background seeds inside the breast, (2) using initial background seeds outside the breast and (3) using only initial foreground seeds. For reducing the computational time, the algorithm is limited to a fixed, experimentally chosen, number of steps, meaning that a result is obtained either when the automaton converges, if it happens in less steps than the maximum number, or when the maximum number of steps is reached. What is more, TbGC introduces a change to the cell evolution rule such that a pixel's label is updated only if its new "strength" is higher than an experimentally chosen threshold value, with the aim of preserving high quality results.

To evaluate the proposed method, the results obtained with TbGC were compared with the ones obtained with the original GrowCut for all the mammographies from the mini-MIAS dataset [15] that contain at least one abnormality, totaling 119 abnormalities. The experiments were run for all three variants of initial background seeds mentioned earlier. The numerical results show an incontestable improvement of TbGC for the last two variants, using a small value for the maximum number of steps, while the results obtained for the first variant are better for the original algorithm, yet close to the ones obtained with TbGC.

In order to achieve the goals stated in Sect. 1, we analyze the structural differences between mini-DDSM [11] and mini-MIAS [15], evaluate the TbGC algorithm on the mini-DDSM dataset on all three variants for background seeds, and compare its results both to the ones obtained with the original GrowCut for mini-DDSM and to the ones obtained for mini-MIAS. The results are presented in Sect. 4.

3.1   Datasets Comparison

The mini-DDSM dataset provides easy access to the original DDSM dataset [9], along with original identification filenames and contour binary masks for abnormalities. It contains a total of 9684 mammographies, split into patient folders. Each patient folder contains both craniocaudal (*CC*) and mediolateral oblique (*MLO*) mammographies for the left and right breasts, along with binary masks for abnormalities, where this is the case. All the patient folders belong to one of the three categories: *Normal, Cancer* and *Benign*, based on the existence of at least one abnormality.

From the total 9684 mammographies, there exist binary contour masks for 1430 malignant abnormalities. Therefore, we evaluate the TbGC algorithm on those mammographies. For a decreased computational time, all the images have been resized at 30% from the original size.

The mini-MIAS dataset contains 322 mammographies, with a total of 119 anomalies. For these images, the dataset also provides the image coordinates of the center of the mass and the approximate radius of a circle that encloses the mass.

The structural differences between mini-DDSM and mini-MIAS are presented in Table 1.

Table 1. Structural differences between mini-DDSM and mini-MIAS.

	mini-DDSM	mini-MIAS
Total number of samples	9684	322
Number of samples containing abnormalities	2832	119
Number of samples used in experiments	1430	119
Image format	PNG	PGM
Orientation of samples	CC and MLO	MLO
Original dimensions	variable, with an approximate mean of 2676 × 1536 pixels	constant, 1024 × 1024 pixels
Resize percentage	30%	-
Resolution per pixel	42, 43.5 or 50 microns	200 microns
Bits per pixel	12 or 16	8
Details for abnormalities	binary mask	coordinates of the center and approximate radius of a circle enclosing the mass

4 Experimental Results

As stated in the previous section, we test the TbGC algorithm on three cases: (1) using initial background seeds inside the breast, (2) using initial background seeds outside the breast and (3) not using initial background seeds. For all the experiments, to simulate the input given by the human expert, we use the mask provided with the dataset as initial foreground seeds. For the first case, we use the contour of a rectangle that encloses the mask provided with the dataset as background seeds, whilst for the second case, we use the black pixels from the unprocessed mammogram as initial background seeds.

In order to find the most suitable value for the maximum number of iterations, we applied both the original GrowCut and the TbGC algorithms on five images for different numbers of iterations, with a threshold value of 0.5 for TbGC and without using background seeds. The results are presented in Fig. 1 for GrowCut and in Fig. 2 for TbGC. The first line in each figure contains the original images, the second line contains the ground-truth images, the third line contains the results obtained in 5 iterations, the fourth line contains the results obtained in 25 iterations, the fifth line contains the results obtained in 50 iterations and the last line presents the results of a complete run of the algorithm (i.e. the algorithm was run until the automaton converged). A complete run consists of approximately 800 iterations for GrowCut and 100 iterations for TbGC.

It is easily noticed that the original GrowCut's segmented area extends outside the breast, all the way to the margin of the mammogram, even for a small number of iterations, while a complete run leads to the entire mammogram being segmented as region of interest. The last line from Fig. 1 proves the importance of the change in the cell evolution rule brought by the Threshold-based GrowCut algorithm - updating a pixel's label only if its new "strength" is higher than a threshold value; while the number of iterations needed for the convergence of the automaton proves that this change also reduces drastically the computational time, even without setting a maximum number of iterations. On the other hand, for TbGC, a small number of iterations results in the center of the tumor not being segmented, as it can be observed in the third line of Fig. 2. Therefore, in order to obtain an accurate comparison between the two algorithms and given not only the visual results, but also the computational time, we decided to set the maximum number of iterations to 25 for the experiments.

To decide on the threshold value to be used for TbGC, we conducted a different set of experiments, running the algorithm on the same images for different threshold values, for 25 iterations, without using background seeds. The results are presented in Fig. 3, where the first line contains the original images, the second line contains the ground-truth images, the third line contains the results obtained with a threshold value of 0.25, the fourth line contains the results obtained with a threshold value of 0.5 and the fifth line contains the results obtained with a threshold value of 0.75. Considering the fact that a threshold value of 0.25 leads to many false positives, while a threshold value of 0.75 leads to many false negatives, we set the threshold value to 0.5 for experiments.

4.1   Numerical Comparison

In order to compare the Threshold-based GrowCut algorithm with the original GrowCut algorithm from a numerical point of view, both algorithms were ran for 25 iterations, using a threshold value of 0.5 for TbGC. For an accurate numerical comparison between GrowCut and TbGC, five metrics were applied: (1) *accuracy* [18], (2) *Precision* [16], (3) *Recall* [16], (4) *Jaccard index* [8] and (5) *Dice index* [5]. We compute the metrics on each of the selected mammographies from the mini-DDSM dataset, then compute the mean of the 1430 resulting values. Table 2 holds the results obtained when using an enclosing square as background seeds

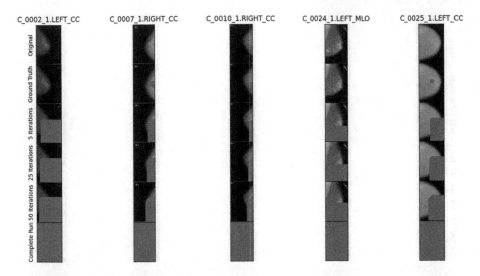

Fig. 1. Results of applying GrowCut for different numbers of iterations.

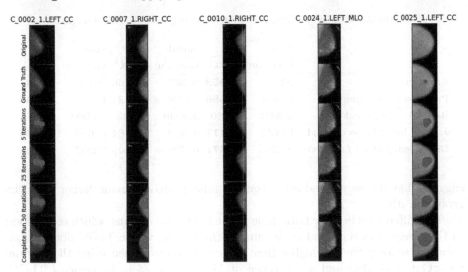

Fig. 2. Results of applying TbGC for different numbers of iterations.

(denoted as "inside"), the results obtained when using the black pixels from the unprocessed mammograms as background seeds (denoted as "outside") and the results obtained when not using background seeds at all (denoted as "none").

In the first two columns of Table 2, which correspond to the the variant where well-defined background seeds are employed, we can observe that the results obtained for both algorithms are fairly close and quite satisfactory: accuracy scores over 98% and recall values over 90%, suggesting that the tumor was almost entirely segmented. However, the values obtained for precision and Jaccard index

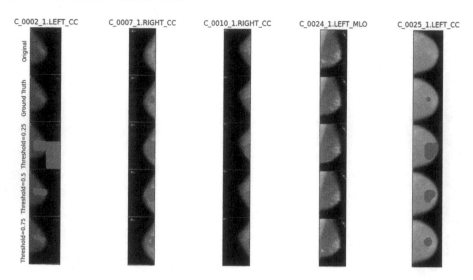

Fig. 3. Results of applying TbGC for different threshold values.

Table 2. Mean of performance metrics computed on 1430 images.

	inside		outside		none	
	GrowCut	TbGC	GrowCut	TbGC	GrowCut	TbGC
Accuracy	0.9845	**0.9858**	0.7365	**0.9166**	0.5959	**0.9044**
Precision for foreground	0.6036	**0.6586**	0.1026	**0.2184**	0.0716	**0.2032**
Recall for foreground	**0.9913**	0.9160	**0.9999**	0.9413	**1.0000**	0.9246
Jaccard Index for foreground	0.6037	**0.6117**	0.1026	**0.2084**	0.0716	**0.1952**
Dice Coefficient for foreground	0.7262	**0.7471**	0.1706	**0.3308**	0.1297	**0.3128**

suggest that the segmented areas contain false positives, being larger than the ground truth.

The differences become noticeable in the next two columns, which correspond to the usage of background seeds outside the breast, where TbGC obtained an accuracy score with 18% higher than the one obtained when using the original GrowCut algorithm and a difference of 11% in precision, in favor of TbGC. Nevertheless, one can observe that the values obtained for precision, Jaccard index and Dice coefficient are considerably lower for this variant than for the one with well-defined background seeds, meaning that the segmented area is much larger than the ground truth.

Yet, the most striking results are presented in the last two columns of Table 2. With an accuracy score with 30% lower for GrowCut than for TbGC and a precision value below 10%, it is clear that the results obtained with the original GrowCut are significantly worse. If we are to look at the last four columns of Table 2, we can observe that the results obtained for the second variant are better, which means that the use of black pixels as background seeds does bring an improvement.

We also want to emphasize the fact that the accuracy obtained by TbGC is over 0.9 for all three cases, while for GrowCut, we can see a difference of almost 0.39 between the first and the third cases. Although the values obtained for the other metrics are not satisfactory, they are obviously better for the Threshold-based GrowCut algorithm (except for the recall value, as already highlighted). Given the numerical comparison between TbGC and GrowCut on the mini-DDSM dataset, we can conclude that the existence and the localization (inside or outside the breast) of the background seeds do impact the segmentation results, but, since the differences in the results obtained with TbGC for the three variants are much lower than the ones in the results obtained with the original GrowCut, we can aver that TbGC is a flexible algorithm in comparison to the original GrowCut.

4.2   Datasets Numerical Comparison

In pursuance of properly studying the impact of a dataset's characteristics on the segmentation results, in this subsection we compare the results obtained with the Threshold-based GrowCut algorithm on two different datasets: mini-DDSM and mini-MIAS. The results obtained for the mini-DDSM dataset are the ones presented in Subsect. 4.1, with the algorithm's configuration introduced in the beginning of this section. On the other hand, the results obtained for the mini-MIAS dataset are the ones presented in our previous paper [12], where the algorithm was run for 5 iterations with a threshold value of 0.5, using a circle that encloses the abnormality, with the coordinates of the center of the mass and the approximate radius in pixels provided with the dataset, as foreground seeds. The most fitting values for the maximum number of iterations and for the threshold value were chosen as a result of a set of experiments similar to the one presented in this section, in Figs. 1, 2 and 3. For the background seeds used in the first variant (inside the breast), a square enclosing the foreground seeds is employed.

Table 3 presents the mean of performance metrics obtained with the Threshold-based GrowCut algorithm when applied on 119 mammographies from the mini-MIAS dataset and on 1430 mammographies from the mini-DDSM dataset, using background seeds inside the breast, using background seeds outside the breast and, respectively, not using background seeds.

The values displayed in Table 3 show a clear improvement for the mini-DDSM dataset, with an approximate increase of 0.35 in precision, 0.31 in Jaccard Index and 0.3 in Dice Coefficient for the case when background seeds inside the breast are employed. However, given the fact that the mask used for mini-DDSM is an exact one, provided with the dataset, while the mask used for mini-MIAS is an approximate one, constructed as a circle with the coordinates of the center and the radius provided with the dataset, and keeping in mind that the contour of a mass is almost never a perfect circle, the better performance of TbGC on mini-DDSM is explained.

Nonetheless, if we look at the middle columns, which hold the results obtained when using the black pixels from the initial mammography as background seeds,

Table 3. Mean of performance metrics computed on 1430 images for mini-DDSM and 119 images for mini-MIAS.

	inside		outside		none	
	mini MIAS	mini DDSM	mini MIAS	mini DDSM	mini MIAS	mini DDSM
Accuracy	0.9797	**0.9858**	**0.9782**	0.9166	**0.9365**	0.9044
Precision for foreground	0.3016	**0.6586**	**0.3063**	0.2184	**0.2157**	0.2032
Recall for foreground	0.8663	**0.9160**	0.7894	**0.9413**	0.8981	**0.9246**
Jaccard Index for foreground	0.3009	**0.6117**	**0.2326**	0.2084	**0.1973**	0.1952
Dice Coefficient for foreground	0.4414	**0.7471**	**0.3615**	0.3308	0.3057	**0.3128**

and at the last two columns, which holds the results obtained when not using background seeds, we can see better accuracy, precision and Jaccard Index scores for the mini-MIAS dataset, whereas the recall score is better for the mini-DDSM dataset. The explanation lies in the maximum number of iterations - going back to Fig. 2, which presents the results obtained when applying TbGC on five mammographies from mini-DDSM for different numbers of iterations, one can see that, for a maximum number of iterations lower than 25, the segmented area would be smaller, thus containing less false positives, yet the center of the tumor would remain unsegmented. On the other hand, as presented in our previous paper, an increased number of iterations applied on mini-MIAS would result in a larger segmented area, containing more false positives.

For all that, we need to mention that the values for precision, Jaccard index and Dice coefficient presented in the last four columns of Table 3 are close for the two datasets, while the differences in accuracy and recall can be linked to the maximum number of iterations employed for each dataset, as previously explained. Everything considered, we can say that TbGC is a generic algorithm that can be applied on structurally different datasets, with the only parameter that needs to be adjusted being the maximum number of iterations.

5   Conclusions and Future Work

In this paper we evaluated the Threshold-based GrowCut algorithm proposed in [12] on the mini-DDSM dataset [11], with the aim of analyzing the impact of a dataset's particularities and of different seed types on the segmentation results, while also validating the proposed approach on a larger number of mammographies. In order for this to happen, first of all, we analyzed the particularities of mini-DDSM and mini-MIAS [15], which was employed in the initial experiments, and made a structural comparison between the two datasets. Secondly, for evaluating the performance of TbGC on mini-DDSM, we compared the results with the ones obtained with the original GrowCut algorithm on three cases: (1) using an automatically generated rectangle enclosing the ground truth as background seeds, (2) using the unprocessed mammogram's black pixels as background seeds and (3) not using background seeds. And, lastly, we compared the numerical results of the Threshold-based GrowCut algorithm when applied to mini-DDSM with the ones obtained when applied to mini-MIAS, presented in our previous paper [12].

The results show that TbGC yields a better segmentation than the original GrowCut when applied to mini-DDSM, providing satisfactory results for small numbers of iterations. Given the same results, we concluded that the existence and the localization of the background seeds do impact the segmentation performance, yet TbGC is much flexible than the original GrowCut. The numerical comparison between the results obtained for mini-DDSM and mini-MIAS proves that the only parameter of TbGC linked to the particularities of a dataset is the maximum number of iterations, while the rest of the algorithm can remain unmodified, and the algorithm employed on any dataset.

We consider that we accomplished our goals. We proved that TbGC is both a generic algorithm that can be used for any dataset with minimum changes, and a flexible one, that can be used with different types of background seeds, and not only did we validate the conclusions presented in the original paper, but we also proved that TbGC obtains better results for all three cases when applied to the mini-DDSM dataset, whilst the initial paper presented better results for the original algorithm when using well-defined background seeds and being applied to the mini-MIAS dataset.

As for future work, we intend to improve the Threshold-based GrowCut algorithm by automatically generating the initial foreground seeds, thus completely removing the need for human intervention.

References

1. Anitha, J., Peter, J.D.: Mammogram segmentation using maximal cell strength updation in cellular automata. Med. Biol. Eng. Comput. **53**(8), 737–749 (2015)
2. Centers for Disease Control and Prevention: What is a mammogram? (2022). Accessed 15 May 2023
3. Cordeiro, F.R., Santos, W.P.D., Silva-Filho, A.G.: Analysis of supervised and semi-supervised growcut applied to segmentation of masses in mammography images. Comput. Methods Biomech. Biomed. Eng. Imaging Vis. **5**(4), 297–315 (2017)
4. Desai, S.D., Megha, G., Avinash, B., Sudhanva, K., Rasiya, S., Linganagouda, K.: Detection of microcalcification in digital mammograms by improved-MMGW segmentation algorithm. In: 2013 International Conference on Cloud & Ubiquitous Computing & Emerging Technologies, pp. 213–218. IEEE (2013)
5. Dice, L.R.: Measures of the amount of ecologic association between species. Ecology **26**(3), 297–302 (1945)
6. Duque, A.E.R., Gómez, D.C.A., Nieto, J.K.A.: Breast lesions detection in digital mammography: an automated pre-diagnosis. In: 2014 XIX Symposium on Image, Signal Processing and Artificial Vision, pp. 1–5. IEEE (2014)
7. Ait lbachir, I., Es-salhi, R., Daoudi, I., Tallal, S., Medromi, H.: A survey on segmentation techniques of mammogram images. In: El-Azouzi, R., Menasché, D.S., Sabir, E., Pellegrini, F.D., Benjillali, M. (eds.) Advances in Ubiquitous Networking 2. LNEE, vol. 397, pp. 545–556. Springer, Singapore (2017). https://doi.org/10.1007/978-981-10-1627-1_43

8. Ge, F., Wang, S., Liu, T.: New benchmark for image segmentation evaluation. J. Electron. Imaging **16**(3), 033011 (2007)
9. Heath, M., Bowyer, K., Kopans, D., Moore, R., Kegelmeyer, P.: The digital database for screening mammography, iwdm-2000 (2001)
10. International Agency for Research on Cancer: Global cancer observatory: Cancer today (2020). Accessed 20 Apr 2022
11. Lekamlage, C.D., Afzal, F., Westerberg, E., Cheddad, A.: Mini-DDSM: mammography-based automatic age estimation. In: 2020 3rd International Conference on Digital Medicine and Image Processing, pp. 1–6 (2020)
12. Moroz-Dubenco, C., Dioşan, L., Andreica, A.: Mammography lesion detection using an improved growcut algorithm. Procedia Comput. Sci. **192**, 308–317 (2021)
13. Raman, V., Sumari, P., Then, H., Al-Omari, S.A.K.: Review on mammogram mass detection by machinelearning techniques. Int. J. Comput. Electr. Eng. **3**(6), 873 (2011)
14. Ramani, R., Vanitha, N.S., Valarmathy, S.: The pre-processing techniques for breast cancer detection in mammography images. Int. J. Image, Graph. Signal Process. **5**(5), 47 (2013)
15. SUCKLING J, P.: The mammographic image analysis society digital mammogram database. Digital MAMMO, pp. 375–386 (1994)
16. Taha, A.A., Hanbury, A.: Metrics for evaluating 3d medical image segmentation: analysis, selection, and tool. BMC Med. Imaging **15**(1), 1–28 (2015)
17. Vezhnevets, V., Konouchine, V.: GrowCut: interactive multi-label ND image segmentation by cellular automata. In: Proceedings of Graphicon, vol. 1, pp. 150–156. Citeseer (2005)
18. Zhang, H., Fritts, J.E., Goldman, S.A.: Image segmentation evaluation: a survey of unsupervised methods. Comput. Vis. Image Understanding **110**(2), 260–280 (2008)

Coherence of COVID-19 Mortality of Spain Versus Western European Countries

Goizalde Badiola, Manuel Grana$^{(\boxtimes)}$, and Jose Manuel Lopez-Guede

Grupo de Inteligencia Computacional, University of the Basque Country,
Bilbao, Spain
manuel.grana@ehu.eus

Abstract. The mortality impact of COVID-19 across European countries is a complex phenomenon that appears to be influenced by political, social, economic, and environmental factors. The western European countries have implemented similar policies, with some specific minor divergences, like in the implementations of lockdowns and vaccination passes, so that similar results were to be expected. We use the wavelet transform coherence (WCT) in order to assess the correlation at diverse time scales among COVID-19 mortality time series. The same process was carried out over the time series of stringency index of implemented population control polices. Specifically, we consider the pairwise WCTs of the COVID mortality and the stringency time series of western European countries versus Spain. We discuss the findings on the WCT plots regarding the temporal inhomogeneity of the plots, and the lack of correspondence between WCT plot dissimilarity and geographical distance of countries relative to Spain. This discussion raises questions about the hypothesis of the transmission of a specific pathogen as the main mechanism underlying the mortality attributed to COVID-19. The synchronization of non-pharmaceutical interventions in the first epoch is highly correlated to the synchronization of the mortality waves in almost countries. As an indication of the impact of political measures on COVID-19 mortality, we compute the overall correlation between second order correlation between mortality time series and stringency index time series, finding a highly significant positive correlation (0.53, $p << 0.05$), raising the question if stronger political measures may have lead to increased COVID-19 mortality.

Keywords: Wavelet coherence · COVID-19 · Propagation

1 Introduction

The COVID-19 virus spread was quick and global in the early stages of the pandemic after the declaration of the WHO of the global health emergency. Simultaneous outbreaks happened in geographically distant locations such as Australia, United Kingdom, Israel, and United States. So the first wave was

P. García Bringas et al. (Eds.): HAIS 2023, LNAI 14001, pp. 721–730, 2023.
https://doi.org/10.1007/978-3-031-40725-3_61

presented in the media as a global synchronous event, though some countries didn't show the sudden first wave in the period of March to May of the year 2020. Many modeling and research efforts were concentrated in the prediction of the number of cases in the early days of the pandemic with no great success [6]. Prediction of initial pseudo-exponential increase was easy with linear models, but after a while the picture turned quite chaotic, as can be ascertaining upon inspection of Fig. 1.

In this study we attempted to understand how the virus has been diffused across nations. A variety of factors, including social, economic, and environmental ones, have an impact on the spread of COVID-19, making it a complex phenomenon. Specifically, it is not evident the positive or negative impact of the diverse policies adopted by different nations which also have adopted slightly different testing and reporting practices. It is challenging to compare COVID-19 mortality data between nations in order to assess the dynamics of the virus transmission.

Despite the challenges posed by the availability and reliability of open access data, research on the diffusion and spread of COVID-19 should yield valuable insights into the dynamics of the pandemic. In a literature search, we did not found papers trying to analyze the patterns and trends of COVID-19 data across multiple countries. We focus on mortality data because we believe is the most definitive representation of the pandemic impact. Other measures, such as cases, can be influenced by the testing policies implemented by the governments.

Wavelet transform coherence (WTC) [9] is a well-established tool that has gained popularity in recent years for its ability to analyze the coherence as a multi-scale correlation measure between two time series data in multiple domains, such as environmental research, brain connectivity, and financial data analysis. Besides, we will also discuss the pandemic propagation dynamics from the point of view of the peaks of the mortality waves. We focus on the data from Spain as the reference country, comparing with western Europe countries, namely: Andorra, Belgium, France, Germany, Ireland, Italy, Netherlands, Portugal, Sweden, Switzerland, and United Kingdom. The study can be extended to greater geographical regions in the future.

The underlying hypothesis that the pandemic effect was due only to the propagation of the virus has two main implications. Firstly it implies that the relation among time series should be modulated by the geographical distance. For instance, coherence plots among distant countries should be dissimilar to coherence plots between neighboring countries at each of the diverse time scales. Secondly, that the relative effects of the pandemic should be similar in time as the pandemic progresses, because the underlying cause is the same. For instance, the shape of the coherence plot among two nations should be a repetition of a basic pattern, corresponding to the various waves of the virus outbreaks.

2   Background

Wavelet transform coherence (WTC) is a time series analysis technique that allows to assess a multi-scale correlation picture among two time series. Essentially, WTC computes coherence a correlation measure among the wavelet transformation coefficients at all possible time scales, thus it allows to detect not only the time instants of greater correlation but also the time scales of these correlations. It is a useful tool in many applications due to its capacity to evaluate non-stationary and complicated signals, and its use is anticipated to increase as new methods and uses are created. It is continually being honed and enhanced through new methods for evaluating complex data [9].

WTC has been applied to weather time series to assess climate change factors such as temperature and precipitation, trying to identify patterns and relationships between different climate variables [3,4]. In recent years, the application of wavelet coherence has also extended to the field of finance, where it has been used to analyze stock market data and identify correlations between different financial assets. This has proven useful in predicting market trends and identifying potential investment opportunities [7]. For instance, analysis of financial data [1] have tried to uncover relations between the COVID-19 outbreak and stock markets in Latin America. In addition, the WTC has also been used in the analysis of physiological signals, such as electroencephalograms (EEGs), to investigate brain function and connectivity [2,5]. The ability to detect localized intermittent periodicities in time-frequency space has proven useful in detecting transient events in brain activity, such as epileptic seizures, sleep spindles or Alzheimer [8].

In this paper, we focus on the visualization of the results of the WTC analysis in order to assess the coherence between COVID-19 related time serics in western Europe countries related to Spain. This analysis can shed some light on the joint dynamics of the pandemic, assessing the existence of propagation synchronization of mortality waves or the influence of the policies imposed by the governments on the actual mortality.

3 Methodology

3.1 Data and Code

The pandemic-related data used in this study has been downloaded in January 1, 2023 from the website ourworldindata.com, which collects a wide range of publicly available databases containing information on various aspects of the pandemic across multiple countries. These databases include data on cases, deaths, testing, vaccination rates, stringency index of political measures and other pertinent pandemic metrics that have been harvested by this website from official sources. The data and the matlab code has been publicised in the Zenodo open access repository (https://doi.org/10.5281/zenodo.7908439).

Figure 1 plots the relative-to-population COVID-19 mortality time series of western Europe countries since January 1st, 2020 until the beginning of 2023 when the data for this study was downloaded. The graph depicts the deaths per million of COVID-19 for each country in the region, smoothed using a 14-day moving average. The figure provides a visual representation of the pandemic impact on Europe.

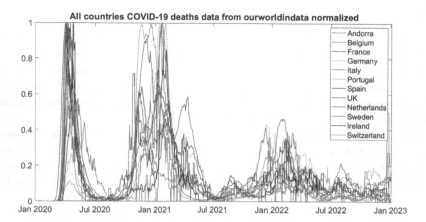

Fig. 1. Relative COVID-19 mortality daily time series of western Europe countries (deaths per million, fourteen days moving average) since January 1st, 2020 until January 1st, 2023. Red font Wn marks the approximate time of the n-th wave peak in the Spanish COVID-19 mortality time series. (Color figure online)

3.2 WTC of COVID-19 Death and Stringency Index Time Series Relative To Spain

Consideration of all possible combinations of WTC among the COVID-19 mortality series of the European countries is a difficult endeavor, hence we have limited the study to the consideration of the WTC of each country against the Spanish time series. The underlying hypothesis is that the geographical relation of the countries with Spain will bear some influence on the shape of the WTC plot, and the similarity among plots.

The coherence between two time series signals at various scales or frequencies is usually depicted visually in a wavelet coherence colormap graphic. The wavelet coherence values are shown as a heatmap, allowing to find pattern of connections between the two signals by visual inspection. In this type of colormap picture, the significance level shows the likelihood that the coherence values between two signals are statistically significant, which means they are not the result of chance or random variation.

4   Results

4.1   WTC Plots

WTC plots show the degree of coherence between signals at several time scales over time. The x-axis correspond to the calendar time, starting in January 2020, ending in the first of January 2023. The y-axis corresponds to the time scale of the coherence, measured in days. Top values of the y-axis are 256 days, corresponding to coherence values that span the entire pandemic. Figure 2 shows the WTC plots computed among the COVID-19 time series of each country with the Spanish time series. We have some observations over these plots:

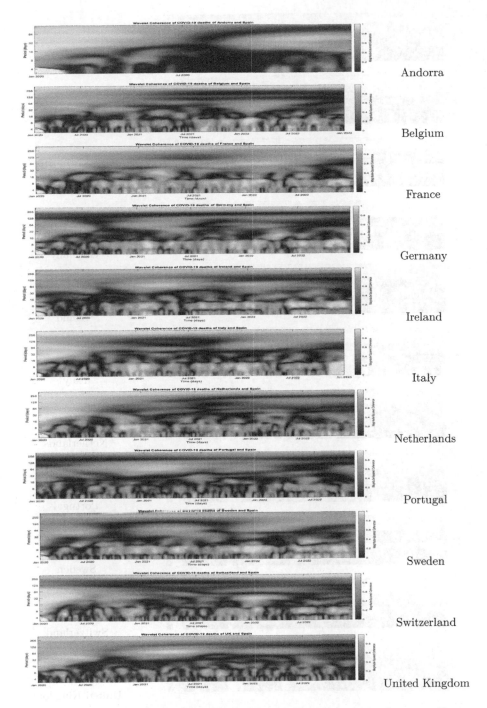

Andorra

Belgium

France

Germany

Ireland

Italy

Netherlands

Portugal

Sweden

Switzerland

United Kingdom

Fig. 2. Wavelet coherence of the COVID-19 mortality time series of western Europe countries with the Spanish time series.

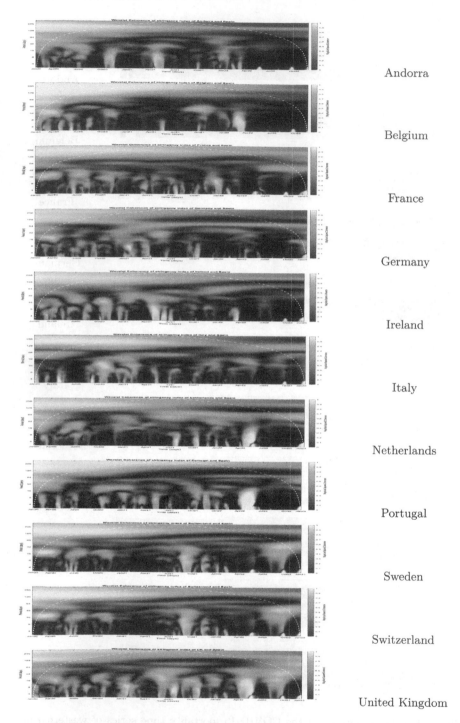

Andorra

Belgium

France

Germany

Ireland

Italy

Netherlands

Portugal

Sweden

Switzerland

United Kingdom

Fig. 3. Wavelet coherence of the COVID-19 stringency time series of western Europe countries with the Spanish time series.

1. The period of March-April-May of the year 2020 shows a high coherence among Spain and almost all other countries. The exceptions are Portugal and Ireland. Despite Portugal being the closest neighboring country, the patterns of the mortality in the first wave of the pandemic were completely different. It is important to note that this strong coherence was not heavily influenced by the geographical distance. Considering mid-term periods of 64 days, almost all countries have high coherence with Spain in the first half of 2020. This highly synchronized coherence disappears after the summer of 2020.
2. Since the autumn of 2020, France, Germany, Ireland, Italy, and Sweden have frequent short term (8 days) peaks of coherence with Spain, while neighboring countries, namely Andorra and Portugal do not have these patterns of coherence.
3. The vaccination campaign starting January 1, 2021, introduced mid term (64 days) coherence of Spain with United Kingdom, Sweden, Portugal, Ireland, but not with Switzerland, Andorra, Belgium, Germany, Italy, and Netherlands. This result is rather independent of the geographical distances, and could be the result of rather different vaccination policies.
4. Most countries (with the exception of Andorra) show long-term coherence (256 days) with Spain, i.e. the overall pattern of mortality was very similar among these countries, due to similar policies of intervention.

Figure 3 shows the WTC plots computed among the stringency time series of each country with the Spanish time series. Some observations:

1. The first two search there is a general coherence among the stringency policies from Spain and other countries. However it tends to disappear in the third year of the pandemic, suggesting a disconnection between countries at the political level.
2. Specifically, there is a high medium coherence at term (one/two months) among Spain and most of the other western Europe countries in the political measures taken.
3. Short term coherences are not equally distributed in the plots of different countries, meaning that short term policy changes were local and with little coordination among countries, due to the diverse socio-economic background.

4.2 Correlation Between WTC Plots

Figures 4 and 5 show a second level correlation analysis, that consists in the computation of the Pearson's Correlation Coefficient (PCC) among the plots shown in Figs. 2 and 3, respectively. Thus, each row/column of the matrix corresponds to the correlation among the WTCs of the corresponding country and the other country with Spain.

WTC plots are treated as a whole, hence the PCC considers each one as a signal. Compressing the relation between two high dimensional signals to a single number implies the loss of much detail and information, however, it allows an immediate appraisal of the similitude between countries.

The intent is to assess if the overall shape of the WTC has some relation with the geographical distance, so that neighboring countries to Spain should have more correlated WTC plots than countries geographically distant from Spain. PCC values above 0.6 are statistically significant (p<0.05). In conclusion, geographical proximity seems to have a secondary role in the similitude among COVID-19 mortality time series, though the central core of the western Europe, namely Germany, France, Belgium, Netherlands, have strong correlation among them. Some countries, like Portugal, have apparently quite different coherence regarding the COVID-19 mortality time series than the stringency index.

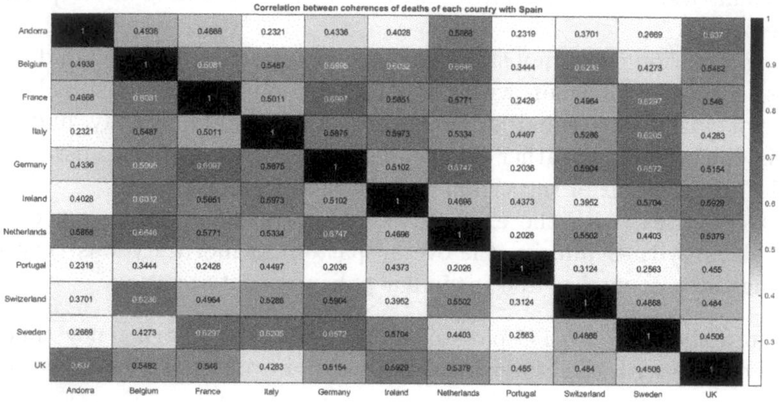

Fig. 4. Correlation between pairs of COVID-19 death WTC plots of western Europe countries with Spain. A single correlation coefficient is computed for each pair of WTC matrices. Each row/column takes as reference the COVID-19 dead WTC plot of the named country with Spain.

4.3   Correlation Among Correlation Matrices

In order to assess indirectly the potential impact of the political measures taken on the COVID-19 mortality, we compute a third order correlation, i.e. the Pearson's Correlation Coefficient among the correlation matrices shown in Figs. 4 and 5. We provide in Table 1 the overall correlation (OC) between them, which is relatively high and positive (0.53) and highly significant ($p << 0.05$). For some countries, like Andorra, this correlation is rather low and non-significative, while for others, like Germany or Portugal it is highly significant.

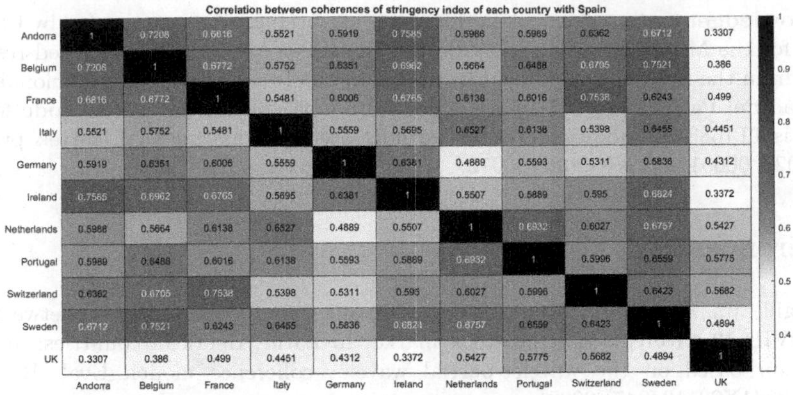

Fig. 5. Correlation between pairs of COVID-19 stringency index WTC plots of western Europe countries with Spain. A single correlation coefficient is computed for each pair of WTC matrices. Each row/column takes as reference the COVID-19 dead WTC plot of the named country with Spain.

Table 1. Correlation between the correlation matrices of deaths and stringency indexes shown in Figs. 4 and 5, respectively. OC is the overall correlation. PCC is the Pearson's Correlation Coefficient. Each column corresponds to the column-wise correlation between these matrices.

	OC	Andorra	Belgium	France	Germany	Italy	Ireland	Netherlands	Portugal	Switzerland	Sweden	UK
PCC	0.53	0.43	0.53	0.65	0.83	0.64	0.57	0.46	0.82	0.75	0.57	0.69
p value	$2,9 \times 10^{-5}$	0.18	0.094	0.03	0.002	0.03	0.07	0.16	0.002	0.009	0.07	0.02

5   Conclusions

The WTC provides a mean to assess the localized coherence between time series at diverse time scales. The WTC of the COVID-19 mortality time series of western Europe countries versus Spain, finds patterns of coherence that are common. Furthermore, a second order correlation between WTC plots gives highly significant correlations between countries, showing the emergence of clusters of countries with rather similar mortality patterns. Carrying out the same analysis over the stringency index time series shows similar clusters. Finally, a third level correlation computed among the stringency and mortality results is highly significant and positive. This result raises the question of whether the implemented political restrictions did in fact contributed to reduce the COVID-19 mortality. In other words, how we can interpret as a positive outcome that increased stringency in population control is highly correlated with increased mortality?. This analysis can be extended to other countries. It can be also of interest to examine each of the pandemic years independently, in order to assess the changing dynamics.

730   G. Badiola et al.

Acknowledgements. The work in this paper has been partially supported by FEDER funds for the MICIN project PID2020-116346GB-I00. Authors have received research funds from the Basque Government as the Grupo de Inteligencia Computacional, Universidad del Pais Vasco, UPV/EHU since 2007 until 2025. The current code for the grant is IT1689-22. Additionally, the authors are participating in Elkartek projects KK-2022/00051 and KK-2021/00070.

References

1. Bilgili, F., Koçak, E., Kuşkaya, S.: Dynamics and co-movements between the COVID-19 outbreak and the stock market in Latin American countries: an evaluation based on the wavelet-partial wavelet coherence model. Eval. Rev. **47**, 0193841X221134847 (2022)
2. Hermans, T., et al.: Partial wavelet coherence as a robust method for assessment of neurovascular coupling in neonates with hypoxic ischemic encephalopathy. Sci. Rep. **13**, 457 (2023). https://doi.org/10.1038/s41598-022-27275-8
3. Huang, Y., Wu, H., Zhu, H.: Time-frequency relationship between R&D intensity, globalization, and carbon emissions in G7 countries: evidence from wavelet coherence analysis. Environ. Sci. Pollut. Res. **28**, 51908–51927 (2021). https://doi.org/10.1007/s11356-021-14369-5
4. Husnain, M.I.u., Nasrullah, Khan, M.A.: Testing dependence patterns of energy consumption with economic expansion and trade openness through wavelet transformed coherence in top energy-consuming countries. Environ. Sci. Pollut. Res. **28**, 1–20 (2021). https://doi.org/10.1007/s11356-021-14046-7
5. Hussain, L., Aziz, W.: Time-frequency spatial wavelet phase coherence analysis of EEG in EC and EO during resting state. Procedia Comput. Sci. **95**, 297–302 (2016). https://doi.org/10.1016/j.procs.2016.09.338. https://www.sciencedirect.com/science/article/pii/S187705091632511X. Complex Adaptive Systems Los Angeles, CA November 2-4, 2016
6. Ioannidis, J.P.A., Cripps, S., Tanner, M.A.: Forecasting for COVID-19 has failed. Int. J. Forecast. **38**(2), 423–438 (2022). https://doi.org/10.1016/j.ijforecast.2020.08.004
7. Rehman, M., Khan, S., Abbas, G., Alhashim, M.: Novel COVID-19 outbreak and global uncertainty in the top-10 affected countries: evidence from wavelet coherence approach. Sustainability **15**, 5556 (2023). https://doi.org/10.3390/su15065556
8. Sankari, Z., Adeli, H., Adeli, A.: Wavelet coherence model for diagnosis of Alzheimer disease. Clinical EEG Neurosci.: EEG Clin. Neurosci. Soc. (ENCS) **43**, 268–278 (2012). https://doi.org/10.1177/1550059412444970
9. Torrence, C., Compo, G.P.: A practical guide to wavelet analysis. Bull. Am. Meteorol. Soc. **79**(1), 61–78 (1998). https://doi.org/10.1175/1520-0477(1998)079<0061:APGTWA>2.0.CO;2. https://journals.ametsoc.org/view/journals/bams/79/1/1520-0477_1998_079_0061_apgtwa_2_0_co_2.xml

A Feature Selection and Association Rule Approach to Identify Genes Associated with Metastasis and Low Survival in Sarcoma

M. Lourdes Linares-Barrera[1], María Martínez-Ballesteros[1]([✉]) [iD],
José M. García-Heredia[2] [iD], and José C. Riquelme[1] [iD]

[1] Departamento de Lenguajes y Sistemas Informáticos, Universidad de Sevilla,
41012 Seville, Spain
marlinbar@alum.us.es, {mariamartinez,riquelme}@us.es
[2] Departamento de Bioquímica Vegetal Biología Molecular, Universidad de Sevilla,
41012 Seville, Spain
jmgheredia@us.es

Abstract. Sarcomas are rare mesodermal tumors of heterogeneous nature and have a higher incidence in children. The relative 5-year survival rate for patients with metastatic sarcoma is usually low. Standard treatment for sarcomas involves surgical resection, and investigating the genetic basis of these tumors through genome-wide analysis is crucial due to their rarity and late diagnosis. This work proposes a methodology that combines preprocessing, feature selection and association rule mining to identify relevant genes and significant relationships in biological data from sarcoma patients. Our study aims to identify the relationships between metastasis-associated genes and patient survival of less than 5 years. The proposed approach was applied to a sarcoma dataset containing data on gene expression, metastasis occurrence, and survival time, revealing a set of biologically relevant gene interactions associated with sarcoma metastasis and low survival rates. The combined use of these techniques can facilitate the identification of biomarkers or gene signatures associated with the disease and provide insight into the underlying biological mechanisms involved in sarcomas.

Keywords: feature selection · association rules · gene expression · sarcoma

1 Introduction

Sarcomas are rare and heterogeneous mesodermal tumors that primarily affect children and adolescents, accounting for over 20% of all pediatric tumors. The standard treatment for sarcomas is surgical resection, and chemotherapy and/or radiation therapy are administered to only a subset of patients. The 5-year relative survival rate for patients with metastatic sarcoma is a mere 15% [18]. Given

P. García Bringas et al. (Eds.): HAIS 2023, LNAI 14001, pp. 731–742, 2023.
https://doi.org/10.1007/978-3-031-40725-3_62

the rarity of the disease and the fact that it is often diagnosed in its later stages, investigating the genetic basis of sarcomas through genome-wide analysis is crucial. The identification of genetic patterns using machine learning techniques could have a significant impact on sarcoma research. These technologies allow for the analysis of large datasets, enabling the discovery of specific genetic patterns and relationships between genes that would not be detectable with traditional methods. This could lead to a better understanding of the molecular mechanisms underlying sarcomas and the identification of novel therapeutic targets [5].

Association rule mining is a powerful technique that could be useful for extracting patterns in gene expression data as it can identify interesting relationships between genes or gene expressions that may not be immediately apparent [13]. By analyzing co-occurrence patterns between genes or gene expressions, association rule mining can help identify groups of genes that are co-expressed, co-regulated, or functionally related. However, one of the main challenges in gene expression data is the high dimensionality in terms of the number of genes and the large imbalance between the number of genes and the number of samples. Feature selection techniques [8] can be useful in this case to reduce the number of features to a manageable subset that is relevant to the problem at hand. By selecting only the most informative genes, feature selection can improve the accuracy and interpretability of machine learning models, and reduce the computational complexity of downstream analyses.

In this study, we propose a methodology that combines preprocessing, feature selection and association rule mining to identify relevant genes in biological data from sarcoma patients and to determine significant relationships among them. Specifically, our analysis focused on selecting a subset of genes that are highly associated with the presence of metastasis and discovering relationships among those genes that contribute to low survival rates. To identify relevant genes, we employed a feature selection technique based on the conditional dependence of variables. This method allowed us to narrow down the subset of genes that are related to metastasis. We then used an association rule algorithm to discover association rules among the selected set of genes that are highly related to metastasis in patients with a survival time of less than 5 years. By combining both techniques, our methodology facilitates the identification of biomarkers or gene signatures associated with sarcoma and provides insights into the underlying biological mechanisms involved in the disease.

The structure of the paper is organized as follows. Section 2 provides a brief overview of related work focused on machine learning techniques based on feature selection and association rules applied to gene expression data. Section 3 describes the proposed methodology in detail. In Sect. 4, the experimental setting used is presented, followed by the reporting of the experimental results and analysis of the selected genes of the proposed methodology. Finally, Sect. 5 discusses the main conclusions of this work.

2 Related Work

Association rules and feature selection are widely used in gene expression data analysis. Association rules identify co-occurrences of genes in different conditions, while feature selection identifies the most informative genes relevant to a phenotype. These techniques have proven effective in identifying biomarkers in various gene expression datasets, including cancer and neurological disorders.

There is a wealth of literature in the field of gene expression analysis that has applied diverse machine learning techniques, particularly in cancer research [10]. In [16], authors present a methodology using AR to identify cancer-related genes, validated through hierarchical cluster analysis, fold-change, and literature review, which successfully characterizes colon cancer patients. In [12], ARs were used to identify genes highly linked to the neurodegenerative disease, based on changes in expression levels between control and patient samples on Alzheimer's disease. The authors in [2] propose a new explainable artificial intelligence strategy based on ARs, which involves pre-processing, knowledge extraction, and functional validation, to identify biologically relevant sequential patterns in longitudinal human gene expression data. In [7], ARs have been used to identify prognostic markers for selecting combined treatments in sarcoma.

Feature selection is a crucial step in analyzing gene expression data due to the challenge of extracting disease-related information from a large amount of redundant data and noise, and eliminating irrelevant genes can help address this issue. Authors in [9] proposed a method to effectively select feature genes from gene expression data by combining double RBF-kernels with weighted analysis. The method outperformed previous methods in terms of accuracy, true positive rate, false positive rate, and runtime when tested on four benchmark datasets. In [15], the authors introduced a methodology for identifying potential biomarkers at the DNA methylation level to distinguish different subtypes of sarcoma. They used a machine learning process to analyze sarcoma samples and employed feature selection and classification algorithms to construct models that could classify sarcoma subtypes based on DNA methylation patterns.

3 Methodology

The objective of the proposed study is to find relevant genetic patterns in sarcoma patients highly related to metastasis and involved in low survival rates using an integrated methodology based on feature selection and association rule mining.

The complete process of the methodology is drawn in Fig. 1. The data analysis methodology applied in this work includes the following steps, which will be described in the subsequent sections:

1. First phase: Preprocessing of data, including filtering, summarization and analysis of differential gene expression (Sect. 3.1).
2. Second phase: Feature selection to select a subset of relevant genes for analysis (Sect. 3.2).

3. Third phase: Application of association rule mining to analyze gene expression data and identify interesting relationships between genes, leading to the identification of potential biomarkers for diseases such as sarcoma (Sect. 3.3).

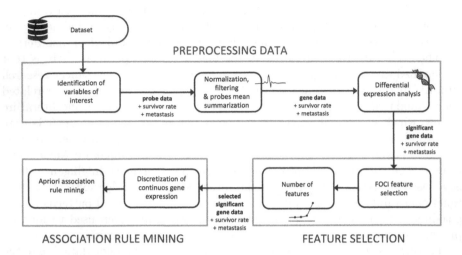

Fig. 1. Methodology proposed to find relevant gene expression patterns related with metastasis and a low survival time.

3.1 First Phase: Preprocessing Data

In the study conducted in this work, we will focus on microarray data. These data are obtained through molecular technology that enables the simultaneous measurement of the expression of thousands of genes from a biological sample. They contain measured values of multiple probes for each patient examined, along with a set of metadata.

Several preprocessing tasks have been conducted to prepare a suitably reduced dataset to be analyzed. The main tasks carried out in the preprocessing phase are detailed as follows.

1. **Identification of variables of interest:** Firstly, we need to select the variables that are of interest in our study. This work focuses on metastasis, survival time, and gene expression values from different probes. The first preprocessing step would involve removing null values and extracting the relevant data. This is crucial to ensure that subsequent analyzes are based on a clean and comprehensive dataset.
2. **Normalization, filtering and summarization:** The next step in the pipeline involves normalizing the data using the log2 technique, which has several benefits including transforming the data to a logarithmic scale, stabilizing variance, and facilitating comparison between experiments.

    Once normalized, we have applied a filtering step to remove data that did not meet certain criteria, such as expression level or variability, in order to eliminate noisy or low-quality data. Specifically, we have removed all probes that exhibited low expression levels on average (log2<5) or displayed minimal variation among patients (log2MAX - log2MIN<1).

After filtering probes, the data is summarized by collecting measurements from multiple probes associated with a gene. This summarization technique provides several advantages, including identifying gene patterns, reducing the dimensionality of the problem, and obtaining a more precise estimation. We used the mean summarization technique to calculate the average gene expression value from multiple probes associated with the same gene. The probes were grouped using a converter from Affymetrix probe to gene symbol. In particular, we have used the biological database The Database for Annotation, Visualization, and Integrated Discovery (DAVID) [6] to obtain the corresponding Affymetrix probe-to-gene symbol notation.

3. **Differential expression analysis:** The preprocessing phase's final stage aims to identify genes with significant changes in expression levels between different biological groups. To identify such genes between patients with and without metastasis, we used the limma package from the Bioconductor project [17], which employs Bayesian statistics to obtain the significance of differentially expressed genes. By fitting a linear model based on the contrast matrix, we estimated the disparity in gene expression between the two study groups, and then identified the differentially expressed genes based on Bayesian statistics. The extracted data represents the genes that are differentially expressed with respect to the two study groups related to metastasis.

3.2   Second Phase: Feature Selection

This works aims at identifying relationships between gene expression values and survival time in patients with metastasis. Therefore, it is necessary to identify the most relevant subset of genes for our study from all the differentially expressed genes that have been extracted in the previous stage.

Therefore, we have applied the FOCI method [3] for the selection of the most relevant subset of attributes for rule extraction. FOCI is a model-free algorithm that does not require tuning parameters, and its consistency is provable under sparsity assumptions. The algorithm has demonstrated excellent performance in both simulated and real datasets, making it a promising tool for variable selection in various applications. This attribute selector works as a forward stepwise feature selection algorithm. The algorithm starts with an empty subset of attributes and, at each iteration, adds the gene that best explains the variable we consider as a response (in our case, metastasis) based on a non-parametric statistic T_n that is based on the notions of conditional dependence (to take into account the relationship between genes as well as the variable's ability to explain metastasis) and nearest neighbors. The algorithm finishes when it reaches the selected number of attributes, returning the subset of genes of the indicated length that present a higher conditional dependence on metastasis. The selection of relevant genes will be used in addition to metastasis and survival data of patients in the extraction of gene patterns through association rules.

The selected number of attributes is a parameter required by FOCI. In order to select the appropriate number of attributes for our analysis, we have considered the point at which the statistic T_n stabilizes, indicating that the addition of more attributes may not improve the accuracy or reliability of the analysis.

3.3   Third Phase: Association Rules Extraction

The well-known Apriori algorithm [1] was applied to discover the association rules in this study. This algorithm requires the discretization of numerical data and the parametrization of the minimum threshold of some quality measures such as support and confidence (Eqs. 1 and 2 described in Sect. 4.2).

The study proposed in this work aims at obtaining relationships among the selected genes in the previous phase and patient survival of less than 5 years. Furthermore, it is interesting to identify whether metastasis is also present in these relationships.

To fulfill this goal, several steps have been conducted:

- As first step, the numerical variables of dataset had to be discretized to convert the continuous variables into categorical variables suitable for association rule mining. On the one hand, the numerical variables associated to genes expression levels were discretized in two intervals to categorize the levels of expression in low (categorized as 0) or high (categorized as 1) using the equal interval width method. On the other hand, the numerical variable related to patient survival time was discretized using fixed interval boundaries to categorize into survival time less than 5 years (categorized as 0) or greater or equal to 5 years (categorized as 1). Metastasis has not been discretized because is already categorized into 0 (absence) or 1 (presence) in the dataset.
- As second step, the Apriori algorithm was applied in the discretized data using minimum support and confidence thresholds. Note that these measures range into the interval 0 to 1, then we are interested in obtaining specific association rules with the highest possible reliability. The minimum and maximum length (number of items) of the association rules have been set to a low number of items, to reduce the set of rules to be found by Apriori. Note that Apriori only creates rules with one item in the consequent of the rule, but the number of items in the antecedent could be higher than 1. Therefore, the selected genes categorized as 0 or 1 in addition to patient survival time categorized as 0 (less than 5 years) have been fixed to appear in the antecedent of the rules. Metastasis with value 1 has been restricted to belong to the consequent of the rules.
- In the final step, we have selected the strongest association rules that contain the survival time along with at least one gene in the antecedent. An example of such a rule that can be derived from our study is:
$\{DSTN = 0 \land ZWINT = 1 \land t\_survivor = 0\} \implies \{metastasis = 1\}$

4   Experimentation

This section provides a description of the dataset selected used in our experimentation, the quality measures applied to evaluate the association rules obtained, and presents and discusses the results obtained in each phase of the proposed methodology detailed in Sect. 3.

4.1   Dataset

For the study, we have selected the gene expression dataset GSE21050 from the French Sarcoma Group (FSG) database, which is available in the public repository Gene Expression Omnibus (GEO) [4,14].

This dataset contains sarcomas that were examined with the aim of characterizing gene expression profiles and identifying possible genetic markers to improve tumor diagnosis. In particular, soft tissue sarcomas with no recurrent chromosomal translocations and for which a frozen tissue of the untreated primary tumor was available. The sarcomas were split into two cohorts. In particular, the dataset contains 310 microarrays sarcoma expression data, survival time of patients, metastasis status, gene CINSARC signature, sample source and diagnosis, among other biological and clinical information. For the study conducted in this work, we have selected the expression data as well as the survival time and metastasis status. The expression values correspond to Affymetrix probes.

4.2   Association Rule Quality Measures

This section presents the most common measures to evaluate the quality of association rules [11].

The support for the rule $(A \Longrightarrow C)$, where A and C denote the antecedents and consequents respectively, measures the percentage of instances in the dataset that contain A and B, simultaneously. $n(A, C)$ denotes the number of instances satisfying both conditions, and N is the total number of instances in the dataset. The support values lie between 0 and 1.

$$sup(A \Longrightarrow C) = \frac{n(A, C)}{N} \tag{1}$$

The confidence is the probability that instances in the dataset that satisfy the antecedent condition (A) also satisfy the consequent condition (C). Like support, confidence also ranges from 0 to 1.

$$conf(A \Longrightarrow C) = \frac{sup(A \Longrightarrow C)}{sup(A)} \tag{2}$$

Lift measures how the co-occurrence of A and C in the dataset exceeds what would be expected if A and C were statistically independent. A lift value greater than one indicates a positive dependence between the two items.

$$lift(A \Longrightarrow C) = \frac{sup(A \Longrightarrow C)}{sup(A)sup(C)} \tag{3}$$

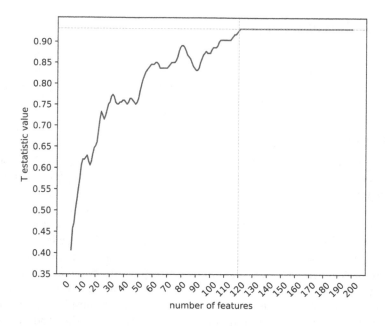

Fig. 2. Number of genes selected using FOCI.

4.3   Preprocessing Results

After completing the pre-processing steps outlined in the first phase of the proposed methodology (Sect. 3.1), we obtained a dataset from 309 patients that contains 1,516 gene expression data points, along with information regarding the metastasis status and the corresponding survival time. In particular, after the filtering and summarization process, we achieved a reduction of the dimensionality from 54,612 probes to 11,901 genes. Additionally, following the differential expression analysis, we obtained a filtering step resulting in 1,516 genes out.

4.4   Feature Selection Results

As described in Sect. 3.2, the number of attributes to be obtained by the FOCI selection feature method in the second phase of our proposal has been determined using the methodology based on the stabilization of the T_n statistic value. As shown in Fig. 2, it can be seen that the T_n value is stabilized when the number of genes reaches 120. Therefore, we have selected this value as the number of genes to be selected by the FOCI method.

Figure 3 displays the volcano plot generated for the genes selected by FOCI. In this plot, the log-fold change of gene expression levels for patients with metastasis is plotted on the x-axis, while the negative log10 p-value is plotted on the y-axis. The most significantly differentially expressed genes are represented by red dots, with a false discovery rate of less than 0.05 used as the cut-off for

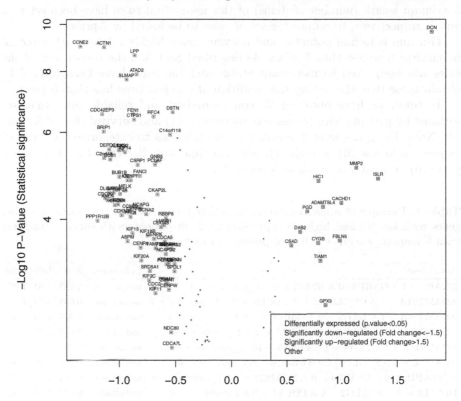

Fig. 3. Volcano plot of the expression levels of the genes selected by FOCI.

statistical significance. Notably, all 120 genes selected by FOCI exhibit p-values lower than 0.05, indicating that they are all statistically significant.

Genes that are significantly up-regulated in patients with metastasis are located towards the right-hand side of the graph and are depicted as purple boxes (fold-change > 1.5 or log2-fold threshold > 0.58). Genes that are significantly down-regulated in metastasis patients are located towards the left-hand side of the graph and are represented as green circles (fold-change < 0.66 or log2-fold threshold < −0.58). Both up-regulated and down-regulated genes are labeled with their corresponding Gene Symbol Identification.

4.5   Association Rules Mining Results

Furthermore, the Apriori algorithm was applied in the third phase of the proposed methodology as described Sect. 3.3 using the discretized and filtered data obtained in the first and second phase (Sects. 3.1 and 3.2) using a minimum support threshold of 0.05, a minimum confidence threshold of 0.9. Note that these measures range into the interval 0 to 1, then we are interested in obtaining specific association rules with the highest possible reliability. The minimum and maximum length (number of items) of the association rules have been set to 3 and 5, respectively, to reduce the set of rules to be found by Apriori.

Our aim is to find potential and relevant genes highly related with sarcoma in survival time less than 5 years. As described Sect. 3.3, the consequent of the rules has been fixed to metastasis status and the rules have been filtered to obtain those that also satisfy the condition of survival time less than 5 years.

In total, we have obtained 57 non redundant and reliable rules that are satisfied by patients with presence of metastasis (1) and survival time < 5 years (0). Note that genes were discretized in two intervals to categorize the levels of expression in low (0) or high (1). Survival time was discretized as less than 5 years (0) or greater or equal to 5 years (1).

Table 1. Example of some association rules that relate relevant relationships among genes with low (0) and high (1) expression levels in patients with survival time less than 5 years ($t\_survivor = 0$) and presence of metastasis.

Antecedent	Consequent	Sup	Lift	Conf
CKAP2 = 1 $\wedge$ GART = 0 $\wedge$ H2AZ1 = 0 $\wedge$ t_survivor = 0	metastasis	0.055	1.64	1.00
ADAMTSL4 = 1 $\wedge$ CDC42EP2 = 0 $\wedge$ DSTN = 0 $\wedge$ t_survivor = 0	metastasis	0.058	1.64	1.00
ADAMTSL4 = 1 $\wedge$ DSTN = 0 $\wedge$ GMNN = 1 $\wedge$ t_survivor = 0	metastasis	0.055	1.64	1.00
ADAMTSL4 = 1 $\wedge$ ISLR = 1 $\wedge$ TOP2A = 1 $\wedge$ t_survivor = 0	metastasis	0.052	1.55	0.94
ACADVL = 1 $\wedge$ C2orf48 = 1 $\wedge$ FBLN5 = 1 $\wedge$ t_survivor = 0	metastasis	0.058	1.48	0.90
ACADVL = 1 $\wedge$ SPDL1 = 1 $\wedge$ TIAM1 = 1 $\wedge$ t_survivor = 0	metastasis	0.061	1.49	0.90
ATP6AP1L = 0 $\wedge$ DPYSL3 = 0 $\wedge$ NCAPG2 = 0 $\wedge$ t_survivor = 0	metastasis	0.061	1.56	0.95
DPYSL3 = 0 $\wedge$ NCAPG2 = 0 $\wedge$ POLA2 = 0 $\wedge$ t_survivor = 0	metastasis	0.074	1.51	0.92
CDC42EP2 = 0 $\wedge$ DPYSL3 = 0 $\wedge$ NCAPG2 = 0 $\wedge$ t_survivor = 0	metastasis	0.074	1.51	0.92

Table 1 presents a subset of the rules obtained that relate relevant relationships among genes in patients with survival time less than 5 years and presence of metastasis divided in three parts. In the first part, we present an example of rules that combines high and low gene expression levels in the antecedent. In the second part, we show an example of rules that present high gene expression levels in the antecedent. In the last part, we display an example of rules that have low gene expression levels in the antecedent. It can be seen that all the expression levels of the genes that appear in the expression levels are consistent with the results obtained in the volcano plot (up or down-regulated) in Fig. 3.

As can be observed, the confidence values of the rules are close to 1, and the lift values are higher than 1. These results indicate that the proposed study was successful in identifying relevant, reliable, and strong relationships among genes with both high and low expression levels in patients with survival times of less than 5 years and the presence of metastasis.

These findings are encouraging, as they may offer potential insights into previously unknown patterns of gene expression that could be relevant to the development and treatment of sarcoma. They could serve as a valuable starting point for further analysis by domain experts and potentially contribute to advancements in our understanding of this disease.

5   Conclusions and Future Works

In this study, we propose a methodology for discovering relevant genes highly associated with metastasis and low survival rates in sarcoma microarrays, based on data processing, feature selection, and association rule mining. Initially, we filtered, grouped, and summarized probes corresponding to the same gene. Subsequently, we applied the FOCI and Apriori algorithms to select potential genes highly associated with metastasis and discover association rules linking high or low expression levels of these selected genes in patients with low survival rates.

The results obtained show the potential and usefulness of the proposed study for expert analysis in the field, providing insights into the complex relationship between gene expression, metastasis, and low survival rates in sarcoma patients. This methodology can also serve as a starting point for future research in the field of sarcoma and other related diseases, paving the way for more targeted and effective treatments.

As future work, we aim to analyze different discretization methods for gene expression data, apply the proposed methodology to various types of omic data, and develop more advanced algorithms for identifying relevant association rules. These efforts could lead to a deeper understanding of the mechanisms underlying sarcoma and other diseases.

Acknowledgements. The authors would like to thank the Spanish Ministry of Science and Innovation for the support under the projects PID2020-117954RB-C22 and TED2021-131311B-C21, and the Junta de Andalucía for projects PYC20 RE 078 USE.

References

1. Agrawal, R., Srikant, R.: Fast algorithms for mining association rules in large databases. In: Proceedings of the International Conference on Very Large Databases, pp. 478–499 (1994)
2. Anguita-Ruiz, A., Segura-Delgado, A., Alcalá, R., Aguilera, C.M., Alcalá-Fdez, J.: eXplainable Artificial Intelligence (XAI) for the identification of biologically relevant gene expression patterns in longitudinal human studies, insights from obesity research. PLoS Comput. Biol. **16**(4), 1–34 (2020)
3. Azadkia, M., Chatterjee, S.: A simple measure of conditional dependence. Ann. Stat. **49**(6), 3070–3102 (2021)
4. Chibon, F., et al.: Validated prediction of clinical outcome in sarcomas and multiple types of cancer on the basis of a gene expression signature related to genome complexity. Nat. Med. **16**(7), 781–787 (2010)
5. Dancsok, A.R., Asleh-Aburaya, K., Nielsen, T.O.: Advances in sarcoma diagnostics and treatment. Oncotarget **8**, 7068–7093 (2016)
6. Dennis, G., et al.: DAVID: database for annotation, visualization, and integrated discovery. Genome Biol. **4**, R60 (2003)

7. García-Heredia, J.M., Pérez, M., Verdugo-Sivianes, E.M., Martínez-Ballesteros, M., Ortega-Campos, S.M., Carnero, A.: A new treatment for sarcoma extracted from combination of miRNA deregulation and gene association rules. Sig. Transduct. Target. Ther. **8**(1), 231 (2023)
8. Jiménez-Navarro, M.J., Martínez-Ballesteros, M., Sousa, I.S., Martínez-Álvarez, F., Asencio-Cortés, G.: Feature-Aware Drop Layer (FADL): a nonparametric neural network layer for feature selection. In: 17th International Conference on Soft Computing Models in Industrial and Environmental Applications (SOCO 2022), pp. 557–566 (2023)
9. Liu, S., et al.: Feature selection of gene expression data for cancer classification using double RBF-kernels. BMC Bioinform. **19**(1), 396 (2018)
10. Macías-García, L., Martínez-Ballesteros, M., Luna-Romera, J., García-Heredia, J., García-Gutiérrez, J., Riquelme-Santos, J.: Autoencoded DNA methylation data to predict breast cancer recurrence: machine learning models and gene-weight significance. Artif. Intell. Med. **110**, 101976 (2020)
11. Martínez-Ballesteros, M., Riquelme, J.C.: Analysis of measures of quantitative association rules. In: Corchado, E., Kurzyński, M., Woźniak, M. (eds.) HAIS 2011. LNCS (LNAI), vol. 6679, pp. 319–326. Springer, Heidelberg (2011). https://doi.org/10.1007/978-3-642-21222-2_39
12. Martínez-Ballesteros, M., García-Heredia, J., Nepomuceno-Chamorro, I., Riquelme-Santos, J.: Machine learning techniques to discover genes with potential prognosis role in Alzheimer's disease using different biological sources. Inf. Fusion **36**, 114–129 (2017)
13. Martínez-Ballesteros, M., Nepomuceno-Chamorro, I., Riquelme, J.C.: Inferring gene-gene associations from quantitative association rules. In: 11th International Conference on Intelligent Systems Design and Applications, pp. 1241–1246 (2011)
14. Peille, A.L., et al.: Prognostic value of *PLAGL*1-specific CpG site methylation in soft-tissue sarcomas. PLoS ONE **8**(11), e80741 (2013)
15. Ren, J., Zhou, X., Guo, W., Feng, K., Huang, T., Cai, Y.D.: Identification of methylation signatures and rules for sarcoma subtypes by machine learning methods. Genet. Res. **2022** (2022)
16. Medina, A.S., Pichardo, A.G., García-Heredia, J.M., Martínez-Ballesteros, M.: Discovery of genes implied in cancer by genetic algorithms and association rules. In: Martínez-Álvarez, F., Troncoso, A., Quintián, H., Corchado, E. (eds.) HAIS 2016. LNCS (LNAI), vol. 9648, pp. 694–705. Springer, Cham (2016). https://doi.org/10.1007/978-3-319-32034-2_58
17. Smyth, G.K.: Limma: Linear models for microarray data. R package version 3.48.3 (2021). https://bioconductor.org/packages/release/bioc/html/limma.html
18. Strassmann, D., et al.: Impact of sarcopenia in advanced and metastatic soft tissue sarcoma. Int. J. Clin. Oncol. **26**(11), 2151–2160 (2021). https://doi.org/10.1007/s10147-021-01997-7

Analysis of Frequency Bands in Electroencephalograms for Automatic Detection of Photoparoxysmal Responses

Fernando Moncada Martins[1]($\boxtimes$) , Victor M. González[1] , José R. Villar[2] ,
Beatriz García López[3] , and Ana Isabel Gómez-Menéndez[3]

[1] Electrical Engineering Department, University of Oviedo, Oviedo, Spain
{uo245868,vmsuarez}@uniovi.es
[2] Computer Science Department, University of Oviedo, Oviedo, Spain
villarjose@uniovi.es
[3] Neurophysiology Department, Burgos University Hospital, Burgos, Spain
{bgarcialo,agomm}@saludcastillayleon.es

Abstract. Photosensitivity is a neurological disorder in which a patient's brain produces epileptic discharges, known as Photoparoxysmal Responses (PPR), as a reaction to certain visual stimuli. The current standardized process of diagnosis used in hospitals consists of submitting the subject to Intermittent Photic Stimulation (IPS) process, attempting to trigger these phenomena. At the same time, the brain's electrical activity is recorded as an electroencephalogram (EEG) while the clinical specialists visually look for the PPRs provoked during the session if any. This research tests a modified version of a frequency-analysis-based method designed by neurophysiologists to predict epileptic activity during IPS by applying the Discrete Fourier Transform to extract spectral components and compare them. The goal is to detect these epileptic phenomena instead of predicting them by classifying EEG windows as PPR or not and flashing frequencies as PPR-triggering or not. The obtained results reveal that this new method cannot outperform those achieved from our previous research on automatic PPR detection. This research is performed with subjects at the Burgos University Hospital, Spain.

Keywords: EEG · Electroencephalography · PPR · Photoparoxysmal Response · Machine Learning · Photosensitivity · Epilepsy

1 Introduction

Photosensitivity is a neurological condition defined as an abnormal sensitivity of the brain to certain visual stimuli, such as light reflections or intermittent

This research has been funded by the Spanish Ministry of Economics and Industry, grant PID2020-112726RB-I00, by the Spanish Research Agency (AEI, Spain) under grant agreement RED2018-102312-T (IA-Biomed), and by the Ministry of Science and Innovation under CERVERA Excellence Network project CER-20211003 (IBERUS) and Missions Science and Innovation project MIG-20211008 (INMERBOT). Also, by Principado de Asturias, grant SV-PA-21-AYUD/2021/50994.

visual patterns, that triggers epileptic activity as a response. These discharges are called Photoparoxysmal Responses (PPRs), and [21] proposed a classification of these phenomena into four different groups depending on the intensity and the spread to different regions of the brain where they were recorded as an electroencephalogram (EEG) –see Fig. 1– that eventually became the standard:

- Type-1: spikes in the occipital region.
- Type-2: spikes followed by a biphasic slow wave in occipital and parietal regions.
- Type-3: spikes followed by a biphasic slow wave in occipital and parietal regions, spreading to frontal regions.
- Type-4: generalized poly-spikes and waves.

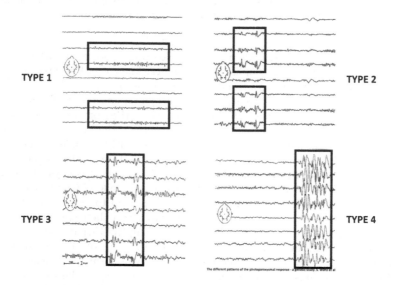

Fig. 1. Examples of the four types of PPRs: **top-left** corresponds to Type-1; **top-right** corresponds to Type-2; **bottom-left** corresponds to Type-3; and **bottom-right** corresponds to Type-4.

As can be seen, each type represents a more dangerous photosensitivity reaction than the previous one, being Type-4 the most severe one, which can lead to epilepsy. However, in real-case scenarios, PPRs morphology varies between individuals or even between sessions from the same subject because they are highly dependent on several clinical variables like medical treatment, sleep quality, time of the day, etc.; making them hard to classify.

This study is a continuation of a previous one [10] where Data Augmentation was applied to improve the balance of the available dataset and, thus, the performance of the Machine Learning algorithms already used to automatically detect PPRs present in EEG recordings. This research proposes a variation of a frequency-based procedure [6] designed by clinical neurophysiologists for PPR prediction to transform it into a PPR detection method. The goal is to compare the performance achieved by the modified version of the aforementioned method [6] against our current technique, proposed in [10], which has achieved the best results on automatic PPR detection so far.

The structure of this study is as follows: the next section introduces a brief state-of-art and related work regarding automated PPR detection; Sect. 3 describes the original frequency analysis technique developed by clinical neurophysiologists on which this study is based; Sect. 4 gives details of the dataset created for this project and the designed experimentation set-up that has been carried out for this study; Sect. 5 includes all the obtained results and the discussion on them; and the final section draws the conclusion of this research.

2   Related Work

Nowadays, the clinical procedure for diagnosing photosensitivity follows a standardized method called Intermittent Photic Stimulation (IPS), first proposed in [14,18]. This process uses a white flashing light to stimulate subjects at different frequency values for a certain period while their brain activity is recorded by EEG. The flashing frequency first increases from a minimum (1 Hz) to a maximum (50–60 Hz) until a PPR is found or the last value is reached; then, the stimulation decreases from the maximum to the minimum and, according to the same criteria, is stopped. The goal is to detect the frequency range in which the subject suffers photosensitivity. Each flashing frequency is performed with the subject's eyes open and closed, and a resting state is placed between subsequent stimulations. The detection of these discharges is currently being performed manually: the clinical staff has to analyze the EEG through a visual inspection and mark each PPR that is triggered during the IPS session.

To the best of our knowledge, only a very few studies address the automatic PPR detection problem: an analysis of the high-frequency components of the brain activity right after a flash of light following a different flashing pattern than the standard IPS procedure was proposed in [16], while [6] focused on the prediction and anticipation of PPRs while performing the IPS procedure by a technique that extracted the Fourier components from the recorded brain activity before the first triggered PPR. The latter method is the one on which the research presented in this paper is based. Besides them, our latest studies published in [9–11] are the only ones that focus on automatic PPR detection by applying different Machine Learning techniques (this series of publications is part of a larger project that analyzes the effects of Virtual Reality on photosensitive patients and proposes the introduction of this technology along with Artificial Intelligence into the photosensitivity diagnosis and evaluation process [11]).

Nevertheless, there are other recent studies focused on the automatic detection of generalized seizures and epilepsy that could perhaps be modified and transferred to the field of photosensitivity due to the connection and similarities between both topics, such as the use of Extreme Gradient Boosting for seizure classification in [20]; the analysis of the fluctuation of EEG channel's higher and lower frequencies in [12]; or the detection of ictal discharges and inter-ictal states by applying the Permutation Rényi Entropy in [8]; while [3] made use of simple Machine Learning techniques like an Artificial Neural Network and K-Nearest Neighbors. Also, more complex Deep Learning techniques are used, like a channel-independent Long Short-Term Memory Network was proposed in [2]. Other studies approached this task from different biological points of view, analyzing other bio-markers and biomedical measures such as electromyography [1,23], electrocardiography (ECG) [4,5,19] or magnetoencephalography (MEG) [15], while combinations of different clinical information are proposed in [6] (EEG + MEG) and [22] (EEG + ECG). Most of these proposals are very recent, even after several decades of research, which means that the detection and prediction of epileptic seizures are far from being solved [13].

3   Frequency Analysis of Paroxysmal Activity

The method proposed in this paper for automatic PPR detection is based on the PPR prediction and anticipation technique proposed by a group of clinical neurophysiologists in [6]. Although it seems to be preferable to predict the epileptic activity before it is triggered than detect it after it happens in such as intense protocol, the reason why we chose to modify this prediction technique to detect PPR activity is that the current clinical protocol for diagnosing photosensitivity requires to trigger the epileptic responses for the clinical specialists to locate these phenomena and mark them in the EEG, which is the task we are trying to help them with.

The original method data was gathered from different patients already diagnosed with photosensitivity who were stimulated using the IPS procedure only at stimulation frequency values of 10, 15, 20 Hz; and the stimulation was paused immediately after an epileptic discharge was triggered for a 20-s rest period of non-epileptic activity. MEG and EEG data were recorded during the sessions.

Given a stimulation trial, a patient was stimulated with a total number of flashes L at a certain flashing frequency f_s (and therefore $T = 1/f_s$, being T the period of time between flashes). Segments $S_{\alpha,i}(t)$ of a duration of less than T were extracted from the original recordings at the instant of each flash as flash-response brain activity, where α corresponds to any recording channel and $i = 1, ..., L$.

Discrete Fourier Transform was computed over each segment $S_{\alpha,i}(t)$, and the complex amplitudes $F^n_{\alpha,i}$ were obtained. From all the spectral components, only those corresponding to the frequencies that are multiples of the stimulation frequency f_s were used; the remaining frequencies were discarded.

Then, a measure called *Phase Clustering Index* C_α^n is calculated for each n frequency component and each α channel following Eq. 1:

$$C_\alpha^n = \frac{\left| \sum_{i=0}^{L} F_{\alpha,i}^n \right|}{\sum_{i=0}^{L} \left| F_{\alpha,i}^n \right|} \tag{1}$$

This study proposed a comparative measure called *Relative Phase Clustering Index* K_α to compare the activity from each frequency component taken into account against the fundamental stimulation frequency component as follows:

$$K_\alpha = \max_n (C_\alpha^n - C_\alpha^1) \tag{2}$$

Equation 2 aims to check if abnormal brain activity is more intense than the fundamental one, known as photic-drive activity. The photic-driving response is a common physiological brain reaction to light flashing during the IPS procedure, which consists of an intensification of brain activity in the occipital region at the same frequency as the current stimulation frequency (i.e. if the patient is receiving a stimulation applied 10 Hz, an intensification 10 Hz brain activity will occur) [7]. If following Eq. 2, $K_\alpha > 1$, it means that there is an anomalous activity in that specific channel α at the frequency corresponding to the component n; otherwise, there is no abnormal activity.

Finally, the average K over all channels K_α is calculated: if this value is higher than 1, then the epileptic activity is starting to emerge. This is the classifier used to predict the triggering of PPRs.

4   Materials and Methods

This section introduces the description of the data set gathered and used in this research in Sect. 4.1, while Sect. 4.2 describes the design of the experiments. The whole process was implemented in Python.

4.1   Dataset Description

The dataset used in this research has been gathered from Burgos University Hospital. The clinical neurophysiologists recorded, annotated, and anonymized 10 sessions from 10 patients diagnosed with different degrees of photosensitivity using their clinical equipment, which is composed of the Natus Nicolet v44 hardware for EEG recording and the Natus Neuroworks software for real-time visualization and annotation.

Each session consisted of a 3-to-5-min continuous recording using an EEG cap while the patient was stimulated by applying the first half of the IPS procedure, corresponding to the ascending standard frequencies 1 Hz up 50 Hz. The sampling rate for the EEG signals 500 Hz; placing up to 19 electrodes according to the 10–20 standardized system [17], as shown in Fig. 2.

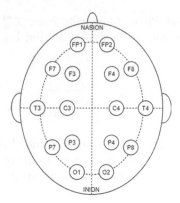

Fig. 2. Position of the 19 electrodes used according to the 10–20 international standardized system. The *Nasion* is located at the center of the frontonasal area; the *Inion* is located at the center of the back of the neck.

The clinical neurophysiologists performed a visual analysis of the EEG recordings and marked each PPR that had been triggered during the stimulation session. For this analysis, they applied the average montage to the recordings because they use it daily. This montage is created by computing the average of all channels at each timestamp and subtracting it from the measured sample at each individual channel.

Finally, the signals were divided using a sliding window of 1-s length and 90% overlapping. Then, each EEG window was manually labeled as PPR or non-PPR following the previously mentioned marks from the clinical staff. Thus, the proportion of the dataset is presented below, where an extreme imbalance between the two classes can be observed:

- Total number of EEG windows: 29190
  - Number of non-PPR windows: 27968 (**95.81%**)
  - Number of PPR windows: 1222 (**4.19%**)

4.2   Experimentation Design

The proposed technique is designed following the workflow shown in Fig. 3. Firstly, EEG windows are preprocessed by removing the average and applying a Notch filter 50 Hz (to remove the power supply component) plus a band-pass filter in the range of 1 to 150 Hz.

A slightly modified version of the original method is proposed in this paper. This approach is designed under the assumption that if spectral analysis of the EEG segments before the triggering of a PPR allows the prediction of such epileptic activity, it could define a PPR bio-marker as well.

Fig. 3. Workflow of the proposed experiment. Original EEG data is windowed and preprocessed. Then, for each stimulation period, EEG windows belonging to that period are divided into sub-segments depending on the frequency value, and the frequency-based classification is applied to classify each window as PPR or not.

The available EEG sessions were recorded while applying the whole first half of the IPS procedure, so more than the three original frequency values were used. Given a certain stimulation period at a flashing frequency f_s within the current EEG recording, each preprocessed window from that period is split into non-overlapped sub-segments of $T = 1/f_s$ length. Then, the frequency analysis technique is applied using these segments as $S_{\alpha,i}(t)$, and the final parameter K is used as the classifier to determine if there is a paroxysmal activity and, thus, a PPR within that window or not. Due to the change of task (from PPR prediction to PPR detection), two different experiments were designed:

Experiment 1: Stimulation Period Detection. This approach consists of detecting if the stimulation applied at a specific frequency value has triggered epileptic activity during its whole period, as shown in Fig. 4. For this experiment, each stimulation period is analyzed independently: EEG windows located in a specific stimulation period are classified as PPR or not following the frequency analysis technique. Once all windows have been classified, two different decision-making statements are applied to determine whether that frequency is PPR-triggering or not: I) if any window is classified as PPR, and II) if more than 50% of the windows are classified as PPR.

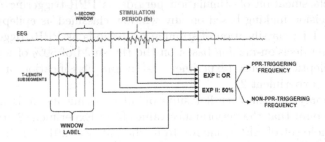

Fig. 4. Application of the frequency analysis technique in Experiment 1: each stimulation period is classified as PPR-triggering or not based on the number of windows located at that period classified as PPRs after being split into sub-segments and analyzed by the frequency-based method.

Experiment 2: Window Detection. This approach consists of classifying each EEG window into PPR or not –see Fig. 5–. For this task, EEG recordings are fully analyzed: windows located at stimulation periods are divided into segments depending on the flashing frequency applied, and the frequency analysis technique is used to classify each EEG window into PPR or not. Resting states between subsequent flashing periods were also analyzed: parameter f_s is fixed 1 Hz, so windows located at resting periods are not divided into sub-segments $S_{\alpha,i}(t)$ and the technique is applied considering it as a unique segment.

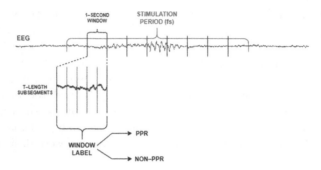

Fig. 5. Application of the frequency analysis technique in Experiment 2: each EEG window is split into sub-segments and the frequency analysis classifies it as PPR or not.

5   Results and Discussion

The results gathered in this research consist of the Accuracy (*Acc*), Sensitivity (*Sens*), and Specificity (*Spec*) values obtained by each experiment. Table 1 shows the results for the three approaches (1.I, 1.II, and 2) carried out for each EEG recording: classification of stimulation periods as PPR-triggering or not after applying decision-making based on any window classified as epileptic response (experiment 1-I); classification of stimulation periods as PPR-triggering or not after applying decision-making based on the threshold of 50% of windows classified as epileptic response (experiment 1-II); and classification of windows as PPR or not (experiment 2).

Before analyzing the overall results of all experiments, it is necessary to take into account that the performance values from Experiment 2 are calculated from the whole set of EEG windows from the dataset (29190 instances), while Experiment 1 classifies the stimulation periods throughout all EEG sessions as a whole (around 150 instances). This high difference in the number of instances between both experiments makes it impossible to correctly compare with each other.

As can be seen, on the one hand, Experiment 2 was by far the best-performing one, which means that the original technique is capable not only of predicting epileptic activity during the IPS procedure but also detecting PPR activity

Table 1. PPR detection results obtained from each experiment. From left to right: experiment 1 (classification of stimulation periods) after ANY-PPR-based decision making; Experiment 1 (classification of stimulation periods) after the 50%-PPR-based decision making; and Experiment 2 (classification of EEG windows).

P_i	Experiment 1: ANY PPR			Experiment 1: 50% PPR			Experiment 2		
	Acc	Sens	Spec	Acc	Sens	Spec	Acc	Sens	Spec
P_1	0.5000	1.0000	0.2222	0.7143	1.0000	0.5556	0.7522	0.8561	0.7473
P_1	0.5000	1.0000	0.2222	0.7143	1.0000	0.5556	0.7522	0.8561	0.7473
P_2	0.3889	1.0000	0.1538	0.5556	1.0000	0.3846	0.7064	0.7541	0.7055
P_3	1.0000	1.0000	1.0000	0.8333	0.8000	1.0000	0.7354	0.5833	0.7526
P_4	0.5625	1.0000	0.2222	0.5625	0.8571	0.3333	0.6605	0.7500	0.6583
P_5	0.1765	0.6667	0.0714	0.4706	0.6667	0.4286	0.6571	0.4898	0.6598
P_6	0.2353	1.0000	0.1875	0.2941	1.0000	0.2500	0.6294	0.3929	0.6315
P_7	0.2778	0.6667	0.2000	0.5000	0.6667	0.4667	0.6659	0.7639	0.6634
P_8	0.1765	0.5000	0.1333	0.2941	0.5000	0.2667	0.6266	0.3023	0.6312
P_9	0.7059	1.0000	0.2857	0.5882	0.7000	0.4286	0.7023	0.7854	0.6963
P_{10}	0.6471	0.9091	0.1667	0.4706	0.5455	0.3333	0.6790	0.5556	0.6994

located at a certain EEG window and classify it after applying modifications more appropriate to the new approach. On the other hand, *Spec* and *Sens* values obtained from Experiment 1 reveal that both approaches are unsuitable for this task because only one PPR misclassification is needed to classify wrong a whole flashing frequency in case I), and although case II) shows a slightly better performance, it is clear that it tends to classify the stimulation periods as PPR-triggering too.

Furthermore, considering that Experiment 2 presents the best performance of the new methodology proposed in this paper, in fact, we can compare it with the results presented in our previous research [10] –see Fig. 6–, which focused on EEG windows classification as PPR or not by applying Machine Learning algorithms. Those performance results are the best ones achieved until now on PPR detection by applying a neural network with one hidden layer with only 10 hidden neurons. As can be seen, our previous method, which achieved performance values of 95% for *Acc*, 85% for *Sens*, and 98% for *Spec*, outperforms the modified technique proposed in this paper.

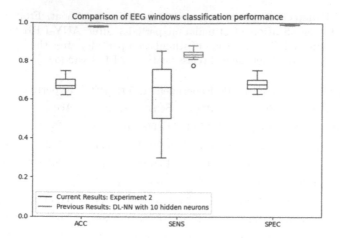

Fig. 6. Comparison of performance results between the proposed frequency-analysis-based method (**blue**) and our best method previously proposed (**red**), a neural network with one hidden layer with only 10 hidden neurons. (Color figure online)

6   Conclusions and Future Work

In this research, we proposed a modified version of a frequency-analysis-based technique for PPR and epileptic activity prediction designed by neurophysiologists specialized in photosensitivity and used it for a different task: automatic PPR detection. For this purpose, windows extracted from the original EEG recordings are divided into sub-segments of variable length, depending on the flashing frequency of the stimulation period they are located at. Then, Discrete Fourier Transform is computed for each segment, and the *Phase Clustering Index* measure is calculated for each component whose corresponding frequency is multiple of the flashing frequency. Finally, the maximum difference between each component when compared to the fundamental flashing frequency component is extracted: if this measure is positive, it means that there is an epileptic activity within that EEG window, and it is classified as a PPR window; otherwise, it is classified as normal.

This process has been applied to two different approaches: 1) classifying flashing frequencies as PPR-triggering or not if I) any or II) more than 50% windows located within that stimulation period are classified as epileptic activity, and 2) detecting PPRs by classifying every window as such phenomenon or not. The results show that the first experiment performed very poorly in both cases, while the second experiment presented better results, although it could not even come close to the results obtained in our previous research.

For future work, since there is still room for improvement for this modified version, a more deep study is needed to make this technique created by clinical specialists more suitable for this new task. Also, Deep Learning models will start to be tested: Convolutional or Recurrent Neural Networks for classifying EEG windows and Generative models –such as Autoencoders or GANs– to artificially generate new samples to balance the dataset. We suppose that these techniques will allow learning the different complex PPR patterns better and easier, achieving higher performances.

Author contributions. Fernando Moncada Martins, Víctor M. González, and José R. Villar designed the methodology and experiments and executed all technical and computer work. Clinical specialists Beatriz García López and Ana Isabel Gómez-Menéndez collected the data from the Burgos University Hospital by finding suitable EEG recordings from photosensitive patients with an appropriate amount of PPRs and anonymizing them.

References

1. Beniczky, S., Conradsen, I., Henning, O., Fabricius, M., Wolf, P.: Automated real-time detection of tonic-clonic seizures using a wearable EMG device. Neurology **90**(5), e428–e434 (2018). https://doi.org/10.1212/WNL.0000000000004893
2. Chakrabarti, S., Swetapadma, A., Pattnaik, P.K.: A channel independent generalized seizure detection method for pediatric epileptic seizures. Comput. Methods Programs Biomed. **209**, 106335 (2021). https://doi.org/10.1016/j.cmpb.2021.106335, https://linkinghub.elsevier.com/retrieve/pii/S0169260721004090
3. Choubey, H., Pandey, A.: A combination of statistical parameters for the detection of epilepsy and EEG classification using ANN and KNN classifier. Signal Image Video Process. **15**(3), 475–483 (2021). https://doi.org/10.1007/s11760-020-01767-4
4. Jahanbekam, A., et al.: Performance of ECG-based seizure detection algorithms strongly depends on training and test conditions. Epilepsia Open **6**(3), 597–606 (2021). https://doi.org/10.1002/epi4.12520
5. Jeppesen, J., et al.: Seizure detection based on heart rate variability using a wearable electrocardiography device. Epilepsia **60**(10), 2105–2113 (2019). https://doi.org/10.1111/epi.16343
6. Kalitzin, S., Parra, J., Velis, D., Lopes da Silva, F.: Enhancement of phase clustering in the EEG/MEG gamma frequency band anticipates transitions to paroxysmal epileptiform activity in epileptic patients with know visual sensitivity. IEEE Trans. Bio-med. Eng. **49**, 1279–86 (2002). https://doi.org/10.1109/TBME.2002.804593
7. Kiloh, L., McComas, A., Osselton, J.: Clinical Electroencephalography. Butterworth-Heinemann, Oxford (2013). https://doi.org/10.1016/B978-1-4831-6768-8.50006-4
8. Mammone, N., Duun-Henriksen, J., Kjaer, T.W., Morabito, F.C.: Differentiating interictal and ictal states in childhood absence epilepsy through permutation rényi entropy. Entropy **17**(7), 4627–4643 (2015). https://doi.org/10.3390/e17074627, https://www.mdpi.com/1099-4300/17/7/4627
9. Martins, F.M., González, V.M., García, B., Álvarez, V., Villar, J.R.: A comparison of machine learning techniques for the detection o type-4 photoparoxysmal responses in electroencephalographic signals. In: Garcia Bringas, P., et al. (eds.) HAIS 2022. Lecture Notes in Computer Science, vol. 13469, pp. 3–13. Springer International Publishing, Cham (2022). https://doi.org/10.1007/978-3-031-15471-3_1
10. Martins, F.M., Suárez, V.M.G., Flecha, J.R.V., López, B.G.: Data augmentation effects on highly imbalanced EEG datasets for automatic detection of photoparoxysmal responses. Sensors **23**(4), 2312 (2023). https://doi.org/10.3390/s23042312, https://www.mdpi.com/1424-8220/23/4/2312

11. Moncada, F., et al.: Virtual reality and machine learning in the automatic photoparoxysmal response detection. Neural Comput. Appl. (2022). https://doi.org/10.1007/s00521-022-06940-z

12. Omidvarnia, A., Warren, A.E., Dalic, L.J., Pedersen, M., Jackson, G.: Automatic detection of generalized paroxysmal fast activity in interictal EEG using time-frequency analysis. Comput. Biol. Med. **133**, 104287 (2021). https://doi.org/10.1016/j.compbiomed.2021.104287

13. Rasheed, K., et al.: Machine learning for predicting epileptic seizures using EEG signals: a review. IEEE Rev. Biomed. Eng. **14**, 139–155 (2021). https://doi.org/10.1109/RBME.2020.3008792

14. Rubboli, G., Parra, J., Seri, S., Takahashi, T., Thomas, P.: EEG diagnostic procedures and special investigations in the assessment of photosensitivity. Epilepsia **45**, 35–39 (2004). https://doi.org/10.1111/j.0013-9580.2004.451002.x

15. Soriano, M.C., et al.: Automated detection of epileptic biomarkers in resting-state interictal meg data. Front. Neuroinf. **11**, 43 (2017). https://doi.org/10.3389/fninf.2017.00043

16. Strigaro, G., Gori, B., Varrasi, C., Fleetwood, T., Cantello, G., Cantello, R.: Flash-evoked high-frequency EEG oscillations in photosensitive epilepsies. Epilepsy Res. **172**, 106597 (2021). https://doi.org/10.1016/j.eplepsyres.2021.106597, https://linkinghub.elsevier.com/retrieve/pii/S0920121121000504

17. International Federation of Clinical Neurophysiology: Report of the committee on methods of clinical examination in electroencephalography. Electroencephalogr. Clin. Neurophysiol. **10**(2) (1958). https://doi.org/10.1016/0013-4694(58)90053-1

18. Trenité, D.G.N., Binnie, C.D., Harding, G.F., Wilkins, A.: Photic stimulation: standardization of screening methods. Epilepsia **40**(9), 75–79 (1999). https://doi.org/10.1111/j.1528-1157.1999.tb00911.x

19. Ufongene, C., Atrache, R.E., Loddenkemper, T., Meisel, C.: Electrocardiographic changes associated with epilepsy beyond heart rate and their utilization in future seizure detection and forecasting methods. Clin. Neurophysiol. **131**(4), 866–879 (2020). https://doi.org/10.1016/j.clinph.2020.01.007

20. Vanabelle, P., Handschutter, P.D., Tahry, R.E., Benjelloun, M., Boukhebouze, M.: Epileptic seizure detection using EEG signals and extreme gradient boosting. J. Biomed. Res. **34**(3), 228 (2020). https://doi.org/10.7555/JBR.33.20190016

21. Waltz, S., Christen, H.J., Doose, H.: The different patterns of the photoparoxysmal response - a genetic study. Electroencephalogr. Clin. Neurophysiol. **83**(2), 138–145 (1992). https://doi.org/10.1016/0013-4694(92)90027-F

22. Yang, Y., et al.: A multimodal AI system for out-of-distribution generalization of seizure detection. IEEE J. Biomed. Health Inf. (2021). https://doi.org/10.1101/2021.07.02.450974

23. Zibrandtsen, I.C., Kidmose, P., Kjaer, T.W.: Detection of generalized tonic-clonic seizures from ear-EEG based on EMG analysis. Seizure **59**, 54–89 (2018). https://doi.org/10.1016/j.seizure.2018.05.001

Textural and Shape Features for Lesion Classification in Mammogram Analysis

Adél Bajcsi[⊠] and Camelia Chira

Babeş–Bolyai University, Cluj-Napoca, Cluj, Romania
{adel.bajcsi,camelia.chira}@ubbcluj.ro
http://www.cs.ubbcluj.ro

Abstract. The efficient analysis of digital mammograms has an important role in the early detection of breast cancer and can lead to a higher percentage of recovery. The process of mammogram classification can be divided into two steps as follows: first, it has to be established if the tissue contains abnormalities, and, second, the nature of the lesion has to be determined. This second step of a computer-aided diagnosis system is important in order to select the best treatment for the patient and to achieve the highest chance of recovery. In general, digital mammogram analysis consists of preprocessing, feature extraction, feature selection and classification. Feature extraction is crucial in identifying informative characteristics that can differentiate between benign and malignant lesions. The two main types of feature extraction methods are shape features and texture features. In the current paper, we present several experiments in order to compare the performance of different feature extraction methods from the two types mentioned previously. As data, images from the Digital Database for Screening Mammography (DDSM) are used, which has precise ground truth for the cancerous tissue. For classification Decision Trees and Random Forest methods are used to evaluate the performance using the different extracted features. The experiments that were carried out show that shape features perform better than texture features to separate benign and malignant abnormalities. Also, some outliers were found causing a decrease in the accuracy of the system and achieving 66% test accuracy using shape features and Random Forest classifier.

Keywords: mammogram analysis · textural features · shape features · DDSM

1 Introduction

In medicine, X-ray imaging is frequently used to analyze the internal structure and potential abnormalities of the human body/organs. Mammography, a type of X-ray imaging, is commonly used to detect and diagnose breast cancer. It is a non-invasive and low-risk diagnostic tool that allows the early detection of breast cancer, which significantly increases the chances of successful treatment

© The Author(s), under exclusive license to Springer Nature Switzerland AG 2023
P. García Bringas et al. (Eds.): HAIS 2023, LNAI 14001, pp. 755–767, 2023.
https://doi.org/10.1007/978-3-031-40725-3_64

and reduces the mortality rate. The growth in digital mammography has greatly contributed to the early detection and diagnosis of breast cancer, a leading cause of mortality among women worldwide [6]. However, there is still much room for improvement in the development of robust and effective feature extraction methods for lesion type detection, which can further enhance the accuracy and reliability of mammographic analysis.

Mammogram analysis is a complex problem, which involves the following steps: preprocessing, segmentation, feature extraction, feature selection and classification. Feature extraction is a crucial step in the process of mammographic analysis, as it enables the identification and characterization of lesions present in digital mammograms. These features may include but are not limited to texture, shape, intensity, and density of the regions of interest.

The current experiments are addressed to compare the performance of different feature extraction methods, specifically using shape and texture features, to improve lesion type detection in digital mammograms. The combination of these features is also considered in this study, as it may provide a more comprehensive and accurate representation of the mammographic images. The experiments use images from the Digital Database for Screening Mammography (DDSM) [10,11] that contain precise ground truth information on cancerous tissue. To evaluate the performance of the different feature extraction methods and achieve optimal accuracy for lesion type detection, decision trees and random forests are used as classification techniques. The novelty of the presented approach consists in the use of feature extraction, feature selection and classification method combination on the dataset (DDMS). Furthermore, in our research we increased the number of input images (1424 instead of 323) compared to [13].

The rest of the paper is organized as follows: in Sect. 2 existing studies are discussed from the literature related to lesion classification. Section 3 details the current approach and Sect. 4 analyzes the achieved results. Finally, in Sect. 5 we present the conclusion of our experiments.

2   Related Work

In recent years, there have been numerous studies [1–4, 7–9, 12, 14] presented in the field of computer-aided diagnosis (CAD) for the early detection of cancerous cells. Breast cancer causes the most deaths among women worldwide [6]; hence, developing accurate and reliable CAD systems has been a major focus of research. With the help of CAD systems, the mortality rate due to breast cancer can be significantly reduced. In the literature, there are studies [1–4, 7–9, 12, 14] focusing on the different steps of a CAD system: preprocessing, segmentation, feature extraction, feature selection, and classification. In the following paragraphs, some of the relevant studies related to feature extraction in mammographic analysis will be discussed.

Various feature extraction methods have been proposed for mammographic analysis. Some use texture features such as Gray-Level Co-Occurrence Matrix (GLCM) [1,4,5,7], Gray-Level Run-Length Matrix (GLRLM) [3–5], and Local Binary Patterns (LBP) [7,8]. Others use shape features such as area, perimeter, compactness, roughness and slope [9,13].

Texture features are frequently used on medical images to capture visual characteristics. These features are derived from second-order statistics that examine the gray levels on the image. The use of GLCM was proposed by Ancy and Nair [1] to extract features from data of Mammographic Image Analysis Society (MIAS) [16]. The computed characteristics were fed to a Support Vector Machine (SVM) classifier to detect tumors in the breast tissue. The system resulted in 81% accuracy score. Farhan et al. [8] have used LBP to differentiate benign and malignant breast lesions. LBP descriptors are proficient in efficiently capturing the grayscale contrast along with local spatial patterns in an image. The authors reported 85% accuracy using logistic regression classifier on MIAS [16]. Saeed et al. [7] proposed the classification of LBP features using Random Forest (RF) classifier using images from the same dataset and achieved 75% accuracy. Chaieb and Kalti [5] published a survey comparing different feature extraction methods and concluded that GLRLM features were the most suitable for identifying breast cancer in mammograms. Based on the results presented in [5], in previous research [3,4] we used GLRLM feature extraction on images from MIAS [16] and DDSM [10,11]. The computed characteristics were used as input to different feature selection (Principal Component Analysis – PCA and genetic algorithm-based – GA method) and classification (Decision Tree – DT and Random Forest – RF) methods to differentiate between normal, benign and malignant tissues. The reported accuracies were 70% on MIAS and 54.1% on DDSM.

In a study by Li et al. [13], contour features were extracted from the mammograms, by defining a 1-dimensional representation of the lesion boundary. The authors obtained 99.33% accuracy using SVM and 323 images from Digital Database for Screening Mammography (DDSM) dataset [10,11]. A similar approach is described in [9], where shape features are classified using an Artificial Neural Network (ANN), achieving an accuracy of 97.24% on the Curated Breast Imaging Subset of DDSM (CBIS-DDSM).

Kumari and Jagadesh [12] introduced an advanced GLCM (AGLCM) by combining texture- (GLCM), intensity- (entropy), and shape features. Using SVM to detect lesions on mammograms from MIAS, the authors obtained an accuracy of 92.4% which outperformed the texture feature extraction methods [1]. This experiment shows how the combination of different features can improve the accuracy of the CAD system.

Ansar et al. [2] proposed a deep learning-based approach for breast cancer detection using a model with Convolutional Neural Networks (CNNs). Their proposed model achieved an accuracy of 86.8% on DDSM. Li et al. [14] proposed a two-view system and achieved 94.7% accuracy.

Experiments clearly show the importance of feature extraction in a mammogram classification system. In the current study, we aim to compare the shape feature extraction method presented in [13] (with outstanding results on DDSM) to GLRLM texture feature extraction method in identifying breast abnormality type in mammograms.

3   Proposed Approach

The objective of the current study is to compare the performance of textural- and shape features in distinguishing between benign and malignant lesions in digital mammograms. Specifically, we use gray-level run-length matrix (GLRLM) texture features and shape (geometrical and contour) features to extract relevant information from mammograms, which are then used as inputs for the classification models. Similarly to [4], feature selection is applied to reduce the dimensionality of the feature set and eliminate any redundant or irrelevant features, which can improve the classification accuracy and efficiency.

3.1   Preprocessing

In the preprocessing step, we use the predefined mask of the lesion to isolate the relevant regions of interest in mammograms. In the first step, the bounding box enclosing the lesion is defined. These bounding boxes are increased to have 25 pixels of padding around the lesion. We presume that this padding helps to capture the surrounding tissue and potential microcalcifications that may be indicative of malignancy – especially for textural feature extraction. The image is cropped based on the resulting bounding box. Next, a same-size binary mask is defined – by using the predefined mask – where 1 marks the pixels belonging to the lesion and 0 marks the pixels belonging to the background.

3.2   Feature Extraction

Feature extraction, as mentioned in Sect. 1, has a key role in computer-aided systems. The classification is highly dependent on its input. Therefore, the process of feature extraction requires a careful selection of appropriate methods and algorithms that can effectively capture the relevant information from the images.

In our proposed approach, we extract texture and shape features from the regions of interest in digital mammograms with the aim of characterizing the lesions. Texture features are extracted using GLRLM [5], which has been shown to effectively capture the texture information in medical – gray-scale – images. These features are quantified by calculating the frequency and distribution of gray-level runs in a given direction. Shape features, on the other hand, are extracted using the mask of the lesion and are categorized as geometrical features and contour features [13]. These characteristics illustrate the size of the lesion and the regularity/irregularity of the border surrounding the lesions. In the following paragraphs, the used feature extraction methods are detailed.

GLRLM [5] is a feature extraction method used to quantify texture features in medical images by calculating the distribution of gray-level runs in a given direction. In case of an image (2-dimensional data) it can be defined in four directions: horizontal, first diagonal, vertical and second diagonal. From the constructed matrices 11 features are extracted – as listed in [3] – describing the relationship between gray levels and their spatial distribution and therefore providing insight into the complex textures present in mammographic images. Taking into account the aforementioned four orientations, a total of 44 characteristics will be derived from an analysis of a mammogram.

Geometrical features are calculated from the mask of a lesion. This set of features includes the perimeter, the area and the compactness (calculated as the perimeter squared divided by the area). These are simple and frequently used features and they are used as a baseline.

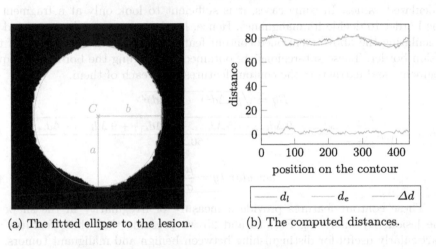

(a) The fitted ellipse to the lesion.   (b) The computed distances.

Fig. 1. Defining contour features of a benign lesion.

Contour features were introduced in [13]. The image (2-dimensional information) is converted into 1-dimensional data. In order to extract details regarding the circularity of a lesion, we try to fit an ellipse to it. First, the center of the ellipse $C(x_c, y_c)$ is defined by the average of white pixel coordinates on the mask. This is also presented in Eq. (1), where N is the total number of white pixels. Next, the width and height of the lesion are defined and used as the minor- (b) and major-axis (a) of the ellipse, as shown in Eq. (2). Figures 1a and 2a illustrate the calculated ellipses.

$$C = \left(\frac{\sum^p x_p}{N}, \frac{\sum^p y_p}{N} \right) \text{, where } p \in \{(x_p, y_p) | mask_{x_p\, y_p} = 1\} \qquad (1)$$

$$a = \max_p x_p - \min_p x_p$$

$$b = \max_p y_p - \min_p y_p \text{ , where } p \in \{(x_p, y_p) | mask_{x_p \, y_p} = 1\} \qquad (2)$$

Based on this information we define points on the ellipse and calculate their distance from C. These distances are saved into a list called d_e. For every point on the ellipse, there is a corresponding point on the boundary of the lesion. In d_l, we save the distances of these points from C. Finally, Δd is defined by the difference between d_l and d_e Eq. (3). Figures 1b and 2b show the calculated distances for a benign and malignant lesion respectively.

$$\Delta d = |d_l - d_e| \qquad (3)$$

After defining Δd, the final features are calculated, namely the root mean roughness Eq. (4), the root mean slope Eq. (5) and the circularity Eq. (6). In Eq. (4) to (6) μ and σ represent the mean and the standard deviation of the calculated values. In some cases, it is sufficient to look only at a fragment of the border to decide its malignancy. Hence, local features are also extracted by calculating the above-mentioned contour features for smaller sub-regions of the lesion border. These sub-regions are obtained by dividing the border into equal segments and extracting the contour features from each of them.

$$Rq = \sqrt{\mu(\Delta d^2) - \mu(\Delta d)^2} \qquad (4)$$

$$R\Delta q = \sqrt{\mu\left[\left(\sum_i \frac{\Delta d_{i-3} - 9\Delta d_{i-2} + 45\Delta d_{i-1} - 45\Delta d_{i+1} + 9\Delta d_{i+2} - \Delta d_{i+3}}{60\Delta d_i}\right)^2\right]} \qquad (5)$$

$$circularity = \frac{\mu(\Delta d)}{\sigma(\Delta d)} \qquad (6)$$

These contour features provide a measure of irregularity in the shape of the lesion. By analyzing Figs. 1b and 2b we presume that these features are particularly useful for distinguishing between benign and malignant tumors.

3.3   Feature Selection

Feature selection involves selecting a subset of the most relevant features from a larger set of extracted features. This is important because it reduces the dimensionality of data and removes irrelevant features, thus simplifying analysis, improving computational efficiency, and increasing the accuracy of the classification model. Various feature selection techniques have been proposed in the literature (more details in survey [5]). In our experiments, we utilize the principal component analysis (PCA) method [4] and a genetic algorithm-based (GA) method [4] to perform feature selection.

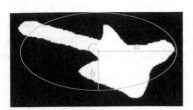

(a) The mask of the lesion. Purple line marks the border of the lesion, while the green one is the fitted ellipse.

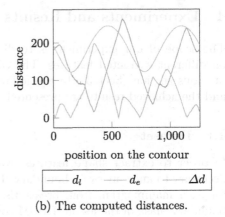

position on the contour

(b) The computed distances.

Fig. 2. Defining contour features of a malignant lesion.

PCA is a mathematical technique that involves transforming data into a new coordinate system, where the features are represented as a set of linearly uncorrelated variables. This method maximizes the variance of data and minimizes the number of variables required to represent it.

GA is a meta-heuristic optimization technique that is inspired by the natural selection process in biology. It involves simulating a population of potential feature subsets. In case of feature selection, the goal is to find the subset of features that maximizes a selected evaluation metric.

3.4 Classification

Classification refers to the process of assigning input data to one of several predefined classes based on a set of rules or models. In the current approach, we utilize two different supervised classification algorithms, namely the Decision Tree (DT) and Random Forest (RF) algorithms because of their interpretability. To construct the models the CART (Classification and Regression Tree) algorithm[1] is used.

The DT algorithm involves recursively splitting the training data into binary partitions based on a set of if-then rules inferred from the input features. The partitioning is performed in a way that the resulting subsets are as homogeneous as possible with respect to the class labels of their members.

On the other hand, the RF algorithm constructs an ensemble of decision trees and aggregates their results to make a final prediction. This approach has been shown to yield higher classification accuracy compared to using a single decision tree, as it reduces the risk of overfitting. In our research, we perform experiments with every possible combination of feature selection and classification, in order to define the best solution.

---

[1] Source: https://scikit-learn.org/stable/modules/tree.html.

4   Experiments and Results

The scope of our experiment is to distinguish the character of lesions based on different extracted features. The constructed system was presented in the previous section (Sect. 3). In the following sections the used data, parameters and the achieved results are presented.

4.1   Dataset

In order to extract shape features from the contour of the abnormality it is necessary to know its exact boundary. Therefore, DDSM [10, 11] is used, because for each mammogram from breast tissue with cancerous cells it contains the boundary mask of the lesion. DDSM contains in total 7809 images: half of them taken from the side and the other half from the top. In the current experiment the mammograms taken from the side are used. Among these samples there are 2465 normal, 712 benign and 728 malignant examples. To build a classifier to distinguish the type of the lesion, the normal images are excluded. Further, to achieve a better result the same number of mammograms are used from each class. Therefore, 1424 images are used in the current experiments (712 examples from each class).

The next step is to split these images into train and test sets. Stratified sampling is used to ensure that the proportion of each set remains the same in both sets. Moreover, if there are more samples from the same patient they will be placed into the same set to prevent bias. 75% of the data (1067) are used to train the model, while 25% (357) to validate to the correctness of the built model.

4.2   Experimental Setup

In Sect. 3 the used methods and the proposed approach are presented. In the following paragraphs, we will further detail the parameter setting for the proposed algorithms.

As mentioned in Sect. 3.2, besides GLRLM features, local contour features are also extracted, by splitting the boundary into smaller segments and applying one of functions presented in Eqs. (4) to (6). As proposed by Li et al. [13], we consider the number of segments (S) to be from $\{2, 4, 6, 8, 10, 12, 14, 16, 18, 20\}$. The value of S also defines the number of extracted features from the 1-dimensional data (Δd).

The parameters of the feature selection methods are selected by running preliminary experiment by following the methodology presented in our previous work [3]. According to these results, the minimum explained variance of the PCA is set to 0.99 and for GA's fitness function a DT is used and the classification accuracy is maximized.

4.3   Results

In the current experiment, we built different systems – detailed in Sect. 3 – for the binary classification problem of determining the type of a lesion. The performance of the proposed method is evaluated using measures such as accuracy, sensitivity, specificity, and f1-score which are commonly used in medical classification problems. The geometrical features are implemented as baseline, and their results are compared to more advanced feature extraction methods.

In our experiments, first, we defined the best shape feature and the optimal number of segments S. The results are presented in Table 1. As we can see Rq (as defined by Eq. (4)) has usually the best performance indifferent from S. We also conducted experiments where all three were used as input to the classifier. We refer to these features as 'combo' in Table 1. This combined feature has slightly better performance than $R\Delta q$ (as defined by Eq. (5)) or $circularity$ (as defined by Eq. (6)) on its own but the results are still behind Rq. Furthermore, based on the information in the same table we decided to use $S = 16$ in further experiments.

Table 1. The achieved accuracies using the different contour features, PCA feature selection and RF classification.

S	Rq	$R\Delta q$	$circularity$	$combo$
2	0.5910	0.5406	0.5546	0.5798
4	0.5742	0.5238	0.5574	0.6022
6	0.5994	0.5686	0.5378	0.6106
8	0.6134	0.5462	0.5350	0.5966
10	0.6050	0.5406	0.5658	0.6190
12	0.6078	0.5966	0.5238	0.6134
14	0.6106	0.5518	0.5518	0.6162
16	0.6498	0.5938	0.55202	0.5966
18	0.6358	0.5938	0.5323	0.6162
20	0.6134	0.5686	0.5322	0.6386

The scope of the current paper was to compare the performance of the textural features against shape features to distinguish benign and malignant lesions of the breast tissue. In the first row of Table 2, the performance of the baseline (geometrical features) is presented for the test set. All of the proposed feature extraction methods outperformed the baseline. Table 2 lists the results for the test set produced by the different feature extraction methods. Hence, we can conclude that the shape features are more suitable for the current classification of cancerous tissue. We conducted an experiment, using the combination of texture- and shape (contour) features and the achieved results are presented in the last row of Table 2.

Table 2. Results of the classification using different feature extraction methods, reported on the test set, using PCA feature selection and RF classification.

Feature extraction	Accuracy	Precision	Recall	F_1
geometry	0.5574	0.5582	0.5574	0.5567
$Rq(S = 16)$	0.6499	0.6515	0.6499	0.6492
GLRLM	0.6359	0.6379	0.6359	0.6349
GLRLM + $Rq(S = 18)$	0.6555	0.6615	0.6555	0.6528

Separate experiments were conducted to decide which classification and feature selection method combination performs the best. Figure 3 shows the performance achieved using Rq and indicates that with the increase in the number of segments the performance of the system also increases. Another observation is that the DT has lower results than RF (with 100 DTs in the ensemble). This can be explained by the "majority rule", that the decision is made based on the opinion of the majority, hence reducing overfitting. Finally, although RF with GA has better accuracy using $S = 16$, by looking at the total picture the classification results using PCA are more stable (the differences are smaller between the segments).

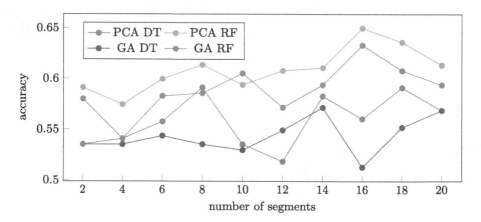

Fig. 3. Accuracy achieved on the test set using Rq computed from different number of segments.

4.4   Discussion

In this subsection, we aim to compare the results reported by the proposed approach (as given in Sect. 4.3) with those of related relevant methods from the literature. In our experiments we are facing the problem of overfitting: on the train set the model can predict with 100% accuracy, but on the test set it has a performance of 65.55%.

Li et al. [13] presented a 99.66% accuracy using the same shape features (more precisely $R\Delta q$) as input to an SVM classifier. The difference in the results can be explained by a different classification method, but also by a different experiment setup as Li et al. used 323 images from the total of 1440 samples with abnormalities from DDSM. Considering this difference we looked in more detail into the dataset and found that there are outliers regarding the regularity/irregularity of the lesions. An example is shown in Fig. 4. Therefore, we will further investigate if the removal of the outliers increase the precision of our system. On the other hand, we will examine other feature extraction methods on these outliers.

Fig. 4. Benign lesion with irregular boundary.

Muramatsu et al. [15] presented a CNN for this binary classification problem and achieved 72.5% by using images from DDSM to train the network. Our results approximate the result of the presented system.

In our previous study [3] we presented 92.23% accuracy using GLRLM features, PCA feature selection and RF classification, but on another dataset (Mammographic Image Analysis Society – MIAS). Another difference, compared to the current study is that the features are extracted from the full preprocessed image, not only from the lesion and its surrounding.

5   Conclusions and Further Work

In the current study we present a computer aided system to define the type of an abnormality in the breast tissue. Our aim was to compare the performance of textural- and shape features for the binary classification of breast cancer. Based on the results of our experiments, we can conclude that using shape features over textural features is more successful in distinguishing benign and malignant lesions. Also, by the combination of textural- and shape features the result increases and slightly outperforms the shape features. In the experiment basic geometrical features were also included, but based on their result we propose to further investigate and combine them with other features. The best results were achieved using a combination of features (Rq of 18 segments and GLRLM), GA feature selection and RF classification. The high train accuracy (100%) and fair test accuracy (65.55%) shows the problem of overfitting. Therefore, in future studies we will look into pruning methods and creating other splits to remove the outliers.

References

1. Ancy, C.A., Nair, L.S.: An efficient cad for detection of tumour in mammograms using SVM. In: 2017 International Conference on Communication and Signal Processing (ICCSP), pp. 1431–1435 (2017). https://doi.org/10.1109/ICCSP.2017.8286621

2. Ansar, W., Shahid, A.R., Raza, B., Dar, A.H.: Breast cancer detection and localization using MobileNet based transfer learning for mammograms. In: Brito-Loeza, C., Espinosa-Romero, A., Martin-Gonzalez, A., Safi, A. (eds.) ISICS 2020. CCIS, vol. 1187, pp. 11–21. Springer, Cham (2020). https://doi.org/10.1007/978-3-030-43364-2_2

3. Bajcsi, A., Andreica, A., Chira, C.: Towards feature selection for digital mammogram classification. Procedia Comput. Sci. **192**, 632–641 (2021). https://doi.org/10.1016/j.procs.2021.08.065

4. Bajcsi, A., Chira, C., Andreica, A.: Extended mammogram classification from textural features. Stud. Univ. Babes-Bolyai Inf. **67**, 5–20 (2023). https://doi.org/10.24193/subbi.2022.2.01

5. Chaieb, R., Kalti, K.: Feature subset selection for classification of malignant and benign breast masses in digital mammography. Pattern Anal. Appl. **22**(3), 803–829 (2019). https://doi.org/10.1007/s10044-018-0760-x

6. Chhikara, B.S., Parang, K.: Global cancer statistics 2022: the trends projection analysis. Chem. Biol. Lett. **10**(1), 451 (2022)

7. Darweesh, M.S., et al.: Early breast cancer diagnostics based on hierarchical machine learning classification for mammography images. Cogent Eng. **8**(1), 1968324 (2021). https://doi.org/10.1080/23311916.2021.1968324

8. Farhan, A.H., Kamil, M.Y.: Texture analysis of mammogram using local binary pattern method. J. Phys: Conf. Ser. **1530**(1), 012091 (2020). https://doi.org/10.1088/1742-6596/1530/1/012091

9. Gurudas, V.R., Shaila, S.G., Vadivel, A.: Breast cancer detection and classification from mammogram images using multi-model shape features. SN Comput. Sci. **3**(5), 404 (2022). https://doi.org/10.1007/s42979-022-01290-y

10. Heath, M., et al.: Current status of the digital database for screening mammography. In: Karssemeijer, N., Thijssen, M., Hendriks, J., van Erning, L. (eds.) Digital Mammography. Computational Imaging and Vision, vol. 13, pp. 457–460. Springer, Netherlands (1998). https://doi.org/10.1007/978-94-011-5318-8_75

11. Heath, M., Bowyer, K., Kopans, D., Moore, R., Kegelmeyer, P.: The digital database for screening mammography. In: Yaffe, M. (ed.) Proceedings of the Fifth International Workshop on Digital Mammography, pp. 212–218. Medical Physics Publishing (2001)

12. Kumari, L.K., Jagadesh, B.N.: A robust feature extraction technique for breast cancer detection using digital mammograms based on advanced GLCM approach. EAI Endorsed Trans. Pervasive Health Technol. **8**(30), e3 (2022). https://doi.org/10.4108/eai.11-1-2022.172813

13. Li, H., Meng, X., Wang, T., Tang, Y., Yin, Y.: Breast masses in mammography classification with local contour features. Biomed. Eng. Online **16**(1), 44 (2017). https://doi.org/10.1186/s12938-017-0332-0

14. Li, H., Niu, J., Li, D., Zhang, C.: Classification of breast mass in two-view mammograms via deep learning. IET Image Process. **15**(2), 454–467 (2021). https://doi.org/10.1049/ipr2.12035

15. Muramatsu, C.: Improving breast mass classification by shared data with domain transformation using a generative adversarial network. Comput. Biol. Med. **119**, 103698 (2020). https://doi.org/10.1016/j.compbiomed.2020.103698
16. Suckling, J., Parker, J., Dance, D.: The mammographic image analysis society digital mammogram database. In: International Congress Series, vol. 1069, pp. 375–378 (1994)

Intent Recognition Using Recurrent Neural Networks on Vital Sign Data: A Machine Learning Approach

Samson Mihirette[1](✉) [iD], Qing Tan[2] [iD], and Enrique Antonio De la Cal Martin[1] [iD]

[1] University of Oviedo, Oviedo, Spain
uo298476@uniovi.es
[2] Athabasca University, Athabasca, Canada

Abstract. The growing importance of technology in daily life has led to a focus on making robots think like humans to enhance the integration of humans and robots in Cyber-Physical Systems (CPS). Cognitive science and psychology offer important knowledge and tools for integrating human-like learning processes into robots. The challenge is to enhance robots with prior knowledge and information, rather than starting the learning process from scratch. The goal of this research is to enable efficient interaction and co-existence of humans, robots, and other agents in CPS. This paper presents a review of the current academic literature on identifying human intentions and feeding robots for their effectiveness when interacting with humans. As a new contribution, this paper also proposes a state-of-the-art solution for human intent recognition studies and focuses our research roadmap on emotion recognition using Vital Signs including electroencephalography (EEG) data (signals) to understand the intent of human action using deep learning techniques. The research also compares the prediction performance of recurrent neural networks (RNN) with other algorithms. Understanding humans' intent using vital signs for effective co-existence of humans in the cyber physical system and how to identify the intent of the agent and ensure that it aligns with the context of the given task or goal based on immediate perceptible visual attributes and dynamic properties (the perception of movement, gaze, vocalization, and emotional state.)

Keywords: Intent Recognition · Vital Signs · EEG Signal · Context Aware

1 Introduction

As the importance of technology in humans' daily life grows exponentially, one of the goals of technology researchers and the industry practitioners is on how to make the role of machines or robots more efficient and integrated within the cyber physical system. More specifically how to make robots think like humans. Instead of viewing robots as a tool for humans to perform a task, enhancing the role of machines close to human behaviour will facilitate the co-existence of humans, robots, and other agents in the Cyber-Physical Systems (CPS).

© The Author(s), under exclusive license to Springer Nature Switzerland AG 2023
P. García Bringas et al. (Eds.): HAIS 2023, LNAI 14001, pp. 768–779, 2023.
https://doi.org/10.1007/978-3-031-40725-3_65

The term CPS refer to systems with integrated computational and physical capabilities that can interact with humans in varies ways, forms, and methods [1]. Several research studies have been conducted on human computer interaction (HCI), Human Robot Interaction (HRI), and Human Machine Interaction to enhance and improve the effective integration of Humans in the CPS. However, there are plenty of research challenges that require a very extensive study on making the interrelationship and integration of agents in the CPS very effective.

The field of Cognitive Science and Psychology provide extensive knowledge and tools on the process of learning in humans and suggest various important attributes robots to have to integrate a more human-like learning process. Integrating key ingredients of human intelligence such as intuitive physics and intuitive psychology will produce significantly more powerful and more human-like learning and thinking abilities than we currently see in the Artificial Intelligence Systems [2].

Human and robot, to co-exist in a system as near equal partners, both cognitive and phenomenological provide aspects need to be considered. The cognitive aspects concern perceptual identification and reciprocal validation, resulting in mutual expectations and understandings. The phenomenological aspects relate to responsiveness that leads to mutual engagement and commitment [3].

The taxonomy and the path our research followed is illustrated in Fig. 1.

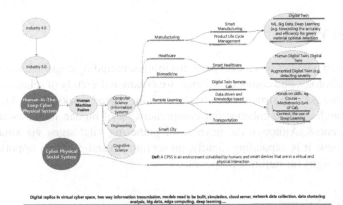

Fig. 1. Taxonomy/findings of the research domains and subdomains for Human Machine Fusion

The scope of our research direction is in understanding the intent of humans, and virtual agents within a remote learning environment so that the interaction will be in each context to accomplish a task or a goal.

1.1 Goals and Motivation of the Research: Human Machine Fusion

The term "Human Machine Fusion" (HMF) is used in this research to describe the incorporation of humans (in the form of human avatars) as co-equal partners in the CPS in various avatar forms, such as virtual, software, and robots. The main objective of HMF is to enhance the relationship between systems and the co-existence of humans and robots in terms of computation, communication, and process control within the CPS. HMF elevates the role of robots as co-equal partners with humans in the cyber physical system, thereby creating advanced integration capabilities. Additionally, HMF can leverage human cognitive capabilities and empower the human factor within technical systems. For instance, in the remote learning domain, HMF, by equipping robots, can provide online students with a close-to-physical experience when collaborating with one another.

HMF takes integration to the next level, by making robots and their cognitive capabilities more equipped with data, knowledge and decision process chains for remote learning, healthcare, and manufacturing domains. Our research uses vital signs to enhance HMF.

Vital signs, (such as temperature, pulse rate, respiratory rate, blood pressure, and brain signals like Electroencephalography (EEG)), are collected from various sensors, including smart watches. These vital signs data offer insight into different aspects of an individual inherent state of mind.

The paper presents a structured flow of content, which includes a review of relevant literature on the significance of vital signs for human intent and state of mind, with respect to cognitive science, health sciences and information technology, a detailed research proposal, an application of deep learning analysis using a dataset of vital signs, and an outlook on future research directions.

2   Related Work

As this research involves diverse range of disciplines, including cognitive science, health science, Psychology, and computer science, we conducted a study of related works. The following is the general structure of our research on related works (Table 1).

Our research aims to enhance our comprehension of human intent awareness and context awareness. Although the practice of gathering vital signs via smart devices is relatively new, it is expanding rapidly, presenting several research opportunities for utilizing vital signs for multiple purposes.

2.1   Cognitive Science

Cognitive science research papers describe different attributes and features that help us comprehend the human learning process, enabling us to apply learning techniques to machines. Understanding these attributes will help the effective utilization of technologies in Artificial Intelligence (AI) more specifically deep learning models. Understanding the core ingredients of human intelligence will help the development of a more effective artificial intelligence systems. Research papers claim that key building blocks such as intuitive physics and psychology are not present in most current learning-based AI systems [2]. Humans always use their prior knowledge to accomplish any given task, however, to accomplish a task, machines use the data that was given to them prior to that task, or they start from the scratch. The cognitive science researchers believe that deep learning models and other learning paradigms can move machines closer to human-like learning and thought if they incorporate psychological ingredients.

Table 1. Category and major findings in the related work

	Summary of the findings in related work
1	Cognitive Science offers insights into the functioning of the human mind, as well as strategies for creating machines that are capable of learning and thinking in a manner like humans
2	Information systems concentrates on understanding the dynamics of human-robot interactions and improving the way data is processed during these interactions
3	The obstacles to achieving human-robot symbiosis, as well as the fundamental components of social cognition and our comprehension of how humans engage in social thinking, are key areas of focus
4	Research aimed at comprehending the correlation between alertness, performance, and human body temperature
5	Studies investigating the impact of oxygen administration on cognitive performance, heart rate, EEG signals, and other vital signs
6	Machine Learning algorithms applicable to our research Deep Learning-based for monitoring human performance and data classification

Cognitive science researchers also explain, in the next generation of robot companionship or robot working partners will need to satisfy social requirements like the famous laws of robotics envisaged by Isaac Asimov. Cognitive scientists explain the human machine fusion in a term symbiotic collaboration of robots and humans. The term human symbiosis is close to the term human machine fusion. Symbiotic collaboration of robots and humans require the integration of the individual partner's intentions into a shared action plan, which may involve continuous negotiation of intentions based on reciprocal understanding of actions [4].

2.2 Health Science

Bruyn et al. [5] study the relationship of one of the vital signs – temperature, they have found out that investigations relating thermal strain indicators, such as core temperature, to cognitive performance are sparse; the majority control and manipulate ambient temperature. Likewise, the isolation of other factors that may interact with heat to affect cognitive performance is infrequent. This report presents findings on the interaction effects of acclimatization, hydration level and operator skill, on human cognitive performance. Temperature as one of the vital signs, can help understand the motive and eventually the intent of humans.

Wright et al. [6] studied body temperature has been reported to influence human performance. Performance is reported to be better when body temperature is high/near its circadian peak and worse when body temperature is low/near its circadian minimum.

Chung et al. [7]Investigated the effect of 30% oxygen administration on verbal cognitive performance, blood oxygen saturation, and heart rate. They developed Two psychological tests were developed to measure the performance level of verbal cognition. The result supports the hypothesis that 30% oxygen administration would lead to increases in verbal cognitive performance.

2.3 Computer Science

Lyra et al. [8] have explained the use of infrared thermography for camera-based skin temperature measurement is becoming more prevalent in medical practice. It has been employed to detect fevers and infections, including in the recent COVID-19 pandemic. Their proposal method can perform real-time vital sign extraction on a low-cost system-on-module and may thus be a useful method for future contactless vital sign measurements.

Li et al. [9] conducted a survey of neurophysiological research carried out between 2009 and 2016. They presented a comprehensive overview of the existing works in emotion recognition using EEG signals. An emotion is a multifaceted psychological state that comprises three distinct components: subjective experience, physiological response, and behavioral or expressive response. Emotions are brief and involve a coordinated set of responses, which may manifest as verbal, behavioral, physiological, and neural mechanisms [9].

Sun et al. [10]context information including surrounding environment and human body can also provide extra clues to recognize emotion more accurately. Inspired by "sequence to sequence model" for neural machine translation, which models input and output sequences by an encoder and a decoder in recurrent neural network (RNN) architecture respectively (Fig. 2).

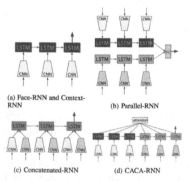

(a) Face-RNN and Context-RNN

(b) Parallel-RNN

(c) Concatenated-RNN

(d) CACA-RNN

Fig. 2. Comparison of RNN-based emotion recognition architectures streams are processed by a CNN feature extractor into corresponding feature stream as LSTM's input [10].

3   Research Proposal

The objective of this study is to develop an advanced solution that can precisely comprehend human intentions by interpreting their state of mind through the analysis of vital signs. By establishing a correlation between human behavior and their mental state, we can gain a deeper understanding of human intentions, which would enable robots to respond appropriately in environments where humans and robots coexist. This comprehension of context would facilitate more effective interactions, leading to the completion of tasks and accomplishments of goals. Our research seeks to investigate AI algorithms and discover a fresh approach that employs human vital signs to recognize intents and enhance robots' cognitive abilities. This pioneering method of interpreting human behavior in human-robot interactions would provide a unique and innovative solution.

This intent recognition solution using dataset that includes multiple features of vital signs data, such as temperature, pulse rate, BPM, blood pressure, and respiratory rate, along with EEG time-series data. EEG is the process of using applied electrodes to derive electrophysiological data and signals produced by the brain. [11] This dataset will be used to classify and predict the emotions and ultimately the intent of humans or subjects during a specific task. Furthermore, we will evaluate the prediction performance of various deep learning models, including Decision Tree, Random Forest, K-Nearest Neighbors, KNN Gaussian Naïve Bayes, and Multinomial Naïve Bayes, to determine the algorithm with the best performance.

Vital signs can be used to understand the state of mind of a person for following real life situations:

- Most organizations continue to work online after the COVID-19 pandemic, and working online will continue to be a norm therefore Vital Signs can be helpful to understand the state of mind of employees working online, during meetings, online discussions, online training, and online brainstorming sessions. By consolidating intent recognitions processes with the help of vital signs and other influencing factors, robots can help improve the online interactions.
- Students in an online or remote lab environment can benefit through an effective interaction between students and robots, robots, and other robots. Understanding intents of students using vital signs and other decision-influencing factors can benefit the co-existence of robots and students and eventually leads to a more human-like interactions with robots.
- Healthcare services will continue to be accessible to patients online and it is extremely important to monitor the vital signs of patients. These vital signs, in addition to a day-to-day healthcare service, they can also be used for a day-to-day operation or tasks. For example, when a patient interacts in an online activity such as shopping, training or another activity, the robots can pick all the intents of the patient using those vital signs and can interact with the patient as equal partners.

4 Methodology

In our literature review we did not find an in-depth study on human intent recognition using vital signs. However, we believe that widely used deep learning algorithm for Natural Language Processing (NLP) can be found useful to achieve our research goal and to produce state-of-the-art deep learning model to classify raw vital signs for the purpose of recognizing human intents, and leveraging the classified data for enhancing machines or robots with adequate information so that the human-machine collaboration will be efficient. From our research recurrent neural network (RNN) has been used successfully to interpret and classify EEG signals which are temporal recordings that exhibit patterns periodically at various skills. It is used in research papers for analyzing brain activities [12] It is also used in analyzing the performance of online game players [13].

4.1 Recurrent Neural Networks (RNN)

Our primary approach will involve employing a recurrent neural network (RNN) to interpret and analyze EEG signals for identifying the emotional states of humans. This will entail stacking multiple 1D convolution layers, followed by gated recurrent unit (GRU) layers. Each 1D convolution layer will utilize multiple filters of exponentially varying lengths, and the stacked GRU layers will be densely connected in a feedforward manner. This methodology will be employed as one of the initial steps in our analysis of EEG sessions for determining human emotional states.

RNN are family of neural networks for processing variable-length sequential data. A RNN maintains a recurrent hidden state whose activation at each time is dependent on that of the previous time step. More formally, given a sequence $x = (x_1, x_2, \ldots, x_T)$

$$h_t = \begin{cases} 0 & t = 0 \\ g(h_{t-1,xt}) & t > 0 \end{cases} \tag{1}$$

where g is a nonlinear function.

In a classical RNN, the recurrent hidden unit of Eq. (1) is updated in the following way:

$$h_t = f(Wx_t + Uh_{t-1} + b) \tag{2}$$

where f is a pointwise nonlinear activation function that is applied to the output of a neural network layer to introduce nonlinearity into the model [12]

However, while using RNN, we will also explore classical ML algorithms, KNN, SMV, K-means and other algorithms and compare their performances.

RNN are a class of neural networks that is powerful for modeling sequence data such as time series or natural language. In analyzing time series data of EEG signals, RNN is very useful (Table 2).

4.2 Experiment and Results

Vital Sign related datasets are available online in a few different flavours and formats. For example, PhysioBank ATM is a self-service repository for time-series data [14]. There are also multiple datasets at GitHub.

To illustrate our research trajectory, we will utilize a dataset containing human vital sign data recorded over a specific period. The dataset includes features such as Heart Rate (BPM), Respiration (BPM), Oxygen Level (SpO2), Temperature (°C), and an output indicating whether the vital signs are categorized as "Normal" or "Abnormal". The health vital sign dataset comprises of 25,500 records, and we are leveraging this dataset to show

Table 2. RNN algorithm pros and cons

Advantages	Drawbacks
Possibility of processing input of any length	Computation being slow
Model size not increasing with size of input	Difficulty of accessing information from a long time ago
Computation considers historical information	Cannot consider any future input for the current state
Weights are shared across time	

our thought process and research direction. The data for these experiments were sourced from a community driven data store hosted on GitHub [15].

In this demonstration, we aim to predict whether an individual's mental state is classified as "Normal" or "Abnormal" using RNN (Recurrent Neural Network) algorithms. This represents the initial phase of our research, which focuses on identifying human intent at a particular time based on the vital sign data we have available. Table 3 shows a partial extract of participants csv file for health vital signs data.

Table 3. Extract of the Human Vital Sign Dataset for multiple participants.

Participant	HR (BPM)	RESP	Sp02(%)	Temp (C)	Output
1	94	21	97	36.2	Normal
2	94	25	97	36.2	Abnormal
3	101	25	93	38	Abnormal
4	55	11	100	35	Abnormal
......	......	......	......	......	......

During the first stage, it came to light that the data contained nil values for certain features, posing an issue. We were faced with two options to address this problem: either remove the data instances with nil values for their features, which resulted in a reduction in dataset size which could potentially harm the model's accuracy. However, the reduction was not substantial in dataset size, removing the instances with nil values was considered not impactful in training the model.

We compile the model using TensorFlow [16] and train it by using Adam optimizer and make the prediction for this demonstration. We also use matplotlib and seaborn for visualization and we are using the confusion matrix and classification report for analyzing the output. The first step is to read the vital signs dataset (a csv file). Then prepressing steps follow such as mapping output value to integers.

The entire process of conducting the experiment, starting from reading the dataset to generating predictions and performing data classification, is summarized in Fig. 3 below. The diagram explains the major three phases of our research work.

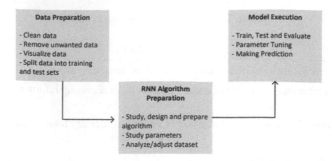

Fig. 3. Deep learning approach taken for analysing the vital signs dataset.

To show the data analysis results, we have included the confusion matrix report generated by applying the algorithm on the vital signs dataset. The predicted values closely aligned with the actual values with accuracy rate 97% as shown in Fig. 4.

The findings obtained from this research successfully fulfill the first objective of applying recurrent neural networks to the human-machine fusion prediction problem. These results will serve as a foundation for the next phase of our research, which aims to identify human intent using human vital signs in more complex datasets, EEG time-series data and utilizing more sophisticated deep learning architectures.

	Predicted	Actual
Abnormal	5867	5849
Normal	1698	1716

```
Classification Report:
_____
                precision    recall  f1-score   support

    Abnormal       0.98      0.99      0.98      5849
      Normal       0.95      0.94      0.95      1716

    accuracy                           0.98      7565
   macro avg       0.97      0.96      0.97      7565
weighted avg       0.98      0.98      0.98      7565
```

Fig. 4. Confusion Matrix – Actual vs Predicted outcomes of RNN model.

In our experiment, for comparative analysis, we have evaluated a LogisticRegression (LR), Linear Discrimination Analysis (LDA), KNeighbhorClassifier (KNN), Decison-TreeClassifier (CART), GuessianNB (NB) and SVC models and use the KFold class to perform the cross-validation configured to shuffle the dataset and set k = 10 and the result of the cross-validation is shown in the boxplot below (Fig. 5).

During our experiment, we explored the effects of varying the number of neighbors in the KNN algorithm, the penalty in Logistic Regression, the choice of solver, the available values for discrimination analysis, the splitter in the Decision Tree Classifier, the 'priors' in GaussianNB, and the regularization parameter in SVC models. Even, additional experiments to observe the impact of adjusting specific parameter values has been deployed. But finally, the default parameters provided by the API has been kept. (Regularization parameter = 1.0, priors = none, splitter = best, solver = svd.) In our future work, we plan to continue evaluating the accuracy of each algorithm by conducting further experiments.

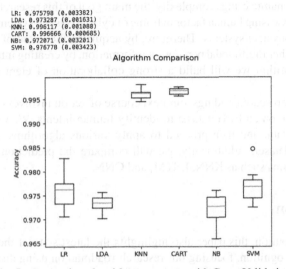

```
LR:   0.975798 (0.003382)
LDA:  0.973287 (0.001631)
KNN:  0.996117 (0.001088)
CART: 0.996666 (0.000685)
NB:   0.972071 (0.003201)
SVM:  0.976778 (0.003423)
```

Fig. 5. Comparing algorithms accuracy with Cross-Validation.

The successful accomplishment of the first objective, which involves the application of recurrent neural networks to the human-machine fusion prediction problem and algorithmic comparative analyses, is evidenced by the findings obtained from this research. These results will provide a basis for the next stage of our investigation, which intends to explore human intent identification in more intricate datasets, such as EEG time-series data, by utilizing more advanced deep learning architectures while incorporating human vital signs.

4.3 Future Work

As a next step of our research work, we will continue to make sure that we get time-series EEG Signals on vital signs, scale those signals to understand the intent of humans. In addition to literature review on EEG signal readings, emotion recognition, and intention recognition, we will follow major steps in identifying the state of mind of humans using Deep Learning (DL) data input, processing, filtering, classifying and prediction steps.

Read EEG dataset that are collected on EEG emotion, human and robot approach behaviours. The preprocessing activities in cleaning up data to prepare for the next RNN algorithms, mapping integer values for labels, train the model, test the model, use functions, feed into the model, visualize, classify, and predict.

In the classification phase, to establish a better performance, we will measure and compare on different types of classification – Decision tree, Random Forest, K-Nearest

Neighbors, KNN Gaussian Naïve Bayes and Multinomial Naïve Bayes to identify the best algorithm that has a best performance.

In the next phase we will also work in combining different modalities or types of information for improving performance. We will be working by combining high level embeddings from the different inputs by concatenating for a better result.

As human dynamic brings complexity, the main goal of this research is to present the possibilities of assessing human factor in frame of cyber-physical systems, the human-in-the-loop cyber-physical systems. Therefore, by acquiring the intent of humans through vital signs and other multimodal perception information, by creating integrated intention recognition algorithm we will build a strong collaboration of elements in the cyber physical system.

Based on our research findings, our next course of action involves conducting information extraction on an EEG dataset to identify human intents. We will begin by preprocessing the data, and then proceed to apply various algorithms, including RNN, to classify the dataset. Additionally, we will compare the prediction performance of different algorithms such as KNN, LSTM, and CNN.

5   Conclusion

As a new contribution, this paper also highlights the latest state-of-the-art solution for human intent recognition, focusing our research roadmap on using deep learning techniques to recognize emotions via vital signs. This approach aims to comprehend human intent through vital signs such as body temperature, respiratory rate, information on EEG signals and others for a more effective co-existence between humans and robots in cyber-physical systems, ensuring that the intent aligns with the context of the task based on perceptible feature attributes and dynamic properties.

Acknowledgement. The research has been funded by the Spanish Ministry of Economics and Industry, grant PID2020-112726RB-I00, by the Spanish Research Agency (AEI, Spain) under grant agreement RED2018–102312-T (IA-Biomed), and by the Ministry of Science and Innovation under CERVERA Excellence Network project CER-20211003 (IBERUS) and Missions Science and Innovation project MIG-20211008 (INMERBOT). Also, by Principado de Asturias, grant SV-PA-21-AYUD/2021/50994. By European Union's Horizon 2020 research and innovation programme (project DIH4CPS) under the Grant Agreement no 872548. And by CDTI (Centro para el Desarrollo Tecnológico Industrial) under projects CER-20211003 and CER-20211022 and by ICE (Junta de Castilla y León) under project CCTT3/20/BU/0002.

References

1. Pasandideh, S., Pereira, P., Gomes, L.: Cyber-physical-social systems: taxonomy, challenges, and opportunities. https://doi.org/10.1109/ACCESS.2022.3167441
2. Lake, B.M., Ullman, T.D., Tenenbaum, J.B., Gershman, S.J.: Building machines that learn and think like people (2017). https://doi.org/10.1017/S0140525X16001837

3. Brinck, I., Balkenius, C.: Recognition in human-robot interaction: the gateway to engagement; recognition in human-robot interaction: the gateway to engagement. In: 2019 Joint IEEE 9th International Conference on Development and Learning and Epigenetic Robotics (ICDL-EpiRob) (2019). https://doi.org/10.1109/DEVLRN.2019.8850691

4. Sandini, G., et al.: Social cognition for human-robot symbiosis-challenges and building blocks (2018). https://doi.org/10.3389/fnbot.2018.00034

5. Bruyn, L., Lamoureux, T.: Literature review: cognitive effects of thermal strain

6. Wright, K.P., Hull, J.T., Czeisler, C.A.: Relationship between alertness, performance, and body temperature in humans. Am. J. Physiol.-Regul. Integrative Comp. Physiol. **283**(6), R1370–R1377 (2002). https://doi.org/10.1152/ajpregu.00205.2002

7. Chung, S.C., Iwaki, S., Tack, G.R., Yi, J.H., You, J.H., Kwon, J.H.: Effect of 30% oxygen administration on verbal cognitive performance, blood oxygen saturation and heart rate. Appl. Psychophysiol. Biofeedback **31**(4), 281–293 (2006). https://doi.org/10.1007/S10484-006-9023-5/FIGURES/5

8. Lyra, S., et al.: A deep learning-based camera approach for vital sign monitoring using thermography images for ICU patients (2021). https://doi.org/10.3390/s21041495

9. Li, Y., Yang, H., Li, J., Chen, D., Du, M.: EEG-based intention recognition with deep recurrent-convolution neural network: performance and channel selection by Grad-CAM. Neurocomputing **415**, 225–233 (2020). https://doi.org/10.1016/J.NEUCOM.2020.07.072

10. Sun, M.-C., Hsu, S.-H., Yang, M.-C., Chien, J.-H.: Context-aware cascade attention-based RNN for video emotion recognition (2018). https://doi.org/10.1109/ACIIAsia.2018.8470372

11. "(2) (PDF) Mental emotional sentiment classification with an EEG-based brain-machine interface. https://www.researchgate.net/publication/329403546_Mental_Emotional_Sentiment_Classification_with_an_EEG-based_Brain-machine_Interface#fullTextFileContent. Accessed 06 Apr 2023

12. Roy, S., Kiral-Kornek, I., Harrer, S.: ChronoNet: a deep recurrent neural network for abnormal EEG identification, January 2018. http://arxiv.org/abs/1802.00308

13. https://www.kaggle.com/datasets/canaria/5-gamers

14. PhysioBank ATM. https://archive.physionet.org/cgi-bin/atm/ATM#input. Accessed 17 Apr 2023

15. Human vital signs | Kaggle. https://www.kaggle.com/datasets/engrarri21/human-vital-signs. Accessed 16 Apr 2023

16. Abadi, M.: Tensorflow: a system for large-scale machine learning. In: OSDI, vol. 16, pp. 265–283 (2016)

Author Index

P. García Bringas et al. (Eds.): HAIS 2023, LNAI 14001, pp. 781–784, 2023.
https://doi.org/10.1007/978-3-031-40725-3

Printed in the United States
by Baker & Taylor Publisher Services